The American Heritage®
Dictionary of Idioms

CHRISTINE AMMER

HOUGHTON MIFFLIN COMPANY Boston New York

Other Books by Christine Ammer

Have a Nice Day! — No Problem! A Dictionary of Clichés
Fruitcakes & Couch Potatoes and Other Delicious Expressions
It's Raining Cats and Dogs and Other Beastly Expressions
Southpaws and Sunday Punches and Other Sporting Expressions
Fighting Words from War, Rebellion and Other Combative Capers
Seeing Red or Tickled Pink: Color Terms in Everyday Language
The HarperCollins Dictionary of Music
Unsung: A History of Women in American Music
The New A to Z of Women's Health

First paperback edition 2003

Library of Congress Cataloging-in-Publication Data
Ammer, Christine.
   The American Heritage dictionary of idioms/Christine Ammer.
      p. cm.
   Includes bibliographical references.
   ISBN 0–395–72774–x (cloth) ISBN 0-618-24953-2 (pbk.)
      1. English language — United States — Idioms — Dictionaries.
   2. English language — United States — Terms and phrases.
   3. Americanisms — Dictionaries. I. Title.
PE2839.A47   1997
423'.I — dc21   97–12390
                                                   CIP
Manufactured in the United States of America

MP 10 9 8 7 6 5 4 3 2 1

Preface

This book is a comprehensive survey of the idioms currently used in American English. An idiom is a set phrase of two or more words that means something different from the literal meaning of the individual words. For instance, the phrase *to change one's tune* has nothing to do with music but means "to alter one's attitude." Similarly, *to hit the nail on the head* often has nothing to do with carpentry but means simply "to be absolutely right." Idioms are the idiosyncrasies of a language. Often defying the rules of logic, they pose great difficulties for non-native speakers. English abounds with phrases such as *if worst comes to worst, far and away,* and *how do you do,* which, if translated literally, make no sense. Indeed, the true test of an idiom is whether it changes meaning when rendered word for word in another language.

In addition to idioms, this book includes common figures of speech, such as *dark horse* and *blind as a bat;* interjections and formula phrases, such as *all the best* and *take care;* emphatic redundancies whose word order cannot be reversed, such as *far and wide* and *cease and desist;* common proverbs, especially ones that often occur in abbreviated form, such as *a bird in the hand;* colloquialisms such as *off the beam* and *out in left field;* and slang phrases such as *push the envelope.*

Each expression is defined and illustrated by at least one sample sentence showing how it is used in context. In most cases the literal meaning of a phrase is omitted; thus the entry *hold up* omits the definition "keep upright" or "support." Wherever possible I have included information regarding the expression's origin or background, along with its date of first appearance. I have given approximate dates for most idioms to allow for their probable use in speech before being written down.

The ultimate origin of many idioms is unknown. Some idioms, such as *by hook or crook,* use familiar words in obscure ways. Some preserve words that are otherwise obsolete, such as *hue* in *hue and cry* and *fell* in *in one fell swoop.* I have tried to explain these lost origins and obscure meanings whenever research can shed light on them. The result is a dictionary that treats almost 10,000 English expressions in greater detail and depth than any other book available today. I hope that all speakers of English will find it both useful and enjoyable.

Heartfelt thanks are due to the many friends and acquaintances who have offered valuable suggestions, advice, and help, especially my husband Dean Ammer. Special mention must be made of Joseph Pickett, Senior Lexicographer, and Susan Chicoski, Associate Editor, of Houghton Mifflin Company, and of their colleagues David A. Jost and Kaethe Ellis for their invaluable expertise. I would also like to thank Jesse Sheidlower of Random House for his generous help dating some of the slang expressions. The dictionary has been vastly improved through their assistance.

— *Christine Ammer*

Guide to Using This Book

Entries

All entry phrases and synonymous variants are given in boldface type at the beginning of an entry before the definition. Related or similar expressions are given in boldface in the text of the entry. Historical precedents and obsolete phrases appear in italic type. Where a phrase has more than one meaning, definitions are numbered, and whenever possible, ordered by frequency of use. Example sentences appear in italic type, quotations in roman type within quotation marks, and cross-references in small capitals.

Alphabetization and Cross-References

Entries are arranged alphabetically, letter by letter up to the comma in the case of inverted or appended elements.

To locate an entry, it sometimes may be hard to decide which word in a phrase will come first in the alphabetical listing. For example, is *as luck would have it* under *as* or *luck*? To help sort out these problems, entries listing cross-references for key words appear alphabetically among the main entries. By checking these key-word entries, readers can locate every phrase treated as an entry in this book. The reader who does not find *as luck would have it* under *as* can look under the entries beginning with the next word, *luck*. If more help is needed, the entry for the word *luck* itself lists all the idioms containing that word which appear elsewhere in the book.

Variants or related expressions that are covered under other entry words appear in parentheses in the cross-references. Thus, at the entry *soft* the reader is referred to HARD (SOFT) SELL, which means that the entry *hard sell* also treats the phrase *soft sell*. Note, however, that words in parentheses are *not* considered part of the alphabetical order, so one should look for *hard sell*, not *hard soft sell*.

Variable Pronouns

Many idioms can be used with different pronouns, as, for example, *clean up his act, clean up her act, clean up my act.* Consequently, the pronouns *one* and *someone* are used in entry words and variants to indicate that the object or possessive pronoun in the idiom may vary according to context. *One* or *one's* means that the antecedent of the pronoun must be the subject of the clause, or in some cases an inanimate noun or a gerund must be the subject. For example, the idiom *hit one's stride* can appear in a sentence such as *She finally hit her stride*, or the idiom *serve one right* can be used in a sentence such as *It serves him right to be thrown off the team.* But note that sentences like *She finally hit his stride* are not possible.

The use of *someone* or *someone's* in the idiom means that the pronoun can be replaced only by a noun or pronoun that does *not* refer to the grammatical subject of the clause. In other words, the action of the verb is directed from one person to another (the "someone"). For example, the idiom *call someone's bluff* implies that you (or he or she or they) can only call someone else's bluff, never your (or his or her or their) own.

Labels

The labels in brackets preceding the date of an idiom's first appearance indicate the degree of formality or offensiveness. The label *colloquial* means that a phrase is used in ordinary speech and informal writing but not in more formal contexts. *Slang* generally refers to phrases that are appropriate only to very informal contexts or are used in irreverent humor. *Vulgar slang* indicates that a phrase is generally considered offensive. The absence of such a label indicates that a term is considered standard English.

Note that these labels are bound to change, as are the idioms themselves. What is slang today may be standard English tomorrow. Furthermore, what is common usage for a time may die out (in this book indicated as *obsolescent*) or it may change its meaning, as the idiom *beg the question* may be doing. As E.B. White put it, "The living language is like a cowpath; it is the creation of the cows themselves, who, having created it, follow it or depart from it according to their whims or their needs. From daily use, the path undergoes change."

Dating

Nearly all entries provide some indication of the idiom's history. For many entries the date when the expression was invented or first used appears within brackets. These dates are often approximate because in many cases a phrase has been used for some time in speech before being recorded in writing. In some cases, as when the expression first appeared in the work of a well-known writer, the precise date and location of its first recorded use are given. Within brackets the abbreviation *c.* (for Latin *circa*) is used to mean "about," as in

"c. 1400." The abbreviation A.D. is used for the years 1 through 1000; B.C. is used to indicate years before A.D. 1.

Quotations

Unless otherwise specified, biblical quotations are from the King James translation of 1611. To avoid the difficulties posed to some readers by the English of earlier writers such as Chaucer, many quotations have had their spelling normalized, and some have been rendered into Modern English.

Sources

Among the principal sources used for dates and citations are, first and foremost, *The Oxford English Dictionary*, Second Edition; *The American Heritage Dictionary of the English Language, Third Edition*; J.E. Lighter, *Historical Dictionary of American Slang*, Volume 1; *The Random House Dictionary of the English Language*, Second Edition; Eric Partridge, *A Dictionary of Catch Phrases, American and British, from the 16th Century to the Present Day*; *Webster's Dictionary of English Usage*; Wolfgang Mieder, *A Dictionary of American Proverbs*; Richard H. Thornton, *An American Glossary*; Mitford M. Mathews, *A Dictionary of Americanisms*; Burton Stevenson, *Home Book of Proverbs, Maxims, and Familiar Phrases*; John Algeo, *Fifty Years Among the New Words*; Clarence Barnhart, Sol Steinmetz, and Robert Barnhart, *The Barnhart Dictionary of New English since 1963* and *The Second Barnhart Dictionary of New English*; and William Safire, "On Language" column, *The New York Times*.

a

aback ♦ See TAKE ABACK.

abide ♦ In addition to the idioms beginning with ABIDE, also see CAN'T STAND (ABIDE).

abide by Accept and act in accordance with a decision or set of rules; also, remain faithful to. For example, *All members must agree to abide by the club regulations,* or *A trustworthy man abides by his word.* An older sense of the verb *abide,* "remain," is still familiar in the well-known 19th-century hymn "Abide with Me," which asks God to stay with the singer in time of trouble. [Early 1500s]

a bit 1. A small amount of anything; also, a short period of time. For example, *Here's a bit of wrapping paper,* or *It'll be ready in a bit,* or *Just wait a bit.* [c. 1600] 2. Somewhat or rather, as in *It stings a bit,* or *Will you have a bit more to eat?* [Second half of 1600s] Also see BIT BY BIT; NOT A BIT.

about ♦ In addition to the idioms beginning with ABOUT, also see AT ABOUT; BEAT ABOUT THE BUSH; BRING ABOUT; CAST ABOUT; COME ABOUT; DO AN ABOUT-FACE; GET ABOUT; GO ABOUT (ONE'S BUSINESS); HOW ABOUT (THAT); JUST ABOUT; KNOCK ABOUT; LAY ABOUT; MAN ABOUT TOWN; MUCK ABOUT; NOSE ABOUT (AROUND); NO TWO WAYS ABOUT IT; ORDER SOMEONE ABOUT; OUT AND ABOUT; SEE ABOUT; SEND SOMEONE ABOUT SOMEONE'S BUSINESS; SET ABOUT; THAT'S ABOUT THE SIZE OF IT; UP AND ABOUT; WHAT ABOUT SOMEONE (SOMETHING).

about time Long past the right time; also, approximately the right time. Thus, *It's about time you went to bed* can mean either that you should have gone to bed much earlier (often stated with emphasis on the word *time*), or that now is the appropriate time for you to retire. [Early 1900s] For a synonym, see HIGH TIME.

about to 1. Ready to, on the verge of, as in *I was about to leave when it began to rain,* or *He hasn't finished yet but he's about to.* This usage was first recorded in Miles Coverdale's 1535 translation of the Bible (Joshua 18:8). 2. **not about to.** Having no intention of doing something, as in *The shop steward was not about to cross the picket line,* or *Are you staying longer?—No, I'm not about to.* [Colloquial; first half of 1900s]

above ♦ In addition to the idioms beginning with ABOVE, also see ALL (NONE) OF THE ABOVE; CUT ABOVE; HEAD AND SHOULDERS ABOVE; OVER AND ABOVE.

above all More than anything else, as in *A winter hike calls for good equipment, but above all it requires careful planning.* This phrase first appears in William Langland's *Piers Ploughman* (1377), in which the narrator exhorts readers to love the Lord God above all. Also see FIRST AND LAST.

above and beyond More than is required. This somewhat redundant expression—*above* and *beyond* here both denote excess—often precedes **the call of duty,** which means exceeding what a particular job requires. Thus *Putting in overtime without pay is above and beyond the call of duty.* Also see OVER AND ABOVE.

aboveboard ♦ See OPEN AND ABOVEBOARD.

above suspicion So trustworthy as never to be suspected of wrongdoing, as in "The wife of Caesar must be above suspicion" (Charles Merivale, *A History of the Romans under the Empire,* 1850). The phrase was given further currency when it was used for the title of a very popular World War II spy film starring Joan Crawford (*Above Suspicion,* 1943). A similar idiom using *above* in the sense of "beyond" is **above the law,** usually describing an individual or business behaving as though exempt from rules or laws that apply to others.

above the law ♦ See under ABOVE SUSPICION.

absence ♦ In addition to the idiom beginning with ABSENCE, also see CONSPICUOUS BY ITS ABSENCE.

absence makes the heart grow fonder Separation intensifies love, as in *After a year in another country she accepted his proposal, so I guess absence makes the heart grow fonder,* or, used ironically, *The boss leaves earlier every day; oh well, absence makes the heart grow fonder.* Although versions of this saying date from Roman times, it only became popular after Thomas Haynes Bayly used it as the last line of a song in *The Isle of Beauty* (1850). The opposite sentiment is expressed by FAMILIARITY BREEDS CONTEMPT.

absent without leave Away without permission or explanation, as in *Her daughter went to the mall but got in trouble for being absent without leave.* The term and its acronym, **AWOL,** originated in the American military during World War I for soldiers absent from duty without permission (leave). It later was transferred to civilian situations, as in *John didn't just cut his Tuesday classes; he went AWOL.*

accidentally on purpose ♦ See ON PURPOSE, def. 2.

accord ♦ See OF ONE'S OWN ACCORD.

according to all accounts ♦ See BY ALL ACCOUNTS.

according to Hoyle In keeping with established rules; on the highest authority, as in *The tax records are in excellent order, all according to Hoyle.* Edmond Hoyle (1679–1769) of England, author of books of rules for card games, was so highly regarded that numerous writers used his name on their own rule books, even for games that had not been invented by the time of Hoyle's death, so that his name became synonymous with any rules.

account ♦ In addition to the idiom beginning with ACCOUNT, also see ALL PRESENT AND ACCOUNTED FOR; BY ALL ACCOUNTS; CALL TO ACCOUNT; GIVE A GOOD ACCOUNT; NO ACCOUNTING FOR TASTES; ON ACCOUNT OF; ON NO ACCOUNT; ON ONE'S OWN AC-COUNT; ON SOMEONE'S ACCOUNT; TAKE ACCOUNT OF; TAKE INTO ACCOUNT; TURN TO GOOD ACCOUNT.

account for 1. Be the determining factor in; cause. For example, *The heat wave accounts for all this food spoilage*, or *Icy roads account for the increase in accidents*. **2.** Explain or justify, as in *Jane was upset because her son couldn't account for the three hours between his last class and his arrival at home*. Both of these related usages are derived from the literal meaning of the phrase, that is, "make a reckoning of an account." [Second half of 1700s]

accustomed to Used to something or someone; having the habit of doing something. For example, *In Spain we gave up our usual schedule and became accustomed to eating dinner at 10 P.M.* Professor Higgins in the musical *My Fair Lady* (1956) ruefully sang the song "I've Grown Accustomed to Her Face" after his protégé Eliza walked out on him. [Second half of 1400s]

ace ♦ In addition to the idioms beginning with ACE, also see HOLD ALL THE ACES; WITHIN AN ACE OF.

ace in the hole A hidden advantage or resource kept in reserve until needed, as in *The prosecutor had an ace in the hole: an eyewitness*. The term comes from stud poker, where each player is dealt one card face down—the so-called hold card— and the rest face up. Should the hole card be an ace, the player has a hidden advantage. *Hole* here simply means "a hiding place." In the 19th-century American West, the expression was used to refer to a hidden weapon, such as a gun concealed in a shoulder holster. By the 1920s it had become a metaphor for any surprise advantage or leverage.

ace it Accomplish something with success, as in *I'm sure he'll ace it when he takes that bar exam*. The verb *ace* originated in tennis with the meaning "to hit an unreturnable serve against an opponent." The idiom **ace it**, however, originated as student slang for getting an "A" on an exam or in a course but soon was extended to other successful accomplishments. [Slang; mid-1900s]

ace out 1. Get the better of, defeat, as in *Our team is bound to ace them out*, or *Those calculus problems aced me out again*. [Slang; mid-1900s] **2.** Take advantage of or cheat someone, as in *John thought they were trying to ace him out of his promised promotion*. [Slang; c. 1920]

Achilles' heel A fatal weakness, a vulnerable area, as in *This division, which is rarely profitable, is the*

company's Achilles' heel. The term alludes to the Greek legend about the heroic warrior Achilles whose mother tried to make him immortal by holding the infant by his heel and dipping him into the River Styx. Eventually he was killed by an arrow shot into his undipped heel. [c. 1800]

acid test A decisive trial to determine worth or quality, as in *Exposure to brilliant sunlight is the acid test for showing this fabric won't fade*. Alluding to a 19th-century chemical test for distinguishing gold from other metals, this term was used figuratively by the early 1900s.

acquaintance ♦ See NODDING ACQUAINTANCE; SCRAPE UP AN ACQUAINTANCE.

acquired taste Something one learns to like rather than appreciates immediately. For example, *Because it is so salty, caviar for many individuals is an acquired taste*, or *With its lack of decorative detail, this china pattern is definitely an acquired taste*. [Mid-1800s]

across ♦ In addition to the idiom beginning with ACROSS, also see COME ACROSS; CUT ACROSS; GET ACROSS; PUT ACROSS; RUN ACROSS.

across the board Applying to all the individuals in a group, as in *They promised us an across-the-board tax cut*, that is, one applying to all taxpayers, regardless of income. This expression comes from horse racing, where it refers to a bet that covers all possible ways of winning money on a race: win (first), place (second), or show (third). The *board* here is the notice-board on which the races and betting odds are listed. Its figurative use dates from the mid-1900s.

act ♦ In addition to the idioms beginning with ACT, also see CATCH IN THE ACT; CLEAN UP (ONE'S ACT); DO A DISAPPEARING ACT; GET IN THE ACT; GET ONE'S ACT TOGETHER; HARD (TOUGH) ACT TO FOLLOW; HIGH-WIRE ACT; IN THE ACT OF; PUT ON AN ACT.

action ♦ In addition to the idioms beginning with ACTION, also see ALL TALK AND NO ACTION; PIECE OF THE ACTION; SWING INTO ACTION.

actions speak louder than words What one does is more important than what one says, as in *Politicians need to be reminded that actions speak louder than words*. This statement, a proverb found in many languages, including ancient Greek, was first worded in precisely this way in English in *Colonial Currency* (1736). Also see ALL TALK; DO AS I SAY, NOT AS I DO.

active duty Full-time service, as in *Julian is 81, but he still comes to the office every day and is very much on active duty*. This term comes from the military, where it stands in opposition to *reserve*, which refers to troops still in the military but not actively engaged. It is occasionally transferred to civilian matters as well. [First half of 1800s]

act of faith Behavior that shows or tests a person's religious or other convictions, as in *Rock climbing with a new, inexperienced partner was a real act of faith*. The term is a translation of the Portuguese *auto da fé*, which referred to the sentencing and execution of heretics (often by burning at the stake) during the Inquisition, when punishing heresy was thought to constitute an assertion of faith. In modern times it is used for more benign circumstances. [Early 1700s]

act of God An unforeseen and uncontrollable natural event, such as a hurricane, fire, or flood. For example, *The publisher shall publish the work within twelve months except in case of delay caused by acts of God such as fires or floods or other circumstances beyond its control*. It most often appears in legal contracts, where it is used to indemnify one party against a disaster that prevents it from carrying out the contract's terms. [Mid-1800s]

act on 1. Also, **act upon**. Conduct oneself in accordance with or as a result of information or another action, as in *I will act on my lawyer's advice*, or *The manager refused to act upon the hotel guest's complaints*. [c. 1800] 2. Influence or affect, as in *The baby's fussing acted on the sitter's nerves*. [c. 1800]

act one's age Behave more maturely. Although the phrase often is used in asking children to act in a more grown-up fashion (*Only babies suck their thumbs; act your age*), it also may refer to an adult who is, sometimes deliberately, acting much younger than might be considered appropriate (*Grandpa, it's time you stopped climbing ladders and acted your age*).

act out 1. Perform or portray something or someone, as in *As she read to the class, the teacher had each child act out a different character in the story*. [c. 1600] 2. Express unconscious feelings or impulses through one's behavior, without being aware of it. For example, *She acted out her anger at her father by screaming at her husband*. This meaning comes from 20th-century psychological theory and usually (but not always) refers to negative or hostile impulses and emotions. The term is sometimes used without an object to mean "misbehave" or "behave disruptively," as in *The child is acting out in class*. [First half of 1900s] In both usages *out* means "openly" or "publicly."

act up 1. Misbehave. For example, *With an inexperienced rider, this horse always acts up*. [c. 1900] 2. Malfunction, as in *I'm not sure what's wrong with my car, but the transmission is acting up*. In both usages *up* means "abnormally."

act upon ▶ See ACT ON.

Adam ▶ See NOT KNOW FROM ADAM.

add fuel to the fire Also, **add fuel to the flames**. Worsen an already bad situation, as by increasing anger, hostility, or passion, as in *Bill was upset, and your making fun of his mishap just added fuel to the fire*. This metaphor dates from Roman times—Livy used it in his history of Rome—and it remains in common use. For similar metaphors, see ADD INSULT TO INJURY; FAN THE FLAMES.

add insult to injury Hurt a person's feelings after doing him or her harm; also, make a bad situation worse. For example, *Not only did the club refuse him, but it published a list of the rejected applicants—that's adding insult to injury*, or *The nearest parking space was half a mile away, and then, to add insult to injury, it began to pour*. The phrase is an ancient one, even older than its often cited use in the Roman writer Phaedrus's fable of the bald man and the fly. A fly bit the head of a bald man, who, trying to crush it, gave himself a heavy blow. The fly then jeered, "You want to avenge an insect's sting with death; what will you do to yourself, who have added insult to injury?" In English it was first recorded in 1748.

addition ▶ See IN ADDITION.

add up 1. Amount to an expected or correct total, as in *These figures don't add up*, meaning they are not correct. [Mid-1800s] 2. Be consistent, make sense, as in *I'm not sure that all this testimony will add up*. [First half of 1900s] 3. Assess, form an opinion of, as in *He looked across the track and added up the competition*. Also see ADD UP TO.

add up to Amount to, signify, as in *The smooth airline connections, luxury hotel, and fine weather added up to the best vacation we'd ever had*. [Early 1900s] Also see ADD UP.

ad hoc For the special purpose or end at hand; also, by extension, improvised or impromptu. The term, Latin for "to this," is most often used for committees established for a specific purpose, as in *The committee was formed ad hoc to address health insurance problems*. The term is also used as an adjective (*An ad hoc committee was formed*), and has given rise to the noun *adhocism* for the tendency to use temporary, provisional, or improvised methods to deal with a particular problem. [Early 1600s]

admiration ▶ See MUTUAL ADMIRATION SOCIETY.

ad nauseam To ridiculous excess, to a sickening degree. For example, *I wish he'd drop the subject; we have heard about budget cuts ad nauseam*. The term, Latin for "to [the point of] nausea," has been used in English since the early 1600s.

a drag A tedious experience, a bore, as in *After several thousand times, signing your autograph can be a drag*. This seemingly modern term was army slang during the Civil War. The allusion probably is to *drag* as something that impedes progress. [Colloquial; mid-1800s]

advance ♦ See IN ADVANCE; MAKE ADVANCES.

advantage ♦ See GET THE ADVANTAGE OF; SHOW TO ADVANTAGE; TAKE ADVANTAGE OF; TO ADVANTAGE.

a far cry ♦ See FAR CRY.

a few A small number of persons or things. This phrase can differ slightly from *few* used alone, which means "not many." For example, *The party was to end at eight, but a few stayed on* indicates that a small number of guests remained, whereas *The party began at eight, and few attended* means that hardly any guests came. [Late 1200s] Also see QUITE A BIT (FEW).

afoul of ♦ See RUN AFOUL OF.

afraid of one's own shadow Very timid and fearful, as in *Richard constantly worries about security; he's afraid of his own shadow.* This hyperbole has been used in English since the early 1500s, and some writers believe it originated in ancient Greece.

after ♦ In addition to the idioms beginning with AFTER, also see DAY AFTER DAY; GET AFTER; GO AFTER; INQUIRE AFTER; KEEP AFTER; LIVE HAPPILY EVER AFTER; LOOK AFTER; MORNING AFTER; NAME AFTER; RUN AFTER; SEE AFTER; SOUGHT AFTER; TAKE AFTER; THROW GOOD MONEY AFTER BAD; TIME AFTER TIME.

after a fashion Also, **after a sort.** Somehow or other; not very well, as in *John can read music, after a fashion,* or *He managed to paint the house after a sort.* The first phrase, in which *fashion* means "a manner of doing something," has been so used since the mid-1800s, when it replaced *in a fashion.* The variant dates from the mid-1500s. Also see IN A WAY; (SOMEHOW) OR OTHER.

after all 1. Despite everything, nevertheless, as in *The plane took off half an hour late but landed on time after all.* 2. After everything else has been considered, ultimately, as in *Mary has final approval of the guest list; after all, it's her wedding.* The two usages are pronounced differently, the first giving stress to the word *after* and the second to the word *all.* Both date from the early 1700s. Also see WHEN ALL IS SAID AND DONE.

after all's said and done ♦ See WHEN ALL IS SAID AND DONE.

after a sort ♦ See AFTER A FASHION.

after a while ♦ See IN A WHILE.

after hours After normal working hours, after closing time; also, after legal or established opening hours. For example, *I haven't time while the shop is open, but I can see you after hours,* or *The restaurant employees sometimes stayed for a meal after hours.* This term originally referred to laws governing business hours. It also gave rise to the term **afterhours club,** for a drinking club that

remained open later than similar establishments. [Mid-1800s]

after one's own heart To one's own personal liking, as in *He's very patient with the slower pupils; he's a teacher after my own heart.* This idiom appears in the King James Bible of 1611 (I Samuel 13:14). [Late 1500s]

after the fact ♦ After an actual occurrence, particularly after a crime. For example, *I know the brakes should have been repaired, but that doesn't help much after the fact.* The use of *fact* for a crime dates from the first half of the 1500s. The word became standard in British law and is still used in this way today. The idiom was first recorded in 1769 in the phrase **accessories after the fact,** referring to persons who assist a lawbreaker after a crime has been committed. Now it is also used more loosely, as in the example above.

again ♦ In addition to the idiom beginning with AGAIN, also see AT IT AGAIN; COME AGAIN; DO SOMETHING OVER AGAIN; EVER AND AGAIN; EVERY NOW AND AGAIN; HERE SOMEONE GOES AGAIN; NOW AND AGAIN; OFF AND ON (OFF AGAIN, ON AGAIN); OVER AGAIN; SOMETHING ELSE AGAIN; TIME AND TIME AGAIN; YOU CAN SAY THAT AGAIN.

again and again Repeatedly, often, as in *I've told you again and again, don't turn up the heat.* This idiom uses repetition for the purpose of emphasis (as does its synonym, OVER AND OVER). Shakespeare used it in *Othello* (1:3): "I have told thee often, and I retell thee again and again." [c. 1600]

against ♦ In addition to the idioms beginning with AGAINST, also see BEAT ONE'S HEAD AGAINST THE WALL; CARDS ARE STACKED AGAINST; COME UP AGAINST; COUNT AGAINST; DEAD SET AGAINST; GUARD AGAINST; HAVE SOMETHING AGAINST; HOLD SOMETHING AGAINST; LIFT A HAND AGAINST; OVER AGAINST; PIT SOMEONE AGAINST; RUN AGAINST; SET AGAINST; SWIM AGAINST; TURN AGAINST; TWO STRIKES AGAINST; UP AGAINST.

against all odds In spite of seeming very unlikely, as in *Against all odds we had a snowstorm in early May,* or *Against all odds the slower team won.* This transfer of a betting term to general usage occurred about 1900.

against one's better judgment Despite serious misgivings or objections, as in *Against my better judgment, I told her to come whenever she pleased.*

against one's will Without one's consent, forcibly, as in *The defendant knew he could not be made to testify against his will.* Originally one meaning of *will* was "acquiescence" or "consent," but this sense survives only in this idiom, which today nearly always implies some use of force. [c. 1400]

against the clock Also, **against time**. In a great hurry, as fast as possible, as in *With her term paper due on Monday, she was racing against the clock to finish it,* or *They were working against time to stay on schedule.* The term comes from various sports in which the contestants do not directly compete against each other but instead are timed individually, the winner being the one who is fastest. Its figurative use dates from the mid-1900s.

against the grain Opposed to one's inclination or preference, as in *We followed the new supervisor's advice, though it went against the grain.* This metaphor refers to the natural direction of the fibers in a piece of wood, called its *grain:* when sawed obliquely, or "against the grain," the wood will tend to splinter. [c. 1600] For a synonym, see RUB THE WRONG WAY.

against the tide ♦ See SWIM AGAINST THE TIDE.

age ♦ See ACT ONE'S AGE; COON'S AGE; GOLDEN AGE; IN THIS DAY AND AGE; OF AGE; RIPE OLD AGE; UNDER AGE.

a goner Something or someone that is dead, doomed, ruined, or past recovery, as in *If this new drug doesn't work, he's a goner,* or *Without a working transmission, my car's a goner.* Synonyms of this idiom, such as **a gone goose** or **chicken** or **gosling,** are no longer heard as much. [Slang; mid-1800s]

a good deal Also, **a great deal.** ♦ See under GOOD DEAL.

ahead ♦ In addition to the idioms beginning with AHEAD, also see COME OUT AHEAD; DEAD AHEAD; FULL SPEED AHEAD; GET AHEAD; GO AHEAD; ONE JUMP AHEAD; QUIT WHILE ONE'S AHEAD.

ahead of one's time In advance of current ideas, customs, or methods, as in *His treatment of light showed this painter to be well ahead of his time,* or *Wearing trousers and smoking cigars marked Amy Lowell as a woman ahead of her time.* This idiom uses *time* in the sense of "era" or "generation," a usage at least a thousand years old. The phrase is usually but not always used to express approval. [First half of 1900s]

ahead of the game In a position of advantage, especially financially; succeeding or winning. For example, *If we can sell 2,000 units of this product by next month, we'll be well ahead of the game.* This idiom uses *ahead of* in the sense of "in advance of," a usage dating from the mid-1700s, and transfers success in gambling (*the game*) to winning in other areas. Also see COME OUT AHEAD.

ahead of time Earlier, sooner, as in *The meeting was scheduled for three o'clock, but most people arrived ahead of time.* [Early 1900s]

aim ♦ In addition to the idiom beginning with AIM, also see TAKE AIM.

aim to Try or intend to do something, as in *We aim to please,* or *She aims to fly to California.* This term derives from *aim* in the sense of "direct the course of something," such as an arrow or bullet. [Colloquial; c. 1600]

air ♦ In addition to the idiom beginning with AIR, also see BREATH OF FRESH AIR; CASTLES IN THE AIR; CLEAR THE AIR; GIVE SOMEONE THE AIR; HOT AIR; IN THE AIR; INTO (OUT OF) THIN AIR; NOSE IN THE AIR; OFF THE AIR; PUT ON AIRS; UP IN THE AIR; WALK ON AIR; WASH (AIR) ONE'S DIRTY LINEN.

air one's grievances Complain publicly, as in *Jane was afraid to complain at work but freely aired her grievances at home.* This figurative exposure to the open air is far from new; to air one's opinions or ideas dates from the early 1800s, and the precise idiom appears in James Joyce's *Ulysses* (1922).

à la Like, in the manner of, as in *He hoped to break all records, à la Babe Ruth.* This expression, an abbreviation of the French à *la mode de* (for "in the manner of"), has been used in English since the late 1500s.

alarm ♦ See FALSE ALARM.

albatross around one's neck A heavy burden of guilt that becomes an obstacle to success, as in *The failed real estate scheme became an albatross around her neck, for now she could not interest other investors in a new project.* This idiom comes from Samuel Coleridge's narrative poem, *The Rime of the Ancient Mariner* (1798), which is based on the widespread superstition that it is unlucky to kill this large white sea bird. In the poem a sailor does kill an albatross, and when the ship then is becalmed near the equator and runs out of water, his shipmates blame him and force him to wear the dead bird around his neck.

aleck ♦ See SMART ALECK.

alert ♦ See ON THE ALERT.

a little 1. A small amount, as in *Will you have some more meat? Yes, just a little.* [Early 1400s] 2. Somewhat or rather, slightly, as in *I am a little annoyed with Harry.* [Late 1300s] For a synonym, see A BIT.

a little bird ♦ See LITTLE BIRD.

a little knowledge ♦ See LITTLE KNOWLEDGE.

alive ♦ In addition to the idioms beginning with ALIVE, also see COME ALIVE; EAT SOMEONE ALIVE; LOOK ALIVE; MORE DEAD THAN ALIVE; SKIN ALIVE.

alive and kicking Also, **alive and well.** Alive and alert; living and healthy. For example, *John's completely recovered; he's alive and kicking,* or *You're quite mistaken; our lawyer is alive and well.* The first expression, sometimes shortened to **live and kicking,** originally was used by fishmongers hawking their wares to convince customers of their freshness and has been considered a cliché since about 1850. The variant originated in the 1960s as a denial of someone's reported death.

alive to Aware of, conscious of, as in *The social worker was alive to all of the mother's worries.* [Mid-1700s]

alive with Teeming with, full of, as in *After the annual stocking, the pond was alive with trout.* [Late 1700s]

all ◆ In addition to the idioms beginning with ALL, also see ABOVE ALL; AFTER ALL; AGAINST ALL ODDS; AS ALL GETOUT; AT ALL; AT ALL COSTS; BE-ALL AND END-ALL; BEAT ALL; BY ALL ACCOUNTS; BY ALL MEANS; BY ALL ODDS; CAP IT ALL; FALL ALL OVER; FIRING ON ALL CYLINDERS; FIRST OF ALL; FOR ALL; FOR ALL I CARE; FOR ALL I KNOW; FOR ALL ONE'S WORTH; FOR ALL THAT; FREE FOR ALL; GET AWAY (FROM IT ALL); GET ONE'S ACT (IT ALL) TOGETHER; GO ALL THE WAY; HAVE ALL ONE'S BUTTONS; HAVE IT ALL OVER SOMEONE; HAVE IT BOTH WAYS (ALL); HIT ON ALL CYLINDERS; HOLD ALL THE ACES; IN A (ALL OF A) DITHER; IN ALL; IN ALL GOOD CONSCIENCE; IN ALL ONE'S BORN DAYS; IN ALL PROBABILITY; (ALL) IN THE SAME BOAT; IT'S ALL DOWNHILL FROM HERE; IT'S ALL OVER WITH; IT TAKES ALL SORTS; JACK OF ALL TRADES; JUMP ALL OVER; KNOW ALL THE ANSWERS; KNOW-IT-ALL; LAUGH ALL THE WAY TO THE BANK; LEAST OF ALL; LET IT ALL HANG OUT; NOT ALL IT'S CRACKED UP TO BE; NOT AT ALL; NOT FOR ALL THE TEA IN CHINA; NO TIME AT ALL; OF ALL THE NERVE; OF ALL THINGS; ONCE AND FOR ALL; ONE AND ALL; PULL OUT ALL THE STOPS; PUT ALL ONE'S EGGS IN ONE BASKET; SEEN ONE, SEEN THEM ALL; TILL ALL HOURS; TO ALL INTENTS AND PURPOSES; (ALL) TO THE GOOD; TURN OUT ALL RIGHT; WALK ALL OVER; WARTS AND ALL; WHEN ALL'S SAID AND DONE; WITH ALL DUE RESPECT; WITH ALL ONE'S HEART; YOU CAN'T WIN THEM ALL.

all along From the start, throughout, from end to end, as in *I've known he was innocent all along.* [c. 1600] Also see ALL ALONG THE LINE.

all along the line Also, **all the way down the line.** At every point, stage, or moment. For example, *We've had problems with this supplier all along the line,* or *He's been very helpful all the way down the line.* The *line* originally referred to a row of troops, but the expression has been used figuratively since the late 1800s. Also see SOMEWHERE ALONG THE LINE.

all and sundry One and all, as in *The salesman gave samples to all and sundry.* [Late 1400s]

all at once 1. All at the same time, as in *We can't get inside all at once, so please wait your turn.* [Late 1300s] 2. Suddenly, unexpectedly, as in *All at once the sky darkened.* For a synonym, see ALL OF A SUDDEN.

all at sea ◆ See AT SEA.

all better Completely healed or cured, as in *Once we've bandaged it up, you'll be all better.* This term is often used to comfort a child who has been hurt. It uses *all* in the sense of "entirely" and *better* in the sense of "cured." The usage has been in the language since A.D. 1000.

all but Almost, nearly, as in *I've all but finished the book.* This expression was used by Andrew Marvell in "Thoughts in a Garden": *"Society is all but rude, To this delicious solitude."* [Late 1500s]

all cylinders ◆ See FIRING ON ALL CYLINDERS.

all ears Eager to hear something, listening attentively, as in *Tell me, who else was invited? I'm all ears.* [Colloquial; late 1700s] Also see ALL EYES.

all else being equal ◆ See OTHER THINGS BEING EQUAL.

alley ◆ In addition to the idiom beginning with ALLEY, also see BLIND ALLEY; RIGHT UP ONE'S ALLEY.

alley cat A promiscuous woman; also, a person of loose morals. For example, *She's constantly picking up men in bars—a real alley cat.* This idiom transfers a stray cat that frequents alleys in search of food to a woman of easy virtue, especially a prostitute seeking customers. [Slang; early 1900s]

all eyes Watching very closely, as in *The buyers at the fashion show were all eyes.* Worded slightly differently (*with all one's eyes*), this idiom dates from the mid-1500s. Also see its counterpart, ALL EARS.

all for Completely in favor of something or someone, as in *I'm all for eating before we leave,* or *The players are all for the new soccer coach.* This colloquial phrase was first recorded in 1864.

all for the best Also, **for the best.** Best in the long run, despite appearances to the contrary. It is often a response to an unhappy outcome, as in *They had to sell their business, but since they weren't making money it's probably for the best,* or *The dress had been sold when she went back, but since it was a little too tight it's all for the best.* [Late 1300s]

all gone Completely finished or used up, as in *There's no milk left; it's all gone.*

all hours Irregular times, as in *You can't come home at all hours and expect your supper to be ready.* The expression can also mean "late at night," as in *College students like to stay up talking until all hours.* It is sometimes amplified into **all hours of the day and night.** [c. 1930]

all in, be 1. Be tired out, exhausted, as in *I can't walk another step; I'm all in.* [Slang; second half of 1800s] 2. In card games, especially poker, be out of money, as in *I'm finished for the night; I'm all in.* It refers to having put *all* of one's money *in* the pot. In his historical dictionary of slang, J.E. Lighter suggests that the gambling usage, first recorded in 1907, may be the source of the first sense.

all in a day's work Also, **all in the day's work.** Expected and normal, as in *He said I had to finish these reports by five o'clock—all in the day's work.* This phrase is sometimes used as an ironic comment on an unpleasant but not abnormal situation. The expression possibly alludes to the nautical term *day's work,* defined in 1789 as the reckoning of a ship's course during the 24 hours from noon to noon. [c. 1800]

all in all Taking everything into account, as in *All in all our trip to Europe was a success.* [First half of 1500s]

all in good time ▶ See IN GOOD TIME.

all in one piece Also, **in one piece.** Entirely undamaged or unharmed, as in *Given all the airport delays and bad weather, we were glad to arrive all in one piece,* or *She was relieved when he returned from Nepal in one piece.* [Early 1800s]

all in the family ▶ See under IN THE FAMILY.

all joking aside Also, **all kidding aside.** Seriously, as in *I know I said I'd quit, but all joking aside this job is too much for one person,* or *All kidding aside, I hate to lose at croquet.* This phrase often accompanies a joking statement.

all kinds of 1. Also, **all manner** or **sorts of.** All or many varieties of something, as in *Before the banquet, they served all kinds of drinks,* or *He sold exotic fruit of all sorts,* or *The museum featured all manner of artifacts.* [Early 1300s] 2. A large amount of something, as in *She has all kinds of money.* This hyperbolic usage is colloquial.

all of 1. The entire amount of something, as in *The baby ate all of his cereal.* This usage is relatively new, the word *of* being included only from about 1800 on. 2. No less than, at least, as in *Although she looked much younger, she was all of seventy.* [First half of 1800s]

all of a sudden Entirely without warning, abruptly, as in *All of a sudden the lights went out.* In Shakespeare's day the common phrase was *of a sudden,* the word *all* being added in the late 1600s. Also see ALL AT ONCE, def. 2.

all of the above Also, **none of the above.** Each one (not any) of the above-named alternatives. For example, *Have you decided to quit and announced your decision, or do you want to find another job first?—None of the above.* These phrases originated as answers to a multiple-choice question on a test but are now also used colloquially, often as a form of avoiding a direct answer. They use *above* in the sense of "preceding," a usage dating from the second half of the 1700s.

all one ▶ See ALL THE SAME, def. 1.

all out With all one's strength, ability, or resources; not holding back. For example, *They are going all out to make the fund-raiser a success.* This seemingly modern term dates from about 1300, when it meant "completely" or "wholly." It now refers to making a great effort and is also used adjectively, as in an **all-out** effort. This usage became current in America in the late 1800s, with reference to races and other kinds of athletic exertion. In the mid-1900s it gave rise to the phrase **to go all out** and was transferred to just about any energetic undertaking. Also see GO WHOLE HOG.

all outdoors, big as ▶ See BIG AS LIFE, def. 3.

all over 1. Everywhere. The phrase may be used alone, as in *I've looked all over for that book,* or *The very thought of poison ivy makes me itch all over.* In addition it can be used as a preposition, meaning "throughout," as in *The news spread all over town.* [Early 1600s] Also see FAR AND WIDE. 2. In all respects, as in *He is his Aunt Mary all over.* Charles Lamb had this usage in a letter (1799) about a poem: "The last lines . . . are Burns all over." [Early 1700s] 3. Also, **all over again.** Again from the beginning. For example, *They're going to play the piece all over,* or *Do you mean you're starting all over again?* [Mid-1500s] 4. Also, **all over with.** Quite finished, completed, as in *By the time I arrived the game was all over,* or *Now that she passed the test, her problems are all over with.* This phrase uses *over* in the sense of "finished," a usage dating from the 1300s. Also see ALL OVER BUT THE SHOUTING; HAVE IT (ALL OVER), def. 4.

all over but the shouting The outcome is a certainty, as in *When Jim hit the ball over the fence, it was all over but the shouting.* The term's first use in print, in 1842, was by Welsh sportswriter Charles James Apperley, but some authorities believe it originated even earlier in the United States for a close political race. Today it is applied to any contest. A common British version is **all over bar the shouting.**

all over one In close physical contact. For example, *Whenever I visit, that dog of Jane's is all over me.* [Early 1900s] Also see FALL ALL OVER ONE; HAVE IT ALL OVER ONE.

all over the place Also, **all over town** or **the world.** ▶ See under ALL OVER, def. 1.

all over with ▶ See ALL OVER, def. 3; IT'S ALL OVER WITH.

allowance ▶ See MAKE ALLOWANCE.

allow for Leave room for, permit, as in *We have enough chairs to allow for forty extra guests,* or *Our denomination allows for a large variety of beliefs.* [Early 1700s] Also see MAKE ALLOWANCE.

all present and accounted for All members or items of a group are here or their whereabouts are known, as in *Is everyone ready to board the bus?—All present and accounted for.* This expression almost certainly originated in the armed forces as a response to roll call. By proper logic, the *and* should be *or.* Nevertheless, the expression is used colloquially to offer assurance that no person or thing is missing.

all right 1. Completely correct, as in *You have a perfect score—your answers are all right.* (It could just as well be put as "all your answers are right.") 2. In proper or working order, in a satisfactory way, as in *The engine is running all right now.* [Late 1800s] Also see TURN OUT ALL RIGHT. 3. In good health, as in *John had the flu, but he's all right now.* [Early 1900s] 4. Not injured, safe, as in *It was just a minor accident and everyone is all right.* [Early 1900s] 5. Very well, yes, as in *Do you want to leave now?—All right,* or *All right, we'll stay home.* [First half of 1800s] Also see ALL RIGHT WITH YOU. 6. Certainly, without a doubt, as in *It's late all right, but it will probably come today.* [Mid-1800s] 7. Hurrah! Good for you, as in *All right! your team has done it again!* [Slang; mid-1900s] 8. Also, **all-right.** Good, satisfactory. For example, *This restaurant is all-right,* or *Harry is an all-right guy.* [Slang; mid-1900s]

all right for you I'm angry with you. This interjection usually accompanies a threat of revenge, as in *All right for you—I won't go out with you again.* [Early 1900s]

all right with one Also, **all right by one.** Agreeable to someone. For example, *If you want to practice now, that's all right with me.* Although *all right* alone has signified acquiescence much longer (see ALL RIGHT, def. 5), the addition of *with someone* (or, sometimes, *by someone*) dates from the mid-1900s.

all roads lead to Rome Many different methods will produce the same result. For example, *So long as you meet the deadline, I don't care how much help you get—all roads lead to Rome.* Based on the fact that the Roman Empire's excellent road system radiated from the capital like the spokes of a wheel, this metaphor was already being used in the 1100s.

all set Ready, in position for some action, as in *I'm all set to leave the country.* This colloquial term uses *set* in the sense of "put in proper position or order." The same meaning appears in the traditional *Ready, get set, go* for starting a race; here *set* means "in position to start."

all sewed up ♦ See SEWED UP.

all's fair in love and war Any conduct is permissible in certain circumstances, as in *Of course he called her—all's fair in love and war.* This maxim, stated in various forms from 1579 on, today some-

times appears altered by an addition or substitution, as in *All's fair in love and the World Series,* or *All's fair in love and war and an election year.*

all shook up Greatly disturbed or upset, as in *His letter left her all shook up.* This slangy idiom uses *shook* instead of the grammatically correct "shaken" (for "agitated") and adds *all* for emphasis. [Second half of 1900s]

all sorts ♦ See ALL KINDS.

all's well that ends well Everything has turned out satisfactorily, even though the outcome has been uncertain. For example, *His lawyer persuaded Jack to plead guilty, but the court merely put him on probation—all's well that ends well.* This proverb, dating from about 1250, gained even more currency as the title of a Shakespeare comedy.

all systems go Everything is ready for proceeding, as in *They've rented a hall and lined up the speakers, so it's all systems go for the rally.* Originating in the late 1960s with reference to launching space missiles and vehicles, this expression has been transferred to general use.

all talk (and no action) Much discussion but no action or results, as in *Don't count on Mary's help—she's all talk,* or *Dave has been saying for months that he'll get a summer job, but he's all talk and no action.* This idiom may have begun life as **all talk and no cider,** which Washington Irving cited as an American proverb in *Salmagundi* (1807). However, similar sayings antedate it by many years—for example, "The greatest talkers are always the least doers" (John Ray, *English Proverbs,* 1670).

all that 1. Too, very, usually employed in a negative context meaning not too, not very. For example, *The new house is not all that different from your old one.* [Mid-1900s] Also see NONE TOO. 2. That and everything else of the kind. For example, *She enjoys wearing nice clothes and perfume and all that.* [c. 1700] Also see AND ALL. 3. See FOR ALL THAT.

all that glitters is not gold Something attractive is not always what it seems, as in *This house is really beautiful, but a close look will show dry rot near the foundation—all that glitters is not gold.* Aesop stated the same idea in two of his fables (c. 600 B.C.), and a version close to the current wording appeared in 1175.

all the 1. Even, more so, as in *Painting the room white will make it all the lighter,* or *They liked her all the better for not pretending,* or *You don't care for dessert? Good, all the more for us.* Used to underscore a comparison, this idiom was used by Shakespeare in *As You Like It* (1:2): "All the better; we shall be the more marketable." [Late 1500s] For a synonym, see SO MUCH THE. 2. The entire amount of, as in *These cousins were all the family he had.* In this usage *all the* is short for *all of the.* [Ninth century A.D.]

all the best 1. Also, **all of the best**. The entire number or amount of the highest quality of something, as in *All of the best fruit was on display,* or *All the best students competed for the award.* 2. Best wishes, as in *I've got to go now—all the best to you and the family.* This idiom, first recorded in 1937, is used as an oral farewell or to close an informal letter or note.

all the better ♦ See ALL THE, def. 1.

all the rage Also, **all the thing**. The current or latest fashion, with the implication that it will be short-lived, as in *In the 1940s the lindy-hop was all the rage.* The use of *rage* reflects the transfer of an angry passion to an enthusiastic one; *thing* is vaguer. [Late 1700s] These terms are heard less often today than the synonym THE THING.

all there Having one's wits about one, mentally competent, as in *John may seem absent-minded, but believe me, he's all there.* This phrase is often used negatively, as **not all there**, for being without one's full faculties. For example, *I wonder about Justin; sometimes it seems as if he's not all there.* [Mid-1800s]

all the same 1. Also, **all one**. Equally acceptable, making no difference. For example, *If it's all the same to you I'd prefer the blue car,* or *Hot or cold, it's all one to me.* [Late 1700s] 2. Also, **just the same**. Nevertheless, still. For example, *John wants to stay another week, but I'm going home all the same,* or *Even if you vote against it, this measure will pass just the same.* [c. 1800]

all the thing ♦ See ALL THE RAGE.

all the time 1. Also, **all the while**. Throughout a specific period, as in *All the time the music was playing she tapped her foot,* or *The baby slept all the while the fire was being put out.* [Late 1400s] 2. Continuously, without interruption, as in *That old refrigerator is running all the time.* 3. Frequently, repeatedly, as in *He goes to that store all the time.*

all the way 1. Also, **the whole way**. The entire distance, from start to finish, as in *He ran all the way home,* or *The baby cried the whole way home.* [Late 1700s] 2. Completely, as in *I'm on your side all the way.* [First half of 1900s] 3. See GO ALL THE WAY.

all the worse ♦ See ALL THE, def. 1.

all things to all people, be Satisfy everyone completely, as in *The trouble with the governor's campaign is that she is trying to be all things to all people.* This proverbial expression is sometimes phrased **be all things to all men**, but today *men* is often replaced by *people* to avoid gender discrimi-

nation. The expression originated in Paul's statement (I Corinthians 9:22): "I am made all things to all men, that I might by all means save some." Today it often appears in a political context, but phrased negatively, as in *He wants to be a good school committee member, but he can't be all things to all people.*

all thumbs Physically awkward, especially with respect to the hands, as in *When it comes to knitting, Mary is all thumbs.* The notion of this idiom derives from a proverb in John Heywood's collection of 1546: "When he should get aught, each finger is a thumb."

all told Added up, in summation, as in *The ferry will hold 80 passengers all told,* or *All told, his proposal makes some good points.* This idiom, first recorded in 1850, uses the verb *tell* in the sense of "count."

all to the good ♦ See TO THE GOOD.

all up Defeated; also, near death. For example, *The home team knew it was all up when their star quarterback was injured,* or *The party lost their way over a week ago and in this sub-zero weather I'm sure it's all up with them.* This idiom uses *up* in the sense of "finished." [Early 1700s] Also see ALL OVER, def. 4.

all very well All right or quite true as far as it goes. For example, *It's all very well for Jane to drop out, but how will we find enough women to make up a team?* This idiom, first recorded in 1853, generally precedes a question beginning with "but," as in the example. Also see WELL AND GOOD.

all well and good ♦ See WELL AND GOOD.

all wet Completely wrong, mistaken, as in *If you think you can beat the system and win at roulette, you're all wet.* The original allusion in this expression in unclear, that is, how moisture or dampness is related to wrongness. [Slang; first half of 1900s]

all wool and a yard wide Genuine, not fake; of excellent quality; also, honorable. For example, *You can count on Ned—he's all wool and a yard wide.* This metaphorical term alludes to a length of highly valued pure-wool cloth that measures exactly a yard (and not an inch less). [Late 1800s]

all work and no play (makes Jack a dull boy) Hard work without time for recreation is not good for one's health, as in *If Harry keeps up that grueling schedule, he's headed for a breakdown—all work and no play isn't healthy.* A proverb included in James Howell's collection of 1659, this phrase remains so familiar that it is often shortened, as in the example.

all year round Throughout the entire year, without regard to seasons. For example, *Thanks to the* *indoor courts we can play tennis all year round.* [Mid-1700s]

alma mater Also, **Alma Mater**. The school or college one attended and, usually, graduated from, as in *During football season I always check to see how my alma mater is doing.* This expression sometimes refers to the institution's official song, as in *I never did learn the words to my college's alma mater.* The term is Latin for "kind mother." [c. 1800]

alone ♦ See GO IT ALONE; LEAVE SOMEONE ALONE; LEAVE WELL ENOUGH ALONE; LET ALONE.

along ♦ In addition to the idioms beginning with ALONG, also see ALL ALONG; ALL ALONG THE LINE; BE ALONG; COME ALONG; FOLLOW ALONG; GET ALONG; GO ALONG; PLAY ALONG; RUN ALONG; STRING ALONG.

along for the ride Participating but not actively, as in *Don't ask me how long this job will take; I'm just along for the ride.* This metaphoric term often is preceded by *just* to emphasize the passive role of the "passenger." [Mid-1900s]

along in years Also, **on in years**. Elderly, old. For example, *Grandma's along in years now and doesn't hear too well,* or *Our dog is not as frisky now that he's getting on in years.* This idiom transfers the length of *along* (and the "onward" of *on*) to the passage of time. [Late 1800s]

alongside of 1. Beside, next to, as in *Tom's canoe lay alongside of mine.* [Late 1700s] **2.** Together with, as in *Her children played alongside of mine all summer long.* [Late 1700s] **3.** Compared to, as in *My car doesn't look like much alongside of Dad's.* [Colloquial; late 1800s]

along the lines of Also, **on the lines of**. Roughly similar or in keeping with. For example, *We told the architect we want a design along the lines of his own house but smaller,* or *Jane asked the caterer for a menu on the lines of the Morgans' wedding reception.* This idiom uses *line* in the sense of "a direction or procedure," a usage dating from the early 1600s.

along with 1. In association with, as in *For his second birthday we sent him a fireman's hat, along with some books,* or *The audience was invited to sing along with the star.* [Early 1700s] **2.** In conjunction with, as in *Along with what I told you before, that's the whole story of what happened.* [Early 1800s] For a synonym, see TOGETHER WITH; also see GO ALONG, def. 2 and 3.

a lot Very many, a large number; also, very much. For example, *A lot of people think the economy is declining,* or *Sad movies always made her cry a lot.* It is sometimes put as **a whole lot** for greater emphasis, as in *I learned a whole lot in his class.* It may also emphasize a comparative indication of amount, as in *We need a whole lot more pizza to*

feed everyone, or *Mary had a lot less nerve than I expected.* [Colloquial; early 1800s]

alpha and omega The beginning and the end, the first and the last, as in *She had to master the alpha and omega of the new computer program before she could even begin.* This idiom and its meaning, based on the first and last letters of the Greek alphabet, appears in the New Testament (Revelation 1:8): "I am Alpha and Omega, the beginning and the ending, saith the Lord," where it is repeated three more times.

also-ran Loser, failure, unsuccessful individual, as in *Jane feared that her candidate, a terrible speaker, would end up as an also-ran,* or *As for getting promotions, Mark counted himself among the also-rans.* This term comes from racing, where it describes a horse that finishes in fourth place or lower or does not finish a race at all. It first appeared in the 1890s in published racing results, and has since been transferred to losers in any kind of competition, and also more broadly to persons who simply don't do well.

ambulance chaser An attorney who seeks to profit from someone's injury or accident; also, an inferior lawyer. For example, *Karen refused to join any law firm that included ambulance chasers.* The practice of suing for damages on behalf of the injured person in exchange for a contingency fee—usually a large percentage of the amount so won—may be older, but this derogatory term began to be used for lawyers who actively sought out individuals injured in accidents who required an ambulance. [Slang; late 1800s]

amends ♦ See MAKE AMENDS.

amiss ♦ See under TAKE THE WRONG WAY.

amount to 1. Add up, develop into, as in *Even though she's careful with her money, her savings don't amount to much,* or *All parents hope that their children will amount to something.* [Mid-1500s] **2.** Be equivalent to, as in *Twenty persons won't amount to a good turnout.* [Late 1300s] Also see AMOUNT TO THE SAME THING.

amount to the same thing Also, **come to the same thing**. Make no difference, be the same, as in *Since it's supposed to rain all day, whether I go outdoors now or later will amount to the same thing,* or *Paying in cash or with a credit card, it comes to the same thing.*

a must A necessity; a requirement. For example, *The Louvre is a must for visitors to Paris,* or *This book is a must for serious students of English.* [Late 1800s]

an apple a day ♦ See APPLE A DAY.

an arm and a leg ♦ See ARM AND A LEG.

ancient history A past event, as in *She's talking about her sea voyage, but that's ancient history,* or *And then there was his divorce, but you don't want to hear ancient history.* This hyperbolic idiom transfers the field of ancient history to a much-repeated tale.

and all Also, **and all that.** Et cetera, and so on; whatever else goes with this statement. For example, *We can't afford eating out, since it's hard to find a babysitter, they charge a lot and all,* or *The contractor will supply the paint and all that.* [First half of 1500s]

and how! Emphatically so. This idiom is an interjection used to stress agreement, as in *Did you enjoy the play?—And how! it was wonderful.* It probably originated as a direct translation of the German *Und wie!* [1920s]

and/or Both or either of two options. For example, *His use of copyrighted material shows that the writer is careless and/or dishonest.* This idiom originated in legal terminology of the mid-1800s.

and so forth Also, **and so on.** And more of the same, also, and others. For example, *At the mall, we shopped, had lunch, shopped some more, and so forth,* or *She planned to buy an entire outfit in blue—dress, shoes, hat, and so on.* The first term dates from the late 1500s, the variant from the early 1700s. Also see AND THE LIKE.

and the like And more of the same, as in *John just loves hot dogs, hamburgers, french fries, and the like.* [c. 1600]

and then some And considerably more, as in *I need all the help I can get and then some,* or *The speaker went on for an hour and then some.* This idiom may originally have come from **and some,** a much older Scottish expression used in the same way. [Early 1900s]

an eye for an eye ♦ See EYE FOR AN EYE.

angels ♦ See FOOLS RUSH IN WHERE ANGELS FEAR TO TREAD; ON THE SIDE OF THE ANGELS.

anger ♦ See MORE IN SORROW THAN IN ANGER.

another ♦ In addition to the idiom beginning with ANOTHER, also see DANCE TO ANOTHER TUNE; HAVE ANOTHER GUESS COMING; HORSE OF A DIFFERENT (ANOTHER) COLOR; ONE GOOD TURN DESERVES ANOTHER; ONE MAN'S MEAT IS ANOTHER MAN'S POISON; ONE WAY OR ANOTHER; SING A DIFFERENT (ANOTHER) TUNE; TOMORROW IS ANOTHER DAY; WEAR ANOTHER HAT.

another county heard from An unexpected person has spoken up or arrived on the scene, as in *Jane's cousin from California decided to contest the will—another county heard from.* This idiom originally alluded to the counting of returns on

election night; it appears in that context in Clifford Odets's play, *Awake and Sing* (1931). However, it may echo the much older phrase, **another Richmond in the field,** alluding to Henry of Richmond (later Henry VII of England), chronicled in Shakespeare's *Richard III* (5:4): "I think there be six Richmonds in the field; five have I slain today." Whatever the origin, today it simply refers to an unforeseen participant or attender.

an ounce of prevention ♦ See OUNCE OF PREVENTION.

answer ♦ In addition to the idioms beginning with ANSWER, also see KNOW ALL THE ANSWERS; TAKE NO FOR AN ANSWER.

answer back ♦ See TALK BACK.

answer for 1. Take responsibility for, take charge of, as in *The new alarm system has to answer for the security of the grounds.* [Late 1200s] 2. Take the blame for, as in *The kids who were caught shoplifting have a lot to answer for.* [c. 1200] 3. To vouch for or sponsor someone, as in *I'll answer for John as a reliable employee.* [Early 1700s]

answer to Explain or justify something to someone, as in *If Mary doesn't help us finish this project, she'll have to answer to the boss.* This expression was at first used mainly for replying to legal charges. [c. A.D. 950]

ante up Pay what is due, contribute; by extension, do one's share. For example, *The trustees were asked to ante up $10,000 each for the new scholarship,* or *Tired of watching Joe sit around while they cleaned up, the roommates told him to ante up or move out.* This expression comes from poker and other betting games, where *to ante* signifies making a bet or contribution to the pot before the cards are dealt. It was being used more loosely by the mid-1800s. Also see RAISE THE ANTE.

ants in one's pants, have 1. Be extremely restless, uneasy, impatient, or anxious, as in *This child just can't sit still; she must have ants in her pants.* This rhyming idiom calls up a vivid image of what might cause one to be jumpy. [Slang; 1920s] 2. Be eager for sexual activity, as in *Bill's got ants in his pants for Rita.* This usage is less common today. [Slang; 1920s]

a number of A collection of persons or things; several. For example, *A number of tours are available,* or *We've visited a number of times.* This idiom often is modified by an adjective giving some idea of quantity, as in *Only a small number are going.* [1300s] Also see ANY NUMBER OF.

any ♦ In addition to the idioms beginning with ANY, also see AT ANY RATE; BY ANY MEANS; GO TO ANY LENGTH; HARDLY ANY; IN ANY CASE; UNDER ANY (NO) CIRCUMSTANCES.

any day 1. No particular time, as in *It doesn't matter when; any day is fine with me.* 2. Also, **any day now**. Quite soon, as in *I might get a call any day,* or *There could be a snowstorm any day now.* 3. Also, **any day of the week**. Every day, as in *I could eat fresh corn any day of the week.* All three senses employ *any* in the sense of "no matter which," a usage dating from A.D. 1000.

any longer 1. With added length, as in *If this skirt were any longer it would sweep the floor.* 2. Still, any more, as in *They don't make this model any longer.* This negative form is often put as NO LONGER.

any number of Many; also, no particular amount of. The meaning here depends on the context. *I can give you any number of reasons for John's absence* means I can offer many reasons. *Any number of subscribers might stay home* means that an unknown number will not attend.

any old No particular, whichever or whatever, as in *Any old brand of detergent suits me.* [Colloquial; mid-1800s]

anyone's guess Something that no one knows for sure, as in *Will it rain next Sunday? That's anyone's guess.* [Mid-1900s] Also see YOUR GUESS IS AS GOOD AS MINE.

any port in a storm Any solution to a difficult situation (is better than none), as in *John's plan isn't ideal, but any port in a storm.* This metaphor was first recorded in 1749.

anything ♦ In addition to the idioms beginning with ANYTHING, also see CAN'T DO ANYTHING WITH; IF ANYTHING; LIKE ANYTHING; NOT ANYTHING LIKE; NOT FOR ANYTHING (IN THE WORLD).

anything but By no means, not at all, as in *He is anything but ambitious for a promotion.* William Wordsworth in his long poem, *The Prelude* (1805–1806), wrote: "Grief call it not, 'twas anything but that."

anything goes Everything is permitted, as in *You're wearing sneakers to the office?—Why not? Anything goes these days.* This idiom began life as **everything goes**, which appeared in George Meredith's novel *The Egoist* (1879). In America *anything* was the preferred word, which gained further currency with Cole Porter's use of the term as the title of his 1934 song and musical comedy, *Anything Goes!*

anything like ♦ See NOT ANYTHING LIKE.

A-one Also, **A-1; A-number-one**. First-class, of the best quality, as in *This is an A-one steak.* The term comes from Lloyd's, the British insurance company, which in its 1775 shipping register designated the condition of a ship's hull by a letter grade (A, B, etc.) and of its cables, anchor, and other equipment by a number grade (1, 2, etc.). By the early 1800s A-1, the best possible grade, was being transferred to anything of superior quality.

apart ♦ In addition to the idiom beginning with APART, also see COME APART; FALL APART; PICK APART; POLES APART; SET APART; TAKE APART; TEAR APART; TELL APART.

apart from Also, **aside from**. Besides, except for. For example, *Apart from jogging occasionally in the park, she gets no exercise,* or *Aside from Sunday dinner with his parents they have not gone out for months.* The first term dates from the early 1600s, the variant from the early 1800s.

appearance ♦ See KEEP UP APPEARANCES; PUT IN AN APPEARANCE.

appear as Act the part of in public, usually alluding to a performance on stage. For example, *She got wonderful reviews when she appeared as Portia.* This idiom uses *appear* in the sense of "to come before the public," a usage dating from the late 1500s.

appetite ♦ See WHET ONE'S APPETITE.

apple ♦ In addition to the idioms beginning with APPLE, also see POLISH THE APPLE; ROTTEN APPLE; UPSET THE APPLECART.

apple a day A small preventive treatment wards off serious problems, as in *He exercises regularly—an apple a day is his motto.* This idiom shortens the proverb **An apple a day keeps the doctor away**, first cited about 1630.

apple of one's eye Special favorite, beloved person or thing, as in *The youngest was the apple of his father's eye.* This term, which rests on the ancients' idea that the eye's pupil is apple-shaped and that eyes are particularly previous, appears in the Bible (Deuteronomy 32:10). [Early 1600s]

apple-pie order Extreme neatness, as in *David keeps his financial records in apple-pie order.* This term is generally believed to be an English corruption of the French *nappes pliées,* "neatly folded linen." [Early 1600s]

apple polisher ♦ See POLISH THE APPLE.

apples and oranges Unlike objects or persons, as in *Assessing the problems of the neighborhood grocery by examining a giant supermarket is comparing apples and oranges.* This metaphor for dissimilarity began as **apples and oysters**, which appeared in John Ray's proverb collection of 1670. It is nearly always accompanied by a warning that one cannot compare such different categories.

appointment ♦ See MAKE AN APPOINTMENT.

approval ♦ See ON APPROVAL; SEAL OF APPROVAL.

apron strings ♦ See TIED TO SOMEONE'S APRON STRINGS.

apropos of Concerning, in connection with, as in *Apropos of keeping in touch, I haven't heard from her in months.* This idiom was a borrowing of the

French à *propos de* ("to the purpose of") in the 17th century. At first it was used without *of* and meant "fitting" or "opportune," as in *Their prompt arrival was very apropos*. By the 1700s it was also being used with *of*, as in the current idiom, for "concerning" or "by way of."

area ◆ See GRAY AREA.

argument ◆ See under PICK A QUARREL.

arm ◆ In addition to the idioms beginning with ARM, also see AT ARM'S LENGTH; BABE IN ARMS; FOREWARNED IS FOREARMED; GIVE ONE'S EYETEETH (RIGHT ARM); LONG ARM OF THE LAW; ONE-ARMED BANDIT; PUT THE ARM ON; SHOT IN THE ARM; TAKE UP ARMS; TALK SOMEONE'S ARM OFF; TWIST SOMEONE'S ARM; UP IN ARMS; WITH ONE ARM TIED BEHIND; WITH OPEN ARMS.

arm and a leg An exorbitant amount of money, as in *These resort hotels charge an arm and a leg for a decent meal*, or *Fixing the car is going to cost an arm and a leg*. According to Eric Partridge, this hyperbolic idiom, which is always used in conjunction with verbs such as "cost," "charge," or "pay," and became widely known from the 1930s on, probably came from the 19th-century American criminal slang phrase, **if it takes a leg** (that is, even at the cost of a leg), to express desperate determination.

armed to the teeth Overly well equipped or prepared, as in *With her elaborate gown and makeup, she was armed to the teeth for her first New York appearance*. The expression *to the teeth* meant "well equipped" in the 14th century, when knights often wore head-to-foot armor. The idiom, however, only gained currency in the mid-1800s, at first still applied to weapons or other military equipment. Today it is used still more figuratively.

arm in arm With one person's arm linked around another's; also, closely allied or intimate, as in *Both couples walked arm in arm around the grounds of the estate*, and *This candidate is arm in arm with the party's liberal wing*. The literal expression dates from the late 1300s, when Chaucer so used it: "They went arm in arm together into the garden" (*Troilus and Cressida*). The figurative usage dates from about 1600. Also see HAND IN HAND.

armor ◆ See CHINK IN ONE'S ARMOR; KNIGHT IN SHINING ARMOR.

around ◆ In addition to the idioms beginning with AROUND, also see BEAT ABOUT (AROUND) THE BUSH; BEEN AROUND; BOSS SOMEONE AROUND; BRING AROUND; CAST ABOUT (AROUND); COME AROUND; ENOUGH TO GO AROUND; EVERY TIME ONE TURNS AROUND; FOOL AROUND; FUCK AROUND; FULL CIRCLE (WHAT GOES AROUND COMES AROUND); GET AROUND; GET AROUND TO; GO AROUND IN CIRCLES; HAND AROUND; HORSE AROUND; KICK AROUND; KID AROUND; KNOCK ABOUT (AROUND); KNOW ONE'S WAY AROUND; MESS AROUND; NOSE ABOUT (AROUND); PAL AROUND WITH; PLAY AROUND; POKE AROUND; PUSH AROUND; RALLY AROUND; ROLL AROUND; RUN AROUND IN CIRCLES; RUN AROUND LIKE A CHICKEN; RUN AROUND WITH; RUN RINGS AROUND; SCREW AROUND; SCROUNGE AROUND; SHOP AROUND; SLEEP AROUND; STICK AROUND; TALK AROUND; TEAR AROUND; THROW ONE'S WEIGHT AROUND; TURN AROUND; TWIST AROUND ONE'S FINGER; UP AND ABOUT (AROUND). Also see under ROUND.

around the bend 1. Around a curve or corner on a road or pathway, as in *Peter's house is just around the bend*. Also see AROUND THE CORNER, def. 1. 2. Also, **round the bend**. Crazy, insane, as in *Throwing out that perfectly good steak? Have you gone round the bend?* [Colloquial; early 1900s]

around the corner 1. On the other side of a street corner, as in *The doctor's office is around the corner from our house*. [First half of 1800s] 2. Nearby, a short distance away, as in *The nearest grocery store is just around the corner*. [Early 1800s] 3. Very soon, imminent, as in *You never know what stroke of luck lies just around the corner*. [First half of 1900s]

arrangements ◆ See MAKE ARRANGEMENTS FOR.

arrears ◆ See IN ARREARS.

arrest ◆ See UNDER ARREST.

arrive at Reach an objective, as in *We arrived at the party right on time*, or *It took Harry only a few minutes to arrive at a solution*. [Early 1500s]

art ◆ See FINE ART; STATE OF THE ART.

as . . . as Also, **so . . . as**. Used with an adjective or adverb to show similarity or equality of one thing with another. The *as . . . as* construction appears in numerous similes, including the idioms *as rich as Croesus*, *as big as life*, *as good as done*. (In this book, when such idioms occur without the first *as*, they can be found under the adjective or adverb, RICH AS . . .; BIG AS . . .; GOOD AS . . .; etc.; those that do not, like *as far as, as long as, as well as*, are found under AS below.) The construction *so . . . as* is often preferred in negative statements like *I couldn't sleep, not so much as a wink*, a usage dating from the 1200s. Also see AS FAR AS.

as all getout To the ultimate degree, as in *She made him furious as all getout*. The American writer Joseph C. Neal had it in his *Character Sketches* (1838): "We look as elegant and as beautiful as get out." Today it always includes *all*. [Colloquial; first half of 1800s]

as a matter of course ◆ See MATTER OF COURSE.

as a matter of fact ◆ See MATTER OF FACT.

as a rule In general, usually, as in *As a rule Irene does not eat meat.* [Mid-1800s]

as a whole All parts or aspects considered, altogether, as in *I like the play as a whole, though the second act seemed somewhat slow.* [Early 1800s] Also see ON THE WHOLE.

as best one can To the ultimate of one's ability, as in *We'll have to get along without it as best we can.* [Mid-1800s] Also see DO ONE'S BEST.

as big as life ◆ See BIG AS LIFE.

as far as Also, **so far as.** To the extent, degree, or amount that. This phrase alone is always used to modify a verb, as in *As far as I can tell it's an authentic antique,* or *It's a good job as far as it goes, but it may need more work,* or *James said that, so far as he can remember, he's never met Mike.* [c. 1300] Also see the subsequent idioms beginning with AS FAR AS.

as far as I can see Also, **so far as I can see.** According to my judgment or understanding, as in *As far as I can see you've got an excellent chance of getting that job.* This idiom was first recorded in 1577.

as far as possible Also, **so far as possible.** To the greatest extent, degree, or amount that is attainable. For example, *I want to drive as far as possible today,* or *It was very complicated, but he promised to explain it so far as possible.*

as far as that goes Also, **so far as that goes; as or so far as that is concerned.** Concerning that, actually, moreover. For example, *As far as that goes, Bill doesn't understand it,* or *My husband has never gotten along with Henry, and so far as that goes, Henry doesn't like him either,* or *As far as that is concerned, Patrice can take care of herself.* Also see AS FOR.

as follows What comes next, usually in the form of a list. For example, *Mary planned her day as follows: returning all phone calls; a department meeting; lunch with her colleagues; library research.* This term is always put in the singular ("follows") even though it applies to numerous items and is frequently followed by a colon. It was first recorded in 1548.

as for Also, **as to.** With regard to, concerning. For example, *As for dessert, I'd better skip it today* and *We are not sure as to how to pay the bill.* A particularly well-known use of this idiom is in Patrick Henry's speech before the Virginia Convention in 1775: "As for me, give me liberty or give me death." Also see AS TO.

as good as ◆ See GOOD AS.

aside ◆ See ALL JOKING ASIDE; LAY ASIDE; SET ASIDE; TAKE ASIDE.

aside from ◆ See under APART FROM.

as if Also, **as though.** As it would be, as in *He decided to accept, as if it really mattered,* or *John scowled as though he were really angry.* The first idiom dates from the late 1500s, the variant from the late 1700s. Also see MAKE AS IF.

as I live and breathe For sure, definitely, as in *As I live and breathe, I've never seen a more beautiful view.* This expression is generally used to emphasize the truth of a statement and has been so used since the mid-1600s, although sometimes it was put simply as **as I live.** However, the complete phrase was also used early on, as in Arthur Murphy's 1756 play *The Apprentice* (2:1): "As I live and breathe, we shall both be taken, for heaven's sake let us make our escape."

as is Just the way it is, with no changes. For example, *We saved a few dollars by buying the floor sample on an as is basis.* This expression is used of goods to be sold that may be slightly worn, damaged, or otherwise less than perfect.

as it were Seemingly, in a way, as in *He was living in a dream world, as it were.* A shortening of "as if it were so," this idiom has been in use since Chaucer's time (he had it in his *Nun's Priest's Tale,* c. 1386). Also see SO TO SPEAK.

ask ◆ In addition to the idioms beginning with ASK, see DON'T ASK; FOR THE ASKING.

askance ◆ See LOOK ASKANCE.

ask a stupid question and you'll get a stupid answer Also, **ask a silly question.** Your query doesn't deserve a proper answer, as in *Am I hungry? ask a stupid question!* One authority believes this idiom is a variant of **ask me no questions and I'll tell you no fibs,** which appeared in Oliver Goldsmith's play *She Stoops to Conquer* (1773) and was frequently repeated thereafter. [Early 1800s]

ask for Also, **ask for it.** To persist in an action despite the likelihood that it will bring trouble on oneself, as in *Speeding as much as he does, he has been asking for a ticket* and *Mary deserved that low grade; in effect, she asked for it by not studying.* [c. 1900] Also see ASK FOR THE MOON.

ask for the moon Make an unreasonable demand, request the unattainable, as in *$1,000 for her birthday? Mary might as well be asking for the moon.* This hyperbolic idiom appeared in the mid-1800s in slightly different form. Charles Dickens had it as **cry for the moon** (in *Bleak House,* 1852) and William Makepeace Thackeray as **wish for the moon** (in *Lovell the Widower,* 1860). Today *ask* is the most common version.

ask out Invite someone to something, such as dinner, the theater, or a date. For example, *We've been asked out to dinner twice this week,* or *Mary felt shy about asking John out.* [Late 1800s]

asleep ◆ In addition to the idiom beginning with ASLEEP, also see FALL ASLEEP.

asleep at the switch Also, **asleep at the wheel.** Inattentive, not doing one's job, as in *At the critical moment the watchman was asleep at the switch and only called the fire department when it was too late.* This term came from 19th-century American railroading, when it was the trainman's duty to switch cars from one track to another by means of manually operated levers. Should he fail to do so, trains could collide. It was later transferred to any lack of alertness. The wheel in the variant is a steering wheel; similarly disastrous results are implied.

as likely as not ♦ See LIKE AS NOT.

as long as 1. For the period of time that, as in *You may keep the book as long as you want,* that is, keep it for whatever time you wish to. [Early 1400s] 2. Also, **so long as.** Since, because, as in *Please pick up some milk as long as you are going to the store,* or *So long as you're here, you might as well stay for dinner.* 3. Also, **so long as; just so.** Provided that, as in *As long as you don't expect it by tomorrow, I'll make the drawing,* or *So long as sales are greater than returns, the company will make a profit,* or *You may have another cookie, just so you don't take the last one.* [Early 1800s]

as luck would have it How things turned out, as it happened, as in *As luck would have it he missed his train,* or *The check arrived in time, as luck would have it.* The *luck* referred to can mean either good fortune or bad. [Late 1500s]

as many 1. The same number of. For example, *He changed jobs four times in as many years* means he changed jobs four times in four years. [c. 1400] 2. **as many as.** A phrase used to qualify the meaning of *many* as a very large number, depending on what follows it. For example, *You can take as many pens as you need.* [Late 1300s] Also see AS . . . AS; AS MUCH AS.

as much The same or virtually the same. For example, *He's resigning? I thought as much* means I thought he was doing just that. [Late 1300s] Also see AS MUCH AS.

as much as 1. The same quantity as. As with AS MANY (def. 2), the meaning of *much* as a large amount here is qualified by what follows. For example, *Please help yourself to as much of the meat as you want* indicates whatever amount you wish. [Late 1100s] 2. Also, **however much, much as.** Even though, no matter how much, as in *As much as I hate to, I must stay home tonight,* or *However much it hurts, you ought to admit you were wrong,* or *Much as Karen would love to see us, she can't get out of her prior commitment.* [Late 1500s] 3. Also, **so much as.** In effect, nearly the same as, as in *Mom as much as told Jane she couldn't go,* or *The clerk so much as accused the customer of shoplifting.* These expressions intensify the meaning of the

verb and indicate that the action is unexpected. [Late 1300s]

as of From, at, or until a given time. For example, *As of five o'clock the store will be closed for inventory,* or *As of last December our meetings have been open to the public,* or *As of now I'm not sure how I'll vote.* This idiom was first used in business but came into more general use. [c. 1900]

as one Also, **as one man** or **woman.** All together, unanimously. For example, *The marchers shouted as one, "We shall overcome!"* or *They replied as one woman, "Of course we'll stay and help."* This term appeared in the Bible (Judges 20:8): "And all the people arose as one man." [Late 1500s] For synonyms, see TO A MAN; WITH ONE VOICE.

as regards ♦ See IN REGARD TO.

ass ♦ In addition to the idiom beginning with ASS, also see BREAK ONE'S ASS; CHEW OUT (ONE'S ASS OFF); COVER ONE'S ASS; DRAG ONE'S ASS; KICK ASS; KICK IN THE PANTS (ASS); KISS ASS; MAKE A FOOL (AN ASS) OF; PAIN IN THE ASS; STICK IT (UP ONE'S ASS); YOU BET YOUR ASS.

ass in a sling, have one's Also, **get one's ass in a sling.** Be (or get) in trouble, in a painfully awkward position, as in *When the news about the slump in sales gets out he'll have his ass in a sling.* Probably originating in the American South, this idiom may refer to so vigorous a kick in the buttocks (for which *ass* is a rude synonym) that the injured person requires a sling of the kind used to support a broken arm. [Vulgar slang; c. 1930]

as soon ♦ See AS SOON AS; JUST AS SOON.

as soon as 1. When, just after, as in *Please call me as soon as dinner is ready,* or *As soon as the sun goes down, the temperature drops dramatically.* [Late 1200s] 2. At the earliest moment that, as in *Telephone me as soon as you can.* It often takes the form **as soon as possible,** meaning at the earliest possible moment, as in *He'll finish the work as soon as possible.* This expression employs *possible* in the sense of "if it can or could be," a usage dating from the late 1600s.

as such 1. In itself, as in *The job as such was easy, but required a lot of time.* [Mid-1600s] 2. In that capacity, as in *In the director's absence the assistants, as such, were in charge.* [c. 1700]

as the crow flies In a straight line, by the shortest route, as in *It's only a mile as the crow flies, but about three miles by this mountain road.* This idiom is based on the fact that crows, very intelligent birds, fly straight to the nearest food supply. [Late 1700s]

as though ♦ See AS IF.

as to 1. According to, as in *They were asked to sort the costumes as to color.* [Mid-1700s] 2. See AS FOR.

astray ◆ See BEST-LAID PLANS GO ASTRAY; GO ASTRAY.

as usual In the normal, habitual, or accustomed way, as in *As usual, he forgot to put away the milk.* This idiom was first recorded in 1716. Also see BUSINESS AS USUAL.

as well 1. In addition, besides, also. For example, *Mary is going to Italy and to France as well,* or *A fine conductor, he plays the violin as well.* [1300s] 2. With an equal or similar result, as in *Since he can't get there in time, he might as well stay at home,* or *It's just as well that you came today, since Harry is here, too.* [1400s]

as well as 1. In as satisfactory or good a way as. For example, *After the operation, she was supposed to walk around as well as she could without limping.* [c. 1400] 2. To the same extent as, as much as. For example, *He is an excellent teacher as well as being a fine musician.* [c. 1440] 3. In addition to, as in *The editors as well as the proofreaders are working overtime.* [c. 1700]

as yet So far, up to now, as in *No one has found a solution as yet.* [Late 1300s]

as you please 1. However you wish, whatever you choose, as in *We can have meat or fish tonight, as you please,* or *Go or don't go — do as you please.* This idiom was introduced about 1500 and inverted what was then the usual order, which was "as it pleases you." 2. Very, extremely, as in *After winning the contract he was smug as you please,* or *She sat there in her new dress, as pretty as you please.* [First half of 1900s]

at about At approximately, as in *We'll start at about nine.* This phrase, most often used with respect to time (as *at about four o'clock*), is sometimes criticized for being redundant. Although one of the two words sometimes can be omitted without changing the meaning — for example, *About four o'clock is when most guests will arrive* — in other instances both are needed, as in *This stock is now selling at about its original offering price.* [Early 1800s]

at a discount At a lower than usual price; also, held in low esteem. For example, *I'm holding off on buying a computer until I can get one at a discount,* or *Liberals are at a discount in the present administration.* The first usage, mainly found in business and commerce, dates from about 1700. The figurative usage is about a century newer.

at all 1. In any way or manner, as in *Is she able to sing at all?* 2. To any extent, as in *Was she at all surprised?* 3. For any reason, as in *Why bother at all?* 4. In the slightest degree, under any circumstances, as in *She simply refused to walk at all.* This construction often occurs in the negative, as in *He was not at all frightened.* All four senses of this phrase date from the mid-1300s.

at all costs Also, **at any cost** or **price**. Regardless of the expense or effort involved, by any means. For example, *Ann told the doctor to preserve her mother's sight at all costs,* or *It seems the company plans to develop the product at any cost,* or *I'm determined to get vacation time at any price.* [Mid-1800s]

at all times Continuously, without interruption, as in *At the airport Mary was warned to keep her carry-on bag in sight at all times.*

at a loss 1. Below cost, as in *The store was doing so badly that it was selling merchandise at a loss.* 2. Puzzled, perplexed, in a state of uncertainty, as in *When his letters were returned unopened, John was at a loss as to what to do next.* This usage was originally applied to hounds who had lost the scent or track of their prey. [Mid-1600s] 3. **at a loss for words.** Unable or uncertain as to what to say. For example, *Father's tirade left us all at a loss for words.* [Late 1600s]

at a low ebb At a low point, in a state of decline or depression. For example, *The current recession has put our business at a low ebb.* This idiom transfers the low point of a tide to a decline in human affairs. [Mid-1600s]

at any cost Also, **at any price.** ◆ See AT ALL COSTS.

at any rate In any event, whatever the case may be; also, at least. For example, *At any rate, I promise to be there even if I'm a little late,* or *It may not pay well, but at any rate it's a job.* [Early 1600s] Also see IN ANY CASE.

at a premium At a higher price than usual owing to scarcity; also, considered more valuable, held in high esteem. For example, *Since that article came out, the firm's stock has been selling at a premium* and *Space is at a premium in most stores.* This idiom uses *premium* in the sense of "bounty" or "bonus." [Mid-1800s] Also see PUT A PREMIUM ON.

at arm's length At a distance, avoiding intimacy or familiarity, as in *Bill hated seeing his colleagues outside the office, preferring to keep all of them at arm's length,* or *She was friendly only when he was safely at arm's length.* Now often used with the verb *keep,* this term for distancing oneself from a person, organization, or issue originated as *at arm's end* but developed its current form by the mid-1600s.

at a sitting At one time, during one period. For example, *The cruise ship could feed about 500 passengers at a sitting,* or *We read the entire poem at a sitting.* Since the word *sitting* implies just that posture, the term means "during a period when one is seated and engaged in a single continuous activity."

at a stretch Also, **at one stretch.** At one time, during one period. For example, *Working quickly, she hoped to finish all the drawings at a stretch.* In contrast to the nearly synonymous AT A SITTING, this idiom, first recorded in 1774, does not imply being seated while engaging in a single continuous activity. Rather, it transfers the meaning of *stretch* as "a continuous length" to "a continuous time period."

at a time ♦ See AT ONE TIME, def. 1.

at a word In immediate response, at an instant. For example, *At a word from the captain they lined up in order.* [c. 1300]

at bat Taking one's turn. For example, *At this conference, with so many interruptions, it's hard to tell which speaker is at bat*, or *I was nervous while waiting to testify, but once at bat I felt better.* This idiom, from baseball, was already being transferred to other enterprises by the 1880s. Also see ON DECK.

at bay Cornered, in distress, as in *Angry bystanders chased the thief into an alley and held him at bay until the police arrived.* This idiom originally came from hunting, where it describes an animal that has been driven back and now faces pursuing hounds. Its use for other situations dates from the late 1500s.

at best Under the most favorable circumstances, as in *At best we'll be just one week behind schedule*, or *Cleaning out the attic is a tedious job at best.* This idiom, formerly also put as **at the best**, today is most often used in situations that are actually far from ideal, as in the examples above. [First half of 1300s] For an antonym, see AT WORST.

at bottom Fundamentally, basically; also, in reality. For example, *He may speak somewhat bluntly, but at bottom he's always honest.* Charles Dickens used this idiom in *Nicholas Nickleby* (1838): "He's a good pony at bottom." [Early 1700s]

at close quarters Crowded, in a confined space, as in *We could use a lot more room; this tiny office puts us at close quarters.* This idiom makes figurative use of *quarters* in the sense of "military lodgings" but originated in 18th-century naval warfare. When the enemy boarded a ship, the crew would retreat behind wooden barriers erected for this purpose and would continue to fire through loopholes. They thus were very near the enemy, fighting **in close quarters.** [c. 1800]

at close range Very nearby, as in *At close range, the rock band was unbearably loud.* Derived from shooting—*range* denotes the distance that a missile or projectile can be made to travel—this expression soon came to mean anything in close proximity.

at cross purposes With aims or goals that conflict or interfere with one another, as in *I'm afraid the two departments are working at cross purposes.* This idiom, first recorded in 1688, may have begun as a 17th-century parlor game called "cross-purposes," in which a series of subjects (or questions) were divided from their explanations (or answers) and

distributed around the room. Players then created absurdities by combining a subject taken from one person with an explanation taken from another.

at death's door On the point of dying, very ill, as in *Whenever she had a bad cold she acted as though she were at death's door.* The association of death with an entry way was first made in English in the late 1300s, and the phrase itself dates from the mid-1500s. Today it is often used as an exaggeration of ill health.

at each other's throats Arguing or fighting. For example, *It was a very dramatic trial, with the prosecutor and the defense attorney constantly at each other's throats.* This idiom, with its vivid image of two persons trying to strangle each other, is often applied to less physical forms of disagreement.

at ease 1. Also, **at one's ease.** Comfortable, relaxed, unembarrassed, as in *I always feel at ease in my grandmother's house.* The related idiom **put at ease** means "make comfortable, reassure," as in *I was worried that the letter would not arrive in time, but the postmaster put me at ease.* [1300s] For the antonym, see ILL AT EASE. 2. In a relaxed position in military ranks. The phrase is often used as a command for troops standing at attention to relax, as in *At ease, squadron.* The command **stand at ease** is slightly different. A British military dictionary of 1802 described it as standing with the right foot drawn back about six inches and one's weight put on it. An American version is to stand with one's feet slightly apart and the hands clasped behind one's back.

at every turn Everywhere; also, continually, at every moment. For example, *He found trash strewn about at every turn*, or *Life holds surprises at every turn.* The *turn* here does not signify change of direction but change of circumstances, and the phrase generally is something of an exaggeration. [Late 1500s]

at face value, take Accept from its outward appearance, as in *You can't always take a manufacturer's advertisements at face value; they're bound to exaggerate.* Literally this idiom has referred to the monetary value printed on a bank note, stock certificate, bond, or other financial instrument since the 1870s. The figurative usage is from the late 1800s.

at fault Responsible for a mistake, trouble, or failure; deserving blame. For example, *At least three cars were involved in the accident, so it was hard to determine which driver was at fault*, or *He kept missing the target and wondered if the sight on his new rifle was at fault.* In Britain this usage was formerly considered incorrect but is now acceptable; in America it has been widespread since the mid-1800s. Also see IN THE WRONG.

at first Initially, at the start, as in *At first the berries were green, but when they ripened they turned bright red.* [Second half of 1500s]

at first blush Also, **at first glance** or **sight.** When first seen. For example, *At first blush we thought it was an elegant restaurant, but it soon became obvious that it was hardly the place for a special dinner,* or *At first glance the contract looked just fine.* All three phrases date from the 1300s. The noun *blush* is used with the obsolete meaning "glimpse" or "momentary view" and in this idiom has nothing to do with showing embarrassment. Also see LOVE AT FIRST SIGHT.

at first hand Directly from the origin, without intervention or intermediary. For example, *I prefer to hear his criticism at first hand, rather than having it passed on by my boss.* This phrase uses *hand* in the sense of "person" (coming directly from one person). [First half of 1700s] Also see AT SECOND HAND.

at full tilt ▸ See FULL TILT.

at gunpoint Also, **at knifepoint.** Under coercion, as in *I'm going to hold him at gunpoint for that raise he promised me last year.* Both these phrases were at first used literally and later also figuratively. [Mid-1900s]

at half-mast Halfway up or down, as in *The church bells tolled off and on all day and the flags were at half-mast.* This term refers to placing a flag halfway up a ship's mast or flagpole, a practice used as a mark of respect for a person who has died or, at sea, as a distress signal. Occasionally the term is transferred to other objects, as in *Tom's pants were at half-mast as he raced around the playground,* or *The puppy's tail was at half-mast.* [First half of 1600s]

at hand 1. Also, **close** or **near at hand.** Within easy reach, nearby, as in *I like to keep my tools close at hand.* [1300s] 2. Also, **on hand.** Nearby in time, soon, as in *The day of judgment is at hand,* or *A change of administration is on hand.* Also see ON HAND.

at heart 1. Fundamentally, basically, as in *He's a good fellow at heart.* It was first recorded in Alexander Pope's *Epistle to a Lady* (1735): "But every Woman is at heart a Rake." 2. In one's deepest feelings, as a great concern, as in *The governor has the party's best interests at heart.* [Early 1700s]

at home 1. In one's own residence, town, or country. For example, *Mary was not at home when I called,* or *Tourists in a foreign country often behave more rudely than they do at home.* This idiom was first recorded in a ninth-century treatise. 2. Ready to receive a visitor, as in *We are always at home to our neighbor's children.* This usage gave

rise to the noun **at-home,** meaning a reception to which guests are invited on a specific day at specific hours (also see OPEN HOUSE). [c. 1600] 3. Also, **at home with.** Comfortable and familiar, as in *Mary always makes us feel at home,* or *I've never been at home with his style of management.* [Early 1500s] Also see AT EASE, def. 1. 4. Also, **at home with.** Proficient, well-versed in, as in *Young John is so much at home with numbers that he may well become a mathematician,* or *Chris is really at home in French.* [Late 1700s] 5. In team sports, playing on one's own field or in one's own town. For example, *The Red Sox always do better at home than they do at away games.*

at issue 1. In question, under discussion; also, to be decided. For example, *Who will pay for the refreshments was the point at issue.* [Early 1800s] 2. In conflict, in disagreement, as in *Physicians are still at issue over the appropriate use of hormone therapy.* This usage, from legal terminology, was defined by Sir William Blackstone (*Commentaries on the Laws of England,* 1768), who said that when a point is affirmed by one side and denied by the other, "they are then said to be *at issue.*"

at it Vigorously pursuing an activity, especially a fight, but also sex or some other activity. For example, *Whenever they play bridge they really go at it* (fight), or *The new job keeps Tom at it day and night* (works hard), or *In the spring the dogs are always at it* (sex). Shakespeare used this seemingly modern idiom for "fighting" in *Troilus and Cressida* (5:3): "They are at it, hark!" [Late 1500s]

at large 1. Free, unconfined, especially not confined in prison, as in *To our distress, the housebreakers were still at large.* [1300s] 2. At length, fully; also, as a whole, in general. For example, *The chairman talked at large about the company's plans for the coming year,* or, as Shakespeare wrote in *Love's Labour's Lost* (1:1): "So to the laws *at large* I write my name" (that is, I uphold the laws in general). This usage is somewhat less common. [1400s] 3. Elected to represent an entire group of voters rather than those in a particular district or other segment—for example, *alderman at large,* representing all the wards of a city instead of just one, or *delegate at large to a labor union convention.* [Mid-1700s]

at last Also, **at long last.** After a long time, finally, as in *At last the speeches ended and dinner was served,* or *Harry's got his degree at long last.* The first term dates from about 1200, the variant from the early 1500s. Also see AT LENGTH, def. 2.

at least 1. Also, **at the least.** According to the lowest possible assessment, no less than. For example, *At least a dozen more chairs are needed,* or *The job* *will take four hours at the least.* [c. 1050] **2.** Anyway, anyhow, as in *At least you got there on time*, or *The children enjoyed the dessert at least.* [c. 1050] For synonyms, see AT ANY RATE; IN ANY CASE.

at leisure 1. Slowly, without haste, as in the famous 16th-century proverb, *Marry in haste and repent at leisure.* **2.** Unemployed, having free time, as in *I'm not looking for another job right now; I want to be at leisure for at least a few months.* This usage has become less common but is still heard. [1300s] Also see AT ONE'S LEISURE.

at length 1. In full, extensively. For example, *The preacher went on at length about sin*, or *I have read at length about these cameras.* [c. 1500] **2.** After a long time, finally, as in *At length the procession ended.* [Early 1500s] Also see IN THE LONG RUN.

at liberty Free, not obligated; also, not occupied. For example, *I am not at liberty to tell you the whole story*, or *"I ... washed when there was a basin at liberty"* (Charlotte Brontë, *Jane Eyre*, 1847). This idiom is often used in a negative context, as in the first example. [First half of 1800s]

at loggerheads Engaged in a quarrel or dispute, as in *The two families were always at loggerheads, making it difficult to celebrate holidays together.* This term may have come from some earlier meaning of *loggerhead*, referring either to a blockhead or stupid person, or to a long-handled iron poker with a bulbshaped end that was heated in the fire and used to melt pitch. If it was the latter, it may have been alluded to as a weapon. [Late 1600s] For a synonym, see AT ODDS.

at long last ◆ See under AT LAST.

at loose ends In an unsettled or uncertain situation. For example, *This whole visit has left me feeling restless, constantly at loose ends*, or *Jane couldn't find a job this year and so is at loose ends for the summer.* [Mid-1800s]

at most Also, **at the most** or **at the outside.** At the largest amount, the furthest limit; also, in the most extreme case. For example, *She'll be finished in two weeks at the most*, or *It'll take two weeks at the outside*, or *At most the chef uses a tiny bit of pepper.* The terms with *most* date from the 1300s; *at the outside* from the mid-1800s. Also see AT BEST.

at odds In disagreement, opposed. For example, *It is only natural for the young and old to be at odds over money matters.* This idiom uses *odds* in the sense of "a condition of being unequal or different," and transfers it to a difference of opinion, or quarrel. [Late 1500s]

at once 1. At the same time, as in *We can't all fit into the boat at once.* [First half of 1200s] Also

see AT ONE TIME, def. 1. **2.** Immediately, as in *Mother told the children to come inside at once.* [First half of 1500s]

at one In agreement, in harmony, as in *John and Pat were at one on every subject except her cat, which made him sneeze*, or *Springtime always makes me feel at one with nature.* [1300s]

at one blow ◆ See AT ONE STROKE.

at one fell swoop ◆ See ONE FELL SWOOP.

at one's ◆ In addition to idioms beginning with AT ONE'S, also see idioms beginning with AT SOMEONE'S.

at one's best In one's most excellent state or condition. For example, *The photographer tried hard to show the bride at her best.* [1500s]

at one's convenience Also, **at one's earliest convenience.** Whenever one wishes; also, as soon as one can. For example, *Pick up the car any time, at your convenience*, or *We need that drawing very soon, so please finish it at your earliest convenience.* The use of *convenience* in the sense of "ease" or "absence of trouble" dates from about 1700.

at one's door Also, **on one's doorstep.** Very nearby, as in *The bus stop was practically on our doorstep*, or *The Mexican currency crisis is literally at our door.* [Early 1900s] Also see LAY AT SOMEONE'S DOOR.

at one's ease ◆ See AT EASE, def. 1.

at one's fingertips Ready at hand, immediately available. This idiom is used both literally, as in *This new dashboard design keeps all the important controls at the driver's fingertips*, and figuratively, as in *Tom was so familiar with the proposal that he had all the details at his fingertips.* [Second half of 1800s]

at one's leisure Whenever one wishes, at one's convenience, as in *At your leisure, please look over this manuscript and give me your comments.* [1400s] Also see AT LEISURE.

at one stroke Also, **at one blow; at a stroke** or **blow; in one stroke** or **blow.** At the same time, with one forceful or quick action. For example, *I managed to please both buyer and seller at one stroke.* The first term is the older version, so used by Chaucer; *at one blow* was used by Shakespeare.

at one's wit's end Also, **at wits' end.** Completely puzzled and perplexed, not knowing what to do. For example, *I've tried every possible source without success, and now I'm at my wit's end.* This idiom, which uses *wit* in the sense of "mental faculties," appeared in *Piers Ploughman* (c. 1377).

at one's word ◆ See TAKE ONE AT ONE'S WORD.

at one time 1. Simultaneously, at the same time, as in *All the boys jumped into the pool at one time.* For synonyms, see AT ONCE, def. 1; AT THE SAME TIME, def. 1. **2.** Formerly, in the past, as in *At one time very few houses in town were on the market.*

at one time or another On various separate occasions. For example, *At one time or another I've considered replacing the furnace, but so far I haven't done so.* [Early 1600s]

at pains, be at Also, **take pains.** Make a special effort or take extra trouble to do something. For example, *Bob was at pains to make a good first impression and wore his best suit,* or *Mary took pains to make sure her speech would interest the audience.* [First half of 1500s]

at peace In a state of agreement or friendliness, not at strife or war; also, in a state of inner harmony or quiet. For example, *Whatever their disagreements, Mexico and Belize have remained at peace,* or *In his last illness he seemed finally to be at peace with himself.* [1300s]

at present Also, **at the present time.** Now, as in *I've not enough cash at present to lend you any,* or *At present the house is still occupied.* This slightly longer way of saying "at this time" formerly was even longer—**at this present** or **at that present**—denoting a more specific time. [Mid-1600s] Also see AT THIS POINT.

at random Without order or fixed purpose, haphazardly, as in *Jackson Pollock dropped paints on canvas seemingly at random.* Originally this phrase meant "very speedily" and "heedlessly." Shakespeare had the present usage in *1 Henry VI* (5:3): "He talks at random; sure the man is mad." [Late 1500s]

at rest **1.** In a state of inactivity or repose, either physical or mental. For example, *The doctor's clear explanation put her mind at rest.* Chaucer used this idiom in *Troilus and Cressida* (c. 1374): "I mine heart set at rest upon this point." Also see LAY AT REST. **2.** Dead, as in *His soul is now at rest with his forebears.* This usage, employing *rest* to refer to death's repose, is less common today. [1300s]

at risk **1.** In danger, as in *Their house's location on the San Andreas Fault puts them at risk in the next major earthquake.* [c. 1900] **2.** Legally responsible to pay for loss or damage, as in *If he can't keep up with the insurance premiums, he is at risk for any liability claims on the property.* [Late 1700s]

at sea **1.** Aboard a ship, on the ocean, as in *Within a few hours the ship would be out at sea.* During World War II a famous American newscaster addressed his radio broadcasts to listeners everywhere, including "all the ships at sea." [1300s] **2.** Also, **all at sea.** Perplexed, bewildered, as in *She was all at sea in these new surroundings.* This idiom transfers the condition of a vessel that has lost its bearings to the human mind. Charles

Dickens used it in *Little Dorrit* (1855): "Mrs. Tickit . . . was so plainly at sea on this part of the case." [Second half of 1700s]

at second hand Received from some source other than the original. For example, *I learned of Mary's divorce at second hand.* This phrase may be applied to information or to previously owned merchandise. [1400s] Also see AT FIRST HAND.

at sight **1.** See ON SIGHT. **2.** On presentation, especially a draft for payment. For example, *These bills are payable at sight.* This usage replaced *on sight* in the late 1600s.

at sixes and sevens Confused, disorganized, disorderly, as in *We've just moved in, and the office is still at sixes and sevens,* or *The new college admissions tests were poorly explained, leaving the students at sixes and sevens.* This ancient term is thought to come from a game of dice in which throwing a six or seven had a particular significance. The name of the game has been lost, but most likely betting on such a throw was very risky, denoting disorder and confusion. [Late 1300s]

at someone's ♦ In addition to idioms beginning with AT SOMEONE'S, also see idioms beginning with AT ONE'S.

at someone's beck and call Required to comply with someone's requests or commands, as in *The boss expects the entire staff to be at his beck and call.* The noun *beck,* now obsolete except in this idiom, meant "a gesture or signal of command, such as a nod or hand movement," whereas *call* signifies "a vocal summons." Also see DANCE ATTENDANCE ON.

at someone's elbow Immediately beside someone, close by, as in *The apprentice was constantly at the master's elbow.* Why this idiom focuses on the elbow rather than the arm, shoulder, or some other body part is not known. Moreover, it can mean either that someone is so nearby as to constitute a nuisance or in order to readily provide assistance. Either can be meant in the example above. [Mid-1500s]

at someone's feet, be Also, **sit at someone's feet.** Be enchanted or fascinated by someone, as in *Dozens of boys are at her feet,* or *Bill sat at his mentor's feet for nearly three years, but he gradually became disillusioned and left the university.* [Early 1700s] For a quite different meaning, see UNDER ONE'S FEET.

at someone's heels Also, **on someone's heels.** Immediately behind, in close pursuit. This idiom is used both literally, as in *Jean's dog was always at her heels,* and figuratively, as in *Although his company dominated the technology, he always felt that his competitors were on his heels.* This idiom appeared in the 14th-century romance *Sir Gawain and the Green Knight*. The expression is sometimes intensified as **hard on someone's heels** or **hot on someone's heels**. Also see ON THE HEELS OF.

at someone's mercy ♦ See AT THE MERCY OF.

at someone's request On being asked to do something, as in *At my request they'll move us to another room*, or *I'm speaking at his request*. [1300s] Also see BY REQUEST.

at someone's service Ready to help someone, at someone's disposal, as in *The tour guide said he was at our service for the rest of the afternoon*. [Second half of 1600s]

at stake At risk to be won or lost, as in *We have a great deal at stake in this transaction*. This phrase uses *stake* in the sense of something that is wagered. Shakespeare used it in *Troilus and Cressida* (3:3): "I see my reputation is at stake." [Late 1500s]

at sword's point Also, **at swords' points**. Antagonistic, hostile, as in *Father and son were at swords' points*. Dating from the days when swords were used to settle quarrels, the idiom today generally signifies only a bitter quarrel.

attach ♦ See NO STRINGS ATTACHED.

attendance ♦ See DANCE ATTENDANCE ON.

attention ♦ See PAY ATTENTION.

at that 1. In addition, besides, as in *The seats were good, and quite cheap at that*. [First half of 1800s] 2. In spite of, nevertheless, as in *Although I had to wait a long time for delivery, it was worth it at that*. [Mid-1800s] 3. As it stands, without further changes, as in *She wasn't happy with her grade in the course but decided to leave it at that*. [Late 1800s]

at that point Also, **at that point in time**. Then, as in *At that point we had finished the first batch of cookies and begun the second*. This phrase refers to a particular time when an event or circumstance occurred, as opposed to "now" (see AT THIS POINT). [Second half of 1900s]

at that rate ♦ See AT THIS RATE.

at that stage ♦ See AT THIS STAGE.

at the crossroads Also, **at a crossroads**. At a point of decision or a critical juncture, as in *Because of the proposed merger, the company is standing at the crossroads*. This phrase, based on the importance accorded to the intersection of two roads since ancient times, has also been used figuratively just about as long. In the 1500s Erasmus quoted from the Greek Theognis's *Elegies* (c. 600 B.C.): "I stand at the crossroads."

at the drop of a hat Immediately, without delay, as in *We were ready to pack our bags and go on va-*cation at the drop of a hat. This phrase probably alludes to signaling the start of a race or other contest by dropping a hat. [Late 1800s]

at the end of one's rope ♦ See END OF ONE'S ROPE.

at the expense of Also, **at one's expense**. 1. Paid for by someone, as in *The hotel bill for the sales force is at the expense of the company*. [Mid-1600s] 2. To the detriment or injury of a person or thing, as in *We can't speed up production at the expense of quality*, or *The laughter was all at Tom's expense*. [Late 1600s]

at the hand of Also, **at the hands of**. Performed by or at the agency of, as in *The slaves suffered greatly at the hands of their new masters*. This idiom was first recorded about 1035. Also see AT HAND.

at the helm In charge, in command, as in *With Charles at the helm, the company is bound to prosper*. This phrase transfers the idea of steering a ship to directing other enterprises. [Early 1500s] Also see the synonym AT THE WHEEL.

at the last minute At the latest possible moment or opportunity. For example, *Jim couldn't get a reservation because he had called at the last minute*. Also see AT THE LATEST; ELEVENTH HOUR.

at the latest No later than. For example, *We have to be in New York by Monday at the latest*. This idiom was first recorded in 1884.

at the least ♦ See under AT LEAST.

at the mercy of 1. Also, **at someone's mercy**. Subject to the power of, helpless against, as in *The captured rebels were at the mercy of the army commander*. [Late 1500s] 2. Without any protection against, as in *On top of Mount Washington we were at the mercy of the elements*. [Late 1600s]

at the most ♦ See under AT MOST.

at the outset Also, **from the outset**. At the start, from the start. For example, *He wanted to explain his position from the outset, but there wasn't time*, or *At the outset the problem seemed simple, but then it became quite complicated*. The noun *outset* is rarely heard today except in these phrases. [Mid-1700s]

at the outside ♦ See under AT MOST.

at the point of ♦ See ON THE POINT OF.

at the ready Available for immediate use, as in *Umbrellas at the ready, we were prepared to brave the storm*. This idiom was originally a military term in which *the ready* denoted the position of a firearm prepared to be raised and aimed or fired. [First half of 1800s]

at the same time 1. Simultaneously, as in *We were all scheduled to leave at the same time*. This idiom was first recorded in 1526. For synonyms, see AT ONCE, def. 1; AT ONE TIME, def. 1. 2. Nevertheless, however, as in *Mary agreed with her mother's criticism, but at the same time she wanted to defend her husband's views.* [c. 1700]

at the top of one's lungs Also, **at the top of one's voice.** With an extremely loud voice. For example, *The babies in the nursery all were crying at the top of their lungs.* The noun *top* here refers to the greatest degree of volume (that is, loudest) rather than high pitch, a usage dating from the mid-1500s.

at the wheel In command, in control. For example, *Ann hated being told what to do; she wanted to be at the wheel by herself.* The analogy here is to the steering wheel of an automobile or other vehicle, or the helm of a vessel. For a synonym, see AT THE HELM.

at the worst ♦ See AT WORST.

at this point Also, **at this point in time** or **at this juncture** or **at this moment.** Now, as in *At this point in time we don't need a new refrigerator.* Even wordier synonyms for "now" than AT PRESENT, all four phrases imply that what is the case now may not always have been so or may not remain so. For example, *At this point she is by far the best athlete on the circuit* implies that she may not have been the best in the past or may not be in the future. Similarly, *Buying a new car seems prudent at this juncture* indicates that this purchase may not have been wise in the past and may not be at some future time. Also see AT THAT POINT.

at this rate Also, **at that rate.** 1. Progressing at this (or that) speed, as in *At this rate we'll never finish in time.* [Mid-1600s] 2. Under these circumstances, in that case. For example, *At this rate they'll never settle their differences.* [Late 1700s]

at this stage Also, **at this** or **that stage of the game.** At this (that) step, phase, or position in a process or activity, as in *I'm not sure if you can help at this stage, but perhaps you can pitch in later,* or *I don't need an assistant at this stage of the game.* The variant uses *game* in the sense of "a particular process or activity." [Early 1800s]

at times Occasionally, sometimes, as in *Away from home for the first time, Mary was homesick at times.* [Early 1500s] Also see AT ONE TIME OR ANOTHER.

at variance Differing, discrepant; also, in a state of conflict. For example, *John's and Mary's answers are at variance* means that their answers do not agree, or *John was at variance with his in-laws* means that he strongly disagreed or quarreled with them. [Early 1500s]

at war Engaged in armed conflict; also, in a state of disagreement. This term may be used literally, usually of nations or smaller groups engaged in armed hostilities, as well as hyperbolically, describing a mild disagreement as "war," and figuratively, for an inner conflict. For example, *The*

Greeks and Turks have been at war for many years (literally); *The two families were at war about the bill for the wedding reception* (hyperbolic); and, as Shakespeare put it in *Measure for Measure* (2:2): "I am at war 'twixt will and will not" (inner conflict of indecision). [Late 1300s]

at will Freely, as one pleases, as in *The grounds are open to the public and one can wander about at will,* or *With this thermostat you can adjust the room temperature at will.* [1300s]

at work 1. Engaged in a job or other activity, as in *The contractor is hard at work on the new building,* or *The little boy was fascinated to see the washing machine at work.* [Early 1600s] 2. At one's office or other place of business, as in *Is it all right if I telephone you at work?* [Late 1800s]

at worst Also, **at the worst.** 1. In the least favorable circumstance; under the most difficult conditions. For example, *Convicted of taking a bribe, the official believed that at worst he would be sentenced to a few months in prison.* [1500s] 2. In the least favorable view or supposition, as in *No harm done; at the worst I'll copy the tax return again.* Chaucer used this sense in *Troilus and Cressida:* "For at the worst, it may yet short our way." [Late 1300s] For the antonym, see AT BEST.

augur well for Also, **augur ill for; bode well** or **ill for.** Have good (or bad) expectations for someone or something. For example, *John's recovery from surgery augurs well for the team* and *The Republican victory in the Congressional elections bodes ill for affirmative action.* The verb *augur* is derived from the Latin word for "soothsayer" (predictor of the future), a meaning perpetuated in this phrase and so used since the late 1700s. The verb *bode* comes from the Old English *bodian,* meaning "to announce or foretell," and is rarely heard today except in this idiom, which dates from about 1700.

avail ♦ In addition to the idiom beginning with AVAIL, also see TO NO AVAIL.

avail oneself of 1. Take advantage of, benefit by. For example, *To get a better mortgage, he availed himself of the employee credit union.* [Late 1500s] 2. Use, employ, as in *I'll avail myself of the first cab to come along.* [Mid-1800s]

avoid like the plague Evade or elude at any cost, shun. For example, *Since Bob was taken into police custody, his friends have been avoiding him and his family like the plague.* This seemingly modern expression dates from the Latin of the early Middle Ages, when Saint Jerome (A.D. 345–420) wrote, "Avoid, as you would the plague, a clergyman who is also a man of business." The plague, a deadly infectious disease in his day, has been largely wiped out, but the term remains current.

away ◆ See BACK AWAY; BANG AWAY; BLOW AWAY; BREAK AWAY; BY FAR (AND AWAY); CARRY AWAY; CART OFF (AWAY); CAST AWAY; CLEAR OUT (AWAY); DIE AWAY; DO AWAY WITH; DRAW AWAY; EAT AWAY; EXPLAIN AWAY; FADE OUT (AWAY); FALL AWAY; FIRE AWAY; FOOL AWAY; FRITTER AWAY; GET AWAY; GET AWAY WITH; GIVE AWAY; GO AWAY; HAMMER AWAY; LAY ASIDE (AWAY); MAKE AWAY WITH; OUT AND AWAY; PASS AWAY; PEG AWAY AT; PISS AWAY; PLUG AWAY AT; PULL AWAY; PUT AWAY; RIGHT AWAY; RUN AWAY; RUN AWAY WITH; SALT AWAY; SEND AWAY; SHY AWAY FROM; SLINK AWAY; SLIP OUT (AWAY); SOCK AWAY; SPIRIT AWAY; SQUARE AWAY; SQUIRREL AWAY; STOW AWAY; TAKE AWAY FROM; TAKE ONE'S BREATH AWAY; TEAR AWAY; THROW AWAY; TUCK AWAY; TURN AWAY; WALK AWAY FROM; WALK OFF (AWAY) WITH; WASTE AWAY; WEAR OFF (AWAY); WHALE AWAY; WHEN THE CAT'S AWAY; WHILE AWAY.

a while back Also, **a while ago.** Some time in the past, as in *I ran into Barbara a while back but didn't get her new address,* or *John wrote me a while ago about his new baby.* This term uses *a while* in the sense of "a short or moderate time," a usage dating from about 1300.

AWOL ◆ See ABSENT WITHOUT LEAVE.

ax ◆ In addition to the idiom beginning with AX, also see GET THE AX.

ax to grind A selfish aim or motive, as in *The article criticized the new software, but the author had an ax to grind, as its manufacturer had fired his son.* This frequently used idiom comes from a story by Charles Miner, published in 1811, about a boy who was flattered into turning the grindstone for a man sharpening his ax. He worked hard until the school bell rang, whereupon the man, instead of thanking the boy, began to scold him for being late and told him to hurry to school. "Having an ax to grind" then came into figurative use for having a personal motive for some action. [Mid-1800s]

b

babe in arms An infant, as in *She's been a family friend since I was a babe in arms.* Although the word "babe" for baby has been used since the 1300s, this phrase describing a child too young to walk (and hence having to be carried) dates only from about 1900.

babe in the woods An innocent or very naive person who is apt to be duped or victimized, as in *She was a babe in the woods where the stock market was concerned.* The term originated in a popular ballad of 1595, "The Children in the Wood,"

about two young orphans who are abandoned in a forest and die.

baby ◆ See THROW OUT THE BABY WITH THE BATH WATER.

back ◆ In addition to the idioms beginning with BACK, also see A WHILE BACK; BEHIND SOMEONE'S BACK; BREAK ONE'S BACK; BREAK THE BACK OF; CALL BACK; CHOKE BACK; COME BACK; CUT BACK; DIE BACK; DOUBLE BACK; DRAW BACK; DROP BACK; EYES IN THE BACK OF ONE'S HEAD; FALL BACK; FALL BACK ON; FALL OVER (BACKWARD); FLAT ON ONE'S BACK; FROM WAY BACK; GET BACK; GET ONE'S BACK UP; GIVE THE SHIRT OFF ONE'S BACK; GO BACK ON ONE'S WORD; HANG BACK; HARK(EN) BACK; HOLD BACK; IN ONE'S OWN BACKYARD; KICK BACK; KNOCK BACK; KNOW LIKE A BOOK (THE BACK OF ONE'S HAND); LEFT-HANDED (BACKHANDED) COMPLIMENT; LIKE WATER OFF A DUCK'S BACK; LOOK BACK; MONKEY ON ONE'S BACK; OFF SOMEONE'S BACK; PAT ON THE BACK; PAY BACK IN SOMEONE'S OWN COIN; PIN SOMEONE'S EARS BACK; PLAY BACK; PLOW BACK; PULL BACK; PUT ONE'S BACK IN IT; PUT ONE'S BACK UP; ROLL BACK; SCRATCH SOMEONE'S BACK; SEE THE BACK OF; SET BACK; SET BACK ON ONE'S HEELS; SET ONE BACK; SET THE CLOCK BACK; SIT BACK; SLAP ON THE BACK; SNAP BACK; STAB IN THE BACK; TAKE ABACK; TAKE A BACK SEAT; TAKE BACK; TALK BACK; THINK BACK; THROW BACK; TURN BACK; TURN ONE'S BACK ON; WHEN SOMEONE'S BACK IS TURNED; WITH ONE ARM TIED BEHIND ONE'S BACK; YOU SCRATCH MY BACK AND I'LL SCRATCH YOURS.

back against the wall ◆ See BACK TO THE WALL.

back alley ◆ See under BACK STREET.

back and fill Vacillate, be undecided, as in *This measure will never be passed if the town meeting continues to back and fill.* This term comes from sailing ships, where it signifies alternately backing and filling the sails, a method used when the wind is running against a ship in a narrow channel. The sail is hauled *back* against the wind and braced so that the tide or current carries the ship forward against the wind. Then the sail must be swung around and *filled,* to keep the ship on course. The term's figurative use for indecisiveness dates from the mid-1800s.

back and forth Also, **backward(s) and forward(s).** To and fro, moving in one direction and then the opposite and so making no progress in either. For example, *The clock pendulum swung back and forth.* The term is also used figuratively, as in *The lawyers argued the point backwards and forwards for an entire week.* [c. 1600]

back away 1. Walk backward, as in *He cautiously backed away from the fire.* 2. Gradually retreat, withdraw, as in *Since he couldn't convince his colleagues, he's backing away from his original idea.*

Both usages employ the verb *back* in the sense of "retreat," dating from the late 1400s. Also see BACK DOWN; BACK OUT.

back burner, on a In a position of low priority. For example, *I haven't forgotten his letter; I've just put it on a back burner for now.* This term alludes to a cook's putting items requiring less attention at the back of the stove. [Colloquial; mid-1900s] Also see FRONT BURNER.

back door 1. An entry at the rear of a building, as in *Deliveries are supposed to be made at the back door only.* [First half of 1500s] 2. A clandestine, unauthorized, or illegal way of operating. For example, *Salesmen are constantly trying to push their products by offering special gifts through the back door.* This term alludes to the fact that the back door cannot be seen from the front. [Late 1500s]

back down 1. Reverse one's upward course, descend. For example, *When she saw the wasps' nest on the roof, she hastily backed down the ladder.* This literal usage usually refers to something one has climbed, such as a ladder or mountain. [Mid-1800s] 2. Also, **back off**. Retreat or yield. For example, *As the watchdog began to snarl the letter carrier backed off,* or *You have a good point; now don't back down when you present it to the board.* [First half of 1900s] Also see BACK AWAY, def. 2.

back in circulation ♦ See IN CIRCULATION.

back in harness ♦ See IN HARNESS.

back number Dated, out of style. For example, *That hat is really a back number;* or *The game has changed so fast that a player who returns to the circuit after several years' absence usually finds he or she is a back number.* This term originally referred to back issues of periodicals, which are no longer newsworthy. [Late 1800s]

back of Also, **at the back of; in back of**. Behind; also, supporting. For example, *The special brands were stored back of the counter;* or "Franklin stood back of me in everything I wanted to do" (Eleanor Roosevelt, quoted by Catherine Drinker Bowen, *Atlantic Monthly*, March 1970). The first term, dating from the late 1600s, was long criticized as an undesirable colloquialism but today is generally considered acceptable. The variants, **at the back of**, from about 1400, and **in back of**, from the early 1900s, also can be used both literally and figuratively and could be substituted for *back of* in either example. Also see BACK OF BEYOND.

back of beyond Extremely remote. For example, *John's about to move to some tiny island, truly back of beyond.* This term, used as a humorous exaggeration, relies on the meaning of *beyond* (or *the beyond*) as "a distant place, beyond human experience." [Early 1800s]

back off 1. See BACK DOWN, def. 2. 2. Relent, abandon one's stand. For example, *The chairman wanted to sell one division but later backed off.* [Mid-1900s]

back of one's hand Rejection or contempt, as in *Unimpressed with him, she gave the back of her hand to his suggestion.* This phrase is usually the object of a verb such as *give* or *show*. [Second half of 1700s] **Back of the hand** similarly means "an insult" in the term **back-handed compliment** (see under LEFT-HANDED COMPLIMENT) but has a quite different meaning in **know like the back of one's hand** (see under KNOW LIKE A BOOK).

back of one's mind The remote part of one's mind or memory, as in *With the idea of quitting in the back of his mind, he turned down the next assignment.* [c. 1900]

back on one's feet ♦ See ON ONE'S FEET.

back order An item not currently in stock but to be sold or delivered when it becomes available, as in *We don't have the shoes in white, but we can make them a back order.* The verb **back-order** means "to obtain such an item," as in *The furniture store is going to back-order the sofa for us.*

back out 1. Move or retreat backwards without turning; same as BACK AWAY, def. 1. 2. Also, **back out of something**. Withdraw from a situation, or break an agreement or engagement. For example, *After the announcement appeared in the papers, Mary found it doubly difficult to back out of her engagement to Todd.* [Early 1800s] Also see GO BACK ON.

backseat driver A passenger who gives unwanted and/or unneeded directions to the driver; also, a person who interferes in affairs without having knowledge, responsibility, or authority for doing so. For example, *Aunt Mary drives us all crazy with her instructions; she's an incurable backseat driver.* This term originated in the United States in the 1920s, when it was first used for a passenger legitimately directing a chauffeur, and it was quickly transferred to figurative use. Also see the synonym MONDAY-MORNING QUARTERBACK and the antonym TAKE A BACK SEAT.

back street Also, **back alley**. A less prominent or inferior location; also, a scene of clandestine or illegal dealings. For example, *The highway department is very slow to clear snow from the back streets,* or *Before they were made legal, abortions were often performed in back alleys.* Although *back street* literally means "one away from the main or business area of a town or city," this term, from the early 1600s, became associated with underhanded dealings, and *back alley,* from the mid-1800s, is always used in this sense.

back the wrong horse Also, **bet on the wrong horse.** Guess wrongly or misjudge a future outcome, as in *Jones garnered only a few hundred votes; we obviously backed the wrong horse,* or *Counting on the price of IBM to rise sharply was betting on the wrong horse.* Transferred from wagering money on a horse that fails to win the race, a usage dating from the late 1600s, this term is widely applied to elections and other situations of uncertain outcome.

back to back 1. With backs close together or touching, as in *In the first and second rows of the bus, the seats were back to back, an unusual arrangement.* This term also can be applied to persons who stand facing in opposite directions and with their backs touching. [Mid-1800s] 2. Consecutively, one after another, as in *I'm exhausted; I had three meetings back to back.* [Mid-1900s]

back to basics Back to fundamental principles, as in *The plans are much too elaborate; to stay in our budget we have to get back to basics.* At first this term was used mainly for schooling that stresses proficiency in reading, writing, and mathematics (also see THREE R'S), but it quickly was transferred to other areas. [1970s]

back to the drawing board Also, **back to square one.** Back to the beginning because the current attempt was unsuccessful, as in *When the town refused to fund our music program, we had to go back to the drawing board,* or *I've assembled this wrong side up, so it's back to square one.* The first term originated during World War II, most likely from the caption of a cartoon by Peter Arno in *The New Yorker* magazine. It pictured a man who held a set of blueprints and was watching an airplane explode. The variant is thought to come from a board game or street game where an unlucky throw of dice or a marker sends the player back to the beginning of the course. It was popularized by British sportscasters in the 1930s, when the printed radio program included a grid with numbered squares to help listeners follow the description of a soccer game.

back to the salt mines Resume work, usually with some reluctance, as in *With my slavedriver of a boss, even on Saturdays it's back to the salt mines.* This term alludes to the Russian practice of punishing prisoners by sending them to work in the salt mines of Siberia. Today the term is only used ironically. [Late 1800s] Also see KEEP ONE'S NOSE TO THE GRINDSTONE.

back to the wall Also, **back against the wall.** In a hard-pressed situation; also, without any way of escape. For example, *In the closing few minutes, our team had its back to the wall but continued to fight gallantly,* or *The bank has him with his back to the wall; he'll have to pay up now.* This term was used originally for a military force that is making a last stand. [First half of 1500s]

back up 1. Move or drive a vehicle backward, as in *He told her to back up into the garage.* [First half of 1800s] 2. Bring or come to a standstill, as in *The water had backed up in the drains,* or *The accident had backed up traffic for miles.* [First half of 1800s] 3. Support or strengthen, as in *The photos were backed up with heavy cardboard so they couldn't be bent,* or *I'll back up that statement of yours.* [Second half of 1700s] 4. Duplicate a file or program so that the original is not lost. For example, *Every computer manual warns you to back up your work frequently in case of a power outage or computer failure.* [Second half of 1900s]

backward ♦ In addition to the idiom beginning with BACKWARD, also see BEND OVER BACKWARD; FALL OVER (BACKWARDS); KNOW LIKE A BOOK (BACKWARDS AND FORWARDS).

backward and forward Also, **backwards and forwards.** 1. Same as BACK AND FORTH. 2. Thoroughly, completely, as in *He read the speech over and over, until he knew it backwards and forwards.* [Late 1500s]

back water Reverse a position, take back a statement, or otherwise retreat, as in *We're sure that the senator will back water on raising taxes.* This term literally refers to a vessel that moves backward in the water because its oars, paddles, or paddlewheel are reversed. It soon was transferred to other kinds of reversal. [Second half of 1700s]

bacon ♦ See BRING HOME THE BACON; SAVE ONE'S BACON.

bad ♦ In addition to the idioms beginning with BAD, also see COME TO AN END (BAD END); FEEL BAD; FROM BAD TO WORSE; GET OFF ON THE WRONG FOOT (TO A BAD START); GIVE A BAD NAME; GIVE BAD MARKS TO; GO BAD; IN A BAD MOOD; IN A BAD WAY; IN BAD FAITH; IN BAD WITH SOMEONE; IN SOMEONE'S BAD GRACES; LEVEL A BAD TASTE IN ONE'S MOUTH; MAKE THE BEST OF (A BAD BARGAIN); NOT A BAD SORT; NOT BAD; POOR (BAD) TASTE; RUN OF (BAD) LUCK; TOO BAD; TURN UP (LIKE A BAD PENNY); WITH BAD GRACE.

bad blood Anger or hostility between persons or groups, as in *There's been bad blood between the two families for years.* This term is based on the old association with blood and emotion, particularly anger. Versions such as *ill blood* preceded it; Charles Lamb was among the first to use the idiom in its current form in an 1823 essay.

bad egg An individual who turns out to be rotten, as in *You can't trust him—he's simply a bad egg.*

Although *egg* had been used for various kinds of person (young, good, bad) since Shakespeare's day, this transfer of a seemingly wholesome food that, when opened, turns out to be rotten took place only in the mid-1800s. An early definition appeared in *The Atheneum* of 1864: "A bad egg . . . a fellow who had not proved to be as good as his promise." In contrast, the schoolyard saying **Last one in is a rotten egg** does not have any special significance other than as a way of urging others to join an activity, jump in the water, or the like. Also see GOOD EGG.

badger game An extortion scheme in which a man is lured into a compromising position, usually by a woman, and then is "discovered" and blackmailed by her associate. For example, *The prosecutor accused the couple of playing the badger game.* The term alludes to the much older sport of badger-baiting, in which a live badger was trapped and put inside a box and dogs were set on it to drag it out. The woman in the scheme is the "badger." [Late 1800s]

bad hair day A day when one's appearance, especially one's hair, does not look attractive. For example, *What have I done to upset Martha? Nothing, she's just having a bad hair day.* Originating as a humorous statement, this term was soon broadened to mean simply having a bad day, that is, a day when everything seems to go wrong. [Late 1980s] Also see NOT ONE'S DAY.

bad luck ♦ See under RUN OF LUCK.

badly off ♦ See BAD OFF.

bad mouth Disparage or criticize unduly, malign, as in *Why do you constantly bad mouth your colleagues?* This term is believed to be of African origin, where the phrase *bad mouth* signifies a curse or evil spell. [1930s]

bad name ♦ See GIVE A BAD NAME.

bad news 1. An unwelcome thing or person, trouble. For example, *That fire was bad news; we were underinsured for the damage,* or *No one wants Mary on the board—she's bad news.* This term transfers literal bad news—the report of an unhappy recent event—to an unwanted or undesirable individual or circumstance. [Slang; 1920s] 2. The amount charged for something, as in *Waiter, bring our check—I want to see the bad news.* [Slang; 1920s]

bad off Also, **badly off**. In unfortunate circumstances, poor. For example, *Her husband's death left her bad off,* or *She had her pension and wasn't too badly off.* The first term is colloquial. [Early 1800s] Also see WELL OFF.

bad sort, a An unpleasant, mean person, as in *We cautioned Bill about his friend, who was clearly a bad sort.* The antonym is a **good sort**, a pleasant,

kind person, as in *She's a good sort, always helping her neighbors.* The latter is stronger than **not a bad sort**, as in *He seems ill-tempered now and then, but he's not a bad sort.* All three terms use *a sort* in the sense of "kind of person." [Second half of 1800s]

bad taste ♦ See LEAVE A BAD TASTE; POOR TASTE.

bad time ♦ See under HAVE A GOOD TIME.

bad trip A frightening or otherwise very unpleasant experience, as in *Given the poor turnout, her book tour was a bad trip.* The term comes from drug slang of the mid-1900s, where it meant experiencing hallucinations, pain, or other terrible effects from taking a drug, especially LSD. It was then extended to any extremely unpleasant experience.

bag ♦ In addition to the idioms beginning with BAG, also see BROWN BAGGER; GRAB BAG; IN THE BAG; LEAVE HOLDING THE BAG; LET THE CAT OUT OF THE BAG; MIXED BAG.

bag and baggage All of one's belongings, especially with reference to departing with them; completely, totally. For example, *The day be quit his job, John walked out, bag and baggage.* Originating in the 1400s, this phrase at first meant an army's property, and to **march off bag and baggage** meant that the departing army was not leaving anything behind for the enemy's use. By the late 1500s, it had been transferred to other belongings.

bag it 1. Pack things in a bag, as in *"Please bag it," the customer said to the checkout clerk.* This usage mainly describes packing groceries or other purchases into a bag. [Colloquial; late 1500s] 2. Abandon something or someone, quit. For example, *The class is not very good, so I've decided to bag it.* This idiom first became widespread among students. [Colloquial; 1960s] 3. Be quiet, stop doing something, go away. For example, *I've heard enough about that, so just bag it!* [Slang; 1960s]

bag of tricks One's stock of resources and stratagems, as in *Mom can fix anything—you never know what she will pull out of her bag of tricks.* Alluding to the magician's bag of equipment for performing magic tricks, this term was first recorded in 1694, when Jean de La Fontaine, in one of his fables, has a fox carry a *sac des ruses* ("bag of tricks").

bail ♦ In addition to the idiom beginning with BAIL, also see MAKE BAIL; OUT ON BAIL; SKIP BAIL.

bail out 1. Empty water out of a boat, usually by dipping with a bucket or other container. For example, *We had to keep bailing out water from this leaky canoe.* [Early 1600s] 2. Rescue someone in an emergency, especially a financial crisis of some kind, as in *They were counting on an inheritance to bail them out.* [Colloquial; 1900s] 3. Jump out of an airplane, using a parachute. For example,

When the second engine sputtered, the pilot decided to bail out. [c. 1930] **4.** Give up on something, abandon a responsibility, as in *The company was not doing well, so John decided to bail out while he could still find another job.* [Second half of 1900s] **5.** See MAKE BAIL.

bait ♦ In addition to the idiom beginning with BAIT, also see FISH OR CUT BAIT; JUMP AT (THE BAIT); RISE TO THE BAIT.

bait and switch A deceptive commercial practice in which customers are induced to visit a store by an advertised sale item and then are told that it is out of stock or that it is far inferior to some more expensive item. For example, *I won't buy a car from this outfit; they're notorious for their bait and switch tactics.* The verb *to bait* has meant to supply a hook or trap with a morsel of food so as to attract a fish or animal since about 1300; the verb *to switch* has meant to change, alter, or transfer from one thing to another since the 1890s. The pairing of the two, however, dates only from the 1920s, although the practice is surely much older. It is called **switch-selling** in Britain.

baker's dozen Thirteen, as in *The new bagel store always gives you a baker's dozen.* The origins of this term are disputed. One theory is that in times when bread was sold by weight, bakers who short-weighted their customers were heavily fined, and for safety's sake they would sell thirteen loaves for the price of twelve. Another theory is that dealers purchasing bread from bakers were allowed by law to receive thirteen loaves for the price of twelve, the thirteenth representing their cut of profit. [Late 1500s]

balance ♦ In addition to the idiom beginning with BALANCE, also see CHECKS AND BALANCES; HANG IN THE BALANCE; OFF BALANCE; ON BALANCE; REDRESS THE BALANCE; STRIKE A BALANCE; TIP THE BALANCE.

balance the books **1.** Add up the debits and credits of an account and determine the difference; also, bring the two sides into equilibrium. For example, *It's Joe's job to balance the books each quarter.* [Late 1500s] **2.** Settle an account by paying what is due, as in *We can't balance the books till your last check clears.* [Early 1700s]

ball ♦ In addition to the idioms beginning with BALL, also see BEHIND THE EIGHT BALL; BREAK ONE'S BALLS; BY THE BALLS; CARRY THE BALL; CORN BALL; CRYSTAL BALL; DROP THE BALL; EYEBALL TO EYEBALL; GET THE BALL ROLLING; HAVE A BALL; HAVE ONE'S EYE ON THE BALL; HAVE SOMEONE BY THE BALLS; ON THE BALL; PLAY BALL; PUT IN MOTHBALLS; SNOWBALL'S CHANCE IN HELL; THAT'S HOW THE BALL BOUNCES; WHOLE BALL OF WAX.

ball and chain A burden and restraint, as in *Karen regarded her job as a ball and chain, but she needed*

the money. The term, dating from the early 1800s, alludes to chaining a heavy iron ball to a prisoner's leg. Later it was transferred to other kinds of restraining burden.

ballgame ♦ See WHOLE NEW BALLGAME.

ballistic ♦ See GO BALLISTIC.

ball of fire A dynamic, energetic, and successful individual, as in *I hope Pat joins us; she's a real ball of fire.* [Slang; early 1800s]

balloon ♦ In addition to the idiom beginning with BALLOON, also see GO OVER (LIKE A LEAD BALLOON); TRIAL BALLOON.

balloon goes up, the The undertaking begins, as in *He's going to announce his candidacy for mayor—the balloon goes up on Monday.* This expression comes from World War I, when British artillery sent up a balloon to notify gunners to open fire, this visual signal being more reliable than courier or telephone. It was soon transferred to signal other kinds of beginning. [1915]

ballot ♦ See STUFF THE BALLOT BOX.

ballpark figure An acceptable, roughly accurate approximation, as in *I know you can't tell me the exact cost; just give me a ballpark figure.* This term alludes to a baseball field, which is always an enclosed space. The expression is basically an extension of the somewhat earlier **in the ballpark,** meaning within a reasonable range, and **out of the ballpark,** beyond a reasonable range. [Slang; late 1960s]

ball's in your court, the It's your responsibility now; it's up to you. For example, *I've done all I can; now the ball's in your court.* This term comes from tennis, where it means it is the opponent's turn to serve or return the ball, and has been transferred to other activities. [Second half of 1900s]

ball up **1.** Roll something into a ball, as in *She loved to knit and was always balling up her yarn.* [Early 1800s] **2.** Confuse or bungle, as in *Jane got all balled up at the beginning of her speech,* or *Henry really balled up that exam.* This term may come from the fact that when a horse is driven over soft or partly thawed snow, the snow becomes packed into icy balls on its hoofs, making it stumble. Another theory is that it alludes to the vulgar term *balls* for testicles. [First half of 1900s]

banana ♦ In addition to the idiom beginning with BANANA, also see DRIVE SOMEONE CRAZY (BANANAS); GO BANANAS; TOP BANANA.

banana oil Nonsense, exaggerated flattery, as in *I should be on television? Cut out the banana oil!* The precise analogy in this idiom is not clear, unless it is to the fact that banana oil, a paint solvent and artificial flavoring agent, has no relation to the fruit other than that it smells like it. Possibly it is a variation on **snake oil**, a term for quack medicine that was extended to mean nonsense. [1920s]

band ♦ See ON THE BANDWAGON; TO BEAT THE BAND.

bang ♦ In addition to the idioms beginning with BANG, also see BEAT (BANG) ONE'S HEAD AGAINST THE WALL; GET A BANG OUT OF; GO OVER BIG (WITH A BANG); MORE BANG FOR THE BUCK.

bang away 1. Strike repeatedly, as in *Mary is always banging away on the piano,* or *The doorbell must be broken; see who is banging away at the door.* [First half of 1800s] Also see BANG OUT. 2. Go ahead; begin or continue. This slangy imperative usually calls merely for energetic action, as in *You can start without me — bang away.* Also see GO TO (IT), def. 3.

bang for the buck ♦ See MORE BANG FOR THE BUCK.

bang into 1. Crash noisily into, collide with, as in *A clumsy fellow, Bill was always banging into furniture.* [Early 1700s] 2. Strike heavily so as to drive in; also, persuade. For example, *I've been banging nails into the siding all day,* or *I can't seem to bang it into his head that time is precious.* The literal usage dates from the mid-1500s, the figurative from the second half of the 1800s. Also see BUMP INTO.

bang one's head against ♦ See BEAT ONE'S HEAD AGAINST.

bang out Produce something loudly or hastily by striking, either a musical instrument or a typing keyboard. For example, *The accompanist banged out the melody on the piano,* or *John planned to bang out his presentation in a couple of hours.* [Late 1800s]

bang up Damage, injure, as in *Banging up the car a second time will make Dad very unhappy,* or *Mother fell down the stairs and was all banged up.* The verb *to bang* alone had this meaning from the 1500s on, *up* being added in the late 1800s. In the early 1800s it gave rise to the colloquial adjective **bang-up,** for excellent or very successful, as in *David did a bang-up job baking the birthday cake.*

bank ♦ In addition to the idiom beginning with BANK, also see BREAK THE BANK; LAUGH ALL THE WAY TO THE BANK.

bank on Rely on, count on. For example, *You can bank on Molly's caterer to do a good job.* This expression alludes to *bank* as a reliable storage place for money. [Late 1800s]

baptism of fire A severe ordeal or test, especially an initial one, as in *This audition would be Robert's baptism of fire.* This term transfers the original religious rite of baptism, whereby holiness is imparted, to various kinds of ordeal. At first it signified the death of martyrs at the stake, and in 19th-century France it was used for a soldier's first experience of combat. Currently it is used more loosely for any difficult first encounter.

bar ♦ In addition to the idiom beginning with BAR, also see BEHIND BARS; NO HOLDS BARRED.

bare bones The mere essentials or plain, unadorned framework of something, as in *This outline gives just the bare bones of the story; details will come later.* This phrase transfers the naked skeleton of a body to figurative use. [c. 1900]

barefaced lie A shameless falsehood. For example, *Bill could tell a barefaced lie with a straight face.* The adjective *barefaced* means "beardless," and one theory is that in the 1500s this condition was considered brazen in all but the youngest males. By the late 1600s *barefaced* also meant "brazen" or "bold," the meaning alluded to in this phrase.

bare hands, with one's With one's hands but without tools, weapons, or other implements. For example, *Jean assembled the new stove with her bare hands.* This phrase, first recorded in 1604, extends the literal meaning, "with uncovered (that is, without gloves) and hence unprotected hands," to "unaided by implements."

bare necessities Just sufficient resources, with nothing to spare. For example, *The room was furnished with just the bare necessities — bed, table, chair.* This idiom uses *bare* in the sense of "mere, and nothing else," a usage dating from about 1200.

bare one's soul Reveal one's most private thoughts and feelings. For example, *Teenagers rarely bare their souls to their parents; they prefer their peers.* This figurative use of the verb *bare,* which literally means "make bare" or "uncover," dates from A.D. 1000.

bare one's teeth Also, **show one's teeth.** Indicate hostility and readiness to fight, as in *His refusal to accept my offer made it clear I'd have to bare my teeth,* or *In this instance, calling in a lawyer is showing one's teeth.* This figurative term transfers the snarl of a dog to human anger. It first was recorded as *show one's teeth* in 1615.

bargain ♦ In addition to the idiom beginning with BARGAIN, also see DRIVE A BARGAIN; INTO THE BARGAIN; MAKE THE BEST OF IT (A BAD BARGAIN); MORE THAN ONE BARGAINED FOR; STRIKE A BARGAIN.

bargain for 1. Also, **bargain over.** Negotiate about something, usually a price. For example, *In open-air markets it is standard practice to bargain for the best price.* [Late 1300s] 2. Also, **bargain on.** Expect, be prepared for, as in *In planning the picnic, we hadn't bargained for bad weather,* or *I hadn't bargained on John's coming along.* [c. 1800] For a synonym, see COUNT ON.

barge in Enter rudely or abruptly, intrude. For example, *Her mother never knocks but just barges in.* The term is also put as **barge into** or **barge in on** to mean interrupt, as in *Who asked you to barge into our conversation?* These phrases use *to barge* in the sense of "bump into" or "knock against," which may allude to the propensity of these clumsy vessels to collide with other craft. [Late 1800s]

bark ♦ In addition to the idioms beginning with BARK, also see TALK ONE'S ARM OFF (THE BARK OFF A TREE).

bark is worse than one's bite, one's A person seems more hostile or aggressive than is the case, as in *Dad sounds very grouchy in the morning, but his bark's worse than his bite.* This phrase was a proverb by the mid-1600s.

bark up the wrong tree Waste one's efforts by pursuing the wrong thing or path, as in *If you think I can come up with more money, you're barking up the wrong tree.* This term comes from the nocturnal pursuit of raccoon-hunting with the aid of dogs. Occasionally a raccoon fools the dogs, which crowd around a tree, barking loudly, not realizing their quarry has taken a different route. [Early 1800s]

barn ♦ See CAN'T HIT THE BROAD SIDE OF A BARN; LOCK THE BARN DOOR AFTER THE HORSE IS STOLEN.

bar none Also, **barring none**. Without exception, as in *This is the best book I've read all year, bar none.* [Mid-1800s]

barrel ♦ See BOTH BARRELS; BOTTOM OF THE BARREL; CASH ON THE BARRELHEAD; LIKE SHOOTING FISH IN A BARREL; LOCK, STOCK, AND BARREL; MORE FUN THAN A BARREL OF MONKEYS; OVER A BARREL; PORK BARREL; ROTTEN APPLE (SPOILS THE BARREL).

base ♦ See GET TO FIRST BASE; OFF BASE; TOUCH BASE.

basis ♦ See ON A FIRST-NAME BASIS.

basket ♦ In addition to the idiom beginning with BASKET, also see PUT ALL ONE'S EGGS IN ONE BASKET.

basket case A person or thing too impaired to function. For example, *The stress of moving twice in one year left her a basket case,* or *The republics of the former Soviet Union are economic basket cases.* Originating in World War I for a soldier who had lost all four limbs in combat and consequently had to be carried in a litter ("basket"), this term was then transferred to an emotionally or mentally unstable person and later to anything that failed to function. [Slang; second half of 1900s]

bat ♦ In addition to the idioms beginning with BAT, also see AT BAT; BLIND AS A BAT; BATS IN ONE'S BELFRY; GO TO BAT FOR; LIKE A BAT OUT OF HELL; RIGHT OFF THE BAT.

bat an eye ♦ See WITHOUT BATTING AN EYE.

bat around 1. Hit something around, often with a baseball bat or other object, as in *We batted the tennis ball around this morning.* Originating in baseball, this term came to be applied to more violent action as well, as in *Jerry left after being batted around by his father.* [Slang; first half of 1900s] 2. Discuss or debate something, as in *We batted the various plans around for at least an hour before we came to a decision.* This usage transfers batting a ball to a back-and-forth exchange of ideas. [Slang; late 1800s] 3. Drift aimlessly, roam, as in *After graduating, they batted around Europe for a year.* [Slang; c. 1900]

bath ♦ See TAKE A BATH; THROW OUT THE BABY WITH THE BATH WATER.

bat one thousand Have a perfect record, as in *In meeting deadlines, she's batting one thousand.* The term comes from baseball statistics, where it signifies getting a hit for every turn at bat. It was transferred to other activities in the 1920s.

bats in one's belfry, have Be crazy or at least very eccentric, as in *Sally thought her aunt's belief in ghosts indicated she had bats in her belfry.* This term in effect likens the bat's seemingly erratic flight in the dark to ideas flying around in a person's head. [Early 1900s]

batten down the hatches Prepare for trouble, as in *Here comes the boss—batten down the hatches.* This term originated in the navy, where it signified preparing for a storm by fastening down canvas over doorways and hatches (openings) with strips of wood called *battens.* [Late 1800s]

bat the breeze ♦ See SHOOT THE BREEZE.

battle ♦ See HALF THE BATTLE; LOSING BATTLE; PITCHED BATTLE.

bawl out 1. Call out loudly, announce, as in *Some of the players were quite hard of hearing, so the rector bawled out the bingo numbers.* [1500s] 2. Scold or reprimand loudly, as in *Her teacher was always bawling out the class for not paying attention.* [c. 1900]

bay ♦ See AT BAY.

be ♦ In addition to the idioms beginning with BE, also see LET BE.

be a credit to ♦ See under DO CREDIT TO.

bead ♦ See DRAW A BEAD ON.

be-all and end-all, the The most important element or purpose, as in *Buying a house became the be-all and end-all for the newlyweds.* Shakespeare used this idiom in *Macbeth* (1:6), where Macbeth muses that "this blow might be the be-all and the end-all" for his replacing Duncan as king. [Late 1500s]

be along Will come, will arrive, as in *John said he'd be along in a few minutes,* or *The doctor's report will be along by the end of the week.* This phrase always indicates a future event. [Colloquial; early 1800s]

beam ♦ See BROAD IN THE BEAM; OFF THE BEAM.

bean ♦ See FULL OF BEANS; NOT HAVE A BEAN; NOT KNOW BEANS; NOT WORTH A DIME (BEAN); SPILL THE BEANS; TOUCH BREAK (BEANS).

bear ♦ In addition to the idioms beginning with BEAR, also see BRING TO BEAR; CROSS AS A BEAR; CROSS TO BEAR; GRIN AND BEAR IT; LOADED FOR BEAR.

bear a grudge Also, **have** or **hold a grudge**. Maintain resentment or anger against someone for a past offense. For example, *They held up my claim for months, but I won't bear a grudge against them,* or *His grandfather was always one to hold a grudge.* [c. 1600]

bear down 1. Press or weigh down on someone or something. For example, *This pen doesn't write unless you bear down hard on it.* [Late 1600s] 2. Try hard, intensify one's efforts, as in *If you'll just bear down, you'll pass the test.* 3. Move forward in a pressing or threatening way, as in *The ferry bore down on our little skiff.* This usage was originally nautical. [Early 1700s]

beard the lion Confront a danger, take a risk, as in *I went straight to my boss, bearding the lion.* This term was originally a Latin proverb based on a Bible story (I Samuel 17:35) about the shepherd David, who pursued a lion that had stolen a lamb, caught it by its beard, and killed it. By Shakespeare's time it was being used figuratively, as it is today. Sometimes the term is amplified to **beard the lion in his den,** which may combine the allusion with another Bible story, that of Daniel being shut in a lions' den for the night (Daniel 6:16–24).

bear fruit Yield results, have a favorable outcome, as in *This new idea of his is bound to bear fruit.* This metaphoric term, first recorded in 1879, transfers the production of fruit by a tree or plant to other kinds of useful yield.

bearings ♦ See GET ONE'S BEARINGS.

bear in mind Also, **keep in mind.** Remember, as in *Bear in mind that I can't walk as fast as you,* or *Keep your constituency in mind when you speak.* [First half of 1500s]

bear one's cross ♦ See CROSS TO BEAR.

bear out Back up or confirm, as in *The results bear out what he predicted,* or *His story bears me out exactly.* [Late 1400s]

bear the brunt Put up with the worst of some bad circumstance, as in *It was the secretary who had to bear the brunt of the doctor's anger.* This idiom uses *brunt* in the sense of "the main force of an enemy's attack," which was sustained by the front lines of the defenders. [Second half of 1700s]

bear up Endure, face a hardship, as in *Jane found it hard to bear up under the strain of her father's illness.* This term is also used as an imperative, as in *Bear up—the trip's almost over.* [c. 1600]

bear with Put up with, make allowance for, as in *He'll just have to bear with them until they decide.* Nicholas Udall used this term in *Ralph Roister Doister* (c. 1553): "The heart of a man should more honour win by bearing with a woman." It may also be used as an imperative, as in *Bear with me—I'm getting to the point.*

beat ♦ In addition to the idioms beginning with BEAT, also see DEAD BEAT; HEART MISSES A BEAT; IF YOU CAN'T BEAT THEM, JOIN THEM; MARCH TO A DIFFERENT BEAT; MISS A BEAT; OFF THE BEATEN TRACK; POUND THE PAVEMENT (A BEAT); TO BEAT THE BAND.

beat a dead horse Also, **flog a dead horse.** Try to revive interest in a hopeless issue. For example, *Politicians who favor the old single-tax idea are beating a dead horse.* From the 1600s on the term *dead horse* was used figuratively to mean "something of no current value," specifically an advance in pay or other debt that had to be worked ("flogged") off. [Second half of 1800s]

beat all Surpass anything, especially in a strange or amazing way, as in *Adam and his cousin Eve eloped—doesn't that beat all!* This phrase appears to have replaced **beat the Dutch.** It is often used in a negative construction, as in the example. [Slang; first half of 1800s] Also see TO BEAT THE BAND.

beat a path to someone's door Come to someone in great numbers, as in *Ever since she appeared on television, agents have been beating a path to her door.* The term *beat a path* alludes to the trampling action of many feet. [Late 1500s]

beat a retreat Also, **beat a hasty retreat.** Reverse course or withdraw, usually quickly. For example, *I really don't want to run into Jeff—let's beat a retreat.* This term originally (1300s) referred to the military practice of sounding drums to call back troops. Today it is used only figuratively, as in the example above.

beat around the bush Also, **beat about the bush.** Approach indirectly, in a roundabout way, or too cautiously. For example, *Stop beating around the bush—get to the point.* This term, first recorded in 1572, originally may have alluded to beating the bushes for game.

beat back Force to retreat or withdraw, as in *His findings beat back all their arguments to the contrary.* This phrase was often used in a military context (and still is), as in *Their armies were beaten back.* [Late 1500s]

beat down 1. Force or drive down; defeat or subdue. For example, "And finally to beat down Satan under our feet" (*The Book of Common Prayer,* 1552). [c. 1400] 2. Strike violently, as in the *The sun kept beating down on us all day long.* [Mid-1800s] 3. **beat someone down.** Make someone lower a price, as in *He's always trying to beat us down.* Economist Jeremy Bentham used this idiom in 1793: "Thus monopoly will beat down prices." [Slang; late 1700s]

beaten track ◆ See OFF THE BEATEN TRACK.

beat hollow ◆ See under BEAT THE PANTS OFF.

beat into one's head Also, **knock** or **drum into one's head**. Force one to learn something. For example, *Hard as I try, I can't seem to beat the correct safe combination into my head*, or *He promised to drum the numbers into my head by morning*, or *Whether we liked it or not, the English department was determined to knock Shakespeare into our heads*. Although *beat* implies violence, the first term, from the early 1500s, usually alludes more to a repeated striking of blows, that is, repetition or drilling; likewise with *drum* (alluding to drumbeats), which dates from the early 1800s.

beat it Go away, as in *We should beat it before the food's all gone*. This term is rude when used as an imperative, as in *Stop pestering me—beat it!* [Slang; late 1800s]

beat off Repulse, drive away by blows, as in *We tried to beat off the flying ants swarming about us*. Originating in the mid-1600s in a military context, this term was being used for other activities by the mid-1700s.

beat one's brains out Make a great mental effort to understand, solve, or remember something, as in *Joe's beating his brains out to finish this puzzle*. Christopher Marlowe used this hyperbolic idiom in *The Massacre of Paris* (1593): "Guise beats his brains to catch us in his trap." Also see RACK ONE'S BRAINS.

beat one's head against the wall Also, **bang** or **run one's head against** or **into a brick wall**. Waste one's time in a hopeless enterprise, as in *I have tried many times to convince him to stop smoking, but I'm beating my head against a brick wall*. The metaphoric phrase alludes to a physical expression of frustration. [Late 1500s] Also see BEAT THE AIR.

beat out **1.** Knock into shape by beating, as in *She managed to beat out all the dents in the fender*. [c. 1600] **2.** Surpass or defeat someone; be chosen over someone. For example, *He got to the head of the line, beating out all the others*. [Colloquial; second half of 1700s] Also see BEAT THE PANTS OFF. **3. beat out of.** Cheat someone of something, as in *He was always trying to beat the conductor out of the full train fare*. [Slang; second half of 1800s]

beats me This baffles or puzzles me, as in *I don't know how he does it—beats me!* This term originally may have alluded to a winning poker hand. It may also be related to the even earlier usage of *beat* for "astonished" or "at a loss." [Slang; mid-1800s]

beat someone at his or her own game Surpass someone in his or her own specialty or undertaking. For example, *Jean knew that if she matched the new store's discount she would keep all her customers and beat the new competitors at their own*

game. The use of *game* for any kind of undertaking or scheme dates from the mid-1200s.

beat the air Also, **beat the wind**. Continue to make futile attempts, fight to no purpose. For example, *The candidates for office were so much alike that we thought our vote amounted to beating the air*. These phrases call up a vivid image of someone flailing away at nothing. [Late 1300s]

beat the band ◆ See TO BEAT THE BAND.

beat the bushes for Look everywhere for something or someone, as in *I've been beating the bushes for a substitute but haven't had any luck*. This term originally alluded to hunting, when beaters were hired to flush birds out of the brush. [1400s] Also see BEAT AROUND THE BUSH.

beat the clock Finish something or succeed before time is up, as in *The paper went to press at five o'clock, and they hurried to beat the clock*. The term comes from various sports or races in which contestants compete within a certain time limit.

beat the drum for Praise, promote, publicize, as in *He's always beating the drum for his division, which actually has done very well*. This term transfers the literal striking of a drum for ceremonial or other purposes to touting the virtues of a person, group, or product. [Mid-1900s]

beat the Dutch ◆ See under BEAT ALL.

beat the living daylights out of Also, **knock** or **lick the hell** or **living daylights** or **shift** or **stuffing** or **tar out of**. Administer a merciless beating to; also, defeat soundly. For example, *The coach said he'd like to beat the living daylights out of the vandals who damaged the gym floor*, or *Bob knocked the stuffing out of that bully*, or *He swore he'd beat the tar out of anyone who tried to stop him*. These colloquial phrases nearly always denote a physical attack. In the first, *daylights* originally (1700) meant "the eyes" and later was extended to any vital (*living*) body organ. Thus Henry Fielding wrote, in *Amelia* (1752): "If the lady says another such words to me . . . I will darken her daylights" (that is, put out her eyes). *Hell* here is simply a swear word used for emphasis. The more vulgar *shit* and the politer *stuffing* allude simply to knocking out someone's insides. *Tar* is more puzzling but has been so used since the late 1800s.

beat the meat Masturbate, as in *He was always beating the meat*. This term, considered vulgar slang, is used for males, since it uses *meat* in the sense of "penis," a usage dating from the late 1500s.

beat the pants off Also, **beat hollow**. Win decisively over someone, outdo. For example, *When it comes to the Patriots' Day parade, Lexington beats the pants off the neighboring towns*, or *This beer beats the other brands hollow*. Both phrases use *beat* in the sense of "surpass." *Pants off* has served as an intensifier since about 1930; the variant dates from about 1775.

beat the rap Escape punishment; win acquittal. For example, *The youngsters were caught shoplifting, but somehow they were able to beat the rap.* The *rap* in this idiom means "the legal charge against one." [Slang; 1920s]

beat time Mark musical time by beating a drum, clapping, tapping the foot, or a similar means. For example, *Even as a baby, Dave always beat time when he heard music.* [Late 1600s]

beat to it 1. Get ahead of someone to obtain something, as in *There was only enough for one, so Jane ran as fast as she could in order to beat Jerry to it.* [Colloquial; c. 1900] 2. Also, **beat to the draw** or **punch.** React more quickly than someone else. For example, *The new salesman tried to serve one of my customers, but I beat him to the draw* and *Bill was determined to get there first and beat everyone else to the punch.* The variants imply aggression to get ahead, *draw* alluding to the drawing of a pistol and *punch* to hitting with the fists. [Second half of 1800s]

beat up 1. Strike repeatedly, as in *She told the police her husband had beaten her up.* [Slang; first half of 1900s] 2. Also, **beat up on.** Attack verbally, as in *That newspaper article really beat up on the town council.* [Slang; late 1900s]

beauty ♦ In addition to the idiom beginning with BEAUTY, also see THAT'S THE BEAUTY OF.

beauty is only skin deep External attractiveness has no relation to goodness or essential quality. This maxim was first stated by Sir Thomas Overbury in his poem "A Wife" (1613): "All the carnall beauty of my wife is but skin-deep."

beaver ♦ See BUSY AS A BEAVER; EAGER BEAVER; WORK LIKE A BEAVER.

be big on ♦ See BIG ON.

be bound to ♦ See BOUND TO.

be busted 1. Also, **go bust.** Become bankrupt, financially ruined. For example, *Who knew that the brokerage firm would be busted?* [Slang; early 1800s] Also see under GO BROKE. 2. Also, **get busted.** Be demoted, as in *If you're caught gambling you'll get busted to private.* This usage originated in the military and still most often denotes a reduction in rank. [c. 1800] 3. Also, **get busted.** Be arrested or turned over to the police, as in *The gang members were sure they'd get busted.* [Mid-1900s]

beck ♦ See AT SOMEONE'S BECK AND CALL.

become ♦ In addition to the idiom beginning with BECOME, also see idioms beginning with GET.

become of Happen to, befall, be the fate of, as in *I haven't seen Joe in a year; what has become of his book?* The King James Bible has this idiom (Gene-

sis 37:20): "We shall see what will become of his dreams." [Late 1500s]

bed ♦ In addition to the idioms beginning with BED, also see EARLY TO BED; GET UP ON THE WRONG SIDE OF BED; GO TO BED WITH; MAKE ONE'S BED AND LIE IN IT; MAKE THE BED; ON ONE'S DEATHBED; PUT TO BED; SHOULD HAVE STOOD IN BED; STRANGE BEDFELLOWS.

bed and board Lodging and meals, as in *Housekeepers usually earn a standard salary in addition to bed and board.* This phrase was first recorded in the *York Manual* (c. 1403), which stipulated certain connubial duties: "Her I take ... to be my wedded wife, to hold to have at bed and at board." Later *bed* was used merely to denote a place to sleep.

bed and breakfast Also, **B and B.** A hotel or other hostelry that offers a room for the night and a morning meal at an inclusive price. For example, *Staying at a bed and breakfast meant never having to plan morning meals.* This term and the practice originated in Britain and have become widespread. [Early 1900s]

bed of roses A comfortable or luxurious position, as in *Taking care of these older patients is no bed of roses.* This metaphor, first recorded in 1635, is often used in a negative context, as in the example. Also see BOWL OF CHERRIES.

be down 1. Be depressed, in low spirits, as in *During the winter months Sue's always down, but spring cheers her up.* [Colloquial; mid-1800s] 2. Be knowledgeable, canny, or sophisticated, as in *He was really down with the new group.* This usage probably originated among jazz musicians. [Slang; mid-1940s]

bee ♦ In addition to the idiom beginning with BEE, also see BIRDS AND THE BEES; BUSY AS A BEAVER (BEE); MAKE A BEELINE FOR; NONE OF ONE'S BUSINESS (BEESWAX).

beef ♦ In addition to the idiom beginning with BEEF, also see WHERE'S THE BEEF.

beef up Strengthen, reinforce, as in *Mary wants us to beef up her part in the play.* This phrase relies on an older slang sense of *beef* as "muscles" or "power." [Colloquial; late 1800s]

bee in one's bonnet A strange idea or notion; also, an idea that is harped on, an obsession. For example, *Bill's got a bee in his bonnet about burglars; he's always imagining strange noises.* This term, which replaced the earlier *have bees in one's head,* transfers the buzzing of a bee inside one's hat to a weird idea in one's head. [Second half of 1600s]

beeline ♦ See MAKE A BEELINE FOR.

been around Been present or active; especially, gained experience or sophistication. For example, *This book isn't new; it's been around for many* *years,* or *This strategy won't fool Bill; he's been around.* [First half of 1900s] Also see GET AROUND.

been had ◆ See BE HAD.

been there, done that ◆ See under SEEN ONE, SEEN THEM ALL.

been to the wars Show signs of rough treatment or injury, as in *That car of yours looks as though it's been to the wars.* This term dates from the late 1300s, when, however, it tended to be used literally. The figurative usage is more recent.

before ◆ In addition to the idioms beginning with BEFORE, also see BUSINESS BEFORE PLEASURE; CART BEFORE THE HORSE; CAST PEARLS BEFORE SWINE; LOOK BEFORE YOU LEAP; PRIDE GOES BEFORE A FALL.

before long Soon, in the near future, as in *The baby will be teething before long.* This idiom was first recorded in 1865.

before the wind Driven ahead, hurried, as in *The bikers are moving before the wind, so it's hard to tell who will come in first.* The literal meaning of this term is nautical, referring to a ship sailing in the same direction as the wind and being propelled forward. Its figurative use dates from the mid-1800s.

before you can say Jack Robinson Also, **quicker than you can say Jack Robinson.** Almost immediately, very soon, as in *I'll finish this book before you can say Jack Robinson.* This expression originated in the 1700s, but the identity of Jack Robinson has been lost. Grose's *Classical Dictionary* (1785) said he was a man who paid such brief visits to acquaintances that there was scarcely time to announce his arrival before he had departed, but it gives no further documentation. A newer version is **before you know it,** meaning so soon that you don't have time to become aware of it (as in *He'll be gone before you know it*).

before you know it ◆ See under BEFORE YOU CAN SAY JACK ROBINSON.

beg ◆ In addition to the idioms beginning with BEG, also see GO BEGGING.

beg, borrow, or steal Obtain by any possible means, as in *You couldn't beg, borrow, or steal tickets to the Olympics.* This term is often used in the negative, to describe something that cannot be obtained; Chaucer used it in *The Tale of the Man of Law.* [Late 1300s]

beggar description Defy or outdo any possible description, as in *The stage set was so elaborate, it beggared description.* This term, alluding to the idea that words are insufficient to do something justice, was already used by Shakespeare in *Antony and Cleopatra* (2:2), "For her own person It beggared all description."

beggars can't be choosers Those in dire need must be content with what they get. For example, *The cheapest model will have to do—beggars can't*

be choosers. This expression was familiar enough to be included in John Heywood's 1546 collection of proverbs.

begin ◆ In addition to the idioms beginning with BEGIN, also see CHARITY BEGINS AT HOME; (BEGIN TO) SEE THE LIGHT; TO START (BEGIN) WITH.

beginner's luck Good fortune in a first attempt or effort, as in *I often use a brand-new recipe for a dinner party; I trust beginner's luck.* [Late 1800s]

beginning of the end, the The start of a bad outcome (ruin, disaster, catastrophe, death), as in *Joe's failing two of his courses was the beginning of the end; he dropped out soon afterward.* This phrase, at first (16th century) used only to describe an approaching death, gained a new meaning after the French lost the battle of Leipzig in 1813 and Talleyrand said to Napoleon, "C'est le commencement de la fin" ("It's the beginning of the end").

begin to see daylight Realize that a task is finally nearing completion, that success or the right solution is near at hand. For example, *I've been working on this experiment for two years and I'm finally beginning to see daylight.* The noun *daylight* has been a metaphor for knowledge and solution since the late 1600s. Also see LIGHT AT THE END OF THE TUNNEL; SEE THE LIGHT.

begin to see the light ◆ See SEE THE LIGHT.

begin with ◆ See START WITH.

beg off Ask to be released from an obligation; turn down an invitation. For example, *He's asked me out to dinner three times already, but I have to beg off again,* or *Mother couldn't take on another committee and so she begged off.* [Early 1700s]

beg the question Take for granted or assume the truth of the very thing being questioned. For example, *Shopping now for a dress to wear to the ceremony is really begging the question—she hasn't been invited yet.* This phrase, whose roots are in Aristotle's writings on logic, came into English in the late 1500s. In the 1990s, however, people sometimes used the phrase as a synonym of "ask the question" (as in *The article begs the question: "What are we afraid of?"*).

beg to differ Disagree with someone, as in *John told me Max was sure to win, but I beg to differ—I don't think he has a chance.* This courteous formula for expressing disagreement echoes similar uses of *beg* in the sense of "ask," such as **I beg your pardon,** so used since about 1600. Also see EXCUSE ME.

be had 1. Be outwitted; also, be cheated, deceived. For example, *This lawyer is a real shyster; you've been had,* or *I've become very cautious about these schemes; it's too costly to be had more than once.* This expression employs the verb *to have* in the sense of getting someone in one's power or at a disadvantage. [Slang; early 1800s] 2. Be bribed or influenced by dishonest means. For example, *Our senator's incorruptible; be cannot be had.* [Slang; early 1800s]

behalf ♦ See IN BEHALF OF.

behavior ♦ See ON ONE'S BEST BEHAVIOR.

behind ♦ In addition to the idioms beginning with BEHIND, also see COME FROM BEHIND; DROP BEHIND; FALL BEHIND; GET BEHIND; POWER BEHIND THE THRONE; PUT BEHIND ONE; WET BEHIND THE EARS; WITH ONE ARM TIED BEHIND ONE'S BACK.

behind bars In prison, as in *All murderers should be put behind bars for life.* The bars here refer to the iron rods used to confine prisoners. [c. 1900]

behind closed doors In secret, privately. For example, *The nominating committee always meets behind closed doors, lest its deliberations become known prematurely.* Also see BEHIND THE SCENES.

behind in 1. Also, **behind on**. Late with; not progressing quickly enough with. For example, *The builders are behind on this project,* or *I can't take time out or I'll be too far behind in my work.* The same idea is also expressed as **behind time,** where *time* means a schedule or appointed time, as in *The bus should have been here; it's behind time.* [Early 1300s] Also see FALL BEHIND. 2. In arrears, owing more than one should. For example, *Jane and Bob are behind in their payments, so the interest will mount up.* [Late 1300s]

behind someone's back Out of one's presence or without someone's knowledge, as in *Joan has a nasty way of maligning her friends behind their backs.* Sir Thomas Malory used this metaphoric term in *Le Morte d'Arthur* (c. 1470): "To say of me wrong or shame behind my back." [Early 1300s]

behind the eight ball In trouble or an awkward position, out of luck, as in *His check bounced, leaving Jim behind the eight ball with his landlord.* The term comes from pocket billiards or pool, where in certain games if the number eight ball is between the "cue ball" and "object ball" the player cannot make a straight shot. [Colloquial; c. 1920]

behind the scenes In secret or private, away from public view, as in *His struggle for the top position took place strictly behind the scenes.* This term alludes to the various activities that go on behind the curtain in theaters, out of the audience's view. [Late 1700s] Also see BEHIND CLOSED DOORS.

behind the times Not keeping up with current fashion, methods, or ideas, as in *Your accounting methods are behind the times.* Charles Dickens used this idiom in *Dombey and Son* (1848): "I'm old-fashioned, and behind the Time." [Mid-1800s]

behind time ♦ See under BEHIND IN.

being ♦ See FOR THE MOMENT (TIME BEING); OTHER THINGS BEING EQUAL.

be in on ♦ See IN ON.

be into Also, **get into**. Be interested in or involved with. For example, *She's really into yoga,* or *Once you retire, it's important to get into some bobby you've always wanted to try.* [Colloquial; mid-1900s]

belabor the point Repeat an argument or other issue over and over, harp on something, as in *We've discussed her decision — let's not belabor the point.* This term dates from the mid-1900s and derives from *belabor* in the sense of "assail with words," a usage dating from the late 1500s.

belfry ♦ See BATS IN ONE'S BELFRY.

believe ♦ In addition to the idioms beginning with BELIEVE, also see LEAD ONE TO BELIEVE; MAKE BELIEVE; YOU'D BETTER BELIEVE IT. Also see SEEING IS BELIEVING.

believe it or not It's true, whether or not you agree, as in *Believe it or not, I finally finished painting the house.* Originating in the 1800s, this phrase gained currency as the title of a cartoon series begun in 1918 by Robert Ripley and continuing to run in American newspapers long after his death in 1949. Each drawing presented a strange but supposedly true phenomenon, such as a two-headed chicken.

believe one's ears Also, **believe one's eyes**. Trust one's own hearing or sight, as in *We couldn't believe our ears when we heard that Gene was accepted at Stanford,* or *I couldn't believe my own eyes when the movie stars walked in.* This expression of incredulity is nearly always stated negatively, as in the examples. [Early 1600s]

believing ♦ See SEEING IS BELIEVING.

bell ♦ In addition to the idiom beginning with BELL, also see CLEAR AS A BELL; RING A BELL; SAVED BY THE BELL; SOUND AS A BELL; WITH BELLS ON.

bell the cat, who will Who has enough courage to do a dangerous job? For example, *Someone has to tell the teacher that her own son started the fire, but who will bell the cat?* This expression originated in one of Aesop's fables as retold by William Langland in *Piers Ploughman* (c. 1377), in which the mice decide to put a bell around the cat's neck as a warning device but then can find none among them who will actually do it.

belly ♦ See GO BELLY UP.

belong ♦ See TO THE VICTOR BELONG THE SPOILS.

below par Also, **under par**. Not up to the average, normal, or desired standard. For example, *I am feeling below par today, but I'm sure I'll recover by tomorrow.* This term employs *par* in the sense of "an average amount or quality," a usage dating from the late 1700s.

below the belt, hit Not behave according to the rules or decency, unfairly, as in *Bringing up my mother's faults — that's really hitting below the belt.* The term comes from boxing, where according to the Marquis of Queensberry Rules (1865) a fighter may punch his opponent only in the upper body or head. For a synonym, see LOW BLOW; also see UNDER ONE'S BELT.

belt ♦ In addition to the idioms beginning with BELT, also see BELOW THE BELT; BIBLE BELT; SUN BELT; TIGHTEN ONE'S BELT; UNDER ONE'S BELT.

belt down Swallow very quickly, as in *After the race, he belted down a whole quart of water.* This phrase is frequently used for guzzling whiskey or some other liquor. [Slang; mid-1800s]

belt out 1. Knock unconscious; beat up, trounce; murder. For example, *The police officer was accused of belting out the teenager before taking him to the station,* or *The hold-up man belted out the storekeeper and fled with the money.* This expression originated in boxing. [Slang; c. 1940] 2. Sing or play music very loudly, as in *She belted out the national anthem before every game.* [Colloquial; c. 1950]

be my guest Do as you wish. For example, *May I drive your car?—Sure, be my guest,* or *Do you mind if I go to the play without you?—No, be my guest.* This expression not only literally invites someone to behave as one's guest (using one's house, belongings, etc.) but also figuratively tells someone to feel free to act as he or she pleases. [Colloquial; c. 1950] Also see FEEL FREE.

bench ♦ See ON THE BENCH; WARM THE BENCH.

bend ♦ In addition to the idioms beginning with BEND, also see AROUND THE BEND; CROOK (BEND) ONE'S ELBOW; ON BENDED KNEE. Also see under BENT.

bend one's elbow ♦ See CROOK ONE'S ELBOW.

bend over backwards Also, **lean over backwards.** Exert oneself to the fullest extent, as in *Dad bent over backwards so as not to embarrass Stasia's new boyfriend.* This phrase transfers the gymnastic feat of a backbend to taking a great deal of trouble for someone or something. [c. 1920] Also see under FALL ALL OVER.

bend someone's ear Talk about a matter at tedious length; monopolize someone's attention. For example, *Aunt Mary is always bending his ear about her financial problems.* This term may have come from the much older *to bend one's ear to someone,* meaning "to listen to someone," although the current phrase implies a less than willing audience. [Colloquial; c. 1940]

benefit ♦ See GIVE THE BENEFIT.

bent on Also, **bent upon.** Determined, resolved, as in *Jamie is bent on winning the math prize.* This phrase, first recorded in 1762, always uses the past participle of the verb *bend* in the sense of "tend toward."

bent out of shape 1. Infuriated, annoyed, as in *Don't let Paul get you bent out of shape—calm*

down. 2. Shocked, astonished, as in *That conservative audience was bent out of shape by his speech.* [Slang; second half of 1900s] Also see IN GOOD CONDITION (SHAPE).

be off 1. Leave, depart, as in *I'm off to the races; wish me luck.* This phrase, first recorded in 1826, was once commonly used as an imperative, meaning "go away"—as in *Be off or I'll call the police*—but today is rare in this context. 2. Be in poor condition; be stale or spoiled; not work properly. For example, *This milk must be off; it tastes sour,* or *The kitchen clock is off by at least five minutes.* [Early 1900s] 3. Be free from work, school, or some other regular occupation, as in *The secretary is off today, but perhaps I can find it.* [Mid-1800s] 4. Decline, as in *The industrial stocks are off 50 points today.* This usage, nearly always applied to securities or other prices, was first recorded in 1929, the year of the great stock market crash.

be on 1. Be taking medication or an illegal drug, as in *Are you on some antibiotic?* or *He was definitely on narcotics when it happened.* [1930s] 2. Be in favor of something or willing to participate, as in *We're going dancing after the play—are you on?* [Colloquial; late 1800s] 3. Be engaged in some action, especially on the stage, as in *Hurry up, you're on in five minutes.* [Late 1700s] 4. Perform extremely well, as in *I can't return Dan's serve—he's really on today.* [Slang; second half of 1900s] 5. Be scheduled, as in *Is tonight's rally still on?* [Colloquial; second half of 1900s] 6. **be on one.** Be at one's expense, either as a treat or the butt of a joke. For example, *This round of drinks is on me,* or *He enjoys a good laugh, even when the joke's on him.* [Colloquial; second half of 1800s] 7. **not be on.** Be unacceptable, not allowable, as in *I can't believe you'd cancel; that's just not on.* This usage is more common in Britain than America. [Colloquial; 1930s] For a synonym, see NOT DONE. Also see BE ON TO.

be oneself 1. Act in one's usual fashion; be in one's normal physical or mental state. For example, *Peter's finally recovered from the accident and is himself again,* or *I was completely distracted; I just wasn't myself.* 2. Act without pretense; be unaffected, sincere. For example, *I really enjoy their company because I can be myself with them.*

be on to 1. Be aware of or have information about, as in *They can't pull that trick again; we're on to them now.* [Colloquial; second half of 1800s] 2. Discover something important or profitable, as in *The researchers claim they are really on to something big.* [Colloquial; mid-1900s]

berth ♦ See GIVE A WIDE BERTH TO.

beside oneself In a state of extreme agitation or excitement, as in *She was beside herself when she found she'd lost her ring,* or *Peter was beside himself* *with joy—he'd won the poetry award.* This phrase appears in the New Testament (Acts 26:24): "Paul, thou art beside thyself; much learning makes the mad." [Late 1400s]

beside the point Also, **beside the mark** or **question.** Irrelevant, off the subject. For example, *Whether you had insurance is beside the point; the accident is your fault.* These terms came into common use in the mid-1800s. Also see NEITHER HERE NOR THERE.

best ♦ In addition to the idioms beginning with BEST, also see ALL FOR THE BEST; ALL THE BEST; AS BEST ONE CAN; AT BEST; AT ONE'S BEST; COME OFF (SECOND-BEST); DO ONE'S BEST; GET THE BETTER (BEST) OF; GIVE IT ONE'S BEST SHOT; HAD BETTER (BEST); HONESTY IS THE BEST POLICY; MAKE THE BEST OF IT; ON ONE'S BEST BEHAVIOR; PUT ONE'S BEST FOOT FORWARD; SECOND BEST; SUNDAY BEST; TO ONE'S (BEST) INTEREST; TO THE BEST OF ONE'S ABILITY; WITH THE BEST OF THEM; WITH THE BEST WILL IN THE WORLD. Also see under BETTER.

best bib and tucker One's finest clothes, dressed up, as in *The men were told to put on their best bib and tucker for the dinner dance.* Although wearing either a bib (frill at front of a man's shirt) or a tucker (ornamental lace covering a woman's neck and shoulders) is obsolete, the phrase survives. [Mid-1700s] For a synonym, see SUNDAY BEST.

best-laid plans go astray, the Also, **the best-laid schemes go astray.** Even very careful designs do not always succeed. For example, *Mary spent all day preparing this elaborate dish but forgot the most important ingredient—oh well, the best-laid plans go astray.* This particular turn of phrase comes from Robert Burn's poem "To a Mouse" (1786): "The best-laid schemes o' mice an' men gang aft a-gley [go often astray]." It is so well known that it is often abbreviated to **the best-laid plans.**

best of both worlds, the Benefits from two seemingly opposed alternatives, as in *Jenny taught in the morning only and worked on her book afternoons, so she had the best of both worlds.* Charles Kingsley used this idiom in *Westward Ho!* (1855): "Make the best of both worlds." Also see MAKE THE BEST OF IT.

best part of something Nearly all of something, the majority, as in *The dentist was late; I waited for the best part of an hour.* The adjective *best* here does not concern quality but quantity. [First half of 1500s] Also see BETTER HALF, def. 1.

best shot ♦ See GIVE IT ONE'S BEST SHOT.

best ♦ In addition to the idioms beginning with BET, also see BACK (BET ON) THE WRONG HORSE; HEDGE ONE'S BETS; YOU BET YOUR ASS.

bête noire A person or thing that is particularly disliked. For example, *Calculus was the bête noire*

of my freshman courses. This phrase, French for "black beast," entered the English language in the early 1800s. For synonyms, see PAIN IN THE NECK; THORN IN ONE'S FLESH.

be that as it may Nevertheless, it may be true but, as in *Be that as it may, I can't take your place on Monday.* This phrase has its roots in *be as be may,* used from Chaucer's time for about four centuries. [Mid-1800s]

be the death of Cause the death of something or someone, as in *This comedian is so funny, he'll be the death of me.* Although this phrase can be used literally, meaning "to kill someone or something," it has also been used hyperbolically (as in the example) since the late 1500s. Shakespeare used it in *1 Henry IV* (2:1): "Since the price of oats rose, it was the death of him."

be the end of one Be one's downfall, as in *His heavy drinking may well be the end of him,* or *That math assignment will be the end of me.* This phrase originally alluded to something that would cause someone's death. Today, while it may be used seriously (as in the first example), it more often is used more lightly (as in the second).

be the making of Be the means or cause of progress or success, as in *Marriage will be the making of him.* This idiom, using *making* in the sense of "advancement," was first recorded about 1470.

bet one's ass Also, **bet one's boots** or **bottom dollar** or **life.** ♦ See YOU BET YOUR ASS.

bet on the wrong horse ♦ See BACK THE WRONG HORSE.

better ♦ In addition to the idioms beginning with BETTER, also see AGAINST ONE'S BETTER JUDGMENT; ALL BETTER; ALL THE BETTER; DISCRETION IS THE BETTER PART OF VALOR; FOR BETTER OR FOR WORSE; GET BETTER; GET THE BETTER (BEST) OF; GO ONE BETTER; HAD BETTER (BEST); KNOW BETTER; SEEN BETTER DAYS; SO MUCH THE BETTER; SOONER THE BETTER; TAKE A TURN FOR THE BETTER; THINK BETTER OF; YOU'D BETTER BELIEVE IT. Also see under BEST.

better half 1. Also, **better part.** The larger amount or majority of something, as in *I won't be long; the better half of this job is complete,* or *I have spent the better part of my life in this city.* Sir Philip Sidney used the first term in *Arcadia* (1580): "I . . . shall think the better half of it already achieved." The variant appears in a well-known proverb, DISCRETION IS THE BETTER PART OF VALOR. 2. Also, **my better half.** One's (my) spouse, as in *I'm not sure if we can go; I'll have to check with my better half.* Originally this expression meant "a close friend or lover," and by the 16th century it referred to either a wife or lover. Sidney used it in this way, again in *Arcadia:* "My dear, my better half (said he), I find I must now leave thee." Today it tends to be used lightly for either husband or wife. [Late 1500s]

better late than never Being tardy is better than not at all, as in *We've been waiting for you for an hour—but better late than never.* This phrase, first recorded about 1200, appears in several early English proverb collections, often with the added **but better never late.** Today it is often used in exasperation over a delay, as in the example.

better off In a more favourable position or financial circumstances. For example, *They were better off flying than driving there,* or *They were better off than most of their neighbors.* This phrase is the comparative form of WELL OFF. [Mid-1800s]

better part of ♦ See BETTER HALF, def. 1.

better safe than sorry Being careful may avoid disaster, as in *I'm not taking any shortcuts—better safe than sorry.* This cautionary phrase appeared as *better sure than sorry* in 1837.

better than 1. Superior to, as in *He's no better than Tom at writing a memo.* [9th century] 2. More than, larger in amount or greater in rate, as in *My new car can do better than 100 miles an hour,* or *The new plan will cut better than 15 percent of costs.* Some authorities consider this usage colloquial and advise that it be avoided in formal writing. [Late 1500s] Also see BETTER HALF, def. 1.

between ♦ In addition to the idioms beginning with BETWEEN, also see BETWIXT AND BETWEEN; COME BETWEEN; DRAW A LINE BETWEEN; FALL BETWEEN THE CRACKS; FEW AND FAR BETWEEN; HIT BETWEEN THE EYES; IN BETWEEN; IN BETWEEN TIMES; READ BETWEEN THE LINES; TAIL BETWEEN ONE'S LEGS.

between a rock and a hard place Also, **between the devil and the deep blue sea** or **Scylla and Charybdis.** Between two equally difficult or unacceptable choices. For example, *Trying to please both my boss and his supervisor puts me between a rock and a hard place.* The *rock and hard place* version is the newest of these synonymous phrases, dating from the early 1900s, and alludes to being caught or crushed between two rocks. The oldest is *Scylla and Charybdis,* which in Homer's *Odyssey* signified a monster on a rock (Scylla) and a fatal whirlpool (Charybdis), between which Odysseus had to sail through a narrow passage. It was used figuratively by the Roman writer Virgil and many writers since. The *devil* in *devil and deep blue sea,* according to lexicographer Charles Earle Funk, referred to a seam around a ship's hull near the waterline, which, if a sailor was trying to caulk it in heavy seas, would cause him to fall overboard. Others disagree, however, and believe the phrase simply alludes to a choice between hellfire with the devil and drowning in deep waters.

between the lines ♦ See READ BETWEEN THE LINES.

between you and me Also, **between ourselves; just between you and me and the bedpost** or **four walls** or **gatepost** or **lamppost.** In strict confidence. For example, *Just between you and me, it was Janet who proposed to Bill rather than vice versa.* This phrase, dating from about 1300, is generally followed by some informative statement that the listener is being asked to keep secret. The variant with *bedpost,* also shortened to *post,* dates from the early 1800s; *four walls,* also shortened to *the wall,* dates from the early 1900s, as does *the gatepost.*

betwixt and between Undecided, midway between two alternatives, neither here nor there. For example, *I'm betwixt and between canceling my trip entirely or just postponing it,* or *Jane is betwixt and between about accepting the offer.* The adverb *betwixt,* originally meaning "by two," is seldom heard except in this expression, first recorded in 1832.

beyond ♦ In addition to the idioms beginning with BEYOND, also see ABOVE AND BEYOND; BACK OF BEYOND; CAN'T SEE BEYOND THE END OF ONE'S NOSE.

beyond a doubt Also, **beyond the shadow of a doubt.** Certainly so, undoubtedly so, as in *Beyond a doubt this is the best view of the valley.* This phrase, along with the earlier **without doubt** (dating from c. 1300), asserts the truth of some statement. W.S. Gilbert's version, in *The Gondoliers* (1889), is: "Of that there is no manner of doubt—no probable, possible shadow of doubt—no possible doubt whatever." In this context *shadow* means "a trace or slight suggestion." Another variant is **beyond a reasonable doubt.** This phrase is often used in court when the judge instructs the jury that they must be convinced of the accused's guilt or innocence beyond a reasonable doubt; *reasonable* here means "logical and rational." Also see BEYOND QUESTION; NO DOUBT.

beyond comparison Also, **without comparison** or **beyond compare.** Too superior to be compared, unrivaled, as in *This view of the mountains is beyond comparison,* or *That bakery is without comparison.* The first term, more common today than the much older variants, was first recorded in 1871. *Without comparison* goes back to 1340, and *without compare* to 1621.

beyond measure To an extreme degree; exceedingly. For example, *Her attitude annoys me beyond measure.* This term was first recorded in 1526.

beyond one's depth ♦ See OUT OF ONE'S DEPTH.

beyond one's means Too costly for one, more than one can afford. For example, *A second vacation this year is well beyond our means.* The noun *means* here signifies "resources at one's disposal," a usage current since Shakespeare's time, as in *Measure for Measure* (2:2): "Let her have needful, but not lavish means." [Late 1800s]

beyond question Also, **beyond all** or **without question.** Definitely, certainly, as in *Beyond question he is the best man for the job.* This idiom indicates that something is so sure it cannot be questioned. So used since the late 1500s, it was also put as **past question,** by Shakespeare and others. Also see BEYOND A DOUBT.

beyond reach ◆ See under IN REACH.

beyond recall Irreversible, irretrievable, as in *We can't repair this screen—it's beyond recall,* or *It's too late to cancel our plans—they're beyond recall.* This idiom employs *recall* in the sense of revoking or annulling something. [Mid-1600s]

beyond reproach Blameless, faultless, as in *Jean's conduct at school is beyond reproach.* The phrase employs the verb *to reproach* in the sense of "censure or rebuke," a usage dating from the early 1500s.

beyond the call of duty ◆ See under ABOVE AND BEYOND.

beyond the pale Outside the bounds of morality, good behavior or judgment; unacceptable. For example, *She thought taking the boys to a topless show was beyond the pale.* The noun *pale,* from the Latin *palum,* meant "a stake for fences" or "a fence made from such stakes." By extension it came to be used for an area confined by a fence and for any boundary, limit, or restriction, both of these meanings dating from the late 1300s. The *pale* referred to in the idiom is usually taken to mean the *English Pale,* the part of Ireland under English rule, and therefore, as perceived by its rulers, within the bounds of civilization.

beyond the shadow of a doubt ◆ See BEYOND A DOUBT.

Bible belt An area noted for religious fundamentalism; specifically, parts of the American South and Midwest. For example, *You wouldn't dare try to sell a sex manual in the Bible belt.* This term alludes to the prevalence of evangelical revivals, strict morals, belief in the literal truth of the Bible, and similar traits. [c. 1920]

bid adieu Say goodbye, take leave of, as in *It's beyond my bedtime, so I bid you all adieu,* or *I'll be glad to bid adieu to these crutches.* French for "goodbye," *adieu* literally means "to God" and was part of *à dieu vous commant,* "I commend you to God." Adopted into English in the 1300s, it was first recorded in Chaucer's *Troilus and Cressida* (c. 1385). Today it is considered quite formal, although it also is used humorously.

bide one's time Wait for the opportune moment, as in *The cat sat in front of the mousehole, biding its time.* This phrase employs the verb *to bide* in the sense of "to wait for," a usage dating from about A.D. 950 and surviving mainly in this locution.

bid up Raise a price by raising one's offer, as in *We were hoping to get an Oriental rug cheaply, but the dealer kept bidding us up.* This phrase is used in business and commerce, particularly at auctions. [Mid-1800s]

big ◆ In addition to the idioms beginning with BIG, also see GO OVER BIG; GREAT (BIG) GUNS; HIT IT BIG; IN A BIG WAY; LITTLE FROG IN A BIG POND; MAKE A FEDERAL CASE (BIG DEAL); TALK BIG; THINK BIG; TOO BIG FOR ONE'S BREECHES; WHAT'S THE (BIG) IDEA. Also see under BIGGER.

big and bold Large and striking, as in *His ties tended to be big and bold in color and pattern,* or *This big and bold design for a book jacket is sure to catch the casual browser's eye.* This phrase, used mostly to describe things rather than persons, is a kind of visual analog of LOUD AND CLEAR.

big as life Also, **large as life.** In person, as in *And there was Mary, big as life, standing right in front of me.* This phrase transfers the same size as in real life (life-size) to an actual appearance. Sometimes this term is embellished with **and quite as natural,** presumably alluding to a likeness of a person or thing that closely resembles the real thing. A similar addition is **and twice as natural,** which doesn't make sense. [Late 1800s] **2.** Also, **larger than life; big as all outdoors.** On a grand scale, as in *The soap opera could well be called a larger-than-life drama,* or *That friend of his was as big as all outdoors.* This phrase can be used either literally, for larger than life-size (second example) or figuratively. The phrase *all outdoors* has been used to compare something or someone to an immensity since the early 1800s.

big bucks A great deal of money, as in *A swimming pool—that means you're spending big bucks.* Buck has been slang for "dollar" since the mid-1800s. [Slang; second half of 1900s]

big cheese Also, **big shot** or **gun** or **wheel** or **enchilada.** An important, powerful person; the boss. For example, *She loved being the big cheese of her company; the big guns in Congress are bound to change the President's bill; you'd better not act like a big shot among your old friends; Harry was the big wheel in his class;* and *You'll have to get permission from the big enchilada.* The first term dates from the late 1800s and its origin is disputed. Some think it comes from the Urdu word *chiz* or *cheez* for "thing," but others hold it plays on the English word "chief." *Big gun* is much older, dating from the early 1800s; *big shot* became very popular in the late 1920s, particularly when used for underworld leaders of gangsters; *big wheel* dates from about the same period. *Big enchilada,* often put as *the big enchilada,* is the newest, dating from the early 1970s.

big daddy 1. An influential man, a big shot (see under BIG CHEESE), as in *You'll have to get permission from big daddy.* [Slang; mid-1900s] 2. A male sweetheart or friend, often a man considerably older than his female companion; a SUGAR DADDY. [Slang; mid-1900s] 3. Grandfather. This usage originated in the South among African-Americans. 4. The largest or most important person or thing of its kind. For example, *The United States has long been the big daddy of the Western Hemisphere,* or *The blue whale was the big daddy of the ocean.* [Slang; 1960s]

big deal 1. A matter of great interest or importance, as in *Performing in Symphony Hall is a big deal for everyone in the chorus.* [c. 1940] Also see under MAKE A FEDERAL CASE OUT OF. 2. So what? Who cares? For example, *So you got the job after all—well, big deal!* This use of the phrase as an ironic interjection dates from approximately the same time.

big enchilada ◆ See under BIG CHEESE.

big fish in a small pond Also, **big frog in a little pond.** A person who is important in a limited arena; someone overqualified for a position or in relation to colleagues. For example, *Steve has both a Ph.D. and an M.D., yet he's content with his practice at a rural hospital; he prefers to be a big fish in a little pond.* The expression *big fish* has been slang for an important or influential person since the early 1800s. The addition of *in a small pond* as a metaphor for an unimportant organization is more recent, as is the substitution of *frog.* Another variant is the proverb *Better a big fish in a little puddle than a little fish in a big puddle.*

bigger ◆ In addition to the idiom beginning with BIGGER, also see EYES ARE BIGGER THAN ONE'S STOMACH.

bigger they come, the harder they fall, the Persons in important positions lose more when they fail, as in *Impeaching a President is very painful—the bigger they come, the harder they fall.* This expression is believed to come from boxing and gained currency when boxer Robert Fitzsimmons used it in a 1902 newspaper interview before fighting the much heavier James J. Jeffries. It was probably derived from similar adages, such as "The bigger the tree, the harder she falls."

big head, have a Be conceited; have an exaggerated sense of one's own importance or ability. For example, *The constant flattery of his subordinates is*

bound *to give Thomas a big head.* [c. 1800] Also see SWELLED HEAD.

big league An area of tough competition and high rewards; the largest or foremost of its kind. For example, *Winning an Oscar put this unknown actress in the big league.* The term alludes to the major (big) leagues of American baseball. [Late 1800s] Also see BIG TIME, def. 2.

big mouth, have a Also, **have** or **be a loud mouth.** Be loquacious, often noisily or boastfully; be tactless or reveal secrets. For example, *After a few drinks, Dick turns into a loud mouth about his accomplishments,* or *Don't tell Peggy anything confidential; she's known for having a big mouth.* [Slang; late 1800s]

big of one Generous of one, as in *It was big of Bill to give his brother his entire paycheck.* This expression may be used either straight-forwardly (as above) or sarcastically, as in *How big of you to save the absolute worst seat for me.* [c. 1940]

big on Enthusiastic about, as in *Dad is big on Christmas with the whole family.* [Slang; mid-1800s]

big shot ◆ See under BIG CHEESE.

big stink A major scandal or furor. For example, *If they don't improve the women's facilities, Marjorie will make a big stink about it.* [Early 1800s]

big time 1. An enjoyable or exciting time, as in *The children came home exhausted but happy; they really had a big time at the circus.* [Mid-1800s] 2. The highest or most important level in any enterprise, as in *I knew that when I made it through the last audition, I was finally in the big time.* [Colloquial; c. 1900] Also see BIG LEAGUE.

big top 1. The main tent of a circus, as in *The highwire act is almost always in the big top.* [c. 1840] 2. Underworld slang for a maximum-security prison, as in *He was sentenced to ten years in the big top.* [1950s]

big wheel ◆ See under BIG CHEESE.

bill ◆ See CLEAN BILL OF HEALTH; FILL THE BILL; FOOT THE BILL; SELL A BILL OF GOODS.

bind ◆ In addition to the idioms beginning with BIND, also see IN A BIND. Also see under BOUND.

bind hand and foot ◆ See BOUND HAND AND FOOT.

bind over Oblige someone to do or not do something; hold on bail or keep under bond. For example, *The sheriff will bind over the murder suspect to the homicide division.* This phrase is nearly always used in a legal context. [Late 1500s]

binge ◆ See GO ON, def. 9.

bird ◆ In addition to the idioms beginning with BIRD, also see CATBIRD SEAT; EARLY BIRD CATCHES THE WORM; EAT LIKE A BIRD; FOR THE BIRDS; FREE AS

A BIRD; KILL TWO BIRDS WITH ONE STONE; LITTLE BIRD TOLD ME; NAKED AS A JAYBIRD; RARE BIRD.

bird has flown, the The individual sought has gone away, as in *Jean hoped to meet her editor at long last, but when she arrived the bird had flown.* This idiom has been used for an escaped prisoner, and more generally, as in 1655 by William Gurnall (*The Christian in Complete Armour*): "Man . . . knows not his time . . . he comes when the bird is flown." [Mid-1600s]

bird in the hand A benefit available now is more valuable than some possibly larger future benefit. For example, *Bob thinks he might do better in a bigger firm, but his wife insists he should stay, saying a bird in the hand.* This expression, which in full is *A bird in the hand is worth two in the bush,* was an ancient Greek proverb. It was well known in English by about 1400 and has been repeated so frequently that it is often shortened.

bird of passage A transient, one who is here today and gone tomorrow. For example, *Mary moves nearly every year; she's a true bird of passage.* This phrase transfers the literal meaning of a migrating bird to human behavior. [Second half of 1700s]

birds and the bees, the A euphemism for sex education, especially when taught informally. For example, *It's time Father told the children about the birds and the bees.* Cole Porter alluded to this expression in his witty song, "Let's Do It, Let's Fall in Love," (1928) when he noted that birds, bees, even educated fleas fall in love. This idiom alludes to sexual behavior in animals to avoid explicit explanation of human behavior. [Second half of 1800s]

bird's eye view An overview, as in *This balcony gives us a bird's eye view of the town,* or *This course gives you a bird's eye view of history—from Eolithic man to the Gulf War in one semester.* This expression can be used literally, for a panoramic view such as a bird might see, as well as figuratively. [c. 1600]

birds of a feather (flock together) Individuals of like character, taste, or background (tend to stay together), as in *The members of the club had no trouble selecting their yearly outing—they're all birds of a feather.* The idea of *like seeks like* dates from ancient Greek times, and "Birds dwell with their kind" was quoted in the apocryphal book of Ecclesiasticus. The full saying in English, **Birds of a feather flock together,** was first recorded in 1545.

birth ◆ See GIVE BIRTH TO.

birthday suit Nakedness, as in *The doorbell rang, and here I was in my birthday suit.* In 18th-century Britain this term originally referred to the clothes one wore on the king's birthday. Later it was jocularly transferred to bare skin, alluding to the condition of a new-born baby.

bit ◆ In addition to the idiom beginning with BIT, also see A BIT; CHAMP AT THE BIT; DO ONE'S BIT; EVERY BIT; NOT A BIT; QUITE A BIT; TAKE THE BIT IN ONE'S MOUTH; TWO BITS.

bit by bit Also, **little by little.** Gradually, by small degrees, slowly. For example, *The squirrels dug up the lawn bit by bit, till we had almost no grass,* or *Little by little be began to understand what John was getting at.* The first term was first recorded in 1849, although *bit* in the sense of "small amount" is much older; the variant dates from the 1400s.

bite ◆ In addition to the idioms beginning with BITE, also see BARK IS WORSE THAN ONE'S BITE; PUT THE BITE ON; SOUND BITE. Also see BITTEN.

bite off more than one can chew Take on more work or a bigger task than one can handle, as in *With two additional jobs, Bill is clearly biting off more than he can chew.* Cautions against taking on too much appear in medieval sources, although this particular metaphor, alluding to taking in more food than one can chew, dates only from about 1870.

bite one's nails Exhibit signs of anxiety, impatience, or nervousness, as in *We'll be biting our nails till the jury comes back.* Biting one's fingernails is a time-honored sign of emotional tension. The Roman satirist Horace described it about 35 B.C.: "As he wrought his verse he would often . . . gnaw his nails to the quick" (*Satires*, Book 1).

bite one's tongue Refrain from speaking out, as in *A new grandmother must learn to bite her tongue so as not to give unwanted advice,* or *I'm sure it'll rain during graduation.—Bite your tongue!* This term alludes to holding the tongue between the teeth in an effort not to say something one might regret. Shakespeare used it in *2 Henry VI* (1:1): "So York must sit and fret and bite his tongue." Today it is sometimes used as a humorous imperative, as in the second example, with the implication that speaking might bring bad luck. [Late 1500s] Also see HOLD ONE'S TONGUE.

bite someone's head off Also, **snap someone's head off.** Scold or speak very angrily to someone, as in *Ask her to step down from the board? She'd bite my head off!* The first expression, dating from the mid-1900s, replaced the much earlier **bite someone's nose off** (16th century); the variant was first recorded in 1886.

bite the bullet Behave bravely or stoically when facing pain or a difficult situation, as in *If they want to cut the budget deficit, they are going to have to bite the bullet and find new sources of revenue.* This phrase is of military origin, but the precise allusion is uncertain. Some say it referred to the treatment of a wounded soldier without anesthesia, so that he would be asked to bite on a lead bullet during treatment. Also, Francis Grose's *Dictionary of the Vulgar Tongue* (1796) holds that grenadiers being disciplined with the cat-o'-nine-tails would bite on a bullet to avoid crying out in pain.

bite the dust Suffer defeat or death, as in *The 1990 election saw both of our senators bite the dust.* Although this expression was popularized by by American Western films of the 1930s, in which either cowboys or Indians were thrown from their horses to the dusty ground, it originated much earlier. Tobias Smollett had it in *Gil Blas* (1750): "We made two of them bite the dust."

bite the hand that feeds you Show ingratitude, turn against a benefactor. For example, *The college gave me a scholarship, so I shouldn't bite the hand that feeds me and criticize its hiring policies.* Used about 600 B.C. by the Greek poet Sappho, this metaphor of a dog biting its master was first recorded in English in 1711.

bitten ♦ See ONCE BITTEN, TWICE SHY; also see BITE.

bitter ♦ In addition to the idioms beginning with BITTER, also see TAKE THE BITTER WITH THE SWEET.

bitter end The last extremity; also, death or ruin. For example, *I'm supporting the union's demands to the bitter end,* or *Even though they fight a lot, I'm sure Mom and Dad will stay together to the bitter end.* The source of this term may have been nautical, a *bitter* being a turn of a cable around posts, or *bitts,* on a ship's deck, and the *bitter end* meaning "the part of the cable that stays inboard." Thus, when a rope is paid out to the bitter end, no more remains. [Mid-1800s]

bitter pill to swallow An unpleasant fact, disappointment, or humiliation that is difficult to endure. For example, *Failing the bar exam was a bitter pill to swallow, but he plans to try again next year.* [Late 1500s]

black ♦ In addition to the idioms beginning with BLACK, also see DIRTY (BLACK) LOOK; IN THE RED (BLACK); LOOK BLACK; PAINT BLACK; POT CALLING THE KETTLE BLACK.

black and blue Badly bruised, as in *That fall down the stairs left me black and blue all over.* Even though multicolored bruises rarely include the color black, this term has been so used since about 1300.

black and white 1. A monochromatic picture, drawing, television image, computer monitor, or film, as opposed to one using many colors, as in *Photos in black and white fade less than those taken with color film.* [Late 1800s] 2. Also, **black or white.** Involving a very clear distinction, without any gradations. For example, *He tended to view everything as a black and white issue—it was either right or wrong—whereas his partner always found*

gray areas. This usage is based on the association of black with evil and white with virtue, which dates back at least 2,000 years. [Early 1800s] Also see GRAY AREA. 3. **in black and white.** Written down or in print, and therefore official. For example, *The terms of our agreement were spelled out in black and white, so there should be no question about it.* This term alludes to black ink or print on white paper. Shakespeare used it in *Much Ado about Nothing* (5:1). [Late 1500s]

black as night Also, **black as coal** or **pitch.** Totally black; also, very dark. For example, *The well was black as night,* or *She had eyes that were black as coal.* These similes have survived while others—black as ink, a raven, thunder, hell, the devil, my hat, the minister's coat, the ace of spades—are seldom if ever heard today. Of the current objects of comparison, *pitch* may be the oldest, so used in Homer's *Iliad* (c. 850 B.C.), and *coal* is mentioned in a Saxon manuscript from A.D. 1000. John Milton used *black as night* in *Paradise Lost* (1667).

black book 1. A list of persons or things out of favor, as in *Tom's in my black book these days.* This usage dates from the 14th century and in time became more ominous. In 1536 the agents of King Henry VIII wrote in a black book the names of those to be censured or punished, specifically "sinful" English monasteries (whose lands Henry wanted to acquire). Today being in someone's black book still signifies being in trouble, at least with that person. Also see BLACK LIST. 2. Also, **little black book.** A personal telephone directory listing girlfriends, or, less often, boyfriends. For example, *Now that he's engaged to Ellen, Jim won't be needing his little black book.* [1930s] 3. A list of measures or facts involved in the unfriendly takeover of one company by another. This usage is employed mainly in business and commerce. [c. 1980]

black eye A mark of shame, a humiliating setback, as in *That there are enough homeless folks to need another shelter is a black eye for the administration.* This metaphor alludes to having discolored flesh around the eye resulting from a blow. The term is also used literally, as in *The mugger not only took Bill's wallet but gave him a black eye.* [Late 1800s]

Black Friday 1. Also **Black Monday, Black Tuesday,** etc. A day of economic catastrophe, as in *We feared there'd be another Black Friday.* This usage dates from September 24, 1869, a Friday when stock manipulators Jay Gould and James Fisk tried to corner the gold market and caused its collapse. The adjective *black* has been appended to similar occasions ever since, including October 29, 1929, the Tuesday of the market collapse that marked the start of the Great Depression, and **Black Monday** of October 19, 1987, when the stock market experienced its greatest fall since the Great Depression. **2.** any day marked by great confusion or activity, as in *It was just my luck to be traveling on Black Tuesday.* This usage, too, is based on the events of 1869, marked by economic chaos. It has since been extended to other kinds of confusion, such as an accident hampering traffic during the evening rush hour.

black hole 1. A wretched prison cell or other place of confinement. For example, *The punishment is solitary confinement, known as the black hole.* This term acquired its meaning in 1756 with the event known as the Black Hole of Calcutta. On the night of June 20, the ruler of Bengal confined 146 Europeans in a prison space of only 14 by 18 feet. By morning all but 23 of them had suffocated to death. Although historians since have questioned the truth of the story, it survives in this usage. **2.** A great void or abyss. For example, *Running a single small newspaper ad to launch a major campaign is useless; it amounts to throwing our money into a black hole.* This usage alludes to a region, so named by astronomers, whose gravitational field is so intense that no electromagnetic radiation can escape from it. [Late 1970s]

black list A list of persons or things considered undesirable or deserving punishment, as in *Japanese beetles are on my black list of garden pests.* The practice of making such lists is quite old. Notorious examples include the late 19th-century black lists of union members whom employers would not hire and the black lists of persons suspected of being Communists as a result of the hearings held by Senator Joseph R. McCarthy in the early 1950s. Today the term is also used more loosely, as in the example. [Early 1600s] Also see BLACK BOOK, def. 1.

black look ♦ See under DIRTY LOOK.

black mark An indication of censure or failure, as in *If you refuse to work late, won't that be a black mark against you?* This phrase alludes to a literal black mark, such as a cross, that was put next to a person's name, indicating that he or she had incurred a rebuke or penalty of some kind. [Mid-1800s]

black out 1. Obliterate with black, as in crossing out words on a page or print on a screen. For example, *They have blacked out all the obscene words in the subtitles to make this movie suitable for youngsters.* This usage may be derived from an earlier meaning, "to stain or defame," which dates from the 15th century (and probably alludes to "blackening" a person's reputation). [Mid-1800s] **2.** Extinguish all lights. For example, *The whole town was asleep, as blacked out as London during the war.* In the early 1900s this expression alluded to the lights in a theater, but from about

1940 on it meant darkening an entire city to hide it from enemy bombers. **3.** Lose consciousness, faint; also, experience a temporary loss of memory. For example, *I couldn't remember a single note of the music; I blacked out completely,* or *The accused man claims he blacked out after his first drink.* This usage is thought to have originated with pilots, who sometimes fainted briefly when pulling out of a power dive. It soon was transferred to other losses of consciousness or memory. [c. 1940]

black sheep The least reputable member of a group; a disgrace. For example, *Uncle Fritz was the black sheep of the family; we always thought he emigrated to Argentina to avoid jail.* This metaphor is based on the idea that black sheep were less valuable than white ones because it was more difficult to dye their wool different colors. Also, in the 16th century, their color was considered the devil's mark. By the 18th century the term was widely used as it is today, for the odd member of a group.

blame ♦ See LAY (THE BLAME) ON; TO BLAME.

blank ♦ In addition to the idiom beginning with BLANK, also see DRAW A BLANK; FILL IN (THE BLANKS).

blank check Unrestricted authority, a free hand, as in *I'll support most of the chairman's agenda, but I'm not ready to give him a blank check for the company's future.* Literally this term signifies a bank check that is signed by the drawer but does not indicate the amount of money, which is filled in by the person to whom it is given. [Late 1800s]

blanket ♦ See SECURITY BLANKET; WET BLANKET.

blast ♦ In addition to the idiom beginning with BLAST, also see FULL BLAST.

blast off 1. Also, **blast away.** Take off or be launched, especially into space, as in *They're scheduled to blast off on Tuesday.* This usage originated with the development of powerful rockets, spacecraft, and astronauts, to all of which it was applied. [c. 1950] **2.** Depart, clear out, as in *This party's over; let's blast off now.* [Slang; early 1950s] **3.** Become excited or high, especially from using drugs, as in *They give parties where people blast off.* [Slang; c. 1960]

blaze ♦ In addition to the idiom beginning with BLAZE, also see HOT AS BLAZES; LIKE GREASED LIGHTNING (BLAZES).

blaze a trail Find a new path or method; begin a new undertaking. For example, *His research blazed a trail for new kinds of gene therapy.* This expression was first used literally in the 18th century for the practice of marking a forest trail by making blazes, that is, marking trees with notches or chips in the bark. [Late 1800s]

bleed ♦ In addition to the idiom beginning with BLEED, also see MY HEART BLEEDS FOR YOU.

bleed someone white Extort money, take someone's last penny. For example, *That contractor would have bled the department white, but fortunately he was apprehended in time.* Presumably this term alludes to losing so much blood that one turns pale (and perhaps also to the idea that money is the life blood of commerce). [First half of 1900s]

blessed event The birth of a baby, as in *When is the blessed event expected?* This expression combines two senses of *blessed*, that is, "happy" and "sacred." Today, however, unless used ironically, it is considered cloyingly sentimental. [1920s]

blessing ◆ In addition to the idiom beginning with BLESSING, also see GIVE THANKS FOR SMALL BLESSINGS; MIXED BLESSING.

blessing in disguise A misfortune that unexpectedly turns into good fortune, as in *Missing the train was a blessing in disguise, for if I hadn't, I wouldn't have met my future wife.* [Mid-1700s]

blind ◆ In addition to the idioms beginning with BLIND, also see FLY BLIND; ROB SOMEONE BLIND; TURN A BLIND EYE.

blind alley A dead end; a position without hope of progress or success. For example, *That line of questioning led the attorney up yet another blind alley.* This term alludes to a street or alley that has no outlet at one end. [Mid-1800s]

blind as a bat Quite blind; also, unaware. For example, *Without my glasses I'm blind as a bat*, or *I had no idea they wanted me to take over his job; I was blind as a bat.* This simile, based on the erroneous idea that the bat's erratic flight means it cannot see properly, has survived even though it is now known that bats have a sophisticated built-in sonar system. [Late 1500s]

blindfolded ◆ See DO BLINDFOLDED.

blind leading the blind Those lacking the skills or knowledge for something are being guided by equally inept individuals. For example, *Bill's teaching his son carpentry; that's a case of the blind leading the blind.* The expression is found in the New Testament as one of Jesus's teachings (Matthew 15:14; Luke 6:39). [c. 1600]

blind side ◆ See under BLIND SPOT.

blind spot Subject about which one is ignorant or biased. For example, *The boss has a blind spot about Henry; he wouldn't fire him for anything*, or *Dad has a blind spot about opera; he can't see anything good about it.* This term uses *blind* in the sense of "covered or hidden from sight." It has two literal meanings: an insensitive part of the retina and an area outside one's field of vision. The phrase has largely replaced **blind side**, which survives mainly in the verb **to blindside**, meaning "to hit someone on an unguarded side" and "to deal an unexpected blow." [Mid-1800s]

blink ◆ See ON THE BLINK.

bliss out Experience great joy or euphoria, as in *Just give me some time to bliss out on the beach.* [Slang; c. 1970]

block ◆ See CHIP OFF THE OLD BLOCK; KNOCK SOMEONE'S BLOCK OFF; ON THE BLOCK; STUMBLING BLOCK.

blood ◆ In addition to the idiom beginning with BLOOD, also see BAD BLOOD; DRAW BLOOD; FLESH AND BLOOD; IN COLD BLOOD; IN ONE'S BLOOD; MAKE ONE'S BLOOD BOIL; MAKE ONE'S BLOOD RUN COLD; NEW BLOOD; OUT FOR (BLOOD); RUN IN THE BLOOD (FAMILY); SCREAM BLOODY MURDER; SHED BLOOD; SPORTING BLOOD; SWEAT BLOOD. Also see under BLEED.

blood is thicker than water Family ties are closer than other relationships. For example, *Nancy will drop everything to help her sister; blood is thicker than water.* Alluding to the fact that water evaporates without leaving a mark whereas blood leaves a stain, this proverb was first recorded about 1412.

blossom into Also, **blossom out**. Develop, flourish, as in *She's blossomed into a fine young woman*, or *His business has blossomed out and he's doing well.* [Second half of 1800s]

blot out Obliterate, wipe out of existence or memory, as in *At least one Indian nation was blotted out as the pioneers moved west*, or *The trauma of the accident blotted out all her memory of recent events.* This idiom, first recorded in 1516, uses the verb *to blot* in the sense of making something illegible by spotting or staining it with ink. The New Testament has it (Acts 3:19): "Repent ye . . . that your sins may be blotted out."

blow ◆ In addition to the idioms beginning with BLOW, also see AT ONE STROKE (BLOW); BODY BLOW; COME TO BLOWS; KEEP (BLOW) ONE'S COOL; LOW BLOW; WAY THE WIND BLOWS.

blow a fuse Also, **blow a gasket**. Lose one's temper, express furious anger. For example, *When his paycheck bounced, John blew a fuse*, or *Tell Mom what really happened before she blows a gasket.* An electric fuse is said to "blow" (melt) when the circuit is overloaded, whereas a gasket, used to seal a piston, "blows" (breaks) when the pressure is too high. The first of these slangy terms dates from the 1930s, the second from the 1940s. Also see BLOW ONE'S TOP; KEEP ONE'S COOL.

blow away 1. Kill, especially by gunshot or explosion. For example, *The unit reported that the whole village was blown away.* This usage became particularly widespread in the 1960s, during the Vietnam War. [Slang; early 1900s] 2. Overcome easily; defeat decisively. For example, *Ann said the test would be easy; she would just blow it away*, or *Jim was sure his crew could blow away their opponents.* [Slang; 1960s] Also see BLOW OFF, def. 5. 3. Impress greatly, overwhelm with surprise, delight, or shock, as in *That music really blew me away.* [Slang; c. 1970] Also see BLOW ONE'S MIND.

blow by blow Described in minute detail, as in *Tell me about last night's party, blow by blow.* This term originated in radio broadcasts during the 1930s, in which the sportscaster gave a detailed account of each punch struck in a boxing match. It soon was transferred to a detailed account of anything at all.

blow hot and cold Change one's mind, vacillate, as in *Jean's been blowing hot and cold about taking a winter vacation.* This expression comes from Aesop's fable (c. 570 B.C.) about a man eating with a satyr on a winter day. At first the man blew on his hands to warm them and then blew on his soup to cool it. The satyr thereupon renounced the man's friendship because he blew hot and cold out of the same mouth. The expression was repeated by many writers, most often signifying a person who could not be relied on. William Chillingworth put it: "These men can blow hot and cold out of the same mouth to serve several purposes" (*The Religion of Protestants,* 1638).

blow in Arrive, especially unexpectedly. For example, *Just when we'd given him up, Arthur blew in.* [Colloquial; late 1800s]

blow it 1. Spoil, botch, or bungle something, as in *That was a great opportunity, but now I've blown it.* [Slang; c. 1940] 2. **blow one's lines.** Make a mistake in speaking one's part in a theatrical production, as in *Ben blew his lines, but Dean came to the rescue.* [Mid-1900s]

blow off 1. Vent one's strong feelings; see BLOW OFF STEAM. 2. Disregard, ignore; evade something important. For example, *If you blow off your homework, you're bound to run into trouble on the exam.* [Slang; second half of 1900s] 3. Overcome, defeat easily, as in *With Rob pitching, we'll have no trouble blowing off the opposing team.* [Slang; 1950s] Also see BLOW AWAY, def. 2. 4. Ignore, abandon, refuse to take part. For example, *The college is blowing off our request for a new student center:* [Slang; mid-1900s]

blow off steam Also, **let off steam.** Air or relieve one's pent-up feelings by loud talk or vigorous activity. For example, *Joan's shouting did not mean she was angry at you; she was just blowing off steam,* or *After spending the day on very exacting work, Tom blew off steam by going for a long run.* This metaphoric term refers to easing the pressure in a steam engine. [Early 1800s]

blow one's brains out Shoot oneself in the head, as in *Blowing one's brains out is more a man's type of suicide; women lean toward poison.* [Early 1800s]

blow one's cool ♦ See under KEEP ONE'S COOL.

blow one's cover Inadvertently give away one's secret identity, as in *Mary came to the annual meeting pretending to be a shareholder and hoped no one would blow her cover.* This expression uses *blow* in the sense of "expose or betray," a usage dating from Shakespeare's day.

blow one's mind 1. Surprise, shock, or amaze one, as in *This jazz group blows my mind,* or *Joe served a jail sentence? That blows my mind.* This term is used rather loosely, as seen in the examples; the first signifies amazement and pleasure, the second shock and dismay. [Slang; 1960s] 2. Alter one's perceptions, especially through drug use, as in *Taking LSD really blows one's mind.* [Slang; 1960s] 3. Make insane, drive crazy, as in *Was it his wife's death that blew his mind?* or *Losing her savings blew her mind.* [1960s]

blow one's own horn Also, **blow one's trumpet.** Brag about oneself, as in *Within two minutes of meeting someone new, Bill was blowing his own horn.* [Late 1500s]

blow one's top 1. Also, **blow one's stack.** Fly into a rage; lose one's composure. For example, *If she calls about this one more time I'm going to blow my top,* or *Warren is generally very easy-going, but today he blew his stack.* The *top* here has been likened to the top of an erupting volcano; the *stack* alludes to a smokestack. [Slang; first half of 1900s] 2. Go crazy, become insane, as in *When she regains consciousness, she just may blow her top.* [Slang; first half of 1900s] Also see FLIP ONE'S LID.

blow someone to Treat someone to something, as in *Let me blow you to dinner.* [Slang; late 1800s]

blow out 1. Extinguish, especially a flame. For example, *The wind blew out the candles very quickly.* [1300s] 2. Lose force or cease entirely, as in *The storm will soon blow itself out and move out to sea.* Also see BLOW OVER. 3. Burst or rupture suddenly, as in *This tire is about to blow out.* This usage alludes to the escape of air under pressure. [Early 1900s] 4. Also, **blow out of the water.** Defeat decisively, as in *With a great new product and excellent publicity, we could blow the competition out of the water.* This term was originally used in mid-19th-century naval warfare, where it meant to blast or shoot another vessel to pieces. It later was transferred to athletic and other kinds of defeat. [Slang; mid-1900s]

blow over Pass away, subside. For example, *The storm will blow over by afternoon,* or *After a couple of years the scandal will blow over.* This term, with its analogy to storm clouds that pass over an area without descending, dates from about 1600.

blow sky-high 1. Destroy by explosion, explode, as in *Once the charge is set, get away fast or you'll be blown sky-high.* [Early 1800s] Also see under BLOW

UP. **2.** Refute completely, as in *The lab report has blown your theory sky-high.* [Mid-1800s]

blow the lid off Also, **blow wide open.** Expose, especially a scandal or illegal activity. For example, *The newspaper's investigation blew the lid off the governor's awarding state contracts to his friends.* [First half of 1900s]

blow the whistle on 1. Expose corruption or other wrongdoing, as in *The President's speech blew the whistle on the opposition's leaking information.* [Colloquial; 1930s] **2.** Put a stop to, as in *The registry decided to blow the whistle on new vanity plates.* The term originally alluded to ending an activity (such as factory work) with the blast of a whistle. [Late 1800s]

blow up 1. Explode or cause to explode. For example, *The squadron was told to blow up the bridge,* or *Jim was afraid his experiment would blow up the lab.* The term is sometimes amplified, as in **blow up in one's face.** [Late 1500s] **2.** Lose one's temper, as in *I'm sorry I blew up at you.* Mark Twain used this metaphor for an actual explosion in one of his letters (1871): "Redpath tells me to blow up. Here goes!" [Colloquial; second half of 1800s] **3.** Inflate, fill with air, as in *If you don't blow up those tires you're sure to have a flat.* [Early 1400s] **4.** Enlarge, especially a photograph, as in *If we blow up this picture, you'll be able to make out the expressions on their faces.* [c. 1930] **5.** Exaggerate the importance of something or someone, as in *Tom has a tendency to blow up his own role in the affair.* This term applies the "inflate" of def. 3 to importance. It was used in this sense in England from the early 1500s to the 1700s, but then became obsolete there although it remains current in America. **6.** Collapse, fail, as in *Graduate-student marriages often blow up soon after the couple earn their degrees.* [Slang; mid-1800s]

blue ♦ In addition to the idioms beginning with BLUE, also see BETWEEN A ROCK AND A HARD PLACE (DEVIL AND DEEP BLUE SEA); BLACK AND BLUE; BOLT FROM THE BLUE; HAVE THE BLUES; INTO THIN AIR (THE BLUE); LIKE GREASED LIGHTNING (A BLUE STREAK); ONCE IN A BLUE MOON; OUT OF A CLEAR BLUE SKY; TALK ONE'S ARM OFF (A BLUE STREAK; UNTIL BLUE IN THE FACE).

blue funk, in a 1. In a state of panic or terror. For example, *Just because the bride's mother is late, you needn't get in a blue funk.* This term originated in the mid-1700s as **in a funk,** the adjective *blue,* meaning "affected with fear or anxiety," being added a century later. **2.** In a state of dejection, sad. For example, *Anne has been in a blue funk since her dog died.* This usage employs *blue* in the sense of "sad"—a meaning that first emerged in the late 1300s. Also see HAVE THE BLUES.

blue in the face Exhausted from anger, strain, or other great effort. For example, *You can argue until you're blue in the face, but I refuse to go.* This expression alludes to the bluish skin color resulting from lack of oxygen, which presumably might result from talking until one was breathless. See also under TALK ONE'S ARM OFF.

blues ♦ See HAVE THE BLUES.

bluff ♦ See CALL SOMEONE'S BLUFF.

blurt out Say abruptly or inadvertently, utter without thinking. For example, *Unfortunately he blurted out how much he hated formal dinners just as his hostess walked in.* [Late 1500s]

blush ♦ See AT FIRST BLUSH.

board ♦ See ACROSS THE BOARD; BACK TO THE DRAWING BOARD; BED AND BOARD; BULLETIN BOARD; BY THE BOARD; GO OVERBOARD; ON BOARD; OPEN AND ABOVEBOARD; ROOM AND BOARD; STIFF AS A BOARD; TREAD THE BOARDS.

boardinghouse reach Reaching across fellow diners for food instead of asking them to pass it. For example, *At holiday meals when the whole family is gathered, Dad always scolds at least one child for his boardinghouse reach.* This term alludes to the formerly common boardinghouse practice of seating all the residents at one large table and to the rudeness of those who simply reached across others to help themselves. Heard less often today, it is not quite obsolete. [c. 1900]

boat ♦ See BURN ONE'S BRIDGES (BOATS); IN THE SAME BOAT; MISS THE BOAT; ROCK THE BOAT.

bob up Appear suddenly or unexpectedly. For example, *I didn't know anyone in the group until Harry bobbed up.* This term uses the verb *bob* in the sense of "to bounce," a usage dating from Chaucer's day. [Late 1800s]

body ♦ In addition to the idioms beginning with BODY, also see COME IN A BODY; KEEP BODY AND SOUL TOGETHER; OVER MY DEAD BODY.

body blow An action that causes severe damage, as in *This last recession dealt a body blow to our whole industry.* This term comes from boxing, where since the 18th century it has been used to refer to a punch that is landing between the opponent's chest and navel. [c. 1900]

body English Movements of the body that express a person's feelings, as in *His body English tells us just how tired he is.* This expression originated about 1900 in such sports as bowling and ice hockey, where a player tries to influence the path of a ball or puck by moving his body in a particular direction. (It was based on the earlier use of *English* to mean "spin imparted to a ball.")

bog down Become stuck, be unable to progress, as in *Their research bogged down because they lacked* *the laboratory expertise.* This expression transfers sinking into the mud of a swamp to being hampered or halted. [First half of 1900s]

boggle the mind Bewilder or astonish with complexity, novelty, or the like, as in *The very magnitude of the Milky Way boggles the mind.* The source of this usage is unclear, as the verb *to boggle* has several other seemingly unrelated meanings—to shy away, to hesitate, to bungle. [Second half of 1900s]

boil ♦ In addition to the idioms beginning with BOIL, also see MAKE ONE'S BLOOD BOIL; WATCHED POT NEVER BOILS.

boil down 1. Simplify, summarize, or shorten, as in *John finally managed to boil his thesis down to 200 pages.* 2. **boil down to.** Be reducible to basic elements, be equivalent to. For example, *What this issue boils down to is that the council doesn't want to spend more money.* These metaphoric usages allude to reducing and concentrating a substance by boiling off liquid. [Late 1800s]

boiling point A climax or crisis; a high degree of fury, excitement, or outrage. For example, *The union's disgust with management has reached the boiling point.* This metaphoric term alludes to the temperature at which water boils. [Second half of 1700s] 2. **have a low boiling point.** Become angry quite readily, as in *Don't tease her anymore—she has a low boiling point.* This phrase means that it takes less heat than usual for a boiling point to be reached. [First half of 1800s] Also see BOIL OVER; MAKE ONE'S BLOOD BOIL.

boil over Erupt in anger, excitement, or other strong emotion. For example, *The mere mention of a tax increase will make Kevin boil over.* This phrase alludes to overflowing while boiling. [Second half of 1800s]

bold ♦ In addition to the idiom beginning with BOLD, also see BIG AND BOLD; MAKE BOLD.

bold as brass Shameless, audacious, impudent. For example, *No one had invited her to the wedding, but she showed up at the church, bold as brass.* This alliterative simile plays on *brass* meaning "shamelessness." [c. 1700]

bolt ♦ In addition to the idioms beginning with BOLT, also see NUTS AND BOLTS; SHOOT ONE'S BOLT.

bolt from the blue, a Also, **a bolt out of the blue.** A sudden, unexpected event. For example, *Bill's dropping his life insurance was a bolt from the blue for his wife.* This metaphoric term alludes to totally unforeseen lightning or thunder from a cloudless (blue) sky. [First half of 1800s]

bolt upright Precisely perpendicular, erect in carriage, as in *She sat bolt upright in her pew.* This expression was used in slightly different form by

Chaucer in the late 1300s: "She was . . . long as a mast and upright as a bolt" (*The Miller's Tale*).

bomb ♦ See TIME BOMB.

bombshell ♦ See DROP A BOMBSHELL.

bone ♦ In addition to the idioms beginning with BONE, also see BARE BONES; CHILLED TO THE BONE; CUT TO THE BONE; FEEL IN ONE'S BONES; FUNNY BONE; MAKE NO BONES ABOUT; PULL A BONER; ROLL THE BONES; SKIN AND BONES; WORK ONE'S FINGERS TO THE BONE.

bone of contention Main issue of a disagreement; something to quarrel about. For example, *Grandfather's will was a bone of contention for the whole family.* This expression alludes to two dogs fighting (contending) over a single bone. In slightly different guise, **bone of dissension,** it was used figuratively in the 16th century and took its present form in the early 1700s.

bone to pick, have a An unpleasant issue or grievance that needs discussion. For example, *Concerning the room assignments, I have a bone to pick with you.* This metaphoric term alludes to a dog worrying a bone. [Early 1500s]

bone up Study intensely, as in *I'll have to bone up on my Spanish if I'm to pass the language requirement.* The verb *bone* alone was used in this sense from the mid-1800s on, *up* being added later. [Slang; late 1800s]

bonnet ♦ See BEE IN ONE'S BONNET.

book ♦ See BALANCE THE BOOKS; BLACK BOOK; BRING TO BOOK; BY THE BOOK; CLOSED BOOK; CLOSE THE BOOKS; COOK THE BOOKS; CRACK A BOOK; HIT THE BOOKS; IN ONE'S BOOK; IN SOMEONE'S BAD GRACES (BOOKS); JUDGE A BOOK BY ITS COVER; KEEP THE BOOKS; KNOW LIKE A BOOK; MAKE BOOK; NOSE IN A BOOK; ONE FOR THE BOOKS; OPEN BOOK; TAKE A LEAF OUT OF SOMEONE'S BOOK; THROW THE BOOK AT; WROTE THE BOOK ON.

boom ♦ See LOWER THE BOOM.

boot ♦ In addition to the idioms beginning with BOOT, also see DIE WITH ONE'S BOOTS ON; GET THE AX (BOOT); KICK (BOOT) OUT; LICK SOMEONE'S BOOTS; PULL ONESELF UP (BY THE BOOTSTRAPS); QUAKE IN ONE'S BOOTS; TO BOOT; TOO BIG FOR ONE'S BREECHES (BOOTS); YOU CAN BET YOUR ASS (BOOTS). Also see under SHOE.

boot out ♦ See KICK OUT.

boot up Start a computer, as in *When you've booted up, it's best not to turn off the computer until you're done for the day.* The term, dating from the late 1970s, was a shortening of **bootstrap,** another computer idiom referring to using one set of instructions to load another set of instructions. Also see LOG IN.

bore to death Also, **bore to tears** or **bore stiff** or **bore the pants off.** Weary someone through extremely dull talk or uninteresting action. For example, *Sam was bored stiff by the opera but didn't dare to admit it,* or *Carol bores the pants off me with her constant talk of remodeling,* or *His books bore me to death.* All four expressions convey the idea of such exasperation that one dies, weeps, stiffens with annoyance, or has one's trousers removed. The verb *bore* has been used in this sense only since about 1750, and its etymology is unknown. The amplifications were added between about 1850 and 1950. Also see under PANTS OFF; TALK ONE'S ARM OFF.

born ♦ In addition to the idioms beginning with BORN, also see IN ALL ONE'S BORN DAYS; NATURAL BORN; NOT BORN YESTERDAY; TO THE MANNER BORN.

born and bred Born and educated in a single locale or social class. For example, *Adam was a Bostonian, born and bred.* Although the two words were paired earlier, the precise locution dates from the mid-1800s.

born under a lucky star Very fortunate, as in *Peter comes out ahead no matter what he tries; he was born under a lucky star.* That stars influence human lives is an ancient idea, and *lucky star* was used by writers from Shakespeare to the present. The precise phrase appears in a compendium of English idioms compiled by J. Burvenich in 1905. Also see THANK ONE'S LUCKY STARS.

born with a silver spoon Born wealthy, or fortunate, or both, as in *Paul can afford to go to medical school; he was born with a silver spoon.* Although some authorities believe this phrase alludes to the custom of godparents giving their godchild a silver spoon, affordable only by rich persons, it is more likely that the spoon has come to symbolize wealth. [c. 1700]

born yesterday ♦ See NOT BORN YESTERDAY.

borrow ♦ In addition to the idiom beginning with BORROW, also see BEG, BORROW OR STEAL; ON BORROWED TIME.

borrow trouble Go out of one's way to do something that may be harmful, as in *Just sign the will—telling her about it ahead of time is borrowing trouble.* [Mid-1800s] Also see ASK FOR, def. 2.

boss around Tell someone what to do, give orders. For example, *David complained that his older sister was always bossing him around.* The use of *boss* in the sense of "to dominate" dates from the mid-1800s, and *around* was added a few decades later.

both ♦ In addition to the idioms beginning with BOTH, also see BEST OF BOTH WORLDS; BURN THE CANDLE AT BOTH ENDS; CUT BOTH WAYS; FOOT IN BOTH CAMPS; HAVE IT BOTH WAYS; PLAY BOTH ENDS AGAINST THE MIDDLE; WORK BOTH SIDES OF THE STREET.

both barrels, with With full force, as in *When I scolded her for stealing, I let her have it with both barrels.* This term alludes to firing with both barrels of a double-barreled shotgun. [Colloquial; mid-1900s]

bother, bothered ♦ See GO TO THE TROUBLE (BOTHER); HOT AND BOTHERED.

both feet on the ground, with In a sensible, realistic, or practical manner. For example, *You can count on Tom not to get cheated in that deal; he has both feet on the ground,* or *Jean is a dreamer; but her husband is a man with his feet on the ground.* There is a related phrase, **have both feet on the ground,** meaning "to be practical or realistic." [Mid-1900s]

bottle ♦ In addition to the idiom beginning with BOTTLE, also see CRACK A BOTTLE; HIT THE BOTTLE; NEW WINE IN OLD BOTTLES.

bottle up Repress, contain, hold back; also, confine or trap. For example, *The psychiatrist said Eve had been bottling up her anger for years,* or *The accident bottled up traffic for miles.* This idiom likens other kinds of restraint to liquid being contained in a bottle. [Mid-1800s]

bottom ♦ In addition to the idioms beginning with BOTTOM, also see AT BOTTOM; FROM HEAD TO TOE (TOP TO BOTTOM); FROM THE BOTTOM OF ONE'S HEART; GET TO THE BOTTOM; HIT (TOUCH) BOTTOM; KNOCK THE BOTTOM OUT OF; ROCK BOTTOM; TOUCH BOTTOM; YOU BET YOUR ASS (BOTTOM DOLLAR).

bottom drops out, the Also, **the bottom falls out.** A collapse occurs, as in *The bottom dropped out of the steel market,* or *When they lost the game, the bottom fell out of their hopes to make the playoffs.* This term alludes to collapsing deeper than the very lowest point, or bottom. [First half of 1600s]

bottom line The ultimate result, the upshot; also, the main point or crucial factor. For example, *The bottom line is that the chairman wants to dictate all of the board's decisions,* or *Whether or not he obeyed the law is the bottom line.* This is an accounting term that refers to the earnings figures that appear on the bottom (last) line of a statement. It began to be transferred to other contexts in the mid-1900s.

bottom of the barrel The least desirable, the dregs, as in *The nominating committee had trouble finding candidates; they were settling for the bottom of the barrel.* The phrase often occurs in **scrape the bottom of the barrel,** meaning "to use the least desirable elements" (because one has no choice), as in *Bringing up that minor legal point proves that you're scraping the bottom of the barrel.* This metaphor for the sediment left by wine in a barrel was already used by Cicero to describe the lowest elements of Roman society. [First half of 1900s]

bottom of the ladder Lowest or most junior position in a hierarchy. For example, *If we hire you, you'll have to begin at the bottom of the ladder.* The rungs of a ladder have been likened to a step-wise progression since the 14th century. Also see LOW MAN ON THE TOTEM POLE.

bottom out Reach the lowest level, as in *The recession appears to have bottomed out.* This verbal use of *bottom* originated in the late 1800s and, with the addition of *out* in the mid-1900s, tends to be used mostly in the context of trade and finance.

bought ♦ See under BUY.

bounce ♦ In addition to the idioms beginning with BOUNCE, also see GET THE AX (BOUNCE); MORE BOUNCE FOR THE OUNCE; THAT'S HOW THE BALL BOUNCES.

bounce around 1. Move around from one person or place to another. For example, *The staff spent the morning bouncing around ideas to improve sales,* or *She had been bouncing around from one job to another.* This term alludes to a ball bouncing among players. [Colloquial; mid-1900s] 2. Treat roughly or unfairly, as in *Quit bouncing me around; I won't stand for it.* This usage is based on a somewhat earlier meaning of *bounce,* "to beat up" or "coerce." [Slang; c. 1970]

bounce back Recover quickly, as in *She had pneumonia, but she bounced back in less than a week.* This expression is a metaphor for the rebound of a ball or some elastic material.

bound ♦ In addition to the idioms beginning with BOUND, also see BY LEAPS AND BOUNDS; DUTY BOUND; HONOR BOUND; OUT OF BOUNDS; WITHIN BOUNDS. Also see under BIND.

bound and determined to Firmly resolved to, as in *He was bound and determined to finish the assignment before taking on another.* This phrase is a redundancy used for emphasis, as *bound* and *determined* here both mean "resolved to." Also see BOUND TO.

bound for On the way to, heading for. For example, *This bus is bound for Broadway.* It is also found in a well-known gospel hymn in which the singer is "bound for the land of Canaan." This phrase stems from the 12th-century meaning of *bound* as "ready" or "prepared."

bound hand and foot Wholly obligated, unable to free oneself. For example, *These rules have us bound hand and foot; we can't even discuss the matter.* This term transfers the literal meaning, having one's hands and feet tied and therefore unable to move, to legal, moral, or social obligations. The expression dates from the 10th century A.D.

bound to, be Be certain or destined to; also, be determined or resolved to. For example, *We are bound to hear from them soon,* or *No matter what they say, she is bound to run for mayor.* This usage is derived from the older sense of *bound* as "obliged." [Mid-1500s]

bound up in Also, **bound up with.** Deeply or inextricably involved in. For example, *Obviously the candidate was bound up with the negotiations on the party platform,* or *She is bound up in her church activities.* This usage appears in the Bible (Genesis 44:30): "His life is bound up in the lad's life." [Late 1500s]

bow ♦ In addition to the idioms beginning with BOW, also see TAKE A BOW; TWO STRINGS TO ONE'S BOW.

bow and scrape Behave obsequiously or too deferentially, as in *In this fashionable store, the salespersons virtually bow and scrape before customers.* This term alludes to the old-fashioned custom of bowing so deeply that one's foot draws back and scrapes the ground. A cliché for a century or more, it may be dying out. [Mid-1600s]

bowl of cherries, life is just a These are happy circumstances; life is wonderful. This phrase is often used ironically, as in *My husband is about to get laid off—life is just a bowl of cherries, right?* Originating as the title of a song (1931) by Lew Brown (lyrics) and composer Ray Henderson, this term expressed the idea that everything was going very well. However, its ironical use was established by the 1970s. Also see BED OF ROSES.

bowl over Astonish, surprise greatly, overwhelm, as in *I was simply bowled over by their wonderful performance.* This term originated in cricket, where it means "to knock all the bails off the wicket." [Mid-1800s]

bow out Depart, withdraw, resign, as in *After five years as chairman, I felt it was time I bowed out,* or *We'll have to beat them; they'll never bow out.* [First half of 1900s]

box ♦ In addition to the idioms beginning with BOX, also see IN A BIND (BOX); ON ONE'S SOAPBOX; PANDORA'S BOX; STUFF THE BALLOT BOX.

box office 1. The office where seats for a play, concert, or other form of entertainment may be purchased, as in *Tickets are available at the box office.* It is so called because originally (17th century) it was the place for hiring a box, a special compartment of theater seats set aside for ladies. [Second half of 1700s] 2. The financial receipts from a performance; also, a show's relative success in attracting a paying audience. For example, *You may not consider it great art, but this play is good box office.* [c. 1900]

box score 1. A detailed summary of actions or an event, as in *The President wanted to base his reelection campaign on his box score.* The term comes from baseball, where since about 1910 it has signified a statistical summary in table form of the essential details of a game. About 1930 it began to be used figuratively, especially by politicians referring to their own record while in office. **2.** In military slang, the number of dead, wounded, or missing in action. For example, *Never mind the details of the battle; just give the lieutenant the box score.* [c. 1950]

box the compass Make a complete turnabout or reversal, as in *With a change of ownership, the editorial page boxed the compass politically, now supporting the Senator.* Originally this was (and continues to be) a nautical term, meaning "repeat the 32 points of the compass in order." In the early 1800s it began to be used figuratively.

boy ◆ In addition to the idiom beginning with BOYS, also see FAIR-HAIRED BOY; MAMA'S BOY; SEPARATE THE MEN FROM THE BOYS; WHIPPING BOY.

boys will be boys One can expect boys to act childishly or misbehave, as in *We told the kids not to eat in the living room, but when we got home there was a big mess there—oh well, boys will be boys.* This term came from a Latin proverb, translated as "Children [boys] are children [boys] and do childish things." In English it was first recorded in 1589.

brace up Also, **brace oneself.** Summon up one's courage or resolve, as in *Brace up, we don't have much farther to go,* or *Squaring his shoulders, he braced himself for the next wave.* This idiom uses *brace* in the sense of "to bolster" or "to strengthen." The first term dates from the early 1700s, the variant from about 1500.

brain ◆ In addition to the idioms beginning with BRAIN, also see BEAT ONE'S BRAINS OUT; BLOW ONE'S BRAINS OUT; HALF A BRAIN; ON ONE'S MIND (THE BRAIN); PICK SOMEONE'S BRAINS; RACK ONE'S BRAINS.

brain drain The departure of educated or talented persons for better pay or jobs elsewhere, as in *The repression of free speech in Germany triggered a brain drain to Britain and America.* The term originated about 1960, when many British scientists and intellectuals emigrated to the United States for a better working climate.

brain someone Hit someone hard on the head. For example, *The roof collapsed and a hunk of plaster brained him,* or *I'll brain you if you don't get to those dishes!* This term is used both literally (first example) and hyperbolically (second example). [Slang; 1930s]

brain trust A group of experts who serve as unofficial but vital advisers. For example, *Each town manager seemed to have his or her own brain trust, which of course changed with every election.* This term, closely associated with President Franklin Roosevelt's advisers on domestic and foreign policy in the early 1930s, was first recorded in 1910.

brake ◆ See PUT THE BRAKE ON.

branch ◆ In addition to the idioms beginning with BRANCH, also see OLIVE BRANCH; ROOT AND BRANCH.

branch off Diverge, subdivide, as in *It's the house on the left, just after the road branches off,* or *English and Dutch branched off from an older parent language, West Germanic.* This term alludes to a tree's growth pattern, in which branches grow in separate directions from the main trunk. [Second half of 1800s] Also see BRANCH OUT.

branch out Separate into subdivisions; strike off in a new direction. For example, *Our software business is branching out into more interactive products,* or *Bill doesn't want to concentrate on just one field; he wants to branch out more.* This term alludes to the growth habits of a tree's limbs. [Early 1700s] Also see BRANCH OFF.

brass ◆ In addition to the idioms beginning with BRASS, also see BOLD AS BRASS; DOUBLE IN BRASS; GET DOWN TO BRASS TACKS.

brass hat A high-ranking official, as in *All the brass hats were invited to the sales conference.* The terms **big brass, top brass,** and **the brass** all refer to high officials considered as a group. For example, *John's one of the top brass in town—he's superintendent of schools.* The origin of this term is disputed. Most authorities believe it originated in the late 19th-century British army, when senior officers had gold leaves on their cap brims. Another theory is that it referred to the cocked hat worn by Napoleon and his officers, which they folded and carried under the arm when indoors. In French these were called *chapeaux à bras* ("hats in arms"), a term the British are supposed to have anglicized as *brass.* By World War I *brass hat* referred to a high-ranking officer in Britain and America, and in World War II it was joined by the other *brass* phrases. After the war these terms began to be used for the top executives in business and other organizations.

brass ring A chance to achieve wealth or success; a prize or reward. For example, "As a businessman he let the brass ring go by too many times. And it got him." This quotation from the *Boston Globe* (July 31, 1995) refers to an executive who was forced to resign. The term comes from the practice of giving a free ride to the person who succeeded in picking a ring out of a box while riding a merry-go-round. [Slang; late 1800s]

brave face, put on a Also, **put up a brave front. 1.** Face adversity cheerfully. For example, *Even though she had been passed over for promotion, she put on a brave face.* **2.** Try to appear brave even though very frightened. For example, *Harry was terrified of animals, but his boss was a dog lover, so he put up a brave front.* [Second half of 1800s]

brave it out 1. Face danger or a difficult situation with courage. For example, *They had far fewer votes than the opposition, but they decided to brave it out.* [Late 1500s] 2. Also, **brazen it out.** Boast or swagger, act with impudent bravado. For example, *They hadn't been invited but decided to stay and brazen it out.* [Mid-1500s]

brave the elements Go out in stormy weather, as in *We've just about run out of food; I'll brave the elements and walk to the store.* The use of *elements* for atmospheric agencies dates from the early 16th century but is rare today except in this expression, which is often used hyperbolically.

breach ♦ See ONCE MORE INTO THE BREACH; STAND IN THE BREACH.

bread ♦ In addition to the idioms beginning with BREAD, also see BREAK BREAD; GREATEST THING SINCE SLICED BREAD; KNOW WHICH SIDE OF BREAD IS BUTTERED; TAKE THE BREAD OUT OF SOMEONE'S MOUTH.

bread and butter 1. The essential, sustaining element, as in *The quality of the schools is the bread and butter of town property values.* This idiom alludes to a basic food, bread spread with butter. [c. 1700] 2. Means of livelihood, as in *John's job is the family's bread and butter.* [First half of 1700s] 3. Ordinary, routine, as in *Don't worry about it; this is just a bread and butter assignment.* [Second half of 1800s]

bread-and-butter letter A thank-you letter from guest to host. For example, *Mother always had to remind the children to send Grandma a bread-and-butter note.* [c. 1900]

break ♦ In addition to the idioms beginning with BREAK, also see GET A BREAK; GIVE SOMEONE A BREAK; MAKE A BREAK FOR IT; MAKE OR BREAK; NEVER GIVE A SUCKER AN EVEN BREAK; TAKE A BREAK; TOUGH BREAK. Also see under BROKE.

break a leg 1. Fracture one or more leg bones, as in *She fell down the stairs and broke her leg in two places.* [c. A.D. 1000] 2. Good luck! as in *Play well, Rob — break a leg!* The origin of this imperative to a performer about to go onstage is unclear; it may have been a translation of the German *Hals und Beinbruch* ("Break your neck and leg"), also of unknown origin. Equally mysterious is the Italian equivalent, *In bocca di lupe,* "Into the mouth of the wolf." [c. 1900]

break away 1. Leave hurriedly, escape, get loose. For example, *The boy tried to break away, but his mother held onto his coat,* or *On the last lap the horse broke away from the pack.* [First half of 1500s] 2. Sever connections with a group. For example, *It was hard for me to break away from that organization, but I knew it was necessary.* 3. Stop doing something, as in *She broke away from work long enough to go out for lunch.*

break bread Have a meal, eat. For example, *It's hard to remain enemies when you've broken bread together.* This term occurs in numerous places in the New Testament, where it sometimes means to share bread and other times to distribute food to others. In later usage it came to refer to the sacramental bread of Communion in Christian services. The latter survives in the spiritual hymn, "Let Us Break Bread Together." [1300s]

break camp Take down a tent and pack up other gear; also, leave a place, move out. For example, *The landlord has to return my rent deposit before I'll break camp.* Originally *camp* denoted a military encampment, but by the mid-1500s the term had been transferred to temporary outdoor sites used by hunters and the like. By the 19th century, the current term was in use. Thus, "It is the hunter's rule to see that the fire is extinguished . . . before breaking camp." (F.H. Guillemard, *Cruise of Marchesa I,* 1886).

break cover Suddenly emerge from a hiding place, as in *The shots distracted our pursuers long enough so that we could break cover and make a run for it.* This term originally alluded to animals being hunted, a frequent usage in the 16th century. Now that hunting is a less common pursuit, it is used for human beings.

break down 1. Demolish, destroy, either physically or figuratively, as in *The carpenters broke down the partition between the bedrooms,* or *The governor's speeches broke down the teachers' opposition to school reform.* [Late 1300s] 2. Separate into constituent parts, analyze. For example, *I insisted that they break down the bill into the separate charges for parts and labor,* or *The chemist was trying to break down the compound's molecules.* [Mid-1800s] 3. Stop functioning, cease to be effective or operable, as in *The old dishwasher finally broke down.* [Mid-1800s] 4. Become distressed or upset; also, have a physical or mental collapse, as in *The funeral was too much for her and she broke down in tears,* or *After seeing all his work come to nothing, he broke down and had to be treated by a psychiatrist.* [Late 1800s]

break even Neither gain nor lose in some venture, recoup the amount one invested. For example, *If the dealer sells five cars a week, he'll break even.* This expression probably came from one or another card game (some authorities say it was faro), where it meant to bet that a card would win and lose an equal number of times. It soon was transferred to balancing business gains and losses. Novelist Sinclair Lewis so used it in *Our Mr. Wrenn* (1914). The usage gave rise to the noun

break-even point, for the amount of sales or production needed for a firm to recoup its investment. [Late 1800s]

break ground Also, **break new ground. 1.** Begin digging into the earth for new construction of some kind. For example, *When will they break ground for the town hall?* This usage alludes to breaking up the land with a plow. [Early 1700s] **2.** Take the first steps for a new venture; advance beyond previous achievements. For example, *Jeff is breaking new ground in intellectual property law.* [Early 1700s]

break in 1. Enter by force, as in *The thieves broke in through the back door.* [Mid-1500s] Also see BREAK INTO. **2.** Also, **break in on.** Interrupt or disturb something unexpectedly, as in *His assistant broke in with the bad news just as we were ready to sign the agreement,* or *He broke in on our private talks.* [Mid-1600s] **3.** Train or instruct someone in a new job or enterprise, as in *Every semester she had to break in a new teaching assistant.* [Late 1700s] **4.** Loosen or soften with use, as in *It takes a while to break in a pair of new shoes.*

break into 1. Make a forcible entry into, as in *The alarm went off as soon as they tried to break into the house.* [1300s] Also see BREAK IN, def. 1. **2.** Interrupt, as in *I couldn't help but break into your conversation.* [Mid-1600s] **3.** Suddenly begin some activity, as in *Without warning she broke into tears.* Also see under BURST INTO. **4.** Enter or be admitted to an occupation or profession, as in *Without connections it is virtually impossible to break into acting.* [Late 1800s]

break it up ◆ See under BREAK UP.

break loose Escape from restraint, as in *The boat broke loose from its moorings,* or *He finally broke loose from the school of abstract expressionism.* This expression also appears in **all hell breaks loose,** which indicates a state of fury or chaos, as in *When Dad finds out you broke his watch, all hell will break loose,* or *When the children saw the dead pigeon in the hall, all hell broke loose.* [Early 1400s]

break of day Dawn, early morning, as in *We'll leave at break of day, as soon as it's light,* or *I feel as though I've been working since the break of day.* This term uses *break* in the sense "burst out of darkness." [First half of 1500s] A synonym from the same period is the noun **daybreak.**

break off 1. Stop abruptly, as in *The trade talks broke off yesterday.* [First half of 1300s] **2.** Separate, sever a connection, as in *The baby broke off the tops of all the flowers,* or *The new sect has broken off from the established church.* [First half of 1500s] **3.** End a relationship or friendship, as in *Mary broke off her engagement to Rob.* [Mid-1600s]

break one ◆ In addition to the idioms beginning with BREAK ONE, also see under BREAK SOMEONE.

break one's ass Also, **break** or **bust one's ass** or **balls** or **butt** or **chops. 1.** Exert oneself to the utmost, try extremely hard, as in *I've been breaking my ass to finish early.* This expression is considered vulgar slang; both *ass,* for backside or buttocks, and *balls,* for male genitals, are rude; *butt,* for buttocks, and *chops,* for either the mouth or the legs, are informal and emphatic but not quite as offensive. For a more polite synonym, see BREAK ONE'S BACK. [Slang; first half of 1900s] **2. break someone's ass.** Also, **bust someone's chops.** Thrash or harass someone, as in *Jim threatened to break Tim's ass,* or *The boss broke his workers' chops to improve service.* [Vulgar slang; mid-1900s]

break one's back Also, **break one's neck.** Make a great effort, work very hard. For example, *I've been breaking my back over this problem for the past week,* or *Don't break your neck to get there; we'll wait for you.* Both versions of this expression, polite equivalents of BREAK ONE'S ASS, transfer the literal fracture of one's back or neck to figurative exertion. However, **break one's neck** has the secondary connotation of proceeding with reckless speed, a sense also conveyed by the term **break-neck pace.** Originally this idiom alluded to literally breaking one's neck by rushing heedlessly along, but it has been used figuratively for the past 300 years. Also see BREAK THE BACK OF.

break one's balls ◆ See under BREAK ONE'S ASS.

break one's fall Interrupt a tumble or descent, as in *It's a long way down over this cliff, with nothing to break your fall.* [Mid-1800s]

break one's neck ◆ See under BREAK ONE'S BACK.

break one's word Violate or fail to observe a promise or contract one has made. For example, *You can trust him implicitly; I've never known him to break his word.* [c. A.D. 1000]

break out 1. Develop suddenly and forcefully. For example, *A fire broke out last night,* or *He broke out in a sweat.* [A.D. 1000] **2.** Be affected with a skin eruption, such as a rash or boils, as in *A teenager's face often breaks out in pimples.* [c. 1300] **3.** Prepare something for consumption, action, or use, as in *Let's break out the champagne,* or *It's such a fine day—let's break out the fishing rods.* [Early 1800s] **4. break out of.** Force out by breaking; also, escape from confinement. For example, *The hurricane broke the glass out of all the windows,* or *He broke out of prison but was soon apprehended.* [Early 1600s] **5.** Isolate a portion of a body of data, as in *Please break out the sales figures from the quarterly report.* [Mid-1900s]

break out of ◆ See BREAK OUT, def. 4.

break ranks Fall out of line or into disorder; also, fail to conform, deviate. For example, *The recruits were warned that they must not break ranks,* or *Harry was told to adhere to the party platform and* *not break ranks.* This idiom uses *rank* in the sense of "soldiers drawn up in line," and the term originally referred to their falling into disarray. The figurative usage dates from the mid-1800s.

break someone ♦ In addition to the idioms beginning with BREAK SOMEONE, also see under BREAK ONE.

break someone of something Cause to discontinue a habit or practice, as in *Mom tried for years to break Betty of biting her nails.* The *Oxford English Dictionary* cites a quotation from W. Wotton's *History of Rome* (1701): "He . . . broke them of their warm Baths," which presumably refers to breaking Romans of their custom of bathing regularly. Today we are more apt to break someone of a bad habit. [Early 1600s]

break someone's heart Cause severe emotional pain or grief. For example, *If the verdict is guilty, it will break her mother's heart.* This hyperbole has appeared in works by Chaucer, Shakespeare, and George Bernard Shaw, among others. In noun form it appears as both **a broken heart** and **heartbreak** (Shaw wrote a play entitled *Heartbreak House,* 1913). Today it also is used ironically, as in *You only scored an A-minus on the final? That breaks my heart!* [Late 1300s]

break someone's serve In tennis and related sports, win a game served by one's opponent, as in *The only way he'll win the match is to break Bill's serve.* The use of *serve,* from the earlier *service,* meaning "starting play" in these sports, dates from the early 1600s.

break someone up ♦ See under BREAK UP, def. 5.

break the back of Overpower, overcome; also, get through the hardest part of. For example, *This new offense has broken the back of the opposing team,* or *We're well over halfway there; we've broken the back of this journey.* [Mid-1800s]

break the bank Ruin one financially, exhaust one's resources, as in *I guess the price of a movie won't break the bank.* This term originated in gambling, where it means that a player has won more than the banker (the house) can pay. It also may be used ironically, as above. [c. 1600]

break the ice 1. Make a start, pave the way, as in *Newton's theories broke the ice for modern physics.* This idiom alludes to breaking ice in a channel so that a ship can pass. [Early 1600s] Also see BREAK GROUND. 2. Relax a tense or very formal situation, as in *Someone at the conference table will have to break the ice.* [Early 1600s]

break the news Make something known, as in *We suspected that she was pregnant but waited for her to break the news to her in-laws.* This term, in slightly different form (*break a matter* or *break a*

business), dates from the early 1500s. Another variant is the 20th-century journalistic phrase, **break a story,** meaning "to reveal a news item or make it available for publication."

break the record 1. Surpass a previous achievement, as in *He was determined to break the record for the high jump.* This usage is applied primarily to sports of various kinds. [1880s] 2. Move very fast, as in *The lecture was so dull that we broke the record getting to the door.* [Second half of 1900s]

break through Penetrate a barrier or obstruction, as in *They broke through the wall to get into the vault,* or *It won't be long before we break through the code and map all human genes.* Used literally for going through a physical barrier since about 1400, this phrase began to be used figuratively in the late 1500s.

break up 1. Divide into many pieces; disintegrate. For example, *Now break up the head of garlic into separate cloves.* [Mid-1700s] 2. Interrupt the continuity of something, as in *A short walk will break up the long morning.* 3. Also, **break it up.** Scatter, disperse, as in *The crowd broke up as soon as they reached the streets.* [Late 1400s] This phrase is also used as an imperative, as in *"Break it up!" shouted the police officer.* [c. 1930] 4. Bring or come to an end, as in *His gambling was bound to break up their marriage.* 5. Also, **break someone up.** Burst into or cause one to burst into an expression of feeling, such as laughter or tears. For example, *His jokes always break me up,* or *That touching eulogy broke us all up,* or *I looked at her and just broke up.* The precise meaning depends on the context. This sense grew out of a usage from the early 1800s that meant "upset" or "disturb." [Colloquial; early 1800s]

break wind Expel intestinal gas, as in *Beans always make him break wind.* [Early 1500s]

break with 1. Separate from, sever relations with. For example, *On this issue the prime minister was forced to break with his cabinet.* [Late 1500s] Also see BREAK OFF, def. 2 and 3. 2. Depart from, reject, as in *The couple broke with tradition and decided to write their own marriage vows.* [Late 1800s]

breast ♦ See KEEP ABREAST OF; MAKE A CLEAN BREAST OF.

breath ♦ In addition to the idiom beginning with BREATH, also see CATCH ONE'S BREATH; HOLD ONE'S BREATH; IN THE SAME BREATH; OUT OF BREATH; SAVE ONE'S BREATH; TAKE ONE'S BREATH AWAY; UNDER ONE'S BREATH; WASTE ONE'S BREATH; WITH BATED BREATH.

breathe ♦ In addition to the idioms beginning with BREATHE, also see AS I LIVE AND BREATHE; BREATHING SPACE; NOT BREATHE A WORD.

breathe down someone's neck 1. Pursue someone closely; pose a threat to one, as in *The immigration authorities were breathing down his neck.* [Mid-1900s] **2.** Watch or supervise someone very closely, as in *The boss is always breathing down our necks.* [Mid-1900s]

breathe easy Also, **breathe easily** or **freely.** Relax, feel relieved from anxiety, stress, or tension. For example, *Now that exams are over with, I can breathe easy,* or *Whenever I'm back in the mountains, I can breathe freely again.* This idiom originally (late 1500s) was put as *breathe again,* implying that one had stopped breathing (or held one's breath) while feeling anxious or nervous. Shakespeare had it in *King John* (4:2): "Now I breathe again aloft the flood." The variant dates from the first half of the 1800s.

breathe life into Also, **breathe new life into.** Revive someone or something. For example, *Cardiopulmonary resuscitation (CPR) shows one how to breathe life into a drowning victim,* or *Her appointment breathed new life into the firm.* This term is used both literally, for reviving a person who has stopped breathing temporarily, and figuratively, for giving new impetus to or renewing some project. Also see BREATH OF FRESH AIR.

breathe one's last Die, as in *Aunt Agatha breathed her last on Tuesday.* This term was used by Shakespeare in *3 Henry VI* (5:2): "Montague has breathed his last." It has survived but today is considered a poetic euphemism.

breathing space 1. Room or time in which to breathe, as in *In that crowded hall, there was hardly any breathing space.* Previously this term was put as **breathing room.** [Mid-1600s] **2.** A rest or pause. For example, *I can't work at this all day; I need some breathing space.* This usage replaced the earlier **breathing while.** [Mid-1600s]

breath of fresh air New and refreshing, as in *His arrival was like a breath of fresh air.* This term transfers the idea of fresh air to a new approach or welcome arrival, and has largely replaced both the earlier *breath of heaven* and *breath of spring,* although the latter is still heard occasionally. [Mid-1800s]

bred ♦ See BORN AND BRED. Also see under BREED.

breed ♦ See FAMILIARITY BREEDS CONTEMPT.

breeze ♦ In addition to the idiom beginning with BREEZE, also see HANDS DOWN (IN A BREEZE); SHOOT THE BREEZE.

breeze in 1. Arrive in a casual way, as in *She breezed in, two hours late.* This phrase transfers the blowing of a light wind to human entrances. [Colloquial; c. 1900] **2.** Win easily, as in *A fine golfer, he breezed in first.* This usage at first alluded to horse racing but soon was transferred to more general use. [c. 1900]

brick ♦ In addition to the idioms beginning with BRICK, also see DROP A BRICK; HIT THE BRICKS; LIKE A CAT ON A HOT BRICK; LIKE A TON OF BRICKS; MAKE BRICKS WITHOUT STRAW; RUN INTO A STONE (BRICK) WALL.

bricks and mortar Basic and essential, as in Matthew Arnold's essay (1865): "Margate, that bricks-and-mortar image of British Protestantism." This phrase transfers essential building materials to other fundamental matters. It also may be used more literally to denote a building or buildings (whether or not made of bricks and mortar), as in *The alumni prefer to see their donations in the form of bricks and mortar.* [Mid-1800s]

bricks shy of a load Mentally impaired, either unintelligent or merely eccentric. For example, *He may be handsome but he's not too bright—a few bricks shy of a load.* This term, transferring a light load to lightweight mental capacity, is usually preceded by either **a few** or a specific number such as **two.** [Slang; 1960s]

bride ♦ See GIVE AWAY (THE BRIDE).

bridge ♦ See BURN ONE'S BRIDGES; CROSS THAT BRIDGE WHEN ONE COMES TO IT; WATER OVER THE DAM (UNDER THE BRIDGE).

brief ♦ See HOLD NO BRIEF FOR; IN BRIEF.

bright ♦ In addition to the idioms beginning with BRIGHT, also see LOOK ON THE BRIGHT SIDE.

bright and early Early in the morning, at dawn, as in *It's a long trip, so we'll have to start out bright and early.* The *bright* here presumably alludes to the brilliance of the dawning sun, which has long been noted by poets. [Early 1800s]

bright-eyed and bushy-tailed Eager and alert, as in *Here is my new kindergarten class, all bright-eyed and bushy-tailed.* The allusion here is to the appearance of a squirrel, which with its beady eyes and bushy tail looks ready for anything. [1930s]

bright idea A clever thought or plan. For example, *John had a bright idea for saving space—we would each have a terminal but share the printer.* This term uses *bright* in the sense of "intelligent" or "quick-witted" and may be employed either straightforwardly, as in the example above, or ironically, as in *Jumping in the pool with your clothes on—that was some bright idea.* [Late 1800s]

bright side A favorable or hopeful aspect, as in *Bob is inclined to look on the bright side of everything.* This idiom uses *bright* in the sense of "lit up with gladness or hope." [First half of 1800s] Also see GLASS IS HALF FULL.

brim ♦ See FILLED TO THE BRIM.

bring about Also, **bring to pass**. Make something happen, accomplish or result in something. For example, *The revised tax code brought about considerable changes in accounting.* The first term dates from the 1400s, and the variant, today considered rather formal, from the first half of the 1500s. Also see BRING ON, def. 1.

bring around Also, **bring round**. **1.** Conduct someone or convey something to others. For example, *Anne brought around the new intern to meet the nursing staff,* or *The clerk will bring round the papers for you to sign.* [Late 1800s] **2.** Also, **bring to**. Restore to health or consciousness. For example, *Some fresh air will help bring him to.* [First half of 1800s] **3.** Convert or persuade someone, as in *The senator was sure he could bring around the other committee members.* [Mid-1800s]

bring down **1.** Cause to fall, collapse, or die. For example, *The pilot won a medal for bringing down enemy aircraft,* or *The bill's defeat was sure to bring down the party.* [c. 1300] **2.** Cause a punishment or judgment, as in *The bomb threats brought down the public's wrath on the terrorists* [Mid-1600s] **3.** Reduce, lower, as in *I won't buy it till they bring down the price,* or *He refused to bring himself down to their level.* This usage may be literal, as in the first example, or figurative, as in the second. [First half of 1500s]

bring down the curtain ♦ See RING DOWN THE CURTAIN.

bring down the house Also, **bring the house down**. Evoke tumultuous applause and cheers, as in *Her solo brought the house down.* This hyperbolic term suggests noise loud enough to pose a threat to the building—an unlikely occurrence. In the late 1800s, British music-hall comedians punned on it: when the audience greeted a joke with silence, they said, "Don't clap so hard; you'll bring down the house (it's a very old house)." [Mid-1700s]

bring forth **1.** Give rise to, introduce. For example, *I may be new, but I can still bring forth any proposals I consider necessary.* [c. 1200] **2.** Give birth; see under BRING INTO THE WORLD.

bring home Get to the heart of a matter, make perfectly clear. For example, *The crash brought home the danger of drinking and driving.* This term uses *home* in the figurative sense of "touching someone or something closely." [Second half of 1800s]

bring home the bacon **1.** Earn a living, provide the necessities of life, as in *Now that she had a job, Patricia could bring home the bacon.* **2.** Be successful, accomplish something of value, as in *George went to Washington and brought home the bacon—he got the funding we needed.* Although the earliest citation for this phrase in the *Oxford*

English Dictionary dates from 1924, the term is widely believed to come from the much older game of catching a greased pig, a popular competition at country fairs in which the winner was awarded the pig.

bring into line ♦ See under FALL IN LINE.

bring into the world Also, **bring forth**. Give birth, as in *It's certainly easier to bring a child into the world when you have a definite means of support,* or "Behold, a virgin shall be with child, and bring forth a son" (Matthew 1:23). Both versions of this term have a somewhat archaic ring. [First half of 1400s]

bring off Accomplish, achieve successfully, as in *We managed to bring off a wonderful performance.* [Early 1900s]

bring on **1.** Cause to happen, produce, as in *His cold brought on an asthma attack.* This usage was first recorded in John Milton's *Samson Agonistes* (1671): "These evils ... I myself have brought them on." Also see BRING ABOUT. **2.** Cause to appear or bring into action, as in *Bring on the jugglers.* [Mid-1800s]

bring out **1.** Expose or reveal; make conspicuous. For example, *His book brought out some new facts about the war,* or *Her photographs bring out the play of light on her subjects.* [Late 1500s] **2.** Nurture or develop a quality, as in *A gifted teacher brings out the best in pupils.* [c. 1700] **3.** Present to the public. For example, *The publisher decided to bring out this dictionary in a single volume,* or *Debutantes traditionally are brought out at a ball.* [c. 1800]

bring round ♦ See BRING AROUND.

bring the house down ♦ See BRING DOWN THE HOUSE.

bring to **1.** Restore to consciousness, as in *I'll see if these smelling salts will bring her to.* Also see BRING AROUND, def. 2. **2.** Cause a vessel to stop by heading into the wind or some other means. For example, *As they neared the anchorage, they brought the boat to.* This usage was first recorded in 1753.

bring to a head Cause to reach a turning point or crisis. For example, *Management's newest policy has brought matters to a head.* The related phrase **come to a head** means "to reach a crisis," as in *With the last break-in, the question of security came to a head.* These phrases allude to the medical sense of *head,* the tip of an abscess that is about to burst. [Mid-1500s]

bring to bear Exert, apply, as in *All his efforts are brought to bear on the new problem,* or *The union is bringing pressure to bear on management.* [Late 1600s]

bring to book Call to account, investigate. For example, *He was acquitted, but one day soon he'll be* *brought to book,* or *As for your records, the IRS is sure to bring you to book concerning your tax deductions.* This term uses *book* in the sense of "a written record," such as an account book or ledger. [c. 1800]

bring to heel Force to obey, subjugate. For example, *The prisoners were quickly brought to heel.* This term transfers commanding a dog to come close behind its master to similar control over human beings or affairs. [Second half of 1800s]

bring to life Enliven or energize a person or thing. For example, *The promise of a big part in the play brought Jane to life,* or *The author's changes really brought this screenplay to life.* [c. 1300] Also see COME TO LIFE.

bring to light Reveal or disclose something previously hidden or secret, as in *After careful investigation all the facts of the case were brought to light.* This term uses *light* in the sense of "public knowledge." [First half of 1500s]

bring to mind Cause to be remembered, as in *The film brought to mind the first time I ever climbed a mountain.* This idiom, first recorded in 1433, appears in Robert Burns's familiar "Auld Lang Syne" (1788), in which the poet asks if old times should never be *brought to mind.* Also see COME TO MIND.

bring to one's knees Make one submit; reduce to a position of subservience. For example, *Solitary confinement usually brings prisoners to their knees.* This particular phrase dates only from the late 1800s, although there were earlier versions alluding to being on one's knees as a gesture of submission.

bring to pass ♦ See BRING ABOUT.

bring to terms Force someone to agree or continue negotiations, as in *The creditors were determined to bring the company to terms.* The *terms* here mean "the conditions for agreement." [First half of 1700s] Also see COME TO TERMS.

bring up 1. Raise from childhood, rear. For example, *Bringing up children is both difficult and rewarding.* [Late 1400s] **2.** Introduce into discussion, mention, as in *Let's not bring up the cost right now.* [Second half of 1800s] **3.** Vomit, as in *She still felt sick but couldn't bring up anything.* This usage was first recorded in Daniel Defoe's *Robinson Crusoe* (1719).

bring up the rear Be last in a line or sequence, as in *As a slow walker, I'm used to bringing up the rear,* or *In test results Tom always brought up the rear.* This term almost certainly came from the military but the earliest citation given by the *Oxford English Dictionary* is from a 1643 religious treatise by Sir Thomas Browne: "My desires onely are . . . to be but the last man, and bring up the Rere in Heaven."

bring up to date Convey information up to the present; also, make one aware of or conform to new ideas, improvements, or styles. For example, *Bring me up to date on the test results,* or *We've been bringing Grandma up to date with a little makeup and some new clothes.* The term *up to date* comes from bookkeeping, where it signifies account entries to the present time. [Late 1800s]

broad ♦ In addition to the idioms beginning with BROAD, also see CAN'T HIT THE BROAD SIDE OF A BARN.

broad daylight Ample and obvious natural light, as in *You don't need your flashlight—it's broad daylight,* or *She was accosted on her own street in broad daylight.* [1300s]

broad in the beam Having broad hips or large buttocks. For example, *I've grown too broad in the beam for these slacks.* This expression originated in the 17th century and described the wideness of a ship. It began to be used for the human body only in the 1920s.

broad shoulders, have Be able to accept considerable responsibility, as in *With his broad shoulders, he can easily handle both departments.* [Second half of 1300s]

broke ♦ See FLAT BROKE; GO BROKE; GO FOR (BROKE); IF IT AIN'T BROKE DON'T FIX IT. Also see under BREAK.

broken reed A weak or unreliable support, as in *I'd counted on her to help, but she turned out to be a broken reed.* The idea behind this idiom, first recorded about 1593, was already present in a mid-15th-century translation of a Latin tract, "Trust not nor lean not upon a windy reed."

broom ♦ See NEW BROOM SWEEPS CLEAN.

broth ♦ See TOO MANY COOKS SPOIL THE BROTH.

brow ♦ See BY THE SWEAT OF ONE'S BROW; CAUSE RAISED EYEBROWS.

brown ♦ In addition to the idioms beginning with BROWN, also see DO UP (BROWN).

brown bagger A person who brings his or her own supplies, as in *The architects of the new office designed a space for brown baggers to eat lunch.* The term originated in the 1930s in Britain for very serious students who carried their books about with them in brown briefcases or bags. That usage crossed the Atlantic within a few decades. However, in America from the 1960s on, it has primarily been used for persons who brought their own liquor in a brown paper bag, either legitimately or surreptitiously, to a public place or restaurant not licensed to sell it, or for those who took their lunch to work.

browned off Very angry, as in *When she locked me out I was really browned off.* This expression originated as Royal Air Force slang for "disgusted" and "depressed" in the late 1930s and had crossed the Atlantic by World War II. It gradually came to be used more widely as a slangy synonym for "infuriated." One theory for its origin, mentioned by Eric Partridge in his slang dictionary, is that it alludes to brass buttons on a uniform turning brown from lack of polishing. Partridge noted, however, that the "predominant Army opinion" was that the word had the same literal meaning as *buggered.*

brownie points Credit for a good deed, as in *John earned a lot of brownie points for doing his boss's report for him.* The term originated with the points earned for various achievements by the youngest group of the Girl Scouts, called Brownies. In the mid-1900s it was transferred to general use.

brown nose Solicit favor obsequiously, toady. For example, *Harry was always brown nosing, but it didn't help his grades.* This term originated in the military in the late 1930s, where it meant "to curry favor"; it alludes to ass-kissing when the backside being kissed is less than clean. Despite its scatological origin, today this slangy term is not considered particularly vulgar.

brown study, in a Daydreaming or deeply contemplative, as in *Margaret sits in the library, in a brown study.* This term dates from the late 1500s, and although by then *in a study* had long meant "lost in thought," the reason for adding *brown* is unclear. Moreover, the present idiom also is ambiguous, some holding that it denotes genuine thoughtfulness and others that it signifies absent-mindedness.

brunt ♦ See BEAR THE BRUNT.

brush ♦ In addition to the idioms beginning with BRUSH, also see GIVE SOMEONE THE AIR (BRUSHOFF); HAVE A BRUSH WITH; TARRED WITH THE SAME BRUSH.

brush aside Disregard, ignore, as in *The teacher brushed aside our questions.*

brush off Dismiss or rebuff, as in *Roberta brushed off the poor reviews with a shrug,* or *You can't brush off a boyfriend and expect him to do you a favor.* This expression, transferring sweeping off crumbs to a curt dismissal, was first recorded about 1820. However, it became common usage only in the 1930s. Also see GIVE SOMEONE THE AIR (BRUSHOFF).

brush up 1. Clean, refurbish, as in *We plan to get the house brushed up in time for the party.* [c. 1600] 2. Also, **brush up on.** Review, refresh one's memory, as in *Nell brushed up on her Spanish before going to Honduras,* or *I'm brushing up my knowledge of town history before I speak at the club.* [Late 1700s]

brute force Also, **brute strength.** Savage violence, unreasoning strength, as in *We hope that reason will triumph over brute force.* Although this expression is also used literally to mean exceptional

physical power, the figurative sense reflects the origin for *brute,* which comes from Latin *brutus,* for "heavy, stupid, unreasoning." [First half of 1700s]

buck ♦ In addition to the idioms beginning with BUCK, also see BIG BUCKS; FAST BUCK; MORE BANG FOR THE BUCK; PASS THE BUCK.

bucket ♦ See DROP IN THE BUCKET; KICK THE BUCKET; RAIN CATS AND DOGS (BUCKETS); WEEP BUCKETS.

buck for Strive for, aim for, as in *She's bucking for Editor of the Year.* Strongly associated with seeking a promotion in the military, this expression originated in the late 1800s and is now applied more widely.

buckle down Set to work, apply oneself with determination, as in *All right, we'll buckle down now and study for exams.* Originating about 1700 as *buckle to,* the expression gained currency with the football song "Buckle Down, Winsocki" (from the Broadway musical comedy *Best Foot Forward,* 1941). [Mid-1800s]

buckle under Give way, collapse owing to stress, as in *One more heavy snowfall and the roof may buckle under,* or *She buckled under the strain of two jobs.* [Late 1500s]

buckle up Fasten a seat belt, as in *All the children must learn to buckle up as soon as they get in a car.* This term came into wide use in the second half of the 1900s, when seat belts became mandatory automobile equipment. Earlier they had been used mainly in airplanes.

buck stops here, the I'll take full responsibility, as in *You needn't call my boss; the buck stops here.* This saying gained fame as a sign on the desk of President Harry S. Truman. It alludes to another expression that means the opposite, PASS THE BUCK. [Mid-1900s]

buck up Cheer up, become encouraged, as in *Buck up! We'll soon have it done,* or *Even the promise of a vacation did not buck her up.* This term was first recorded in 1844.

bud ♦ See NIP IN THE BUD.

buddy up Be very friendly, as in *He is always wanting to buddy up with me, but I don't really like him.* [Slang; early 1900s]

buff ♦ See IN THE BUFF.

bug ♦ In addition to the idioms beginning with BUG, also see CUTE AS A BUTTON (BUG'S EAR); PUT A BUG IN SOMEONE'S EAR; SNUG AS A BUG IN A RUG; WHAT'S EATING (BUGGING) YOU.

bugger off ♦ See BUG OFF.

bug off Also, **bugger off.** Go away, as in *Bug off before I call the police.* Both terms are often used as an imperative, as in the example, and the variant is heard more in Britain than in America. [Slang; c. 1900] For a synonym, see BUZZ OFF.

bug out 1. Bulge, as in *The news will make her eyes bug out with astonishment.* This expression was originally used literally for bulging eyes and later used more loosely as a sign of astonishment. [Colloquial; mid-1800s] 2. Leave, run out, as in *This conference is a bore; I think I'll bug out.* This usage originated as military slang for deserting and today is used more loosely. [Slang; c. 1950]

build ♦ In addition to the idioms beginning with BUILD, also see LIGHT (BUILD) A FIRE UNDER. Also see under BUILT.

build down Reduce, diminish, as in *Owing to increased vigilance, traffic in narcotics is finally building down.* This term, the antonym of BUILD UP, came into use about 1980 with regard to reducing the stockpile of nuclear weapons and soon was applied more widely.

build in Also, **build into.** Construct or include as an integral part; also, make automatic, concomitant, or inherent. For example, *Frank Lloyd Wright liked to build in as much furniture as possible, not just bookcases but desks, tables, and the like,* or *We've got to build some slack into the schedule for this project.* The literal usage referring to physical objects dates from the late 1920s. The figurative arose a decade or so later. Both are frequently used in past participle form, that is, **built in.**

build on Also, **build upon.** Add as an extension; use as a basis or foundation. For example, *They decided to build on an addition,* or *She was building all her hopes on passing the exam.* John Locke had this idiom in his treatise on government (1689): "Sovereignty built on 'property' . . . comes to nothing." [Late 1600s]

build on sand Use an unstable foundation, as in *If you buy nothing but high-risk stocks, your portfolio will be built on sand.* This metaphor appears in the New Testament, where Jesus likens those who do not heed his sayings to a foolish man who builds his house on sand, which then is washed away by rain, flood, and wind (Matthew 7:24–27). [c. 1600]

build up 1. Fill an area with houses or other buildings, urbanize. For example, *We want to protect the wetlands against those who want to build up the area.* [c. 1400] 2. Gradually develop, increase in stages. For example, *I want to build up my endurance for the race.* [Early 1700s] 3. Accumulate or collect, as in *A lot of rust has built up on the farm machinery.* [Mid-1900s] 4. Increase, strengthen, develop toward, as in *The sound built up until it was nearly deafening,* or *His argument was building up to a grand climax.* [c. 1930] 5. Establish or enhance a reputation; praise or flatter. For example, *Months before the official campaign could begin, they had been building up the senator's image.* [c. 1930]

built ♦ See MADE (BUILT) TO ORDER; NOT BUILT THAT WAY; ROME WASN'T BUILT IN A DAY. Also see under BUILD.

bulk ♦ See IN BULK.

bull ♦ In addition to the idioms beginning with BULL, also see COCK AND BULL STORY; HIT THE BULL'S-EYE; SHOOT THE BREEZE (BULL); TAKE THE BULL BY THE HORNS.

bullet ♦ See BITE THE BULLET; SWEAT BULLETS.

bulletin board Also, **electronic bulletin board.** A computer service that provides facilities for people to leave messages by phone or telecomputing. For example, *The National Writers Union has a bulletin board through which members communicate via their modems.* Both the device and the term, alluding to the older board for posting notices, date from the late 1970s.

bull in a china shop An extremely clumsy person, as in *Her living room, with its delicate furniture and knickknacks, made him feel like a bull in a china shop.* The precise origin for this term has been lost; it was first recorded in Frederick Marryat's novel, *Jacob Faithful* (1834).

bull session An informal discussion, as in *College students love late-night bull sessions about anything and everything, from professors to poetry to politics.* This expression originally referred to an exchange of opinions and anecdotes, including stories of sexual prowess, by men, and then came to be used more broadly. [Slang; c. 1915]

bullshit artist Also, **bull artist.** A person who habitually exaggerates, flatters, or talks nonsense. For example, *Don't believe a word of it—he's a bullshit artist.* Both versions are considered vulgar slang. The first dates from the 1940s, the second from the World War I period.

bum ♦ In addition to the idioms beginning with BUM, also see ON THE BLINK (BUM).

bum around 1. Loaf, wander idly, as in *After graduating he decided to bum around Europe for a year.* [Mid-1800s] 2. Frequent bars or nightclubs, as in *Her father accused her of bumming around half the night and threatened to cut off her allowance.* In the mid-1800s *to bum* was slang for going on a drinking spree. A century later, with the addition of *around,* it simply meant going to saloons or clubs.

bum out 1. Depress, sadden, dispirit, as in *He's been really bummed out since his girlfriend moved to California.* [Slang; late 1960s] 2. Annoy, irritate, vex, as in *That haircut will really bum out his parents.* [Slang; c. 1970] 3. Fail badly, as in *I got through the midterm, but I bummed out totally on the final exam.* This usage is student slang. [Late 1960s]

bump ♦ In addition to the idioms beginning with BUMP, also see GOOSE PIMPLES (BUMPS); LIKE A BUMP ON A LOG.

bump into 1. Also, **bump against**. Collide, come in contact with; same as BANG INTO. For example, *It's easy to bump into furniture in the dark*. [Mid-1800s] 2. Encounter, meet by chance, as in *While I was downtown, I bumped into George*. [Colloquial; 1880s] Also see RUN INTO.

bump off Kill, murder, as in *The convict bragged about bumping off his partner*, or *The first fighter plane bumped off three enemy aircraft*. This term was at first principally criminal slang and somewhat later military jargon. [Slang; c. 1900]

bump up 1. Suddenly increase, as in *Oil-producing nations decided to bump up the price of oil*. This term is used mainly for prices or other figures. [Colloquial; 1930s] 2. Give a promotion. For example, *Kevin hoped to be bumped up to first class*, or *After five years, she expected they would bump her up to vice-president*. [Slang; second half of 1900s]

bum rap A false accusation or conviction; also, unfair criticism or action. For example, *He claimed he was in prison on a bum rap*, or *The theater critics gave her last play a bum rap*. This expression originated in the 1920s as underworld slang, and by the mid-1900s it was also used figuratively for other kinds of injustice.

bum's rush Forcible ejection, abrupt dismissal. For example, *When Henry started shouting, the bouncer gave him the bum's rush*, or *Within hours of being fired, Alice was given the bum's rush*. This idiom uses *bum* in the sense of "a vagrant or tramp." [Slang; early 1900s]

bum steer False or misleading information; poor advice. For example, *Gene felt his doctor had given him a bum steer, as he hadn't lost any weight on the diet*. [Slang; c. 1920]

bundle ♦ In addition to the idiom beginning with BUNDLE, also see MAKE A BUNDLE.

bundle of nerves Extremely jittery, tense, or fearful person, as in *For months after the accident, Aunt Jane was a bundle of nerves*. [1930s]

burden of proof Obligation of proving a disputed charge or allegation. For example, *Are you sure you mailed the tax return on time? The burden of proof's on you*. A legal term dating from the late 1500s, it has also been used more loosely in recent times.

burn ♦ In addition to the idioms beginning with BURN, also see CRASH AND BURN; EARS ARE BURNING; FIDDLE WHILE ROME BURNS; (BURN) IN EFFIGY; KEEP THE HOME FIRES BURNING; MONEY BURNS A HOLE IN ONE'S POCKET; MONEY TO BURN; SLOW BURN.

burn at the stake Execute someone by tying to a stake and burning; also, punish severely. This expression refers to a method used in the Middle Ages for putting heretics to death, but now it is used as a hyperbolic metaphor for harsh punishment, as in *She was sure she'd be burned at the stake*

for losing the contract. In fact, *the stake* can be used loosely for any extreme punishment. William Makepeace Thackeray so used it in *Henry Esmond* (1852): "'I know I would go to the stake for you,' said Harry."

burn down 1. Completely consume by fire, burn to the ground, as in *Their house burned down and they had nowhere to go*. [Mid-1800s] 2. Diminish for lack of fuel, as in *The fire will soon burn down*. [Late 1800s]

burned up ♦ See BURN UP.

burn in effigy ♦ See IN EFFIGY.

burning question An urgent or crucial issue under heated discussion. For example, *Real estate taxes are always a burning question for the town leaders*. This term has exact equivalents in French (*question brûlante*) and German (*brennende Frage*). [Mid-1800s]

burn into Make an indelible impression on, as in *An event like the Holocaust burns into the minds of all the survivors*, or *The scene was burned into her memory*. This expression alludes to such processes as etching or engraving, where a caustic substance bites into a solid plate to make a design. [Early 1800s]

burn off 1. Dissipate by heat, as in *The sun will soon burn off the morning fog*. 2. Clear land by burning vegetation, as in *They've decided to burn off part of the field to prepare it for another planting*. This practice has long been common in many parts of the world, but the precise term dates only from the first half of the 1800s.

burn one's bridges Also, **burn one's boats**. Commit oneself to an irreversible course. For example, *Denouncing one's boss in a written resignation means one has burned one's bridges*, or *Turning down one job before you have another amounts to burning your boats*. Both versions of this idiom allude to ancient military tactics, when troops would cross a body of water and then burn the bridge or boats they had used both to prevent retreat and to foil a pursuing enemy. [Late 1800s] Also see CROSS THE RUBICON.

burn oneself out ♦ See BURN OUT, def. 3.

burn one's fingers Harm oneself, as in *I'm staying away from risky stocks; I've burned my fingers often enough*. Some believe this expression came from a legend about a monkey who gets a cat to pull its chestnuts out of the fire (see CAT'S PAW); others hold it is from an English proverb: "Burn not thy fingers to snuff another's candle" (James Howell, *English Proverbs,* 1659). [c. 1700]

burn out 1. Stop functioning because something, such as fuel, has been used up. For example, *There's nothing wrong with the lamp; the light bulb just burned out*. [Late 1300s] 2. **be burned out**.

Lose one's home, place of work, or school as the result of a fire. For example, *Hundreds of tenants are burned out every year because of negligent landlords.* 3. Also, **burn oneself out.** Make or become exhausted or disaffected, especially with one's work or schooling. For example, *Many young lawyers burn themselves out after a few years of 70-hour weeks.* This metaphoric term alludes to a fire going out for lack of new fuel. Robert Southey used it in an 1816 essay: "The spirit of Jacobinism was burnt out in France." [1970s]

burn rubber Drive very fast, as in *We'll have to burn rubber to get there in time.* In this bit of automotive jargon, the *rubber* refers to tires that heat up when they rotate suddenly at great speed. [Slang; mid-1900s]

burn someone up ♦ See BURN UP, def. 1.

burn the candle at both ends Exhaust one's energies or resources by leading a hectic life. For example, *Joseph's been burning the candle at both ends for weeks, working two jobs during the week and a third on weekends.* This metaphor originated in France and was translated into English in Randle Cotgrave's *Dictionary* (1611), where it referred to dissipating one's wealth. It soon acquired its present broader meaning.

burn the midnight oil Stay up late working or studying, as in *The semester is almost over and we're all burning the midnight oil before exams.* This expression alludes to the oil in oil lamps. [Early 1600s]

burn to a cinder Also, **burn to a crisp.** Destroy by fire; overcook. For example, *If I stay in the sun too long, I'll be burnt to a cinder,* or *He's an awful cook—dinner was burnt to a crisp.* Although both expressions can be used literally, they also function as hyperbole, as in the examples.

burn up 1. **burn someone up.** Make angry or very irritated, as in *Arthur was really burned up at his son for denting the new car,* or *Those careless drivers just burn me up.* [Colloquial; c. 1920] 2. Travel very fast, as in *This car will burn up the road.* [1940s] 3. Easily surpass or outdo, as in *They'll burn up the other teams.* [Slang; late 1970s]

burst at the seams Be filled to or beyond normal capacity. For example, *On her wedding day the church was bursting at the seams,* or *That was a wonderful meal, but I'm bursting at the seams.* This expression alludes to rupturing the seams of a garment too tight for the wearer and is widely used hyperbolically. Also see COME APART AT THE SEAMS.

burst into 1. Also, **burst out in** or **into.** Break out into sudden activity. For example, **burst into flames** means "break out in a fire," as in *This dry woodpile may well burst into flames.* A version of this term, which dates from the 16th century, was used figuratively by John Milton: "Fame is the

spur . . . But the fair guerdon [reward] when we hope to find, and think to burst out into sudden blaze" (*Lycidas,* 1637). 2. Also, **burst out.** Give sudden utterance to. For example, **burst into tears, laughter, song, speech** or **burst out crying, laughing, singing,** etc. mean "begin suddenly to weep, laugh, sing," and so on, as in *When she saw him, she burst into tears,* or *I burst out laughing when I saw their outfits,* or *When they brought in the cake, we all burst into song.* These terms have been so used since the late 1300s.

burst out ♦ See under BURST INTO.

burst with Be overfull with something, be unable to contain oneself with an emotion. For example, *Jane's award made her parents burst with pride,* or *Harry is bursting with the news about his promotion.* [Early 1600s]

bury one's head in the sand ♦ See HIDE ONE'S HEAD IN THE SAND.

bury the hatchet Make peace; settle one's differences. For example, *Toward the end of the year, the roommates finally decided to bury the hatchet.* Although some believe this term comes from a Native American custom for declaring peace between warring tribes, others say it comes from **hang up one's hatchet,** a term dating from the early 1300s (well before Columbus landed in the New World). The word *bury* replaced *hang up* in the 1700s.

bush ♦ See BEAT AROUND THE BUSH; BEAT THE BUSHES FOR; BRIGHT-EYED AND BUSHY-TAILED.

bushel ♦ See HIDE ONE'S LIGHT UNDER A BUSHEL.

business ♦ In addition to the idiom beginning with BUSINESS, also see FUNNY BUSINESS; GET DOWN TO (BUSINESS); GO ABOUT (ONE'S BUSINESS); HAVE NO BUSINESS DOING; LAND-OFFICE BUSINESS; LIKE MAD (NOBODY'S BUSINESS); MAKE IT ONE'S BUSINESS; MEAN BUSINESS; MIND ONE'S OWN BUSINESS; MONKEY BUSINESS; NONE OF ONE'S BUSINESS; OUT OF BUSINESS; SEND SOMEONE ABOUT HIS OR HER BUSINESS; THE BUSINESS.

business as usual The normal course of some activity, as in *The fire destroyed only a small section of the store, so it's business as usual.* This term originated as an announcement that a commercial establishment was continuing to operate in spite of fire, construction, or some similar interruption. It had been extended to broader use by 1914, when Winston Churchill said in a speech: "The maxim of the British people is 'Business as usual,'" which became a slogan for the rest of World War I. Today it may be used in this positive sense and also pejoratively, as in *Never mind that most civilians are starving to death—the ministry regards its job to be business as usual.* [Late 1800s]

busman's holiday Free time spent in much the same pursuit as one's work. For example, *Weather permitting, the lifeguard spent all her days off at the* beach—*a real busman's holiday.* The term alludes to a bus driver spending his day off taking a long bus ride. [Late 1800s]

bust ◆ In addition to the idioms beginning with BUST, also see BREAK (BUST) ONE'S ASS; GO BROKE (BUST).

bust a gut Also, **burst a gut. 1.** Exert oneself to the utmost. For example, *He was busting a gut trying to please her.* This hyperbolic term alludes to hurting one's mid-section through physical straining. The first slangy term dates from the early 1900s, the variant from about 1700. For a synonym, see BREAK ONE'S ASS. **2.** Explode with strong feeling, especially laughter or anger. For example, *Gene almost bust a gut laughing,* or *The foreman will burst a gut when he learns that the machine isn't repaired.* The former dates from the late 1800s, the latter from about 1940.

bust one's ass ◆ See BREAK ONE'S ASS.

busy ◆ In addition to the idioms beginning with BUSY, also see GET BUSY.

busy as a beaver Also, **busy as a bee.** Hardworking, very industrious, as in *With all her activities, Sue is always busy as a bee,* or *Bob's busy as a beaver trying to finish painting before it rains.* The comparison to beavers dates from the late 1700s, the variant from the late 1300s. Also see EAGER BEAVER; WORK LIKE A BEAVER.

busy work Activity meant to take up time but not actually be productive. For example, *We have to put in an eight-hour day, even if we do nothing but busy work.* [c. 1840]

but ◆ In addition to the idioms beginning with BUT, also see ALL BUT; ALL OVER BUT THE SHOUTING; ANYTHING BUT; CAN'T HELP BUT; CLOSE BUT NO CIGAR; EVERYTHING BUT THE KITCHEN SINK; GONE BUT NOT FORGOTTEN; IT NEVER RAINS BUT IT POURS; LAST BUT NOT LEAST; NO IFS OR BUTS; NOTHING BUT; SADDER BUT WISER; SEPARATE BUT EQUAL; SLOW BUT SURE; SPIRIT IS WILLING BUT THE FLESH IS WEAK; THERE BUT FOR THE GRACE OF GOD.

but for Except for, were it not for. For example, *But for the afternoon shower, it was a perfect day,* or *But for the children, they would have gotten a divorce long ago.* [c. 1200]

but good Emphatically, thoroughly, as in *Ruth decided to clean up the whole yard but good.* The word *but* in this colloquialism functions as an intensive. Also see AND HOW.

butter ◆ In addition to the idioms beginning with BUTTER, also see BREAD AND BUTTER; BREAD-AND-BUTTER LETTER; KNOW WHICH SIDE OF BREAD IS BUTTERED.

butterflies in one's stomach Fluttering sensations caused by a feeling of nervous anticipation. For example, *I always get butterflies in my stomach before making a speech.* This term likens a nervous feeling to that resulting from swallowing live butterflies that fly about inside one. [c. 1900]

butter up Excessively praise or flatter someone, usually to gain a favor. For example, *If you butter up Dad, he'll let you borrow the car.* This term transfers the oily, unctuous quality of butter to lavish praise. [c. 1700]

butter wouldn't melt in one's mouth Be overly coy or demure; be insincere. For example, *She looked quite innocent, as though butter wouldn't melt in her mouth, but we knew better.* Already a proverb in John Heywood's collection of 1546, this metaphoric expression alleges that one is literally so cool that butter inside the mouth would not melt.

butt in Interfere, interrupt, intrude. For example, *Mom is always butting in on our conversations,* or *It's against the law for employers to butt in on personal matters.* This term alludes to the thrusting of an animal with its horns. [Slang; 1890s]

button ◆ In addition to the idioms beginning with BUTTON, also see CUTE AS A BUTTON; HAVE ALL ONE'S BUTTONS; ON THE BUTTON; PUSH (PRESS) SOMEONE'S BUTTONS; PUSH THE PANIC BUTTON.

buttonhole someone Accost or detain a person in conversation. For example, *The reporter tried to buttonhole the senator, but she got away.* This term is a metaphor for literally grasping someone by a buttonhole on his or her clothing. [Mid-1800s]

button one's lip ◆ See BUTTON UP, def. 2.

button up 1. Close securely, fasten, as in *The house was all buttoned up,* or *Button up your coat—it's very cold.* [Late 1500s] **2.** Also, **button one's lip.** Hold one's tongue, keep quiet. For example, *Please button your lip about the surprise.* A variant of this usage, **button one's mouth,** dates from the 17th century. [Mid-1800s] **3.** Finish successfully, as in *I've got this report all buttoned up.* [c. 1940]

buy into Purchase a membership, a share, or an interest in something. For example, *I'd love to buy into this partnership, but I can't afford it.* [First half of 1600s]

buy it 1. Suffer a severe reversal, as in *If they can't raise the money in time, they'll buy it.* [Slang; mid-1900s] **2.** Be killed; die. For example, *By the time we could get to the hospital, he had bought it.* Originating during World War I as military slang, this term later was extended to peacetime forms of death. A later slang equivalent is **buy the farm,** dating from about 1950. For example, *He'll soon buy the farm riding that motorcycle.* According to J.E. Lighter, it alludes to training flights crashing in a farmer's field, causing the farmer to sue the government for damages sufficient to pay off the farm's mortgage. Since the pilot usually died in such a crash, he in effect bought the farm with his life. **3.** Believe it; see BUY SOMETHING.

buy off Pay to get rid of a claim or opposition, or to avoid prosecution, as in *He was caught trying to buy off the opposing candidate.* [First half of 1600s]

buy out Purchase the entire stock, business rights, or interests of a concern. For example, *A rival store owner offered to buy out my grandfather, but he refused.* [Late 1200s]

buy something Believe something; accept as true or satisfactory. For example, *You think he's a millionaire? I just won't buy that.* [Slang; 1920s]

buy the farm ♦ See under BUY IT.

buy time Increase the time available for a specific purpose. For example, *Renting an apartment buys them time to look around for a new house.*

buy up Purchase all that is available, as in *They want to buy up all the land in this area.* This term was first recorded in a law enacted under Henry VIII: "They buy up all manner of fish."

buzz off Go away, leave. For example, *The store owner told the teenagers to buzz off and find another place to hang out.* This curt imperative dates from World War I. Also see BUG OFF.

by a hair Also, **by a hairbreadth** or **whisker.** Very narrowly. For example, *His serve was out by a hair,* or *We made our flight by a hairbreadth,* or *Dad missed hitting the pole by a whisker.* The first two hyperboles are the very narrowest margin date from the 1300s and 1400s respectively; *whisker* meaning "a small amount" was first recorded in 1913. Also see BY THE SKIN OF ONE'S TEETH; HANG BY A HAIR.

by all accounts Also, **according to all accounts.** From all reports available, from what everyone is saying. For example, *By all accounts the party was a great success,* or *They spent a fortune on their cruise, according to all accounts.* These phrases rely on *account* in the sense of "a particular report or description of some event." [Late 1700s]

by all means 1. Also, **by all manner of means.** In every possible way, as in *I plan to make use of him by all means.* [Late 1400s] **2.** Also, **by all manner of means.** Without fail, at any cost, as in *Losing the contract is to be avoided by all means.* [c. 1600] **3.** Certainly, yes, as in *Are you coming tonight?— By all means, I'll be there.* [Late 1600s] Also see BY ANY MEANS; BY NO MEANS.

by all odds By far, as in *She is by all odds the best player on the team.* This idiom uses *odds* in the sense of "the amount by which one thing excels or exceeds." [Mid-1800s]

by a long shot ♦ See under LONG SHOT.

by a mile ♦ See MISS BY A MILE.

by and by After a while, soon, as in *She'll be along by and by.* The expression probably relies on the meaning of *by* as a succession of quantities (as in "two by two"). This adverbial phrase came to be used as a noun, denoting either procrastination or the future. William Camden so used it for the former (*Remains,* 1605): "Two anons and a by and by is an hour and a half." And W.S. Gilbert used it in the latter sense when Lady Jane sings plaintively that little will be left of her "in the coming by and by," that is, as she grows old (*Patience,* 1881). [Early 1500s]

by and large For the most part, generally speaking, as in *By and large the novel was a success.* This expression originated in 17th-century seamanship, where it referred to sailing into the wind and then off it, which made it easier to steer. By the early 1700s the term had been broadened to mean "in one direction and another," whence its present meaning of "in general." For a synonym, see FOR THE MOST PART.

by any means In any possible way, no matter how, as in *By any means I've got to get there.* [Late 1400s] Also see BY HOOK OR CROOK; BY MEANS OF; BY NO MEANS.

by any stretch Beyond ordinary limits, especially of the imagination. For example, *She could not, by any stretch of the imagination, be considered a great actress.* The phrase sometimes is put in the negative, **by no stretch,** as in *By no stretch can that work be called an opera.* [Late 1700s]

by a thread ♦ See HANG BY A THREAD.

by chance Casually, accidentally, as in *I ran into Bill purely by chance.* [c. 1300] Also see BY COINCIDENCE.

by choice Deliberately, as a matter of preference. For example, *No one told me to come; I'm here by choice.* This expression replaced the earlier *with choice,* used from about 1500.

by coincidence Through an accidental simultaneous occurrence, as in *By coincidence both researchers discovered the same solution.* [Mid-1600s] Also see BY CHANCE.

by definition According to prior determination, as a given. For example, *This antibiotic is by definition the most effective now on the market.* [1970s]

by degrees Gradually, by successive steps or stages. For example, *By degrees he began to delegate more and more of his duties to his staff.* [Mid-1500s] Also see BY INCHES.

by design On purpose, deliberately, as in *Whether by luck or by design, his application was accepted.* This term, originally put as *on design,* uses *design* in the sense of "plan." [First half of 1600s]

by dint of By means of, as in *By dint of hard work he got his degree in three years.* The word *dint,* which survives only in this expression, originally meant "a stroke or blow," and by the late 1500s signified the force behind such a blow. The current term preserves the implication of vigorous or persistent means.

by far Also, **far and away**. To the greatest degree, by a large margin. For example, *She is by far the most experienced member of the cast*, or, as Anthony Trollope wrote, "He was far and away the cleverest of his party" (*The Duke's Children*, 1880). The first term dates from the late 1700s, the variant from the mid-1800s. Also see BY HALF.

by fits and starts ♦ See FITS AND STARTS.

bygones ♦ See LET BYGONES BE BYGONES.

by half Considerably, a great deal, as in *He was too good a cook by half for this small restaurant*. [c. A.D. 1000] Contrast BY HALVES.

by halves Imperfectly, reluctantly, or halfheartedly, as in *You really can't paint a portrait by halves*. [Mid-1500s]

by hand With a hand or hands, manually (as opposed to a machine or some other means). For example, *This letter was delivered by hand*, or *You can make these drawings by hand, but computer graphics are more efficient*. [Mid-1500s]

by heart Also, **by rote**. From memory; also, mechanically. For example, *Betty had trouble learning the song by heart, but her teacher insisted on it*, or *Japanese schools put heavy emphasis on learning by rote*. These terms are often put as **know by heart** or **learn by rote**. The first term was already used by Chaucer (in *Troilus and Cressida*). The variant, also dating from the 1300s, often implies mere memorization without deeper understanding. Both phrases remain in use, although this form of learning is no longer so widespread as it once was. Also see COMMIT TO MEMORY.

by hook or crook By any means possible, in one way or another. For example, *The car broke down, but I'll get there by hook or crook*. This term has a disputed origin. A widely held theory is that it comes from the custom of allowing commoners to take as much wood from royal forests as they could reach with a shepherd's crook and cut down with a billhook. [1300s] Also see the synonym BY ANY MEANS.

by inches Also, **inch by inch**. Gradually, bit by bit, as in *We found ourselves in rush hour traffic, moving by inches*. Shakespeare used this term in *Coriolanus* (5:4): "They'll give him death by inches." Despite the increasing use of metric measurements, it survives, often as an exaggeration of the actual circumstance. The phrase **to inch along**, first recorded in 1812, means "to move bit by bit," as in *There was a long line at the theater, just inching along*.

by Jove Also, **by cracky**. Used to express surprise or emphasis. For example, *By Jove, I was glad to see her*, or *It was a great day, by cracky*. These mild oaths are euphemisms, the first for "by Jesus" or "by God" (Jove is another name for Jupiter, the principal Roman god), and the folksy variant *by cracky* for "by Christ." Both idioms may be dying out.

by leaps and bounds Rapidly, or in fast progress, as in *The corn is growing by leaps and bounds*, or *School enrollment is increasing by leaps and bounds*. This term is a redundancy, since *leap* and *bound* both mean "spring" or "jump," but the two words have been paired since Shakespeare's time and are still so used.

by means of Through the use of, owing to, as in *We plan to pay for medical school by means of a second mortgage*, or *He'll succeed by means of sheer persistence*. [Early 1400s] Also see BY DINT OF.

by mistake Erroneously, as in *He took my coat by mistake*. [c. 1700]

by no means Also, **not by any means**. In no way, certainly not. For example, *He is by no means a weak opponent*, or *Not by any means will I go along with that decision*. [Late 1400s]

by no stretch ♦ See BY ANY STRETCH.

by one's bootstraps ♦ See under PULL ONESELF UP.

by oneself Alone, unaccompanied; also, unassisted. For example, *She enjoyed being by herself much of the time*, or *Brian can pick up his toys by himself*. [c. A.D. 1000]

by one's wits ♦ See LIVE BY ONE'S WITS.

by reason of Because of, owing to, as in *By reason of a crop failure, the price of coffee is bound to rise*. This expression is considered quite formal today. [c. 1300]

by request Also, **on** or **upon request**. In response to being asked to do something. For example, *The band is playing our favorite song by request*. This usage replaced *at request*. [Late 1600s]

by rights Justly, in fairness, as in *By rights he should have been chosen first*. Originally put as *by right*, this term was first recorded about 1315.

by storm ♦ See TAKE BY STORM.

by surprise ♦ See TAKE BY SURPRISE.

by the balls ♦ See HAVE ONE BY THE BALLS.

by the board Fallen out of use, discarded. This expression usually is put as **go by the board**, as in *With all the crime around here, the practice of leaving the house unlocked has gone by the board*. The *board* here is the board of a ship, and the expression has been used since about 1630 to signify something that has fallen overboard and been carried away. [Mid-1800s]

by the book Strictly according to the rules, as in *Our trip leader is going by the book, allowing us to wander off only for short periods.* Shakespeare already used the term figuratively in *Romeo and Juliet* (1:5): "You kiss by the book." Also see BY THE NUMBERS.

by the bye Also, **by the by.** Incidentally, in passing, as in *By the bye, my wife is coming too,* or *Exactly where do you live, by the by?* The *bye* or second *by* in this term originally meant "a side path," whence the current sense of "off the track" or "of secondary importance." [Early 1500s] Also see BY THE WAY.

by the day Also, **by the hour** or **week** or **month** or **year.** According to a specific time period, as in *I'm renting this car by the day,* or *He's being paid by the hour.* This usage generally describes some kind of rate. [1400s]

by the dozen Also, **by the hundred** or **thousand.** According to a definite quantity, as in *She's buying tapes by the dozen.* This usage is generally employed for some kind of rate. A 1950 film about efficiency expert Frank Gilbreth and his family was entitled *Cheaper by the Dozen.* [c. 1300]

by the numbers In a strict sequence, step-by-step; also, mechanically. For example, *The only way to assemble this computer is to do it by the numbers,* or *Writing a novel is not something one can do by the numbers.* This expression has nothing to do with actual numerical figures (like BY THE DOZEN) but uses *numbers* in the sense of a strict order or sequence.

by the same token 1. In the same way, for the same reason. For example, *He has a good ear for music, and by the same token he finds it easy to pronounce foreign words.* This phrase today is used in a general way to connect statements that have some logical association with one another. [Mid-1400s] 2. As a corroborating circumstance, as in *Boston's population has grown very fast, and by the same token its urban problems have also increased.* [Late 1800s]

by the seat of the pants ♦ See SEAT OF THE PANTS.

by the short hairs Under one's complete control. This expression is often used with *get* or *have,* as in *She had her husband by the short hairs.* It is in effect a euphemism for HAVE SOMEONE BY THE BALLS, the hairs in question being public hair. [Colloquial; second half of 1800s]

by the skin of one's teeth Just barely, very narrowly, as in *Doug passed the exam by the skin of his teeth.* A related term appears in the Bible (Job 19:20), where Job says, "I am escaped with the skin of my teeth," presumably meaning he got away with nothing at all. Today the phrase using

by is used most often to describe a narrow escape. [c. 1600] Also see SQUEAK THROUGH.

by the sweat of one's brow By hard work, as in *The only way he'll succeed is by the sweat of his brow.* This figurative usage appears in the Bible (Genesis 31:9), where Adam's punishment for eating fruit in Eden is "In the sweat of thy face shalt thou eat bread"—that is, he will have to work for his bread, or living. [c. 1600]

by the way 1. In passing, incidentally, as in *She's my wife's cousin, and by the way, a good friend.* [Mid-1500s] 2. Parenthetically, in addition, as in *We saw Mary last week, and by the way, did Tom call you?* [Early 1600s]

by turns Alternately, one after another, as in *She is by turns cheerful, serious, and sad.* [First half of 1500s]

by virtue of Also **in virtue of.** On the grounds of, by reason of, as in *By virtue of a large inheritance she could easily afford not to work.* [Early 1300s]

by way of 1. Through, via, as in *I'm flying to Australia by way of Hawaii.* [Mid-1400s] 2. As a means of, as in *He paid our fares by way of apology.* [Late 1300s]

by weight According to weight rather than height, volume, or some other measure. For example, *In Europe bread often is sold by weight rather than by the loaf.* [c. A.D. 1000]

by word of mouth ♦ See WORD OF MOUTH.

byways ♦ See HIGHWAYS AND BYWAYS.

C

cabin fever Distress or anxiety caused by prolonged confinement in a small or remote place, as in *We've been snowed in for a week and everyone has cabin fever.* Originating in the West, this term at first alluded to being penned up in a remote cabin during a long winter but has since been applied more broadly. [Late 1800s]

caboodle ♦ See WHOLE KIT AND CABOODLE.

cahoots ♦ See under IN LEAGUE WITH.

Cain ♦ See RAISE CAIN.

cake ♦ See EAT ONE'S CAKE AND HAVE IT, TOO; FLAT AS A PANCAKE; ICING ON THE CAKE; NUTTY AS A FRUITCAKE; PIECE OF CAKE; SELL LIKE HOT CAKES; SLICE OF THE PIE (CAKE); TAKE THE CAKE.

calculated risk A chance taken after careful estimation of the probable outcome, as in *Taking their dispute to arbitration was definitely a calculated risk.* This term uses *calculated* in the sense of "planned with forethought," a usage from the mid-1800s. Its pairing with *risk* dates from World

War II, when the chances for losing bombers were taken into account before a bombing mission was sent out. After the war the term was transferred to other undertakings where taking a chance to succeed had to be weighed against the costs of failure.

calf ♦ See KILL THE FATTED CALF; PUPPY (CALF) LOVE.

call ♦ In addition to the idioms beginning with CALL, also see ABOVE AND BEYOND (THE CALL OF DUTY); AT SOMEONE'S BECK AND CALL; CLOSE CALL; DRESSING (CALLING) DOWN; NO CALL FOR; ON CALL; PAY A CALL; POT CALLING THE KETTLE BLACK; TOO CLOSE TO CALL; UNCALLED FOR; WAKE-UP CALL; WITHIN CALL.

call a halt Order something stopped, as in *It was getting too dark to see the ball, so the referee called a halt to the match,* or *They'd played the march four times, so the conductor called a halt to the rehearsal.* [Late 1800s]

call a spade a spade Speak frankly and bluntly, be explicit, as in *You can always trust Mary to call a spade a spade.* This term comes from a Greek saying, *call a bowl a bowl,* that was mistranslated into Latin by Erasmus and came into English in the 1500s. Also see TELL IT LIKE IT IS.

call back 1. Ask someone to return; also, ask that something be returned, as in *He passed the first audition and was waiting to be called back,* or *These screws are defective; the manufacturer has called them back.* [Late 1500s] 2. **call someone back.** Telephone someone in return, as in *May I call you back next week?* [Early 1900s]

call down 1. Invoke, as from heaven; for example, *He called down the wrath of God.* [Early 1800s] 2. **call someone down.** Scold or reprimand, as in *The conductor called her down for playing out of tune.* [Mid-1800s] For a synonym, see DRESS DOWN, def. 1.

call for 1. Go to get someone or something, as in *John said he'd call for Mary at eight,* or *Someone's at the door, calling for the package.* [First half of 1600s] 2. Summon someone or something. For example, *The audience called for the playwright,* or *The judge called for the verdict.* [First half of 1500s] 3. Require, demand, as in *This job calls for a lot of patience.* [First half of 1700s] Also see NO CALL FOR; UNCALLED FOR.

call in 1. Summon for help or consultation, as in *We've decided to call in a specialist to look at Father.* [Second half of 1600s] 2. Withdraw from circulation, as in *We're calling in all the old models.* [Late 1500s] 3. Communicate by telephone, as in *In this office salesmen must call in once a day.* [Mid-1900s]

call in question Also, **call into question.** Dispute, challenge; also, cast doubt on. For example, *How can you call her honesty into question?* This usage was first recorded in John Lyly's *Euphues* (1579):

"That ... I should call in question the demeanour of all."

call in sick Telephone one's employer or school that one is ill and cannot come to work or attend. For example, *Ben called in sick and told his boss he would miss the meeting.* [Mid-1900s]

call it a day Stop a particular activity for the rest of the day, as in *It's past five o'clock so let's call it a day.* Similarly, **call it a night** means "to stop something for the rest of the night," as in *One more hand of bridge and then let's call it a night.* The original phrase was *call it half a day,* first recorded in 1838, which referred to leaving one's place of employment before the work day was over. The first recorded use of *call it a day* was in 1919, and of *call it a night* in 1938. Also see CALL IT QUITS.

call it quits Stop working, abandon something, give up, as in *John is calling it quits for now* or *This ground is far too stony for a garden so I'm calling it quits.* This idiom comes from **cry quits,** dating from the 1600s and meaning "declare even" or "get even." The verb *call* was substituted in the late 1800s. Also see CALL IT A DAY.

call names Verbally abuse someone, use offensive epithets, as in *The teacher told the children to stop calling names.* This idiom was first recorded in the late 1600s but Shakespeare used a similar expression earlier in *Richard III* (1:3): "That thou hadst called me all these bitter names."

call of duty ♦ See under ABOVE AND BEYOND.

call off 1. Summon away, restrain, as in *Please call off your dog.* [Early 1600s] 2. Cancel some plan or undertaking, as in *She decided to call off their engagement,* or *In case of rain the picnic will be called off.* [Late 1800s]

call of nature Need to urinate or defecate, as in *He left to answer the call of nature.* This euphemism may be dying out. [Mid-1800s]

call on Also, **call upon.** 1. Make a request, ask for, choose, as in *We are calling upon you to run for chairman,* or *The teacher called on Joe to answer.* [c. 1400] 2. Pay a brief visit, as in *The salesman said he'd call on me in the morning.* Shakespeare had this usage in *Antony and Cleopatra* (1:4): "I'll call upon you ere you go to bed." [Late 1500s]

call one's own Claim or regard something as one's possession or under one's control, as in *Victorian wives had almost nothing to call their own.* This expression, dating from about 1600, today is often used in a negative context, as in the example. It also appears in **can't call one's time one's own,** which dates from the 18th century and means one spends much of one's time in someone else's service, as in *The hours in this job are terrible; I can't call my time my own.*

call on the carpet Summon for a scolding or rebuke, as in *Suspecting a leak to the press, the governor called his press secretary on the carpet.* This term began as **on the carpet**, which in the early 1700s referred to a cloth (carpet) covering a conference table and therefore came to mean "under consideration or discussion." In 19th-century America, however, *carpet* meant "floor covering," and the expression, first recorded in 1902, alluded to being called before or reprimanded by a person rich or powerful enough to have a carpet.

call out 1. Summon into action or service, as in *The governor called out the militia.* [Mid-1400s] 2. Challenge to a fight, as in *To avenge the insult, Arthur called him out.* This term originated with dueling and is dying out. [Early 1800s]

call someone's bluff Expose someone's deception, invite a showdown, as in *I don't believe they have enough capital; I'm going to call their bluff.* This term comes from poker, where bluffing (pretending) that one has better cards than one's opponents is an intrinsic part of the game, and calling someone's bluff means forcing them to show their cards. By the late 1800s it was being applied to other enterprises. Also see SHOW ONE'S HAND.

call the shots Exercise authority, be in charge, as in *It's up to the boss to call the shots.* This term probably alludes to determining accuracy in target practice. [Mid-1900s] Also see CALL THE TUNE.

call the tune Make important decisions, exercise authority, as in *Nancy said that it's her turn to call the tune.* The full term is **Who pays the piper calls the tune,** meaning whoever bears the cost of an enterprise should have authority over it. [Late 1800s] Also see the synonym CALL THE SHOTS.

call to account 1. Hold answerable, as in *One day soon we'll be called to account for the child's behavior.* [Mid-1500s] 2. Challenge or contest, as in *The IRS is bound to call us to account on these deductions.* [First half of 1800s]

call to mind Remember, recall, as in *I've tried but I can't call his name to mind.* This idiom was first recorded in 1472.

call to order Formally open a meeting; also, bid people to obey the rules. For example, *The chairman used his gavel to call everyone to order,* or *The judge called the spectators to order and threatened to make them leave.* [Early 1800s]

call up 1. Summon to military service, as in *He was called up for active duty.* [Late 1600s]. 2. Cause to remember, bring to mind, as in *These stories call up old times.* [c. 1700] Also see CALL TO MIND. 3. Telephone someone, as in *I'll call up the theater and find out about tickets.* [Late 1800s] 4. Retrieve data from a computer memory, as in *I asked him*

to call up the last quarter's sales figures. [Second half of 1900s]

call upon ♦ See CALL ON.

camel ♦ See under LAST STRAW.

camp ♦ In addition to the idioms beginning with CAMP, also see BREAK CAMP; FOOT IN BOTH CAMPS; HAPPY CAMPER.

camp follower 1. A civilian who follows or settles near a military camp, especially a prostitute who does so. For example, *The recruits were told not to associate with camp followers.* [Early 1800s] 2. A person who sympathizes with a cause or group but does not join it. For example, *She's only a camp follower so we can't count on her for a contribution.*

camp it up Make an extravagant, affected, or vulgar display, as in *Amateur actors often camp it up, trying to be more dramatic.* Originating in the 1950s as slang for flamboyant behavior stereotypically associated with gay men, this term began to be used more loosely by about 1970. Also see HAM IT UP.

camp out Sleep outdoors; also, stay somewhere for an unusually long time. For example, "We camped out in a field this night" (George Washington, Journal, March 18, 1748). In the early 1900s, the expression was extended to figurative uses, meaning simply "to stay somewhere for an unusually long time," as in *She camped out at the stage door, hoping for an autograph.*

can ♦ In addition to the idioms beginning with CAN, also see AS BEST ONE CAN; BEFORE YOU CAN SAY JACK ROBINSON; BITE OFF MORE THAN ONE CAN CHEW; CARRY THE CAN; CATCH AS CATCH CAN; GAME THAT TWO CAN PLAY, GET THE AX (CAN); IN THE CAN; MORE THAN ONE CAN SHAKE A STICK AT; NO CAN DO; YOU CAN BET YOUR ASS; YOU CAN LEAD A HORSE TO WATER; YOU CAN SAY THAT AGAIN; YOU NEVER CAN TELL. Also see under CAN'T.

canary ♦ See LOOK LIKE THE CAT THAT ATE THE CANARY.

cancel out Neutralize the effect of, offset, render void. For example, *Anne's kindness to her neighbor could not cancel out her irritability.* The verb *cancel* was used in this way by itself from the late 1400s; *out* was added in the early 1900s.

candle ♦ See BURN THE CANDLE AT BOTH ENDS; GAME IS NOT WORTH THE CANDLE; HOLD A CANDLE TO.

can do with Also, **could do with.** Might profit from, needs, as in *This room can do with a good cleaning,* or *Harry could do with a new suit.* [Colloquial; late 1700s] Also see DO WITH.

canned laughter Also, **canned music.** Pre-recorded sound effects that can be played repeatedly, as in *That canned laughter doesn't make his jokes any* *funnier,* or *Canned music is greatly reducing the number of musical jobs available.* O. Henry had the term in his story, *Cabbages and Kings* (1903): "We'll export canned music to the Latins." Canned laughter today is often used in broadcasting to simulate the reaction of a nonexistent live audience. [c. 1900]

cannot ♦ See under CAN'T.

canoe ♦ See PADDLE ONE'S OWN CANOE.

can of worms A complex unexpected problem or unsolvable dilemma, as in *Tackling the budget cuts is sure to open a can of worms.* This expression alludes to a container of bait used for fishing, which when opened reveals an inextricable tangle of worms. [1920s]

can't ♦ In addition to the idioms beginning with CAN'T, also see BEGGARS CAN'T BE CHOOSERS; IF YOU CAN'T BEAT THEM, JOIN THEM; YOU CAN'T BE SERIOUS; YOU CAN'T TAKE IT WITH YOU; YOU CAN'T WIN THEM ALL. Also see under CAN.

can't abide ♦ See CAN'T STAND.

can't but Also, **cannot but.** ♦ See CAN'T HELP.

can't complain Used as a response meaning fairly good or well, to questions such as "How are you?" or "How is business?" For example, *How've you been?—Can't complain.* This term means that nothing serious is wrong. [Mid-1800s]

can't do anything with Unable to cope with or manage someone or something. For example, *I can't do anything with my hair,* or *My teenage daughter is very difficult—I can't do anything with her.* This expression uses *do* in the sense of "deal with," a usage dating from the early 1500s.

can't fight City Hall Unable to overcome bureaucratic rules, as in *Brad couldn't get a permit without going through channels—you can't fight City Hall!* This term transfers the seat of city government to a more general sense of bureaucracy in any sphere. [Mid-1800s]

can't help Also, **can't help but** or **cannot but.** Be unable to do otherwise. For example, *I can't help thinking that the keys will turn up eventually,* or *He couldn't help but believe he would pass the entrance exam,* or *I cannot but applaud his efforts.* The first of these phrases, *can't help,* is always followed by a present participle whereas the others take an infinitive. [c. 1700]

can't hit the broad side of a barn Have very poor aim. For example, *That rookie can't hit the broad side of a barn, let alone strike anyone out* or, as put in *The New Republic* (February 19, 1990): "Their missiles couldn't hit the broad side of a barn." This hyperbolic term, dating from the mid-1800s, at first denoted poor marksmanship. Around

1900 it also began to be used in baseball, for a pitcher with poor aim.

can't make head or tail of Also **can't make heads or tails of.** Fail to understand, be quite confused about, as in *I can't make head or tail of these directions.* A version of this term dates back to Roman times, when Cicero wrote *Ne caput nec pedes* ("neither head nor feet") to describe confusion. In the current idiom the precise allusion is unclear: *head* and *tail* may mean top and bottom, beginning and end, or the two sides of a coin. [Second half of 1600s]

can't make a silk purse out of a sow's ear Be unable to turn something ugly or inferior into something attractive or of value, as in *No matter how expensive his clothes, he still looks sloppy—you can't make a silk purse out of a sow's ear.* This expression was already a proverb in the mid-1500s.

can't punch one's way out of a paper bag Be inept, as in *Ask him to program the VCR? He can't punch his way out of a paper bag.* This hyperbolic term for extreme ineptitude originally was an expression of contempt for a weak or cowardly boxer. [Slang; c. 1910]

can't see beyond the end of one's nose. Also, **can't see farther than the end of one's nose.** Lack foresight, envisioning only immediate events or problems, as in *Thomas hasn't hired an orchestra for the Christmas concert; he just can't see beyond the end of his nose.* This expression originated as a French proverb that was frequently cited in English from about 1700 on. Alexander Pope used a similar expression in his *Essay on Man* (1734): "Onward still he goes, Yet ne'er looks forward further than his nose."

can't seem to Be apparently unable to, as in *No matter how hard I try, I can't seem to concentrate on this book.* This phrase gives added emphasis to a negative statement, as in the example. [Late 1800s]

can't see the forest for the trees Also, **can't see the wood for the trees.** Focus only on small details and fail to understand larger plans or principles, as in *Alex argues about petty cash and overlooks the budget—he can't see the forest for the trees.* This expression was already a proverb in John Heywood's 1546 collection.

can't stand Also, **can't abide** or **bear** or **stomach.** Thoroughly dislike; be unable to put up with something or someone. For example, *I can't stand the sight of her; she's obnoxious,* or *I can't bear to leave the country,* or *I can't stomach a filthy kitchen.* The oldest of these synonymous expressions is **can't abide,** which Shakespeare used in *2 Henry IV* (3:2): "She could not abide Master Shallow." **Can't stand** dates from the early 1600s; **can't bear**

dates from about 1700 and often but not always is used with an infinitive; **can't stomach** dates from the late 1600s and today is less common than the others.

can't wait Be very eager, anxious, or impatient, as in *We can't wait for the baseball season to begin* or *I can't wait to see Dad—it's been a year.* While the literal sense of being unable to wait (for lack of time) is much older, this figurative usage dates only from about 1930.

cap ♦ In addition to the idioms beginning with CAP, also see FEATHER IN ONE'S CAP; HAT (CAP) IN HAND; IF THE SHOE (CAP) FITS, WEAR IT; PUT ON ONE'S THINKING CAP; SET ONE'S CAP FOR. Also see under HAT.

cap and gown Ceremonial dress worn at graduation exercises; by extension, the academic community (also see TOWN AND GOWN). For example, *Mary was very proud when she received her cap and gown for commencement.* [Mid-1800s]

cap in hand ♦ See under HAT IN HAND.

capital ♦ See MAKE CAPITAL OUT OF.

cap it all 1. Also, **cap it all off.** Finish or complete something, as in *To cap it all off they served three kinds of dessert.* 2. Surpass or outdo something, as in *This last story of Henry's caps them all.* Both usages employ *cap* in the sense of "topping" something. [First half of 1800s]

captive audience Listeners or onlookers who have no choice but to attend. For example, *It's a required course and, knowing he has a captive audience, the professor rambles on endlessly.* This expression, first recorded in 1902, uses *captive* in the sense of "unable to escape."

carbo load Consume a large amount of carbohydrate food, as in *Karen began carbo loading three days before the road race.* This term, a clipping of "carbohydrate loading," originated among marathon runners, who were advised to build up their strength before a race by eating quantities of foods like spaghetti. [1970s]

carbon copy A person or thing that closely resembles another, as in *Our grandson is a carbon copy of his dad.* Originally this term meant a copy of a document made by using carbon paper. The linguistic transfer to other kinds of duplicate survived the demise of carbon paper (replaced by photocopiers, computer printers, and other more sophisticated devices). [c. 1870]

card ♦ In addition to the idioms beginning with CARD, also see HOLD ALL THE ACES (THE TRUMP CARD); HOUSE OF CARDS; IN THE CARDS; LAY ONE'S CARDS ON THE TABLE; PLAY ONE'S CARDS CLOSE TO ONE'S CHEST; PLAY ONE'S CARDS RIGHT; TRUMP CARD; WILD CARD.

card in Sign in to one's place of business by use of a magnetic card, as in *I told him I'd card in for him if he was late tomorrow.* Similarly, **card out** means to sign out of one's place of business, as in *I want to sneak out early, so could you please card out for me at the end of the day?* This term arose in the 1940s with the invention of automated check-in systems.

cards are stacked against Many difficulties face someone or something, as in *The cards are stacked against the new highway project.* This term originated in gambling, where **to stack the cards** or **stack the deck** means to arrange cards secretly and dishonestly in one's own favor or against one's opponent. [Mid-1800s]

card up one's sleeve Also, **ace up one's sleeve.** A hidden or secret advantage or resource, as in *Before we make a decision, let's see if management has another card up its sleeve,* or *You can count on John to have an ace up his sleeve.* The practice of storing something in one's sleeve dates from the 16th century, when clothes rarely had pockets. The current term comes from gambling, where a dishonest player might so conceal an ace or other winning card. [Mid-1800s]

care ♦ In addition to the idiom beginning with CARE, also see COULDN'T CARE LESS; DEVIL-MAY-CARE; FOR ALL (I CARE); IN CARE OF; IN CHARGE (THE CARE OF); TAKE CARE; TAKE CARE OF; TENDER LOVING CARE; THAT'S (TAKES CARE OF) THAT.

career ♦ See CHECKERED CAREER.

care package A gift package of food or other items not readily available to the recipient, as in *While I was in college, Mom sent me a care package of homemade cookies just about every month.* This term originated after World War II with CARE, an organization founded to send needed food, clothing, and other items to war-torn nations. By the 1960s the term had been transferred to sending packages of treats to children at camp, students away at school, and the like.

carpe diem Enjoy the present and don't worry about the future, as in *It's a beautiful day, so forget tomorrow's test—carpe diem!* Latin for "seize the day," an aphorism found in the Roman writer Horace's *Odes,* this phrase has been used in English since the early 1800s.

carpet ♦ See CALL ON THE CARPET; RED CARPET. Also see under RUG.

carried away ♦ See CARRY AWAY.

carrot and stick Reward and punishment used as persuasive measures, as in *Management dangled the carrot of a possible raise before strikers, but at the same time waved the stick of losing their pension benefits.* This term alludes to enticing a horse or donkey to move by dangling a carrot before it and, either alternately or at the same time, urging it forward by beating it with a stick. [Late 1800s]

carry ♦ In addition to the idioms beginning with CARRY, also see FETCH AND CARRY; (CARRY) OFF SOMEONE'S FEET.

carry a torch for Also, **carry the torch for.** Continue to feel the pain of unreciprocated love for, as in *Jane has been carrying the torch for Bill for at least a year.* The *torch* in this term alludes to the heat of love or passion. [1920s]

carry a tune Accurately sing a melody, as in *Dean loves to listen to music but he can't carry a tune.* [Early 1800s]

carry away Move or excite greatly. This expression is usually used in the passive, **be carried away**, as in *The eulogy was so touching we were carried away,* or *Take it easy; don't get carried away and overdo.* [Late 1500s]

carry coals to Newcastle Do or bring something superfluous or unnecessary, as in *Running the sprinkler while it's raining, that's carrying coals to Newcastle.* This metaphor was already well known in the mid-1500s, when Newcastle-upon-Tyne had been a major coal-mining center for 400 years. It is heard less often today but is not yet obsolete.

carry forward 1. Also, **carry over.** Transfer a bookkeeping entry to the next column, page, another account, or the next accounting period, as in *Let's carry forward this loss to the next quarter for a saving in taxes,* or *She made an error in carrying over this column.* The first term dates from the first half of the 1800s; the variant dates from the mid-1700s. 2. Make progress in, advance, as in *His successor hoped to carry forward his work.* Also see CARRY ON.

carrying charge 1. Interest charged on the balance owed when paying on an installment plan, as in *What is the carrying charge for this credit card?* The term denotes the amount charged for carrying the remaining debt. [Late 1800s] 2. The cost incurred when an asset is unproductive, as when aircraft are grounded during a strike, real estate cannot be developed owing to zoning laws, or similar circumstances. For example, *The carrying charge for owning this building may send us into bankruptcy.*

carry off 1. Handle successfully, win, as in *It was a difficult situation, but he managed to carry it off gracefully,* or *They carried off first prize.* [First half of 1800s] 2. Cause the death of someone, as in *The new African virus carried off an entire village.* This usage is less common today. [Late 1600s]

carry on 1. Maintain, conduct, as in *The villagers carried on a thriving trade,* or *They carried on a torrid love affair.* [c. 1600] 2. Continue or progress,

persevere, as in *I'm sure you can carry on without me.* [Mid-1600s] 3. Behave in an excited, improper, or silly manner, as in *They laughed and sang and carried on rather noisily.* [Early 1800s] 4. Flirt, engage in an illicit love affair, as in *She accused her friend of carrying on with her husband.* [Early 1900s]

carry out 1. Accomplish, bring to a conclusion, as in *They carried out the mission successfully.* Shakespeare had this term in *King Lear* (5:1): "And hardly shall I carry out my side, Her husband being alive." [Late 1500s] 2. Put in practice or effect, as in *We will carry out the new policy,* or *Please carry out my instructions.* [Mid-1800s]

carry over 1. See CARRY FORWARD, def. 1. 2. To keep something, usually merchandise, for a subsequent period. For example, *We'll carry over this summer's bathing suits for next winter's resort season.* 3. Persist from one time or situation to another, as in *His leadership in sports carried over to the classroom.* [Late 1800s]

carry the ball Take charge, advance a cause, as in *In our lab any of the assistants can carry the ball.* This usage comes from such sports as football, where the ball-carrying player gives the team yardage or a touchdown. By the early 1900s it was being transferred to other endeavors.

carry the can Take responsibility or accept blame, as in *Joan felt she was always carrying the can for her boss's errors.* [Slang; second half of 1900s]

carry the day Win, prevail, as in *At auctions the wealthiest bidders usually carry the day.* [Late 1600s]

carry the torch ♦ See CARRY A TORCH.

carry through 1. Continue with or persevere to the end, as in *She carried the project through despite being ill.* Shakespeare used this idiom in *King Lear* (1:4): "My good intent may carry through itself." [c. 1600] 2. Survive or persist, as in *His excellent technique carries through all his work.* 3. Also, **carry one through.** Enable to endure; sustain. For example, *His faith helped carry him through this last ordeal.* [Mid-1700s]

carry too far Also, **carry to excess.** Extend too much in a single direction, as in *One can carry the concept of mercy too far; these young thugs should be punished,* or *Humor in a sermon can be carried to excess.* [Early 1700s]

carry weight Also, **carry authority** or **conviction.** Exert influence, authority, or persuasion, as in *No matter what the President says, his words always carry weight.* Shakespeare combined two of these expressions in *Henry VIII* (3:2): "Words cannot carry authority so weighty." [c. 1600]

cart ♦ In addition to the idioms beginning with CART, also see UPSET THE APPLECART.

cart before the horse, put the Reverse the proper order of things or events, as in *Don't put the cart before the horse and give away the punch line.* This expression has been used since antiquity but was first recorded in English in 1520.

cart off Also, **cart away.** Transport or remove in an unceremonious way, as in *The police carted them all off to jail,* or *We'll call the town to cart away this trash.* This term owes its meaning to *cart,* a humble conveyance compared to a carriage. [Second half of 1800s]

case ♦ In addition to the idiom beginning with CASE, also see BASKET CASE; GET DOWN TO BRASS TACKS (CASES); HAVE A CASE ON; IN ANY CASE; IN CASE OF; IN NO CASE; IN THE CASE OF; JUST IN CASE; MAKE A FEDERAL CASE; OFF SOMEONE'S BACK (CASE); OPEN AND SHUT CASE.

case in point A relevant example or illustration of something, as in *A case in point was the collision of a cyclist with a pedestrian crossing the designated bike path.* [Mid-1700s]

cash ♦ In addition to the idioms beginning with CASH, also see COLD CASH.

cash cow A dependable source of profit, as in *The small-appliance division is this company's cash cow.* Although this precise term dates only from about 1970, **milch cow** was used in exactly the same way from 1601.

cash in 1. Settle an account, close a matter, quit, as in *I'm simply going to cash in and leave,* or *The countries of the former Soviet Union have cashed in.* [Late 1800s] 2. Profit handsomely, as in *When the stock price went up, we really cashed in.* This phrase often is extended to **cash in on,** meaning to take advantage of. [Early 1900s] 3. Also, **cash in one's chips.** Die, as in *If this new treatment fails, Bob may be cashing in his chips before long.* This usage was a transfer from quitting a poker game. [Slang; late 1800s]

cash on the barrelhead Immediate payment, as in *They won't extend credit; it's cash on the barrelhead or no sale.* The lexicographer Charles Earle Funk surmised that this term originated in the days when upended barrels served as both seats and tables in bars, and customers were required to pay for their drinks immediately, literally putting their money on the top (head) of a barrel.

cast ♦ In addition to the idioms beginning with CAST, also see DIE IS CAST.

cast about 1. Also, **cast around.** Seek, make a search, as in *We cast about for the necessary tools, but couldn't find them in the garage.* [Late 1600s] 2. Devise means, contrive, as in *They cast about for new ways to increase revenue.* This usage was first recorded in 1867.

cast adrift ♦ See CAST LOOSE.

cast away 1. Also, **cast aside.** Discard, reject, as in *He picked a book, then cast it aside,* or *She cast away all thoughts of returning home.* [Early 1400s] 2. Squander, waste, as in *She cast away a fortune on jewelry.* Shakespeare used this idiom in *King John* (2:1): "France, hast thou yet more blood to cast away?" [Early 1500s]

cast doubt on Cause something or someone to be questioned. For example, *The prosecutor cast doubt on the wife's alibi.* This idiom uses *cast* in the sense of "throw," a usage dating from the early 1200s.

cast down 1. Throw down, hurl to the ground, as in *She cast down her coat on the grass.* [Late 1400s] 2. Bend down, lower, as in *He cast down his eyes.* [Late 1300s]

cast in one's lot ♦ See CAST ONE'S LOT.

cast in stone Also, **etched in stone.** Definite, fixed, as in *We may choose to stay longer—our plans aren't cast in stone,* or *When Carl sets an agenda you can safely assume it's etched in stone.* Both expressions allude to sculpture, with the first, from the early 1500s, using the verb *cast* in the sense of pouring and hardening some material into a final form, and the second cutting or corroding a permanent design.

cast in the same mold Bearing a close resemblance, as in *All his detective stories are cast in the same mold.* This term uses the verb *to cast* in the sense of forming an object by running molten metal into a mold. [Late 1500s]

castles in the air Also, **castles in Spain.** Dreams about future success, as in *Musing about the best-seller list, she was apt to build castles in the air.* The first term dates from the late 1500s. The variant, **castles in Spain** (or *chateaux en Espagne*), was recorded in the *Roman de la Rose* in the 13th century and translated into English about 1365.

cast loose Also, **cast adrift.** Let go, freed, as in *After Rob was suspended from boarding school, he was cast loose with nowhere to go,* or *Selling her home meant she was cast adrift with no financial ties or responsibilities.* Originally a nautical term for releasing a vessel, this idiom was being used figuratively by the late 1500s.

cast off 1. Discard, reject, as in *He cast off his clothes and jumped in the pool.* This term was already used figuratively in Miles Coverdale's translation of the Bible (1535): "Thy mother . . . that hath cast off her housebonds and her children" (Ezekiel 16:45). 2. Let go, set loose, as in *He cast off the line and the boat drifted from the dock.* [Second half of 1600s] 3. In knitting, to finish the last row of stitches, that is, take the stitches off the needle and form a selvage. For example, *Your* *sweater is finished; I just have to cast off.* [Late 1800s] Also see CAST ON, def. 1.

cast on 1. Make the first stitches in knitting, putting them on the needle, as in *Once you learn how to cast on, you can use either simple or complicated stitches.* [Mid-1800s] 2. Hastily put on clothes, as in *He cast on his coat and ran out.* This usage is dying out. [Early 1800s]

cast one's lot with Also, **cast** or **throw in one's lot with.** Join or side with, no matter what the outcome, as in *Bill cast his lot with the new company.* [First half of 1500s]

cast out Forcibly drive out, expel, as in *We have to cast out these old-fashioned ideas and methods.* [Late 1200s]

cast pearls before swine Give something of value to someone who won't appreciate it, as in *The old professor felt that lecturing on Dante to unruly undergraduates would be casting pearls before swine.* This term comes from the New Testament (Matthew 7:6), appearing in Tyndale's translation (1526). It was repeated often by writers from Shakespeare to Dickens and remains current.

cast the first stone Also, **throw the first stone.** Be quick to blame, criticize, or punish, as in *She's always criticizing her colleagues, casting the first stone no matter what the circumstances.* The term comes from the New Testament (John 8:7), where Jesus defends an adulteress against those who would stone her, saying "He that is without sin among you, let him first cast a stone at her." Also see PEOPLE WHO LIVE IN GLASS HOUSES; POT CALLING THE KETTLE BLACK.

cat ♦ In addition to the idioms beginning with CAT, also see ALLEY CAT; BELL THE CAT; CURIOSITY KILLED THE CAT; FAT CAT; GRIN LIKE A CHESHIRE CAT; LET THE CAT OUT OF THE BAG; LIKE A CAT ON A HOT BRICK; LOOK LIKE SOMETHING THE CAT DRAGGED IN; LOOK LIKE THE CAT THAT ATE THE CANARY; MORE THAN ONE WAY TO SKIN A CAT; NOT ENOUGH ROOM TO SWING A CAT; PLAY CAT AND MOUSE; RAIN CATS AND DOGS; WHEN THE CAT'S AWAY.

catbird seat A situation of advantage or superiority, as in *His promotion put Charles in the catbird seat.* This term is thought to allude to that noisy bird's habitual high perch. It was popularized in the 1940s by sportscaster Red Barber.

catch ♦ In addition to the idioms beginning with CATCH, also see EARLY BIRD CATCHES THE WORM; GET (CATCH) THE DRIFT; TAKES ONE TO KNOW ONE (A THIEF TO CATCH A THIEF). Also see under CAUGHT.

catch as catch can By whatever means or in any way possible, as in *There was no formal language program; one simply learned Spanish catch as catch can.* This term, in slightly varying versions but with the same meaning, dates from the late 1300s.

catch at Snatch, grasp, as in *The beggars kept catching at their coats.* [c. 1600] Also see GRASP AT STRAWS.

catch a Tartar Seek out something or someone that turns out to be unexpectedly unpleasant or formidable, as in *Now that she finally agreed to meet with you, you just might find that you've caught a Tartar.* In this term, *Tartar* signifies a difficult or sometimes violent individual, referring to Turkic and Mongolian invaders of Asia in the Middle Ages. [Mid-1600s]

catch cold Also, **catch one's death (of cold).** Become infected with a cold virus, contract a bad cold, as in *Jane manages to catch cold on every important business trip,* or *Put on your hat or you'll catch your death.* The first term originally (16th century) meant becoming chilled by exposure to cold and took on its present meaning in the late 1600s. The hyperbolic variant, often shortened, is somewhat newer.

catch fire 1. Be ignited, as in *This wood is dry enough to catch fire.* [c. 1600] Also see SET ON FIRE. 2. Become inflamed with enthusiasm or passion, as in *His ideas caught fire all over the country.* [Early 1700s]

catch in the act ♦ See under CATCH REDHANDED.

catch it Also, **get it.** Receive a punishment or scolding, as in *If I forget anything on the shopping list, I'll catch it,* or *I'm really going to get it when I turn in my paper late.* [Colloquial; early 1800s]

catch napping Surprise, take unawares. This term is often used in the passive, as in *The United States was really caught napping the day the Japanese bombed Pearl Harbor.* It originated in the mid-1500s as **to be taken napping.** Also see under OFF GUARD.

catch off guard ♦ See under OFF GUARD.

catch on 1. Understand, as in *Aunt Mary doesn't catch on to any jokes.* The verb *to catch* alone was used with this meaning from Shakespeare's time, *on* being added in the late 1800s. Also see GET IT, def. 2. 2. Become popular, as in *This new dance is really beginning to catch on.* [Late 1800s]

catch one's breath 1. Resume normal breathing after physical exertion of some kind, as in *These stairs are steep; wait a minute till I catch my breath.* This phrase once meant the same as HOLD ONE'S BREATH—that is, stop breathing momentarily—a usage no longer current. [Early 1800s] 2. Relax, take a rest, as in *Events have been moving so fast I'd like to stop and catch my breath.* [First half of 1900s]

catch one's death (of cold) ♦ See under CATCH COLD.

catch red-handed Also, **catch in the act.** Apprehend someone in the course of wrong-doing, as in *The boys were trying to steal a car and the police* *caught them red-handed,* or *He tried to cheat on the exam, but his teacher walked in and caught him in the act.* The first term referred to blood on a murderer's hands and originally signified only that crime. Later it was extended to any offense. The variant (*catch in the act*) is a translation of the Latin *in flagrante delicto,* part of the Roman code and long used in English law.

catch sight of ♦ See SUDDENLY or UNEXPECTEDLY, as in *When I first caught sight of the Alps, I was overwhelmed.* [First half of 1800s]

catch someone's eye Attract someone's attention, as in *That window display really catches my eye.* [Early 1800s]

catch some rays Sunbathe, as in *I want a good tan so I think I'll go catch some rays.* [Slang; second half of 1900s]

catch some z's Take a nap, go to sleep, as in *I stayed up all night studying so I'd better catch some z's.* This term alludes to the buzzing sound of snoring. [Slang; second half of 1900s]

catch the drift ♦ See GET THE DRIFT.

Catch-22 A no-win dilemma or paradox, similar to DAMNED IF I DO, DAMNED IF I DON'T. For example, *You can't get a job without experience, but you can't get experience unless you have a job—it's Catch-22.* The term gained currency as the title of a 1961 war novel by Joseph Heller, who referred to an Air Force rule whereby a pilot continuing to fly combat missions without asking for relief is regarded as insane, but is considered sane enough to continue flying if he does make such a request.

catch up 1. Suddenly snatch or lift up, as in *The wind caught up the kite and sent it high above the trees.* [First half of 1300s] **2.** Also, **catch up with.** Come from behind, overtake. This usage can be either literal, as in *You run so fast it's hard to catch up with you,* or figurative, as in *The auditors finally caught up with the embezzler.* [Mid-1800s] **3.** Become involved with, enthralled by, as in *We all were caught up in the magical mood of that evening.* [Mid-1600s] **4.** Also, **catch up on** or **with.** Bring or get up to date, as in *Let's get together soon and catch up on all the news,* or *Tonight I have to catch up with my correspondence.* [First half of 1900s]

cat got one's tongue A comment made when someone is unaccountably or unusually quiet, as in *We haven't heard from you all morning—has the cat got your tongue?* Often put as a question, this term originally was used mainly with a child who did something wrong and refused to answer any questions. Today it is used more generally to ask anyone to speak. [Mid-1800s]

cat's paw A dupe or tool for another, a sucker, as in *You always try to make a cat's paw of me, but I refuse to do any more of your work.* This term alludes to a very old tale about a monkey that persuades a cat to pull chestnuts out of the fire so as to avoid burning its own paws. The story dates from the 16th century and versions of it (some with a dog) exist in many languages.

caught ♦ In addition to the idioms beginning with CAUGHT, also see under CATCH.

caught dead, wouldn't be Also, **wouldn't be seen dead.** Would have nothing to do with, detest, as in *I wouldn't be caught dead in that outfit,* or *He'd not be seen dead drinking a cheap wine.* This hyperbole is always put negatively. [Colloquial; first half of 1900s]

caught flat-footed Caught unprepared, taken by surprise, as in *The reporter's question caught the President flat-footed.* This usage comes from one or another sport in which a player should be on his or her toes, ready to act. [c. 1900]

caught in the middle Also, **caught in the cross-fire.** Between two opposing sides, as in *The writers are often caught in the middle between editor and publisher, who are political opponents,* or *When parents don't get along, the children are often caught in the cross-fire.* Long used in military situations, these terms began to be used figuratively in the second half of the 1800s.

caught short Found to be lacking something one needs, especially money, as in *Can you pay the check? I seem to be caught short.* This idiom uses *short* in the sense of "lacking money," a usage dating from the early 1500s.

caught with one's pants down, be Be surprised in an embarrassing or guilty posture, as in *We spent a lot of time preparing for the inspection; we didn't want to get caught with our pants down.* This phrase presumably alludes to someone's pants being lowered to attend to bathroom needs but is not considered particularly vulgar. It is similar to OFF GUARD and, if wrongdoing is discovered, CATCH RED-HANDED. [Colloquial; early 1900s]

cause ♦ In addition to the idioms beginning with CAUSE, also see LOST CAUSE.

cause a commotion Also, **cause a stir.** Give rise to a disturbance, raise a fuss. For example, *The opening debate was so bitter it caused a commotion in the legislature,* or *Her entrance always caused a stir.*

cause raised eyebrows Also, **raise eyebrows.** Cause surprise or disapproval, as in *At school his purple hair usually causes raised eyebrows.* This transfer of a physical act (raising one's eyebrows) to the feelings it may express took place in the early 1900s. Lytton Strachey used the term in *The Eminent Victorians* (1918): "The most steady-going churchman hardly raises an eyebrow at it now."

caution ♦ See THROW CAUTION TO THE WINDS.

cave in 1. Fall in, collapse, as in *The earthquake made the walls cave in.* [Early 1700s] 2. Give in, admit defeat, as in *The prosecutor's questions soon made the witness cave in.* [Early 1800s] 3. Collapse, faint, or die from exhaustion, as in *After a twenty-mile hike I caved in.* [Mid-1800s]

cease ♦ In addition to the idiom beginning with CEASE, also see WONDERS WILL NEVER CEASE.

cease and desist Stop, leave off doing something, as in: "Bliss excavated at least once on his own and Dr. Brand . . . told him to cease and desist" (Douglas Preston quoting Frank Hibben, *The New Yorker,* June 12, 1995). This legal term is a redundancy, since *cease* and *desist* mean virtually the same thing, but often appears in legal documents to avoid possible misinterpretation. [c. 1920]

ceiling ♦ See GLASS CEILING; HIT THE CEILING.

cent ♦ See FOR TWO CENTS; NOT WORTH A DIME (RED CENT); PUT IN ONE'S TWO CENTS.

center ♦ In addition to the idiom beginning with CENTER, also see DEAD CENTER; FRONT AND CENTER.

center of attraction, the Something or someone that attracts the most interest or curiosity. For example, *The Ferris wheel is always the center of attraction at our carnival,* or *Jan is the center of attraction wherever she goes.* This expression comes from physics, where since about 1770 it has denoted the point to which bodies tend by gravity or the action of centripetal force.

century ♦ See TURN OF THE CENTURY.

ceremony ♦ See STAND ON (CEREMONY).

certain ♦ See FOR CERTAIN.

chain ♦ In addition to the idioms beginning with CHAIN, also see BALL AND CHAIN; PULL SOMEONE'S CHAIN.

chain reaction A series of events in which each influences or gives rise to the next event, as in *If one person collects substantial damages by suing a company, you can expect a chain reaction of such lawsuits.* The term originated in the physical sciences, first (1920s) chemistry and later (1940) physics; in the latter it denotes a process of nuclear fission. By the 1940s it had been transferred to more general use.

chain smoker One who smokes continually by lighting a new cigarette from the one being finished, as in *Before they forbade smoking, bridge tournaments often attracted players who are chain smokers.* [c. 1930]

chair ♦ See MUSICAL CHAIRS.

chalk up 1. Score or earn, as in *She chalked up enough points to be seeded first in the tournament.* This term alludes to recording accounts (and later,

scores) in chalk on a slate. [c. 1700] 2. Credit or ascribe, as in *They chalked their success up to experience.* [First half of 1900s]

champ ♦ In addition to the idiom beginning with CHAMP, also see LIKE A CHAMP.

champ at the bit Show impatience at being held back or delayed, as in *The dismissal bell hadn't rung, but they were champing at the bit to leave.* This term transfers the action of a horse that impatiently bites the bit in its mouth to human behavior. [Mid-1600s]

chance ♦ In addition to the idioms beginning with CHANCE, also see BY CHANCE; CHINAMAN'S CHANCE; EYE TO THE MAIN CHANCE; FAT CHANCE; FIGHTING CHANCE; JUMP AT (THE CHANCE); NOT HAVE AN EARTHLY CHANCE; ON THE (OFF) CHANCE; SNOWBALL'S CHANCE IN HELL; SPORTING CHANCE; STAND A CHANCE; TAKE A CHANCE; TAKE ONE'S CHANCES.

chance it Take the risk or hazard of, as in *I don't know if there's a later bus but let's chance it.* The verb *to chance* alone was so used for a time, as in *Let's just chance the rain—I'm not buying a new umbrella!* [Late 1800s] Also see TAKE A CHANCE.

chance on Also, **chance upon.** Happen upon, find or meet accidentally, as in *In Paris we chanced on a wonderful little restaurant,* or *Andrew chanced upon his karate teacher in the health-food store.* [Mid-1500s]

change ♦ In addition to the idioms beginning with CHANGE, also see FOR A CHANGE; LEOPARD CANNOT CHANGE ITS SPOTS; PIECE OF CHANGE; RING THE CHANGES.

change hands Pass from one owner to another. For example, *This house seems to change hands every other year,* or *The contract is valid only when money changes hands.* [Second half of 1600s]

change horses in midstream, don't Also, **don't swap horses in midstream.** It's unwise to alter methods or choose new leaders during a crisis, as in *I don't hold with getting a new manager right now— let's not swap horses in midstream.* This expression was popularized (although not originated) by Abraham Lincoln in a speech in 1864 when he discovered that the National Union League was supporting him for a second term as President.

change off Alternate, or take turns. This phrase is used either for two individuals alternately performing a task, as in *Lifting cement blocks is such heavy work that they decided to change off periodically,* or for one person alternately performing two task, as in *I can concentrate on this book only for short periods so I frequently change off and work in the garden.* Also see CHANGE OF PACE.

change of heart Altered feelings or attitude, as in *Paul didn't like his new job, but a raise prompted a*

change of heart and he became quite enthusiastic.
[Early 1800s]

change of life Also, **the change.** Menopause. For example, *After nine pregnancies, she was actually looking forward to the change of life,* or *She became quite moody during the change.* [c. 1820]

change of pace A shift in normal routine, a variation in usual activities or pattern, as in *She's smiling in that one photo, just for a change of pace,* or *After six hours at my desk I need a change of pace, so I'm going for a swim.* This term originated in a number of sports where strategy can involve altering the speed of, for example, a pitched or struck ball or a horse's gait. By the mid-1900s it was being transferred to other enterprises.

change one's mind Alter one's views or intentions, as in *I can always change my mind about going on this trip.* [Early 1600s]

change one's stripes ♦ See under LEOPARD CANNOT CHANGE ITS SPOTS.

change one's tune Also, **sing another** or **a different tune.** Reverse one's views or behavior, switch sides, as in *When she realized she was talking to the bank president, she quickly changed her tune,* or *I bet Dan will sing a different tune when he finds out what the salary is.* A version of this term, *sing another song,* dates from about 1300, and it has been theorized that it alludes to itinerant minstrels who changed the words of their songs to please their current audience. The first locution was already in use by 1600. Also see DANCE TO ANOTHER TUNE.

change the subject Deliberately talk about another topic, as in *If someone asks you an embarrassing question, just change the subject.* This term uses *subject* in the sense of "a topic of conversation," a usage dating from the late 1500s.

channel ♦ In addition to the idiom beginning with CHANNEL, also see GO THROUGH CHANNELS.

channel surfing Switching from one television station (channel) to another frequently, either to search for an interesting program or to keep track of several programs at once. For example, *What did you see on TV last night?—Nothing much; I was just channel surfing.* The term transfers the surfer's search for good waves to the viewer's search for programs. This practice became widespread with the use of remote-control devices for changing channels while remaining seated some distance from the television set. [1980s] A 1990s version is **Internet surfing,** a similar process for searching cyberspace.

chapter and verse The precise authority backing up a statement or view; established rules for or detailed information about something. For example, *You can't withdraw a card after you've played it; I'll cite you the rules, chapter and verse.* The term alludes to the chapter and verse of a quotation from the Bible, long regarded as an ultimate authority. [Early 1600s]

character ♦ See IN CHARACTER; OUT OF CHARACTER.

charge ♦ In addition to the idioms beginning with CHARGE, also see CARRYING CHARGE; GET A BANG (CHARGE) OUT OF; IN CHARGE; IN CHARGE OF; TAKE CHARGE.

charge off 1. Hurriedly depart, run away, as in *After a few minutes, she charged off to the next exhibit.* This term alludes to the military meaning of *charge,* "attack impetuously." [Early 1500s] 2. Also, **charge against.** Consider or count as an accounting loss or expense, as in *I'm charging off this purchase to overhead,* or *Let's charge the new computer against office supplies.* [Late 1800s] Also see WRITE OFF. 3. Attribute to, blame something for, as in *We can charge off these errors to inexperience.*

charge up Excite, agitate, stimulate, as in *The new preacher can really charge up the congregation,* or *Planning Beth's wedding got her mom all charged up.* This term originally was used for narcotic stimulation but now is used more broadly. [Slang; early 1900s]

charge with 1. Impose a duty or task on, as in *He was charged with getting this message to the commissioners.* [c. 1300] 2. Accuse of a crime, as in *He was charged with creating a disturbance.* [Mid-1500s]

charity begins at home Be generous to your family before helping others. For example, *She spends hours and hours on volunteer work and neglects the children, forgetting that charity begins at home.* This proverb was first recorded in English, in slightly different form, in John Wycliffe's *Of Prelates* (c. 1380): "Charity should begin at himself."

charley horse Cramp or stiffness in a muscle, most often in the thigh, as in *After working in the garden I frequently get a bad charley horse.* First used in the 1880s among baseball players, the term was soon extended to more general use. Its true origin is disputed. Among the more likely theories proposed is that it alludes to the name of either a horse or an afflicted ball player who limped like one of the elderly draft horses formerly employed to drag the infield.

charm ♦ In addition to the idioms beginning with CHARM, also see (CHARM THE) PANTS OFF; WORK LIKE A CHARM.

charmed life An existence that seems protected by extreme good luck, as in *Robert came out of that accident without a scratch; he must lead a charmed life.* The adjective *charmed* once meant "magical," which is no doubt what Shakespeare had in mind when he used the term in *Macbeth* (5:8): "Let fall thy blade on vulnerable crests, I bear a charmed life, which must not yield To one of woman born." Later it was extended to anyone who narrowly escaped from danger or was similarly lucky. [Late 1500s]

charm the pants off ♦ See under PANTS OFF.

chase ♦ See AMBULANCE CHASER; CUT TO THE CHASE; GIVE CHASE; GO FLY A KITE (CHASE YOURSELF); LEAD A MERRY CHASE; RUN (CHASE) AFTER; WILD GOOSE CHASE.

chat up 1. Talk flirtatiously to, as in *Leave it to Charlie to chat up the girls.* This usage is mostly but not entirely British. [Late 1800s] 2. Engage in light, friendly talk, as in *He was soon chatting up all the board members.* [Mid-1900s]

cheap ♦ In addition to the idioms beginning with CHEAP, also see DIRT CHEAP; ON THE CHEAP.

cheap at twice the price Very inexpensive, a good value for the money. For example, *Pete got a $3,000 rebate on his new car—it was cheap at twice the price.* For a synonym see DIRT CHEAP.

cheap shot An unfair or unsporting verbal attack, as in *You called him an amateur? That's really taking a cheap shot.* The term originated in sports, especially American football, where it signifies deliberate roughness against an unprepared opponent. [Slang; second half of 1900s]

cheap skate A stingy person, as in *He's a real cheap skate when it comes to tipping.* This idiom combines *cheap* (for "penurious") with the slang usage of *skate* for a contemptible or low individual. It has largely replaced the earlier **cheap John.** [Slang; late 1800s]

cheat on Be sexually unfaithful to, as in *They broke up right after she found he was cheating on her.* [Colloquial; 1920s]

check ♦ In addition to the idioms beginning with CHECK, also see BLANK CHECK; CLAIM CHECK; DOUBLE CHECK; GET A CHECKUP; IN CHECK; PICK UP (THE CHECK); RAIN CHECK; REALITY CHECK; RUBBER CHECK.

checkered career A background that includes many changes, especially of employment. For example, *Heather's had a checkered career, hopping from one city to another and one job to another.* This expression, first recorded in 1881, uses *checkered* in the sense of "constantly alternating," much like the squares on a checkerboard.

check in 1. Record one's arrival at a hotel, conference, or other function, as in *I asked the hotel if we could check in early.* [Early 1900s] Also see CHECK INTO, def. 2. 2. Die, as in *With the plane rapidly losing fuel, the pilot was sure he'd check in.* [Slang; early 1900s] Also see CHECK OUT.

check into 1. Investigate something, as in *I don't know when they open but I'll check into it.* Also see CHECK OUT. 2. Register one's arrival at, as in *She was about to check into the hospital.* Also see CHECK IN, def. 1.

check off Mark as entered, or examined and passed, as in *He checked off their names as they arrived.* [Early 1800s]

check on Also, **check up on; check over.** Investigate, scrutinize, or inspect, as in *I'll check on the brakes and make sure they're all right,* or *We need to check up on his work from time to time,* or *Let's check over the books together.* [Late 1800s] Also see CHECK OUT, def. 6.

check out 1. Record one's departure from a hotel by paying the bill, or from a conference or other function, as in *As soon as my bags are packed I'll check out of the motel.* [Early 1900s] 2. Leave hurriedly, make a quick exit, as in *The minute I get paid I'm checking out.* [Slang; 1920s] 3. Die, as in *When he got cholera, he was sure he'd check out.* [Slang; 1920s] 4. Withdraw an item after recording the withdrawal, as in *I'll check out the tapes on your library card.* [1930] 5. Record, total the prices, and receive payment for a purchase, as in *The cashier checked out and bagged my groceries in record time.* 6. **check something** or **someone out.** Investigate or evaluate something or someone; observe carefully. For example, *I don't know if you'll like the film; check it out yourself,* or *That man who's staring is probably just checking us out.* [Slang; mid-1900s] 7. Pass close inspection, as in *That rattle made me suspicious, but the repairman said the machine checked out completely.*

check over ♦ See CHECK ON.

checks and balances System whereby each branch of an organization can limit the powers of the other branches, as in *The union has used a system of checks and balances to prevent any large local from dominating its policies.* This system was enacted through the Constitution of the United States in order to prevent any of its three branches from dominating the Federal government. The term is occasionally transferred to other mechanisms for balancing power.

check up ♦ See under CHECK ON.

cheek ♦ In addition to the idiom beginning with CHEEK, also see TONGUE IN CHEEK; TURN THE OTHER CHEEK.

cheek by jowl Side by side, close together, as in *In that crowded subway car we stood cheek by jowl, virtually holding one another up.* This term dates from the 16th century, when it replaced **cheek by cheek.**

cheer ♦ In addition to the idioms beginning with CHEER, also see THREE CHEERS.

cheer on Encourage, as in *The crowd was cheering on all the marathon runners.* Originating in the 1400s simply as *cheer,* this usage was augmented by *on* in the early 1800s.

cheer up Become or make happy, raise the spirits of, as in *This fine weather should cheer you up.* This term may also be used as an imperative, as Shakespeare did (*2 Henry IV,* 4:4): "My sovereign lord, cheer up yourself." [Late 1500s]

cheese ◆ In addition to the idioms beginning with CHEESE, also see BIG CHEESE.

cheesed off Angry, fed up, annoyed, as in *I'm cheesed off about watering their plants twice a week.* This term was originally military slang and sometimes put simply as **cheesed.** [Slang; mid-1900s]

cheese it Stop, look out, as in *Cheese it! Here come the cops!* This term, generally stated as an imperative, may have been a replacement for the earlier "Stop at once." Eric Partridge speculated that it may have been a corruption of *Cease!* but its true origin is not known. [Slang; mid-1800s]

chest ◆ See OFF ONE'S CHEST; PLAY ONE'S CARDS CLOSE TO ONE'S CHEST.

chestnut ◆ See OLD CHESTNUT.

chew ◆ In addition to the idioms beginning with CHEW, also see BITE OFF MORE THAN ONE CAN CHEW.

chew out Scold harshly, as in *Dad will chew you out for taking the car without permission.* Originating in the military, this slangy term began to be used during World War I and soon spread to civilian life. Several vulgar versions, such as **chew someone's ass out,** should be avoided in polite speech. Also see EAT OUT, def. 2.

chew the cud Also, **chew over.** Ponder over, meditate, as in *John tends to chew the cud before he answers,* or *Let me chew that over and let you know.* The first term, first recorded in 1382, transfers the appearance of a patiently ruminating cow to a person deep in thought. The variant was first recorded in 1696.

chew the fat Also, **chew the rag.** Chat in a friendly, leisurely way, as in *Let's get together for coffee and chew the fat,* or *John and Dave spend hours just chewing the rag.* Before the 1880s in Britain, *chew the fat* meant "to grumble or complain," and *chew the rag* also has been used in this way. Today both expressions are largely synonyms for a friendly talk or gossip session. Why this idiom uses *fat* and *rag* is not known, but some speculate that *fat* refers to juicy items of gossip and *rag* to ladies' sewing circles and the cloth they worked on while chatting.

chicken ◆ In addition to the idioms beginning with CHICKEN, also see COUNT ONE'S CHICKENS; GO TO BED WITH (THE CHICKENS); LIKE A CHICKEN WITH ITS HEAD CUT OFF, NO SPRING CHICKEN.

chicken feed Trifling amount of money, as in *I'm not going to mow lawns for $5 an hour—that's chicken feed.* This expression alludes to the fact that chickens can be fed corn and wheat grains too small for other uses. [Slang; early 1800s]

chicken out Back out from fear, lose one's nerve, as in *In the end I chickened out and took the easier route down the mountain.* Chicken is a popular synonym for "cowardly," a usage arising in the 1600s and 1700s but then apparently abandoned until the 20th century. [Slang; c. 1930]

chickens come home to roost The consequences of doing wrong always catch up with the wrongdoer, as in *Now that you're finally admitting your true age, no one believes you—chickens come home to roost.* The fact that chickens usually come home to rest and sleep has long been known, but the idea was used figuratively only in 1809, when Robert Southey wrote, "Curses are like young chickens, they always come home to roost" (*The Curse of Kehama*).

chicken shit 1. Contemptibly petty or insignificant. For example, *He has spent his life making up chicken shit rules that nobody follows anyway.* This expression gained currency during World War II, when it was often applied to the enforcement of petty and disagreeable military regulations. [Vulgar slang; c. 1930] 2. Cowardly, as in *You're not too chicken shit to come along, are you?* [Vulgar slang; mid-1940s]

chicken with its head cut off ◆ See LIKE A CHICKEN WITH ITS HEAD CUT OFF.

chief cook and bottlewasher A person in charge of numerous duties, both vital and trivial, as in *We have no secretaries or clerks; the department head is chief cook and bottlewasher and does it all.* [Slang; c. 1840]

child ◆ In addition to the idiom beginning with CHILD, also see SECOND CHILDHOOD.

child's play Something easily done, a trivial matter. For example, *Finding the answer was child's play for Robert,* or *The fight we had was child's play compared to the one I had with my mother!* Originating in the early 1300s as **child's game,** the idiom was already used in its present form by Chaucer in *The Merchant's Tale*: "It is no child's play to take a wife."

chilled to the bone Also, **chilled to the marrow.** Extremely or bitterly cold, as in *After skiing in the wind for five hours straight, I was chilled to the bone.* These hyperboles replaced the earlier idea of one's blood freezing and are more picturesque than the current synonym *frozen.*

chill out Calm down or relax, as in *Don't let it bother you—just chill out,* or *Rex decided to come home and chill out for a while.* [Slang; 1970s.] Also see COOL IT.

chime in 1. Join in harmoniously or in unison, either literally (with music) or figuratively (joining a conversation to express agreement). For example, *In this passage I want the altos to chime in with the tenors,* or *When Mary agreed, her sister chimed in that she'd join her.* The literal usage was first recorded in 1681, the figurative in 1838. **2. chime in with.** Be in agreement or compatible with, as in *His views chime in with the paper's editorial stance.* [Early 1700s]

chin ♦ See KEEP ONE'S CHIN UP; LEAD WITH ONE'S CHIN; TAKE IT ON THE CHIN.

china, China ♦ In addition to the idiom beginning with CHINA, also see BULL IN A CHINA SHOP; NOT FOR ALL THE TEA IN CHINA.

Chinaman's chance Also, **ghost of a chance.** An extremely slim chance, a hopeless undertaking. Both versions are most often put negatively, as in *He hasn't a Chinaman's chance of finishing the work in time,* or *They haven't a ghost of a chance to get as far as the playoffs.* The first term, now considered offensive, dates from the late 1800s when many Chinese immigrants came to work in California and were resented because they worked for lower wages. Its precise allusion is unclear. The variant, which relies on the meaning of *ghost* as an insubstantial shadow, dates from the mid-1800s. Also see the synonyms CHANCE; SNOWBALL'S CHANCE IN HELL.

chink in one's armor A vulnerable area, as in *Putting things off to the last minute is the chink in Pat's armor and is bound to get her in trouble one day.* This term relies on *chink* in the sense of "a crack or gap," a meaning dating from about 1400 and used figuratively since the mid-1600s.

chip ♦ In addition to the idioms beginning with CHIP, also see CASH IN (ONE'S CHIPS); IN THE MONEY (CHIPS); LET THE CHIPS FALL WHERE THEY MAY; WHEN THE CHIPS ARE DOWN.

chip in 1. Contribute money, help, or advice, as in *If we all chip in we'll have enough to buy a suitable gift,* or *Everyone chipped in with ideas for the baby shower.* Mark Twain used this term in *Roughing It* (1872): "I'll be there and chip in and help, too." [Mid-1800s] **2.** In poker and other games, to put up chips or money as one's bet. For example, *I'll chip in another bundred but that's my limit* or, as Bret Harte put it in *Gabriel Conroy* (1876): "You've jest cut up thet rough with my higher emotions, there ain't enough left to chip in on a ten-cent ante." [Mid-1800s]

chip off the old block A person who closely resembles a parent, as in *Like her mother, Karen has very little patience—a chip off the old block.* This term, with its analogy to a chip of stone or wood that closely resembles the larger block it was cut from, dates from ancient times (Theocritus, *Idyls,* c. 270 B.C.). In English it was already a proverb by the 17th century, then often put as *chip of the old block.*

chip on one's shoulder A belligerent attitude or grievance, as in *Mary is easily offended; she always has a chip on her shoulder.* This term actually was defined in a newspaper article (*Long Island Telegraph,* May 20, 1830): "When two churlish boys were determined to fight, a chip would be placed on the shoulder of one and the other demanded to knock it off at his peril." [Early 1800s]

chip and dip Also, **chip'n dip.** A snack food or an appetizer consisting of potato chips, crackers, or raw vegetables (like carrot sticks) that are used to scoop up a dip, a savory creamy mixture. For example, *There wasn't much to eat; all they served was a chip and dip.* The term is also used for the utensils employed for this dish—a plate for the crackers and a small bowl for the dip. [Mid-1900s]

choice ♦ See BY CHOICE; HOBSON'S CHOICE; OF CHOICE; PAYS YOUR MONEY AND TAKES YOUR CHOICE. Also see under CHOOSE.

choke back Suppress, as in *He choked back his tears.* [Late 1800s]

choke off 1. Put a stop to, throttle, as in *Higher interest rates are choking off the real estate boom.* [Early 1800s] **2.** Stop someone from speaking or complaining, as in *Throughout the debate the congressman had to be choked off to give the other candidate a chance to speak.* [Slang; late 1800s]

choke up 1. Block a channel or other passage, as in *Vegetation choked up the creek like a dam.* [Late 1600s] **2.** Be too emotional or upset to speak, as in *She became so emotional about winning that she choked up and was unable to give an interview.* **3.** Become too nervous or tense in a critical situation to perform, as in *He's fine during practice but in a match he tends to choke up.* This usage, also put as *to choke* alone, is especially common in sports. [Colloquial; mid-1900s]

choose ♦ In addition to the idiom beginning with CHOOSE, also see BEGGARS CAN'T BE CHOOSERS; PICK AND CHOOSE. Also see under CHOICE.

choose up Select players and form sides for a game or team, as in *Jean was always afraid she'd be last when it was time to choose up.* [First half of 1900s]

chops ♦ See BREAK ONE'S ASS (CHOPS); LICK ONE'S CHOPS.

chord ♦ See STRIKE A CHORD.

chorus ♦ See IN CHORUS.

chow down Eat, as in *He's always ready to chow down at dinner time*. Originally military slang, this term is now more widely used. The noun *chow* in the sense of food, originating from either Chinese or pidgin English in the 18th century, also appears in such terms as **chow line**, a line of people waiting for food, and **chow time**, mealtime. [Slang; mid-1900s].

chump change A trivial sum of money, a trivial matter. For example, *Dave was sick of working for chump change; he wanted a decent salary*, or *Don't put that on the agenda; it's chump change*. This expression uses *chump* in the sense of "a fool or sucker who should be ignored." [Slang; 1960s] Also see CHICKEN FEED.

church ♦ See POOR AS A CHURCHMOUSE.

churn out Produce in an abundant and automatic manner, as in *He churned out a novel every six months*. This idiom transfers the turning of milk into butter to other kinds of production. [Early 1900s]

cinder ♦ See BURNED TO A CINDER.

circle ♦ See FULL CIRCLE; GO AROUND (IN CIRCLES); RUN AROUND (IN CIRCLES); RUN RINGS (CIRCLES) AROUND; VICIOUS CIRCLE.

circulation ♦ See IN CIRCULATION; OUT OF CIRCULATION.

circumstance ♦ See EXTENUATING CIRCUMSTANCES; UNDER THE CIRCUMSTANCES.

circus ♦ See THREE-RING CIRCUS.

civil tongue ♦ See KEEP A CIVIL TONGUE IN ONE'S HEAD.

claim ♦ In addition to the idiom beginning with CLAIM, also see LAY CLAIM TO; STAKE A CLAIM.

claim check A receipt for property that has been left or deposited, as in *Give me your claim check and I'll pick up your laundry for you*. This term most often refers to a receipt for such items as laundry (left for washing), clothes (for dry cleaning), a car (for servicing), or baggage (for short-term storage). [First half of 1900s]

clam ♦ In addition to the idiom beginning with CLAM, also see HAPPY AS THE DAY IS LONG (AS A CLAM).

clamp down on Also, **put the clamps on**. Become stricter or more repressive; put a stop to. For example, *The company was clamping down on expenses like business lunches*, or *It's time we put the clamps on polluters*. [Mid-1900s]

clam up Refuse to talk or respond, as in *Whenever she asks her teenager about his activities, he clams up*. This term alludes to the tightly closed valves of a live clam. [Slang; early 1900s]

clap eyes on ♦ See under LAY EYES ON.

class ♦ See CUT CLASS.

clay ♦ In addition to the idiom beginning with CLAY, also see FEET OF CLAY.

clay pigeon A person easily duped or taken advantage of, as in *You're a clay pigeon for all of those telephone fund-raisers*. The term alludes to the clay pigeon of trapshooting, which replaced the use of live birds in this sport in the 1860s. Its transfer to figurative use in the first half of the 1900s probably is explained by the much older slang use of *pigeon* for "dupe." Also see FALL GUY.

clean ♦ In addition to the idioms beginning with CLEAN, also see COME CLEAN; HAVE A CLEAR (CLEAN) CONSCIENCE; KEEP ONE'S NOSE CLEAN; MAKE A CLEAN BREAST OF; MAKE A CLEAN SWEEP; NEW BROOM SWEEPS CLEAN; TAKE TO THE CLEANERS; WIPE THE SLATE CLEAN.

clean as a whistle Completely, entirely, thoroughly, as in *He chopped off the branch, clean as a whistle*. The allusion in this simile is unclear. It may have been a replacement for the 18th-century **clear as a whistle**, which alluded to the pure, clean sound of a whistle (it has few overtones). However, it was adopted to describe something thoroughly done. [Early 1800s]

clean bill of health A report confirming the absence of fault or guilt in a person or thing, as in *Jeff checked every component and gave the computer a clean bill of health*, or *He had a foolproof alibi so the police had to give him a clean bill of health*. This term comes from a 17th-century practice of requiring ships to produce a medical document (*bill*) attesting to the absence of infectious disease on board before landing.

clean breast ♦ See MAKE A CLEAN BREAST OF.

clean hands, have Be innocent or guiltless, as in *John's got clean hands; he had nothing to do with it*. It is sometimes worded as **one's hands are clean**, meaning "one has done nothing wrong," as in *Don't look at me—my hands are clean*. This metaphor for freedom from wrongdoing dates back to at least 1600.

clean house 1. Wipe out corruption or inefficiency, as in *It's time the Republican Party cleaned house*. This usage is most often applied to an organization. [Slang; c. 1900] 2. Punish, give a beating, as in *Whenever he was drunk he threatened to clean house on one and all*. [Slang; c. 1900]

cleanliness is next to godliness Being clean is a sign of spiritual purity or goodness, as in *Don't forget to wash your ears—cleanliness is next to godliness*. This phrase was first recorded in a sermon by John Wesley in 1778, but the idea is ancient, found in Babylonian and Hebrew religious tracts. It is still invoked, often as an admonition to wash or clean up.

clean out 1. See CLEAN UP, def. 1. **2.** Empty something of its contents, leave bare. For example, *The crows cleaned out the whole field of corn,* or *At the shop's first sale the customers cleaned out the entire stock of shoes.* [Mid-1800s] **3.** Deprive of money or other material resources. This usage originated in gambling, where it signified losing one's last stake. Charles Dickens had it in *Oliver Twist* (1838): "He has cleaned me out, but I can go and earn some more." [Early 1800s] **4.** Drive out by force, as in *The new CEO tried to get away with cleaning out all employees over the age of 60.* [Mid-1800s]

clean slate A fresh start; another chance after wiping out old offenses or debts. This idiom often appears as **wipe the slate clean.** For example, *Henry's boss assured him that the matter was finished and he could start with a clean slate,* or *He wished he could wipe the slate clean, but it was too late to salvage the relationship.* This expression alludes to the slate boards on which school work or tavern bills were recorded in easily wiped-off chalk. Since 1850 or so the term has been used figuratively, and it has long outlived the practice of writing on slate.

clean someone's clock Beat, thrash, or defeat someone decisively, as in *He's much bigger than you and could easily clean your clock.* This term originated in the military. The use of *clock* is unclear but possibly alludes to hitting someone in the face (for "clockface"). [Slang; mid-1900s]

clean sweep ♦ See MAKE A CLEAN SWEEP.

clean up 1. Also, **clean out.** Make clean or orderly, as in *She cleaned up the cellar after the flood,* or *Dad said be cleaned out the garage.* [First half of 1800s] **2.** Also, **wash up.** Wash or tidy oneself, as in *Do I have time to clean up before dinner?* **3.** Settle or dispose of, as in *He cleaned up all the bills that had arrived during his vacation.* **4.** Bring to a certain standard of order or morality, as in *This script won't do; we'll have to clean up the language.* Applied to personal behavior, it also is put as **clean up one's act,** as in *He'll have to clean up his act and obey the rules.* [c. 1900] **5.** Succeed, especially financially, as in *We had fantastic luck at the races and really cleaned up.* [Slang; first half of 1800s] **6.** Also, **clean up on.** Defeat or vanquish, kill, as in *We're cleaning up all the other teams,* or *With enough ammunition we could clean up on this pocket of snipers.* [Slang; mid-1800s]

clear ♦ In addition to the idioms beginning with CLEAR, also see COAST IS CLEAR; FREE AND CLEAR; HAVE A CLEAR CONSCIENCE; IN THE CLEAR; LOUD AND CLEAR; OUT OF A CLEAR BLUE SKY; SEE ONE'S WAY (CLEAR); STEER CLEAR OF.

clear as a bell Pure as the sound of a bell; also, readily understood. For example, *Did you understand the message I left you?—Yes, clear as a bell.* This simile, which alludes to the bell's clarity owing to lack of overtones, was already a proverb in John Ray's *English Proverbs* (1670).

clear as crystal ♦ See CRYSTAL CLEAR.

clear as mud Murky, obscure, totally unclear, as in *The translation of these directions is clear as mud.* This ironic phrase always indicates that something is far from clear. [Early 1800s]

clear away ♦ See CLEAR OUT, def. 1.

clear off 1. See CLEAR OUT, def. 1. **2.** Become clear after cloudiness, fog, etc., as in *I hope this fog clears off before morning.* This phrase, first recorded in 1816, is heard less often today, *clear* alone often sufficing (*I hope the fog clears*). Also see CLEAR UP.

clear one's name Also, **clear oneself.** Prove someone (or oneself) innocent. For example, *She not only wanted to be acquitted, she wanted to clear her name entirely.* This locution employs the verb *clear* in the sense of "purify" or "wash away a stain." [Late 1400s]

clear out 1. Also, **clear away** or **off.** Remove the contents, take something or someone away, as in *I'll clear out this closet so you can use it,* or *Let me clear away these things,* or *Please clear off the table.* The first phrase dates from the mid-1600s, the second from the mid-1700s, and the third from the early 1700s. Sometimes *away* and *out* are omitted, as in *Let me clear these things,* or *Please clear the table.* Also see CLEAN UP, def. 1. **2.** Depart suddenly or run away, as in *We cleared out before our landlord could stop us.* [Early 1800s] **3.** Drive or force out, as in *The police cleared out the restaurant in no time.* [Mid-1800s]

clear the air Eliminate confusion, dispel controversy or emotional tension, as in *His letter has cleared the air; we now know where he stands.* This idiom alludes to an atmosphere cleared of sultriness by a storm. [Late 1800s]

clear the decks Prepare for action, as in *I've finished all these memos and cleared the decks for your project,* or *Clear the decks—here comes the coach.* This expression originated in naval warfare, when it described preparing for battle by removing or fastening down all loose objects on the ship's decks. [Second half of 1800s]

clear the table ♦ See CLEAR OUT, def. 1.

clear up 1. Clarify, explain, solve, as in *Let's try to clear up this misunderstanding.* [Late 1600s] **2.** Become clear, as in *After the storm, it cleared up* *very quickly.* [Early 1600s] **3**. Return something to a normal condition, cure, as in *This new salve will clear up your rash.*

clear with Obtain approval or permission. For example, *Before you proceed, you'll have to clear it with the main office.* [Mid-1900s]

climb the walls Show extreme frustration, impatience, or anxiety, as in *That long, boring banquet made me want to climb the walls,* or *If he says that one more time I'll be ready to climb the walls.* Although describing a military maneuver dating from ancient times, this slangy phrase has been used figuratively to express strong negative feeling only since about 1970. Also see under DRIVE SOMEONE CRAZY.

clinging vine An overly dependent person, as in *A clinging vine since her marriage, she's never made a decision on her own.* Nearly always applied to a woman (or wife), this metaphor for a climbing plant today criticizes dependency rather than, as in former times, praising the vine's fruitfulness.

clip someone's wings Restrain or reduce someone's freedom, as in *Hiding his car keys—you're really clipping his wings.* This metaphor for clipping a bird's wings to prevent its flying away dates from ancient Roman times. Christopher Marlowe used it in *The Massacre at Paris* (1590): "Away to prison with him, I'll clip his wings."

clock ♦ In addition to the idioms beginning with CLOCK, also see AGAINST THE CLOCK; BEAT THE CLOCK; CLEAN SOMEONE'S CLOCK; LIKE CLOCKWORK; SET BACK (THE CLOCK); STOP SOMEONE'S CLOCK; STOP THE CLOCK.

clock in Begin work, as in *She clocked in late again.* Also, **clock out**, end work, as in *Please wait for me; I forgot to clock out.* The allusion here is to punching a time clock, a device that punches the time on a card to record when an employee arrives and departs. [Late 1800s]

clock is ticking, the The time (for something to be done) is passing quickly; hurry up. For example, *The clock is ticking on that project.* This allusion to a stopwatch is often used as an admonition to speed something up. It also is used in more specific form—**one's biological clock is ticking**—meaning that a woman may soon be too old to bear a child, as in *Her biological clock is ticking—she just turned forty.*

clock up Record accumulated hours, miles, or points. For example, *It won't be easy to clock up 1,000 flying hours,* or *Brian clocked up a record number of baskets this year.* [Mid-1900s]

close ♦ In addition to the idioms beginning with CLOSE, also see AT CLOSE QUARTERS; AT CLOSE RANGE; BEHIND CLOSED DOORS; DRAW TO A CLOSE; KEEP (A CLOSE) WATCH; NEAR (CLOSE) TO ONE'S HEART; PLAY ONE'S CARDS CLOSE TO ONE'S CHEST; SAIL CLOSE TO THE WIND; TOO CLOSE FOR COMFORT; TOO CLOSE TO CALL.

close at hand ♦ See AT HAND.

close but no cigar A narrowly missed success, as in *That ball was definitely out—close but no cigar.* This interjection alludes to awarding a cigar to the winner of some competition, such as hitting a target. [Slang; early 1900s]

close call Also, **close shave**. Narrow escape, near miss. For example, *That skier just missed the tree—what a close call,* or *That was a close shave, nearly leaving your passport behind.* The first phrase dates from the late 1800s and comes from sports, alluding to an official's decision (*call*) that could have gone either way. The second, from the early 1800s, alludes to the narrow margin between closely shaved skin and a razor cut. (This latter usage replaced the much earlier equation of a *close shave* with miserliness, based on the idea that a close shave by a barber meant one would not have to spend money on another shave quite so soon.) Also see TOO CLOSE FOR COMFORT.

closed book, a A secret, mystery, or puzzle, as in *I can't figure her out; she's a closed book to me.* This term alludes to information one can't obtain or comprehend (because the book is closed). [Early 1900s]

closed door **1**. An obstacle or restriction, as in *There are no closed doors in the new field of gene therapy.* [First half of 1900s] **2. close one's doors**. See CLOSE DOWN. Also see BEHIND CLOSED DOORS; CLOSE THE DOOR.

close down **1**. Also, **close one's doors; shut down**. Go out of business, end operations. For example, *If the rent goes up we'll have to close down,* or *After fifty years in business the store finally closed its doors,* or *The warehouse had a clearance sale the month before it shut down for good.* Also see CLOSE UP, def. 2. **2**. Force someone to go out of business, as in *The police raided the porn shop and closed it down.* Both usages date from the early 1900s, but *shut down* was first recorded in 1877.

close in **1**. Surround, enclose, envelop, as in *The fog closed in and we couldn't see two yards in front of us,* or *She felt the room was closing in.* [c. 1400] **2**. Also, **close in on** or **upon**. Draw in, approach, as in *The police closed in on the suspect.* [Early 1800s]

close one's eyes to Also, **shut one eyes to**. Deliberately ignore, refuse to notice. For example, *Jill closed her eyes to the danger and pushed off downhill,* or *The professor shut her eyes to students who* *read a book during her lecture.* [Early 1700s] For a synonym see TURN A BLIND EYE.

close out 1. Also, **close something out.** Dispose of a stock of goods; end a business. For example, *We are closing out all our china,* or *They've decided to close out their downtown branch.* This expression is most often used in business and commerce but occasionally refers to other matters. [Late 1800s] **2. close someone out.** Prevent someone's entry or inclusion, as in *No one will tell us about the merger— we've been closed out.* [Second half of 1900s]

close ranks Unite, work together, as in *The members decided to close ranks and confront the president.* This expression, dating from the late 1700s, comes from the military, where it denotes bringing troops into close order so there are no gaps in the fighting line. (A slightly earlier form was **close lines.**) It has been used figuratively since the mid-1800s.

close shave ♦ See CLOSE CALL.

closet ♦ See COME OUT OF THE CLOSET; SKELETON IN THE CLOSET.

close the books Stop financial transactions; end a matter. For example, *The entire estate went at the auction, so we can close the books on it,* or *He was glad to close the books on this case.*

close the door on Also, **shut the door on.** End or exclude from consideration, discussion, or action. For example, *His lack of qualifications closed the door on further promotions,* or *Last quarter's poor sales figures have shut the door on any expansion plans.*

close the sale Also, **close the deal; close on a sale** or **deal.** Complete a transaction, as in *Jack was delighted to close the sale.* This term applies to such transactions as the sale of a house, also put as **closing on a house,** as well as negotiations leading up to a sale. The latter was also put as to **close a bargain,** a phrase used by Charles Dickens and other 19th-century writers: "He closed the bargain directly it reached his ears," *Nicholas Nickleby,* 1838.

close to home Also, **where one lives.** Affecting one intimately and personally, as in *That description of orphans really was too close to home,* or *The teacher's criticisms of her work got her where she lives.* The noun *home* here means "the heart of something," a usage dating from the late 1800s; the variant was first recorded in 1860. Both of these colloquialisms are sometimes preceded by *hit,* that is, something is said to **hit close to home** or **hit one where one lives,** as in *That remark about their marriage hit close to home.* Also see TOO CLOSE FOR COMFORT (TO HOME).

close up Also, **close up shop.** Stop doing business, temporarily or permanently; also, stop working. For example, *The bank is closing up all its overseas*

branches, or *That's enough work for one day—I'm closing up shop and going home.* [Late 1500s]

cloth ♦ See OUT OF WHOLE CLOTH; SACKCLOTH AND ASHES.

clothing ♦ See WOLF IN SHEEP'S CLOTHING.

cloud ♦ In addition to the idioms beginning with CLOUD, also see HEAD IN THE CLOUDS; ON CLOUD NINE; SILVER LINING, EVERY CLOUD HAS; UNDER A CLOUD.

cloud-cuckoo land An idealized mythical domain, as in *That idea about flying cars is straight out of cloud-cuckoo land.* This expression originated as a translation from the Greek of Aristophanes' play *The Birds,* where it signifies the realm built by the birds to separate the gods from humankind. It came into use in the 1820s. During the 19th century it began to be used for a place of wildly fanciful dreams, unrealistic expectations, or the like, and it also acquired the connotation of "crazy" (from *cuckoo,* slang for "crazy" since about 1900). Also see LA-LA LAND; NEVER-NEVER LAND.

cloud over Also, **cloud up. 1.** Become overcast with clouds, as in *It's clouding over now, so it may rain soon,* or *It was too hot and sunny, but after a while the sky clouded up and we ventured outside.* [Mid-1700s] **2.** Become opaque, misty, or dim, as in *I'm sweating so much that my eyeglasses are clouded over.*

clover ♦ See LIKE PIGS IN CLOVER.

club ♦ See JOIN THE CLUB.

clue in Also, **clue up.** Give someone guiding information, as in *It's time someone clued us in on what's happening,* or *I hope they clue us up soon.* This expression, which uses the verb *clue* in the sense of "inform," is sometimes put simply as *clue* (as in *I'll clue you—this isn't going to work*). [Colloquial; mid-1900s] Also see NOT HAVE A CLUE.

clutch ♦ See GRASP (CLUTCH) AT STRAWS.

coal ♦ See CARRY COALS TO NEWCASTLE; RAKE OVER THE COALS.

coast is clear, the No observers or authorities are present; one can proceed safely. For example, *Let's make sure the coast is clear before we set up this surprise party.* This expression may have originated among pirates and smugglers who were referring to the absence of coast guards, or with regard to a coastal military invasion, but no citations bear out these theories. By the late 1500s the term was used purely figuratively.

coattails ♦ See ON SOMEONE'S COATTAILS.

cobbler ♦ See STICK TO ONE'S LAST.

cock and bull story An unbelievable tale that is intended to deceive; a tall tale. For example, *Jack told us some cock and bull story about getting lost.* This expression may come from a folk tale involving these two animals, or from the name of an English inn where travelers told such tales. W.S. Gilbert used it in *The Yeomen of the Guard* (1888), where Jack Point and Wilfred the Jailer make up a story about the hero's fictitious death: "Tell a tale of cock and bull, Of convincing detail full." [c. 1600]

cock a snook Thumb one's nose, as in *As soon as the teacher turned her back, the boys cocked a snook at her.* This expression was first recorded in 1791 and the precise source of *snook*, here used in the sense of "a derisive gesture," has been lost. It is more widely used in Britain but is not unknown in America.

cocked ♦ See GO OFF HALF-COCKED; KNOCK INTO A COCKED HAT.

cockles of one's heart ♦ See WARM THE COCKLES OF ONE'S HEART.

cock of the walk A conceited, bossy person, as in *Since his last promotion he's been acting like the cock of the walk—he's unbearable.* This expression alludes to the rooster's proud strut about the barnyard, asserting his rule over hens and chicks. [Mid-1800s]

cog ♦ In addition to the idiom beginning with COG, also see SLIP A COG.

cog in the wheel Also, **cog in the machine.** One who holds a minor but necessary post in a large organization, as in *Frank knew he was just a cog in the wheel of this giant corporation.* This term alludes to the role of the mechanical *cog*, one of the teeth on a wheel or gear that, by engaging other teeth, transmits or receives motion. Used figuratively since about 1930, it sometimes is put as **small cog in a large wheel,** emphasizing a person's lack of importance.

coin ♦ In addition to the idiom beginning with COIN, also see OTHER SIDE OF THE COIN; PAY BACK (IN SOMEONE'S OWN COIN).

coin money Also, **mint money.** Make a great deal of money easily or very quickly. For example, *With a monopoly on the market he could coin money,* or *These highly motivated realtors just about enable the agency to mint money.* This hyperbolic expression dates from the mid-1800s.

cold ♦ In addition to the idioms beginning with COLD, also see BLOW HOT AND COLD; CATCH COLD; COME IN FROM THE COLD; IN A COLD SWEAT; IN COLD BLOOD; IN COLD STORAGE; IN THE COLD LIGHT OF DAY; KNOCK OUT (COLD); LEAVE ONE COLD; MAKE ONE'S BLOOD RUN COLD; OUT COLD; OUT IN THE COLD; POUR COLD WATER ON; STONE COLD; STOP COLD.

cold cash Also, **hard cash.** Actual currency (bills and coins); money immediately available, paid at the time of a purchase. For example, *Will you lower the price if I pay in cold cash instead of using a credit card?* or *We have only a limited amount of hard cash—the rest is in accounts receivable.* [First half of 1900s]

cold comfort Slight or no consolation. For example, *He can't lend us his canoe but will tell us where to rent one—that's cold comfort.* The adjective *cold* was being applied to *comfort* in this sense by the early 1300s, and Shakespeare used the idiom numerous times.

cold feet, get Also, **have cold feet.** Retreat from an undertaking; lose one's nerve. For example, *I got cold feet when I learned the trip involves whitewater rafting,* or *Don't count on including her—she's been known to have cold feet in the past.* The origin of this term has been lost. In early 17th-century Italy it meant to be short of money, but that sense has never been used in English. [Late 1800s]

cold fish A hard-hearted, unfeeling individual, one who shows no emotion, as in *Not even the eulogy moved him; he's a real cold fish.* This expression was used by Shakespeare in *The Winter's Tale* (4:4): "It was thought she was a woman, and was turn'd into a cold fish." However, it came into wider use only in the first half of the 1900s.

cold hands, warm heart Not showing one's feelings does not signify lack of feeling. For example, *Dan rarely sends flowers or anything, but he's a case of cold hands, warm heart.* Why a literally cold hand should indicate sympathy or affection is not really clear, but this expression has been so used since about 1900, and the Germans have an identical saying (*kalte Hand, warmes Herz*).

cold shoulder Deliberate coldness or disregard, a slight or snub. For example, *When I said hello to her in the library, she gave me the cold shoulder and walked away.* This term, which first appeared in writings by Sir Walter Scott and others, supposedly alludes to the custom of welcoming a desired guest with a meal of roasted meat, but serving only a cold shoulder of beef or lamb—a far inferior dish—to those who outstayed their welcome. [Early 1800s]

cold shower A surprisingly chilly reception, reaction, or response, as in *The small voter turnout was a cold shower to the League of Women Voters.* The allusion in this term is to the unexpected and not always pleasant effect of an ice-cold shower. [Second half of 1900s]

cold snap Also, **cold spell.** A short period of unusually cold weather, as in *The recent cold snap has threatened the crop.* The first expression presumably likens *snap* in the sense of "a sudden bite or cut" to sudden unexpected cold. The variant is more obvious, *spell* having been used in the sense of "a bout or turn at something" since the early 1700s. [Early 1800s]

cold storage ♦ See IN COLD STORAGE.

cold sweat ♦ See IN A COLD SWEAT.

cold turkey Immediate, complete withdrawal from something, especially an addictive substance; also, without planning or preparation. For example, *My bad shoulder forced me to quit playing tennis cold turkey,* or *I'd never done any rock climbing, but decided to try it cold turkey.* This term may have come from the earlier expression TALK TURKEY (for blunt speaking). At first used strictly for abrupt withdrawal from drugs or alcohol, it soon was transferred to quitting any habit or activity. [Early 1900s]

collar ♦ See HOT UNDER THE COLLAR.

collected ♦ See COOL, CALM, AND COLLECTED.

collector's item An object of great interest, value, or rarity, as in *This necklace is a collector's item.* Originating in the early 1900s as **collector's piece**, a usage still common in Britain, the term in its present form is occasionally transferred to persons as well, as in *The Beach Boys became a collector's item on the tour* [c. 1930]

color ♦ In addition to the idiom beginning with COLOR, also see FALSE COLORS; HORSE OF A DIFFERENT COLOR; LEND COLOR TO; LOOK THROUGH ROSE-COLORED GLASSES; UNDER FALSE COLORS; WITH FLYING COLORS.

color of someone's money, see the Prove that you can pay, as in *Before we talk any more about this car, let's see the color of your money.* This term probably originated in gambling or betting. [Slang; early 1900s]

comb ♦ See FINE-TOOTH COMB.

come ♦ In addition to the idioms beginning with COME, also see BIGGER THEY COME; CROSS A BRIDGE WHEN ONE COMES TO IT; DREAM COME TRUE; EASY COME, EASY GO; FIRST COME, FIRST SERVED; FULL CIRCLE, COME; GET ONE'S COMEUPPANCE; (COME) TO THE POINT; HOW COME; IF THE MOUNTAIN WON'T COME TO MUHAMMAD; IF WORST COMES TO WORST; JOHNNY-COME-LATELY; KNOW ENOUGH TO COME IN OUT OF THE RAIN; MAKE A COMEBACK; OF AGE, COME; ON THE SCENE, COME; OUT OF NOWHERE, COME; PUSH COMES TO SHOVE; SHIP COMES IN, WHEN ONE'S; TILL THE COWS COME HOME; WHAT GOES AROUND COMES AROUND; WHEN IT COMES DOWN TO. Also see under COMING.

come about 1. Also, **come to pass**. Happen, take place, as in *How did this quarrel come about?* or *When did this new development come to pass?* Shakespeare used the first term, first recorded in 1315, in *Hamlet* (5:2): "How these things came about." The variant, dating from the late 1400s, appears often in the Bible, as in, "And it came to pass . . . that there went out a decree from Caesar Augustus" (Luke 2:1). 2. Also, **go about**. In sailing, to change tack (direction), as in *It's important to duck under the boom when we come about.* [Mid-1500s]

come across 1. Also, **come upon; run across**. Meet or find by chance, as in *I came across your old letters today,* or *He came upon her looking in the store window.* or *If I run across it, I'll call you.* The first term dates from the 1800s. The first variant was used by Oliver Goldsmith in *She Stoops to Conquer* (1773): "You are to go sideways till you come upon Crack-Skull Common." The second variant was used by Mark Twain in *Tramp Abroad* (1880): "If I don't run across you in Italy, you hunt me up in London." 2. Also, **come across with**. Pay or give what is expected or demanded, as in *He finally came across with some food,* or *The landlord wants the rent, so come across.* [Colloquial; late 1800s] 3. Make a particular impression, as in *He comes across as a very sincere person,* or *Her meaning doesn't really come across; she'll have to revise the speech.* [Colloquial; first half of 1900s] Also see GET ACROSS; PUT ACROSS.

come again? What did you say? as in *Come again? I can't believe you said that.* This expression takes the literal meaning of the phrase—return—to ask someone to repeat a statement, either because it wasn't heard clearly or because its truth is being questioned. [Colloquial; second half of 1800s]

come alive Also, **come to life**. 1. Become vigorous or lively. For example, *It took some fast rhythms to make the dancers come alive,* or *As soon as he mentioned ice cream, the children came to life.* The adjective *alive* has been used in the sense of "vivacious" since the 1700s. Also, the variant originally (late 1600s) meant "to recover from a faint or apparent death." [Colloquial; first half of 1900s] 2. Appear real or believable, as in *It's really hard to make this prose come to life.* Also see LOOK ALIVE.

come along 1. Accompany or go with someone. For example, *Are you coming along with us today?* [Late 1600s] 2. Advance toward a goal, make progress, as in *How are you coming along with your piano lessons?* 3. Appear or materialize, as in *I'm hoping another offer will come along soon.*

come a long way Make considerable progress or improvement, as in *That's good, Rob—you've certainly come a long way.* This usage, which transfers the "distance" of *a long way* to progress, gained considerable currency in the 1960s and 1970s in an advertising slogan for Virginia Slims cigarettes addressed especially to women: "You've come a long way, baby."

come and get it Come and eat, the meal is ready, as in *She called to the children, "Come and get it!"* Originating in the British armed forces, this term passed to other English-speaking armies in the late 1800s and was taken up as a dinner summons by various groups who shared meals in a camp, among them cowboys, lumbermen, and construction workers. It occasionally is used facetiously for other summons, especially for sexual favors. For example, "'Come and get it,' she said and going to the bed, she lay down . . . and beckoned to him" (James Hadley Chase, *You're Dead Without Money*, 1972).

come and go 1. Arrive and depart, either briefly or repeatedly; go to and fro. Shakespeare had it in *The Merry Wives of Windsor* (2:2): "He may come and go between you both." [Late 1300s] 2. Alternately appear and disappear, as in *This rash is odd; it comes and goes*. [Mid-1300s] Also see COMING OR GOING; EASY COME, EASY GO.

come apart at the seams Also, **come unglued** or **unstuck**. Become extremely upset; break down. For example, *After he lost his job Brad seemed to come apart at the seams*, or *The proposed bank merger is coming unglued*, or *When her last play flopped she became completely unstuck*. This idiom transfers physical to emotional disintegration. [Slang; mid-1900s]

come around Also, **come round**. 1. Make a circuit; also, arrive casually or visit. For example, *The milkman comes around every day at this time*, or *You should come round more often*. [Early 1800s] Also see COME BY, def. 2. Change in a favorable way, as in *I was sure you would come around and see it my way*. [Early 1800s] 3. Recover consciousness, be restored to a normal condition, as in *The smelling salts quickly made her come round*. [Mid-1800s]

come at 1. Get hold of, attain, as in *You can come at a classical education with diligent study*. [Mid-1300s] 2. Rush at, make for, attack, as in *They came at him in full force*. [Mid-1600s]

come back 1. Return to or regain past success or popularity, as in *It's hard to come back from two sets down and win the match*, or *Long hemlines are coming back this fall*. [Early 1900s] 2. Return to one's mind, as in *Her name came back to me after I saw her picture*. [Late 1800s] 3. Retort or reply; also, retaliate. For example, *No matter how many insults he flings, I can always come back with another*. [Late 1800s]

come between Divide, cause to be antagonized, as in *I wouldn't want to come between husband and wife*. This idiom transfers the literal meaning of the phrase, "to intervene" (as in *Volume 6 should come between Volumes 5 and 7*), to figurative interference.

come by 1. Acquire, obtain, as in *A good assistant is hard to come by*. This usage, dating from about 1600, superseded the earlier sense of acquiring

something with considerable effort. A variant is **come by honestly**, meaning "to obtain in some honorable or logical way." For example, *I'm sure she didn't come by that large bonus honestly*, or *He does have an unusual gait but he came by it honestly; his father's is the same*. 2. Stop in, visit, as in *Please come by whenever you're in the neighborhood*. [Late 1800s]

come clean Confess everything, as in *If you come clean about what happened I will promise to keep it to myself*. [Slang; early 1900s]

come down 1. Lose wealth or position, as in *After the market crashed, the Tates really came down in the world*. A 1382 translation of the Bible by followers of John Wycliffe had this term: "Come down from glory, sit in thirst" (Jeremiah 48:18). 2. Become reduced in size or amount, be lowered, as in *Interest rates will have to come down before the economy recovers*. [Mid-1600s] 3. Be handed down by inheritance, tradition, or a higher authority. For example, *This painting has come down to us from our great-grandparents*, or *These stories have come down through the generations*, or *An indictment finally came down*. [c. 1400] 4. Also, **go down**. Happen, occur, as in *What's coming down tonight?* [Slang; 1960s]

come down on Also, **come down upon**. 1. Also, **come down hard on**. Punish or reprimand severely. For example, *My professor is going to come down on me for not completing the paper*, or *The judge promised to come down hard on drug dealers*. [Early 1600s] Also see LIKE A TON OF BRICKS. 2. Oppose, voice one's opposition, as in *The President came down on the new budget cuts, promising to veto them*. [Late 1800s] 3. **come down on the side of**. Make a choice or decision in favor of, plump for, as in *I'll come down on the side of those who are needy*.

come down the pike Appear, become prominent, as in *He was the best writer to come down the pike in a long time*. The noun *pike* here is short for "turnpike" or "road." [Slang; mid-1900s]

come down to Also, **come right down to**. Amount to or be reduced to, as in *It all comes down to a matter of who was first in line*, or *When it comes right down to it, you have to admit he was mistaken*. [Late 1800s] Also see BOIL DOWN, def. 2.

come down with Become ill with, as in *The whole family came down with the flu*. [Late 1800s]

comedy of errors A complex or humorous series of events, as in *Mary and John went to the Smiths', while the Smiths went to the Parkers', and the Parkers wondered why no one answered the door at John and Mary's—a true comedy of errors*. The term borrows the title of Shakespeare's play, *The Comedy of Errors*, about two sets of twin brothers, master and slave, who are separated in infancy, and the mixups occurring when they arrive in the same place many years later. [c. 1600]

come forward Present oneself, offer one's services, as in *The boss asked for more help, but no one was inclined to come forward.* [Early 1800s]

come from 1. See COME OUT OF. 2. Arrive from someone or somewhere, as in *This package just came from Alice,* or *Where did these chairs come from?* [c. 1300] Also see WHERE ONE IS COMING FROM.

come from behind Also, **come up from behind.** Advance from the rear or from a losing position, as in *You can expect the Mets to come from behind before the season is over,* or *The polls say our candidate is coming up from behind.* This idiom, which originated in horse racing, was first transferred to scores in various sports and later to more general use.

come full circle ♦ See FULL CIRCLE.

come hell or high water ♦ See HELL OR HIGH WATER

come home to roost ♦ See CHICKENS COME HOME TO ROOST.

come in 1. Arrive, become available for use or begin to produce, as in *Has the new fall line come in yet?* or *The latest reports are coming in now,* or *This well has just begun to come in.* [Late 1800s] 2. Also, **come in on.** Join an enterprise, as in *Do you want to come in on our venture?* [Mid-1800s] 3. Be one of those who finish a contest or race, as in *My horse came in last.* [Late 1800s] 4. Perform or function, as in *This mixer comes in very handy,* or *Where does my department come in?* [Late 1800s] Also see COME IN HANDY. 5. Enter into an account, issue, or list, as in *Where does this question come in?* or *Please explain where in this long process I come in.* This usage dates from Shakespeare's time and appears in *The Tempest* (2:1): "Widow? A pox on that! How came that widow in?" Also see subsequent entries beginning with COME IN; COME INTO; THIS IS WHERE I CAME IN.

come in for Receive, be subjected to, as in *His last book came in for some heavy criticism.* [Mid-1800s]

come in from the cold Also, **come in out of the cold.** Return to shelter and safety, be welcomed into a group. For example, *Bill was fed up with traveling on his own for the company and hoped they'd let him come in from the cold,* or *After years of not being invited to join, Steve was finally asked to come in out of the cold.* This phrase, generally used figuratively, gained currency in the 1960s with John LeCarré's best-selling spy novel, *The Spy Who Came in from the Cold,* about a longtime British spy in the cold war who longed to abandon the dirty tricks of his profession. Also see COME IN OUT OF THE RAIN.

come in handy Be useful or convenient, as in *This check will really come in handy.* [Mid-1800s] Also see COME IN, def. 4.

come in out of the rain, know enough to Show common sense. Alluding to having enough sense to seek shelter, this hyperbolic phrase is often used in the negative, as in *Peter doesn't know enough to come in out of the rain.* [Late 1800s]

come into 1. Inherit, acquire, as in *She expected to come into a fortune when she turned twenty-one.* [Early 1700s] 2. Accede to power or office, as in *He came into office in 1820 and served three terms.* [Early 1800s] 3. **come into one's own.** Get rightful possession of something; achieve rightful recognition. For example, *The serial composers have finally come into their own.* [Early 1900s]

come of ♦ See COME OUT OF.

come of age ♦ See OF AGE.

come off 1. Happen, occur, as in *The trip came off on schedule.* [Early 1800s] 2. Acquit oneself, reach the end. This usage always includes a modifier, as in *Whenever challenged he comes off badly,* or *This model is doomed to come off second-best.* [Mid-1600s] 3. Succeed, as in *Our dinner party really came off.* [Mid-1800s] 4. See COME OFF IT.

come off it Stop acting or speaking foolishly or pretentiously, as in *Oh come off it! you're no smarter than they are.* This term, often used as an imperative, dates from the late 1800s, when it was usually put simply as **come off.**

come on 1. Move forward, progress, develop. For example, *We stopped as soon as darkness began to come on.* [Early 1600s] 2. Hurry up, as in *Come on now, it's getting late.* This imperative to urge someone forward has been so used since about 1450. 3. Also, **come upon.** Meet or find unexpectedly, as in *We came on him while walking down the street,* or *I came upon an old friend in the bookstore today.* [Second half of 1700s] 4. Make a stage entrance, as in *After the next cue she comes on from the right.* [Early 1800s] 5. Please oblige me, as in *Come on, that's no excuse for leaving,* or *Come on, you'll really like this restaurant.* [Colloquial; first half of 1900s] 6. Convey a specific personal image, as in *He comes on like a go-getter but he's really rather timid.* [Slang; c. 1940] 7. Also, **come on strong.** Behave or speak in an aggressive way, as in *Take it easy; you're coming on awfully strong.* [c. 1940] 8. Also, **come on to.** Make sexual advances, as in *She reported her boss for coming on to her.* This usage probably was derived from the earlier use of the noun *come-on* for a sexual advance. [Slang; 1950s]

come one's way Present itself, happen to, as in *I sure hope another opportunity like that will come her way.* [First half of 1900s]

come on in Please enter, as in *Come on in, the door's open.* This phrase is simply a friendly request to enter one's house or some other place. The related **come on in, the water's fine** originated as an encouragement (or, sometimes, a command) to a reluctant or fearful swimmer but has been extended to other activities, as in *Come on in, the water's fine — this is a great office to work in!*

come on strong ♦ See COME ON, def. 7.

come on to ♦ See COME ON, def. 8.

come out 1. Become known, be discovered, as in *The whole story came out at the trial.* [c. 1200] **2.** Be issued or brought out, as in *My new book is coming out this month.* [Late 1500s] **3.** Make a formal debut in society or on the stage, as in *In New York, debutantes come out in winter.* [Late 1700s] **4.** End up, result, as in *Everything came out wrong.* [Mid-1800s] Also see COME OUT AHEAD. **5. come out for** or **against.** Declare oneself publicly in favor of or opposed to someone or something, as in *The governor came out for a tax cut,* or *Many senators came out against the bill.* [Late 1800s] **6.** Also, **come out of the closet.** Reveal that one is homosexual, as in *The military has specific policies regarding soldiers who come out of the closet while enlisted.* [Mid-1900s] Also see the subsequent entries beginning with COME OUT.

come out ahead Succeed, make a profit. For example, *By the end of the year we expect to come out ahead.* Also see AHEAD OF THE GAME.

come out for ♦ See COME OUT, def. 5.

come out in the wash, it will A problem will be solved or difficulties will disappear. For example, *Don't worry about the fight you got into — it'll all come out in the wash.* Cervantes had this metaphoric use of laundry for cleaning up a mess or difficulty in *Don Quixote* (*Todo saldrá en la colada*) and it has been repeated ever since. [Early 1600s]

come out of Also, **come from** or **come of.** Issue, proceed, or result from, as in *What good can come out of all this wrangling?* or *Where are these questions coming from?* or *What do you think will come of this change?* The first term dates from the early 1600s, the second from the early 1200s, and the third from the late 1500s. Also see WHERE ONE IS COMING FROM.

come out of nowhere ♦ See OUT OF NOWHERE.

come out of the closet ♦ See COME OUT, def. 6.

come out with Also, **come right out with. 1.** Put into words; speak frankly. For example, *He always comes right out with the truth,* or *She can always come out with a pun.* The first term dates from the mid-1400s, the variant from the second half of the 1800s. **2.** Make public, publish, as in *I don't*

know why they're coming out with yet another biography of Truman. [Late 1500s]

come over 1. Change sides or positions, as in *He's decided to come over to their side.* [Second half of 1500s] **2.** Happen to or affect, as in *Why are you leaving? What's come over you?* or *A sudden fit of impatience came over her.* [First half of 1900s] **3.** Pay a casual visit, as in *I want to show you my garden, so please come over soon.* This usage employs *come over* in the sense of "crossing an intervening space" (from somewhere to one's home). [c. 1600]

come round ♦ See COME AROUND.

come through 1. Also, **come through with.** Do what is required or anticipated; succeed. For example, *My parents really came through for me when I needed help,* or *He came through with flying colors.* [Late 1800s] **2.** Become manifested or be communicated, as in *He tried to keep a straight face but his true feelings came through nevertheless.* [Mid-1900s] **3.** Be approved, as in *If the second mortgage comes through, we can afford to redecorate.*

come to 1. Recover consciousness, as in *She fainted but quickly came to.* [Second half of 1500s] **2.** Arrive at, learn, as in *I came to see that Tom had been right all along.* [c. 1700] **3.** See AMOUNT TO, def. 2. **4.** See WHEN IT COMES TO. **5.** Stop a sailboat or other vessel by bringing the bow into the wind or dropping anchor, as in "The gale having gone over, we came to" (Richard Dana, *Two Years Before the Mast,* 1840). [Early 1700s] Also see the subsequent entries beginning with COME TO.

come to a halt Also, **come to a standstill.** Stop, either permanently or temporarily. For example, *The sergeant ordered the men to come to a halt,* or *With the strike, construction came to a standstill.* Both terms employ *come to* in the sense of "arrive at" or "reach," a usage dating from the 10th century. Also see COME TO, def. 2.

come to a head ♦ See BRING TO A HEAD.

come to an end 1. Conclude, terminate, as in the familiar proverb, *All things come to an end,* stated by Geoffrey Chaucer in *Troilus and Cressida* (c. 1374). **2. come to a bad end; come to no good.** Have a bad outcome or die in an unpleasant way. For example, *I always suspected this venture would come to no good,* or *Her parents feared he would come to a bad end.* **3. come to** or **meet an untimely end.** Die at a young age, terminate much sooner than desired or expected. For example, *The blow was fatal, causing the young boxer to meet an untimely end,* or *Our partnership came to an untimely end when I became too ill to work.* Also see DEAD END.

come to blows Begin to fight. For example, *It hardly seems worth coming to blows over a dollar!*

Thomas Hobbes had it in *Leviathan* (1651): "Their controversie must either come to blowes, or be undecided." This term is also put as **fall to blows,** especially in Britain. [Late 1500s]

come to grief Meet with disaster or failure. For example, *The icy runway caused at least one light plane to come to grief.* [Mid-1800s]

come to grips with Confront squarely, deal decisively with, as in *Her stories help the children come to grips with upsetting events.* This term, sometimes put as **get to grips with,** employs *grip* in the sense of a "tight hold." [Mid-1900s]

come to life ♦ See COME ALIVE.

come to light Be clearly revealed or exposed, as in *New facts about evolution have come to light with the latest fossil discoveries in Africa.* Miles Coverdale had this idiom in his translation of the Bible (Ezekiel 16:57): "And before thy wickednesse came to light." [First half of 1500s]

come to mind Be recollected, occur to one, as in *A new idea just came to mind.* This phrase replaced the earlier **come in mind,** which dates from the late 1300s. Also see BRING TO MIND; CALL TO MIND; ENTER ONE'S MIND.

come to no good ♦ See COME TO AN END, def. 2.

come to nothing Also, **come to naught.** Fail, as in *All his efforts have come to nothing,* or *The last round of peace talks came to naught.* The first term dates from the mid-1500s, the variant from the early 1600s.

come to one's senses Return to thinking or behaving sensibly and reasonably; recover consciousness. For example, *I wish he'd come to his senses and stop playing around.* This term employs *senses* in the sense of "normal or sane mental faculties," and in the earliest recorded use (1637) it meant "recover from a swoon." Its broader present-day meaning dates from the mid-1800s. The related **bring someone to his or her senses** was used by John Gay in his *Beggars' Opera* (1727). Also see TAKE LEAVE (OF ONE'S SENSES).

come to pass ♦ See COME ABOUT.

come to terms 1. Reach an agreement, as in *The landlord and his tenants soon came to terms regarding repairs.* [Early 1700s] 2. **come to terms with.** Reconcile oneself to, as in *He'd been trying to come to terms with his early life.* [Mid-1800s]

come to that ♦ See WHEN IT COMES TO.

come to the point ♦ See TO THE POINT.

come to the same thing ♦ See AMOUNT TO THE SAME THING.

come to think of it Remember or consider on reflection. For example, *Come to think of it, I've got*

to send in my order now, or *I was going to lend him a saw, but come to think of it, he already has one.* [First half of 1800s]

come true Happen as predicted, be realized or fulfilled, as in *Her marriage is my fondest dream come true.* [Early 1800s]

come under 1. Fit into a category or classification, as in *This document comes under the heading "classified."* [Mid-1600s] 2. Be the responsibility or province of, as in *My department comes under your jurisdiction.* [Early 1700s]

come unglued Also, **come unstuck.** ♦ See COME APART AT THE SEAMS.

come up 1. Arise, present itself, as in *This question never came up.* [Mid-1800s] 2. Rise (from a lower place to a higher one) as in *We'll leave as soon as the sun comes up.* [9th century] 3. Also, **come up to.** Approach, come near, as in *He came up and said hello,* or *The dog came right up to Nora.* [Early 1700s] 4. Also, **come up to.** Rise in status or value, be equal to, as in *His paintings will never come up to his teacher's,* or *This officer came up through the ranks.* [c. 1600] A variant is **come up** or **rise in the world,** used for someone who has risen in rank, wealth, or status; for example, *He has really come up in the world — be now owns a yacht,* or *I could see at once that she was a woman who would rise in the world.* Also see the subsequent idioms beginning with COME UP.

come up against Encounter, especially an obstacle or problem. For example, *I've never come up against anything I can't handle,* or *Dealing with Malcolm is like coming up against a brick wall.*

come up in the world ♦ See COME UP, def. 4.

come upon ♦ See COME ACROSS, def. 1; COME ON, def. 3.

come up roses 1. Turn out extremely well, as in *I had my doubts about this project, but now it's coming up roses.* [Slang; c. 1960] 2. **come up smelling like roses.** Emerge untarnished from a difficult situation, have no stain on one's character, as in *He was suspended for a month but still came up smelling like roses.* Eric Partridge believed this usage originally was **fall into shit and come up smelling like roses,** but the vulgar initial phrase is now generally omitted. [Slang; first half of 1900s]

come up to ♦ See COME UP, def. 3 and 4.

come up with Produce, supply; also, discover. For example, *Henry always comes up with the wrong answer,* or *We're hoping they come up with a cure in time to help Aunt Alice.* [First half of 1900s]

come what may No matter what happens, as in *Come what may, I'll be home in time for dinner.* This phrase, in slightly different form, **come what**

will, dates from the 16th century and has almost exact equivalents in French, Italian, and German.

come with the territory Accompany specific circumstances, as in *You may not like the new coach, but he comes with the territory,* or *As the editor, you may not like listening to complaints, but it comes with the territory.* This term uses *territory* in the sense of "sales district," and the phrase originally meant that traveling sales personnel had to accept whatever problems or perquisites they found in their assigned region. Today it is applied in many other contexts. [Second half of 1900s]

comfort ♦ See COLD COMFORT; CREATURE COMFORTS; TOO CLOSE FOR COMFORT.

comfortable as an old shoe, as Familiar and very much at ease, as in *Kathy's really enjoying her third summer at the same camp – for her it's comfortable as an old shoe.* This simile was once put **as easy as an old shoe,** first recorded in J. T. Brockett's *North Country Glossary* (1825). It was most often applied to friends, as in the proverb **Old shoes are easy, old friends are best,** but today it is used more broadly for easy familiarity in any situation.

coming ♦ In addition to the idioms beginning with COMING, also see GET WHAT'S COMING TO ONE; HAVE ANOTHER GUESS COMING; HAVE IT COMING; WHERE ONE IS COMING FROM. Also see under COME.

coming and going, have someone Catch someone both ways, give someone no way out. For example, *If Jane accepted the transfer she would have to move, but if she turned it down she would have to travel more—they had her coming and going.* Also see COMING OR GOING.

coming or going, not know if one is Be in a state of mental confusion, as in *He has so much to do that he doesn't know if he's coming or going.* This idiom was first recorded in 1924.

coming out of one's ears Overabundant, more than can be managed, as in *We miscalculated— new orders are coming out of our ears.* [Slang; mid-1900s] Also see EMBARRASSMENT OF RICHES.

comings and goings Movements, activities, as in *He's in and out of the office; I can't keep up with his comings and goings,* or *In her job on the school board, Mrs. Smith keeps track of all the comings and goings in town.*

command ♦ In addition to the idiom beginning with COMMAND, also see HAVE A GOOD COMMAND.

command performance An occasion that one is obliged to attend, as in *My boss's invitations to dinner are always a command performance.* This term originally (late 1800s) denoted a theatrical or musical performance presented at the behest of a sovereign or head of state. By the 1930s it was also

used figuratively for any more or less obligatory occasion or performance.

commission ♦ See IN COMMISSION; ON COMMISSION; OUT OF COMMISSION.

commit to memory Learn by heart, memorize, as in *The director insisted that the altos commit their part to memory by Tuesday.* First recorded in 1875, this phrase today is often replaced by the shorter *memorize.*

common ♦ In addition to the idioms beginning with COMMON, also see IN COMMON.

common cause A joint interest, as in "The common cause against the enemies of piety" (from John Dryden's poem, *Religio laici, or a Layman's Faith,* 1682). This term originated as **to make common cause (with),** meaning "to unite one's interest with another's." In the mid-1900s the name **Common Cause** was adopted by a liberal lobbying group.

common ground Shared beliefs or interests, a foundation for mutual understanding. For example, *The European Union is struggling to find common ground for establishing a single currency.* [1920s]

common touch, the The ability to appeal to the ordinary person's sensibilities and interests. For example, *The governor is an effective state leader who also happens to have the common touch.* This phrase employs *common* in the sense of "everyday" or "ordinary." [c. 1940]

commotion ♦ See CAUSE A COMMOTION.

company ♦ In addition to the idioms beginning with COMPANY, also see KEEP SOMEONE COMPANY; MISERY LOVES COMPANY; PART COMPANY; TWO'S COMPANY.

company man A male worker more loyal to management than to his fellow workers; also, one who informs on fellow employees. For example, *He'll never join in a strike; he's a company man.* Dating from the 1920s, a period of considerable labor unrest, this term uses *company* in the sense of "a business concern" and was often applied as a criticism by supporters of labor unions.

company manners One's best behavior, as in *George never interrupts when we have guests; he has fine company manners.* This term employs *company* in the sense of "guests." An older variant, **Tell me thy company and I'll tell thee thy manners,** uses *company* in the sense of "companions." The current term implies that one is more mindful of politeness with invited guests.

compare ♦ In addition to the idiom beginning with COMPARE, also see BEYOND COMPARE.

compare notes Exchange information, observations, or opinions about something, as in *Michael and Jane always compare notes after a department* *meeting.* This term originally referred to written notes. [c. 1700]

complain ◆ See CAN'T COMPLAIN.

compliment ◆ See LEFT-HANDED COMPLIMENT; PAY A COMPLIMENT; RETURN THE COMPLIMENT.

concern ◆ See AS FAR AS THAT GOES (IS CONCERNED); TO WHOM IT MAY CONCERN.

conclusion ◆ See FOREGONE CONCLUSION; JUMP TO A CONCLUSION.

condition ◆ See IN CONDITION; MINT CONDITION; ON CONDITION THAT; OUT OF CONDITION.

confidence ◆ In addition to the idiom beginning with CONFIDENCE, also see IN CONFIDENCE; TAKE INTO ONE'S CONFIDENCE.

confidence game Also, **confidence trick; con game.** A swindle in which the victim is defrauded after his or her trust has been won. For example, *The police warned of a confidence game in which people were asked to turn over valuables for a so-called appraisal,* or *The typical confidence trick is easy to spot if you know what to look for,* or *I almost let myself be taken in by her con game—she seemed so sincere.* These terms, which use *confidence* in the sense of "trust," date from the mid-1800s. They also gave rise to **confidence man** (or **con man**) for the swindler.

conk out 1. Stop functioning, fail, as in *The engine finally conked out.* [Colloquial; early 1900s] 2. Fall asleep, as in *Every evening he conked out in front of the television set.* [1940s] 3. Faint or collapse, as in *I don't know if it was the heat, but she suddenly conked out.* [1920s] 4. Die, as in *He's paranoid about conking out and he's only twenty!* [Late 1920s]

conniption ◆ See HAVE A FIT (CONNIPTION).

conquer ◆ See DIVIDE AND CONQUER.

conscience ◆ See HAVE A CLEAR CONSCIENCE; IN CONSCIENCE.

consequence ◆ See IN CONSEQUENCE; OF CONSEQUENCE.

consideration ◆ See IN CONSIDERATION OF; TAKE INTO ACCOUNT (CONSIDERATION); UNDER CONSIDERATION.

conspicuous by its absence Also, **conspicuous by one's absence.** Glaringly obvious by the fact of not being there. For example, *One agenda item concerning publicity is conspicuous by its absence,* or *The bride's father was conspicuous by his absence.* The idea is ancient; it was expressed by the Roman writer Tacitus, concerning the absence of Junia's brother and husband at her funeral procession. [Mid-1800s]

conspiracy of silence A tacit or explicit agreement to keep something secret. For example, *In*

this state's medical society there is a conspiracy of silence regarding incompetent practitioners. This term was first used as a complaint about lack of attention, but today it more often refers to remaining silent about something unfavorable or criminal. [Late 1800s].

contempt ◆ See FAMILIARITY BREEDS CONTEMPT.

content ◆ See TO ONE'S HEART'S CONTENT.

contention ◆ See BONE OF CONTENTION.

contradiction in terms A statement that seems to contradict itself, with one part of it denying another. For example, *I've always believed that "a poor millionaire" was a contradiction in terms.* [Late 1700s]

contrary ◆ See ON THE CONTRARY; TO THE CONTRARY.

control ◆ See OUT OF CONTROL; SPIN CONTROL.

convenience ◆ See AT ONE'S CONVENIENCE.

conventional wisdom A widely held belief on which most people act. For example, *According to conventional wisdom, an incumbent nearly always wins more votes than a new candidate.* This term was invented by John Kenneth Galbraith, who used it in *The Affluent Society* (1958) to describe economic ideas that are familiar, predictable, and therefore accepted by the general public. Today it is used in any context where public opinion has considerable influence on the course of events.

conversation ◆ In addition to the idiom beginning with CONVERSATION, also see MAKE CONVERSATION.

conversation piece An unusual object that arouses comment or interest, as in *That bust of Aunt Nettie is ugly but it's an excellent conversation piece.* In the early 1700s this same term was used for a particular kind of painting that represented a group, often a family, arranged as though they were conversing with one another. Later in the century the term was extended to any object that stimulates conversation.

conviction ◆ See COURAGE OF ONE'S CONVICTIONS.

cook ◆ In addition to the idioms beginning with COOK, also see CHIEF COOK AND BOTTLEWASHER; SHORT ORDER (COOK); TOO MANY COOKS SPOIL THE BROTH; WHAT'S COOKING.

cookie ◆ See HAND IN THE TILL (COOKIE JAR); THAT'S HOW THE BALL BOUNCES (COOKIE CRUMBLES); TOSS ONE'S COOKIES.

cook someone's goose Ruin someone, upset someone's plans. For example, *He thinks he'll get away with stealing my idea, but I'm going to cook his goose.* The origin of this phrase has been lost, but there are numerous fanciful theories; one concerns a besieged town that displayed a goose to show it had enough food, causing the attackers to set it on fire. The first recorded use of this colloquial phrase was in 1851.

cook the books Falsify a company's financial records, as in *An independent audit showed that they've been cooking the books for years.* This slangy phrase was first recorded in 1636.

cook up Fabricate, concoct, as in *She's always cooking up some excuse.* [Colloquial; mid-1700s]

cook with gas Also, **cook on the front burner.** Do very well, make rapid progress. For example, *The first half is finished already? Now you're cooking with gas,* or *Two promotions in two years—she's really cooking on the front burner!* The first of these metaphoric phrases alludes to gas stoves, which began to replace slower wood-burning stoves about 1915. The variant, which alludes to something on a stove's front burner receiving more attention, is heard less often today. [Slang; 1940s] Also see BACK BURNER.

cool ♦ In addition to the idioms beginning with COOL, also see KEEP COOL; KEEP ONE'S COOL; PLAY IT COOL.

cool as a cucumber Calm and composed, self-possessed, as in *Despite the mishap Margaret was cool as a cucumber.* This idiom may be based on the fact that in hot weather the inside of cucumbers remains cooler than the air. [c. 1600] For a synonym, see COOL, CALM, AND COLLECTED.

cool, calm, and collected Calm and composed, self-possessed. For example, *No matter what the board decides, you have to appear cool, calm, and collected in front of the stockholders.* This alliterative synonym for COOL AS A CUCUMBER dates from the late 1800s.

cool down Also, **cool off.** 1. Effect a lower temperature, especially of the body following vigorous exercise. For example, *After a race the coach makes the entire team do stretches to cool down,* or *Let's take a dip to cool off.* These phrases date from A.D. 1000 with reference to the weather or cooking (as in *First let the eggs cool off*). The first gained renewed currency with the exercise boom of the late 1900s. 2. See COOL OFF, def. 2.

cool it 1. Calm down, relax, as in *John was beginning to seethe, but I told him to cool it.* [Slang; c. 1950] 2. Stop what one is doing, especially stop talking or behaving conspicuously, as in *We'd be wise to cool it until the scandal blows over.* It is also used as an imperative, as in *Cool it! We'll be in trouble if anyone hears you.* [Slang; c. 1950]

cool off 1. See COOL DOWN. 2. Also, **cool down** or **out.** Calm down, become less ardent, angry, or agitated, as in *We can't discuss it until you've cooled off.* The verb *cool* alone has been used in this sense

since approximately A.D. 1000; *off* and *down* were added in the late 1800s, and Davy Crockett's *Almanac* (1836) had: "Resting a while, just long enough to cool out a little." 3. Also, **cool out.** Kill someone, as in *Did you know they threatened to cool off his brother?* [Slang; first half of 1800s]

cool one's heels Wait or be kept waiting, as in *I've been cooling my heels in the doctor's waiting room for at least an hour.* This term originally meant to cool one's feet when they become hot from walking, and began to be used ironically for being forced to rest (or wait) in the early 1600s.

cool out ♦ See COOL OFF, def. 2 and 3.

coon's age Also, **a dog's age.** A very long time, as in *I haven't seen Sam in a coon's age,* or *It's been a dog's age since I went to the ballpark.* The first phrase rests on the mistaken idea that raccoons ("coons") live a long time. The variant may reflect a similar assumption but the true origin is not known. [c. 1835] Also see DONKEY'S YEARS.

coop ♦ See FLY THE COOP.

cop a feel Surreptitiously fondle someone in a sexual manner. For example, *The female clerks complained that Mr. Hardy was always trying to cop a feel.* This term uses the verb *cop* in the sense of "get hold of." [Slang; 1930s]

cop a plea 1. Plead guilty or confess to a crime in exchange for a lighter sentence; also, plead guilty to a lesser charge in exchange for not being tried for a more serious charge. For example, *Arnold decided he was better off copping a plea than facing a jury.* [Colloquial; 1920s] 2. Plead for mercy; make excuses. For example, *He copped a plea about not knowing his way around.* [Slang; c. 1940]

cop out Back out of a responsibility or commitment; also, take the easy way out. For example, *Don't count on him; he's been known to fake illness and cop out,* or *She'll cop out and let her assistant do all the work.* These meanings are derived from the underworld slang use of *cop out* for backing down or surrendering. [Late 1950s]

core ♦ See ROTTEN TO THE CORE.

corner ♦ In addition to the idiom beginning with CORNER, also see AROUND THE CORNER; CUT CORNERS; FOUR CORNERS OF THE EARTH; IN A TIGHT CORNER; OUT OF THE CORNER OF ONE'S EYE; PAINT ONESELF INTO A CORNER; TURN THE CORNER.

corner the market Buy all or most of a commodity or stock so that its price goes up. For example, *In a famous maneuver the Hunt brothers cornered the market in silver.* This idiom uses *corner* in the sense of "drive would-be buyers into a corner." [Early 1800s]

correct ♦ See STAND CORRECTED.

corridors of power The offices of powerful leaders. For example, *As clerk to a Supreme Court justice, Jim thought he'd get his foot inside the corridors of power.* This term was first used by C.P. Snow in his novel *Homecomings* (1956) for the ministries of Britain's Whitehall, with their top-ranking civil servants. Later it was broadened to any high officials.

cost ♦ See ARM AND A LEG, COST AN; AT ALL COSTS; COUNT THE COST; PRETTY PENNY, COST A.

cotton to 1. Take a liking to, get along with, as in *This dog doesn't cotton to strangers.* Although this verbal phrase comes from the noun for the fabric, the semantic connection between these parts of speech is unclear. [Early 1800s] 2. Also, **cotton on to.** Come to understand, grasp, as in *She didn't really cotton on to what I was saying.* [Colloquial; early 1900s]

cough up 1. Hand over or relinquish, especially money; pay up. For example, *It's time the delinquent members coughed up their dues.* [Slang; late 1800s] 2. Confess or divulge, as in *Pretty soon she'd cough up the whole story about last night.* This idiom transfers the act of vomiting to telling the entire truth. [Slang; late 1800s]

could ♦ See CAN (COULD) DO WITH; SEE WITH HALF AN EYE, COULD. Also see under CAN; COULDN'T.

couldn't ♦ In addition to the idioms beginning with COULDN'T, also see HURT A FLEA, COULDN'T. Also see under CAN'T.

couldn't care less Also, **could care less.** Be completely indifferent. For example, *Pick whatever dessert you want; I couldn't care less,* or *I could care less about the editor's opinion.* This expression originated about 1940 in Britain and for a time invariably used *couldn't.* About 1960 *could* was occasionally substituted, and today both versions are used with approximately equal frequency, despite their being antonyms.

counsel ♦ See KEEP ONE'S OWN COUNSEL.

count ♦ In addition to the idioms beginning with COUNT, also see DOWN FOR THE COUNT; EVERY MINUTE COUNTS; OUT FOR (THE COUNT); STAND UP AND BE COUNTED.

count against Be disadvantageous to, as in *His earnings this year will count against his Social Security benefits.* This idiom uses *count* in the sense of "make a reckoning," in this case negative. [Early 1900s]

count down 1. Count backward from any number to zero to indicate time, as in *The final seconds before take off were counted down: 10, 9, 8, etc.* The *down* in this term refers to the decreasing size of the numbers. This usage originated in connection with the firing of missiles and spacecraft and has since been broadened to such events as the roll call of states at a political convention. [c. 1950] 2. Make final preparations for an event, as in *Hong Kong was counting down to the day when it became part of mainland China.* This usage is derived from def. 1. [Late 1950s]

counter ♦ See RUN COUNTER TO; UNDER THE COUNTER.

count for 1. Have importance or worth, as in *Doesn't his long tenure count for anything?* or *Does this tournament count for computer points?* This usage employs *count* in the sense of "enter into a reckoning." [Mid-1800s] 2. **count for nothing.** Have no influence or effect, as in *All his work counts for nothing since they've dropped the project.* This idiom was first recorded in 1861.

count in Include, as in *Can all the members be counted in?* or *I'd love to come; count me in.* [Mid-1800s]

count noses Also, **count heads.** Reckon up the number of those present. For example, *The theater seemed only half-full, so the producer decided to count noses,* or *Our tour leader was always careful to count heads before the bus started off.* This idiom was originally put as **tell noses.** [Mid-1600s]

count off 1. Count aloud from one end of a line of persons to the other, each person counting in turn. For example, *The soldiers counted off one by one.* This usage and the practice it describes come from the military. 2. Place in a separate group by counting, as in *The office counted off the telephone books for each delivery route.*

count on Also, **count upon.** Rely on, depend on, as in *You can always count on Kent to be punctual,* or *Carol was counting upon getting a raise in spring.* [First half of 1600s]

count one's chickens before they hatch Make plans based on events that may or may not happen. For example, *You might not win the prize and you've already spent the money? Don't count your chickens before they hatch!* or *I know you have big plans for your consulting business, but don't count your chickens.* This expression comes from Aesop's fable about a milkmaid carrying a full pail on her head. She daydreams about buying chickens with the milk's proceeds and becoming so rich from selling eggs that she will toss her head at suitors; she then tosses her head and spills the milk. Widely translated from the original Greek, the story was the source of a proverb and was used figuratively by the 16th century. Today it is still so well known that it often appears shortened and usually in negative cautionary form (**don't count your chickens**).

count out 1. Declare a boxer (or other contestant) to have lost, as in *Paul was counted out in the first round.* This term alludes to *count* in the sense of "ten seconds," the time allowed for a boxer to rise after being knocked down (if he does not rise in time, he is "out"). The earliest recorded use of the term was for a cockfight in 1808; its use for boxing came about a century later. Also see DOWN FOR THE COUNT. **2.** Exclude, leave out of consideration, as in *As for skiing this winter, you'll have to count me out.* [Colloquial; mid-1800s] Also see COUNT IN. **3.** Apportion; also, recalculate. For example, *They counted out four pieces of music for each band member,* or *When Peggy got her change she counted out all the pennies.* [Mid-1800s]

country cousin One whose lack of sophistication or rural ways may amuse or embarrass city dwellers. For example, *The sightseeing guide geared his tour toward country cousins who had never been to a large city before.* This term, which literally means "a cousin who lives in the country," has been used in this figurative way since the second half of the 1700s, although the idea is much older (such persons were stock figures of fun in Restoration comedies of the late 1600s and early 1700s).

count to ten Calm down, get hold of oneself. For example, *Before you tell him what you think of him, count to ten.* Often used as an imperative, this phrase in effect means that if one takes the time to count from one to ten one can regain one's composure.

courage ♦ In addition to the idiom beginning with COURAGE, also see DUTCH COURAGE; PLUCK UP (ONE'S COURAGE).

courage of one's convictions, have the Behave according to one's beliefs. For example, *Carl wouldn't give his best friend any of the test answers; he had the courage of his convictions.* This expression is believed to have originated as a translation of the French *le courage de son opinion* ("the courage of his opinion"), dating from the mid-1800s and at first so used. By the late 1800s it had changed to the present form.

course ♦ In addition to the idiom beginning with COURSE, also see CRASH COURSE; IN DUE COURSE; MATTER OF COURSE; OF COURSE; PAR FOR THE COURSE; RUN ITS COURSE; STAY THE COURSE.

course of true love never ran smoothly, the Lovers often face difficulties, as in *Every time he tells me that he and his wife are fighting, I say the same thing—you know about the course of true love.* The full term is a quotation from Shakespeare's *A Midsummer Night's Dream* (1:1): "The course of true love never did run smooth." Over the years it

has become so familiar that today it is often shortened, as in the example.

court ♦ See BALL'S IN YOUR COURT; DAY IN COURT; FRIEND IN COURT; HOLD COURT; KANGAROO COURT; LAUGH OUT OF COURT; PAY COURT TO.

cousin ♦ See COUNTRY COUSIN; FIRST COUSIN; KISSING COUSINS; SECOND COUSIN.

cover ♦ In addition to the idioms beginning with COVER, also see BLOW ONE'S COVER; BREAK COVER; JUDGE A BOOK BY ITS COVER; (COVER A) MULTITUDE OF SINS; TAKE COVER; UNDER COVER.

cover for 1. Also, **cover up for.** Conceal a wrongdoing or wrongdoer, as in *Bill was supposed to be on duty but went to a ballgame and Alan agreed to cover for him* or *I covered up for my friend when her mother called to find out where she was.* [1960s] Also see COVER UP, def. 2. **2.** Substitute for someone, act on someone's behalf, as in *Mary was asked to cover for Joe while he was on jury duty.* [c. 1970] **3. cover for something.** Provide protection against some hazard, as in *This policy covers the house for fire but not for theft.* This idiom employs the verb *to cover* in the sense of "protect" or "shield," a usage dating from the 13th century.

cover girl An attractive woman whose photograph is featured on a magazine cover; also, a woman attractive enough to be so featured. For example, *All models hope to be cover girls some day,* or *She's gorgeous—a real cover girl.* [c. 1910]

cover ground Also, **cover the ground** or **a lot of ground. 1.** Go a given extent or considerable distance, especially at a satisfactory speed. For example, *She really knows how to cover ground with her studies,* or *This outfielder covers a lot of ground.* [Early 1800s] **2.** Deal with or accomplish in a certain way, as in *This history text covers the ground quite well.* [Late 1800s] Also see COVER THE FIELD.

cover one's ass Also, **cover one's hide or oneself.** Make excuses or otherwise take action to avoid being blamed, punished, or harmed. For example, *The first thing you learn in the army is to cover your ass,* or *Jane is ingenious at finding ways to cover her hide.* The first phrase, considered vulgar slang, dates from the 1960s; the variants are more polite.

cover one's tracks Conceal one's whereabouts, activities, intentions, or the evidence of one's involvement. For example, *No one knows much about where he's been—he's very good at covering his tracks.* This term transfers hiding one's footprints to more general activities. [1870s] Also see COVER UP, def. 2.

cover story 1. A featured story in a magazine that concerns the illustration on the cover, as in *The earthquake is this week's cover story for all the news magazines.* [Mid-1900s] **2.** A false story intended to mislead or deceive; also, an alibi. For example, *Their cover story while investigating local repair services was that they had just bought the house and were having problems,* or *The suspect gave the police some cover story about being held up.* [Mid-1900s]

cover the field Also, **cover the territory** or **waterfront.** Be comprehensive. For example, *The review course will cover the field very well,* or *Bob's new assignment really covers the territory,* or *The superintendent's speech covered the waterfront on the drug problem.* These expressions all employ the verb *cover* in the sense of "extend over" or "include," a usage dating from the late 1700s, with the nouns (*field, ground, territory, waterfront*) each meaning "whole area."

cover up 1. Wrap up or enfold in order to protect. For example, *Be sure to cover up the outdoor furniture in case of rain,* or *It's cold, so be sure to cover up the baby.* [Late 1800s] 2. Conceal something, especially a crime, as in *The opposition accused the President of covering up his assistant's suicide.* [c. 1920]

cow ♦ In addition to the idiom beginning with cow, also see CASH COW; HOLY COW; SACRED COW; TILL THE COWS COME HOME.

cow college An agricultural college; any small, relatively unknown rural college. For example, *He's never published a paper, but he might do all right in some cow college.* This term uses *cow* in the somewhat pejorative sense of "provincial." [c. 1910]

cozy up Try to get on friendly or intimate terms, ingratiate oneself. For example, *That new woman is always cozying up to one or another club member so she'll be asked to join.* [Mid-1900s]

crack ♦ In addition to the idioms beginning with CRACK, also see BY JOVE (CRACKY); FALL BETWEEN THE CRACKS; GET CRACKING; HARD NUT TO CRACK; HAVE A CRACK AT; MAKE A CRACK; NOT ALL IT'S CRACKED UP TO BE; PAPER OVER (THE CRACKS).

crack a book Open a book to study or read, as in *He passed the exam without cracking a book.* This expression employs the verb *to crack* in the sense of "to open," a slang usage that dates from the early 1700s. [Colloquial; c. 1930]

crack a bottle Open a bottle so as to drink its contents, as in *Let's celebrate by cracking a bottle of champagne!* This seemingly modern colloquialism was first recorded in H. Kelly's *School for Wives* (1773): "When shall we crack a bottle together?"

crack a joke Make a joke, say something humorous, as in *You can count on Grandpa to crack a joke on every occasion.* This expression uses the verb *to crack* in the now obsolete sense of "briskly pronounce" or "boast." [Early 1700s]

crack a smile Smile, as in *Betty was a very serious person; she rarely cracked a smile.* This colloquialism transfers *crack* in the sense of "break" to breaking a serious facial expression into a smile.

crack down Act more forcefully to regulate, repress, or restrain. For example, *The police cracked down on speeding.* [1930s]

cracked up 1. Past tense of CRACK UP. 2. **cracked up to be.** Reputed to be. This expression is always used in a negative way, as in *I don't think this book is all it's cracked up to be.* It relies on the now obsolete use of *to crack up* to mean "to praise extravagantly." It appeared in *The Kentuckian*: "He is not the thing he is cracked up for" (May 28, 1829). [Early 1800s] 3. Under the influence of crack (a form of cocaine). For example, "Who's cracked up, who's cracked out, and who's dead?" (*World News Tonight*, ABC-TV, May 12, 1992). [1980s]

crack of dawn Very early morning, daybreak. For example, *I got up at the crack of dawn.* The *crack* in this term alludes either to the suddenness of sunrise or to the small wedge of light appearing as the sun rises over the horizon. Originally the term was usually put as **crack of day.** [Late 1800s]

crack the whip Behave in a domineering and demanding way toward one's subordinates. For example, *He's been cracking the whip ever since he got his promotion.* This expression, first recorded in 1647, alludes to drivers of horse-drawn wagons who snapped their whips hard, producing a loud cracking noise. Its figurative use dates from the late 1800s.

crack up 1. Suffer an emotional breakdown, become insane, as in *He might crack up under the strain.* This usage alludes to the result of cracking one's skull; from the early 1600s *to crack* alone was used in this way. [Slang; early 1900s] 2. Damage or wreck a vehicle or vessel. For example, *I'm always afraid that I'll crack up the car.* 3. Experience a crash, as in *We cracked up on the freeway in the middle of the ice storm.* 4. Also, **crack someone up.** Burst or cause to burst out laughing, as in *The audience cracked up,* or *That joke really cracked me up.* [Slang; c. 1940] Also see BREAK UP, def. 6. All of these expressions derive from *crack* in the sense of "break into pieces" or "collapse," a usage dating from the late 1600s. Also see CRACKED UP.

cradle ♦ See FROM THE CRADLE TO THE GRAVE; ROB THE CRADLE.

cramp someone's style Restrict or prevent someone from free action or expression, as in *It really cramps my style when Mom hovers around me while I'm making dinner.* Although in 1819 Charles Lamb complained that using different inks cramped his style of writing, the present sense of this colloquial term dates only from the early 1900s.

crank in Factor in, integrate, as in *We'll have to crank in both state and federal taxes when we make our plans.* [Slang; 1960s]

crank letter Also, **crank call.** An irrational, fanatical, or hostile letter or telephone call. For example, *The office was flooded with mail, including a lot of crank letters,* or *Harriet was upset enough by the crank calls to notify the police.* This expression employs *crank* in the sense of "irrational person." The first term dates from the mid-1900s, the variant from the 1960s.

crank out Produce, especially mechanically or rapidly, as in *I don't know how he can crank out a novel a year.* [Colloquial; mid-1900s]

crank up 1. Get started, as in *The theater season is cranking up with four benefit performances.* This expression transfers the literal sense of *crank,* "operate a motor by turning a crank," to starting any activity. [Slang; 1930s] **2.** Stimulate or intensify one's efforts. For example, *We've got to crank up enthusiasm for this new product,* or *Close to the election the campaign really cranked up.* [Slang; mid-1900s]

cranny ♦ See NOOK AND CRANNY.

crap ♦ In addition to the idioms beginning with CRAP, also see CUT THE COMEDY (CRAP); FULL OF CRAP.

crap around 1. Waste time, act foolishly, as in *Stop crapping around and get to work.* This usage derives from *crap* in the sense of "defecate." [Vulgar slang; 1930s] **2.** Trifle with, as in *It's time that we all stopped crapping around with the environment.* [Vulgar slang; 1940s]

crap out 1. Back down, quit, *When it got to the point of putting up some money, Jack crapped out.* This expression originated in the game of craps, where it means to make a first throw (of the dice) of two, three, or twelve, thereby losing. [Slang; 1920s] **2.** Go to sleep. This usage was military slang for sleeping during work hours or during a crap game. [Slang; c. 1940] **3.** Die, as in *He's really sick; he could crap out any time.* This usage is less common than def. 1 or def. 2. [Slang; 1920s]

crap up 1. Burden or clutter up, as in *Jane crapped up the garden with plastic pink flamingos.* [c. 1946] **2.** Ruin or foul up, as in *I've really crapped up this speech; can I just start over again?* This idiom employs *crap* in the sense of "defecate." [Vulgar slang; c. 1950]

crash and burn 1. Fail utterly, as in *Dale crashed and burned three times before passing the bar exam.* This idiom alludes to a car or airplane that has crashed and caught fire. [Slang; 1970s] **2.** In skate-

boarding and other sports, be taken out of competition by a collision, accident, or fall, as in *Although she was favored to win the downhill race, she crashed and burned on her first run.* [Slang; 1980s]

crash course A short, intensive training course, as in *Daisy planned to take a crash course in cooking before she got married.* [Colloquial; mid-1900s]

crash pad A free, temporary lodging place, as in *The company maintains several crash pads for employees from out-of-town divisions.* This expression originally referred to a place affording runaways, drug addicts, and the like somewhere to *crash* in the sense of "sleep." In time it also was used more broadly, as in the example. [Slang; 1960s]

crash the gate Gain admittance, as to a party or concert, without being invited or without paying. For example, *The concert was outdoors, but heavy security prevented anyone from crashing the gate.* This term originally applied to persons getting through the gate at sports events without buying tickets. By the 1920s it was extended to being an uninvited guest at other gatherings and had given rise to the noun *gatecrasher* for one who did so. [Early 1900s]

craw ♦ See STICK IN ONE'S CRAW.

crazy ♦ In addition to the idioms beginning with CRAZY, also see DRIVE SOMEONE CRAZY; LIKE CRAZY.

crazy about, be Also, **be mad about.** Be immoderately fond of or infatuated with, as in *I'm crazy about lobster,* or *George is mad about his new saxophone.* The first expression dates from the early 1900s. The second, with *mad,* is much older; Shakespeare had it as **mad for** in *All's Well That Ends Well* (5:3): "madde for her"; and *mad about* was common by the mid 1700s.

crazy like a fox Seemingly foolish but actually very shrewd and cunning. For example, *You think Bob was crazy to turn it down? He's crazy like a fox, because they've now doubled their offer.* This usage gained currency when humorist S.J. Perelman used it as the title of a book (1944). [Early 1900s] Also see SLY AS A FOX.

cream of the crop, the The best or choicest of anything, as in *The apples from this orchard are definitely the cream of the crop.* The noun *cream* has been used to mean "the best" since the 16th century. The French equivalent of the present term, *la crème de la crème* ("the cream of the cream") was familiar in English by 1800.

create a scene ♦ See MAKE A SCENE.

creature comfort Something that contributes to physical comfort, such as food, clothing, or housing. For example, *Dean always stayed in the best hotels; he valued his creature comforts.* This idiom was first recorded in 1659.

credibility gap Distrust of a public statement or position, as in *The current credibility gap at City Hall is the result of miscommunication between the mayor's office and the press.* This term originated about 1960 in connection with the American public's disinclination to believe government statements about the Vietnam War. It soon was extended to individuals and corporations as well as government agencies to express a lack of confidence in the truth of their statements, or perception of a discrepancy between words and actions.

credit ♦ See DO SOMEONE PROUD (CREDIT TO); EXTEND CREDIT TO; GET CREDIT FOR; GIVE CREDIT WHERE CREDIT IS DUE.

creek ♦ See UP A CREEK.

creep ♦ In addition to the idiom beginning with CREEP, also see MAKE ONE'S FLESH CREEP; THE CREEPS.

creep up on Advance slowly or stealthily, as in *The cat crept up on the bird,* or *Autumn is creeping up on us.* This expression is recorded in slightly different form—**creep in** or **creep on**—from the 15th century on. One of the *Hymns to the Virgin and Christ* (c. 1430) has "Now age has cropen [crept] up on me ful stille."

crew cut A closely cropped haircut, usually for a male, as in *The boys all think crew cuts are cooler in summer.* This term presumably originated in the navy (*crew* referring to a ship's crew), where such a haircut was mandatory. [c. 1940]

cricket ♦ See NOT CRICKET.

crime does not pay Lawbreakers do not benefit from their actions. For example, *Steve didn't think it mattered that he stole a candy bar, but he's learned the hard way that crime does not pay.* This maxim, originating as a slogan of the F.B.I. and given wide currency by the cartoon character Dick Tracy, was first recorded in 1927. There have been numerous jocular plays on it, as in Woody Allen's screenplay for *Take the Money and Run* (1969): "I think crime pays. The hours are good, you travel a lot."

crisp ♦ See BURN TO A CINDER (CRISP).

crocodile tears An insincere display of grief, as in *When the play's star broke her leg, her understudy wept crocodile tears.* This term comes from the mistaken notion that crocodiles weep while eating their prey, one held in ancient Roman times. The actual term was picked up by Shakespeare and many other writers after him, and remains current. [Late 1500s]

Croesus ♦ See RICH AS CROESUS.

crook ♦ In addition to the idioms beginning with CROOK, also see BY HOOK OR CROOK.

crook one's elbow Also, **bend one's elbow**. Drink liquor, especially a great deal. For example, *Bill is*

known to crook his elbow now and then, or *Uncle Joe rather overdoes it with bending his elbow.* Both slangy expressions allude to the motion of lifting a drink to one's lips, which involves bending the elbow. The first dates from about 1820, and the second from about 1900.

crop ♦ In addition to the idioms beginning with CROP, also see CREAM OF THE CROP.

crop out Rise to the surface, become visible or evident, as in *These superstitions crop out time and again.* This term originated in mining, where a stratum or vein of ore is said to crop out when it comes to the surface. [Mid-1800s]

crop up Appear unexpectedly or occasionally, as in *One theory that crops up periodically is the influence of sunspots on stock prices,* or *We hope new talent will crop up in the next freshman class.* [Mid-1800s]

cross ♦ In addition to the idioms beginning with CROSS, also see AT CROSS PURPOSES; AT THE CROSSROADS; CAUGHT IN THE MIDDLE (CROSS-FIRE); DOT ONE'S I'S AND CROSS ONE'S T'S; DOUBLE CROSS; GET ONE'S WIRES CROSSED; LOOK CROSS-EYED AT.

cross a bridge when one comes to it Also, **cross that bridge when you come to it**. Deal with a situation when, and not before, it occurs. For example, *If we can't sell the house—well, we'll cross that bridge when we come to it.* The ultimate origin of this proverb, a caution not to anticipate trouble and often put as **don't cross a bridge till you come to it,** has been lost. The earliest recorded use is in Henry Wadsworth Longfellow's *The Golden Legend* (1851): "Don't cross the bridge till you come to it, is a proverb old and of excellent wit."

cross as a bear Grumpy, ill-humored, annoyed, as in *Stay away from Claire; she's cross as a bear this morning.* Unlike the earlier **cross as two sticks,** this survives even though the adjective *cross* for "ill-tempered" is otherwise not used much in America. It is sometimes amplified as **cross as a bear with a sore head.** [Early 1700s]

cross my heart and hope to die Attest to the truth of something; solemnly assure someone that the truth has been spoken. For example, *I did lock the door—cross my heart and hope to die!* This phrase most likely originated as a religious oath based on the sign of the cross; it is generally accompanied by hand gestures such as crossing one's hands over one's breast and then pointing the right hand skyward (a variant is **cross my heart and point to God**). Today most often uttered by children, it was first recorded in 1908.

cross one's fingers Also, **keep one's fingers crossed. 1.** Wish for luck by crossing two fingers of one hand. For example, *I'm crossing my fingers* that I get the job, or *Keep your fingers crossed that the hurricane goes out to sea.* This superstitious statement presumably alludes to the much older practice of making the sign of the cross to ward off evil. [Early 1900s] **2.** Tell a white lie that doesn't matter. For example, *I told Mom I didn't eat any cookies but I had my fingers crossed.* The childish belief that if one keeps one's fingers crossed one may lie with impunity probably comes from children's games in which one was "safe" if one crossed one's fingers, and the ultimate allusion may be the same as in def. 1.

cross one's mind Also, **pass through one's mind.** Suddenly occur to one, as in *It never crossed my mind that they would turn the proposal down,* or *It passed through her mind that he might have gotten lost.* [Mid-1700s]

cross over 1. Change from one field or affiliation to another, as in *Graham Greene crossed over from the Anglican to the Roman Catholic Church,* or *If he doesn't run I'm going to cross over to the Democratic Party.* [First half of 1900s] **2.** Also, **cross over to the other side.** Die, as in *It's a year since my grandmother crossed over to the other side.* [c. 1930]

cross someone's palm with silver Pay for a service; pay in advance. For example, *I'll give you all the details, but first cross my palm with silver.* This phrase alludes to the old practice of placing silver coins across a gypsy fortuneteller's hand before having one's fortune told. Today it is sometimes used in a jocular way to ask for a bribe or a tip, as in the example. [c. 1700] Also see GREASE SOMEONE'S PALM.

cross someone's path Encounter or meet someone, especially unexpectedly. For example, *John didn't know her name, so he was hoping she would cross his path again soon,* or *She swore she would scream if a snake crossed her path.* This phrase originally implied that such an encounter meant obstructing or thwarting a person, but in current usage this is not necessarily true. [Early 1600s]

cross swords Fight, either verbally or physically. For example, *At every policy meeting the two vice-presidents crossed swords.* This phrase alludes to the ancient form of combat using swords. Also see AT SWORD'S POINT.

cross the Rubicon Irrevocably commit to a course of action, make a fateful and final decision. For example, *Once he submitted his resignation, he had crossed the Rubicon.* This phrase alludes to Julius Caesar's crossing the Rubicon River (between Italy and Gaul) in 49 B.C., thereby starting a war against Pompey and the Roman Senate. Recounted in Plutarch's *Lives: Julius Caesar* (c. A.D. 110), the crossing gave rise to the figurative English usage by the early 1600s.

cross to bear A burden or trial one must put up with, as in *Alzheimer's is a cross to bear for the whole family,* or in a lighter vein, *Mowing that huge lawn once a week is Brad's cross to bear.* This phrase alludes to the cross carried by Jesus to his crucifixion. Today it may be used either seriously or lightly. [Second half of 1500s]

cross up 1. Betray, double-cross, cheat, as in *Jack crossed up his buddies and told the police they had broken in.* Originally this usage often was put simply as **to cross.** [Early 1800s] **2.** Confuse, muddle, as in *We all planned to meet at the restaurant but several of us got crossed up as to time and place.*

crow ♦ In addition to the idiom beginning with CROW, also see AS THE CROW FLIES; EAT CROW.

crowd ♦ See FOLLOW THE CROWD; THREE'S A CROWD.

crown jewels 1. A prized possession or asset, as in *The Iliad and Odyssey are the crown jewels of ancient literature,* or *The software products are the company's crown jewels.* This usage transfers the value of royal jewels to some other object. [Late 1800s] **2.** Also, **family jewels.** The male genitals, especially the testicles. For example, *She gave the would-be mugger a hard kick in the family jewels.* A slang euphemism, the term dates from the 1970s, and the variant from the early 1900s.

crow over Exult loudly about, especially over someone's defeat. For example, *In most sports it's considered bad manners to crow over your opponent.* This term alludes to the cock's loud crow. [Late 1500s]

crumble ♦ See THAT'S HOW THE BALL BOUNCES (COOKIE CRUMBLES).

crunch numbers Perform numerous calculations or process a large amount of numerical data. For example, *Preparing John's presentation to the Federal Reserve Board required many hours of crunching numbers.* This term originated with the computer age and indeed still applies mostly to the operations of computers. [Slang; second half of 1900s]

crunch time A period when pressure to succeed is great, often toward the end of an undertaking. For example, *It's crunch time—we only have two more days to finish.* This term employs *crunch* in the sense of "a critical situation or test." [Slang; 1970s]

crush ♦ See HAVE A CRUSH ON.

crust ♦ See UPPER CRUST.

crux of the matter Also, **heart of the matter.** The basic, central or critical point of an issue. For example, *In this trial the bloodstains represent the crux of the matter,* or *We think the second clause is the heart of the matter.* Although *crux* is Latin for "cross," in English it means "difficulty" or "puzzle," and it is from the latter that this expression is thought to be derived. The variant employs *heart* in the sense of "a vital part" (as it is in the body). The first term dates from the late 1800s, the variant from the early 1500s.

cry, crying ♦ In addition to the idioms beginning with CRY, also see BURST INTO (OUT CRYING); FAR CRY; FOR CRYING OUT LOUD; HUE AND CRY; IN FULL SWING.

cry for Also, **cry out for; have a crying need for.** Be in urgent need of, as in *This wall cries for a second coat of paint,* or *This car is crying out for a good washing,* or *There is a crying need for order in this house.* The figurative use of *cry for,* literally meaning "implore" or "weep for," dates from the late 1500s, as does the use of *crying* for "demanding attention." The first variant, alluding to actually shouting out one's needs or desires, dates from the second half of the 1800s.

cry havoc Sound an alarm or warning, as in *In his sermon the pastor cried havoc to the congregation's biases against gays.* The noun *havoc* was once a command for invaders to begin looting and killing the defenders' town. Shakespeare so used it in *Julius Caesar* (3:1): "Cry 'Havoc' and let slip the dogs of war." By the 19th century the phrase had acquired its present meaning.

crying shame, a An unfortunate situation, as in *It's a crying shame that Bob can't find a job.* This term may well come from the now obsolete *to cry shame upon,* meaning "express vigorous disapproval or censure," current from about 1600 to the mid-1800s.

crying towel A figurative towel for wiping the tears of a self-pitying individual. For example, *So you didn't make the first team? Get out the crying towel.* This expression is always used sarcastically. [Slang; 1920s]

cry off Break or withdraw from a promise or agreement, as in *We thought we'd bought the car, but the owner cried off at the last minute.* [Late 1700s]

cry one's eyes out Also, **cry one's heart out.** Weep inconsolably. For example, *Wendy was so homesick that she was crying her eyes out,* or *At funerals Ruth always cries her heart out.* [c. 1700]

cry on someone's shoulder Tell one's problems to someone so as to gain sympathy or consolation, as in *When James had a problem at the office he generally cried on his sister's shoulder.* It is also put as **a shoulder to cry on,** as in *When Mom came home, Jane had a shoulder to cry on.* [Late 1930s]

cry out for ♦ See CRY FOR.

cry over spilt milk, don't Also, **no use crying over spilt milk.** Don't regret what cannot be undone or rectified, as in *The papers you wanted went out in last week's trash, so don't cry over spilt milk.*

This metaphor for the inability to recover milk once it has been spilled is very old indeed, already appearing as a proverb in James Howell's *Paroimiografia* (1659). It is sometimes shortened to **spilt milk.**

crystal ball A means of predicting the future, as in *So what does your crystal ball say about the coming election?* The term is a figurative use of the crystal or glass ball used by fortune-tellers. [c. 1900]

crystal clear, be Also, **be clear as crystal.** Be easy to understand, have a very obvious meaning. For example, *The directions for installing the door are crystal clear,* or *Her intentions are clear as crystal.* Allusions to crystal's very high degree of transparency have been made since the 15th century.

cry uncle Also, **say uncle.** Concede defeat, as in *The Serbs want the Bosnians to cry uncle,* or *If you say uncle right now, I'll let you go first in the next game.* This phrase originated about 1900 as an imperative among schoolchildren who would say, "Cry uncle when you've had enough (of a beating)." By the mid-1900s it was being used figuratively, as in the examples.

cry wolf Raise a false alarm, as in *Helen's always crying wolf about attempted break-ins, but the police can never find any evidence.* This term comes from the tale about a young shepherd watching his flock who, lonely and fearful, called for help by shouting "Wolf!" After people came to his aid several times and saw no wolf, they ignored his cries when a wolf actually attacked his sheep. The tale appeared in a translation of Aesop's fables by Roger L'Estrange (1692), and the expression has been applied to any false alarm since the mid-1800s.

cuckoo ♦ See CLOUD-CUCKOO LAND.

cucumber ♦ See COOL AS A CUCUMBER.

cudgel one's brains ♦ See RACK ONE'S BRAINS.

cue in Give information or instructions, for example, *She said she'd cue us in on their summer plans.* This verbal use of the noun *cue* in the sense of "guiding suggestion" dates from the 1920s.

cuff ♦ See OFF THE CUFF; ON THE CUFF.

culture shock A state of confusion and anxiety experienced by someone upon encountering an alien environment. For example, *It's not just jet lag—it's the culture shock of being in a new country.* This term was first used by social scientists to describe, for example, the experience of a person moving from the country to a big city. It is now used more loosely, as in the example. [Late 1930s]

culture vulture An individual with a consuming or excessive interest in the arts. For example, *A relentless culture vulture, she dragged her children to every museum in town.* This slangy term may have been originated by Ogden Nash, who wrote: "There is a vulture Who circles above The carcass of culture" (*Free Wheeling*, 1931). [1940s]

cup ◆ In addition to the idiom beginning with CUP, also see IN ONE'S CUPS.

cupboard is bare, the The desired resources are not available, as in *The schools are asking for a budget increase but the cupboard is bare*. This metaphoric expression may have come from the nursery rhyme: "Old Mother Hubbard, went to the cupboard, to fetch her poor dog a bone, And when she went there, the cupboard was bare, and so the poor dog had none" (Sarah Catherine Martin, *The Comic Adventures of Old Mother Hubbard*, 1805).

cup of tea, one's Something that is in accord with one's liking or taste. For example, *Quiz shows are just my cup of tea*, or *Baseball is not her cup of tea*. The origin of this metaphorical expression has been lost, but the positive version— "he's my cup of tea"—has been used since the late 1800 and the negative—**not one's cup of tea**—since the 1920s.

cure ◆ See KILL OR CURE; OUNCE OF PREVENTION (IS WORTH A POUND OF CURE); SURE CURE.

curiosity killed the cat It's best to mind one's own business. For example, *Don't ask about his divorce—curiosity killed the cat*. This cautionary expression sounds like the moral of some fable or folktale, but any such origin for it has been lost. The first recorded use was in O. Henry's *Schools and Schools* (1909).

curl one's hair ◆ See MAKE ONE'S HAIR STAND ON END (CURL).

curl up 1. Assume a position with the legs drawn up; settle down for sleep in this posture. For example, *I love to curl up with a good book*. [c. 1900] 2. **curl up and die**. Retreat, collapse, die, as in *At first the horse was ahead but in the home stretch she curled up and died*, or *I'll just curl up and die if he shows up*. This colorful expression for collapsing or dying is often used hyperbolically (second example). [Early 1900s] 3. **curl someone up**. Kill someone, as in *The sheriff said he'd curl up that outlaw*. This usage originated as cowboy slang in the second half of the 1800s.

curry favor Seek gain or advancement by fawning or flattery, as in *Edith was famous for currying favor with her teachers*. This expression originally came from the Old French *estriller fauvel*, "curry the fallow horse," a beast that in a 14th-century allegory stood for duplicity and cunning. It came into English about 1400 as *curry favel*—that is, curry (groom with a currycomb) the animal—and in the 1500s became the present term.

curtain ◆ In addition to the idioms beginning with CURTAIN, also see DRAW THE CURTAIN; RAISE THE CURTAIN; RING DOWN THE CURTAIN.

curtain raiser Preliminary event, as in *This limited attack on the chairman is just a curtain raiser for the concerted effort to oust him*. This term literally refers to a short play or skit presented before the main theatrical production. It began to be transferred to other preliminaries about 1940.

curtains for, be. Also, **it's curtains.** Be the end, especially death. For example, *If he hadn't worn a bullet-proof vest, it would have been curtains for him*, or *It's curtains if she doesn't finish on time*. This expression is a metaphor for the falling curtain signifying the end of a performance. [Slang; c. 1900]

curve ◆ See THROW A CURVE.

customer ◆ See UGLY CUSTOMER.

cut ◆ In addition to the idioms beginning with CUT, also see (CUT) DOWN TO SIZE; FISH OR CUT BAIT; HAVE ONE'S WORK CUT OUT; LIKE A CHICKEN WITH ITS HEAD CUT OFF; MAKE (CUT) A LONG STORY SHORT; UNKINDEST CUT; YOU COULD CUT IT WITH A KNIFE.

cut above Someone or something that is superior to examples of a similar nature, as in *This book is a cut above his previous one*. This idiom uses *cut* in the sense of "a higher degree or stage." [Early 1800s]

cut across Go beyond, transcend, as in *The new regulations cut across class lines*. This figurative use of *cut across*, which literally means "run through" or "intersect," dates from the 1920s.

cut a deal Offer or arrange an agreement or compromise, as in *The administration is hoping to cut a deal with Japan*. This expression uses *deal* in the sense of "business transaction." [Colloquial; 1970s]

cut adrift Separated or detached; freed. For example, *The dissenters were cut adrift from the denomination*. This expression alludes to cutting the rope of a floating vessel so that it drifts without direction or purpose. The figurative use of *adrift* dates from the late 1600s.

cut a long story short ◆ See MAKE A LONG STORY SHORT.

cut and dried Ready-made, predetermined and not changeable. For example, *The procedure is not quite cut and dried—there's definitely room for improvisation*. This expression originally alluded to herbs for sale in a shop, as opposed to fresh, growing herbs. [c. 1900]

cut and paste Describing a patched-up job or trivial work. For example, *The revision was easy, just cut and paste*, or *The new assistant had expected some training, but all she got was cut and* *paste*. This term alludes to simple artwork done by small children—cutting out pictures and gluing them to paper. [Mid-1900s]

cut and run Clear out, escape, desert, as in *He wished he could just cut and run*. This term originally (about 1700) meant to cut a vessels anchor cable and make sail at once. By the mid-1800s it was being used figuratively. Charles Dickens had it in *Great Expectations* (1861): "I'd give a shilling if they had cut and run." Also see CUT OUT, def. 7.

cut a wide swath Draw a lot of attention, make a considerable display, as in *Although he was new to the company, he cut a wide swath*. This metaphoric use of making a big sweep of the scythe in cutting grass survives despite the mechanization of farming and the declining use of the noun *swath*. [Mid-1800s]

cut back 1. Shorten by cutting, prune, as in *It's time we cut back these bushes*. [1860s] 2. Reduce, decrease, as in *They are going to cut back defense spending*, or *We have to cut back production*. [c. 1940] Also see CUT TO THE BONE.

cut both ways Have a mixed effect, have advantages and disadvantages. For example, *Their solution will cut both ways; it'll take longer but is permanent*. This metaphoric expression alludes to a double-edged sword. [c. 1600]

cut capers Also, **cut a caper**. Frolic or romp, as in *The children cut capers in the pile of raked leaves*. The noun *caper* comes from the Latin for "goat," and the allusion is to act in the manner of a young goat clumsily frolicking about. The expression was first recorded in Shakespeare's *Twelfth Night* (1:3): "Faith, I can cut a caper."

cut class Absent oneself from a class or other, usually mandatory event, as in *If he cuts one more class he'll fail the course*. [Late 1700s]

cut corners Do something in the easiest or least expensive way; also, act illegally. For example, *Cutting corners in production led to a definite loss in product quality*, or *If the accountant cuts corners the auditors are sure to find out*. This term alludes to rounding a corner as closely as possible in order to shorten the distance traversed and/or save time. [Late 1800s]

cut dead ♦ See CUT ONE DEAD.

cut down 1. Kill, as in *The troops were cut down one by one as they crossed the field*. [Early 1800s] 2. Also, **cut down on**. Reduce, decrease, as in *I want to cut down my caffeine intake*, or *We have to cut down on our expenses*. [Mid-1800s] 3. **cut down to size; knock down to size**. Reduce the self-importance of, humble, as in *He's so arrogant—I wish someone would cut him down to size*,

or *She really got knocked down to size when her class ranking slipped*. [Early 1900s]

cute as a button Also, **cute as a bug's ear**. Pretty or attractive in a dainty way, as in *That baby is cute as a button*. *Cute* originally was a shortening of *acute*, for "sharp-witted and clever," but in the early 1800s it also took on its current meaning. Other than that buttons and bug's hearing organs can be small, there is no good explanation for these similes.

cut ice ♦ See CUT NO ICE.

cut in 1. Move oneself between others, take a place ahead of one's proper turn. For example, *She was very aggressive, always cutting in the cafeteria line*. [Early 1600s] 2. Also, **cut in on** or **into**. Interrupt a conversation; also, interpose oneself between dancing partners and replace one of them. For example, *Before Walter was done talking, Marion cut into his conversation*, or *Jane was quite pleased when Arthur cut in on their dance*. [First half of 1800s] 3. Also, **cut in on**. Include in a profitable business deal or share of the profit, as in *Do you want to be cut in on this deal?* or *We plan to cut you in on this moneymaker*. [Slang; late 1800s]

cut into ♦ See CUT IN.

cut it 1. Also, **cut that**. Stop, as in *I won't stand for that—cut it!* or *If you don't cut that, I'll tell*. [Slang; first half of 1800s] Also see CUT IT OUT. 2. Manage, tolerate, as in *I don't know how he can cut it*. [Slang; c. 1900] 3. Be effective, prove satisfactory, as in *She's getting old and can no longer cut it*. [Late 1900s] For a synonym see CUT THE MUSTARD. Also see the subsequent entries beginning with CUT IT.

cut it fine Do something closely with a very slight margin, as in *Tom always cut it fine, arriving at the last minute*. This term uses *fine* in the sense of "narrow." [Late 1800s]

cut it out Stop, desist, as in *Cut it out, stop teasing your sister*. [c. 1900] Also see CUT IT, def. 1.

cut loose 1. Speak or act without restraint, as in *He cut loose with a string of curses*. [Early 1800s] 2. Leave, clear out, as in *Let's cut loose right now*. [Slang; 1960s]

cut no ice Have no effect, make no impression, as in *That excuse cuts no ice with me*. This term predates modern refrigeration, when ice was obtained by cutting it from a large block with a sharp tool. [Late 1800s]

cut off 1. Separate from others, isolate, as in *The construction debris cut off the workers from the canteen*, or *The new sect was cut off from the church*. [Late 1500s] 2. Stop suddenly, discontinue, as in *He quickly cut off the engine*, or *The drama was cut* *off by a news flash about tornado warnings.* [Late 1500s] **3.** Shut off, bar, *Their phone was cut off when they didn't pay the bill,* or *Tom's father threatened to cut off his allowance.* [c. 1600] **4.** Interrupt the course or passage of, intercept, as in *The operator cut us off,* or *The shortstop cut off the throw to the plate.* [Late 1500s] **5.** Also, **cut off with a shilling** or **cent.** Disinherit, as in *Grandfather cut him off with a shilling.* This usage dates from the early 1700s; the purpose of bequeathing one shilling (a small sum) was to indicate that the heir had not been overlooked but was intentionally being disinherited. In America *cent* was substituted from about 1800 on.

cut off one's nose to spite one's face Injure oneself out of pique. For example, *Staying home because Meg was invited first is cutting off your nose to spite your face.* Similar hyperboles appeared in several Latin proverbs; in English the expression was first recorded in 1561.

cut off with a shilling ◆ See CUT OFF, def. 5.

cut of one's jib One's general appearance or personality, as in *I don't like the cut of Ben's jib.* In the 17th century the shape of the jib sail often identified a vessel's nationality, and hence whether it was hostile or friendly. The term was being used figuratively by the early 1800s, often to express like or dislike for someone.

cut one's losses Withdraw from a losing situation, as in *They decided to close down the unprofitable branch and cut their losses.* This expression uses *cut* in the sense of "reduce" (also see CUT DOWN, def. 2).

cut one's teeth on Also, **cut one's eyeteeth on.** Get one's first experience by doing, or learn early in life, as in *I cut my teeth on this kind of layout* or *He cut his eyeteeth on magazine editing.* This term alludes to the literal verb **to cut teeth,** meaning "to have teeth first emerge through a baby's gums," a usage dating from the late 1600s.

cut out 1. Excise, remove as if by cutting; also, form or shape as if by cutting or carving. For example, *Young children love cutting out pictures from magazines,* or *The first step is cutting out the dress pattern.* The first usage dates from about 1400, the second from the mid-1500s. **2.** Oust, replace, or supplant someone, as in *He cut out all her other boyfriends.* [Mid-1600s] **3.** Also, **cut out for.** Suited or fitted by nature, as in *Dean's not cut out for lexicography.* [Mid-1600s] **4.** Also, **cut out for.** Assigned beforehand, prepared, predetermined, as in *We have our work cut out for us.* [Early 1600s] **5.** Deprive, as in *He threatened to cut her out of his will.* [Early 1800s] **6.** Stop, cease, as in *He cut out the motor,* or *Cut out that noise!* [c.

1900] Also see CUT IT OUT. **7.** Leave, especially in a hurry; also, run away. For example, *I'm cutting out right now,* or *At the first hint of a police raid they cut out.* [Slang; first half of 1800s] Also see CUT AND RUN.

cut out of whole cloth ◆ See OUT OF WHOLE CLOTH.

cut short Abbreviate, stop abruptly, as in *The thunderstorm cut short our picnic,* or *She cut her short, saying she'd already heard the story of their breakup.* Shakespeare used this term to mean "put a sudden end to someone's life": "Rather than bloody war shall cut them short" (*2 Henry VI,* 4:4), a less common usage today. The broader usage dates from the mid-1600s.

cut someone dead Pretend not to see or recognize someone, as in "Any fellow was to be cut dead by the entire school" (Benjamin Disraeli, *Vivien Grey,* 1826). This idiom, in the first half of the 1600s, began as *to cut someone*; in the early 1800s *dead* was added for greater emphasis.

cut someone's throat 1. Be the means of someone's ruin, as in *Joe would cut her throat if she got in his way.* One can also **cut one's own throat,** that is, spoil one's own chances, as in *Alice cut her own throat by her repeated absences.* This hyperbolic term alludes to actual murder (or suicide). [c. 1500] **2. cut one another's throats.** Engage in destructive competition. For example, *With their price war the two stores were cutting each other's throats.* This usage gave rise, by 1880, to the idiom **cutthroat competition,** for vicious competitive practices.

cut teeth ◆ See CUT ONE'S TEETH.

cut the comedy Also, **cut the crap.** Stop talking or behaving foolishly, as in *Cut the comedy! We have work to do,* or *It's time you cut the crap and got to work.* The first of these slangy imperatives dates from the early 1900s, the ruder variant from the 1920s.

cut the ground from under Unexpectedly withdraw support or destroy one's foundation, trip someone up. For example, *Overriding his veto, Congress cut the ground from under the President.* This metaphoric phrase alludes to removing the solid earth from under someone. [Mid-1800s]

cut the mustard Perform satisfactorily, as in *We need a better catcher; this one just doesn't cut the mustard.* The origin of this expression is disputed. Some believe it alludes to *mustard* in the sense of the best or main attraction (owing to its spicing up food), whereas others believe it is a corruption of PASS MUSTER. Still others hold that it concerns the preparation of mustard, which involves adding vinegar to mustard seed to "cut" (reduce) its bitterness. The expression is often in negative form, as in the example. [Slang; c. 1900]

cutting edge, at the Also, **on the cutting edge.** In the forefront, in a position of greatest advantage or importance. For example, *In my youth I was at the cutting edge of medical research,* or *Our company is on the cutting edge of gene therapy.* This metaphoric phrase alludes to the sharp edge of a knife or other cutting tool. [c. 1950]

cut to the bone Severely reduced, as in *During the Depression Grandmother's housekeeping money was cut to the bone.* The phrase *to the bone,* literally meaning "through the flesh to the inmost part or core," dates from about 1400. This expression in effect means that everything extraneous has been cut away so that only bone remains.

cut to the chase Get to the point, get on with it, as in *We don't have time to go into that, so let's cut to the chase.* This usage alludes to editing (cutting) film so as to get to the exciting chase scene in a motion picture. [Slang; 1920s]

cut to the quick Deeply wound or distress, as in *His criticism cut her to the quick.* This phrase uses *the quick* in the sense of a vital or a very sensitive part of the body, such as under the fingernails. It also appeared in such older locutions as **touched to the quick,** for "deeply affected," and **stung to the quick,** for "wounded, distressed," both dating from the early 1500s. The current expression was considered a cliché from about 1850 on.

cut up 1. Divide into smaller parts, break the continuity of, as in *These meetings have cut up my whole day.* [c. 1800] 2. Severely censure or criticize, as in *The reviewer cut up the book mercilessly.* [Mid-1700s] 3. **be cut up.** Be distressed or saddened, as in *I was terribly cut up when she left.* [Mid-1800s] Charles Dickens used this idiom in *A Christmas Carol* (1844): "Scrooge was not so dreadfully cut up by the sad event." 4. Behave in a playful, comic, or boisterous way, as in *On the last night of camp the children usually cut up.* [Late 1800s] 5. **cut up rough.** Act in a rowdy, angry, or violent way, as in *After a beer or two the boys began to cut up rough.* [Slang; first half of 1800s]

cylinder ♦ See FIRING ON ALL CYLINDERS.

d

daddy ♦ See BIG DADDY; GRANDDADDY OF THEM ALL; SUGAR DADDY.

dagger ♦ In addition to the idiom beginning with DAGGERS, also see LOOK DAGGERS.

daggers drawn, at Also, **with daggers drawn.** About to or ready to fight, as in *Are Felix and Oscar still at daggers drawn over the rent?* Although daggers today are rarely if ever used to avenge an insult or issue a challenge to a duel, this idiom remains current. Its figurative use dates from about 1800.

daily dozen Physical exercise, as in *Helen walks two miles every morning—that's her daily dozen.* This term originally referred to a set of twelve specific calisthenic exercises to be performed every day. They were devised by a famous Yale University football coach, Walter Camp (1859–1925), and came into general use in the early 1900s. Despite the physical fitness craze of the late 1900s, these exercises and their name are no longer taken literally, but the term survives in a very general way.

daisy ♦ In addition to the idiom beginning with DAISY, also see FRESH AS A DAISY; PUSH UP DAISIES.

daisy chain 1. A series of connected events, activities, or experiences. For example, *The daisy chain of lectures on art history encompassed the last 200 years.* This metaphorical term alludes to a string of the flowers linked together. [Mid-1800s] 2. A line or circle of three or more persons engaged in simultaneous sexual activity. For example, *A high-class call girl, she drew the line at daisy chains.* [Vulgar slang; 1920s] 3. A series of securities transactions intended to give the impression of active trading so as to drive up the price. For example, *The SEC is on the alert for unscrupulous brokers who are engaging in daisy chains.* [1980s]

dam ♦ See WATER OVER THE DAM.

damage ♦ In addition to the idioms beginning with DAMAGE, also see DO ONE WRONG (DAMAGE); THE DAMAGE.

damage control Measures to minimize or curtail loss or harm. For example, *As soon as they discovered the leak to the press, the senator's office worked night and day on damage control.* Used literally since the 1950s, specifically for limiting the effect of an accident on a ship, this term began to be used figuratively in the 1970s.

damaged goods A person, especially an unmarried woman who is no longer a virgin, as in *A person who has sex before marriage is not considered damaged goods in this day and age.* This pejorative expression transfers the reduced value of materials (stock, provisions, etc.) marred in some way to women who have had a sexual experience. [Early 1900s]

damn ♦ In addition to the idioms beginning with DAMN, also see DO ONE'S DAMNEDEST; GIVE A DAMN; NOT WORTH A DIME (TINKER'S DAMN).

damned if I do, damned if I don't A situation in which one can't win. For example, *If I invite Aunt Jane, Mother will be angry, and if I don't, I lose Jane's friendship—I'm damned if I do and damned* *if I don't*. Eric Partridge suggested this idiom may have come from the emphatic **I'm damned if I do,** meaning "I definitely will not do something," but despite the similar wording the quite different meaning argues against this theory. [Colloquial; first half of 1900s] Also see CATCH-22.

damn well Also, **damned well**. Certainly, without doubt; emphatically. For example, *You damn well better improve your grades,* or *I know damned well that he's leaving me out.* The *damn* in this phrase is mainly an intensifier.

damn with faint praise Compliment so feebly that it amounts to no compliment at all, or even implies condemnation. For example, *The reviewer damned the singer with faint praise, admiring her dress but not mentioning her voice.* This idea was already expressed in Roman times by Favorinus (c. A.D. 110) but the actual expression comes from Alexander Pope's *Epistle to Doctor Arbuthnot* (1733): "Damn with faint praise, assent with civil leer, and, without sneering, teach the rest to sneer."

damper ♦ See PUT A DAMPER ON.

dance ♦ In addition to the idioms beginning with DANCE, also see LEAD A CHASE (DANCE); SONG AND DANCE.

dance attendance on Wait on attentively and obsequiously, obey someone's every wish or whim. For example, *He expected his secretary to dance attendance on him so she quit her job.* This expression alludes to the old custom of making a bride dance with every wedding guest. In the 1500s it was used first to mean "await" an audience with someone, but by about 1600 it had acquired its present meaning. Also see AT SOMEONE'S BECK AND CALL.

dance to another tune Change one's manner, behavior, or attitude. For example, *He'll be dancing to another tune when he finds out that the board means business.* Also see CHANGE ONE'S TUNE.

dander ♦ See GET ONE'S BACK (DANDER) UP.

dandy ♦ See FINE AND DANDY.

dangerous ♦ See LITTLE KNOWLEDGE IS A DANGEROUS THING; LIVE DANGEROUSLY.

dare say ♦ See I DARE SAY.

dark ♦ In addition to the idioms beginning with DARK, also see IN THE DARK; KEEP SOMEONE IN THE DARK; LEAP IN THE DARK; SHOT IN THE DARK; WHISTLE IN THE DARK.

darken someone's door Come unwanted to someone's home, as in *I told him to get out and never darken my door again.* The verb *darken* here refers to casting one's shadow across the *threshold,* a word that occasionally was substituted for *door.* As an imperative, the expression is associated with Victorian melodrama, where someone (usually a young woman or man) is thrown out of the parental home for some misdeed, but it is actually much older. Benjamin Franklin used it in *The Busybody* (1729): "I am afraid she would resent it so as never to darken my doors again."

dark horse A little known, unexpectedly successful entrant, as in *You never can tell—some dark horse may come along and win a Senate seat.* This metaphoric expression originally alluded to an unknown horse winning a race and was so used in a novel by Benjamin Disraeli (*The Young Duke,* 1831). It soon began to be transferred to political candidates, among the first of whom was James K. Polk. He won the 1844 Democratic Presidential nomination on the eighth ballot and went on to win the election.

dash off 1. Write or sketch hastily, as in *I'm just going to dash off a letter.* [Early 1700s] 2. Hurry away, depart hastily, as in *He dashed off as though he was being chased.* This usage employs the verb *dash* in the sense of "impetuously run" or "rush," a usage dating from about 1300.

dash someone's hopes Destroy someone's plans, disappoint or disillusion. For example, *That fall dashed her hopes of a gold medal.* This term uses *dash* in the sense of "destroy," a usage surviving only in this idiom. [Second half of 1500s]

date ♦ In addition to the idiom beginning with DATE, also see BRING UP TO DATE; DOUBLE DATE; MAKE A DATE; OUT OF DATE; TO DATE; UP TO DATE.

date rape Sexual intercourse forced by the victim's social escort. For example, *Date rape is much more common on college campuses than was previously realized.* This term originated in the 1980s, when awareness of the phenomenon increased exponentially.

Davy Jones's locker Also, **Davy's locker**. The bottom of the sea, especially the grave of those who die at sea. For example, *Caught out at sea during the hurricane, they thought they were heading for Davy Jones's locker.* This term, first recorded in 1726, alludes to **Davy Jones,** a name given to the evil spirit of the sea. The ultimate origin of both *Davy* and *Jones* is disputed. A logical theory is that *Jones* referred to the biblical Jonah who was swallowed by a whale, and *Davy* was a corruption of a West Indian word for "devil."

dawn ♦ In addition to the idiom beginning with DAWN, also see CRACK OF DAWN; LIGHT DAWNED.

dawn on Also, **dawn upon**. Become evident or understood, as in *It finally dawned on him that he was expected to call them,* or *Around noon it dawned upon me that I had never eaten breakfast.* This expression transfers the beginning of daylight to the beginning of a thought process. Harriet Beecher Stowe had it in *Uncle Tom's Cabin*

(1852): "The idea that they had either feelings or rights had never dawned upon her." [Mid-1800s]

day ◆ In addition to the idioms beginning with DAY, also see ALL IN A DAY'S WORK; ANY DAY; APPLE A DAY; BAD HAIR DAY; BREAK OF DAY; BY THE DAY; CALL IT A DAY; CARRY THE DAY; DIFFERENT AS NIGHT AND DAY; DOG DAYS; EVERY DOG HAS ITS DAY; FIELD DAY; FOR DAYS ON END; FOREVER AND A DAY; FROM THIS DAY FORWARD; GOOD DAY; HAD ITS DAY; HAPPY AS THE DAY IS LONG; HEAVENLY DAYS; IN ALL ONE'S BORN DAYS; IN THE COLD LIGHT OF DAY; IN THIS DAY AND AGE; LATE IN THE DAY; MAKE A DAY OF IT; MAKE ONE'S DAY; NAME THE DAY; NIGHT AND DAY; NINE-DAY WONDER; NOT GIVE SOMEONE THE TIME OF DAY; NOT ONE'S DAY; ONE OF THESE DAYS; ORDER OF THE DAY; PASS THE TIME (OF DAY); PLAIN AS DAY; RAINY DAY; RED-LETTER DAY; ROME WASN'T BUILT IN A DAY; SALAD DAYS; SAVE THE DAY; SEEN BETTER DAYS; SEE THE LIGHT OF DAY; THAT'LL BE THE DAY; THE OTHER DAY; THOSE WERE THE DAYS; TIME OF DAY; TOMORROW IS ANOTHER DAY; WIN THROUGH (THE DAY).

day after day Also, **day in, day out.** For many days, continuously; also, every day. For example, *Day after day the rain spoiled our vacation,* or *Day in, day out, all I ever do is work.* [First half of 1800s]

day and night ◆ See under NIGHT AND DAY.

day by day On each successive day, daily, as in *Day by day he's getting better.* Percy Bysshe Shelley used this expression, first recorded in 1362, in *Adonais* (1821): "fear and grief . . . consume us day by day."

day in, day out ◆ See DAY AFTER DAY.

day in court, have one's Have an opportunity to be heard, as in *By asking Rob for an explanation the professor showed he was willing to let him have his day in court.* This expression transfers the idea of a hearing in a court of law to more general use.

daylight ◆ In addition to the idiom beginning with DAYLIGHT, also see BEAT THE LIVING DAYLIGHTS OUT OF; BEGIN TO SEE DAYLIGHT; IN BROAD DAYLIGHT; LET DAYLIGHT THROUGH; SCARE OUT OF ONE'S WITS (THE LIVING DAYLIGHTS OUT OF).

daylight robbery Charging exorbitant prices, as in *The amount you're asking for this couch is daylight robbery.* [Mid-1900s] Also see HIGHWAY ROBBERY.

day off A day away from work, school, or a similar obligation; a free day. For example, *Sophie always used her day off to do errands.* [Late 1800s]

days are numbered, one's Also, **its days are numbered.** The usefulness or life of someone or something is nearly ended. For example, *When they announced the layoffs, she knew her days at the company were numbered,* or *My car's days are numbered—the transmission is shot.* A version of this expression appears in the Bible (Daniel 5:26):

"God hath numbered thy kingdom and finished it." It came into common use in the late 1800s.

day to day Also, **from day to day. 1.** Continuously, without interruption, on a daily basis. For example, *Running this office day to day is not an easy task.* [Late 1800s] **2. live from day to day.** Be interested only in immediate concerns, without thought for the future. For example, *Jean lives from day to day, planning nothing in advance.* Also see LIVE FOR THE MOMENT.

dead ◆ In addition to the idioms beginning with DEAD, also see BEAT A DEAD HORSE; CAUGHT DEAD; CUT SOMEONE DEAD; DROP DEAD; KNOCK DEAD; MORE DEAD THAN ALIVE; OVER MY DEAD BODY; QUICK AND THE DEAD; STOP COLD (DEAD); TO WAKE THE DEAD. Also see under DEATH.

dead ahead Directly or straight in front of one, as in *There's the house, dead ahead.* The use of *dead* in the sense of "straight" dates from the last quarter of the 1800s.

dead and buried Also, **dead and gone.** Long forgotten, no longer in use, as in *That argument is dead and buried,* or *No point in worrying about regulations that are long dead and gone.* This figurative use of "having died" is usually applied to some issue. [Late 1800s]

dead as a doornail Also, **dead as a dodo** or **herring.** Totally or assuredly dead; also finished. For example, *The cop announced that the body in the dumpster was dead as a doornail,* or *The radicalism she professed in her adolescence is now dead as a dodo,* or *The Equal Rights Amendment appears to be dead as a herring.* The first, oldest, and most common of these similes, all of which can be applied literally to persons or, more often today, to issues, involves *doornail,* dating from about 1350. Its meaning is disputed but most likely it referred to the costly metal nails hammered into the outer doors of the wealthy (most people used the much cheaper wooden pegs), which were clinched on the inside of the door and therefore were "dead," that is, could not be used again. *Dead as a herring* dates from the 16th century and no doubt alludes to the bad smell this dead fish gives off, making its death quite obvious. *Dead as a dodo,* referring to the extinct bird, dates from the early 1900s.

dead beat 1. Defeated; also exhausted. For example, *That horse was dead beat before the race even began,* or, as Charles Dickens put it in *Martin Chuzzlewit* (1843): "Pull off my boots for me . . . I am quite knocked up. Dead beat." [Slang; first half of 1800s] **2.** Also, **deadbeat.** A lazy person or loafer; also, one who does not pay debts. For example, *Her housemate knew she was a deadbeat, shirking her share of the chores,* or *He's a deadbeat;*

don't count on getting that money back. [Slang; second half of 1800s]

dead drunk Completely intoxicated, as in *I can't remember a thing about last night; I was dead drunk.* This phrase, first recorded in 1599, alludes to the immobility and insensibility of actual death.

dead duck 1. A person doomed to failure or death; a hopeless case. For example, *If they can't find a heart to transplant soon, he's a dead duck.* [1940s] 2. A useless, worthless, or outmoded person or thing. For example, *They didn't interview the outgoing senator; to the press he's a dead duck.* Some speculate that this slangy term comes from an old saying, "Never waste powder on a dead duck," first recorded in 1829.

dead end 1. A passage that has no exit, as in *This street's a dead end, so turn back.* [Late 1800s] 2. An impasse or blind alley, allowing no progress to be made. For example, *This job is a dead end; I'll never be able to advance.* [c. 1920]

dead from the neck up Extremely stupid, as in *That news commentator sounds dead from the neck up.* This expression alludes to being "brain-dead." [Early 1900s]

dead heat A contest in which the competitors are equally matched and neither can win; a tie. For example, *The two companies are in a dead heat to get a new personal computer on the market.* This term comes from 18th-century British horse racing and is still part of racing terminology. It later was transferred to other kinds of competition.

dead horse ♦ See BEAT A DEAD HORSE.

dead in one's tracks ♦ See under STOP COLD.

dead in the water Unable to function or move; inoperable. For example, *Without an effective leader, our plans for expansion are dead in the water.* Originally referring to a crippled ship, this colloquialism was soon applied more broadly.

dead letter 1. An unclaimed or undelivered letter that is eventually destroyed or returned to the sender. For example, *She moved without leaving a forwarding address, so her mail ended up in the dead letter office.* [c. 1700] 2. A statute or directive that is still valid but in practice is not enforced. For example, *The blue laws here are a dead letter; all the stores open on Sundays and holidays.* [Second half of 1600s]

dead loss 1. A total loss, as in *They've changed the currency, so these old coins are a dead loss.* [Early 1700s] 2. A worthless person or thing; also, an utter waste of time. For example, *With an injured knee he's a dead loss to the team,* or *It rained every day, so our week at the beach was a dead loss.* [1920s]

dead man ♦ See DEAD SOLDIER.

dead of The period of greatest intensity of something, such as darkness or cold. For example, *I love looking at seed catalogs in the dead of winter, when it's below zero outside.* The earliest recorded use of **dead of night**, for "darkest time of night," was in Edward Hall's *Chronicle* of 1548: "In the dead of the night . . . he broke up his camp and fled." **Dead of winter,** for the coldest part of winter, dates from the early 1600s.

dead on one's feet Also, **dead tired.** Extremely weary, as in *Mom was in the kitchen all day and was dead on her feet,* or *I'd love to go, but I'm dead tired.* The use of *dead* for "tired to exhaustion" dates from the early 1800s, and *dead on one's feet,* conjuring up the image of a dead person still standing up, dates from the late 1800s.

dead ringer A person or thing that closely resembles another; an exact counterpart. For example, *Brian's a dead ringer for his Dad,* or *That red bike is a dead ringer for Mary's.* [Late 1800s]

dead set against Completely opposed to, as in *His parents were dead set against John's taking a year off from college. Set against* has been used to mean "opposed to" since the 1400s. *Dead* acquired the meaning "utterly" in the 16th century.

dead soldier Also, **dead man.** An empty liquor, wine, or beer bottle, as in *Their trash barrel's full of dead soldiers; they must drink a lot,* or *That dead man sticking out of your pocket alerted the officer to the fact that you'd been drinking. Dead man* has been slang for "empty bottle" since the late 1600s but has been largely replaced by *dead soldier,* dating from the late 1800s.

dead tired ♦ See DEAD ON ONE'S FEET.

dead to rights In the act of committing an error or crime, red-handed. For example, *They caught the burglars dead to rights with the Oriental rugs.* This phrase uses *to rights* in the sense of "at once." [Slang; mid-1800s]

dead to the world Sound asleep or unconscious, as in *The alarm clock went off but Joseph was dead to the world.* [Late 1800s]

dead weight A heavy or oppressive burden, as in *That police record will be a dead weight on his career.* This term alludes to the unrelieved weight of an inert mass. [Early 1700s]

deaf ♦ In addition to the idiom beginning with DEAF, also see FALL ON DEAF EARS; STONE DEAF; TURN A DEAF EAR.

deaf as a post Also, **deaf as an adder.** Unable to hear or to listen, as in *Speak louder, Grandpa's deaf as a post.* The first simile has its origin in John Palsgrave's *Acolastus* (1540): "How deaf an ear I intended to give him . . . he were as good to tell his tale to a post." It has largely replaced *deaf as an adder,* alluding to an ancient belief that adders cannot hear; it is recorded in the Bible (Psalms 58:3–5).

deal ♦ In addition to the idioms beginning with DEAL, also see BIG DEAL; CLOSE THE SALE (DEAL); CUT A DEAL; DONE DEAL; GOOD DEAL; MAKE A FEDERAL CASE (BIG DEAL); NO DEAL; RAW DEAL; SQUARE DEAL; SWEETEN THE KITTY (DEAL); WHEEL AND DEAL.

deal in 1. Also, **deal with**. Be occupied or concerned with, as in *Jim deals in generalities,* or *This book deals with idioms.* The first term dates from the late 1500s, the variant from about 1300. 2. Do business or trade in something, as in *They deal in diamonds.* [Late 1500s] Also see DEAL WITH. 3. **deal someone in**. Also, **deal one a hand**. Include someone, give someone a share, as in *I hope they'll deal me in on this new enterprise.* This usage comes from card games, where *to deal* has meant "to distribute cards" since the 16th century. [Early 1900s]

deal out 1. Distribute, as in *He dealt out more and more work.* [Late 1300s] Also see DEAL IN, def. 3. 2. **deal someone out**. Exclude someone, as in *I don't have time for this project, so deal me out.* This usage is the opposite of DEAL IN, def. 3.

deal with 1. See DEAL IN, def. 1. 2. Do business with someone, as in *I like dealing with this company.* [Late 1600s] Also see DEAL IN, def. 2. 3. Take action in, handle, administer, dispose of, as in *The committee will deal with this matter.* [Second half of 1400s] 4. Act in a specified way toward someone, as in *He dealt extremely fairly with his competitors.* [c. 1300]

dear ♦ In addition to the idiom beginning with DEAR, also see FOR DEAR LIFE; NEAREST AND DEAREST.

dear me Also, **oh dear**. A polite exclamation expressing surprise, distress, sympathy, etc. For example, *Dear me, I forgot to mail it,* or *Oh dear, what a bad time you've been having.* These usages may originally have invoked God, as in **dear God** or **oh God,** which also continue to be so used. [Late 1600s]

death ♦ In addition to the idioms beginning with DEATH, also see AT DEATH'S DOOR; BE THE DEATH OF; BORE TO DEATH; CATCH COLD (ONE'S DEATH); FATE WORSE THAN DEATH; IN AT THE DEATH; KISS OF DEATH; LOOK LIKE DEATH (WARMED OVER); MATTER OF LIFE AND DEATH; PUT TO DEATH; SCARE OUT OF ONE'S WITS (TO DEATH); SIGN ONE'S OWN DEATH WARRANT; THRILL TO PIECES (TO DEATH); TICKLED PINK (TO DEATH); TO DEATH. Also see under DEAD.

death and taxes, certain as Also, **sure as death and taxes**. Bound to occur, inevitable, as in *His business is going to fail, certain as death and taxes.* This phrase was invented by Benjamin Franklin in a letter (1789) and has been repeated ever since,

the government's recurring need for revenue probably assuring its continued popularity.

death knell Something that indicates impending failure, as in *His low scores sounded the death knell for his ambitions.* The noun *knell,* used for the ringing of a bell since at least A.D. 1000, is rarely heard today except in this figurative phrase.

death of ♦ See BE THE DEATH OF.

death on Very effective against; also, very fond of. For example, "He is a wonderful fielder and sure death on bunts" (Christy Mathewson, *Pitching,* 1912), or *The boss is death on tardiness,* or *She's death on the latest fashions.* [Slang; early 1800s]

debt ♦ See HEAD OVER HEELS (IN DEBT).

deck ♦ In addition to the idiom beginning with DECK, also see CLEAR THE DECKS; HIT THE DECK; ON DECK.

deck out Decorate, dress up, as in *They were all decked out in their best clothes.* [Mid-1700s]

declare war on Also, **declare war against**. Announce one's intent to suppress or eradicate something or someone. For example, *The police have declared war on drug dealing in the neighborhood,* or *Several gangs have declared war against each other.* This usage transfers the literal sense of the term, "to state formally one's intention to carry on hostilities against another power," to a somewhat smaller scale.

deep ♦ In addition to the idioms beginning with DEEP, also see BEAUTY IS ONLY SKIN DEEP; BETWEEN A ROCK AND A HARD PLACE (DEVIL AND DEEP BLUE SEA); GO OFF THE DEEP END; IN DEEP; STILL WATERS RUN DEEP.

deep down At bottom, basically. For example, *Deep down she was a rebel,* or *Although he would never admit it, deep down he was very fond of her.* [c. 1900]

deep end ♦ See GO OFF THE DEEP END.

deep pocket Also, **deep pockets**. A source of substantial wealth or financial support, as in *The college relies on the deep pocket of one particular alumna.* This term alludes to money-filled pockets. [Slang; 1970s]

deep six 1. Also, **give** or **get the deep six**. Burial at sea. For example, *When the torpedo hit our boat, I was sure we'd get the deep six.* This expression alludes to the customary six-foot depth of most graves. [Early 1900s] 2. Disposal or rejection of something, as in *They gave the new plan the deep six.* This usage comes from nautical slang of the 1920s for tossing something overboard (to its watery grave; see def. 1). It was transferred to more general kinds of disposal in the 1940s and gave rise to the verb *to deep-six,* for "toss overboard" or "discard."

deep water ♦ See IN DEEP, def. 2.

default ♦ See IN DEFAULT OF.

defensive ♦ See ON THE DEFENSIVE.

defiance ♦ See IN DEFIANCE OF.

degree ♦ See BY DEGREES; THIRD DEGREE; TO SOME DEGREE; TO THE NTH DEGREE.

deliver ♦ In addition to the idiom beginning with DELIVER, also see SIGNED, SEALED, AND DELIVERED.

deliver the goods Do what is required, come up to expectations. For example, *Kate delivered the goods and got us the five votes we needed.* This phrase alludes to delivering an order of groceries or other items. [Colloquial; second half of 1800s]

demand ♦ See IN DEMAND; MAKE DEMANDS ON; ON DEMAND.

dent ♦ See MAKE A DENT IN.

depth ♦ See IN DEPTH; OUT OF ONE'S DEPTH.

description ♦ See BEGGAR DESCRIPTION.

desert ♦ In addition to the idiom beginning with DESERT, also see JUST DESERTS.

desert a sinking ship Abandon a failing enterprise before it is too late. For example, *After seeing the company's financial statement, he knew it was time to desert a sinking ship.* This metaphoric expression alludes to rats, which leave a vessel when it founders in a storm or runs aground so as to escape drowning. It was transferred to human behavior by about 1600.

deserve ♦ See ONE GOOD TURN DESERVES ANOTHER.

design ♦ See BY DESIGN; HAVE DESIGNS ON.

desire ♦ See LEAVE A LOT TO BE DESIRED.

desist ♦ See CEASE AND DESIST.

detail ♦ See IN DETAIL.

determine ♦ See BOUND AND DETERMINED.

device ♦ See LEAVE TO SOMEONE'S OWN DEVICES.

devil ♦ In addition to the idioms beginning with DEVIL, also see BETWEEN A ROCK AND A HARD PLACE (DEVIL AND DEEP BLUE SEA); FULL OF IT (THE DEVIL); GIVE SOMEONE HELL (THE DEVIL); GIVE THE DEVIL HIS DUE; GO TO HELL (THE DEVIL); LUCK OF THE DEVIL; PLAY THE DEVIL WITH; RAISE CAIN (THE DEVIL); SPEAK OF THE DEVIL.

devil and deep blue sea ♦ see under BETWEEN A ROCK AND A HARD PLACE.

devil of a Also, **one devil** or **the devil of a; hell of a.** Infernally annoying or difficult, as in *This is a devil of an assembly job,* or *She had one devil of a time getting through the traffic,* or *I had a hell of a morning sitting in that doctor's office.* The first expression dates from the mid-1700s. The variant is a couple of decades newer and its precise meaning depends on the context. For example, *We had a hell of a time getting here* invariably means we had a very difficult or annoying time, but *He is one hell*

of a driver could mean that he is either very good or very bad (see HELL OF A, def. 2).

devil's advocate One who argues against a cause or position either for the sake of argument or to help determine its validity. For example, *My role in the campaign is to play devil's advocate to each new policy before it's introduced to the public.* This term comes from the Roman Catholic Church, where *advocatus diaboli* (Latin for "devil's advocate") signifies an official who is appointed to present arguments against a proposed canonization or beatification. It was transferred to wider use in the mid-1700s.

devil take the hindmost, the Let everyone put his or her own interest first, leaving the unfortunate to their fate. For example, *I don't care if she makes it or not—the devil take the hindmost.* This expression, first recorded in 1608, probably originated as an allusion to a children's game in which the last (coming "hindmost") is the loser, and came to mean utter selfishness.

devil to pay, the Serious trouble resulting from some action, as in *There'll be the devil to pay if you let that dog out.* This expression originally referred to trouble resulting from making a bargain with the devil, but later was broadened to apply to any sort of problem. A variant, **the devil to pay and no pitch hot,** first recorded in 1865, gave rise to the theory that the expression was originally nautical, since *pay* also means "to waterproof a seam by caulking it with pitch," and *no pitch hot* meant it was a particularly difficult job, since cold pitch is hard to use. However, the original expression is much older and is the one that survives. [c. 1400]

diamond in the rough Also, **a rough diamond.** A person of exceptional character or potential but lacking polish and refinement. For example, *Jack is intelligent and trustworthy but lacks manners—he's a diamond in the rough.* [Early 1600s]

dibs ♦ See HAVE DIBS ON.

dice ♦ See LOAD THE DICE; NO DEAL (DICE).

dice are loaded, the ♦ See under LOAD THE DICE.

dick ♦ See EVERY TOM, DICK, AND HARRY.

die ♦ In addition to the idioms beginning with DIE, also see CURL UP (AND DIE); DO OR DIE; IT'S TO DIE; NEVER SAY DIE.

die away Also, **die down.** Gradually diminish, fade, or subside; slowly come to an end. For example, *As they moved higher up, their voices died away,* or *The rain seems to be dying down.* The first term, from the late 1600s, today is most often applied to a diminishing sound and was originally used to describe the wind slowing down or ceasing to blow. The variant dates from the first half of the 1800s.

die down ♦ See DIE AWAY.

die for Also, **be dying for**. Long for, desire excessively, as in *I'm dying for some ice cream*. This hyperbolic usage dates from the late 1500s. Also see DIE TO.

die hard Take a long time to cease to exist or be dropped from consideration. For example, *Old prejudices die hard*, or *The more radical parts of this proposal will die hard*. This idiom alludes to struggling against physical death. [Late 1700s]

die in harness ♦ See DIE WITH ONE'S BOOTS ON.

die is cast, the The decision or course of action has been determined and cannot be changed. For example, *Now that I've announced my resignation, the die is cast*. This expression comes from the Latin *Iacta alea est*, "the dice have been thrown," which according to Suetonius was said by Julius Caesar when he crossed the Rubicon and invaded Italy in 49 B.C. In English it dates from the first half of the 1600s.

die laughing Experience extreme amusement, as in *When his pants fell down, I thought I'd die laughing*. This hyperbolic expression was used by Shakespeare in *The Taming of the Shrew* (3:2): "Went they not quickly, I should die with laughing." Also see SPLIT ONE'S SIDES.

die off Perish one by one, as in *A celibate community, the Shakers are dying off*. [Late 1600s]

die out Gradually become extinct, as in *As technology advances, and Western culture spreads, many folk traditions are dying out*. [Mid-1800s]

diet ♦ See ON A DIET.

die to Also, **be dying to**. Long greatly to do something, as in *I'm dying to go to Alaska*. [c. 1700] Also see DIE FOR.

die with one's boots on Also, **die in harness**. Expire while working, keep working to the end, as in *He'll never retire—he'll die with his boots on*, or *She knows she'll never get promoted, but she wants to die in harness*. Both phrases probably allude to soldiers who died on active duty. Until the early 1600s the noun *boot* denoted a piece of armor for the legs, which may have given rise to this usage; and Shakespeare used *harness* in the sense of armor when he wrote: "At least we'll die with harness on our back" (*Macbeth* 5:5).

differ ♦ See BEG TO DIFFER. Also see under DIFFERENCE; DIFFERENT.

difference ♦ See MAKE A DIFFERENCE; SPLIT THE DIFFERENCE. Also see under DIFFERENT.

different ♦ In addition to the idioms beginning with DIFFERENT, also see HORSE OF A DIFFERENT COLOR; KETTLE OF FISH, DIFFERENT; MARCH TO A DIFFERENT DRUMMER; SING A DIFFERENT TUNE; WEAR ANOTHER (DIFFERENT) HAT.

different as night and day Also, **different as day and night**. Totally unlike. For example, *Although they are sisters, they are as different as night and day*. Also see NIGHT AND DAY.

different strokes for different folks ♦ See under NO ACCOUNTING FOR TASTES.

dig down Pay with money from one's own pocket; be generous. For example, *We've got to dig down deep to make the next payment*. [Colloquial; c. 1940]

dig in 1. Excavate trenches to defend oneself in battle and hold one's position, as in *The battalion dug in and held on*. This usage gained currency in the trench warfare of World War I. [Mid-1800s] 2. Also, **dig in one's heels**. Adopt a firm position, be obstinate and unyielding. For example, *Arthur refused to argue the point and simply dug in*, or *The dog dug in its heels and refused to move*. [Colloquial; late 1800s] 3. Begin to work intensively, as in *If we all dig in it'll be done before dark*. [Colloquial; second half of 1800s] 4. Also, **dig into**. Begin to eat heartily, as in *Even before all the food was on the table they began to dig in*, or *When the bell rang, the kids all dug into their lunches*. [Colloquial; early 1900s]

dig one's own grave Seriously harm oneself, cause one's own ruin or downfall. For example, *If Sam pursues that course, he'll be digging his own grave*. [First half of 1900s]

dig out 1. Extract, remove, as in *He was determined to dig out every bit of metal he could find*. [Late 1300s] 2. Find by searching for, as in *He dug out his first contract from the file*. [Mid-1800s]

dig up 1. Search out, find, obtain, as in *I'm sure I can dig up a few more supporters*. [Mid-1800s] 2. **dig up some dirt** or **the dirt**. Find derogatory information about someone or something. For example, *The editor assigned him to dig up all the dirt on the candidates*. The slangy use of the noun *dirt* for "embarrassing or scandalous information" dates from about 1840, but this metaphoric expression is a century newer.

dilemma ♦ See HORNS OF A DILEMMA.

dim ♦ See TAKE A DIM VIEW.

dime ♦ In addition to the idiom beginning with DIME, also see DROP A DIME; GET OFF THE DIME; NOT WORTH A DIME; ON A DIME.

dime a dozen So plentiful as to be valueless. For example, *Don't bother to buy one of these—they're a dime a dozen*. The dime was declared the American ten-cent coin in 1786 by the Continental Congress. [First half of 1900s]

dine ♦ In addition to the idiom beginning with DINE, also see EAT (DINE) OUT; WINE AND DINE.

dine out on Be invited to dinner because of something one knows about and can discuss. For example, "In a couple of years you will be dining out on this murder" (Ngaio Marsh, *A Man Lay Dead*, 1934). [First half of 1900s] Also see EAT OUT; SING FOR ONE'S SUPPER.

dint ♦ See BY DINT OF.

dip into 1. Investigate superficially, as in *He began to dip into Chaucer*, or *She's just dipping into psychology*. This expression alludes to plunging briefly into a liquid. [Late 1600s] 2. Withdraw something in small amounts, usually money, as in *I'll have to dip into my savings*. This usage employs *dip into* in the sense of plunging one's hand or a ladle into a pot, water, or the like for the purpose of taking something out. [Early 1800s]

dip one's toes into Also, **get one's toes into** or **wet**. Begin to do something novel or unfamiliar, as in *I have been dipping my toes into Asian cooking*, or *She's eager to go to Europe and has been getting her toes wet by getting travel information*. [Late 1900s] Also see GET ONE'S FEET WET.

direction ♦ See STEP IN THE RIGHT DIRECTION.

dirt ♦ In addition to the idiom beginning with DIRT, also see DIG UP (DIRT); DISH THE DIRT; EAT CROW (DIRT); HIT THE DECK (DIRT); PAY DIRT; TREAT LIKE DIRT. Also see under DIRTY.

dirt cheap Very inexpensive, as in *Their house was a real bargain, dirt cheap*. Although the idea dates back to ancient times, the precise expression, literally meaning "as cheap as dirt," replaced the now obsolete *dog cheap*. [Early 1800s]

dirty ♦ In addition to the idioms beginning with DIRTY, also see DOWN AND DIRTY; WASH ONE'S DIRTY LINEN IN PUBLIC.

dirty joke A smutty story, as in *Teenagers love to tell dirty jokes*. The use of *dirty* in the sense of "obscene" or "indecent" dates from the late 1500s, but its application to a joke began only in the 20th century. The same sense also appears in such expressions as **dirty book**, for a pornographic book; **dirty old man**, for a middle-aged or elderly lecher; and **dirty word** or **talk dirty**, for a lewd, offensive expression or sexually explicit conversation.

dirty look, give a Scowl at someone, look disapproving. For example, *When I started to tell the story, Carol gave me a really dirty look*. This expression has largely replaced the earlier and more formal **black look**. [Colloquial; 1920s]

dirty one's hands Also, **get one's hands dirty** or **soil one's hands**. Do something shameful or illegal. For example, *He refused to dirty his hands and*

give jobs to the big campaign donors, or *Getting one's hands dirty by lying to the boss will be severely punished*, or *She would not soil her hands by cheating*. This expression is a metaphor for literally defiling or soiling oneself. [Mid-1600s]

dirty tricks Undercover or clandestine operations and deceitful stratagems in politics and espionage. For example, *This campaign has been dominated by the dirty tricks of both sides*. The adjective *dirty* here is used in the sense of "unethical" or "unfair." The term originally was applied to covert intelligence operations carried out by the Central Intelligence Agency, whose planning directorate was nicknamed "department of dirty tricks." It later was extended to underhanded activity intended to undermine political opponents and commercial rivals. [1940s]

dirty work An unpleasant, distasteful, or thankless task or job. For example, *Jane complained that she had to do all the dirty work while her colleagues took long vacations*. [First half of 1900s]

discount ♦ See AT A DISCOUNT.

discretion ♦ In addition to the idiom beginning with DISCRETION, also see THROW CAUTION (DISCRETION) TO THE WINDS.

discretion is the better part of valor It is better to be prudent than merely courageous, as in *I'm signing up for the easy course first; discretion is the better part of valor*. This proverb, a synonym of LOOK BEFORE YOU LEAP, was first recorded in 1477. Charles Churchill put it in poetic form: "Even in a hero's heart, Discretion is the better part" (*The Ghost*, 1762). Shakespeare also used a form of it: "The better part of valor is discretion" (*1 Henry IV*, 5:4).

disguise ♦ See BLESSING IN DISGUISE.

dish ♦ In addition to the idioms beginning with DISH, also see DO THE DISHES. Also see under DISHWATER.

dish out 1. Deal out, dispense, as in *He dishes out advice to one and all*. This expression alludes to serving food from a dish. [Colloquial; first half of 1600s] 2. **dish it out**. Dispense abuse or punishment, as in *He can dish it out with the best of them, but he can't take it*. [Slang; c. 1930]

dish the dirt Spread gossip or scandal, as in *Sally was notorious for dishing the dirt*. [Slang; 1920s]

dishwater ♦ See DULL AS DISHWATER.

dispense with 1. Manage without, forgo, as in *We can dispense with the extra help*. Shakespeare had this idiom in *Timon of Athens* (3:2): "Men must learn now with pity to dispense." [c. 1600] 2. Get rid of, do away with, as in *The European Union is trying to dispense with tariff barriers*. [Late 1500s] 3. Exempt one from a law, promise, or obligation, as in *He asked the court to dispense with swearing on the Bible.* This usage originally applied to religious obligations (to which the Pope granted *dispensation*). [Early 1500s]

disposal ♦ See PUT AT SOMEONE'S DISPOSAL.

dispose of 1. Attend to, settle, deal with, as in *He quickly disposed of the problem.* [Early 1600s] **2.** Transfer, part with, as by giving away or selling. For example, *They wanted to dispose of the land as soon as possible.* [Second half of 1600s] **3.** Get rid of, throw out, as in *Can we dispose of the trash in this barrel?* Oliver Goldsmith had this idiom in *She Stoops to Conquer* (1773): "I'm disposing of the husband before I have secured the lover." [Mid-1600s] **4.** Kill or destroy; also, humorously, consume. For example, *The king was determined to dispose of his enemies,* or *John disposed of the cake in no time.* [Second half of 1800s]

dispute ♦ See IN DISPUTE.

distance ♦ See GO THE DISTANCE; KEEP ONE'S DISTANCE; SPITTING DISTANCE.

ditch ♦ See LAST-DITCH EFFORT.

divide and conquer Also, **divide and govern** or **rule.** Win by getting one's opponents to fight among themselves. For example, *Divide and conquer was once a very successful policy in sub-Saharan Africa.* This expression is a translation of the Latin maxim, *Divide et impera* ("divide and rule"), and began to appear in English about 1600.

do, doing ♦ In addition to the idioms beginning with DO, also see CAN DO WITH; CAN'T DO ANYTHING WITH; DO YOU READ ME?; HARD WAY (DO IT THE); HAVE NO BUSINESS DOING; HAVE NOTHING TO DO WITH; HAVE TO DO WITH; HOW DO YOU DO; JUST AS SOON DO; LEAD ONE TO (DO); LEFT HAND DOESN'T KNOW WHAT RIGHT HAND IS DOING; MAKE DO; NO CAN DO; NOTHING DOING; TAKE DOING; THAT WILL DO; TWO WRONGS DO NOT MAKE A RIGHT; UP AND ABOUT (DOING); WHAT DO YOU KNOW; WHAT'S NEW (DOING). Also see under DOES; DONE; DON'T.

do a disappearing act Vanish, as in *As soon as the teacher came outside, Mary did a disappearing act.* This expression describes a sudden disappearance as if by magic and presumably alludes to a magician's performance. [Colloquial; early 1900s]

do a double take ♦ See DOUBLE TAKE.

do a job on Also, **do a number on.** Damage, harm, as in *The cat really did a job on the upholstery,* or *The teacher did a number on the class with that assignment.* This slangy idiom uses *job* (or *number*) in the sense of "something negative."

do an about-face Also, **do a flip-flop** or **one-eighty.** Reverse one's opinion or course of action. For example, *The board did an about-face on acquiring more land,* or *We expected Dad to do a flip-*

flop concerning our vacation plans, or *They had relied on Jim to vote for Harry, but he did a one-eighty and cast his vote for the incumbent.* The first term, alluding to the army command to turn around, dates from the first half of the 1900s, and the variants from the second half of the 1900s (the last refers to a 180-degree change of direction).

do any good Improve a situation or effect a favorable result, as in *Tell me if this new medicine does any good.* [Early 1700s] A negative version, **do no good,** is slightly older (late 1600s); for example, *All his explanations will do no good.*

do as I say Obey my instructions, as in *Never mind about the other mothers—you do as I say.* This admonitory order is sometimes followed by a self-deprecating phrase, **Do as I say, not as I do,** meaning "don't imitate my behavior but obey my instructions." This order first appeared in John Selden's *Table-Talk* (c. 1654): "Preachers say, 'Do as I say, not as I do.'"

do away with 1. Make an end of, eliminate. For example, *The town fathers have decided to do away with the old lighting system.* **2.** Demolish, destroy, kill, as in *The animal officer did away with the injured deer lying by the side of the road.* In the 13th century both usages were simply put as *do away,* the *with* being added only in the late 1700s.

do blindfolded Also, **do standing on one's head.** Perform very easily, as in *Dave said he could do the income tax return blindfolded,* or *An excellent carpenter, he could do just about anything standing on his head.* For a synonymous hyperbolic expression, see WITH ONE ARM TIED.

do by Behave with respect to, treat, as in *John was determined to do well by his children.* This idiom was first recorded about 1175.

dock ♦ See IN THE DOCK.

do credit to ♦ See DO ONE PROUD, def. 1.

doctor ♦ See JUST WHAT THE DOCTOR ORDERED.

dodo ♦ See under DEAD AS A DOORNAIL.

does, doesn't ♦ See EASY DOES IT; HANDSOME IS AS HANDSOME DOES; HOW DOES THAT GRAB YOU?; LEFT HAND DOESN'T KNOW WHAT THE RIGHT HAND IS DOING; THAT DOES IT.

do for 1. Bring about the death, defeat, or ruin of, as in *He swore he'd do for him.* This usage is often put in the passive voice (see DONE FOR). [First half of 1700s] **2.** Care or provide for, take care of, as in *They decided to hire a housekeeper to do for Grandmother.* This usage today is more common in Britain than in America. [Early 1500s]

dog ♦ In addition to the idioms beginning with DOG, also see COON'S (DOG'S) AGE; EVERY DOG HAS ITS DAY; GO TO POT (THE DOGS); HAIR OF THE DOG; HANG-DOG LOOK; HOT DOG; IN THE DOGHOUSE; LET

SLEEPING DOGS LIE; PUT ON THE DOG; RAIN CATS AND DOGS; SEE A MAN ABOUT A DOG; SHAGGY DOG STORY; SICK AS A DOG; TAIL WAGGING THE DOG; TEACH AN OLD DOG NEW TRICKS; THROW TO THE WOLVES (DOGS); TOP BANANA (DOG).

dog-and-pony show An elaborate presentation to gain approval for a product or policy. For example, *The administration loved putting on a dog-and-pony show for every minor change of policy.* This term alludes to a traveling variety show. [1950s]

dog days Hot, sultry summer weather; also, a period of stagnation. For example, *It's hard to get much work done during the dog days,* or *Every winter there's a week or two of dog days when sales drop dramatically.* The term alludes to the period between early July and early September, when Sirius, the so-called Dog Star, rises and sets with the sun. The ancient Romans called this phenomenon *dies caniculares,* which was translated as "dog days" in the first half of the 1500s.

dog eat dog Ruthless acquisition or competition, as in *With shrinking markets, it's dog eat dog for every company in this field.* This contradicts a Latin proverb which maintains that dog does *not* eat dog, first recorded in English in 1543. Nevertheless, by 1732 it was put as "Dogs are hard drove when they eat dogs" (Thomas Fuller, *Gnomologia*).

doghouse ♦ See IN THE DOGHOUSE.

dog in the manger One who prevents others from enjoying something despite having no use for it. For example, *Why be a dog in the manger? If you aren't going to use those tickets, let someone else have them.* This expression alludes to Aesop's fable about a snarling dog that prevents horses from eating fodder that is unpalatable to the dog itself. [Mid-1500s]

dog it 1. Do less than is required; loaf or shirk. For example, *I'm afraid our donors are dogging it this year.* This expression originated in sports and soon was transferred to other endeavors. [Slang; c. 1900] 2. Move slowly, as in *We just dogged it along from California to Oregon.* 3. Run away, as in *Let's dog it out of here right now.* This usage originated in American underworld slang in the 1920s, where it meant "to back down in cowardly fashion," and acquired its present sense about 1930. 4. Same as PUT ON THE DOG.

do good Act in an upright, moral way; engage in philanthropy. For example, *Social workers are trained to help people to help themselves, not simply going around doing good.* This term was first recorded in A.D. 725. Also see DO ANY GOOD; DO ONE GOOD.

dog's age ♦ See under COON'S AGE.

dog's life A miserably unhappy existence, as in *He's been leading a dog's life since his wife left him.*

This expression was first recorded in a 16th-century manuscript and alludes to the miserable subservient existence of dogs during this era. By the 1660s there was a proverb: "It's a dog's life, hunger and ease."

do in 1. Tire out, exhaust, as in *Running errands all day did me in.* [Colloquial; early 1900s] Also see DONE IN. 2. Kill, as in *Mystery writers are always thinking of new ways to do their characters in.* [Slang; early 1900s] Also see def. 4. 3. Ruin utterly; also cheat or swindle. For example, *The five-alarm fire did in the whole block,* or *His so-called friend really did him in.* [First half of 1900s] 4. **do oneself in.** Commit suicide, as in *She was always threatening to do herself in.* [Slang; first half of 1900s]

do justice to 1. Treat fairly or adequately, with full appreciation, as in *That review doesn't do the play justice.* This expression was first recorded in John Dryden's preface to *Troilus and Cressida* (1679): "I cannot leave this subject before I do justice to that Divine Poet." 2. **do oneself justice.** Execute in accordance with one's abilities, as in *She finally got a position in which she could do herself justice.* [Second half of 1800s]

doldrums ♦ See IN THE DOLDRUMS.

dollar ♦ In addition to the idiom beginning with DOLLARS, also see FEEL LIKE A MILLION DOLLARS; LOOK LIKE A MILLION DOLLARS; YOU CAN BET YOUR ASS (BOTTOM DOLLAR).

dollars to doughnuts, it's It's a virtual certainty, as in *It's dollars to doughnuts that the team will make the playoffs.* This metaphoric term pits dollars against doughnuts as in a bet. [Colloquial; late 1800s]

dolled up Also, **all dolled up.** Dressed or fixed up smartly and, often, ostentatiously, usually for a special occasion. For example, *There's no need to get all dolled up—it's just a picnic,* or *They dolled up the classroom for parents' night.* This expression alludes to a person or object being as attractive as a pretty doll. It is also put verbally, **to doll up,** as in *I wanted to doll up my apartment before the guests arrived.* [Colloquial; c. 1900] Also see GUSSIED UP.

done ♦ In addition to the idioms beginning with DONE, also see EASIER SAID THAN DONE; GOOD AS DONE; HAVE DONE (WITH); NO SOONER SAID (THAN DONE); NOT DONE; OVER AND DONE WITH; SEEN ONE, SEEN THEM ALL (BEEN THERE, DONE THAT); WHAT'S DONE IS DONE; WHEN ALL'S SAID AND DONE. Also see under DO.

done deal An irrevocable agreement, as in *Once you've signed the lease, it's a done deal.* This slangy expression, first recorded in 1979, may have come from *done thing,* originating in the late 1600s.

done for 1. Exhausted, worn out, as in *This old computer is just about done for.* [Colloquial; c. 1800]

Also see DONE IN. **2.** Doomed to death or destruction, as in *Before he went to the hospital it seemed as if he was done for.* [Colloquial; mid-1800s]

done in Exhausted, very tired, as in *After that hike I felt absolutely done in.* [Colloquial; early 1900s] Also see DONE FOR, def. 1.

done to a T ♦ See TO A T.

donkey's years A long time, as in *I haven't seen her in donkey's years.* This expression punningly alludes to the considerable length of the animal's ears. [Early 1900s]

do no good ♦ See under DO ANY GOOD.

don't ask A phrase used to fend off questions about a situation one finds awkward, unpleasant, or unsatisfactory. For example, *How did we do in the bridge tournament? Don't ask!* [Colloquial; 1960s] For a similar phrase, see FORGET IT.

don't change horses at midstream ♦ See CHANGE HORSES AT MIDSTREAM.

don't cross that bridge till you come to it ♦ see CROSS A BRIDGE WHEN ONE COMES TO IT.

don't hold your breath ♦ See HOLD ONE'S BREATH.

don't let the grass grow under one's feet Act now, don't delay. For example, *Write your applications today; don't let the grass grow under your feet.* This expression alludes to waiting so long that grass can grow. [c. 1600]

don't mention it ♦ See under YOU'RE WELCOME.

don't put off ♦ See PUT OFF.

do one ♦ Also see DO SOMEONE.

do one good **1.** Be of benefit to one, as in *I'm sure some fresh air will do her good.* [Late 1400s] **2.** Also, **do one's heart good.** Please, gratify, give satisfaction. For example, *It does my heart good to see the young couple so happy.*

do one's best Also, **do one's level best** or **one's damnedest.** Perform as well as one can, do the utmost possible, as in *I'm doing my best to balance this statement,* or *She did her level best to pass the course,* or *He did his damnedest to get done in time.* The first term dates from the 16th century, but the addition of *level,* here meaning "very," occurred only in the mid-1800s; the variant dates from the late 1800s.

do one's bit Also, **do one's part.** Make an individual contribution to an overall effort. For example, *You can always rely on Anne to do her bit,* or *I'm anxious to do my part as a board member.* [Early 1900s]

do one's duty **1.** Do one's tasks or what is expected of one. For example, *He was only doing his duty when he made the children finish their work.* [Early 1500s] **2.** Defecate or urinate, as in *Please keep the dog outdoors until he does his duty.* This euphemism for attending to such needs is heard less often today. [1930s]

do oneself in ♦ See DO IN, def. 4.

do one's heart good ♦ See DO ONE GOOD.

do one's homework Be well prepared, as in *Steve had done his homework before the meeting and could answer all of the client's questions.* This usage transfers a school assignment to a broader context. [c. 1930]

do one's thing Also, **do one's own thing.** Pursue one's interests or inclination; do what one does best or enjoys the most. For example, *I really give him credit for doing his thing and not being discouraged by what the critics say,* or *Phyllis is busy doing her own thing, running the magazine and publishing books.* Although this colloquialism became closely associated with the counterculture of the 1960s, it is actually much older. In one of his essays (1841) Ralph Waldo Emerson wrote: "But do your thing and I shall know you." However, it came into wide use only during the mid-1900s.

door ♦ See AT DEATH'S DOOR; AT ONE'S DOOR; BACK DOOR; BEAT A PATH TO SOMEONE'S DOOR; BEHIND CLOSED DOORS; CLOSE THE DOOR ON; DARKEN ONE'S DOOR; FOOT IN THE DOOR; KEEP THE WOLF FROM THE DOOR; LAY AT SOMEONE'S DOOR; LEAVE THE DOOR OPEN; LOCK THE BARN DOOR; NEXT DOOR TO; OPEN DOORS; OPEN THE DOOR TO; SEE SOMEONE OUT (TO THE DOOR); SHOW SOMEONE OUT (TO THE DOOR); SHOW SOMEONE THE DOOR; WOLF AT THE DOOR.

do or die Exert supreme effort because failure is close at hand, as in *Carol was going to set up the computer, do or die.* This hyperbolic expression in effect says one will not be deterred by any obstacle. [c. 1600]

doornail ♦ See DEAD AS A DOORNAIL.

doorstep ♦ See under AT ONE'S DOOR (ON ONE'S DOORSTEP).

door to door **1.** Calling at each house, apartment, store, etc. in an area, in order to deliver, sell, or ask for something. For example, *We were asked to go door to door to collect enough signatures.* [c.1900] **2.** Sent from a place of origin or pickup to a place of delivery. For example, *They quoted me a price for door to door, as well as a lower one if I would pick up the goods myself.* This usage is nearly always applied to a shipment of merchandise.

do out of Cheat or deprive someone of something. For example, *Jane tried to do me out of my inheritance but the lawyer wouldn't let her.* [Early 1800s]

do over Also, **do something over.** **1.** Also, **do over again.** Repeat something, as in *This setup won't work; I'll have to do it over again.* **2.** Redecorate, as in *We've decided to do over the living room.* [Early 1900s]

dope out **1.** Work or figure out, as in *I've been trying to dope out this new computer program.* [Slang;

c. 1900] **2.** Also, **dope up.** Use narcotics or psychotropic drugs, as in *They said the fraternity initiation may involve doping up.* The first term dates from the early 1900s, the variant from about 1970.

do's and don'ts Rules or customs concerning some activity, as in *It's important to know the do's and don'ts of diplomatic receptions.* This expression alludes to what one should and should not do or say. [c. 1900]

dose of one's own medicine Also, **taste of one's own medicine.** Repayment or retaliation, as in *It's time we gave them a dose of their own medicine and simply forget to call them back,* or *Joe was upset at being left out, but they were just giving him a taste of his own medicine.* [Late 1800s]

do someone ♦ Also see DO ONE.

do someone proud 1. Also, **do credit to someone.** Be a source of honor, distinction, or pride. For example, *She did us proud, handling the problem with such aplomb,* or *Your new title does you credit.* [Early 1800s] **2.** Treat someone or oneself generously or extravagantly, as in *You really did us proud with that banquet.* [Early 1800s]

do someone wrong Also, **do someone damage** or **harm.** Injure someone; be unfaithful or disloyal; act unjustly or unfairly toward someone. For example, *John's done me wrong, and I intend to tell him so,* or *She did him real damage when she started that rumor.* The first term dates from the late 1300s; the substitutions of *damage* and *harm* are newer. However, while these locutions are still current, a more common modern usage is to turn them into verbal phrases—that is, *wrong someone, harm someone, damage someone.*

do something over ♦ See DO OVER.

dot ♦ In addition to the idiom beginning with DOT, also see ON THE DOT; SIGN ON THE DOTTED LINE.

do tell A phrase used to express surprise about something, as in *Jane's getting married again? Do tell.* This expression does not necessarily ask the speaker to provide more details but merely expresses one's astonishment. [Colloquial; first half of 1800s] For a synonym, see YOU DON'T SAY.

do the dishes Wash the plates, glasses, and silverware used at a meal. For example, *If you walk the dog, I'll do the dishes.*

do the honors Act as a host or hostess, performing introductions and otherwise attending to guests. For example, *At home Mary leaves it to Bill to do the honors when they have guests.* This expression uses *honors* in the sense of "courtesy." [Mid-1600s]

do the spadework Make the preliminary preparations or do the preliminary research for something. For example, *The department head did all the spadework for this agreement.* This expression

transfers the heavy spading required to prepare for planting to other kinds of preparation. [c. 1900]

do the trick Also, **turn the trick.** Bring about a desired result, succeed. For example, *One more turn with the wrench should do the trick,* or *Bill wanted to finish all the errands in one day but he couldn't quite turn the trick.* The first expression dates from the early 1800s; the variant, from the first half of the 1900s, should not be confused with TURN A TRICK.

do time Serve a prison sentence, as in *Many of the gang members did time while they were still teenagers.* This expression originated as underworld slang and is now standard usage. [c. 1860]

dot the i's and cross the t's Be meticulous and precise, fill in all the particulars, as in *Laura had dotted all the i's and crossed the t's, so she wondered what she'd done wrong.* This expression presumably began as an admonition to schoolchildren to write carefully and is sometimes shortened. William Makepeace Thackeray had it in a magazine article (*Scribner's Magazine,* 1849): "I have . . . dotted the i's." [Mid-1800s]

double ♦ In addition to the idioms beginning with DOUBLE, also see LEAD A DOUBLE LIFE; ON THE DOUBLE; SEE DOUBLE.

double back Reverse one's course, go back the way one has come. For example, *The officer lost the suspect, who had doubled back on him.* This term, at first put simply as *to double,* is used largely to describe a way of evading pursuit. [Late 1500s]

double bill ♦ See DOUBLE FEATURE.

double cross A deliberate betrayal; violation of a promise or obligation, as in *They had planned a double cross, intending to keep all of the money for themselves.* This usage broadens the term's earlier sense in sports gambling, where it alluded to the duplicity of a contestant who breaks his word after illicitly promising to lose. Both usages gave rise to the verb *double-cross.* [Late 1800s]

double date A social engagement in which two couples go together, as in *They went on a double date with her brother and his girlfriend.* [c. 1920]

double Dutch 1. Language that cannot be understood, gibberish, as in *They might have been speaking double Dutch, for all I understood.* This usage dates from the 1870s (an earlier version, however, had it as **high Dutch**) and is heard less often today than the synonym DOUBLE TALK. **2.** A game of jump rope in which players jump over two ropes swung in a crisscross fashion.

double duty Fulfilling two functions at the same time, as in *Our pickup truck does double duty, since it is used for the business and for family outings.*

double feature Also, **double bill.** A program consisting of two full-length films shown for the price of a single ticket. For example, *It was a double feature and lasted five hours*, or *The women's conference had a double bill, first speakers from China and then visiting guests from the rest of the world*. This expression is occasionally loosely used for other paired events (as in the second example). [c. 1930]

double in brass Serve in two capacities, as in *In this company everyone is asked to double in brass occasionally*. This expression was originally used in the traveling circus, where, for example, a clown was also expected to play an instrument in the street parade. The original allusion, however, is to an instrumentalist who plays more than one instrument in an ensemble, a practice particularly common among players of brass instruments. [Late 1800s]

double life ♦ See LEAD A DOUBLE LIFE.

doublespeak ♦ See DOUBLE TALK, def. 2.

double standard A set of principles establishing different provisions for one group than another; also, specifically, allowing men more sexual freedom than women. For example, *She complained that her father had a double standard—her brothers were allowed to date, but she was not, even though she was older*. [Mid-1900s]

double take, do a Show a delayed reaction to an unusual remark or circumstance; also, look at something or someone again. For example, *He did a double take when his ex-wife appeared at his wedding*. [1930s]

double talk 1. Meaningless speech, gibberish mixing real and invented words. For example, *Some popular songs are actually based on double talk*. [1930s] 2. Also, **doublespeak**. Deliberately ambiguous and evasive language. For example, *I got tired of her double talk and demanded to know the true story*, or *His press secretary was very adept at doublespeak*. This usage dates from the late 1940s, and the variant from about 1950.

double up 1. Bend over suddenly, as in pain or laughter. For example, *She doubled up with a cramp*. [Late 1800s] 2. Share accommodations meant for one person, as in *The hotel ran out of rooms, so we had to double up*. [Late 1700s]

doubt ♦ See BEYOND A DOUBT; CAST DOUBT ON; GIVE THE BENEFIT OF THE DOUBT; NO DOUBT; SHADOW OF A DOUBT.

doubting Thomas One who is habitually doubtful. For example, *He was a doubting Thomas about the coming merger, not believing it would ever happen*. The term alludes to the disciple Thomas, who doubted Jesus's resurrection until he had firsthand evidence of it (John 20:24–29).

do unto others as you would have them do unto you Behave toward others as you would like to

have them behave toward you, as in *Of course I'll help him out; it's a case of do unto others, and I may be in the same boat one day*. This so-called **golden rule** is stated in just about every ancient writing about behavioral precepts (including the New Testament, Talmud, Koran, and the Analects of Confucius). Among the earliest appearances in English is Earl Rivers' translation of a saying of Socrates (*Dictes and Sayenges of the Philosophirs*, 1477): "Do to other as thou wouldst they should do to thee, and do to none other but as thou wouldst be done to." It is so well known that it is often shortened.

do up 1. Fasten up or put up; also, dress up. For example, *Let's do up all the gifts in matching paper*, or *Please help me do up the collar button*, or *Jane did up her hair for the dance*, or *The children were all done up in their best outfits*. [c. 1800] 2. **do something up brown** or **do it up brown**. Do something thoroughly or very well, as in *They really did it up brown for the dinner party*. The allusion here is unclear, but it may be to wrapping a package in brown paper. [Mid-1800s]

do well 1. Prosper, thrive, succeed, as in *He's done well in the market*. [c. 1300] 2. **do well to do something**. Fare better or act prudently by doing something, as in *She would do well to ask permission before she leaves*. [Late 1400s]

do with Put up or manage with, as in *I can do with very little sleep*. [Early 1800s] Also see CAN DO WITH; HAVE TO DO WITH.

do without Manage in spite of being without something. For example, *They will just have to do without a vacation this year*, or *There was no telephone in the cabin, but we soon learned to do without*. [Early 1700s]

down ♦ In addition to the idioms beginning with DOWN, also see BACK DOWN; BATTEN DOWN THE HATCHES; BEAR DOWN; BEAT DOWN; BE DOWN; BELT DOWN; BOG DOWN; BOIL DOWN TO; BREAK DOWN; BREATHE DOWN ONE'S NECK; BRING DOWN; BRING DOWN THE HOUSE; BUCKLE DOWN; BUILD DOWN; BURN DOWN; CALL DOWN; CAST DOWN; CAUGHT WITH ONE'S PANTS DOWN; CHOW DOWN; CLAMP DOWN; CLOSE DOWN; COME DOWN; COME DOWN ON; COME DOWN TO; COME DOWN WITH; COOL DOWN; COOL OFF (DOWN); COUNT DOWN; CRACK DOWN; CUT DOWN; DEEP DOWN; DIE AWAY (DOWN); DIG DOWN; DRAW DOWN; DRESSING DOWN; FACE DOWN; FALL DOWN; FLAG DOWN; GET DOWN TO BRASS TACKS; GO DOWN (DOWNHILL); GO DOWN THE LINE; HAND DOWN; HANDS DOWN; HIT SOMEONE WHEN DOWN; HOLD DOWN; IT'S ALL DOWNHILL; JUMP DOWN SOMEONE'S THROAT; KEEP DOWN; KNOCK BACK (DOWN); KNOCK DOWN DRAG OUT; KNOCK DOWN WITH A FEATHER; KNUCKLE DOWN;

LAY DOWN; LAY DOWN THE LAW; LEAD DOWN THE GARDEN PATH; LET DOWN EASY; LET ONE'S HAIR DOWN; LET SOMEONE DOWN; LET THE SIDE DOWN; LIE DOWN (ON THE JOB); LIVE DOWN; LOOK DOWN ON; MARK DOWN; MIX DOWN; MOW DOWN; NAIL DOWN; PIN DOWN; PIPE DOWN; PLAY DOWN; PLUNK DOWN; PULL DOWN; PUT DOWN; PUT DOWN ROOTS; PUT ONE'S FOOT DOWN; RAM DOWN SOMEONE'S THROAT; RING DOWN THE CURTAIN; RUB DOWN; RUN DOWN; SCALE DOWN; SELL DOWN THE RIVER; SEND DOWN; SET DOWN; SETTLE DOWN; SHAKE DOWN; SHOOT DOWN; SHOUT DOWN; SHUT DOWN; SIMMER DOWN; SIT DOWN; SLAP DOWN; SLOW DOWN; SPLASH DOWN; STAND DOWN; STARE DOWN; STEP DOWN; STRIKE DOWN; SUIT DOWN TO THE GROUND; TAKE DOWN; TAKE DOWN A NOTCH; TAKE LYING DOWN; TALK DOWN TO; TEAR DOWN; THE LOWDOWN ON; THROW DOWN THE GAUNTLET; THUMBS UP (DOWN); TIE DOWN; TONE DOWN; TOUCH DOWN; TRACK DOWN; TRADE DOWN; TURN DOWN; TURN UPSIDE DOWN; UPS AND DOWNS; VOTE DOWN; WASH DOWN; WATER DOWN; WEAR DOWN; WEIGH DOWN; WHEN IT COMES (DOWN) TO; WHEN THE CHIPS ARE DOWN; WIND DOWN; WRITE DOWN.

down and dirty 1. Vicious, not governed by rules of decency, as in *The candidates are getting down and dirty early in the campaign.* [Slang; early 1980s] 2. Very earthy, uninhibitedly sexual. For example, "L.A. club people rarely get down and dirty on a dance floor" (*The New Yorker,* May 21, 1990). [Late 1980s]

down and out Lacking funds or prospects; destitute, penniless. For example, *After losing his job, car, and home, he was completely down and out.* This term probably originated in boxing, where it alludes to the fighter who is knocked down and stays down for a given time, thereby losing the bout. [c. 1900] Also see DOWN FOR THE COUNT.

down cold, have Learn or accomplish perfectly. For example, *I have this song down cold.* The slangy use of *cold* for "completely" dates from the late 1800s and the phrase itself from about 1900.

down for the count Defeated, finished, doomed, as in *I doubt if he'll ever leave the hospital; his illness really has him down for the count.* This expression alludes to the losing boxer, unable to get to his feet before the umpire has counted to ten (*the count*). [1920s]

downhill all the way Also, **all downhill from here.** 1. Easy from this point, without obstacles the rest of the way. For example, *Once we had the basic design, it was downhill all the way.* 2. Deteriorating or declining from this point on, as in *When the cancer couldn't be removed, it was downhill all the way for him.* The usage therefore needs to be clarified by the context to indicate which of

these opposite meaning is intended. The figurative use of *downhill* dates from the late 1500s. Also see GO DOWNHILL.

down in the dumps Also, **down in the mouth.** Discouraged, depressed, or sad, as in *She's been down in the dumps ever since she lost the match,* or *What's wrong with him? He's so down in the mouth about everything.* The noun *dumps* has been used for "a state of depression" since the early 1500s, and *down in the mouth,* alluding to the downturned corners of the mouth as a sign of misery, dates from the mid-1600s.

down on Hostile or negative toward, ill-disposed to. For example, *All the reviewers were down on this play,* or *Ever since he was injured, he's been down on skiing.* [Mid-1800s] Also see DOWN ON ONE'S LUCK.

down one's alley ♦ See RIGHT UP ONE'S ALLEY.

down one's neck ♦ See BREATHE DOWN SOMEONE'S NECK.

down one's nose ♦ See LOOK DOWN ONE'S NOSE.

down on one's luck Afflicted by misfortune, as in *They've been down on their luck ever since they moved out West.* [Colloquial; second half of 1800s]

down someone's throat ♦ see JUMP DOWN SOMEONE'S THROAT; RAM DOWN SOMEONE'S THROAT.

down the drain On the way to being lost or wasted; disappearing. For example, *Buying new furniture when they can't take it with them is just pouring money down the drain,* or *During the Depression huge fortunes went down the drain.* This metaphoric term alludes to water going down a drain and being carried off. [Colloquial; c. 1920] For a synonym, see DOWN THE TUBES.

down the hatch Drink up, as in *"Down the hatch,"* said Bill, as they raised their glasses. This phrase, often used as a toast, employs *hatch* in the sense of "a trap door found on ships." [Slang; c. 1930]

down the line 1. Also, **all along the line.** All the way, throughout. For example, *We've found numerous errors down the line.* The first term dates from the mid-1900s, the variant from the second half of the 1800s. 2. Also, **down the road.** At a future point or end. For example, *Somewhere down the road I think he'll be elected to high office.* [Second half of 1900s]

down the pike ♦ See COME DOWN THE PIKE.

down the road ♦ See DOWN THE LINE, def. 2.

down the tubes Also, **down the tube.** Into a state of failure or ruin, as in *If he failed the test, his chances went down the tubes.* [Colloquial; 1960s] Also see DOWN THE DRAIN.

down to ♦ In addition to the idioms beginning with DOWN TO, also see COME DOWN TO; GET DOWN TO.

down to earth Back to reality. For example, *It's time the employees were brought down to earth concerning the budget.* P.G. Wodehouse had this idiom in *Very Good, Jeeves!* (1930): "I had for some little time been living . . . in another world. I now came down to earth with a bang." [Late 1920s] **2.** Also, **down-to-earth.** Realistic or interested in everyday occurrences, as in *She is a very down-to-earth person, not at all involved with the glamour of Hollywood.* [1930s]

down to size ♦ See CUT DOWN, def. 3.

down to the ground Thoroughly, completely, as in *This new job suits him down to the ground.* [Colloquial; second half of 1800s]

down to the wire To the last minute; to the very end. For example, *We're just about down to the wire with this project.* This term comes from horseracing, where it was long the practice to stretch a wire across and above the track at the finish line. It was extended to figurative use about 1900.

down with 1. Ill with, as in *He's down with the flu.* The *down* here alludes to being felled by illness. Also see COME DOWN WITH. **2.** Depose, do away with, as in *Down with the king!* This imperative dates from the early 1500s. **3.** Lower or put something down, as in *Down with the mainsail.* [Mid-1600s] **4. be** or **get down with.** Be close friends with, as in *I'm down with that crowd.* [Slang; late 1900s]

do you read me? Do you understand me? For example, *I'm sick of all these meetings—do you read me?* This phrase originally applied to messages received by radio or telephone. [c. 1930]

dozen ♦ See BAKER'S DOZEN; BY THE DOZEN; DAILY DOZEN; DIME A DOZEN; SIX OF ONE, HALF DOZEN OF THE OTHER.

doze off Fall into a light sleep, as in *Watching the ballet always made her doze off.* [Mid-1800s]

drab ♦ See DRIBS AND DRABS.

drag ♦ In addition to the idioms beginning with DRAG, also see A DRAG; IN DRAG; KNOCK DOWN, DRAG OUT; LOOK LIKE SOMETHING THE CAT DRAGGED IN; MAIN DRAG; WILD HORSES WOULDN'T DRAG ME.

drag in Introduce unnecessarily or forcefully. For example, *The defense tried to drag in every scrap of evidence, relevant or not.* [Mid-1800s] Also see LOOK LIKE SOMETHING THE CAT DRAGGED IN.

drag on Also, **drag out.** Prolong or be prolonged tediously. For example, *The speech dragged on for another hour,* or *He dragged out the story in an excruciating manner.* [First half of 1800s]

drag one's ass 1. Also, **drag ass** or **drag it** or **drag tail.** Leave, depart, as in *I'm dragging my ass out of this place,* or *It's really late, let's drag ass!* [Vulgar slang; 1920s] **2.** Also, **drag one's tail.** Move or act with deliberate slowness, as in *Hurry up, stop dragging your tail.* [Vulgar slang; c. 1930] For a more polite synonym, see DRAG ONE'S FEET.

drag one's feet Also, **drag one's heels.** Act or work with intentional slowness, deliberately hold back or delay. For example, *The British had been dragging their feet concerning a single European currency.* This metaphor for allowing one's feet to trail dates from the mid-1900s.

dragon lady A domineering or belligerent woman, as in *They called her the neighborhood dragon lady—she was always yelling at the children.* This slangy term was originally the name of a villainous Asian woman in Milton Caniff's popular cartoon strip *Terry and the Pirates* (1934–1973), which ran in many newspapers. It was transferred to more general use in the mid-1900s.

drag queen A male transvestite; also, a female impersonator. For example, *He was surprised to find out that Roxanne was actually a drag queen.* This term uses the slang noun *drag* in the sense of "female attire worn by a man" (a usage dating from about 1870; also see IN DRAG). [Offensive slang; c. 1940]

drain ♦ See BRAIN DRAIN; DOWN THE DRAIN.

draw ♦ In addition to the idioms beginning with DRAW, also see BACK TO THE DRAWING BOARD; BEAT TO IT (THE DRAW); DAGGERS DRAWN; LUCK OF THE DRAW; QUICK ON THE DRAW.

draw a bead on Take careful aim, as in *The debater drew a bead on his opponent.* This term, dating from about 1830, alludes to the bead on a revolver or rifle, that is, a small knob in the foresight. [c. 1930]

draw a blank Fail to find or remember something, as in *He looks familiar but I've drawn a blank on his name.* This expression alludes to drawing a lottery ticket with nothing on it (so one cannot win a prize). [Early 1800s]

draw a line between Also, **draw the line between.** Define a limit between two groups, courses of action, or the like. For example, *Legally it's important to draw a line between private and public enterprises,* or *We'll have to draw the line between our department's different jurisdictions.* This metaphoric idiom was first recorded in 1793. Also see DRAW THE LINE AT.

draw and quarter Punish severely, as in *Mom'll draw and quarter me if even one scratch appears on her new car.* This expression alludes to two brutal forms of execution practiced in the past. In one the victim was drawn by a horse to a gallows, hanged, and then cut into four pieces and scattered; in the other the victim was hanged, disemboweled while still alive (*drawn*), and then beheaded and dismembered. In both the victim was said to be **hanged, drawn, and quartered.** Today the term is usually used hyperbolically.

draw an inference Conclude, as in *From his wording, we can draw the inference that he disapproves.* This idiom is a long-winded way of saying *infer.* [Late 1600s]

draw a veil over Conceal or avoid discussing something; keep from public knowledge. For example, *Louise drew a veil over the accounting errors.* [c. 1700]

draw away 1. Pull off or back, as in *He drew his chair away from the fire.* **2.** Move ahead of competitors, as in *On the last lap Jim drew away from the other runners.*

draw back 1. Retreat, as in *The heckler drew back into the crowd to avoid being identified.* [c. 1300] **2.** Withdraw from an undertaking, as in *I was too deeply committed to draw back now.* [Mid-1800s]

draw blood Injure someone physically or emotionally. For example, *The bullet skimmed his shoulder and barely drew any blood,* or *That reviewer really knows how to draw blood.* This term alludes to drawing blood for diagnostic purposes.

draw down Deplete by consuming or spending, as in *The government worries about drawing down our oil reserves.*

drawer ♦ See TOP DRAWER.

draw fire Encounter criticism, as in *His recent article was bound to draw fire.* This expression uses the verb *draw* in the sense of "attract" or "provoke," and transfers *fire* in the sense of "gunfire" to a somewhat milder attack.

draw in Induce to enter or participate; inveigle. For example, *They tried to draw in as many new members as possible,* or *I refused to be drawn in to his scheme.* [Mid-1500s]

drawing board ♦ See BACK TO THE DRAWING BOARD.

drawing card A feature or event that attracts a large audience. For example, *This Italian tenor is always a good drawing card. Card* in this idiom refers to a large poster containing an advertisement for something, often some sort of entertainment. [Late 1800s]

draw in one's horns ♦ See PULL IN ONE'S HORNS.

draw in the reins Come to a halt, back down. For example, *During a recession, many businesses are forced to draw in the reins on expansion.* This expression transfers the means of stopping a horse to other kinds of restraint.

draw on 1. Approach, as in *As evening draws on, we'll make our way back to the house.* [First half of 1500s] **2.** Put on a piece of clothing, as in *She drew on her gloves.* [Early 1700s] **3.** Also, **draw upon.** Make use of something or someone. For example, *This dictionary draws on many different sources,* or

The chairman was good at drawing upon the various members for their expertise. [Mid-1600s]

draw out 1. Pull out, extract, remove, as in *She drew out her pen,* or *Let's draw some money out of the bank.* [c. 1300] **2.** Prolong, protract, as in *This meal was drawn out over four hours.* The related expression **long-drawn-out** means "greatly extended or protracted," as in *The dinner was a long-drawn-out affair.* [1500s] **3.** Induce to speak freely, as in *The teacher was good at drawing out the children.* [Late 1700s]

draw straws Also, **draw lots.** Decide by a lottery using straws of different lengths. For example, *Let's draw straws to see who will write the first draft.* The *lots* version dates from the 1400s, whereas *straws* dates from the 1800s. Both have replaced the still older **draw cuts.** Another variant is **draw the short straw,** meaning to be the one so selected for a particular task.

draw the curtain 1. Pull a curtain back or to one side to let in more light or to discover what is behind it. For example, *The sun was so pleasant I drew the curtains.* [c. 1500] **2.** Block or conceal something. For example, *Let's draw the curtain over this matter; no one needs to know more.* [c. 1500] Also see DRAW A VEIL.

draw the line at Refuse to go any further than, as in *I draw the line at giving them more money.* This expression alludes to a line drawn at a stopping point of some kind. [Late 1700s]

draw up 1. Compose or write out in a set form, as in *The lawyer drew up the contract.* [First half of 1600s] **2.** Arrange in order or formation, put in position, as in *The bandleader drew up his players,* or *The officer drew up the troops.* [c. 1600] **3.** Bring or come to a halt, as in *The car drew up to the curb.* [Early 1800s] **4. draw oneself up.** Assume an erect posture to express dignity or indignation. For example, *She drew herself up and protested.* [Mid-1800s]

dream ♦ In addition to the idioms beginning with DREAM, also see LIKE A DREAM; PIPE DREAM; SWEET DREAMS; WOULDN'T DREAM OF.

dream come true, a A wild fancy or hope that is realized. For example, *Winning a trip to Paris is a dream come true.*

dream up Invent, concoct, as in *Count on her to dream up some explanation for her absence.* This expression replaced the somewhat earlier **dream out.** [c. 1940]

dress down 1. Scold, reprimand, as in *The sergeant will dress down the entire unit.* In the 15th century the verb *dress* alone was used in the sense of "punish," *down* being added several centuries later. It also gave rise to the noun **dressing down** for punishment with blows or words. For example, *The*

teacher gave the girls a severe dressing down.
2. Wear informal clothes, as in *It's best to dress down for a party like a barbecue.* [Mid-1900s] For the antonym, see DRESS UP.

dressed to kill Also, **dressed to the nines.** Elaborately attired, as in *For the opening of the restaurant she was dressed to kill,* or *At the opera everyone was dressed to the nines.* The first of these hyperbolic expressions dates from the early 1800s and uses *kill* in the sense of "to a great or impressive degree." The phrase *to the nines* in the sense of "superlative" dates from the late 1700s and its original meaning has been lost, but the most likely theory is that it alludes to the fact that *nine,* the highest single-digit numeral, stands for "best." Also see GUSSIED UP.

dress up 1. Wear formal or elaborate clothes, as in *I love to dress up for a party.* [Late 1600s] For the antonym, see DRESS DOWN, def. 2. **2.** Put on a costume of some kind, as in *The children love dressing up as witches and goblins.* [Late 1800s] **3.** Adorn or disguise something in order to make it more interesting or appealing. For example, *She has a way of dressing up her account with fanciful details.* [Late 1600s]

dribs and drabs Bits and pieces, negligible amounts, as in *There's not much left, just some dribs and drabs of samples.* The noun *drib* is thought to be a shortening of *driblet,* for "drop" or "tiny quantity," dating from the early 1700s, whereas *drab* meaning "a small sum of money" dates from the early 1800s.

drift ♦ See GET THE DRIFT.

drink ♦ In addition to the idioms beginning with DRINK, also see DRIVE SOMEONE CRAZY (TO DRINK); EAT, DRINK, AND BE MERRY; INTO THE DRINK; MEAT AND DRINK TO; NURSE A DRINK.

drink like a fish Consume large amounts of alcoholic beverages, as in *He always drinks like a fish at holiday dinners.* The expression, first recorded in the mid-1600s, alludes to the way fish obtain oxygen, which causes them to be open-mouthed and appear to be constantly drinking.

drink to Salute a person or occasion with a toast, as in *Let's drink to our continued success.* [Early 1500s]

drive a hard bargain Be severe in negotiating a transaction, make an agreement to one's advantage. For example, *It's more than I planned to pay, but you drive a hard bargain.* This expression, first recorded in 1836, uses the verb *drive* in the sense of "forcefully carry through."

drive at Mean to do or say, as in *I don't understand what he's driving at.* Today this idiom, first recorded in 1579, is used mainly with the participle *driving.*

drive home Make clearly understood, make a point, as in *The network news programs drive home the fact that violence is part of urban life.* This expression uses the verb *drive* in the sense of "force by a blow or thrust" (as in driving a nail). Samuel Hieron used it in *Works* (1607): "That I may ... drive home the nail of this exhortation even to the head."

driven ♦ See PURE AS THE DRIVEN SNOW.

driver ♦ See BACKSEAT DRIVER; IN THE DRIVER'S SEAT.

drive someone crazy Also, **drive someone mad** or **bananas** or **bonkers** or **nuts** or **up the wall; drive someone to drink.** Greatly exasperate someone, annoy to distraction. For example, *His habitual lateness drives me crazy,* or *Apologizing over and over drives me bananas,* or *These slovenly workmen drive me up the wall,* or *Your nagging is driving me to drink.* All of these hyperbolic expressions describe a person's extreme frustration, supposedly to the point of insanity (*crazy, mad, nuts, bonkers,* and *bananas* all mean "insane"); *up the wall* alludes to climbing the walls to escape and *to drink* to imbibing alcohol to induce oblivion.

drive to drink ♦ See under DRIVE CRAZY.

driving force The impetus, power, or energy behind something in motion, as in *He was clearly the driving force in the new administration.* This term transfers the force that sets in motion an engine or vehicle to other enterprises. Ralph Waldo Emerson was among the first to use it figuratively (*English Traits,* 1856): "The ability of its journals is the driving force."

drop ♦ In addition to the idioms beginning with DROP, also see AT THE DROP OF A HAT; BOTTOM DROPS OUT OF; GET THE DROP ON; HEAR A PIN DROP; LET DROP; WAIT FOR THE OTHER SHOE TO DROP.

drop a bombshell Make an unexpected or shattering announcement. For example, *Bill dropped a bombshell when he said he was quitting.* This expression, which alludes to the destruction caused by a falling bomb, dates from World War I.

drop a brick Also, **drop a clanger.** Say something indiscreet, commit a social gaffe. For example, *John dropped a brick when he called her by his ex-wife's name.* [Slang; 1920s]

drop a dime Inform on or betray someone, as in *No one can cheat in this class — someone's bound to drop a dime and tell the teacher.* This expression, alluding to the ten-cent coin long used for making a telephone call, originated as underworld slang for phoning the police to inform on a criminal and occasionally is extended to any kind of betrayal. [1960s]

drop a line Correspond, write a short letter or note. For example, *I hope you'll drop me a line* *soon.* This idiom uses *line* in the sense of "a few words in writing," a usage first recorded in 1647.

drop back Step back, retreat. For example, *When it was time for a group picture, Mary dropped back.*

drop behind Fall short of the normal pace or progress. For example, *The teacher said Greg was dropping behind the class and needed extra help.*

drop by Also, **drop in** or **over**. Pay a brief, casual, and usually unannounced visit. For example, *I asked her to drop by whenever she was in the neighborhood,* or *Joan loves to have friends drop in,* or *We'd love to drop over but we haven't time on this trip.* The first term dates from the first half of the 1900s; *drop in* is from the mid-1600s and *drop over* from the late 1800s.

drop dead An expression of anger, rejection, or indignation toward someone. For example, *I should do all that work for you? Drop dead!* This rude imperative is usually hyperbolic, that is, the speaker is not literally asking someone to die on the spot. [c. 1930] Curiously, the adjective (and adverb) **drop-dead** is not at all insulting. Rather, it means "dazzling" or "awe-inspiring," as in *She wore a drop-dead outfit that all the other women admired.* This usage originated in slangy journalism in the 1960s.

drop in one's tracks Collapse from weariness or illness; also, die suddenly. For example, *I packed all day until I could have dropped in my tracks,* or *Grandfather's died; he just dropped in his tracks.* The phrase **in one's tracks** has meant "where one is at the moment," and by extension, "instantly," since the early 1800s.

drop in someone's lap Give to someone suddenly or without warning. What is given may be desirable, as in *I'm just going to drop the promotion in her lap this afternoon,* or it may be burdensome, as in *They simply dropped the employment problem in our laps.* The former usage dates from the mid-1500s, the latter from the mid-1900s.

drop in the bucket A very small quantity, especially one that is too small. For example, *These contributions are just a drop in the bucket; the new church wing will cost thousands more.* John Wycliffe's followers used this seemingly modern phrase in their translation of the Bible (1382), and it also appears in the 1611 King James version (Isaiah 40:15): "Behold, the nations are as a drop of a bucket, and are counted as the small dust of the balance."

drop like a hot potato ♦ See HOT POTATO.

drop like flies Rapidly collapse, die, or drop out, usually referring to a group rather than an individual. For example, *The words were so difficult that the spelling bee contestants were dropping like flies.*

The simile *like flies* has meant "in large numbers," as it does in this expression, since about 1600.

drop names Refer to important persons as acquaintances in order to impress the listener. For example, *Her habit of dropping names made everyone very skeptical about her veracity.* [Mid-1900s]

drop off 1. Fall asleep, as in *When I looked at Grandma, she had dropped off.* [Early 1800s] 2. Decrease; also, become less frequent. For example, *Sales have dropped off markedly,* or *Over the year her visits dropped off.* [Early 1800s] 3. Deliver, unload, as in *Bill dropped off the package at the office.* 4. Die, as in *He is so ill he could drop off any time.* [Early 1800s]

drop out Withdraw from participation in a group such as a school, club, or game; also, withdraw from society owing to disillusionment. For example, *He couldn't afford the membership dues and had to drop out,* or *She planned to drop out from college for a year.* [Late 1800s]

drop the ball Make an error; miss an opportunity. For example, *She really dropped the ball when she forgot to call back,* or *He dropped the ball, turning down their offer.* This expression comes from sports where a player who fails to catch a ball is charged with an error. Its use for more general kinds of mistakes dates from about 1950.

drown ♦ In addition to the idioms beginning with DROWN, also see LIKE A DROWNED RAT.

drown one's sorrows Drink liquor to escape one's unhappiness. For example, *After the divorce, she took to drowning her sorrows at the local bar.* The notion of drowning in drink dates from the late 1300s.

drown out Overwhelm with a louder sound, as in *Their cries were drowned out by the passing train.* [Early 1600s]

drug on the market A commodity whose supply greatly exceeds the demand for it. For example, *Now that asbestos is considered dangerous, asbestos tile is a drug on the market.* The use of the noun *drug* in the sense of "something overabundant" (as opposed to a medicine or narcotic) dates from the mid-1600s, but the first record of the full expression, put as **drug in the market,** dates only from the 1830s.

drum into someone's head ♦ See BEAT INTO SOMEONE'S HEAD.

drummer ♦ See MARCH TO A DIFFERENT BEAT (DRUMMER).

drum out Expel or dismiss publicly and in disgrace, as in *They drummed him out of the club.* This usage, which alludes to dismissal from a military service to the beat of a drum, began to be applied to civilian expulsions in the mid-1700s.

drum up 1. Bring about by persistent effort, as in *I'm trying to drum up more customers,* or *We have to drum up support for this amendment.* This expression alludes to making repeated drumbeats. [Mid-1800s] 2. Devise, invent, obtain, as in *He hoped to drum up an alibi.* [Mid-1800s]

drunk as a lord Also, **drunk as a fiddler** or **skunk; falling-down** or **roaring drunk.** Extremely intoxicated, as in *He came home drunk as a lord.* The three similes have survived numerous others. The first was considered proverbial by the mid-1600s and presumably alludes to the fact that noblemen drank more than commoners (because they could afford to). The *fiddler* alludes to the practice of plying musicians with alcohol (sometimes instead of pay), whereas *skunk,* dating from the early 1900s, was undoubtedly chosen for the rhyme. The most graphic variant alludes to someone too drunk to keep his or her balance, as in *He couldn't make it up the stairs; he was falling-down drunk.* And *roaring drunk,* alluding to being extremely noisy as well as intoxicated, was first recorded in 1697. Also see DEAD DRUNK.

druthers ♦ See HAVE ONE'S DRUTHERS.

dry ♦ In addition to the idioms beginning with DRY, also see CUT AND DRIED; HANG OUT TO DRY; HIGH AND DRY; KEEP ONE'S POWDER DRY; WELL'S RUN DRY.

dry as dust Dull, boring, as in *This text is dry as dust; it's putting me to sleep.* [c. 1500]

dry behind the ears ♦ See under WET BEHIND THE EARS.

dry out Undergo a cure for alcoholism, as in *After years of constant drinking, he realized that he needed to dry out.* [1960s]

dry run A trial exercise or rehearsal, as in *Regard this as a dry run for tonight's ceremony.* This term, using *dry* in the sense of "unproductive," was at first employed mainly in the military for simulated bombings in which no bombs were dropped. [c. 1940]

dry up 1. Gradually become unproductive, as in *After two collections of short stories, his ability to write fiction dried up.* Also see WELL'S RUN DRY. 2. Stop talking; also, cause to stop talking. For example, *Dry up! You've said enough.* [Slang; mid-1800s]

duck ♦ In addition to the idioms beginning with DUCK, also see DEAD DUCK; GET ONE'S DUCKS IN A ROW; LAME DUCK; LIKE WATER OFF A DUCK'S BACK; SITTING DUCK; TAKE TO (LIKE A DUCK TO WATER); UGLY DUCKLING.

duck out Leave hurriedly or secretly; evade responsibility. For example, *If I can I'll duck out of the office early,* or *He simply ducked out on his entire family.* This slangy expression originated in the late 1800s simply as *duck, out* being added about 1930.

duck soup An easily accomplished task or assignment, a cinch to succeed, as in *Fixing this car is going to be duck soup.* This expression gained currency as the title of a hilarious popular movie by the Marx Brothers (1933). The original allusion has been lost. [Early 1900s]

dudgeon ♦ See IN HIGH DUDGEON.

due ♦ In addition to the idiom beginning with DUE, also see GIVE CREDIT (WHERE IT'S DUE); GIVE SOMEONE HIS OR HER DUE; GIVE THE DEVIL HIS DUE; IN DUE COURSE; PAY ONE'S DUES; WITH ALL DUE RESPECT.

due to 1. Likely to, announced as, as in *Betty bought more of the stock, believing it was due to rise,* or *The play is due to open next week.* [Early 1900s] 2. Attributable to, because of, as in *Due to scanty rainfall, we may face a crop failure.* This usage has been criticized by some authorities, but today it is widely considered standard. [Early 1900s] Also see ON ACCOUNT OF. 3. Owing or payable to, as in *We must give our staff whatever vacation is due to them.*

dull ♦ In addition to the idiom beginning with DULL, also see NEVER A DULL MOMENT.

dull as dishwater Boring, tedious, as in *That lecture was dull as dishwater.* The original simile, **dull as ditchwater,** dating from the 1700s, alluded to the muddy water in roadside ditches. In the first half of the 1900s, perhaps through mispronunciation, it became *dishwater,* that is, the dingy, grayish water in which dirty dishes had soaked.

dumb bunny A stupid person, as in *She was a bit of a dumb bunny but very nice.* This expression implies some toleration or endearment of the person. [c. 1920]

dumps ♦ See DOWN IN THE DUMPS.

dust ♦ In addition to the idiom beginning with DUST, also see BITE THE DUST; DRY AS DUST; IN THE DUST; MAKE THE DUST FLY; SHAKE THE DUST FROM ONE'S FEET; THROW DUST IN SOMEONE'S EYES; WATCH MY DUST; WHEN THE DUST HAS SETTLED.

dust off 1. Restore to use. For example, *I've dusted off last year's menu for the party.* This usage alludes to cleaning and thereby renewing some object. [Mid-1900s] 2. Pitch a baseball dangerously close to the batter's head, as in *I'm sure he dusted him off on purpose.* [Slang; 1920s] 3. Finish off, kill; also, easily defeat. For example, *They vowed to dust off the old man,* or *We'll dust off this team in no time.* [Slang; c. 1940] 4. Thrash, beat up, as in *If he didn't hand over his wallet, they threatened to dust him off.* [Slang; 1920s]

Dutch ◆ In addition to the idioms beginning with DUTCH, also see BEAT ALL (THE DUTCH); DOUBLE DUTCH; IN DUTCH.

Dutch courage False courage acquired by drinking liquor, as in *He had a quick drink to give him Dutch courage.* This idiom alludes to the reputed heavy drinking of the Dutch, and was first referred to in Edmund Waller's *Instructions to a Painter* (1665): "The Dutch their wine, and all their brandy lose, Disarm'd of that from which their courage grows."

Dutch treat An outing or date in which each person pays his or her own expenses. For example, *Her parents agreed that she might date if it were a Dutch treat.* The related expression **go Dutch** means "to go on a date with each person paying their own way," as in *Students often elect to go Dutch.* The first term dates from about 1870, and the variant from the early 1900s.

Dutch uncle A stern, candid critic or adviser, as in *When I got in trouble with the teacher again, the principal talked to me like a Dutch uncle.* This expression, often put as **talk to one like a Dutch uncle,** presumably alludes to the sternness and sobriety attributed to the Dutch. [Early 1800s]

duty ◆ In addition to the idiom beginning with DUTY, also see ABOVE AND BEYOND (THE CALL OF DUTY); ACTIVE DUTY; DO ONE'S DUTY; DOUBLE DUTY; HEAVY DUTY; OFF DUTY; ON DUTY.

duty bound Obliged, as in *You're duty bound to help your little brother.* [c. 1900]

dwell on Also, **dwell upon.** Linger over; ponder, speak or write at length. For example, *Let's not dwell on this topic too long; we have a lot to cover today.* [c. 1500]

dying ◆ See under DIE.

e

each ◆ In addition to the idioms beginning with EACH, also see AT EACH OTHER'S THROATS; MADE FOR (EACH OTHER).

each and every one Also, **every last one; every single one.** Every individual in a group, as in *Each and every student must register by tomorrow,* or *I've graded every last one of the exams,* or *Every single one of his answers was wrong.* All of these phrases are generally used for emphasis. The first, although seemingly redundant, has replaced *all and every,* first recorded in 1502. The first variant dates from the late 1800s, and both it and the second are widely used. Also see EVERY TOM, DICK, AND HARRY. **Every mother's son** (late 1500s) and

every man Jack (mid-1800s) are earlier versions that refer only to males.

each other Also, **one another.** Each one the other, one the other, as in *The boys like each other,* or *The birds were fighting one another over the crumbs.* Both of these phrases indicate a reciprocal relationship or action between the subjects preceding (*the boys, the birds*). Formerly, many authorities held that *each other* should be confined to a relationship between two subjects only and *one another* used when there are more than two. Today most do not subscribe to this distinction, which was never strictly observed anyway. [Late 1300s] Also see AT EACH OTHER'S THROATS.

eager beaver An exceptionally zealous person, one who habitually takes on more tasks or works harder than others. For example, *Bill is a real eager beaver, always volunteering to stay late.* This expression became especially popular during World War II, applied to recruits anxious to impress their commanding officers by such behavior. [First half of 1900s]

eagle eye Unusually keen sight; also, keen intellectual vision. For example, *Antiques dealers have an eagle eye for valuable objects,* or *A good manager has an eagle eye for employee errors.* [Late 1500s]

ear ◆ In addition to the idioms beginning with EAR, also see ALL EARS; BELIEVE ONE'S EARS; BEND SOMEONE'S EAR; CAN'T MAKE A SILK PURSE OUT OF SOW'S EAR; COMING OUT OF ONE'S EARS; CUTE AS A BUTTON (BUG'S EAR); FALL ON DEAF EARS; FLEA IN ONE'S EAR; HAVE SOMEONE'S EAR; IN ONE EAR AND OUT THE OTHER; LEND ONE'S EAR; MUSIC TO ONE'S EARS; OUT ON ONE'S EAR; PIN SOMEONE'S EARS BACK; PLAY BY EAR; PRICK UP ONE'S EARS; PUT A BUG IN SOMEONE'S EAR; TURN A DEAF EAR; UP TO ONE'S EARS; WALLS HAVE EARS; WET BEHIND THE EARS.

early ◆ In addition to the idioms beginning with EARLY, also see BRIGHT AND EARLY.

early bird catches the worm Also, **early bird gets the worm.** One who arrives first has the best chance for success, as in *She's always the first one in line and does well at these auctions—the early bird catches the worm!* This proverbial saying, first recorded in English in 1605, is so familiar that it is often shortened to **early bird,** a term also used in the sense of "early riser," as in *You can call me at seven—I'm an early bird,* as well as "early diner" (*This restaurant has early-bird specials at lower prices*).

early on At an early stage in a process or course of events, as in *He started using computers very early on.* [1920s]

early to bed, early to rise (makes a man healthy, wealthy, and wise) Prudent habits pay off, as in

With *final exams coming, you'd best remember,* *early to bed and early to rise.* This ancient rhyming proverb, so familiar that it is often abbreviated as in the example, was long ascribed to Benjamin Franklin, who quoted it in this form in *Poor Richard's Almanack.* However, slightly different versions existed in English in the mid-1400s and in Latin even earlier.

earn ♦ In addition to the idioms beginning with EARN, also see PENNY SAVED IS A PENNY EARNED.

earnest ♦ See IN EARNEST.

earn one's keep Also, **be worth one's keep** or **salt.** Work well enough to deserve what one is paid, as in *Get a job—it's time you earned your keep,* or *With that batting average he's not worth his salt.* The *keep* in this phrase refers to "room and board," which in former times sometimes constituted the only reward for working (on a farm, in a home, etc.). The *salt* stands for "salary" and alludes to the ancient Roman practice of paying soldiers an allowance to buy salt. [First half of 1800s]

earn one's stripes Gain a position through hard work and accumulated experience. For example, *She'd earned her stripes by serving for years as the governor's secretary and personal aide.* This expression alludes to a military promotion or award, indicated by strips of chevron or braid added to the recipient's uniform and known as *stripes* since the early 1800s.

ears are burning, one's Be disconcerted by what one hears, especially when one is being talked about. For example, *Were your ears burning? Jim was telling us about your exploits.* Similarly, **make one's ears burn** means "to embarrass," as in *Mom's stories about us as babies make my ears burn.* These expressions allude to one's ears turning red from blushing.

earth ♦ See DOWN TO EARTH; ENDS OF THE EARTH; FOUR CORNERS OF THE EARTH; MOVE HEAVEN AND EARTH; NOT HAVE AN EARTHLY CHANCE; ON EARTH; RUN TO EARTH; SALT OF THE EARTH.

ear to the ground, have one's Also, **keep one's ear to the ground.** Be or remain well informed; be on the watch for new trends and information. For example, *She knew she'd succeed as a reporter if she kept her ear to the ground.* This graphic expression probably alludes to listening for distant hoofbeats by putting one's ear close to the ground. [Late 1800s]

ease ♦ In addition to the idioms beginning with EASE, also see AT EASE; ILL AT EASE. Also see under EASILY; EASY.

ease off 1. Also, **ease up.** Lessen in severity, relax; abate. For example, *I wish you'd ease off on Harold; he's doing the best he can,* or *The wind's eased up, so*

I think the storm is just about over. [Late 1800s] Also see LET UP. **2.** Fall away, gradually decrease, as in *The market's easing off, so we may get some stocks more cheaply.* [Late 1800s]

ease out Extract or remove someone or something gradually or gently. For example, *He carefully eased the car out of the garage,* or *We were trying to ease him out of office without a public scandal.* [Mid-1900s]

easier said than done Also, **more easily said than done.** Describing something more readily talked about than accomplished, as in *Keeping the cats off the sofa is easier said than done.* This expression also was put as **sooner** or **better said than done.** Today, the variant (*more easily*) is still heard less often than the original. [c. 1450]

easily ♦ See BREATHE EASY (EASILY); EASIER (MORE EASILY) SAID THAN DONE.

easy ♦ In addition to the idioms beginning with EASY, also see BREATHE EASY; FREE AND EASY; GET OFF (EASY); GO EASY; LET SOMEONE DOWN EASY; ON EASY STREET; TAKE IT EASY.

easy as pie Also, **easy as falling** or **rolling off a log.** Capable of being accomplished with no difficulty, as in *This crossword puzzle is easy as pie.* The first term presumably alludes to consuming pie (since making pie requires both effort and expertise). The variants most likely allude to standing on a log that is moving downstream, a feat in which falling off is a lot easier than remaining upright. Mark Twain had it in *A Connecticut Yankee in King Arthur's Court* (1889): "I could do it as easy as rolling off a log." The first colloquial term dates from the early 1900s, the colloquial variants from the 1830s. For a synonym, see PIECE OF CAKE.

easy come, easy go Readily won and readily lost, as in *Easy come, easy go—that's how it is for Mark when he plays the stock market.* This phrase states a truth known since ancient times and expressed in numerous proverbs with slightly different wording (**lightly come, lightly go; quickly come, quickly go**). The adverb *easy* was substituted in the early 1800s.

easy does it Go carefully, don't hurry, as in *That chest is heavy, so easy does it.* [1920s] Also see GO EASY.

easy money Money obtained readily, with little effort and, often, illegally. For example, *Winning the lottery—that's easy money!* or *I was wary of making easy money with the insider tips I'd been given.* [c. 1900] Also see FAST BUCK.

easy on the eyes Also, **easy to look at.** Attractive, beautiful, as in *That model is definitely easy on the eyes.* [Colloquial; c. 1900]

easy sledding Effortless progress, as in *It's easy sledding from here on.* This expression alludes to coasting smoothly down a hill and was first recorded as **smooth sledding** in 1898. Also see SMOOTH SAILING and the antonym TOUGH SLEDDING.

easy street, on A condition of financial security and comfort, as in *If he actually makes partner, he will be on easy street.* [Colloquial; c. 1900] Also see FAT CITY.

eat ◆ In addition to the idioms beginning with EAT, also see DOG EAT DOG; PROOF OF THE PUDDING IS IN THE EATING; WHAT'S EATING YOU.

eat and run Depart immediately after consuming a meal; also, leave in a hurry. For example, *Sorry, but I'll have to eat and run* or *I'll miss the last train*, or *Jim runs a meeting so efficiently that in effect it's eat and run.* [Colloquial; first half of 1900s]

eat away at Destroy gradually, erode; also, worry one constantly. For example, *The sea has been eating away at the outer banks for years*, or *The fact that he failed the test is eating away at him.* [Early 1800s]

eat crow Also, **eat dirt** or **humble pie**. Be forced to admit a humiliating mistake, as in *When the reporter got the facts all wrong, his editor made him eat crow.* The first term's origin has been lost, although a story relates that it involved a War of 1812 encounter in which a British officer made an American soldier eat part of a crow he had shot in British territory. Whether or not it is true, the fact remains that *crow* meat tastes terrible. The two variants originated in Britain. *Dirt* obviously tastes bad. And *humble pie* alludes to a pie made from *umbles*, a deer's undesirable innards (heart, liver, entrails). [Early 1800s] Also see EAT ONE'S WORDS.

eat high off the hog ◆ See HIGH OFF THE HOG.

eat in Have a meal at home, as in *Are we eating in tonight?* [Colloquial; second half of 1900s] Also see EAT OUT, def. 1.

eat like a bird Eat very little, as in *Jan is very thin—she eats like a bird.* This simile alludes to the mistaken impression that birds don't eat much (they actually do, relative to their size), and dates from the first half of the 1900s. An antonym is **eat like a horse**, dating from the early 1700s, and alluding to the tendency of horses to eat whatever food is available. For example, *I never have enough food for Ellen—she eats like a horse!*

eat one's cake and have it, too Also, **have one's cake and eat it, too**. Have a dual benefit, consume something and still possess it, as in *Doug was engaged to Ann and still dating Jane; he was trying to eat his cake and have it, too.* This metaphoric expression is often put negatively, as it already was

in John Heywood's proverb collection of 1546: "You cannot eat your cake and have your cake."

eat one's hat Declare one's certainty that something will not happen or is untrue. This hyperbolic expression almost always follows an if-clause, as in *If he's on time, I'll eat my hat,* that is, "I'll consume my headgear if I'm wrong." Charles Dickens used it in *Pickwick Papers* (1837): "If I knew as little of life as that, I'd eat my hat and swallow the buckle whole." [First half of 1800s]

eat one's heart out Feel bitter anguish, grief, worry, jealousy, or another strong negative emotion. For example, *She is still eating her heart out over being fired,* or *Eat your heart out—my new car is being delivered today.* This hyperbolic expression alludes to strong feelings gnawing at one's heart. [Late 1500s]

eat one's words Be forced to retract something one has said, as in *The incumbent won easily, so I had to eat my words.* This expression was already proverbial in John Ray's *English Proverbs* (1670). [Second half of 1500s]

eat out 1. Have a meal outside one's home, usually at a restaurant. For example, *We're almost out of groceries, so let's eat out tonight.* [Second half of 1900s] For the antonym, see EAT IN. 2. **eat someone out** Also, **eat someone up**. Rebuke or scold someone sharply, as in *He was always eating out the kids,* or *Why are you eating me up? I haven't done anything wrong.* This slangy synonym for CHEW OUT probably originated as a euphemism for EAT SOMEONE'S ASS OUT. It dates from the 1940s, the variant from the 1840s. Also see the subsequent entries beginning with EAT OUT.

eat out of someone's hand Be manipulated or dominated by another, be submissive, as in *He had the press eating out of his hand.* This metaphoric expression alludes to a tame animal eating out of one's hand. [Early 1900s]

eat shit Also, **eat crap**. Submit to degrading treatment, as in *He refused to eat shit from the coach.* James T. Farrell had the one term in *Grandeur* (1930), "They don't eat nobody's crap," and Mario Puzo the other in *Dark Arena* (1955), "He'd eaten shit all week." [Vulgar slang; second half of 1800s]

eat someone alive Overwhelm or defeat someone thoroughly, make short work of someone. For example, *Lacking experience in manufacturing, he was eaten alive by his competitors.* This slangy hyperbole dates from the early 1900s. A newer slangy variant is **eat someone's lunch,** dating from the mid-1900s. For example, *It was a decisive victory; he ate the incumbent's lunch.*

eat someone out ◆ See EAT OUT, def. 2.

eat someone out of house and home Eat so much as to deplete someone's resources, as in *The kids are eating her out of house and home.* This hyperbole was well known by the time Shakespeare used it (*2 Henry IV,* 2:1): "He hath eaten me out of house and home."

eat someone's ass out Rebuke or scold harshly, as in *Watch it or the sergeant will eat your ass out.* This expression became widespread especially in the armed forces. [Vulgar slang; c. 1940]

eat someone's lunch ♦ See under EAT SOMEONE ALIVE.

eat someone up ♦ See EAT OUT, def. 2.

eat up 1. Consume completely, as in *No television until you eat up your dinner,* or *This quarter's expenses have eaten up all my spare cash.* The literal use (first example) dates from the early 1500s, the figurative from the early 1600s. 2. Enjoy avidly, as in *She simply eats up the publicity.* [Late 1800s] 3. Believe unquestioningly, be gullible, as in *He'll eat up whatever the broker tells him.* [Slang; early 1900s] 4. Defeat completely, as in *This new fighter just eats up every opponent.* [Slang; c. 1830] 5. See EAT OUT, def. 2.

ebb ♦ In addition to the idiom beginning with EBB, also see AT A LOW EBB.

ebb and flow A decline and increase, constant fluctuations. For example, *He was fascinated by the ebb and flow of the Church's influence over the centuries.* This expression alludes to the inward and outward movement of ocean tides. [Late 1500s]

edge ♦ In addition to the idioms beginning with EDGE, also see CUTTING EDGE; GET A WORD IN EDGE-WISE; HAVE THE EDGE ON; ON EDGE; ON THE EDGE; OVER THE EDGE; SET ONE'S TEETH ON EDGE; TAKE THE EDGE OFF; THIN EDGE OF THE WEDGE.

edge in Work into a limited space or time; move gradually or hesitantly; insert. For example, *The train was crowded but I managed to edge in,* or *Everyone was talking at once and he barely managed to edge in a word.* [Mid-1600s] Also see GET A WORD IN EDGEWISE.

edge out Surpass or defeat by a small margin, as in *She edged out her opponent on the home stretch.* [Late 1800s]

edgewise ♦ See GET A WORD IN EDGEWISE.

educated guess, an A speculation based on past experience or knowledge, as in *I'm not sure how much meat we need to feed twelve, but I'll make an educated guess and say six pounds.* [Mid-1900s]

eel ♦ See SLIPPERY AS AN EEL.

effect ♦ See IN EFFECT; INTO EFFECT; TAKE EFFECT; TO THAT EFFECT.

effigy ♦ See IN EFFIGY.

effort ♦ See ALL OUT (EFFORT); LAST-DITCH EFFORT.

egg ♦ In addition to the idioms beginning with EGG, also see BAD EGG; GOOD EGG; GOOSE EGG; KILL THE GOOSE THAT LAYS THE GOLDEN EGGS; LAY AN EGG; PUT ALL ONE'S EGGS IN ONE BASKET; WALK ON EGGS.

egg in your beer A bonus, something for nothing, as in *What do you want—egg in your beer?* This expression dates from about 1940 and became widespread during World War II. The origin is unknown, since adding egg to beer does not improve the taste.

egg on Incite, urge ahead, provoke, as in *Jack is always egging me on to drive faster,* or *Seemingly quiet, Margo actually eggs on Donald to quarrel with his staff.* This expression has nothing to do with hen's eggs but comes from an Old Norse word, *eggja,* "to edge." Both *edge on* and *egg on* were used interchangeably, but today the latter is preferred. [c. 1200]

egg on one's face, have Look foolish or be embarrassed, as in *If you ask any more personal questions, you'll end up with egg on your face.* This expression possibly alludes to dissatisfied audiences pelting performers with raw eggs. [Colloquial; mid-1900s]

ego trip Behavior or activities undertaken mainly out of vanity or for self-gratification. For example, *She's really on an ego trip, trying out for the lead.* [1960s]

eight ♦ See BEHIND THE EIGHT BALL.

eke out 1. Supplement, make last, as in *The survivors eked out their food and water until they were rescued.* [Late 1500s] 2. Get with great difficulty or effort, as in *The soil was terrible but they managed to eke out a living by rotating crops.* [Early 1800s]

elbow ♦ In addition to the idioms beginning with ELBOW, also see AT SOMEONE'S ELBOW; CROOK ONE'S ELBOW; OUT AT THE ELBOWS; RUB ELBOWS WITH.

elbow grease Strenuous physical effort, as in *You'll have to use some elbow grease to get the house painted in time.* This term alludes to vigorous use of one's arm in cleaning, polishing, or the like. It soon was extended to any kind of hard work, and Anthony Trollope used it still more figuratively (*Thackeray,* 1874): "Forethought is the elbowgrease which a novelist . . . requires." [First half of 1600s]

elbow room Enough space to move about, as in *Two hundred on the stage? There won't be any elbow room.* This term alludes to having enough room to extend one's elbows. [Late 1500s]

element ♦ See BRAVE THE ELEMENTS; IN ONE'S ELEMENT.

elephant ♦ See SEE THE ELEPHANT; WHITE ELEPHANT.

eleventh hour The latest possible time, as in *We turned in our report at the eleventh hour.* This term is thought to allude to the parable of the laborers (Matthew 20: 1–16), in which those workers hired at the eleventh hour of a twelve-hour working day were paid the same amount as those who began in the first hour. [Early 1800s]

else ♦ See IN SOMEONE'S (ELSE'S) SHOES; OR ELSE; SOMETHING ELSE; SOMETHING ELSE AGAIN.

embarrassment of riches An overabundance of something, too much of a good thing, as in *All four of them have their own cars but there's no room in the driveway—an embarrassment of riches.* This term originated in 1738 as John Ozell's translation of a French play, *L'Embarras des richesses* (1726).

empty ♦ In addition to the idioms beginning with EMPTY, also see GLASS IS HALF FULL (HALF EMPTY); RUNNING ON EMPTY.

empty calories Food that has little or no nutritional value. For example, *Snacking on beer and potato chips makes for a lot of empty calories.* [1960s]

empty nest The home of parents whose children have grown up and moved out. For example, *Now that they had an empty nest, Jim and June opened a bed-and-breakfast.* This expression, alluding to a nest from which baby birds have flown, gave rise to such related ones as **empty-nester,** for a parent whose children had moved out, and **empty-nest syndrome,** for the state of mind of parents whose children had left. [c. 1970]

empty suit An unimportant person; also, a phony. For example, *Don't pay any attention to him—he's just an empty suit,* or *She acts as though she knows what she's doing, but she's really an empty suit.* This graphic expression calls up the image of an empty suit of clothes. [c. 1970]

enchilada ♦ See BIG CHEESE (ENCHILADA); WHOLE BALL OF WAX (ENCHILADA).

end ♦ In addition to the idioms beginning with END, also see ALL'S WELL THAT ENDS WELL; AT LOOSE ENDS; AT ONE'S WIT'S END; BE-ALL AND END-ALL; BEGINNING OF THE END; BITTER END; BURN THE CANDLE AT BOTH ENDS; CAN'T SEE BEYOND THE END OF ONE'S NOSE; COME TO AN END; DEAD END; GO OFF THE DEEP END; HAIR STAND ON END; HOLD ONE'S END UP; IN THE END; LIGHT AT THE END OF THE TUNNEL; MAKE ENDS MEET; NEVER HEAR THE END OF; ODDS AND ENDS; ON END; ON THE RECEIVING END; PLAY BOTH ENDS AGAINST THE MIDDLE; PUT AN END TO; REAR END; SHORT END (OF THE STICK); TAIL END; WRONG END OF THE STICK.

endangered species A group threatened with extinction or destruction. For example, *Workers willing to put in overtime without extra pay are an endangered species,* or *With the new budget cuts, public television has become an endangered species.* This expression, originally referring to species of plants or animals in danger of dying out, began in the 1980s to be extended to anything or anyone becoming rare.

end game The final stage of some process, as in *The book discussed the diplomatic end game resulting in the treaty.* This term, dating from about 1880, comes from chess, where it denotes the stage of a game when most of the pieces have been removed from the board. In the mid-1900s it began to be transferred to other activities.

end in itself A purpose or goal desired for its own sake (rather than to attain something else). For example, *For me, writing books is an end in itself; they don't really make that much money.* This expression employs the noun *end* in the sense of "final cause or purpose," a usage dating from the early 1500s.

end justifies the means, the A good outcome excuses any wrongs committed to attain it. For example, *He's campaigning with illegal funds on the theory that if he wins the election the end will justify the means,* or *The officer tricked her into admitting her guilt—the end sometimes justifies the means.* This proverbial (and controversial) observation dates from ancient times, but in English it was first recorded only in 1583.

end of one's rope, at the Also, **at the end of one's tether.** At the limits of one's resources, abilities, endurance, or patience. For example, *If that loan doesn't come through, we'll be at the end of our rope,* or *The workmen are driving me crazy; I'm at the end of my tether.* This expression alludes to a tied-up animal that can graze only as far as the rope (or tether) permits. [Late 1600s]

end of the line Also, **end of the road.** The conclusion or final outcome. For example, *The editorial pointed out that it was the end of the line for the President; he'd never be reelected,* or *It was obviously the end of the road for this television series.* This idiom alludes to the point where a road or line stops. [c. 1900]

end run Evasive action, as in *The new department head was making an end run around the old hands who opposed her appointment.* This term comes from American football, where it denotes an offensive play in which the ball carrier runs around one end of the opposing team's line. [Mid-1900s]

ends of the earth, the The utmost limit, as in *She would go to the ends of the earth for him.* This usage was once literal (referring to the farthest reaches of the planet) but now is used only figuratively.

end to end 1. In a row with the ends touching. For example, *The logs were laid end to end.* [Mid-1800s] 2. **from end to end.** Throughout the length of something, as in *We hiked the Appalachian Trail from end to end.* [First half of 1600s]

end up Arrive at, result in, finish. For example, *He thought he'd end up living in the city,* or *We don't know how Nancy will end up.* [First half of 1900s] Also see WIND UP.

English ♦ See BODY ENGLISH; IN PLAIN ENGLISH.

en masse In one group or body; all together. For example, *The activists marched en masse to the capitol.* This French term, with exactly the same meaning, was adopted into English about 1800.

enough ♦ In addition to the idioms beginning with ENOUGH, also see FAIR ENOUGH; HAD ENOUGH; LEAVE WELL ENOUGH ALONE; NOT ENOUGH ROOM TO SWING A CAT; SURE ENOUGH; (ENOUGH) TO WAKE THE DEAD.

enough is enough One should be satisfied; stop, there should be no more. For example, *No more speeches—enough is enough,* or as Robert Southey put it (*The Doctor,* 1834): "As for money, enough is enough; no man can enjoy more." This expression already appeared in John Heywood's proverb collection of 1546 and is often used as an interjection (first example).

enough rope, give someone Allow someone to continue on a course and then suffer its consequences. For example, *The auditor knew something was wrong but decided to give the chief accountant enough rope.* This expression, a shortening of **enough rope to hang oneself,** was already proverbial in John Ray's *English Proverbs* (1678).

enough said Say no more; also, I agree completely. For example, *She didn't even bother to call—enough said?* or *You'll bring the wine—enough said.* [Mid-1800s]

enough to sink a ship Also, **enough to sink a battleship.** A more than sufficient amount, as in *They brought enough food to sink a ship.* [Colloquial; mid-1900s]

en route On or along the way, as in *We'll pick up Dan en route to the restaurant,* or *We can finish our discussion en route.* This French term was adopted into English in the late 1700s.

enter into 1. Participate in, take an active role or interest in, as in *We had to think twice before we entered into these negotiations.* [Late 1700s] 2. Become party to (a contract), bind oneself, as in *The nations entered into a new agreement.* [First half of 1500s] 3. Become a component, form a part of, as in *Finances soon entered into the discussion.* [Early 1700s] 4. Also, **go into.** Consider, investigate, as in *The report entered into the effect of high interest rates,* or *Let's not go into that.* [Mid-1500s]

enter on Also, **enter upon.** Set out, begin, as in *We are entering on a new era,* or *They entered upon the most difficult part of the research.* [Early 1600s]

enter one's mind Also, **enter one's head.** Occur to one, come into one's consciousness. This expression is most often used negatively, as in *It didn't enter my mind that he'd want to join us,* or *Run for office? It never entered my head.*

enterprise ♦ See FREE ENTERPRISE.

enter the lists Also, **enter the fray.** Engage in a fight or competition, as in *He said he'd be willing to enter the lists well before the primaries,* or *Whenever people disagreed, she was eager to enter the fray.* The first term uses the noun *lists* in the sense of "a barrier around the arena enclosing medieval jousting tournaments" and was being used figuratively by the late 1500s. The variant uses *fray* in the sense of "a noisy skirmish or battle," a usage from the late 1300s.

envy ♦ See GREEN WITH ENVY.

equal In addition to the idioms beginning with EQUAL, also see OTHER THINGS BEING EQUAL; SEPARATE BUT EQUAL.

equal to Adequate or fit in ability or extent, as in *I'm not sure I'm equal to the task.* [Late 1600s] Also see FEEL UP TO; UP TO.

errand ♦ See FOOL'S ERRAND; RUN AN ERRAND.

error ♦ See COMEDY OF ERRORS; TRIAL AND ERROR.

escape ♦ In addition to the idiom beginning with ESCAPE, also see NARROW ESCAPE.

escape notice Elude attention or observation, as in *It must have escaped the editor's notice so I'll write again.* [c. 1700]

etched in stone ♦ See CAST IN STONE.

eternal triangle A relationship involving three lovers, such as two women involved with one man or two men with one woman. For example, *The plot of the murder mystery revolved around the eternal triangle of a husband, wife, and another woman.* [c. 1900]

eve ♦ See ON THE EVE OF.

even ♦ In addition to the idioms beginning with EVEN, also see BREAK EVEN; GET EVEN; NEVER GIVE A SUCKER AN EVEN BREAK; ON AN EVEN KEEL.

evening ♦ See GOOD DAY (EVENING).

even money Equal odds that something will occur, as in *It's even money that he'll get the contract.* The term comes from gambling, where it signifies equal odds in a bet. [Late 1800s]

even so Nevertheless, still, that being the case. For example, *That may be true, but even so we will investigate further,* or *She claimed it contained no garlic, but even so I could taste it.* [Late 1300s]

even-steven Exactly equal; also, with nothing due or owed on either side. For example, *I've paid it all back, so now we're even-steven.* This rhyming phrase is used as an intensive for *even*. [Mid-1800s]

event ♦ See BLESSED EVENT; IN ANY CASE (EVENT); IN CASE (IN THE EVENT); IN THE UNLIKELY EVENT.

ever ♦ In addition to the idiom beginning with EVER, also see HARDLY EVER; LIVE HAPPILY EVER AFTER.

ever and again Now and then, occasionally. For example, *We visit her ever and again.* This phrase has largely replaced the earlier **ever and anon**, dating from the late 1500s, but is less common than EVERY NOW AND THEN. [Late 1800s]

every ♦ In addition to the idioms beginning with EVERY, also see AT EVERY TURN; EACH AND EVERY; FINGER IN THE (EVERY) PIE; LIVING SOUL, EVERY; NOOK AND CRANNY, EVERY.

every bit 1. All of something, as in *Eat every bit of that broccoli!* **2.** In all ways, equally. For example, *He is every bit as smart as his sister.* Also see EVERY LITTLE BIT HELPS.

every cloud has a silver lining ♦ see SILVER LINING.

every dog has its day Even the lowliest will sometimes come to the fore, as in *They may not listen to me now, but just wait, every dog has its day.* This proverbial saying alludes to the lowly status dogs once held. [Mid-1500s] Also see HAD ITS DAY.

every inch Completely, wholly, as in *He was every inch a leader,* or *I had to argue this case every inch of the way.* [Early 1400s]

every last one ♦ See EACH AND EVERY.

every little bit helps Any contribution can be useful, as in *He can only give us one day, but every little bit helps.* This expression, with slightly different wording (*everything helps*), dates from the late 1500s.

every man for himself Each individual puts his or her own interests foremost. For example, *In this company no one helps anyone—it's every man for himself.* In Chaucer's day this dictum was stated approvingly, meaning "if you don't look out for yourself, no one else will," but today such selfishness is usually censured. Despite the wording, the term applies to either sex.

every man has his price Any person can be bribed in some way, as in *They had trouble persuading her to join, but when they offered her a car—well, every man has his price.* This cynical observation was first recorded in 1734 but may be much older, and it applies to either sex.

every minute counts Also, **every moment counts**. Time is of the essence. For example, *Hurry up with those tools—every minute counts,* or *In performing surgery every moment counts.* This idiom uses *count* in the sense of "to enter into the reckoning" (and hence be important).

every nook and cranny ♦ See NOOK AND CRANNY.

every now and then Also, **every now and again; every once in a while; every so often.** Occasionally, from time to time; also, periodically. For example, *Every now and then I long for a piece of chocolate,* or *We take long walks every now and again,* or *Every once in a while he'll call,* or *Every so often she washes the car.* The first term dates from the first half of the 1700s, the last from the mid-1900s. Also see FROM TIME TO TIME; ONCE IN A WHILE.

everyone ♦ See entries under EVERY MAN.

every other Every second one in a series, as in *I'm supposed to take this pill every other day.* [c. 1400]

every single one ♦ See EACH AND EVERY.

every so often ♦ See EVERY NOW AND THEN.

everything ♦ In addition to the idiom beginning with EVERYTHING, also see HOLD EVERYTHING.

everything but the kitchen sink Also, **everything under the sun.** Including just about everything, whether appropriate or not. For example, *Our new car has every feature—everything but the kitchen sink.* This hyperbolic term may date from the early 1900s but only became widespread in the mid-1900s. The variant employs *under the sun* in the sense of "everything on earth," a usage dating from about A.D. 1000.

every time one turns around Very often; too often. For example, *Every time I turn around he's asking for more money,* or *Something in this house breaks down every time I turn around.*

every Tom, Dick, and Harry Also, **every mother's son; every man Jack.** Everyone, all ordinary individuals, as in *This model should appeal to every Tom, Dick, and Harry.* The use of masculine names in this way dates from Shakespeare's time (he used *Tom, Dick, and Francis* in *1 Henry IV*), but the current one dates from the early 1800s. The two variants are largely British usage but occasionally are used in America. The first is recorded as early as 1583, whereas the second dates from the first half of the 1800s.

everywhere ♦ See ALL OVER (EVERYWHERE); HERE, THERE, AND EVERYWHERE.

every which way In all directions, as in *Papers were blowing every which way.* [Colloquial; mid-1800s]

evidence ♦ See IN EVIDENCE; MUCH IN EVIDENCE.

evil eye The power to cause injury or misfortune, as in *The tomatoes died shortly after planting—I must have an evil eye.* The source of this expression is the ancient superstitious belief that some individuals could inflict harm on others simply by looking at them. Today the term is generally used figuratively or ironically, as above, and also in the

example   126

form **give someone the evil eye,** which means "glare malevolently at someone." For example, *Helen gave his cat the evil eye, hoping it would stay out of her garden.* [Late 1300s]

example ◆ See FOR EXAMPLE; MAKE AN EXAMPLE OF; SET AN EXAMPLE.

except for Also, **with the exception of.** Other than, were it not for. For example, *Except for Jack, everyone came to the party,* or *With the exception of the weather, everything went extremely well.* [c. 1600]

exception ◆ In addition to the idioms beginning with EXCEPTION, also see EXCEPT FOR (WITH THE EXCEPTION OF); MAKE AN EXCEPTION; TAKE EXCEPTION TO.

exception proves the rule, the An instance that does not obey a rule shows that the rule exists. For example, *John's much shorter than average but excels at basketball—the exception proves the rule.* This seemingly paradoxical phrase is the converse of the older idea that every rule has an exception. [Mid-1600s]

excess ◆ See CARRY TOO FAR (TO EXCESS); IN EXCESS OF.

exchange ◆ See IN EXCHANGE.

excuse me 1. Also, **I beg your pardon, pardon me.** Forgive me, as in *Excuse me, please let me pass,* or *Pardon me for asking,* or *I beg your pardon, I don't think so.* These phrases are used as an apology for interrupting a conversation, bumping into someone, asking a speaker to repeat something, politely disagreeing with something said, and so on. The first dates from about 1600, the first variant from about 1800, the second from the mid-1700s. 2. Also, **excuse oneself.** Allow or ask to leave or be released from an obligation. For example, *Please excuse me, I have to leave now,* or *I asked the judge to excuse me from jury duty.* [1920s]

exert oneself Put oneself to strenuous effort, as in *We exerted ourselves mightily to raise funds.* [First half of 1700s]

exhibition ◆ See MAKE AN EXHIBITION OF ONESELF.

expect ◆ See WHEN LEAST EXPECTED.

expedition ◆ See FISHING EXPEDITION.

expense ◆ See AT THE EXPENSE OF; GO TO THE TROUBLE (EXPENSE); MONEY (EXPENSE) IS NO OBJECT.

explain away Dismiss or minimize the importance of something, especially something detrimental. For example, "His words were taken down, and though he tried to explain them away, he was sent to the Tower" (Thomas Macaulay, *The History of England,* 1855). [c. 1700]

explain oneself 1. Clarify what one has said or done, as in *If you have a few minutes, I'll try to explain myself.* [First half of 1600s] 2. Demand or give an explanation or excuse for something

wrong one has done. For example, *You're three hours late—can you explain yourself?*

express oneself Reveal or portray one's feelings or views through speech, writing, some form of art, or behavior. For example, *I find it hard to express myself in Italian,* or *Helen expresses herself through her painting,* or *Teenagers often express themselves through their attire, haircuts, and the like.* [Mid-1500s]

extend credit to Also, **extend someone credit.** Allow a purchase on credit; also, permit someone to owe money. For example, *The store is closing your charge account; they won't extend credit to you any more,* or *The normal procedure is to extend you credit for three months, and after that we charge interest.* This idiom uses the verb *extend* in the sense of "offer" or "provide," a usage dating from the mid-1500s.

extent ◆ See TO SOME DEGREE (EXTENT).

extenuating circumstances A situation or condition that provides an excuse for an action, as in *Although Nancy missed three crucial rehearsals, there were extenuating circumstances, so she was not dismissed.* This expression was originally legal terminology, denoting circumstances that partly excuse a crime and therefore call for less punishment or damages. [c. 1600]

eye ◆ In addition to the idioms beginning with EYE, also see ALL EYES; APPLE OF ONE'S EYE; BELIEVE ONE'S EARS (EYES); BIRD'S-EYE VIEW; BLACK EYE; BRIGHT-EYED AND BUSHY-TAILED; CATCH SOMEONE'S EYE; CLOSE ONE'S EYES; CRY ONE'S EYES OUT; EAGLE EYE; EASY ON THE EYES; EVIL EYE; FEAST ONE'S EYES ON; GIVE SOMEONE THE ONCE-OVER (EYE); GREEN-EYED MONSTER; HAVE AN EYE FOR; HAVE ONE'S EYE ON; HIT BETWEEN THE EYES; HIT THE BULL'S-EYE; IN A PIG'S EYE; IN ONE'S MIND'S EYE; IN THE EYE OF THE WIND; IN THE PUBLIC EYE; IN THE TWINKLING OF AN EYE; KEEP AN EYE ON; KEEP AN EYE OUT; KEEP A WEATHER EYE; KEEP ONE'S EYE ON THE BALL; KEEP ONE'S EYES OPEN; LAY EYES ON; LOOK CROSS-EYED AT; LOOK SOMEONE IN THE FACE (EYE); MAKE EYES AT; MORE THAN MEETS THE EYE; MY EYE; NAKED EYE; ONE EYE ON; OPEN ONE'S EYES; OUT OF THE CORNER OF ONE'S EYE; PRIVATE EYE; PULL THE WOOL OVER SOMEONE'S EYES; RUN ONE'S EYES OVER; SEE EYE TO EYE; SEE WITH HALF AN EYE; SIGHT FOR SORE EYES; STARS IN ONE'S EYES; THROW DUST IN SOMEONE'S EYES; TURN A BLIND EYE; UP TO ONE'S EARS (EYES); WITH AN EYE TO; WITH ONE'S EYES OPEN; WITHOUT BATTING AN EYE.

eyeball to eyeball Face to face; especially, about to begin a conflict. For example, *We are eyeball to eyeball with the enemy,* or *In the playoffs we go eyeball to eyeball with the Yankees,* or *In the first debate our candidate's going eyeball to eyeball with his* *opponent.* This term was originally used only in a military context but later entered civilian language, particularly in political or sports confrontations. [Colloquial; c. 1950]

eyebrow ♦ See CAUSE RAISED EYEBROWS.

eye for an eye, an Punishment in which the offender suffers what the victim has suffered, exact retribution, as in *Joe believed in an eye for an eye; stealing his client would have to be avenged.* This idiom is a quotation from the Bible, which has "Life shall go for life, eye for eye, tooth for tooth" (Deuteronomy 19:21); the idea is contradicted in the New Testament (see TURN THE OTHER CHEEK).

eye opener, an 1. A startling or shocking revelation, as in *The first sentence of his speech was a real eye opener.* This expression alludes to widening one's eyes with surprise. [Mid-1800s] 2. A strong alcoholic drink taken early in the morning, as in *After a late night and little sleep, he generally needed an eye opener to jolt him awake.* This usage alludes to the alleged wakening effect of such a beverage. [Early 1800s]

eyes are bigger than one's stomach, one's Someone wants more than he or she can handle, as in *He's thinking of acquiring a third business, but we think his eyes are bigger than his stomach.* This expression alludes to someone taking more food than he or she can digest. [Late 1500s]

eyes in the back of one's head, have Be more aware of what is happening than is generally realized. For example, *Even when he's away he always knows what the staff are doing—he has eyes in the back of his head,* or *With such hostile colleagues she needs to have eyes in the back of her head.* [Mid-1500s]

eyes open, with ♦ See KEEP ONE'S EYES OPEN; OPEN ONE'S EYES.

eyeteeth ♦ See GIVE ONE'S EYETEETH.

eye to, with an With a view of, with a plan for. For example, *With an eye to expansion, we'll have to be careful with expenses,* or *She always operates with an eye to the future.* [Late 1300s]

eye to eye ♦ See SEE EYE TO EYE.

eye to the main chance, have an Look out for one's own best interest. For example, *Tom is watching the company's progress very closely; he always has an eye to the main chance.* [c. 1600]

f

face ♦ In addition to the idioms beginning with FACE, also see AT FACE VALUE; BLUE IN THE FACE; BRAVE FACE; DO AN ABOUT-FACE; EGG ON ONE'S FACE; FEED ONE'S FACE; FLY IN THE FACE OF; HIDE ONE'S FACE; IN SOMEONE'S FACE; IN THE FACE OF; IN YOUR FACE; KEEP A STRAIGHT FACE; LAUGH OUT OF THE OTHER SIDE OF ONE'S MOUTH (FACE); LONG FACE; LOOK SOMEONE IN THE FACE; LOSE FACE; MAKE A FACE; ON THE FACE OF IT; PLAIN AS DAY (THE NOSE ON YOUR FACE); POKER FACE; PUT ONE'S FACE ON; RED IN THE FACE; SAVE FACE; SET ONE'S FACE AGAINST; SHOW ONE'S FACE; SLAP IN THE FACE; STARE IN THE FACE; STUFF ONE'S FACE; TALK ONE'S ARM OFF (UNTIL BLUE IN THE FACE); THROW IN SOMEONE'S FACE; TO SOMEONE'S FACE.

face down 1. With the upper surface put down, as in *Please put these papers face down.* This usage appears to come from card-playing. [First half of 1600s] The antonym, "with the upper surface uppermost," is **face up.** 2. Overcome, intimidate, or browbeat someone in a bold confrontation. This verbal expression dates from the 16th century. Shakespeare used it in *The Comedy of Errors* (3:1): "Here's a villain that would face me down."

face it ♦ See FACE UP TO.

face the music Confront unpleasantness, especially the consequences of one's errors. For example, *When the check bounced, he had to face the music.* The precise allusion in this expression has been lost. Most authorities believe it refers to a theater's pit orchestra, which an actor must face when he faces what can be a hostile audience, but some hold it comes from the military, where a formal dismissal in disgrace would be accompanied by band music. [Second half of 1800s] Also see FACE UP TO.

face to face 1. In each other's presence, opposite one another; in direct communication. For example, *The two chairmen sat face to face,* or *It's time his parents met the teacher face to face.* [Mid-1300s] 2. Confronting each other, as in *We were face to face with death during the avalanche.* [Late 1800s]

face up ♦ See under FACE DOWN.

face up to Also, **face it.** Confront or accept an unpleasant or difficult situation. For example, *Jane had to face up to the possibility of being fired,* or *Face it—you were wrong.* [Late 1700s] Also see FACE THE MUSIC.

face value ♦ See AT FACE VALUE.

face with Confront, as in *When he was faced with the evidence, he admitted it.* [Late 1500s]

fact ♦ In addition to the idiom beginning with FACT, also see AFTER THE FACT; HARD FACTS; IN FACT; IS THAT A FACT; MATTER OF FACT.

factor in Figure in, include as a basic element. For example, *In preparing the schedule we factored in vacation and sick days.* This term comes from mathematics. [Mid-1900s]

facts of life Knowledge of sexual reproduction, as in *Some people feel that the facts of life should not be taught in school.* [Late 1800s] Also see BIRDS AND THE BEES.

fade away ◆ See FADE OUT, def. 2.

fade out 1. Gradually disappear or become inaudible; also, cause to disappear or become inaudible gradually. For example, *He let the final chord fade out completely before he played the next movement.* The antonym is **fade in**, "to appear gradually or become audible," as in *The images on the screen faded in until they could be seen clearly.* These terms originated in the motion-picture and broadcasting industries, where they apply to images and sounds. [c. 1915] 2. Also, **fade away.** Quietly depart, as in "Florence Scape, Fanny Scape and their mother faded away to Boulogne" (William Makepeace Thackeray, *Vanity Fair,* 1848). [Mid-1800s]

fail ◆ See WITHOUT FAIL; WORDS FAIL ME.

faint ◆ See DAMN WITH FAINT PRAISE.

fair ◆ In addition to the idioms beginning with FAIR, also see ALL'S FAIR IN LOVE AND WAR; PLAY FAIR; TURNABOUT IS FAIR PLAY.

fair and square Just and honest, as in *He won the race fair and square.* This redundant expression—*fair* and *square* mean essentially the same thing—probably owes its long life to its rhyme. [Early 1600s]

fair enough That's reasonable; I agree. For example, *I'll wait just one more day.—Fair enough, you've been very patient.* [Colloquial; early 1900s]

fair game A legitimate target for attack or ridicule. For example, *On his talk show, authors are considered fair game.* This expression alludes to hunting. [Early 1800s]

fair-haired boy A favorite, a person who is given special treatment. For example, *Today the attorney general is the governor's fair-haired boy.* This term alludes to the preference of blond ("fair") hair over dark hair. [Late 1800s]

fair play Conformity to established rules; upright conduct and equitable conditions. For example, *The coach insists on fair play.* Shakespeare used this idiom in *King John* (5:2): "According to the fair play of the world, let me have audience." [Late 1500s] Also see TURNABOUT IS FAIR PLAY.

fair sex Girls or women, as in *Many women would object to being called the fair sex nowadays.* This euphemism uses *fair* in the sense of "physically beautiful" and is probably dying out. [Mid-1600s]

fair shake, a An equitable bargain or opportunity, as in *You can always count on the boss to give his crew a fair shake.* This expression probably alludes to the shaking of dice. [Colloquial; early 1800s]

fair to middling Mediocre, pretty good, so-so, as in *I asked them how they liked their new home and John answered, "Fair to middling."* This phrase, often a replay to an inquiry about one's health, business, or the like, is redundant, since *fair* and *middling* both mean "moderately good." [Mid-1800s] Also see CAN'T COMPLAIN.

fair-weather friend A person who is dependable in good times but is not in times of trouble. For example, *You can't rely on Sarah—she's strictly a fair-weather friend.* This expression likens *fair weather* to good times. [Early 1700s]

fairy ◆ In addition to the idiom beginning with FAIRY, also see TOOTH FAIRY.

fairy godmother A generous benefactor, as in *An anonymous fairy godmother donated the money for the new organ.* This expression alludes to a stock character in fairy tales such as *Cinderella,* who gives unexpected and much needed assistance. [Late 1800s]

faith ◆ See ACT OF FAITH; IN BAD (GOOD) FAITH; IN FAITH; LEAP OF FAITH; ON FAITH; PIN ONE'S HOPES (FAITH) ON.

fall ◆ In addition to the idioms beginning with FALL, also see BOTTOM DROPS (FALLS) OUT; BREAK ONE'S FALL; EASY AS PIE (FALLING OFF A LOG); LET DROP (FALL); LET THE CHIPS FALL WHERE THEY MAY; RIDE FOR A FALL; TAKE THE FALL.

fall all over oneself Also, **fall over backwards.** Make an inordinate effort to do something, try very hard or eagerly. For example, *They fell all over themselves to be helpful, but only got in the way,* or *She fell over backwards trying to please her boss, but it got her nowhere.* The first of these hyperbolic expressions dates from the late 1800s, the second from the mid-1900s.

fall apart Collapse, break down, either physically or mentally and emotionally. For example, *This chair is about to fall apart,* or *After his wife died, he fell apart.* For synonyms for the latter usage, see COME APART AT THE SEAMS; GO TO PIECES.

fall asleep Go to sleep; also, cease paying attention. For example, *As soon as the lights were dimmed he fell asleep,* or *His lectures are so dull that I fall asleep.* The literal usage, which uses the verb *fall* in the sense of "succumb," dates from about 1300; the figurative is several centuries newer. Also see ASLEEP AT THE SWITCH.

fall away 1. Also, **fall off.** Withdraw one's friendship, support, or allegiance. For example, *After the divorce, her friends slowly fell away.* [Early 1500s] 2. Also, **fall off.** Gradually decline in size or strength, as in *The breeze slowly fell away,* or, as Shakespeare put it (*King Lear,* 1:2): "Love cools, friendship falls off, Brothers divide." [Early 1500s] **3.** Drift from an established faith, cause, or principles. For example, *I fell away from the Catholic Church when I was a teenager.* [Early 1500s]

fall back 1. Give ground, retreat, as in *The troops fell back before the relentless enemy assault,* or *He stuck to his argument, refusing to fall back.* [c. 1600] **2.** Recede, as in *The waves fell back from the shore.* [c. 1800]

fall back on Also, **fall back upon.** Rely on, have recourse to, as in *I fall back on old friends in time of need,* or *When he lost his job he had to fall back upon his savings.* [Mid-1800s]

fall behind Also, **get behind. 1.** Lag, fail to keep up, as in *You really must keep up with the others; if you fall behind you could get lost.* [First half of 1500s] **2.** Be financially in arrears, as in *He fell behind in his payments.* [Mid-1800s]

fall between the cracks Also, **fall through the cracks** or **between two stools.** Be neglected or overlooked; also, not fit either of two alternatives. For example, *Please make sure that either our department or yours deals with this account, lest it fall between the cracks,* or *Trying to be both teacher and parent, she fell between two stools.* The variant using *stools,* with its image of a person falling to the ground between two chairs instead of sitting down on one or the other, was already a proverb in ancient times; in English it was first recorded about 1390.

fall by the wayside Fail to continue, drop out, as in *At first she did well on the tour, but with all the pressure she soon fell by the wayside.* This phrase appeared in William Tyndale's translation of the New Testament (1526; Luke 8:5).

fall down Fail to meet expectations; lag in performance. For example, *It was disappointing to see him fall down on the job.* This expression transfers a literal drop to a figurative one. [Second half of 1800s]

fall flat Fail, prove to be ineffective, as in *His jokes nearly always fell flat—no one ever laughed at them.* [First half of 1800s]

fall for 1. Become attracted to, as in *I was sure he'd fall for her.* [Slang; early 1900s] **2.** Be deceived or swindled by, as in *He fell for the con artist's scheme and lost a great deal of money.* [Slang; early 1900s]

fall from grace Experience reduced status or prestige, cease to be held in favor, as in *The whole department has fallen from grace and may well be dissolved entirely.* This expression originally alluded to losing the favor of God. Today it is also used more loosely, as in the example. [Late 1300s]

fall guy 1. A scapegoat, one who is blamed for the actions of others. For example, *He refused to be the*

fall guy for his colleagues. This expression uses *fall* in the sense of "consequences" or "blame," which originated in prison slang. [Slang; early 1900s] Also see TAKE THE FALL. **2.** An easy victim, one who is readily duped. For example, *His friends had marked him as the fall guy—they knew he would believe their ruse.* [Slang; early 1900s]

fall in 1. Take one's place in formation or in the ranks, as in *The sergeant ordered the troops to fall in.* A related expression is **fall into,** as in *They all fell into their places.* [Early 1600s] Also see FALL INTO. **2.** Sink inward, cave in, as in *The snow was so heavy that we feared the roof would fall in.* [Early 1700s] Also see under DROP IN; the subsequent idioms beginning with FALL IN; FALL INTO.

falling down drunk ‣ See under DRUNK AS A LORD.

fall in line Also, **fall into line.** Adhere to established rules or predetermined courses of action. For example, *This idea falls in line with the entire agenda,* or *It wasn't easy to get all the tenants to fall into line concerning the rent hike.* A related term is **bring into line,** meaning "to make someone fit established rules," as in *It was her job to bring her class into line with the others.* These terms employ *line* in the sense of "alignment," a usage dating from about 1500.

fall in love Become enamored. This expression may be used either literally, as in *John and Mary fell in love on their first date,* or hyperbolically, as in *I fell in love with that antique chest.* [First half of 1500s]

fall in place Also, **fall into place.** Fit well; also, become organized. For example, *With the last witness's testimony, the entire sequence of events fell in place,* or *When the architect's plans were complete, the construction schedule fell into place.* This idiom uses *place* in the sense of "proper position," a usage dating from the mid-1500s.

fall into 1. Enter or engage in, be drawn into, as in *I told Dad not to fall into conversation with them.* [Late 1400s] **2.** See FALL IN, def. 1. **3.** Be naturally divisible into, as in *These students fall into three categories.* [First half of 1600s] **4. fall into error** or **sin.** Be drawn into bad behavior, as in *I fell into error when I started spending time with the wrong crowd.* This usage, like FALL FROM GRACE, originally alluded to religious concerns. It is now used less often and more loosely. [Late 1100s] **5. fall into a trap.** Be deceived, unknowingly become involved in something. For example, *By admitting I had free time, I fell into the trap of having to help him with his work.* Also see under FALL IN; FALL IN LINE; FALL IN PLACE.

fall in with 1. Agree with, be in harmony with, as in *We happily fell in with his plans.* [First half of 1600s] **2.** Associate with, become acquainted with (especially by chance), as in *On the cruise we fell in with a couple from Boston.* [Late 1500s]

fall off ♦ See FALL AWAY.

fall off the wagon ♦ See OFF THE WAGON.

fall on Also, **fall upon**. 1. Attack suddenly and viciously, as in *They fell on the guards and overpowered them.* [c. 1400] 2. Meet with, encounter, as in *They fell on hard times.* [Late 1500s] 3. Find by chance, discover, as in *We fell upon the idea last Saturday night.* [Mid-1600s] 4. Be the responsibility or duty of someone, as in *It fell on Clara to support the entire family.* [Mid-1800s] Also see the subsequent idioms beginning with FALL ON.

fall on deaf ears Be ignored or disregarded, as in *Any advice we give them about remodeling seems to fall on deaf ears.* This expression transfers physical inability to hear to someone who does not want to listen. [1400s] Also see TURN A DEAF EAR.

fall on one's face Also, **fall flat on one's face**. Make a blunder or error of judgment, as in *Holly fell on her face whenever she forecast earnings,* or *That weatherman keeps falling flat on his face with his predictions.* This term, first recorded in 1614, originally had the literal meaning of "prostrate oneself in reverence." The present colloquial usage, however, transfers a physical fall to various kinds of bungling.

fall on one's feet Also, **land on one's feet**. Overcome difficulties, be restored to a sound or stable condition. For example, *Don't worry about Joe's losing his job two years in a row—he always falls on his feet,* or *The company went bankrupt, but the following year it was restructured and landed on its feet.* This term alludes to the cat and its remarkable ability to land on its paws after falling from a great height. [Mid-1800s]

fall out 1. Leave one's place in military ranks, as in *After inspection they were ordered to fall out.* [First half of 1800s] 2. Also, **have a falling-out**. Disagree, quarrel, as in *The brothers fell out over their inheritance,* or *They no longer speak—they had a falling-out some years ago.* [First half of 1500s] 3. Happen, result, as in *Let us know how it falls out in the end.* [Second half of 1500s]

fall over ♦ See under FALL ALL OVER ONESELF.

fall short Prove inadequate or insufficient. For example, *His skills fell short of the required standard.* [Late 1500s]

fall through Fail, miscarry, as in *The proposed amendment fell through,* or *I hope our plans won't fall through.* [Late 1700s]

fall through the cracks ♦ See FALL BETWEEN THE CRACKS.

fall to Energetically begin an activity, set to work, as in *As soon as they had the right tools, they fell to*

work on the house. This expression is also often used to mean "begin to eat." Charles Dickens so used it in *American Notes* (1842): "We fall-to upon these dainties." [Late 1500s]

fall under 1. Be classified as, as in *These scores fall under choral music.* [Mid-1400s] 2. Be subject to, as in *This precinct falls under the city's jurisdiction.* [Second half of 1500s]

false ♦ In addition to the idioms beginning with FALSE, also see LULL INTO (FALSE SENSE OF SECURITY); PLAY FALSE; RING FALSE.

false alarm A warning signal that is groundless, made either by mistake or as a deliberate deception. For example, *The rumor that we were all going to get fired was just a false alarm,* or *Setting off a false alarm is a criminal offense.* This expression, first recorded in 1579, today is often used for a report of a nonexistent fire.

false colors Pretense, misrepresentation, or hypocrisy; deceptive statements or actions. For example, *She's sailing under false colors—she claims to be a Republican, but endorses Democratic legislation.* This term alludes to the practice of pirate ships **sailing under false colors**—that is, running a particular flag specifically to lure another vessel close enough to be captured. [Late 1600s]

false start A wrong beginning, as in *After several false starts she finally managed to write the first chapter.* The term originated in racing, where it refers to beginning a race before the starting signal has been given. The expression was soon transferred to other kinds of failed beginning. [Early 1800s]

false step A stumble or blunder, as in *Making a down payment without securing a mortgage was clearly a false step.* This term transfers physical stumbling or tripping to other enterprises. [c. 1700]

familiar ♦ See HAVE A FAMILIAR RING.

familiarity breeds contempt Long experience of someone or something can make one so aware of the faults as to be scornful. For example, *Ten years at the same job and now he hates it—familiarity breeds contempt.* The idea is much older, but the first recorded use of this expression was in Chaucer's *Tale of Melibee* (c. 1386).

family ♦ See IN A FAMILY WAY; IN THE FAMILY; RUN IN THE BLOOD (FAMILY).

famine ♦ See FEAST OR FAMINE.

famous last words A phrase used to express disbelief, rejection, or self-deprecation. For example, *They said we'd get an extra bonus at Christmas—famous last words!* or *This book is bound to make the best-seller list—famous last words!* This expression alludes to grandiose statements about human affairs that prove to be untrue, such as

"This is the war to end all wars," or "We must make the world safe for democracy." [Late 1930s]

fan ♦ In addition to the idiom beginning with FAN, also see SHIT WILL HIT THE FAN.

fancy ♦ See FLIGHT OF FANCY; FOOTLOOSE AND FANCY-FREE; TAKE A FANCY TO; TICKLE ONE'S FANCY.

fan the flames Intensify or stir up feelings; exacerbate an explosive situation. For example, *She already found him attractive, but his letters really fanned the flames,* or *His speech fanned the flames of racial dissension.*

far ♦ In addition to the idioms beginning with FAR, also see AS FAR AS; AS FAR AS POSSIBLE; AS FAR AS THAT GOES; BY FAR; CARRY TOO FAR; FEW AND FAR BETWEEN; GO FAR; GO SO FAR AS TO; GO TOO FAR; SO FAR; SO FAR SO GOOD.

far afield Wide-ranging, at a distance, as in *I started out identifying wild mushrooms, but since then I've gone far afield in other branches of botany.* [c. 1400]

far and away ♦ See under BY FAR.

far and near Everywhere, at a distance and nearby. For example, *People came from far and near to see the Pope.* [c. A.D. 1000]

far and wide For a great distance, over a large area. For example, *They searched far and wide for the lost child,* or *The message went out far and wide.* [c. A.D. 900]

far be it from one to One will not do or say something. This disclaimer may be true or false, depending on the speaker or the context. For example, *Far be it from him to disagree* may be used as a straightforward indication that he is unlikely to disagree, or it may be used ironically to indicate that he actually disagrees quite strongly. [Late 1300s] For a phrase used similarly, see GOD FORBID.

far cry from, a 1. Also, **far from.** Very different from, as in *Thinking someone is stupid is a far cry from saying so,* or *Far from being neutral, Jack regarded him as his friend.* The first term may have originated as calculating the distance of one's enemies by shouting, but it has been used figuratively (signifying difference rather than distance) since the early 1800s. The variant, dating from the mid-1600s, is most often used with a participle, as in the example (*being*). 2. **far from it.** An interjection expressing strong denial, as in *I thought you were bored.—Far from it, I enjoyed the evening.*

far from ♦ See under FAR CRY FROM.

far gone Extremely advanced, referring to some progressive action or condition. For example, *These trees are too far gone to be saved,* or *He's had a lot to drink and is too far gone to drive himself home.* [Mid-1500s]

farm ♦ In addition to the idiom beginning with FARM, also see BUY IT (THE FARM).

farm out Assign something to an outsider; subcontract something. For example, *The contractor was so busy he had to farm out two jobs to a colleague,* or *When their mother was hospitalized, the children had to be farmed out to the nearest relatives.* This term originally referred to letting or leasing land. Today it usually refers to subcontracting work or the care of a dependent to another. In baseball it means "to assign a player to a lesser (*farm*) league," as opposed to a BIG LEAGUE. [Mid-1600s]

far out 1. Unusual or eccentric; very advanced. For example, *Painting blindfolded, that's far out,* or *Her child-rearing theories are far out.* 2. An interjection meaning "great" or "cool," as in *All he could say when he won the lottery was "Far out!"* Originally a slang term for daringly creative jazz, this expression has been applied to other art forms and undertakings. [Colloquial; mid-1900s]

farther ♦ See CAN'T SEE BEYOND (FARTHER THAN) THE END OF ONE'S NOSE.

fashion ♦ See AFTER A FASHION; IN FASHION.

fast ♦ In addition to the idioms beginning with FAST, also see GET NOWHERE (FAST); HARD AND FAST; PULL A FAST ONE; STAND ONE'S GROUND (FAST); THICK AND FAST.

fast and furious Swiftly, intensely and energetically, as in *The storm moved in fast and furious,* or *The sale was going fast and furious, attracting large crowds.* This phrase is also often applied to intense gaiety, as when it was first recorded in Robert Burn's poem "Tam o' Shanter" (1793): "The mirth and fun grew fast and furious."

fast and loose ♦ See PLAY FAST AND LOOSE.

fast buck Money made quickly and easily and, often, dishonestly. For example, *He's all right, but his partner is just out for a fast buck.* This expression gave rise to **fast-buck artist** for an individual, especially a swindler, intent on making money quickly. [Slang; mid-1900s] Also see EASY MONEY.

fast lane Also, **life in the fast lane.** A lifestyle that involves free spending and self-indulgence, and sometimes also dissipation and danger. For example, *They're finding that life in the fast lane can be very stressful.* This term alludes to the highway express lane used by faster vehicles to pass slower ones. [Colloquial; c. 1970] Also see FAST TRACK.

fast track A situation involving high pressure, competition, and, especially, rapid success or advancement. For example, *He was definitely on a fast track, becoming a partner after only five years in the firm,* or *This company was on the fast track in software development.* This term alludes to a dry, hard horse track that enables horses to run at high speeds. [Colloquial; mid-1960s] Also see FAST LANE.

fat ♦ In addition to the idioms beginning with FAT, also see CHEW THE FAT; KILL THE FATTED CALF.

fat cat A wealthy and privileged person, as in *This neighborhood, with its million-dollar estates, is full of fat cats.* This term originally meant "a rich contributor to a political campaign," and while this usage persists, it now is often applied more broadly, as in the example. [Colloquial; 1920s]

fat chance Very little or no possibility, as in *A fat chance he has of coming in first,* or *You think they'll get married? Fat chance!* A related expression is a **fat lot,** meaning "very little or none at all," as in *A fat lot of good it will do her.* The first of these slangy sarcastic usages dates from the early 1900s, the second from the 1890s.

fat city Also, **Fat City.** A condition or circumstance marked by considerable prosperity or having a superior advantage. For example, *With that new job she'll be in fat city.* [Slang; 1960s] Also see EASY STREET.

fate ♦ In addition to the idioms beginning with FATE, also see SEAL ONE'S FATE; TEMPT FATE.

fate worse than death, a A highly undesirable occurrence, a misfortune, as in *Dean thinks driving daily during rush hour is a fate worse than death.* Formerly applied quite seriously to a woman's loss of virginity, this idiom today is used hyperbolically and far more loosely. [1600s]

fat farm A clinic or resort where people go to lose weight, as in *She spends all her vacations at a fat farm but it hasn't helped so far.* This is a somewhat derisive term for such an establishment. [Colloquial; 1960s]

father ♦ See LIKE FATHER, LIKE SON.

fat is in the fire, the A course of action with inevitable bad consequences has begun; there's trouble ahead. For example, *Now the fat's in the fire—the boss arrived early and will see we haven't even started work.* This expression, with its allusion to fat dropping into a fire and causing a burst of flames, was already a proverb in John Heywood's 1546 collection.

fat lot ♦ See under FAT CHANCE.

fat of the land, the The best or richest of anything, as in *The tiny upper class lived off the fat of the land while many of the poor were starving.* This expression alludes to *fat* in the sense of "the best or richest part." The Bible has it as *eat the fat of the land* (Genesis 45:18).

fatted calf ♦ See KILL THE FATTED CALF.

fault ♦ See AT FAULT; FIND FAULT; TO A FAULT.

favor ♦ See CURRY FAVOR; IN FAVOR OF; IN FAVOR WITH; IN ONE'S FAVOR; OUT OF FAVOR; RETURN THE COMPLIMENT (FAVOR).

favorite son A person valued by his or her hometown or organization for his or her achievements, usually political, as in *Mary hoped they would treat her as a favorite son and nominate her for state senator.* This term was originally employed for a candidate nominated for office by his own locality. Today this usage may ignore gender, as in the example. [c. 1780]

fear ♦ See FOOLS RUSH IN WHERE ANGELS FEAR TO TREAD; FOR FEAR OF; NEVER FEAR; PUT THE FEAR OF GOD IN.

feast one's eyes on Be delighted or gratified by the sight of, as in *I'm feasting my eyes on this new sculpture—it's wonderful.* This metaphoric expression may have been originated by Shakespeare, who used it in Sonnet 47: "With my love's picture then my eye doth feast."

feast or famine Also, **either feast or famine.** Either too much or too little, too many or too few. For example, *Free-lancers generally find it's feast or famine—too many assignments or too few,* or *Yesterday two hundred showed up at the fair, today two dozen—it's either feast or famine.* This expression, which transfers an overabundance or shortage of food to numerous other undertakings, was first recorded in 1732 as **feast or fast,** the noun *famine* being substituted in the early 1900s.

feather ♦ In addition to the idioms beginning with FEATHER, also see BIRDS OF A FEATHER; FUSS AND FEATHERS; IN FINE FEATHER; KNOCK DOWN WITH A FEATHER; LIGHT AS A FEATHER; MAKE THE DUST (FEATHERS) FLY; RUFFLE SOMEONE'S FEATHERS; SHOW THE WHITE FEATHER; TAR AND FEATHER.

feather in one's cap, a An act or deed to one's credit; a distinctive achievement. For example, *Getting all three factions to the bargaining table would be a feather in his cap.* This expression alludes to the practice of putting a feather on a soldier's cap for every enemy he kills, an early practice of some Native American tribes and many other peoples. [Early 1600s]

feather one's nest Acquire wealth for oneself, especially by taking advantage of one's position or using the property of others. For example, *Bill's many profitable consulting assignments enabled him to feather his nest quite comfortably.* This expression alludes to birds making a soft nest for their eggs. [Mid-1500s]

fed to the gills Also, **fed to the teeth; fed up.** Disgusted, unable or unwilling to put up with something. For example, *I'm fed to the gills with these delays* (*the gills* here is slang for "mouth"), or *He* *was fed to the teeth with her excuses*, or *I'm fed up—let's leave right now*. Of these colloquial expressions, *fed up*, alluding to being overfull from having overeaten, dates from about 1900, and the others from the first half of the 1900s. Also see UP TO ONE'S EARS.

feed ♦ In addition to the idioms beginning with FEED, also see BITE THE HAND THAT FEEDS YOU; CHICKEN FEED; OFF ONE'S FEED; PUT ON THE FEED BAG.

feed one's face Also, **stuff one's face**. Eat greedily, overeat, as in *When Dave comes home he's apt to feed his face*, or *She won't lose any weight if she keeps stuffing her face like that*. [Slang; c. 1900]

feed someone a line 1. Also, **feed someone lines**. Cue an actor with his or her next line (or lines), or tell someone what to say, as in *Some contestants become tongue-tied, so someone has to feed them a line*, or *Eric still has trouble learning a part; he needs someone to feed him his lines*. 2. Also, **hand someone a line**. Lead someone on, deceive with glib or exaggerated talk. For example, *He really fed them a line about his important new position*, or *Don't hand me a line—I know exactly how much you paid for it*. [Early 1900s]

feed the kitty Contribute money to a pool or reserve, as in *I can't make a big donation this year, but I'm willing to feed the kitty something*. This term, originating in gambling, incorporates a pun, since *kitty* can mean "cat" as well as "pool." [Late 1800s]

feel ♦ In addition to the idioms beginning with FEEL, also see (FEEL) AT HOME; COP A FEEL; GET THE FEEL OF; (FEEL) PUT UPON. Also see FEELINGS.

feel bad Also, **feel bad about**. Experience regret, sadness, embarrassment, or a similar unpleasant emotion. For example, *I feel bad about not attending the funeral*, or *The teacher's scolding made Bobby feel bad*. [First half of 1800s]

feel blue Be depressed or sad, as in *I was really feeling blue after she told me she was leaving*. The use of *blue* to mean "sad" dates from the late 1300s. See also BLUE FUNK, def. 2; HAVE THE BLUES.

feeler ♦ See PUT OUT FEELERS.

feel for 1. Grope, reach for with one's hands, as in *It was pitch dark, and I felt for the doorknob*. [Early 1700s] 2. **feel for someone**. Sympathize with or feel sorry for someone, as in *Tom was so upset that I felt for him*. This usage was put as *feel with* by Shakespeare: "It resounds as if it felt with Scotland" (*Macbeth*, 4:3). Both senses of *feel for* are present in the somewhat sarcastic **I feel for you but I can't quite reach you**, meaning "Too bad, but I don't really feel sorry for you."

feel free Be uninhibited about doing or saying something. For example, *Feel free to borrow the car whenever you need it*, or *You want to state the case? Feel free*. For a synonym, see BE MY GUEST.

feelings ♦ See HARD FEELINGS; MIXED FEELINGS; NO HARD FEELINGS; RUN HIGH, (FEELINGS); SINKING FEELING.

feel in one's bones Have an intuition or hunch about something, as in *I'm sure he'll succeed—I can feel it in my bones*. This expression alludes to the age-old notion that persons with a healed broken bone or with arthritis experience bone pain before rain, due to a drop in barometric pressure, and therefore can predict a weather change. [c. 1600]

feel like Have an inclination or desire for, as in *I feel like going out tonight*, or *Do you feel like steak for dinner?* [Colloquial; early 1800s]

feel like oneself 1. Also, **feel oneself**. Sense oneself as being in a normal state of health or spirits. For example, *I'm finally over the flu and feel like myself again*, or *He doesn't know what's wrong but he doesn't feel himself*. The antonym is **not feel oneself**, that is, "feel unwell." [Mid-1800s] Also see FEEL UP TO. 2. **feel like new**. Also, **feel like a new person**. Have a renewed sense of well-being, especially after something has happened, such as recovery from illness or receiving good news. For example, *The surgery went very well, and he now feels like new*, or *I am so relieved at the news, I feel like a new person*. 3. **feel like a million**. Be in the best of health or good spirits. For example, *After winning that prize I feel like a million*. The *million* alludes to a million dollars. Also see LOOK LIKE A MILLION DOLLARS; ON TOP OF THE WORLD.

feel like death ♦ See LOOK LIKE DEATH.

feel like two cents ♦ See FOR TWO CENTS.

feel no pain Be intoxicated, as in *After six beers he was feeling no pain*. This expression alludes to being oblivious to pain because of the consumption of a large amount of liquor. [Slang; mid-1900s]

feel oneself ♦ See FEEL LIKE ONESELF.

feel one's oats 1. Feel frisky or animated, as in *School was out, and they were feeling their oats*. This usage alludes to the behavior of a horse after having been fed. [Early 1800s] 2. Display self-importance, as in *He was feeling his oats, bossing everyone around*. [Mid-1800s]

feel one's way Proceed cautiously, as in *Until we know who we're dealing with, we'll have to feel our way*. This expression alludes to groping by touch when one is unable to see. [Early 1600s] Also see FEEL FOR, def. 1.

feel out Try cautiously or indirectly to ascertain someone's viewpoint or the nature of something. For example, *We'd better feel out the author before* *we commit him to a publicity tour.* This term alludes to physical groping. [Late 1800s] Also see TAKE THE PULSE OF.

feel out of place ♦ See under OUT OF PLACE.

feel put upon ♦ See PUT UPON.

feel someone up Touch or fondle someone sexually, as in *She complained that her boss tried to feel her up.* [Early 1900s]

feel the pinch Be affected by hardship, especially straitened finances. For example, *This job pays much less, so we're bound to feel the pinch.* [Mid-1800s]

feel up to Consider oneself capable or able to do something, as in *Do you feel up to a three-mile run?* or *I don't feel up to another evening out.* [Late 1800s] Also see EQUAL TO; UP TO.

feet ♦ In addition to the idioms beginning with FEET, also see AT SOMEONE'S FEET; BOTH FEET ON THE GROUND; COLD FEET; DEAD ON ONE'S FEET; DON'T LET THE GRASS GROW UNDER ONE'S FEET; DRAG ONE'S FEET; FALL ON ONE'S FEET; GET ONE'S FEET WET; GET THE LEAD OUT OF (ONE'S FEET); GET TO ONE'S FEET; HAVE TWO LEFT FEET; HOLD SOMEONE'S FEET TO THE FIRE; OFF ONE'S FEET; ON ONE'S FEET; PUT ONE'S FEET UP; RUSH OFF ONE'S FEET; SHAKE THE DUST FROM ONE'S FEET; SIX FEET UNDER; STAND ON ONE'S FEET; TAKE THE LOAD OFF (ONE'S FEET); THINK ON ONE'S FEET; UNDER ONE'S FEET; VOTE WITH ONE'S FEET. Also see under FOOT.

feet of clay A failing or weakness in a person's character, as in *The media are always looking for a popular idol's feet of clay.* This expression comes from the Bible (Daniel 2:31–33), where the prophet interprets Nebuchadnezzar's dream of a statue with a head of gold and feet of iron clay. [c. 1600]

feet on the ground ♦ See BOTH FEET ON THE GROUND.

fell ♦ See ONE FELL SWOOP.

fellow ♦ See HALL FELLOW WELL MET; REGULAR GUY (FELLOW); STRANGE BEDFELLOWS.

fence ♦ In addition to the idioms beginning with FENCE, also see MEND ONE'S FENCES; ON THE FENCE; STRADDLE THE FENCE.

fence in Also, **hem in**. Restrict or confine someone, as in *He wanted to take on more assignments but was fenced in by his contract,* or *Their father was old-fashioned and the children were hemmed in by his rules.* Both expressions transfer a literal form of enclosure to a figurative one. The first gained currency from a popular song in the style of a cowboy folk song by Cole Porter, "Don't Fence Me In" (1944), in which the cowboy celebrates open land and starry skies. The variant is much older, dating from the late 1500s.

fence with Avoid answering directly, try to evade, as in *The mayor was very clever at fencing with the press about his future plans.* This expression transfers the parry and thrust of fencing to a verbal exchange. [Second half of 1600s]

fend for oneself ♦ See SHIFT FOR ONESELF.

ferret out Uncover and bring to light by searching, as in *Sandy was a superb reporter, tireless in ferreting out whatever facts were needed for her story.* This expression alludes to hunting with ferrets, weasel-like animals formerly used to drive rabbits out of their burrows. [c. 1600]

fetch and carry Do errands and other menial tasks, as in *She was hired as administrative assistant, but all she does is fetch and carry for the department's supervisor.* This expression originally alluded to dogs that were taught to carry various objects for their masters. It has been applied to humans since the late 1700s.

fever ♦ See CABIN FEVER; RUN A FEVER.

few ♦ In addition to the idioms beginning with FEW, also see A FEW; BRICKS SHY OF A LOAD, (A FEW); OF FEW WORDS; PRECIOUS FEW; QUITE A BIT (FEW).

few and far between At wide intervals, scarce, as in *Supporters of the amendment are few and far between.* This expression originally was used very literally for physical objects such as houses appearing at widely separated intervals. Today it is also used more loosely. [Mid-1600s]

few bricks shy of a load ♦ See BRICKS SHY OF A LOAD.

few words ♦ See OF FEW WORDS.

fiddle ♦ In addition to the idiom beginning with FIDDLE, also see FIT AS A FIDDLE; HANG UP (ONE'S FIDDLE); PLAY SECOND FIDDLE.

fiddle while Rome burns Occupy oneself with unimportant matters and neglect important ones during a crisis. For example, *The account was falling through, but he was more worried about missing his golf game—talk about fiddling while Rome burns!* This expression alludes to the legend that the Emperor Nero played his fiddle while watching the conflagration of Rome. [Mid-1600s]

field ♦ In addition to the idiom beginning with FIELD, also see COVER THE FIELD; FAR AFIELD; OUT IN LEFT FIELD; PLAY THE FIELD; TAKE THE FIELD.

field day A time of great pleasure, activity, or opportunity, as in *The press had a field day with this sensational murder trial.* This colloquial expression, dating from the 1700s, originally referred to a day set aside for military maneuvers and exercises, and later was extended to a similar day for sports and games. Since the early 1800s it has been used more loosely.

fifth ♦ In addition to the idioms beginning with FIFTH, also see TAKE THE FIFTH.

fifth column A secret subversive group that works against a country or organization from the inside, as in *The right-to-life movement has established a fifth column among freedom-of-choice activists.* This term was invented by General Emilio Mola during the Spanish Civil War in a radio broadcast on October 16, 1936, in which he said that he had *una quinta columna* ("a fifth column") of sympathizers for General Franco among the Republicans holding the city of Madrid, and it would join his four columns of troops when they attacked. The term was popularized by Ernest Hemingway and later extended to any traitorous insiders.

fifth wheel An extra and unnecessary person or thing, as in *He was the only one without a date, so he felt like a fifth wheel.* This expression, which alludes to an unneeded wheel on a four-wheel vehicle, may have originated as long ago as 1631, when Thomas Dekker wrote *Match Me in London:* "Thou tiest but wings to a swift gray Hounds heel, And addest to a running Chariot a fifth wheel."

fifty-fifty ♦ See under GO HALVES.

fig ♦ See under NOT GIVE A DAMN.

fight ♦ In addition to the idioms beginning with FIGHT, also see CAN'T FIGHT CITY HALL.

fight fire with fire Combat an evil or negative circumstances by reacting in kind. For example, *When the opposition began a smear campaign, we decided to fight fire with fire.* Although ancient writers from Plato to Erasmus cautioned that one should not add fire to fire, this warning is not incorporated in the idiom, which was first recorded in Shakespeare's *Coriolanus.*

fighting chance A possibility of winning, but only with a struggle. For example, *It's going to be hard to beat that record, but I think he has a fighting chance.* [Late 1800s]

fighting words A statement bound to start a quarrel or fight. It is often expressed as **them's fighting words**, as in *You say your father's smarter than mine? Them's fighting words.* The ungrammatical use of *them's* for "those are" emphasizes the folksy tone of this colloquialism, first recorded in Ring Lardner's *Gullible's Travels* (1917).

fight it out Settle a dispute by fighting, either physically or verbally. For example, *The two sides couldn't agree on a budget but were determined to fight it out to the end.* [Mid-1500s]

fight off Defend against, drive back, as in *I've been fighting off a cold all week.* This figurative use of

the term, originally meaning "to repel an enemy," dates from the early 1800s.

fight shy of Avoid meeting or confronting someone, as in "I have . . . had to fight shy of invitations that would exhaust time and spirits" (Washington Irving, *Life and Letters*, 1821). This usage may allude to a military reluctance to meet or engage with the enemy. [Late 1700s]

fight tooth and nail Engage in vigorous combat or make a strenuous effort, using all one's resources. For example, *I'm going to fight tooth and nail for that promotion.* This expression, with its allusion to biting and scratching, was first recorded in 1576.

figment of one's imagination Something made up, invented, or fabricated, as in "The long dishevelled hair, the swelled black face, the exaggerated stature were figments of imagination" (Charlotte Brontë, *Jane Eyre*, 1847). This term is redundant, since *figment* means "product of the imagination." [Early 1800s]

figure ♦ In addition to the idioms beginning with FIGURE, also see BALLPARK FIGURE; IN ROUND NUMBERS (FIGURES); IT FIGURES.

figure in 1. Include, add in. For example, *Did you figure in the travel expense?* 2. Play a part in, as in *His speaking ability definitely figured in his being chosen for the lead,* or *Their reduced income figures in all their recent decisions.*

figure on 1. Depend on, count on, as in *We figured on your support.* 2. Take into consideration, expect, as in *We figured on his being late.* 3. Plan, as in *We'll figure on leaving at noon.* All three colloquial usages date from about 1900.

figure out 1. Discover or determine, as in *Let's figure out a way to help.* [Early 1900s] 2. Solve or decipher, as in *Can you figure out this puzzle?* [Early 1800s]

figure up Calculate, total, as in *Please figure up just how many feet of lumber we need.* [Late 1800s]

file ♦ See IN SINGLE FILE; ON FILE; RANK AND FILE.

fill ♦ In addition to the idioms beginning with FILL, also see BACK AND FILL; GET ONE'S FILL OF. Also see under FULL.

filled to the brim As full as possible; also, completely satisfied. For example, *We're filled to the brim with excitement.* This expression transfers the idea of a container filled to the very top. W.S. Gilbert used it in the comic opera *The Mikado* (1885): "Three little maids from school are we, Filled to the brim with girlish glee." [c. 1600]

fill in 1. Complete something, especially by supplying more information or detail. For example, *Be sure to fill in your salary history.* It is also put as

fill in the blanks, as in *We'll rely on Mary to fill in the blanks.* Yet another related usage is **fill someone in,** as in *I couldn't attend, so will you fill me in?* The first term dates from the mid-1800s; the others from the first half of the 1900s. Also see FILL OUT. **2.** Also, **fill in for.** Take someone's place, substitute for. For example, *The understudy had to fill in at the last minute,* or *I can't come but my wife will fill in for me.* Also see FILL SOMEONE'S SHOES.

fill out 1. Complete by supplying required information, especially in writing. For example, *Please fill out the application form,* or *I don't quite understand this drawing, so fill out the details.* [Late 1800s] **2.** Become enlarged, distended, rounded in outline. For example, *The wind filled out the sails,* or *He's put on weight and really filled out.* Applied to objects, this expression dates from about 1700, but to persons or animals becoming fatter, only from the late 1800s.

fill someone's shoes Assume someone's position or duties, especially in a satisfactory way. For example, *It'll be hard to find someone to fill her shoes when she retires,* or *John expects his son to fill his shoes at the store.* Also see IN SOMEONE'S SHOES.

fill the bill Serve a particular purpose well, as in *I was afraid there wasn't enough chicken for everyone, but this casserole will fill the bill,* or *Karen's testimony just fills the bill, so we're sure to get a conviction.* This expression alludes to adding less-known performers to a program (or *bill*) in order to make a long enough entertainment. [First half of 1800s]

filthy lucre Money; originally, money obtained dishonestly. For example, *She didn't like the job but loved the filthy lucre in the form of her weekly paycheck.* This term comes from the Bible (Titus 1:11), where it refers to those who teach wrongly for the sake of money. In time it came to be used loosely, and usually jokingly, for money in general, and in the mid-1900s gave rise to the jocular slang term **the filthy** for "money." Although both versions may be dying out, the expression **filthy rich,** for "extremely wealthy," survives.

final ◆ See IN THE FINAL ANALYSIS.

find ◆ In addition to the idioms beginning with FIND, also see GOOD MAN IS HARD TO FIND; HARD WAY (FIND OUT THE).

finders, keepers A phrase meaning that whoever finds something is entitled to keep it. For example, *Someone left a dollar bill in this rented car—finders, keepers.* This expression alludes to an ancient Roman law to that effect and has been stated in numerous different ways over the centuries. The modern version, often stated as **Finders keepers, losers weepers,** dates from the mid-1800s and is no longer a legal precept.

find fault Criticize, express dissatisfaction with, as in *She was a difficult traveling companion, constantly finding fault with the hotel, meal service, and tour guides.* [Mid-1500s]

find it in one's heart Persuade oneself to do something, as in *They were an hour late, but I couldn't find it in my heart to scold them.* This expression, today generally put in the negative, alludes to searching self-examination. [Mid-1400s]

find one's bearings ◆ See GET ONE'S BEARINGS.

find oneself 1. Become aware of what one wishes and can best do in life. For example, *At last he's found himself—he really loves teaching.* The same idea was sometimes put as to **find one's feet,** transferring a baby's new ability to stand or walk to a person becoming conscious of his or her abilities. [Late 1800s] **2.** Discover where one is; also, how one is feeling. For example, *He suddenly found himself on the right street,* or *To my surprise I find myself agreeing with you.* [Mid-1400s]

find one's way Reach a destination, especially with some difficulty or not as a matter of course. For example, *She finally found her way to the remote cabin,* or *Some slang phrases have found their way into standard English.* The literal use of this term dates from the 1200s, the figurative from the early 1800s.

find out 1. Discover through examination or inquiry, as in *You can find out his phone number by looking in the book.* [Mid-1500s] **2.** Expose, detect the true nature or character of, especially in an offense. For example, *Cheaters risk being found out.* [c. 1700]

find true north Get on the right course, proceed in the right direction, as in *We'd better find true north before our competitors do.* This term alludes to locating the position of the North Pole from a particular point. [Slang; late 1900s]

fine ◆ In addition to the idioms beginning with FINE, also see COME ON IN (THE WATER'S FINE); CUT IT FINE; IN FINE FEATHER.

fine and dandy All right, excellent, as in *What you're proposing is fine and dandy with the rest of us.* This redundant colloquialism (*fine* and *dandy* both mean "excellent") today is more often used sarcastically in the sense of "not all right" or "bad," as in *You don't want to play bridge? Fine and dandy, you've left me without a partner.*

fine art Something requiring highly developed techniques and skills, as in *He's turned lying into a fine art,* or *The contractor excels in the fine art of demolition.* This term alludes to the *fine arts,* such as music, painting, and sculpture, which require both skill and talent. It is now often used to describe anything that takes skill to do. [First half of 1800s]

fine-tooth comb A method of searching or investigating in minute detail, as in *He examined the figures with a fine-tooth comb but found no errors.* The practice of using a comb with close-set teeth to comb out head lice was transferred to various kinds of investigation in the late 1800s.

finger ♦ In addition to the idiom beginning with FINGER, also see AT ONE'S FINGERTIPS; BURN ONE'S FINGERS; CROSS ONE'S FINGERS; GIVE SOMEONE THE FINGER; LAY A FINGER ON; LET SLIP (THROUGH THE FINGERS); NOT LIFT A FINGER; POINT THE FINGER AT; PUT ONE'S FINGER ON; PUT THE FINGER ON; SNAP ONE'S FINGERS AT; STICKY FINGERS; TWIST AROUND ONE'S FINGER; WORK ONE'S FINGERS TO THE BONE.

finger in the pie, have a Have an interest in or meddle in something. For example, *When they nominated me for the board, I'm sure Bill had a finger in the pie.* Another form of this idiom is **have a finger in every pie**, meaning "to have an interest in or be involved in everything," as in *She does a great deal for the town; she has a finger in every pie.* The precise origin of this metaphor, which presumably alludes either to tasting every pie or being involved in their concoction, has been lost. [Late 1500s]

fingertips ♦ See AT ONE'S FINGERTIPS.

finish ♦ See FROM SOUP TO NUTS (START TO FINISH); IN AT THE DEATH (FINISH).

finishing touch A small change or addition that serves to complete something. For example, *The room still needed a few finishing touches, such as a flower arrangement.* This expression is sometimes put as **a finishing stroke**. [c. 1700]

fire ♦ In addition to the idioms beginning with FIRE, also see ADD FUEL TO THE FIRE; BALL OF FIRE; BAPTISM OF FIRE; CATCH FIRE; CAUGHT IN THE CROSS-FIRE; DRAW FIRE; FAT IS IN THE FIRE; FIGHT FIRE WITH FIRE; GET ON (LIKE A HOUSE AFIRE); HANG FIRE; HOLD ONE'S FIRE; HOLD SOMEONE'S FEET TO THE FIRE; IRONS IN THE FIRE; KEEP THE HOME FIRES BURNING; LIGHT A FIRE UNDER; LINE OF FIRE; MISS FIRE; NO SMOKE WITHOUT FIRE; ON FIRE; OPEN FIRE; OUT OF THE FRYING PAN INTO THE FIRE; PLAY WITH FIRE; SET ON FIRE; SET THE WORLD ON FIRE; SPREAD LIKE WILDFIRE; TRIAL BY FIRE; UNDER FIRE; WHERE'S THE FIRE. Also see under FIRING.

fire away Start to talk or ask questions. For example, *You've got more questions? Well, fire away.* This expression originated in the 1600s as a military command to discharge firearms and was being transferred to other actions by the late 1700s. Also see FIRE OFF.

fire off Say or write and send away rapidly, as in *He fired off three more questions,* or *She fired off a letter of complaint to the president.* This expression originally (from about 1700) was, and still is, used in the sense of "discharge a weapon or ammunition," as in *The police were instructed to fire off canisters of tear gas.* The figurative use dates from the late 1800s.

fire on all cylinders Also, **hit** or **click on all cylinders**. Function very well, as in *Once we figured out how to use the new software, the department was firing on all cylinders,* or "So the best infielder takes time to fit into the infield of a Big League club and have it hit on all four cylinders again" (Christy Mathewson, *Pitching in a Pinch,* 1912). This term transfers the functioning of an internal combustion engine, which works best when all its cylinders ignite, to broader use. [Early 1900s]

fire up **1.** Inflame with enthusiasm, anger, or another strong emotion, as in *Her speech fired up the crowd in favor of her proposals.* This expression dates from the early 1800s, when it referred literally to starting a fire in a furnace or boiler; its figurative use dates from the late 1800s. **2.** Light a pipe, cigar, or cigarette, as in *Do you mind if I fire up?* [Late 1800s] A more common term, however, is LIGHT UP, def. 2. **3.** Start the ignition of an engine, as in *Whenever he tried to fire up the motor, it stalled.* [Mid-1900s]

firing line, on the In the forefront of any activity or pursuit, especially a controversy. For example, *At the sales conference they asked so many questions that Anne felt she was on the firing line.* This expression originally meant the line of positions from which gunfire is directed at a target and is still so used in a military context. Today it is also used more loosely. [Late 1800s]

first ♦ In addition to the idioms beginning with FIRST, also see AT FIRST; AT FIRST BLUSH; AT FIRST HAND; CAST THE FIRST STONE; GET TO FIRST BASE; IF AT FIRST YOU DON'T SUCCEED; IN THE FIRST PLACE; IN THE (FIRST) FLUSH OF; LOVE AT FIRST SIGHT; NOT KNOW BEANS (THE FIRST THING); OF THE FIRST WATER; ON A FIRST-NAME BASIS.

first and foremost Also, **first of all.** Most important, primarily; also, to begin with. For example, *First and foremost, I want to thank our sponsors,* or *What we need, first and foremost, is a new secretary,* or *We have to deal, first of all, with the early history.* The first term, dating from the late 1300s, is redundant, since *first* and *foremost* mean virtually the same thing. Both it and the variant, which dates from the mid-1500s, are used to give emphasis to the initial item in a list of several. Also see FIRST OFF; FIRST THING.

first and last Under all circumstances, always, as in *She was an artist first and last.* (For a synonym, see ABOVE ALL.) This expression, first recorded in 1589, should not be confused with the similar-sounding **from first to last**, which means "from start to finish" or "throughout," as in *We cheered them on from first to last.*

first blush ♦ See AT FIRST BLUSH.

first come, first served Those who precede others will have their needs attended to earliest, as in *So many people showed up that we may not have enough food to go around, so let it be "first come, first served."* The idea is very old, but the first recorded use of this precise phrase was in 1545. Also see EARLY BIRD CATCHES THE WORM.

first cousin A close relation or resemblance to someone or something, as in *This new machine is a first cousin to the previous model.* The figurative use of *cousin,* which literally means "the child of one's aunt or uncle," dates from the 1300s.

first hand ♦ See AT FIRST HAND.

first of all ♦ See FIRST AND FOREMOST.

first off From the start, immediately. For example, *He said to wash the car first off,* or *Why wasn't she told first off?* [Colloquial; late 1800s] Also see under FIRST AND FOREMOST; FIRST THING.

first thing Before anything else; without delay. For example, *Tom was supposed to call him first thing in the morning.* [Late 1500s] Also see under FIRST AND FOREMOST; FIRST OFF.

first things first The most important task gets priority, as in *I very much wanted to see that movie, but first things first—the paper's due tomorrow.* This adage was first recorded in 1545.

fish ♦ In addition to the idioms beginning with FISH, also see BIG FISH IN A SMALL POND; COLD FISH; DRINK LIKE A FISH; GOLDFISH BOWL; KETTLE OF FISH; LIKE SHOOTING FISH IN A BARREL; NEITHER FISH NOR FOWL; NOT THE ONLY FISH IN THE SEA; OTHER FISH TO FRY; SMELL FISHY.

fish for 1. Try to obtain something through artifice or indirectly. For example, *He was always fishing for compliments,* or, as William Makepeace Thackeray put it in *Vanity Fair* (1848): "The first woman who fishes for him, hooks him." [Mid-1500s] 2. Search for something, as in *I've fished for it in all the drawers.* [First half of 1700s]

fishing expedition An attempt to find useful information by asking questions at random. For example, *The sales force was told to go on a fishing expedition to find out what they could about the company's competitors.* This expression was taken up by lawyers to describe interrogating an adversary in hopes of finding relevant evidence and is now used more broadly still. [c. 1930]

fish in troubled waters Try to take advantage of a confused situation. For example, *He often buys up stock in companies declaring bankruptcy; fishing in troubled waters generally pays off.* This term, first recorded in 1568, expresses the even older notion that fish bite more readily when seas are rough.

fish or cut bait Either proceed with an activity or abandon it completely. For example, *You've been putting off calling him for hours; either fish or cut bait.* This expression, often uttered as an imperative, alludes to a fisherman who should either be actively trying to catch fish or cutting up bait for others to use. It was first recorded in the *Congressional Record* (1876), when Congressman Joseph P. Cannon called for a vote on a bill legalizing the silver dollar: "I want you gentlemen on the other side of the House to 'fish or cut bait.'" A vulgar synonym from the 1940s is **shit or get off the pot.**

fish out 1. Also, **fish up.** Discover and retrieve something from a pile or store. For example, *She finally fished out the right letter from the files,* or *He fished up a scandal for the paper to run in the early edition.* This usage likens pulling fish from the sea to finding something. [Mid-1600s] 2. Deplete the fish in a body of water by fishing, as in *This stream is completely fished out.*

fish out of water, a A person away from his or her usual environment or activities. For example, *Using a computer for the first time, Carl felt like a fish out of water,* or *On a hiking trail, Nell was a fish out of water.* This expression alludes to the fact that fish cannot survive for long on dry land. [Late 1300s]

fish story An improbable, boastful tale, as in *He came up with some fish story about his winnings at the track.* This expression alludes to the tendency of fishermen to exaggerate the size of their catch. [Early 1800s]

fist ♦ See HAND OVER FIST.

fit ♦ In addition to the idioms beginning with FIT, also see GIVE SOMEONE FITS; HAVE A FIT; IF THE SHOE FITS; SEE FIT TO; SURVIVAL OF THE FITTEST.

fit as a fiddle In excellent form or health. For example, *He's not just recovered, he's fit as a fiddle.* The original allusion of this simile has been lost. Its survival is probably due to the pleasant sound of its alliteration. [Early 1600s]

fit in 1. Also, **fit into.** Provide a place or time for. For example, *We can't fit in another appointment—there's no time,* or *That tree won't fit into the hole you've dug.* [Late 1600s] 2. **fit in with.** Be suited to, belong. For example, *I just don't fit in with this group,* or *Her mood fitted in with the sad occasion.*

fit like a glove Be the right size and well suited; also, be in conformity with. For example, *That position fits him like a glove.* Tobias Smollett used this simile, rather incongruously, in *Humphry Clinker* (1771): "The boots . . . fitted me like a glove." [Second half of 1700s] Also see TO A T.

fit out Also, **fit up.** Equip or supply what is needed, as in *They promised to fit out the expedition free of charge.* This expression, dating from the late 1600s, originally was confined to furnishing a ship or other vessel with supplies, repairs, and the like. By the 1720s it was being used more broadly, as it still is.

fits and starts, by Also, **in fits and starts.** With irregular intervals of action and inaction, spasmodically, as in *The campaign is proceeding by fits and starts.* This expression began in the late 1500s as *by fits,* the noun *fit* meaning a "paroxysm" or "seizure"; *starts* was added about a century later.

fit to be tied Furious, enraged, as in *I've been waiting for two hours and am fit to be tied.* This expression implies anger so extreme that it requires physical restraint. [Late 1800s]

fit to kill Excessively, immoderately, as in *She was dressed up fit to kill.* [Colloquial; mid-1800s] Also see DRESSED TO KILL.

five ♦ See HIGH FIVE; NINE TO FIVE; TAKE FIVE.

fix ♦ In addition to the idioms beginning with FIX, also see GET A FIX; GET A FIX ON; IF IT AIN'T BROKE DON'T FIX IT; IN A FIX.

fix someone's wagon Get even with someone, get revenge on someone, spoil someone's chance of success. For example, *He may think he can win the election, but these ads will fix his wagon,* or *After what he did to her, her family's out to fix his wagon.* This term uses *fix* in the sense of "punish someone" or "put someone in an awkward position," a usage dating from about 1800. The *wagon* was added in the 1900s, presumably making the phrase refer to putting sand in a wagon axle or similar sabotage.

fix up 1. Repair, refurbish, or renew. For example, *They're busy fixing up their house,* or *We fixed ourselves up before we ventured outside.* [Late 1700s] 2. **fix someone up.** Provide or furnish someone with something, as in *He can fix you up with a new car,* or *Can you fix up my friend with a date for the dance?* [Colloquial; c. 1930] 3. Smooth over or settle, as in *You'd think they could fix up these small differences.* [Late 1800s]

fizzle out Fail, end weakly, especially after a hopeful beginning. For example, *The enthusiasm for reform has fizzled out in this state.* The word *fizzle* dates from the early 1500s and meant "to break wind without making noise." Later it was applied to hissing noises, such as those made by wet fireworks, and then to any endeavor that ends in disappointment. [Colloquial; mid-1800s]

flag down Signal to stop, as in *The police were flagging down all cars.* This expression uses the verb *flag* in the sense of "catch the attention of, as by

waving a flag," a usage dating from the mid-1800s; *down* was added in the first half of the 1900s.

flake out 1. Drop from exhaustion, faint. For example, *After running the marathon, he simply flaked out on the ground.* This expression possibly is derived from a now obsolete meaning of *flake,* "to become flabby or fall in folds." [Slang; c. 1940] 2. Lie down, go to sleep, as in *Homeless persons flaked out in doorways.* [Slang; early 1940s] 3. Lose one's nerve, as in *Please don't flake out now.* [Slang; 1950s] 4. Go crazy; also, cause someone to go crazy. For example, *She just flaked out and we had to call an ambulance,* or *This project is flaking us out.* The usages in def. 3 and 4 probably are derived from the adjective *flaky,* meaning "eccentric." [c. 1970] 5. Die, as in *He flaked out last night.* [1960s] 6. Surprise, astonish, as in *She said she'd just been made a partner, and that flaked me out.* This usage appears to be a variant of FREAK OUT. [c. 1970]

flame ♦ See ADD FUEL TO THE FIRE (FLAMES); BURST INTO (FLAMES); FAN THE FLAMES; GO UP IN FLAMES; SHOOT DOWN (IN FLAMES).

flare up Suddenly become angry, as in *She flared up at the slightest provocation.* This metaphoric expression, dating from the mid-1800s, transfers a sudden burst of flame to sudden rage.

flash ♦ In addition to the idiom beginning with FLASH, also see IN A FLASH; QUICK AS A WINK (FLASH).

flash in the pan An effort or person that promises great success but fails. For example, *His second novel proved to be a flash in the pan,* or *We had high hopes for the new director, but she was a flash in the pan.* This metaphoric term alludes to the 17th-century flintlock musket, which could be fired only when the flash of the priming powder in the lockpan ignited the charge in the bore. When it failed to ignite, there was only a flash in the pan and the gun did not shoot.

flat ♦ In addition to the idioms beginning with FLAT, also see CAUGHT FLAT-FOOTED; FALL FLAT; IN NO TIME (NOTHING FLAT); LEAVE FLAT.

flat as a pancake Extremely level, especially too much so. For example, *There are no hills; this terrain is flat as a pancake.* This simile dates from the 1500s and has survived its contemporary, **flat as a flounder.** It is sometimes used, either disparagingly or ruefully, to describe a small-breasted woman.

flat broke Also, **stone** or **stony broke.** Completely penniless. For example, *I can't help you—I'm flat broke,* or *He's stone broke again.* The first term dates from the mid-1800s and uses *flat* in the sense of "completely" or "downright." The variant dates from the late 1800s.

flat-footed ♦ See CAUGHT FLAT-FOOTED.

flat on one's back 1. Sick in bed. For example, *The flu has put her flat on her back.* 2. Helpless, without recourse, defeated, as in *I wish I could help but the recession has put me flat on my back.*

flat out 1. In a direct manner, bluntly. For example, *He told the true story flat out.* [Colloquial; mid-1900s] 2. At top speed, as in *She was running flat out to catch the train.* [Slang; c. 1930]

flatter oneself Be gratified vainly by one's own achievement; exaggerate one's good points. For example, *He flattered himself that his presentation at the sales conference was a success,* or *She flattered herself that she was by far the best skater at the rink.* This usage is often put negatively, as in *Don't flatter yourself—we haven't won the contract yet.* [Late 1500s]

flea ◆ In addition to the idioms beginning with FLEA, also see HURT A FLY (FLEA).

flea in one's ear, a An annoying hint or a stinging rebuke, as in *He has a flea in his ear about their relationship,* or *If he doesn't bring the right equipment, I'll put a flea in his ear.* This expression originated in French and has been used in English since the 1400s.

flea market A market, usually held outdoors, where used goods and antiques are sold. For example, *We picked up half of our furniture at flea markets.* The term is a direct translation of the French *marché aux puces* and presumably implies that some of the used clothes and furniture might be flea-infested. [1920s]

flesh ◆ In addition to the idioms beginning with FLESH, also see GO THE WAY OF ALL FLESH; IN PERSON (THE FLESH); MAKE ONE'S FLESH CREEP; NEITHER FISH NOR FOWL (FLESH); PEDDLE FLESH; POUND OF FLESH; PRESS THE FLESH; SPIRIT IS WILLING BUT THE FLESH IS WEAK; THORN IN ONE'S FLESH.

flesh and blood 1. Human beings, especially with respect to their failings or weaknesses. For example, *I can't do everything—I'm only flesh and blood.* [c. 1600] 2. **one's own flesh and blood.** One's blood relatives, kin, as in *She can't cut her own flesh and blood out of her will.* [c. 1300]

flesh out Also, **put flesh on the bones of.** Give substance to, provide with details, amplify. For example, *The editor told her to flesh out the story,* or *You need to put flesh on the bones of these characters.* This metaphoric expression, alluding to clothing a nude body or adding flesh to a skeleton, was in the mid-1600s put simply as *to flesh,* the adverb *out* being added about two centuries later.

flex one's muscles Show off one's strength or power, as in *The boys love flexing their muscles,* or *The new department head has decided to flex her muscles.* [Early 1900s]

flies ◆ See AS THE CROW FLIES; DROP LIKE FLIES; NO FLIES ON SOMEONE; TIME FLIES. Also see under FLY.

flight ◆ In addition to the idioms beginning with FLIGHT, also see PUT TO FLIGHT; TAKE FLIGHT.

flight of fancy An unrealistic idea or fantastic notion, a pipe dream. For example, *She engaged in flights of fancy, such as owning a million-dollar house.* This idiom uses *flight* in the sense of "a soaring of the imagination," a usage dating from the mid-1600s.

fling ◆ In addition to the idiom beginning with FLING, also see LAST FLING.

fling oneself at someone Also, **fling or throw oneself at someone's head.** Try openly to make someone love one. For example, *She was constantly phoning him and inviting him over, really flinging herself at him,* or *Mom said she should stop throwing herself at his head.*

flip one's lid Also, **flip one's wig; flip out.** React very strongly or wildly, as with anger, surprise, or excitement; also, go crazy. For example, *I'm going to flip my lid if he doesn't show up,* or *She really-flipped out when she realized that she had won first prize,* or *I think Rob has flipped his wig.* These slangy expressions, with their allusion to losing the top of one's head, date from the 1930s and 1940s.

flip through Browse through, as in *She flipped through the magazine while she waited.* This expression uses *flip* in the sense of "turn over pages."

flog ◆ See BEAT A DEAD HORSE.

floor ◆ See GROUND FLOOR; MOP UP THE FLOOR WITH; SINK THROUGH THE FLOOR; TAKE THE FLOOR; WALK THE FLOOR.

flotsam and jetsam 1. Discarded odds and ends, as in *Most of our things have been moved to the new house, but there's still some flotsam and jetsam to sort.* [Mid-1800s] 2. Destitute, homeless individuals, as in *The mayor was concerned about the flotsam and jetsam of the inner city.* [Second half of 1900s] Both words originated in 17th-century sailing terminology. *Flotsam* literally meant "wreckage or cargo that remains afloat after a ship has sunk." *Jetsam* meant "goods thrown overboard from a ship in danger of sinking in order to give it more buoyancy." Both literal meanings remain current, although the distinction between them is often forgotten.

flow ◆ See EBB AND FLOW; GO WITH THE FLOW.

flunk out 1. Expel or be expelled from a school because one's work does not meet the required standard. For example, *He flunked out of Harvard after just one year.* [Slang; early 1800s.] 2. Fail at anything, as in *The camera ran out of film so we flunked out as photographers.* [Slang; late 1800s]

fly, flying ◆ In addition to the idioms beginning with FLY or FLYING, also see GET OFF THE GROUND

(TO A FLYING START); GO FLY A KITE; HIGH FLYER; LET FLY; MAKE THE DUST FLY; NOT HURT A FLY; ON THE FLY; SEND FLYING; WHEN PIGS FLY; WITH FLYING COLORS. Also see UNDER FLIES; FLIGHT.

fly at Attack fiercely, assault. For example, *The dogs flew at each other's throats.* [Late 1500s]

fly blind Feel one's way, proceed by guesswork, as in *There are no directions for assembling this furniture, so I'm flying blind.* This hyperbolic expression dates from World War II, when it was used by pilots who could not see the horizon and therefore had to rely on instruments. It was transferred to broader use soon afterward.

fly high Be elated, as in *They were flying high after the birth of their first baby.* This expression alludes to a high pitch of feeling. [Mid 1600s]

flying start ♦ See under GET OFF THE GROUND.

fly in the face of Also, **fly in the teeth of.** Act in direct opposition to or defiance of. For example, *This decision flies in the face of all precedent,* or *They went out without permission, flying in the teeth of house rules.* This metaphoric expression alludes to a physical attack. [Mid-1500s]

fly in the ointment A drawback or detrimental factor. For example, *The new library is wonderful but there's a fly in the ointment: their catalog isn't complete yet.* This term probably alludes to a biblical proverb (Ecclesiastes 10:1): "Dead flies cause the ointment of the apothecary to send forth a stinking savour." [c. 1600]

fly off the handle Lose one's temper, as in *Tom flies off the handle at the slightest setback.* This metaphoric expression alludes to the loosened head of a hammer flying off after a blow. [Early 1800s]

fly on the wall An unseen observer or listener, as in *I wish I could be a fly on the wall when she tells him she's pregnant.* [Mid-1900s]

fly the coop Escape, run away, as in *After years of fighting with my mother, my father finally flew the coop.* This term originally meant "escape from jail," known as the *coop* in underworld slang since the late 1700s. [Late 1800s]

foam at the mouth Be extremely angry, as in *She was foaming at the mouth over the judge's ruling.* This hyperbolic term uses the verb *foam* in the sense of "froth at the mouth," a usage generally applied to animals such as horses and dating from about A.D. 950. [1400s]

fob off 1. Sell or dispose of goods by fraud or deception, as in *They tried to fob off the zircon as a diamond.* [c. 1600] 2. Put off or appease by deceitful means, as in *We needed her help but were fobbed off by promises.* [c. 1600]

foe ♦ See FRIEND OR FOE.

fog ♦ See IN A FOG.

fold ♦ In addition to the idioms beginning with FOLD, also see RETURN TO THE FOLD.

fold one's tent Quietly depart, as in *It's late, so let's fold our tents.* This term is a partial quotation of Henry Wadsworth Longfellow's poem "The Day is Done" (1844): "And the night shall be filled with music, And the cares that infest the day, Shall fold their tents, like the Arabs, And quietly steal away."

fold up 1. Fail, especially go out of business. For example, *Three stores on Main Street have folded up.* 2. Collapse, break down. For example, *When she told him about the dog's death, she folded up.* This idiom alludes to closing or bringing an object into more compact form. [Early 1900s]

folk ♦ See JUST FOLKS.

follow ♦ In addition to the idioms beginning with FOLLOW, also see AS FOLLOWS; CAMP FOLLOWER; HARD ACT TO FOLLOW.

follow along Move or proceed in accord or in unison with someone. For example, *The children followed along with the song,* or *They followed along with the crowd.*

follow in someone's footsteps Also, **follow in someone's tracks.** Follow someone's example or guidance. For example, *Dean hoped his son would follow in his footsteps and become an economist,* or *Jane tried to follow in her mentor's tracks.* [Mid-1500s]

follow one's nose Go straight ahead, as in *To get to the restaurant, just follow your nose down Baker Avenue.* [Late 1600s]

follow out Bring to a conclusion, carry out. For example, *The second volume simply followed out the theories presented in the first,* or *He instructed them to follow out their orders to the letter.* This idiom is dying out. [Mid-1700s]

follow suit Imitate or do as someone else has done, as in *Bill decided to leave for the rest of the day, and Mary followed suit.* This term comes from card games in which one must play a card from the same suit as the one led. [Mid-1800s]

follow the crowd Go along with the majority, do what most others are doing. For example, *Make your own decision—don't just follow the crowd.*

follow through 1. In sports such as tennis or golf, carry a stroke to completion after striking the ball. For example, *You don't follow through on your backhand, so it goes into the net.* [Late 1800s] 2. Carry an object, project, or intention to completion; pursue fully. For example, *She followed through on her promise to reorganize the department.* Also see FOLLOW UP, def. 1.

follow up 1. Carry to completion. For example, *I'm following up their suggestions with concrete proposals.* Also see FOLLOW THROUGH. 2. Increase the effectiveness or enhance the success of something by further action. For example, *She followed up her interview with a phone call.* [Late 1700s]

food for thought An idea or issue to ponder, as in *That interesting suggestion of yours has given us food for thought.* This metaphoric phrase, transferring the idea of digestion from the stomach to mulling something over in the mind, dates from the late 1800s, although the idea was also expressed somewhat differently at least three centuries earlier.

fool ♦ In addition to the idioms beginning with FOOL, also see MAKE A FOOL OF; NOBODY'S FOOL; NO FOOL LIKE AN OLD FOOL; NOT SUFFER FOOLS GLADLY; PLAY THE FOOL; TAKE FOR (A FOOL). Also see under FOOLISH.

fool and his money are soon parted, a A silly or stupid person readily wastes money. For example, *Albert is known for giving waiters enormous tips — a fool and his money are soon parted.* This proverbial expression has been cited again and again since the mid-1500s.

fool around 1. Also, **monkey around.** Engage in idle or casual activity, putter. For example, *Jim loved to fool around with his computer,* or *She was monkeying around with some figures in hopes of balancing the budget.* [Second half of 1800s] 2. Engage in frivolous activity, waste time. For example, *Instead of studying, he spends all his spare time fooling around.* Also see FOOL AWAY. 3. Engage in flirting or casual sexual acts; also, engage in adultery. For example, *He caught the two teenagers fooling around in the basement.* [1830s]

fool away Squander, waste money or time, as in *He was fooling away the entire afternoon.* [Early 1600s] Also see FOOL AROUND, def. 2.

foolish ♦ See PENNY WISE AND POUND FOOLISH.

fool's errand A fruitless mission or undertaking, as in *Asking the bank for yet another loan was clearly a fool's errand.* [c. 1700]

fool's paradise State of delusive contentment or false hope. For example, *Joan lived in a fool's paradise, looking forward to a promotion she would never get.* This expression was first recorded in 1462.

fools rush in where angels fear to tread Ignorant or inexperienced individuals get involved in situations that wiser persons would avoid, as in *I've never heard this symphony and here I am conducting it — oh well, fools rush in where angels fear to tread,* or *He tried to mediate their unending argument — fools rush in.* This expression, so well known it is sometimes shortened as in the second example, is a quotation from Alexander Pope's *Essay on Criticism* (1709): "No place so sacred from such fops is barr'd . . . Nay, fly to altars; there

they'll talk you dead; For fools rush in where angels fear to tread."

foot ♦ In addition to the idioms beginning with FOOT, also see BOUND HAND AND FOOT; CAUGHT FLAT-FOOTED; GET OFF ON THE WRONG FOOT; NOT TOUCH WITH A TEN-FOOT POLE; ONE FOOT IN THE GRAVE; ON FOOT; ON THE RIGHT FOOT; PLAY FOOTSIE; PUT ONE'S BEST FOOT FORWARD; PUT ONE'S FOOT DOWN; PUT ONE'S FOOT IN IT; SET FOOT; SHOE IS ON THE OTHER FOOT; SHOOT ONESELF IN THE FOOT; WAIT ON HAND AND FOOT. Also see under FEET.

foot in both camps, have a Support or have good relations with two opposing sides. For example, *He had a foot in both camps, making donations to candidates in both parties.* In this expression *camp* alludes to encampments of enemy troops in a battle. [First half of 1900s]

foot in one's mouth, put one's Say something foolish, embarrassing, or tactless. For example, *Jane put her foot in her mouth when she called him by her first husband's name.* This notion is sometimes put as having **foot-in-mouth disease,** as in *He has a bad case of foot-in-mouth disease, always making some tactless remark.* The first expression dates from about 1900. The variant, dating from the mid-1900s, is a play on the *foot-and-mouth* (sometimes called *hoof-and-mouth*) *disease* that afflicts cattle, causing eruptions to break out around the mouth and hoofs.

foot in the door, get one's Achieve an initial stage; succeed with a first step. For example, *I think I could do well in an interview once I get my foot in the door with an appointment.* This term alludes to the door-to-door salesperson or canvasser who blocks the door with one foot so it cannot be closed.

footloose and fancy-free Having no attachments, especially romantic ones, and free to do as one pleases. For example, *When I was in my twenties, footloose and fancy-free, I would travel at the drop of a hat.* Both of these words have long been used separately; their pairing dates only from the 1900s.

footstep ♦ See FOLLOW IN SOMEONE'S FOOTSTEPS.

foot the bill Pay the bill, settle the accounts, as in *The bride's father was resigned to footing the bill for the wedding.* This expression uses *foot* in the sense of "add up and put the total at the foot, or bottom, of an account." [Colloquial; early 1800s]

for ♦ In addition to the idioms beginning with FOR, also see ALL FOR; AS FOR; BUT FOR; DO FOR; DONE FOR; EXCEPT FOR; GO FOR; GOING FOR; GOOD FOR; IN FOR; OUT FOR; UNCALLED FOR; WHAT FOR.

for a change For the sake of variety or novelty, as in *Let's take a taxi for a change,* or *So you're on time *for a change.* This phrase is sometimes used in a straightforward way, as in the first example, or to express the same sentiment as ABOUT TIME, that is, "it's high time something different happened," as in the second example. [First half of 1900s]

for all 1. Also, **for all that.** In spite of, notwithstanding. For example, *For all her protests she still loved the attention,* or *He's too old for the part but he did a good job for all that.* [Early 1300s] 2. **for all one cares** or **knows.** So far as one knows; also, one doesn't really care or know. These phrases are employed like a negative. For example, *He can buy ten houses for all I care,* meaning one doesn't care at all, or *For all I know she's gone to China,* meaning one doesn't really know where she is. [Mid-1700s]

for all intents and purposes ♦ See TO ALL INTENTS AND PURPOSES.

for all one is worth 1. To the utmost of one's power or ability, as in *Coming onto the homestretch she ran for all she was worth.* [Second half of 1800s] 2. **for all** or **for what it's worth; for whatever it's worth.** Even though it may not be important or valuable. For example, *Here's my opinion, for what it's worth,* or *For whatever it's worth I've decided to take the train.* [Late 1800s]

for all that ♦ See under FOR ALL.

for all the world 1. In all respects, precisely, as in *She looked for all the world like Greta Garbo.* [Late 1300s] 2. Also, **not for the world.** Not for anything, not at any price. For example, *I wouldn't give up chocolate for all the world,* or *Not for the world would I reveal your secret.* This hyperbolic expression is generally part of a negative statement. [First half of 1800s] For a synonym, see NOT FOR LOVE OR MONEY.

for a loop ♦ See KNOCK FOR A LOOP.

for a song Very cheaply, for little money, especially for less than something is worth. For example, "I know a man . . . sold a goodly manor for a song" (Shakespeare, *All's Well That Ends Well,* 3:2). This idiom alludes to the pennies given to street singers or to the small cost of sheet music. [Late 1500s]

for a wonder Surprisingly, strange to say, as in *For a wonder he didn't argue with the waiter about the bill.* [Late 1700s]

for better or for worse Under good or bad circumstances, with good or bad effect. For example, *For better or for worse he trusts everyone.* This term became widely familiar because it appears in the marriage service of the Book of Common Prayer (1549): "With this ring I thee wed, for richer or poorer, in sickness and in health, for better or worse, til death do us part." [Late 1300s]

forbid ♦ See GOD FORBID

forbidden fruit Unlawful pleasure or enjoyment; illicit love. For example, *After Mary moved in with John, Tom began courting her—forbidden fruit is sweet, I guess,* or *Smoking behind the woodshed, that's a case of forbidden fruit.* This expression alludes to Adam and Eve's violation of God's commandment not to touch fruit from the tree of knowledge, which resulted in their expulsion from the Garden of Eden (Genesis 3:6). In the form **forbidden fruit is sweet** it appeared in numerous early English proverb collections.

force ♦ In addition to the idioms beginning with FORCE, also see BRUTE FORCE; DRIVING FORCE; IN FORCE; JOIN FORCES; RECKON WITH (FORCE TO BE RECKONED WITH).

for certain Also, **for sure.** Without doubt. For example, *I can't tell for certain if this is the right color,* or *I know for sure that she has a new car.* The first term dates from the early 1300s. The variant, dating from the late 1500s, is also used colloquially to express agreement or assert the truth of a statement, as in *Mary is really bossy.—That's for sure,* or *Are you coming to the party?—For sure I am.*

force someone's hand Compel someone to act or speak prematurely or against his or her will. For example, *He didn't want to decide just then, but the board forced his hand.* This expression probably alludes to the **hand** (the cards) held in a game such as whist or poker, in which a player is compelled to play some card from his hand or to reveal his hand. [Mid-1800s]

force to be reckoned with ♦ See under RECKON WITH.

for chicken feed ♦ see CHICKEN FEED.

for crying out loud An exclamation of anger or exasperation, as in *For crying out loud, can't you do anything right?* This term is a euphemism for "for Christ's sake." [Colloquial; early 1900s]

for days on end ♦ See ON END.

for dear life Also, **for one's life.** Desperately, urgently, so as to save one's life. For example, *When the boat capsized, I hung on for dear life,* or *With the dogs chasing them they ran for their lives,* or *She wanted that vase but I saw it first and hung on to it for dear life.* These expressions are sometimes hyperbolic (that is, one's life may not actually be in danger). The first dates from the mid-1800s, the variant from the first half of the 1600s. Also see FOR THE LIFE OF ONE.

fore ♦ In addition to the idioms beginning with FORE, also see TO THE FORE.

fore and aft Both front and back, everywhere, as in *The children clung to the teacher fore and aft.* This expression is nautical terminology for the bow, or front, and the stern, or back, of a vessel. Today it is also used more broadly. [First half of 1600s]

foregone conclusion, a 1. An outcome regarded as inevitable, as in *The victory was a foregone conclusion.* 2. A conclusion formed in advance of argument or consideration, as in *The jury was warned to consider all of the evidence and not base their decision on a foregone conclusion.* This idiom probably was invented by Shakespeare (*Othello*, 3:3) but scholars are not agreed as to his precise meaning. [c. 1600]

foremost ♦ See FIRST AND FOREMOST.

forest ♦ See CAN'T SEE THE FOREST FOR THE TREES.

forever and a day 1. For a very long time, as in *He's been working on that book forever and a day.* This hyperbolic expression probably originated as a corruption of the now obsolete *for ever and ay.* Shakespeare used it in *The Taming of the Shrew* (4:4): "Farewell for ever and a day." Today it is mainly a substitute for "very long time." [c. 1600] 2. Incessantly, ceaselessly, as in *Will this racket never end? It's been going on forever and a day.* [Colloquial; first half of 1900s]

forewarned is forearmed Knowledge in advance enables one to be prepared, as in *Let me know when he's in town so I can take the phone off the hook—forewarned is forearmed.* This expression originated as a Latin proverb, *Praemonitus, praemunitus,* which was translated into English by the early 1500s. It soon was put to broader use than its original military applications.

for example Also, **for instance**. As an illustration of something, as in *Dress casually, in blue jeans, for example,* or *This program has problems—for instance, it's hard to retrieve lost data.* The first expression, which dates from the late 1500s, is used throughout this book to illustrate how an idiom is used. The variant dates from the mid-1600s.

for fear of Also, **for fear that**. In order to avoid or prevent, in case of. For example, *They closed all the windows for fear of rain.* The variant is always used before a clause, as in *She wouldn't let her children climb trees for fear that they would fall.* The first term dates from the late 1400s, the second from about 1600.

for free Without charge, gratis, as in *You can't expect the doctor to treat you for free.* [Colloquial; c. 1900]

for fun 1. Also, **in fun**. As a joke, not seriously. For example, *For fun the children told the teacher it was a holiday,* or *Their teasing was just in fun.* [Mid-1800s] 2. **for the fun of it; for kicks**. For pleasure or excitement. For example, *He played basketball for the fun of it,* or *They drove around for hours, just for kicks.* Also see FOR THE HELL OF IT.

forget ♦ In addition to the idioms beginning with FORGET, also see FORGIVE AND FORGET.

forget it Overlook it, it's not important; you're quite mistaken. This colloquial imperative is used in a variety of ways. For example, in *Thanks so much for helping—Forget it, it was nothing,* it is a substitute for "don't mention it" or YOU'RE WELCOME; in *Stop counting the change—forget it!* it means "stop doing something unimportant"; in *You think assembling this swingset was easy—forget it!* it means "it was not at all easy"; and in *Forget it—you'll never understand this theorem* it means that the possibility of your understanding it is hopeless. [c. 1900]

forget oneself Lose one's reserve, temper, or self-restraint; do or say something out of keeping with one's position or character. For example, *A teacher should never forget herself and shout at the class.* Shakespeare used it in *Richard II* (3:2): "I had forgot myself: am I not king?" [Late 1500s]

forgive and forget Both pardon and hold no resentment concerning a past event. For example, *After Meg and Mary decided to forgive and forget their differences, they became good friends.* This phrase dates from the 1300s and was a proverb by the mid-1500s. For a synonym, see LET BYGONES BE BYGONES.

for God's sake Also, **for goodness sake**. ♦ See FOR THE SAKE OF, def. 3.

for good Also, **for good and all**. Permanently, forever. For example, *I'm moving to Europe for good.* [1500s] Also see FOR KEEPS.

for good measure In addition to the required amount. For example, *Whenever she bakes she adds a little more cinnamon for good measure,* or *He didn't argue with my price, so I gave him some extra supplies for good measure.*

for heaven's sake ♦ See FOR THE SAKE OF, def. 3.

for keeps 1. For the winner to retain, as in *You can't take the marbles back; we were playing for keeps.* [Mid-1800s] 2. For an indefinitely long time, forever, as in *She is leaving town for keeps.* 3. In earnest, seriously, as in *We're separating for keeps.* [Late 1800s]

fork over Also, **fork out** or **up**. Hand over, pay up. For example, *It's time you forked over what you owe,* or *He forked out a hundred for that meal,* or *Fork up or we'll sue.* [Slang; early 1800s]

for love or money ♦ See NOT FOR LOVE OR MONEY.

form ♦ In addition to the idiom beginning with FORM, also see IMITATION IS THE SINCEREST FORM OF FLATTERY; RUN TO FORM; TRUE TO FORM.

form an opinion Make up one's mind or decide what one thinks about something. For example, *I* *need more facts before I can form an opinion about this issue,* or *Don't tell me your views; I want to form my own opinion.*

for one Also, **for one thing.** As the first of several possible instances. For example, *Everything seemed to go wrong; for one, we had a flat tire, and then we lost the keys,* or *I find many aspects of your proposal to be inadequate; for one thing, you don't specify where you'll get the money.* For one can also be applied to a person, as in *He doesn't like their behavior, and I for one agree with him.*

for one's money According to one's opinion, choice, or preference. For example, *For my money, a trip to Europe is not worth the trouble or expense.* [Second half of 1500s]

for one's pains In return for the trouble one has taken, as in *And all he got for his pains was a failing grade.* This expression is nearly always used ironically to indicate that the return was not appropriate to the effort made. [First half of 1500s]

for one's part Also, **on one's part; on the part of one.** 1. So far as one is concerned, as regards one's share in the matter. For example, *You may want to go out, but for my part I want to stay home,* or *On the part of the others, they expect a small share of the profits.* [Mid-1400s] 2. Regarding or with respect to the one specified, as in *For the Confederates' part, a daring strategy accounted for their victory at Chancellorsville,* or, as Thomas Macaulay put it in *History of England* (1849): "No excess of tyranny on the part of a prince can justify active resistance on the part of a subject." [c. 1400]

for one's sake ◆ See FOR THE SAKE OF.

for one thing ◆ See FOR ONE.

for openers Also, **for starters.** To begin with. For example, *Out of 50 possible jurors they eliminated 30, for openers,* or *She believed him, which indicated, for starters, that she was very gullible.* The word *starters* is also used for the appetizer or first course of a meal, as in *For starters we had shrimp cocktail.* [Mid-1900s]

for Pete's sake Also, **for pity's sake.** ◆ See FOR THE SAKE OF, def. 3.

for real Actually so, genuine, as in *Are your plans to move away for real?* [Slang; mid-1900s]

for shame Also, **shame on you.** An expression that condemns someone for being dishonorable or disgraceful. For example, *"For shame," said Carol to the puppy, "You shouldn't have done that,"* or *"Shame on you for cheating," the teacher said.* [c. 1300]

for short Also, **short for.** As an abbreviation. For example, *Richard prefers to be called Dick for short,* or *The Fed is short for the Federal Reserve Board of Governors.* [Mid-1800s]

for show For the sake of appearances of display. For example, *They put on a lavish buffet, mainly for show,* or *The police pretended to jail the informer, for show.* [c. 1700]

for starters ◆ See FOR OPENERS.

for sure ◆ See FOR CERTAIN.

fort ◆ See HOLD THE FORT.

forth ◆ See AND SO FORTH; BACK AND FORTH; BRING FORTH; HOLD FORTH; PUT FORTH; SET FORTH.

for that matter As for that, so far as that is concerned, as in *For that matter I'm not too hungry.* William Congreve used it in *The Old Batchelour* (1693; 4:22): "No, no, for that matter, when she and I part, she'll carry her separate maintenance." [Late 1600s]

for the asking On request, without charge, as in *My brother is a lawyer, so for us his advice is free for the asking,* or *If you want to borrow the tractor, it's yours for the asking.* This expression dates from the early 1800s, although slightly different versions of it (such as *at one's asking*) have been used since the late 1500s.

for the best ◆ See ALL FOR, def. 2.

for the birds Worthless, not to be taken seriously, no good. For example, *This conference is for the birds—let's leave now.* This term has been said to allude to horse droppings from which birds would extract seeds. This seemingly fanciful theory is borne out by a more vulgar version of this idiom, **shit for the birds.** [Slang; first half of 1900s]

for the hell of it Also, **for the heck of it; just for the hell of it.** For no particular reason; on a whim. For example, *We drove by the old place just for the hell of it.* In the first variant, *heck* is a euphemism for *hell.* [First half of 1900s] Also see FOR FUN, def. 2.

for the life of one Although trying hard, as in *I can't for the life of me remember his name.* This expression is always used hyperbolically, that is, one's life is not at all endangered. [Late 1700s]

for the love of 1. For the sake of, in consideration of. For example, *She signed up for all these volunteer jobs for the love of praise.* [c. 1200] 2. **for the love of Pete** or **Mike** or **God.** An exclamation of surprise, exasperation, or some similar feeling, as in *For the love of Pete, give me the money!* James Joyce used this idiom in *Ulysses* (1922): "For the love of Mike listen to him." *Pete* and *Mike* are euphemisms for God. [Early 1900s] Also see FOR THE SAKE OF, def. 3.

for the moment Also, **for the present; for the time being.** Temporarily, during the period under consideration, for now. For example, *For the moment I am tied up, but I'll get to it next week,* or *This room arrangement will do for the present,* or *Jim* *will act as secretary for the time being.* The first term dates from the late 1800s, the first variant from the mid-1500s, and the second variant from the late 1400s.

for the most part In general, usually. For example, *For the most part she is very good-humored,* or *The committee members agree for the most part.* [Late 1300s] Also see the synonyms BY AND LARGE; ON THE WHOLE.

for the present ♦ See FOR THE MOMENT.

for the record ♦ See GO ON RECORD; JUST FOR THE RECORD.

for the sake of 1. Also **for one's sake.** Out of consideration or regard for a person or thing; for someone's or something's advantage or good. For example, *For Jill's sake we did not serve meat,* or *We have to stop fighting for the sake of family unity.* [Early 1200s] 2. For the purpose or motive of, as in *You like to quarrel only for the sake of an argument* [Early 1200s]. 3. **for God's sake.** Also **for goodness** or **heaven's** or **Pete's** or **pity's sake.** An exclamation showing surprise, impatience, anger, or some other emotion, depending on the context. For example, *For God's sake, I didn't expect to see you here,* or *Hurry up, for goodness sake,* or *For heaven's sake, how can you say such a mean thing?* or *For pity's sake, finish your dinner.* The variants are euphemisms for God. [c. 1300] For a synonym, see FOR THE LOVE OF, def. 2.

for the time being ♦ See FOR THE MOMENT.

fortune ♦ See MAKE A FORTUNE.

for two cents For nothing; for a petty sum. For example, *For two cents I'd quit the club entirely.* Similarly, **like two cents,** means "of little or no value or importance, worthless," as in *She made me feel like two cents.* The use of *two cents* in this sense is thought to be derived from a similar British use of *twopence* or *tuppence,* which dates from about 1600. The American coin was substituted in the 1800s, along with **two bits,** slang for 25 cents and also meaning "a petty sum." Similarly, **put in one's two cents** or **two cents' worth,** meaning "to express one's unsolicited opinion for whatever it is worth," dates from the late 1800s.

forty winks A brief nap, as in *There's just time for forty winks before we have to leave.* This expression supposedly was first recorded in 1828 and relies on *wink* in the sense of "sleep," a usage dating from the 14th century.

forward ♦ See BACKWARD AND FORWARD; CARRY FORWARD; COME FORWARD; FROM THIS DAY FORWARD; KNOW LIKE A BOOK (BACKWARDS AND FORWARDS); LOOK FORWARD; PUT FORWARD; PUT ONE'S BEST FOOT FORWARD; SET FORWARD.

for what it's worth ♦ See under FOR ALL ONE IS WORTH.

foul ♦ In addition to the idioms beginning with FOUL, also see RUN AFOUL OF.

foul one's nest Also, **foul one's own nest.** Hurt one's own interests, as in *With his constant complaints about his wife, he's only fouling his own nest.* This metaphoric expression transfers a bird's soiling of its nest to human behavior. [Mid-1200s]

foul play Unfair or treacherous action, especially involving violence. For example, *The police suspected he had met with foul play.* This term originally was and still is applied to unfair conduct in a sport or game and was being used figuratively by the late 1500s. Shakespeare used it in *The Tempest* (1:2): "What foul play had we, that we came from thence?"

foul up Blunder or cause to blunder; botch, ruin. For example, *He's fouled up this report, but I think we can fix it,* or *Our plans were fouled up by the bad weather.* This expression is widely believed to have originated as a euphemism for FUCK UP. [Colloquial; c. 1940]

four ♦ In addition to the idioms beginning with FOUR, also see BETWEEN YOU AND ME AND (THE FOUR WALLS); ON ALL FOURS.

four corners of the earth, the The far ends of the world; all parts of the world. For example, *Athletes came from the four corners of the earth to compete in the Olympics.* This expression appeared in the Bible (Isaiah 11:12): "And gather the dispersed of Judah from the four corners of the earth." Although the idea that the earth is a flat plane with actual corners has long been discarded, the term has survived.

four-letter word Any of several short English words that are generally regarded as vulgar or obscene. For example, *No four-letter words are permitted in this classroom.* This expression is applied mostly to words describing excretory or sexual functions. [First half of 1900s]

fowl ♦ See NEITHER FISH NOR FOWL.

fox ♦ See CRAZY LIKE A FOX; SLY AS A FOX.

frame of mind Mental or emotional attitude or mood, as in *You have to be in the right frame of mind to enjoy hiking in the rain.* This idiom was first recorded in 1665.

fray ♦ See ENTER THE LISTS (FRAY).

freak out 1. Experience or cause to experience hallucinations, paranoia, or other frightening feelings as a result of taking a mind-altering drug. For example, *They were freaking out on LSD or some other drug.* [Slang; mid-1960s] 2. Behave or cause to behave irrationally and uncontrollably, with enthusiasm, excitement, fear, or madness. For example, *The band's wild playing made the audience freak out*, or *It was such a close accident, it really freaked me out*, or *She freaked out and ended up in the psychiatric ward*. [Slang; 1960s] Also see FLIP ONE'S LID; WIG OUT.

free ♦ In addition to the idioms beginning with FREE, also see BREATHE EASY (FREELY); FEEL FREE; FOOTLOOSE AND FANCY-FREE; FOR FREE; GET OFF (SCOT-FREE); HOME FREE; MAKE FREE WITH; OF ONE'S OWN ACCORD (FREE WILL).

free agent 1. A person not under compulsion or constraint, not responsible to any authority for his or her actions. For example, *After he quit his job, he decided to pursue the same line of work as a free agent*. Originally used to describe a person subject to the philosophic concept of **free will** (as opposed to determinism), this expression was first recorded in 1662. Later it was extended to mean "someone not under obligation to an authority." 2. A professional athlete who is free to sign a contract with any team. For example, *After he was released from the Yankees, he was a free agent and could shop around for the team that offered the most money*. [Second half of 1900s]

free and clear Without any legal encumbrance, such as a lien or mortgage. For example, *After the mortgage was paid off they owned the house free and clear*. [Mid-1800s]

free and easy 1. Casual, relaxed, as in *His style of writing is free and easy*. In the 1930s and 1940s this phrase gained currency as part of a slogan for a brand of cigarettes, which were said to be "free and easy" to inhale. [c. 1700] 2. Careless, sloppy, morally lax, as in *This administration was free and easy with the taxpayers' money*, or *These girls hate to be considered free and easy*. [First half of 1900s]

free as a bird At liberty, without obligations, as in *Can you join us tonight?—Yes, I'm free as a bird*, or *He's free as a bird—he can travel wherever he chooses*. [c. 1700]. Also see FOOTLOOSE AND FANCY-FREE.

free enterprise Also, **private enterprise**. An undertaking on one's own behalf, especially a shady or illegal one. For example, *The city treasurer didn't bother with competitive bids; the spirit of free enterprise just led him to his brother-in-law*, or *The sergeant indulged in a little private enterprise, selling cigarettes on the black market*. This sarcastic application of a term that has meant, since about 1885, the freedom of private businesses to operate competitively for profit with a minimum of government control, dates from the mid-1900s.

free fall A rapid, uncontrolled decline, as in *The markets threatened to go into free fall and we came close to outright panic*. This term transfers the aeronautical meaning of a free fall, that is, "a fall through the air without any impedance, such as a parachute," to other kinds of precipitous drop. [Second half of 1900s]

free hand Also, **free rein**. Freedom to do or decide as one sees fit. For example, *The teacher gave her assistant a free hand with the class*, or *They gave me free rein to reorganize the department*. The first expression dates from the late 1800s, the second from the mid-1900s.

free lunch Something acquired without due effort or cost. For example, *In politics there is no free lunch; every favor calls for repayment*. This expression alludes to the custom of taverns offering food free of charge to induce customers to buy drinks. It was soon extended to other kinds of gift but is often used in a negative way, as in the example. [First half of 1800s]

free rein ♦ See FREE HAND.

freeze one's blood ♦ See MAKE ONE'S BLOOD RUN COLD.

freeze out Shut out or exclude by unfriendly treatment; force to retire or withdraw from membership, a job, or the like. For example, *They tried to freeze me out of the conversation*, or *After Bill was frozen out of the case, they hired a new lawyer*. [Mid-1800s]

fresh ♦ In addition to the idioms beginning with FRESH, also see BREATH OF FRESH AIR.

fresh as a daisy Well rested, energetic, as in *I'm finally over my jet lag and feel fresh as a daisy*. This simile may allude to the fact that a daisy's petals fold at night and open in the morning. [Late 1700s]

fresh out of Also, **clean out of**. Recently or completely used up or unavailable. For example, *Sorry, I'm fresh out of sugar and can't lend you any*, or *We're clean out of small change*. [Colloquial; late 1800s]

friday ♦ See BLACK FRIDAY; GIRL FRIDAY; THANK GOD (IT'S FRIDAY).

friend ♦ In addition to the idiom beginning with FRIEND, also see FAIR-WEATHER FRIEND; MAKE FRIENDS.

friend in court Also, **friends in high places**. A person or persons who can help by virtue of their important position. For example, *With a friend in court, he has a good chance of getting the contract*, or *Jim thinks he can get out of paying the fine; he has friends in high places*. This expression alludes to the power of a person at the royal court. With the decline of monarchies, *high places* came into more common use. [c. 1400]

frighten ♦ See SCARE OUT OF ONE'S WITS.

fritter away Squander or waste little by little; wear down gradually. For example, *She frittered away her salary on odds and ends and saved nothing.* This expression was first recorded in Alexander Pope's *Dunciad* (1728): "How prologues into prefaces decay, And these to notes are fritter'd quite away."

fritz ♦ See ON THE BLINK (FRITZ).

fro ♦ See TO AND FRO.

frog in one's throat Hoarseness or phlegm in the throat, as in *Can you understand me? I've got a frog in my throat.* This expression probably owes its origin to the froglike croaks produced by a person with a sore throat. [c. 1900]

frog in a small pond ♦ See under BIG FISH IN A SMALL POND.

from bad to worse Unacceptable and getting more so, on a steady downward course. For example, *Mary's grades have gone from bad to worse.* [Mid-1500s] Also see IF WORST COMES TO WORST.

from first to last ♦ See under FIRST AND LAST.

from hand to hand ♦ See HAND TO HAND.

from hand to mouth ♦ See HAND TO MOUTH.

from head to toe Also, **from head to heels** or **foot**; **from tip** or **top to toe**. Over the entire body, in its entirety. For example, *He was dressed in black from head to toe,* or *She ached all over, from tip to toe.* These expressions date from ancient times. The alliterative *head to heels* originated about 1400, and Shakespeare had "from top to toe" in *Hamlet* (1:2).

from Missouri, I'm I'm extremely skeptical so you'll have to prove it. For example, *You won the lottery? Come on, I'm from Missouri.* The full expression, **I'm from Missouri and you'll have to show me,** dates from about 1880. Some authorities believe it alludes to the Missouri Compromise of 1820, whereby Missouri was admitted to the Union as a slave state and slavery was forbidden in certain other areas, but the connection, if any, is not clear.

from pillar to post From one thing or place to another, hither and thither. For example, *After Kevin joined the Air Force, the family kept moving from pillar to post.* This expression began life in the early 1400s as *from post to pillar,* an order no longer used, and is thought to allude to the banging about of a ball in the game of court tennis.

from rags to riches From being poor to being wealthy, especially through one's own efforts. For example, *The invention catapulted the scientist from rags to riches.* Horatio Alger (1834–1899) popularized this theme in some 130 best-selling novels, in which the hero, through hard work and thrift, pulled himself out of poverty to wealth and happiness.

from scratch From the very beginning, from the outset; from nothing. For example, *I knew we'd have a problem from scratch.* Similarly, **to start from scratch** means "to start from the very beginning," as in *After the business failed, they decided to reorganize and start from scratch.* This term comes from racing, where a competitor starts from the line scratched into the ground (whereas others may start ahead with a handicap). [Mid-1800s] Also see FROM THE GROUND UP; FROM THE WORD GO.

from soup to nuts Also, **from A to Z** or **start to finish** or **stem to stern**. From beginning to end, throughout, as in *We went through the whole agenda, from soup to nuts,* or *She had to learn a whole new system from A to Z,* or *It rained from start to finish,* or *We did over the whole house from stem to stern.* The first expression, with its analogy to the first and last courses of a meal, appeared in slightly different forms (such as *from potage to cheese*) from the 1500s on; the precise wording here dates only from the mid-1900s. The second expression alludes to the first and last letters of the Roman alphabet; see also ALPHA AND OMEGA. The third comes from racing and alludes to the entire course of the race; it dates from the mid-1800s. The last variant is nautical, alluding to the front or *stem,* and rear or *stern,* of a vessel.

from the bottom of one's heart Most sincerely, unreservedly. For example, *I want to thank all of my supporters from the bottom of my heart,* or *She wished, from the bottom of her heart, that her daughter would get well.* In English this term appeared in the Anglican Book of Common Prayer's Communion service (1545): "If one . . . be content to forgive from the bottom of his heart"; in Latin it dates back to Virgil.

from the cradle to the grave From birth to death, throughout life, as in *This health plan will cover you from cradle to grave.* Richard Steele used the term in *The Tatler* (1709): "A modest fellow never has a doubt from his cradle to his grave." [c. 1700]

from the ground up From the very beginning; also, completely, thoroughly. For example, *We've had to learn a new system from the ground up,* or *The company changed all of the forms from the ground up.* This expression alludes to the construction of a house, which begins with the foundation.

from the horse's mouth From a reliable source, on the best authority. For example, *I have it from the horse's mouth that he plans to retire next month.* Also put as **straight from the horse's mouth,** this expression alludes to examining a horse's teeth to determine its age and hence its worth. [1920s]

from the outset ◆ See AT THE OUTSET.

from the sublime to the ridiculous From the beautiful to the silly, from great to puny. For example, *They played first Bach and then an ad jingle—from the sublime to the ridiculous.* The reverse, **from the ridiculous to the sublime,** is used with the opposite meaning. Coined by Tom Paine in *The Age of Reason* (1794), in which he said the two are so closely related that it is but one step from one to the other, the phrase has been often repeated in either order.

from the word go From the start, as in *I've had trouble with this computer from the word go.* This expression probably alludes to the start of a race, signaled by the word *go.* [Early 1800s] For a synonym, see FROM SCRATCH.

from this day forward Also, **from this day on; from now on.** Beginning today and continuing forever, as in *They promised to follow instructions from this day forward,* or *From now on I'll do what you say.* The first rather formal expression for this concept dates from about 1500. The second was used in the past tense by Thomas Hobbes in *Odyssey* (1675): "From that day on, centaurs and men are foes." The last version is the most common today.

from time to time Occasionally, once in a while. For example, *From time to time we play bridge with the Carters.* [Late 1300s] Also see AT TIMES; EVERY NOW AND THEN; ONCE IN A WHILE.

from way back Since long ago; for a long time. For example, *This painting has been in the family from way back,* or *We know the Smiths from way back.* [Colloquial; late 1800s]

front ◆ In addition to the idioms beginning with FRONT, also see BRAVE FACE (FRONT); IN FRONT OF; OUT FRONT; UP FRONT.

front and center In the most prominent position, as in *You couldn't miss John—he was front and center in that presentation.* This expression alludes to the best and usually most expensive seats in a theater.

front burner, on a Also, **on the front burner.** A position of relatively great importance or high priority. For example, *The boss said this project is now on a front burner.* This expression alludes to a cook's putting the items requiring the most attention at the front of the stove. [1960s] Also see BACK BURNER.

front office The policy-making or executive individuals in an organization, as in *I'll have to check with the front office before I can give you a discount.* This term was originally underworld slang for police headquarters or the main detective bureau. It soon was extended to other administrative offices and their personnel. [c. 1900]

frosting on the cake ◆ See ICING ON THE CAKE.

frown on Regard with disapproval or distaste, as in *Pat frowns on bad language.* This idiom transfers the disapproving facial expression to the thought it expresses. [Late 1500s]

fruit ◆ See BEAR FRUIT; FORBIDDEN FRUIT.

fruitcake ◆ See NUTTY AS A FRUITCAKE.

fry, frying ◆ See OTHER FISH TO FRY; OUT OF THE FRYING PAN; SMALL FRY.

fuck around 1. Also, **fart around.** Engage in frivolous activity, as in *Stop fucking around and get the job done,* or *I'm tired of farting around—let's go home.* [Vulgar slang; 1920s] 2. **fuck someone around.** Cheat, treat badly or make trouble for someone, as in *Stop fucking me around; I know what you're up to.* [Vulgar slang; mid-1900s] 3. Be sexually promiscuous, as in *Doesn't he have a reputation for fucking around?* [Vulgar slang; c. 1930]

fuck off 1. Go away, get out of here, as in *Fuck off or I'll call the police.* This idiom is used only as a command. [Vulgar slang; 1920s] 2. Spend time idly, loaf or shirk one's duty. For example, *After twelve years of school some kids feel they're entitled to fuck off,* or *You're always fucking off instead of working.* [Vulgar slang; 1940s] 3. **be fucked off.** To be furious, as in *They didn't show up, and I am really fucked off.* [Vulgar slang; c. 1940] Also see PISS OFF.

fuck over Treat unfairly, take advantage of, as in *This so-called reform is really fucking over the homeless.* [Vulgar slang; c. 1960]

fuck up 1. Ruin, botch, spoil. For example, *Don't tell me you're going to fuck up again.* It is also put as **be fucked up,** meaning "be ruined or spoiled," as in *This entire project is fucked up.* This vulgar usage dates from the early 1900s but did not become widespread until about 1940. 2. Act carelessly or foolishly, mess up, as in *I'm sorry, I really fucked up when I invited them.* [Vulgar slang; c. 1940] 3. Break down, fail, as in *If the flash mechanism fucks up again, I won't get a picture.* [Vulgar slang; c. 1980] 4. **be fucked up.** Be very confused or mentally ill; also, intoxicated. For example, *He was so fucked up they had to hospitalize him,* or *What a party—I sure got fucked up.* [Vulgar slang; 1940s]

fuck you Also **get fucked; go fuck yourself.** A curse meaning "go to hell." For example, *Fuck you—go get your own dinner!* or *Get out of here, get fucked!* or, as John Dos Passos had it in *1919* (1931): "Joe got sore and told him to go fuck himself." The first and third of these vulgar curses date from the late 1800s, and the second from about 1950. Also see GIVE THE FINGER.

fuel ◆ See ADD FUEL TO THE FIRE.

full ◆ In addition to the idioms beginning with FULL, also see GLASS IS HALF FULL; HAVE ONE'S

HANDS FULL; IN FULL SWING; TO THE FULL. Also see under FILL.

full blast Also, **at full blast**. At full power, with great energy; also, as loud as possible. For example, *The committee is working full blast on the plans*, or *The fanfare featured the trumpets at full blast*. This expression transfers the strong currents of air used in furnaces to anything being done at full power. [Late 1700s]

full circle, come Also, **go full circle**. Complete an entire cycle; return to the original position or condition. For example, *After a whole year of debate we have come full circle on this issue*. Shakespeare may have originated this expression in *King Lear* (5:3): "The wheel is come full circle." A 20th-century idiom with a similar meaning is **what goes around comes around**, as in *I knew if I helped her now, she would help me later—what goes around comes around*.

full-court press An all-out effort to exert pressure. For example, *She'd learned over the years how to deliver a full-court press of guilt*. The term alludes to a basketball tactic in which the defenders put pressure on the opposing team over the entire court, trying to disrupt their dribbling and passing. [Late 1900s]

full of beans 1. Lively, energetic, in high spirits, as in *The children were full of beans today, looking forward to their field trip*. This expression has no valid explanation. [c. 1840] 2. Also, **full of prunes**. Acting foolish, talking nonsense, as in *One cup of coffee won't hurt you—you're full of prunes*. [c. 1930] Also see FULL OF CRAP.

full of crap Also, **full of bull; full of shit**. Talking nonsense or rubbish, as in *She doesn't know what she's talking about; she's full of crap*. All of these expressions alluding to excrement are considered vulgar. [First half of 1900s] Also see FULL OF IT, def. 2; HOT AIR.

full of hot air ♦ See HOT AIR.

full of it 1. Also, **full of the devil**. Mischievous, naughty. For example, *The youngsters were full of it today, giving the teacher a hard time*, or *Bill is full of the devil, hiding his roommate's clothes and teasing him mercilessly*. 2. Talking nonsense, as in *He claims to have fixed the dock, but I think he's full of it*. This usage is a euphemism for ruder idioms like FULL OF CRAP.

full of oneself Conceited, self-centered, as in *Ever since she won the prize Mary's been so full of herself that no one wants to talk to her*. This expression uses *full of* in the sense of "engrossed with" or "absorbed with," a usage dating from about 1600.

full speed ahead Also, **full steam ahead**. As fast and as strongly as possible. For example, *There's only one way we'll get there on time, so go full speed ahead*, or *Production would go full steam ahead as soon as the orders were confirmed*. It is also put as **with a full head of steam**, as in *She was traveling with a full head of steam—she was due there at noon*. These expressions all allude to the steam engine, where *full steam* signifies that a boiler has developed maximum pressure. They became well known through an order allegedly given by Admiral David Farragut at the battle of Mobile Bay (1864): "Damn the torpedoes! Full steam ahead!"

full swing ♦ See IN FULL SWING.

full tilt, at As fast or forcefully as possible, as in *Running full tilt on that very uneven ground, she was bound to trip and fall* or *Trying to keep up with new orders, the factory was running at full tilt*. Originally referring to the combatants' thrust of a sword or lance, this term has been used figuratively since about 1700.

full well Very well, exceedingly well, as in *You know full well how much this costs*. [c. 1700]

fun ♦ In addition to the idiom beginning with FUN, also see FOR FUN; LIKE FUN; MAKE FUN OF; MORE FUN THAN A BARREL OF MONKEYS. Also see under FUNNY.

fun and games Activity for pure pleasure or diversion. For example, *This job isn't all fun and games, you know*, or *We're just out for fun and games tonight*. [Early 1900s]

funeral ♦ See IT'S YOUR FUNERAL.

funny ♦ In addition to the idioms beginning with FUNNY, also see under FUN.

funny bone 1. A point on the elbow where the ulnar nerve runs close to the surface and produces a sharp tingling sensation when knocked against the bone. For example, *Ouch! I just banged my funny bone*. The expression is a pun on *humerus* (pronounced the same as *humorous*), the Latin name for the long bone of the arm. [Early 1800s] 2. A sense of humor, as in *That comedian really tickles my funny bone*. This expression is derived from def. 1.

funny business Deceit, treachery, unethical conduct. For example, *We suspect their outfit has been up to some funny business*. [Colloquial; c. 1880]

funny money Counterfeit money; also, money from an obscure or questionable source. For example, *The police warned storekeepers that some funny money was being passed around town*. This expression probably endures because of its rhyme. [1930s]

fur ♦ See MAKE THE DUST (FUR) FLY.

furious ♦ See FAST AND FURIOUS.

further ♦ See WITHOUT FURTHER ADO.

fury ♦ See HELL HAS NO FURY LIKE A WOMAN SCORNED.

fuse ♦ See BLOW A FUSE.

fuss ♦ In addition to the idiom beginning with FUSS, also see KICK UP A FUSS; MAKE A FUSS.

fuss and feathers Needless commotion and display, as in *There was so much fuss and feathers over the award ceremony that I decided not to attend.* This expression probably survives because of its appealing alliteration. [Mid-1800s]

future ♦ See IN THE NEAR FUTURE.

futz around Also, **futz with.** Waste time or effort on frivolities, play around. For example, *He spent all morning futzing around with the report,* or *No more futzing with the car—we have to go now.* This term may be a shortening and corruption of the Yiddish *arumfartzen,* for "fart around." [Slang; 1920s]

g

gab ♦ See GIFT OF GAB.

gaff ♦ See STAND THE GAFF.

gain ♦ In addition to the idiom beginning with GAIN, also see ILL-GOTTEN GAINS; NO PAIN, NO GAIN; NOTHING VENTURED, NOTHING GAINED.

gain ground 1. Advance, make progress; also, win acceptance. For example, *The new conservation policy is gaining ground among the voters.* This expression alludes to a military advance in which an army literally takes territory from the enemy. Its figurative use dates from about 1800. For an antonym, see LOSE GROUND. 2. **gain ground on** or **upon.** Encroach on, advance at the expense of. For example, *Door-to-door canvassing helped them gain ground on the opposition.*

gallery ♦ See PLAY TO THE GALLERY; ROGUES' GALLERY.

game ♦ In addition to the idioms beginning with GAME, also see AHEAD OF THE GAME; AT THIS STAGE (OF THE GAME); BADGER GAME; BEAT SOMEONE AT HIS OR HER OWN GAME; CALL SOMEONE'S BLUFF (GAME); CONFIDENCE GAME; END GAME; FAIR GAME; FUN AND GAMES; GIVE AWAY (THE GAME); LOSING BATTLE (GAME); NAME OF THE GAME; ONLY GAME IN TOWN; PLAY A WAITING GAME; PLAY GAMES; PLAY THE GAME; WAITING GAME; WHOLE NEW BALL GAME.

game is not worth the candle, the The returns from an activity or enterprise do not warrant the time, money or effort required. For example, *The office he is running for is so unimportant that the game's not worth the candle.* This expression, which began as a translation of a term used by the French essayist Michel de Montaigne in 1580, alludes to gambling by candlelight, which involved the expense of illumination. If the winnings were not sufficient, they did not warrant the expense. Used figuratively, it was a proverb within a century.

game is up, the Also, **the jig is up.** The trick or deception has been exposed. For example, *When they took inventory they realized what was missing, and the game was up for the department head.* This expression dates from the mid-1800s and uses *up* in the sense of "over" or "lost." The variant employs *jig* in the sense of "trickery," a usage dating from about 1600.

game that two can play, that's a Also, **two can play at that game.** Another can behave in the same way or do the same thing. For example, *He refused to tell us whether he would go or stay, but that's a game two can play.* This expression is generally used as a threat of retaliation. [Early 1800s]

gander ♦ See TAKE A GANDER AT.

gang ♦ In addition to the idiom beginning with GANG, also see LIKE GANGBUSTERS.

gang up 1. Also, **gang up with.** Act together as a group. For example, *The residents ganged up to make the neighborhood safer.* [Colloquial; c. 1920] 2. **gang up on** or **against.** Join in opposition or attack against, as in *The big kids were always ganging up on the little ones,* or *They all ganged up against the substitute teacher.* [1920s]

garden ♦ In addition to the idiom beginning with GARDEN, also see LEAD DOWN THE GARDEN PATH.

garden variety Ordinary, common, as in *I don't want anything special in a VCR—the garden variety will do.* This term alludes to a common plant as opposed to a specially bred hybrid. [Colloquial; 1920]

gas ♦ In addition to the idiom beginning with GAS, also see COOK WITH GAS; RUN OUT OF STEAM (GAS).

gasket ♦ See under BLOW A FUSE.

gasp ♦ See LAST GASP.

gas up Supply a vehicle with gasoline, as in *I want to be sure to gas up before we go.* James M. Cain used this term in *The Postman Always Rings Twice* (1934): "I went to gas up a car." [Colloquial; c. 1930] Also see TANK UP.

gate ♦ See CRASH THE GATE; GIVE SOMEONE THE AIR (GATE).

gather ♦ See ROLLING STONE GATHERS NO MOSS.

gauntlet ♦ See RUN THE GAUNTLET; THROW DOWN THE GAUNTLET.

gear ♦ See HIGH GEAR; SLIP A COG (GEAR).

gee whiz An expression of surprise, dismay, or enthusiasm. For example, *Gee whiz, Dad, I thought you'd let me borrow the car,* or *Gee whiz, they finally won the Series!* This term is thought to be a euphemism for "Jesus Christ." [Slang; 1870s]

gender gap A broad difference between men and women, as in *There is still an enormous gender gap in the wages of unskilled labor.* This expression at first referred to the difference between men and women in voting preferences. It has since been extended to other areas. [1970s]

general ♦ See IN GENERAL; ON (GENERAL) PRINCIPLE.

generation gap A broad difference in values and attitudes between one generation and another, especially between parents and their children. For example, *There's a real generation gap in their choice of music, restaurants, clothing—you name it.* [1960s]

generous to a fault ♦ See TO A FAULT.

get ♦ In addition to the idioms beginning with GET, also see BE (GET) BUSTED; CATCH (GET) IT IN THE NECK; COME AND GET IT; DIP (GET) ONE'S TOES INTO; EARLY BIRD CATCHES (GETS) THE WORM; GIVE AS GOOD AS ONE GETS; GROUND FLOOR, GET IN ON THE; IT TAKES GETTING USED TO; LAY (GET) ONE'S HANDS ON; LET SOMETHING GET OUT; MARCHING ORDERS, GET ONE'S; PLAY HARD TO GET; SQUEAKY WHEEL GETS THE GREASE; TELL SOMEONE WHERE TO GET OFF; WHEN THE GOING GETS TOUGH; YOU GET WHAT YOU PAY FOR. Also see under BECOME; GIVE; HAVE.

get a bang out of Also **get a charge** or **kick out of.** Get a feeling of excitement from, get a thrill from. For example, *I get a bang out of taking the kids to the amusement park,* or *I get a charge out of her imitations.* The first two terms allude to the jolt of an electrical charge. The first dates from the 1920s; Damon Runyon had it in *Guys and Dolls* (1929): "He seems to be getting a great bang out of the doings." The second dates from the mid-1900s. The third probably alludes to the stimulating effect of a strong alcoholic drink—*kick* was used in this sense from the 1840s on—but the precise wording dates from the early 1900s. Cole Porter used it for one of his most popular songs, "I Get a Kick Out of You" (1934).

get about 1. Also **get around.** Move around, be active, especially after an illness. For example, *At 85 Jean still gets around very well,* or *Arthritis makes it hard for him to get about.* [Mid-1800s] **2.** Become known, circulate, as in *The news of her engagement got about very quickly.* [Early 1800s] Also see GET AROUND, def. 4. **3.** Be socially active, as in *After her husband died, she didn't get about much for a year.* Also see GET AROUND, def. 3 and 4.

get a break Obtain a favorable opportunity; get special consideration or treatment. For example, *The understudy finally got a break when the star became ill,* or *The new price is higher, but you are getting a break on service.* [c. 1900] Also see GIVE SOMEONE A BREAK.

get a charge ♦ See GET A BANG.

get across 1. Also, **get it across.** Make understandable or clear, as in *I tried to get my point across,* or *He'll have to get it across to the others.* [Late

1800s] **2.** Also, **come across.** Be convincing, impress on others, as in *How can I get across to the students?* or *The headmaster's announcement comes across as a criticism of the faculty.* [c. 1920] Also see PUT ACROSS.

get a dirty look ♦ See DIRTY LOOK.

get a fix Obtain a needed dose of something, especially but not necessarily a narcotic drug. For example, *Heroin addicts will do anything to get their fix,* or *Chris referred to her daily swim in the pool as her chlorine fix.* The noun *fix* has been used for a narcotic dose since the 1930s, and was extended to other compulsively sought things about two decades later. Also see GET A FIX ON.

get a fix on Also, **have a fix on; get** or **have a handle on; get** or **have a grasp of.** Obtain (or have) a clear determination or understanding of something. For example, *I was finally able to get a fix on the specifics of this problem,* or *No one in the press room had a handle on Balkan history,* or *Do you have a grasp of the situation?* Similarly, **give a fix** means "provide a clear understanding," as in *This briefing will give us a fix on the current situation.* The usages with *fix* and *handle* are colloquialisms dating from the 1920s; those with *grasp* are more formal and date from the late 1600s.

get a free hand ♦ See FREE HAND.

get after Urge or scold someone about doing something. For example, *Dad should get after Billy to mow the lawn,* or *Mary got after Jane for forgetting her house key.* Also see KEEP AFTER.

get a grip on Also, **have a grip on.** Obtain mastery or control over something or someone. For example, *Get a grip on yourself or the reporters will give you a hard time,* or, as Arthur Conan Doyle put it in *Sherlock Holmes* (1894): "I have a grip on the essential facts of the case." This expression transfers a firm physical hold to emotional or intellectual control. [Late 1800s]

get a hand ♦ See GIVE A HAND, def. 2.

get a handle on ♦ See under GET A FIX ON.

get ahead 1. Succeed or make progress, especially in one's career or in society. For example, *She put in many hours of overtime in order to get ahead.* [c. 1800] **2.** Save a little money, as in *After we settle the hospital bill, we hope to get ahead enough to buy a new car.* **3. get ahead of.** Move in front of, as in *I got ahead of her in line.* **4. get ahead of.** Outdo, surpass, as in *We were determined to get ahead of the competition.* Also see AHEAD OF THE GAME.

get a head start ♦ See HEAD START.

get a kick out of ♦ See GET A BANG OUT OF.

get a life Acquire some interests or relationships of one's own. For example, *Stop sitting around and complaining—get a life.* [Slang; late 1900s]

get a line on Also, **have a line on.** Acquire information about something or someone, come to know. For example, *Sue got a line on some possible tennis partners,* or *The realtor has a line on a number of vacant apartments.* Similarly, **give someone a line on** means "provide information about," as in *The librarian gave me a line on the books I would need.* This idiom uses *line* in the sense of "a direct course." [c. 1900] Also see GET A FIX ON.

get a load of Look at or listen to, as in *Get a load of Mike feeding the baby,* or *Through those thin walls we really got a load of their fight.* [Slang; early 1900s]

get along 1. Also, **get on.** Be or continue to be on harmonious terms. For example, *She finds it hard to get along with her in-laws,* or *He gets on well with all of his neighbors except one.* The use of *along* dates from the late 1800s; the use of *on* dates from the early 1800s. A colloquial synonym for *get along well* is **get on like a house on fire,** in effect comparing increasingly good relations to the rapid progress of a fire. 2. Also, **get on.** Manage, fare with some success; also, prosper. For example, *I can just get along in this town on those wages,* or *Her way of getting on in the world was to marry a rich man.* The use of *on* dates from the late 1700s; the variant dates from the early 1800s. 3. **get along without.** Manage without something, as in *With that new car loan, he can't get along without a raise.* [Early 1800s] 4. Also, **get on.** Progress; advance, especially in years. For example, *How are you getting along with the refinishing?* or *Dad doesn't hear too well; he's getting on, you know.* [Late 1700s] Also see ALONG IN YEARS; GET ON, def. 5. 5. **get along with you.** Go away; also, be quiet, drop the subject, as in "Leave me. Get along with you" (Charles Dickens, *Barnaby Rudge,* 1837). [First half of 1800s] Also see GET ON.

get a move on Also, **get cracking** or **going** or **rolling.** Hurry up; also, start working. For example, *Get a move on, it's late,* or *Let's get cracking, kids,* or *It's time we got going,* or *The alarm went off ten minutes ago, so get rolling.* The first colloquial expression dates from the late 1800s. The second term, also colloquial, employs the verb *to crack* in the sense of "travel with speed," a usage dating from the early 1800s, but the idiom dates only from the first half of the 1900s. The third term dates from the late 1800s and also has other meanings; see GET GOING. **Get rolling** alludes to setting wheels in motion and dates from the first half of the 1900s. Also see GET BUSY; GET ON THE STICK.

get an in with Also, **have an in with.** Acquire (or have) influence with someone in authority. For example, *The only way they'll allow us to film the play is if we get an in with the director,* or *We should*

have no problem, since Dad has an in with the inspector. This idiom employs the noun *in* in the sense of "an introduction to someone of power, fame, or authority," a usage dating from the 1920s.

get another guess ♦ See HAVE ANOTHER GUESS.

get a rise out of Elicit an angry or irritated reaction, as in *His teasing always got a rise out of her.* This expression alludes to the angler's dropping a fly in a likely spot in the hope that a fish will rise to this bait.

get around 1. Also, **get round.** Circumvent or evade, as in *He managed to get around the rules for visiting hours.* [Late 1800s] 2. Also, **get round.** Convince or win over by flattery or cajoling, as in *Karen knew just how to get around her father,* or *I'll try to get round him but I'm not sure it'll work.* [Mid-1800s] 3. Travel from place to place; also, be active socially. For example, *It's hard to get around without a car,* or *Mary is never without a date — she really gets around.* [First half of 1900s] Also see GET ABOUT, def. 1. 4. Become known, circulate, as in *Reports of her resignation got around quickly.* [c. 1950] Also see GET ABOUT, def. 2. 5. **get around to** or **get round to.** Find the time or occasion for, as in *Dean never gets around to cleaning up the garage.* [Late 1800s]

get at 1. Touch, reach successfully, as in *Mom hid the peanut butter so we couldn't get at it.* [Late 1700s] 2. Try to make understandable; hint at or suggest. For example, *I think I see what you're getting at.* [Late 1800s] 3. Discover, learn, ascertain, as in *We must get at the facts of the case.* [Late 1700s] 4. Bribe or influence by improper or illegal means, as in *He got at the judge, and the charges were dismissed.* [Colloquial; mid-1800s] 5. Start on, begin work on, attend to, as in "Get at your canvassing early, and drive it with all your might" (Mark Twain, letter to his publishers, 1884). [Colloquial; late 1800s]

get a thing about ♦ See HAVE A THING ABOUT.

get away 1. Break free, escape, as in *The suspect ran down the street and got away,* or *I wanted to come but couldn't get away from the office.* [c. 1300] A variant is **get away from it all,** meaning "to depart and leave one's surroundings or problems or work behind." For example, *Joe is taking a few days off — he needs to get away from it all.* 2. Start out or leave quickly, as in *The greyhounds got away from the starting gate,* or *I thought I had the answer but it got away from me.* 3. Go, move off. For example, *Get away from my desk!* or *Get away — I don't want you near that hot stove.* [Late 1700s] Also see GET AWAY WITH.

get away with 1. Escape the consequences or blame for, as in *Bill often cheats on exams but usually gets away with it.* [Late 1800s] 2. **get away**

with murder. Escape the consequences of killing someone; also, do anything one wishes. For example, *If the jury doesn't convict him, he'll have gotten away with murder,* or *He talks all day on the phone—the supervisor is letting him get away with murder.* [First half of 1900s]

get a word in edgewise Also, **get a word in edgeways.** Insert oneself into a conversation or express one's opinion despite competition from other speakers. For example, *So many people had questions for the lecturer that it was hard to get a word in edgewise,* or *Nancy loves to talk, and I couldn't get a word in edgeways.* This idiom, often put in the negative, transfers an object with its edge foremost to inserting conversation. [Late 1700s]

get back 1. Also **get back to.** Return to a person, place, or condition. For example, *What time will you get back?* or *I hope he'll get back to the subject of this report.* [c. 1600] **2.** Recover something, as in *When will I get this book back?* [c. 1800]

get back at Take revenge on, as in *Watch out for Peter; he's sure to get back at you.* Similarly, **get one's own back** means simply "get revenge," as in *She finally saw a chance to get her own back.* The first expression dates from the late 1800s, the second from the early 1900s.

get back to ♦ See GET BACK, def. 1.

get behind 1. See FALL BEHIND. **2.** Support someone or something; also, help to promote someone or something. For example, *We must find as many workers as we can to get behind the union.* **3.** Enjoy, appreciate, as in *Norma just can't get behind ballet.* [Slang; c. 1970]

get better 1. Improve, as in *I just started studying Japanese, and I hope to get better soon.* **2.** Recover one's health, as in *The doctor said I could expect to get better within a couple of days.* Also see GET WELL.

get busy Start working, become active, as in *Stop dawdling; get busy,* or *We'd better get busy on this paper.* [c. 1900] Also see GET A MOVE ON; GET GOING; GET ON THE STICK.

get by 1. Move past, as in *There isn't room for this car to get by.* **2.** Manage to succeed or get along; also, barely succeed. For example, *He's getting by even though he only works half-time,* or *If he applied himself, Paul could be getting A's, but instead he's just getting by.* [Early 1900s] **3.** Be unnoticed; also, get approval or pass inspection. For example, *I wonder if these errors will get by the proofreader,* or *He hoped the paint job would get by.* [Early 1900s]

get cold feet ♦ See COLD FEET.

get cracking ♦ See under GET A MOVE ON.

get credit for Receive acknowledgment or praise for some accomplishment, as in *Bill got all the credit for attracting a big audience.* Similarly, **give**

credit for means "acknowledge" or "praise," as in *We should give the pianist credit for her work in the program.* [Mid-1700s]

get down 1. Descend; bring down; also, swallow. For example, *He's getting down from the ladder,* or *Can you get the cat down from the tree?* or *I can't seem to get this pill down.* [Late 1500s] **2. get down to.** Give one's attention to, as in *Let's get down to work,* or *It's time we got down to business.* [Late 1800s] For the most important variants, see under GET DOWN TO BRASS TACKS. **3. get down on.** See DOWN ON. **4. get someone down.** Discourage or depress someone. For example, *Don't let Mary's troubles get you down,* or *Day after day of rain really gets me down.* [c. 1930] **5.** Describe in writing, as in *Can you get down all he's saying?* **6.** Lose one's inhibitions, enjoy oneself fully. For example, *At our reunion we got down with all our old friends.* [Slang]

get down to brass tacks Also, **get down to bedrock** or **the nitty gritty** or **cases.** Deal with the essentials; come to the point. For example, *Stop delaying and get down to brass tacks,* or *We really need to get down to bedrock,* or *He has a way of getting down to the nitty gritty,* or *Let's get down to cases.* The origin of the first phrase, dating from the late 1800s, is disputed. Some believe it alludes to the brass tacks used under fine upholstery, others that it is Cockney rhyming slang for "hard facts," and still others that it alludes to tacks hammered into a sales counter to indicate precise measuring points. The noun *bedrock* has signified the hard rock underlying alluvial mineral deposits since about 1850 and has been used figuratively to denote "bottom" since the 1860s. The noun *nitty-gritty* dates from the mid-1900s and alludes to the detailed ("nitty") and possibly unpleasant ("gritty") issue in question. The noun *cases* apparently alludes to the game of faro, in which the "case card" is the last of a rank of cards remaining in play; this usage dates from about 1900. Also see TO THE POINT.

get going 1. See GET A MOVE ON. **2. get something going.** Start something, get something into full swing. For example, *Once we get production going we'll have no more problems.* This usage also appears in **when the going gets tough, the tough get going,** meaning that difficulties spur on capable individuals; the first *tough* here means "difficult," whereas the second means "strong-minded, resolute." For example, *That problem won't stop Tom; when the going gets tough, the tough get going.* Also see SWING INTO ACTION. **3.** Make someone talkative or active, as in *Once he got her going on her grandchildren, there was no stopping her.* [Colloquial; late 1800s]

get goose pimples ♦ See GOOSE PIMPLES.

get gray hair from Be very worried or upset by. For example, *I know I'm going to get gray hair from his driving.* Similarly, **give gray hair to** means "to worry someone," as in *The boy's love of rock climbing gave his parents gray hair.* This idiom alludes to the notion that extreme anxiety or grief can cause one's hair to turn gray. [Early 1600s]

get hold of Grasp, obtain; also, get in touch with. For example, *If you can just get hold of one end, I'll get the other,* or *Jane had no luck getting hold of the book she needed,* or *I've phoned a dozen times but I can't seem to get hold of him.* [c. 1300] Also see LAY HOLD OF.

get in 1. Enter a place, as in *We managed to get in just before the doors closed.* [First half of 1500s] 2. Arrive, as in *We got in late last night.* [Early 1600s] 3. Be elected to office or become accepted, as in a club. For example, *Marge asked the club if she could get in.* The variant **get into** takes an object, as in *Things changed after he got into office.* [Late 1500s] 4. Succeed in including, delivering, or finishing something, as in *Can you get in that last paragraph?* or *I hope you'll get it in on time.* Also see GET IN WITH.

get in a snit ♦ See IN A SNIT.

get in a stew ♦ See IN A STEW.

get in bad with Also, **get in good with.** ♦ See IN BAD WITH; IN GOOD WITH.

get in on ♦ see IN ON. Also see GET INTO THE ACT; (GET IN ON THE) GROUND FLOOR.

get in one's hair ♦ See IN ONE'S HAIR.

get in someone's face ♦ See IN SOMEONE'S FACE.

get in the way ♦ See IN THE WAY.

get into 1. Become involved in, as in *He got into trouble by stealing cars,* or *I don't want to get into the long history of this problem.* [Early 1700s] 2. Put on clothes, as in *Wait till I get into my suit.* [Late 1600s] 3. Take possession of one, cause to act differently or inappropriately, as in *You're leaving it to the animal shelter? What has got into you?* or *I don't know what gets into you children.* [Late 1800s] 4. See BE INTO. Also see subsequent entries beginning with GET INTO.

get into bed with ♦ See GO TO BED WITH.

get into hot water ♦ See HOT WATER.

get into one's head Also, **get** or **take it into one's head.** From an impression, idea, or plan. For example, *What strange idea has she got into her head?* or *He took it into his head that you want to quit.* [Late 1600s] Also see GET THROUGH ONE'S HEAD.

get into the act Also, **get in the act.** Become involved in some activity or venture, as in *Everybody wants to get into the act on this offer,* or *I'm sure his agent plans to get in the act and start negotiations.* This expression alludes to inserting oneself into a performance. [Mid-1900s]

get into the swing of things Become active, make progress. For example, *She only started work last week, but she quickly got into the swing of things.* [Late 1800s]

get into trouble ♦ See IN TROUBLE WITH.

get in touch ♦ See IN TOUCH.

get involved Become associated, especially in an emotional or sexual way. For example, *He joined the company last year but never really got involved in the work,* or *It's been two years since Tom got involved with Jean.*

get in with Become involved or associated with, as in *She got in with the right crowd,* or *These loans got me in deeper and deeper with the bank.* [Late 1600s]

get it 1. See CATCH IT. 2. Understand something, as in *He claims his plan is reasonable, but I'm not sure I get it.* This synonym for CATCH ON was popularized during the 1980s through a televised political debate in which presidential nominee Ronald Reagan told his opponent, **You just don't get it, do you?** This particular phrase has since been repeated in numerous contexts where one is expressing exasperation at someone's failure to understand something. The phrase is also put in the past tense, **got it,** meaning "understood." For example, *We're leaving tomorrow.—OK, got it.* [Colloquial; late 1800s] Also see GET THE MESSAGE.

get it on 1. Become filled with energy or excitement; enthusiastically begin. For example, *If you're ready to start rehearsing, let's get it on.* [Slang; c. 1950] 2. Engage in sexual intercourse, as in *They were about to get it on when the doorbell rang.* [Slang; 1970s]

get lost Go away, as in *Get lost, we don't want you around.* This rather rude slangy imperative dates from the 1940s.

get mileage out of Make use of, obtain service from, as in *The chorus got a lot of mileage out of that publicity,* or *You won't get much mileage out of that old TV set.* This expression alludes to the number of miles of travel yielded by a given amount of fuel, a tire, or other auto equipment. [Colloquial; mid-1900s]

get nowhere Also, **not get anywhere.** Make no progress, as in *I've tried to put this together, but I'm getting nowhere with it.* This expression is sometimes intensified as **get nowhere fast,** as in *I tried phoning but got nowhere fast.* [Early 1900s] Also see GET SOMEWHERE; GET THERE.

get off 1. Dismount, leave a vehicle, as in *She got off the horse right away,* or *Let's get off the train at the next stop.* [Late 1600s] 2. Start, as on a trip; leave. For example, *We got off at the crack of dawn.* [Mid-1700s] 3. Fire a round of ammunition; also, send away. For example, *He got off two shots,* *but the deer fled*, or *I got off that letter just in time*. **4.** Escape from punishment; also, obtain a lesser penalty or release for someone. For example, *He apologized so profusely that he was sure to get off*, or *The attorney got her client off with a slap on the wrist*. This sense is sometimes amplified to **get off easy** or **get off lightly**. Where there is no punishment at all, the expression is sometimes put as **get off scot-free**, originally meaning "be free from paying a fine or tax (*scot*)," dating from the 1500s. [Mid-1600s] **5.** Remove, take off, as in *I can't seem to get this paint off the car.* [Second half of 1600s] **6.** Succeed in uttering, especially a joke. For example, *Carl always manages to get off a good one before he gets serious.* [Mid-1800s] **7.** Have the effrontery to do or say something. For example, *Where does he get off telling me what to do?* [Colloquial; early 1900s] **8.** Experience orgasm, as in *She never did get off.* [Slang; first half of 1900s] **9.** Also, **get off of one.** Stop bothering or criticizing one, as in *Get off me right now!* or *If you don't get off of me I'm walking out.* [Slang; c. 1940] Also see GET OFF ON; OFF ONE'S BACK.

get off on 1. Feel the effects of or take a mind-altering drug. For example, *He was getting off on crack.* [Slang; 1930s] **2.** Enjoy, derive intense pleasure from, as in *I really get off on good jazz.* [Slang; c. 1970]

get off one's chest ▶ See OFF ONE'S CHEST.

get off one's tail Also, **get off one's butt.** Stop loafing and start doing something. For example, *Get off your tail and help your mother*, or *I should get off my butt, but I'm exhausted.* Neither slangy expression, with its allusion to the buttocks, is considered polite.

get off on the wrong foot ▶ See under ON THE RIGHT FOOT.

get off scot-free ▶ See GET OFF, def. 4.

get off someone's back ▶ See OFF SOMEONE'S BACK.

get off the dime Take action, especially following a time of indecision or delay. For example, *It's time this administration got off the dime and came up with a viable budget.* This expression originated in the 1920s in dancehalls as an imperative for dancers to get moving. By 1926 it had been extended to other activities.

get off the ground Make a start, get underway, as in *Because of legal difficulties, the construction project never got off the ground.* This expression, alluding to flight, dates from the mid-1900s. The similar-sounding **get off to a flying start**, meaning "make a successful start," alludes not to flight but to a quick start in a race, a usage from the late 1800s. For example, *He's off to a flying start with his dissertation.*

get off the hook ▶ See OFF THE HOOK.

get on 1. Also, **get upon.** Climb on, mount. For example, *They say one should get back on a horse as soon as one's fallen off.* [Early 1600s] **2.** See GET ALONG, def. 1. **3.** See GET ALONG, def. 2. **4.** See GET ALONG, def. 4. Also see ALONG IN YEARS. **5. get on in the world** or **company,** etc. Prosper or succeed, as in *Her inheritance has helped her get on in society*, or *Dad asked if Bill was getting on in the company.* [Early 1800s] **6. get on with it.** Move ahead, pursue one's work. For example, *We've spent enough time talking about it; now let's get on with it.* [Early 1800s] **7. get on for.** Advance toward an age, amount, time, and so on. For example, *It's getting on for noon, so we'd better eat lunch.* This usage is often put in the participial form, **getting on for.** [Mid-1800] **8.** See TURN ON, def. 3. Also see the subsequent entries beginning with GET ON.

get one down ▶ See GET DOWN, def. 4.

get one's ▶ In addition to the idioms beginning with GET ONE'S, also see GET SOMEONE'S.

get one's 1. Get one's due punishment or reward, as in *If they put off their schoolwork to go to the ball game, sooner or later they'll get theirs*, or *The union members were prepared to go on strike; they were determined to get theirs.* The punishment version is earlier, dating from about 1900. **2.** Be killed, as in "He'd got *his*. I knew it by the way his head rolled in my hands" (Rudyard Kipling, *Diversity of Creatures,* 1913). This usage originated in the military. [c. 1900]

get one's act together Also, **get one's shit** or **it all together.** Start to behave more appropriately or effectively; get organized. For example, *Once Joe gets his act together he'll get a raise*, or *You'd better get it all together before the boss comes back.* The variant using *shit* is considered vulgar. [Slang; second half of 1900s] Also see GET ONE'S DUCKS IN A ROW.

get one's bearings Also, **find one's bearings.** Figure out one's position or situation relative to one's surroundings. For example, *She's still new to the company and needs time to find her bearings*, or *I'll be along soon; just wait till I get my bearings.* Naturally, one can also **lose one's bearings,** as in *After we missed the turnpike exit, we completely lost our bearings.* These phrases use *bearings* in the sense of "relative position," a usage dating from the 1600s.

get one's comeuppance Receive the treatment one deserves, especially punishment or retribution. For example, *She behaved badly, but I'm sure she'll get her comeuppance soon.* The exact relationship of *comeuppance* to the verb *come up* in its common senses—"rise" and "present itself"—is no longer clear. [Mid-1800s]

get one's ducks in a row Also, **have one's ducks in a row.** Complete one's preparations, become efficient and well organized, as in *I'm trying to get my ducks in a row before I go to Europe.* This synonym for GET ONE'S ACT TOGETHER probably alludes to lining up target ducks in a shooting gallery. [Slang; 1970s]

get one's feet on the ground Also, **have** or **keep one's feet on the ground.** ◆ See BOTH FEET ON THE GROUND.

get one's feet wet Embark on a new venture, start into new territory. For example, *I've only had a few cello lessons—I've barely gotten my feet wet.* This expression alludes to the timid swimmer slowly getting into the water. [Late 1500s]

get one's fill Also, **have one's fill.** Be satisfied; have enough (or more than enough) of something. For example, *I love opera—I can never get my fill of it,* or *He's had his fill of dirty jobs.* This expression alludes to having enough (or too much) to eat. [Mid-1500s] Also see FED TO THE GILLS.

get one's hands dirty ◆ See DIRTY ONE'S HANDS.

get one's hands on ◆ See LAY HANDS ON.

get one's head examined Also, **have one's head examined.** One is crazy or absolutely wrong. For example, *You like this food? Go get your head examined,* or *If you believe that story, you should have your head examined.* This hyperbolic and usually jocular expression of disagreement may, thought Eric Partridge, allude to the now discredited field of phrenology, which holds that the configurations of the skull reveal mental and emotional characteristics. [Early 1900s]

get one's money's worth Receive good value, as in *They performed four extra songs, so we really got our money's worth,* or *We got our money's worth at the beach—there wasn't a cloud in the sky.* This expression often but not always refers to a monetary expenditure.

get one's own back ◆ See GET BACK AT.

get one's teeth into ◆ See SINK ONE'S TEETH INTO.

get one's walking papers ◆ See WALKING PAPERS.

get one's way Also, **get** or **have one's own way.** Be allowed to or make others do as one wishes. For example, *Two-year-olds often scream until they get their own way,* or *All right, I give in—have it your own way.* [Late 1500s]

get one's wires crossed Also, **have one's wires crossed.** Become or be confused or mistaken about something, as in *If you think there's a meeting today, you really have your wires crossed; it's not till next month.* This expression transfers a wrongly wired telephone or telegraph connection to human misunderstanding. [Colloquial; early 1900s]

get on someone's good side Win someone's approval or support, as in *Kate offered to walk the dog in order to get on her aunt's good side.* [c. 1930] Also see IN GOOD WITH.

get on someone's nerves Irritate someone, as in *His fidgeting gets on the teacher's nerves,* or, as T.S.

Eliot put it in *The Elder Statesman* (1959): "How it used to get on my nerves, when I saw you always sitting there with your nose in a book." [c. 1900]

get on the bandwagon ◆ See ON THE BANDWAGON.

get on the stick Start working, as in *I have to get on the stick and start preparing dinner.* This synonym for GET GOING OR GET BUSY alludes to getting a car going by manipulating the gearshift, or *stick.* [Slang; early 1900s]

get on with it ◆ See GET ON, def. 6.

get out 1. Leave, escape, as in *With good conduct he'll get out of prison in a few months,* or *In case of a fire, we just want to get out alive.* [c. 1300] This phrase is also used as an imperative, ordering someone to depart. For example, *Get out! You've no business being in here.* [c. 1700] Also see GET OUT OF, def. 1. 2. Become known, as in *Somehow the secret got out.* [Late 1800s] Also see OUT IN THE OPEN. 3. **get something out.** Publish something, as in *Once we get out the newsletter, we can concentrate on other projects.* [Late 1700s] 4. Produce a sound, as in *The singer had a sore throat and could hardly get out a note.* [First half of 1800s] Also see the subsequent idioms beginning with GET OUT.

get out from under ◆ See OUT FROM UNDER.

get out of 1. Emerge or escape from, as in *I hate to get out of bed on cold mornings,* or *He'll be lucky to get out of this mess.* [First half of 1500s] Also see GET OUT, def. 1. 2. Go beyond, as in *The cat had climbed into the tree; she'd gotten well out of my reach.* [First half of 1600s] Also see OUT OF CONTROL; OUT OF SIGHT. 3. Evade or avoid, as in *He tried to get out of answering their questions,* or *Please get out of the way so we can pass.* [Late 1800s] Also see OUT OF THE WAY. 4. Elicit or draw out something from someone. For example, *I can't get a straight answer out of him,* or *Getting a contribution out of her is like pulling teeth.* [First half of 1600s] 5. Get rid of something, remove, as in *Get these cats out of the house,* or *I can't get this melody out of my head.* Also see OUT OF ONE'S SYSTEM. 6. Extract from, obtain from. For example, *You can get a lot of juice out of these oranges,* or *She got little or nothing out of this investment.* It is also put as **get the most out of,** meaning "use to the greatest advantage," as in *He gets the most out of his staff.* [Second half of 1600s] Also see GET A BANG OUT OF; GET A RISE OUT OF; GET MILEAGE OUT OF.

get out of one's face ◆ See under IN SOMEONE'S FACE, def. 2.

get out of one's system ◆ See OUT OF ONE'S SYSTEM.

get out of someone's sight ◆ See OUT OF SIGHT, def. 1.

get out of the way ◆ See OUT OF THE WAY.

get out while the getting is good Leave while one can or has the chance to, as in *He just had a* good offer from a rival firm and decided to get out while the getting is good. This colloquial phrase uses GET OUT in the sense of "escape" or "depart."

get over 1. Overcome, surmount, as in *We have finally gotten over our biases.* [Late 1600s] 2. Recover from, as in *I just got over the flu,* or *I hope the children get over their parents' divorce quickly.* [c. 1700] This usage sometimes appears as **get over it,** as on a bumper sticker following the 1992 presidential election: "Bush Lost, Get Over It." 3. Also, **get over with.** Complete, have done with, especially something unpleasant. For example, *When I finally got the proofreading over, I was ready for a day off,* or *I'm glad to get all that dental work over with.* It also is put as **get it over with,** as in *I might as well sign the check and get it over with.* The first usage dates from the late 1800s, the second from the early 1800s.

get physical Make physical contact, either forcefully or sexually. For example, *Stop pushing—there's no need to get physical,* or *Thirteen is too young to get physical in that way.* [Slang; second half of 1900s]

get ready Also, **make ready.** Become prepared or make preparations for something. For example, *It'll take me another hour to get ready for the painter,* or *Jane promised to make the room ready for our guests.* [Late 1500s] Also see GET SET.

get real Be realistic, understand what's going on, as in *You think you'll win the lottery if you buy one ticket a week? Get real!* [Slang; second half of 1900s]

get religion Be converted; also, decide to behave in an upright, ethical way. For example, *After the children were born, John got religion and joined the church,* or *After years of total selfishness, she suddenly got religion and is doing all kinds of volunteer work.* [Second half of 1700s]

get rid of Also, **be rid of.** Eliminate, discard, or free oneself from. For example, *It's time we got rid of these old newspapers,* or *He kept calling for months, but now we're finally rid of him.* The first expression dates from the mid-1600s, the second from the 1400s. Also see GET OUT OF, def. 5.

get right Understand accurately or do correctly, as in *If I get it right, you're not leaving until tomorrow,* or *The faucet works perfectly; the plumber finally got it right.* [First half of 1900s]

get rolling ♦ See GET A MOVE ON.

get round ♦ See GET AROUND, def. 1 and 2.

get set Prepare to go, as in *Get set; the taxi's coming.* This phrase is also a synonym for GET READY. Also see under ALL SET.

get sick 1. Also, **take sick** or **ill.** Become ill, as in *It's just my luck to get sick on vacation,* or *When was she taken ill?* [Ninth century] 2. Become disgusted, as in *We got sick as we learned how much money* was wasted, or *I get sick when I hear about his debts.* [Early 1500s] Also see MAKE ONE SICK. 3. Also, **get sick to one's stomach; be sick.** Become nauseated, vomit, as in *If you eat any more candy you'll get sick,* or *Sick to her stomach every morning? She must be pregnant.* [Early 1600s]

get someone's back up Also, **get someone's dander up; put** or **set someone's back up.** Make angry, as in *Bill's arrogance really got my back up,* or *The foolish delays at the bank only put her back up.* **Get one's back up** and **get one's dander up** mean "become angry," as in *Martha is quick to get her dander up.* The *back* in these phrases alludes to a cat arching its back when annoyed, and *put* and *set* were the earliest verbs used in this idiom, dating from the 1700s; *get* is more often heard today. The origin of *dander,* used since the early 1800s, is disputed; a likely theory is that it comes from the Dutch *dander,* for "thunder." Also see GET SOMEONE'S GOAT; RAISE ONE'S HACKLES.

get someone's goat Annoy or anger someone, as in *By teasing me about that article I wrote, he's trying to get my goat, but I won't let him.* The origin of this expression is disputed. H.L. Mencken held it came from using a goat as a calming influence in a racehorse's stall and removing it just before the race, thereby making the horse nervous. However, there is no firm evidence for this origin. [c. 1900]

get someone's number Also, **have someone's number.** Determine or know one's real character or motives, as in *You can't fool Jane; she's got your number.* This expression uses *number* in the sense of "a precise appraisal." Charles Dickens had it in *Bleak House* (1853): "Whenever a person proclaims to you, 'In worldly matters I'm a child,' . . . that person is only crying off from being held accountable . . . and you have got that person's number." [Mid-1800s]

get someone wrong Misunderstand someone, as in *I think you got him wrong.* This expression is often put as **Don't get me wrong,** used to clarify one's feelings, views, or the like, as in *Don't get me wrong—I'm happy about the outcome.* [Colloquial; c. 1900] Also see MAKE NO MISTAKE.

get something into one's head ♦ See GET INTO ONE'S HEAD.

get something on someone Also, **have something on someone.** Obtain or possess damaging knowledge about someone. For example, *They hoped to get something on the candidate,* or *Once Tom had something on his boss, he knew he would not be pressured again.* [c. 1920] Also see BE ON TO.

get somewhere Make progress. For example, *The foundation has been laid, so we're finally getting somewhere.* Also see GET NOWHERE; GET THERE.

get straight Also, **have straight.** Understand correctly or make something clear, as in *Now let's get* *it straight—you'll take over at four*, or *Do I have it straight about when you're leaving?* This expression uses *straight* in the sense of "in proper order" or "not confused." [c. 1920]

get stuffed An only slightly politer version of FUCK YOU. For example, *When the taxi cut in front of him, he yelled at the driver, "Get stuffed!"* [Vulgar slang; mid-1900s]

get the advantage of Also, **get** or **have the advantage over**. Be in a superior position to, as in *He had the advantage over me, since I couldn't even remember his name, let alone his position.* [Mid-1500s] Also see GET THE BETTER OF; GET THE DROP ON.

get the air ♦ See GIVE SOMEONE THE AIR.

get the ax Also, **get the boot** or **bounce** or **can** or **heave-ho** or **hook** or **sack**. Be discharged or fired, expelled, or rejected. For example, *He got the ax at the end of the first week*, or *The manager was stunned when he got the boot himself*, or *We got the bounce in the first quarter*, or *The pitcher got the hook after one inning*, or *Bill finally gave his brother-in-law the sack.* All but the last of these slangy expressions date from the 1870s and 1880s. They all have variations using **give** that mean "to fire or expel someone," as in *Are they giving Ruth the ax?* **Get the ax** alludes to the executioner's *ax*, and **get the boot** to literally *booting* or kicking someone out. **Get the bounce** alludes to being *bounced* out; **get the can** comes from the verb *can*, "to dismiss," perhaps alluding to being sealed in a container; **get the heave-ho** alludes to *heave* in the sense of lifting someone bodily, and **get the hook** is an allusion to a fishing hook. **Get the sack**, first recorded in 1825, probably came from French though it existed in Middle Dutch. The reference here is to a workman's *sac* ("bag") in which he carried his tools and which was given back to him when he was fired. Also see GIVE SOMEONE THE AIR.

get the ball rolling Also, **keep the ball rolling**. Start an undertaking; also, keep an undertaking from flagging. For example, *Let's get the ball rolling by putting up some posters*, or *The hostess kept the ball rolling, talking to each of the guests in turn.* This expression originated in one or another sport in which it was important to keep a ball moving. [Colloquial; late 1700s] Also see GET THE SHOW ON THE ROAD.

get the better of Also, **get the best of**; **have the better** or **best of**. Become superior to or master someone or something; win out. For example, *John's common sense got the better of his pride, and he apologized*, or *Her older sister was always trying to get the best of her*, or *He was determined to have the better of his competitors.* [c. 1600] Also see GET THE DROP ON.

get the business ♦ See THE BUSINESS.

get the can ♦ See under GET THE AX.

get the drift Also, **catch the drift**. Understand the general meaning or purport. For example, *I didn't get the drift—do they want to go or not?* or *Over all the noise he barely managed to catch the drift of their conversation.* The noun *drift* has been used for "purport" since the early 1500s.

get the drop on Also, **get** or **have the jump on**. Achieve a distinct advantage over someone, especially through early or quick action; get a head start. For example, *Their book on electronic communication has the drop on all the others*, or *We really got the jump on the competition.* The first of these slangy expressions dates from the mid-1800s and originally alluded to pointing one's gun at someone before he pointed his at you. It was transferred to more general use by about 1900. The second, which uses *jump* in the sense of "start," dates from about 1900.

get the feel of Also, **have the feel of**. Become or be accustomed to or learn about; acquire skill in. For example, *It took me a while to get the feel of the new car*, or *After a few months Jack had the feel of his new position.* This idiom transfers the sense of touch to mental perception. [Mid-1900s]

get the goods on Also, **have the goods on**. Acquire or possess confidential information about someone, especially of a damaging or incriminating kind. For example, *"Trouble is, they've got the goods on me"* (Owen Johnson, *The Lawrenceville Stories*, 1909). [Slang; 1870s] Also see GET ON ONE.

get the hang of Learn the proper way of doing, using or handling something; acquire the knack of something. For example, *I finally got the hang of this computer program.* [Colloquial; mid-1800s]

get theirs ♦ See GET ONE'S.

get the jump on ♦ See GET THE DROP ON.

get the lead out Also, **get the lead out of one's feet** or **pants**. Hurry up, move faster. For example, *Get the lead out of your pants, kids, or we'll be late*, or even more figuratively, *Arthur is the slowest talker—he can't seem to get the lead out and make his point.* This expression implies that lead, the heaviest of the base metals, is preventing one from moving. [Slang; first half of 1900s]

get the message Also, **get the picture**. Understand or infer the real import or substance of something. For example, *He gestured to the waiter, who got the message and brought the bill*, or *Kate got the picture and decided to keep her mouth shut about the error.* [Mid-1900s] Also see GET IT.

get the most out of ♦ See GET OUT OF, def. 6.

get the nod Receive approval or assent, as in, *The contestant got the nod from the judges.* Similarly **give the nod** means "to show approval or assent." These expressions allude to the quick inclination of the head to indicate approval. [First half of 1900s]

get the picture ♦ See under GET THE MESSAGE.

get there Achieve success, as in *He always wanted to be a millionaire, and he finally got there.* In this expression, *there* indicates one's goal. The participial form of this phrase, **getting there,** means "making progress toward a goal," as in *I haven't finished the book, but I'm getting there.* [Late 1800s] Also see GET SOMEWHERE.

get the runaround Be treated evasively or misleadingly, especially in response to a request. For example, *Every time I ask about next year's plans I get the runaround.* The related expression **give the runaround** means "to treat evasively or misleadingly," as in *He gives her the runaround whenever she asks for time off.* [Early 1900s]

get the sack ♦ See under GET THE AX.

get the show on the road Start an undertaking; begin work. For example, *After months of training, the astronauts were eager to get the show on the road.* This synonym of GET GOING alludes to a theatrical production going on tour. Also see GET THE BALL ROLLING.

get the upper hand ♦ See UPPER HAND.

get the worst of it Also, **have the worst of it.** Be defeated, experience a disadvantage, or suffer the most harm. For example, *In any argument Joe usually gets the worst of it,* or *If we play the last three games as scheduled, our team is bound to have the worst of it,* or *The car got the worst of it, and no one was hurt.* These phrases survive many older ones (such as **go to the worst** and **come by the worst**) in which *worst* is used in the sense of "defeat," a usage dating from about 1500. Also see GET THE BETTER (BEST) OF.

get through 1. Reach the end, finish, complete, as in *Now that our computer system is working again, I should get through by mid-afternoon.* It is also put as **get through with,** as in *As soon as we get through with painting the kitchen, I'll call you.* [Mid-1600s] 2. Succeed in passing or surviving something, as in *This epidemic is awful, but I'm sure we'll get through it somehow.* [Mid-1700s] 3. Also, **get through to someone.** Make contact with or reach someone, as in *After trying to reach them all night, we got finally through,* or *He tried to get through to the family.* [Late 1800s] 4. Also **get through to.** Make oneself understood, as in *Am I getting through to you?* [Colloquial; mid-1900s]

get through one's head Understand, believe, or be convinced. For example, *Bill cannot get it through his head that John is moving out.*

get through to ♦ See GET THROUGH, def. 3 and 4.

getting there ♦ See under GET THERE.

get to 1. Arrive at, reach, as in *When we get to the store we'll talk to the manager.* 2. Begin doing something or start to deal with something. For example, *We got to reminiscing about college days,* or *Let's get to this business right now.* [Mid-1800s] 3. Bribe someone, as in *We're sure the dealer got to one of the narcotics agents.* [Slang; 1920s] 4. Influence or affect, especially adversely, as in *This loud music really gets to me,* or *Mother's crying always gets to him.* [Colloquial; 1960s] Also see GET UNDER SOMEONE'S SKIN.

get to first base Also, **reach first base.** 1. Succeed in the initial phase of something; meet with preliminary approval. For example, *They were delighted that they'd gotten to first base in the negotiations.* This term alludes to the *first base* of baseball, which is the first step toward scoring a run for the batter's team. [c. 1900] 2. Reach the initial stage of sexual intimacy, such as kissing. For example, *Mary is so shy that I can't even get to first base with her.* [1920s]

get together 1. Accumulate, gather, as in *Go get all the firewood together.* [c. 1400] 2. Come together, assemble, as in *Let's get together next week.* The variant **get together with** means "meet with someone," as in *I can't get together with them today but I'll have time next week.* [Late 1600s] 3. Arrive at an agreement, as in *The jury was unable to get together on a verdict.* 4. **get something** or **oneself together.** See under GET ONE'S ACT TOGETHER.

get to one's feet Also, **get on one's feet.** Stand up, as in *They all got to their feet when the President came in.* [Early 1700s]

get to the bottom of Find the basic underlying quality or cause of something. For example, *He was determined to get to the bottom of the problem.* [Late 1700s] Also see AT BOTTOM.

get to the heart of Find or determine the most important or essential facts or meaning. For example, *It's important to get to the heart of the matter before we make any decisions.* The noun *heart* has been used in the sense of "a vital part" since the early 1500s.

get to the point ♦ See TO THE POINT.

get tough with Become harsh, severe, unyielding with someone. For example, *We have to get tough with these people or we'll get nowhere.* [c. 1930]

get under someone's skin 1. Irritate someone, as in *She really knows how to get under my skin with her nagging.* This expression no doubt alludes to burrowing or stinging insects that cause itching or similar skin irritations. [Late 1800s] 2. Obsess someone or affect someone's deep feelings, as in *Jean's really gotten under his skin; he misses her terribly.* Cole Porter used this sense in his love song, "I've Got You Under My Skin" (1936).

get up 1. Arise from bed; also, sit or stand up. For example, *Once I get up and have coffee, I'm ready to* *work.* One of Irving Berlin's earliest hit songs was "Oh! How I Hate to Get Up in the Morning" (1918). [Mid-1300s] **2.** Ascend, mount, as in *I hate to get up on a ladder.* [First half of 1500s] **3.** Create or organize, as in *She got up the petition against zoning.* [Late 1500s] **4.** Dress or adorn, as in *She plans to get herself up in a bizarre outfit.* This usage is most often put in the form of the past participle (*got up*), as in *The wedding albums were got up with ruffles and lace.* [Late 1700s] **5.** Draw on, create in oneself, as in *I finally got up the nerve to quit*, or *Joe got up his courage and told the boss he was leaving.* [Early 1800s] Also see GET SOMEONE'S BACK UP; also see the subsequent idioms beginning with GET UP.

get up one's nerve ◆ See GET UP, def. 5.

get up on the wrong side of bed Be in a grouchy, irritable state, as in *What's got into Max today? Did he get up on the wrong side of bed?* This expression alludes to the ancient superstition that it was bad luck to put one's left foot down first, and was so used in a number of 17th-century plays. By the early 1800s it was associated more with ill humor than misfortune.

get up steam Prepare to work hard, summon up energy. For example, *If we can just get up steam we can finish in no time.* This expression alludes to producing enough steam to work an engine. [Early 1800s] Also see under FULL SPEED AHEAD.

get used to ◆ See IT TAKES GETTING USED TO; USED TO.

get well Recover from illness, as in *I hope you get well soon.* This idiom uses *well* in the sense of "in good health," a usage dating from the mid-1500s.

get what's coming to one Receive what one deserves or is due, especially something unpleasant, such as a punishment or rebuke. For example, *When they suspended Steve for cheating, he was only getting what was coming to him.*

get wind of Learn of; hear a rumor about. For example, "If my old aunt gets wind of it, she'll cut me off with a shilling" (William Makepeace Thackeray, in *Paris Sketch Book*, 1840). This expression alludes to an animal perceiving a scent carried by the wind. [First half of 1800s]

get wise to Also **be wise to.** See through the deception of; also, become aware of. For example, *It took a while, but she finally got wise to Fred's lies*, or *I'm wise to the fact that her clothes come from a thrift shop.* [Colloquial; mid-1800s]

get with it ◆ See WITH IT.

ghost ◆ In addition to the idiom beginning with GHOST, also see CHINAMAN'S (GHOST OF A) CHANCE; GIVE UP THE GHOST.

ghost town A once thriving town that has been completely abandoned, as in *Many of the old min-*

ing communities are ghost towns now. This idiom implies that there are no living people left in town. [First half of 1900s]

gift ◆ In addition to the idiom beginning with GIFT, also see LOOK A GIFT HORSE IN THE MOUTH.

gift of gab Talent for verbal fluency, especially the ability to talk persuasively. For example, *His gift of gab made him a wonderful salesman.* [Late 1700s]

gilded cage The encumbrances or limitations that often accompany material wealth, as in *She had furs, jewelry, whatever money could buy, but was trapped in a gilded cage.* This metaphoric expression indicating that riches cannot buy happiness was popularized (and possibly coined) in a song, "A Bird in a Gilded Cage" (1900; lyrics by Arthur J. Lamb, music by Harry von Tilzer), about a young girl marrying for wealth instead of love and paying for luxury with a life of regret.

gild the lily Add unnecessary adornment or supposed improvement. For example, *Offering three different desserts after that elaborate meal would be gilding the lily.* This expression is a condensation of Shakespeare's metaphor in *King John* (4:2): "To gild refined gold, to paint the lily . . . is wasteful and ridiculous excess." [c. 1800]

gills ◆ See FED TO THE GILLS; GREEN ABOUT THE GILLS.

gird one's loins Also, **gird up one's loins.** Prepare oneself for action, as in *I'm girding up my loins for that crucial interview.* This expression comes from the Bible (Proverbs 31:17) and originally alluded to tucking up the traditional long robe into a girdle (that is, a belt) so it will not hamper physical activity. [c. 1600]

girl Friday Also, **gal Friday.** An efficient and faithful female assistant, as in *I'll have my girl Friday get the papers together.* The expression plays on **man Friday,** a name for a devoted male servant or assistant. The name *Friday* comes from Daniel Defoe's *Robinson Crusoe*, whose shipwrecked hero named the young native who became his faithful companion for the day of the week when he found him. In the mid-1900s *Friday* was applied to a male servant and then a woman secretary or clerk who works for a man. The expression *girl Friday* gained currency through a motion picture starring Cary Grant and Rosalind Russell, *His Girl Friday* (1940). Today it tends to be considered condescending and, applied to a woman, sexist.

give ◆ In addition to the idioms beginning with GIVE, also see HARD TIME (GIVE SOMEONE A); INDIAN GIVER; NEVER GIVE A SUCKER AN EVEN BREAK; NOT CARE (GIVE) A RAP; NOT GIVE SOMEONE THE TIME OF DAY; WHAT'S COOKING (GIVES). Also see under idioms beginning with GET and HAVE.

give a bad name to Also, **give someone** or **something a bad name.** Spoil the reputation of, as in

Late deliveries are giving the company a bad name. The use of *bad name* (sometimes put as *ill name*) dates from about 1400, and the proverb "He that hath a ill name is half hanged" was included in numerous collections from 1546 on.

give a break ♦ See GIVE SOMEONE A BREAK.

give a damn ♦ See NOT GIVE A DAMN.

give a good account of oneself Behave or perform creditably, as in *Harry gave a good account of himself over the last few months,* or *The company will probably give a good account of itself in the next quarter.* This expression transfers a financial reckoning to other affairs. [c. 1600]

give a hand 1. Also, **lend a hand.** Help a person, as in *Let me give you a hand with those chairs,* or *Jane is always willing to lend a hand with refreshments.* [Mid-1800s] 2. Also, **give a big hand.** Give an enthusiastic round of applause, as in *Please give her a hand.* One can also be given applause or **get a big hand,** as in *This speaker always gets a big hand.* [Early 1800s]

give a hang ♦ See NOT GIVE A DAMN.

give a hard time ♦ See HARD TIME.

give a hoot ♦ See NOT GIVE A DAMN.

give a leg up ♦ See LEG UP.

give and take 1. The practice of compromise, as in *Every contract involves some give and take.* This expression was first recorded in 1778, although the verbal idiom, **to give and take,** was used from the early 1500s. 2. Lively exchange of ideas or conversation, as in *The legislature is famous for raucous give and take.* [Second half of 1800s]

give an inch and they'll take a mile Make a small concession and they'll take advantage of you. For example, *I told her she could borrow the car for one day and she's been gone a week—give an inch!* This expression, in slightly different form, was already a proverb in John Heywood's 1546 collection, "Give him an inch and he'll take an ell," and is so well known it is often shortened (as in the example). The use of *mile* dates from about 1900.

give a pain ♦ See PAIN IN THE NECK.

give a piece of one's mind ♦ See PIECE OF ONE'S MIND.

give as good as one gets Return in kind, retaliate, as in *In an argument Laura can give as good she gets,* or *Don't worry about the bullies in Bobby's class—he can give as good as he gets.* The general idea of this expression dates from the late 1600s, but the precise wording was first recorded only in 1952.

give a shit ♦ See under NOT GIVE A DAMN.

give away 1. Make a gift of, bestow, as in *I decided to give away all my plants.* [c. 1400] 2. Present a bride to the groom in a marriage ceremony, as in *Her father gave Karen away.* [c. 1700] 3. Reveal or make something known, often unintentionally; also, betray or expose someone. For example, *She gave away her true feelings,* or *He gave away his accomplices.* This idiom is sometimes put as **give oneself away,** as in *If you don't want the family to know about your gambling, don't give yourself away by spending your winnings.* [Late 1800s]

give a wide berth Avoid, as in *After Jane told on them, they gave her a wide berth.* This expression alludes to giving a vessel enough room to swing at anchor so as to avoid a collision. [Mid-1800s]

give bad marks to Judge unsatisfactory, as in *They gave bad marks to the President's program.* This expression transfers the marking used in evaluating schoolwork to other endeavors. [Late 1800s]

give birth to 1. Bear a child, as in *She gave birth to her first child exactly at midnight.* [Early 1800s] 2. Also, **give rise to.** Be the cause or origin of. For example, *His hobby gave birth to a very successful business,* or *The economic situation gave rise to widespread dissatisfaction.* The first term dates from the early 1700s, the second from the late 1700s.

give chase Pursue, as in *The police gave chase to the robber.* [c. 1700]

give color to ♦ See LEND COLOR TO.

give credit 1. Also, **extend credit.** Trust someone to pay at some future time what he or she owes. For example, *I haven't enough cash this month, so I hope they'll give me credit.* This use of *credit* dates from the mid-1500s. 2. Acknowledge an accomplishment, as in *They really should give her credit for the work she's done.* [Late 1700s] The phrase is sometimes amplified to **give credit where credit is due,** meaning the acknowledgment should be to the person who deserves it. This expression was probably coined by Samuel Adams in a letter (October 29, 1777), which put it: "Give credit to whom credit due." It is sometimes put **give someone their due,** as in *We should really give Nancy her due for trying to sort out this mess.*

give free rein to ♦ See under FREE HAND.

give ground Yield to a stronger force, retreat, as in *He began to give ground on that point, although he didn't stop arguing entirely.* This expression originated in the 1500s, when it alluded to a military force retreating and so giving up territory to the enemy. By the mid-1600s it was being used figuratively.

give in 1. Hand in, submit, as in *She gave in her report today.* [Early 1600s] 2. Relent, cease opposition, yield, as in *I'll give in on this point,* or *You can have the car—I give in to your arguments.* [Early 1600s]

give it one's best shot Make one's hardest or most enthusiastic attempt, as in *I don't know if I* *can do it, but I'll give it my best shot.* This expression employs *shot* in the sense of "attempt," a usage dating from the mid-1700s.

give it to Punish or reprimand, as in *Dad really gave it to Tom for coming in so late.* This expression, implying a physical or verbal attack, dates from the late 1500s. Also see GIVE SOMEONE HELL. In more recent times the expression gave rise to **give it to someone straight,** meaning "to tell someone something candidly and directly." For example, *I asked the doctor to give it to us straight about Mother's condition.*

give me a break ♦ See GIVE SOMEONE A BREAK, def. 2.

give notice 1. Inform or warn someone of something, as in *He's prompt about giving us notice of any discrepancy in the accounts.* [Late 1500s] 2. Tell one's employer one is quitting, as in *Our housekeeper gave notice last week.* This usage, first recorded in 1765, originally alluded to any kind of termination, such as a housing lease, but today is most often used for leaving employment.

given to Tending toward, inclined to, as in *She was given to eating crackers in bed.* [Late 1500s]

give off Send out, emit, as in *Certain chemical changes give off energy,* or *This mixture gives off a very strange odor.* [Early 1800s]

give of oneself Give time and energy to an unselfish pursuit. For example, *The minister's sermons always emphasize giving of oneself to the less fortunate.* [c. 1920]

give one ♦ See below and also under GIVE SOMEONE.

give oneself airs ♦ See PUT ON AIRS.

give oneself away ♦ See GIVE AWAY, def. 3.

give oneself up 1. Surrender, as in *They gave themselves up to the police.* [Second half of 1500s] 2. Devote or abandon oneself completely, as in *She gave herself up to her research.* [Second half of 1500s] Also see GIVE UP.

give one's eyeteeth Also, **give one's right arm.** Go to any lengths to obtain, as in *She'd give her eyeteeth for a mink coat,* or *He'd give his right arm for a new car.* These hyperbolic expressions both allude to something precious, the eyeteeth (or canines) being useful for both biting and chewing and the right arm a virtual necessity for the 90 percent of the population who are righthanded. Both date from the first half of the 1900s, when the first replaced **give one's eyes,** from the mid-1800s.

give or take Plus or minus a small amount, approximately, more or less. For example, *We have ten acres of land, give or take a bit,* or *It should take a couple of hours, give or take.* [Mid-1900s]

give out 1. Allow to be known, declare publicly, as in *They gave out that she was ill.* [Mid-1300s] 2. Send forth, emit, as in *The machine gave out a*

steady buzzing. [Mid-1400s] 3. Distribute, as in *They gave out surplus food every week.* [c. 1700] 4. Stop functioning, fail; also, become exhausted or used up. For example, *The motor gave out suddenly,* or *My strength simply gave out.* [First half of 1500s]

give over 1. Hand over, entrust, as in *They gave over all the papers to the library.* [Late 1400s] 2. Also, **give oneself over.** Devote or surrender to a particular purpose or use, as in *The whole day was given over to merrymaking,* or *He gave himself over to grief.* [Late 1400s]

give pause Cause one to hesitate, as in *The high monthly installment payments gave me pause,* or, as Shakespeare put it in *Hamlet* (3:1): "For in that sleep of death what dreams may come . . . Must give us pause." [c. 1600]

give rein to ♦ See under FREE HAND.

give rise to ♦ See GIVE BIRTH TO, def. 2.

give short shrift ♦ See SHORT SHRIFT.

give someone ♦ See below, or under GIVE ONE, or look up the expression by its other words, as GIVE THE BENEFIT OF THE DOUBT.

give someone a break 1. Give someone a chance or special consideration. For example, *She begged the professor for an extension on her term paper, saying "Please give me a break."* [c. 1900] Also see GET A BREAK. 2. **give me a break.** Stop trying to fool or upset or bother me. For example, *Don't tell me the party's been postponed again—give me a break!* This interjection is usually uttered with semihumorous exasperation. [Slang; late 1900s]

give someone a ring 1. Also, **give someone a buzz.** Call someone on the telephone, as in *Give me a ring next week,* or *Bill said he'd give her a buzz.* Both these expressions allude to the sound of a telephone's ring. [Colloquial; c. 1920] 2. Present a lover with an engagement ring, as in *I think he's giving her a ring tonight.* [First half of 1800s]

give someone enough rope ♦ See ENOUGH ROPE.

give someone fits ♦ See HAVE A FIT.

give someone heart failure Frighten or startle someone very much, as in *You nearly gave me heart failure when you told me you were quitting.* It is also put as **have heart failure,** meaning "be frightened or startled," as in *I just about had heart failure when I heard about her accident.* These hyperbolic terms allude to the life-threatening physical condition in which the heart fails to pump blood at an adequate rate or stops altogether. Also see HEART MISSES A BEAT.

give someone hell Also, **give someone the devil.** Scold someone harshly. For example, *The boss gave them hell for not finishing in time,* or *Mom will give her the devil if she doesn't get home soon.* Also see GIVE IT TO, def. 1.

give someone his or her due ◆ See under GIVE CREDIT, def. 2.

give someone his or her head Also, **let someone have his or her head**. Allow someone to proceed as he or she wishes, give someone freedom. For example, *He usually gave his assistant his head when it came to scheduling appointments*, or *Sometimes it's wise for parents to let a teenager have his head*. This expression alludes to loosening a horse's reins and letting it go where it wants to. [Second half of 1500s]

give someone the air Also, **give someone the brushoff** or **the gate** or **the old heave-ho**. Break off relations with someone, oust someone, snub or jilt someone, especially a lover. For example, *John was really upset when Mary gave him the air*, or *His old friends gave him the brushoff*, or *Mary cried and cried when he gave her the gate*, or *The company gave him the old heave-ho after only a month*. In the first expression, which dates from about 1920, *giving air* presumably alludes to being blown out. The second, from the first half of the 1900s, alludes to *brushing* away dust or lint. The third, from about 1900, uses *gate* in the sense of "an exit." The fourth alludes to the act of *heaving* a person out, and is sometimes used to mean "to fire someone from a job" (see GET THE AX). All these are colloquialisms, and all have variations using *get*, **get the air** (etc.), meaning "to be snubbed or told to leave," as in *After he got the brushoff, he didn't know what to do*.

give someone the evil eye ◆ See under EVIL EYE.

give someone the once-over Also, **give someone the eye**. Look or stare at someone with interest. For example, *The new coach gave the team the once-over before introducing himself*, or *He gave her the eye and she blushed*. The first expression, a colloquialism, generally implies a quick but comprehensive survey or assessment. The variant, a slangy usage sometimes amplified to **give the glad eye** often signifies an inviting glance. [Early 1900s] Also see MAKE EYES AT.

give something a whirl Make a brief or experimental try, as in *I've never made a pie but I'll give it a whirl*. [Colloquial; late 1800s]

give thanks for small blessings Express gratitude for a minor favor or advantage, as in *My bag didn't get on the plane but it did arrive in time—give thanks for small blessings*. This expression is usually uttered when one encounters an unexpected bit of good fortune.

give the back of one's hand ◆ See BACK OF ONE'S HAND.

give the benefit of the doubt Regard someone as innocent until proven otherwise; lean toward a favorable view of someone. For example, *Let's give her the benefit of the doubt and assume that she's right*. [Mid-1800s]

give the business ◆ See THE BUSINESS.

give the creeps ◆ See THE CREEPS.

give the devil his due Give credit to what is good in a disagreeable or disliked person. For example, *I don't like John's views on education, but give the devil his due, he always has something important to say*, or *I don't like what the new management has done, but give the devil his due, sales have improved*. [Late 1500s]

give the eye Also, **give the once-over**. ◆ See GIVE SOMEONE THE ONCE-OVER.

give the finger Make an obscene gesture by closing one's fist and extending one's middle finger upward, generally interpreted as FUCK YOU. For example, *Herb has a dangerous habit of giving the finger to motorists who cut in front of him*. Although from about 1890 to 1920 this term was used in the sense of "disappoint or snub someone," that meaning seems to have died out. [Second half of 1900s]

give the go-ahead ◆ See GO AHEAD, def. 1.

give the lie to Show to be false, refute, as in *His black eye gave the lie to his contention that he hadn't been fighting*. [First half of 1500s]

give the shakes ◆ See THE SHAKES.

give the shirt off one's back Give anything and everything one possesses. For example, *Tom is truly generous—he'll give you the shirt off his back*. This hyperbolic idiom was first recorded in 1771.

give the slip Escape or evade someone. For example, *He saw the rival gang approaching but managed to give them the slip*. [Mid-1500s]

give the time of day ◆ See NOT GIVE SOMEONE THE TIME OF DAY.

give the word Also, **say the word**. Give an order, tell or show when something is to be done, as in *If you want us to move out, just give the word*, or *When you want the car, just say the word*. The first expression, dating from about 1400, originally alluded to uttering a password in response to a sentinel's challenge. The second is even older, appearing in an early translation of the biblical books of Genesis and Exodus: "And God said the word to Abraham."

give the works ◆ See THE WORKS.

give to understand Lead one to think, as in *I was given to understand that the President was coming here*. [Mid-1500s]

give up 1. Surrender, as in *The suspect gave himself up*. [1100s] **2.** Stop doing or performing something, as in *They gave up the search*, or *She gave up smoking almost thirty years ago*. [c. 1600] **3.** Part with, relinquish, as in *They gave up their New York* *apartment,* or *We gave up all hope of finding the lost tickets.* [Mid-1500s] **4.** Lose hope for, as in *We had given you up as lost.* [Late 1500s] **5.** Admit defeat, as in *I give up—what's the right answer?* [c. 1600] **6. give up on.** Abandon, lose one's faith in, as in *I gave up on writing a novel,* or *She gave up on religion years ago.* [Colloquial; second half of 1900s] Also see GIVE ONESELF UP TO.

give up the ghost Die, as in *At ten o'clock he gave up the ghost.* This expression, which employs *ghost* in the sense of "the soul or spirit," may itself be dying out. [Late 1300s]

give vent to Express an emotion, as in *He didn't dare give vent to his annoyance in front of her parents.* [Late 1500s]

give voice to Say or express, especially an opinion or feeling. For example, *The faculty gave voice to their anger over the dean's tenure decisions.* This term once meant "to vote." Its present sense dates from the mid-1800s.

give way **1.** Retreat or withdraw, as in *The army gave way before the enemy.* [Early 1500s] **2.** Yield the right of way; also, relinquish ascendancy, as in *The cars must give way to the parade,* or *The children were called inside as day gave way slowly to night.* [Early 1700s] **3.** Collapse, fail, break down, as in *The ladder gave way,* or *His health gave way under the strain.* [Mid-1600s] **4.** Also, **give way to.** Yield to urging or demand, as in *At the last minute he gave way and avoided a filibuster,* or *The owners gave way to their demands for a pay increase.* [Mid-1700s] **5.** Also, **give way to.** Abandon oneself, lose self-control, as in *She gave way to hysteria,* or *Don't give way to despair.* [First half of 1800s]

give way to ♦ See GIVE WAY, def. 4 and 5.

give what for ♦ See WHAT FOR.

glad ♦ In addition to the idioms beginning with GLAD, also see GIVE SOMEONE THE ONCE-OVER (GLAD EYE); NOT SUFFER FOOLS GLADLY.

glad hand A warm and hearty but often insincere welcome or greeting, as in *Politicians are apt to give the glad hand to one and all.* [Slang; late 1800s]

glad rags Stylish clothes, as in *Let's put on our glad rags and go out on the town.* [Slang; late 1800s]

glance ♦ See AT FIRST BLUSH (GLANCE).

glass ♦ In addition to the idioms beginning with GLASS, also see PEOPLE WHO LIVE IN GLASS HOUSES.

glass ceiling An unacknowledged discriminatory barrier to advancement, especially for women and minorities. For example, *Harriet knew she'd never be promoted—she would never get through the glass ceiling.* [1980s]

glasses ♦ See SEE THROUGH ROSE-COLORED GLASSES.

glass is half full, the A person views the situation optimistically or hopefully. For example, *Betty*

was not upset by the last-minute change, since it gave her extra time—*she always sees the glass as half full.* The opposite—that is, the pessimistic view—is put as **the glass is half empty.** Also see BRIGHT SIDE.

glitter ♦ See ALL THAT GLITTERS IS NOT GOLD.

glory ♦ See IN ONE'S GLORY.

gloss over Make attractive or acceptable by deception or superficial treatment. For example, *His resumé glossed over his lack of experience,* or *She tried to gloss over the mistake by insisting it would make no difference.* [Mid-1600s]

glove ♦ See FIT LIKE A GLOVE; HAND IN GLOVE; HANDLE WITH KID GLOVES; HANG UP (ONE'S GLOVES); WITH THE GLOVES OFF.

glutton for punishment Someone who habitually takes on burdensome or unpleasant tasks or unreasonable amounts of work. For example, *Rose agreed to organize the church fair for the third year in a row—she's a glutton for punishment.* This expression originated as *a glutton for work* in the late 1800s, *punishment* being substituted about a century later.

gnash one's teeth Express a strong emotion, usually rage, as in *When Jonah found out he was not going to be promoted, he gnashed his teeth.* This expression is actually redundant, since *gnash* means "to strike the teeth together." Edmund Spenser used it in *The Faerie Queene* (1590): "And both did gnash their teeth." [Late 1500s]

go, goes, going ♦ In addition to the idioms beginning with GO, GOES, and GOING, also see ALL OUT, GO; ALL SYSTEMS GO; ANYTHING GOES; AS FAR AS THAT GOES; BESTLAID PLANS GO ASTRAY; COLD TURKEY, GO; COME AND GO; COMING AND GOING; COMING OR GOING; COMINGS AND GOINGS; DOWN THE DRAIN, GO; DUTCH TREAT (GO DUTCH); EASY COME, EASY GO; FROM THE WORD GO; GET A MOVE ON (GOING); GET GOING; HAVE A CRACK (GO) AT; HAVE A GOOD THING GOING; HAVE GOING FOR; HEART GOES OUT TO; HEAVY GOING; HERE GOES; HERE SOMEONE GOES AGAIN; LET GO; MAKE A GO OF; NO DEAL (NO GO); ON THE GO; OUT THE WINDOW, GO; PAY AS YOU GO; RARING TO GO; SHOW MUST GO ON; TAKE (GO INTO) EFFECT; TOUCH AND GO; WHAT GOES AROUND COMES AROUND; WHERE DO WE GO FROM HERE. Also see under GONE.

go about **1.** Also, **go around.** Move here and there, to and fro; also, circulate. For example, *She's been going about telling everyone the news,* or *A report went around that the dollar was dropping.* [c. 1300] **2.** Set about, undertake, as in *I'm not sure how to go about making a pie.* [Late 1600s] **3. go about one's business.** Proceed with one's own proper occupation or concern. For example, *Don't* bother with that—just go about your business. [Late 1600s]

go after Pursue, try to get, as in *The officer went after the burglar*, or *Ed was going after a new job with a vengeance*. [Mid-1400s]

go against Oppose, be in conflict with, as in *Does this legislation go against their best interest?* [c. 1600] Also see AGAINST THE GRAIN.

go ahead 1. Move forward rapidly or act without restraint; also, continue something. For example, *If you want to borrow the tractor, go ahead*. This expression is often put as **go ahead with**, as in *Are you going ahead with the house party?* The term dates from the mid-1600s and gave rise to **give the go-ahead**, meaning "give permission to move or act in some way." 2. **go ahead of**. Make one's way to the front of, as in *They went ahead of me to see the purser*. [Mid-1700s]

go all out ♦ See ALL OUT.

go all the way 1. Continue on a course to the end, as in *The town agreed to put in a sewer but would not go all the way with widening the street*. [First half of 1900s] Also see GO THE DISTANCE. 2. Engage in sexual intercourse, as in *Her mother told her some boys will always try to make her go all the way*. [Slang; second half of 1900s]

go along 1. Move on, proceed, as in *She was going along, singing a little song*. This expression is also used as an imperative meaning "be off" or "get away from here," as in *The police ordered them to go along*. [First half of 1500s] 2. Also, **go along with**. Cooperate, acquiesce, agree. For example, *Don't worry about enough votes—we'll go along*, or *I'll go along with you on that issue*. [c. 1600] 3. Accompany someone, as in *I'll go along with you until we reach the gate*. [c. 1600] This usage gave rise to the phrase **go along for the ride**, meaning "to accompany someone but without playing an active part," as in *I won't be allowed to vote at this meeting so I'm just going along for the ride*.

go a long way ♦ See GO FAR.

go a long way toward Have considerable effect or influence on. For example, *This argument goes a long way toward proving the scientists are wrong*, or, as Eudora Welty put it in *The Ponder Heart* (1954): "It went a long way toward making him touchy about what Uncle Daniel had gone and done." This idiom, then put as *go a great way toward*, was first recorded in 1697.

go and This phrase is an intensifier, that is, it heightens the action indicated by the verb that follows it. For example, *Don't go and eat all the leftover chicken* is stronger than "Don't eat all the leftover chicken." Similarly, Thomas Gray put it in a letter (1760): "But now she has gone . . . and married that Monsieur de Wolmar." Sometimes

the *and* is omitted, as in *Go tell Dad dinner is ready*, or *Go fly a kite*, colloquial imperatives telling someone to do something. [c. 1300]

go ape Become wildly excited or enthusiastic. For example, *The audience went ape over the band*. This idiom is a modern version of the older GO BERSERK. It fancifully equates frenzy with an ape's behavior. [Second half of 1900s] Also see GO BANANAS.

go around 1. Also, **go round**. Satisfy a demand or need, as in *Is there enough food to go around?* [Mid-1800s] 2. Same as GO ABOUT, def. 1. 3. **go around with**. Same as GO WITH, def. 1. 4. **go** or **run around in circles**. Engage in excited but useless activity. For example, *Bill ran around in circles trying organize us but to no avail*. This idiom was first recorded in 1933. For **what goes around comes around**, see under FULL CIRCLE.

go astray Wander off the right path or subject; also, wander into evil or error. For example, *it was hard to follow the lecturer's gist, since he kept going astray*, or *The gang members made him go astray, and he ended up in court*. This expression alludes to sheep or other animals that stray from the rest of the flock. Indeed, Handel's oratorio *Messiah* (1741) has this chorus: "All we like sheep have gone astray, Every one to his own way." [c. 1300]

goat ♦ See GET SOMEONE'S GOAT; SEPARATE THE SHEEP FROM THE GOATS.

go at Attack, especially with energy; also, proceed vigorously. For example, *The dog went at the postman's legs*, or *Tom went at the woodpile, chopping away*. This idiom is sometimes put as **go at it**, as in *When the audience had settled down, the lecturer went at it with renewed vigor*. [First half of 1800s]

go away Depart, leave a place, travel somewhere. For example, *They went away this morning*, or *Are you going away this winter?* This expression also can be used as an imperative ordering someone to leave: *Go away!* It can also be used figuratively to mean "disappear," as in *This fever just doesn't go away*. [c. 1200]

go back 1. Return, retrace one's steps; also, return to a former condition. For example, *I'm going back to the haunts of my youth*, or *We want to go back to the old way of doing things*. [First half of 1500s] 2. Extend backward in space or time, as in *Our land goes back to the stone wall*, or *The family name goes back to Norman times*. [Second half of 1600s] Also see GO BACK ON.

go back on Fail to honor or keep, as in *You can't go back on your word*, or *One should never go back on a promise*. [Mid-1800s]

go bad Spoil, decay; also, turn to crime. For example, *You can tell from the smell that this milk has gone bad*, or *If he keeps running around with that street gang, he's sure to go bad*. [Late 1800s]

go ballistic Become extremely upset or angry, as in *Dad will go ballistic when he sees you dented the new car.* This expression, a variation on GO BE-SERK, originally alluded to a guided missile going out of control. [Slang; mid-1980s]

go bananas Act crazy, as in *When it comes to animal rights, some people go bananas.* According to the lexicographer J. E. Lighter, this expression may allude to the similar GO APE, in that apes and other primates are closely associated with eating bananas. [Slang; second half of 1900s]

go begging Be in little or no demand, as in *At this time of year barrels of apples go begging.* [Late 1500s]

go belly-up Fail, go bankrupt, as in *This company's about to go belly-up.* This expression alludes to the posture of a dead fish in the water. [Slang; early 1900s] Also see GO BROKE.

go berserk Erupt in furious rage, become crazily violent. For example, *When they announced the gymnast's score, her coach went berserk.* This expression is believed to allude to the name of Norse warriors renowned for their ferocity in battle and for wearing no armor but a bearskin shirt (or *berserkar*). [Late 1800s] Also see GO APE.

go broke Also, **go bust.** Undergo financial collapse, lose most or all of one's money. For example, *The company's about to go broke,* or *The producer of that movie went bust.* The first expression dates from the mid-1600s; the second, slangier variant dates from the mid-1800s.

go by 1. Elapse, pass, as in the popular song, "As Time Goes By" (by Herman Hupfeld, 1931), or *He just went by our house.* [c. 1600] 2. Ignore, fail to notice or take advantage of, as in *You shouldn't let this opportunity go by.* [Early 1500s] For the related **go by the board,** see BY THE BOARD. 3. Rely on, believe, as in *I'm going by the numbers on this list,* or *We'll have to go by what she tells us.* 4. **go by the name of.** Be known by or use a specific name. For example, *She continued to go by her maiden name, Mary Smith.* [Late 1500s]

God ◆ In addition to the idioms beginning with GOD, also see ACT OF GOD; FOR GOD'S SAKE; HONEST TO GOD; LAP OF THE GODS; MILLS OF GODS GRIND SLOWLY; MY GOD; PUT THE FEAR OF GOD IN; SO HELP ME (GOD); THANK GOD; THERE BUT FOR THE GRACE OF GOD; TIN GOD.

God forbid ◆ Also, **heaven forbid.** May God prevent something from happening or being the case. For example, *God forbid that they actually encounter a bear,* or *Heaven forbid that the tornado pulls off the roof.* This term, in which *heaven* also stands for "God," does not necessarily imply a belief in God's direct intervention but merely expresses a strong wish. [c. 1225] For a synonym, see PERISH THE THOUGHT.

God knows Also, **goodness knows; heaven knows.** 1. Truly, certainly, definitely, as in *God knows I need a winter coat.* This expression, which originated about 1300 as **God wot,** does not necessarily imply that God is all-knowing but merely emphasizes the truth of the statement it accompanies. The variants using *goodness* and *heaven* are euphemisms that avoid taking God's name in vain. [Second half of 1500s] 2. Also, **God only knows.** Only God knows, that is, neither I nor anyone else knows, as in *God knows where I've stored those photos,* or *God only knows how many people will join the march.* [Second half of 1500s]

go down 1. Descend to a lower level; drop below the horizon, fall to the ground, or sink. For example, *Don't let the baby go down the stairs alone,* or *The sun went down behind the hill,* or *I was afraid the plane would go down,* or *The ship went down and all hands were lost.* [c. 1300] 2. Experience defeat or ruin, as in *They went down fighting,* or *The boxer went down in the first round.* [Late 1500s] 3. Decrease, subside, as in *After Christmas prices will go down,* or *As soon as the swelling goes down it won't hurt as much.* [Second half of 1600s] 4. Be swallowed, as in *This huge pill just won't go down,* or *Your wine goes down very smoothly.* [Second half of 1500s] 5. Be accepted or believed, as in *How did your speech at the convention go down?* When it takes an object, it is put as **go down with,** as in *It's hardly the truth but it still goes down with many voters.* [c. 1600] 6. Also, **go down in history.** Be recorded or remembered, as in *This event must go down in her book as one of the highlights of the year,* or *This debate will go down in history.* [Late 1800s] 7. Occur, take place, as in *Really crazy behavior was going down in the sixties.* [Slang; mid-1900s] Also see COME DOWN, def. 4. 8. Be sent to prison, as in *He went down for a five-year term.* [Slang; c. 1900] 9. In the game of bridge, fail to fulfill one's contract (that is, take fewer than the required number of tricks), as in *We had bid four hearts and the bad distribution made us go down.* [Early 1900s] Also see the subsequent idioms beginning with GO DOWN.

go downhill Deteriorate, worsen, as in *Ever since the recession began, the business has been going downhill.* The figurative use of *downhill* for "decline" dates from the mid-1800s. Also see DOWN-HILL ALL THE WAY.

go down in history ◆ See GO DOWN, def. 6.

go down the drain ◆ See DOWN THE DRAIN.

go Dutch ◆ See under DUTCH TREAT.

go easy 1. Act or proceed with caution, as in *Go easy moving that bookcase,* or *Go easy on the subject of layoffs.* [Late 1800s] Also see EASY DOES IT; TAKE IT EASY. 2. **go easy with** or **on; go light on.**

Use sparingly, as in *Go easy with the makeup; a little lipstick is enough,* or *Go light on the salt.* [Colloquial; early 1900s]

goes to show ♦ See IT GOES TO SHOW.

go far Also, **go a long way.** Be sufficient for nearly all that is required; also, last for a long time. For example, *This turkey will go far to feed the people at the shelter,* or *She can really make that small amount of cash go a long way.* [Early 1400s] Also see GO A LONG WAY TOWARD; GO SO FAR AS TO.

go fly a kite Also, **go chase yourself** or **climb a tree** or **jump in the lake** or **sit on a tack** or **soak your head.** Go away and stop bothering me, as in *Quit it, go fly a kite,* or *Go jump in the lake.* All of these somewhat impolite colloquial imperatives date from the first half of the 1900s and use *go* as described under GO AND.

go for 1. Go in order to get, as in *I'll go for the paper,* or *He went for the doctor.* This usage, dating from the late 1500s, gave rise to the 20th-century noun *gofer,* a person who is habitually sent on routine errands. **2.** Be equivalent to or valued as; also, pass for, serve as. For example, *All our efforts are going for very little,* or *That silver went for a lot of money,* or *That sofa can go for a bed.* [Mid-1500s] **3.** Aim or try for, especially making a vigorous effort. For example, *They're going for the league championship.* This idiom is also put as **go for it,** as in *When Steve said he'd like to change careers, his wife told him to go for it.* The related phrase **go for broke** means "to commit all one's available resources toward achieving a goal," as in *Our competitors are going for broke to get some of our accounts.* The first expression dates from the mid-1500s; the two colloquial variants from the first half of the 1900s. Also see ALL OUT; GO OUT FOR. **4.** Attack, as in *We have to tie up our dog, because he loves to go for letter carriers.* A hyperbolic variant, **go for the jugular,** is used for an all-out attack on the most vital part, as in *In political arguments he always goes for the jugular.* The jugular is a blood-vessel whose rupture is life-threatening. [Colloquial; late 1800s] **5.** Have a special liking for, as in *I really go for progressive jazz.* [Colloquial; first half of 1900s] **6.** Be valid for or applicable to, as in *Kevin hates broccoli, and that goes for Dean, too.* [Early 1900s] Also see HAVE GOING FOR ONE.

go for nothing Be useless, serve no purpose. For example, *He lost the case, so all our efforts on his behalf went for nothing.* [Late 1500s] Also see GO FOR, def. 2.

go great guns ♦ See GREAT GUNS, def. 1.

go halfway Also, **meet someone halfway.** Compromise, give up something for the sake of an agreement. For example, *The Smiths are willing to go halfway and pay their share for snow-plowing,* or

I'll make peace with Nancy if she'll just meet me halfway. [Late 1500s]

go halves Also, **go fifty-fifty.** Share equally. For example, *Ann suggested that they go halves on the rent,* or *The brothers are going fifty-fifty in their new business.* The first term dates from the late 1600s, the variant from the early 1900s.

go hand in hand ♦ See HAND IN HAND.

go hard with Fare ill, be to one's harm or disadvantage. For example, *If this case gets to a jury, it will go hard with the defendant.* [First half of 1500s]

go haywire Become wildly confused, out of control, or crazy. For example, *The plans for the party have gone haywire,* or *His enemies accused the mayor of going haywire.* This term alludes to the wire used for bundling hay, which is hard to handle and readily tangled. [First half of 1900s]

go hog wild Become crazy with excitement, as in *The crowd went hog wild as soon as the band began to play.* Why this expression should allude to the craziness of hogs is no longer known. [Colloquial; c. 1900]

go in 1. Enter, especially into a building. For example, *It's cold out here, so can we go in?* [Tenth century A.D.] **2.** Be obscured, as in *After the sun went in, it got quite chilly.* [Late 1800s] **3. go in with.** Join others in some venture. For example, *He went in with the others to buy her a present.* [Late 1800s] Also see the subsequent idioms beginning with GO IN.

go in for 1. Have a particular interest in or liking for, as in *He really goes in for classical music.* [Mid-1800s] **2.** Take part in, especially as a specialty. For example, *She's going in for tennis this year.* [Mid-1800s]

going for one ♦ See HAVE GOING FOR ONE.

going, going, gone No longer available, as in *If you want this last doughnut speak up—going, going, gone!* This expression, used by auctioneers to indicate the acceptance of a final bid for an item, is occasionally used more loosely, as in the example. It is beloved by baseball announcers when describing a home run as it approaches and clears the outfield wall. [c. 1800]

going my way ♦ See GO ONE'S WAY, def. 2.

going on Also, **going on for.** Approaching, especially an age or time. For example, *She's twelve, going on thirteen,* or *It's going on for midnight.* The first term dates from the late 1500s, the variant from the mid-1800s. Also see GO ON.

going to About to, will, as in *I'm going to start planting now,* or *Do you think it's going to rain?* or *We thought the train was going to stop here.* This phrase is used with a verb (*start, rain, stop* in the examples) to show the future tense. Occasionally the verb is omitted because it is understood. For example, *That wood hasn't dried out yet but it's going to soon,* or *Will you set the table?—Yes, I'm going to.* [1400s] Also see GO TO.

go in one ear and out the other ♦ See under IN ONE EAR.

go into 1. Enter somewhere or something; also fit inside something. For example, *Don't go into this building,* or *The tractor is too big to go into the shed.* [c. A.D. 1000] 2. Enter a particular state or condition, as in *She's about to go into hysterics,* or *I'm afraid he went into a coma.* [Second half of 1600s] 3. Enter a profession or line of work, as in *She decided to go into politics.* [Early 1800s] For synonyms, see GO IN FOR, def. 2; TAKE UP. 4. Investigate or discuss, especially in detail. For example, *We haven't time to go into the entire history of the project.* [Early 1800s] Also see ENTER INTO, def. 4. Also see the subsequent entries beginning with GO INTO.

go into a huddle Gather together privately to talk about or plan something, as in *The attorneys went into a huddle with their client before asking the next question.* Although *huddle* has been used since the 16th century in the sense of "a crowded mass of things," the current usage comes from football, where the team goes into a huddle to decide on the next play. [Mid-1900s]

go into a tailspin Lose emotional control, collapse, panic. For example, *If she fails the bar exam again, she's sure to go into a tailspin.* This expression alludes to the downward movement of an airplane out of control, in which the tail describes a spiral. [Early 1900s]

go into effect ♦ See IN EFFECT, def. 3.

go it alone Undertake a project, trip, or responsibility without the aid or presence of others. For example, *If you decide not to help, I'll just go it alone.* [Mid-1800s]

gold, golden ♦ In addition to the idioms beginning with GOLD or GOLDEN, also see ALL THAT GLITTERS IS NOT GOLD; GOOD AS GOLD; HEART OF GOLD; SILENCE IS GOLDEN; WORTH ONE'S WEIGHT IN GOLD.

golden age A period of prosperity or excellent achievement, as in *Some consider the baroque period the golden age of choral music.* The expression dates from the mid-1500s, when it was first applied to a period of classical Latin poetry.

golden handcuffs Financial benefits that an employee will lose upon resigning, as in *The company's presented all the middle managers with golden handcuffs, so they can't afford to leave.* This slangy business expression dates from the 1970s.

golden handshake Generous severance pay to an employee, often as an incentive for early retire-

ment. For example, *With a dwindling school population, the town decided to offer golden handshakes to some of the teachers.* This slangy business term dates from the mid-1900s. A close relative is **golden parachute**, a generous severance agreement for an executive in the event of sudden dismissal owing to a merger or similar circumstance. This expression first appeared about 1980.

golden rule ♦ See under DO UNTO OTHERS.

goldfish bowl A situation affording no privacy, as in *Being in a goldfish bowl comes with the senator's job—there's no avoiding it.* The glass bowl allowing one to view goldfish from every direction was transferred first, in the 1920s, to a police interrogation room equipped with a one-way mirror. By the mid-1900s the expression was being used more broadly.

gold mine A rich, plentiful source of wealth or some other desirable thing, as in *That business proved to be a gold mine,* or *She's a gold mine of information about the industry.* [First half of 1800s]

go light on ♦ See GO EASY, def. 2.

go native Adopt another people's way of life, especially that of a culture from a less developed country. For example, *Ben's decided to go native, sleeping in a hammock and eating all kinds of strange foods.* This expression is closely associated with the often contemptuous view British colonists had of indigenous peoples. [c. 1900]

gone ♦ In addition to the idioms beginning with GONE, also see A GONER; ALL GONE; DEAD AND BURIED (GONE); FAR GONE; GOING, GOING, GONE; HERE TODAY, GONE TOMORROW; TO HELL AND GONE. Also see under GO.

gone coon, a Also, **a gone goose**. A person in a hopeless situation, one who is doomed; a DEAD DUCK. For example, *When he passed me, I knew I was a gone goose.* These terms have survived such synonyms as *gone chick, gone beaver, gone horse,* and *gone gander.* Stephen Crane used the first in *The Red Badge of Courage* (1894): "I'm a gone coon this first time." [Slang; early 1800s]

gone goose ♦ See GONE COON.

gone with the wind Disappeared, gone forever, as in *With these unforeseen expenses, our profits are gone with the wind.* This phrase became famous as the title of Margaret Mitchell's 1936 novel, which alludes to the Civil War's causing the disappearance of a Southern way of life. It mainly serves as an intensifier of *gone.*

good ♦ In addition to the idioms beginning with GOOD, also see BAD (GOOD) SORT; BUT GOOD; DO ANY GOOD; DO GOOD; DO ONE GOOD; FOR GOOD; FOR GOOD MEASURE; GET ON SOMEONE'S GOOD SIDE; GET OUT WHILE THE GETTING IS GOOD; GIVE A

GOOD ACCOUNT OF ONESELF; GIVE AS GOOD AS ONE GETS; HAVE A GOOD COMMAND OF; HAVE A GOOD MIND TO; HAVE A GOOD THING GOING; HAVE A GOOD TIME; HOLD GOOD; ILL WIND (THAT BLOWS NOBODY ANY GOOD); IN ALL GOOD CONSCIENCE; IN BAD (GOOD) FAITH; IN (GOOD) CONDITION; IN DUE COURSE (ALL IN GOOD TIME); IN GOOD; IN GOOD HANDS; IN GOOD PART; IN GOOD REPAIR; IN GOOD SPIRITS; IN GOOD TIME; IN GOOD WITH; IN SOMEONE'S GOOD GRACES; KEEP (GOOD) TIME; MAKE GOOD; MAKE GOOD TIME; MAKE SOMEONE LOOK GOOD; MISS IS AS GOOD AS A MILE; NEVER HAD IT SO GOOD; NO GOOD; NO NEWS IS GOOD NEWS; NOT THE ONLY FISH (OTHER GOOD FISH) IN THE SEA; ONE GOOD TURN DESERVES ANOTHER; ON GOOD TERMS; ON ONE'S BEST (GOOD) BEHAVIOR; PUT IN A GOOD WORD; PUT TO GOOD USE; SHOW SOMEONE A GOOD TIME; SHOW TO (GOOD) ADVANTAGE; SO FAR SO GOOD; STAND IN GOOD STEAD; TAKE IN GOOD PART; THROW GOOD MONEY AFTER BAD; TO GOOD PURPOSE; TOO GOOD TO BE TRUE; TOO MUCH OF A GOOD THING; TO THE GOOD; TURN TO (GOOD ACCOUNT); UP TO NO GOOD; WELL AND GOOD; WHAT'S THE GOOD OF; WITH GOOD GRACE; WORLD OF GOOD; YOUR GUESS IS AS GOOD AS MINE. Also see under GOODNESS; GOODS.

good and Very, as in *I'll go when I'm good and ready,* or *Mike was good and mad at Tom.* This phrase is used to intensify the words that follow. [Colloquial; early 1800s]

good as, as Practically, in effect, almost the same as, as in *He as good as promised to buy a new car,* or *The house is as good as sold.* This idiom is very widely used to modify just about any verb, adverb, or adjective. However, it has been used so often with certain words that together they themselves now make up idioms (see the following entries beginning with GOOD AS).

good as done, as Virtually finished or accomplished, as in *Your printing job is as good as done.* This idiom was first recorded in 1530.

good as gold, as Completely genuine; also, well behaved. For example, *Her credit is as good as gold,* or *The children were good as gold.* With this alliterative idiom the initial *as* is sometimes dropped, and nearly always so when behavior is referred to. [Late 1600s]

good as one's word, as Completely trustworthy, dependable, as in *The boss said we could leave early on Friday and she was as good as her word.* [Second half of 1500s]

good day Also, **good afternoon** or **evening** or **morning**. Formal ways of saying "Hello" or "Goodbye." For example, *He began rather oddly by addressing the audience with "Good day,"* or *"Good afternoon, ladies," said the sales clerk as we walked out.* All these greetings represent an abbreviation

of the now obsolete *God give you a good day (afternoon, etc.),* which dates from about 1200. Also see GOOD NIGHT.

good deal, a Also, **a great deal.** 1. A large but indefinite quantity, as in *He has a good* (or *great*) *deal of money;* also, to a large extent or degree, as in *"I bled . . . a great deal"* (from Daniel Defoe's *Robinson Crusoe,* 1719). Also see GOOD MANY. 2. A very successful transaction or business agreement; a bargain. For example, *The new agent got him a great deal,* or *Only $50,000 for all that land? That's a good deal.* [Colloquial; mid-1800s]

good egg, a Also, **a good scout.** An amiable, basically nice person. For example, *You can always count on her to help; she's a good egg,* or *His friends all think Dad's really a good scout.* This colloquial antonym of BAD EGG dates from the early 1900s, as did the variant.

good evening ♦ See under GOOD DAY.

good faith ♦ See under IN BAD FAITH.

good for 1. Beneficial to, as in *Milk is good for children.* [Tenth century A.D.] 2. Financially reliable, able to pay or repay, as in *They know he's good for a big tip.* [Mid-1800s] 3. Able to serve or continue to function, as in *This furniture's good for at least ten more years,* or *I hope you're not tired—I'm good for another three miles or so.* [Mid-1800s] 4. Equivalent in value; also, valid for. For example, *These cou-pons are good for a 20 percent discount,* or *This contract is good for the entire life of the book.* [Second half of 1800s] 5. **good for someone.** An expression of approval, as in *Good for Bill—he's sold the car,* or *Good for you! You passed the exam.* This usage differs from the others in that orally a slight emphasis is placed on *you* or whoever is being mentioned. [Mid-1800s]

good graces ♦ See IN ONE'S GOOD GRACES.

good grief An exclamation expressing surprise, alarm, dismay, or some other, usually negative emotion. For example, *Good grief! You're not going to start all over again,* or *Good grief! He's dropped the cake.* The term is a euphemism for "good God." [Early 1900s]

good head on one's shoulders, have a Be intelligent or shrewd; have good sense or good judgment. For example, *We can depend on George to figure it out—he has a good head on his shoulders.* This term originated in the 1500s as *have an old head on young shoulders,* alluding to the wisdom of age and physical youth. It took its present form in the 1800s.

good life, the A wealthy, luxurious style of living. For example, *Aunt Agatha left them a fortune, so now they're enjoying the good life.* [Mid-1900s]

good luck 1. Good fortune or a happy outcome, especially by chance. For example, *It was sheer good* *luck that brought this offer my way,* or, as Shakespeare put it in *The Merry Wives of Windsor* (3:5): "As good luck would have it, comes in one Mistress Page." [Late 1400s] **2.** Also, **good luck to you.** I wish you success. This term is used both straightforwardly, as in *Good luck on your journey,* and sarcastically, implying that what someone is undertaking is not likely to succeed, as in *If you think you'll find that long-lost letter, good luck to you.*

good many, a Also, **a great many.** A large number of, as in *A good many checks have come in already,* or *We saw only a few hikers on the trail, when we had thought there would be a great many.* The first term dates from the early 1800s, the variant from the late 1600s. Also see A LOT; QUITE A BIT (FEW).

good mind ♦ See HAVE A GOOD MIND.

good morning ♦ See under GOOD DAY.

good nature A cheerful, obliging disposition, as in *Ted is known for his good nature—he's always willing to help.* [Mid-1400s]

goodness ♦ In addition to the idioms beginning with GOODNESS, also see FOR THE SAKE OF, def. 3; GOD (GOODNESS) KNOWS; HONEST TO GOD (GOODNESS); MY GOD (GOODNESS).

goodness gracious Also, **good gracious; gracious sakes.** Exclamation of surprise, dismay, or alarm, as in *Goodness gracious! You've forgotten your ticket.* Both *goodness* and *gracious* originally alluded to the good (or grace) of God, but these colloquial expressions, which date from the 1700s, are not considered either vulgar or blasphemous.

goodness knows ♦ See GOD KNOWS.

good night 1. Expression of farewell used when parting at night or when going to sleep, as in *He stood at the door, saying good night to each of the departing guests,* or *Mother came to tuck the children in and kiss them good night.* [Late 1300s] **2.** Exclamation of surprise or irritation, as in *Good night, Joe!—You can't mean what you said,* or *Good night, Anne—it's time you learned how to throw a ball.* [Late 1800s]

good riddance Also, **good riddance to bad rubbish.** A welcome loss or departure. This expression is often used as an exclamation. For example, *The principal has finally retired, and most of the teachers are saying, "Good riddance!"* or *When Jean decided to give up her violin her relieved family quietly said, "Good riddance to bad rubbish."* [Late 1700s]

goods ♦ See DAMAGED GOODS; DELIVER THE GOODS; GET THE GOODS ON; SELL A BILL OF GOODS; STRAIGHT GOODS.

good Samaritan A compassionate person who unselfishly helps others, as in *In this neighborhood you can't count on a good Samaritan if you get in trouble.* This expression alludes to Jesus's parable about a Samaritan who rescues and cares for a stranger who had been robbed and badly hurt and had been ignored by a priest and a Levite (Luke 10:30–35). The Samaritans were considered a heretical group by other Jews, so by using a Samaritan for the parable, Jesus chose a person whom his listeners would find least likely to be worthy of concern. [c. 1600]

good scout ♦ See GOOD EGG.

good sort ♦ See under BAD SORT.

good thing ♦ See HAVE A GOOD THING GOING.

good time ♦ See HAVE A GOOD TIME.

good-time Charlie Affable, convivial fellow, as in *Joe was a typical good-time Charlie, always ready for a party.* [Colloquial; 1920s]

good turn A favor, an act of good will, as in *Pat did her a good turn by calling in a second surgeon.* [First half of 1400s]

good word ♦ See PUT IN A GOOD WORD.

good works Acts of charity, kindness, or good will, as in *She spent much of her life in doing good works, especially for the homeless.* This expression, also put as *good work,* originally had the theological meaning of an act of piety. Today it is used in a more general context. [c. A.D. 1000]

goody two-shoes A prudish, self-righteous individual, a goody-goody. For example, *Phyllis was a real goody two-shoes, tattling on her friends to the teacher.* This expression alludes to the main character of a nursery tale, *The History of Goody Two-Shoes* (1765), who was so pleased when receiving a second shoe that she kept saying "Two shoes." The *goody* in the story is short for *goodwife* but means "goody-goody" in the idiom.

goof around Fool or play around, engage in horseplay, as in *The boys were goofing around in the schoolyard.* [Slang; 1920s]

go off 1. Explode, detonate; also, make noise, sound, especially abruptly. For example, *I heard the gun go off,* or *The sirens went off at noon.* This expression developed in the late 1500s and gave rise about 1700 to the related **go off half-cocked,** now meaning "to act prematurely" but originally referring to the slipping of a gun's hammer so that the gun fires (goes off) unexpectedly. **2.** Leave, depart, especially suddenly, as in *Don't go off mad,* or *They went off without saying goodbye.* [c. 1600] **3.** Keep to the expected plan or course of events, succeed, as in *The project went off smoothly.* [Second half of 1700s] **4.** Deteriorate in quality, as in *This milk seems to have gone off.* [Late 1600s] **5.** Die. Shakespeare used this sense in *Macbeth* (5:9): "I would the friends we missed were safely arrived.—Some must go off." **6.** Experience orgasm. D.H. Lawrence used this slangy sense in *Lady Chatterley's Lover* (1928): "You couldn't go off at the same time. . . ." This usage is probably rare today. Also see GET OFF, def. 8. **7. go off on a tangent.** See under ON A TANGENT. **8. go off one's head.** See OFF ONE'S HEAD. Also see subsequent idioms beginning with GO OFF.

go off half-cocked ♦ See GO OFF, def. 1.

go off the deep end 1. Become unduly excited, overwrought, or angry. For example, *When he heard about John's smashing into his car, he went off the deep end.* [c. 1920] Also see IN DEEP, def. 2. **2.** Be irrationally carried away, act irresponsibly or heedlessly. For example, *Just because you like her looks doesn't mean you should go off the deep end and propose.* [c. 1920] In both of these colloquial usages *deep end* alludes to the deep end of a swimming pool.

goof off Shirk work or responsibility, loaf; fool around. For example, *We were supposed to be studying but we were really goofing off,* or *If you ever feel like goofing off, please call me.* This idiom was a synonym of GOOF UP during World War II, a usage that has died out. [Slang; 1920] Also see GOOF AROUND.

goof on Make fun of, mock, as in *He was always goofing on his little brother.* [Slang; mid-1900s]

goof up Blunder, make a mistake, spoil. For example, *I really goofed up and got all the dates wrong.* This expression emerged in the military during World War II, along with the synonymous GOOF OFF. Quite often *up* is omitted, as in *Sorry, I goofed.* [Slang; c. 1940]

go on 1. Happen, take place, as in *What's going on here?* [Early 1700s] **2.** Continue, as in *The show must go on.* [Late 1500s] **3.** Keep on doing; also, proceed, as in *He went on talking,* or *She may go on to become a partner.* [Second half of 1600s] **4.** Act, behave, especially badly. For example, *Don't go on like that; stop kicking the dog.* [Second half of 1700s] **5.** Also, **go on and on; run on.** Talk volubly, chatter, especially tiresomely. For example, *How she does go on!* The first usage dates from the mid-1800s; *run on* appeared in Nicholas Udall's *Ralph Roister Doister* (c. 1553): "Yet your tongue can run on." **6.** An interjection expressing disbelief, surprise, or the like, as in *Go on, you must be joking!* [Late 1800s] **7.** Approach; see GOING ON. **8.** Use as a starting point or as evidence, as in *The investigator doesn't have much to go on in this case.* [Mid-1900s] **9. go on something.** Begin something, as in **go on line,** meaning "start to use a computer," or **go on a binge,** meaning "begin to overdo, especially drink or eat too much."

go on and on 1. See GO ON, def. 5. **2.** Continue without stopping, last for a long time, as in *This trail goes on and on,* or *The movie went on and on.* This usage was first recorded in 1938.

go one better Outdo or surpass someone, as in *He went one better than his teacher and came up with five more famous scientists.* This expression originated in gambling games, where it meant "to offer a higher stake than one's opponent." [Mid-1800s]

go one's way Also, **go one's own way. 1.** Do what one pleases, especially differing from what others are doing, as in *You go your way and I'll go mine,* or *He always insisted on going his own way.* This expression, dating from about 1400, originally alluded to moving on in a particular direction. It can still do so, as in *The delivery truck went on its way.* By the late 1500s it was also being used figuratively. **2.** Proceed according to one's plans or wishes, as in *Let's hope things will go my way this time.* Applied to both events and people's actions, this thought is often expressed as **everything's going one's way** or **going my way.** For example, *With her husband in charge, everything's going her way,* or *I trust you'll be going my way when we vote on this issue.*

go on line ♦ See GO ON, def. 9.

go on record Embrace a position publicly. For example, *I want to go on record in favor of the mayor's reelection.* It is also put as **for the record,** as in *For the record, we support sending troops there.* The *record* in both signifies either publication or public knowledge. Both expressions date from the first half of the 1900s, although slightly different phrases, such as **put on record,** are older. Also see JUST FOR THE RECORD; OFF THE RECORD.

goose ♦ In addition to the idioms beginning with GOOSE, also see COOK SOMEONE'S GOOSE; GONE COON (GOOSE); KILL THE GOOSE THAT LAID THE GOLDEN EGGS; SAUCE FOR THE GOOSE; WILD GOOSE CHASE.

goose egg Zero, nothing, especially a score of zero. For example, *Our team did badly, earning goose egg,* or *My income from writing this year was goose egg.* This expression is an Americanization of the earlier British *duck's egg.* [Mid-1800s]

goose pimples Also, **goose bumps** or **flesh.** Temporary rough skin caused by small raised bumps. For example, *Horror movies always give me goose pimples,* or *She tends to get goose bumps whenever she goes to the dentist.* This expression likens the skin of a plucked goose to the condition of human skin when a person is cold or afraid. [Early 1800s]

go out 1. Be extinguished, as in *All the lights went out.* [c. 1400] **2.** Die; also, faint. For example, *I want to go out before I become senile,* or *At the sight of blood he went out like a light.* The first usage dates from about 1700 and was at first put as *go out of the world.* For the variant, see under OUT COLD. **3.** Take part in social life outside the home, as in *We go out a lot during the holiday season.* This usage dates from the second half of the 1700s and gave rise to **go out with someone,** meaning "to date someone." **4.** Stop working, as in *To show their support of the auto workers, the steel workers went out too.* This expression is short for **go out on strike.** [Late 1800s] **5.** Become unfashionable, as in *Bell-bottom pants went out in the 1970s but made a comeback in the 1990s.* This usage is sometimes amplified to **go out of fashion** or **go out of style,** as in *This kind of film has gone out of fashion,* or *These boots are going out of style.* [Late 1400s] **6.** Cease to function as before. This sense appears in **go out of print,** said of a book that will no longer be printed. Also see the subsequent idioms beginning with GO OUT.

go out for Seek to become a participant in, as in *I'm going out for soccer.* [First half of 1900s] Also see GO FOR, def. 3; GO IN FOR, def. 2.

go out of fashion Also, **go out of style.** ♦ See under GO OUT, def. 5.

go out of one's mind Lose one's mental stability, become insane, as in *After he heard that the ore he had mined was worthless, the prospector went out of his mind.* This phrase is often used as a humorous exaggeration, as in *I'm going out of my mind reading these proofs.* The phrase **out of one's mind** dates from the late 1300s, and was used with *go* shortly thereafter. Also see LOSE ONE'S MIND.

go out of one's way Inconvenience oneself or take extra trouble to do something beyond what is required. For example, *He went out of his way to introduce me to everyone there,* or *She went out of her way to be kind.* This usage alludes to deviating from one's intended path or normal procedures. [Mid-1700s]

go out the window ♦ See OUT THE WINDOW.

go out with ♦ See GO OUT, def. 3; GO WITH.

go over **1.** Examine, review. For example, *They went over the contract with great care,* or *I think we should go over the whole business again.* This term originated in the late 1500s, then meaning "consider in sequence." **2.** Gain acceptance or approval, succeed, as in *I hope the play goes over.* This term is sometimes elaborated to **go over big** or **go over with a bang** for a big success, and **go over like a lead balloon** for a dismal failure. [Early 1900s] **3.** Rehearse, as in *Let's go over these lines one more time.* [Second half of 1700s]

go overboard Show excessive enthusiasm, act in an excessive way. For example, *It's easy to go overboard with a new stock offering,* or *She really went overboard, hiring the most expensive caterer.* [Mid-1900s]

go over someone's head ♦ See OVER ONE'S HEAD.

go places Make progress, succeed, as in *I suspect they'll be going places with the new product,* or *Now*

that she has her doctorate I'm sure she'll go places. [Colloquial; early 1900s]

go public Become a publicly held company, that is, issue ownership shares in the form of stock. For example, *As soon as the company grows a little bigger and begins to show a profit, we intend to go public.* [Mid-1900s]

go right Succeed, happen correctly, as in *If everything goes right, we should be in Canada by Tuesday,* or *Nothing has gone right for me today.* This idiom uses *right* in the sense of "in a satisfactory state," a usage dating from the mid-1600s.

go right through one ♦ See under GO THROUGH ONE.

go so far as to Also, **go as far as to.** Proceed to the point of doing something. For example, *I wouldn't go so far as to call him incompetent, but he does need supervision,* or *Would she go as far as to sell the house before she's found another?*

go south Deteriorate or decline, as in *The stock market is headed south again.* This expression is generally thought to allude to compasses and two-dimensional maps where north is up and south is down. However, among some Native Americans, the term was a euphemism for dying, and possibly this sense led to the present usage. [Slang; first half of 1900s] Also see GO WEST.

gospel truth Something that is unquestionably true. For example, *Every word he uttered was the gospel truth.* The word *gospel,* which comes from the Old English *god spel,* "good news," has been used to describe something that is thought to be as true as the biblical gospel (that is, undeniably true) since the 13th century. The current idiom originated in the 1600s, when it referred to biblical truths, and has been applied to truth of a more general nature since the late 1800s. Also see TAKE AS GOSPEL.

go stag Go unaccompanied by a person of the opposite sex to a social event, as in *John decided to go stag to his roommate's party,* or *Some of the girls are going stag to the dance.* Although this term originally applied only to men attending an event without a woman companion, it is now applied to women as well. [c. 1900]

go steady Date one person exclusively, as in *Parents often don't approve of their children's decision to go steady.* This usage may be obsolescent. [Slang; c. 1900] Also see GO TOGETHER, def. 2; GO WITH, def. 1.

go straight Become a law-abiding person; abandon crime. For example, *Once he got out on probation, he swore he would go straight.* The use of *straight* in the sense of "honest" dates from the 1500s and probably alludes to the opposite of *crooked,* used in the sense of "dishonest" from the 13th century on.

got a thing going ♦ See HAVE A THING GOING.

go the distance Carry through a course of action to completion. For example, *He said he's willing to go the distance with this project.* This expression originated in boxing, where it means "to last for all the rounds that have been scheduled." In baseball the same term means "to pitch an entire game." For a synonym, see ALL THE WAY, def. 1.

go the limit ♦ See GO WHOLE HOG.

go the way of all flesh Die, as in *Our dog's gone the way of all flesh and I'm not sure we'll get another.* This expression is actually a misquotation from the Bible, which has it *to go the way of all the earth* (I Kings 2:2; Joshua 22:14), also meaning "to die."

go through 1. Examine carefully, as in *I went through all the students' papers.* [Mid-1600s] 2. Experience, undergo, suffer, as in *We went through hell trying to find an answer.* [Early 1700s] 3. Perform; also, rehearse for performance. For example, *I went through the sonata in ten minutes,* or *Let's go through the third act again.* [Mid-1700s] 4. Use up, complete, as in *The children went through all the milk we bought in one day.* [Mid-1900s] 5. Succeed, be approved, as in *I'm sure this new deal will go through.* [Late 1800s] 6. **go through with.** Complete, carry out, as in *They got engaged last year, but I'm not sure they'll go through with the wedding.* [Mid-1500s]

go through channels Use the correct procedure, especially in a hierarchy or bureaucracy. For example, *You'll have to go through channels for approval of this expenditure.* This term uses *channel* in the sense of "a conduit." [Mid-1900s]

go through one 1. Use as an intermediary, as in *Bob can't release that; you'll have to go through the main office.* Also see GO THROUGH CHANNELS. 2. Also, **go right through one (like a dose of salts).** Be rapidly excreted without being digested. For example, *I don't know why, but Thai cooking goes right through me,* or *That banana drink went through Dad like a dose of salts.*

go through the mill ♦ See THROUGH THE MILL.

go through the motions Do something perfunctorily, or merely pretend to do it. For example, *The team is so far behind that they're just going through the motions,* or *She didn't really grieve at his death; she just went through the motions.* [c. 1800]

go through the roof 1. Also, **hit the ceiling** or **roof.** Lose one's temper, become very angry, as in *Marge went through the roof when she heard she'd been fired.* [Colloquial; first half of 1900s] 2. Reach new or unexpected heights, as in *After the war; food prices went through the roof.* [Colloquial; first half of 1900s]

go through with ♦ See GO THROUGH, def. 6.

got it ♦ See under GET IT.

go to 1. See GOING TO. 2. Also, **go toward.** Contribute to a result, as in *Can you name the bones that go to make the arms and legs?* or *The director has a good eye for seeing what will go toward an entire scene.* [c. 1600] 3. Begin, start, as in *By the time she went to call, she'd forgotten what she wanted to say.* The related idiom **go to it** means "get started, get going." P.G. Wodehouse used it in *Louder & Funnier* (1932): "Stoke up and go to it." [First half of 1700s]

go to any length Also, **go to great lengths.** Take a great deal of trouble for something, go to extremes. For example, *He'll go to great lengths to make a perfect chocolate cake,* or, as Benjamin Disraeli put it in *Coningsby* (1844): "He would go . . . [to] any lengths for his party."

go to bat for Take the side of, support, defend. For example, *Dad will always go to bat for his kids.* This term originated in baseball, where it means simply substituting for another batter, but it is the idea of helping one's team in this way that has been transferred to more general use. [Slang; early 1900s]

go to bed with 1. Engage in sex with; see GO ALL THE WAY, def. 2. 2. **go to bed with the chickens.** Retire very early, as in *She made the children go to bed with the chickens.* The *chickens* here alludes to the fact that domestic fowl generally go to sleep at sundown. 3. Also, **get in** or **into bed with.** From a close association with, as in *There's always the danger that the inspectors will get in bed with the industries they're supposed to be inspecting.* This usage simply extends the sexual relationship of def. 1 to broader use. 4. **go to bed.** Start printing a newspaper or other publication. The allusion here is that the morning newspaper is usually printed sometime during the night before. For example, *It's too late for your story; the paper went to bed half an hour ago.* [Mid-1800s]

go together 1. Be mutually suitable, appropriate, or harmonious, as in *Pink and purple can go together well,* or *I don't think champagne and meatloaf go together.* [c. 1600] 2. Date on a regular basis, keep company. For example, *Are Bill and Ann still going together?* [Late 1800s] Also see GO STEADY; GO WITH.

go to hell Also, **go to the devil** or **dickens.** Go to everlasting torment, ruin, or perdition. For example, *Nancy did not mince words but simply told him to go the devil,* or *Go to hell, Tom, I won't give you another cent.* These phrases are often uttered as angry imperatives to order someone to go away. *Hell, devil,* and *dickens* (a euphemism for "devil") all refer to the underworld, the residence of the devil, from which a person would never return.

go to it ♦ See GO TO, def. 3.

go too far Exceed some limit, as in *I wouldn't go too far with those remarks or they'll turn on you,* or

If Jane goes too far, she'll be sent to her room. [Second half of 1500s]

go to one's head 1. Make one dizzy or drunk, as in *Wine always goes to her head.* [c. 1900] 2. Make one proud or vain, as in *All this money is going to his head.* [Early 1900s]

go to pieces Experience an emotional or mental breakdown, as in *When she heard of his death she went to pieces.* [Late 1800s] For a synonym, see FALL APART, def. 2.

go to pot Also, **go to the dogs.** Deteriorate, decline; come to a bad end. For example, *My lawn has gone to pot during the drought,* or *The city schools are going to the dogs.* The first of these colloquial expressions dates from the late 1500s and alludes to inferior pieces of meat being cut up for the stewpot. The second, from the 1600s, alludes to the traditional view of dogs as inferior creatures. Also see RACK AND RUIN; RUN TO SEED.

go to show Help to indicate or serve as evidence. For example, *His research goes to show that the medication is ineffective.* This term was first recorded in 1842.

go to the devil ▶ See GO TO HELL.

go to the dogs ▶ See under GO TO POT.

go to the expense ▶ See GO TO THE TROUBLE.

go to the mat Fight until one side or another is victorious, as in *The governor said he'd go to the mat for this bill.* This term comes from wrestling and evokes the holding of an opponent when both contestants are down on the mat, the padded floor-covering used in matches. It has been used figuratively since about 1900.

go to the trouble Also, **take the trouble; go to the bother** or **the expense.** Make the effort or spend the money for something. For example, *He went to the trouble of calling every single participant,* or *She took the trouble to iron all the clothes,* or *Don't go to the bother of writing them,* or *They went to the expense of hiring a limousine.* [Second half of 1800s] Also see PUT ONESELF OUT.

go to the wall 1. Lose a conflict, be defeated; also, yield. For example, *In spite of their efforts, they went to the wall,* or *When it's a matter of family versus friends, friends must go to the wall.* [Late 1500s] 2. Fail in business, go bankrupt. For example, *First one branch and then another did poorly, and the store finally went to the wall.* [First half of 1800s] 3. Take an extreme position, hold out to the end. For example, *The President went to the wall to defend his choice to head the FBI.* For a synonym, see GO TO THE MAT.

go to town Also, **go to town on.** 1. Do something efficiently and energetically. For example, *She really went to town, not only developing and printing the film but making both mat and frame.* [Early 1900s] 2. Act without restraint, overindulge, as in *He went to town on the hors d'oeuvres, finishing nearly all of them.* [Early 1900s] 3. Be successful, as in *After months of hard work, their business is really going to town.* [Mid-1900s]

go to waste Fail to be used or taken advantage of. For example, *I hate to see such talent go to waste,* or *We bought so much food that some will be going to waste.* [c. 1500]

go to ▶ See HAVE TO.

go under 1. Suffer defeat or destruction; fail. For example, *We feared the business would go under after the founder died.* [Mid-1800s] 2. Lose consciousness. For example, *Ether was the first anesthetic to make patients go under quickly and completely.* This usage dates from the 1930s. 3. Submerge, sink, as in *This leaky boat is about to go under.*

go up 1. Be put up, as in *New buildings are going up all over town.* 2. Rise; increase. For example, *His temperature is going up at an alarming rate,* or *The costs of construction are going up all the time.* [Late 1800s] 3. Also, **be gone up.** Be destroyed, ruined, done for; also, die, be killed. For example, *If we're not back in a week, you'll know we've gone up,* or *In spite of our efforts, the plans for a new library are gone up.* [Slang; mid-1800s] 4. Forget one's lines on the stage or make a mistake in performing music. For example, *Don't worry, you know your part and you won't go up,* or *He went up in the last movement of the sonata.* [Slang; 1960s] Also see the subsequent idioms beginning with GO UP.

go up in flames Also, **go up in smoke.** Be utterly destroyed, as in *This project will go up in flames if the designer quits,* or *All our work is going up in smoke.* This idiom transfers a fire to other kinds of destruction. [Early 1900s]

go west Die, as in *He declared he wasn't ready to go west just yet.* This expression has been ascribed to a Native American legend that a dying man goes to meet the setting sun. However, it was first recorded in a poem of the early 1300s: "Women and many a willful man, As wind and water have gone west."

go whole hog Also, **go the limit.** Do something completely or thoroughly; proceed as far as possible. For example, *Instead of just painting the room, why not go whole hog and redecorate it completely?* or *Let's go the limit and dig up the entire garden.* Although the precise source of *whole hog* is disputed, this colloquialism was first recorded in 1828 (in *Japhet* by Frederick Marryat) as **go the whole hog.** Today the article is usually omitted. **Go the limit,** also a colloquialism, dates from the mid-1900s. Also see ALL OUT.

go wilding Also, **go out wilding.** Go on a rampage, as in *The convention delegates have arrived in town, and after deliberating all day they are ready* *to go out wilding at night.* This term originally referred to teenage gang violence directed against randomly chosen victims, impulsive mugging or rape, and similar terrorizing. It also has been transferred to unruly but less violent outings, as in the example. [1980s]

go with 1. Also, **go out with.** Accompany; also, date regularly. For example, *When I leave, do you want to go with me?* or *Jerry has been going out with Frieda for two years.* [Mid-1500s] **2.** Be associated with, as in *His accent goes with his background.* [c. 1600] **3.** Take the side of someone, as in *I'll go with you in defending his right to speak freely.* [Mid-1400s] Also see GO ALONG, def. 2. **4.** Also, **go well with.** Look good with, match. For example, *This chair goes well with the rest of the furniture,* or *That color doesn't go with the curtains.* [Early 1700]

go without saying Be self-evident, a matter of course. For example, *It goes without saying that success is the product of hard work.* This expression is a translation of the French *cela va sans dire.* [Second half of 1800s]

go with the flow Also, **go with the tide.** Move along with the prevailing forces, accept the prevailing trend, as in *Rather than striking out in new directions, I tend to go with the flow,* or *Pat isn't particularly original; she just goes with the tide.* The *flow* in the first and more colloquial term, which dates from the late 1900s, alludes to the ebb and flow of tides and probably gained currency because of its appealing rhyme.

gown ♦ See CAP AND GOWN; TOWN AND GOWN.

go wrong 1. Go astray, make a mistake. For example, *We made a left turn and somehow went wrong from then on,* or *You won't go wrong if you follow the directions in the dress pattern.* [c. 1300] **2.** Take to evil ways, become a criminal, as in *As soon as he turned thirteen, Billy fell in with a gang and began to go wrong.* [c. 1500] **3.** Fail, turn out badly, as in *Everything about this party has gone wrong.* [Late 1500s] **4.** Fail to work properly, as in *The car starts fine, but as soon as you put it in gear, the transmission goes wrong.* [Late 1800s]

grab ♦ In addition to the idiom beginning with GRAB, also see HOW DOES THAT GRAB YOU; UP FOR GRABS.

grab bag A miscellaneous collection, as in *The meeting amounted to a grab bag of petty complaints.* This term alludes to a container offered at a party or fair, where one dips in for a party favor or prize without knowing what one will get. [Mid-1800s]

grace ♦ See FALL FROM GRACE; IN SOMEONE'S BAD GRACES; IN SOMEONE'S GOOD GRACES; SAVING GRACE; SAY GRACE; THERE BUT FOR THE GRACE OF GOD; WITH GOOD GRACE.

gracious ♦ See GOODNESS GRACIOUS.

grade ♦ See MAKE THE GRADE.

grain ♦ See AGAINST THE GRAIN; WITH A GRAIN OF SALT.

grand ♦ In addition to the idioms beginning with GRAND, also see LIKE GRAND CENTRAL STATION.

granddaddy of them all The first, oldest, or most respected of its kind, as in *That computer is the granddaddy of them all.* [Colloquial; c. 1900]

grand slam A sweeping success or total victory, as in *This presentation gave us a grand slam—every buyer placed an order.* This term originated in the early 1800s in the card game of whist (forerunner of contract bridge), where it refers to the taking of all thirteen tricks. It later was extended to bridge and various sports, where it has different meanings: in baseball, a home run hit with runners on all the bases, resulting in four runs for the team; in tennis, winning all four national championships in a single calendar year; in golf, winning all four major championships. In the 1990s the term was used for four related proposals presented on a ballot at once.

grandstand play, make a Show off, act ostentatiously, as in *His colleagues were annoyed with Tom for constantly making a grandstand play at sales conferences.* This expression was first used for a baseball play made to impress the crowd in the grandstand (the section of high-priced seats at ballparks). [Second half of 1800s] For a synonym, see PLAY TO THE GALLERY.

grand tour A comprehensive tour, survey, or inspection. For example, *They took me on a grand tour of their new house,* or *The new chairman will want to make a grand tour of all the branches.* Starting in the late 1600s this term was used for a tour of the major European cities, considered essential to a well-bred man's education. In the mid-1800s it was extended to more general use.

granted ♦ See TAKE FOR GRANTED.

grape ♦ See SOUR GRAPES.

grasp ♦ In addition to the idiom beginning with GRASP, also see GET A FIX ON (GRASP OF).

grasp at straws Also, **clutch at straws.** Make a desperate attempt at saving oneself. For example, *He had lost the argument, but he kept grasping at straws, naming numerous previous cases that had little to do with this one.* This metaphoric expression alludes to a drowning person trying to save himself by grabbing at flimsy reeds. First recorded in 1534, the term was used figuratively by the late 1600s.

grass ♦ In addition to the idioms beginning with GRASS, also see DON'T LET THE GRASS GROW UNDER ONE'S FEET; PUT OUT TO GRASS; SNAKE IN THE GRASS.

grasshopper ♦ See KNEE-HIGH TO A GRASSHOPPER.

grass is always greener on the other side, the A different situation always seems better than one's own. For example, *Bob always thinks the grass is greener elsewhere, which accounts for his constant job changes.* This expression, an ancient proverb cited by Erasmus in the 15th century, is so well known that it is often shortened.

grass widow A woman who is separated from her husband, either by divorce or temporary absence. For example, *She's a grass widow these days, with Herb traveling to golf tournaments all over the country.* The expression dates from the 16th century, when it referred to the mother of an illegitimate child, *grass* presumably alluding to the open-air setting of the child's conception.

grave ♦ See DIG ONE'S OWN GRAVE; FROM THE CRADLE TO THE GRAVE; ONE FOOT IN THE GRAVE; TURN IN ONE'S GRAVE.

gravy train, ride the Experience excessive ease, success, or profit, especially undeservedly. For example, *Now that his brother is paying all his bills, Jim is riding the gravy train.* The word *gravy* has long meant "easy profits," and the term is believed to come from 19th-century railroad slang, although the earliest recorded use dates from the early 1900s. W.C. Handy used it in one of his famous blues songs written in 1914, in which he bemoans falling off the gravy train. Also see EASY STREET.

gray ♦ In addition to the idioms beginning with GRAY, also see GET GRAY HAIR FROM.

gray area Indeterminate territory, undefined position, neither here nor there. For example, *There's a large gray area between what is legal and what is not.* This term, which uses *gray* in the sense of "neither black nor white" (or halfway between the two), dates only from the mid-1900s.

gray matter Brains, intellect, as in *If you'd only use your gray matter, you'd see the answer in a minute.* This expression refers to actual brain tissue that is gray in color. Agatha Christie's fictional detective, Hercule Poirot, constantly alludes to using *the little gray cells* for solving a crime. [Late 1800s]

grease ♦ In addition to the idioms beginning with GREASE, also see ELBOW GREASE; LIKE GREASED LIGHTNING; SQUEAKY WHEEL GETS THE GREASE.

grease someone's palm Also, **oil someone's palm** or **hand.** Give someone money in exchange for a favor; also, bribe someone. For example, *If you want your luggage to make the plane, be sure to grease the porter's palm.* This term uses *grease* in the sense of "enrich." [First half of 1500s]

grease the wheels Also, **oil the wheels.** Make things run smoothly, as in *You can count on Ben to grease the wheels so we'll be waited on promptly.* This metaphoric expression transfers literal lubrication to figurative. [Mid-1600s]

greasy spoon A cheap restaurant, especially one serving short-order fried foods. For example, *College students short of cash tend to eat a lot in that greasy spoon.* This expression also implies that the restaurant is not very clean. [c. 1900]

great ♦ In addition to the idioms beginning with GREAT, also see GOOD (GREAT) DEAL; GOOD (GREAT) MANY; GO TO ANY LENGTH (GREAT LENGTHS); HAVE A GOOD (GREAT) MIND TO; MAKE GREAT STRIDES; NO GREAT SHAKES; SET (GREAT) STORE BY.

great deal ♦ See GOOD DEAL.

greatest thing since sliced bread Also, **best thing since sliced bread.** An excellent new invention, as in *Harry swears that this new program is the greatest thing since sliced bread.* This phrase, used either straightforwardly or sarcastically, alludes to the convenience of buying bread that is already sliced. [Mid-1900s]

great guns 1. Very energetically or successfully. This colloquial expression usually occurs in the phrase **go great guns,** as in *They're going great guns with those drawings.* The expression comes from British naval slang of the late 1700s, when *blowing great guns* meant a violent gale. Harry Truman used the term in *Dear Bess* (1945): "We have been going great guns in the last day or two." **2. great gun.** Also **big gun.** An important person, as in *All the great guns came to the reception.* This usage is heard less often today. [Slang; early 1800s] Also see BIG CHEESE. **3. Great guns!** An expletive expressing surprise or astonishment, as in *Great guns! You're not leaving now?* [Late 1800s]

great many ♦ See under GOOD MANY.

great minds run in the same channel, all Intelligent persons think alike or come up with similar ideas. For example, *I see you brought your tennis racket—thank goodness for great minds.* This term is often uttered (sometimes jokingly) when two persons seem to find the same answer simultaneously, and is frequently shortened. [Late 1500s]

great shakes ♦ See NO GREAT SHAKES.

great white hope Something or someone that is expected to succeed. For example, *Mark is the great white hope of the international division.* This expression dates from the early 1900s, when heavyweight boxing champion Jack Johnson, who was black, seemed invincible and the term was used for any white opponent who might defeat him. It gained currency as the title of a Broadway play and later (1970) a film. By then it had been transferred to anyone of whom much was expected.

Greek to me, it's Also, **it's all Greek to me.** It is beyond my comprehension, as in *This new computer program is all Greek to me.* This expression was coined by Shakespeare, who used it literally in *Julius Caesar* (1:2), where Casca says of a speech by Seneca, deliberately given in Greek so that some would not understand it, "For mine own part, it was Greek to me." It soon was transferred to anything unintelligible.

green ♦ In addition to the idioms beginning with GREEN, also see GRASS IS ALWAYS GREENER.

green about the gills Also, **green around the gills.** Looking ill or nauseated, as in *After that bumpy ride she looked quite green about the gills.* The use of *green* to describe an ailing person's complexion dates from about 1300, and *gills* has referred to the flesh around human jaws and ears since the 1600s. Although in the 1800s *white* and *yellow* were paired with *gills* to suggest illness, the alliterative *green* has survived them.

green-eyed monster Jealousy, as in *Bella knew that her husband sometimes succumbed to the green-eyed monster.* This expression was coined by Shakespeare in *Othello* (3:3), where Iago says: "O! beware, my lord, of jealousy; it is the green-eyed monster which doth mock the meat it feeds on." It is thought to allude to cats, often green-eyed, who tease their prey. Also see GREEN WITH ENVY.

green light, the Permission to go ahead, as in *The chief gave us the green light for starting this project.* This term originated in the late 1800s for the signal used by railroads to indicate that a train could proceed. It was transferred to more general use in the first half of the 1900s.

green thumb A knack for making plants grow well, as in *Just look at Louise's plants—she really has a green thumb.* This term presumably alludes to the stained fingers of an avid gardener. [First half of 1900s]

green with envy Full of desire for someone's possessions or advantages; extremely covetous. For example, *Her fur coat makes me green with envy.* Shakespeare described envy as *the green sickness* (*Anthony and Cleopatra*, 3:2), but the current phrase, dating from the mid-1800s, is the one most often heard. Also see GREEN-EYED MONSTER.

grey ♦ See GRAY.

grief ♦ See COME TO GRIEF; GOOD GRIEF.

grievance ♦ See AIR ONE'S GRIEVANCES.

grin and bear it Put up good-humoredly with adversity, with good humor, as in *It's no fun being sick for the holidays, but you might as well grin and bear it.* Also put as *grin and abide* in the 19th century, this expression became so well known that Sam Walter Foss (1858–1911) made a pun on it in his poem, "The Firm of Grin and Barrett": "Never yet was any panic Scared the firm of Grin and Barrett."

grind ♦ In addition to the idiom beginning with GRIND, also see AX TO GRIND; MILLS OF THE GODS GRIND SLOWLY.

grindstone ♦ See NOSE TO THE GRINDSTONE.

grind to a halt Also, **come to a grinding halt.** Gradually come to a standstill or end. For example, *Once the funding stopped, the refurbishing project ground to a halt,* or *She's come to a grinding halt with that book she's writing.* This expression alludes to a clogged engine that gradually stops or a ship that runs aground.

grin like a Cheshire cat Smile broadly, especially in a self-satisfied way. For example, *John ended the set with a beautiful serve, an ace, and couldn't help grinning like a Cheshire cat.* The ultimate origin of this expression, appearing in print since the late 1700s, is disputed, but its most famous exponent was Lewis Carroll, in whose *Alice's Adventures in Wonderland* the grinning cat gradually vanished from view, with its grin the last part to vanish.

grip ♦ See COME TO GRIPS WITH; GET A GRIP ON; IN THE GRIP OF; LOSE ONE'S GRIP.

grist for the mill Something that can be used to advantage, as in *These seemingly useless data will be grist for the mill when he lodges a complaint.* This expression alludes to *grist,* the amount of grain that can be ground at one time. [Late 1500s]

grit one's teeth Summon up one's strength to face unpleasantness or overcome a difficulty. For example, *Gritting his teeth, he dove into the icy water.* This expression uses *grit* in the sense of both clamping one's teeth together and grinding them with effort. [Late 1700s]

groove ♦ See IN THE GROOVE.

gross one out Disgust or revolt one, as in *Chewing gum in church grosses me out,* or *His explicit language grossed her out.* [Slang; mid-1900s]

ground ♦ In addition to the idioms beginning with GROUND, also see BOTH FEET ON THE GROUND; BREAK GROUND; COMMON GROUND; COVER GROUND; COVER THE FIELD (GROUND); CUT THE GROUND FROM UNDER; DOWN TO THE GROUND; EAR TO THE GROUND; FROM THE GROUND UP; GAIN GROUND; GET OFF THE GROUND; GIVE GROUND; HAPPY HUNTING GROUND; HIT THE GROUND RUNNING; LEAVE THE GROUND; LOSE GROUND; ON ONE'S HOME GROUND; RUN INTO THE GROUND; RUN TO EARTH (GROUND); STAMPING GROUND; STAND ONE'S GROUND; WORSHIP THE GROUND SOMEONE WALKS ON.

ground floor, get in on the Participate in the beginning of a venture, thereby gaining some advantage. For example, *Investors were eager to get in on the ground floor of the new development.* [First half of 1800s]

ground rules Basic procedures of conduct, as in *The press secretary sets the ground rules for all of the President's press conferences.* The term comes from baseball, where it refers to specific rules for a particular ballpark, which are based on special conditions such as a very high outfield fence or a field obstruction of some kind. It began to be transferred to more general use in the mid-1900s.

grow ♦ In addition to the idioms beginning with GROW, also see ABSENCE MAKES THE HEART GROW FONDER; LET THE GRASS GROW UNDER ONE'S FEET.

growing pains Problems that arise in beginning or enlarging an enterprise, as in *The company is undergoing growing pains but should be viable by next year.* This expression, which dates from the late 1800s, originally referred to the joint and limb aches experienced by youngsters who are growing rapidly. By about 1900 it was being used figuratively.

grow into 1. Develop so as to become, as in *The army makes a boy grow into a man.* [Mid-1500s] 2. Develop or change so as to fit, as in *He'll soon grow into the next shoe size,* or *She has grown into her job.* [Early 1800s]

grow on Also, **grow upon**. 1. Gradually become more evident. For example, *A feeling of distrust grew upon him as he learned more about the way the account was handled.* [c. 1600] 2. Gradually become more pleasurable or acceptable to, as in *This music is beginning to grow on me.* Jane Austen had it in *Pride and Prejudice* (1796): "Miss Bennet's pleasing manners grew on the good-will of Mrs. Hurst." [c. 1700]

grow out of 1. Develop or come into existence from. For example, *This article grew out of a few scribbled notes,* or *Their mutual trust grew out of long acquaintance.* 2. Also, **outgrow**. Become too large or mature for, as in *The baby's outgrown of all her dresses.*

grow up 1. Become an adult, as in *Sam wants to be a policeman when he grows up.* [First half of 1500s] 2. Come into existence, arise, as in *Similar social problems grew up in all the big cities.* [Late 1500s] 3. Become mature or sensible, as in *It's time you grew up and faced the facts.* This usage may also be in the form of an imperative (as in *Don't bite your nails—grow up!*) [Mid-1900s]

grudge ♦ See BEAR A GRUDGE; NURSE A GRUDGE.

guard ♦ See OFF GUARD; STAND GUARD.

guess ♦ See ANYONE'S GUESS; EDUCATED GUESS; HAVE ANOTHER GUESS COMING; I SUPPOSE (GUESS) SO; YOUR GUESS IS AS GOOD AS MINE.

guess again ♦ See HAVE ANOTHER GUESS COMING.

guest ♦ See BE MY GUEST.

gum up Ruin or bungle something, as in *The front office has gummed up the sales campaign thoroughly.* This idiom is also put as **gum up the works**, as in *John's changes in procedures have gummed up the works in the shipping department.* [Slang; c. 1900]

gun ♦ In addition to the idiom beginning with GUN, also see AT GUNPOINT; BIG CHEESE (GUN); GREAT GUNS; HIRED GUN; HOLD A GUN TO SOMEONE'S HEAD; JUMP THE GUN; SMOKING GUN; SON OF A BITCH (GUN); STICK TO ONE'S GUNS; UNDER THE GUN.

gun for 1. Pursue relentlessly so as to overcome or destroy. For example, *He was sure they were gunning for him and asked for police protection,* or *The senator felt that the reporters were gunning for him with that article about his brother.* [Slang; late 1800s] 2. Go after in earnest, try hard to obtain. For example, *He's been gunning for a raise all year.* [Slang; mid-1900s]

gung ho Also, **gung-ho**. Extremely enthusiastic or dedicated, as in *She was gung ho about her new job.* This expression was introduced in 1942 as a training slogan for a U.S. Marine battalion, derived from what an American officer thought were Mandarin Chinese words for "work together." It was actually an abbreviation for the name of Chinese industrial cooperatives.

gussied up Also, **all gussied up**. Dressed up, as in *Dana loves to get all gussied up and go to a fine restaurant.* The origin of this expression is not clear, though possibly it relates to the earlier use of the noun *gussie* (derived from a proper name) for an effeminate man. [Slang; mid-1900s]

gut ♦ In addition to the idiom beginning with GUT, also see BUST A GUT; HATE SOMEONE'S GUTS; HAVE THE GUTS.

gut it out Also, **tough it out**. Show pluck and perseverance in the face of opposition or adversity. For example, *I know it's hard but we'll just have to gut it out,* or *His boss has a terrible temper, but Joe is determined to tough it out.* The first term dates from the mid-1900s; the variant was first recorded in 1860.

gutter ♦ See IN THE GUTTER.

h

habit ♦ See KICK A HABIT.

hackles ♦ See RAISE SOMEONE'S HACKLES.

had ♦ In addition to the idioms beginning with HAD, also see under HAVE.

had, to be ♦ See BE HAD.

had better Also, **had best**. Ought to, should. For example, *You had better finish this one before starting another,* or *We had best be going.* [Mid-1400s] Also see YOU'D BETTER BELIEVE IT.

had enough ♦ See HAVE HAD ENOUGH.

had it ♦ See HAVE HAD IT.

had its day, has Is no longer useful or popular or successful, as in *Some people think the railroad has had its day.* This expression is the antonym of **have its** (or **one's**) **day,** meaning "to experience success or prosperity," as in *Every dog has its day,* a proverb dating from the 16th century. Both terms use *day* in the sense of "a propitious or opportune time."

had one's fill Also, **have one's fill.** ♦ See GET ONE'S FILL.

had rather Also, **had sooner.** Would prefer. For example, *I had rather you let me do the driving,* or *He'd sooner switch than fight.* This idiom today is often replaced by WOULD RATHER. [Late 1500s] Also see JUST AS SOON.

hail ♦ In addition to the idiom beginning with HAIL, also see WITHIN CALL (HAIL).

hail from Come from, originate from, as in *He hails from Oklahoma.* This term originally referred to the port from which a ship had sailed. [Mid-1800s]

hair ♦ In addition to the idioms beginning with HAIR, also see BAD HAIR DAY; BY A HAIR; BY THE SHORT HAIRS; FAIR-HAIRED BOY; GET GRAY HAIR FROM; HANG BY A THREAD (HAIR); HIDE OR HAIR; IN SOMEONE'S HAIR; LET ONE'S HAIR DOWN; MAKE ONE'S HAIR STAND ON END; PUT LEAD IN ONE'S PENCIL (HAIR ON ONE'S CHEST); SPLIT HAIRS; TEAR ONE'S HAIR; TURN A HAIR.

hair of the dog that bit you Whatever made you ill used as a remedy, especially alcohol as a hangover cure. For example, *A little hair of the dog will cure that hangover in no time.* This expression, already a proverb in John Heywood's 1546 compendium, is based on the ancient folk treatment for dogbite of putting a burnt hair of the dog on the wound. It is often shortened, as in the example.

hair shirt A self-imposed punishment or penance, as in *I apologized a dozen times—do you want me to wear a hair shirt forever?* This term, mentioned from the 13th century on, alludes to wearing a coarse, scratchy hair shirt, the practice of religious ascetics. Its figurative use dates from the mid-1800s.

hale and hearty In robust good health, as in *After her long bout with pneumonia, I was glad to see her hale and hearty.* This redundant expression, since both *hale* and *hearty* here mean "healthy," probably survives owing to its pleasing alliteration. [Mid-1800s]

half ♦ In addition to the idioms beginning with HALF, also see AT HALF-MAST; BETTER HALF; BY HALF; GLASS IS HALF FULL; GO HALFWAY; GO OFF (HALF-COCKED); IN HALF; NOT BAD (HALF BAD); SIX OF ONE, HALF DOZEN OF THE OTHER; TIME AND A HALF; WITH HALF AN EYE. Also see under HALFWAY; HALVES.

half a heart, with With only moderate enthusiasm, as in *After his transfer he worked with half a heart, looking forward to early retirement.* [Mid-1800s] For an antonym, see WITH ALL ONE'S HEART.

half a loaf is better than none Something is better than nothing, even if it is less than one wanted. For example, *He had asked for a new trumpet but got a used one—oh well, half a loaf is better than none.* This expression, often shortened, was already a proverb in 1546, where it was explicitly put: "For better is half a loaf than no bread."

half a mind An inclination that is not definite or resolute. For example, *I've half a mind to drop the course,* or *He went out with half a mind to walk all the way there.* [First half of 1700s] Also see HAVE A GOOD MIND TO.

half of it Only part of something, as in *You saw them together, but that's just the half of it; she's moved in with him.* This phrase, signifying the most important portion (more than half), is often put negatively as **not the half of it,** as in *You thought they played badly? That's not the half of it, because they've been kicked out of the league.* [First half of 1900s]

half the battle A successful beginning, as in *You've got the shopping list done—that's half the battle.* This expression is an abbreviation of an 18th-century proverb, "The first blow is half the battle."

halfway ♦ See GO HALFWAY.

halt ♦ See CALL A HALT; COME TO A HALT; GRIND TO A HALT.

halves ♦ See BY HALVES; GO HALVES. Also see under HALF.

hammer ♦ In addition to the idioms beginning with HAMMER, also see UNDER THE HAMMER.

hammer and tongs Forcefully, with great vigor. For example, *She went at the weeds hammer and tongs, determined to clean out the long neglected flowerbed.* Often put as **go at it hammer and tongs,** this phrase alludes to the blacksmith's tools. [c. 1700]

hammer away at Keep at something continuously, as in *The reporters hammered away at the candidate.* This phrase employs *hammer* in the sense of "beat repeatedly," a usage dating from the mid-1600s.

hammer out Work out with considerable effort, as in *It took weeks of negotiations to hammer out an acceptable compromise.* This usage likens intellectual effort to shaping metal with the blows of a hammer. [Mid-1700s]

ham up Exaggerate or overdo, especially with extravagant emotion, as in *Hamming up the eulogy was disgraceful, especially since he didn't even know the deceased.* It is also put as **ham it up,** meaning "overact," as in *She loves to ham it up in front of the class*. This idiom probably alludes to the *hamfat* (lard) used to remove stage makeup, mentioned in the minstrel song, "The Ham-Fat Man." From this *hamfatter* came to mean "an inexpert and flamboyant actor," and was in the late 1800s shortened to *ham*. The idiom here was first recorded in 1933.

hand ♦ In addition to the idioms beginning with HAND, also see AT FIRST HAND; AT HAND; AT SECOND HAND; AT THE HAND OF; BACK OF ONE'S HAND; BARE HANDS; BIRD IN THE HAND; BITE THE HAND THAT FEEDS YOU; BOUND HAND AND FOOT; BY HAND; CATCH RED-HANDED; CHANGE HANDS; CLEAN HANDS; COLD HANDS, WARM HEART; DEAL IN (ONE A HAND); DIRTY ONE'S HANDS; EAT OUT OF SOMEONE'S HAND; FEED (HAND) SOMEONE A LINE; FORCE SOMEONE'S HAND; FREE HAND; FROM HAND TO HAND; GIVE A HAND; GLAD HAND; GREASE SOMEONE'S PALM (HAND); HANG HEAVY ON ONE'S HANDS; HAT IN HAND; HAVE A HAND IN; HAVE ONE'S HANDS FULL; HEAVY HAND; HELPING HAND; IN GOOD HANDS; IN HAND; IN ONE'S HANDS; IN THE HANDS OF; IRON HAND; KEEP ONE'S HAND IN; KNOW LIKE A BOOK (THE BACK OF ONE'S HAND); LAY HANDS ON; LEFT HAND DOESN'T KNOW WHAT THE RIGHT HAND IS DOING; LEFT-HANDED COMPLIMENT; LEND A HAND; MANY HANDS MAKE LIGHT WORK; OFF ONE'S HANDS; ON A PLATTER, HAND; ON HAND; ON ONE'S HANDS; ON THE ONE HAND; ON THE OTHER HAND; OUT OF CONTROL (HAND); OUT OF HAND; PLAY INTO THE HANDS OF; PUTTY IN SOMEONE'S HANDS; RAISE A HAND AGAINST; RIGHT-HAND MAN; RUB ONE'S HANDS; SHAKE HANDS; SHOW OF HANDS; SHOW ONE'S HAND; SIT ON ONE'S HANDS; SLEIGHT OF HAND; TAKE IN HAND; TAKE INTO ONE'S HANDS; TAKE ONE'S LIFE (IN ONE'S HANDS); TAKE THE LAW INTO ONE'S HANDS; THROW IN ONE'S HAND; THROW UP ONE'S HANDS; TIE ONE'S HANDS; TIME ON ONE'S HANDS; TIP ONE'S HAND; TO HAND; TRY ONE'S HAND; TURN ONE'S HAND TO; UPPER HAND; WAIT ON HAND AND FOOT; WASH ONE'S HANDS OF; WITH ONE ARM (HAND) TIED.

hand and foot ♦ See BOUND HAND AND FOOT; WAIT ON SOMEONE HAND AND FOOT.

hand down 1. Bequeath to one's heirs, as in *The silver and jewels have been handed down from generation to generation in that family*. [Late 1600s] 2. Make and pronounce an official decision, especially the verdict of a court. For example, *The judge wasted no time in handing down a sentence of contempt of court*. [First half of 1900s] Also see HAND ON; HAND OVER.

hand in glove On intimate terms, in close association, as in *The internist is hand in glove with the surgeon, so you'd better get a second opinion*. This metaphoric expression for a close fit was already included in John Ray's 1678 collection of proverbs, when it was put *hand and glove*.

hand in hand In cooperation, jointly, as in *Industrial growth and urbanization often go hand in hand*. This phrase, often put as **go hand in hand with**, was first recorded in 1576.

hand in the till, with one's Also, **with one's fingers in the till; have one's hand in the cookie jar.** Stealing from one's employer. For example, *He was caught with his hand in the till and was fired immediately*, or *They suspected she had her hand in the cookie jar but were waiting for more evidence*. The noun *till* has been used for a money box or drawer since the 15th century; *cookie jar*, perhaps alluding to the "sweets" of money, dates only from about 1940.

hand it to Give credit to, congratulate, as in *You've got to hand it to her; she knows what she's doing*. [c. 1900]

handle ♦ In addition to the idioms beginning with HANDLE, also see FLY OFF THE HANDLE; GET A FIX (HANDLE) ON.

handle to one's name A nickname or title, as in *He was knighted and now had a handle to his name*, or *His gluttony earned him a handle to his name, Big Mouth*. [First half of 1800s]

handle with gloves Also, **handle with kid gloves.** Treat with great care or very gently, as in *She has a terrible temper, so try to handle her with kid gloves*. This usage probably alludes to the antonym, **handle without gloves**, meaning "to treat harshly." Gloves made of kidskin, the hide of a young goat, are soft and pliable, whence the transfer to delicate treatment. [Second half of 1800s]

hand on Turn over to another, as in *When you've read it, please hand it on to Sam*. This term can also be used in the sense of "bequeath" (see HAND DOWN, def. 1). [Second half of 1800s]

hand out Distribute, as in *The teacher handed out the test papers*. [Late 1800s] For a synonym, see PASS OUT, def. 1.

hand over Release or relinquish to another's possession or control. For example, *You may as well hand over the money*, or *He decided to hand the store over to his children*. [c. 1800] For a synonym, see TURN OVER, def. 5.

hand over fist Rapidly, at a tremendous rate, as in *He's making money hand over fist*. This expression is derived from the nautical **hand over hand**, describing how a sailor climbed a rope. [First half of 1800s]

hand over hand ♦ See HAND OVER FIST.

hands are tied ♦ See TIE ONE'S HANDS.

hands down 1. Also, **in a breeze; in a walk.** Easily, without effort, as in *she won the election hands down*, or *They won in a breeze, 10–0*, or *The top *players get through the first rounds of the tournament in a walk.* All of these expressions originated in sports. **Hands down,** dating from the mid-1800s, comes from horse racing, where jockeys drop their hands downward and relax their hold when they are sure to win. **In a breeze,** first recorded in a baseball magazine in 1910, alludes to the rapid and easy passage of moving air; **in a walk,** also from baseball, alludes to taking a base on balls, that is, reaching first base without having hit a pitched ball because of the pitcher's mistakes. **2.** Unquestionably, without a doubt, as in *Hands down, it was the best thing I've ever done.*

handshake ♦ See GOLDEN HANDSHAKE.

hands off An order to stop touching or interfering with something, as in *Hands off the cake, children!* This idiom is also put as **keep one's hands off,** as in *She knew she had to keep her hands off so he could learn to tie his shoes by himself.* [Mid-1500s]

handsome is as handsome does How one acts is more important than how one looks. For example, *He may be homely, but he's the kindest man I've ever met — handsome is as handsome does.* This expression already appeared in John Ray's 1670 collection of proverbs.

hands up A direction or order to hold one's hands high, as in *Hands up or I'll shoot!* This imperative is used by police officers and criminals so that they can see if someone is holding a weapon. [Second half of 1800s]

hand to hand **1.** In close combat; also, at close quarters. For example, *If the enemy came any closer they would soon be fighting hand to hand.* This expression, dating from about 1400, is usually restricted to military contexts but occasionally sees more general use. **2. from hand to hand.** From one person to another; through a succession of persons. For example, *The instructions were passed from hand to hand until everyone had seen them,* or *Over the generations the family albums went from hand to hand.* [Mid-1500s]

hand to mouth, from With only the bare essentials, existing precariously. For example, *After she lost her job she was living from hand to mouth.* This expression alludes to eating immediately whatever is at hand. [c. 1500]

hand to on a silver platter Also, **serve up on a plate.** Provide with something valuable for nothing, or give an unearned reward to; also, make it easy for. For example, *She did no work at all, expecting to have everything handed to her on a silver platter,* or *just ask them — they'll serve up the data on a plate.* Both terms allude to being elaborately served at the table. [Early 1900s] Also see BORN WITH A SILVER SPOON.

handwriting on the wall Also, **writing on the wall.** A warning or presentiment of danger, as in *The company was losing money, and seeing the handwriting on the wall, she started to look for another job.* This expression comes from the Bible (Daniel 5:5–31), in which the prophet interprets some mysterious writing that a disembodied hand has inscribed on the palace wall, telling King Belshazzar that he will be overthrown.

handy ♦ See COME IN HANDY.

hang, hanged ♦ In addition to the idioms beginning with HANG and HANGED, also see DRAW AND QUARTER (HANGED, DRAWN AND QUARTERED); GET THE HANG OF; I'LL BE HANGED; LEAVE HANGING; LET IT ALL HANG OUT; NOT GIVE A DAMN (HANG); THEREBY HANGS A TALE; TIME HANGS HEAVY.

hang a left Also, **hang a right.** Make a left (or right) turn, as when driving an automobile. For example, *Hang a left at the traffic light and then hang a right at the next intersection.* [Slang; mid-1900s]

hang around **1.** Spend time idly, loiter, as in *Every afternoon they could be found hanging around the mall.* [Mid-1800s] Also see HANG OUT, def. 4. **2.** Keep company or consort with someone, as in *The younger campers loved to hang around the older ones.* [Mid-1800s] Also see HANG OUT, def. 5.

hang back Be reluctant to move ahead, hold back. For example, *They hung back at the entrance, fearful that they wouldn't be admitted,* or *We hung back to let our parents go in first.* [Second half of 1500s]

hang by a thread Also, **hang by a hair.** Be in a risky or unstable situation, as in *His promotion was hanging by a thread,* or *With the lead actor sick, the success of our play hung by a hair.* This expression, already proverbial in the early 1500s, alludes to Damocles, who vexed King Dionysius with constant flattery. The king invited him to a banquet where Damocles found himself seated under a naked sword suspended by a single hair, symbolizing his insecure position at the court.

hanged, drawn, and quartered ♦ See DRAW AND QUARTER.

hanged for a sheep as a lamb, might as well be Might just as well be punished for a big misdeed as a small one. For example, *I might as well be hanged for a sheep as a lamb and have a third piece of cake — I've gone off my diet anyhow.* Already a proverb in John Ray's 1678 collection, this expression alludes to the old punishment for stealing sheep, which was hanging no matter what the age or size of the animal.

hang fire Delay, as in *The advertising campaign is hanging fire until they decide how much to spend on it.* This expression originally referred to the 17th-century flintlock musket, where the priming powder ignited but often failed to explode the main charge, a result called *hanging fire*. [c. 1800]

hang in Also, **hang in there**. Keep at something, persevere. For example, *We decided to hang in until we had figured out why the experiment failed*, or *Hang in there! You'll soon catch on to the language.* [Slang; mid-1900s]

hang in the balance Be in a precarious condition or in a state of suspense. For example, *The doctor said her life was hanging in the balance.* This expression alludes to the suspended balance scale where an object is placed in one pan and weights are added one by one to the other pan until the two are balanced. [First half of 1400s]

hang it Also, **hang it all**. An expression of annoyance, probably a euphemism for *hell* or *damn*. For example, *Hang it! I locked my keys inside the car*, or *Hang it all, you don't need to push me.*

hang loose Relax, take it easy, as in *Just hang loose and it will all work out.* [Slang; mid-1900s]

hang on 1. **hang on to**. Cling tightly to something, retain, as in *Hang on to those papers before they blow away.* [Mid-1800s] Also see HANG ON TO YOUR HAT. 2. Continue persistently, persevere, as in *This cough is hanging on much longer than I expected*, or *He was hanging on, hoping business would improve when interest rates went down.* This usage was sometimes embellished to **hang on by one's eyelashes** or **eyebrows** or **eyelids**, meaning "to persist at any cost." [Second half of 1800s] 3. Keep a telephone connection open, as in *Please hang on, I'll see if he's in.* [First half of 1900s] 4. Wait for a short time, be patient, as in *Hang on, I'm getting it as fast as I can.* [First half of 1900s] 5. Depend on, as in *Our plans hang on their decision about the new park.* [Colloquial; second half of 1900s] 6. Blame on, as in *They'll try to hang that robbery on the same gang, but I don't think they'll succeed.* [Colloquial; first half of 1900s] 7. **hang one on**. Get very drunk, as in *Come on, let's go and hang one on.* [Slang; mid-1900s] Also see the subsequent idioms beginning with HANG ON.

hang one on ‣ See HANG ON, def. 7.

hang one's head Express shame or contrition. For example, *No need to hang your head—you've done the best you can.* [c. 1200]

hang on someone's words Listen very attentively to someone. For example, *You don't need to hang on his words—just remember the gist of it.* It is also put as **hang on to every word**, as in *Whenever Mother read their favorite book to them, the children hung on to every word.*

hang on to your hat Also, **hold your hat**. An expression warning someone of a big surprise. For example, *Hang on to your hat, we're about to go*

public, or *Hold your hat — we just won the lottery.* This expression may allude, according to lexicographer Eric Partridge, to a wild ride on a rollercoaster. [Colloquial; first half of 1900s]

hang out 1. Protrude downward, as in *The dog's tongue was hanging out*, or *The branches hung out over the driveway.* [c. 1400] 2. Display a flag or sign of some kind, as in *They hung out the flag on every holiday.* [Mid-1500s] 3. Reside, live, as in *I've found a place downtown, and I'll be hanging out there beginning next week.* [c. 1800] 4. Spend one's free time in; also, loiter, pass time idly. For example, *They hung out around the pool parlor*, or *They spent the evening just hanging out.* [Slang; mid-1900s] 5. **hang out with**. Keep company with, appear in public with, as in *She's hanging out with her ex-boyfriend again.* [Slang; second half of 1900s] Also see the subsequent idioms beginning with HANG OUT; LET IT ALL HANG OUT.

hang out one's shingle Open an office, especially a professional practice, as in *Bill's renting that office and hanging out his shingle next month.* This American colloquialism dates from the first half of the 1800s, when at first lawyers, and later also doctors and business concerns, used shingles for signboards.

hang out to dry Abandon someone to danger, as in *The squadron withdrew and just let us hang out to dry.* This expression alludes to hanging wet laundry on a clothesline. [Slang; 1960s]

hang over 1. Remain suspended or unsettled, as in *They plan to let the vote hang over until the next session.* This usage alludes to something suspended or floating in the air. [c. 1200] 2. Also, **hang over one's head**. Threaten or be imminent, as in *I've got that test hanging over me*, or *A stiff fine is hanging over his head.* [Mid-1500s] Also see HANG BY A THREAD.

hang together 1. Stand united, stick together, as in *We must all hang together and tell the same story.* [c. 1400] 2. Cohere, constitute a consistent whole. For example, *The plot lines in that movie don't hang together.* [Mid-1500s]

hang tough Remain firmly resolved, as in *We're going to hang tough on this point and not give in.* This slangy idiom uses *tough* in the sense of "aggressively unyielding," a usage dating from the first half of the 1900s.

hang up 1. Suspend on a hook or hanger, as in *Let me hang up your coat for you.* [c. 1300] 2. Also, **hang up on**. Replace a telephone receiver in its cradle; end a phone conversation. For example, *She hung up the phone*, or *He hung up on her.* [Early 1900s] 3. Delay or hinder; also, become halted or snagged, as in *Budget problems hung up the project for months*, or *Traffic was hung up for* *miles*. [Second half of 1800s] **4.** Have or cause to have emotional difficulties; as in *Being robbed at gunpoint can hang one up for years to come.* [Slang; early 1900s] **5. hung up on.** Obsessed with, as in *For years the FBI was hung up on Communist spies.* [First half of 1900s] **6. hang up one's sword** or **gloves** or **fiddle.** Quit, retire, as in *He's hanging up his sword next year and moving to Florida.* The noun in these expressions refers to the profession one is leaving—*sword* for the military, *gloves* for boxing, and *fiddle* for music—but they all are used quite loosely as well, as in the example. **7. hang up one's hat.** Settle somewhere, reside, as in "Eight hundred a year, and as nice a house as any gentleman could wish to hang up his hat in" (Anthony Trollope, *The Warden*, 1855).

happily ◆ See LIVE HAPPILY EVER AFTER.

happy ◆ In addition to the idioms beginning with HAPPY, also see MANY HAPPY RETURNS; TRIGGER HAPPY.

happy as the day is long Also, **happy as a lark; happy as a clam (at high tide).** Extremely glad, delighted, very cheerful, as in *He was happy as the day is long,* or *When she heard the news she was happy as a lark,* or *Once I got the test results I was happy as a clam at high tide.* The first of these similes dates from the late 1700s. The second alludes to the lark's beautiful, seemingly very happy, song. The third, from the early 1800s, alludes to the fact that clams can only be dug at low tide and therefore are safe at high tide; it is often shortened to **happy as a clam.**

happy camper A satisfied participant, a contented person, as in *She loved the challenge of her new job; she was one happy camper.* This expression is also often put in the negative, as in *She hated the heat and humidity of the southern summer; she was not a happy camper.* [Slang; mid-1900s]

happy hour A period in the late afternoon or early evening when a bar or lounge features drinks at reduced prices. For example, *The hotel bar has a happy hour from five to seven every day.* [1960s]

happy hunting ground A place where one can find or do what one wishes without restriction. For example, *The North Shore is a happy hunting ground for antique collectors.* This term alludes to the Native American idea of an afterlife where hunters find unlimited game. [Early 1800s]

happy medium The midway point between two extremes. For example, *We need to find a happy medium between overdoing the holiday season and ignoring it entirely.* This expression, first recorded in 1778, was once known as **the golden mean** and is based on ancient mathematical principles.

hard ◆ In addition to the idioms beginning with HARD, also see BETWEEN A ROCK AND A HARD

PLACE; COLD (HARD) CASH; COME DOWN (HARD) ON; DIE HARD; DRIVE A (HARD) BARGAIN; GO HARD WITH; NO HARD FEELINGS; PLAY HARDBALL; PLAY HARD TO GET; SCHOOL OF HARD KNOCKS; TOUGH (HARD) ROW TO HOE.

hard act to follow Also, **tough act to follow.** An outstanding performance or individual. For example, *Lucy was a terrific group leader—hers is a hard act to follow,* or *Bob's record is excellent—it will be a tough act to follow.* This expression, dating from about 1900, was originally used for a particularly good vaudeville act that made the next act look poor by comparison. It soon was extended to other enterprises.

hard and fast Defined, fixed, invariable, as in *We have hard and fast rules for this procedure.* This term originally was applied to a vessel that has come out of water, either by running aground or being put in dry dock, and is therefore unable to move. By the mid-1800s it was being used figuratively.

hard as nails Unyielding, callous, unsympathetic, as in *Don't ask her for a contribution—she's hard as nails.* This expression has replaced the 14th-century simile *hard as flint stone* and presumably alludes to the rigidity of nails.

hard bargain ◆ See under DRIVE A HARD BARGAIN.

hard cash ◆ See COLD CASH.

harden one's heart Feel no sympathy for, as in *We can't afford to give them more; we'll just have to harden our hearts when they ask.* [Late 1300s]

hard feelings ◆ See NO HARD FEELINGS.

hard hat A working-class ultraconservative. For example, *They were counting on a large number of votes from the hard hats.* This term alludes to the rigid protective headgear worn by construction workers, who were noted for their conservatism during the tumultuous 1960s. [c. 1960]

hard hit, be Be adversely affected or be severely stricken, as in *The walk-in clinics were hard hit by the new insurance laws.* This idiom must be differentiated from the similar-sounding adjective *hard-hitting,* alluding to strenuous exertion, as in *They were a hard-hitting team.* [Second half of 1800s]

hard line A firm, uncompromising policy or position. For example, *The President was taking a hard line on the budget.* [c. 1960]

hard liquor Distilled alcoholic beverages, such as gin or whiskey. For example, *We're serving wine and beer but no hard liquor.* The *hard* here refers to their high alcoholic content, which is also true for **hard cider,** although the latter is not distilled but has simply fermented.

hard luck Misfortune, adversity, as in *He's had a lot of hard luck in his day.* This expression is also used in the phrase **hard-luck story**, a tale of one's misfortune that is related in order to get sympathy (or a donation). For example, *We can't ignore her hard-luck story, even if you doubt that it's true.* [Second half of 1500s] Also see TOUGH BREAK.

hardly ever Also, **rarely ever, scarcely ever.** Very seldom, almost never, as in *This kind of thief is hardly ever caught,* or *He rarely ever brings up his wartime experiences.* The *ever* in these expressions, first recorded in 1694, serves as an intensifier.

hard nut to crack Also, **tough nut to crack.** A difficult problem; also, an individual who is difficult to deal with. For example, *This assignment is a hard nut to crack,* or *It won't be easy getting her approval; she's a tough nut to crack.* This metaphoric expression alludes to hard-shelled nuts like walnuts. [Early 1700s]

hard of hearing Somewhat deaf, having a partial loss of hearing. For example, *You'll have to speak distinctly; Dad's a little hard of hearing.* The use of *hard* in the sense of "difficulty in doing something" survives only in this expression. [Mid-1500s]

hard on 1. Also, **hard upon, hard by.** In close proximity, as in *The police were hard on the heels of the thieves,* or *It was hard upon three o'clock,* or *Their house is hard by ours.* The variants are used less than *hard on.* [Second half of 1700s] 2. **be hard on.** Deal severely with, cause damage to. For example, *He asked the teacher not to be too hard on those who forgot the assignment,* or *That cat has really been hard on the upholstery.* [Second half of 1600s] Also see HARD TIME, def. 2.

hard on someone's heels ♦ See AT SOMEONE'S HEELS.

hard pressed Overburdened, put upon, as in *With all these bills to pay we find ourselves hard pressed.* [c. 1800]

hard put, be Find something very difficult, as in *The show was so bad that I was hard put to conceal my dismay,* or *Manufacturers will be hard put to meet the new standards.* [c. 1700]

hard row to hoe ♦ See TOUGH ROW TO HOE.

hard sell 1. An aggressive, high-pressure sales practice or promotion, as in *Used-car salesmen tend to give you a hard sell.* This expression gave rise to the antonym **soft sell**, a low-key sales approach that relies on gentle persuasion. [Colloquial; c. 1950] 2. A difficult sales prospect, one who resists sales pressure. For example, *Those brokers who call us at dinnertime find me a hard sell— I usually just hang up on them.* [Late 1900s]

hard time 1. Also, **hard times.** A period of difficulty or hardship, especially financial hardship. For example, *Since Mom died, Christmas has been a hard time for Dad,* or *It's been hard times for both of them since they split up.* It is also put as **have a**

hard time, as in *I'm having a hard time finishing this book.* Charles Dickens used *Hard Times* as the title of a novel about poverty (1854). A more recent version is **have a time of it**, which despite its ambiguity (not specifying either "good" or "bad") nearly always means "experiencing difficulty"; for example, *We had quite a time of it in that hurricane.* [Late 1300s] 2. **give someone a hard time.** Annoy or harass someone. For example, *Don't let him give you a hard time; he's often late himself.* [Colloquial; early 1900s]

hard up In need, poor, as in *Unemployment is rising and many families are hard up,* or *With widespread emigration, Russia is finding itself hard up for scientists and other professional people.* [Colloquial; early 1800s]

hard way, the By bad or difficult experiences; also, by one's own efforts. For example, *Bill found out the hard way that interest on his credit-card debt can mount up fast,* or *No one can teach you how—you'll just have to learn it the hard way.* This expression comes from shooting craps (a dice game), where it refers to making an even-numbered point such as six by throwing doubles (two three's). Since there are more unmatching combinations that can produce the same number (four and two, five and one), the odds against throwing doubles are higher, hence the difficulty. [Early 1900s]

hare ♦ See MAD AS A HATTER (MARCH HARE); RUN WITH (THE HARE).

hark back Return to a previous point, as in *Let us hark back briefly to my first statement.* This expression originally alluded to hounds retracing their course when they have lost their quarry's scent. It may be dying out. [First half of 1800s]

harm ♦ See DO ONE WRONG (HARM); OUT OF HARM'S WAY.

harness ♦ See DIE WITH ONE'S BOOTS ON (IN HARNESS); IN HARNESS.

harp on Dwell on; talk or write about to a tedious and excessive extent. For example, *She kept harping on the fact that she had no household help at all.* This expression is a shortening of **harp on the same string**, meaning "to play the same note over and over." It was first recorded in 1518.

has ♦ See under HAVE.

hash ♦ In addition to the idiom beginning with HASH, also see MAKE A HASH OF; SETTLE SOMEONE'S HASH; SLING HASH.

hash over Also, **hash out.** Discuss carefully, review, as in *Let's hash over these plans again,* or *The department was hashing out the new syllabus.* This idiom uses the verb *hash* in the sense of "cut into small pieces," a usage dating from the mid-1700s.

haste ♦ In addition to the idiom beginning with HASTE, also see MAKE HASTE.

haste makes waste Proceeding too quickly can spoil an enterprise, as in *Stop trying to rush through three things at once—haste makes waste, you know.* This rhyming warning, first recorded in this exact form in 1575, was in John Ray's 1678 proverb collection, where the full text was: "Haste makes waste, and waste makes want, and want makes strife between the goodman and his wife."

hat ♦ In addition to the idioms beginning with HAT, also see AT THE DROP OF A HAT; BRASS HAT; EAT ONE'S HAT; HANG ON TO YOUR HAT; HANG UP (ONE'S HAT); HARD HAT; HATS OFF TO; KEEP UNDER ONE'S HAT; KNOCK INTO A COCKED HAT; PASS THE HAT; PULL OUT OF A HAT; TAKE ONE'S HAT OFF TO; TALK THROUGH ONE'S HAT; THROW ONE'S HAT IN THE RING; WEAR ANOTHER HAT. Also see under CAP.

hatch ♦ See BATTEN DOWN THE HATCHES; COUNT ONE'S CHICKENS BEFORE THEY HATCH; DOWN THE HATCH.

hatchet ♦ In addition to the idioms beginning with HATCHET, also see BURY THE HATCHET.

hatchet job ♦ See HATCHET MAN, def. 2.

hatchet man 1. A person assigned or hired to carry out a disagreeable task or unscrupulous order. For example, *When it came to firing an employee, Arthur was his boss's hatchet man.* This expression originally referred to a hired assassin but in the mid-1900s was transferred to less nefarious enterprises. 2. A person who attacks the reputation of others, especially a journalist hired to do so, as in *You can count on Mary's column to destroy the mayor—she's the perfect hatchet man.* This usage gave rise to **hatchet job,** meaning "harsh destructive criticism." [Mid-1900s]

hate ♦ In addition to the idiom beginning with HATE, also see SOMEBODY UP THERE LOVES (HATES) ME.

hate someone's guts Thoroughly despise someone, as in *I hate Peter's guts.* The *guts* here refers to a person's inner essence. [Slang; c. 1900]

hat in hand Also, **cap in hand.** In a humble manner. For example, *They went to her, hat in hand, asking for a change of assignment.* This expression alludes to removing one's headgear as a sign of respect and has survived the era of doffing one's hat. [c. 1700]

hat in the ring ♦ See THROW ONE'S HAT IN THE RING.

hats off to Congratulations to, as in *Hats off to Claire! She's set a new record for the mile.* This expression alludes to taking off one's hat as a sign of respect. [Mid-1800s]

hatter ♦ See MAD AS A HATTER.

hat trick An extremely clever or adroit maneuver, as in *It looked as though the party was going to*

achieve a hat trick in this election. The term originated in cricket, where it refers to three wickets taken by a bowler in three consecutive balls, traditionally rewarded with the presentation of a hat. It later was transferred to ice hockey, soccer, and baseball, where it denotes three consecutive successes (goals, hits), and then to more general use.

haul ♦ In addition to the idioms beginning with HAUL, also see LONG HAUL; RAKE (HAUL) OVER THE COALS.

haul off 1. Draw back slightly, in preparation for some action. For example, *He hauled off and smacked his brother in the face.* [c. 1800] 2. Also, **haul out.** Shift operations to a new place, move away. For example, *The group gradually hauled off to the West Coast,* or *The train hauled out just as I arrived.* [Second half of 1800s]

haul over the coals ♦ See RAKE OVER THE COALS.

haul up 1. Come to a halt, stop, as in *We hauled up in front of the hotel.* 2. Bring someone before a superior or other authority, call someone to account. For example, *This was the third time he'd been hauled up before the judge.* [Mid-1800s]

have ♦ In addition to the idioms beginning with HAVE, also see entries beginning with GET, HAD, and KEEP.

have a ball Enjoy oneself enormously, as in *It was a great trip—I had a ball.* This idiom uses the noun *ball* in the sense of "a gala dance." [Slang; 1920s]

have a big mouth ♦ See BIG MOUTH.

have a bone to pick ♦ See BONE TO PICK.

have a brush with Have an encounter or come in conflict with, as in *This was not the first time that Bob had a brush with the law.* This expression alludes to the noun *brush* in the sense of "a hostile collision," a usage dating from about 1400.

have a case on Also, **have a crush on.** Be infatuated with someone, as in *He's had a case on her for years,* or *Teenage girls often have a crush on this teacher.* The first slangy term dates from the mid-1800s; the second, a colloquialism, dates from the late 1800s.

have a clear conscience Also, **have a clean conscience.** Feel free of guilt or responsibility. For example, *I have a clear conscience—I did all I could to help.* This idiom is also put as **one's conscience is clear** or **clean,** as in *His conscience is clean about telling the whole story.* The adjective *clear* has been used in the sense of "innocent" since about 1400; *clean* was so used from about 1300.

have a clue ♦ See NOT HAVE A CLUE.

have a crack at Also, **get** or **have a go** or **shot** or **whack at; take a crack at.** Make an attempt or have a turn at doing something. For example, *Let me have a crack at assembling it,* or *I had a shot at it* *but failed,* or *Dad thinks he can—let him have a go at it,* or *Dave had a whack at changing the tire,* or *Jane wants to take a crack at it.* The oldest of these colloquialisms is *have a shot at,* alluding to firing a gun and first recorded in 1756; *crack* and *go* date from the 1830s, and *whack* from the late 1800s.

have a crush on ♦ See HAVE A CASE ON.

have a familiar ring Sound or seem as though one has already heard of something. For example, *That story has a familiar ring; I'm sure I've read it before.*

have a fit Also, **have fits** or **a conniption fit; take** or **throw a fit; have kittens.** Become extremely upset. For example, *She'll have a fit when she sees Anne wearing the same dress,* or *Mom had a conniption fit when she heard about the broken mirror,* or *Don't take a fit—the car's not really damaged,* or *Jill was having kittens over the spoiled cake.* One can also **give someone a fit** or **fits,** as in *His dithering about punctuation is enough to give me fits.* **Fit** and **fits,** along with **conniption fit,** have been used in hyperbolic expressions to denote a bout of hysterics since the 1830s; **throw a fit** was first recorded in 1906, and **have a fit** in 1924; **have kittens,** alluding to being so upset as to bear kittens, also dates from about 1900.

have against ♦ See HAVE SOMETHING AGAINST.

have a go at ♦ See HAVE A CRACK AT.

have a good command of Have the ability to use or control; have mastery of. For example, *She has a remarkably good command of Japanese,* or *He had a good command of his emotions.* [Mid-1600s]

have a good day ♦ See HAVE A NICE DAY.

have a good head on one's shoulders ♦ See GOOD HEAD ON ONE'S SHOULDERS.

have a good mind to Be strongly inclined to, as in *She had a good mind to tell him everything.* A slightly weaker form of this idiom is **have a mind to,** as in *I have a mind to spend my next vacation in the desert.* Formerly this idiom was sometimes put as **have a great mind to.** [c. 1400] Also see HALF A MIND.

have a good thing going Have matters arranged to one's benefit or profit. For example, *Joe's got a good thing going with this new franchise.* It also may be put as **make a good thing of,** meaning "make something work to one's benefit," as in *If we work hard we can make a good thing of this job.* The first term dates from the second half of the 1900s, the second from the early 1800s. Also see HAVE GOING FOR ONE.

have a good time Enjoy oneself, as in *I hope you have a good time at the beach.* This idiom, also used as an imperative, dates from 16th-century England, where it was popular until the late 1600s

and died out. Samuel Pepys, in a diary entry of March 1, 1666, wrote, "I went and had as good a time as heart could wish." In America it continued to be used, and in the 1800s it reappeared in British speech as well. Also see HARD TIME; SHOW ONE A GOOD TIME.

have a grasp of ♦ See under GET A FIX ON.

have a hand in 1. Also, **take a hand in.** Participate, be involved, as in *I'd like to have a hand in planning the publicity.* [Late 1500s] **2. have** or **keep one's hand in.** Be actively engaged or remain in practice doing something. For example, *He works as stage manager, director, understudy—he has a hand in every aspect,* or *Write a few pages every day, just to keep your hand in.* [Mid-1700s]

have a hard time ♦ See HARD TIME.

have a head for Also, **have a good** or **strong head for. 1.** Be able to tolerate, as in *Nell has no head for liquor,* or *Luckily I have a good head for heights.* [Early 1800s] **2.** Have a mental aptitude for, as in *She has a good head for figures and straightened out the statistics in no time.* [Early 1900s]

have a heart Be merciful, show pity; also, be reasonable. For example, *Have a heart—I can't pay you back until next month,* or *Have a heart and stop your arguing now.* This expression is often put as an imperative, as in the examples. [c. 1900] Also see HARDEN ONE'S HEART.

have a hold over Also, **have a hold on.** Have a controlling influence over. For example, *Blackmailers have a hold over their victims,* or, as Shakespeare put it in *The Merchant of Venice* (4:1): "The law has yet another hold on you." [Late 1500s]

have all one's buttons Also, **have all one's marbles.** Be completely sane and rational. For example, *Grandma may be in a wheelchair, but she still has all her buttons,* or *I'm not sure he has all his marbles.* These slangy expressions date from the mid-1800s, as do the antonyms **lose** or **be missing some of one's buttons** or **marbles,** meaning "become (or be) mentally deficient."

have a lot going for ♦ See HAVE GOING FOR ONE.

have a lot on one's plate Also, **have too much on one's plate.** Have a great deal (or too much) to cope with, as in *What with the new baby and the new house, they have a lot on their plate,* or *I can't take that on now; I've got too much on my plate already.* This expression transfers a loaded or overloaded dinner plate to other activities. [First half of 1900s]

have a mind to ♦ See HAVE A GOOD MIND TO.

have an edge on Also, **have the edge on.** Have an advantage over, as in *Our team has an edge on them,* or *In this competition our town has the edge.* The use of *edge* here alludes to the power to cut, transferred to a margin of superiority. [Late 1800s]

have a nerve Also, **have some nerve**. Have audacity, show effrontery. For example, *You have a nerve telling me what to do*, or *She had some nerve, criticizing the people who donated their time*. The related **have the nerve** is used with an infinitive, as in *He had the nerve to scold his boss in public*. This idiom uses *nerve* in the sense of "courage" or "audacity." [Late 1800s]

have an eye for 1. Be discriminating or perceptive about something, as in *She has an eye for decorating*. [c. 1700] 2. **have eyes for**. Also, **have eyes only for**. Be attracted to or desire someone or something (exclusively). For example, *It's obvious she has eyes for him*, or *He has eyes only for the top award*. [Early 1800s]

have a nice day Also, **have a good day; have a good one**. A cordial goodbye to you. For example, *Thanks for the order, have a nice day*, or *See you next week—have a good day*, or *The car's ready for you—have a good one*. These expressions have become synonymous with a polite farewell. The first originated about 1920 but, like the variants, became widespread only after 1950.

have another guess coming Also, **have another think coming**. Be mistaken and therefore have to reconsider or rethink one's answer. For example, *If you think you can fool me, you have another guess coming*, or *John thinks he convinced me; well, he has another think coming*. A related idiom is **guess again**, often used in the imperative, as in *You think that car cost $20,000? Guess again!* [Colloquial; first half of 1900s]

have an out Have a means of escape or an excuse, as in *I'm supposed to go to the meeting, but I have an out—Sam invited me first to come to his wedding*. One can also **give someone an out**, as in *She was hoping someone would give her an out; otherwise she'd be stuck visiting relatives all afternoon*. [Slang; early 1900s]

have a penchant for Have a tendency or taste for. For example, *He has a penchant for saying the wrong thing*, or *She has a strong penchant for baroque music*. [Second half of 1600s]

have a right to Have a just or legal claim on something or on some action, as in *The accused has a right to legal counsel*. The related **have the right to** is often used with infinitives, as in *You have the right to remain silent*. [Late 1300s] The antonym, dating from the mid-1600s, is **have no right to**, as in *He has no right to push you aside*. Also see IN THE RIGHT.

have a say in 1. Also, **have a voice in**. Have the right or power to influence or make a decision about something. For example, *I want to have a say in this matter*, or *Citizens want to have a voice in their local government*. [c. 1600] 2. **have one's say**. Express one's views, as in *As soon as I've had*

my say I'll sit down. [Late 1600s] 3. **have the say**. Be in command, as in *The general has the say over which troops will be sent*. [Early 1800s]

have a screw loose Be mentally unstable or eccentric, as in *Anyone who approves that purchase must have a screw loose*. This term likens a mental weakness to a machine in which a part is not securely fastened. An antonym is **have one's head screwed on right**; for example, *She's very capable; she has her head screwed on right*. [Slang; early 1800s]

have a shot at ◆ See HAVE A CRACK AT.

have a stake in Have a share, interest, or involvement in something or someone. For example, *Every member had a stake in the business*, or *She knew that she had a stake in her children's future*. This term uses *stake* in the sense of "something to gain or lose," as in gambling. [Late 1700s]

have at Attack; also, make an attempt at. For example, *Urging the dog on, he said, "Go on, Rover, have at him,"* or *It's time to have at straightening out these files*. [Late 1300s]

have a thing about Be obsessed or preoccupied with something. For example, *He has a thing about disorder in the garage*, or *Bob has a thing about brunettes*. [Slang; first half of 1900s]

have a thing going ◆ See HAVE A GOOD THING GOING; HAVE GOING FOR ONE.

have a time of it ◆ See under HARD TIME, def. 1.

have a way with Have success in dealing with, as in *She has a way with young children*. [c. 1700]

have a weakness for Be susceptible to; also, like or enjoy. For example, *She has a weakness for older men*, or *Bill has a weakness for fine wine*. [c. 1700]

have a whack at ◆ See HAVE A CRACK AT.

have a word with Speak with, discuss with, as in *Jerry asked to have a word with you*, or *I must have a word with Bill about the repairs*. This expression, from the late 1400s, was at one time used interchangeably with HAVE WORDS WITH, but it no longer is.

have a yen for Crave or desire, as in *I have a yen for a thick juicy steak*. The *yen* in this expression comes from the Chinese *yan*, meaning "a craving" (probably for opium). The term was first recorded in English in 1906.

have designs on Contrive a secret plot or scheme, especially with selfish motives. For example, *I think he has designs on my job*, or *Mary has designs on her sister's boyfriend*. This term uses *design* in the sense of "a crafty plan," a usage dating from about 1700.

have dibs on Have a first claim on something, as in *If you don't want it, I have dibs on the next available apartment*. This term was originally schoolyard slang. [c. 1930]

have done Stop or cease, as in *Have done—enough of this nonsense.* This idiom is also put as **have done with,** as in *This arrangement won't work; let's find a new one and have done with it.* The past participle *done* has been used in the sense of "finished" since about 1300. Also see HAVE TO DO WITH.

have eyes only for ♦ See HAVE AN EYE FOR, def. 2.

have fits ♦ See HAVE A FIT.

have going for one Have in one's favor or of benefit to one. For example, *They have enough going for them that their new store should be a success,* or *Mary is very talented; she has a lot going for her.* [Mid-1900s] Also see HAVE A GOOD THING GOING.

have got to ♦ See HAVE TO.

have had enough Want no more of something, as in *I've had enough of their quarreling.* This phrase uses *enough* in the sense of "an adequate amount," which is intended ironically to mean "a more than sufficient amount." [c. 1700] For synonyms, see FED TO THE GILLS; HAVE HAD IT, def. 1.

have had it **1.** Also, **have had it up to here.** Have endured all one can, as in *I've had it with their delays,* or *She has had it up to here with her hour-long commute.* **2.** Be in a state beyond remedy, repair, or salvage, as in *That old coat has had it.* **3.** Be dead, as in *His heart just stopped; he'd had it.* All three colloquial usages, which appear to be shortenings of HAVE HAD ENOUGH, date from the mid-1900s.

have in common ♦ See IN COMMON.

have in one's hands ♦ See IN ONE'S HANDS.

have it **1.** Receive or learn something, as in *I have it on the best authority that he's running again.* [Late 1600s] **2.** Possess a solution, understand, as in *Is this the new phone number? Do I have it straight?* or *I think I have it now.* [Mid-1800s] **3.** Take it, as in *There's some ice cream left; go ahead and have it.* This usage is always put as an imperative. [Second half of 1300s] **4.** Have the victory, win, as in *We've counted the votes and the nays have it.* The related expressions **have it over someone** or **have it all over someone** mean "to be superior to someone." For example, *Jane has it all over Mary when it comes to reading aloud.* [Early 1900s] **5. let someone have it.** Give a beating, scolding, or punishment. For example, *When she gets home Dad will let her have it.* [Mid-1800s] **6. have it off.** Have sexual intercourse, as in *The two dogs were having it off in the backyard.* [Colloquial; early 1900s] Also see the subsequent idioms beginning with HAVE IT; NOT HAVE IT.

have it both ways Achieve two mutually exclusive objectives, as in *Bill wants to have it both ways—to enjoy Christmas at home and to travel with his friends.* The related **have it all** means "to get everything one wants," as in *It's too bad we can't have it all—the wisdom of experience and the fresh enthusiasm of youth.* [Early 1900s]

have it coming Deserve what one receives, as in *You may not like being reprimanded, but you have to admit you had it coming,* or *When he won the Nobel Prize, everyone said he'd had it coming for a long time.* [c. 1900]

have it in for Intend to harm, especially because of a grudge. For example, *Ever since he called the police about their dog, the neighbors have had it in for Tom.* [Mid-1800s]

have it in one Have the ability to accomplish something. As Sir Arthur Conan Doyle put it in *A Study in Scarlet* (1887), "I know well that I have it in me to make my name famous."

have it made Be sure of success; also, have achieved success. For example, *Since he knows all the important people, John has it made,* or *Karen was accepted every place she applied—she has it made.* [Colloquial; mid-1900s]

have it out Settle decisively, especially in an argument or discussion. For example, "I shall double-lock myself in with him and have it out before I die" (Charles Dickens, *Nicholas Nickleby,* 1839). [Early 1800s]

have kittens ♦ See HAVE A FIT.

have no business ♦ See NONE OF ONE'S BUSINESS.

have no heart for Also, **not have the heart for.** Lack enthusiasm for, as in *After the dog died he had no heart for taking long walks,* or *I should go through the family albums, but I don't have the heart for it.* [Mid-1600s] Also see HEART IN IT.

have none of ♦ See under NOT HAVE IT.

have no stomach for ♦ See NO STOMACH FOR.

have nothing on Also, **not have anything on.** **1.** Have no advantage over something or someone, as in *This car has nothing on my old one.* [c. 1900] **2.** Have no damaging information or proof of wrongdoing about someone, as in *The police had nothing on him and so were forced to let him go.* This usage is the antonym of **have something on someone,** as in *Blackmail requires that you have something on someone wealthy.* [c. 1920] **3.** Have nothing scheduled for a certain time, as in *We have nothing on tonight, so why don't you come over?* This expression, and its antonym, **have something on,** are abbreviations of *have nothing* (or *something*) *going on.* **4.** Be naked, as in *Please bring in the mail; I just took a bath and don't have anything on.*

have nothing to do with Also, **not have anything to do with.** **1.** Be irrelevant, be unrelated, as in *Their visit has nothing to do with the holiday.* [Early 1600s] **2.** Avoid, as in *Dad insisted that we have nothing to do with the neighbors,* or *I won't* *have anything to do with people who act like that.* [Early 1600s] Also see HAVE TO DO WITH.

have no time for ♦ See NO TIME FOR.

have no truck with Have no dealings with, as in *The doctor said he wanted no truck with midwives.* This term was first recorded in 1868, although *truck* in the sense of "dealings" dates from the early 1600s.

have no use for 1. Not require something, as in *I don't smoke, so I have no use for a lighter.* [c. 1600] 2. Dislike something or someone, as in *I have no use for people who won't answer letters.* [Second half of 1800s]

haven't ♦ See under NOT HAVE.

have on 1. **have something on.** See HAVE NOTHING ON, def. 3. 2. **have someone on; put someone on.** Deceive or fool someone, as in *There was no answer when I called; someone must be having me on,* or *You can't mean you're taking up ballet—you're putting me on!* [Colloquial; mid-1800s]

have one's ass in a sling ♦ See ASS IN A SLING.

have one's cake and eat it, too ♦ See EAT ONE'S CAKE.

have one's day ♦ See under HAD ITS DAY.

have one's druthers Have one's choice, as in *If I had my druthers I'd go to London first.* The noun *druthers* is a contraction of "would rather." [Slang; late 1800s]

have oneself Enjoy something, as in *Be sure to have yourself a good nap,* or *They were having themselves a great time at the fair.* The *oneself* in this colloquial expression adds emphasis to the verb *have.*

have one's eye on 1. Also, **keep an eye on.** Look at, especially attentively or continuously; watch. For example, *The teacher has his eye on the boys in the back row,* or *Please keep an eye on the stew.* [First half of 1400s] Also see KEEP AN EYE OUT FOR. 2. Also, **have an eye to.** Have as one's objective, as in *We had our eyes on that birthday cake,* or *The Republicans have an eye to a big majority in the House.* The first usage dates from the mid-1600s, the second from the early 1500s. 3. Also, **with an eye to.** With a view to, regarding as an objective, as in *With an eye to her inheritance, she was very attentive to her aunt.* [Mid-1800s] Also see HAVE AN EYE FOR.

have one's hands full Be extremely busy, as in *With the new baby she really has her hands full.* [Second half of 1400s]

have one's head in the sand ♦ See HIDE ONE'S HEAD.

have one's head screwed on right ♦ See under HAVE A SCREW LOOSE.

have one's heart in it ♦ See HEART IN IT.

have one's moments Also, **have its moments.** Experience or undergo brief periods of distinction. For example, *It wasn't an outstanding performance, but it had its moments,* or "Even a mailman has his moments" (*Saturday Evening Post,* April 9, 1927). [Early 1900s]

have one's own way ♦ See GET ONE'S WAY.

have one's say ♦ See HAVE A SAY IN, def. 2.

have one's way with Have sex with someone, as in *He wanted to have his way with her.* This usage is nearly always used of a man trying to get a woman to have sex. It may be dying out. [Early 1900s]

have one's wits about one Also, **keep one's wits about one.** Remain alert or calm, especially in a crisis. For example, *After the collision I had my wits about me and got his name and license number,* or *Being followed was terrifying, but Kate kept her wits about her and got home safely.* [Early 1600s]

have one's work cut out for one Face a difficult task, as in *This is a very large house to manage, so I have my work cut out for me.* This expression alludes to cloth cut out to make a garment. [c. 1600]

have on the ball ♦ See ON THE BALL.

have out ♦ See HAVE IT OUT.

have pity on ♦ See TAKE PITY ON.

have pull with Have a means of gaining advantage with, have influence on, as in *She had pull with several of the board members.* [Colloquial; late 1800s]

have rocks in one's head ♦ See ROCKS IN ONE'S HEAD.

have someone by the balls Have someone at one's mercy, as in *You have to pay up—they've got you by the balls.* The *balls* here allude to the male genitals. [Vulgar slang; early 1900s]

have someone's ear Obtain someone's attention, especially favorable attention. For example, *Harry has the boss's ear and could put in a good word about you.* [Early 1700s]

have someone's hide ♦ See TAN SOMEONE'S HIDE.

have someone's number ♦ See GET SOMEONE'S NUMBER.

have something against Be opposed to, especially for a particular reason. For example, *Do you have something against this plan?* or *Annie must have something against Mary, because she's always so surly when they're together.*

have something coming ♦ See HAVE IT COMING.

have something going ♦ See HAVE A GOOD THING GOING; HAVE GOING FOR ONE.

have something on ♦ See under HAVE NOTHING ON.

have something to show for ♦ See HAVE TO SHOW FOR.

have the better of ♦ See GET THE BETTER OF.

have the blues Also, **feel blue.** Feel depressed or sad, as in *After seeing the old house in such bad shape, I had the blues for weeks,* or *Patricia tends to* *feel blue around the holidays.* The noun *blues,* meaning "low spirits," was first recorded in 1741 and may come from *blue devil,* a 17th-century term for a baleful demon, or from the adjective *blue* meaning "sad," a usage first recorded in Chaucer's *Complaint of Mars* (c. 1385). The idiom may have been reinforced by the notion that anxiety produces a livid skin color. Also see BLUE FUNK.

have the courage of one's convictions ♦ See COURAGE OF ONE'S CONVICTIONS.

have the edge on ♦ See HAVE AN EDGE ON.

have the feel of ♦ See GET THE FEEL OF.

have the goods on ♦ See GET THE GOODS ON.

have the guts Possess the courage, as in *Does he have the guts to dive off the high board?* This expression replaces the earlier and now obsolete sense of *stomach* as "courage," a usage from the early 1500s. [Slang; late 1800s]

have the heart to ♦ See NOT HAVE THE HEART TO. Also see HAVE A HEART; HEART IN IT.

have the last laugh ♦ See LAST LAUGH.

have the makings of Have the abilities or qualities needed to become something, as in *She has the makings of a fine teacher,* or, as Shakespeare put it in *Henry VIII* (4:1): "She had all the royal makings of a Queen." [Late 1500s]

have the say ♦ See HAVE A SAY IN, def. 3.

have to Also, **have got to.** Be obliged to, must. For example, *We have to go now,* or *He has got to finish the paper today.* The use of *have* as an auxiliary verb to indicate obligation goes back to the 16th century; the variant using *got* dates from the mid-1800s.

have to do with Be concerned or associated with; deal with. For example, *This book has to do with the divisions within the church.* [1100s] For the antonym, see HAVE NOTHING TO DO WITH.

have to show for Be able to exhibit as a result of one's work or expenditure. For example, *I've been working all day and I have absolutely nothing to show for it,* or *He has some very fine paintings to show for the vast amount of money he's spent.* This idiom was first recorded in 1727.

have two left feet ♦ See TWO LEFT FEET.

have words with Quarrel with, scold, as in *If Pete keeps on pushing Billy I'm going to have words with him.* This phrase dates from the late 1700s, although the use of *words* for an altercation is much older. Also see HAVE A WORD WITH.

havoc ♦ See CRY HAVOC; PLAY HAVOC.

haw ♦ See HEM AND HAW.

hawk ♦ See WATCH LIKE A HAWK.

hay ♦ See HIT THE HAY; MAKE HAY WHILE THE SUN SHINES; ROLL IN THE HAY; THAT AIN'T HAY.

haystack ♦ See NEEDLE IN A HAYSTACK.

haywire ♦ See GO HAYWIRE.

hazard ♦ See OCCUPATIONAL HAZARD.

haze ♦ See IN A FOG (HAZE).

head ♦ In addition to the idioms beginning with HEAD, also see BEAT INTO SOMEONE'S HEAD; BEAT ONE'S HEAD AGAINST THE WALL; BIG HEAD; BITE SOMEONE'S HEAD OFF; BRING TO A HEAD; CAN'T MAKE HEAD OR TAIL OF; COUNT NOSES (HEADS); DO BLINDFOLDED (STANDING ON ONE'S HEAD); ENTER ONE'S MIND (HEAD); EYES IN THE BACK OF ONE'S HEAD; FROM HEAD TO TOE; GET INTO ONE'S HEAD; GET ONE'S HEAD EXAMINED; GET THROUGH ONE'S HEAD; GIVE SOMEONE HIS OR HER HEAD; GOOD HEAD ON ONE'S SHOULDERS; GO TO ONE'S HEAD; HANG ONE'S HEAD; HANG OVER (ONE'S HEAD); HAVE A HEAD FOR; HAVE A SCREW LOOSE (HEAD SCREWED ON RIGHT); HIDE ONE'S HEAD; HIDE ONE'S HEAD IN THE SAND; HIT THE NAIL ON THE HEAD; HOLD A GUN TO SOMEONE'S HEAD; HOLD ONE'S HEAD HIGH; IN OVER ONE'S HEAD; KEEP ONE'S HEAD; LAUGH ONE'S HEAD OFF; LIKE A CHICKEN WITH ITS HEAD CUT OFF; LOSE ONE'S HEAD; MAKE ONE'S HEAD SPIN; NEED LIKE A HOLE IN THE HEAD; NOT RIGHT IN THE HEAD; OFF ONE'S HEAD; OFF THE TOP OF ONE'S HEAD; ON ONE'S HEAD; ON THE BLOCK (PUT ONE'S HEAD); OVER ONE'S HEAD; PRICE ON ONE'S HEAD; PUT IDEAS IN SOMEONE'S HEAD; PUT OUR HEADS TOGETHER; REAR ITS UGLY HEAD; ROCKS IN ONE'S HEAD; ROOF OVER ONE'S HEAD; SCRATCH ONE'S HEAD; SHAKE ONE'S HEAD; SOFT IN THE HEAD; SWELLED HEAD; TALK SOMEONE'S ARM (HEAD) OFF; THROW ONESELF (AT SOMEONE'S HEAD); TOUCHED IN THE HEAD; TROUBLE ONE'S HEAD; TURN ONE'S HEAD; UPSIDE THE HEAD; USE ONE'S HEAD.

head above water, keep one's Stay out of trouble, especially financial difficulties; also, keep up with work or other demands. For example, *With new bills coming in every day they're barely keeping their heads above water,* or *The work's piling up, but I manage to keep my head above water.* This expression alludes to keeping oneself from drowning. [Early 1700s] Also see IN DEEP.

head and shoulders above Greatly superior to, as in *This book is head and shoulders above her first one.* This expression transfers physical stature to other kinds of status. [Mid-1800s]

head for Proceed or go in a certain direction, as in *I'm heading for town,* or *I believe Karen and Jane are heading for a big quarrel.* This expression, which uses *head* in the sense of "advance toward," is occasionally amplified with a figurative destination, especially in the American West. For example, **head for the hills** means "to run away to high and safer ground" or "to flee from danger." It is often used facetiously, as in *Here comes that old* bore—*head for the hills!* **Head for the setting sun** alludes to where a wanted man or outlaw went when a law-enforcement agent was close behind him, that is, farther west, and **head for the last roundup** means "to die." [Early 1800s]

head in the clouds, have one's Be absentminded or impractical, as in *She must have had her head in the clouds when she made the reservations, because they never heard of us,* or *He'll never be able to run the business—he's always got his head in the clouds.* This idiom uses *in the clouds* in the sense of "fanciful" or "unreal," a usage dating from the mid-1600s.

head in the sand ♦ See HIDE ONE'S HEAD.

head off Block the progress or completion of; also, intercept. For example, *They worked round the clock to head off the flu epidemic,* or *Try to head him off before he gets home.* [First half of 1800s] This expression gave rise to **head someone off at the pass,** which in Western films meant "to block someone at a mountain pass." It then became a general colloquialism for intercepting someone, as in *Jim is going to the boss's office—let's head him off at the pass.*

head on 1. With the face or front first, as in *The two bicycles collided head on.* [Early 1800s] 2. In direct conflict, in open opposition, as in *They decided to meet the opposition head on.*

head or tail ♦ See CAN'T MAKE HEAD OR TAIL.

head out 1. Depart, begin a journey, as in *The ship was heading out to sea,* or *When do you head out again?* 2. **head out after.** Follow or pursue, as in *Since they knew the way, we headed out after them,* or *A police car headed out after the car thieves.*

head over heels Completely, thoroughly, as in *They fell head over heels in love.* This expression originated in the 1300s as *heels over head* and meant literally being upside down. It took its present form in the 1700s and its present meaning in the 1800s.

heads or tails An expression used when tossing a coin to decide between two alternatives, as in *Let's just flip a coin to decide who pays—do you want heads or tails?* Each person involved chooses a different side of the coin, either "heads" or "tails," and whichever side lands facing up is considered the winner. This usage, dating from the late 1600s, is sometimes turned into **Heads I win, tails you lose,** meaning "I win no matter what," which probably originated in an attempt to deceive someone. [Mid-1800s]

head start An early start that confers an advantage, as in *This year we'll get a head start on the competition by running more ads.* The expression comes from racing, where it was used for a horse being given an advantage of several lengths over

the others. Its extension to other areas dates from the early 1900s.

heads up A warning to watch out for potential danger, as in *Heads up, that tree is coming down now!* The expression is generally in the form of an interjection. [c. 1940]

heads will roll Someone will be severely punished, as in *If no one meets the chairman's plane, heads will roll.* This hyperbolic expression alludes to the punishment of being beheaded.

head up Be in charge of, lead, as in *She headed up the commission on conservation.* [Colloquial; mid-1900s]

headway ♦ See MAKE HEADWAY.

health ♦ See CLEAN BILL OF HEALTH.

hear ♦ In addition to the idioms beginning with HEAR, also see ANOTHER COUNTY HEARD FROM; HARD OF HEARING; NEVER HEAR THE END OF; NOT HAVE IT (HEAR OF IT); UNHEARD OF.

hear a peep out of Hear the slightest noise from, as in *I don't want to hear another peep out of those children.* This expression is often used negatively, as in *I didn't hear another peep out of them.* [c. 1900]

hear a pin drop, can Be able to hear even the smallest noise because of the quiet, as in *When he came onstage you could have heard a pin drop.* This hyperbolic expression dates from the early 1800s.

hear from 1. Receive a letter, call, or other communication from someone, as in *I haven't heard from my daughter in two weeks.* [Early 1300s] 2. Be reprimanded by, as in *If you don't get home on time, you'll be hearing from your father.* [Late 1800s]

hear, hear An expression used to express approval, as in *Whenever the senator spoke, he was greeted with cries of "Hear! hear!"* This expression was originally *Hear him! hear him!* and used to call attention to a speaker's words. It gradually came to be used simply as a cheer. [Late 1600s]

hear of Be informed about, as in *I'd never heard of that jazz singer before, but she was very good.* [Late 1500s] Also see NOT HAVE IT (HEAR OF IT).

hear oneself think, can't Be unable to concentrate because there is too much noise. For example, *There was so much noise from the jackhammers we couldn't hear ourselves think.* [Early 1900s]

hear out Listen to someone's discourse until the end, allow someone to speak fully, as in *Please hear me out before you jump to any conclusions.* [First half of 1600s]

heart ♦ In addition to the idioms beginning with HEART, also see ABSENCE MAKES THE HEART GROW FONDER; AFTER ONE'S OWN HEART; AT HEART; BREAK SOMEONE'S HEART; BY HEART; CHANGE OF HEART; COLD HANDS, WARM HEART; CROSS MY HEART; CRY

ONE'S EYES (HEART) OUT; CUT TO THE QUICK (HEART); DO ONE (ONE'S HEART) GOOD; EAT ONE'S HEART OUT; FIND IT IN ONE'S HEART; FROM THE BOTTOM OF ONE'S HEART; GET TO THE HEART OF; GIVE SOMEONE HEART FAILURE; HALF A HEART; HARDEN ONE'S HEART; HAVE A HEART; HAVE NO HEART FOR; HEAVY HEART; IN ONE'S HEART OF HEARTS; LOSE HEART; LOSE ONE'S HEART TO; NEAR TO ONE'S HEART; NOT HAVE THE HEART TO; OPEN ONE'S HEART; POUR OUT ONE'S HEART; SET ONE'S HEART ON; SICK AT HEART; STEAL SOMEONE'S HEART; STEEL ONE'S HEART AGAINST; TAKE HEART; TAKE TO HEART; TO ONE'S HEART'S CONTENT; WARM HEART; WARM THE COCKLES OF ONE'S HEART; WEAR ONE'S HEART ON ONE'S SLEEVE; WITH ALL ONE'S HEART; YOUNG AT HEART.

heart and soul The entirety of one's energies or affections. For example, *He put heart and soul into his music.* [Late 1700s]

heart goes out to, one's One's sympathy is extended to someone, as in *She's had a terrible time of it; my heart goes out to her.* [Late 1700s]

heart in it, have one's Also, **put one's heart in it.** Be emotionally involved in something, undertake something enthusiastically, as in *Nancy puts her heart in her teaching.* This expression may also be put negatively as **one's heart is not in it,** as in *She decided to quit; her heart just wasn't in this kind of work.* [Late 1700s] Also see HAVE NO HEART FOR.

heart in one's mouth, have one's Be extremely frightened or anxious, as in *When the plane was about to take off, my heart was in my mouth.* This usage alludes to the heart beating so violently that it appears to leap upward. [Mid-1500s]

heart in the right place, have one's Be well-intentioned, *Her plan to reconcile them didn't succeed, but she had her heart in the right place.* [Early 1800s]

heart is set on ♦ See SET ONE'S HEART ON.

heart misses a beat, one's Also, **one's heart skips a beat** or **stands still.** One is startled, frightened, or very excited. For example, *Her heart missed a beat when she heard her name called out in the list of finalists,* or *When the bear appeared in front of us, my heart skipped a beat,* or *My heart stands still at the very thought of flying through a thunderstorm.* All these hyperbolic expressions can also be used with **make,** meaning "to cause one to be startled" as in *That blast from the ship's whistle made my heart skip a beat.*

heart not in it ♦ See under HEART IN IT.

heart of gold A very kind and good nature, as in *Bill is very generous; he has a heart of gold.* This expression alludes to gold in the sense of "something valued for its goodness." [Late 1500s]

heart of stone A very cold and unfeeling nature, as in *You'll get no sympathy from her; she has a heart of stone.* This idea dates from ancient times and in English appeared in the Bible (Job 41:24). [Early 1600s]

heart of the matter ♦ See CRUX OF THE MATTER.

heart on one's sleeve ♦ See WEAR ONE'S HEART ON ONE'S SLEEVE.

heart's content ♦ See TO ONE'S HEART'S CONTENT.

heart sinks, one's One's courage or hope fails; one is very disappointed or dejected. For example, *An hour before the picnic I heard thunder and my heart sank.* This expression was first recorded in 1605 but was preceded in the 15th century by **one's heart is at one's heels,** or **in one's hose,** or **in one's shoes.** The present (and only surviving) usage was first recorded in 1605.

heart stands still ♦ See HEART MISSES A BEAT.

heart to heart Candidly, sincerely, as in *We need to talk heart to heart about her coming marriage.* This expression is nearly always applied to a conversation of some kind. [Mid-1900s]

hearty ♦ See HALE AND HEARTY.

heat ♦ In addition to the idioms beginning with HEAT, also see DEAD HEAT; IN HEAT; IN THE HEAT OF THE MOMENT; TAKE THE HEAT OUT OF; TURN UP THE HEAT.

heat up Become acute or intense, as in *If inflation heats up, the interest rate will surely rise,* or *The debate over the budget was heating up.* [Early 1200s]

heave-ho, give the ♦ See under GET THE AX; GIVE SOMEONE THE AIR.

heave into sight Rise or seem to rise into view. For example, *We waited and waited, and finally the rest of our party heaved into sight.* This expression was at first used for ships rising over the horizon. [Late 1700s]

heaven ♦ In addition to the idioms beginning with HEAVEN, also see FOR ONE'S (HEAVEN'S) SAKE; GOD (HEAVEN) FORBID; GOD (HEAVEN) KNOWS; IN SEVENTH HEAVEN; IN THE NAME OF (HEAVEN); MANNA FROM HEAVEN; MOVE HEAVEN AND EARTH; PENNIES FROM HEAVEN; SEVENTH HEAVEN; STINK TO HIGH HEAVEN; THANK GOD (HEAVEN).

heaven knows ♦ See GOD KNOWS.

heavenly days An exclamation similar to **for heaven's sake.** See under FOR ONE'S SAKE, def. 3.

heavy ♦ In addition to the idioms beginning with HEAVY, also see HOT AND HEAVY; MAKE HEAVY WEATHER OF; PLAY THE HEAVY; TIME HANGS HEAVY.

heavy going Also, **heavy weather.** 1. Difficult, as in *Tom found calculus heavy going,* or *It's going to be heavy weather for us from here on.* The first expression originally referred to a road or path that was hard to negotiate; the variant alludes to bad weather at sea. [Mid-1800s] **2. make heavy weather of.** Make hard work or a fuss over something, especially unnecessarily. For example, *They made heavy weather of the differences between their proposals, which actually seemed much alike.* This use of *weather* likens a commotion to a storm. [Mid-1900s]

heavy hand, with a 1. In a clumsy manner, as in *You can't use that delicate equipment with a heavy hand.* [Mid-1600s] **2.** Overbearingly or severely, as in *Children brought up with a heavy hand often rebel in later years.* [Late 1800s]

heavy heart, with a In a sad or miserable state, unhappily, as in *He left her with a heavy heart, wondering if she would ever recover.* The adjective *heavy* has been used in the sense of "weighed down with grief or sadness" since about 1300. Its antonym *light* dates from the same period. The latter use survives only in **light heart,** meaning "freedom from the weight of sorrow"—that is, "a happy feeling." For example, *She left for Europe with a light heart, knowing that the kids would be fine.*

heavy hitter An important or influential individual or organization. For example, *This publishing house is one of the heavy hitters in the textbook industry.* This expression originated in sports such as boxing, where it literally meant "hitting hard," and was transferred to other enterprises in the mid-1900s.

hedge one's bets Lessen one's chance of loss by counterbalancing it with other bets, investments, or the like. For example, *I'm hedging my bets by putting some of my money in bonds in case there's another drop in the stock market.* This term transfers *hedge,* in the sense of "a barrier," to a means of protection against loss. [Second half of 1600s]

heel ♦ See ACHILLES' HEEL; AT SOMEONE'S HEELS; BRING TO HEEL; COOL ONE'S HEELS; DIG IN (ONE'S HEELS); DRAG ONE'S FEET (HEELS); HEAD OVER HEELS; KICK UP ONE'S HEELS; ON THE HEELS OF; OUT AT THE ELBOWS (HEELS); SET BACK ON ONE'S HEELS; SHOW ONE'S HEELS; TAKE TO ONE'S HEELS; TO HEEL; TURN ON ONE'S HEEL.

hell ♦ In addition to the idioms beginning with HELL, also see (ALL HELL) BREAK LOOSE; DEVIL (HELL) OF A; FOR THE HELL OF IT; GIVE SOMEONE HELL; GO TO HELL; HOT AS HELL; LIKE A BAT OUT OF HELL; LIKE HELL; MAD AS A HORNET (HELL); NOT A HOPE IN HELL; RAISE CAIN (HELL); ROAD TO HELL IS PAVED WITH GOOD INTENTIONS; SHOT TO HELL; SNOWBALL'S CHANCE IN HELL; TILL HELL FREEZES OVER; TO HELL AND GONE; TO HELL WITH; WHAT THE HELL.

hell-bent for leather Moving recklessly fast, as in *Out the door she went, hell-bent for leather.* The use of *hell-bent* in the sense of "recklessly deter-

mined" dates from the first half of the 1800s. *Leather* alludes to a horse's saddle and to riding on horseback; this colloquial expression may be an American version of the earlier British army jargon **hell for leather,** first recorded in 1889.

hell has no fury like a woman scorned No anger is worse than that of a jilted woman. For example, *Nancy has nothing good to say about Tom—hell has no fury, you know.* This term is a shortening of William Congreve's lines, "Heav'n has no rage, like love to hatred turn'd, nor Hell a fury like a woman scorn'd" (*The Mourning Bride,* 1697). Similar lines appear in several plays of the same period. Today the proverb is often shortened even more, as in the example.

hell of a Also, **one hell of a 1.** See DEVIL OF A. **2.** This phrase is used as an intensive to emphasize certain qualities about the noun it modifies. By itself the idiom is ambiguous, for its exact meaning depends on the context. For example, *He is a hell of a driver* can mean either that he is very skillful or that he is a terrible driver. Similarly, *We had one hell of a time* can mean either that we enjoyed ourselves greatly or that we had an awful or difficult time. [Second half of 1700s]

hell on wheels Tough, aggressive, wild, or mean, as in *Watch out for the boss—he's hell on wheels this week.* This expression originated with the building of the Union Pacific Railroad in the 1860s, when it denoted the last town on the line, which was carried on freight cars as the track was extended. The town consisted mainly of tents occupied by construction gangs, liquor dealers, gamblers, and other camp followers known for their rough and often vicious ways.

hell or high water, come Also, **in spite of hell or high water.** No matter what difficulty or obstacle, as in *I'm going to finish this week, come hell or high water.* This colloquial expression, alluding to the destructive forces of hellfire or flood, was first recorded in 1915 but is thought to be older.

hell to pay Great trouble, as in *If we're wrong there'll be hell to pay.* [c. 1800]

helm ♦ See AT THE HELM.

help ♦ In addition to the idioms beginning with HELP, also see CAN'T HELP BUT; EVERY LITTLE BIT HELPS; NOT IF ONE CAN HELP IT; SO HELP ME.

helping hand ♦ See under LEND A HAND.

help oneself 1. Make an effort on one's own behalf. Shakespeare used this expression in *2 Henry IV* (3:2): "She is old, and cannot help herself," and it also appears in the old proverb, *God (or heaven) helps those who help themselves.* [First half of 1500s] Also see CAN'T HELP. **2.** Serve oneself, as in *The food's in the kitchen; just help yourself.* When it takes an object this phrase is put as **help oneself**

to, as in *I helped myself to more meat.* It also is used as a euphemism for stealing, as in *She simply helped herself to the hotel towels and left.* The first usage dates from the late 1600s; the second, a colloquialism, from the mid-1800s.

help out Give additional assistance, as in *I offered to help out with the holiday rush at the store.* [Early 1600s]

hem and haw Be hesitant and indecisive; avoid committing oneself, as in *When asked about their wedding date, she hemmed and hawed,* or *The President hemmed and hawed about new Cabinet appointments.* This expression imitates the sounds of clearing one's throat. [Late 1700s]

hem in ♦ See FENCE IN.

hen ♦ See MAD AS A HORNET (WET HEN); SCARCE AS HEN'S TEETH.

herd ♦ See RIDE HERD ON.

here ♦ In addition to the idioms beginning with HERE, also see BUCK STOPS HERE; DOWNHILL ALL THE WAY (FROM HERE); HAVE HAD IT (UP TO HERE); NEITHER HERE NOR THERE; SAME HERE; WHERE DO WE GO FROM HERE.

here and now 1. At this moment, as in *We must reach a decision here and now.* [Early 1800s] 2. **the here and now.** This life, the present, as in *We'd better think of the here and now before worrying about future generations.* [Early 1900s]

here and there 1. In various places, as *She's lived here and there, never for more than a year in one city.* [c. 1300] 2. In various directions, hither and thither, as in *She turned her eyes here and there, looking for him in the audience.* [Late 1200s] Also see HERE, THERE, AND EVERYWHERE.

here goes 1. An expression or exclamation declaring one's resolution to do something, as in *This hill is steeper than any I've skied before, but here goes!* This usage is sometimes amplified to **here goes nothing,** meaning one is starting something that one doubts will succeed, as in *I've never tried this before, but here goes nothing.* [Early 1800s] 2. **here one goes again.** Someone is repeating the same action or speech, especially an undesirable one. For example, *Here he goes again, criticizing all his colleagues,* or *The power's out—here we go again.* [Colloquial; mid-1900s]

here's to One salutes someone or something. For example, *Here's to Bill on his retirement,* or *Here's to the new project.* This phrase, nearly always used as a toast to someone or something, is a shortening of *here's a health to* and has been so used since the late 1500s. Shakespeare had it in *Romeo and Juliet* (5:3): "Here's to my Love."

here, there, and everywhere In every possible place. For example, *Flags hung here, there, and*

everywhere, making it a colorful occasion. [Late 1500s]

here today, gone tomorrow Lacking permanence, fleeting. For example, *His book attracted a great deal of attention but quickly went out of print— here today and gone tomorrow.* Originally alluding to the briefness of the human lifespan, this phrase was first recorded in John Calvin's *Life and Conversion of a Christian Man* (1549): "This proverb that man is here today and gone tomorrow."

here to stay Permanent or established, as in *I'm afraid the uncertainty about energy costs is here to stay.* [First half of 1900s]

herring ♦ See DEAD AS A DOORNAIL (HERRING); RED HERRING.

he who hesitates is lost One who cannot come to a decision will suffer for it, as in *I couldn't make up my mind, and now the offer has expired—he who hesitates is lost.* Although the idea is undoubtedly older, the present wording is a misquotation or an adaptation from Joseph Addison's play *Cato* (1712): "The woman that deliberates is lost."

hide ♦ In addition to the idioms beginning with HIDE, also see COVER ONE'S ASS (HIDE); TAN ONE'S HIDE.

hide and seek ♦ See PLAY HIDE AND SEEK.

hide nor hair, neither Also, **hide or hair.** No trace of something lost or missing. For example, *I haven't seen hide nor hair of the children.* This expression alludes to the entire outer coat of an animal. [Mid-1800s]

hide one's face Also, **hide one's head.** Feel shame or embarrassment. For example, *You needn't hide your face—you're not to blame,* or *Whenever the teacher singled her out for something, shy little Mary hid her head.* This idiom alludes to the gesture indicative of these feelings. [Late 1500s]

hide one's head in the sand Also, **bury one's head in the sand.** Refuse to face something by pretending not to see it. For example, *For years we have been hiding our heads in the sand, refusing to admit that the store is losing money,* or *When it comes to a family quarrel, Dean just buries his head in the sand.* This expression, transferred to human behavior in the early 1600s, alludes to the belief that ostriches burrow in sand thinking they will not be seen because they cannot see. In fact, however, when they do this, they are consuming sand and gravel to aid their digestive system.

hide one's light under a bushel Show extreme modesty, as in *Even after Paul won the scholarship he went on hiding his light under a bushel.* This expression, which does not necessarily express approval of this behavior, has its origin in the New Testament (Matthew 5:15): "Neither do men light a candle, and put it under a bushel, but on a candlestick." [Early 1600s]

hide out Go into or stay in hiding, especially from the authorities. For example, *The cattle thieves hid out in the canyon,* or *He decided to hide out from the press.* [Late 1800s]

high ♦ In addition to the idioms beginning with HIGH, also see BLOW SKY-HIGH; FLY HIGH; FRIEND IN COURT (HIGH PLACES); HELL OR HIGH WATER; HIT THE HIGH SPOTS (POINTS); HOLD ONE'S HEAD HIGH; IN HIGH DUDGEON; KNEE-HIGH TO A GRASSHOPPER; ON HIGH; ON ONE'S HIGH HORSE; RIDE HIGH; RUN HIGH; STINK TO HIGH HEAVEN; THINK A LOT (HIGHLY) OF; TURN ON (GET HIGH).

high and dry Stranded, as in *They walked out on the party, leaving me high and dry.* This expression originally alluded to a ship that had run aground or was in dry dock. Its figurative use dates from the late 1800s.

high and low Everywhere, as in *We searched high and low but couldn't find the ring,* or *He hunted high and low for a parking space.*

high and mighty Conceited, haughty, as in *She was too high and mighty to make her own bed.* This expression originally alluded to high-born rulers and was being transferred to the merely arrogant by the mid-1600s.

high as a kite Intoxicated, as by alcohol, as in *After three beers she's high as a kite.* The adjective *high* has been used in the sense of "drunk" since the early 1600s; the addition of *kite* dates from the early 1900s. The phrase is now used of disorientation due to any drug.

high gear A state of maximum activity, energy, or force. For example, *His mind was in high gear as he studied for the medical exam,* or *The political campaign is finally moving into high gear.* This expression alludes to the high gear of an engine transmission, used at the fastest speeds.

high hopes ♦ See IN HOPES OF.

high horse ♦ See ON ONE'S HIGH HORSE.

high jinks Playful or rowdy activity, often involving mischievous pranks. For example, *All sorts of high jinks go on at summer camp after "lights out."* About 1700 this term denoted a gambling game accompanied by much drinking, but by the mid-1800s it acquired its present meaning.

high off the hog, eat Also, **live high on the hog.** Prosper, live luxuriously, as in *When Aunt Ida dies and they inherit her estate, they'll be eating high off the hog,* or *Since their loan was approved, they've been living high on the hog.* It alludes to the choicest cuts of meat, which are found on a pig's upper flanks. [Late 1800s]

high on 1. Under the influence of alcohol or a drug. For example, *I think he got high on mari-*

juana before he came to the party. [c. 1930] 2. Very enthusiastic about, as in *They were high on video games.* [1940s]

high places, friends in ♦ See under FRIEND IN COURT.

high seas Open waters of an ocean or sea, beyond the territorial jurisdiction of a country. For example, *Commercial fishermen are being forced to go out on the high seas in order to make a living.* [c. 1100]

high sign A secret signal intended to warn or inform, as in *Dad gave us the high sign when it was time to leave.* This expression presumably alludes to a gesture such as a hand wave. [c. 1900]

hightail it Go as fast as possible, especially in leaving; rush off. For example, *With the police now searching for them, they hightailed it out of town,* or *When Jane remembered it was his birthday, she hightailed it to the bakery for a cake.* This expression alludes to the raised tail of a rabbit or other animal that is fleeing. [Colloquial; late 1800s]

high time The appropriate time for something; also, past the appropriate time. For example, *It's high time we did something about Martha's dog,* or *It's high time you children were in bed.* The precise meaning of this term depends on the tone of voice and/or the context. For a synonym, see ABOUT TIME.

high-water mark The peak of something, especially an achievement. For example, *This composition is the high-water mark of his entire output.* This expression alludes to the highest mark left on shore by the tide. [Mid-1800s]

highway robbery The exaction of an exorbitantly high price or fee. For example, *You paid ten dollars for that meat? That's highway robbery.* This term, used figuratively since the late 1800s, alludes to literal robbery of travelers on or near a public road.

high-wire act A risky job or operation, as in *The university press is not allowed to either make or lose money—that's a high-wire act.* This expression alludes to the aerialist performing on a tightrope stretched high above the ground. [Colloquial; mid-1900s]

hike ♦ See TAKE A HIKE.

hill ♦ See DOWNHILL ALL THE WAY; GO DOWNHILL; HEAD FOR (THE HILLS); MAKE A MOUNTAIN OUT OF A MOLEHILL; NOT WORTH A DIME (HILL OF BEANS); OLD AS ADAM (THE HILLS); OVER THE HILL.

hilt ♦ See TO THE HILT.

hindmost ♦ See DEVIL TAKE THE HINDMOST.

hinge on Also, **hinge upon.** Depend or be contingent on, as in *This plan hinges on her approval.* This expression employs the verb *hinge* in the sense of "to hang," as a door would hang on a hinge, a usage dating from the early 1700s.

hint ♦ See TAKE A HINT.

hip ♦ See SHOOT FROM THE HIP.

hired gun 1. A person, especially a professional killer, employed to kill someone, as in *They thought the murder had been done by a hired gun.* The noun *gun* has been slang for a professional criminal since the mid-1800s. **2.** A person with special knowledge or expertise who is employed to resolve a complex problem. For example, *The legal team was looking for a hired gun to handle the antitrust angle of the case.* [Slang; 1960s]

hired hand Also, **hired man** or **girl.** A person engaged to assist with farm or domestic chores, as in *We need extra hired hands during the harvest,* or *She was looking for a hired girl to do the laundry.* This use of *hired* dates from the 1200s and referred to someone employed for wages as opposed to a slave or serf. The use of *girl* now may be offensive.

hire out Obtain work; also, grant the services or temporary use of for a fee, as in *He hired out as a cook,* or *They hired out the cottage for the summer.* [Second half of 1700s]

history ♦ See ANCIENT HISTORY; GO DOWN (IN HISTORY); MAKE HISTORY; (HISTORY) REPEATS ITSELF.

hit ♦ In addition to the idioms beginning with HIT, also see (HIT) BELOW THE BELT; CAN'T HIT THE BROAD SIDE OF A BARN; HEAVY HITTER; MAKE A HIT; PINCH HITTER; SMASH HIT.

hit a snag Encounter a problem or obstacle. For example, *We've hit a snag with this building project.* The noun *snag* has been used in the sense of "a sharp or rough projection," such as would im pede passage, since the 1500s.

hit below the belt ♦ See BELOW THE BELT.

hit between the eyes Make someone suddenly aware of something, have a sudden impact on. For example, *News of their divorce hit me right between the eyes.* [Colloquial; early 1900s]

hit bottom Also, **touch bottom.** Reach the worst or lowest point. For example, *When he lost his job again they knew they had hit bottom,* or *When wheat prices touch bottom, the farmers will be up in arms.* [Second half of 1800s]

hitch a ride Also, **thumb a ride.** Solicit a free ride, especially by hitchhiking. For example, *I've no car; can I hitch a ride home with you?* or *He was hoping to thumb a ride to the stadium.* The verb *hitch* here alludes to walking unevenly, presumably to hop into a car or truck; raising one's *thumb* is the traditional signal for stopping a car on the road. [First half of 1900s]

hitch one's wagon to a star Aim high, as in *Bill's hitching his wagon to a star—he plans to be a partner by age thirty.* This metaphoric expression was invented by essayist Ralph Waldo Emerson in 1870.

hither and thither Also, **hither and yon.** Here and there, as in *I've been wandering about, hither and thither,* or *Ruth went hither and yon, searching for her sister.* These old words for "here" and "there" are rarely heard outside these expressions, which themselves may be dying out. [c. A.D. 725]

hit it big Score a major success, especially a profit, as in *Some investors hit it big in the stock market.* The adverb *big* here means "with great success." [Slang; late 1800s]

hit it off Get along well together, as in *I was so glad that our parents hit it off.* In the 17th century this phrase was put simply as *hit it,* the adverb *off* being added only in the mid-1800s.

hit on 1. Also, **hit upon.** Discover, happen to find, as in *I've hit upon a solution to this problem.* [c. 1700] **2.** Make sexual advances to someone, especially unwanted ones, as in *You can't go into that bar without being hit on.* [Slang; mid-1900s]

hit on all cylinders ♦ See FIRE ON ALL CYLINDERS.

hit one's stride 1. Achieve a steady, effective pace, as in *After the first few laps around the track he hit his stride.* This expression comes from horse racing, *stride* alluding to the regular pace of the horse. [Early 1900s] **2.** Attain a maximum level of competence, as in *Jack didn't really hit his stride until he started college.* [First half of 1900s]

hit one where one lives ♦ See under CLOSE TO HOME.

hit or miss Haphazardly, at random. For example, *She took dozens of photos, hit or miss, hoping that some would be good.* [c. 1600]

hit out Make a violent verbal or physical attack; also, strike aimlessly. For example, *The star hit out at the press for their lukewarm reviews,* or *The therapist said patients often hit out in frustration.* [First half of 1800s]

hit parade A listing of the most popular or best items or individuals of some kind, as in *The library has a veritable hit parade of videos.* This expression dates from the 1930s, when it was the name of a weekly radio show featuring the most popular songs as indicated by record sales.

hit the books Study with concentrated effort, as in *At exam time we all hit the books.* [Slang; first half of 1900s]

hit the bottle Also, **hit the booze** or **sauce.** Drink alcoholic beverages, especially a great deal, as in *I don't know if it will be a problem, but he hits the bottle every weekend,* or *She hardly ever hits the booze, but when she does, watch out,* or *It doesn't show in her work, but she hits the sauce every night.* These slangy expressions date from the late 1800s and early 1900s.

hit the bricks Go out on strike, as in *The union voted to hit the bricks as soon as their contract expired.* [Slang; 1940s]

hit the bull's-eye Also, **hit the mark** or **the nail on the head.** Be absolutely right, as in *Your remark about finances hit the bull's-eye,* or *Jane hit the* mark with her idea for shuffling personnel, or The governor's speech on attracting new businesses hit the nail on the head. The round black center of a target has been called a *bull's-eye* since the 17th century; *mark* similarly alludes to a target; and the analogy to driving home a nail by hitting it on its head dates from the 16th century. Also see OFF THE MARK.

hit the ceiling Also, **hit the roof.** Explode in anger, as in *Jane hit the ceiling when she saw her grades,* or *Dad hit the roof when he didn't get his usual bonus.* The first expression dates from the early 1900s; the second is a version of a 16th-century locution, *up in the house roof* or *house-top,* meaning "enraged."

hit the deck Also, **hit the dirt.** Fall to the ground, usually for protection. For example, *As the planes approached, we hit the deck,* or *We heard shooting and hit the dirt.* In the early 1900s the first expression was nautical slang for "jump out of bed," or "wake up," and somewhat later, "get going." The current meaning dates from the 1920s.

hit the fan ♦ See SHIT WILL HIT THE FAN.

hit the ground running Seize an opportunity; begin at full speed. For example, *As soon as the front office gave its approval for the new department, we hit the ground running.* The origin of this term is disputed. It may come from troops dropped into a combat zone, from stowaways jumping off a freight train as it nears the station, or from Pony Express riders avoiding delay when they changed mounts.

hit the hay Also, **hit the sack.** Go to bed, as in *I usually hit the hay after the eleven o'clock news,* or *I'm tired, let's hit the sack.* The first colloquial expression dates from the early 1900s, the variant from about 1940.

hit the high spots Also, **hit the high points.** Pay attention only to the most important places or parts. For example, *We only had a week in New York, but we managed to hit the high spots,* or *His speech was brief, but he hit all the high points.* This idiom alludes to running a dustcloth or paintbrush over an uneven surface and touching only the raised portions. [c. 1900]

hit the jackpot Be highly successful, especially unexpectedly; win, especially a lot of money. For example, *She hit the jackpot at the auction; that platter turned out to be genuine Meissen.* This term comes from a form of poker in which a hand can be opened only if one holds at least a pair of jacks (or higher). Often a number of hands must be dealt before anyone can open, and since players must put in money for each round, the *jackpot,* or total amount held, is apt to be quite large. [Early 1900s]

hit the mark ♦ See HIT THE BULL'S-EYE.

hit the nail on the head ♦ See HIT THE BULL'S-EYE.

hit the road Also, **hit the trail.** Set out, as on a trip. For example, *Come on, it's time to hit the road,* or *Jack hit the trail at dawn.* [Late 1800s]

hit the roof ♦ See HIT THE CEILING.

hit the sack ♦ See HIT THE HAY.

hit the spot Give total satisfaction, as in *This beer really hits the spot.* This expression gained enormous currency with a 1930s advertising jingle, in which a popular soda was said to *hit the spot.* [Slang; mid-1800s]

hit up for Ask for a loan or favor, as in *He hit me up for ten bucks,* or *I hit Doug up for a job.* [Slang; early 1900s]

hit upon ♦ See HIT ON.

Hobson's choice An apparently free choice that actually offers no alternative. For example, *My dad said if I wanted the car I could have it tonight or not at all—that's Hobson's choice.* This expression alludes to Thomas Hobson of Cambridge, England, who rented horses and allowed each customer to take only the horse nearest the stable door. [Mid-1600s]

hoe ♦ See TOUGH ROW TO HOE.

hog ♦ See GO HOG WILD; GO WHOLE HOG; HIGH OFF THE HOG; ROAD HOG.

hold ♦ In addition to the idioms beginning with HOLD, also see (HOLD) AT BAY; BEAR (HOLD) A GRUDGE; GET HOLD OF; HANG (HOLD) ON TO YOUR HAT; HAVE A HOLD OVER; LAY HOLD OF; LEAVE HOLDING THE BAG; NO HOLDS BARRED; ON HOLD; (HOLD THE) PURSE STRINGS; STAND (HOLD) ONE'S GROUND; TAKE HOLD.

hold a candle to, not Also, **not fit to** or **cannot hold a candle to.** Be inferior to someone or something, as in *This hotel can't hold a candle to the Palace,* or *This new friend of his is not fit to hold a candle to his former buddies.* This expression was already a proverb in John Heywood's collection of 1546 and alludes to holding a candle to provide light for someone, at that time considered a menial chore.

hold against Think badly of someone because of some fault or occurrence. For example, *Even if you're late, I won't hold it against you,* or *She backed right into his new car, so he's bound to hold it against her.* Also see BEAR A GRUDGE.

hold a grudge ♦ See BEAR A GRUDGE.

hold a gun to someone's head Exert pressure on someone, as in *How could I refuse when she was holding a gun to my head?* This hyperbolic expression dates from the first half of the 1900s. Also see AT GUNPOINT; HOLD ONE'S FEET TO THE FIRE.

hold all the aces Also, **hold all the trumps.** Be in a winning position, as in *We can't argue with Jeff; he* *holds all the aces,* or *If Jean refuses, he'll reveal that he holds all the trumps and force her to give in.* These expressions allude to card games in which the ace or a trump card outranks all the others. Also see PLAY ONE'S CARDS RIGHT; TRUMP CARD.

hold at bay ♦ See AT BAY.

hold back Also, **keep back.** 1. Retain in one's possession or control, as in *He held back vital information,* or *I managed to keep back my tears.* [First half of 1500s] 2. Restrain oneself, as in *She held back from joining the others,* or *I wanted to denounce him right there, but I kept back for fear of making a scene.* The first usage dates from the second half of the 1500s, the variant from the early 1800s. 3. Impede the progress of, as in *The barriers held back traffic during the funeral procession,* or *Her daughter was kept back and had to repeat first grade.*

hold court Be surrounded by and command the attention of admirers, subordinates, or hangers-on. For example, *After a match Judy generally held court in the locker room.* This expression alludes to royalty convening courtiers as well as a judge convening a court of law.

hold down 1. Also, **keep down.** Limit, restrain, as in *Please hold down the noise.* [First half of 1500s] Also see KEEP DOWN. 2. Work at or discharge one's duties satisfactorily, as in *He managed to hold down two jobs at the same time.* [Colloquial; late 1800s]

hold everything Also, **hold it.** Stop, wait. These expressions are usually used in the imperative, as in *Hold everything, we can't unload the truck yet,* or *Hold it, you've gone far enough.* [First half of 1900s]

hold forth Speak in public, especially at great length. For example, *Barbara loved to hold forth on the latest discoveries in astronomy.* [Second half of 1600s]

hold good Also, **hold true.** Be valid, apply. For example, *Does that version of events still hold good?* or *The account he gave ten years ago holds true today.* Shakespeare used these terms frequently. [c. 1300]

hold it ♦ See HOLD EVERYTHING.

hold no brief for Refuse to support, dislike, as in *I hold no brief for liars.* This term is a negative version of the legal expression **hold a brief for,** meaning "to support or defend a position by argument." The noun *brief* has been used in this way since the 1200s.

hold off 1. Keep at a distance, resist, delay, as in *This payment should hold off the creditors.* [Early 1400s] 2. Stop or delay from action, as in *Let's hold off until we know more.* [c. 1600]

hold on 1. Also, **hold on to.** Maintain one's grip, cling, as in *Hold on to your hat in this wind,* or *The early Christians held on to their beliefs despite*

strong opposition. [Early 1500s] 2. Continue to do something, persist, as in *Please hold on for a while longer.* [Late 1800s] 3. Stop, wait, as in *Hold on! We can't go past this gate.* [Mid-1800s] 4. Remain on a telephone line, as in *If you can hold on a minute I'll go and find her.* [Late 1800s]

hold one's breath 1. Be excited, anxious, or nervous. For example, *The election was so close that I held my breath until the final results were in,* or *I'm holding my breath until everyone's been heard from.* This expression alludes to the interruption of normal breathing; the literal usage dating from the early 1700s. 2. **not hold one's breath.** An expression used to mean one is *not* awaiting something, as in *I'm hoping to hear if I got the job, but I'm not holding my breath.* It often is put as an imperative, **don't hold your breath,** meaning "don't expect it, it's not likely," as in *They may get married this summer, but don't hold your breath.* This expression in effect implies it is unwise to stop breathing until a particular event occurs, since it may never come to pass. [Slang; mid-1900s]

hold one's end up Also, **keep one's end up.** Do one's share. For example, *John always holds his end up, but Jerry is less reliable,* or *Let's hope she can keep up her end.* In these expressions *end* alludes to one of two sides of something that must be lifted by two persons. [Mid-1900s]

hold one's fire Refrain from comment or criticism, especially for the time being. For example, *Hold your fire, Jim, she's not finished yet,* or *Nancy decided to hold her fire until she had more information.* This expression alludes to refraining from shooting a gun and originated in the military.

hold one's head high Also, **hold one's head up; hold up one's head.** Behave proudly; maintain one's dignity. For example, *After the bankruptcy Mr. Jones still held his head high,* or *Grandma told Brian he could hold his head up because he'd tried extremely hard,* or *After that newspaper article, I'm not sure I'll ever hold up my head again.* All these expressions allude to a posture of pride. [Second half of 1500s]

hold one's horses Slow down, be patient, as in *Dad told Kevin to hold his horses on Christmas shopping, since it was only July,* or *Hold your horses, I'm coming.* This expression alludes to a driver making horses wait by holding the reins tightly. [Slang; c. 1840]

hold one's own Do reasonably well despite opposition, competition, or criticism. For example, *The team held its own against their opponents,* or *Rumors often hold their own against facts.* [First half of 1300s]

hold one's peace ♦ See under HOLD ONE'S TONGUE.

hold one's temper Also, **keep one's temper.** Refrain from expressing violent anger, maintain composure or poise. For example, *Billy has to learn to hold his temper when he's frustrated,* or *If the chairman can keep his temper, the matter will get settled.* [c. 1700] For an antonym, see LOSE ONE'S TEMPER.

hold one's tongue Also, **hold** or **keep one's peace.** Keep quiet, remain silent, as in *If you don't hold your tongue you'll have to go outside,* or *Jenny kept her peace about the wedding.* The idiom with *tongue* uses *hold* in the sense of "restrain," while the others use *hold* and *keep* in the sense of "preserve." Chaucer used the first idiom in *The Tale of Melibus* (c. 1387): "Thee is better hold thy tongue still, than for to speak." The variant appears in the traditional wedding service, telling anyone who knows that a marriage should not take place to "speak now or forever hold your peace." [First half of 1300s] Also see KEEP QUIET.

hold on to ♦ See HOLD ON, def. 1.

hold on to your hat ♦ See HANG ON TO YOUR HAT.

hold out 1. Extend, stretch forth; also, present or offer something. For example, *He held out his hand and she took it,* or *The new policy held out promise of major changes in the welfare program.* These usages date from the first half of the 1500s and of the 1600s respectively. 2. Last, continue to be in supply or service, as in *The food is holding out nicely.* [Late 1500s] Also see HOLD UP, def. 4. 3. Continue to resist, as in *The garrison held our for another month.* [Second half of 1700s] 4. Withhold cooperation, agreement, or information, as in *We've asked for a better deal, but they've been holding out for months.* It is also put as **hold out on,** as in *They were still holding out on some of the provisions,* or *He's not telling us what happened; he's holding out on us.* 5. **hold out for.** Insist on obtaining, as in *The union is still holding out for a better contract.* [c. 1900]

hold out on ♦ See HOLD OUT, def. 4.

hold over 1. Postpone or delay, as in *Let's hold this matter over until the next meeting.* [Mid-1800s] 2. Keep something in a position or state beyond the normal period, as in *The film was to be held over for another week.* [First half of 1900s] 3. Continue in office past the normal period, as in *The committee chair held over until they could find a suitable replacement.* [Mid-1600s] 4. **hold something over someone.** Have an advantage or use a threat to control someone. For example, *They knew he'd been caught shoplifting and were sure to hold it over him.* [Second half of 1800s]

hold someone's feet to the fire Also, **keep someone's feet to the fire.** Pressure someone to consent to or undertake something, as in *The only way you'll get him to agree is to hold his feet to the fire.* This idiom alludes to an ancient test of courage or form of torture in which a person's feet were so

placed. It began to be used figuratively in the second half of the 1900s. Also see HOLD A GUN TO SOMEONE'S HEAD.

hold still for Also, **stand still for.** Accept or tolerate something, as in *Do you think he'll hold still for your decision?* These terms are often put negatively, as in *The town won't hold still for another increase in property taxes,* or *The teacher won't stand still for this kind of behavior.* The first expression employs *hold* in the sense of "sustain a particular position or attitude," a usage dating from about 1300.

hold sway over Dominate, have a controlling influence over, as in *He held sway over the entire department.* This idiom uses the noun *sway* in the sense of "power" or "dominion," a usage dating from the late 1500s.

hold the bag ♦ See LEAVE HOLDING THE BAG.

hold the fort Assume responsibility, especially in another's absence; also, maintain a secure position. For example, *Harry did a good job of holding the fort until his boss recovered,* or *Can you hold the fort in the kitchen?* This expression has been traced to an order given by General William Tecumseh Sherman in 1864, which was repeated as "Hold the fort [against the enemy at Allatoona] at all costs, for I am coming."

hold the line Maintain the existing position or state of affairs. For example, *We'll have to hold the line on spending until our profits rise.* This term alludes to former military tactics, in which a line of troops was supposed to prevent an enemy breakthrough. Eventually, it was transferred to civilian enterprises. [Mid-1900s]

hold the phone Stop what one is doing, as in *Hold the phone! There's no sense in continuing this argument.* This expression is often put as an imperative, as in the example. [Colloquial; second half of 1900s] Also see HOLD EVERYTHING.

hold the purse strings ♦ See PURSE STRINGS.

hold to Remain loyal or faithful to, abide by, as in *She held to her resolutions,* or *He held to his view that the interest rate should be lowered.* [c. 1200] Also see STICK BY; STICK TO.

hold true ♦ See under HOLD GOOD.

hold up 1. Offer or present as an example, as in *The teacher held Bernie's essay up as a model for the class to follow.* [c. 1600] 2. Obstruct or delay, as in *We were held up in traffic.* [c. 1900] 3. Rob, as in *He was held up in a dark alley, with no help nearby.* This usage, which gave rise to the noun *holdup* for a robbery, alludes to the robbers' demand that the victims hold their hands high. [Late 1800s] 4. Also, **hold out.** Continue to function without losing force or effectiveness, endure. For example, *We held up through that long bitter* *winter,* or *The nurse was able to hold out until someone could relieve her.* [Late 1500s] **5.** See HOLD ONE'S HEAD HIGH.

hold water Stand up to critical examination, be sound and valid, as in *This argument just won't hold water,* or *Her reasons for quitting don't hold water.* This metaphoric expression alludes to a container that can hold water without leaking. [c. 1600]

hold with Agree with, support, as in *I don't hold with that view of the situation.* [c. 1300]

hold your ♦ See under HOLD ONE'S.

hole ♦ In addition to the idioms beginning with HOLE, also see ACE IN THE HOLE; BLACK HOLE; IN A BIND (HOLE); IN THE HOLE; MONEY BURNS A HOLE IN ONE'S POCKET; NEED LIKE A HOLE IN THE HEAD; PICK HOLES IN; SQUARE PEG IN A ROUND HOLE.

hole in one A perfect achievement, as in *Tim scored a hole in one on that test.* The term alludes to a perfect stroke in golf, where one drives the ball from the tee into the hole with a single stroke. [c. 1900]

hole in the wall A small, modest, or obscure place, as in *My new apartment is just a hole in the wall,* or *Believe it or not, that little hole in the wall is a great restaurant.* This graphic term is often used disparagingly. [First half of 1800s]

hole up Take refuge or shelter, hide, as in *I spent most of the cruise holed up in my cabin.* This usage alludes to animals hibernating in winter or hiding from attack in caves or holes. [Late 1800s]

holiday ♦ See BUSMAN'S HOLIDAY.

hollow ♦ See BEAT THE PANTS OFF (HOLLOW).

holy cow Also, **holy mackerel** or **Moses** or **moly** or **smoke.** An exclamation of surprise, astonishment, delight, or dismay, as in *Holy cow, I forgot the wine,* or *Holy mackerel, you won!* or *Holy Moses, here comes the teacher!* or *Holy smoke, I didn't know you were here too.* The oldest of these slangy expletives uses *mackerel,* dating from about 1800; the one with *Moses* dates from about 1850 and *cow* from about 1920. None has any literal significance, and *moly* is a neologism devised to rhyme with "holy" and possibly a euphemism for "Moses."

holy of holies A place of awe or sacredness, as in *The corporate board room is the holy of holies here.* This expression is a translation of the Hebrew term for the sanctuary inside the tabernacle of the Temple of Jerusalem, where the sacred Ark of the Covenant was kept (Exodus 26:34). Its figurative use dates from the second half of the 1800s.

holy terror An exasperating individual, as in *He was only five, but he was a holy terror, running wild through the house and throwing whatever he could lay his hands on.* The adjective *holy* here is an intensifier. [Late 1800s]

home ♦ In addition to the idioms beginning with HOME, also see AT HOME; BRING HOME; BRING HOME THE BACON; CHICKENS COME HOME TO ROOST; CLOSE TO HOME; DRIVE HOME; EAT SOMEONE OUT OF HOUSE AND HOME; MAKE ONESELF AT HOME; NOBODY HOME; NOTHING TO WRITE HOME ABOUT; TILL THE COWS COME HOME.

home free In a secure or comfortable position, especially because of being certain to succeed. For example, *Once I meet the schedule I'll be home free,* or *I think we have enough support for this measure—we're home free.* This expression probably alludes to safely reaching baseball's *home plate,* meaning one has scored a run. [Mid-1900s]

home in on Move toward or focus on a goal, as in *He began with a couple of jokes before homing in on the main subject of his talk.* This expression originally alluded to a vessel, aircraft or missile being guided to its target by a radio beam or some other means. [c. 1920]

home run A highly successful achievement; also, doubling one's profits. For example, *We scored a home run with that drug stock, buying it at 15 and selling at 30.* This expression originated in the mid 1800s in baseball, where it refers to a pitched ball batted so far that the batter can round all three bases and reach home plate, scoring a run. Its figurative use dates from the mid-1900s.

home truth A key or basic truth, especially one that is discomforting to acknowledge. For example, *It's time you told a few home truths here, such as where your campaign finances actually came from.* This expression uses *home* in the sense of "the very heart of a matter." [c. 1700]

homework ♦ See DO ONE'S HOMEWORK.

honest ♦ In addition to the idioms beginning with HONEST, also see COME BY (HONESTLY); OPEN (HONEST) AND ABOVEBOARD.

honest to God Also, **honest to goodness** or **Pete; honest Injun.** Truly, really, as in *Honest to God, I didn't know it was yours,* or *Honest to goodness, we had exactly the same experience,* or *I promise I'll finish in time, honest to Pete,* or *Honest Injun, I didn't take your wallet.* These colloquial assertions date from about 1900, except for *honest Injun,* dating from the late 1800s and today considered offensive.

honeymoon is over, the The initial harmonious period in a new relationship has ended, as in *After the first ninety days, the honeymoon between the new President and the press was over.* The figurative use of *honeymoon* (literally referring to the first month of marriage) dates from the late 1500s.

honor ♦ In addition to the idiom beginning with HONOR, also see DO THE HONORS; IN HONOR OF; ON ONE'S HONOR; WORD OF HONOR.

honor bound Obliged by one's personal integrity, as in *She was honor bound to admit that it was her work and not her sister's.* Also see ON ONE'S HONOR.

hoof it 1. Go on foot, as in *The car's being repaired—we'll have to hoof it.* [First half of 1600s] 2. Dance, as in *He was always a good dancer, and he's still able to hoof it.* [Slang; 1920s]

hook ♦ In addition to the idioms beginning with HOOK, also see BY HOOK OR CROOK; OFF THE HOOK; ON ONE'S OWN ACCOUNT (HOOK).

hook, line, and sinker Without reservation, completely, as in *He swallowed our excuse hook, line, and sinker.* This expression, first recorded in 1865, alludes to a fish swallowing not only the baited hook but the leaden sinker and the entire fishing line between them.

hook or crook ♦ See BY HOOK OR CROOK.

hook up 1. Assemble or wire a mechanism, as in *Dick helped us hook up the stereo system.* [1920s] 2. Connect a mechanism with a main source, as in *The computer had not yet been hooked up to the mainframe.* [1920s] 3. **hook up with.** Form a tie or association, as in *She had hooked up with the wrong crowd.* [Slang; mid-1900s]

hooky ♦ See PLAY HOOKY.

hoop ♦ See JUMP THROUGH HOOPS.

hoot ♦ See NOT GIVE A DAMN (HOOT).

hop ♦ In addition to the idioms beginning with HOP, also see MAD AS A HORNET (HOPS).

hope ♦ In addition to the idioms beginning with HOPE, also see GREAT WHITE HOPE; IN HOPES OF; LIVE IN (HOPE OF); NOT A HOPE IN HELL; PIN ONE'S HOPES ON; WHILE THERE'S LIFE, THERE'S HOPE.

hope against hope Hope or wish for with little reason or justification, as in *I'm hoping against hope that someone will return my wallet.* This expression, based on the biblical "Who against hope believed in hope" (Romans 4:18), was first recorded in 1813.

hope springs eternal People will keep on hoping, no matter what the odds. For example, *I keep buying lottery tickets—hope springs eternal.* This expression was coined by Alexander Pope (*An Essay on Man,* 1732) and quickly became proverbial.

hopped up 1. Relating to a motor, especially a car engine, whose power has been increased. For example, *Kids loved to ride around in hopped-up cars.* [Slang; mid-1900s] Also see SOUP UP. 2. Stimulated with, or as if with, a narcotic. For example, *Their idea of a good time is to get all hopped up on marijuana or worse.* This slangy usage dates from the 1920s but may be related to the late 19th-century use of the noun *hop* for a narcotic, especially opium.

hopping mad Enraged, furious, as in *I was hopping mad when they left my name off the list.* This expression conjures up an image of jumping up and down with rage. [Colloquial; early 1800s]

hop, skip, and a jump A short distance, as in *It's just a hop, skip, and a jump from my house to yours.* This expression, dating from the early 1700s, originally referred to an exercise or game involving these movements, but by the mid-1800s was also being used figuratively for the short distance so covered.

hop to it Begin to do something quickly and energetically, as in *We've got to hop to it and get our shopping done.* [Colloquial; first half of 1900s]

hop up ♦ See HOPPED UP.

horizon ♦ See ON THE HORIZON.

horn ♦ In addition to the idioms beginning with HORN, also see BLOW ONE'S OWN HORN; LOCK HORNS; PULL IN ONE'S HORNS; TAKE THE BULL BY THE HORNS.

hornet ♦ See MAD AS A HORNET; STIR UP A HORNET'S NEST.

horn in on Intrude, join without being invited. For example, *She has a rude way of horning in on our conversations.* This expression alludes to an ox or bull pushing in with its horns. [c. 1900]

horns of a dilemma, on the Faced with two equally undesirable alternatives. For example, *I'm on the horns of a dilemma: if I sell the house now I have no place to live, but if I wait I may not get as good a price.* This term was first recorded about 1600, but the idea of being caught on either one horn or the other (of an animal) was already expressed in Roman times.

horror ♦ See under THROW UP ONE'S HANDS.

horse ♦ In addition to the idioms beginning with HORSE, also see BACK THE WRONG HORSE; BEAT A DEAD HORSE; CART BEFORE THE HORSE; CHANGE HORSES IN MIDSTREAM; CHARLEY HORSE; DARK HORSE; EAT LIKE A BIRD (HORSE); FROM THE HORSE'S MOUTH; HOLD ONE'S HORSES; IF WISHES WERE HORSES; LOOK A GIFT HORSE IN THE MOUTH; ONE-HORSE RACE; ON ONE'S HIGH HORSE; WAR HORSE; WILD HORSES COULDN'T DRAG; WORK LIKE A BEAVER (HORSE); YOU CAN LEAD A HORSE TO WATER.

horse around Indulge in frivolous activity or play. For example, *The boys were horsing around all afternoon.* This term presumably alludes to *horseplay,* which has meant "rough or boisterous play" since the late 1500s. [First half of 1900s]

horse of a different color, a Also, **a horse of another color.** Another matter entirely, something else. For example, *I thought that was her boyfriend but it turned out to be her brother—that's a horse of a different color.* This term probably derives from a phrase coined by Shakespeare, who wrote "a horse of that color" (*Twelfth Night,* 2:3), meaning "the same matter" rather than a different one.

By the mid-1800s the term was used to point out difference rather than likeness.

horse sense Sound practical sense, as in *She's got too much horse sense to believe his story.* The exact allusion in this term, which dates from the mid-1800s, is disputed, since some regard horses as rather stupid. However, they tended to be viewed more positively in the American West, where the term originated.

horse trading Negotiation marked by hard bargaining and shrewd exchange. For example, *The restaurant owner is famous for his horse trading; he's just exchanged a month of free dinners for a month of free television commercials.* This expression alludes to the notorious shrewdness of **horse traders**, who literally bought and sold horses. [c. 1820]

hot ♦ In addition to the idioms beginning with HOT, also see BLOW HOT AND COLD; LIKE A CAT ON HOT BRICKS; LIKE HOT CAKES; MAKE IT HOT FOR; PIPING HOT; STRIKE WHILE THE IRON'S HOT.

hot air Empty, exaggerated talk, as in *That last speech of his was pure hot air.* It is also put as **full of hot air,** as in *Pay no attention to Howard—he's full of hot air.* This metaphoric term transfers heated air to vaporous talk. [Late 1800s]

hot and bothered In a state of agitated excitement, flustered, as in *She was all hot and bothered before her big opening.* [c. 1920]

hot and heavy 1. Very enthusiastic and excited, as in *That was a hot and heavy debate.* This slangy expression employs *hot* in the sense of "characterized by intense feeling," a usage dating from the tenth century A.D., and *heavy* in the sense of "serious." 2. Passionate, lustful, as in *They were awfully young to be so hot and heavy about their romance.* This slangy term employs *hot* in the sense of "sexually aroused," a usage dating from about 1500.

hot as blazes Also, **hot as hell.** Extremely warm, as in *It was hot as blazes in that room,* or *I'm hot as hell and would love a cold shower.* The first of these hyperbolic similes dates from the mid-1800s, the second from the early 1900s.

hot dog A person who performs showy, often dangerous stunts, especially but not exclusively in sports; also, a showoff. For example, *He was a shameless hot dog on the tennis court, smashing every ball,* or *She was a hot dog behind the wheel, screeching her wheels at every turn.* The relation of this term to the edible hot dog is unknown. [Colloquial; c. 1900] 2. Also, **hot diggety dog; hot diggety.** An interjection expressing delight or enthusiasm, as in *Hot dog! What a great gift,* or *Hot diggety! We got the best concert tickets after all.* [Slang; c. 1900]

hotfoot it Go in haste, walk fast or run. For example, *I'll have to hotfoot it to the airport if I'm to meet them.* [Slang; c. 1900]

hot line A telephone line that gives quick and direct access to a source of information or help. For example, *Our state has an AIDS hot line in every country.* This term was originally (and is still) used for a direct link between heads of government for use during a crisis, but was quickly extended to wider applications. [1950s]

hot number Also, **hot stuff.** Someone or something that is currently popular or fashionable; also, someone or something unconventional or daring. For example, *That new song is going to be a hot number,* or *He really thinks he's hot stuff.* These slangy expressions use *hot* in the sense of "recent" or "fresh," a usage dating from the 1300s, although *hot stuff* dates from the 1700s and *hot number* from about 1900.

hot off the press Newly printed; sensational and exciting. For example, *I've got it hot off the press—he's resigning,* or *This design is hot off the press.* [c. 1900]

hot on 1. Also, **hot for.** Enthusiastic about, as in *She's really hot on golf,* or *He's hot for another skiing vacation.* This seemingly modern slangy usage was first recorded in 1667. Also see MAKE IT HOT FOR. 2. Also, **hot at.** Very good, impressive, as in *He's hot at anything involving numbers.* This expression, first recorded in 1573, is frequently used in the negative, as in *I'm not so hot at new computer programs.*

hot potato A problem so controversial and sensitive that it is risky to deal with. For example, *Gun control is a political hot potato.* This term, dating from the mid-1800s, alludes to the only slightly older expression **drop like a hot potato,** meaning "to abandon something or someone quickly" (lest one be burned). The idiom alludes to the fact that cooked potatoes retain considerable heat because they contain a lot of water.

hot rod An automobile modified to increase its speed and acceleration, as in *Kids love to tinker with cars and try to convert them into hot rods.* [Mid-1900s] Also see HOPPED UP.

hot seat, in the In a position of extreme stress or discomfort, as when subjected to harsh criticism. For example, *When merger negotiations broke down, he was in the hot seat with the stockholders.* This expression extends *hot seat* in the sense of "the electric chair" (for effecting an execution) to wider use. [c. 1930]

hot stuff ♦ See HOT NUMBER.

hot to trot 1. Ready and willing, eager. For example, *We should let them start putting up posters; they're hot to trot.* 2. Sexually avid, lascivious, as in *He's hot to trot and asked her out almost as soon as he met her.* Both slangy usages allude to a horse eager to get going.

hot under the collar Angry, as in *She is quick to get hot under the collar, but once the problem is ironed out she forgets it entirely.* This expression alludes to the heat of anger. [c. 1900]

hot water Trouble or difficulty, as in *She's deep in political hot water,* or *We got in hot water over the car deal,* or *He's finally paid his tuition and is out of hot water with the school.* This metaphoric term alludes to water hot enough to burn one. [First half of 1500s] Also see IN TROUBLE WITH.

hound ♦ See RUN WITH (THE HARE, HUNT WITH THE HOUNDS).

hour ♦ See AFTER HOURS; ALL HOURS; AT THE TOP OF THE HOUR; BY THE DAY (HOUR); ELEVENTH HOUR; FOR DAYS (HOURS); HAPPY HOUR; KEEP LATE HOURS; ON THE HOUR; SMALL HOURS.

house ♦ In addition to the idiom beginning with HOUSE, also see BOARDINGHOUSE REACH; BRING DOWN THE HOUSE; CLEAN HOUSE; EAT SOMEONE OUT OF HOUSE AND HOME; GET ON (LIKE A HOUSE AFIRE); KEEP HOUSE; ON THE HOUSE; OPEN HOUSE; PEOPLE WHO LIVE IN GLASS HOUSES; PUT ONE'S HOUSE IN ORDER; SAFE AS HOUSES.

house of cards A weak and fragile structure, plan, or organization, as in *Her scheme to reorganize the school sounds like another house of cards,* or *Jerry built his entire business on what turned out to be a house of cards.* This metaphoric expression alludes to the structure made by balancing playing cards against one another. [First half of 1600s]

how ♦ In addition to the idioms beginning with HOW, also see AND HOW.

how about What is your thought, feeling, or desire concerning. For example, *How about a cup of tea?* or *How about joining us for lunch?* It is also put as **how about it,** as in *How about it? Do you want to come along?* [Mid-1800s] Also see WHAT ABOUT.

how about that? Isn't that surprising, remarkable, or pleasing. For example, *They're engaged—how about that?* [Colloquial; first half of 1900s]

how are you? ♦ See HOW DO YOU DO?

how come? How is it that, as in *How come you're not attending the conference?* Sometimes **how come** follows a statement and asks the question "why" or "in what way," as in *You're not going? How come?* The related phrase **how so?** functions the same way, as in *You say she's changed her mind—how so?* **How come** is short for *how did it come about that* and dates from the mid-1800s; **how so,** short for *how is it so* or *how is it that,* dates from about 1300.

how does that grab you? What do you think of that? For example, *They want to put his name at the top of the masthead—how does that grab you?* This expression employs the verb *grab* in the sense of "excite one's interest or attention." [Slang; early 1900s]

how do you do? A conventional greeting used mostly after being introduced to someone, as in *And this is our youngest—say "How do you do" to Mr. Smith.* Although it is a question, it requires no reply. Originally, in the 1600s, this expression was an inquiry after a person's health or standing, *how do you do* meaning "how do you fare?" Today we usually express this as **How are you?** or **How are you doing?** or **How goes it?** or **How's it going?** Even more general are the slangy locutions **How are things?** or **How's tricks?** All of these greetings date from the first half of the 1900s.

however much ♦ See AS MUCH AS, def. 2.

how goes it ♦ See HOW DO YOU DO?

howling success A tremendous triumph, as in *Their first play was a howling success.* This colloquial expression employs *howling* in the sense of "very pronounced" or "glaring," a usage dating from the mid-1800s.

how so? ♦ See under HOW COME?

how's that Also, **how's that again.** What did you say? Please repeat it. For example, *How's that? I didn't quite hear you.*

how's tricks? ♦ See HOW DO YOU DO?

how the land lies ♦ See LAY OF THE LAND.

how the wind blows ♦ See WAY THE WIND BLOWS.

Hoyle ♦ See ACCORDING TO HOYLE.

huddle ♦ See GO INTO A HUDDLE.

hue and cry A public clamor, as of protest or demand. For example, *The reformers raised a hue and cry about political corruption.* This redundant expression (*hue* and *cry* both mean "an outcry"), dating from the 1200s, originally meant "an outcry calling for the pursuit of a criminal." By the mid-1500s it was also being used more broadly, as in the example.

huff ♦ In addition to the idiom beginning with HUFF, also see IN A HUFF.

huff and puff Make noisy, empty threats; bluster. For example, *You can huff and puff about storm warnings all you like, but we'll believe it when we see it.* This expression uses two words of 16th-century origin, *huff,* meaning "to emit puffs of breath in anger," and *puff,* meaning "to blow in short gusts," and figuratively, "to inflate" or "make conceited." They were combined in the familiar nursery tale, "The Three Little Pigs," where the wicked wolf warns, "I'll huff and I'll puff and I'll blow your house down"; rhyme has helped these idioms survive.

human ♦ See MILK OF HUMAN KINDNESS.

humble ♦ See EAT CROW (HUMBLE PIE).

humor ♦ See OUT OF SORTS (HUMOR).

hump ♦ See OVER THE HUMP.

hundred ♦ See BY THE DOZEN (HUNDRED).

hung up ♦ See under HANG UP.

hunt ♦ See HAPPY HUNTING GROUND; HIGH AND LOW, (HUNT); RUN WITH (THE HARE, HUNT WITH THE HOUNDS).

hurry up and wait Move quickly and then have to wait for something or someone. For example, *We did our share in good time, but the others were several days behind so we couldn't finish—it was another case of hurry up and wait.* This expression dates from the 1940s and probably originated in the armed services.

hurt ♦ See NOT HURT A FLY.

hush money A bribe paid to keep something secret, as in *No amount of hush money will keep that scandal from coming out.* [c. 1700]

hush up Keep from public knowledge, suppress mention of. For example, *They tried to hush up the damaging details.* [First half of 1600s]

Hyde ♦ See JEKYLL AND HYDE.

i

i ♦ See DOT THE I'S AND CROSS THE T'S.

I beg your pardon ♦ See under BEG TO DIFFER.

ice ♦ See BREAK THE ICE; CUT NO ICE; ON ICE; ON THIN ICE; PUT ON ICE; TIP OF THE ICEBERG.

icing on the cake Also, **frosting on the cake.** An additional benefit to something already good. For example, *All these letters of congratulation are icing on the cake,* or *After that beautiful sunrise, the rainbow is just frosting on the cake.* This metaphoric expression alludes to the sweet creamy coating used to enhance a cake. [Mid-1900s]

I dare say 1. I venture to assert or affirm, as in *I dare say my point of view will be heard.* [c. 1300] **2.** Also, **I daresay.** I presume or assume to be likely, as in *I daresay you'll be invited.* This usage is more common in Britain than in America. [Mid-1700s]

idea ♦ See BRIGHT IDEA; PUT IDEAS IN SOMEONE'S HEAD; WHAT'S THE IDEA.

idiot box A television set, as in *There they sit in front of the idiot box, hour after hour.* This slangy and pejorative expression dates from about 1960.

if ♦ In addition to the idioms beginning with IF, also see AS IF; DAMNED IF I DO, DAMNED IF I DON'T; MAKE AS IF TO; NO IFS OR BUTS; NOTHING IF NOT; (IF) PUSH COMES TO SHOVE; WHAT IF.

if anything If at all, if in any degree. For example, *If anything, we have too much food rather than too little.* [Early 1800s]

if at first you don't succeed, try, try again Don't let a first-time failure stop further attempts. For example, *I know it's hard at first to shift gears without stalling but if at first you don't succeed . . .* This seemingly ancient adage was first recorded only in 1840 but has become so well known that it is often shortened.

if it ain't broke don't fix it Don't meddle with something that's functioning adequately. For example, *So long as they like our proposal let's not change it; if it ain't broke don't fix it.* This folksy and deliberately ungrammatical expression dates from the mid-1900s. For a synonym, see LEAVE WELL ENOUGH ALONE.

if only I wish that. For example, *If only I had known you were coming I would have met your plane,* or *If only it would snow on Christmas Eve.* [c. A.D. 1000] For a synonym, see WOULD THAT.

if the mountain won't come to Muhammad, Muhammad must go to the mountain If one can't have one's way, one must give in. For example, *Since you can't come here for the holiday, I'll go to your house—if the mountain won't come to Muhammad, Muhammad must go to the mountain.* This expression is based on a tale that Muhammad once sought proof of his teachings by ordering a mountain to come to him. When it did not move, he maintained that God had been merciful, for if it had indeed moved they all would have been crushed by it. [Late 1500s]

if the shoe fits, wear it Also, **if the cap fits, wear it.** If something applies to you, accept it, as in *These problems are hard to solve, and most people would need help, so if the shoe fits, wear it!* This expression originated as *if the cap fits,* which alluded to a fool's cap and dates from the early 1700s. Although this version has not died out entirely, *shoe* today is more common and probably gained currency through the Cinderella fairy tale, in which the prince sought her out by means of the slipper she lost at the ball.

if wishes were horses If one could readily have what one wanted, life would be easy. For example, *Wendy would love a brand-new car for her sixteenth birthday but—if wishes were horses.* This expression is a shortening of **If wishes were horses, beggars would ride,** first recorded about 1628 in a collection of Scottish proverbs.

if worst comes to worst Also, **if worse comes to worst.** In the least favorable situation, if the worst possible outcome occurs. For example, *If worst comes to worst and the budget is not approved, the government will shut down,* or *Go ahead and go to* school with a cold; if worse comes to worst the teacher will send you home. This expression is nearly always followed by a solution. [Late 1500s]

if you can't beat 'em, join 'em Also, **if you can't lick 'em, join 'em.** If you can't defeat your opponents you might be better off by switching to their side. For example, *Seeing that no one else was willing to stick with the old software program, Marcia learned the new one, noting if you can't beat 'em, join 'em,* or *I opposed a new school library, but the town voted for it, so I'll support it—if you can't lick 'em, join 'em.* This expression dates from about 1940 and originally alluded to political opponents. The opposite idea is expressed in an advertising slogan used in the 1960s and 1970s by a cigarette company, in which the smoker would fight rather than switch brands.

if you can't stand the heat, get out of the kitchen If the pressure or stress is too great, leave or give up. For example, *It'll take a lot of weekend overtime to finish, so if you can't stand the heat, get out of the kitchen.* This folksy adage has been ascribed to President Harry S. Truman, who certainly said it and may have originated it. [c. 1950]

ignorance is bliss What you don't know won't hurt you. For example, *She decided not to read the critics' reviews—ignorance is bliss.* Although its truth may be dubious at best, this idea has been expressed since ancient times. The actual wording, however, comes from Thomas Gray's poem, "Ode on a Distant Prospect of Eton College" (1742): "Where ignorance is bliss, 'tis folly to be wise."

ill ◆ In addition to the idioms beginning with ILL, also see under GET SICK.

ill at ease Uncomfortable, uneasy, as in *Large parties made him feel ill at ease.* [c. 1300] For an antonym, see AT EASE.

I'll be hanged 1. I am very surprised, as in, *Well, I'll be hanged; there's Susan.* 2. **I'll be hanged if I.** Under no circumstances will I, as in *I'll be hanged if I let you do that.* Both of these hyperbolic colloquial usages allude to being executed by hanging.

I'll be seeing you Also, **see you.** Goodbye, as in *I have to go now; I'll be seeing you,* or *All right, see you.* These colloquial formulas do not necessarily imply a future meeting. [Late 1800s]

ill-gotten gains Benefits obtained in an evil manner or by dishonest means, as in *They duped their senile uncle into leaving them a fortune and are now enjoying their ill-gotten gains.* [Mid-1800s]

I'll say Absolutely, I strongly agree. For example, *Did you enjoy the film?—I'll say.* This phrase is generally used alone and for emphasis. [First half of 1900s] For a synonym, see YOU CAN SAY THAT AGAIN.

ill wind that blows no one any good, it's an A loss or misfortune usually benefits someone. For

example, *They lost everything when that old shed burned down, but they got rid of a lot of junk as well—it's an ill wind.* This expression appeared in John Heywood's 1546 proverb collection and remains so well known that it is often shortened. It also gave rise to a much-quoted pun about the difficulty of playing the oboe, describing the instrument as *an ill wind that nobody blows good.*

image ◆ See SPITTING IMAGE.

imagination ◆ See FIGMENT OF ONE'S IMAGINATION.

I'm from Missouri ◆ See FROM MISSOURI.

immemorial ◆ See TIME IMMEMORIAL.

impose on 1. Force something on someone; also, levy a tax or duty. For example, *Don't try to impose your ideas on me,* or *The British crown imposed a tariff on tea.* [Late 1500s] 2. Force oneself on others; take unfair advantage of. For example, *Am I imposing on you if I stay overnight?* or *He's always imposing on us, dropping in unexpectedly with numerous friends.* [Early 1600s]

impression ◆ See MAKE AN IMPRESSION; UNDER THE IMPRESSION.

improve on Make beneficial additions or changes to, as in *The company is trying to improve on the previous model.* [Late 1600s]

in ◆ In addition to the idioms beginning with IN, also see under OUT OF.

in a bad light ◆ See IN A GOOD LIGHT.

in a bad mood In an irritable or depressed state of mind. For example, *Dad's in a bad mood, so don't ask for anything right now.* The antonym, **in a good mood,** refers to a cheerful, well-disposed state of mind, as in *When the boss is in a good mood our whole day goes well.* The phrase *in a mood,* meaning "disposed" or "inclined," dates from about A.D. 1000. Also see IN THE MOOD.

in a bad way In trouble; also, deteriorating. For example, *If he can't get that bank loan he'll be in a bad way,* or *The business is in a bad way, with profits declining every month.* [Early 1800s]

in a big way To a great extent, conspicuously. For example, *I could go for a hamburger in a big way,* or *This hotel chain is expanding in a big way.* [Slang; late 1800s]

in a bind Also, **in a box** or **hole** or **jam** or **tight corner** or **tight spot.** In a difficult, threatening, or embarrassing position; also, unable to solve a dilemma. For example, *He's put us in a bind: we can't refuse, but at the same time we can't fill the order,* or *Jim's in a box; he can't afford to pay what he owes us,* or *He quit without giving notice and now we're really in a hole,* or *We always end up in a jam during the holiday season,* or *He's in a tight corner with those new customers,* or *We'll be in a tight spot unless we can find another thousand dollars.* All these colloquial terms allude to places from which one can't easily extricate oneself. The phrase using *bind* was first recorded in 1851; *box*, 1865; *jam*, 1914; *tight spot*, 1852. Also see IN A FIX.

in a breeze ♦ See under HANDS DOWN.

in absentia While not present, as in *He was tried and convicted in absentia*, or *He was awarded his degree in absentia*. This expression is Latin for "in absence"; its use in English dates from the late 1800s.

in a cold sweat Feeling nervous or terrified, as in *When I looked over the cliff, I broke out in a cold sweat*. This expression refers to perspiring accompanied by a feeling of cold, which can be induced by acute fear as well as by fever. [Late 1700s]

in addition 1. Also, as well as. For example, *They study their instruments and, in addition, theory and music history*. 2. **in addition to**. Over and above, besides, as in *In addition to a new muffler, the truck needs new brakes*. [c. 1900]

in a dither Also, **all of a dither; in a flutter** or **tizzy**. In a state of tremulous agitation, as in *Planning the wedding put her in a dither*, or *He tried to pull himself together, but he was all of a dither*, or *She showed up in such a flutter that our meeting was useless*. The noun *dither* dates from the early 1800s and goes back to the Middle English verb *didderen*, "to tremble"; *in a flutter* dates from the mid-1700s; *in a tizzy* dates from about 1930 and is of uncertain origin.

in advance 1. Beforehand, ahead of time. For example, *He insisted on being paid half his fee in advance*. 2. **in advance of**. In front of, as in *The point man moved in advance of the squad*. [Mid-1600s]

in a fix Also, **in a pickle** or **spot**. In a difficult or embarrassing situation, in a dilemma. For example, *I was really in a fix when I missed the plane*, or *Lost and out of gas—how did we get in such a pickle?* or *John had lost all his money in the crap game—now he was in a spot*. The first of these colloquial usages dates from the early 1800s; *pickle* in the sense of a mess or quandary, sometimes put as **in a pretty pickle**, dates from the 1500s; *spot*, also put as **in a bad spot** or **tough spot**, dates from the early 1900s. Also see IN A BIND; IN DEEP, def. 2; IN THE SOUP; IN TROUBLE; ON THE SPOT.

in a flash Also, **in a jiffy** or **second** or **trice**. Quickly, immediately. For example, *I'll be with you in a flash*, or *He said he'd be done in a jiffy*, or *I'll be off the phone in a second*, or *I felt a drop or two, and in a trice there was a downpour*. The first idiom alludes to a flash of lightning and dates from about 1800. The word *jiffy*, meaning "a short time," is of uncertain origin and dates from the late 1700s (as does the idiom using it); *a second*, literally one-sixtieth of a minute, has been used vaguely to mean "a very short time" since the

early 1800s; and *trice* originally meant "a single pull at something" and has been used figuratively since the 1500s.

in a flutter ♦ See IN A DITHER.

in a fog Also, **in a haze**. Preoccupied, not paying attention; also, at a loss, confused. For example, *After the accident he went about in a fog, even though he had not been injured*, or *Millie always seems to be in a haze; she never knows what's going on*. These expressions allude to fog or haze obscuring one's view; the *fog* usage dates from about 1600, *haze* from about 1800.

in a good light Under favorable circumstances, as in *They thought he'd make a wonderful mayor, but they'd only seen him in a good light*, or *The book portrayed their actions in a good light*. Both this expression and its antonym, **in a bad light**, transfer physical light in which something can (or cannot) be seen clearly to figurative use. The literal terms date from the early 1500s.

in a hole ♦ See IN A BIND.

in a huff In an offended manner, angrily, as in *When he left out her name, she stalked out in a huff*. This idiom transfers *huff* in the sense of a gust of wind to a burst of anger. [Late 1600s] Also see IN A SNIT.

in a jam ♦ See IN A BIND.

in a lather Also, **in a state**. Agitated and anxious, as in *Don't get yourself in a lather over this*, or *She was in a state over the flight cancellation*. The first term alludes to the frothy sweat of a horse, the second to an upset state of mind. [Early 1800s] For a synonym, see IN A STEW.

in all All together, considering everything, as in *There are four cars in all*, or *They won ten games and lost two, doing very well in all*. [Late 1300s] Also see ALL IN ALL.

in all one's born days Ever, as in *I've never seen so much snow, not in all my born days*. This folksy colloquial usage literally means "since I was born." [Mid-1700s]

in all probability Also, **in all likelihood**. Most likely, almost certainly. For example, *In all probability we'll be home for Christmas*. This expression was first recorded in 1617, the variant in 1664.

in a manner of speaking In a way; so to speak. For example, *He was, in a manner of speaking, asked to leave the group*. [Late 1800s]

in and of itself Intrinsically, considered alone. For example, *In and of itself the plan might work, but I doubt that it will be approved*. It is also put simply as **in itself**, as in *This account may be true in itself*. [First half of 1600s]

in a nutshell Concisely, in a few words, as in *Here's our proposal—in a nutshell, we want to sell the* *business to you.* This hyperbolic expression alludes to the Roman writer Pliny's description of Homer's *Iliad* being copied in so tiny a hand that it could fit in a nutshell. For a time it referred to anything compressed, but from the 1500s on it referred mainly to written or spoken words.

in any case Also, **at all events; in any event.** No matter what happens, certainly; also, whatever the fact is, anyway. For example, *In any case, I plan to go,* or *Call me tomorrow, at all events,* or *He may not be getting a raise, but in any event his boss thinks highly of him.* **In any case** dates from the second half of the 1800s, **at all events** from about 1700, and **in any event** from the 1900s. For an antonym, see IN NO CASE.

in a pig's eye Under no condition, not at all, as in *In a pig's eye he'll pay me back,* or *You think he's competent? In a pig's eye!* This expression, a euphemism for *in a pig's ass,* is generally used as a strong negative. [Slang; late 1800s]

in a pinch In an emergency, when hardpressed, as in *This music isn't what I would have chosen, but it will do in a pinch.* This term dates from the late 1400s, when it was put as *at a pinch* (a usage still current in Britain); *pinch* alludes to straitened circumstances.

in arms ♦ See BABE IN ARMS; UP IN ARMS.

in arrears Late or behind, especially in payment of money. For example, *He's been in arrears on his rent so often that he may be evicted.* [First half of 1600s]

in a rut In a settled or established habit or course of action, especially a boring one. For example, *We go to the seashore every summer—we're in a rut,* or *After ten years at the same job she says she's in a rut.* This expression alludes to having a wheel stuck in a groove in the road. [Early 1800s]

in a sense Also, **in some sense.** Sort of, in some ways but not others. For example, *In a sense our schools are the best in the state, but the test scores don't always show that,* or *In some sense I agree with you, but not entirely.* [Late 1500s] Also see IN A WAY.

inasmuch as Also, **insomuch as. 1.** Since, because of the fact that, as in *Inasmuch as I have to go anyhow, I'll pick up the book for you,* or *Insomuch as they are friends, we can seat them together.* The first usage dates from the late 1300s, the second from the late 1400s. **2.** Also, **insofar as.** To the extent or degree that, as in *You will become a good pianist only inasmuch as you keep practicing,* or *He's lost interest insomuch as he has stopped attending church altogether,* or *Insofar as this is a temporary measure, we can't complain.* [Late 1500s]

in a snit In a state of agitation or irritation, as in *He is in a snit over the guest list.* It is also put as **get in** or **into a snit,** as in *She tends to get in a snit every time*

things don't go her way. The origin of this expression is uncertain. [Colloquial; first half of 1900s]

in a state ♦ See under IN A LATHER.

in a stew Agitated, alarmed, or anxious. For example, *Mary was in a stew about how her cake was going to turn out.* It is also put as **get in** or **into a stew,** as in *Every Saturday the minister got in a stew about Sunday's sermon.* This expression transfers the mixture of meat and vegetables constituting a stew to overheated mixed emotions. [c. 1800]

in a tight corner Also, **in a tight spot.** ♦ See under IN A BIND.

in a tizzy ♦ See IN A DITHER.

in at the death Also, **in at the finish** or **kill.** Involved in or present at the end, especially a disastrous end but sometimes merely the climax of an important event. For example, *He had a hand in their breakup, but he didn't want to be in at the death,* or *They've done really well this year, and we want to be in at the kill.* These expressions originally alluded to hunters and hounds being present at the death of a fox they had run to ground. [First half of 1700s]

in a walk ♦ See under HANDS DOWN.

in a way To a certain extent, with reservations; also, in some respects. For example, *In a way I like the new styles,* or *You're right, in a way, but we have to consider the price.* [Mid-1800s]

in awe of, be Also, **stand in awe of.** Respect and revere someone or something, experience a feeling of solemn wonder, as in *All of us are in awe of his many achievements.* This expression dates from about A.D. 1000 and originally meant "fear something or someone." Later *awe* came to mean "dread mingled with respect," and eventually it signified reverence alone.

in a while Also, **after a while.** After a period of time, usually a moderately short time. For example, *Go ahead, I'll be along in a while,* or *After a while we turned off the television and went for a walk.* [c. 1300]

in a word ♦ See IN BRIEF.

in a world of one's own ♦ See IN ONE'S OWN WORLD.

in back of ♦ See BACK OF.

in bad ♦ See IN BAD WITH.

in bad faith With the intention of deceiving someone or doing harm, as in *I'm sure they were acting in bad faith and never planned to pay us.* This expression was first recorded in 1631. The antonym, **in good faith,** meaning "sincerely and honestly," as in *I signed that contract in good faith,* dates from about 1350.

in bad with, be Be disliked; be out of favor. For example, *She was afraid she would be in bad with* *her new supervisor.* [Colloquial; c. 1900] Also see IN GOOD WITH.

in behalf of Also, **on behalf of.** **1.** For someone else, as someone's agent or representative. For example, *In behalf of the board, I want to thank you for your help,* or *Joan was speaking on behalf of the entire staff.* [c. 1300] **2.** For someone's benefit or interest, as in *He was collecting the dues in my behalf.* [Late 1500s] Some authorities insist that *in behalf of* be used only to mean "for someone's benefit" and *on behalf of* only to mean "as someone's agent." In practice, however, the terms are so often used interchangeably that this distinction no longer has a basis.

in between In an intermediate situation, as in *My roommates disagreed and I was caught in between.* [Late 1500s]

in between times During an intervening period, as in *He has written several books, and in between times he teaches.*

in black and white ♦ See BLACK AND WHITE, def. 3.

in brief Also, **in short; in a word.** Concisely, in few words, to sum up. All three phrases usually precede or follow a summary statement, as in *In brief, we didn't get much out of his speech,* or *There was no agenda; in short, they could discuss whatever they wanted to,* or *The sun was shining, the sky was clear—in a word, it was a beautiful day.* The first expression dates from the early 1400s; **in short** dates from the 1300s but the present usage dates from the 1700s; the hyperbolic **in a word** (since there is nearly always more than one word) dates from the late 1500s.

in bulk **1.** Unpackaged, loose, as in *It's cheaper to buy rice in bulk.* [Late 1600s] **2.** In large amounts or volume, as in *The ship was carrying wheat in bulk.* [Mid-1700s]

in cahoots ♦ See IN LEAGUE WITH.

in care of Through someone, by way of someone, as in *I sent the gift in care of your parents.* This phrase indicates that something is to be delivered to someone at someone else's address. [Mid-1800s] Also see IN CHARGE, def. 3.

in case **1.** Also, **just in case.** If it should happen that. For example, *In case he doesn't show up, we have a backup speaker.* The variant also is used without a following clause to mean simply "as a precaution," as in *I took an umbrella just in case.* [c. 1400] **2.** **in case of; in the event of.** If there should happen to be. For example, *Here is a number to call in case of an emergency,* or *In the event of a power failure, we'll have to shift our plans.* Similarly, **in that case** means "if that should happen," as in *You're alone in the store? In that case I'll bring your lunch.* The first usage dates from the early 1700s,—the second (with *event*) from about

1600, and the third from the mid-1800s. Also see IN ANY CASE; IN NO CASE; IN THE CASE OF.

in cement Firmly settled or determined; unalterable. For example, *Their policy on taxes was set in cement despite opposition.* For a synonym, see CAST IN STONE.

inch ♦ In addition to the idioms beginning with INCH, also see BY INCHES; EVERY INCH; GIVE AN INCH; WITHIN AN ACE (INCH) OF.

inch along ♦ See under BY INCHES.

in character Consistent with someone's general personality or behavior. For example, *Her failure to answer the invitation was completely in character.* This usage dates from the mid-1700s, as does the antonym, **out of character,** as in *It was out of character for him to refuse the assignment.*

in charge **1.** In a position of leadership or supervision, as in *Who's in charge here?* or *He's the agent in charge at the ticket counter.* [Early 1500s] **2.** **in charge of.** Having control over or responsibility for, as in *You're in charge of making the salad.* [Late 1500s] **3.** **In the charge of; in the care of.** Under someone's care or supervision, as in *We left the children in the charge of their grandparents.* [Mid-1800s]

inch by inch ♦ See BY INCHES.

in check Restrained from moving or acting; under control. For example, *The first division held the enemy in check,* or *Mary kept her emotions in check.* This term replaced **at check** and **out of check,** which date from the mid-1500s.

in chorus All together, in unison, as in *The voters answered the legislators in chorus.* This expression transfers group singing to simultaneous utterance of any kind. [c. 1800]

in circles ♦ See GO AROUND IN CIRCLES.

in circulation Also, **into circulation.** In business or social life, especially after a period of absence. For example, *After a month in the hospital Bill was eager to get back in circulation.* The antonym is **out of circulation,** as in *Since we had twins we've been out of circulation, but we're hoping to get out more often soon.* These expressions, dating from the first half of the 1900s, employ *circulation* in the sense of "making the rounds among people," a usage dating from the 1600s.

inclined to Tending or disposed toward, as in *I'm inclined to give him the benefit of the doubt.* [Mid-1300s]

in clover Prosperous, living well. For example, *After we make our first million, we'll be in clover.* This expression alludes to cattle happily feeding on clover. Slightly different versions are **like pigs in clover** and **rolling in clover.** [c. 1700]

in cold blood In a purposely ruthless and unfeeling manner; as in *The whole family was murdered in cold blood.* This expression alludes to the notion that blood is the seat of emotion and is hot in passion and cold in calm. The term therefore means *not* "in the heat of passion," but "in a calculated, deliberate manner." [Late 1500s]

in cold storage In a state of abeyance or postponement. For example, *We can't consider these design changes now; let's put them in cold storage for a year or so.* This expression alludes to the literal storage of food, furs, or other objects in a refrigerated place. [Colloquial; late 1800s]

in commission ◆ See under OUT OF COMMISSION.

in common Shared characteristics, as in *One of the few things John and Mary have in common is a love of music.* [Mid-1600s] **2.** Held equally, in joint possession or use, as in *This land is held in common by all the neighbors.* [Late 1300s]

in concert Together, jointly, as in *They worked in concert on the script,* or *When mind is in concert with body, one can accomplish a great deal.* This expression uses *concert* in the sense of "an agreement of two or more persons." [Early 1700s]

in condition Also, **in good condition** or **shape; in shape.** Physically fit; also, in a state of readiness. For example, *I've got to get in condition before the next road race,* or *This project's in good shape now,* or *Is this report in shape to show to the president?* The first expression dates from the late 1700s; the use of *shape* for "a state of health or repair" dates from the mid-1800s. The antonyms of these expressions, **out of condition** and **out of shape,** date from the mid-1800s. For example, *Their stock was out of condition and not suitable for selling,* or *I'm so out of shape that I can barely run a mile.*

in confidence Also, **in strict confidence.** Privately, on condition that what is said will not be revealed. For example, *The doctor told her in confidence that her mother was terminally ill,* or *He told us in strict confidence that Gail was pregnant.* This idiom was first recorded in 1632. Also see TAKE INTO ONE'S CONFIDENCE.

in conscience Also, **in all good conscience.** In all truth or fairness, as in *I can't in conscience say that the meeting went well,* or *In all good conscience we can't support their stand on disarmament.* [Late 1500s]

in consequence As a result, therefore, as in *She was away for years and in consequence has few friends here.* The prepositional phrase **in consequence of** means "as a result of," as in *In consequence of this finding, there is sure to be further investigation.* [Late 1600s]

in consideration of **1.** In view of, on account of, as in *We turned back in consideration of the worsening weather.* [First half of 1500s] **2.** In return for, as in *She received an honorarium in consideration of her key contributions.* [c. 1600]

in creation ◆ See under ON EARTH.

incumbent on Also, **incumbent upon.** Imposed as an obligation or duty on, obligatory for. For example, *He felt it was incumbent on us all to help the homeless.* [Mid-1500s]

indeed ◆ See FRIEND IN NEED IS A FRIEND INDEED.

in deep **1.** Seriously involved; far advanced. For example, *He was in deep with the other merchants and couldn't strike out on his own,* or *She used her credit cards for everything, and before long she was in deep.* **2. in deep water.** Also, **in over one's head.** In trouble, with more difficulties than one can manage, as in *The business was in deep water after the president resigned,* or *I'm afraid Bill got in over his head.* These metaphoric expressions transfer the difficulties of being submerged to other problems. The first appears in Miles Coverdale's 1535 translation of the Book of Psalms (68:13): "I am come into deep waters." The second, which also can signify being involved with more than one can understand, dates from the 1600s. Also see OVER ONE'S HEAD.

in default of Through the failure, absence, or lack of, as in *In default of a better solution, we'll have to make do with this one.* This term was originally put as *for default of,* but John Gower had the current wording in *Confessio Amantis* (1397): "The fish, if it be dry, might in default of water die." [Late 1200s]

in defiance of In spite of, with outright disregard for, as in *They went on strike in defiance of union policy.* This term was first recorded in 1750.

in demand Sought after, as in *The general was in demand as an after-dinner speaker.* [Early 1800s]

in depth Profoundly, thoroughly, as in *It will take years to cover the entire subject in depth.* [Mid-1900s]

in detail With close attention to particulars; thoroughly. For example, *She explained her theory in detail.* It is also put as **go into detail,** meaning "to investigate thoroughly," as in *You know what I mean, so I needn't go into detail.* The first expression dates from about 1600, the second from the late 1800s.

Indian file ◆ See SINGLE FILE.

Indian giver One who takes or demands back one's gift to another, as in *Jimmy wanted to take back Dan's birthday present, but Mom said that would make him an Indian giver.* This term, now considered offensive, originally alluded to the Native American practice of expecting a gift in return for one that is given. [Colloquial; early 1800s]

Indian summer A period of mild, sunny weather occurring in late autumn, usually following a seasonable cold spell. For example, *We had two whole days of Indian summer this year, and then it turned cold again.* [Late 1700s]

in dispute Disagreed about, in controversy. For example, *This parcel of land is in dispute, claimed by several persons,* or *The origin of this phrase is in dispute.* [Mid-1600s]

in drag Wearing clothes normally worn by the opposite sex, as in *All of the actors in the revue were in drag.* This expression originally alluded to male actors wearing women's apparel on stage, especially for comic purposes, but also refers to crossdressing by homosexuals. [Colloquial; c. 1870]

in due course Also, **in due course of time; in due time; in time; all in good time.** After an appropriate interval, in a reasonable length of time. For example, *In due course we'll discuss the details of this arrangement,* or *In due time the defense will present new evidence,* or *You'll learn the program in time,* or *We'll come up with a solution, all in good time.* Chaucer used **in due time** in the late 1300s, and the other usages arose over the next few centuries. However, also see IN GOOD TIME for another meaning.

in Dutch In trouble or disfavor, as in *If I don't finish on time I'll really be in Dutch.* This expression may allude to the stern reprimands of a DUTCH UNCLE. [Slang; c. 1850]

In earnest 1. With purposeful or sincere intent, as in *We settled down to study in earnest.* [c. A.D. 1000] 2. Also, **in dead earnest.** Serious, determined, as in *We thought he was joking, but he was in earnest,* or *I'm in dead earnest about selling the business.* In the variant, from the late 1800s, *dead* means "completely" or "thoroughly" and is used purely for emphasis. [c. A.D. 1000]

in effect 1. For all practical purposes, as in *This testimony in effect contradicted her earlier statement.* [Late 1500s] 2. In or into operation, as in *This law will be in effect in January.* Related phrases include **go into effect** and **take effect,** which mean "become operative," as in *This law goes into effect January 1,* or *It takes effect January 1.* Similarly, **put into effect** means "make operative," as in *When will the judge's ruling be put into effect?* [Late 1700s] Also see IN FORCE, def. 2.

in effigy Symbolically. For example, *That umpire was completely unfair—let's burn him in effigy.* Now used only figuratively, this term formerly signified a way of carrying out the sentence of a criminal who had escaped, such as **burn in effigy** or **hang in effigy.** A dummy was made of the criminal or a detested political figure and subjected to the prescribed punishment. [c. 1600]

in escrow In trust with a third party for delivery after certain conditions are fulfilled. For example, *Our down payment on the house is in escrow until the current owner makes the promised repairs.* This legal term dates from the late 1800s.

in essence Basically, by nature, as in *He is in essence a very private person* or *In essence, they were asking the wrong question.* This term employs *essence* in the sense of "intrinsic nature," a usage dating from the mid-1600s.

in evidence 1. Also, **much in evidence.** Plainly visible, conspicuous, as in *The car's new dents were very much in evidence.* [Second half of 1800s] 2. As testimony in a court of law, as in *The attorney submitted the photograph in evidence.* [c. 1700]

in excess of Greater than, more than, as in *The book sold in excess of a million copies.* [Early 1600s]

in exchange Also, **in exchange for.** In return (for something or someone), as in *Jim lent Bill his motorcycle, and Bill offered his car in exchange,* or *At the party, the guests were given cookies in exchange for the ones they brought.* [Late 1500s]

in fact Also, **in point of fact.** In reality, in truth; actually. For example, *She was, in fact, eager to join the club,* or *In point of fact, his parents never had much influence on him.* The first term dates from about 1700, and the variant from about 1800.

in fashion Also, **in style.** ♦ See under GO OUT, def. 5.

in favor of Also, **in one's favor.** 1. In support of, approving, as in *We are in favor of her promotion,* or *All the reviews were in his favor.* [Mid-1500s] 2. To the advantage of, as in *The court decided in favor of the defendant.* [Mid-1500s] 3. Inscribed or made out to the benefit of, as in *The check was made out in favor of the charity.* [Mid-1500s] 4. Out of a preference for, as in *The commissioner turned down the new road in favor of improved sewers.* [Late 1800s]

in favor with Held in friendly regard by, as in *She's really in favor with the press.* This idiom uses *favor* in the sense of "approval." The same is true of the antonym, **out of favor with,** as in *He was out of favor with the board.* [Early 1500s] Also see IN FAVOR OF.

inference ♦ See DRAW AN INFERENCE.

in fine feather Also, **in good** or **high feather.** In excellent form, health, or humor. For example, *He was in fine feather, joking with all his visitors.* These expressions all allude to a bird's healthy plumage, a usage dating from the late 1500s and no longer very common.

influence ♦ See UNDER THE INFLUENCE.

in for 1. Guaranteed to get or have, as in *We're in for a difficult time.* [Late 1500s] 2. **in for it.** Certain to encounter trouble or punishment, as in

When Harry finds out we left early, we'll be in for it. [Late 1600s] **3.** Involved or entered for some purpose, as in *We're in for the profits.* [Mid-1800s] Also see HAVE IT IN FOR; IN FOR A PENNY.

in for a penny, in for a pound Once involved, one must not stop at half-measures. For example, *All right I'll drive you all the way there—in for a penny, in for a pound.* This term originally meant that if one owes a penny one might as well owe a pound, and came into American use without changing the British monetary unit to *dollar*. [Late 1600s] For a synonym, see HANGED FOR A SHEEP.

in force 1. In full strength, in large numbers, as in *Demonstrators were out in force.* This usage originally alluded to a large military force. [Early 1300s] **2.** Operative, binding, as in *This rule is no longer in force.* This usage originally alluded to the binding power of a law. [Late 1400s]

information ♦ See under GOLD MINE.

in front of 1. Facing someone or a group, as in *He was shy about speaking in front of a large audience.* [Early 1600s] **2.** In someone's presence, as in *Let's not fight in front of the children.* [Mid-1800s]

in full Completely, as in *His talk covered the subject in full,* or *The debt was repaid in full.* [Mid-1500s]

in full swing Also, **in full cry.** In full operation, at the highest level of activity. For example, *After the strike it would be some time before production was in full swing,* or *His supporters were out in full cry.* The first expression, dating from the mid-1800s, alludes to the vigorous movement of a swinging body. The second employs *full cry* in the sense of "vigorous pursuit," a usage dating from the late 1500s that may be dying out.

in general 1. Referring to a group of persons or a subject as a whole, as opposed to particular ones. For example, *I am speaking about contracts in general,* or *Girls in general mature at a younger age than boys.* [Late 1300s] For an antonym, see IN PARTICULAR. **2.** For the most part; commonly, usually. For example, *In general the children behaved very well,* or *Our winters are quite mild in general.* [Early 1700s]

in good condition Also, **in good shape.** ♦ See IN CONDITION.

in good faith ♦ See under IN BAD FAITH.

in good hands In competent or safe care. For example, *I know the children are in good hands when they visit my mother.* The term *good hand* has been used in the sense of "skill" or "ability" since the late 1300s.

in good part 1. take in good part. Accept good-naturedly or with good grace; without taking offense. For example, *She took her brother's teasing in*

good part. [Mid-1500s] **2.** Mostly, to a great extent, as in *Their failure is in good part the result of poor management.* Also see FOR THE MOST PART.

in good spirits Also, **in high spirits.** Happy, cheerful, as in *Jane was in good spirits today.* [Early 1700s] However, *high spirits* also can indicate liveliness and vivacity, as in *The children were in high spirits at the prospect of a trip to the circus.*

in good stead ♦ See STAND IN GOOD STEAD.

in good time 1. See IN DUE COURSE. **2.** In a short time, quickly; also, earlier than expected. For example, *We want to get home in good time for the broadcast,* or *They submitted the bids in good time.* [Late 1500s]

in good with, be Also, **be in with; get on someone's good side.** Be in someone's favor, be well liked by someone. For example, *He's in good with the higher-ups so we can expect approval of our application,* or *I'd love to be in with that popular crowd, but I don't quite know how,* or *I don't know how he got on her good side after that fight they had.* The first two terms date from the 1900s, the third from the late 1600s. Also see IN BAD WITH; IN FAVOR WITH; IN SOMEONE'S GOOD GRACES.

in half In two equal or roughly equal parts. For example, *Let's cut this sheet in half.* [Late 1500s]

in hand 1. Accessible at the present time, as in *The company has very little cash in hand.* [Late 1300s] **2.** Under one's control or authority, as in *The police had the situation well in hand.* [Early 1600s] **3.** In process, being settled, as in *He was willing to give full attention to the matter in hand.* [Late 1300s] Also see IN ONE'S HANDS.

in harness On duty or at work. For example, *Despite his illness he's determined to continue in harness.* It also is put as **be back in harness,** meaning "to return to duty or work," as in *After a long vacation she's finally back in harness.* This expression alludes to horses harnessed to perform work. [First half of 1800s] Also see DIE WITH ONE'S BOOTS ON (IN HARNESS).

in heat In a state of sexual excitement immediately preceding ovulation. For example, *Our cat's in heat so we have to keep her inside.* This expression applies to most female mammals and indicates the period when the animal is fertile and most receptive to mating. [Mid-1700s]

in high dudgeon Furiously, resentfully, as in *He stormed out in high dudgeon.* This term is the only surviving use of the word *dudgeon,* whose origin has been lost. [c. 1600]

in honor of In celebration of, as a mark of respect for, as in *We are holding a banquet in honor of the president.* [c. 1300]

in hopes of Also, **in hopes that; in the hope of** or that; **in high hopes of** or that. Expecting and wishing for, as in *We met in the hope of finding a vacancy,* or *They met in the hope of bringing about a peaceful settlement.* The phrases with *that* are used with clauses, as in *In hopes that something good might come of it, he began to work,* or *We are in high hopes that a cure for leukemia will be found soon.* [c. 1600]

initiative ♦ See ON ONE'S OWN ACCOUNT (INITIATIVE); TAKE THE INITIATIVE.

in itself ♦ See under IN AND OF ITSELF.

injury ♦ See ADD INSULT TO INJURY.

in keeping with Conforming to, in harmony with, as in *The new wing is in keeping with the house's original architecture,* or *His actions are not in keeping with his words.* This expression uses *keeping* in the sense of "harmony," as does its antonym, **out of keeping with,** as in *The funeral arrangements were out of keeping with the family's wishes.* [c. 1800] Also see IN KEY; IN LINE.

in key In harmony with other factors, in a matching style, as in *This furniture is perfectly in key with the overall design.* This term uses *key* in the musical sense, that is, "a scheme of notes related to one another." The antonym, **out of key,** means "not in harmony with other factors," or "unsuitable," as in *He is out of key with his time.* [c. 1900]

in kind 1. With produce or commodities rather than money. For example, *I edited Bob's book for payment in kind; he gave me voice lessons in exchange.* [c. 1600] 2. In the same manner or with an equivalent, as in *He returned the insult in kind.* [Early 1700s]

in large measure ♦ See under IN SOME MEASURE.

in league with Also, **in cahoots with.** In close cooperation or in partnership with, often secretly or in a conspiracy. For example, "For anybody on the road might be a robber, or in league with robbers" (Charles Dickens, *A Tale of Two Cities,* 1859), or *We suspect that the mayor is in cahoots with the construction industry.* The first term dates from the mid-1500s. The variant, a colloquialism dating from the early 1800s, may come from the French *cahute,* "a small hut or cabin," and may allude to the close quarters in such a dwelling.

in left field ♦ See OUT IN LEFT FIELD.

in lieu of ♦ See INSTEAD OF.

in light of Also, **in the light of; in view of.** In consideration of, in relationship to. For example, *In light of recent developments, we're postponing our meeting,* or *In the light of the weather forecast we've canceled the picnic,* or *He got a special bonus in view of all the extra work he had done.* The first

two of these terms date from the late 1600s, the third from about 1800.

in limbo 1. In a condition of oblivion or neglect, as in *They kept her application in limbo for months.* [Early 1600s] 2. An intermediate or transitional state, as in *After his editor left the firm, his book was in limbo.* [Early 1600s] Both usages allude to the theological meaning of *limbo,* that is, a place outside hell and heaven to which unbaptized infants and the righteous who died before Christ's coming were traditionally consigned.

in line 1. Also, **in line with.** In conformity or agreement; within ordinary or proper limits. For example, *The new policy was intended to keep prices in line with their competitors,* or *It's up to the supervisor to keep the nurses in line.* Also see FALL IN LINE. 2. Also, **on line.** Waiting behind others in a row or queue. For example, *The children stood in line for their lunches,* or *There were at least 50 persons on line for opera tickets.* 3. **in line for.** Next in order for, as in *He is next in line for the presidency.* All of these terms employ *line* in the sense of "an orderly row or series of persons or objects," a usage dating from the 1500s.

in love ♦ See FALL IN LOVE.

in luck Fortunate, enjoying success, as in *You're in luck—we found your car keys.* [Mid-1800s]

in memory of As a reminder of or memorial to. For example, *In memory of Grandma we put flowers on her grave every Easter,* or *In memory of our happy times here we've planted a little garden.* [First half of 1300s]

in mind ♦ See BEAR IN MIND; PUT ONE IN MIND OF.

in name only Also, **only in name.** Nominally, not actually. For example, *He's the chief executive in name only; his vice-president makes all the decisions,* or *Theirs was a marriage only in name; they lived on different continents.* [Late 1300s]

in no case Never, under no circumstances, as in *She should in no case be told that he has a terminal illness.* [First half of 1400s] For an antonym, see IN ANY CASE.

in nothing flat ♦ See under IN NO TIME.

in no time Also, **in no time at all; in less than no time; in nothing flat.** Almost instantly, immediately, as in *The train will be here in no time at all,* or *He'll be finished in less than no time,* or *I'll be there in nothing flat.* All these hyperbolic terms equate a very short time with "at once." [First half of 1800s]

in no uncertain terms Emphatically, definitely so. For example, *Jane told them in no uncertain terms that she wanted no part of their practical joke.* The double negative in this idiom serves for emphasis. [Mid-1900s] Also see IN SO MANY WORDS.

in on, be Also, **get in on.** Be or become a participant; be or become one of a group who have information. For example, *Is she in on our secret?* or *I'd like to get in on this venture.* [c. 1920] Also see BARGE IN ON; GROUND FLOOR (GET IN ON THE); IN GOOD WITH.

in one blow ♦ See AT ONE STROKE.

in one breath ♦ See IN THE SAME BREATH.

in one ear and out the other Quickly forgotten, as in *Their advice to her just went in one ear and out the other.* This expression, a proverb in John Heywood's 1546 collection, conjures up a graphic image of sound traveling through one's head. [Late 1300s]

in one fell swoop ♦ See ONE FELL SWOOP.

in one piece ♦ See ALL IN ONE PIECE.

in one's ♦ In addition to the idioms beginning with IN ONE'S, also see under IN SOMEONE'S; OUT OF ONE'S.

in one's behalf ♦ See IN BEHALF OF.

in one's blood Also, **in the blood.** Part of one's essential nature. For example, *The whole family loves music; it's in their blood,* or *Sailing somehow gets in your blood.* Also see RUN IN THE BLOOD.

in one's book According to one's opinion or way of thinking. For example, *In my book he's a wonderful father.* This expression alludes to a book containing a personal list of some kind. [Slang; mid-1900s] Also see BLACK BOOK.

in one's cups Drunk, as in *You can't believe anything he says when he's in his cups.* [Early 1600s]

in one's element In an environment naturally suited to or associated with one; doing what one enjoys. For example, *He's in his element when he's doing woodworking.* This term alludes to one's natural abode, as does the antonym, **out of one's element** (used by Daniel Defoe in *Robinson Crusoe,* 1719: "When they came to make boards . . . they were quite out of their element"). [Late 1500s] Also see IN ONE'S GLORY.

in one's eyes ♦ See IN ONE'S MIND'S EYE; IN THE EYES OF.

in one's favor ♦ See IN FAVOR OF.

in one's glory At one's best, happiest, or most gratified. For example, *She was in her glory playing her first big solo,* or *In the classroom, this teacher's in his glory.* [c. 1800] Also see IN ONE'S ELEMENT.

in one's hands Also, **in the hands of one.** In one's responsibility, charge, or care. For example, *The disposition of the property is in his hands,* or *Let's put this part of that project in Christine's hands.* [c. 1400] For the antonym, see OFF ONE'S HANDS. Also see IN THE HANDS OF; ON ONE'S HANDS; TAKE ONE'S LIFE (IN ONE'S HANDS); TAKE INTO ONE'S HANDS; TAKE THE LAW INTO ONE'S OWN HANDS.

in one's heart of hearts According to one's truest, innermost feelings, especially when secret. For example, *It's a wonderful job offer; but in my heart of hearts I don't want to leave this area.* [Late 1500s]

in one's interest Also, **in the interest of one; in one's own interest; in one's best interest.** For one's benefit or advantage, as in *It's obviously in their interest to increase profits,* or *Is this policy in the interest of the townspeople?* or *I suspect it's in your own best interest to quit now.* [Early 1700s]

in one's mind's eye In one's imagination or memory. For example, *I can just see the old farm in my mind's eye.* This term pairs *mind* and *eye* in the sense of "a mental view." [Early 1400s]

in one's name ♦ See IN THE NAME OF.

in one's own backyard In one's own domain, in a position very close to one. For example, *You didn't expect to find a first-class organist in your own backyard.* [Mid-1900s] Also see CLOSE TO HOME.

in one's own right Through one's own skills or qualifications, as in *He's a fine violinist in his own right,* or *She has a fortune in her own right.* This term originally alluded to a legal title or claim, as in *She was queen in her own right,* but has been used more loosely since about 1600.

in one's own world Also, **in one's own little world; in a world of one's own.** In deep thought or concentration. For example, *Luanne was really in her own world at the meeting this morning,* or *Like many mathematicians, Bill lives in his own little world,* or *Bob's in a world of his own when he's listening to music.* [Late 1500s]

in one's pocket 1. In one's power or possession, under one's influence. For example, *The defense lawyer had the jury in his pocket.* [Mid-1800s] 2. **in each other's pockets.** In very close proximity or mutual dependence, as in *Bert and Harry work in the same office, live in the same house, belong to the same clubs—they're constantly in each other's pockets.* [Mid-1900s]

in one's prime ♦ See PRIME OF LIFE.

in one's right mind In a healthy mental state; sane and rational. For example, *No one in his right mind would ski down this icy slope.* This expression is often used in a negative construction, as in the example. The positive sense appears in the New Testament (Mark 5:15), where a deranged man whom Jesus helped is now "sitting, and clothed, and in his right mind." The antonym **out of one's mind,** as in *You must be out of your mind to swim in that icy stream,* is from the same period. [c. 1600] Also see GO OUT OF ONE'S MIND.

in one's shell Also, **into one's shell.** In a quiet or withdrawn state. For example, *Jim is extremely shy; if you try to get him to talk he immediately goes* *into his shell.* This usage alludes to the shell as a protective covering and dates from about 1800, as does the antonym, **out of one's shell,** as in *Once Anne is out of her shell she's very articulate.* However, the same expression was also used from the 1500s on to denote being young and inexperienced, alluding to a baby bird that had not quite emerged from its shell.

in one stroke ♦ See AT ONE STROKE.

in one's tracks ♦ See DROP IN ONE'S TRACKS; FOLLOW IN ONE'S TRACKS; STOP COLD (DEAD IN ONE'S TRACKS).

in one's way 1. Also, **in one's own way.** According to one's personal manner. For example, *She's brusque but kind in her own way,* or *Both of them are generous in their way.* This phrase is often used to limit an expression of praise, as in the examples. [c. 1700] 2. Also, **put in one's way; put in the way of.** Before one, within reach or experience, as in *That venture put an unexpected sum of money in my way,* or *He promised to put her in the way of new business.* [Late 1500s] 3. **in someone's way** Also, **in the way.** In a position to obstruct, hinder, or interfere with someone or something. For example, *That truck is in our way,* or *You're standing in the way; please move to one side.* [c. 1500]

in orbit Thrilled, delighted, as in *Dean's in orbit over his son's success.* This expression alludes to the successful launching into orbit of a satellite or other spacecraft. [Slang; late 1900s]

in order 1. In proper sequence or arrangement, as in *The children lined up in order of size,* or *Are the letters all in order?* [c. 1400] 2. Suitable, correct, appropriate, as in *A few words on this subject are in order now.* [Mid-1800s] 3. See IN SHORT ORDER. 4. **in order that.** So that, to the end or purpose that, as in *In order that Bob can meet my husband, we've come early.* [Early 1700s] 5. **in order to.** For the purpose of, as a means to, as in *We'll have to hire more help in order to finish on time.* This usage always precedes a verb, such as *finish* in the example. [c. 1700]

in other words Putting it differently, usually more simply or explicitly. For example, *The weather was terrible, the plane took off several hours after the scheduled time, and then fog prevented their landing—in other words, they never got to the wedding at all.* [Mid-1800s]

in over one's head ♦ See under IN DEEP, def. 2.

in part Also, **in large** or **small part.** To some extent, not wholly, somewhat. For example, *We didn't get to Chicago, in part because we didn't have time,* or *Jerry was the one to blame, in large part because he was the one who hired the contractor,* or *The attorney himself was in small part responsible for this witness.* [Late 1300s]

in particular Especially; also, separately, individually, in detail. For example, *The chancellor talked about the curriculum, the core courses in particular,* or *The orchestra was outstanding, the strings in particular.* [c. 1500]

in passing Incidentally, by the way, as in "It may be remarked in passing" (Charlotte Brontë, *Shirley,* 1849). [Mid-1800s]

in perpetuity For all time, forever, as in *This land was given to the state in perpetuity.* [First half of 1400s]

in person Also, **in the flesh.** In one's physical presence, as in *He applied for the job in person,* or *I couldn't believe it, but there she was, in the flesh.* The first expression dates from the mid-1500s. The variant, from the 1300s, was long used to allude to the bodily resurrection of Jesus, but later acquired its looser meaning. Charles Dickens has it in *Our Mutual Friend* (1865): "The minutes passing on, and no Mrs. W. in the flesh appearing."

in phase Also, **in sync.** In a correlated or synchronized way; in accord, in harmony. For example, *If everyone were in phase we could step up the schedule,* or *John and Pat often say the same thing at the same time; their minds are perfectly in sync.* Both versions of this idiom refer to physical phenomena. The first, dating from the second half of the 1800s, alludes to being at the same stage in a series of movements. The second, a slangy abbreviation of *synchronization* dating from the mid-1900s, alludes to exact coincidence in the time or rate of movement. Also see IN STEP; PHASE IN; for the antonym, see OUT OF PHASE.

in place 1. In the appropriate or usual position or order. For example, *With everything in place, she started the slide show.* [Mid-1500s] Also see PUT SOMEONE IN HIS OR HER PLACE. 2. In the same spot, without advancing or retreating, as in *While marching in place, the band played six more numbers.*

in place of ♦ See IN SOMEONE'S SHOES; INSTEAD OF.

in plain English In clear, straightforward language, as in *The doctor's diagnosis was too technical; please tell us what he meant in plain English.* [c. 1500] Also see IN SO MANY WORDS.

in play 1. In action or operation. For example, *A number of conflicting forces were in play, so the outcome was uncertain.* It is also put as **bring into play,** meaning "to put into action," as in *The surprise witness brought new evidence into play.* [Mid-1600s] 2. In sports, in a position to be legally or feasibly played, as in *The ball is now in play.* [Late 1700s] 3. In business, in a position for a possible corporate takeover, as in *After a news item said the* *company was in play, the price of its stock began to rise.* [Colloquial; second half of 1900s]

in pocket Having funds; also, having a particular amount of extra funds that constitute a profit. For example, *Tom's in pocket this week so let him treat us all,* or *After a day at the races she was a hundred dollars in pocket.* [Mid-1700s] Also see IN ONE'S POCKET.

in point 1. Relevant or pertinent, as in *That is a case in point.* [Mid-1600s] 2. **in point of.** With reference to, in the matter of, as in *In point of the law, he is obviously wrong.* [c. 1600] 3. **in point of fact.** See under IN FACT.

in practice 1. Actually, in fact, especially as opposed to theoretically or IN PRINCIPLE. For example, *In practice this contraption seems to work, although no one knows how or why.* [Second half of 1500s] Also see PUT INTO PRACTICE. 2. In the exercise of a particular profession, as in *She's an obstetrician and has been in practice for at least ten years.* [c. 1700] 3. In a state of being exercised so as to maintain one's skill, as in *This trumpeter is always in practice.* [Early 1600s] For an antonym, see OUT OF PRACTICE.

in principle Fundamentally, in general, but not necessarily in all particulars. For example, *The diplomats accepted the idea in principle but would rely on experts to work out all the details.* [Early 1800s]

in print 1. In printed or published form, as in *You can find this information in print.* This usage dates from the late 1400s, almost from the time of the first printing press. 2. Offered for sale by a publisher, as in *The library has a list of all the books in print.* The antonym for this usage is **out of print**, describing material no longer offered for sale by a publisher, as in *Most of his books are out of print.* [Late 1800s]

in private Not in public; secretly, confidentially. For example, *The hearings will be conducted in private,* or *May I speak to you in private?* [Late 1500s] For an antonym, see IN PUBLIC.

in progress Going on, under way, happening, as in *She's got another book in progress,* or *The game was already in progress when I tuned in.* [c. 1600]

in proportion ◆ See OUT OF PROPORTION.

in public Openly, open to public view or access. For example, *They've never appeared together in public.* [c. 1450] For an antonym, see IN PRIVATE.

in question Under consideration, referring to the subject being discussed, as in *No new facts have been discovered about the period in question.* Shakespeare used this idiom in *Cymbeline* (1:1): "His father … had, besides the gentleman in question, two other sons." [c. 1600] Also see CALL IN QUESTION.

in quest of ◆ See IN SEARCH OF.

inquire after Ask about the health or condition of someone or something. For example, *She was inquiring after you in particular.* [c. 1600]

in reach Also, **within reach**. Within one's means or powers or understanding. For example, *The legatees were extremely greedy, taking whatever of their aunt's came within reach,* or *Don't price this item too high; it should be in reach of the average customer.* This expression dates from the mid-1500s, as do the antonyms **out of reach** and **beyond reach**, meaning "unattainable"; for example, *This plan is out of reach for most subscribers,* or *His explanation is beyond my reach.*

in reality Actually, in fact, as in *He may seem slow to you, but in reality he's very intelligent.* [Second half of 1600s]

in reason Also, **within reason**. Inside the bounds of good sense, justification, or practicality. For example, *We need to keep our prices in reason,* or *He promised to do what he can to help us, within reason.* [Late 1500s]

in reference to ◆ See IN REGARD TO.

in regard to Also, **as regards; in** or **with reference to; with regard to; in** or **with respect to**. Concerning, about. For example, *In regard to your letter, forget it,* or *As regards your subscription, I'm not sure why it was canceled,* or *In reference to your inquiry, we'll have to pass it on to the board,* or *We have a few questions with regard to your recent offer,* or *With respect to your latest request, we'll be happy to oblige.* The word *reference* has been used in this idiom since the late 1500s, *regard* from the second half of the 1400s, and *respect* from the first half of the 1500s. Also see RELATIVE TO.

in relation to ◆ See RELATIVE TO.

in reserve Kept back, set aside, or saved. For example, *We have a fair amount of cash in reserve,* or *The coach decided to keep the best player in reserve until the last quarter.* [Late 1600s]

in residence Committed to live and work in a certain place, often for a specific length of time. For example, *He loved being the college's poet in residence.* This expression, dating from the 1300s, originally referred to ecclesiastical clerics whose presence was required in a specific church. It was extended to other appointments in the mid-1800s.

in respect to Also, **with respect to**. ◆ See IN REGARD TO.

in retrospect Looking backward, reflecting on the past. For example, *In retrospect, he regarded his move as the best thing he'd ever done.* This idiom employs *retrospect* in the sense of "a view of the past." [Second half of 1600s]

in return Also, **in return for.** In repayment or reciprocation for something, as in *I did her many favors and got nothing in return*, or *In return for your patience, I promise to do a really good job.* [c. 1600]

inroads ♦ See MAKE INROADS INTO.

in round numbers Also, **in round figures.** As an approximate estimate. For example, *How much will the new highway cost, in round numbers?* or *In round figures a diamond of this quality is worth five thousand dollars, but it depends on the market at the time of selling.* This idiom, which uses *round* in the sense of "whole" or "rounded off," is sometimes used very loosely, as Thomas Hardy did in *Far from the Madding Crowd* (1874): "Well, ma'am, in round numbers, she's run away with the soldiers." [Mid-1600s] Also see BALLPARK FIGURE.

ins and outs 1. The intricate details of a situation or process. For example, *It takes a newcomer some time to learn the ins and outs of the legislative process*, or *David really knows the ins and outs of how this engine works.* This usage alludes to the tortuous windings and turnings of a road or path. [Second half of 1600s] 2. Those with position and influence and those without, especially those in office versus those who are not, as in "Juan stood well both with Ins and Outs" (Byron, *Don Juan*, 1823). [Mid-1700s]

in search of Also, **in quest of.** Looking for, seeking, as in *They went to California in search of gold*, or *I went to the library in quest of a quiet place to read.* The first term dates from the mid-1400s, the second from the second half of the 1500s.

in season 1. At the right time, opportunely, as in "The two young men desired to get back again in good season" (Charles Dickens, *Martin Chuzzlewit*, 1844). 2. Available and ready for eating, or other use; also, legal for hunting or fishing. For example, *Strawberries are now in season*, or *Let me know when trout are in season and I'll go fishing with you.* Both usages date from the 1300s, as does the antonym **out of season**, used for "inopportunely," "unavailable," and also for "not in fashion." For example, *Sorry, oysters are out of season this month*, or *This style used to be very popular, but it's been out of season for several years.*

in secret Unknown to others, privately. For example, *They met in secret*, or, as Shakespeare put it in *Love's Labour's Lost* (5:2): "One word in secret." [Second half of 1400s]

in seventh heaven In a state of bliss, as in *John was in seventh heaven when the director praised his speech.* Used figuratively since the early 1800s, this term alludes to the dwelling place of God in highest of the seven concentric spheres that surround the earth in the system recognized by both Muslims and ancient Jews.

in shape ♦ See IN CONDITION.

in short ♦ See IN BRIEF.

in short order Quickly, without delay, as in *The children got ready in short order to go to the mall.* [First half of 1800s]

in short supply Less than is needed, lacking. For example, *Skilled operators were in short supply*, or *The hotels are all full, and beds are in short supply.* [First half of 1900s]

inside ♦ In addition to the idioms beginning with INSIDE, also see ON THE INSIDE; STEP IN (INSIDE).

inside of Within, in less than the whole of, referring especially to a period of time. For example, *They promised to return it inside of a month.* Although some authorities believe *inside* alone conveys the same meaning, the full term is widely used. [Early 1800s]

inside out 1. With the inner surface turned out or revealed, as in *He wore his shirt inside out.* This expression dates from about 1600 and was soon used figuratively, as in *He turned the verses inside out and revealed their hidden sense.* 2. Extremely well, thoroughly, especially alluding to knowing something. For example, *He knows this system inside out.* [First half of 1900s]

inside track, the A position of special advantage, as in *His relationship with Walter put him on the inside track with the company.* This metaphoric expression, which alludes to the inner, shorter track of a race course, has been used figuratively since the mid-1800s.

in sight 1. Within one's range of vision, as in *The sailboat was still in sight on the horizon.* [c. 1200] 2. Also, **in one's sight** or **sights.** Before one's eyes; also, within one's awareness. For example, *In the world's sight he was at fault*, or *Harold had that promotion firmly in his sights.* [c. 1200]

in single file ♦ See SINGLE FILE.

insofar as ♦ See INASMUCH AS, def. 2.

in so many words In those precise words; also, plainly, directly. For example, *He didn't tell me in so many words, but I understood that he planned to apply*, or, as Charles Dickens put it in *Sketches by "Boz"* (1836): "That the Lord Mayor had threatened in so many words to pull down the London Bridge." [Late 1600s]

in some measure Somewhat, to a certain extent, as in *In some measure we owe these privileges to our parents.* Shakespeare used this term in *A Midsummer Night's Dream* (1:2): "I will condole in some measure." Similarly, **in large measure**, dating from the same period, means "to a considerable extent," as in *In large measure the two sides agree.* [c. 1600]

in someone's ◆ In addition to the idioms beginning with IN SOMEONE'S, also see under IN ONE'S.

in someone's bad graces Also, **in someone's bad books.** Out of favor with someone. For example, *Harry's tardiness put him in the teacher's bad graces,* or *Making fun of the director is bound to get you in his bad books.* The use of *grace* in the sense of "favor" dates from the 1400s; the use of *books* dates from the early 1800s. Also see BLACK BOOK, def. 1; IN SOMEONE'S GOOD GRACES.

in someone's face 1. In front of or against someone directly, as in *He slammed the door in her face.* [First half of 1400s] Also see IN THE FACE OF. 2. Also, **get in someone's face.** Annoy or pester someone. For example, *He's always getting in my face when I'm trying to meet a deadline.* Closely related is the imperative, **get out of my face,** meaning "stop annoying me," as in *Get out of my face before I punch you!* [Slang; 1920s] Also see IN YOUR FACE; THROW IN SOMEONE'S FACE.

in someone's good graces Also, **in someone's good books; in the good graces of.** In someone's favor or good opinion, as in *Ruth is back in her mother's good graces,* or *Bill is anxious to get in the boss's good books,* or *She was always in the good graces of whoever happened to be in charge.* The use of *good grace* dates from the 1400s, *grace* alluding to the condition of being favored; *good books* dates from the early 1800s. One antonym is **out of someone's good graces,** as in *Walking out on his speech got him out of the professor's good graces.* Another is IN SOMEONE'S BAD GRACES.

in someone's hair Annoying or bothering someone. For example, *She was constantly in my hair, overseeing everything I did,* or *Dad was working on taxes, and the children were getting in his hair.* This expression alludes to entangling one's hair. [Mid-1800s] The antonym, **out of someone's hair,** is often used as an imperative, as in *Get out of my hair!* [c. 1900]

in someone's shoes Also, **in someone else's shoes; in someone's place** or **stead.** Acting for another person or experiencing something as another person might; in another's position or situation. For example, *If you were in my shoes, would you ask the new secretary for a date?* or *In your shoes I wouldn't accept the offer,* or *Can you go to the theater in my place?* or *He was speaking in her stead.* The idioms alluding to *shoes,* with their image of stepping into someone's shoes, date from about 1700 and are generally used in a conditional clause beginning with *if. Stead,* dating from the 1300s, and *place,* from the 1500s, are used more loosely. Also see FILL SOMEONE'S SHOES; PUT SOMEONE IN HIS OR HER PLACE; TAKE SOMEONE'S PLACE.

in someone's stead ◆ See IN SOMEONE'S SHOES; INSTEAD OF.

insomuch as ◆ See INASMUCH AS.

in spades Considerably, in the extreme; also, without restraint. For example, *They were having money problems, in spades,* or *Jan told him what he really thought of him, in spades.* This expression alludes to spades as the highest-ranking suit in various card games, such as bridge, and transfers "highest" to other extremes. [Colloquial; 1920s]

in specie 1. In coin, as in *The balance was to be paid only in specie.* [First half of 1600s] 2. In a similar manner, in kind, as in *They repaid the offense in specie.* [Mid-1500s] Both usages are derived from the Latin *in specie,* meaning "in the actual form."

in spite of Regardless of, in defiance of, as in *They kept on in spite of their fears.* [c. 1400]

instance ◆ See under FOR EXAMPLE.

in state With pomp and ceremony, as in *The foreign leaders were dining in state at the White House.* This expression, dating from the late 1600s, also appears in **lie in state,** said of a dead body ceremoniously exposed to public view before being interred. This latter usage, dating from about 1700, is generally confined to important public figures, as in *His Majesty lay in state in the palace.*

instead of Also, **in lieu of; in place of; in someone's stead.** In substitution for, rather than. For example, *She wore a dress instead of slacks,* or *They had a soprano in lieu of a tenor,* or *In place of soft drinks they served fruit juice,* or *The chairman spoke in her stead.* **Instead of** dates from about 1200; **in lieu of,** which borrows *lieu,* meaning "place," from French, dates from the late 1200s; **in place of** dates from the 1500s; and **in someone's stead** from the 1200s. Also see under IN SOMEONE'S SHOES.

in step 1. Moving to a rhythm or conforming to the movements of others, as in *The kids marched in step to the music.* [Late 1800s] 2. **in step with.** In conformity or harmony with, as in *He was in step with the times.* The antonym to both usages is **out of step,** as in *They're out of step with the music,* or *His views are out of step with the board's.* [Late 1800s] Also see IN PHASE; OUT OF PHASE.

in stitches Laughing uncontrollably, as in *Joke after joke had me in stitches.* Although the precise idiom dates only from about 1930, Shakespeare had a similar expression in *Twelfth Night* (3:2): "If you desire the spleen, and will laugh yourselves into stitches, follow me." *Stitches* here refers to the sharp local pain (known as **a stitch in the side**) that can make one double over, much as a fit of laughter can.

in stock Available for sale or use, on hand, as in *We have several dozen tires in stock.* The antonym, **out of stock,** means "not available for sale," usually only temporarily. For example, *This item is out of stock now, but we expect a new order next week.* [Early 1600s]

in store 1. In readiness, in preparation for future use, as in *I'm keeping several videos in store for your visit.* Edmund Spenser used this idiom in *The Faerie Queene* (1590): "Then for her son . . . In her own hand the crown she kept in store." [1300s] 2. **in store for.** Forthcoming for, awaiting, as in *There's trouble in store for you.* [Mid-1600s]

In stride ▪ See TAKE IN STRIDE.

in style ▪ See under GO OUT, def. 5.

in substance 1. In reality, essentially, as in *The Archbishop of Salzburg was in substance a temporal authority as well.* [Late 1300s] 2. In essence, basically, as in *I don't remember all the details, but in substance this was the plan.* [Late 1400s]

insult ▪ See ADD INSULT TO INJURY.

Intent ▪ See TO ALL INTENTS AND PURPOSES.

interest ▪ See IN ONE'S INTEREST; TAKE AN INTEREST; VESTED INTEREST; WITH INTEREST.

interim ▪ See IN THE INTERIM.

in terms of 1. As measured or indicated by, on the basis of. For example, *How far is it in terms of miles?* This usage originated in mathematics, where it alludes to numerical units. [Mid-1700s] 2. In relation to, with reference to, as in *This film offers nothing in terms of satisfactory entertainment.* [Late 1800s]

in that For the reason that, because, as in *In that you will be busy for the next few weeks, let's go over your paper now.* [Mid-1400s]

in that case ▪ See IN CASE, def. 2.

in the act 1. In the process of doing something. For example, *The police caught the robber in the act,* or *I was in the act of closing the window.* [Second half of 1600s] 2. Performing sexual intercourse, as in *Her father caught them in the act.* [Late 1500s]

in the aggregate Considered as a whole, as in *Our profits in the aggregate have been slightly higher.* [Late 1700s]

in the air ▪ In addition to the following idiom, also see CASTLES IN THE AIR; LEAVE HANGING (IN THE AIR); NOSE IN THE AIR; UP IN THE AIR.

in the air 1. In circulation, in people's thoughts. For example, *There's a rumor in the air that they're closing,* or *Christmas is in the air.* [Second half of 1800s] Also see IN THE WIND. 2. See UP IN THE AIR. [Mid-1700s]

in the altogether Also, **in** or **stripped to the buff; in the raw.** Naked, nude, as in *The art class wanted a model to pose in the altogether,* or *She was stripped to the buff when the doorbell rang,* or *He always sleeps in the raw.* The first of these colloquial terms dates from the late 1800s. **In the buff,** a seemingly modern locution dates from the 1600s, *buff* alluding to a soft, undyed leather, *buffskin,* that also gave its name to the color. The use of *raw,* presumably also alluding to raw (undressed) leather, dates from the early 1900s.

in the back ▪ See EYES IN THE BACK OF ONE'S HEAD; STAB IN THE BACK.

in the bag Assured of success, virtually accomplished or won. For example, *The coach thought the trophy was in the bag,* or *Our new contract is in the bag.* The precise allusion in this idiom is unknown. One writer believes it refers to a completed transaction, that is, an item bought and wrapped in a bag. However, it may well refer to the game bag in which hunters place small game such as birds. [c. 1920] Also see under WRAP UP.

in the balance ▪ See HANG IN THE BALANCE.

in the ballpark Also, **out of the ballpark.** ▪ See under BALLPARK FIGURE.

in the bargain ▪ See INTO THE BARGAIN.

in the black ▪ See under IN THE RED.

in the blood ▪ See IN ONE'S BLOOD.

in the bud ▪ See NIP IN THE BUD.

in the buff ▪ See IN THE ALTOGETHER.

in the can 1. In the lavatory, as in *He can't come to the phone; he's in the can.* The related **on the can** means "sitting on the toilet." The noun *can* is used for both the room and the toilet. [Slang; c. 1900] 2. Completed, as in *About a hundred pages of her next book are in the can.* This usage originated in filmmaking to describe a completed motion picture, when film was literally put into a can or canister. [Slang; c. 1930] 3. As an out-of-the-money finisher in a horse race, where a horse comes in fourth or worse. For example, *He had no luck that day—every bet ended up in the can.* [1960s]

in the cards Likely or certain to happen, as in *I don't think Jim will win—it's just not in the cards.* This term, originally put as **on the cards,** alludes to the cards used in fortunetelling. [Early 1800s]

in the care of ▪ See IN CHARGE, def. 3.

in the case of ▪ Regarding, in the matter of, in that instance. For example, *In the case of James, they decided to promote him to the next grade.* [Late 1300s] Also see IN CASE, def. 2.

in the chips ▪ See IN THE MONEY.

in the circumstances ▪ See UNDER THE CIRCUMSTANCES.

in the clear 1. Free from danger or suspicion of wrongdoing, as in *The evidence showed that the suspect was actually in the clear.* [1920s] 2. Having enough money to make a profit, as in *When they added up the box-office returns, they found they were several thousand dollars in the clear.* [Slang; 1920s]

in the clouds ♦ See HEAD IN THE CLOUDS.

in the cold light of day Dispassionately, unemotionally, especially at a later time. For example, *They had a terrible fight about the mixup, but in the cold light of day they realized they were both at fault.* This expression transfers the illumination of daylight to rational understanding and uses *cold* to emphasize the lack of passion.

in the course of Also, **during the course of.** In the process or progress of, as in the famous phrase from the *Declaration of Independence* (1776), "When in the course of human events, it becomes necessary for one people to dissolve the political bands . . ." These phrases have been criticized as needlessly wordy (*in* or *during* alone are adequate), but they have an emphatic rhythm that keeps them alive. [Mid-1600s]

in the dark 1. In secret, in concealment, as in *This agreement was concluded in the dark.* [Early 1600s] 2. In a state of ignorance, uninformed, as in *I was in the dark about their plans.* This metaphor often appears in the locution **keep someone in the dark,** meaning "deliberately keep someone uninformed," as in *They kept me in the dark about their plans.* [Late 1600s] For an antonym, see IN THE KNOW.

in the dock On trial, especially in a criminal case. For example, *The accused stood in the dock through the entire proceeding.* This expression employs *dock* in the sense of "an enclosed place for the defendant in a court of law," a usage dating from the late 1500s, and is used even in American courts where no such enclosure exists.

in the doghouse In disfavor, in trouble, as in *Jane knew that forgetting the check would put her in the doghouse.* This expression alludes to relegating a dog that misbehaves to its outdoor kennel. [c. 1900]

in the doldrums Depressed; dull and listless. For example, *Dean's in the doldrums for most of every winter.* This expression alludes to the maritime doldrums, a belt of calms and light winds north of the equator in which sailing ships were often becalmed. [Early 1800s] Also see DOWN IN THE DUMPS.

in the driver's seat Also, **in the saddle.** In control, in a position of authority. For example, *With the boss on vacation, Mr. Burns was in the driver's seat and enjoying it,* or *She waited until after the elec-*

tion, knowing that she'd be in the saddle then. The first expression dates from the 1800s, the second from the early 1600s. Also see AT THE HELM.

in the dumps ♦ See DOWN IN THE DUMPS.

in the dust, leave someone Leave one far behind, as in a race or competition. For example, *This marketing strategy will leave the others in the dust.* This metaphoric colloquialism alludes to the dust raised by a fast-moving horse or vehicle.

in the end Eventually, ultimately, as in *All will turn out well in the end.* [Mid-1500s]

in the event of Also, **in the event that.** ♦ See under IN CASE, def. 2.

in the eye ♦ In addition to the idiom beginning with IN THE EYE, also see IN ONE'S MIND'S EYE; IN THE PUBLIC EYE; LOOK ONE IN THE FACE (EYE).

in the eye of 1. In the center or focal point of something, as in *They were right in the eye of this controversy.* This term employs *eye* in the sense of "a central spot," a usage dating from the mid-1700s. 2. **in the eyes of.** In the view or opinion of, from the standpoint of. For example, *In the eyes of his fans Elvis could do no wrong,* or *In the eyes of the law he was a fugitive.* The *eyes* here allude to their function, seeing. [Late 1500s]

in the face ♦ In addition to the idiom beginning with IN THE FACE, also see BLUE IN THE FACE; FLY IN THE FACE; LOOK ONE IN THE FACE; RED IN THE FACE; SLAP IN THE FACE; STARE IN THE FACE; TALK SOMEONE'S ARM OFF (UNTIL BLUE IN THE FACE).

in the face of 1. Despite the opposition of, notwithstanding, as in *In the face of published statistics, they insist there is no flu epidemic.* [Early 1800s] Also see FLY IN THE FACE OF. 2. When confronted with, as in *It is hard for brokers to be cheerful in the face of a falling stock market.* [Late 1800s]

in the family way Pregnant, as in *Mary's in the family way again.* This euphemistic expression dates from the late 1700s and may be dying out.

in the final analysis Also, **in the last analysis.** When all things are considered. For example, *In the final analysis we must find ways to improve our sales,* or *I can, in the last analysis, talk only about my own work.* This expression was at first put as *in the ultimate analysis.* [Late 1700s]

in the first place 1. From the beginning, at the outset, before anything else. For example, *Why didn't you tell me in the first place that you've decided to leave?* or *He could have bought a new one in the first place.* 2. As the first of several items in order of importance. This phrase is usually accompanied by **in the second place, third place,** and so on, as in *I'm not joining the health club because, in the first place, I don't like their hours, and in the* *second place, I can't afford the dues.* [First half of 1600s] Also see FOR ONE.

in the flesh ♦ See IN PERSON.

in the flush of Also, **in the first** or **full flush of.** During a sudden rush of a strong positive feeling regarding something, as in *In the first flush of victory he decided to take all his friends to dinner.* This expression employs *flush* in the sense of "a bout of emotion or passion." [c. 1600]

in the fullness of time Within the appropriate or destined time, as in *We'll know if it's a boy or a girl in the fullness of time.* This expression employs *fullness* in the sense of "a complete or ample measure or degree." [Early 1600s]

in the groove Performing very well, excellent; also, in fashion, up-to-date. For example, *The band was slowly getting in the groove,* or *To be in the groove this year you'll have to get a fake fur coat.* This idiom originally alluded to running accurately in a channel, or groove. It was taken up by jazz musicians in the 1920s and later began to be used more loosely. A variant, **back in the groove,** means "returning to one's old self," as in *He was very ill but now he's back in the groove.* [Slang; mid-1800s]

in the gutter Appropriate to or from a squalid, degraded condition. For example, *The language in that book belongs in the gutter:* An antonym, **out of the gutter,** means "away from vulgarity or sordidness," as in *That joke was quite innocent; get your mind out of the gutter.* This idiom uses *gutter* in the sense of "a conduit for filthy waste." [Mid-1800s]

in the hands of In the possession of; in the custody or under the authority of. For example, *In the hands of the decorator the hall was completely transformed.* [Late 1200s] Also see IN HAND; IN ONE'S HANDS.

in the heat of In the most intense or active stage of some activity or condition. For example, *One never knows how soldiers will behave in the heat of battle,* or *In the heat of the moment she accepted his proposal,* or *In the heat of the negotiations he forgot to call his wife.* [Late 1500s]

in the hole 1. In debt; in trouble, especially financial trouble. For example, *Joan is too extravagant; she's always in the hole,* or *Buying all these Christmas presents will put us in the hole for the next few months.* [Colloquial; early 1800s] Also see IN A BIND. 2. In trouble in a competitive sport. For example, *At three balls and no strikes, the pitcher's in the hole,* or *The batter's got two strikes on him; he's in the hole.* [Slang; late 1800s] 3. In a card game, scoring lower than zero. For example, *Only one hand's been dealt and I'm already three points in the hole.* This expression alludes to the practice of circling a minus score in the old game of euchre.

The antonym for all three usages is **out of the hole,** as in *It took careful financial management to get Kevin out of the hole,* or *An experienced pitcher often can manage to get out of the hole.* Also see ACE IN THE HOLE.

in the hope ♦ See under IN HOPES OF.

in the hot seat ♦ See HOT SEAT.

in the interest of ♦ See IN ONE'S INTEREST.

in the interim In the meantime, as in *Arthur's in Israel, so in the interim Judy will handle their business.* [Second half of 1500s]

in the know Privy to special or secret information, as in *Not too many people are in the know about this project.* [Late 1800s]

in the lap of luxury ♦ See LAP OF LUXURY.

in the least Also, **in the slightest.** At all, in the smallest degree. These terms are nearly always used in a negative context. For example, *I don't care in the least what you do with the money,* or *It doesn't matter in the slightest whether or not you attend.* [c. 1600] They may also be put as **not in the least** or **not in the slightest,** as in *I am not in the least worried about the outcome,* or *The heat doesn't bother me in the slightest.* **In the least** dates from about 1600; **in the slightest** has been used in the sense of "emphatically unimportant or trifling" since the late 1500s.

in the limelight Also, **in the spotlight.** At the center of public attention or notoriety. For example, *John loves being in the limelight,* or *The reporters made sure the attractive new actress would be in the spotlight.* Both terms come from the theater and allude to focusing light on an important person, the first from a lighting device used from about 1840 on, the second from the early 1900s. Also see IN THE PUBLIC EYE; STEAL THE SHOW.

in the long run Over a lengthy period of time, in the end. For example, *He realized that in the long run, their argument wouldn't seem so awful.* This expression, which originated as *at the long run* in the early 1600s, presumably alludes to a runner who continues on his course to the end. Economist John Maynard Keynes used it in a much-quoted quip about economic planning: "In the long run we are all dead." The antonym, **in the short run,** meaning "over a short period of time," dates only from the 1800s. The novelist George Eliot used both in a letter (October 18, 1879): "Mrs. Healy's marriage is surely what you expected in the long or short run."

in the loop Provided with information and included in a decision-making process. For example, *She's new to the board, but be sure to keep her in the loop.* This expression uses *loop* in the sense of "a circle of individuals among whom information or responsibility circulates." The antonym out of the loop, meaning "left out of such a circle," dates from the same period. For example, *The chairman was consistently leaving Chris out of the loop.* [1970s]

in the lurch ♦ See LEAVE SOMEONE IN THE LURCH.

in the main For the most part, chiefly, as in *It was an excellent conference in the main.* [First half of 1600s]

in the making In the process of developing or growing, being made, as in *The editor believed this election signified history in the making.* This term is frequently used to describe the course of events, as in the example. [Mid-1600s]

in the market for Wanting to possess, eager to have, seeking. For example, *The crowd was in the market for more entertainment,* or *I'm sure he's in the market for another fast car.* [Early 1900s]

in the middle of 1. Also, in the midst of. During, while engaged in, as in *He stopped him in the middle of his speech,* or *I'm in the midst of calculating my income tax.* The first expression dates from about 1600, the second from about 1500. Also see IN THE MIDST. 2. in the middle of nowhere. In a very remote location, as in *We found a great little hotel, out in the middle of nowhere.* [Early 1900s]

in the midst 1. Also, in one's midst. Surrounded by, among, as in *I saw a familiar face in the midst of the crowd,* or *To think there was a Nobel Prize winner in our midst!* [c. 1500s] 2. See IN THE MIDDLE OF, def. 1.

in the money 1. Also, in the chips. Rich, affluent. For example, *When he's in the money, he's extremely generous to his friends,* or *After that box-office bonanza, she's in the chips.* The *chips* in the variant presumably allude to poker chips. [Colloquial; late 1800s] 2. Placing first, second or third in a contest on which a bet has been placed, especially a horse race. For example, *My luck held today, and I ended up in the money.* [c. 1900]

in the mood Disposed or inclined toward something, as in *I'm in the mood for a good long walk.* This phrase is also put in the negative, *I'm not in the mood to argue.* [Late 1500s]

in the mouth ♦ See DOWN IN THE DUMPS (MOUTH); LOOK A GIFT HORSE IN THE MOUTH.

in the name of 1. By the authority of, as in *Open up, in the name of the law!* [Late 1300s] 2. On behalf of, as in *She made a donation in her daughter's name.* [Late 1300s] 3. in God's or heaven's name; in the name of God or heaven. With appeal to, as in *In the name of God, stop that noise!* or *What in heaven's name are you doing?* [c. A.D. 900] 4. Under the designation of, as in *They burned witches at the stake in the name of piety.* [Late 1300s]

5. Under the possession or ownership of, as in *The certificate of ownership was rightfully in my name.* [Mid-1900s] 6. in one's own name. On one's own behalf, as in *Mary signed the check for John in her own name.* [Late 1800s]

in the near future Very soon, within a short time. For example, *We'll be needing a new car in the near future.* This term employs *near* in the sense of "close at hand," a usage dating from about 1300. Also see AT HAND, def. 2.

in the neck ♦ See PAIN IN THE NECK.

in the neighborhood of Also, in the region of. Approximately, about, as in *They paid in the neighborhood of a million dollars,* or *I don't know exactly what the exchange rate is—somewhere in the region of 95 yen to the dollar.* The first expression dates from the mid-1800s, the variant from the mid-1900s.

in the nick of time Also, just in time. At the last moment, as in *The police arrived in the nick of time,* or *He got there just in time for dinner.* The first term began life as in the nick and dates from the 1500s, when *nick* meant "the critical moment" (a meaning now obsolete). The second employs *just* in the sense of "precisely" or "closely," a usage applied to time since the 1500s. Also see IN TIME, def. 1.

in the offing In the near or immediate future; soon to come. For example, *Jan was delighted that exams were finished and graduation was in the offing.* This expression originally meant "in the part of the ocean visible between shore and horizon"; its figurative use dates from the late 1700s. Also see IN THE WIND.

in the picture, be Understand, be informed about or be involved in a particular situation or activity. For example, *The new ambassador wanted to be in the picture for every event, small or large.* This term is also used in such locutions as put someone in the picture, meaning "to inform or include someone," as in *Put me in the picture about the new staff,* or out of the picture, meaning "to be left ignorant of or excluded from some activity," as in *The local authorities were out of the picture when it came to drug dealers.* [Early 1900s] Also see GET THE MESSAGE (PICTURE).

in the pink In good health, as in *We're glad to hear Bob's in the pink again.* In the 1500s *pink* meant "the embodiment of perfection," but the current idiom dates only from about 1900.

in the pipeline 1. In process, under way, as in *The blueprints for the new machine are in the pipeline, but it will take months to get approval.* [Colloquial; 1940s] Also see IN THE WORKS. 2. Budgeted for something but not yet spent, as in *There's $5 million more in the pipeline for the city schools.* [Colloquial; second half of 1900s]

in the public eye Under the attention and scrutiny of the public, as in *The rock star's activities were very much in the public eye.* This usage, which is similar to IN THE LIMELIGHT, dates from the late 1800s. It should not be confused with the similar-sounding **in the eyes of the public,** which means "in the opinion or views of the general public" (as in *In the eyes of the public the mayor was guilty of perjury*). Also see IN THE EYE OF, def. 2.

in the raw ♦ See IN THE ALTOGETHER.

in the red In debt, as in *Joshua can't keep track of funds, so half the time his company is in the red.* This expression alludes to the bookkeeping practice of marking debits in red ink and credits in black. It survives even in the age of computerized accounts. So does the antonym, **in the black,** for being financially solvent or out of debt, as in *Bill was happy to say they were in the black.* [Early 1900s]

in there pitching Exerting one's best effort, trying actively. For example, *After the flood, everyone was in there pitching to clean up the streets.* This metaphor alludes to the pitcher's important role in baseball. [Colloquial; c. 1940]

in the right, be Have the support of fact, justice; or reason. For example, *Nancy's parents were in the right when they took her teacher to task,* or, as Shakespeare put it in *Richard III* (5:3): "He was in the right, and so indeed it is." [Late 1400s] Also see the antonym IN THE WRONG.

in the rough ♦ See DIAMOND IN THE ROUGH.

in the round Visible from all sides, as in *Jerry's done an excellent job in this interview, really portraying the senator in the round.* This expression, which dates from about 1800, was at first used for a free-standing piece of sculpture (as opposed to a relief on a wall), and a century later for a theatrical stage (called **theater-in-the-round**) so placed that the audience could see a performance from all sides. Since the 1920s it has also been used figuratively for someone or something seen three-dimensionally, as in the example.

in the running 1. Entered as a competitor in a contest. For example, *Is Mary in the running for this election?* The antonym, **out of the running,** means "not entered as a competitor," as in *Ian is out of the running for the job now that he's living in another state.* [Mid-1800s] 2. Having a chance to win, as in *Mary's still in the running for the promotion.* Again, **out of the running** means the opposite, as in *He's too old—he's out of the running.* [Mid-1800s] Both usages allude to the entry and chances of a horse in a race.

in the saddle ♦ See IN THE DRIVER'S SEAT.

in the same boat Also, **all in the same boat.** In a similar situation, in the same position. For example, *Everyone's got too much work—we're all in the same boat.* This expression alludes to the risks shared by passengers in a small boat at sea. [Mid-1800s]

in the same breath 1. Also, **in one breath.** At or almost at the same time. For example, *Ed complains about having too much homework and in the same breath talks about going out every night,* or *The twins said, in one breath, "More cake, please."* [Mid-1800s] 2. **not in the same breath.** Not to be compared. For example, *Karen's a good runner, but you can't speak of her in the same breath as an Olympic athlete.* Also see IN THE SAME LEAGUE.

in the same league On the same level of skill, in the same class, as in *As a woodworker, Bill wishes he were in the same league as Carl, who is a master carpenter.* This metaphoric expression alludes to the leagues of baseball clubs, categorized as major or minor. It is often put negatively as **not in the same league,** as in *This restaurant is not in the same league as the French café across the street.* [Early 1900s]

in the same mold ♦ See CAST IN THE SAME MOLD.

in the second place ♦ See under IN THE FIRST PLACE.

in the short run ♦ See under IN THE LONG RUN.

in the soup In trouble, as in *She mailed all the checks with the wrong postage, and now she's really in the soup.* [Slang; late 1800s]

in the street ♦ See under ON THE STREET.

in the swim Actively participating, in the thick of things, as in *He was new in town, but he soon got in the swim at school.* This expression alludes to the fishing term for a large number of fish in one area, a so-called *swim.* [Mid-1800s]

in the teeth of 1. Straight into, confronting, as in *The ship was headed in the teeth of the gale.* [Late 1200s] 2. In opposition to or defiance of, as in *She stuck to her position in the teeth of criticism by the board members.* [Late 1700s] Also see FLY IN THE FACE OF. 3. Facing danger or threats, as in *The tribe was in the teeth of starvation.* [Early 1800s]

in the throes In the midst of, especially of a difficult struggle. For example, *The country was in the throes of economic collapse,* or *We were in the throes of giving a formal dinner when my in-laws arrived.* The noun *throe,* meaning "a severe pang or spasm of pain," was at first used mainly for such physical events as childbirth or dying. Today it is used both seriously (first example) and more lightly (second example). [Mid-1800s]

in the twinkling of an eye In an instant, as in *The breakup of Yugoslavia created many warring nations in the twinkling of an eye.* This hyperbolic expression, which alludes to the very brief time it takes for an eye to blink, is heard less often today. [c. 1300]

in the unlikely event If something improbable should occur. For example, *In the unlikely event that I'm held up, please cover for me,* or *In the unlikely event that we should have snow in May, we're still well equipped to cope with it.* Also see under IN CASE, def. 2.

in the wake of 1. Following directly on, as in *In the wake of the procession, a number of small children came skipping down the aisle.* This usage alludes to the waves made behind a passing vessel. [c. 1800] 2. In the aftermath of, as a consequence of, as in *Famine often comes in the wake of war.* [Mid-1800s]

in the way 1. See IN ONE'S WAY, def. 3. 2. **in the way of.** In the nature of, as in *He was getting nothing in the way of pay,* or *They had nothing in the way of an alibi.* [Mid-1600s]

in the wind Likely to occur, as in "He knew Gattis had guessed what was in the wind and was pretty unhappy about it" (Clive Egleton, *A Different Drummer,* 1985). This metaphoric expression alludes to perceiving something being brought or blown by the wind. [Late 1500s] Also see GET WIND OF; SOMETHING IN THE WIND.

in the wings Also, **waiting in the wings.** Nearby in the background, available on short notice. For example, *Some police were in the wings in case of trouble at the rally,* or *There are at least a dozen young managers waiting in the wings for Harold to retire.* This expression alludes to the theater, where a player waits in the wings or backstage area, unseen by the audience, for his or her turn to come on stage. [Second half of 1800s]

in the works In preparation, under development. For example, *The agent said there was a movie deal in the works,* or *He assured her that a follow-up campaign was in the works.* [Second half of 1900s] Also see IN THE PIPELINE.

in the world ♦ See COME UP (IN THE WORLD); ON EARTH; NOT HAVE A CARE IN THE WORLD; WITH THE BEST WILL IN THE WORLD.

in the worst way Desperately, very much, as in *He wanted a new trumpet in the worst way.* This usage replaced *worst kind.* [Colloquial; second half of 1800s]

in the wrong Mistaken, to blame. For example, *The teacher was clearly in the wrong but refused to admit it,* or *Since he had driven straight through a red light, Jack was the one in the wrong.* [c. 1400]

in thing, the ♦ See under THE THING.

in this day and age Now, in the present, as in *In this day and age divorce is a very common occurrence.* This phrase is redundant, since *this day* and *this age* both mean "now". [Early 1900s]

in time ♦ In addition to the idiom beginning with IN TIME, also see AT THIS POINT (IN TIME); IN DUE TIME; IN GOOD TIME; IN THE NICK OF (JUST IN) TIME; ON TIME; STITCH IN TIME.

in time 1. Before a time limit expires, early enough, as in *His speech begins at eight, so we've arrived in time.* It is often put as **in time for,** as in *Please come in time for dinner.* [Second half of 1400s] Also see IN GOOD TIME. 2. Eventually, within an indefinite period, as in *In time you'll see that Dad was right.* [c. 1450] Also see IN DUE COURSE. 3. In the proper musical tempo or rhythm, as in *It's important to dance in time to the music.* [c. 1700]

into ♦ In addition to the idioms beginning with INTO, also see BE INTO.

into account ♦ See TAKE INTO ACCOUNT.

into effect ♦ See IN EFFECT, def. 2.

in token of As a sign or symbol of, as in *He gave her a ring in token of his love,* or *In token of our esteem, we dedicate this hospital wing to Dr. Lurie.* [Early 1500s]

into line ♦ See FALL IN LINE.

into one's head ♦ See BEAT INTO ONE'S HEAD; GET INTO ONE'S HEAD.

into question ♦ See CALL IN QUESTION.

into the bargain Also, **in the bargain.** In addition, over and above what is expected. For example, *The new researcher was an excellent chemist and a good programmer in the bargain,* or *It was very cold, and then rain and sleet were added into the bargain.* These expressions transfer *bargain* in the sense of "a business agreement" to what is anticipated.

into the blue ♦ See under INTO THIN AIR.

into the drink Into the water, especially the ocean. For example, *One more wave and I thought I'd fall off the boat into the drink.* [Slang; c. 1830]

into thin air Also, **into the blue.** Completely disappeared, as in *The report was here on my desk and now it's gone, vanished into thin air;* or *I don't know where they've gone—into the blue, for all I know.* Both of these hyperbolic expressions, often preceded by *vanish* as in the first example, use the rarefied atmosphere far above the earth as a metaphor for an unknown location. Shakespeare wrote of ghosts that "melted ... into thin air" (*The Tempest,* 4:1). An antonym for both is **out of thin air,** meaning "from an unknown place or source." For example, *She made up this excuse out of thin air,* or *The car appeared out of thin air.*

However, **out of the blue** is not precisely an antonym (see under OUT OF A CLEAR BLUE SKY).

in touch, be Also, **be in touch with**. Be in communication or contact (with), as in *Be sure to be in touch once you've arrived*, or *Our representative is really in touch with her constituents*. A related idiom is **get in touch**, meaning "initiate contact," as in *We tried to get in touch with you but you were out of town*, and **keep or stay in touch**, meaning "remain in communication or contact," as in *With Jim stationed in Korea, it was hard to keep in touch*, or *Do stay in touch with us*. This idiom transfers physical touch to communication. [Late 1800s]

in tow In one's charge or close guidance; along with one. For example, *The older girl took the new student in tow*, or *Peter always had his family in tow*. This expression alludes to the literal meaning of being pulled along. [Early 1700s]

in trouble with In difficulties with someone, especially an authority. For example, *If they don't shovel their walk, they'll be in trouble with their neighbors*. This idiom is also put as **get in** or **into trouble with**, as in *Watch what you say or you'll get into trouble with the teacher*. [Mid-1500s] Also see HOT WATER; IN A FIX.

in trust In the possession or care of a trustee, as in *The money was held in trust for the children's education*. This expression implies having confidence in someone (the trustee). [Mid-1500s]

in tune Also, **in tune with**. 1. In agreement in musical pitch or intonation, as in *It's hard to keep a violin in tune during damp weather*, or *Dave is always in tune with the other instrumentalists*. [Mid-1400s] 2. In concord or agreement, as in *He was in tune with the times*. [Late 1500s] The antonyms for both usages, dating from the same periods, are **not in tune** and **out of tune**, as in *That trumpet's not in tune with the organ*, or *The lawyer was out of tune with his partners*.

in turn Also, **in turns**. In the proper order or in sequence; also, one at a time. For example, *Each generation in turn must deal with the same budget problems*, or *Someone must be awake at all times, so let's sleep in turns*. [Late 1500s] Also see OUT OF TURN; TAKE TURNS.

in two shakes Also, **in two shakes of a lamb's tail** Very quickly, very soon, as in *I'll be with you in two shakes*, or *She'll be finished in two shakes of a lamb's tail*. The longer idiom alludes to the friskiness of lambs; the shorter one may be an abbreviation of the longer one, or it may refer to the shaking of dice or any two quick movements. [Early 1800s]

in unison 1. In complete agreement, harmonizing exactly. For example, *Their opinion was in unison with ours*. [Early 1800s] 2. Saying the same thing at the same time, simultaneously, as in *The whole class answered in unison*. [Late 1800s] Both usages allude to the unison of music, a single identical pitch.

in up to ♦ See UP TO ONE'S EARS.

in vain To no avail, useless, as in *All our work was in vain*. [c. 1300] Also see TAKE SOMEONE'S NAME IN VAIN.

invent the wheel ♦ See REINVENT THE WHEEL.

in view 1. Also, **within view**. Visible, in sight, as in *The end of the project is in view*, or *The mountains are just within view*. [Mid-1500s] 2. Under consideration, as in *Let's keep this suggestion in view while we talk about the project*. [Mid-1600s] 3. As an end or goal one aims at. For example, *With the coming election in view, we should present a united front on the issues*. [Early 1700s] Also see IN VIEW OF.

in view of 1. See IN LIGHT OF. 2. Also, **with a view to**. Considering, in prospect or anticipation of, as in *In view of their hostile relations, both countries began mobilizing*, or *Dan started saving money with a view to going to law school*. [c. 1700]

involve ♦ See GET INVOLVED WITH.

in wait ♦ See LIE IN WAIT.

in waiting In attendance, especially on a royal personage. For example, *The prelates who were in waiting asked him to take the last rites*. This usage has become less common with the diminution of royalty and royal courts but still survives. [Late 1600s]

in with, be 1. Be in league or association with, as in *She was in with the wrong crowd*. It is also put as **keep in with**, meaning "to remain in league or association with," as in *He really kept in with his high school friends even while he was in college*. [Late 1600s] 2. See IN GOOD WITH.

in your face Defiantly confrontational; also, an exclamation of contempt. For example, *This show is not suitable for youngsters; its attitude about sex is in your face*, or *In your face, mister!* This slangy expression originated in the 1970s in basketball as a phrase of contempt used against the opposing team and was extended to other areas by the mid-1980s.

iota ♦ See NOT ONE IOTA.

Irish ♦ See LUCK OF THE DEVIL (IRISH).

iron ♦ In addition to the idioms beginning with IRON, also see PUMP IRON; STRIKE WHILE THE IRON'S HOT.

iron hand Rigorous control, as in *He ruled the company with an iron hand*. This usage is sometimes put as **iron hand in a velvet glove**, meaning "firm but seemingly gentle control," as in *She runs the town with an iron hand in a velvet glove*. [c. 1700]

iron out Work out, resolve, settle. For example, *They managed to iron out all the problems with the* new production process, or *John and Mary finally ironed out their differences*. This expression uses ironing wrinkled fabric as a metaphor for smoothing differences. [Mid-1800s]

irons in the fire, too many Too many activities or undertakings at once. For example, *Bill's got too many irons in the fire to cope with moving this year*. This expression originally referred to the blacksmith heating too many irons at once and therefore spoiling some in the forging. [Mid-1500s]

I see Also, **I see what you mean**. I understand, as in *I see, you'd rather go running in the morning while it's cool*, or *It's too early to run an ad? I see what you mean*. This idiom uses *see* in the sense of "perceive" or "comprehend," a usage dating from 1300. Also see AS FAR AS I CAN SEE.

Is my face red! ♦ See under RED IN THE FACE.

issue ♦ See AT ISSUE; TAKE ISSUE WITH.

is that a fact? Also, **is that so?** Phrases indicating that one is following what another person is saying. These expressions, which require no reply, can be used either straightforwardly, as in *You mean you've flown to Paris three times just this month? Is that a fact?* or sarcastically, expressing disbelief or contempt, as in *Just wait, I'll be promoted over you before the year is out.*—*Oh yeah, is that so?* [Late 1800s]

I suppose so Also, **I guess so**. I reluctantly agree, as in *Do you want tickets to the concert?*—*I suppose so*, or *Do you think it's going to rain?*—*I guess so*. [Mid-1500s]

it ♦ In addition to the idioms beginning with IT, also see THAT DOES IT.

itch for, have an Also, **itch to**. Have a persistent restless craving for, as in *Dean has an itch for excitement*, or *Chris is itching to go around the world*. [Late 1500s]

itchy palm Also, **itching palm**. A desire for money, greed; also, wanting a bribe. For example, *The porter has an itchy palm; he wants a big tip*, or *The mayor was known for his itchy palm*. This expression alludes to placing money in the palm of the hand. [Late 1500s]

it figures Also, **that figures**. It's (or that's) reasonable; it makes sense. For example, *Hanging it upside down sounds like a weird idea, but it figures*, or *It figures that they won't be coming this year*, or *So she's complaining again; that figures*. This idiom alludes to reckoning up numbers. [Colloquial; mid-1900s]

it never rains but it pours When something occurs it often does so to excess. For example, *First Aunt Sue said she and Uncle Harry were coming for the weekend and then my sister and her children said they were coming too*—*it never rains but it*

pours. This expression may have come from either a book by Queen Anne's physician, John Arbuthnot, or an article by Jonathan Swift, both entitled *It Cannot Rain But It Pours* and both published in 1726.

I told you so I warned you in advance, especially of a bad outcome. For example, *It's too bad your guests didn't get along with each other, but remember, I told you so*.

it's about time Also, **it's high time**. ♦ See ABOUT TIME; HIGH TIME.

it's all downhill Also, **it's all uphill from here**. ♦ See under DOWNHILL ALL THE WAY.

it's all over with Something or someone is completely finished, defeated, or dead. The precise meaning of this phrase depends on the context. In *This loss means that it's all over with the company*, it refers to defeat, whereas in *The vet can do no more; it's all over with the dog*, it refers to the dog's death, either approaching or actual. Also see ALL UP (WITH).

it's an ill wind ♦ See ILL WIND.

it's a small world One encounters the same people, events or situations in unexpected places. For example, *I never thought I'd run into Samantha at a ball game*—*it's a small world*. [c. 1900]

it's a zoo Also, **what a zoo**. This is a place or situation of confusion and/or disorder. For example, *Mary's got all these house guests with children and pets*—*it's a zoo*, or *We're in the midst of moving our office and files are all over the place*—*what a zoo!* [Slang; late 1800s]

it's no use ♦ See NO USE.

it stands to reason It's reasonable or to be expected. For example, *It stands to reason that if we leave late we'll arrive late*. [Early 1600s]

it's to die Also, **it is to die for**. It's extraordinary; it's deeply appreciated and/or greatly desired. For example, *Her performance, it's to die!* or *That mink coat*—*it's to die for!* This hyperbole is usually put as an exclamation. [Slang; 1970s]

it's to laugh Also, **it is to laugh**. It is absurd, laughable, as in *You think the trial will be over in a week*—*it's to laugh!* This expression is usually put as an exclamation, as in the example. [Second half of 1900s]

it's your funeral Also, **it's or it's not his or her or my or our or their funeral**. One must take the consequences of one's destructive or foolish actions. This expression is used to show one's contempt or lack of sympathy for another's actions. For example, *Suppose they do get pulled over for taking a joy ride*—*It's their funeral*, or *I don't care whether you quit your job*—*it's not my funeral*. This hyperbolic term implies that an action is so bad it will result in death. [Slang; mid-1800s]

it takes all sorts Many different kinds of people make up the world. For example, *I would never go swimming in April, but it takes all sorts,* or *Gordon insists on wearing sunglasses indoors and out—I guess it takes all sorts.* This expression, originating in the 1600s as *It takes all sorts to make a world,* is often used in remarking one's own difference from others or tolerating someone else's peculiarity. Also see NO ACCOUNTING FOR TASTES.

it takes getting used to One needs to become accustomed to something. For example, *We've always had a small car, so driving a big van like this—well, it takes getting used to.* This idiom employs *used to* in the sense of "accustomed to," a usage dating from the first half of the 1500s.

it takes one to know one The person who expressed criticism has similar faults to the person being criticized. This classic retort to an insult dates from the early 1900s. For example, *You say she's a terrible cook? It takes one to know one!* For a synonym, see POT CALLING THE KETTLE BLACK. A near equivalent is the proverbial **it takes a thief to catch a thief,** meaning "no one is better at finding a wrongdoer than another wrongdoer." First recorded in 1665, it remains current.

it takes two to tango The active cooperation of both parties is needed for some enterprises, as in *We'll never pass this bill unless both parties work out a compromise—it takes two to tango.* This expression dates from the 1920s, when the Latin American tango became a very popular dance. It was popularized by the singer Pearl Bailey in her 1952 hit song of that name written by Al Hoffman and Dick Manning.

ivory tower A place or attitude of retreat, remoteness from everyday affairs, as in *What does the professor know about student life, living as he does in an ivory tower?* This term is a translation of the French *tour d'ivoire,* which the critic Saint-Beuve used to describe the attitude of poet Alfred de Vigny in 1837. It is used most often in reference to intellectuals and artists who remain complacently aloof.

j

jack ♦ In addition to the idioms beginning with JACK, also see BEFORE YOU CAN SAY JACK ROBINSON.

jack off ♦ See JERK OFF.

jackpot ♦ See HIT THE JACKPOT.

Jack Robinson ♦ See BEFORE YOU CAN SAY JACK ROBINSON.

jack up Raise or increase, as in *The cartel is jacking up oil prices again.* This term alludes to the literal meaning of *jack up,* that is, "hoist with a jack." [Colloquial; c. 1900]

jam ♦ See under GET IN A BIND.

jaybird ♦ See NAKED AS A JAYBIRD.

jazz up 1. Enliven, make more interesting, as in *They jazzed up the living room with a new rug,* or *They decided to include a comedy act to jazz up the program.* 2. Modify so as to increase its performance, as in *Peter wanted to jazz up his motorbike with a stronger engine.* Both usages are colloquialisms from the mid-1900s. Also see JUICE UP.

Jekyll and Hyde A personality alternating between good and evil behavior, as in *You never know whether Bob will be a Jekyll or a Hyde.* This expression comes from Robert Louis Stevenson's *The Strange Case of Dr. Jekyll and Mr. Hyde* (1886). Also see LEAD A DOUBLE LIFE.

jerk around Take unfair advantage of, manipulate or deceive, as in *Leave me alone; quit jerking me around!* or *He was jerking you around when he said he was home all evening.* [Slang; mid-1900s]

jerk off Also, **jack off.** Masturbate, as in *His roommate was always jerking off.* [Vulgar slang; first half of 1900s]

jetsam ♦ See FLOTSAM AND JETSAM.

jib ♦ See CUT OF ONE'S JIB.

jiffy ♦ See under IN A FLASH.

jig is up ♦ See GAME IS UP.

jinks ♦ See HIGH JINKS.

job ♦ See DO A JOB ON; HATCHET MAN (JOB); LIE DOWN (ON THE JOB); ON THE JOB; PUT-UP JOB; SNOW JOB; SOFT JOB.

jockey for position Maneuver or manipulate for one's own benefit, as in *The singers are always jockeying for position on stage.* This expression, dating from about 1900, originally meant maneuvering a race horse into a better position for winning. It was transferred to other kinds of manipulation in the mid-1900s.

Joe Six-pack A lower-middle-class male. For example, *I don't think opera will appeal to Joe Six-pack; he'd prefer a rock concert.* This disparaging term, first recorded in 1977, conjures up the image of a man in undershirt and construction helmet who will down all of a six-pack (six cans or bottles of beer sold in a package) in an evening.

John Doe 1. Also, **John Q. Public; Joe Blow; Joe Doakes; Joe Zilch.** An average undistinguished man; also, the average citizen. For example, *This television show is just right for a John Doe,* or *It's up to John Q. Public to go to the polls and vote.* Originally used from the 13th century on legal documents as an alias to protect a witness, *John Doe* acquired the sense of "ordinary person" in the 1800s. The variants date from the 1900s. Also see JOE SIX-PACK. **2.** Also, **Jane Doe.** An unknown individual, as in *The police found a John Doe lying on the street last night,* or *The judge issued a warrant for the arrest of the perpetrators, Jane Doe no. 1 and Jane Doe no. 2.* [Second half of 1900s]

John Hancock Also, **John Henry.** One's signature, as in *Just put your John Hancock on the dotted line.* This expression alludes to John Hancock's prominent signature on the Declaration of Independence. The variant simply substitutes a common name for "Hancock." [Mid-1800s]

Johnny-come-lately A newcomer, as in *She may be a Johnny-come-lately on the board, but she's doing a fine job with publicity.* [1830s]

Johnny-on-the-spot A person who is available when needed, as in *He always is there at the right time, a real Johnny-on-the-spot.* [Late 1800s]

John Q. Public ♦ See under JOHN DOE.

join forces Act together, combine efforts. For example, *The public relations people joined forces to get better coverage for their candidates.* This expression originally referred to combining military forces. [Mid-1500s]

joint ♦ See CLIP JOINT; NOSE OUT OF JOINT; OUT OF JOINT.

join the club A phrase used to express sympathy for a common experience. For example, *You waited three hours for the doctor? Join the club!* [c. 1940]

joke ♦ See CRACK A JOKE; DIRTY JOKE; NO JOKE; SICK JOKE; STANDING JOKE; TAKE A JOKE.

joking ♦ See ALL JOKING ASIDE.

Jones ♦ See DAVY JONES'S LOCKER; KEEP UP (WITH THE JONESES).

jowl ♦ See CHEEK BY JOWL.

joy ♦ See BURST WITH (JOY); PRIDE AND JOY.

judge ♦ In addition to the idiom beginning with JUDGE, also see SOBER AS A JUDGE. Also see JUDGMENT.

judge a book by its cover, one can't One can't rely on outward appearances to know what something or someone is really like. For example, *He seems very quiet, but you can't judge a book by its cover.* [First half of 1900s]

judgment ♦ See AGAINST ONE'S BETTER JUDGMENT; SNAP JUDGMENT.

jugular ♦ See GO FOR, def. 4.

juice ♦ In addition to the idiom beginning with JUICE, also see STEW IN ONE'S OWN JUICE.

juice up **1.** Give something energy, spirit, or interest. For example, *They tried to juice up the party by playing loud music.* **2.** Change something to improve its performance, as in *That old jeep's motor got juiced up in the shop,* or *Lowering interest rates*

is one way to juice up the economy. [Slang; second half of 1900s]

jump ♦ In addition to the idioms beginning with JUMP, also see GET THE DROP (JUMP) ON; GO FLY A KITE (JUMP IN THE LAKE); HOP, SKIP AND A JUMP; NOT KNOW WHICH WAY TO JUMP; ONE JUMP AHEAD OF; SKIP (JUMP) BAIL.

jump all over someone Also, **jump** or **land on someone.** Scold, reprimand or criticize someone. For example, *Brian jumped all over his son for being late,* or *The editor jumped on Dennis for getting the names wrong,* or *He was always landing on me for something or other.* The first metaphoric term dates from the mid-1800s, the second from the late 1800s. Also see JUMP DOWN SOMEONE'S THROAT.

jump at Also, **jump at the chance; jump at the bait.** Take prompt advantage of, respond quickly to an opportunity. For example, *When Dad said he'd help pay for my vacation, I jumped at the offer,* or *When the lead singer became ill, Sheila jumped at the chance to replace her,* or *They offered a large reward, hoping that someone would jump at the bait.* [Mid-1700s]

jump bail ♦ See SKIP BAIL.

jump down someone's throat Strongly criticize, reprimand or disagree with someone. For example, *Just because I admitted to being there, you needn't jump down my throat.* [Late 1800s] Also see JUMP ALL OVER SOMEONE.

jump in Also **jump in with both feet** or **into the ring.** Enter into something enthusiastically; also, act precipitately. For example, *When Don found out what his job was to be, he was ready to jump in immediately,* or *As soon as they asked me to join, I jumped in with both feet,* or *When buying securities, Anne's apt to jump into the ring, no matter what the risks.* The first two usages allude to jumping into water; the third alludes to entering the fray of the boxing ring.

jumping-off place or **point** **1.** A starting point for a journey or venture, as in *This tiny village is the jumping-off place for our trek into the desert.* This usage probably alludes to jumping into the water. [Early 1800s] **2.** A very remote spot; also, the last place to be reached. For example, *This was the jumping-off point for the first gold miners in Alaska.* [Early 1800s]

jump on ♦ See JUMP ALL OVER SOMEONE.

jump out of one's skin Be extremely startled or frightened. For example, *When he crept up on me so quietly, I nearly jumped out of my skin.* [Early 1900s]

jump the gun Start doing something too soon, act too hastily. For example, *The local weather bureau jumped the gun on predicting a storm; it didn't happen for another two days.* This expression alludes to starting a race before the starter's gun has gone off, and supplants the earlier **beat the pistol,** which dates from about 1900. [Mid-1900s]

jump the track Suddenly switch from one thought or activity to another. For example, *Joe was describing his trip to Australia and, jumping the track, began complaining about the airline,* or *They couldn't decide on the next step and now the whole reorganization plan has jumped the track.* This expression alludes to a train going off the rails. [Colloquial; early 1900s]

jump through hoops Do just about anything to please someone. For example, *The boss expects the entire staff to jump through hoops for him,* or *This violinist will jump through hoops for the conductor.* This metaphoric expression alludes to trained circus animals jumping through hoops. [Early 1900s]

jump to a conclusion Form an opinion or judgment hastily, as in *Wait till you have the facts; don't jump to a conclusion.* [c. 1700]

juncture ♦ See AT THIS POINT (JUNCTURE).

jungle ♦ See LAW OF THE JUNGLE.

junk food Prepackaged snack food that is high in calories but low in nutritional value; also, anything attractive but negligible in value. For example, *Nell loves potato chips and other junk food,* or *When I'm sick in bed I often resort to TV soap operas and similar junk food.* [c. 1970]

junk mail Third-class mail, such as unsolicited advertisements and flyers, that is sent indiscriminately. For example, *While we were on vacation the front hall filled up with junk mail.* [c. 1950]

jury is still out, the No decision has been made; the public's opinion is not known. For example, *As for a possible merger, the jury is still out,* or *The jury is still out on the new spring fashions.* This expression alludes to the jury that decides a legal case. [Colloquial; mid-1900s]

just ♦ In addition to the idioms beginning with JUST, also see ALL (JUST) THE SAME; GET IT (YOU JUST DON'T); TAKE IT (JUST SO MUCH). Also see under JUSTICE.

just about Almost, very nearly, as in *This job is just about done,* or *At just about midnight we'll uncork the champagne.* This phrase is sometimes used alone, as in *Are you finished yet?—Just about.* It uses *about* in the sense of "nearly," a usage dating from the early 1600s.

just a minute Also, **just a moment. 1.** Wait a little bit. This expression is used before explaining oneself, as in *Just a minute, I didn't mean that he was wrong,* or to stop someone from something, as in *Just a moment, I was here first.* Also see HOLD EVERYTHING. **2.** Only a very short time, as in *I'll be with you in just a minute.*

just as 1. In precisely the same way as. For example, *He's signing his name just as he's always done*

it. [Early 1600s] **2.** Also, **just so.** To the same degree as. For example, *Jim's running just as fast as his friend,* or *He intended to give them just so much work as they could do in a day.* [Late 1600s] Also see JUST SO.

just as soon Also, **as soon.** Rather, more readily; also, equally. For example, *I'd just as soon you took care of it,* or *I would as soon recover before I go and babysit,* or *I'd as soon have the lamb as the beef.* [Late 1500s]

just deserts A deserved punishment or reward, as in *He got his just deserts when Mary jilted him.* This idiom employs *desert* in the sense of "what one deserves," a usage dating from the 1300s but obsolete except in this expression.

just folks Friendly, unpretentious. For example, *Politicians meeting the public like to pretend they are just folks, but that's not always true.* [First half of 1900s]

just for the record Let's get things straight; also, let me make myself clear. For example, *Just for the record, we never endorsed this idea,* or *Just for the record, I didn't vote for him.* This usage employs *record* in the sense of "public knowledge." [Mid-1900s] Also see GO ON RECORD; SET (THE RECORD) STRAIGHT.

justice ♦ See DO JUSTICE TO; MISCARRIAGE OF JUSTICE; POETIC JUSTICE.

just in case ♦ See IN CASE, def. 1.

just in time ♦ See IN THE NICK OF TIME.

just like that 1. Suddenly and, sometimes, unexpectedly. For example, *The alarm went off, just like that,* or *And then they walked out, just like that.* **2.** Also, **like that.** Very friendly or intimate with one another. For example, *Bill and his boss often see each other socially; they are just like that,* or *Joe and Jane are always together; they're like that.* This expression is usually emphasized by the speaker's holding up two fingers and either keeping them together or crossing them to show the closeness or intimacies of the parties being discussed. [Colloquial; early 1900s]

just now 1. Exactly at this time, as in *Harry isn't here just now; can he call you back?* [Late 1600s] **2.** Only a moment ago, as in *As she was saying just now, they are fully booked.* [Early 1600s]

just one of those things A random occurrence that can't be explained. For example, *It wasn't their fault that the show failed; it was just one of those things.* This expression was given greater currency as the title and refrain of one of Cole Porter's most popular songs ("Just One of Those Things," 1935). [c. 1930] Also see ONE OF THOSE DAYS.

just so 1. Precisely in that way, very carefully and appropriately, as in *The children had to be dressed just so for their aunt's wedding.* [Mid-1700s] **2.** I agree, that is correct, as in *The house was a mess.—Just so; I told her to clean the place up.* [Mid-1700s] **3.** See JUST AS, def. 2. **4.** See AS LONG AS, def. 3.

just the same ♦ See ALL ONE, def. 2.

just the ticket Also, **that's the ticket.** Exactly what is needed; exactly right. For example, *This van is just the ticket for carrying all our luggage,* or *That's the ticket—you're handling that chain saw very well.* The second phrase dates from the early 1800s, and the first is slightly newer. The exact allusion is disputed—it could be to a winning lottery ticket, a price tag for merchandise, or, as one writer suggests, a corruption of the French word *etiquette* for "appropriate behavior." For a synonym, see WAY TO GO.

just what the doctor ordered Exactly what was needed. For example, *This steak is just what the doctor ordered,* or *You've been a great help in our office—just what the doctor ordered.* This expression alludes to a physician's prescription for a cure. [First half of 1900s]

k

kangaroo court A self-appointed tribunal that violates established legal procedure; also, a dishonest or incompetent court of law. For example, *The rebels set up a kangaroo court and condemned the prisoners to summary execution,* or *That judge runs a kangaroo court—he tells rape victims they should have been more careful.* This expression is thought to liken the jumping ability of kangaroos to a court that jumps to conclusions on an invalid basis. [Mid-1800s]

keel ♦ In addition to the idiom beginning with KEEL, also see ON AN EVEN KEEL.

keel over Collapse, as if in a faint; also, faint. For example, *When she heard the awful news, she keeled over.* This term alludes to a vessel rolling on its keel and capsizing. [Mid-1800s]

keen about, be Be enthusiastic about. For example, *He's been keen about this whole endeavor for a long time.* It is also put as **be keen on,** which has the additional meaning "to be ardent about or in love with," as in *Jim's been keen on Jane for years.* With other adverbs, such as *keen at* and *keen of, keen* has been so used since the early 1500s; the current locutions, however, date from the mid-1800s.

keep ♦ In addition to the idioms beginning with KEEP, also see EARN ONE'S KEEP; FINDERS KEEPERS, LOSERS WEEPERS; FOR KEEPS; IN KEEPING; (KEEP SOMEONE) IN THE DARK.

keep abreast of Stay or cause to stay up to-date with, as in *He's keeping abreast of the latest weather reports,* or *Please keep me abreast of any change in his condition.* This term alludes to the nautical sense of *abreast,* which describes ships keeping up with each other. [Late 1600s]

keep a civil tongue in one's head Speak politely, as in *The teacher won't allow swearing; she says we must keep a civil tongue in our heads.* This expression uses *tongue* in the sense of "a manner of speaking," a usage dating from the 1400s. An early cautionary version was "Keep a good tongue in your head, lest it hurt your teeth" (1595).

keep after Make a persistent effort regarding; also, persistently urge someone to do something. For example, *We'll have to keep after the cobwebs,* or *He won't get anything done unless you keep after him.* Also see KEEP AT, def. 2.

keep a low profile Stay out of public notice, avoid attracting attention to oneself. For example, *Until his appointment becomes official, Ted is keeping a low profile.* This expression alludes to *profile* in the sense of "a visible contour," a usage dating from the 1600s. [Late 1900s]

keep an eye on ♦ See HAVE ONE'S EYE ON, def. 1.

keep an eye out for Also, **keep a sharp lookout for.** Be watchful for something or someone, as in *Keep an eye out for the potholes in the road,* or *They told him to keep a sharp lookout for the police.* The first expression, sometimes amplified to **keep a sharp eye out for,** dates from the late 1800s, the variant from the mid-1700s. Also see HAVE ONE'S EYE ON, def. 1; KEEP A WEATHER EYE; KEEP ONE'S EYES OPEN; LOOK OUT.

keep a sharp lookout ♦ See KEEP AN EYE OUT FOR.

keep a stiff upper lip Show courage in the face of pain or adversity. For example, *I know you're upset about losing the game, but keep a stiff upper lip.* This expression presumably alludes to the trembling lips that precede bursting into tears. [Early 1800s]

keep a straight face Don't show one's feelings, especially refrain from laughing. For example, *The school orchestra played so many wrong notes that I had trouble keeping a straight face.* [Late 1800s]

keep at **1.** Persevere or persist at doing something. For example, *If you keep at your math, you'll soon master it.* It is also put as **keep at it,** as in *He kept at it all day and finally finished the report.* [Early 1800s] **2. keep at someone.** Nag, harass, or annoy someone, as in *You have to keep at Carl if you want him to do the work,* or *He keeps at Millie all the time.* Also see KEEP AFTER.

keep at arm's length ♦ See AT ARM'S LENGTH.

keep a weather eye out Also, **keep a weather eye on** or **open.** Be extremely watchful or alert, as in

We should keep a weather eye on our competitors in case they start a price war. The precise allusion in this expression is disputed, but presumably it refers to watching for a storm. [Early 1800s]

keep back ♦ See HOLD BACK.

keep body and soul together Stay alive, support life, as in *He earns barely enough to keep body and soul together.* This expression alludes to the belief that the soul gives life to the body, which therefore cannot survive without it. Today it most often is applied to earning a living. [Early 1700s]

keep company 1. Also, **keep company with**. Associate with; also, carry on a courtship. For example, *He keeps company with a wild bunch,* or *Jack and Françoise kept company for two years before they married.* [Mid-1500s] 2. **keep someone company**. Accompany or remain with someone, as in *Mary kept Mother company while she shopped,* or *Do you want me to stay and keep you company?* This term was originally put as **bear someone company**. [c. 1300]

keep cool Also, **keep a cool head; stay cool; be cool; take it cool**. Remain calm and under control, as in *Keep cool, they'll soon show up,* or *Be cool, the surprise is not spoiled,* or *You have to keep a cool head in these volatile situations,* or *Sit tight, take it cool, they won't bother you again.* All these terms employ *cool* in the sense of "not heated by strong emotion," a usage dating from the late 1300s or even earlier. The first three expressions are colloquial and date from the second half of the 1800s; both of the last two are slang, and the very last (**take it cool**) is the oldest, first recorded in 1841. Also see KEEP ONE'S COOL; PLAY IT COOL.

keep down 1. Hold under control, repress; also, retain food. For example, *Keep your voice down,* or *They vowed to keep down the insurgency,* or *With morning sickness, she had a hard time keeping down her breakfast.* [Late 1500s] 2. Prevent from increasing or succeeding, as in *The government was determined to keep prices down,* or *Joyce felt that her lack of an advanced degree kept her down in terms of promotions.* [Early 1800s]

keep from 1. Withhold; also, prevent. For example, *What information are you keeping from me?* or *Please keep your dog from running through our garden.* [c. 1340] 2. Restrain oneself, hold oneself back, as in *I can hardly keep from laughing.* [c. 1340]

keep house Manage a household, especially do the housework. For example, *It's difficult to find time to keep house when you work full-time.* [c. 1600]

keeping up with the Joneses ♦ See KEEP UP, def. 1.

keep in mind ♦ See BEAR IN MIND.

keep in the dark ♦ See IN THE DARK, def. 2.

keep in touch ♦ See IN TOUCH.

keep in with ♦ See IN WITH.

keep it up Continue to do or maintain something, as in *They were playing loud music, and they kept it up all night long.* [Mid-1700s] Also see KEEP UP, def. 4.

keep late hours Stay awake until late at night. For example, *Never call Ethel before noon; she keeps late hours and sleeps all morning.*

keep off 1. Ward off, avert, as in *She used a bug spray to keep off the mosquitoes.* [Mid-1500s] 2. Stay away from, not touch or trespass on; also, prevent from touching or trespassing. For example, *They put up a sign asking the public to keep off their property,* or *Please keep your feet off the sofa.* [Late 1500s] Also see HANDS OFF.

keep on 1. Continue, persist, as in *They kept on singing all night.* [Late 1500s] 2. Maintain an existing situation, as in *After Mr. Brown died, the housekeeper wondered if she would be kept on.* [Mid-1600s] 3. Cause to stay on or remain attached, as in *Keep your coat on; it's cold in here.* [Late 1800s]

keep one's chin up Be stalwart and courageous in a difficult situation, as in *Don't let the loan officer intimidate you; keep your chin up,* or *Despite all the difficulty, he kept his chin up.* This expression alludes to a posture of firm resolution. [First half of 1900s]

keep one's cool Retain one's composure and poise, as in *Billy keeps his cool, no matter what the situation.* This slangy usage dates from the mid-1900s, as do the antonyms **blow one's cool** and **lose one's cool**, as in *Try not to blow your cool in front of the team,* or *Dad lost his cool when he saw Jim playing with matches.* Also see KEEP COOL.

keep one's distance Stay away; also, remain emotionally remote. For example, *It's wise to keep one's distance from any wild animal,* or *Since the family argued with him, Harry's been keeping his distance.* [Late 1500s]

keep oneself to oneself ♦ See under KEEP TO ONESELF.

keep one's end up ♦ See HOLD ONE'S END UP.

keep one's eye on the ball Remain alert and attentive, as in *The research director told her students to keep their eye on the ball when it came to accurate footnotes.* This expression alludes to numerous sports in which players must watch a ball's path. [c. 1900]

keep one's eyes open Also, **keep one's eyes peeled** or **skinned**. Be watchful and observant. For example, *We should keep our eyes open for a change in the wind's direction,* or *Keep your eyes peeled for the teacher.* The first phrase dates from the late 1800s; the second and third, both colloquial and alluding to the lids not covering the eyes, date from the mid-1800s and 1830s, respectively.

keep one's fingers crossed ◆ See CROSS ONE'S FINGERS.

keep one's hand in ◆ See under HAVE A HAND IN.

keep one's hands off ◆ See HANDS OFF.

keep one's head 1. Stay calm, retain self-control, as in *When the rowboat capsized, George yelled that everyone should keep their head and hold onto the boat.* This usage dates from the early 1600s and is about two centuries older than the antonym, *lose one's head,* meaning "to become confused and agitated," as in *Whenever the stock market goes down sharply, people seem to lose their heads and sell.* 2. **keep one's head above water.** See HEAD ABOVE WATER.

keep one's mouth shut Be quiet; don't reveal confidential information. For example, *The teachers told us to keep our mouths shut during the entire presentation,* or *You can't tell Carol anything; she's incapable of keeping her mouth shut.* Also see HOLD ONE'S TONGUE.

keep one's nose clean Stay out of trouble. For example, *Dad told Brian to keep his nose clean from now on or he'd cut off his allowance.* [Colloquial; late 1800s]

keep one's nose to the grindstone ◆ See NOSE TO THE GRINDSTONE.

keep one's own counsel Say little or nothing about one's opinions or intentions. For example, *Betty is notorious for keeping her own counsel; you never know what she really thinks.* This expression employs *counsel* in the sense of "a secret," a usage dating from about 1300.

keep one's powder dry Stay alert, be careful, as in *Go ahead and take on the opposition, but keep your powder dry.* This colloquial expression, which originally alluded to keeping gunpowder dry so that it would ignite, has been used figuratively since the 1800s but today is less common than TAKE CARE.

keep one's shirt on Stay calm, be patient; not give way to temper or excitement. For example, *Keep your shirt on, Bob, they'll be here in time for the wedding.* [Colloquial; mid-1800s]

keep one's temper ◆ See HOLD ONE'S TEMPER.

keep one's wits about one ◆ See HAVE ONE'S WITS ABOUT ONE.

keep one's word Honor one's promises, as in *You can count on Richard; he'll keep his word.* This expression employs *word* in the sense of "a promise," a usage dating from the late 1500s. For an antonym, see GO BACK ON.

keep pace Also, **keep up.** Go at the same rate as others, not fall behind. For example, *The teacher*

told his mother that Jimmy was not keeping up with the class. Shakespeare had the first term in *A Midsummer Night's Dream* (3:2): "My legs cannot keep pace with my desires." [Late 1500s]

keep posted Supply with up-to-date information, as in *Keep me posted about your new job.* This usage alludes to the accounting practice of posting the latest figures in a ledger. [Early 1800s]

keep quiet Also, **keep still.** 1. Also, **be quiet** or **still.** Remain silent; same as HOLD ONE'S TONGUE. For example, *Please keep quiet about the party.* Also see KEEP ONE'S MOUTH SHUT. 2. Refrain from moving, stay in the same position; same as HOLD STILL. For example, *The doctor gave the young boy a toy to keep him quiet while on the examining table,* or *It's hard for the baby to keep still unless he's sleeping.* [Late 1300s]

keep tabs on Observe carefully, keep a record of. For example, *I hate having my boss keep tabs on my every move,* or *We've got to keep tabs on outgoing mail so we can keep track of postage.* This expression uses *tab* in the sense of "an account." [Late 1800s] Also see KEEP TRACK.

keep the ball rolling ◆ See GET THE BALL ROLLING.

keep the lid on ◆ See PUT THE LID ON.

keep the peace Maintain public order; prevent strife. For example, *President Clinton ordered troops to Bosnia to keep the peace.* This expression dates from the 1400s and was originally used more in the first sense, that is, of police keeping public order. It gained extra currency in the second half of the 1900s when military forces were sent to diverse places — Lebanon, Haiti, Bosnia — to stop warring factions.

keep the wolf from the door Ward off starvation or financial ruin. For example, *In many countries people are working simply to keep the wolf from the door, and owning a car or washing machine is just a dream,* or *Gail would take any job now, just to keep the wolf from the door.* This term alludes to the wolf's fabled ravenousness. [Mid-1500s]

keep time 1. Maintain the correct tempo and rhythm of music; also, mark the rhythm by foot-tapping, hand movements, or the like. For example, *The children love to keep time by clapping their hands.* This usage dates from the late 1500s and is occasionally put figuratively, as Ben Jonson did in *Cynthia's Revels* (1699): "Slow, slow, fresh fount, keep time with my salt tears." 2. Also, **keep good time.** Indicate the correct time, as in *This inexpensive watch does not keep good time.* [Late 1800s]

keep to 1. Adhere to, conform to, as in *Let's keep to the original purpose of this will.* [Early 1600s] 2. Confine oneself to, as in *Whenever she didn't feel well, she kept to her bed.* Also see KEEP TO ONESELF.

keep to oneself 1. Also, **keep oneself to oneself.** Shun the company of others value one's privacy, as in *She kept to herself all morning,* or, as Doris Lessing put it in *In Pursuit of the English* (1960): "She keeps herself to herself so much." [Late 1600s] 2. Refrain from revealing, hold secret, as in *He promised to keep the news to himself.* Also see the synonym KEEP UNDER ONE'S HAT.

keep track Remain informed, follow the course of, as in *Are you keeping track of the time?* This usage alludes to following a literal track, as of footsteps. The antonym, **lose track,** alludes to straying or wandering from a track, as in *I've lost track — what day are you leaving?* [Late 1800s]

keep under one's hat Preserve the secrecy of something, as in *I'll tell you about it if you promise to keep it under your hat.* This usage alludes to hiding a secret in one's head, covered by a hat. [Late 1800s]

keep under wraps ♦ See UNDER WRAPS.

keep up 1. Also, **keep up with.** Proceed at the same pace, continue alongside another, as in *We try to keep up with the times.* [First half of 1600s] This usage, also put as KEEP PACE, appears in the phrase **keeping up with the Joneses,** which was coined in 1913 by cartoonist Arthur R. Momand for the title of a series in the *New York Globe.* It means "trying to match the lifestyle of one's more affluent neighbors or acquaintances." For example, *Their buying a new van is just another attempt to keep up with the Joneses.* 2. Support, sustain, as in *They're trying to keep up their spirits while they wait for news of the crash.* [Late 1600s] Also see KEEP ONE'S CHIN UP. 3. Maintain in good condition, as in *Joan really kept up the property.* [Mid-1500s] This usage also appears in the idiom **keep up appearances,** meaning "to maintain a good front, make things look good even if they're not," as in *She was devastated by his bad prognosis but is trying hard to keep up appearances for their children.* [Mid-1700s] 4. Persevere, carry on, prolong, as in *Keep up the good work,* or *How long will this noise keep up?* [Early 1500s] Also see KEEP IT UP. 5. Also, **keep up with; keep up on.** Stay in touch, remain informed. For example, *Ann and I haven't seen each other since college, but we keep up through our annual Christmas letters,* or *We subscribe to three papers so as to keep up on current events.* [c. 1900] 6. **keep someone up.** Cause someone to remain out of bed, as in *He's keeping up the children beyond their bedtime.* [Mid-1700s]

keep watch Also, **keep a watch** or **close watch on; watch over.** Observe with continuous attention, especially to act as a sentinel or for protection. For example, *Afraid that the wolves would return, she kept watch while the others slept,* or *They kept a close*

watch on the harbor, looking for signs of enemy ships, or, according to the Gospel of St. Luke (2:8): "And there were in the same country shepherds . . . keeping watch over their flock by night." [Late 1300s] Also see KEEP AN EYE OUT FOR.

keep your . . . ♦ See under KEEP ONE'S.

keg ♦ See SITTING ON A POWDER KEG.

kettle ♦ In addition to the idiom beginning with KETTLE, also see POT CALLING THE KETTLE BLACK.

kettle of fish 1. Also, **a fine** or **pretty kettle of fish.** An unpleasant or messy predicament, as in *They haven't spoken in years, and they're assigned to adjoining seats — that's a fine kettle of fish.* This term alludes to the Scottish riverside picnic called *kettle of fish,* where freshly caught salmon were boiled and eaten out of hand. [Early 1700s] 2. **a different** or **another kettle of fish.** A very different matter or issue, not necessarily a bad one. For example, *They're paying for the meal? That's a different kettle of fish.* [First half of 1900s]

key ♦ In addition to the idiom beginning with KEY, also see IN KEY; UNDER LOCK AND KEY.

key up Make intense, excited, or nervous. For example, *The excitement of the gallery opening has really keyed her up.* This usage alludes to *key* in the sense of "wind up a spring-driven mechanism such as a clock." [Late 1800s]

kibosh ♦ See PUT THE KIBOSH ON.

kick ♦ In addition to the idioms beginning with KICK, also see ALIVE AND KICKING; FOR FUN (KICKS); GET A BANG (KICK) OUT OF.

kick a habit Also, **kick it; kick the habit.** Overcome or give up habitual use, especially of narcotics. For example, *Smoking is addictive; it's not easy to kick,* or *If he doesn't kick the habit, he may not make it through school.* This idiom uses *kick* in the sense of "get rid of." [First half of 1900s]

kick around 1. Treat badly, abuse, as in *I'm sick and tired of being kicked around by my supervisor.* [Colloquial; first half of 1900s] 2. Also, **kick about.** Move from place to place, as in *They spent three years kicking around the country on their bikes,* or *We've no address; we're just kicking about until we find somewhere to settle.* [Colloquial; early 1800s] 3. Also, **kick about.** Consider, think about or discuss; examine or try out. For example, *Let's kick this scenario around for a while and see what we come up with,* or *We've been kicking about various schemes to make money.* [Colloquial; first half of 1900s] 4. Be available or unused, as in *This old computer has been kicking around for months — no one seems to want it.* [c. 1900]

kick ass Also, **kick butt.** Punish or discipline harshly; also, defeat soundly. For example, *That foreman's furious; he's going to kick ass before the* *day is over,* or *Our team is out to kick butt today.* [Vulgar slang; 1940s]

kick back 1. Recoil unexpectedly and violently, as in *This rifle kicks back a lot when you fire it.* [Early 1800s] **2.** Return stolen property to the owner, as in *The pawnbroker kicked back the paintings to the gallery.* [Colloquial; first half of 1900s] **3.** Pay back a part of one's earnings, as in *The workers were forced to kick back half their pay to the agent.* [Colloquial; first half of 1900s]

kick in 1. Contribute one's share, as in *We'll kick in half if you take care of the rest.* [Colloquial; c. 1900] **2.** Also, **kick off.** Die, as in *No one knows when he'll kick in,* or *He finally kicked off yesterday.* [Slang; first half of 1900s] Also see KICK THE BUCKET. **3.** Begin to operate, as in *Finally the motor kicked in and we could get started.* This usage was first recorded in 1908.

kick in the pants, a 1. Also, **a kick in the teeth.** A humiliating setback or rebuff. For example, *That rejection was a real kick in the pants,* or *That review was a kick in the teeth.* A third, vulgar variant of these colloquial terms is **a kick in the ass.** Versions of this last expression—**kick in the breech, kick in the behind**—have been used since the early 1800s. **2.** A cause of enjoyment, as in *That show was a real kick in the pants.* This meaning is virtually the opposite of def. 1 and can be differentiated from it only by the context. [1960s]

kick it ♦ See KICK A HABIT.

kick off 1. Start, begin, as in *They kicked off the celebration with a parade.* This term alludes to starting play by kicking the ball in soccer, football, and similar sports. [Mid-1800s] **2.** See KICK IN, def. 2.

kick oneself Berate oneself, reproach oneself, as in *I've been kicking myself all day for forgetting the keys.* [Late 1800s]

kick out 1. Also, **boot out.** Throw out, dismiss, especially ignominiously. For example, *George said they'd been kicked out of the country club,* or *The owner booted them out of the restaurant for being loud and disorderly.* This idiom alludes to expelling someone with a KICK IN THE PANTS. [Late 1600s] **2.** Supply, especially in a sorted fashion, as in *The bureau kicked out the precise data for this month's production.* [Slang; late 1900s]

kick over the traces Break loose from restraint, misbehave. For example, *There's always one child who'll kick over the traces as soon as the bell rings.* This metaphoric expression alludes to the straps attaching a horse to a vehicle, which the animal sometimes gets a leg over in order to kick more freely and thereby refuse to move forward. [Mid-1800s]

kick the bucket Die, as in *All of my goldfish kicked the bucket while we were on vacation.* This moder-

ately impolite usage has a disputed origin. Some say it refers to committing suicide by hanging, in which one stands on a bucket, fastens a rope around one's neck, and kicks the bucket away. A more likely origin is the use of *bucket* in the sense of "a beam from which something may be suspended"; because pigs were suspended by their heels from such beams after being slaughtered, the term **kick the bucket** came to mean "to die." [Colloquial; late 1700s]

kick the habit ♦ See KICK A HABIT.

kick up Malfunction, cause trouble or pain, as in *My grandmother's arthritis is kicking up again.* [Colloquial; first half of 1900s] Also see ACT UP; also subsequent entries beginning with KICK UP.

kick up a fuss Also, **kick up a row** or **storm.** Create a disturbance; start a fight. For example, *The soup was cold, and Aunt Mary began to kick up a fuss, calling for the manager,* or *There's no need to kick up a row; the boys will leave quietly,* or *If they fire him, Carl is ready to kick up a storm.* These expressions all employ *kick up* in the sense of "raise dust or dirt," a usage dating from the mid-1700s.

kick up one's heels Enjoy oneself, as in *When she retires, she plans to kick up her heels and travel.* This expression originated about 1600 with a totally different meaning, "to be killed." The modern sense, alluding to a prancing horse or exuberant dancer, dates from about 1900.

kick upstairs Promote someone to a higher but less desirable position, especially one with less authority. For example, *Paul never forgave the company for kicking him upstairs at age 55.* This expression alludes to its antonym, **kick downstairs,** simply meaning "eject." [Mid-1900s]

kid ♦ In addition to the idioms beginning with KID, also see HANDLE WITH (KID) GLOVES. Also see KIDDING.

kid around Engage in good-humored fooling, joking, or teasing. For example, *He's always kidding around with the other boys.* [First half of 1900s]

kidding ♦ See ALL JOKING (KIDDING) ASIDE; NO KIDDING.

kid gloves ♦ See HANDLE WITH KID GLOVES.

kid stuff Something very easy or uncomplicated, as in *That new computer program is kid stuff.* This usage alludes to something suitable for young children, or "kids." [c. 1920]

kid the pants off ♦ See PANTS OFF.

kill ♦ In addition to the idioms beginning with KILL, also see CURIOSITY KILLED THE CAT; DRESSED TO KILL; FIT TO KILL; IN AT THE DEATH (KILL); LADY KILLER; MAKE A KILLING; RUN OUT (KILL) THE CLOCK.

kill off 1. Render extinct, eliminate completely, as in *The plague killed off entire villages and towns.*

[c. 1600] **2.** Represent as dead, as in *This mystery writer kills off a new victim in almost every chapter.* [Mid-1800s]

kill or cure Either remedy a disease or kill the patient, as in *The copy chief did not like her headline for the drug, "Kill or Cure."* This expression dates from the mid-1700s, when it was already being used half-jokingly.

kill the fatted calf Prepare for a joyful occasion or a warm welcome. For example, *When Bill comes home from his trip to Korea we're going to kill the fatted calf.* This expression alludes to the parable of the prodigal son (Luke 15:11–32), whose father welcomed him by serving the choicest calf after his return. [Early 1600s]

kill the goose that lays the golden eggs Destroy a source of riches through stupidity or greed, as in *If he never gives his loyal customers a break on some items in his store, he'll kill the goose that lays the golden eggs.* This expression, already a proverb in the late 1400s, alludes to Aesop's fable about a farmer whose goose lays one golden egg a day, and who kills the goose in the mistaken belief that he'll get all the eggs at once.

kill time Pass time aimlessly. For example, *There was nothing to do, so I sat around killing time until dinner was ready.* This idiom was first recorded about 1768.

kill two birds with one stone Achieve two ends with a single effort, as in *As long as I was in town on business, I thought I'd kill two birds and visit my uncle too.* This expression is so well known that it is often shortened, as in the example. [c. 1600]

kill with kindness Overwhelm or harm someone with mistaken or excessive benevolence. For example, *Aunt Mary constantly sends Jane chocolates and cake and other goodies, even though she's been told Jane's on a diet—nothing like killing with kindness.* This expression originated as *kill with kindness as fond apes do their young* (presumably crushing them to death in a hug) and was a proverb by the mid-1500s.

kilter ‣ See OUT OF KILTER.

kin ‣ See KITH AND KIN.

kind ‣ In addition to the idiom beginning with KIND, also see ALL KINDS OF; IN KIND; NOTHING OF THE KIND; OF A KIND; TWO OF A KIND.

kindly ‣ See TAKE KINDLY TO.

kindness ‣ See KILL WITH KINDNESS; MILK OF HUMAN KINDNESS.

kind of Also, **sort of.** Rather, somewhat, as in *I'm kind of hungry,* or *The bird looked sort of like a sparrow.* [Colloquial; c. 1800] This usage should not be confused with **a kind of** or **a sort of,** which

are much older and refer to a borderline member of a given category (as in *a kind of a shelter* or *a sort of a bluish color*). Shakespeare had this usage in *Two Gentlemen of Verona* (3:1): "My master is a kind of a knave." Also see OF A KIND.

kindred spirit Also, **kindred soul.** An individual with the same beliefs, attitudes or feelings as oneself. For example, *Dean and I are kindred spirits when it comes to spending money—we're both tight.* [Mid-1800s]

king ‣ In addition to the idiom beginning with KING, also see LIVE LIKE A KING.

king's ransom A huge sum of money, as in *That handmade rug must have cost a king's ransom.* This metaphoric expression originally referred to the sum required to release a king from captivity. [Late 1400s]

kiss and make up Settle one's differences, reconcile, as in *The two friends decided to kiss and make up.* This colloquial expression has largely replaced *kiss and be friends,* dating from the 1400s. [Mid-1900s]

kiss and tell Betray a confidence, as in *A real lady doesn't kiss and tell.* This idiom originally alluded to betraying an amorous or sexual intimacy. First recorded in 1695, it is still so used, as well as more loosely, as in *Don't ask how I voted; I don't kiss and tell.*

kiss ass Also, **kiss up to.** Seek or gain favor by fawning or flattery, as in *I am not going to kiss ass to get the raise I deserve,* or *If I could find a good way to kiss up to the publisher, my book would be well promoted.* The first, a vulgar slangy usage, was first recorded in 1705 as *kiss arse,* which is still the British usage. The variant, a euphemistic blend of *kiss ass* and SUCK UP TO, dates from the late 1900s.

kiss good-bye Be forced to regard as lost, ruined, or hopeless, as in *Now that both kids are sick, we'll have to kiss our vacation in Florida good-bye.* This usage ironically alludes to a genuine good-bye kiss. [Colloquial; c. 1900] Also see KISS OFF, def. 2.

kissing cousins Two or more things that are closely akin or very similar. For example, *They may be made by different manufacturers, but these two cars are kissing cousins.* This metaphoric term alludes to a distant relative who is well known enough to be greeted with a kiss. [c. 1930]

kiss of death An action or relationship that is ultimately ruinous. For example, *Some regard a royal divorce as a kiss of death to the monarchy.* This term alludes to the betrayal of Jesus by Judas Iscariot, who kissed him as a way of identifying him to the soldiers who came to arrest him (Matthew 26: 47–49). It dates only from about 1940 but was previously called a **Judas kiss.**

kiss off 1. Dismiss or reject, as in *He kissed off their offer*. This usage alludes to kissing something goodbye [Slang; c. 1900] 2. Be forced to give up or regard as lost, as in *You can kiss off that promotion*. [Slang; late 1940s] 3. Get out, go away, as in *She told the reporters to kiss off*. [Slang; early 1900s]

kit and caboodle ♦ See WHOLE KIT AND CABOODLE.

kitchen ♦ See EVERYTHING BUT THE KITCHEN SINK; IF YOU CAN'T STAND THE HEAT, GET OUT OF THE KITCHEN.

kite ♦ See GO FLY A KITE; HIGH AS A KITE.

kith and kin Friends and family, as in *Everyone was invited, kith and kin as well as distant acquaintances*. This expression dates from the 1300s and originally meant "countrymen" (*kith* meant "one's native land") and "family members." It gradually took on the present looser sense.

kitten ♦ See HAVE A FIT (KITTENS); WEAK AS A KITTEN.

knee ♦ In addition to the idiom beginning with KNEE, also see BRING TO ONE'S KNEES; ON BENDED KNEE.

knee-high to a grasshopper Quite young, as in *I haven't seen him since I was knee-high to a grasshopper*. This hyperbolic expression, dating from about 1850 and alluding to someone's youth, replaced the earlier *knee-high to a mosquito* or *bumblebee* or *splinter*.

knell ♦ See DEATH KNELL.

knife ♦ See AT GUNPOINT (KNIFEPOINT); UNDER THE KNIFE; YOU COULD CUT IT WITH A KNIFE.

knight in shining armor A rescuer or defender, as in *What this political party needs is a knight in shining armor to change its tarnished image*. This metaphoric expression alludes to a medieval knight. [Mid-1900s]

knock ♦ In addition to the idioms beginning with KNOCK, also see BEAT (KNOCK) INTO SOMEONE'S HEAD; BEAT (KNOCK) THE LIVING DAYLIGHT'S OUT OF; (KNOCK) DOWN TO SIZE; (KNOCK) OFF SOMEONE'S FEET; SCHOOL OF HARD KNOCKS.

knock about Also, **knock around**. 1. Be rough or brutal with, maltreat, as in *He was known to knock his wife about on a regular basis*. [c. 1800] 2. Wander from place to place, as in *They were knocking around Europe all summer*. [Colloquial; c. 1830] 3. Discuss or consider, as in *They met to knock about some new ideas*. [Mid-1900s] Also see KICK AROUND.

knock back Also, **knock it back**. Gulp down an alcoholic beverage, as in *He knocked back glass after glass of wine*, or *I hear you've been knocking it back a bit*. [First half of 1900s]

knock cold ♦ See KNOCK OUT, def. 1.

knock dead Greatly amuse, astonish, or thrill someone, as in *This new song will knock them dead*. This slangy hyperbolic expression was first recorded in 1889. Also see KNOCK THE SOCKS OFF.

knock down 1. Take apart for storage or shipping, as in *We need to knock down this chest to ship it safely overseas*. [Mid-1900s] 2. Declare sold at an auction, as by striking a blow with a gavel. For example, *That was the last bid, and the first edition was knocked down for only three hundred*. [Mid-1700s] 3. Reduce the price of, as in *They knocked it down by another hundred dollars*, or *An overabundant harvest will knock down corn prices*. [Colloquial; mid-1800] 4. Earn as wages, as in *She knocks down a hundred grand a year*. [Slang; 1920s] 5. Steal, embezzle, as in *He was caught knocking down the box-office receipts*. This usage may be obsolescent. [Slang; mid-1800s] Also see KNOCK OVER, def. 2.

knock down with a feather ♦ See under KNOCK FOR A LOOP.

knock for a loop Also, **throw for a loop; knock down** or **over with a feather; knock sideways**. Overcome with surprise or astonishment, as in *The news of his death knocked me for a loop*, or *Being fired without any warning threw me for a loop*, or *Jane was knocked sideways when she found out she won*. The first two of these hyperbolic colloquial usages, dating from the first half of the 1900s, allude to the comic-strip image of a person pushed hard enough to roll over in the shape of a loop. The third hyperbolic term, often put as *You could have knocked me down with a feather*, intimating that something so light as a feather could knock one down, dates from the early 1800s; the fourth was first recorded in 1925.

knock into a cocked hat Debunk, render useless or unbelievable. For example, *His findings knocked our theory into a cocked hat*. This expression alludes to a style of hat with the brim turned up on three sides—the three-cornered (tricorne) hat worn by officers in the American Revolution—giving it a distorted look. [Early 1800s]

knock it off Quit or stop doing something, as in *Knock it off, boys! That's enough noise*. This term is often used as an imperative. [Colloquial; c. 1900] Also see KNOCK OFF.

knock off 1. Take a break or rest from, stop, especially quit working. For example, *He knocked off work at noon*, or *Let's knock off at five o'clock*. [Colloquial; mid-1600s] Also see KNOCK IT OFF. 2. Also, **knock out**. Dispose of or produce easily or hastily, finish, as in *A writer of detective novels, he knocks off a book a year*, or *We can knock out a rough drawing in a few minutes*. The first colloquial usage dates from the early 1800s, the variant from the mid-1800s. 3. Get rid of, reduce, as in *She knocked off twelve pounds in a month*, or *They* knocked off one-third of the original price. [Colloquial; early 1800s] **4.** Kill, murder, as in *They decided to knock off the old lady.* [Slang; early 1900s] Also see KNOCK SOMEONE'S BLOCK OFF. **5.** Copy or imitate, especially without permission, as in *They are knocking off designer Swiss watches and selling them for a few dollars.* [Colloquial; late 1800s] **6.** Hold up, rob, as in *The gang knocked off two liquor stores in half an hour.* [Slang; early 1900s] Also see KNOCK THE SOCKS OFF.

knock oneself out 1. Make a great effort, as in *I was knocking myself out to finish on time.* This expression also is put negatively, **Don't knock yourself out,** meaning "don't exert yourself; it's not worth that much effort." [c. 1930] **2.** Enjoy yourself, have a good time, as in *You're off to Europe? Knock yourself out.* [Slang; mid-1900s] Both usages allude to knocking oneself unconscious (see KNOCK OUT). For a synonym see BREAK ONE'S ASS.

knock on wood Also, **touch wood.** Express a wish that something will or will not occur, as in *This last round of treatment should have cured her, knock on wood.* This expression alludes to an ancient superstition that literally knocking on or touching wood will ward off evil spirits. [c. 1900]

knock out 1. Also, **knock out cold.** Render unconscious by a blow or some other means. For example, *It was just a swinging door, but it knocked her out,* or *Just one of those sleeping pills can knock you out cold.* [Late 1500s] **2.** Make tired, exhaust, as in *That sightseeing tour knocked me out.* **3.** Render useless or inoperative, as in *The storm knocked out the power.* **4.** See KNOCK OFF, def. 2. **5.** See KNOCK ONESELF OUT.

knock over 1. Astonish, overcome, as in *Their resemblance completely knocked me over.* [Mid-1800s] Also see KNOCK FOR A LOOP. **2.** Steal or burgle, as in *They knocked over one bank and headed for another.* [Slang; 1920s]

knock over with a feather ♦ See under KNOCK FOR A LOOP.

knock someone's block off Beat up someone, as in *If he doesn't leave at once, I'll knock his block off.* This hyperbolic term employs *block* in the sense of "head," a usage dating from the 1600s. The idiom, however, dates only from about 1900. Also see BEAT THE LIVING DAYLIGHTS OUT OF.

knock someone's socks off ♦ See KNOCK THE SOCKS OFF.

knock the bottom out of Also, **knock the props out from under.** Render invalid, undermine. For example, *The discovery of another planet that might support life knocks the bottom out of many theories,* or *Jane's skilled debating knocked the props out from under her opponent.* The first ex-

pression dates from the late 1800s, the variant from the first half of the 1900s.

knock the living daylights out of Also, **knock the shit or stuffing or tar out of.** ♦ See BEAT THE LIVING DAYLIGHTS OUT OF.

knock the socks off Also **knock someone's socks off. 1.** Overwhelm, bedazzle, or amaze someone, as in *The young pianist knocked the socks off of the judges,* or *That display will knock their socks off.* [Slang; mid-1800s] **2.** Also, **knock the spots off.** Surpass or outdo completely, defeat. For example, *These large chains have been knocking the socks off the small independent grocers,* or *Our team knocked the spots off them.* The *spots* most likely allude to target practice with playing cards where the object is to shoot through all the pips, spots, or marks indicating the suit or numerical value of a playing card, but one authority holds that they were used in a horse-breeding context and meant "to be in the vanguard." [Mid-1800s]

knock together Make or assemble quickly or carelessly, as in *We knocked together the bookcases in about half an hour.* [Late 1800s]

knock up 1. Make pregnant, as in *The young girl said she was afraid of getting knocked up.* [Slang; early 1800s] **2.** Injure or damage, as in *This coffee table got all knocked up in the moving van.*

knot ♦ See TIE INTO KNOTS; TIE THE KNOT.

know ♦ In addition to the idioms beginning with KNOW, also see BEFORE YOU KNOW IT; (KNOW) BY HEART; COME IN OUT OF THE RAIN, KNOW ENOUGH TO; COMING OR GOING, KNOW IF ONE'S; FOR ALL; (I KNOW); GOD KNOWS; (KNOW) INSIDE OUT; IN THE KNOW; IT TAKES ONE TO KNOW ONE; LEFT HAND DOESN'T KNOW WHAT RIGHT HAND IS DOING; NOT KNOW BEANS; NOT KNOW FROM ADAM; NOT KNOW WHERE TO TURN; NOT KNOW WHICH WAY TO JUMP; THING OR TWO, KNOW; WHAT DO YOU KNOW; WHAT HAVE YOU (WHO KNOWS WHAT); WHICH IS WHICH, KNOW; YOU KNOW.

know all the answers Also, **know a thing or two; know it all; know one's way around.** Be extremely knowledgeable or experienced. These idioms may be used somewhat differently, expressing overconfidence, as in *Helen always knew all the answers, or thought she did,* or competence, as in *Bob knows a thing or two about battery technology,* or ruefulness, as in *I thought I knew it all about plants and then I got poison ivy,* or genuine expertise, as in *John knows his way around tax forms.* The first term dates from the early 1900s, the second from the later 1700s, the third from the later 1800s, and the fourth, also put as **know one's way about,** dates from the 1500s. Also see KNOW ONE'S STUFF; KNOW THE ROPES; under TRICKS OF THE TRADE.

know a thing or two ♦ See KNOW ALL THE ANSWERS.

know beans ♦ See NOT KNOW BEANS.

know better Be able to recognize something as wrong or not possible, as in *Mary should know better than to leave her child alone in the house,* or *Try to get in without a ticket? You know better than that.* [c. 1700]

know by heart ♦ See BY HEART.

know by sight Recognize someone or something by appearance but not know the name or other details. For example, *I know a lot of people by sight from the tennis courts.* [1200s]

know enough to come in out of the rain ♦ See COME IN OUT OF THE RAIN.

know from Adam ♦ See NOT KNOW FROM ADAM.

know if one is coming or going ♦ See COMING OR GOING.

know it all ♦ See KNOW ALL THE ANSWERS.

knowledge ♦ See LITTLE KNOWLEDGE IS A DANGEROUS THING; TO THE BEST OF (ONE'S KNOWLEDGE).

know like a book Also, **know like the back of one's hand** or **know backwards and forwards.** Be extremely familiar with or knowledgeable about; understand perfectly. For example, *I know Greg like a book—I'm sure he'll come,* or *I know this town like the back of my hand,* or *John knew his part backwards and forwards.* The first of these hyperbolic idioms, dating from the early 1800s, has a close cousin in **read like a book,** which means "to discern someone's intent," as in *I can read Greg like a book;* also see under OPEN BOOK. The second (*back of hand*) dates only from the mid-1900s. Also see BACKWARDS AND FORWARDS, def. 2; INSIDE OUT, def. 2; KNOW ALL THE ANSWERS.

know one's own mind Be certain about what one wants; be decisive. For example, *Don't ask him; he's so tired that he doesn't know his own mind,* or *She certainly knows her own mind when it comes to giving stage directions.* This term was first recorded in 1824.

know one's place Behave suitably for one's position, rank, or status. This idiom often has the sense of "to behave humbly, not criticize ones' superiors," as in *Sorry, I know my place and I can't tell you more about my supervisor's plans.* [Late 1500s] Also see PUT ONE IN ONE'S PLACE.

know one's stuff Also, **know one's onions.** Be experienced or knowledgeable in one's field or in the matter at hand. For example, *Patrice knows her stuff when it comes to Mexican history,* or *We need a handyman who knows his onions.* The allusion in the variant is unclear. [First half of 1900s]

know one's way around ♦ See under KNOW ALL THE ANSWERS.

know only too well ♦ See under ONLY TOO.

know the ropes Be informed about the details of a situation or task. For example, *Don't worry about Sara's taking over that reporter's job—she already knows the ropes.* This expression alludes to sailors learning the rigging so as to handle a sailing vessel's ropes. It was being used figuratively by the late 1800s. The same allusion is present in **show someone the ropes,** meaning "to familiarize someone with the details," as in *Tom's very experienced—he'll show you the ropes.*

know the score Also, **know what's what.** Understand what is happening; be familiar with the real story or the full situation. For example, *It will take the new legislators some time to know the score,* or *When it comes to teaching youngsters to read, Nell knows what's what.* The first expression, dating from about 1930, alludes to *score* as a tally of points in a game. The variant dates from about 1400.

know where one stands 1. Be aware of one's position relative to others, or how one is regarded by others, as in *I'd love to know where I stand with the new board.* 2. Be aware of one's own opinion or feelings about something, as in *He knows where he stands on the issue of public housing.*

know which side of one's bread is buttered Be aware of where one's best interests lie, as in *Jerry always helps out his boss; he knows which side of his bread is buttered.* This expression alludes to the more favorable, or buttered, side of bread and has been used metaphorically since the early 1500s.

knuckle ♦ In addition to the idioms beginning with KNUCKLE, also see RAP SOMEONE'S KNUCKLES.

knuckle down 1. Apply oneself seriously to some task or goal, as in *The professor insisted that we knuckle down and get our papers in by Friday.* Both this term and the rhyming synonym **buckle down** date from the 1860s, but the precise allusion in either is unclear. 2. See KNUCKLE UNDER.

knuckle under Also, **knuckle down.** Give in, acknowledge defeat, as in *The dean refused to knuckle under to the graduate students' demands,* or *He was forced to knuckle down before their threats of violence.* Presumably this idiom alludes to a kneeling position with hands on the ground, knuckles down. [Mid-1700s].

L

labor of love Work done for one's satisfaction rather than monetary reward. For example, *The research took three years but it was a labor of love.* This expression appears twice in the New Testament (Hebrews 6:10, Thessalonians 1:3), referring to those who do God's work as a labor of love. [c. 1600]

lace into Also, **light into**. Attack, assail, as in *He laced into me for arriving late*, or *She lit into him for forgetting the tickets*. The first of these colloquial terms employs *lace* in the sense of "beat up or thrash," a usage dating from the late 1500s. The idiom with *light* dates from the late 1800s and stems from the verb *alight*, meaning "descend."

ladder ♦ See BOTTOM OF THE LADDER.

ladies' man Also **lady's man**. A man who enjoys and attracts the company of women. For example, *Because women seemed to seek him out at parties, Brian got the reputation for being quite a ladies' man*. [Late 1700s]

laid up 1. Also, **sick in bed**. Ill and confined to bed, as in *I was laid up for a week with the flu*, or *Sally can't come outside; she's sick in bed*. [Mid-1500s] 2. Put in a safe place, as in *The ship was laid up in dock with engine trouble*, or *The hikers were laid up in a cave during the storm*. [Mid-1600s] Also see under LAY IN; LAY SOMEONE LOW.

la-la land 1. Los Angeles, California (often abbreviated L.A.). This expression pokes fun at the alleged eccentricities of the city's inhabitants. For example, *What do you expect? Frederick has lived in la-la land for ten years and it has rubbed off on him*. [Slang; c. 1980] 2. A state of being out of touch with reality, as in *I don't know what's going on with Amy she seems to be in la-la land*. [Slang; c. 1980] Also see CLOUD-CUCKOO LAND; NEVER-NEVER LAND.

lam ♦ See ON THE LAM.

lamb ♦ See HANGED FOR A SHEEP (AS A LAMB); IN TWO SHAKES (OF A LAMB'S TAIL); LIKE A LAMB TO THE SLAUGHTER.

lame duck An elected officeholder whose term of office has not yet expired but who has failed to be re-elected and therefore cannot garner much political support for initiatives. For example, *You can't expect a lame duck President to get much accomplished; he's only got a month left in office*. This expression originated in the 1700s and then meant a stock-broker who did not meet his debts. It was transferred to officeholders in the 1860s. The **Lame Duck Amendment**, 20th to the U.S. Constitution, calls for Congress and each new President to take office in January instead of March (as before), thereby eliminating the lame-duck session of Congress.

land ♦ In addition to the idioms beginning with LAND, also see CLOUD-CUCKOO LAND; FALL (LAND) ON ONE'S FEET; FAT OF THE LAND; LA-LA LAND; LAY OF THE LAND; NEVER-NEVER LAND.

land in Also, **land up**. Arrive at, end in something. For example, *This situation could land you in a ter-*

rible mess, or *I never thought I'd land up with a reward for excellence*. These expressions both employ *land* in the sense of "to end," a usage dating from the late 1600s.

land-office business A thriving, expanding, or very profitable concern or volume of trade. For example, *After the storm they did a land-office business in snow shovels and rock salt*. This term, dating from the 1830s, alludes to the throng of applicants to government land offices through which Western lands were sold. It has been used for other booming business since the mid-1800s.

land on ♦ See under JUMP ALL OVER; for **land on one's feet**, see FALL ON ONE'S FEET.

land up ♦ See LAND IN.

lane ♦ See FAST LANE; LOVERS' LANE.

lap ♦ In addition to the idioms beginning with LAP, also see DROP IN SOMEONE'S LAP.

lap of luxury, in the In affluent circumstances, equipped with anything money can buy. For example, *Jane grew up in the lap of luxury*. This expression alludes to the *lap* as a place of comfort. [Late 1700s]

lap of the gods, in the Beyond one's control, in the hands of providence. For example, *She's done what she can to expedite matters; now it's in the lap of the gods*. This expression is a translation from Homer's *Iliad*, in which Automedon, the charioteer of Achilles and Patroclos, said the battle's outcome was "in the lap of the gods." *Lap of the gods* has also been translated as *knees of the gods*.

lap up Take in or receive very eagerly, as in *She loves to travel—she just laps it up*, or *The agency is lapping up whatever information their spies send in*. This expression alludes to an animal drinking greedily. [Late 1800s]

large ♦ See AT LARGE; BIG (LARGE) AS LIFE; BY AND LARGE; COG IN THE (A LARGE) WHEEL; IN SOME (LARGE) MEASURE; LOOM LARGE; WRIT LARGE.

large as life Also, **larger than life**. ♦ See BIG AS LIFE.

lark ♦ In addition to the idiom beginning with LARK, also see HAPPY AS THE DAY IS LONG (AS A LARK).

lark it up Also, **lark about**. Have a noisy, exuberant good time. For example, *We were larking it up when the supervisor walked in*, or *He's always larking about at night*. These expressions employ *lark* in the sense of "to frolic," a usage dating from the early 1800s. Also see CUT UP.

lash out Make a sudden blow or fierce verbal attack. For example, *The mule lashed out with its hind legs*, or *After listening to Dad's criticism of his driving, Arthur lashed out at him*. [Second half of 1500s]

last ♦ In addition to the idioms beginning with LAST, also see AT LAST; AT THE LAST MINUTE;

BREATHE ONE'S LAST; EACH AND EVERY (LAST ONE); FAMOUS LAST WORDS; FIRST AND LAST; HEAD FOR (THE LAST ROUNDUP); IN THE FINAL (LAST) ANALYSIS; ON ONE'S LAST LEGS; SEE THE LAST OF; STICK TO ONE'S LAST; TO THE LAST.

last analysis ‣ See FINAL ANALYSIS.

last but not least Last in sequence but not least in importance, as in *Last but not least, I want to thank all the people who sent me copies of my article in the paper.* [Late 1500s]

last-ditch effort A desperate final attempt, as in *We're making a last-ditch effort to finish on time.* This expression alludes to the military sense of *last ditch,* "the last line of defense." Its figurative use dates from the early 1800s.

last fling A final enjoyment of freedom. For example, *He's planning to have one last fling before joining the army.* This expression employs *fling* in the sense of "a brief period of indulging one's impulses," a usage dating from the first half of the 1800s.

last gasp The moment before death; also, the end. For example, "Fight till the last gasp" (Shakespeare, *1 Henry VI,* 1:2), or *He was determined to stay at the party until the last gasp.* This idiom alludes to taking one's last breath, literally (first example) or figuratively (second example). [Late 1500s]

last laugh, have the Succeed in the end, after some earlier reverses. For example, *We'll have the last laugh when they learn we got the contract.* This expression, alluding to laughing at the loser, appeared in slightly different form in the mid-1500s and gave rise to the modern proverbial phrase, **He who laughs last laughs best** (or **He laughs best who laughs last**).

last resort A final expedient or recourse to achieve some end or settle a difficulty. For example, *If you don't improve, we'll try this new medication as a last resort.* This term originally referred to a court of law from which there was no appeal. [Late 1600s]

last straw, the The final annoyance or setback, which even though minor makes one lose patience. For example, *I could put up with his delays and missed deadlines, but when he claimed the work was unimportant—that was the last straw!* This term is a shortening of **the straw that broke the camel's back,** which conveys a vivid image of an overloaded animal being given one slight additional weight. The expression dates from the mid-1800s, and replaced the earlier *the last feather that breaks the horse's back.*

last word, the 1. The final statement in a verbal argument, as in *Karen is never satisfied unless she has the last word.* [Late 1800s] 2. A conclusive or authoritative statement or treatment; also, the power or authority of ultimate decision. For example, *This report is considered to be the last word on genetic counseling,* or *In financial matters, the treasurer has the last word.* [Late 1800s] 3. The latest: thing; the newest, most fashionable of its kind. For example, *Our food processor is the last word in kitchen gadgetry.* [c. 1930]

latch onto Also, **latch on to.** 1. Get hold of, grasp; also, understand, grasp mentally. For example, *They latched onto a fortune in the fur trade,* or *Carol quickly latched on to how the sewing machine works.* [c. 1930] 2. Attach oneself to, join in with, as in *Rob didn't know the way so he latched on to one of the older children.* [c. 1930]

late ‣ In addition to the idioms beginning with LATE, also see AT THE LATEST; BETTER LATE THAN NEVER; JOHNNY-COME-LATELY; KEEP LATE HOURS; OF LATE; THE LATEST; TOO LITTLE, TOO LATE. Also see under LATER.

late in life In old age. For example, *Isn't it rather late in life for your grandmother to go trekking in Nepal?*

late in the day Far advanced; also, too far advanced. For example, *It's late in the day to change the kitchen layout, since we've already ordered the cabinets,* or *It's a bit late in the day for apologizing.* [Late 1700s]

later ‣ See In addition to the idiom beginning with LATER, also see SOONER OR LATER. Also see under LATE.

later on Subsequently, afterward, as in *They served the main course, and later on, the dessert,* or *When can I use the sewing machine?—Later on, when I'm done.* [Late 1800s]

lather ‣ See IN A LATHER.

laugh ‣ In addition to the idioms beginning with LAUGH, also see CANNED LAUGHTER; DIE LAUGHING; IT'S TO LAUGH; LAST LAUGH; NO JOKE (LAUGHING MATTER); SHAKE WITH LAUGHTER.

laugh all the way to the bank Also, **cried all the way to the bank.** Exult in a financial gain from something that had either been derided or thought worthless. For example, *You may not think much of this comedian, but he's laughing all the way to the bank.* Despite the seeming difference between *laugh* and *cry,* the two terms are virtually synonymous, the one with *cry* being used ironically and *laugh* straightforwardly. [c. 1960]

laugh and the world laughs with you Keep your sense of humor and people will sympathize with you, as in *She's always cheerful and has dozens of friends; laugh and the world laughs with you.* This expression actually is part of an ancient Latin saying that concludes, *weep and the world weeps with you.* The current version, with the ending **weep and you weep alone** (meaning "you'll get no sympathy in your sorrow"), first appeared in 1883 in Ella Wilcox's poem "Solitude." O. Henry used a slightly different version: "Laugh, and the world laughs with you; weep, and they give you the laugh" (*The Count and the Wedding Guest*, 1907).

laugh at Treat lightly, scoff at. For example, *He said the other children all laughed at his jacket*, or *They stopped laughing at his theory when it proved to be correct*. [Late 1300s]

laughing matter ♦ See under NO JOKE.

laugh off Also, **laugh away**. Dismiss as ridiculous or trivial, as in *He laughed off the suggestion that his career was over*. [Early 1700s]

laugh one's head off ♦ See SPLIT ONE'S SIDES.

laugh out of court Dismiss with ridicule or scorn, as in *When he told them the old car could be repaired, they laughed him out of court*. This expression, which originally referred to a case so laughable or trivial that a court of law would dismiss it, originated in ancient Roman times but has been used in English, without its former legal significance, since the late 1800s.

laugh out of the other side of one's mouth Also, **laugh on the wrong side of one's mouth** or **face**. Change from happiness to sadness, disappointment, or vexation. For example, *He'll be laughing out of the other side of his mouth when he learns that he'll have to pay for the business trip he sought*. [Late 1700s]

laugh up one's sleeve Rejoice or exult secretly, hide one's amusement, as in *When she tripped over her bridal train, her sister couldn't help laughing up her sleeve*. This expression replaced the earlier *laugh in one's sleeve*, used by Richard Sheridan in *The Rivals* (1775): "'Tis false, sir, I know you are laughing in your sleeve." The expression, which alludes to hiding one's laughter in big loose sleeves, was already a proverb in the mid-1500s.

laundry ♦ See WASH ONE'S DIRTY LINEN (LAUNDRY).

laurel ♦ See LOOK TO ONE'S LAURELS; REST ON ONE'S LAURELS.

law ♦ In addition to the idioms beginning with LAW, also see ABOVE SUSPICION (THE LAW); LAY DOWN THE LAW; LETTER OF THE LAW; LONG ARM OF THE LAW; MURPHY'S LAW; POSSESSION IS NINE POINTS OF THE LAW; TAKE THE LAW INTO ONE'S HANDS; UNWRITTEN LAW.

law and order Strict enforcement of laws, especially for controlling crime. For example, *Our candidate is always talking about law and order*. The concept behind this term was stated by Aristotle. Today, however, it also carries the implication of infringing on civil rights in the course of too arduous law enforcement. [Late 1500s]

law of averages The idea that probability will influence all occurrences in the long term, that one will neither win nor lose all of the time. For example, *If it rains every day this week, by the law of averages we're bound to get a sunny day soon*. This

colloquial term is a popular interpretation of a statistical principle, Bernoulli's theorem, formulated in the late 1600s.

law of the jungle Survival of the strongest, as in *The recent price war among airlines was governed by the law of the jungle*. This term, alluding to the jungle as a place devoid of ethics where brutality and self-interest reign, was first used by Rudyard Kipling in *The Jungle Book* (1894).

law unto oneself A person who is totally independent, especially one who ignores established rules. For example, *You can't tell Marge how to punctuate; she's a law unto herself*. [Second half of 1800s]

lay ♦ In addition to the idioms beginning with LAY, also see LET IT LAY. Also see under LAID; LIE; PUT.

lay about one 1. Strike blows on all sides, as in *When the dogs cornered the old man, he laid about him with his cane*. [Early 1400s] 2. Act vigorously, make strenuous efforts, as in *When there was an opportunity for profit, he laid about him*. [c. 1600]

lay a finger on Also, **put a finger on**. Barely touch, as in *You'd better not lay a finger on those documents!* or *If you lay a finger on me, I'll sue*. This expression is nearly always used as a prohibition. [Mid-1800s] Also see PUT ONE'S FINGER ON.

lay an egg Fail, especially in a public performance; make a humiliating error. For example, *Carol really laid an egg last night when she forgot her lines*, or, as *Variety* had it in October 1929: "Wall Street Lays An Egg." The term originated in the late 1800s in vaudeville and was extended to nontheatrical failures in the early 1900s.

lay aside 1. Give up, abandon, as in *He laid aside all hopes of winning first prize*. [First half of 1400s] 2. Also, **lay away; lay by**. Set apart for a reason, save for the future, as in *They lay aside enough to pay the rent*, or *Because coffee prices were rising, she laid by enough for a month*, or *The store laid away the winter coat I wanted*. [Early 1700s] The first variant gave rise, about 1970, to the term **layaway plan**, in which merchandise is *laid away* for a buyer who pays a deposit and receives it when payment is made in full. Also see LAY DOWN, def. 4; SET ASIDE.

lay at rest Also, **lay to rest; set at rest**. Satisfy, settle, as in *I'll take care of it; you can set your mind at rest*, or *The arbitrator is sure to lay these questions to rest*. [Late 1300s] Also see AT REST; LAY TO REST.

lay at someone's door Impute or lay the blame on someone; make someone responsible for something (usually discreditable). For example, *That this law failed to pass can be laid at your door, Senator*. [c. 1700]

lay a wager ♦ See under LAY ODDS.

lay away ♦ See LAY ASIDE, def. 2.

lay by ♦ See LAY ASIDE, def. 2.

lay claim to Assert one's right to or ownership of, as in "What claim lays she to thee?" (Shakespeare, *The Comedy of Errors*, 3:2). [Late 1500s] Also see STAKE A CLAIM.

lay down 1. Give something up, surrender, as in *They laid down their arms*. [c. 1300] 2. Formulate, specify, as in *The club laid down new membership rules*. [Late 1400s] 3. Also, **lay down one's life**. Sacrifice one's life, as in *He would willingly lay down his life for his children*. [c. 1600] 4. Store for the future, as in *It was a great vintage year for burgundy, and Mark laid down several cases*. [Early 1800s] Also see LAY ASIDE, def. 2.

lay down the law Assert something positively and often arrogantly, state something dogmatically. For example, *Dad laid down the law about locking up the house*. This colloquial expression, first recorded in 1762, uses LAY DOWN in the sense of def. 2.

lay eyes on Also, **clap** or **set eyes on**. Look at, see, as in *As soon as I laid eyes on him I knew he would be perfect for the lead in our play*, or *I'd never set eyes on such a beautiful gown*. The first term dates from the early 1200s and the third from the late 1300s; the second, using *clap* in the sense of "a sudden movement," dates from the first half of the 1800s.

lay for Be waiting to attack; also, lie in wait for, as in *The gang members were laying for him in that dark alley*, or *The reporters were laying for the Vice President when he came out of the meeting*. [Late 1400s]

lay hands on 1. Also, **get one's hands on**. Get someone or something in one's grasp, especially to do harm. For example, *Tom's gone off with the keys again; just wait till I lay my hands on him*. [c. A.D. 1000] 2. Also, **get** or **lay** or **put one's hands on**. Find, obtain, as in *As soon as I lay hands on the book, I'll call you*, or *He couldn't seem to put his hands on last year's sales figures*. Also see GET HOLD OF.

lay hold of Grasp, seize on, as in *He clutched at branches, shrubs, anything he could lay hold of to break his fall*. [First half of 1500s] Also see GET HOLD OF.

lay in Also, **lay up**. Stock or store for future use, as in *We laid in supplies for the winter*, or *Are you sure you've laid up enough material?* The first term dates from the late 1500s, the second from about 1400. Also see LAY ASIDE, def. 2; LAY DOWN, def. 4.

lay into 1. Attack physically, *The boys ganged up and laid into Bobby*. 2. Scold vigorously, as in *The teacher laid into her aide when she learned he had left the children alone in the schoolyard*. [Early 1800s] Also see PITCH INTO.

lay it on the line ♦ LAY ON THE LINE.

lay it on thick Also, **lay it on with a trowel**. Exaggerate, overstate; also, flatter effusively. For example, *Jane laid it on thick when she said this was the greatest book she'd ever read*, or *Tom thought he'd get the senator to waive the speaker's fee if he just laid it on with a trowel*. This idiom alludes to applying a thick coat of paint or plaster. [c. 1600]

lay low ♦ See LAY SOMEONE LOW; LIE LOW.

lay odds Make a bet on terms favorable to the other party, as in *I'll lay odds that it will rain before the week is out*. [c. 1600] The closely related **lay a wager** means "make a bet," as in *He laid a wager that Don would be late*. [c. 1300]

lay off 1. Terminate a person from employment. For example, *When they lost the contract, they had to lay off a hundred workers*. This expression formerly referred to temporary dismissals, as during a recession, with the idea that workers would be hired back when conditions improved, but with the tendency of businesses to downsize in the 1990s it came to mean "terminate permanently." [First half of 1800s] 2. Mark off the boundaries, as in *Let's lay off an area for a flower garden*. [Mid-1700s] 3. Stop doing something, quit, as in *Lay off that noise for a minute, so the baby can get to sleep*, or *She resolved to lay off smoking*. [Early 1900s] 4. Stop bothering or annoying someone, as in *Lay off or I'll tell the teacher*. [Slang; c. 1900] 5. Place all or part of a bet with another bookmaker so as to reduce the risk. For example, *Some bookmakers protect themselves by laying off very large bets with other bookmakers*. [Mid-1900s]

lay of the land, the The nature, arrangement, or disposition of something, the general state of affairs, as in *Once we know the lay of the land, we can plan our advertising campaign*. A related expression is **how the land lies**, as in *Let's be cautious till we know how the land lies*. This usage originated in Britain about 1700 as *the lie of the land* and is still so used there.

lay on 1. Cover with, apply; also, use. For example, *He decided to lay on a second coat of primer*, or *She laid on a thick Southern accent*. [c. 1600] Also see LAY IT ON THICK. 2. Inflict blows, attack, as in "Lay on, Macduff; and damn'd be him that first cries, 'Hold, enough!'" (Shakespeare, *Macbeth*, 5:8). [Early 1200s] 3. Impose or cast something on someone, as in *The government laid a tax on landholders*, or *Dad had a way of laying the guilt for his shortcomings on his partners*. This usage is also found in **lay** or **put the blame on someone**, as in *Nancy could always find someone to lay the blame on*, or *Jerry put the blame on Bill*. [1300s]

lay one's cards on the table Also, **put one's cards on the table**. Be open and honest, reveal one's position or intentions, as in *John laid his cards on the table and told her how much they could afford*. This expression alludes to showing the hand one holds. [c. 1900] Also see SHOW ONE'S HAND.

lay oneself out ♦ See PUT ONESELF OUT.

lay on the line 1. Make ready for payment, as in *They laid hundreds of thousands of dollars on the line to develop the new software*. [c. 1900] 2. **lay it on the line**. Speak frankly and firmly, make something clear. For example, *The professor laid it on the line: either hand in a term paper or fail the course*. [c. 1920] 3. Put something at risk, as in *The troops sent overseas were laying their lives on the line*. [Mid-1900s]

lay open Expose; also, make vulnerable to. For example, *The audit laid open some suspicious dealings*, or *She had not laid herself open to any charge of wrongdoing*. The first usage dates from the mid-1500s, the second from the mid 1800s. Also see LEAVE OPEN.

lay out 1. Make a detailed plan, design, or explanation, as in *They laid out the exact dimensions in order to construct the new display*, or *Robert laid out next year's plans for his staff*. [Mid-1700s] 2. Prepare a dead body for burial, as in *He died that morning and was laid out for the wake by afternoon*. [Late 1500s] 3. Rebuke harshly, as in *She laid me out for breaking the vase*. [Slang; late 1800s] 4. Knock unconscious or to the ground, render helpless, as in *He laid him out with one good punch*. [Late 1800s] 5. Expend, spend, as in *She laid out a fortune on jewelry*. [Mid-1400s] 6. Display or arrange, especially in a particular order, as in *He asked her to lay out the merchandise in an attractive way*. [Mid-1400s]

lay over 1. Postpone, as in *This issue will have to be laid over until our next meeting*. [Late 1800s] 2. Make a stop in the course of a journey, as in *They had to lay over for two days in New Delhi until the next flight to Katmandu*. This sense gave rise to the noun **lay-over** for such a stopover. [Late 1800s]

lay someone low Overcome someone, as in *He laid him low with one good punch*, or *The flu laid us low for two weeks*. [1300s] Also see LIE LOW.

lay to rest 1. See LAY AT REST. 2. Bury someone, as in *She wanted to be laid to rest beside her husband*. This usage replaced the earlier **go to rest**. [Late 1800s]

lay up ♦ See LAID UP; LAY IN.

lay waste Ravage, ruin, as in *The hurricane laid waste the entire seashore*. Originally referring to the devastation caused by attackers, this term has come to be used more generally.

lead ♦ In addition to the idioms beginning with LEAD, also see ALL ROADS LEAD TO ROME; BLIND LEADING THE BLIND; GET THE LEAD OUT OF; GO OVER (LIKE A LEAD BALLOON); PUT LEAD IN ONE'S PENCIL; YOU CAN LEAD A HORSE TO WATER.

lead a chase Also, **lead a merry chase** or **dance**. Mislead someone; waste someone's time. For example, *Mary refuses to commit herself and is leading John a merry chase*, or *Harry led us all a dance; we were waiting at the hotel and he'd gone to the movies*. [First half of 1500s]

lead a dog's life ♦ See DOG'S LIFE.

lead a double life Live as if one were two persons, usually one good and one bad. For example, *They learned that his frequent travels were actually fictitious, and he was leading a double life, with a second home on the other side of town*. This phrase is frequently used for a married person who establishes a second household with a lover. [Late 1800s] Also see JEKYLL AND HYDE.

lead by the nose Dominate or control someone, as in "The Moor . . . will tenderly be led by the nose as asses are" (Shakespeare, *Othello*, 1:3). This expression alludes to an animal being led by a ring passed through its nostrils. [Late 1500s]

lead down the garden path Also, **lead up the garden path**. Deceive someone. For example, *Bill had quite different ideas from Tom about their new investment strategy; he was leading him down the garden path*. This expression presumably alludes to the garden path as an intentional detour. [Early 1900s] Also see LEAD ON.

leading light An important or influential individual, as in *Jim was a leading light in his community*. This expression, alluding to moral guidance, dates from about 1870, but terms such as a *shining light* have been used for an outstanding person since the first half of the 1500s.

leading question A question worded so as to elicit particular information or a particular answer, as in *When are you selling the business?* This example assumes that the person is going to sell the business, an action that may not have been established or revealed. This expression originated with a specific meaning in law, that is, "a question that guides a witness toward a desired answer." In court, this practice is called **leading a witness** and is forbidden. [Mid-1800s]

lead off Begin, start, go first. For example, *We have a panel of three speakers, so will you lead off?* [c. 1800]

lead on Entice someone into proceeding, mislead; also, deceive someone, especially pretending romantic interest. For example, *He's leading her on to reveal more of her family history*, or *She's just leading him on; she has a serious boyfriend at home*. [Late 1500s]

lead one to Cause one to do something. For example, *This report leads me to believe that we're in an economic recession*, or *Her unexpected pregnancy led her to take a leave of absence*. [First half of 1500s]

lead-pipe cinch A certainty, an assured success. For example, "An engagement ain't always a lead-pipe cinch" (O. Henry, *The Sphinx Apple,* 1907). This colloquial expression is of disputed origin. It may allude to the *cinch* that tightly holds a horse's saddle in place, which can make it easier for the rider to succeed in a race; or it may allude to a *cinch* in plumbing, in which a lead pipe is fastened with a band of steel to another pipe or a fixture, making a very secure joint. [Late 1800s]

lead the way 1. Act as a guide, go in advance of others. For example, *We asked Tom to lead the way, since he'd hiked this mountain before.* [c. 1200] 2. Be first or most prominent in some field or action, as in *Our teacher led the way in finding new methods of teaching algebra.* [Late 1600s]

lead up the garden path ◆ See LEAD DOWN THE GARDEN PATH.

lead up to Prepare gradually for, result in gradually, as in *These events clearly led up to the coup,* or *His remarks led up to the main point of the speech, that he was going to resign next year.* [Mid-1800s]

lead with one's chin Take a risk, behave without caution. For example, *Gordon always says exactly what he thinks; he never minds leading with his chin.* This term alludes to a boxer leaving his chin, a vulnerable point, unprotected. [Mid-1900s]

leaf ◆ In addition to the idiom beginning with LEAF, also see QUAKE IN ONE'S BOOTS (LIKE A LEAF); TAKE A LEAF OUT OF SOMEONE'S BOOK; TURN OVER A NEW LEAF.

leaf through Turn pages, as in browsing or searching for something. For example, *There she sat, leafing through the various catalogs.* This expression employs *leaf* in the sense of "turn over the leaves of a book," a usage dating from the mid-1600s.

league ◆ See BIG LEAGUE; IN LEAGUE WITH; IN THE SAME LEAGUE.

lean on 1. Rely on, depend on, as in *He's leaning on me for help.* [Mid-1400s] 2. Exert pressure on one, especially to obtain something or make one do something against his or her will. For example, *The gangsters were leaning on local storekeepers to pay them protection money.* [Colloquial; Mid-1900s]

lean over backwards ◆ See BEND OVER BACKWARDS.

leap ◆ In addition to the idioms beginning with LEAP, also see BY LEAPS AND BOUNDS; LOOK BEFORE YOU LEAP; QUANTUM LEAP. Also see under JUMP.

leap in the dark An act whose results cannot be predicted. For example, *Given today's high divorce rate, he considered marriage a leap in the dark.* [Late 1600s]

leap of faith A belief or trust in something intangible or incapable of being proved. For example, *It required a leap of faith to pursue this unusual step of transplanting an animal's heart into a human patient.*

learn ◆ In addition to the idioms beginning with LEARN, also see BY HEART, LEARN; LITTLE KNOWLEDGE (LEARNING) IS A DANGEROUS THING; LIVE AND LEARN.

learn by heart Also, **learn by rote.** ◆ See under BY HEART.

learn one's lesson Profit from experience, especially an unhappy one. For example, *From now on she'd read the instructions first; she'd learned her lesson.* Also see HARD WAY.

learn to live with Get used to or accustom oneself to something that is painful, annoying, or unpleasant. For example, *The doctor said nothing more could be done about improving her sight; she'd just have to learn to live with it,* or *Pat decided she didn't like the new sofa but would have to learn to live with it.*

lease ◆ See NEW LEASE ON LIFE.

least ◆ In addition to the idioms beginning with LEAST, also see AT LEAST; IN THE LEAST; LAST BUT NOT LEAST; TO SAY THE LEAST.

least of all Especially not. For example, *No one cared, least of all the manager,* or *None of them will attend, least of all Jim.* [Late 1800s]

least resistance, line of Also, **path of least resistance.** The easiest method, way, or course of action. For example, *He tends to do what most people seem to want, taking the line of least resistance.* This term employs *resistance* in the sense of "the physical opposition of one thing or force to another," a usage dating from the early 1600s. It has been used figuratively since about 1900.

leather ◆ See HELL-BENT FOR LEATHER.

leave ◆ In addition to the idioms beginning with LEAVE, also see ABSENT WITHOUT LEAVE; (LEAVE) HIGH AND DRY; (LEAVE) OUT IN THE COLD; TAKE IT OR LEAVE IT; TAKE LEAVE OF; TAKE ONE'S LEAVE. Also see under LET.

leave a bad taste in one's mouth Make a lingering bad impression on one, as in *The argument left a bad taste in my mouth, so after that I avoided talking politics.* This expression transfers the bad taste left by consuming bitter or otherwise unpleasant food to a distasteful experience. [Mid-1800s]

leave alone ◆ See LEAVE SOMEONE ALONE.

leave a lot to be desired Also, **leave a great deal** or **much to be desired.** Be imperfect or unsatisfactory. For example, *His account of the election leaves a lot to be desired.* This usage can also be put in a more positive way, that is, **leave nothing to be desired,** meaning "to be perfectly satisfactory," as in *His account leaves nothing to be desired.* [Late 1700s]

leave flat Forsake or abandon completely, especially without warning. For example, *He didn't tell her he wasn't picking her up; he just left her flat.*

[Colloquial; c. 1900] Also see HIGH AND DRY; LEAVE IN THE LURCH.

leave hanging Also, **leave hanging in the air** or in **midair.** Keep undecided, uncertain, or in suspense. For example, *Since we hadn't found a big enough hall, we left the final date hanging,* or *She couldn't figure out a good ending for the book, so her audience was left hanging in midair.*

leave holding the bag Abandon someone, force someone to bear the responsibility or blame. For example, *Her friends said they were too busy to help with cleaning up, and left Lucy holding the bag.* This expression is often put as **be left holding the bag,** as in *When they quit the clean up committee. Lucy was left holding the bag.* This idiom grew out of the earlier *give one the bag (to hold),* which dates from about 1600 and alludes to being left with an empty bag while others have taken the valuable contents. Also see LEAVE IN THE LURCH.

leave in the lurch Abandon or desert someone in difficult straits. For example, *Jane was angry enough to quit without giving notice, leaving her boss in the lurch.* This expression alludes to a 16th-century French dice game, *lourche,* where to incur a *lurch* meant to be far behind the other players. It later was used in cribbage and other games, as well as being used in its present figurative sense by about 1600.

leave no stone unturned Make every possible effort, use every possible source or resource. For example, *To raise ten thousand dollars to keep the shelter open, we must leave no stone unturned.* This expression alludes to an ancient Greek legend about a general who buried a large treasure in his tent when he was defeated in battle. Those seeking the treasure consulted the Oracle of Delphi, who advised them to move every stone. The present form dates from the mid-1500s.

leave off 1. Stop, cease; also, stop doing or using. For example, *Mother told the children to leave off running around the house,* or *Please use a bookmark to show where you left off reading.* [c. 1400] 2. **leave something off.** Omit, as in *We found she had left off our names.*

leave one cold Disappoint one, fail to interest one. For example, *This book leaves me cold.* This expression, first recorded in 1853, employs *cold* in the sense of "unenthusiastic" or "indifferent," a usage dating from the late 1100s.

leave open 1. Keep undecided or unscheduled, as in *We don't know how much fabric will be needed; let's leave that open,* or *The doctor leaves Fridays open for consultation.* This expression uses *open* in the sense of "undetermined," a usage dating from the mid-1500s. 2. **leave oneself open.** Remain vulnerable to; also, remain willing to consider. For

example, *Her actions left her open to widespread criticism,* or *I left myself open to further suggestions about how to proceed.* Also see under LAY OPEN.

leave out Omit, fail to include, as in *This sentence doesn't make sense; a key word has been left out.* [Late 1400s]

leave out in the cold ▶ See OUT IN THE COLD.

leave out of account ▶ See TAKE INTO ACCOUNT.

leave someone alone Also, **let someone alone.** Refrain from disturbing or interfering with someone. For example, *She'll manage very well if you just leave her alone,* or *Stop teasing the dog; let him alone.* [c. 1400] Also see LEAVE ONE IN PEACE; LET ALONE; LET BE.

leave someone in peace Avoid disturbing or bothering someone, as in *It's best to leave Dean in peace when he's paying the bills.* This expression uses *peace* in the sense of "undisturbed," a usage dating from the early 1200s. Also see LEAVE SOMEONE ALONE; LET BE.

leave someone in the lurch ▶ See LEAVE IN THE LURCH.

leave someone to his or her resources Let one rely on oneself to do what he or she likes or to get out of trouble. For example, *Left to his own resources, my four-year-old might well turn the hose on the dog,* or *Refusing to pay for Lydia's traffic ticket, Dad insisted on leaving her to her resources.*

leave the door open Allow for further action or discussion. For example, *This will's terms leave the door open for fighting among the heirs.* This metaphoric expression transfers the invitation implied by an open door to future events. Also see OPEN THE DOOR TO.

leave to someone's own devices Allow someone to do as he or she wishes. For example, *Left to his own devices, he would hire someone to do the yard work.* This expression uses *device* in the sense of "a plan or scheme." [Late 1800s]

leave to someone's tender mercies Submit to another's power or discretion, especially to an unsympathetic individual. Today this expression is always used ironically, as in *We left him to the tender mercies of that stiffnecked, arrogant nurse.* It alludes to a biblical passage (Proverbs 12:10): "A righteous man regardeth the life of his beast; but the tender mercies of the wicked are cruel."

leave well enough alone Also, **let well enough alone.** Do not try to change something lest you make it worse. For example, *This recipe has turned out fine in the past, so leave well enough alone.* The idea behind this expression dates from ancient Greek times, specifically Aesop's fable about a fox who refused a hedgehog's offer to take out its ticks lest, by removing those that are full, other hungry ones will replace them. Put as *let well* *alone* from the early 1700s, it was first recorded as *let well enough alone* in 1827. Also see LET SLEEPING DOGS LIE.

leave without a leg to stand on ◆ See WITHOUT A LEG TO STAND ON.

leave word Leave a message, as in *Please leave word at the desk when you check out,* or *I left word about my plans with the secretary; didn't she tell you?* This expression employs *word* in the sense of "information," a usage dating from the 10th century.

left ◆ In addition to the idioms beginning with LEFT, also see HANG A LEFT; OUT IN LEFT FIELD; RIGHT AND LEFT; TAKE UP WHERE ONE LEFT OFF; TWO LEFT FEET.

left field ◆ See OUT IN LEFT FIELD.

left hand doesn't know what the right hand is doing, the The actions are uncoordinated, especially when they are contrary, as in *Purchasing has placed the order and accounting says we can't pay for more supplies this month; the left hand doesn't know what the right hand is doing.* Today this expression is nearly always used as a criticism. But, it first appeared in the New Testament (Matthew 6:3) in an approving sense, when Jesus recommended not publicizing one's good deeds — *not letting the left hand know what the right hand does.* [Early 1600s]

left-handed compliment Also, backhanded compliment. An insult in the guise of an expression of praise. For example, *She said she liked my hair, but it turned out to be a left-handed compliment when she asked how long I'd been dyeing it.* This expression uses *left-handed* in the sense of "questionable or doubtful," a usage dating from about 1600.

left wing The liberal or radical faction of a political group, as in *Many consider him a leader of the Democratic Party's left wing.* This expression originated in the seating practice of European legislatures, whereby those holding liberal views were assigned to the left side of the house. [First half of 1800s]

leg ◆ In addition to the idiom beginning with LEG, also see ARM AND A LEG; BREAK A LEG; ON ONE'S LAST LEGS; PULL SOMEONE'S LEG; SHAKE A LEG; STRETCH ONE'S LEGS; TAIL BETWEEN ONE'S LEGS; WITHOUT A LEG TO STAND ON.

leg up, a 1. The act of assisting someone, giving someone a boost. For example, *Studying with Jane, who knows French history well, will give you a leg up for the final exam.* This usage alludes to helping a person get on a horse by getting a foot in the stirrup. [First half of 1800s] 2. A position of advantage, as in *Because of the advertising campaign, we had a leg up on the competition.*

leisure ◆ See AT LEISURE; AT ONE'S LEISURE.

lend a hand Also, lend a helping hand. Be of assistance, as in *Can you lend them a hand with putting up the flag,* or *Peter is always willing to lend a helping hand around the house.* [Late 1500s]

lend color to Embellish, especially to give the appearance of truth. For example, *I'm sure he lied about reaching the summit; that detailed account about losing his pack merely lent color to the story.* This expression uses *color* in the sense of "appearance of authenticity." [Late 1700s]

lend itself to Adapt to, be suitable for. For example, *The Bible lends itself to numerous interpretations,* or *This plot of land lends itself to a variety of uses.* [Mid-1800s]

lend one's ear Also, lend an ear. Pay attention, listen, as in "Friends, Romans, countrymen, lend me your ears" (Shakespeare, *Julius Caesar,* 3:2). This idiom may be obsolescent. [Late 1300s]

length ◆ See AT ARM'S LENGTH; AT LENGTH; GO TO ANY LENGTH.

leopard cannot change its spots, a Also, the tiger cannot change its stripes. One can't change one's essential nature. For example, *He's a conservative, no matter what he says; the leopard cannot change its spots.* These metaphoric expressions both originated in an ancient Greek proverb that appears in the Bible (Jeremiah 13:23): "Can the Ethiopian change his skin, or the leopard his spots?" It was first recorded in English in 1546.

less ◆ In addition to the idiom beginning with LESS, also see COULDN'T CARE LESS; IN (LESS THAN) NO TIME; MORE OR LESS; MUCH LESS.

lesser of two evils The somewhat less unpleasant of two poor choices. For example, *I'd rather stay home and miss the picnic altogether than run into those nasty people — it's the lesser of two evils.* This expression was already a proverb in ancient Greek and appeared in English by the late 1300s. Chaucer used it in *Troilus and Cressida.*

lesson ◆ See LEARN ONE'S LESSON; TEACH A LESSON.

less than Not at all or hardly at all. For example, *He had a less than favorable view of the matter,* or *She had a less than adequate grasp of the subject.* This expression uses *less* in the sense of "a smaller quantity, number, or extent than is implied," a usage dating from about A.D. 1000. The same sense appears in **less than no time,** a hyperbolic term for a very short time (as in *Don't worry, he'll be here in less than no time*) that dates from about 1800.

let ◆ In addition to the idioms beginning with LET, also see BLOW (LET) OFF STEAM; GIVE (LET) SOMEONE HAVE HIS OR HER HEAD; (LET SOMEONE) HAVE IT; LIVE AND LET LIVE. Also see under LEAVE.

let alone 1. See LEAVE SOMEONE ALONE. 2. Not to mention, as in *We have no room for another house guest, let alone an entire family.* [c. 1800]

let be Leave undisturbed, refrain from interfering with. For example, *Stop fussing with the tablecloth; let it be,* or, as A.E. Houseman put it in *A Shropshire Lad* (1896): "Will you never let me be?" [Second half of 1100s] Also see LEAVE SOMEONE ALONE; LEAVE SOMEONE IN PEACE.

let bygones be bygones What's done is done; don't worry about the past, especially past errors or grievances. For example, *Bill and Tom shook hands and agreed to let bygones be bygones.* [First half of 1600s]

let daylight through or **into** Shoot or stab a person, especially fatally. For example, *Stick up your hands or I'll let daylight through you.* This idiom alludes to making a hole in someone's body. [Slang; early 1700s]

let down 1. Cause to descend, lower, as in *They let down the sails.* [Mid-1100s] 2. Also, **let up.** Slacken, abate, as in *Sales are letting down in this quarter,* or *They didn't let up in their efforts until the end.* The first term dates from the mid-1800s, the variant from the late 1700s. 3. See LET SOMEONE DOWN. Also see LET ONE'S HAIR DOWN.

let down easy ♦ See under LET SOMEONE DOWN.

let down one's hair ♦ See LET ONE'S HAIR DOWN.

let drop Also, **let fall.** Utter a word or hint, either casually or inadvertently. For example, *He let drop the fact that he'd decided to run for office,* or *She let fall some bits of gossip about the other teachers.* [Late 1500s]

let fly Discharge a missile or fire a weapon; also, attack verbally. For example, *He let fly a rotten egg at the speaker,* or *They let fly some insults laced with four-letter words.* The first usage dates from about A.D. 1000, the second from the late 1500s.

let go 1. Allow to escape, set free, as in *The police decided to let him go.* [c. 1300] 2. Also, **let go of.** Release one's hold on, as in *Please let go of my sleeve,* or *Once he starts on this subject, he never lets go.* [Early 1400s] 3. **let it go.** Allow it to stand or be accepted. For example, *Let it go; we needn't discuss it further.* This usage is sometimes amplified to **let it go at that,** meaning "allow matters to stand as they are." [Late 1800s] 4. Cease to employ, dismiss, as in *They had to let 20 workers go.* 5. Also, **let oneself go.** Behave without restraint, abandon one's inhibitions; also, neglect one's personal hygiene and appearance. For example, *When the music began, Jean let herself go and started a wild dance,* or *After her husband's death she let herself go, forgetting to bathe and staying in*

her nightgown all day. The first sense dates from the late 1800s, the second from the early 1900s.

let grass grow ♦ See DON'T LET THE GRASS GROW UNDER ONE'S FEET.

let in on Allow someone to know about or participate in something, as in *I'm going to let you in on a little secret.* This idiom was first recorded in 1904.

let it all hang out Be totally candid in expressing feelings and opinions; hold nothing back. For example, *The psychiatrist urged him not to spare any details, to let it all hang out.* [Slang; late 1960s]

let it lay Also, **leave her lay.** Allow it to rest; leave it alone. For example, *Don't discuss their gift anymore; let it lay.* The use of *her* in the variant is a slangy version of "it." [Slang; first half of 1900s]

let it rip Also, **let her rip.** Go ahead, proceed unchecked. For example, *Once you get the tractor started, let it rip.* The use of *her* in the variant comes from a tradition of referring to vehicles as feminine. [Mid-1800s]

let me see Also, **let's see.** I'm thinking about it or trying to remember, as in *Let me see, I'll be in Boston tomorrow and the next day.* This idiom was first recorded in 1520.

let off 1. Release by exploding; see BLOW OFF STEAM. 2. Allow to go free or escape; excuse from punishment. For example, *They let her off from attending graduation,* or *The headmaster let him off with a reprimand.* [Early 1800s] Also see OFF THE HOOK.

let off steam ♦ See BLOW OFF STEAM.

let on 1. Reveal one's true feelings or a fact, allow something to be known, as in *Don't let on that you met her before.* This usage is probably a shortening of *let it on someone.* [c. 1700] 2. Pretend, as in *He let on that he was very angry, but in fact he didn't care a bit.* [First half of 1800s] Also see LET IN ON.

let oneself go ♦ See LET GO, def. 5.

let one's hair down Also, **let down one's hair.** Drop one's reserve or inhibitions, behave casually or informally, as in *Whenever the two sisters get together, they let their hair down and discuss all their problems.* This expression alludes to the practice of women taking down their pinned-up long hair only in the privacy of the bedroom. [c. 1900]

let out 1. Allow to GET OUT; also see GET OUT OF. 2. Make known, reveal, as in *I thought it was a secret—who let it out?* [First half of 1800s] Also see LET THE CAT OUT OF THE BAG. 3. Come to a close, end, as in *What time does school let out?* [Late 1800s] 4. Increase the size of a garment, as in *May's coat needs to be let out across the shoulders.* This usage refers to opening some of the seams. [Late 1700s]

let ride Also, **let slide.** Allow something to be ignored or to take or continue in its natural course. For example, *Bill disagreed with Mary's description, but he let it ride,* or *He had a way of letting things slide.* The first term, alluding to things moving along as though they were riding a horse or vehicle, dates from the early 1900s; the variant, using *slide* in the sense of "pass by," dates from the late 1500s. Also see under LET SLIP.

let sleeping dogs lie Allow inactive problems to remain so, as in *Jane knew she should report the accident but decided to let sleeping dogs lie.* This injunction to avoid stirring up trouble was already a proverb in the 13th century. It alludes to waking up a fierce watchdog and has been stated in English since the late 1300s.

let slide ♦ See LET RIDE; LET SLIP.

let slip 1. Also, **let slip** or **slide by; let slide.** Miss an opportunity; waste time. For example, *We forgot to buy a ticket and let our big chance slip by,* or *He let the whole day slide by.* The first term dates from the mid-1500s, the variant from the late 1500s. 2. Also, **let slip out.** Reveal something, usually inadvertently, as in *He let it slip out that he had applied for the vacant position.* [Mid-1800s] 3. **let slip through one's fingers.** Fail to seize an opportunity, as in *We could have won the trophy but we let it slip through our fingers.* [First half of 1600s]

let someone ♦ In addition to the idioms beginning with LET SOMEONE, also see under LET ONE.

let someone down 1. Fail to support someone; also, disappoint someone. For example, *I was counting on John to come, but he let me down,* or *The team didn't want to let down the coach.* [Late 1400s] A British phrase with the same meaning is **let the side down,** alluding to some kind of competition (sports, politics) and dating from the mid-1900s. It is occasionally used in America. 2. **let someone down easy.** Convey bad or disappointing news in a considerate way, so as to spare the person's self-respect. For example, *The teacher knew that Paul would have to repeat the course and that there was no way to let him down easy.* [Colloquial; mid-1700s] Also see LET DOWN.

let someone have it ♦ See HAVE IT, def. 5.

letter ♦ In addition to the idiom beginning with LETTER, also see BREAD AND BUTTER LETTER; CRANK CALL (LETTER); DEAD LETTER; FOUR-LETTER WORD; POISON-PEN LETTER; RED-LETTER DAY; TO THE LETTER.

letter of the law The precise wording rather than the spirit or intent. For example, *Since it was the first time he'd broken the rules, the school decided to ignore the letter of the law and just give him a warning.* [Late 1500s]

let the cat out of the bag Give away a secret, as in *Mom let the cat out of the bag and told us Karen was engaged.* This expression alludes to the dishonest practice of a merchant substituting a worthless cat for a valuable pig, which is discovered only when the buyer gets home and opens the bag. [Mid-1700s] Also see PIG IN A POKE.

let the chips fall where they may No matter what the consequences, as in *I'm going to tell the truth about what happened, and let the chips fall where they may.* This metaphoric term alludes to chopping wood and is usually joined to a statement that one should do what is right (that is, the woodcutter should pay attention to the main task of cutting logs and not worry about small chips). [Late 1800s]

let the grass grow under one's feet ♦ See DON'T LET THE GRASS GROW UNDER ONE'S FEET.

let the side down ♦ See under LET SOMEONE DOWN, def. 1.

let up 1. See LET DOWN, def. 2. 2. Cease, stop entirely, as in *The rain has let up so we can go out.* [Late 1700s] 3. **let up on.** Be or become more lenient with, take the pressure off, as in *Why don't you let up on the child?* [Late 1800s]

let well enough alone ♦ See LEAVE WELL ENOUGH ALONE.

level ♦ In addition to the idioms beginning with LEVEL, also see DO ONE'S (LEVEL) BEST; ON THE LEVEL.

level best ♦ See under DO ONE'S BEST.

level off Move toward stability or consistency, as in *Prices have leveled off.* This idiom transfers a physical flattening to a figurative one. [Mid-1900s]

level with someone Speak frankly and openly to someone, as in *His companions advised him to level with the customs inspector.* [Colloquial; early 1900s] Also see ON THE LEVEL.

liberty ♦ See AT LIBERTY; TAKE THE LIBERTY OF.

lick and a promise, a A superficial effort made without care or enthusiasm. For example, *I haven't time to do a good job of vacuuming, just enough for a lick and a promise.* This expression is believed to allude to the quick lick a cat or other animal might give itself and a promise to do more or better at some future time. [Mid-1800s]

lick into shape Also, **whip into shape.** Bring into satisfactory condition or appearance, as in *The garden looks neglected, but Dad will soon lick it into shape,* or *We need at least three more practices before the team is whipped into shape.* The expression using lick, which some think alludes to how bears treat their cubs, dates from about 1600. The variant alludes to the forceful use of a whip to accomplish something.

lick one's chops Also, **lick one's lips.** Anticipate with great pleasure. For example, *The kids were licking their chops as Mother described the family vacation plans,* or *I couldn't help but lick my lips when she talked about the menu.* Both expressions allude to anticipating a tasty morsel of food. The second is the older, dating from about 1500 and used interchangeably with *lick one's fingers,* now seldom heard. The first also served as 1930s jazz slang for warming up, *chops* meaning "the jaw or mouth" (a usage dating from the 1300s).

lick one's wounds Recuperate from injuries or hurt feelings. For example, *They were badly beaten in the debate and went home sadly to lick their wounds.* This expression alludes to an animal's behavior when wounded. It was originally put as *lick oneself clean* or *whole,* dating from the mid-1500s.

lick someone's boots Act with extreme servility, as in *This man wanted every employee to lick his boots, so he had a hard time keeping his staff.* Shakespeare used this idiom in the form of *lick someone's shoe* in *The Tempest* (3:2). [Late 1500s]

lick the stuffing out of Also, **lick the tar out of.** ♦ See under BEAT THE LIVING DAYLIGHTS OUT OF.

lid ♦ See BLOW THE LID OFF; FLIP ONE'S LID; PUT THE LID ON.

lie ♦ In addition to the idioms beginning with LIE, also see BAREFACED LIE; GIVE THE LIE TO; (LIE) IN STATE; LAY OF THE LAND (HOW THE LAND LIES); LET SLEEPING DOGS LIE; LIVE A LIE; MAKE ONE'S BED AND LIE IN IT; TAKE LYING DOWN; WHITE LIE.

lie down Also, **lie down on the job.** Be remiss or lazy. For example, *They fired Max because he was always lying down on the job.* This expression alludes to lying down in the sense of "resting." [Early 1900s]

lie in 1. Be in confinement for childbirth, as in *She thought she'd be lying in by next week.* This usage is probably dying out. The name of Boston's Lying-In Hospital was changed to Women's Hospital in the 1970s. [Mid-1400s] 2. Also, **lie in one's hands** or **in one's power.** Rest or depend on something or someone, as in *The solution lies in research,* or *The decision lies in the President's hands,* or *It does not lie in my power to turn this situation around.* [Mid-1300s] Also see LIE IN WAIT; LIE THROUGH ONE'S TEETH.

lie in state ♦ See under IN STATE.

lie in wait Remain hidden while preparing to attack, as in *The opposition was quietly lying in wait for the incumbent to make his first big mistake.* This expression originally alluded to physical attacks and is now often used figuratively. [Mid-1400s] Also see LAY FOR.

lie low Also **lay low.** Keep oneself or one's plans hidden; bide one's time; act later. For example, *The* children lay low, hoping their prank would soon be forgotten, or *The senator decided to lay low until his opponent had committed herself to raising taxes.* This expression calls up the image of a hunter concealed in the brush, waiting for game. [Colloquial; late 1800s]

lie through one's teeth Also, **lie in one's teeth.** Utter outrageous falsehoods, as in *He was lying through his teeth when he said he'd never seen her before; they've known each other for years.* This expression presumably alludes to a particular facial grimace one assumes when lying. [c. 1300]

lieu ♦ See under INSTEAD OF.

lie with Be decided by, dependent on, or up to. For example, *The choice of restaurant lies with you.* Starting about 1300 this phrase meant "to have sexual intercourse with," a usage that is now obsolete. [Late 1800s]

life ♦ In addition to the idioms beginning with LIFE, also see BET ONE'S ASS (LIFE); BIG AS LIFE; BREATHE NEW LIFE INTO; BRING TO LIFE; CHANGE OF LIFE; CHARMED LIFE; COME ALIVE (TO LIFE); DOG'S LIFE; FACTS OF LIFE; FOR DEAR LIFE; FOR THE LIFE OF; GET A LIFE; GOOD LIFE; LATE IN LIFE; LAY DOWN (ONE'S LIFE); LEAD A DOUBLE LIFE; LIGHT OF ONE'S LIFE; MATTER OF LIFE AND DEATH; NEW LEASE ON LIFE; NOT ON YOUR LIFE; OF ONE'S LIFE; ONCE IN A LIFETIME; PRIME OF LIFE; RISK LIFE AND LIMB; RUN FOR IT (ONE'S LIFE); STAFF OF LIFE; STORY OF MY LIFE; TAKE SOMEONE'S LIFE; TO SAVE ONE'S LIFE; TO THE LIFE; TRUE TO (LIFE); VARIETY IS THE SPICE OF LIFE; WALK OF LIFE; WHILE THERE'S LIFE THERE'S HOPE; YOU BET (YOUR LIFE).

life and death ♦ See MATTER OF LIFE AND DEATH.

life is too short Do not waste time on unimportant matters or unworthy emotions, such as anger or anxiety. For example, *I could get my revenge by snubbing Tom, but life's too short,* or *Don't spend all day waiting for his call—life is too short.* This phrase, possibly echoing the ancient Latin proverb, *Ars longa, vita brevis* ("Art is long-lasting, life is short"), is often used to dismiss an unimportant or unworthy concern. [Mid-1800s]

life of Riley Also, **life of Reilly.** An easy life, as in *Peter had enough money to take off the rest of the year and live the life of Riley.* This phrase originated in a popular song of the 1800s, "Is That Mr. Reilly?" by Pat Rooney, which described what its hero would do if he suddenly came into a fortune.

life of the party A lively, amusing person who is the center of attention at a social gathering. For example, *Eileen was the life of the party, telling one good story after another.* [First half of 1800s]

lift a finger ♦ See NOT LIFT A FINGER.

lift a hand against ◆ See RAISE A HAND AGAINST.

lift off Begin flight, as in *The spacecraft was due to lift off at ten o'clock*. The *off* in this idiom means "off the ground." [Late 1800s]

lift the curtain ◆ See RAISE THE CURTAIN.

light ◆ In addition to the idioms beginning with LIGHT, also see BEGIN TO SEE DAYLIGHT (SEE THE LIGHT OF DAY); BRING TO LIGHT; COME TO LIGHT; GO LIGHT ON; GREEN LIGHT; HEAVY (LIGHT) HEART; HIDE ONE'S LIGHT; IN A GOOD (BAD) LIGHT; IN THE COLD LIGHT OF DAY; IN THE LIGHT OF; LACE (LIGHT) INTO; LEADING LIGHT; MAKE LIGHT OF; MANY HANDS MAKE LIGHT WORK; ONCE OVER LIGHTLY; OUT COLD (LIKE A LIGHT); SEE THE LIGHT; SHED LIGHT ON; SWEETNESS AND LIGHT; TRAVEL LIGHT; TRIP THE LIGHT FANTASTIC.

light a fire under Also, **build a fire under**. Urge or goad to action, as in *If we don't light a fire under that committee, they'll never do any work*. This hyperbolic colloquialism uses *light* in the sense of "ignite," a usage dating from the mid-1100s.

light as a feather Extremely lightweight. This simile can be used to refer either to physical weight, as in *This load is light as a feather*, or to texture, as in *This cake is light as a feather*. [Mid-1500s]

light at the end of the tunnel The end of a difficult situation or task, the solution to a difficult problem. For example, *It's taken three years to effect this merger, but we're finally seeing the light at the end of the tunnel*. This metaphoric expression dates from the 1800s, but became widespread only in the mid-1900s.

light dawned, the Understanding came at last, as in *They couldn't figure out where they went wrong, but then the light dawned—they'd turned right instead of left*. This expression transfers the beginning of dawn to human perception. [c. 1800]

lighten up Become or cause to become less serious or gloomy, and more cheerful. For example, *Lighten up, Sam—it'll turn out all right*. This slangy expression transfers reducing a physical weight to a change of mood or attitude.

light heart ◆ See under HEAVY HEART.

light into ◆ See LACE INTO.

lightly ◆ See GET OFF (LIGHTLY); ONCE OVER LIGHTLY.

lightning ◆ In addition to the idiom beginning with LIGHTNING, also see LIKE GREASED LIGHTNING; QUICK AS A WINK (LIGHTNING).

lightning never strikes twice in the same place The same misfortune will never recur, as in *Go ahead and try your luck investing in options again; lightning never strikes twice*. This saying is based on a long-standing myth, which has been proved to be untrue. Nevertheless, it is so well

known it is often shortened, as in the example. [Mid-1800s]

light on Also, **light upon**. Happen upon, come across, discover. For example, *John was delighted to light on a new solution to the problem*, or *We were following the path when suddenly we lit upon a cave*. [Second half of 1400s]

light out Leave hastily, run away, as in *Here comes the teacher—let's light out*. This slangy idiom may allude to the nautical sense, that is, to move or lift anything along. [Slang; mid-1800s]

light up 1. Become or cause to become more animated or cheerful, as in *Her laughter lit up the whole room*, or *His face lit up when he saw her*. This expression transfers physical illumination to human moods. Also see LIGHTEN UP. [Mid-1700s] 2. Start smoking a cigar, cigarette, or pipe, as in *The minute he got outside the church he lit up*. [Colloquial; mid-1800s]

like ◆ In addition to the idioms beginning with LIKE, also see AND THE LIKE; AVOID LIKE THE PLAGUE; COME UP (SMELLING LIKE) ROSES; CRAZY LIKE A FOX; DRINK LIKE A FISH; DROP LIKE FLIES; DUTCH UNCLE, TALK TO LIKE A; EAT LIKE A BIRD; FEEL LIKE; (LIKE A) FISH OUT OF WATER; FIT LIKE A GLOVE; FLY ON THE WALL, WOULD LIKE TO BE A; GET ON (LIKE A HOUSE AFIRE); GO OUT (LIKE A LIGHT); GO OVER (LIKE A LEAD BALLOON); GRIN LIKE A CHESHIRE CAT; (DROP LIKE A) HOT POTATO; JUST LIKE THAT; KNOW LIKE A BOOK; LIVE LIKE A KING; LOOK LIKE A MILLION DOLLARS; LOOK LIKE DEATH; LOOK LIKE SOMETHING THE CAT DRAGGED IN; LOOK LIKE THE CAT THAT ATE THE CANARY; MAKE OUT LIKE A BANDIT; MANNA FROM HEAVEN, LIKE; MIND LIKE A STEEL TRAP; NEED LIKE A HOLE IN THE HEAD; NO FOOL LIKE AN OLD FOOL; NOT ANYTHING LIKE; NO TIME LIKE THE PRESENT; OUT LIKE A LIGHT; PACKED IN LIKE SARDINES; SLEEP LIKE A LOG; SOMETHING LIKE; SPREAD LIKE WILDFIRE; STICK OUT (LIKE A SORE THUMB); SWEAR LIKE A TROOPER; TAKE TO (LIKE A DUCK TO WATER); TELL IT LIKE IT IS; TREAT LIKE DIRT; TURN UP LIKE A BAD PENNY; WAIL LIKE A BANSHEE; WATCH LIKE A HAWK; WORK LIKE A BEAVER; WORK LIKE A CHARM.

like a bat out of hell Moving extremely fast, as in *She ran down the street like a bat out of hell*. This expression presumably alludes to the rapid darting movement of bats and, Charles Earle Funk theorized, their avoidance of such light as might be cast by the fires of hell. [c. 1900] For a synonym, see LIKE GREASED LIGHTNING.

like a bump on a log Unmoving, inactive, stupidly silent. For example, *Harry just sat there like a bump on a log while everyone else joined in the fun*. This simile presumably alludes to the immobility of such a protuberance. [Colloquial; mid-1800s]

like a cat on hot bricks Also, **like a cat on a hot tin roof.** Restless or skittish, unable to remain still, as in *Nervous about the lecture he had to give, David was like a cat on hot bricks.* The first expression replaced a still earlier one, *like a cat on a hot bake-stone,* which appeared in John Ray's *Proverbs* (1678). The second was popularized as the title of Tennessee Williams's play, *Cat on a Hot Tin Roof* (1955).

like a champ Very well, very successfully, as in *He got through that audition like a champ.* This expression, in which *champ* is short for *champion,* alludes to the winner of a sporting competition. [Slang; c. 1960]

like a chicken with its head cut off In a frenzied manner, distractedly, crazily. For example, *She ran around the station looking for her lost bag like a chicken with its head cut off.* This graphic simile alludes to the fact that the body of a chicken whose head has been cut off sometimes totters about crazily before succumbing.

like a drowned rat Also, **wet as a drowned rat.** Soaking wet and utterly bedraggled, as in *When she came in out of the rain she looked like a drowned rat.* This simile appeared in Latin nearly 2,000 years ago, and in English about the year 1500.

like a fish out of water ♦ See FISH OUT OF WATER.

like a house afire ♦ See under GET ALONG, def. 1.

like a lamb to the slaughter Also, **as lambs to the slaughter.** Innocently and helplessly, without realizing the danger. For example, *She agreed to appeal to the board, little knowing she would go like a lamb to the slaughter.* This expression appears in several biblical books (Isaiah, Jeremiah), and the simile itself was used by Chaucer.

like anything Extremely, vigorously, as in *She cried like anything when the dog died.* This idiom probably substitutes *anything* for a swear word. [Colloquial; late 1600s]

like a shot Very rapidly, as in *When they asked for volunteers, he raised his hand like a shot.* This expression alludes to the rapidity of gunfire. [Colloquial; late 1800s]

like as not Also, **as like as not; as likely as not.** In all probability, with an even chance, as in *Like as not it'll rain by afternoon,* or *Likely as not the governor will run for a second term.* In the first two terms, *like* is short for *likely* in the sense of "probably," that is, "It is as likely as it is not likely." [Late 1800s]

like as two peas in a pod Very similar, bearing a close resemblance. For example, *They're not even sisters, but they're like as two peas in a pod.* This expression alludes to the seeds contained in a pea pod, which do indeed look very much alike. [Late 1500s]

like a ton of bricks Very heavily, without subtlety. For example, *If he doesn't like your work, he'll come down on you like a ton of bricks.* This expression, often coupled with COME DOWN ON (def. 1), replaced the earlier *thousand of brick* or *hundred of brick.* The allusion in all these is to the considerable weight of such a load. [Early 1900s]

like clockwork Also, **regular as clockwork.** With extreme regularity, as in *Ruth arrives every Wednesday morning just like clockwork,* or *You can count on his schedule, which is regular as clockwork,* or *Their assembly line runs like clockwork.* This idiom alludes to the mechanical and therefore very regular action of a clock. [Second half of 1600s]

like crazy Also, **like mad; like nobody's business.** With exceeding enthusiasm or speed, without restraint. For example, *We shopped like crazy and bought all our furniture in one day,* or *Once he's out of the town limits he drives like mad,* or *The choir sang the Hallelujah Chorus like nobody's business.* The first terms employ *crazy* and *mad* in the sense of "lunatic" as a hyperbole for lack of restraint; the third implies that no *business* could be conducted in such an extraordinary fashion. The first and third date from the 1920s, the second from the mid-1600s.

like death warmed over ♦ See LOOK LIKE DEATH.

like father, like son In the same manner from generation to generation, as in *Kevin decided to run for mayor—like father, like son.* This ancient proverb has been stated in English in slightly varying versions since the 1300s, sometimes appearing with a counterpart, **like mother, like daughter.** Thomas Draxe had it in *Bibliotheca* (1616): "Like father, like son; like mother, like daughter." Also see CHIP OFF THE OLD BLOCK; FOLLOW IN SOMEONE'S FOOTSTEPS.

like fun Not really, certainly not. For example, *She said she'd been skiing for years—like fun she had!* or *Do I want to eat raw oysters—like fun I do.* This expression originated in the early 1800s with a quite different meaning, "energetically" or "vigorously," a sense now obsolete. Its present sense dates from the 1900s. Also see FOR FUN.

like gangbusters Energetically, forcefully, loudly. For example, *This is a soft passage—the horns shouldn't come in like gangbusters.* This expression alludes to a popular radio series entitled *Gangbusters,* which featured explosive sound effects, such as gunfire and sirens, at the beginning of each episode. [Slang; late 1930s]

like greased lightning Also, **like a blue streak; like the wind; like blazes.** Very fast indeed, as in *He climbed that ladder like greased lightning,* or *She kept on talking like a blue streak,* or *The children ran like the wind when they heard there'd be free ice* *cream.* The likening of speed to lightning dates from the 1500s, and *grease* was added in the early 1800s to further accentuate the idea of haste. The first variant, *blue streak,* also dates from the early 1800s and alludes to something resembling lightning. The *wind* in the second variant has been a metaphor for swiftness since ancient Roman times. The *blazes* in the last variant, first recorded in 1925, alludes to fire or lightning.

like hell 1. Recklessly, extremely, as in *We ran like hell to catch the train.* [Mid-1800s] 2. Not at all, on the contrary, as in *You think I'll call her stupid? Like hell I will!* or *Like hell I can't say that to Bob.* [Late 1800s]

like hot cakes, go Also, **sell like hot cakes.** Be a great commercial success, as in *I'm sure this new line of coats will go like hot cakes,* or *She was thrilled that her new book was selling like hot cakes.* This term alludes to *hot cakes,* another name for griddle cakes or pancakes, which are so popular at church sales, food fairs, and similar events that they tend to sell as quickly as they are cooked. [Mid-1800s]

like it or lump it Also, **if you don't like it you can lump it.** Whether or not you want to, as in *Like it or lump it, we're staying home this summer.* The origin of *lump* in this idiom is unclear; one writer believes it to be a euphemism for STUFF IT, a not unreasonable conjecture. [Early 1800s]

likely as not ♦ See LIKE AS NOT. Also see under UNLIKELY.

like mad ♦ See LIKE CRAZY.

like nobody's business ♦ See LIKE CRAZY.

like nothing on earth ♦ See ON EARTH, def. 2.

like pigs in clover Extremely contentedly, as in *They had a handsome pension and lived like pigs in clover.* This expression alludes to pigs being allowed to eat as much clover, a favorite food, as they wish. It appeared in the *Boston Gazette* of January 7, 1813: "Canadians! then in droves come over, And live henceforth like pigs in clover." [Early 1800s]

like pulling teeth Very difficult, especially to extract information from someone. For example, *It's like pulling teeth to get a straight answer from him.*

like rolling off a log ♦ See EASY AS ROLLING OFF A LOG.

like shooting fish in a barrel Ridiculously easy, as in *Setting up a computer nowadays is like shooting fish in a barrel.* This hyperbolic expression alludes to the fact that fish make an easy target inside a barrel (as opposed to swimming freely in the sea). [Early 1900s]

likes of, the Also, **the like of one.** An equivalent or very similar person or thing; an equal or match. For example, *I've never seen the likes of this before,* or *We'll never see his like again.* This expression

today is almost always put in a negative context. [Mid-1500s]

like something the cat dragged in ♦ See LOOK LIKE SOMETHING THE CAT DRAGGED IN.

like that 1. In that way or manner, having those characteristics, as in *I told him not to talk to her like that,* or *I wish I could, like Dick, tell you what I really think, but I'm not like that.* [Late 1800s] 2. See JUST LIKE THAT.

like to Also, **liked to.** Come close to, be on the point of. For example, *We like to froze to death,* or *He liked to have never got away.* This expression, now considered a colloquialism from the American South, dates from the early 1400s and was used several times by Shakespeare.

like water off a duck's back Readily and without apparent effect. For example, *The scathing reviews rolled off him like water off a duck's back.* This expression alludes to the fact that duck feathers shed water. [Early 1800s]

lily ♦ See GILD THE LILY.

limb ♦ See OUT ON A LIMB; RISK LIFE AND LIMB.

limbo ♦ See IN LIMBO.

limit ♦ See GO WHOLE HOG (THE LIMIT); SKY'S THE LIMIT; THE LIMIT.

line ♦ In addition to the idioms beginning with LINE, also see ALL ALONG (THE LINE); ALONG THE LINES OF; BLOW IT (ONE'S LINES); BOTTOM LINE; CHOW DOWN (LINE); DOWN THE LINE; DRAW A LINE; DRAW THE LINE AT; DROP A LINE; END OF THE LINE; FALL IN LINE; FEED SOMEONE A LINE; FIRING LINE; GET A LINE ON; GO ON (LINE); HARD LINE; HOLD THE LINE; HOOK, LINE, AND SINKER; HOT LINE; IN LINE; LAY ON THE LINE; LEAST RESISTANCE, LINE OF; MUFF ONE'S LINES; ON LINE; OUT OF LINE; PARTY LINE; READ BETWEEN THE LINES; SIGN ON THE DOTTED LINE; SOMEWHERE ALONG THE LINE; STEP OUT OF LINE; TOE THE LINE.

linen ♦ WASH ONE'S DIRTY LINEN IN PUBLIC.

line of fire, in the In the path of an attack, as in *Whenever Audrey and Jeff quarrel, I take care to get out of the line of fire.* This expression, dating from the mid-1800s, originally referred to the path of a bullet or other projectile, a meaning also still current. Also see FIRING LINE.

line one's pockets Accept a bribe or other illicit payment, as in *The mayor and his cronies found dozens of ways to line their pockets.* This expression dates from the mid-1500s, when it was also put as *line one's purse.*

line up 1. Arrange in or form a line, as in *Betty lined up the books on the shelf,* or *The children lined up for lunch.* [Late 1800s] 2. Organize, make ready, make the arrangements for, as in *They lined* up *considerable support for the bill,* or *Nancy was supposed to line up a hall for the concert.* [c. 1900]

lining ♦ See SILVER LINING.

lion ♦ In addition to the idiom beginning with LION, also see BEARD THE LION; THROW TO THE WOLVES (LIONS).

lion's share The greater part of most of something, as in *Whenever they won a doubles match, Ethel claimed the lion's share of the credit,* or *As usual, Uncle Bob took the lion's share of the cake.* This expression alludes to Aesop's fable about a lion, who got all of a kill because its fellow hunters, an ass, fox, and wolf, were afraid to claim their share. [Late 1700s]

lip ♦ In addition to the idioms beginning with LIP, also see BUTTON UP (ONE'S LIP); KEEP A STIFF UPPER LIP; LICK ONE'S CHOPS (LIPS); PASS ONE'S LIPS.

lips are sealed, one's One will reveal nothing, especially about a secret. For example, *You can trust me with the details of the lawsuit—my lips are sealed.* [Early 1900s]

lip service Verbal but insincere expression of agreement or support. It is often put as **pay** or **give lip service,** as in *They paid lip service to holding an election next year, but they had no intention of doing so.* [Mid-1600s]

list ♦ See BLACK LIST; ENTER THE LISTS; SUCKER LIST.

listen in 1. Hear or overhear the conversation of others; eavesdrop. It is also put as **listen in on,** as in *She listened in on her parents and learned they were planning a surprise party.* [Early 1900s] 2. Tune in and listen to a broadcast, as in *Were you listening in the other night when they played Beethoven's Fifth?* [1920s]

listen to reason Pay heed to sensible advice or argument, as in *We can't let him rush into that job—it's time he listened to reason.* [Mid-1700s]

little ♦ In addition to the idioms beginning with LITTLE, also see A LITTLE; EVERY LITTLE BIT HELPS; IN ONE'S OWN (LITTLE) WORLD; MAKE LITTLE OF; PRECIOUS FEW (LITTLE); THINK LITTLE OF; TO LITTLE PURPOSE; TOO LITTLE, TOO LATE.

little bird told one, a A source one cannot or will not identify gave this information, as in *How did you learn they were getting a divorce?—Oh, a little bird told me.* Versions of this idiom date from ancient times and appear in numerous proverb collections.

little by little ♦ See BIT BY BIT.

little frog in a big pond Also, **small frog in a large pond.** An unimportant or unqualified individual in a large organization or other setting. For example, *Coming from a small school, Sandy felt lost at the state university—a little frog in a big pond.*

This phrase is the counterpart of BIG FISH IN A SMALL POND.

little knowledge is a dangerous thing, a Also, **a little learning is a dangerous thing.** Knowing a little about something tempts one to overestimate one's abilities. For example, *I know you've assembled furniture, but that doesn't mean you can build an entire wall system; remember, a little knowledge.* This maxim, originally a line from Alexander Pope's *An Essay on Criticism* (1709), has been repeated with slight variations ever since. It is still heard, although less frequently, and sometimes shortened, as in the example.

little pitchers have big ears Young children often overhear something they should not. For example, *Don't use any swear words around Brian—little pitchers have big ears.* This metaphoric expression, which likens the curved handle of a pitcher to the human ear, was already in John Heywood's proverb collection of 1546.

live ♦ In addition to the idioms beginning with LIVE, also see ALIVE (LIVE) AND KICKING; AS I LIVE AND BREATHE; CLOSE TO HOME (WHERE ONE LIVES); (LIVE FROM) DAY TO DAY; FAT OF THE LAND, LIVE OFF THE; HIGH OFF THE HOG, LIVE; IN ONE'S POCKET (LIVE IN EACH OTHER'S POCKETS); LEARN TO LIVE WITH; PEOPLE WHO LIVE IN GLASS HOUSES.

live and learn Profit from experience, as in *I ignored the garden book, planted my beans in March, and they all rotted—live and learn.* [Second half of 1500s]

live and let live Show tolerance for those different from yourself. For example, *I'm not going to tell my sister what to do—live and let live, I say.* [First half of 1600s]

live by one's wits Manage by clever expedience rather than hard work or wealth. For example, *Alan's never held a steady job but manages to live by his wits.* This expression uses *wits* in the sense of "keen mental faculties." [c. 1600]

live dangerously Take numerous risks, be daring, as in *Bill never knows if he'll have enough money to pay the next month's rent—he likes to live dangerously.* This expression figured in the work of such 19th-century German writers as Nietzsche, who regarded it as an admirable course of action. Today it is often used with mildly humorous effect, as in the example. [c. 1900]

live down Overcome or reduce the shame of a mistake, misdeed, or the like. It is often put in the negative, as in *I'm afraid I'll never live down that tactless remark I made.* [Mid-1800s]

live for the moment Concentrate on the present, with little or no concern for the future. For example, *Instead of putting aside funds for the children's* education, Jane and Jim live for the moment, spending whatever they earn. [Mid-1900s] Also see FOR THE MOMENT; DAY TO DAY, def. 2.

live from day to day ♦ See DAY TO DAY, def. 2.

live from hand to mouth ♦ See HAND TO MOUTH.

live happily ever after Spend the rest of one's life in happiness, as in *In her romantic novels the hero and heroine end up marrying and then live happily ever after.* This hyperbolic phrase ends many fairy tales. [Mid-1800s]

live high off the hog ♦ See HIGH OFF THE HOG.

live in 1. Reside in one's place of employment or schooling, as in *They wanted a babysitter who could live in,* or *Joe was planning to live in at the college.* This expression is used primarily for domestic servants or students. [Late 1800s] Also see LIVE OUT. 2. **live in something.** Continue in existence, memory, or some feeling. This sense appears in such phrases as **live in the past,** meaning "to concentrate on past memories," or **live in hope of,** meaning "to continue anticipating that something will happen." For example, *Alice lived in the past; she had no interest in current events,* or *Jim lived in hope of getting a teaching post.* Also see LIVE IN SIN.

live in each other's pockets ♦ See IN ONE'S POCKET, def. 2.

live in sin Cohabit outside marriage, as in *Bill and Anne lived in sin for years before they got married.* This term, dating from the early 1800s, is mostly used in a jocular fashion today, when customs and views are more liberal in this regard. Also see LIVE TOGETHER.

live it up Enjoy oneself, often extravagantly. For example, *They came into some money and decided to live it up with a trip around the world.* [Colloquial; mid-1900s]

live like a king Also, **live like a prince.** Enjoy a lavish style of living, as in *He spared no expense, preferring to live like a king as long as he could,* or *Since they got their inheritance, the Andersons are living like princes.* This expression continues to be used despite the much smaller role royalty plays in the present day. [Mid-1500s]

live on 1. Be financially supported by, subsist on, as in *His pension is too small to live on.* [Mid-1600s] 2. Continue to survive, especially unexpectedly, as in *They thought the cancer would kill her, but Lucy lived on for another twenty years.* 3. Remain in human memory, as in *This book will live on long after the author's death.*

live on borrowed time ♦ See ON BORROWED TIME.

live on the edge ♦ See ON THE EDGE.

live out 1. Complete or survive the end of a period of time, as in *Grandpa wants to live out his days in*

a warmer climate. [First half of 1500s] 2. Reside away from one's place of employment, as in *She's a fine housekeeper, but insists on living out.* This expression is used primarily for domestic help. [Mid-1800s] Also see LIVE IN, def. 1. 3. **live out of.** Lead a lifestyle characterized by a particular item. This phrase appears in such idioms as **live out of a suitcase,** meaning "to travel so much that one has no time to unpack one's belongings," or **live out of cans,** meaning "to eat only canned food for lack of other foods or time to prepare them." For example, *Traveling for months on end, he got very tired of living out of a suitcase,* or *We had neither gas nor electricity for a week and had to live out of cans.*

live through Endure, survive. This idiom is used both seriously, as in *Those who have lived through a depression never forget what it was like,* or hyperbolically, as in *That speech was endless—I thought I'd never live through it.*

live together Cohabit, especially when not married. For example, "I . . . am only concerned that their living together before the marriage took place should be so generally known" (Jane Austen, *Pride and Prejudice,* 1813). [c. 1800] Also see LIVE IN SIN.

live up to 1. Live or act in accordance with; also, measure up to. For example, *Children rarely live up to their parents' ideals,* or *This new technology has not lived up to our expectations.* [Late 1600s] 2. Carry out, fulfill, as in *she certainly lived up to her end of the bargain.* [First half of 1800s]

live wire A highly alert or energetic person. For example, *Sally's a real live wire; she brightens up any gathering.* This metaphoric term transfers a wire carrying electric current to a lively individual. [c. 1900]

live with 1. Cohabit with, live as if married to, as in *I don't approve of my daughter living with her boyfriend.* [Mid-1700s] Also see LIVE TOGETHER. 2. Put up with, come to terms with, as in *I think I can live with this new agreement.* [Colloquial; first half of 1900s] Also see LEARN TO LIVE WITH. 3. **live with oneself.** Keep one's self-respect, as in *I don't know how he can live with himself after violating their trust.* [Mid-1900s]

living daylights ♦ See BEAT THE LIVING DAYLIGHTS.

living end, the The utmost in any situation, something quite extraordinary as in *When he threw the stereo out the window—well, that was the living end!* or *That performance was the living end.* [Colloquial; late 1930s]

living soul A person. For example, *Every living soul in this town has a stake in the decision to ban smoking,* or *The place was empty—not a living soul to be found.* [First half of 1600s]

load ♦ In addition to the idioms beginning with LOAD, also see BRICKS SHY OF A LOAD; CARBO LOAD; GET A LOAD OF; TAKE THE LOAD OFF.

loaded for bear Fully prepared for action; also, spoiling for a fight. For example, *Bill tackled his new sales route loaded for bear,* or *When Martin was three hours late, his wife was loaded for bear.* This term, dating from the mid-1800s, alludes to the heavy charge of powder or lead that hunters use for large animals like a bear.

loaded question A question heavy with meaning or emotional impact, as in *When he inquired after Helen's ex-husband, that was a loaded question.* This term employs *loaded* in the sense of "charged with hidden implication." [Mid-1900s]

load off one's feet ♦ See TAKE THE LOAD OFF.

load off one's mind, a Relief from a mental burden or anxiety, as in *Good news about the baby took a load off my mind.* This expression uses *load* in the sense of "a figurative burden." [Mid-1800s]

load the dice Rig the odds so there is little chance for another person to win; cheat. For example, *There's no way we can win this contest; they've loaded the dice.* This expression is also put as **the dice are loaded,** as in *There's no point in trying; the dice are loaded.* This expression alludes to adding weight to one side or another of dice so that they will always come up with certain numbers facing upward. [Late 1800s]

loaf ♦ See HALF A LOAF IS BETTER THAN NONE.

local yokel A native or inhabitant of a particular locale, as in *She's only gone out with local yokels, so she's not used to more sophisticated men.* This disparaging rhyming term was first used by troops stationed away from home. [Slang; mid-1900s]

lock ♦ In addition to the idioms beginning with LOCK, also see UNDER LOCK AND KEY.

locker ♦ See DAVY JONES'S LOCKER.

lock horns Become embroiled in conflict, as in *At the town meeting Kate and Steve locked horns over increasing the property tax.* This expression alludes to how stags and bulls use their horns to fight one another. [First half of 1800s]

lock in 1. Enclose, surround, as in *The ship was completely locked in ice.* [c. 1400s] 2. Also, **lock into.** Fix firmly in position, commit to something. This phrase often occurs as **be locked in** or **into,** as in *She felt she was locked in a binding agreement,* or *Many of the stockholders are locked into their present positions.* [Mid-1900s]

lock out 1. Keep out, prevent from entering. For example, *Karen was so angry at her brother that she locked him out of the house.* [Late 1500s] Shakespeare had it in *The Comedy of Errors* (4:1): "For locking me out of my doors by day." 2. Withhold

work from employees during a labor dispute, as in *The company threatened to lock out the strikers permanently.* [Mid-1800s]

lock, stock, and barrel The entirety; all of something. For example, *Jean moved out of the house, lock, stock, and barrel.* This expression alludes to the three elements of a firearm—the lock or firing mechanism, the stock or handle, and the barrel or tube. [Early 1800s]

lock the barn door after the horse has bolted Also, **lock the stable door after the horse is stolen.** Take precautions after damage has occurred. For example, *After the burglary they installed an alarm system, but it's locking the barn door,* or *Deciding to negotiate now after they've been fired—that's a matter of locking the stable door after the horse is stolen.* These expressions of action that is useless because it comes too late have long been proverbs in many languages and first appeared in English in the mid-1300s.

lock up 1. Close a house or place of work, fastening all the doors and windows, as in *The attendant locks up at eleven o'clock every night,* or *Did you remind Abby to lock up?* [Late 1500s] 2. Invest in something not easily converted into cash, as in *Most of their assets were locked up in real estate.* [Late 1600s] 3. **lock someone up.** Confine or imprison someone, as in *The princes were locked up in the Tower of London.* [c. 1300]

log ♦ In addition to the idiom beginning with LOG, also see EASY AS PIE (ROLLING OFF A LOG); LIKE A BUMP ON A LOG; SLEEP LIKE A LOG.

loggerheads ♦ See AT LOGGERHEADS.

log in Also, **log on.** Enter into a computer the information needed to begin a session, as in *I logged in at two o'clock,* or *There's no record of your logging on today.* These expressions refer especially to large systems shared by numerous individuals, who need to enter a username or password before executing a program. The antonyms are **log off** and **log out,** meaning "to end a computer session." All these expressions derive from the use of *log* in the nautical sense of entering information about a ship in a journal called a *log book.* [c. 1960]

loin ♦ See GIRD ONE'S LOINS.

lone wolf A person who prefers to do without the company or assistance of others. For example, *Her nursery school teacher described Beth as a lone wolf, an assessment her parents found astonishing.* This expression alludes to the tendency of some species of wolf to hunt alone rather than in packs. [c. 1900]

long ♦ In addition to the idioms beginning with LONG, also see ALL DAY (LONG); AS LONG AS; AT (LONG) LAST; BEFORE LONG; COME A LONG WAY; (LONG) DRAWN OUT; GO A LONG WAY TOWARD;

HAPPY AS THE DAY IS LONG; IN THE LONG RUN; MAKE A LONG STORY SHORT; SO LONG. Also see under LONGER.

long ago A time well before the present, the distant past. For example, *I read that book long ago,* or *The battles of long ago were just as fierce.* [Second half of 1300s]

long and short of it, the The substance or gist of something, as in *The first page of this report will give you the long and short of it.* This expression, originally stated as *the short and long of it,* dates from about 1500, the present order being established by the end of the 1600s.

long arm of the law, the The far-reaching power of the authorities. For example, *You'll never get away with leaving work early; the long arm of the law is bound to catch you.* This expression began as *Kings have long arms* (or *hands*) and was listed as a proverb in 1539. The current version, now often used lightly, was first recorded in 1908.

longer ♦ See ANY LONGER; NO LONGER.

long face A facial expression showing sadness or disappointment, as in *Greg's long face was a clear indication of his feelings.* [Late 1700s]

long haul 1. A considerable distance over which something must travel or be carried. For example, *It's a long haul from my house to yours.* This usage dates from the late 1800s, as does the antonym, **short haul,** as in *The movers charge just as much for a short haul as for a long one.* 2. A considerable length of time, an extended period, as in *This investment is one for the long haul.* It is often put as **over the long haul,** as in *Over the long haul we needn't worry about production.* [c. 1930] Also see IN THE LONG RUN.

long in the tooth Getting on in years, old, as in *Aunt Aggie's a little long in the tooth to be helping us move.* This expression alludes to a horse's gums receding with age and making the teeth appear longer. [Mid-1800s]

long shot, a A remote possibility of success, as in *It's a long shot that Joan will actually finish the marathon,* or *He may be a good programmer, but he's a long shot for that job.* This expression alludes to the inaccuracy of early firearms, which when shot over a distance rarely hit the target. It is commonly used in horseracing for a bet made at great odds. A related phrase is **not by a long shot,** meaning "not even remotely," as in *I'll never make it to California in three days, not by a long shot.* [Late 1800s]

long suit One's strong point or advantage, as in *Organizing has never been Nancy's long suit.* This expression alludes to whist, bridge, and other card games in which holding numerous cards in a single suit may convey a strong advantage. [c. 1900]

long time no see It's been a long time since we met, as in *Hi Bob! Long time no see.* This jocular imitation of broken English originated in the pidgin English used in Chinese and Western exchange. [Late 1800s]

look ♦ In addition to the idioms beginning with LOOK, also see (LOOK ON THE) BRIGHT SIDE; DIRTY LOOK; MAKE SOMEONE LOOK GOOD; TAKE A LOOK AT; THINGS ARE LOOKING UP.

look after Also, **look out for; see after.** Take care of, attend to the safety or well-being of, as in *Please look after your little brother,* or *We left Jane to look out for the children,* or *Please see after the luggage.* The first expression dates from the second half of the 1300s, the second from the mid-1900s, and the third from the early 1700s.

look a gift horse in the mouth Be critical or suspicious of something received at no cost. For example, *Dad's old car is full of dents, but we shouldn't look a gift horse in the mouth.* This term, generally expressed as a cautionary proverb (*Don't look a gift horse in the mouth*), has been traced to the writings of the 4th-century cleric, St. Jerome, and has appeared in English since about 1500. It alludes to determining the age of a horse by looking at its teeth.

look alive Act lively, hurry up, as in *Look alive! This job has to be finished today.* This phrase, often used as an imperative, today is more common in Britain than in America. [Mid-1800s]

look as if butter wouldn't melt ♦ See BUTTER WOULDN'T MELT.

look askance View with mistrust, as in *They looked askance at him when he said he'd just made a million in the stock market.* The precise feeling conveyed by this expression has varied since it was first used in the 1500s, from envy to contempt to suspicion, although the literal meaning was "look obliquely, with a side glance." The present sense dates from about 1800. Also see LOOK SIDEWAYS.

look back 1. Remember or think about the past, as in *When Mom looked back on the early days of their marriage, she wondered how they'd managed with so little money* [Late 1500s] 2. **not look back; never look back.** Never show signs of interrupted progress, never return to past circumstances. For example, *Once he'd won the Pulitzer Prize, he never looked back.* [Late 1800s]

look before you leap Think of the consequences before you act, as in *You'd better check out all the costs before you buy a cellular phone—look before you leap.* This expression alludes to Aesop's fable about the fox who is unable to climb out of a well and persuades a goat to jump in. The fox then climbs on the goat's horns to get out, while the goat remains trapped. [c. 1350]

look black Appear threatening or unfavorable, as in *The future looked black for Henry after he dropped out of school.* This expression employs *black* in the sense of "boding ill," a usage dating from about 1700. Also see under DIRTY LOOK.

look blank Be expressionless, appear dumbstruck or overwhelmed. For example, *When I asked her how to get to the hospital, she looked blank.* [c. 1700]

look daggers Glare, stare fiercely, as in *When she started to discuss their finances, he looked daggers at her.* This metaphoric term, likening an angry expression to a dagger's thrust, dates from ancient times and has appeared in English since about 1600.

look down on Also, **look down one's nose at.** Regard with contempt or condescension, consider oneself superior to. For example, *When it comes to baking, Beth is a purist—she looks down on anyone who uses a mix,* or *Seniors have a way of looking down their noses at juniors.* The first expression dates from about 1700, the second from about 1900.

look for 1. Search for; also, seek out. For example, *A search party was sent to look for the lost fliers,* or *Those kids are just looking for trouble.* [Late 1500s] 2. Expect, anticipate, as in *Look for a change of weather in March.* [Early 1500s]

look forward to Eagerly anticipate, as in *I'm looking forward to their visit,* or *Jim looked forward to the day when he could retire.* [First half of 1700s]

looking ♦ See LOOK (LOOKING) TO; LOOK (LOOKING) UP.

look in on Pay a brief visit, as in *I'm just going to look in on Gail and the new baby; I won't stay long.* [c. 1600] Also see LOOK SOMEONE IN THE FACE.

look into Also, **see into.** Investigate, as in *He promised to look into the new law,* or *We must see into the matter of the missing checks.* The first term dates from the late 1500s, the variant from the mid-1800s.

look like 1. Have the appearance of, as in *This letter looks like an acceptance.* [c. 1400] 2. **It looks like.** It seems likely that, as in *It looks like they'll invite us to dinner.* [Colloquial; c. 1900] Also see the subsequent idioms beginning with LOOK LIKE.

look like a million dollars Appear attractive or prosperous. For example, *The painter did a good job—the house looks like a million dollars.* The related **feel like a million dollars** means "feel healthy," as in *Helen came back from her winter vacation feeling like a million dollars.* [c. 1920]

look like death Also, **look** or **feel like death warmed over.** Look or feel very ill or exhausted. For example, *After two nights without sleep, Bill looked like death warmed over,* or *This cold makes me feel like death.* [Colloquial; 1930s]

look like something the cat dragged in Appear completely bedraggled, as in *After running around in the rain for hours, I looked like something the cat dragged in.* This expression alludes to a cat's bringing home birds or mice it has killed or savaged. [c. 1920]

look like the cat that ate the canary Also, **look like the cat that swallowed the canary.** Appear smug and self-satisfied. For example, *After she hit her third winning shot, Jeannie looked like the cat that ate the canary.* [Second half of 1800s]

look on 1. Also, **look upon.** Regard in a certain way, as in *I looked on him as a second father,* or *We looked upon her as a worthy successor.* [Early 1600s] 2. Be a spectator, watch, as in *She rode the horse around the ring as her parents looked on.* [Late 1500s] 3. Also, **look on with.** Read from someone's book, paper, or music at the same time, as in *I forgot my score; can I look on with you?* [Late 1800s]

look on the bright side ♦ See BRIGHT SIDE.

lookout ♦ See KEEP AN EYE OUT FOR (SHARP LOOKOUT); ON THE LOOKOUT. Also see entries beginning with LOOK OUT.

look out Also, **watch out.** Be careful, be watchful, as in *Look out that you don't slip and fall on the ice,* or *Watch out! There's a car coming.* [c. 1600] Also see LOOK OUT FOR.

look out for 1. See to the welfare of, as in *Mary was assigned to look out for the youngsters on the playground.* Similar to LOOK AFTER, this expression appears in such terms as **look out for number one,** meaning "see to one's own best interests," as in *Looking out for number one is Barbara's first priority.* Versions of this expression, such as **take care of number one,** date from 1700. 2. Be careful of or watchful for something or someone, as in *Look out for broken glass on the floor,* or *Look out for Mary—she'll be coming any minute.* [Second half of 1600s] Also see LOOK OUT.

look over Also, **look up and down.** Examine or inspect something or someone. For example, *Jerry was looking over the books when he found an error,* or *They looked the new boy up and down.* The first expression dates from the mid-1400s, the variant from the late 1800s.

look sharp Get moving, be alert, as in *The coach told the team they would have to look sharp if they wanted to win.* This colloquial expression, dating from the early 1700s, originally meant "to keep a strict watch" but acquired its present sense in the early 1800s.

look sideways at Glance at suspiciously or amorously, as in *I'm sure the detective was looking sideways at me, and it made me very nervous,* or *They were looking sideways at each other, and I don't* *think it was innocent.* [Mid-1800s] Also see LOOK ASKANCE.

look someone in the face Also, **look someone in the eye.** Face someone directly and forthrightly. These expressions imply honesty—or at least the appearance of honesty—in what is said, as in *Can you look me in the face and tell me you don't want that prize?* or *John looked me in the eye and told me he didn't break the window.* The first term was first recorded in 1566, the variant in 1931. Also see STARE IN THE FACE.

look the other way Deliberately overlook something, especially something of an illicit nature. For example, *They're not really entitled to a discount but the sales manager decided to look the other way.* This expression uses *the other way* in the sense of "away from what is normal or expected."

look through rose-colored glasses ♦ See SEE THROUGH ROSE-COLORED GLASSES.

look to 1. Pay attention to, take care of, as in *You'd best look to your own affairs.* [c. 1300] 2. Anticipate or expect, as in *We look to hear from her soon.* [c. 1600] 3. **look to be.** Seem to be, promise to be, as in *This looks to be a very difficult assignment.* [Mid-1700s]

look to one's laurels Protect one's preeminent reputation or position, especially against a threat of being surpassed. For example, *Your opponent's done very well in the practice, so you'd better look to your laurels in the actual game.* This idiom alludes to *laurels* as the traditional material for making a victor's crown. [Late 1800s]

look up 1. Search for in a book or other source, as in *I told her to look up the word in the dictionary.* [Late 1600s] 2. Call on or visit, as in *I'm going to look up my friend in Chicago.* [Mid-1800s] 3. Become better, improve, as in *Business is finally looking up.* [c. 1800] 4. **look up to.** Admire, respect, as in *The students really looked up to Mr. Jones.* [Early 1700s]

look up and down ♦ See under LOOK OVER.

look up to ♦ See LOOK UP, def. 4.

look who's talking You're in no position to criticize, as in *I wish Kate would be on time for once.—You do? Look who's talking!* This colloquial idiom dates from the mid-1900s, although another version, **you can't talk,** is a century or so older.

loom large Appear imminent in a threatening, magnified form. For example, *The possibility of civil war loomed large on the horizon,* or *Martha wanted to take it easy for a week, but the bar exam loomed large.* This term employs *loom* in the sense of "come into view," a usage dating from the late 1500s.

loop ♦ See IN THE LOOP; KNOCK FOR A LOOP.

loose ♦ In addition to the idioms beginning with LOOSE, also see AT LOOSE ENDS; BREAK LOOSE; CAST LOOSE; CUT LOOSE; FOOTLOOSE AND FANCY-FREE; HANG LOOSE; HAVE A SCREW LOOSE; LET LOOSE; ON THE LOOSE; PLAY FAST AND LOOSE.

loose cannon One who is uncontrolled and therefore a serious and unpredictable danger. For example, *We can't trust her to talk to the press—she's a loose cannon.* This metaphoric expression alludes to cannon mounted on the deck of a sailing ship, which if dislodged during combat or a storm could cause serious damage to both vessel and crew by sliding about. Its figurative use dates from the first half of the 1900s.

loose ends Unfinished details, incomplete business. For example, *We've not quite finished the project; there are still some loose ends.* This expression alludes to the ends of a rope or cable that should be fastened. [Mid-1800s] Also see AT LOOSE ENDS.

lord ♦ In addition to the idiom beginning with LORD, also see DRUNK AS A LORD.

lord it over Domineer over, act arrogantly toward, as in *After Mary was elected president, she tried to lord it over the other girls.* [Late 1500s] Also see QUEEN IT.

lose ♦ In addition to the idioms beginning with LOSE, also see GET (LOSE) ONE'S BEARINGS; KEEP (LOSE) ONE'S COOL; KEEP (LOSE) TRACK; WIN SOME, LOSE SOME. Also see under LOSING; LOST.

lose face Be embarrassed or humiliated, especially publicly. For example, *Terry lost face when his assistant was promoted and became his boss.* Both this expression and the underlying concept come from Asia; the term itself is a translation of the Chinese *tiu lien* and has been used in English since the late 1800s. Also see SAVE FACE.

lose ground Fail to hold one's position; fall behind, deteriorate. For example, *The Democrats were losing ground in this district,* or *We thought Grandma was getting better, but now she's quickly losing ground.* This expression originally referred to territory lost by a retreating army. [Second half of 1700s]

lose heart Become discouraged, as in *The rescuers worked hard for the first few hours, but then they lost heart.* This term uses *heart* in the sense of "courage" or "spirit." [Mid-1800s] Also see LOSE ONE'S HEART TO.

lose it ♦ See LOSE ONE'S GRIP; LOSE ONE'S TEMPER.

lose no time ♦ See LOSE TIME, def. 2.

lose one's bearings ♦ See under GET ONE'S BEARINGS.

lose one's buttons ♦ See under HAVE ALL ONE'S BUTTONS.

lose one's cool ♦ See under KEEP ONE'S COOL.

lose oneself in Become deeply absorbed or involved in, as in *Doctors are notorious for losing* *themselves in their work.* This expression alludes to becoming so absorbed as to forget oneself. [c. 1600]

lose one's grip Also **lose it.** **1.** Fail to maintain control or one's ability to function, as in *Ted wasn't running things the way he used to, and his boss thought he might be losing his grip,* or *I thought I was losing it when I couldn't remember the words to that old song.* The first term dates from the mid-1800s, the slangy variant from the mid-1900s. **2.** Fail to keep one's composure, as in *When Billy broke the window, Dad just lost his grip and let him have it,* or *I just can't deal with this many visitors—I must be losing it.* [Slang; first half of 1900s] Also see LOSE ONE'S TEMPER.

lose one's head ♦ See under KEEP ONE'S HEAD, def. 1.

lose one's heart to Fall in love with, as in *I totally lost my heart to the new puppy.* This expression uses *heart* in the sense of "the seat of love or affection." [First half of 1600s]

lose one's lunch Vomit, as in *When Anne saw the wound, she thought she'd lose her lunch.* This expression does not usually refer to a specific meal and probably survives because of alliteration. [Colloquial; c. 1940]

lose one's marbles ♦ See under HAVE ALL ONE'S BUTTONS.

lose one's mind Also, **lose one's reason.** Go crazy, lose one's sanity, as in *I thought she'd lost her mind when she said she was going ice-fishing,* or *That assignment is enough to make me lose my reason.* The first expression dates from the late 1500s; the second employs *reason* in the sense of "unimpaired mental faculties," a usage dating from the late 1300s. Also see under GO OUT OF ONE'S MIND; HAVE ALL ONE'S BUTTONS.

lose one's nerve Become frightened or timid, lose courage. For example, *I wanted to ski down the expert slope but then I lost my nerve.* This expression employs *nerve* in the sense of "courage or boldness." [Early 1900s]

lose one's shirt Face financial ruin, go bankrupt, as in *He lost his shirt in the last recession.* This expression implies one has lost even one's shirt. [Early 1900s]

lose one's temper Also, **lost it.** Give way to violent anger, lose self-control. For example, *When she found out what Ann had done, she lost her temper,* or *He arrived without that important check, and then I just lost it completely.* The first term dates from the early 1800s; the second slangy locution dates from the mid-1900s.

lose one's touch No longer be able to do or handle something skillfully. For example, *I used to make beautiful cakes but I seem to have lost my touch,* or *Dad had a real knack for letting someone down gently,*

but he's lost his touch. This expression alludes to the older sense of *touch* as a musician's skill on an instrument or an artist's skill in using a brush or chisel. [First half of 1900s] Also see LOSE TOUCH.

lose out **1.** Fail to succeed, be defeated, as in *The election's over, and you've lost out.* [Mid-1800s] **2.** Also, **lose out on** or **in.** Miss an opportunity to participate, as in *We came so late that we lost out on our chance to see her dance,* or *The Republicans lost out in last fall's elections.* [Colloquial; mid-1900s] Also see MISS OUT ON.

loser ♦ See under FINDERS, KEEPERS.

lose sight of Overlook, fail to take into account, as in *We must not lose sight of our main objective,* or *Beverly never lost sight of her humble beginnings.* This metaphoric expression alludes to physical sight. [Early 1700s] For an antonym, see BEAR IN MIND.

lose sleep over Worry about, as in *It's too bad the experiment failed, but I'm not going to lose sleep over it.* This expression, often put negatively, alludes to actual insomnia caused by anxiety. [First half of 1900s]

lose the thread Cease to follow the sense of what is said. For example, *It was such a long story that I soon lost the thread.* This expression uses *thread* in the sense of "something that connects the various points of a narrative." [Mid-1900s]

lose time **1.** Operate too slowly. For example, *My watch loses time,* or *This clock loses five minutes a day.* This usage is always applied to a timepiece. [Mid-1800s] **2.** Waste time, delay, as in *We wanted to paint the entire porch today, but we lost time trying to find a color that matched the house.* This expression is sometimes put negatively as **lose no time,** meaning "act immediately" or "not delay," as in *We must lose no time in getting him to the hospital.* [Late 1500s] Also see MAKE UP FOR LOST TIME.

lose touch Fail to keep in contact or communication, as in *The two sisters lost touch years ago,* or *Please don't lose touch with me after you move away.* [Late 1800s] For an antonym, see IN TOUCH.

lose track ♦ See under KEEP TRACK.

losing battle, a Also, **a losing game.** A failing effort or activity. For example, *He's fighting a losing battle against putting on weight,* or *We think his candidacy is a losing game.* These expressions, alluding to actual unsuccessful battles or games, have been used figuratively since the early 1600s. Also see LOST CAUSE.

loss ♦ See AT A LOSS; CUT ONE'S LOSSES; DEAD LOSS.

lost ♦ In addition to the idioms beginning with LOST, also see GET LOST; HE WHO HESITATES IS LOST; MAKE UP FOR LOST TIME; NO LOVE LOST; YOU'VE LOST ME. Also see LOSE.

lost cause A hopeless undertaking, as in *Trying to get him to quit smoking is a lost cause.* In the 1860s this expression was widely used to describe the Confederacy. [Mid-1800s] Also see LOSING BATTLE.

lost in the shuffle Failing to stand out among others, as in *In that huge economics class Jane's afraid she'll get lost in the shuffle.* This metaphoric term alludes to mixing playing cards before dealing them. [c. 1900]

lost in thought Concentrating on or pondering over something. For example, *Gwen didn't hear a word you said; she was lost in thought.*

lost on one Have no effect or influence on one, as in *Ned's attempts at humor were lost on Meg,* or *David's kindness was not lost on his aunt.* This expressions uses *lost* in the sense of "wasted." [c. 1600] Also see YOU'VE LOST ME.

lot ♦ See A LOT; CARRY (A LOT OF) WEIGHT; CAST ONE'S LOT WITH; FAT CHANCE (LOT); HAVE (A LOT) GOING FOR ONE; HAVE A LOT ON ONE'S PLATE; LEAVE A LOT TO BE DESIRED; QUITE A BIT (LOT); THINK A LOT OF.

loud ♦ In addition to the idioms beginning with LOUD, also see ACTIONS SPEAK LOUDER THAN WORDS; BIG (LOUD) MOUTH; FOR CRYING OUT LOUD; OUT LOUD; THINK ALOUD; (LOUD ENOUGH) TO WAKE THE DEAD.

loud and clear Easily audible and understandable. For example, *They told us, loud and clear, what to do in an emergency,* or *You needn't repeat it—I hear you loud and clear.* This expression gained currency in the military during World War II to acknowledge radio messages (**I read you loud and clear**) although it originated in the late 1800s.

loud mouth ♦ See BIG MOUTH.

louse up Spoil, ruin, bungle. For example, *The bad weather loused up our plans,* or *Your change of mind really loused me up.* This slangy expression originated in World War I, when infestation with lice was the common lot of soldiers in the trenches; its figurative use dates from the 1930s.

lousy with Abundantly supplied, as in *He's lousy with money.* Like LOUSE UP, this expression alludes to being infested with lice. [First half of 1800s]

love ♦ In addition to the idioms beginning with LOVE, also see ALL'S FAIR IN LOVE AND WAR; COURSE OF TRUE LOVE; FALL IN LOVE; FOR THE LOVE OF; LABOR OF LOVE; MAKE LOVE; MISERY LOVES COMPANY; NO LOVE LOST; NOT FOR LOVE OR MONEY; PUPPY LOVE; SOMEBODY UP THERE LOVES ME.

love affair 1. An intimate sexual relationship, as in *They had a torrid love affair many years ago.* This expression dates from about 1600, when it referred merely to the experiences connected with being in love. The current sense dates from the second half of the 1800s. 2. A strong enthusiasm, as in *We can't ignore America's love affair with the automobile.* [Mid-1900s]

love at first sight An instantaneous attraction to someone or something. For example, *With Peter and Constance, it was a case of love at first sight,* or *When Dave saw that car, it was love at first sight.* This expression was already used by Chaucer for romantic attraction in *Troilus and Cressida:* "She loved right from the first sight." The transfer to objects dates from the first half of the 1900s.

lovers' lane A secluded road or area sought out by lovers seeking privacy. For example, *The police loved to embarrass youngsters parked in lovers' lane.* [Late 1800s]

loving ♦ See TENDER LOVING CARE.

low ♦ In addition to the idioms beginning with LOW, also see AT A LOW EBB; (LOW) BOILING POINT; HIGH AND LOW; KEEP A LOW PROFILE; LAY SOMEONE LOW; LIE LOW.

low blow An unscrupulous attack; an insult. For example, *When my roommate moved out without a word of warning, leaving me to pay the entire rent, that was a low blow,* or *She wanted to win the argument, but bringing up his failed marriage was a low blow.* This term alludes to the illegal practice of hitting an opponent in boxing BELOW THE BELT. [c. 1950]

low boiling point ♦ See BOILING POINT, def. 2.

lower one's sights Reduce one's goals or aspirations, as in *Once he got the job I'd applied for, I had to lower my sights.* This expression alludes to taking aim through the sights of a firearm. Also see RAISE ONE'S SIGHTS; SET ONE'S SIGHTS ON. [Second half of 1900s]

lower the boom on Scold harshly or punish severely; also, put a stop to something. For example, *If you're caught smoking in school, the principal is bound to lower the boom on you,* or *The new radar equipment enabled the police to lower the boom on speeding.* This expression refers to the boom of a sailboat—a long spar that extends from the mast to hold the foot of the sail. In a changing wind, the boom can swing wildly, leaving one at risk of being struck. [Slang; first half of 1900s]

low man on the totem pole Low in rank, least important person, as in *I just joined the board so I'm low man on the totem pole.* This slangy expression is thought to have been invented by the American comedian Fred Allen about 1940 and caught on despite its lack of application to a genuine totem pole.

low profile ♦ See KEEP A LOW PROFILE.

luck ♦ In addition to the idioms beginning with LUCK, also see AS LUCK WOULD HAVE IT; BEGINNER'S LUCK; DOWN ON ONE'S LUCK; GOOD LUCK; HARD

LUCK; IN LUCK; OUT OF LUCK; PUSH ONE'S LUCK; RUN OF LUCK; TAKE POT LUCK; TOUGH BREAK (LUCK); TRY ONE'S HAND (LUCK).

luck into ♦ See LUCK OUT.

luck of the devil Also, **luck of the Irish.** Extraordinarily good fortune, as in *You've the luck of the devil—that ball landed just on the line,* or *Winning the lottery—that's the luck of the Irish.* These superstitious attributions of good fortune date from the first half of the 1900s.

luck of the draw Pure chance, as in *It isn't anyone's fault—it's just the luck of the draw.* This expression alludes to the random drawing of a playing card. [Mid-1900s]

luck out Also, **luck into.** Gain success or something desirable through good fortune. For example, *We lucked out and found the same rug for half the price,* or *Nell and Dave lucked into a terrific apartment.* [Colloquial; mid-1900s]

lucky ♦ See BORN UNDER A LUCKY STAR; STRIKE IT RICH (LUCKY); THANK ONE'S LUCKY STARS.

lull into Deceive into trustfulness, as in *The steadily rising market lulled investors into a false sense of security.* The earliest recorded version of this term referred to wine: "Fitter indeed to bring and lull men asleep in the bed of security" (Philemon Holland, *Pliny's Historie of the World,* 1601). Today it still often appears with the phrase **a false sense of security.**

lump ♦ In addition to the idiom beginning with LUMP, also see LIKE IT OR LUMP IT.

lump in one's throat A feeling of constriction in the throat caused by emotion, as in *The bride's mother had a lump in her throat.* This expression likens the sense of a physical swelling to the tight sensation caused by strong feelings. [Mid-1800s]

lunch ♦ See EAT SOMEONE ALIVE (SOMEONE'S LUNCH); FREE LUNCH; LOSE ONE'S LUNCH; OUT TO (LUNCH).

lung ♦ See AT THE TOP OF ONE'S LUNGS.

lurch ♦ See LEAVE IN THE LURCH.

luxury ♦ See LAP OF LUXURY.

lying down ♦ See TAKE LYING DOWN. Also see LIE DOWN.

m

mad ♦ In addition to the idioms beginning with MAD, also see CRAZY (MAD) ABOUT; DRIVE SOMEONE CRAZY (MAD); HOPPING MAD; LIKE CRAZY (MAD); STARK RAVING MAD.

mad about Also, **mad for.** ♦ See CRAZY ABOUT.

mad as a hatter Also, **mad as a March hare.** Crazy, demented, as in *She is throwing out all his clothes;*

she's mad as a hatter. This expression, dating from the early 1800s, alludes to exposure to the chemicals formerly used in making felt hats, which caused tremors and other nervous symptoms. The variant, dating from the 14th century, alludes to the crazy behavior of hares during rutting season, mistakenly thought to be only in March.

mad as a hornet Also, **mad as hell** or **hops** or **a wet hen.** Very angry, enraged as in *Mary was mad as a hornet when her purse was stolen,* or *Upset? Dan was mad as hell,* or *The teacher was mad as a wet hen.* The use of *mad* for "angry" dates from about 1300, but these similes are of much more recent vintage (1800s, early 1900s). The allusions to a *hornet,* which can launch a fierce attack, and *hell,* with its furious fires, are more obvious than the other variants. *Mad as hops* was first recorded in 1884 and is thought to have been the writer's version of HOPPING MAD; *mad as a wet hen,* first recorded in 1823, is puzzling, since hens don't really mind water.

made ♦ In addition to the idioms beginning with MADE, also see HAVE IT MADE. Also see under MAKE.

made for each other Also, **made for one another.** Perfectly suited, as in *Pat and Peter were just made for each other,* or, as Samuel Richardson put it in *Clarissa* (1751): "Her features are all harmony, and made for one another." The use of *made for* in the sense of "fitted for" dates from the late 1100s.

made of money Very rich, as in *Afford a limousine? Do you think I'm made of money?* This hyperbolic expression uses *made of* in the sense of "composed of," a usage dating from about 1200.

made to measure Also, **tailor-made.** Fashioned to fit a particular need or purpose, very suitable. For example, *Jane finds her new position is made to measure for her,* or *This bridge club is tailor-made for Max.* Originally referring to clothes made to fit a particular person very precisely, these terms have been used figuratively since the mid-1900s. Also see MADE TO ORDER.

made to order Also, **built to order.** Very suitable, as in *Her new assignment was built to order for her.* In its literal use, this idiom refers to an item fashioned according to particular instructions. [Mid-1900s]

madness ♦ See METHOD IN ONE'S MADNESS.

mad rush A wild hurry, as in *I was in a mad rush to get to the bank on time to cash my check,* or *Why the mad rush? We have lots of time before the concert starts.* The use of *in a rush* for "being in a hurry" dates from the second half of the 1800s, and *mad,* for "frenzied," serves merely as an intensifier.

maiden voyage The first experience, as in *This tennis tournament is my maiden voyage in statewide* *competition*. This term, originally meaning the first voyage of a ship, was first recorded in 1901, but the use of *maiden* to signify "the first time" dates from the mid-1500s.

main ◆ In addition to the idioms beginning with MAIN, also see EYE TO THE MAIN CHANCE; IN THE MAIN; MIGHT AND MAIN.

main drag The principal street of a city or town, as in *Several stores on the main drag have closed*. This slangy term was first recorded in 1851.

main squeeze 1. One's boss, the highest authority, an important person. For example, *Who's the main squeeze in this company?* This slangy term was first recorded in 1896, and the precise allusion is unclear. 2. One's sweetheart, as in *Nancy is his main squeeze*. This slangy usage, first recorded in 1970, alludes to the "squeeze" of a hug.

make ◆ In addition to the idioms beginning with MAKE, also see ABSENCE MAKES THE HEART GROW FONDER; ALL WORK AND NO PLAY MAKES JACK A DULL BOY; CAN'T MAKE A SILK PURSE OUT OF A SOW'S EAR; CAN'T MAKE HEAD OR TAIL OF; KISS AND MAKE UP; MANY HANDS MAKE LIGHT WORK; MIGHT MAKES RIGHT; ON THE MAKE; PRACTICE MAKES PERFECT; PUT IN (MAKE) AN APPEARANCE; PUT THE MAKE ON; RUN FOR IT, MAKE A; THAT MAKES TWO OF US; TWO WRONGS DO NOT MAKE A RIGHT; WHAT MAKES ONE TICK. Also see under MADE.

make a beeline for Go straight to, as in *He made a beeline for the refreshments*. In this expression, *beeline* means "the shortest distance between two points," alluding to the route of worker bees bringing nectar and pollen back to the hive. [c. 1830]

make a break for Also, **make a run for**. Run toward something. For example, *As soon as it ended, they made a break for the door*, or *I'll have to make a run for the plane*. The noun *break* here means "escape," and both terms may be put as **make a break** or **run for it**, meaning "to escape or get away quickly." For example, *With the guards asleep, he decided to make a break for it*, or *The rain's stopped; let's make a run for it*. [c. 1840]

make a bundle Also, **make a pile**. Make a great deal of money, as in *When the market went up they made a bundle*, or *He made a pile from that department store*. The first term, dating from about 1900, comes from the somewhat earlier use of *bundle* for a roll of banknotes. The variant, alluding to a heap of money, was first recorded in 1864.

make a clean breast of Confess fully; as in *Caught shoplifting, the girls decided to make a clean breast of it to their parents*. This expression, first recorded in 1752, uses *clean breast* in the sense of baring of one's heart, the breast long considered the seat of private or secret feelings.

make a clean sweep 1. Remove or eliminate unwanted persons or things, as in *The new owners made a clean sweep of the place, intending to replace all the equipment*. This phrase replaced the much older **general sweep**. [Mid-1800s] Also see NEW BROOM SWEEPS CLEAN. 2. Win overwhelmingly, as in *Our candidate made a clean sweep of all the districts*. This usage is most often found with reference to success in a sports competition or election.

make a comeback Also, **stage a comeback**. Achieve a success after retirement or failure, as in *After years in mediocre movies, she made a comeback on Broadway*, or *The humble hamburger is about to stage a comeback*. [Colloquial; c. 1920] Also see COME BACK, def. 1.

make a crack Utter an impudent, sarcastic, or ironic remark, as in *She's constantly making cracks about the store's management*. The noun *crack* here alludes to a hunter's shot at game. [Slang; late 1800s]

make a date Arrange a meeting with someone, as in *Let's get the department heads together and make a date for lunch next week*, or *I've made a date with Jean; can you join us?* At first alluding only to social engagements, especially with a member of the opposite sex, this term, first recorded in 1876, is now used more broadly.

make a day of it Also, **make a night of it**. Devote a day (or night) to some pleasurable pursuit, as in *Now that we're at the beach, let's make a day of it*, or *Since they missed the seven o'clock train, they decided to make a night of it*. [Mid-1600s]

make a dent in Begin to accomplish or consume something, as in *I've barely made a dent in this pile of correspondence*, or *Help us put a dent in this pie*. This metaphoric expression alludes to striking a blow to make a physical indentation in something.

make a difference 1. Distinguish or discriminate. This phrase appears in the Bible (Leviticus 11:47): "To make a difference between the unclean and the clean." [Late 1500s] 2. Also, **make the difference**. Cause a change in effect, change the nature of something, as in *His score on this test will make the difference between passing and failing*, or *These curtains sure make a difference in the lighting*. 3. Be important, matter, as in *Her volunteer work made a difference in many lives*. The antonym of this usage is **make no difference**, as in *It makes no difference to me if we go immediately or in an hour*. This usage appeared long ago in slightly different versions. Miles Coverdale's translation of the Bible of 1535 had *it is no difference*, and the converse, *it makes great difference*, was first recorded about 1470.

make advances 1. Attempt to make someone's acquaintance or make overtures, as in *The ambassador knew that the ministers would soon make advances to him*. [Late 1600s] 2. Approach amorously or sexually, as in *His wife accused him of making* *advances to the nanny.* [c. 1700] Also see MAKE A PASS AT.

make a face Grimace, distort the facial features, as in *The teacher told Joan to stop making faces at Mary.* This expression was first recorded in 1570.

make a federal case of Also, **make a big deal of.** Give undue importance to an issue, as in *I'll pay you back next week—you needn't make a federal case of it,* or *Jack is making a big deal of filling out his passport application.* The first hyperbolic expression, almost always used in a negative context, alludes to taking a legal action before a high (federal) court. The second alludes to an important business transaction (see BIG DEAL, def. 1).

make a fool of Also, **make an ass** or **monkey out of.** Cause someone or oneself to look foolish or stupid. For example, *John doesn't mind making a fool of himself at parties,* or *They made an ass of me by giving me the wrong instructions,* or *Just watch him make a monkey out of this amateur chess player.* The use of *fool* and *ass* date from the early 1600s; the latter is sometimes put more rudely as **make a horse's ass of,** alluding to a horse's behind. The use of *monkey* dates from about 1900.

make a fortune Also, **make a small fortune.** Earn a great deal of money, as in *He made a fortune on the stock market.* Similar expressions are **be worth a fortune** or **small fortune,** as in *Now that their parents have died, they're worth a small fortune.* **Make a fortune** dates from about 1700, and its use with *small* from the second half of the 1800s.

make a fuss 1. Cause a needless commotion or display, as in *I'm sure he'll be here soon; please don't make a fuss.* It is also often put as **make a fuss about** or **over,** as in *He's making a fuss about nothing,* or *If you make a fuss over the small budget items, what will it be like when we discuss the big ones?* The idiom dates from about 1800, although the use of *fuss* in this sense is a century older. 2. **make a fuss over someone.** Treat someone with excessive attention, solicitude, or affection, as in *Whenever they visit Grandma she makes a fuss over the children.* [1920s]

make a go of Achieve success in, as in *He has made a go of his new business.* This expression was first recorded in 1877.

make a hash of Also, **make a mess of.** Ruin or spoil something, as in *They've made a hash of their financial affairs,* or *She thought he'd make a mess of the garden.* The first term, first recorded in 1833, uses *hash* in the sense of "a jumble of mangled fragments"; the variant, using *mess* in the sense of "a muddle" or "a state of confusion," was first recorded in 1862.

make a hit 1. Also, **be a hit.** Achieve (or be) a success, especially a popular one, as in *She made a big*

hit in this performance, or *In out-of-town tryouts the play was already a hit.* This seemingly modern term, which transfers the literal meaning of *hit* as "a stroke or blow," has been around since the early 1800s. It was used then, as now, for theatrical performances, books, songs, and the like 2. In underworld slang, commit a murder, as in *Known for his deadly accuracy, he was about to make his third hit.* This usage also has been extended to such terms as **hit list,** a roster of persons to be killed, and **hit man,** a killer who is usually hired by someone else. [Second half of 1900s]

make a hole in ♦ See under PICK APART.

make a killing Enjoy a large and quick profit, as in *They made a killing in real estate.* This expression alludes to a hunter's success. [Slang; late 1800s]

make a laughingstock of Lay open to ridicule, as in *They made a laughingstock of the chairman by inviting him to the wrong meeting-place,* or *She felt she was making a laughingstock of herself, always wearing the wrong clothes for the occasion.* The noun *laughingstock* replaced the earlier *mockingstock* and *sportingstock,* now obsolete. The idiom was first recorded in 1667.

make a living Earn enough to support oneself, as in *Can he make a living as a freelance trumpeter?* This term was first recorded in 1632.

make allowance for Also, **make allowances for.** Take into account extenuating circumstances, as in *We have to make allowance for Jeff; he's very new to the business,* or *Grandma is always making allowances for the children's bad manners.* [c. 1700]

make a long story short Get to the point, as in *To make a long story short, they got married and moved to Omaha.* Although the idea of abbreviating a long-winded account is ancient, this precise phrase dates only from the 1800s. Henry David Thoreau played on it in a letter of 1857: "Not that the story need be long, but it will take a long time to make it short."

make amends Compensate someone for a grievance or injury, as in *They must make amends for the harm they've caused you.* This expression was first recorded in 1330.

make a monkey out of ♦ See under MAKE A FOOL OF.

make a mountain out of a molehill Exaggerate trifling difficulties, as in *If you forgot your racket you can borrow one—don't make a mountain out of a molehill.* This expression, alluding to the barely raised tunnels created by moles, was first recorded in John Fox's *The Book of Martyrs* (1570).

make a name for oneself Achieve distinction, become prominent or well known, as in *Martha is making a name for herself as an excellent chef.* The earliest recorded use of this term was in John Wycliffe's followers' translation of the Bible (II

Samuel 8:13): "Forsooth David made to him a name." Also see MAKE ONE'S MARK.

make an appearance ♦ See PUT IN AN APPEARANCE.

make an appointment 1. Assign someone to a particular office or position, as in *When the head of White House security resigned, it was up to the President to make an appointment.* [Mid-1800s] **2.** Schedule a meeting with someone, as in *Do I need to make another appointment with the doctor?* [Mid-1700s]

make an ass of ♦ See MAKE A FOOL OF.

make an end of ♦ See PUT AN END TO.

make an example of Punish someone so as to be a warning to others, as in *The teacher made an example of the boy she caught cheating,* or *The judge imposed a tough sentence to make an example of the car thieves.* This usage is first recorded in John Wycliffe's followers' translation of the Bible (c. 1382).

make an exception Exempt someone or something from a general rule or practice, as in *Because it's your birthday, I'll make an exception and let you stay up as late as you want.* This expression was first recorded about 1391.

make an exhibition of oneself Show off or otherwise embarrass oneself in public, as in *When Mike has too much to drink he's apt to make an exhibition of himself.* The first recorded use of this term was in Charles Dickens's *A Child's History of England* (1853).

make a night of it ♦ See under MAKE A DAY OF IT.

make an impression Produce a strong effect on one. This phrase is often qualified with an adjective such as *good, bad, strong,* or the like. For example, *He tried to make a good impression on his girlfriend's parents,* or *Be careful or you'll make a bad impression on the jury,* or *You made quite an impression with that speech.* [Mid-1600s]

make a note of Write down so as to remember; also, remember. For example, *I'll make a note of the fact that the tires are low.* Shakespeare used this term in slightly different form in *The Two Gentlemen of Verona* (2:7): "Go with me to my chamber to take a note of what I stand in need."

make a nuisance of oneself Bother or annoy others, as in *That child is making a nuisance of himself.*

make a pass at 1. Flirt or make advances to someone, especially of a sexual nature, as in "Men seldom make passes at girls who wear glasses" (Dorothy Parker, *Not So Deep As A Well,* 1936). [1920s] **2.** Also, **take a pass at.** Make an attempt, as in *I've made a pass at opening it but had no luck,* or *Jake, will you take a pass at changing the oil?* This usage employs *pass* in the sense of a

"jab" or "poke." [Colloquial; 1900s] Also see MAKE A STAB AT.

make a pig of oneself Overeat, as in *I really made a pig of myself at the buffet.* [Colloquial; 1940s] Also see PIG OUT.

make a pile ♦ See MAKE A BUNDLE.

make a pitch for Say or do something in support of someone or something, as in *That announcer really made a pitch for Sunday's concert,* or *Her agent's been making a pitch for her books all over town.* This expression originally alluded to an inflated sales talk that was "pitched" (in the sense of "thrown") at the listener. [Slang; late 1800s]

make a play for Try to attract someone's interest, especially romantic interest. For example, *Bill has been making a play for Anne, but so far it hasn't gotten him anywhere.* [Slang; c. 1900]

make a point of Treat something as important or essential, as in *She made a point of thanking everyone in the department for their efforts.* This expression uses *point* in the sense of "an objective or purpose." [Late 1700s] Also see MAKE ONE'S POINT.

make a practice of Habitually do something, as in *Bill makes a practice of checking the oil and gas before every long trip.* [c. 1900]

make arrangements for Plan or prepare for someone or something, as in *Who is making all the arrangements for our sales meeting?* This expression employs *arrangements* in the sense of "measures or preparations for a particular purpose," a usage dating from the late 1700s.

make a run for ♦ See MAKE A BREAK FOR.

make a scene Also, **create a scene; make an uproar.** Make a public disturbance or excited emotional display. For example, *Joan made a scene when the restaurant lost her dinner reservation,* or *Ted made an uproar over losing his luggage.* **Make a scene** was first recorded in 1831; the variant employs *uproar* in the sense of "a noisy commotion," a usage first recorded in 1548.

make as if Also, **make as though; make like.** Behave as if, pretend that. For example, *Jean made as if she really liked the soup,* or *Dad made as though he had not heard them,* or *She makes like she's a really important person.* The first two usages date from the early 1500s; the third, a colloquialism, dates from the late 1800s.

make a silk purse ♦ See CAN'T MAKE A SILK PURSE OUT OF A SOW'S EAR.

make a stab at Try to do something, as in *I don't know the answer but I'll make a stab at it.* This expression derives from *stab* in the sense of "a vigorous thrust." [Late 1800s] Also see MAKE A PASS AT, def. 2.

make a stand Hold firm against something or someone, as in *The government was determined to make a stand against all forms of terrorism.* This idiom transfers the early meaning of holding ground against an enemy to other issues. [c. 1600]

make a statement Create a certain impression; communicate an idea or mood without using words. For example, *The furnishings here make a statement about the company.* [Mid-1900s]

make a stink Also, **raise a stink.** Create a great fuss; complain, criticize, or otherwise make trouble about something. For example, *They promised to fix the printer today; you needn't make a stink about it,* or *The parents were raising a stink about the principal's new rules.* This idiom transfers an offensive odor to a public fuss. [Mid-1800s] Also see MAKE A SCENE.

make a virtue of necessity Do the best one can under given circumstances, as in *Since he can't break the contract, Bill's making a virtue of necessity.* This expression first appeared in English in Chaucer's *The Knight's Tale:* "Then is it wisdom, as it thinketh me, to make virtue of necessity." Also see MAKE THE BEST OF.

make away with 1. Carry off, steal, as in *The burglars made away with all their jewelry.* [Late 1600s] 2. Use up, consume, as in *The boys made away with all the sandwiches.* This usage was first recorded in 1843. 3. Kill, destroy, as in *We decided to make away with the old horse.* [c. 1500] Also see DO AWAY WITH, def. 2.

make bail Put up security as an assurance that someone released from prison will appear for trial, as in *He didn't think he could make bail for his brother.* The use of *bail* for "security" was first recorded in 1495.

make believe Pretend, as in *Let's make believe we're elves.* This expression in effect means making oneself believe in an illusion. [Early 1700s]

make bold Also, **make so bold as.** Dare, presume, take the liberty of doing something, as in *Let me make bold and ask you to back me as a member,* or *I will not make so bold as to criticize a respected scholar.* This expression was frequently used by Shakespeare but is heard less often today. [Late 1500s]

make book Accept bets on a race, game, or contest, as in *No one's making book on the local team.* This expression uses *book* in the sense of "a record of the bets made by different individuals." [Mid-1800s]

make bricks without straw Perform a task without essential materials or means, as in *Writing a report without the current data is making bricks without straw.* This expression alludes to straw as a material necessary in early brick manufacturing. [Early 1600s]

make capital out of Use profitably, turn to account, as in *The challengers made capital out of the President's signing a bill that increased taxes.* This expression, first recorded in 1855, uses *capital* in the sense of "material wealth used to create more wealth."

make conversation Engage someone in talking purely for its own sake, make small talk, as in *She had a real talent for making conversation with strangers.* [c. 1920]

make demands on Urgently require something of someone, as in *Her mother's illness has made considerable demands on her time.* [Late 1300s]

make do Get along with the means available, especially insufficient means. For example, *We'll just have to make do with one potato apiece.* [c. 1900]

make ends meet Manage so that one's financial means are enough for one's needs, as in *On that salary Enid had trouble making ends meet.* This expression originated as **make both ends meet,** a translation from the French *joindre les deux bouts* (by John Clarke, 1639). The *ends,* it is assumed, allude to the sum total of income and expenditures. However, naval surgeon and novelist Tobias Smollett had it as "make the two ends of the year meet" (*Roderick Random,* 1748), thought to go back to the common practice of splicing rope ends together in order to cut shipboard expenses.

make eyes at Ogle, flirt with, as in *To her sister's disgust, she was always making eyes at the boys.* Although slightly different versions, such as *throw the eye at,* are much older, this precise locution was first recorded in William Makepeace Thackeray's *Henry Esmond* (1852): "She used to make eyes at the Duke of Marlborough." See also GIVE SOMEONE THE ONCE-OVER.

make fast work of ♦ See MAKE SHORT WORK OF.

make for 1. Have or cause to have a particular effect; also, help promote or further. For example, *That letter of yours will make for hard feelings in the family,* or *This system makes for better communication.* [Early 1500s] 2. Go toward, as in *They turned around and made for home.* This usage originated in the late 1500s, but was not widely used until the 1800s. Also see MADE FOR.

make free with Take liberties with, treat very familiarly, as in *That reporter makes free with the truth,* or *It's best not to make free with one's employees.* This term was first recorded in 1714.

make friends Form a friendship, foster cordial feelings, as in *I hope Brian will soon make friends at school,* or *She's done a good job of making friends with influential reporters.* [c. 1600]

make fun of Also, **poke fun at; make sport of.** Mock, ridicule, as in *The girls made fun of Mary's shoes,* or *They poked fun at Willie's haircut,* or *I wish you wouldn't make sport of the new boy.* The first term dates from the early 1700s, the second from the mid-1800s, and the third from the early 1500s.

make good 1. Carry out successfully, make sure of, as in *He made good his escape.* This usage was first recorded in 1606. 2. Fulfill, as in *She made good her promise.* This usage was first recorded in Miles Coverdale's 1535 translation of the Bible (II Chronicles 6:16): "Make good unto my father, David . . . that which thou hast promised him." 3. Compensate for, make up for, as in *They made good the loss.* This usage first appeared in William Langland's *Piers Ploughman* (1377). 4. Succeed, as in *He made good as a writer.* [c. 1900]

make good time Travel far in a short time, as in *We made good time, getting to Vermont in only four hours.* [Late 1800s]

make great strides Advance considerably, make good progress, as in *He made great strides in his study of Latin.* Since its earliest recorded use in 1600, this expression has taken a number of forms—*make a wide stride, take strides, make rapid strides.* All of them transfer a long walking step to other kinds of progress.

make haste Also, **make it snappy.** Hurry up, move or act quickly, as in *If you don't make haste we'll be late,* or *Make it snappy, kids.* The first expression was first recorded in Miles Coverdale's 1535 translation of the Bible (Psalms 39:13): "Make haste, O Lord, to help me." The variant dates from the early 1900s and uses *snappy* in the sense of "resembling a sudden jerk." The oxymoron **make haste slowly,** dating from the mid-1700s, is a translation of the Latin *festina lente.* It is used either ironically, to slow someone down (as in *You'll do better if you make haste slowly*), or to comment sarcastically on a lack of progress (as in *So far the committee has been making haste slowly*).

make hay while the sun shines Take advantage of favorable circumstances, as in *Car sales have finally improved so we're making hay while the sun shines.* This expression alludes to optimum dry weather for cutting grass. [Early 1500s]

make head or tail of ♦ See CAN'T MAKE HEAD OR TAIL OF.

make headway Advance, make progress, as in *We haven't made any headway with this project.* This expression, first recorded in 1887, uses *headway* in the nautical sense of "a vessel's forward movement."

make heavy weather ♦ See under HEAVY GOING.

make history Do something memorable or spectacular enough to influence the course of history, as in *That first space flight made history.* [Mid-1800s]

make inroads into Encroach on, advance at another's expense, as in *The Japanese rapidly made inroads into the computer-chip market.* The noun *inroad* originally meant "an invasion." [Late 1600s]

make it 1. Also, **make it to.** Reach a certain point or goal, as in *Do you think she'll make it to graduation?* or *We finally made it to Chicago.* [c. 1900] 2. Succeed; also, win acceptance. For example, *When he won the prize he realized he'd finally made it,* or *Jane longed to make it with the crowd from Society Hill.* [Colloquial; mid-1900s] 3. Also, **make it with.** Have sexual intercourse, as in *Tom bragged that he'd made it with Sue last night.* [Colloquial; mid-1900s]

make it hot for Cause trouble or discomfort for someone, as in *They made it so hot for Larry that he had to resign,* or *The police were making it hot for shoplifters.* This seemingly modern idiom was first recorded in 1618.

make it one's business Undertake a self-appointed task, as in *I'll make it my business to find out their plans.* This phrase was first recorded in 1642.

make it snappy ♦ See MAKE HASTE.

make it up ♦ See under MAKE UP.

make it with ♦ See MAKE IT, def. 3.

make light of Also, **make little of.** Treat as unimportant, as in *He made light of his allergies,* or *She made little of the fact that she'd won.* The first term, which uses *light* in the sense of "trivial," was first recorded in William Tyndale's 1526 Bible translation (Matthew 22:5), in the parable of the wedding feast, where the invited guests reject the king's invitation: "They made light of it and went their ways." The variant dates from the early 1800s. For an antonym, see MAKE MUCH OF.

make like of ♦ See MAKE AS IF.

make little of ♦ See MAKE LIGHT OF.

make love 1. Court, engage in amorous caressing, as in *Romance was in the air, and she hoped he would make love to her.* [Late 1500s] 2. Have sexual intercourse, as in *They'd been making love well before they married.* This usage today is the more common of the two. [Mid-1900s]

make mincemeat of Also, **make hamburger of.** Thrash, beat decisively, as in *That bully will make mincemeat of my son,* or *The other team will make hamburger out of us.* This idiom alludes to finely chopping up meat. The first term dates from about 1700, the variant from the first half of the 1900s.

make mischief Cause trouble, as in *Don't listen to her gossip—she's just trying to make mischief.* This idiom was first recorded in 1884, but the related noun *mischief-maker,* a person who causes trouble especially by tale-bearing, dates from about 1700.

make much of Treat or consider as very important; also, pay someone a lot of favorable attention. For example, *Bill made much of the fact that he'd been to Europe three times,* or *Whenever Alice came home for a visit they made much of her.* [c. 1300]

make my day ◆ See MAKE ONE'S DAY.

make no bones about Act or speak frankly about something, without hesitation or evasion. For example, *Tom made no bones about wanting to be promoted,* or *Make no bones about it—she's very talented.* Versions of this expression date back to the mid-1400s and the precise allusion is no longer known. Some believe it meant a boneless stew or soup that one could eat without hesitation; others relate it to dice, originally made from bones, that were thrown without hesitation or fuss.

make no difference ◆ See MAKE A DIFFERENCE, def. 3.

make no mistake Have no doubt, certainly, as in *Make no mistake—I'll vote Republican no matter who runs.* [Mid-1800s] Also see GET SOMEONE WRONG.

make nothing of 1. Regard as unimportant, make light of, as in *He made nothing of walking three miles to buy a newspaper.* This expression was first recorded in 1632. 2. **can make nothing of.** Fail to accomplish, understand, or solve something, as in *I could make nothing of that long speech.* [Late 1600s]

make off 1. Depart in haste, run away, as in *The cat took one look at Richard and made off.* [c. 1700] 2. **make off with.** Take something away; also, steal something, as in *I can't write it down; Tom made off with my pen,* or *The burglars made off with the stereo and computer as well as jewelry.* [Early 1800s]

make one's bed and lie in it Suffer the consequences of one's actions. For example, *It's unfortunate that it turned out badly, but Sara made her bed and now she must lie in it.* The earliest English citation for this oftrepeated proverb is in Gabriel Harvey's *Marginalia* (c. 1590): "Let them ... go to their bed, as themselves shall make it." The idiom alludes to times when a permanent bed was a luxury, and most people had to stuff a sack with straw every night for use as a bed. There are equivalents in French, German, Danish, and many other languages.

make one's blood boil Enrage one, as in *Whenever Jim criticizes his father, it makes my blood boil.* Although this term did not appear in print until 1848, the term *the blood boils,* meaning "one gets angry," dates from the 1600s.

make one's blood run cold Also, **freeze one's blood.** Cause one to shiver from fright or horror, as in *The radiator's clanking at night made George's blood run cold,* or *Movies about vampires always freeze my blood.* [Early 1800s] Also see MAKE ONE'S FLESH CREEP.

make one's day Give one great pleasure, as in *Hearing you won first prize just made my day.* This phrase, which uses *make* in the sense of "secure success in," was first recorded in 1909.

make one's ears burn ◆ See EARS ARE BURNING.

make oneself at home Be at ease, act as though one were in one's own home. For example, *I have to make a phone call but please make yourself at home,* or *Tim has a way of making himself at home just about anywhere.* This expression was first recorded in 1860. Also see AT HOME, def 3.

make oneself scarce Depart quickly, go away, as in *The children saw Mrs. Frost coming and made themselves scarce.* This idiom applies *scarce* in the sense of "seldom seen" to removing one's presence. [c. 1800]

make one's flesh creep Also, **make one's skin crawl.** Cause one to shudder with disgust or fear, as in *That picture makes my flesh creep,* or *Cockroaches make my skin crawl.* This idiom alludes to the feeling of having something crawl over one's body or skin. The first term appeared in Jonathan Swift's *Gulliver's Travels* (1727): "Something in their countenance made my flesh creep with a horror I cannot express." The variant dates from the late 1800s.

make one's hair stand on end Also, **make one's hair curl.** Terrify one, as in *The very thought of an earthquake makes my hair stand on end,* or *Diving off a high board is enough to make my hair curl.* The first term, first recorded in 1534, alludes to goose pimples prompted by fear, which cause the hairs around them to stand up. The variant dates from the mid-1900s.

make one's head spin Cause one to be giddy, dazed, or confused, as in *The figures in this tax return make my head spin.* This phrase employs *spin* in the sense of "rapidly gyrating," a usage applied to the brain or head since about 1800.

make one sick Disgust one, as in *Your constant complaining makes me sick.* This expression transfers the sensations of physical illness to strong negative sentiments. [c. 1800]

make one's mark Achieve distinction, as in *Terry soon made his mark as an organist.* This expression transfers a written or printed symbol to a strong impression. [Mid-1800s] Also see MAKE A NAME FOR ONESELF.

make one's mouth water Cause one to eagerly anticipate or long for something, as in *Those travel folders about Nepal make my mouth water.* This metaphoric term alludes to salivating when one anticipates food and has been used figuratively since the mid-1600s, whether it refers to food, as in *The sight of that chocolate cake made her mouth water,* or not.

make one's peace with Reconcile oneself to, bring about friendly relations with, as in *He's repented and made his peace with God.* This expression was first recorded about 1315. Also see MAKE PEACE.

make one's point Effectively express one's idea, as in *I see what you mean about skateboards being dangerous—you've made your point.* This expression uses *point* in the sense of "an important or essential argument or suggestion." Also see MAKE A POINT OF; TAKE ONE'S POINT. [c. 1800]

make one's way 1. Go in a particular direction or to a particular destination, as in *I'm making my way to the china department,* or *How are we going to make our way through this underbrush?* This usage was first recorded about 1400. 2. Also, **make one's own way.** Advance in life by one's own efforts, *His family hasn't much money so he'll just have to make his own way in the world.* [c. 1600]

make or break Cause either total success or total ruin, as in *This assignment will make or break her as a reporter.* This rhyming expression, first recorded in Charles Dickens's *Barnaby Rudge* (1840), has largely replaced the much older (16th-century) alliterative synonym **make or mar,** at least in America.

make out 1. Discern or see, especially with difficulty, as in *I can hardly make out the number on the door.* [Mid-1700s] 2. Manage, get along, as in *How did you make out with the accountant?* This usage was first recorded in 1820. 3. Engage in sexual foreplay or intercourse, as in *Bill and Jane were making out on the sofa,* or *Joe bragged that he made out last night.* [Slang; early 1900s] 4. Understand, as in *I can't make out what she is trying to say.* [Mid-1600s] Also see CAN'T MAKE HEAD OR TAIL OF. 5. Establish or prove, as in *He made out that he was innocent.* [Colloquial; mid-1600s] 6. Imply or suggest. This usage often occurs with an infinitive, as in *Are you making me out to be a liar?* [Colloquial; mid-1600s] 7. Write out, draw up; fill in a written form. For example, *He made out the invoices,* or *Jane started making out job applications.* This usage was first recorded in 1465.

make out like a bandit Succeed extremely well, as in *He invested in real estate and made out like a bandit.* This expression likens other forms of success to that of a triumphant robber. It may, however, come from an intermediate source, that is, the use of *bandit* (or *one-armed bandit*) for a slot machine, which is far more profitable for the house than for gamblers. [Slang; c. 1970]

make over 1. Redo, renovate, as in *We're making over the playroom into an additional bedroom.* [Late 1600s] 2. Change or transfer ownership, usually through a legal document, as in *She made over the house to her daughter.* This usage was first recorded in 1546.

make peace Bring about friendly relations or a state of amity; end hostilities. For example, *The United Nations sent a task force to make peace between the two warring factions,* or *Mom was good at making peace among the children.* [Mid-1100s] Also see MAKE ONE'S PEACE WITH.

make ready ◆ See GET READY.

make rounds ◆ See MAKE THE ROUNDS, def. 2.

make sail ◆ See SET SAIL.

make sense 1. Be understandable. This usage, first recorded in 1686, is often used in a negative context, as in *This explanation doesn't make sense.* 2. Be reasonable, wise, or practical, as in *It makes sense to find out first how many will attend the conference.* This term employs *sense* in the meaning of "what is reasonable," a usage dating from 1600. In Britain it is also put as **stand to sense.**

make short work of Complete or consume quickly, as in *The children made short work of the ice cream,* or *They made short work of cleaning up so they could get to the movies.* This term, first recorded in 1577, in effect means "to turn something into a brief task."

make someone look good Cause someone to appear in a favorable light, as in *Harry's staff does most of the important work and makes him look good.*

make something of 1. Render important or useful; improve. For example, *Dad hoped Tim would make something of himself.* [Late 1700s] 2. Give undue importance to something, especially a problem or disagreement, as in *Ann decided to make something of it when Bob said women's studies is not a real discipline.* This usage sometimes is put as **make something out of nothing,** as in *So what if Jim had coffee with your girlfriend—don't make something out of nothing.* For an antonym, see MAKE NOTHING OF, def. 1.

make sport of ◆ See MAKE FUN OF.

make stick Make effective or permanent, as in *They tried to appeal but our lawyers made the verdict stick.* This idiom uses *stick* in the sense of "adhere." [First half of 1900s]

make sure 1. Make certain, establish something without doubt, as in *Make sure all the doors are locked.* It is also put as **make sure of,** as in *Before you make that speech, make sure of your facts.* This usage was first recorded in 1565. 2. **make sure of.** Act so as to be certain of something, as in *He* *wanted to make sure of his own district before seeking support elsewhere.* This usage was first recorded in 1673.

make the bed Rearrange a bed and its coverings to its condition before it was slept in. For example, *Mom taught us all to make the bed before we got dressed.* Also see MAKE ONE'S BED AND LIE IN IT.

make the best of it Also, **make the best of a bad bargain.** Adapt as well as possible to a bad situation, bad luck, or similar circumstances, as in *Jeff ended up in a cabin without his friends, but decided to make the best of it,* or *She got the worst possible position, but Dad told her to make the best of a bad bargain.* The first term dates from the first half of the 1600s. The second appeared in John Ray's proverb collection of 1670 and coexisted for a time with variants such as *make the best of a bad game* and *make the best of a bad market,* which have died out.

make the dust fly Also, **make the feathers** or **fur fly.** Stir matters up, cause a commotion or disturbance. For example, *When she saw the dog sleeping on her new bedspread, she really made the dust fly,* or *As soon as he learns who dented his car, he'll make the feathers fly,* or *She'd better not interfere or he'll make the fur fly.* The first usage alludes to the results of a vigorous house-cleaning effort. The two variants, both dating from the early 1800s, allude to what happens when a hunting dog is set on a bird or rabbit.

make the grade Satisfy the requirements, qualify; also, succeed. For example, *Angela hoped her work in the new school would make the grade,* or *Barbara certainly has made the grade as a trial lawyer.* This expression uses *grade* in the sense of "accepted standard." [c. 1900]

make the most of Use to the greatest advantage, as in *She planned to make the most of her trip to Europe,* or *The class quickly made the most of the teacher's absence.* This expression was first recorded in 1526.

make the rounds 1. Follow a given circuit, as in *The watchman makes the rounds every hour,* or *The gossip soon made the rounds of the school.* Versions of this expression, such as **go the rounds, follow the rounds, march the rounds,** date from about 1600. **2. make rounds.** Visit each hospitalized patient who is under the care of a specific physician, as in *The surgery residents make rounds with their chief every morning.* [c. 1900]

make the scene Put in an appearance, take part in an event, as in *I'll miss most of the party, but I hope to make the scene before midnight.* This expression employs *scene* in the sense of "a place where an action occurs." [Slang; mid-1900s]

make the sparks fly Start a fight or argument, as in *If Mary finds out he went to the races without her, that will make the sparks fly.* In this idiom, the small particles of a fire called *sparks* are transferred to an inflammatory situation. [Early 1900s]

make time 1. Proceed rapidly, as in *We have to make time if we don't want to miss the first part of the movie.* This usage alludes to compensating for lost time. [First half of 1800s] Also see MAKE GOOD TIME. **2. make time for.** Arrange one's schedule for doing something or seeing someone, as in *Harold always manages to make time for tennis,* or *I'm pretty busy, but I can make time for you tomorrow morning.* **3. make time with.** Court or flirt with someone, as in *Jerry is trying to make time with Beth.* [Slang; first half of 1900s]

make tracks Move or leave in a hurry, as in *If we're going to catch the first show, we'd better make tracks.* This term alludes to the foot-prints left by running. [Slang; early 1800s]

make up 1. Put together, construct or compose, as in *The druggist made up the prescription,* or *The tailor said he could make up a suit from this fabric.* This usage was first recorded in 1530. **2.** Constitute, form, as in *One hundred years make up a century.* [Late 1500s] **3.** Change one's appearance; apply cosmetics. For example, *He made himself up as an old man.* [c. 1800] **4.** Devise a fiction or falsehood; invent. For example, *Mary is always making up stories for her children,* or *Is that account true or did you make it up?* This usage was first recorded in 1828. **5.** Compensate for, provide for a deficiency, as in *Can you make up the difference in the bill?* or *What he lacks in height he makes up in skill.* This usage was first recorded in 1538. Also see MAKE UP FOR LOST TIME. **6.** Repeat a course, take a test or do an assignment at a later time because of previous absence or failure. For example, *Steve will have to make up calculus this summer,* or *The professor is letting me make up the exam tomorrow.* **7.** Also, **make it up.** Resolve a quarrel, as in *The Sweeneys argue a lot but they always make up before going to sleep,* or *Will you two ever make it up?* The first usage was first recorded in 1699, the variant in 1669. **8.** Put in order, as in *We asked them to make up the room for us,* or *Can you make up another bed in this room?* [Early 1800s] Also see the subsequent idioms beginning with MAKE UP.

make up for lost time Also, **make up ground.** Hurry to compensate for wasted time, as in *They married late but hoped to make up for lost time,* or *We're behind in the schedule, and we'll just have to make up ground as best we can.* The first term was first recorded in 1774; the variant dates from the late 1800s.

make up one's mind Decide between alternatives, come to a decision, as in *I had trouble making up my mind about which coat I liked best.* This expression dates from the early 1800s, although a similar usage appeared two centuries earlier in Shakespeare's *King John* (2:1): "I know she is not for this match made up."

make up to Make ingratiating or fawning overtures to, flirt with, as in *She was always making up to the boss's assistant.* This usage was first recorded in 1781.

make use of Utilize, use, as in *I hope readers will make use of this dictionary.* This expression dates from the late 1500s. Shakespeare had it in *The Two Gentlemen of Verona* (2:4).

make waves Cause a disturbance or controversy, as in *We've finally settled our differences, so please don't make waves.* This expression alludes to causing turbulence in the water. [Slang; mid-1900s] Also see ROCK THE BOAT.

make way 1. Allow room for passage, move aside, as in *Please make way for the wheelchair.* This expression was first recorded about 1200. 2. Also, **make way for.** Leave room for a successor or substitute, as in *It's time he retired and made way for some younger professor.* [Mid-1700s] 3. Progress, advance, as in *Is this enterprise making way?* [Late 1500s] For a synonym, see MAKE HEADWAY.

make whoopee ♦ See WHOOP IT UP.

make with Use, concern oneself with, as in *Why are you making with that strange outfit?* or *Let's go—make with the feet!* This expression is a translation of the Yiddish *mach mit.* [Slang; first half of 1900s]

mama's boy A sissy, especially a boy or man excessively attached to his mother. For example, *The children called Tom a mama's boy because he ran home with every little problem.* This sexist expression has survived despite its pejorative tone. [Colloquial; mid-1800s]

man ♦ In addition to the idioms beginning with MAN, also see AS ONE (MAN); COMPANY MAN; DEAD SOLDIER (MAN); DIRTY JOKE (OLD MAN); EVERY MAN FOR HIMSELF; EVERY MAN HAS HIS PRICE; GIRL (MAN) FRIDAY; HATCHET MAN; HIRED HAND (MAN); LADIES' MAN; LOW MAN ON THE TOTEM POLE; MARKED MAN; NEW PERSON (MAN); NO MAN IS AN ISLAND; ODD MAN OUT; (MAN) OF FEW WORDS; ONE MAN'S MEAT IS ANOTHER MAN'S POISON; OWN MAN; RIGHT-HAND MAN; SEE A MAN ABOUT A DOG; TO A MAN. Also see under MEN.

man about town A man who frequently attends fashionable social functions, as in *Fred is quite the man about town these days.* This expression, first

recorded in 1734, uses *town* in the sense of "a sophisticated place" as opposed to rural settings.

manger ♦ See DOG IN THE MANGER.

man in the street Also, **woman in the street.** An ordinary, average person, as in *It will be interesting to see how the man in the street will answer that question.* This expression came into use in the early 1800s when the votes of ordinary citizens began to influence public affairs. Today it is used especially in the news media, where reporters seek out the views of bystanders at noteworthy events, and by pollsters who try to predict the outcome of elections.

manna from heaven An unexpected aid, advantage, or assistance, as in *After all the criticism in the media, that favorable evaluation was like manna from heaven.* This expression alludes to the food (*manna*) that miraculously appears to feed the Israelites on their journey from Egypt to the Promised Land (Exodus 16:15).

manner ♦ See ALL KINDS (MANNER OF); BY ALL (MANNER OF) MEANS; COMPANY MANNERS; IN A MANNER OF SPEAKING; TO THE MANNER BORN.

man of few words ♦ See under FEW WORDS.

man of his word A man who keeps promises, who can be trusted, as in *You can count on Rudy—he's a man of his word.* This expression, which uses *word* in the sense of "a promise or undertaking," was first recorded in 1542.

man of the moment ♦ See OF THE MOMENT.

man of the world Also, **woman of the world.** A sophisticated person, experienced in social conventions. For example, *You can discuss anything with him—he's a man of the world,* or *She's a woman of the world and understands these delicate issues.* The first expression dates from about 1200 and originally meant "a man of the secular world" or "a married man" (that is, not a priest). Shakespeare applied this latter sense in *As You Like It* (5:3) where Audrey, at the prospect of marriage, says: "I hope it is no dishonest desire to be a woman of the world." Henry Fielding in *Tom Jones* (1749) also echoed this earlier sense: "A man of the world that is to say, a man who directs his conduct in this world as one, who being fully persuaded there is no other, is resolved to make the most of this." By the mid-1800s the idea of sophistication had replaced this meaning.

many ♦ In addition to the idioms beginning with MANY, also see AS MANY; GOOD (GREAT) MANY; IN SO MANY WORDS; IRONS IN THE FIRE, TOO MANY; SO MANY; TOO MANY COOKS SPOIL THE BROTH.

many a Numerous ones, as in *Many a little boy has wanted to become a fireman.* This adjective is always used with a singular noun, a usage dating from about 1200. Also see MANY IS THE.

many hands make light work More helpers make a task easier, as in *We need a few more volunteers to move the furniture — many hands make light work, you know.* This proverb was first recorded in English in the early 1300s in a knightly romance known as *Sir Bevis of Hampton.* It appeared in practically all proverb collections from 1546 on. For the converse, see TOO MANY COOKS SPOIL THE BROTH.

many happy returns Also, **many happy returns of the day.** Happy birthday and many more of them, as in *I came by to wish you many happy returns.* This expression was first recorded in a letter of 1779 where the writer meant "Happy New Year," but the present meaning has persisted since the second half of the 1800s.

many is the There are a great number of, as in *Many is the time I've told her to be careful,* or *Many is the child who's been warned against strangers.* This phrase, always used at the beginning of a sentence and with a singular noun, was first recorded in 1297. Also see MANY A.

map ♦ See PUT ON THE MAP; WIPE OFF THE MAP.

marble ♦ See HAVE ALL ONE'S BUTTONS (MARBLES).

march ♦ In addition to the idiom beginning with MARCH, also see STEAL A MARCH ON.

marching orders, get one's Be ordered to move on or proceed; also, be dismissed from a job. For example, *The sales force got their marching orders yesterday, so now they'll be on the road with the new product,* or *It's too bad about Jack — the boss gave him his marching orders Friday.* This expression originally alluded to a military command. [Colloquial; late 1700s]

march to a different beat Also, **march to a different drummer.** Act independently, differ in conduct or ideas from most others, as in *Joe wanted to be married on a mountain top — he always marches to a different beat,* or *Sarah has her own ideas for the campaign; she marches to a different drummer.* This idiom, alluding to being out of step in a parade, is a version of Henry David Thoreau's statement in *Walden* (1854): "If a man does not keep pace with his companions, perhaps it is because he hears a different drummer." It came into wide use in the mid-1900s.

marines ♦ See TELL IT TO THE MARINES.

mark ♦ In addition to the idioms beginning with MARK, also see BESIDE THE POINT (MARK); BLACK MARK; GIVE BAD MARKS TO; HIGH-WATER MARK; HIT THE BULL'S-EYE (MARK); MAKE ONE'S MARK; OFF THE MARK; QUICK OFF THE MARK; TOE THE LINE (MARK);

UP TO PAR (THE MARK); WIDE OF THE MARK; X MARKS THE SPOT.

mark down Reduce the price of something, as in *If they mark down these shoes, I'll buy two pairs.* The *mark* here alludes to the label indicating a price. [Mid-1800s]

marked man, a Also, **a marked woman.** A person singled out as an object of suspicion, hostility, or vengeance. For example, *As a witness to the robbery, he felt he was a marked man,* or *After her fiasco at the meeting, she was a marked woman — no one would hire her.* This idiom was first recorded in 1833.

market ♦ See CORNER THE MARKET; DRUG ON THE MARKET; FLEA MARKET; IN THE MARKET FOR; ON THE MARKET; PLAY THE MARKET; PRICE OUT OF THE MARKET.

mark my words Pay attention to what I say, as in *Mark my words, that man is not to be trusted.* This admonition first appeared in Miles Coverdale's 1535 translation of the Bible (Isaiah 28:23).

mark time Wait idly for something to occur, as in *We were just marking time until we received our instructions.* This idiom alludes to the literal meaning of marching in place to the *time,* or beat, of music. [Early 1800s]

mark up 1. Deface by drawing, cutting, or another means of covering something with marks. For example, *John was punished for marking up his desk,* or *These shoes really mark up the floor.* 2. Raise the price of something, as in *This small shop marks up its merchandise much more than department stores do.* [Second half of 1800s]

mast ♦ See AT HALF-MAST.

master ♦ See PAST MASTER.

mat ♦ See GO TO THE MAT; WELCOME MAT.

match ♦ See MEET ONE'S MATCH; MIX AND MATCH; WHOLE BALL OF WAX (SHOOTING MATCH).

matter ♦ In addition to the idioms beginning with MATTER, also see CRUX OF THE MATTER; FOR THAT MATTER; GRAY MATTER; MINCE MATTERS; MIND OVER MATTER; NO JOKE (LAUGHING MATTER); NO MATTER; THE MATTER.

matter of course, a Something that is expected, as in *It was a matter of course that police officers received special training.* It is also put as **as a matter of course,** meaning "as part of a standard procedure," as in *The employer checked John's references as a matter of course.* First recorded only in 1809, this idiom uses *course* in the sense of "the natural or logical order of events."

matter of fact, a Something that is literally or factually true, as in *The records showed it to be a matter of fact that they were married in 1960.* This idiom often occurs in the phrase **as a matter of fact,** as in *As a matter of fact, you are absolutely right.* **Matter of fact** was first recorded in 1581, and originally was a legal term distinguishing the facts of a case from the law, called *matter of law,* applying to it. It began to be applied to other concerns in the late 1600s.

matter of life and death, a A very urgent issue, situation, or circumstance. This expression can be used either literally, as in *She told the doctor to hurry as it was a matter of life and death,* or hyperbolically, as in *Don't worry about finishing on time—it's hardly a matter of life and death.* First recorded in 1849, it alludes to such urgency that someone's life depends on it. Although *a matter of life or death* would make more sense, it is rarely put that way.

matter of opinion, a A question on which people hold different views, as in *I rather like that design, but really, it's a matter of opinion,* or *The quality of that new stock issue is a matter of opinion.* This expression was first recorded in 1843.

max out 1. Exhaust one's options, capacity, or the like by producing or performing to the maximum, as in *The weight lifter maxed out at 180 kilograms.* [Slang; late 1900s] 2. Reach a point at which no more growth, improvement, or benefit is possible, as in *The salary for this job maxes out at $90,000.* [Slang; late 1900s] 3. Relax, take things easy, as in *Let's go to the beach and max out.* [Slang; late 1900s]

may ♦ See BE THAT AS IT MAY; COME WHAT MAY; LET THE CHIPS FALL WHERE THEY MAY; TO WHOM IT MAY CONCERN.

me ♦ See DEAR ME; SO HELP ME.

meal ♦ In addition to the idiom beginning with MEAL, also see SQUARE MEAL.

meal ticket A person or thing depended on as a source of income, as in *Magic Johnson was a real meal ticket for his team,* or *Her interpersonal skills will be her meal ticket when she goes into sales.* This metaphoric expression alludes to the earlier practice of handing out tickets that entitle their holder to a meal. [Early 1900s]

mean ♦ In addition to the idioms beginning with MEAN, also see under MEANS.

mean business Be in earnest. For example, *He really means business with this deadline.* This idiom uses *business* in the sense of "a serious endeavor." [Mid-1800s]

means ♦ See BEYOND ONE'S MEANS; BY ALL MEANS; BY ANY MEANS; BY MEANS OF; BY NO MEANS; END JUSTIFIES THE MEANS.

mean to Intend to, as in *I meant to go running this morning but got up too late,* or *I'm sorry I broke it—I didn't mean to.* This idiom was first recorded in 1560.

measure ♦ In addition to the idiom beginning with MEASURE, also see BEYOND MEASURE; FOR GOOD MEASURE; IN SOME MEASURE; MADE TO MEASURE; TAKE SOMEONE'S MEASURE.

measure up 1. Be the equal of, as in *Is he a good enough actor to measure up to the other members of the cast?* [Early 1900s] 2. Have the qualifications for, be of high enough quality for, as in *His latest book hasn't measured up to the reviewers' expectations.* [First half of 1900s]

meat ♦ In addition to the idioms beginning with MEAT, also see BEAT THE MEAT; ONE'S MAN'S MEAT IS ANOTHER MAN'S POISON.

meat and drink to one A source of great satisfaction or delight, as in *Good music is meat and drink to her.* This metaphoric expression, transferring basic sustenance to satisfaction, appeared as early as 1533, in John Frith's *A Boke Answering unto Mr. Mores Letter:* "It is meat and drink to this child to play."

meat and potatoes The fundamental part or parts of something, as in *This paragraph is the meat and potatoes of the contract.* This metaphoric term transfers what some regard as basic fare to the basics of an issue. [Mid-1900s]

medicine ♦ See DOSE OF ONE'S OWN MEDICINE; TAKE ONE'S MEDICINE.

medium ♦ See HAPPY MEDIUM.

meet ♦ In addition to the idioms beginning with MEET, also see GO (MEET) HALFWAY; MAKE ENDS MEET; MORE THAN MEETS THE EYE.

meeting of the minds Agreement, concord, as in *The teachers and the headmaster had a meeting of the minds regarding smoking in school.* This expression uses *meet* in the sense of "arrive at mutual agreement," as clergyman Edward B. Pusey did in a letter of 1851: "Devout minds, of every school . . . meet at least in this."

meet one's match Encounter someone equal in ability to oneself, as in *The chess champion was about to meet his match in a computer.* This expression originated about 1300 as *find one's match,* but the alliterative *meet* was being used by the mid-1500s and has survived.

meet one's Waterloo Suffer a major defeat, as in *Our team's done well this season but is about to meet its Waterloo.* This term alludes to Napoleon's defeat at Waterloo, Belgium, in 1815, marking the end of his military domination of Europe. It was being transferred to other kinds of defeat by the mid-1800s.

meet the requirements Satisfy the conditions, as in *This grade of lumber does not meet our require-*

ments, or *Lynn did not meet the requirements for this position.* This expression uses *meet* in the sense of "satisfy," a usage dating from the early 1800s. Also see MEASURE UP, def. 2.

meet up with Encounter, especially by accident, as in *We hadn't gone far along the trail when we met up with another mule train.* [Colloquial; late 1800s]

meet with Encounter or experience, as in *The housing bill met with their approval,* or *Drunk and homeless, he's bound to meet with a bad end.* [Mid-1400s]

mellow out Become genial or pleasant, calm down, relax, as in *The teacher mellowed out when they explained what had happened.* This expression uses *mellow* in the sense of "ripening," with the connotation of softness and sweetness. [Slang; late 1900s]

melt ♦ In addition to the idiom beginning with MELT, also see BUTTER WOULDN'T MELT.

melt in one's mouth Taste very good, as in *This cake is wonderful—it just melts in one's mouth.* This expression, first recorded in 1693, at first alluded to the tenderness of some food that therefore did not require chewing, but it had acquired its present meaning by about 1850. Also see BUTTER WOULDN'T MELT.

memory ♦ See COMMIT TO MEMORY; IN MEMORY OF.

men ♦ See ALL THINGS TO ALL PEOPLE (MEN); SEPARATE THE MEN FROM THE BOYS. Also see under MAN.

mend ♦ In addition to the idioms beginning with MEND, also see ON THE MEND.

mend one's fences Improve poor relations; placate personal, political, or business contacts. For example, *The senator always goes home weekends and spends time mending his fences.* This metaphoric expression dates from an 1879 speech by Senator John Sherman in Mansfield, Ohio, to which he said he had returned "to look after my fences." Although he may have meant literally to repair the fences around his farm there, media accounts of the speech took him to mean campaigning among his constituents. In succeeding decades the term was applied to nonpolitical affairs as well.

mend one's ways Improve one's behavior, as in *Threatened with suspension, Jerry promised to mend his ways.* This expression, transferring a repair of clothes to one of character, was first recorded in 1868, but 150 or so years earlier it had appeared as *mend one's manners.*

mention ♦ See NOT TO MENTION; YOU'RE WELCOME (DON'T MENTION IT).

mercy ♦ See AT THE MERCY OF.

merit ♦ See ON ITS MERITS.

merrier, merry ♦ See LEAD A MERRY CHASE; MORE THE MERRIER.

mess ♦ In addition to the idioms beginning with MESS, also see GET INTO TROUBLE (A MESS); MAKE A HASH (MESS) OF.

message ♦ See GET THE MESSAGE.

mess around ♦ See FOOL AROUND.

mess up 1. Create disorder in; muddle or ruin. For example, *On rainy days the children really mess up the house,* or *He had a way of messing up his own business.* [c. 1900] 2. Make a mistake, especially from nervousness or confusion, as in *He messed up and took the wrong dossier to the meeting,* or *Jill swore she would never mess up again.* [Colloquial; early 1900s] 3. Beat up, manhandle, as in *Joe got messed up in a barroom brawl.* [Slang; early 1900s]

mess with Interfere or associate with; also, annoy, bother. For example, *Our group won't mess with those street musicians,* or *I told him not to mess with me or there would be trouble.* [Colloquial; c. 1900]

met ♦ See HAIL FELLOW WELL MET. Also see under MEET.

meter is running, the Costs or other consequences are accumulating, as in *We'd better come to a decision soon, for the meter is running.* This metaphoric expression alludes to the fare mounting up on a taxi meter. [Late 1900s]

method in one's madness An underlying purpose in crazy behavior, as in *Harry takes seemingly random trips around the country but there's method to his madness—he's checking on real estate values.* This expression comes from Shakespeare's *Hamlet* (2:2): "Though this be madness, yet there is method in it." For a modern equivalent, see CRAZY LIKE A FOX.

mice ♦ See BEST-LAID PLANS OF MICE AND MEN; WHEN THE CAT'S AWAY, MICE WILL PLAY. Also see under MOUSE.

midair ♦ See under LEAVE HANGING.

middle ♦ See CAUGHT IN THE MIDDLE; IN THE MIDDLE OF; PLAY BOTH ENDS AGAINST THE MIDDLE.

middling ♦ See FAIR TO MIDDLING.

midnight oil ♦ See BURN THE MIDNIGHT OIL.

midstream ♦ See CHANGE HORSES MIDSTREAM.

might and main, with Strenuously, vigorously, as in *She pulled on the rope with all her might and main.* This expression is redundant, since the noun *main* also means "strength" or "power." It survives only in this phrase, which may also be dying out. [Late 1200s]

might makes right Superior strength can enforce one's will or dictate justice, as in *The generals dismissed the parliament and imprisoned the premier—might makes right in that country,* or *The* big boys wouldn't let the little ones use the basketball, a case of might makes right. This expression was first recorded in English about 1327.

mighty ◆ See HIGH AND MIGHTY.

mildly ◆ See PUT IT MILDLY.

mile ◆ In addition to the idioms beginning with MILE, also see MISS BY A MILE; MISS IS AS GOOD AS A MILE; STICK OUT (LIKE A MILE).

mile a minute, a Very rapidly, as in She was talking a mile a minute about the accident. This expression, alluding to the literal speed of 60 miles per hour, dates from the mid-1900s, when that speed was considered very fast, but it has survived into times of much greater velocity.

miles and miles A considerable distance; also, a large interval, by far. For example, We drove for miles and miles before we saw a gas station, or She was miles and miles a better pianist than her brother. This usage was first recorded in 1889.

milk ◆ In addition to the idiom beginning with MILK, also see CRY OVER SPILT MILK.

milk of human kindness, the Compassion, sympathy, as in There's no milk of human kindness in that girl—she's totally selfish. This expression was invented by Shakespeare in Macbeth (1:5), where Lady Macbeth complains that her husband "is too full of the milk of human kindness" to kill his rivals.

mill ◆ See GRIST FOR THE MILL; MILLS OF THE GODS GRIND SLOWLY; RUN OF THE MILL; THROUGH THE MILL; TILT AT WINDMILLS.

million ◆ See FEEL LIKE ONESELF (A MILLION DOLLARS); LOOK LIKE A MILLION DOLLARS; ONE IN A MILLION.

mills of the gods grind slowly One's destiny is inevitable even if it take considerable time to arrive. For example, I'm sure he'll be wealthy one day, though the mills of the gods grind slowly. This expression comes from ancient Greek, translated as "The mills of the gods grind slowly, but they grind small." In English it appeared in George Herbert's Jacula Prudentum (1640) as "God's mill grinds slow but sure."

millstone around one's neck A heavy burden, as in Julie finds Grandma, who is crabby, a millstone around her neck. The literal hanging of a millstone about the neck is mentioned as a punishment in the New Testament (Matthew 18:6), causing the miscreant to be drowned. Its present figurative use was first recorded in a history of the Quakers (c. 1720).

mince matters Also, **mince words**. Moderate or restrain one's language to be polite or avoid giving offense. Today these phrases are nearly always put negatively, as in Not to mince matters, I feel he should resign, or Don't mince words—say what you mean. The usage dates from the mid-

1500s and transfers cutting something such as meat into small pieces to minimizing the harsh impact of words.

mincemeat ◆ See MAKE MINCEMEAT OF.

mind ◆ In addition to the idioms beginning with MIND, also see BACK OF ONE'S MIND; BEAR IN MIND; BLOW ONE'S MIND; BOGGLE THE MIND; BRING TO MIND; CALL TO MIND; CHANGE ONE'S MIND; COME TO MIND; CROSS ONE'S MIND; FRAME OF MIND; GO OUT OF ONE'S MIND; GREAT MINDS; HALF A MIND; HAVE A GOOD MIND TO; IN ONE'S MIND; IN ONE'S MIND'S EYE; IN ONE'S RIGHT MIND; KNOW ONE'S OWN MIND; LOAD OFF ONE'S MIND; LOSE ONE'S MIND; MAKE UP ONE'S MIND; MEETING OF THE MINDS; NEVER MIND; OF TWO MINDS; ONE-TRACK MIND; ON ONE'S MIND; OPEN MIND; OUT OF SIGHT (OUT OF MIND); PIECE OF ONE'S MIND; PRESENCE OF MIND; PREY ON (ONE'S MIND); PUT ONE IN MIND OF; READ SOMEONE'S MIND; SPEAK ONE'S MIND; TO MY MIND.

mind like a steel trap, have a Be very quick to understand something, as in Aunt Ida may be old, but she still has a mind like a steel trap. This simile likens the snapping shut of an animal trap to a quick mental grasp.

mind of one's own, have a Think independently, reach one's own opinions or conclusions. For example, You can't tell Karen what she should wear—she has a mind of her own. Also see KNOW ONE'S OWN MIND.

mind one's own business Keep from meddling, pay attention to one's own affairs, as in If she would only mind her own business, there would be a lot fewer family quarrels. Already described as a wise course by the ancients (Seneca had it as Semper meum negotium ago, "I always mind my own business"), this precept has been repeated in English since about 1600.

mind one's p's and q's Practice good manners, be precise and careful in one's behavior and speech, as in Their grandmother often told the children to mind their p's and q's. The origin of this expression, first recorded in 1779, is disputed. Among the more interesting theories advanced is that bartenders kept track of customers' consumption in terms of pints (p's) and quarts (q's) and the phrase referred to an honest accounting; that school-children were taught to be careful in distinguishing the letters p and q; and that French dancing masters cautioned pupils about the correct performance of the figures pieds and queues (either abbreviated or mispronounced in English as p's and q's).

mind over matter Willpower can overcome physical obstacles, as in Margaret was determined to go to the wedding even on crutches—mind over matter. This idea was already expressed by Virgil in the Aeneid (c. 19 B.C.) as Mens agitat molem,

"Mind moves matter," and it appeared in various forms in English by 1700.

mind the store Attend to local or family matters, as in *Ask Dad for permission; he's minding the store while Mom's away.* This expression transfers looking after an actual business to more general activities. [Colloquial; second half of 1900s]

mine ♦ See BACK TO THE SALT MINES; GOLD MINE; YOUR GUESS IS AS GOOD AS MINE.

mint condition, in In excellent condition, unblemished, perfect, as in *This car is in mint condition.* This expression alludes to the condition of a freshly minted coin. [c. 1900]

mint money ♦ See COIN MONEY.

minute ♦ See AT THE LAST MINUTE; EVERY MINUTE COUNTS; JUST A MINUTE; MILE A MINUTE; WAIT A MINUTE.

miscarriage of justice An unfair decision, especially one in a court of law. For example, *Many felt that his being expelled from the school was a miscarriage of justice.* This expression, which uses *miscarriage* in the sense of "making a blunder," was first recorded in 1875.

mischief ♦ See MAKE MISCHIEF.

misery ♦ In addition to the idiom beginning with MISERY, also see PUT SOMEONE OUT OF HIS OR HER MISERY.

misery loves company Fellow sufferers make unhappiness easier to bear, as in *She secretly hoped her friend would fail, too—misery loves company.* Words to this effect appeared in the work of Sophocles (c. 408 B.C.) and other ancient writers; the earliest recorded use in English was about 1349.

miss ♦ In addition to the idioms beginning with MISS, also see HEART MISSES A BEAT; HIT OR MISS; NEAR MISS; NOT MISS A TRICK.

miss a beat Hesitate momentarily, out of embarrassment or confusion. This expression is most often used in a negative context, as in *He sidestepped the reporter's probe into his personal life without missing a beat,* or *Not missing a beat, she outlined all the reasons for her decision.* This expression alludes to the regular beat of musical time. [Mid-1900s]

miss by a mile Fall short, fail by a considerable amount, as in *Your guess as to the winner missed by a mile.* This expression employs *miss* in the sense of "fail to hit something aimed at," a usage dating from the late 1400s, and *by a mile* for a great distance or interval, so used since Shakespeare's day.

miss fire Fail to achieve the anticipated result, as in *Recycling cardboard seemed like a good idea but it missed fire.* First recorded in 1727, this phrase originally described a firearm failing to go off and has been used figuratively since the mid-1800s.

miss is as good as a mile, a Coming close to success but failing is no better than failing by a lot, as in *He was beaten by just one vote, but a miss is as good as a mile.* This proverbial expression, first recorded in 1614, is a shortening of the older form, "An inch of a miss is as good [or bad] as a mile of a miss."

miss much ♦ See under NOT MISS A TRICK.

Missouri ♦ See FROM MISSOURI.

miss out on Lose a chance for, fail to achieve, as in *Ruth came late to the party and missed out on all the fun,* or *Trudy missed out on the promotion.* [First half of 1900s] Also see LOSE OUT, def. 2.

miss the boat 1. Fail to take advantage of an opportunity, as in *Jean missed the boat on that club membership.* This expression, which alludes to not being in time to catch a boat, has been applied more widely since the 1920s. 2. Fail to understand something, as in *I'm afraid our legislator missed the boat on that amendment to the bill.* [Mid-1900s] Also see MISS THE POINT.

miss the point Overlook or fail to understand the essential or important part of something, as in *Chris missed the point of Gwen's complaint, thinking she was opposed to the date of the next meeting.* This expression employs *point* in the sense of "the salient portion," a usage dating from the late 1300s.

mistake ♦ In addition to the idiom beginning with MISTAKE, also see BY MISTAKE; MAKE NO MISTAKE.

mistake for Take someone or something for someone or something else, as in *I'm sorry, I mistook you for her sister,* or *Don't mistake that friendly smile for good intentions; he's a tough competitor.* [c. 1600]

mix and match Combine different items in a number of ways. For example, *The store displayed skirts, blouses, and slacks in colors that one could mix and match.* [Mid-1900s]

mixed bag A heterogeneous collection of people, items, activities, or the like; an assortment. For example, *The school offers a mixed bag of after-school activities—team sports, band practice, a language class.* This idiom calls up the image of a sack full of different items. [First half of 1900s]

mixed blessing Something that has both good and bad features, as in *Being accepted by the college was a mixed blessing, since she couldn't afford the tuition.* [First half of 1900s]

mixed feelings A partly positive and partly negative reaction to something, as in *I have mixed feelings about this trip; I'd love to go but don't want to ride in that tiny car.*

mix it up Get in a fight, as in *The driver got out and began to mix it up with the other driver.* This expression uses *mix* in referring to physical mingling. [c. 1900]

mix up 1. Confuse, confound, as in *His explanation just mixed me up even more*, or *I always mix up the twins*. [c. 1800] **2.** Involve or implicate. This usage is usually put in the passive, as in *He got mixed up with the wrong crowd*. [Mid-1800s]

mold ♦ See CAST IN THE SAME MOLD.

molehill ♦ See MAKE A MOUNTAIN OUT OF A MOLEHILL.

moment ♦ In addition to the idiom beginning with MOMENT, also see AT THIS POINT (MOMENT); EVERY MINUTE (MOMENT) COUNTS; FOR THE MOMENT; HAVE ONE'S MOMENTS; JUST A MINUTE (MOMENT); LIVE FOR THE MOMENT; NEVER A DULL MOMENT; NOT FOR A MOMENT; OF THE MOMENT; ON THE SPUR OF THE MOMENT; WEAK MOMENT.

moment of truth A critical or decisive time, at which one is put to the ultimate test, as in *Now that all the bills are in, we've come to the moment of truth—can we afford to live here or not?* This expression, a translation of the Spanish *el momento de la verdad*, signifies the point in a bullfight when the matador makes the kill. It was first used in English in Ernest Hemingway's story *Death in the Afternoon* (1932).

Monday-morning quarterback A person who criticizes or passes judgment from a position of hindsight, as in *Ethel was a Monday-morning quarterback about all the personnel changes in her department—she always claimed to have known what was going to happen*. This expression, first recorded in 1932, alludes to fans who verbally "replay" Sunday's football game the next day, the *quarterback* being the team member who calls the plays.

money ♦ In addition to the idioms beginning with MONEY, also see COIN MONEY; COLOR OF ONE'S MONEY; EASY MONEY; EVEN MONEY; FOOL AND HIS MONEY ARE SOON PARTED; FOR ONE'S MONEY; FUNNY MONEY; GET ONE'S MONEY'S WORTH; HUSH MONEY; IN THE MONEY; MADE OF MONEY; NOT FOR LOVE OR MONEY; ON THE MONEY; PAY YOUR MONEY AND TAKE YOUR CHOICE; PIN MONEY; POCKET MONEY; PUT MONEY ON; PUT ONE'S MONEY WHERE ONE'S MOUTH IS; ROLLING IN IT (MONEY); RUN FOR ONE'S MONEY; SPEND MONEY LIKE WATER; THROW GOOD MONEY AFTER BAD; TIME IS MONEY.

money burns a hole in one's pocket One can't keep from spending whatever money one has. For example, *As soon as she gets paid she goes shopping; money burns a hole in her pocket*. This hyperbolic expression, which alleges that one must take out the money before it actually burns a hole, was stated only slightly differently by Thomas More (c. 1530): "A little wanton money . . . burned out the bottom of his purse."

money is no object Also, **expense is no object**. It doesn't matter how much it costs, as in *Get the very best fur coat you can find—money is no object*.

In this expression *no object* means "something not taken into account or presenting no obstacle." It was first recorded as *salary will be no object* in a 1782 newspaper advertisement for someone seeking a job. Both *money* and *expense* were so described by the mid-1800s.

money talks Wealth has great influence, as in *Big contributors to campaigns are generally rewarded with important posts—in politics money talks*. The idea behind this idiom was stated by Euripides in the fifth century B.C., and some 2,000 years later Erasmus spoke of "the talking power of money" (*Adagia*, 1532). The precise current locution, however, only began to be used about 1900.

money to burn More than enough money for what is required or expected, as in *After they paid off the creditors, they still had money to burn*. This hyperbolic expression implies one has so much that one can afford to burn it. [Late 1800s] This sense of the verb *burn* is occasionally used in other phrases, such as **time to burn** ("more than enough time"), but not very often.

monkey ♦ In addition to the idioms beginning with MONKEY, also see FOOL (MONKEY) AROUND; MAKE A FOOL (MONKEY) OF; MORE FUN THAN A BARREL OF MONKEYS; THROW A MONKEY WRENCH.

monkey business Silly, mischievous, or deceitful conduct, as in *The teacher told the children to cut out the monkey business and get to work*, or *I don't trust that lawyer—there's some monkey business going on*. This expression transfers the tricks of monkeys to human behavior. [Late 1800s]

monkey on one's back 1. Drug addiction, as in *He'd had a monkey on his back for at least two years*. [Slang; first half of 1900s] **2.** A vexing problem or burden, as in *This project has proved to be a monkey on my back—there seems to be no end to it*. Both usages allude to being unable to shake off the animal from one's back.

monster ♦ See GREEN-EYED MONSTER.

month ♦ In addition to the idiom beginning with MONTH, also see BY THE DAY (MONTH); (FOR MONTHS) ON END.

month of Sundays, a A long time, as in *I haven't seen Barbara in a month of Sundays*. This expression, which would literally mean thirty weeks, has been used hyperbolically since it was first recorded in 1832. One writer suggests it originally connoted a long *dreary* time, since games and other kinds of amusement used to be forbidden on Sunday.

mood ♦ See IN A BAD MOOD; IN THE MOOD.

moon ♦ See ASK FOR THE MOON; ONCE IN A BLUE MOON; PROMISE THE MOON.

moot point A debatable question, an issue open to argument; also, an irrelevant question, a matter of no importance. For example, *Whether Shakespeare actually wrote the poem remains a moot point among critics,* or *It's a moot point whether the chicken or the egg came first.* This term originated in British law where it described a point for discussion in a *moot,* or assembly, of law students. By the early 1700s it was being used more loosely in the present sense.

mop up 1. Clear an area of remaining enemy troops after a victory, as in *They left behind just one squadron to mop up.* [c. 1900] 2. Perform the minor tasks that conclude a project or activity, as in *Go ahead, I'll mop up these last invoices.* [First half of 1900s] Both usages transfer the task of housecleaning with a mop to other kinds of cleanup.

mop up the floor with Also, **wipe the floor with.** Defeat thoroughly, overwhelm, as in *The young boxer said he was sure to mop up the floor with his opponent,* or *I just know we'll wipe the floor with the competition.* [Late 1800s]

moral support Emotional or psychological backing, as opposed to material help. For example, *There's not much I can do at the doctor's office, but I'll come with you to give you moral support.* [Late 1800s]

more ♦ In addition to the idioms beginning with MORE, also see BITE OFF MORE THAN ONE CAN CHEW; IRONS IN THE FIRE, MORE THAN ONE; WEAR ANOTHER (MORE THAN ONE) HAT; WHAT IS MORE.

more and more Increasingly, to a steadily growing extent or degree. For example, *As night came on, we were getting more and more worried,* or *More and more I lean toward thinking he is right.* [c. 1200]

more bang for the buck Also, **more bounce to the ounce.** More value for one's money, a greater return on an investment. For example, *Buying a condominium is better than renting for years and years; more bang for the buck,* or *We always get the largest packages of dog food—more bounce to the ounce.* The first term originated in the late 1960s in the military for expenditures for firepower and soon was extended to mean an increased financial return or better value. The variant originated in the mid-1900s as an advertising slogan for a carbonated soft drink.

more dead than alive Exhausted, in poor condition, as in *By the time I got off that mountain I was more dead than alive.* This idiom may be used either hyperbolically or literally. [c. 1900]

more fun than a barrel of monkeys Very amusing or diverting, as in *That video game was more fun than a barrel of monkeys.* This expression, first recorded in 1895, alludes to the playful behavior of these primates.

more in sorrow than in anger Saddened rather than infuriated by someone's behavior. For example, *When Dad learned that Jack had stolen a car, he looked at him more in sorrow than in anger.* This expression first appeared in 1603 in Shakespeare's *Hamlet* (1:2), where Horatio describes to Hamlet the appearance of his father's ghost: "A countenance more in sorrow than in anger."

more often than not Also, **often as not.** Fairly frequently, more than or at least half the time, as in *More often than not we'll have dinner in the den,* or *Dean and Chris agree on travel plans, often as not.* [First half of 1900s]

more or less 1. Approximately, as in *The truck will hold nine yards of dirt, more or less.* This usage was first recorded in 1589. 2. Basically, essentially, as in *We more or less agree on the substance of the letter.* This usage was first recorded about 1225.

more power to someone Best wishes to someone, as in *He's decided to climb Mount Everest—well, more power to him.* [Mid-1800s] For a more recent synonym, see RIGHT ON.

more sinned against than sinning Less guilty than those who have injured one, as in *It's true she took the money but they did owe her quite a bit—in a way she's more sinned against than sinning.* This expression comes from Shakespeare's *King Lear* (3:2), where the King, on the heath during a storm, so describes his plight.

more than meets the eye A hidden significance, greater than is first apparent, as in *This agreement involves more than meets the eye.* [Mid-1800s]

more than one bargained for An unexpected outcome, especially an unfavorable one, as in *Serving on the board this year has involved more work than I bargained for.* This expression alludes to a higher than anticipated cost for a transaction. [Mid-1800s]

more than one can shake a stick at A large quantity, more than one can count, as in *Our town has more banks than you can shake a stick at* This idiom presumably refers to brandishing a stick as a weapon, but the precise allusion is unclear. [Colloquial; c. 1800]

more than one way to skin a cat More than one method to reach the same end, as in *We can get around that by renting instead of buying a computer—there's more than one way to skin a cat.* This expression may be an American version of the earlier British **more ways of killing a cat,** but why the death of a cat should be alluded to at all is not clear. [Second half of 1800s]

more the merrier, the The larger the number involved, the better the occasion. For example, *John's invited all his family to come along, and why not? The more the merrier.* This expression was first recorded in 1530, when it was put as "The more the merrier; the fewer, the better fare" (meaning "with fewer there would be more to eat"), an observation that made its way into numerous proverb collections.

morning ♦ In addition to the idiom beginning with MORNING, also see GOOD DAY (MORNING); MONDAY-MORNING QUARTER-BACK.

morning after, the The unpleasant results of an earlier activity, especially overindulgence in alcohol. For example, *A headache is just one of the symptoms of the morning after.* This expression originated in the late 1800s as a synonym for a hangover (and was often put as *the morning after the night before*). By the mid-1900s, however, it was also being used more loosely for the aftereffects of staying up late.

mortar ♦ See BRICKS AND MORTAR.

moss ♦ See ROLLING STONE GATHERS NO MOSS.

most ♦ See AT MOST; FOR THE MOST PART; MAKE THE MOST OF.

mothballs ♦ See PUT IN MOTHBALLS.

mother ♦ In addition to the idiom beginning with MOTHER, also see NECESSITY IS THE MOTHER OF INVENTION.

mother of The best or greatest of a type, as in *That was the mother of all tennis matches.* This expression originated during the Gulf War as a translation of Iraqi leader Saddam Hussein's term *umm al-ma'arik*, for "major battle"; the Arabic "mother of" is a figure of speech for "major" or "best." It was quickly adopted and applied to just about any person, event, or activity. [Slang; late 1980s]

motion ♦ See GO THROUGH THE MOTIONS; SET IN MOTION; SET THE WHEELS IN MOTION.

mountain ♦ See IF THE MOUNTAIN WON'T COME TO MUHAMMAD; MAKE A MOUNTAIN OUT OF A MOLEHILL.

mouse ♦ See PLAY CAT AND MOUSE; POOR AS A CHURCHMOUSE; QUIET AS A MOUSE. Also see under MICE.

mouth ♦ In addition to the idiom beginning with MOUTH, also see BAD MOUTH; BIG MOUTH; BUTTER WOULDN'T MELT IN ONE'S MOUTH; DOWN IN THE DUMPS (MOUTH); FOAM AT THE MOUTH; FOOT IN ONE'S MOUTH; FROM THE HORSE'S MOUTH; HAND TO MOUTH; HAVE ONE'S HEART IN ONE'S MOUTH; KEEP ONE'S MOUTH SHUT; LAUGH OUT OF THE OTHER SIDE OF ONE'S MOUTH; LEAVE A BAD TASTE IN ONE'S MOUTH; LOOK A GIFT HORSE IN THE MOUTH; MAKE ONE'S MOUTH WATER; MELT IN ONE'S MOUTH; NOT OPEN ONE'S MOUTH; OUT OF THE MOUTHS OF BABES; PUT ONE'S MONEY WHERE ONE'S MOUTH IS; PUT WORDS IN SOMEONE'S MOUTH; RUN OFF AT THE MOUTH; SHOOT OFF ONE'S MOUTH; TAKE THE BIT IN ONE'S MOUTH; TAKE THE BREAD OUT OF SOMEONE'S MOUTH; TAKE THE WORDS OUT OF SOMEONE'S MOUTH; WORD OF MOUTH.

mouthful ♦ See SAY A MOUTHFUL.

mouth off 1. Complain or express one's opinions loudly and indiscreetly, as in *She was always mouthing off about the other members.* [Slang; 1960s] 2. Speak impudently, talk back, as in *He got in trouble by mouthing off to his teacher.* [Slang; 1960s]

move ♦ In addition to the idioms beginning with MOVE, also see GET A MOVE ON; ON THE MOVE. Also see under MOVER.

move a muscle Bestir oneself even slightly. This idiom is usually put negatively, either with implied criticism, as in *She won't move a muscle to help get dinner,* or not, as in *When I saw the deer, I stayed quite still, not daring to move a muscle.* It was first recorded in 1889.

move heaven and earth Exert the utmost effort, as in *I'd move heaven and earth to get an apartment here.* This hyperbolic expression was first recorded in 1792.

move in 1. Begin to occupy a residence or working place, as in *We are scheduled to move in next month,* or *Helen is moving in with her sister.* [Late 1800s] 2. **move in on.** Intrude on; also, try to take over or get control of. For example, *Their sales force is moving in on our territory,* or *The police moved in on the gang.* [Mid-1900s]

move on Continue moving or progressing; also go away. For example, *It's time we moved on to the next item on the agenda,* or *The police ordered the spectators to move on.* [First half of 1800s]

mover ♦ In addition to the idiom beginning with MOVER, also see PRIME MOVER.

mover and shaker A person who wields power and influence in a particular activity or field, as in *He's one of the movers and shakers in the art world.* At first the two nouns referred specifically to God, alluding to the belief that a divine force was responsible for all events. The current usage refers only to human beings. [Second half of 1800s]

move up Also, **move up in the world.** Advance, rise to a higher level, succeed, as in *Gene hoped he would move up in the new division,* or *That new house and car show they are moving up in the world.* Also see COME UP, def. 4.

mow down 1. Destroy in great numbers, especially in battle, as in *The machine gun mowed them down as they advanced.* [Late 1500s] 2. Overwhelm, as in *He mowed down the opposition with his arguments.* This usage, like the first, alludes to *mowing,* the cutting of grass with a scythe or other implement.

much ♦ In addition to the idioms beginning with MUCH, also see AS MUCH; AS MUCH AS; MAKE MUCH OF; NOT MISS A TRICK (MUCH); NOT THINK MUCH OF; NOT UP TO MUCH; PRETTY MUCH; SO MUCH; SO MUCH FOR; SO MUCH THE BETTER; (MUCH) SOUGHT

AFTER; TAKE IT (JUST SO MUCH); TAKE ON (TOO MUCH); TOO MUCH OF A GOOD THING; WITHOUT SO MUCH AS.

much ado about nothing A big fuss over a trifle, as in *Jerry had everyone running around looking for his gloves—much ado about nothing.* Although this expression is best remembered as the title of Shakespeare's comedy, the phrase *much ado* was already being used for a big commotion or trouble in the early 1500s.

much as ♦ See AS MUCH AS, def. 2.

much less And certainly not, as in *He rarely talks about his outside activities, much less his family.* The earliest record of this idiom is in John Milton's *Paradise Lost* (1671): "The world thou hast not seen, much less her glory."

much sought after ♦ See SOUGHT AFTER.

muck up Bungle, damage, make a mess of, as in *Don't let him write the review; he's sure to muck it up.* This idiom alludes to the verb *muck* in the sense of "spread manure on." [Early 1900s] For a synonym, see FOUL UP.

mud ♦ See CLEAR AS MUD; NAME IS MUD; SLING MUD AT.

muddle through Blunder through something, manage but awkwardly, as in *The choir never knows how to line up, but we muddle through somehow.* [Early 1900s]

muddy the waters Confuse the issue, as in *Bringing up one irrelevant fact after another, he succeeded in muddying the waters.* This metaphoric expression, alluding to making a pond or stream turbid by stirring up mud from the bottom, was first recorded in 1837.

mule ♦ See STUBBORN AS A MULE.

mull over Ponder, think about, as in *She mulled over the offer for some time and then turned it down.* [Late 1800s]

multitude of sins, cover a Compensate for numerous evils, as in *You may not be offering to help with the fair, but that big donation covers a multitude of sins.* This expression originated in the New Testament (I Peter 4:8): "And above all things have fervent charity among yourselves: for charity shall cover the multitude of sins."

mum's the word Say nothing about this, it's a secret, as in *Mum's the word on tonight's surprise party.* This expression dates from about 1700, but *mum*, meaning "silence," is much older. In *2 Henry VI* (1:2) Shakespeare wrote, "Seal up your lips, and give no words but mum."

murder ♦ In addition to the idiom beginning with MURDER, also see GET AWAY WITH (MURDER); SCREAM BLOODY MURDER.

murder will out Certain news cannot be suppressed, as in *He's being charged with embezzlement and fraud—murder will out, you know.* This

expression already appeared in Chaucer's *The Nun's Priest's Tale:* "Murder will out that we see day by day." [Late 1300s]

Murphy's law If anything can go wrong, it will, as in *We may think we've covered all the details for the benefit, but remember Murphy's law.* The identity of Murphy, if ever a real person, is unknown. Some think it alludes to (but was not invented by) a feckless Irishman named Murphy. [c. 1940]

muscle ♦ In addition to the idiom beginning with MUSCLE, also see FLEX ONE'S MUSCLES; MOVE A MUSCLE.

muscle in Also, **muscle in on.** Forcibly intrude on or interfere with something, as in *The children were determined not to allow the school bully to muscle in,* or *No more muscling in on our policy decisions!* [Colloquial; 1920s]

museum piece An elderly or old-fashioned item or person, as in *When are you going to sell that museum piece of a car?* or *Aunt Jane comes from another era—she's a real museum piece.* This expression originated about 1900 for an article valuable enough for museum display but began to be used disparagingly from about 1915.

music ♦ In addition to the idiom beginning with MUSIC, also see FACE THE MUSIC.

musical chairs, play Move around from position to position, such as the jobs in an organization. For example, *Bob took over for Tom, who took over for Mary, who got Bob's title—the boss loves to play musical chairs with the staff.* This expression alludes to the children's game in which children walk around a number of seats while music plays, and there is one less chair than players. When the music stops the players must sit down, and the player who is left standing is eliminated. Then another chair is removed, and the game goes on until only one player is left sitting. [c. 1900]

music to one's ears Very pleasing information, excellent news, as in *So they're getting married? That's music to my ears.*

must ♦ See A MUST; SHOW MUST GO ON.

mustard ♦ See CUT THE MUSTARD.

muster ♦ In addition to the idiom beginning with MUSTER, also see PASS MUSTER.

muster in Enlist in military service. For example, *They were mustered in at Fort Dix.* The antonym is **muster out,** meaning "to leave or be discharged from military service," as in *He was mustered out and given a dishonorable discharge.* [First half of 1800s]

mutual admiration society A relationship in which two people have strong feelings of esteem for each other and often exchange lavish compliments. The term may signify either genuine or pretended admiration, as in *Each of them praised the other's book—it was a real mutual admiration society.* The expression was invented by Henry David Thoreau in his journal (1851) and repeated by Oliver Wendell Holmes and others.

my eye Like hell, that's nonsense, as in *You were at the library all day? My eye, you were!* This slangy expression of disbelief was first recorded in 1842. From about 1800 to the 1930s the same term was used to indicate surprise (*My eye, she's been promoted after all.*) but this usage seems to be obsolete.

my God Also, **my goodness.** Expressions of shock, surprise, or dismay, as in *My God, don't tell me he's dying,* or *My goodness, what an awful outfit.* The first term dates from about 1800; *goodness* in the variant is a euphemism for *God.*

my heart bleeds for you I don't feel at all sorry for you, I don't sympathize, as in *You only got a five percent raise? My heart bleeds for you.* Originating in the late 1300s, this hyperbolic expression of sympathy has been used ironically since the mid-1700s.

my name is mud ◆ See under NAME IS MUD.

n

nail ◆ In addition to the idioms beginning with NAIL, also see BITE ONE'S NAILS; FIGHT TOOTH AND NAIL; HARD AS NAILS; HIT THE BULL'S-EYE (NAIL ON THE HEAD); ON THE NAIL.

nail down Establish conclusively, as in *The reporter nailed down the story by checking all the facts.* This metaphoric expression alludes to fixing or fastening something down with nails. [c. 1600]

nail in one's coffin Something that might hasten or contribute to one's death, as in *Every cigarette you smoke is another nail in your coffin.* This expression, alluding to fastening down a coffin lid, is today almost always used for a harmful habit such as tobacco use (giving rise to the slang term **coffin nail** for a cigar or cigarette). The idea was first expressed in an ode by Pindar (the pseudonym of John Wolcot) in 1792: "Care to our coffin adds a nail, no doubt."

naked as a jaybird Bare, unclothed, as in *I came straight out of the shower, naked as a jaybird.* This simile replaced the 19th-century *naked as a robin* and is equally unclear, since neither bird is normally stripped of its feathers. Further, the bird it refers to is more often called simply "jay" rather than "jaybird," yet the latter is always part of the simile. [c. 1940]

naked eye Sight unassisted by an instrument such as a microscope or telescope. For example, *These insects are too small to be seen with the naked eye.* This expression was first recorded in 1664.

naked truth Plain unadorned facts, without concealment or embellishment. For example, *What I've told you is the naked truth.* This expression supposedly alludes to a fable in which Truth and Falsehood went bathing, Falsehood then dressed in Truth's clothes, and Truth, refusing to take another's clothes, went naked. [Late 1500s]

name ◆ In addition to the idioms beginning with NAME, also see CALL NAMES; CLEAR ONE'S NAME; DROP NAMES; GIVE A BAD NAME; GO BY (THE NAME OF); HANDLE TO ONE'S NAME; IN NAME ONLY; IN THE NAME OF; MAKE A NAME FOR ONESELF; ON A FIRST-NAME BASIS; TAKE SOMEONE'S NAME IN VAIN; TO ONE'S NAME; WORTHY OF THE NAME; YOU NAME IT.

name after Also, **name for.** Give someone or something the name of another person or place. For example, *They named the baby after his grandfather,* or *The mountain was named for President McKinley.*

name is mud, one's One is in trouble, disgraced, or discredited, as in *If they find out I broke it, my name will be mud,* or *If his estimate is completely wrong, his name will be mud.* A popular theory for this expression's origin derives it from Dr. Samuel Mudd, the physician who was convicted as conspirator after he set the broken ankle of President Lincoln's assassin, John Wilkes Booth. But the expression was first recorded in 1823, when *mud* was slang for a stupid person or fool, a usage dating from the early 1700s. Later the term *mud* simply alluded to discredit.

name names Specify persons by name, especially those who are accused of something. For example, *More than one person was involved in the robbery, and his lawyer said he would get a shorter sentence if he named names.* It is also put negatively, **name no names,** as in *Some of our neighbors disobey the town's leash law, but I'm naming no names.* The negative form was first recorded in 1792.

name of the game, the The crux of the matter; also, the main goal. For example, *Getting them to admit they're wrong—that's the name of the game,* or *Parents don't approve of a coach who insists that winning any way one can is the name of the game.* This rhyming idiom uses *name* in the sense of "identity." [Mid-1900s]

name the day Fix the date for a wedding, as in *Her parents pressed her to name the day.* This expression was first recorded in 1766. However, similar usages for specifying a time, such as *name the time,* date from the late 1500s.

napping ◆ See CATCH NAPPING.

narrow ♦ In addition to the idiom beginning with NARROW, see STRAIGHT AND NARROW.

narrow escape A barely successful flight from or avoidance of danger or trouble, as in *He had a narrow escape, since the bullet came within inches of his head.* This expression uses *narrow* in the sense of "barely sufficient." [Late 1500s] For a newer synonym, see CLOSE CALL.

nary a Not one, as in *There's nary a mention of taxes in that speech,* or *Nary an officer could be seen.* This archaic-sounding contraction of "never a" remains in current use. [Mid-1700s]

natural ♦ See under BIG AS LIFE.

nature ♦ See CALL OF NATURE; GOOD NATURE; SECOND NATURE.

naught ♦ See COME TO NOTHING (NAUGHT).

near ♦ In addition to the idioms beginning with NEAR, also see FAR AND NEAR; IN THE NEAR FUTURE; NOT ANYTHING LIKE (ANYWHERE NEAR).

near at hand ♦ See AT HAND.

nearest and dearest One's closest and fondest friends, companions, or relatives, as in *It's a small gathering—we're inviting only a dozen or so of our nearest and dearest.* This rhyming expression has been used ironically since the late 1500s, as well as by Shakespeare in 1 *Henry IV* (3:2): "Why, Harry, do I tell thee of my foes, which art my nearest and dearest enemy?"

near miss A narrowly avoided mishap; also, an attempt that falls just short of success. For example, *It was a near miss for that truck, since the driver had crossed the center strip into oncoming traffic,* or *Her horse kept having a near miss in every race, so she decided to sell it.* This expression originated during World War II, when it signified a bomb exploding in the water near enough to a ship to damage its hull. Soon afterward it acquired its present meanings.

near thing Something just barely effected, as in *That election was a near thing—he won by a handful of votes.* [Mid-1700s]

near to one's heart Also, close to one's heart. Loved by or important to one, as in *This last painting was very near to her heart,* or *His first grandson is close to his heart.* [Late 1800s]

necessity ♦ In addition to the idiom beginning with NECESSITY, also see MAKE A VIRTUE OF NECESSITY; OF NECESSITY.

necessity is the mother of invention Inventiveness and ingenuity are stimulated by difficulty. For example, *The first prisoner to tie together bedsheets to escape knew that necessity was the mother of invention.* This proverb first appeared in English in 1519 in slightly different form, "Need

taught him wit," and exists in many other languages as well.

neck ♦ In addition to the idioms beginning with NECK, also see ALBATROSS AROUND ONE'S NECK; BREAK ONE'S BACK (NECK); BREATHE DOWN SOMEONE'S NECK; DEAD FROM THE NECK UP; MILLSTONE AROUND ONE'S NECK; PAIN IN THE NECK; RISK LIFE AND LIMB (ONE'S NECK); SAVE SOMEONE'S BACON (NECK); STICK ONE'S NECK OUT; UP TO ONE'S EARS (NECK).

neck and neck So close that the advantage or lead shifts from one to the other or is virtually indistinguishable, as in *The two are neck and neck in developing a new operating system for the computer.* The term comes from horse racing, where the necks of two horses in competition appear to be side by side. [Early 1800s] For a synonym, see NIP AND TUCK.

neck of the woods A neighborhood or region, as in *He's one of the wealthiest men in our neck of the woods.* Originally (mid-1800s) alluding to a forest settlement, this colloquial term is now used more loosely, for urban as well as rural locales.

need ♦ In addition to the idiom beginning with NEED, also see CRY FOR (CRYING NEED FOR); FRIEND IN NEED IS A FRIEND INDEED.

needle ♦ In addition to the idiom beginning with NEEDLE, also see ON PINS AND NEEDLES.

needle in a haystack An item that is very hard or impossible to locate, as in *Looking for that screw in Dean's workshop amounts to looking for a needle in a haystack.* Originating in the early 1500s, with *meadow* instead of *haystack,* this metaphor exists in many other languages as well.

needless to say Very likely or obvious, self-evident, as in *Needless to say, the availability of assault weapons is closely connected with crime.* Although nonsensical at first glance (if unnecessary to say, why say it?), this phrase is generally used for emphasis. It originated as *needless to speak* in the early 1500s. Also see GO WITHOUT (SAYING).

need like a hole in the head Have neither a need nor a desire for something, as in *I needed that extra work like I need a hole in the head.* This expression has such ancestors as "As much need of it as he has of the pip [a disease] or of a cough," from John Ray's *English Proverbs* (1678), and "As much need of it as a toad of a side pocket," from Francis Grose's *Dictionary of the Vulgar Tongue* (1785). [Slang; c. 1940]

neither fish nor fowl Also, neither fish nor flesh; neither fish, flesh, nor fowl. Not one or the other, not something fitting any category under discussion. For example, *They felt he was neither fish nor fowl—not qualified to lead the department, yet not appropriate to work as a staff member either.* This expression appeared in slightly different form in

John Heywood's 1546 proverb collection ("Neither fish, nor flesh, nor good red herring") and is thought to allude to food for monks (*fish*, because they abstained from meat), for the people (*flesh*, or meat), and for the poor (*red herring*, a very cheap fish).

neither here nor there Unimportant, irrelevant, as in *You pay for the movie and I'll get the dinner check, or vice versa—it's neither here nor there.* This expression was first recorded in 1583. Also see BESIDE THE POINT.

neither hide nor hair ♦ See HIDE OR HAIR.

neither rhyme nor reason ♦ See RHYME OR REASON.

Nellie ♦ See NERVOUS NELLIE.

nerve ♦ See BUNDLE OF NERVES; GET ON SOMEONE'S NERVES; GET UP (ONE'S NERVE); HAVE A NERVE; LOSE ONE'S NERVE; OF ALL THE NERVE; WAR OF NERVES.

nervous Nellie An unduly timid or anxious person, as in *He's a real nervous Nellie calling the doctor about every little symptom.* This term does not allude to a particular person named Nellie; rather, the name was probably chosen for the sake of alliteration. [Colloquial; c. 1920]

nervous wreck An individual suffering from extreme agitation or worry, as in *Pat was a nervous wreck until her mother arrived at the wedding.* This expression is nearly always used hyperbolically. [Colloquial; c. 1900] Also see BASKET CASE.

nest ♦ See EMPTY NEST; FEATHER ONE'S NEST; FOUL ONE'S NEST; STIR UP A HORNET'S NEST.

never ♦ In addition to the idioms beginning with NEVER, also see BETTER LATE THAN NEVER; IT NEVER RAINS BUT IT POURS; LIGHTNING NEVER STRIKES TWICE; NOW OR NEVER; WATCHED POT NEVER BOILS; WONDERS WILL NEVER CEASE; YOU NEVER CAN TELL.

never a dull moment Something is always changing or happening, as in *First Lauren spits up, then she coughs, then she sneezes—never a dull moment with this baby!* This expression was first recorded in 1889.

never fear Don't worry that a thing will or won't occur, be confident, as in *I'll get there, never fear.* This phrase was used by Christopher Marlowe in *Doctor Faustus* (c. 1590): "'Tis but a surfeit; never fear, man."

never give a sucker an even break Don't allow a person who's easily duped a fair chance, as in *He's always trying to give out expired coupons for his store, firmly believing in never giving a sucker an even break.* Probably a direct quotation, it has been attributed to showman P. T. Barnum (responsible for the oft-quoted "There's a sucker born every minute"); and comedian W. C. Fields (who popularized it in one of his films); and the-

ater manager Edward Francis Albee, the most probable of the three. [Slang; early 1900s]

never had it so good, one One is better off now than one has ever been before, as in *She keeps complaining about her new job, but the truth is that she's never had it so good.* [Colloquial; first half of 1900s]

never hear the end of Be incessantly reminded of, as in *If you do not send a wedding present to them you will never hear the end of it from your mother.*

never mind 1. Don't worry about something, don't trouble yourself, it doesn't matter. For example, *Never mind what I said, it wasn't important,* or *Never mind, you can always take the driver's test again.* This expression employs *mind* in the sense of "care about something," a usage dating from the late 1700s. 2. Also, **never you mind.** Don't concern yourself with that, it's none of your business, as in *Never you mind where I plan to buy the new TV.* [Early 1800s]

never miss a trick ♦ See NOT MISS A TRICK.

never-never land A fantasy land, an imaginary place, as in *I don't know what's gotten into Marge—she's way off in never-never land.* This expression gained currency when James Barrie used it in *Peter Pan* (1904) for the place where Peter and the Lost Boys live. However, in the second half of the 1800s Australians already were using it for vast unsettled areas of their continent (*the outback*), and there the term became popular through Mrs. Aeneas Gunn's *We of the Never Never* (1908). In Australia it still refers to north-west Queensland or northern Australia in general. Elsewhere it simply signifies a fantasy or daydream.

never put off until tomorrow ♦ See under PUT OFF.

never say die Don't ever give up, do not despair, as in *This stage set doesn't look too promising, but never say die, it may still work out.* This maxim today is often used ironically and deprecatingly, for something that has already failed. [Early 1800s]

never say never Nothing is impossible, anything can happen, as in *Mary said Tom would never call her again, but I told her, "Never say never."* This expression was first recorded in Charles Dickens's *Pickwick Papers* (1837).

new ♦ In addition to the idioms beginning with NEW, also see BREAK (NEW) GROUND; BREATHE NEW LIFE INTO; FEEL LIKE (NEW); NOTHING NEW UNDER THE SUN; RING IN THE NEW YEAR; TEACH AN OLD DOG NEW TRICKS; TURN OVER A NEW LEAF; WHAT'S COOKING (NEW); WHOLE NEW BALLGAME.

new ballgame ♦ See WHOLE NEW BALLGAME.

new blood Additional, fresh individuals regarded as an invigorating force, as in an organization. For example, *The board could really use some new blood next year.* This metaphoric expression, first recorded in 1853, alludes to a blood transfusion and employs *new* in the sense of "fresh."

new broom sweeps clean, a A fresh leader or administration gets rid of the old and brings in New ideas and personnel. For example, *Once he takes office, you can be sure the President will replace most of the people on the staff—a new broom sweeps clean.* This term was already in John Heywood's 1546 proverb collection, was used figuratively by Shakespeare, and exists in many other languages as well.

Newcastle ◆ See CARRY COALS TO NEWCASTLE.

new leaf ◆ See TURN OVER A NEW LEAF.

new lease on life A fresh start; renewed vigor and good health, as in *Since they bought his store Dad has had a new lease on life.* This term with its allusion to a rental agreement dates from the early 1800s and originally referred only to recovery from illness. By the mid-1800s it was applied to any kind of fresh beginning.

new man ◆ See under FEEL LIKE ONESELF.

new one ◆ See under THAT'S ONE ON ME.

new person ◆ See under FEEL LIKE ONESELF.

news ◆ See BAD NEWS; BREAK THE NEWS; NO NEWS IS GOOD NEWS.

new woman ◆ See under FEEL LIKE ONESELF.

new wrinkle A clever device or expedient, a novelty, as in *The players added a new wrinkle to victory celebrations by tossing their shirts to the crowd after the game.* In the form of simply *a wrinkle*, this expression dates from the mid-1700s, *new* being added two centuries later.

next ◆ In addition to the idioms beginning with NEXT, also see CLEANLINESS IS NEXT TO GODLINESS.

next door to Very close to, as in *The old dog was next door to death.* This metaphoric expression, alluding to an adjacent house, was first recorded in 1529.

next to 1. Adjacent to, as in *The car next to mine has a flat tire.* [Late 1300s] 2. Following in order or degree, as in *Next to skiing, she likes hiking.* [Early 1500s] 3. Almost, practically, as in *It's next to impossible to predict the outcome,* or *I earned next to nothing last year.* [Second half of 1600s]

nick ◆ See IN THE NICK OF TIME.

nickel ◆ See NOT WORTH A DIME (PLUGGED NICKEL).

night ◆ In addition to the idioms beginning with NIGHT, also see BLACK AS NIGHT; CALL IT A DAY (NIGHT); DEAD OF (NIGHT); DIFFERENT AS NIGHT AND DAY; GOOD NIGHT; MAKE A DAY (NIGHT) OF IT; SHIPS THAT PASS IN THE NIGHT.

night and day Also **day and night**. Continually, without stopping. This phrase is used either literally, as in *The alarm is on night and day,* or hyperbolically, as in *We were working day and night on these drawings.* Shakespeare put it **by night and day** in *The Comedy of Errors* (4:2): "Time comes stealing on by night and day."

night owl A person who habitually stays up late and is active at night, as in *You can call her after midnight, for she's a night owl.* This colloquial term, originally used in the late 1500s for an owl that is active at night, was transferred to nocturnal human beings in the mid-1800s.

nine ◆ See DRESSED TO KILL (TO THE NINES); ON CLOUD NINE; POSSESSION IS NINE POINTS OF THE LAW; WHOLE NINE YARDS.

nip and tuck Very close so that the advantage or lead of competitors keeps shifting, as in *It was nip and tuck whether they would deal with the bill before Congress adjourned.* The precise allusion in this term has been lost. [Early 1800s] Also see NECK AND NECK.

nip in the bud Halt something at an early stage, or thoroughly check something. For example, *By arresting all the leaders, they nipped the rebellion in the bud.* This metaphoric expression, alluding to a spring frost that kills flower buds, was first recorded in a Beaumont and Fletcher play of 1606–1607.

no ◆ In addition to the idioms beginning with NO, also see ALL TALK (AND NO ACTION); ALL WORK AND NO PLAY; BY NO MEANS; CLOSE BUT NO CIGAR; COME TO AN END (TO NO GOOD); CUT NO ICE; DO ANY (NO) GOOD; FEEL NO PAIN; HELL HAS NO FURY; HOLD NO BRIEF FOR; IN NO CASE; IN NO TIME; IN NO UNCERTAIN TERMS; LEAVE NO STONE UNTURNED; LESS THAN (NO TIME); LONG TIME NO SEE; LOSE (NO) TIME; MAKE NO BONES ABOUT; MAKE NO DIFFERENCE; MAKE NO MISTAKE; MONEY IS NO OBJECT; NONE OF ONE'S (HAVE NO) BUSINESS; POINT OF NO RETURN; PULL NO PUNCHES; ROLLING STONE GATHERS NO MOSS; SHADOW OF A DOUBT, NO; TAKE NO FOR AN ANSWER; THERE'S NO TELLING; TO LITTLE (NO) PURPOSE; TO NO AVAIL; UNDER ANY (NO) CIRCUMSTANCES; UP TO NO GOOD; YES AND NO.

no accounting for tastes, there's Individual likes and dislikes defy explanation, as in *They painted their house purple—there's really no accounting for tastes.* This expression, first put as *no disputing about tastes*, dates from the mid-1600s; the present wording was first recorded in 1794. A mid-20th-century synonym that originated in the American South is **different strokes for different folks.** For a far older synonym, see ONE MAN'S MEAT.

nobody ◆ In addition to the idioms beginning with NOBODY, also see LIKE CRAZY (NOBODY'S BUSINESS).

nobody home 1. No one is paying attention, as in *She threw the ball right past him, yelling "Nobody home!"* **2.** The person being discussed is mentally impaired and so cannot understand, as in *When the woman did not answer, he concluded it was a case of nobody home.* Both usages transfer the absence of someone in a dwelling to absent-mindedness or mental deficiency, and are thought to have been invented by cartoonist and journalist Thomas Aloysius Dorgan ("TAD") around 1900. He often embellished his column with such punning amplifications as "Nobody home but the telephone and that's in the hands of the receiver," or "Nobody home but the oyster and that's in the stew."

nobody's fool A person who cannot be duped or taken advantage of, as in *You can't put anything over on Ryan—he's nobody's fool.* [Early 1900s]

no buts ‣ See NO IFS OR BUTS.

no call for Also, **no call to.** No requirement or reason for doing something, as in *There was no call for your condescending suggestions; she knew quite well what to do.* This idiom, first recorded in 1779, uses *call* in the sense of "duty" or "need." The variant is always used with a verb, as in *There was no call to get the police involved because it's a simple dispute between neighbors.*

no can do It's impossible; I can't do this. For example, *When Bill asked me to write a speech, I told him bluntly no can do.* This colloquial phrase was first recorded in 1914.

nod ‣ In addition to the idiom beginning with NOD, also see GET THE NOD.

nodding acquaintance Superficial knowledge of someone or something, as in *I have a nodding acquaintance with the company president,* or *She has a nodding acquaintance with that software program.* This expression alludes to knowing someone just well enough to nod or bow upon meeting him or her. [Early 1800s]

no dice Also, **no go; no soap.** No, certainly not; also, impossible. For example, *Anthony wanted to borrow my new coat, but Mom said no dice,* or *We tried to rent the church for the wedding, but it's no go for the date you picked,* or *Jim asked Dad to help pay for the repairs, but Dad said no soap.* All of these slangy expressions indicate refusal or an unsuccessful attempt. *No dice,* from the 1920s, alludes to an unlucky throw in gambling; *no go,* alluding to lack of progress, dates from about 1820; and **no soap** dates from about 1920 and possibly alludes to the phrase **it won't wash,** meaning "it won't find acceptance." Also see NOTHING DOING; WON'T WASH.

nod off Fall asleep momentarily, doze, as in *Grandma spends a lot of time in her rocking chair, nodding off now and then.* This expression alludes to the quick involuntary dropping of one's head from an upright position when drowsy or napping. The verb *nod* alone was so used from the mid-1500s. Also see DROP OFF, def. 1.

no doubt 1. Probably, most likely, as in *No doubt you've heard the news about Mother.* [Early 1300s] **2.** Also, **without doubt** or **a doubt.** Certainly, without question, as in *He's guilty, no doubt, but he doesn't deserve such a long sentence,* or *That basketball player is without doubt the tallest man I've ever seen.* [Early 1300s] Also see BEYOND A DOUBT.

no end 1. A large number, a great deal, as in *He made no end of campaign promises.* This expression sometimes is put as **no end to** or **no end of,** meaning "no limit to" or "an incalculable amount of," as in *There is no end to the junk mail we get,* or *There are no end of books in this house.* [c. 1600] **2.** Immensely, exceedingly, as in *This situation puzzles us no end.* [c. 1900]

no flies on one One is wide awake; there is nothing slow or dull about one. For example, *She may be new to this field, but there are no flies on her.* This slangy expression, which alludes to flies settling on a sluggish animal, was being used in Australia in the 1840s but did not appear in America until the last decades of the 1800s.

no fool like an old fool, there's An old fool is the worst kind of fool, as in *He's marrying a woman fifty years his junior—there's no fool like an old fool.* This adage, now considered somewhat offensive for stereotyping old people, appeared in John Heywood's 1546 proverb collection and has been repeated ever since.

no go ‣ See NO DICE.

no good Unsatisfactory, inadequate; also, no use. For example, *This work is no good; it'll have to be done over;* or *It's no good complaining since there's nothing we can do,* or *I tried to appeal to his sense of generosity, but it did no good.* [Mid-1800s] Also see COME TO AN END (TO NO GOOD), def. 2; DO ANY (NO) GOOD.

no great shakes Nothing out of the ordinary, mediocre, as in *I'm afraid the new pitcher is no great shakes,* or *What I did with this decorating project was no great shakes.* This term possibly alludes to the shaking of dice, which most often yields a mediocre result, but there is no evidence to support this theory. [Early 1800s]

no hard feelings No resentment or anger, as in *I hope there are no hard feelings about excluding your group.* This idiom uses *hard* in the sense of "severe" or "harsh," a usage dating from about A.D. 1000.

no holds barred Without any restrictions, as in *Telephone companies are entering the market for*

Internet users with no holds barred. This expression comes from wrestling, where certain holds are illegal, or *barred,* and has been used figuratively since about 1940.

no ifs or buts Also, **no ifs, ands, or buts.** No reservations, restrictions, or excuses, as in *You'd better be there tomorrow, and no ifs, ands, or buts about it.* This expression uses the conjunctions to stand for the conditions and objections that they introduce. The earliest phrase to appear was *ifs and ands* in the 1600s. This phrase is actually an emphatic redundancy, for *and* often meant "if." *But* was tacked on to this pair soon afterward.

no joke Also, **no laughing matter.** A serious issue, as in *Missing the last flight out was no joke,* or *This outbreak of flu is no laughing matter.* The first term dates from about 1800, and the variant from the second half of the 1500s.

no kidding Truly, seriously, as in *No kidding, I really did lose my wallet.* [Colloquial; first half of 1900s]

no longer Not any more, as in *They no longer make this model of blender.* [c. 1300]

no love lost Dislike, ill will, hate, as in *There's no love lost between Bob and Bill.* This term originated in the 1500s and until about 1800 could indicate either extreme love or extreme hate. The former was meant in "No love between these two was lost, each was to the other kind" (*Reliques of Ancient English Poetry,* 1765). Today, however, the term signifies ill will exclusively.

no man is an island Human beings necessarily depend on one another, as in *You can't manage this all by yourself; no man is an island.* This expression is a quotation from John Donne's *Devotions* (1624): "No man is an Island, entire of it self; every man is a piece of the Continent, a part of the main."

no matter 1. It's not important, as in *She wasn't home when I came by, but no matter.* [Mid-1500s] 2. Also, **no matter what.** Regardless, it makes no difference, as in *No matter what I say, she'll do what she likes,* or *The car must be repaired, no matter what.* [Mid-1500s]

no matter how you slice it Regardless of how one views something, as in *No matter how you slice it, he's still guilty of perjury.* This expression uses *slice* in the sense of "cut apart." [Colloquial; first half of 1900s]

none ♦ In addition to the idioms beginning with NONE, also see ALL (NONE) OF THE ABOVE; BAR NONE; NOT HAVE IT; (HAVE NONE OF); SECOND TO NONE.

none of one's business Not one's concern, as in *How much I earn is none of your business.* This expression employs *business* in the sense of "one's affairs," a usage dating from about 1600. (Also see MIND ONE'S OWN BUSINESS.) A slangy, jocular variant from about 1930 is **none of one's beeswax.** The related verb phrase **have no business** is used to indicate that one should not meddle or interfere, as in *He has no business discussing the will with outsiders.*

none of the above ♦ See under ALL OF THE ABOVE.

none other than That very person or thing, the same as. For example, *In the elevator I ran into none other than the woman we'd been talking about,* or *It turned out to be none other than Jim in a clown costume.* [Late 1800s]

none the wiser Knowing no more than before, as in *He tried to explain the tax structure, but in the end I was none the wiser.* [Early 1800s]

none the worse for 1. Not harmed from, as in *He was none the worse for walking the entire ten miles,* or *This carpet may be old, but it's none the worse for wear.* [Early 1800s] 2. Be improved by, as in *The dog would be none the worse for a good brushing.* [Early 1800s]

none too Also, **not too.** Not very, as in *The application arrived none too soon,* or *I'm afraid this secretary is not too smart,* or *He was here not too long ago.* The first usage was first recorded in 1885; the variant dates from about 1920. Also see NOT ALL THAT.

no news is good news Having no information means that bad developments are unlikely, as in *I haven't heard from them in a month, but no news is good news.* This proverbial phrase may have originated with King James I of England, who allegedly said "No news is better than evil news" (1616).

nonsense ♦ See STUFF AND NONSENSE.

no offense Please don't feel insulted, I don't mean to offend you, as in *No offense, but I think you're mistaken.* This expression, first recorded in 1829, generally accompanies a statement that could be regarded as insulting but is not meant to be, as in the example.

nook and cranny, every Everywhere, as in *I've searched for it in every nook and cranny, and I still can't find it.* This metaphoric idiom pairs *nook,* which has meant "an out-of-the-way corner" since the mid-1300s, with *cranny,* which has meant "a crack or crevice" since about 1440. Neither noun is heard much other than in this idiom.

no pain, no gain Suffering is needed to make progress, as in *I've worked for hours on those irregular French verbs, but no pain, no gain.* Although this idiom is often associated with athletic coaches who urge athletes to train harder, it dates from the 1500s and was already in John Ray's proverb collection of 1670 as "Without pains, no gains."

no picnic Difficult, no fun, as in *Recovering from abdominal surgery is no picnic.* This expression, alluding to a picnic as a pleasant occasion, was first recorded in 1888.

no problem 1. Also, **no sweat; not to worry.** There's no difficulty about this, don't concern yourself. For example, *Of course I can change your tire—no problem,* or *You want more small change? no sweat,* or *We'll be there in plenty of time, not to worry.* The first of these colloquial terms dates from about 1960 and the second from about 1950. The third, originating in Britain in the 1930s and using *not to* with the sense of "don't," crossed the Atlantic in the 1970s. **2.** You're welcome, as in *Thanks for the ride, Dad.—No problem.* [Late 1900s]

nor ‣ See HIDE NOR HAIR; NEITHER FISH NOR FOWL; NEITHER HERE NOR THERE; RHYME OR REASON (NEITHER RHYME NOR REASON).

nose ‣ In addition to the idioms beginning with NOSE, also see BROWN NOSE; CAN'T SEE BEYOND THE END OF ONE'S NOSE; COUNT NOSES; CUT OFF ONE'S NOSE; FOLLOW ONE'S NOSE; KEEP ONE'S NOSE CLEAN; LEAD BY THE NOSE; LOOK DOWN ON (ONE'S NOSE); NO SKIN OFF MY NOSE; ON THE NOSE; PAY THROUGH THE NOSE; PLAIN AS DAY (THE NOSE ON YOUR FACE); POKE ONE'S NOSE INTO; RUB SOMEONE'S NOSE IN IT; THUMB ONE'S NOSE; TURN UP ONE'S NOSE; UNDER ONE'S NOSE; WIN BY A NOSE.

nose about Also, **nose around.** Look for something, especially something private or hidden. For example, *She was always nosing about the kitchen, looking in all the cupboards,* or *The detective nosed around the apartment.* [Second half of 1800s]

nose in Also, **nose into. 1.** Advance cautiously, front end first, as in *We nosed the boat into her berth,* or *The car nosed in very slowly.* [Mid-1900s] **2.** Pry, snoop, as in *He was nosing into our finances again.* [First half of 1900s] Also see NOSE ABOUT; POKE ONE'S NOSE INTO.

nose in a book, have one's Be constantly reading, as in *Walter is known for having his nose in a book.* This expression graphically depicts immersing oneself in reading. [Mid-1900s]

nose in the air, have one's Be haughty or disdainful, as in *Ever since we moved in, our next-door neighbor has had her nose in the air.* The related phrase **with one's nose in the air** means "haughtily," as in *She thinks she's so smart; she's always walking around with her nose in the air.* Also see TURN UP ONE'S NOSE AT.

nose into ‣ See NOSE IN.

nose out 1. Defeat by a narrow margin, as in *She barely nosed out the incumbent.* This expression, alluding to a horse's winning with its nose in front, has been used figuratively since the mid-1900s. **2.** Discover, especially something hidden

or secret, as in *This reporter has a knack for nosing out the truth.* This usage alludes to following the scent of something. [Early 1600s]

nose out of joint, have one's Be upset or irritated, especially when displaced by someone. For example, *Ever since Sheila got promoted he's had his nose out of joint.* Similarly, **put one's nose out of joint** indicates the cause of the upset, as in *The boss's praise of her assistant put Jean's nose out of joint.* The earliest form of this idiom, first recorded in 1581, was **thrust one's nose out of joint,** with *put* appearing shortly thereafter. Presumably all these expressions allude to the face-distorting grimace made by one who is displeased.

nose to the grindstone, keep one's Stay hard at work, as in *We expect John to get good grades again, since he really keeps his nose to the grindstone.* This expression, first recorded in 1539, alludes to a tool that must be sharpened by being held to a grindstone.

no shit Really, do you mean it, as in *You took her to a prizefight? No shit!* This vulgar slangy interjection is used to express surprise, disbelief, or scornful acknowledgment of the obvious.

no sir Also, **no sirree.** Certainly not. This emphatic denial is used without regard to the gender of the person addressed. For example, *No sir, I'm not taking her up on that,* or *Live here? No sirree.* [Mid-1800s]

no skin off one's nose Not harmful or bothersome to one, as in *I don't care if you stay home—it's no skin off my nose.* This expression probably arose in boxing, but there is no evidence to prove it. [Early 1900s]

no smoke without fire, there's Also, **where there's smoke there's fire.** A suspicion or rumor usually has a basis in fact, as in *When the sales figures continued strong but the company still wasn't making money, he suspected something was wrong—there's no smoke without fire.* First stated in the late 1300s, this expression appeared in numerous proverb collections from 1546 on and remains current today.

no soap ‣ See under NO DICE.

no sooner said than done Accomplished immediately, as in *He said we should leave and, no sooner said than done.* This expression employs *no sooner . . . than* in the sense of "at once," a usage dating from the mid-1500s.

no spring chicken No longer a young person, as in *Sally's no spring chicken, but she plays a fine game of tennis.* This unflattering expression, often applied to women, has been used since the early 1700s, although *spring* was omitted from the earliest citation (1711).

no stomach for, have Dislike, be unable to tolerate, as in *Pat has no stomach for violent movies.* This expression uses *stomach* in the sense of "appetite" or "relish for." [Early 1700s]

no strings attached Without conditions or restrictions, as in *They give each of the children $10,000 a year with no strings attached.* This expression dates from the mid-1900s, although *string* in the sense of "a limitation" has been used since the late 1800s.

no such thing 1. Nothing like that, nothing of the kind, as in *We've been looking for a car without air-conditioning, but no such thing is available.* [Mid-1500s] 2. On the contrary, certainly not, as in *You thought I was quitting? No such thing!* [Mid-1700s]

no sweat ♦ See under NO PROBLEM.

not ♦ In addition to the idioms beginning with NOT, also see ALL THAT GLITTERS IS NOT GOLD; (NOT) ALL THERE; (NOT) AT ALL; BELIEVE IT OR NOT; CAUGHT DEAD, NOT BE; (NOT A) CHINAMAN'S CHANCE; COMING OR GOING, NOT KNOW IF; DO AS I SAY (NOT AS I DO); GAME IS NOT WORTH THE CANDLE; HEART (NOT) IN IT; HOLD ONE'S BREATH, NOT; (NOT) IN THE LEAST; (NOT) IN THE MOOD; IT'S (NOT) YOUR FUNERAL; LAST BUT NOT LEAST; LIKE AS NOT; LIVING SOUL, NOT A; MINCE MATTERS, NOT TO; MORE OFTEN THAN NOT; (NOT) MOVE A MUSCLE; NO PROBLEM (NOT TO WORRY); (NOT TO) SNEEZE AT; (NOT) TAKE NO FOR AN ANSWER; (NOT) THE HALF OF IT; (NOT) TURN A HAIR; TWO WRONGS DO NOT MAKE A RIGHT; WASTE NOT, WANT NOT; WHETHER OR NOT; WITHOUT A (NOT A) LEG TO STAND ON; WON'T (WILL NOT) HEAR OF. For verbal phrases also see under CAN'T; COULDN'T; WOULDN'T.

not a bad sort ♦ See BAD SORT.

not a bit Not at all, not in the least, as in *She was not a bit interested.* [Mid-1700s]

not able ♦ See under CAN'T or under main phrase.

not about to ♦ See ABOUT TO, def. 2.

not a Chinaman's chance Also, **not a ghost of a chance.** ♦ See under CHINAMAN'S CHANCE.

not a hope in hell Also, **not a prayer.** No chance at all, as in *There's not a hope in hell that we have a winning bid,* or *If you don't watch the conductor you won't have a prayer of coming in on time.* The first term was first recorded in 1923, the second in 1941. Both allude to the chance for heavenly salvation. Also see SNOWBALL'S CHANCE IN HELL.

not a leg to stand on ♦ See WITHOUT A LEG TO STAND ON.

not a living soul ♦ See LIVING SOUL.

not all it's cracked up to be It is disappointing, it does not live up to its reputation, as in *The restaurant wasn't all it's cracked up to be.* This term uses *crack up* in the sense of "to praise," which

survives only in this expression. [Colloquial; early 1800s]

not all that ♦ See ALL THAT, def. 1.

not all there ♦ See ALL THERE.

not anything like Also, **nothing like; not anywhere near; nowhere near.** Quite different from, far from; also, not nearly. For example, *The town's library isn't anything like the university's library,* or *His outfit was nothing like his brother's,* or *It isn't anything like as cold as it was last winter,* or *That movie isn't anywhere near as exciting as I thought it would be,* or *Her diamond is nowhere near as big as mine.* The phrases with *like* date from the late 1700s, and those with *near* from the mid-1400s.

not at all ♦ See AT ALL, def. 4.

not bad Also, **not half bad; not so** or **too bad; not too shabby.** Fairly good, as in *Not bad, said the conductor, but we need to play the scherzo again,* or *The movie wasn't half bad, but Jerry wanted to go home,* or *Our garden's not too bad this year,* or *How are things going?—Not too shabby.* All of the terms involving *bad,* which imply that something is less bad than it might be, date from the mid-1700s. The last variant, using *shabby* in the sense of "inferior," is slang of the late 1900s.

not bat an eye ♦ See BAT AN EYE.

not be caught dead ♦ See CAUGHT DEAD.

not born yesterday More experienced and less naive than one appears to be, as in *Don't think you can fool me; I wasn't born yesterday.* This term gained currency from the title of Garson Kanin's popular Broadway play, *Born Yesterday,* which was made into an even more popular film. In both, Judy Holliday played a stereotypical dumb blonde who shows more common sense than her sophisticated acquaintances. [Early 1800s]

not breathe a word Not reveal a secret, keep concealed, as in *You must promise not to breathe a word of what I'm about to tell you.* This phrase relies on the verb *breathe* as meaning "to utter," a usage dating from the late 1500s.

not built that way Not so disposed or inclined, as in *I can't apologize for something I didn't do—I'm just not built that way.* [Late 1800s]

not by a long shot ♦ See LONG SHOT.

not by any means ♦ See BY NO MEANS.

notch ♦ See TAKE DOWN A NOTCH.

not cricket Unfair, unsportsmanlike, as in *It's not cricket to let him go without notice.* This term, in which the sport of cricket is equated with upright behavior, survives in America despite the relative unfamiliarity of the sport there. [Mid-1800s]

not done Socially unacceptable, improper, as in *Bringing along two friends without asking, that's not done.* [First half of 1900s]

note ◆ See BREAD AND BUTTER LETTER (NOTE); COMPARE NOTES; MAKE A NOTE OF; OF NOTE; STRIKE THE RIGHT NOTE; TAKE NOTE; TAKE NOTES.

no telling ◆ See THERE'S NO TELLING.

not enough room to swing a cat Very little space, cramped quarters, as in *There's not enough room to swing a cat in this tent.* This expression, first recorded in 1771, is thought to allude to the cat-o'-nine-tails, or "cat," a whip with nine lashes widely used to punish offenders in the British military.

not feel oneself ◆ See NOT ONESELF.

not for all the tea in China Not at any price, never, as in *I wouldn't give up my car, not for all the tea in China.* This term originated in Australia and alludes to the presumed huge quantity of tea in China. [Late 1800s] Also see FOR ALL THE WORLD; NOT FOR LOVE OR MONEY.

not for a moment Never, not in the least, as in *Not for a moment did I believe he was telling the truth.* This expression employs *moment* in the sense of "the tiniest length of time," a usage dating from the mid-1300s.

not for love or money Never, under no circumstances, as in *I'd never visit them again, not for love or money.* A version of this expression, which alludes to these two powerful persuasive forces, was recorded in A.D. 971.

not give a damn Also, **not give a fig** or **hang** or **hoot** or **rap** or **shit.** Not care about, be indifferent to, as in *I don't give a damn about him,* or *She doesn't give a fig if he comes or not.* The nouns in all these terms signify something totally worthless. Although probably in oral use for much longer, *damn* is first recorded in this negative form in the late 1700s and the worthless item it is used to denigrate is a curse. *Fig* has denoted something small and worthless since about 1400, and *hang* since the mid-1800s; *hoot* has been used for the smallest particle since the later 1800s; *rap,* also for the smallest particle, since the first half of the 1800s, and *shit,* for excrement, since about 1920. All but the first of these terms are colloquial and the last (using *shit*) is vulgar.

not give someone the time of day Ignore someone, refuse to pay the slightest attention to someone, as in *He's tried to be friendly but she won't give him the time of day.* This expression, first recorded in 1864, alludes to refusing even to answer the question, "What time is it?"

not half bad ◆ See NOT BAD.

no thanks to ◆ See THANKS TO.

not have a bean Be destitute or penniless, as in *He doesn't have a bean, but she's set on marrying him. Bean* has been a slang term for a guinea or a sovereign coin since the early 1800s. The precise expression was first recorded in 1928.

not have a clue ◆ Have no idea or inkling about something, as in *Jane doesn't have a clue as to why John won't call her,* or *Do you know what's wrong with the boiler?—No, I haven't a clue.* This usage was first recorded in 1928.

not have an earthly chance Also, **stand no earthly chance.** Have no chance whatever, as in *She doesn't have an earthly chance of getting into medical school,* or *Bill stands no earthly chance of winning the lottery.* The use of *no earthly* in the sense of "no conceivable" dates from the mid-1700s.

not have anything on ◆ See HAVE NOTHING ON.

not have it Also, **have none of; not** or **won't** or **wouldn't hear of.** Not allow; refuse to tolerate, accept, or endure. For example, *Mary wanted to have the reception at home, but her mother would not have it,* or *I'll have none of your backtalk,* or *The minister wouldn't hear of a change in the worship service.* [Late 1500s] The related **not having any,** for wanting no part of (as in *Fund-raising? I'm not having any!*) was first recorded in 1902.

not have one's heart in it see under HEART IN IT.

not have the heart to Be unable to bring oneself to say or do something, as in *He didn't have the heart to tell her the cat had died.* [Mid-1600s] Also see HAVE A HEART.

not having any ◆ See under NOT HAVE IT.

nothing ◆ In addition to the idioms beginning with NOTHING, also see COME TO NOTHING; COUNT FOR (NOTHING); GO FOR NOTHING; HAVE NOTHING ON; HAVE NOTHING TO DO WITH; HERE GOES (NOTHING); IN NO TIME (NOTHING FLAT); LEAVE A LOT (NOTHING) TO BE DESIRED; MAKE NOTHING OF; MAKE SOMETHING OF (NOTHING); MUCH ADO ABOUT NOTHING; NOT KNOW BEANS (FROM NOTHING); NOT TO MENTION (SAY NOTHING OF); STOP AT NOTHING; SWEET NOTHINGS; THINK NOTHING OF; WANT FOR NOTHING.

nothing but Only, as in *She thinks of nothing but money.* This term was first recorded about 1380.

nothing doing Certainly not, as in *Can I borrow your down coat?—Nothing doing.* This colloquial interjection was first recorded in 1910. Also see, NO DICE.

nothing if not Above all else, as in *He was nothing if not discreet.* Shakespeare used this idiom in *Othello* (2:1): "I am nothing if not critical." [c. 1600]

nothing like ◆ See NOT ANYTHING LIKE.

nothing new under the sun Everything has been seen before, as in *Those designs take me back to the 1950s—there really is nothing new under the sun.* This world-weary view was already expressed in 1382 in the Bible translation attributed to John Wycliffe's followers: "No thing under the sun is new" (Ecclesiastes 1:9).

nothing of the kind Also, **nothing of the sort. 1.** No, certainly not, as in *Did you push Charlie?—*

Nothing of the kind! or *Do you think the kids were trying to shoplift?—Nothing of the sort.* [Second half of 1800s] 2. Not at all like what is mentioned or expected, as in *They thought we would look them up, but we'd intended nothing of the kind.* [Second half of 1800s]

nothing short of The equivalent of, the same as, as in *His accusation is nothing short of slander.* This term is slightly stronger than **little short of,** meaning "almost the same as," as in *Her claim is little short of stupid.* The first term dates from about 1800, the second from about 1830. Also see SHORT OF.

nothing to do with ♦ See HAVE NOTHING TO DO WITH.

nothing to it, there's It's not at all difficult, it's easy, as in *Of course I can fix the faucet—there's nothing to it.* This hyperbolic term was first recorded in 1934.

nothing to sneeze at ♦ See NOT TO BE SNEEZED AT.

nothing to speak of Not much, nothing worth mentioning, as in *What's been happening in the stock market?—Nothing to speak of,* or *They've done nothing to speak of about publicity.* This expression was first recorded in 1582.

nothing to write home about Ordinary or unremarkable, as in *The restaurant was all right but nothing to write home about.* This idiom originated in the late 1800s, possibly among troops stationed far from home, and became widespread during World War I.

nothing ventured, nothing gained One must take risks to achieve something, as in *They quit their jobs, packed up, and moved to Wisconsin, saying "nothing ventured, nothing gained."* Although this adage has appeared in slightly different form since the late 1300s, it was first recorded in this form only in 1624. For another version, see NO PAIN, NO GAIN.

not hurt a fly Also, **not hurt a flea.** Not cause harm to anyone, be gentle and mild, as in *Paul's the kindest man—he wouldn't hurt a flea,* or *Bert has a temper but it's all talk; he wouldn't hurt a fly.* Both *fly* and *flea* are used in the sense of "a small insignificant animal." [Early 1800s]

notice ♦ See ESCAPE NOTICE; GIVE NOTICE; SHORT NOTICE; SIT UP AND TAKE NOTICE; TAKE NOTE (NOTICE).

not if one can help it Only without one's agreement, only if one cannot prevent it. For example, *Is he taking a second job?—Not if his wife can help it,* or *He's not riding on the back of that motorcycle, not if I can help it.* This idiom uses *help* in the sense of "prevent" or "cause to be otherwise." [Mid-1800s]

not if you paid me Under no circumstances, as in *I wouldn't jump off the high diving board, not if you paid me.* [Late 1800s]

no time at all ♦ See IN NO TIME.

no time for, have Can't be bothered with, dislike, as in *Dad has no time for her temper tantrums.* This expression alludes to unwillingness to spend time with someone or something.

no time like the present, there's Do or say it now, as in *Go ahead and call him—there's no time like the present.* This adage was first recorded in 1562. One compiler of proverbs, John Trusler, amplified it: "No time like the present, a thousand unforeseen circumstances may interrupt you at a future time" (*Proverbs Exemplified,* 1790).

not in the least ♦ See IN THE LEAST.

not know beans Also, **not know the first thing; not know from nothing.** Be ignorant about something, as in a poem published in the *Yale Literary Magazine* in 1855: "When our recent Tutor is heard to speak, This truth one certainly gleans, Whatever he knows of Euclid and Greek, In Latin he don't know beans." The *beans* in this colloquial phrase, dating from the early 1800s, signify something small and worthless; not knowing *the first thing* about something clearly shows one doesn't know anything about it at all; and the third slangy phrase, with its double negative, implies stupidity as well as ignorance, as in *Poor girl, just starting out and she doesn't know from nothing.*

not know enough to come in in out of the rain ♦ See COME IN OUT OF THE RAIN.

not know someone from Adam Be unable to recognize someone, as in *Although I have worked here for two months, I've never seen the department head; I wouldn't know her from Adam.* This term refers to the biblical story about the world's first human being. As at least one writer has pointed out, differentiating someone from Adam makes little sense since he had no name and wore only a fig leaf. [Mid-1800s]

not know where to turn Also, **not know which way to jump** or **turn.** Have no idea of how to get help or what course to take. For example, *With all these offers coming in, he didn't know where to turn,* or *When her car was towed, Meg was distraught and did not know which way to jump.* The first phrase dates from about 1400.

not know whether one is coming or going ♦ See under COMING OR GOING.

not let the grass grow under one's feet ♦ See DON'T LET THE GRASS GROW.

not lift a finger Refuse to exert oneself to help or perform an action. For example, *Dad won't lift a finger to help them financially,* or *Early in the war, America officially would not lift a finger.* [Mid-1900s]

not miss a trick Also, **never miss a trick; not miss much.** Not fail to be aware of what is going on. For example, *When it comes to the commodities market,*

Mark never misses a trick, or *Dad may seem absentminded, but he doesn't miss much.* The first phrase dates from the early 1900s; the variant employs *miss* in the sense of "fail to perceive," a usage dating from the late 1600s.

not move a muscle ♦ See MOVE A MUSCLE

not my cup of tea ♦ See CUP OF TEA.

not one iota Not even the smallest amount, as in *He got not one iota of thanks for his efforts.* This usage appeared in slightly different form in the New Testament (Matthew 5:18): "One jot [iota] . . . shall in no wise pass from the law till all be fulfilled." (The noun *jot* comes from the Greek *iota*.)

not one's day, this is Also, **just one of those days.** Nothing is going right for one today. For example, *The car wouldn't start, it rained unexpectedly—this is not my day,* or *The phone has rung nonstop all morning; it's just one of those days.* [c. 1920]

not oneself Not feeling physically or mentally well, as in *I think there's something wrong; he's not himself,* or *She seemed to be improving last week, but she's just not feeling herself today.* Also see FEEL LIKE ONESELF.

not on your life Certainly not, as in *Go hanggliding? Not on your life.* The first recorded use of this interjection was in 1896.

not open one's mouth Also, **shut one's mouth; not say** or **utter a word.** Be silent, repress one's feelings or opinions, keep a secret. For example, *Don't worry, I'm not going to open my mouth on this issue,* or *She promised not to say a word about it to anyone.* Also see HOLD ONE'S TONGUE; KEEP ONE'S MOUTH SHUT.

not put something past someone Consider someone capable of doing something, especially something bad. For example, *I wouldn't put it past him to tell a lie or two.* This expression uses *past* in the sense of "beyond." [Late 1800s]

not right in the head Mentally unsound, as in *Physically, she's quite healthy for ninety, but we suspect she's not right in the head.* This usage was first recorded as *right in his wits* in 1662.

not see beyond one's nose ♦ See CAN'T SEE BEYOND THE END OF ONE'S NOSE.

not suffer fools gladly Refuse to tolerate stupidity, as in *Chris can be intimidating at these meetings; she does not suffer fools gladly.* This expression comes from the New Testament (II Corinthians 11:19), where Paul sarcastically says, "For ye suffer fools gladly, seeing ye yourselves are wise." [c. 1600]

not take no for answer ♦ See TAKE NO FOR AN ANSWER.

not the half of it ♦ See HALF OF IT.

not the only fish in the sea Also, **lots** or **plenty of good fish in the sea; not the only pebble on the beach.** Plenty of other suitable persons, especially for a romantic relationship. For example, *When Bob walked out on Sally, all we could tell her was that he was not the only fish in the sea,* or *Bill knew she wasn't the only pebble on the beach but he was determined to win her over.* Both *fish* and *pebble* here refer to something available in large quantities. The expressions using *fish* have been used to comfort jilted lovers since the early 1500s. The variant using *pebble* was first recorded in a poem of 1896 by Henry Braistead: "If you want to win her hand Let the maiden understand That she's not the only pebble on the beach."

not think much of Have little regard for, have a low opinion of, as in *Bill doesn't think much of the carpentry work in that house.* The phrase *not much* has been used in this sense since the mid-1800s.

not to be sneezed at Also, **nothing to sneeze at.** Not to be ignored or dismissed, as in *It's a great honor, not to be sneezed at,* or *That salary of his is nothing to sneeze at.* This expression presumably alludes to turning up one's nose in disdain. [c. 1800]

not to mention Also, **not to speak of; to say nothing of.** In addition to, besides what's already been said. For example, *I don't think the voters will want that big program, not to mention the cost,* or *Dave teaches trumpet and trombone, not to speak of other brass instruments,* or *Their house is worth at least a million, to say nothing of their other assets.*

not touch with a ten-foot pole Stay far away from, avoid completely, as in *Ronald wouldn't touch raw oysters with a ten-foot pole.* This expression dates from the mid-1700s, when it began to replace the earlier *not to be handled with a pair of tongs.* In the 1800s *barge-pole* was sometimes substituted for *ten-foot pole,* but that variant has died out.

not to worry ♦ See NO PROBLEM.

not turn a hair ♦ See TURN A HAIR.

not up to ♦ See UP TO.

not worth a damn Also, **not worth a plugged nickel** or **red cent** or **bean** or **hill of beans** or **fig** or **straw** or **tinker's damn.** Worthless, as in *That car isn't worth a damn,* or *My new tennis racket is not worth a plugged nickel.* As for the nouns here, a *damn* or curse is clearly of no great value (also see NOT GIVE A DAMN); a *plugged nickel* in the 1800s referred to a debased five-cent coin; a *cent* denotes the smallest American coin, which was *red* when made of pure copper (1800s); a *bean* has been considered trivial or worthless since the late 1300s (Chaucer so used it), whereas *hill of beans* alludes to a planting method whereby four or five beans are put in a mound (and still are worthless); and both *fig* and *straw* have been items of no worth since about 1400. A *tinker's dam,* first recorded in 1877, was a wall of dough raised around a spot where a metal pipe is being repaired so as to hold solder in place until it hardens, whereupon the dam is discarded. However, *tinker's damn* was first recorded in 1839 and probably was merely an intensification of "not worth a damn," rather than having anything to do with the *dam.*

no two ways about it No room for difference of opinion, no alternative, as in *We have to agree on the nomination, and no two ways about it.* [Early 1800s]

no use, it's 1. It's impossible; it can't succeed. For example, *It's no use; these pieces just don't fit.* [c. 1800] **2.** Also, **it's no use to man or beast.** It's worthless, it serves no purpose, as in *This car is so old it's no use to man or beast.* Also see HAVE NO USE FOR.

no use crying over spilt milk ♦ See CRY OVER SPILT MILK.

now ♦ In addition to the idioms beginning with now, also see ANY DAY (NOW); EVERY NOW AND THEN; HERE AND NOW; JUST NOW.

now and again Also, **now and then.** ♦ See EVERY NOW AND THEN.

no way Also, **there is no way.** Certainly not; never. For example, *No way can I forget what he did,* or *Are you coming along?—No way!* or *There's no way our candidate can lose.* This colloquial expression dates from the mid-1900s, but an earlier adverb, *noway,* dates from the 1300s.

nowhere ♦ In addition to the idiom beginning with NOWHERE, also see GET NOWHERE; IN THE MIDDLE (OF NOWHERE); OUT OF NOWHERE.

nowhere near ♦ See under NOT ANYTHING LIKE.

no-win situation A situation certain to end in failure or disappointment, as in *If the inlaws visit them or they visit the in-laws, either way they see it as a no-win situation.* [c. 1960]

no wonder Also, **small wonder.** It's not at all (or hardly) surprising, as in *With the goalie out with a sprained ankle, it's no wonder you lost the game,* or *If he finished off all of the turkey, small wonder he has a stomachache.* [c. A.D. 900]

now or never, it's It must be done now or not at all, as in *If you plan to state your case to the boss, it's now or never.* This phrase was first recorded in 1560.

now that Seeing that, since, as in *Now that you're here, you might as well stay for dinner.* This usage was first recorded in 1530. For a synonym, see AS LONG AS.

now you're talking Good for you, you're saying the right thing, as in *You've decided to enter the contest? Now you're talking!* [Mid-1800s]

nth ♦ See TO THE NTH DEGREE.

nuisance ♦ See MAKE A NUISANCE OF ONESELF.

null and void Canceled, invalid, as in *The lease is now null and void.* This phrase is actually redundant, since *null* means "void," that is, "ineffective." It was first recorded in 1669.

number ♦ In addition to the idiom beginning with NUMBER, also see A NUMBER OF; ANY NUMBER OF; BACK NUMBER; BY THE NUMBERS; CRUNCH NUMBERS; DAYS ARE NUMBERED; DO A JOB (NUMBER) ON; GET (HAVE) SOMEONE'S NUMBER; HOT NUMBER; IN ROUND NUMBERS; LOOK OUT FOR (NUMBER ONE); OPPOSITE NUMBER; SAFETY IN NUMBERS.

number is up, one's One is in grave difficulty or near death. For example, *She knew her number was up when she saw the look on her supervisor's face,* or *He looks terrible; I think his number's up.* In the earliest use of this phrase, in the early 1800s, *number* referred to an unfavorable lottery number, but in other citations it could be any number whereby one is identified, such as the number on a military dog tag.

nurse a drink Consume a drink slowly, especially in order to conserve it. For example, *He nursed one drink for the whole evening.* This idiom alludes to holding a glass very carefully, as one might a child. [c. 1940]

nurse a grudge Bear resentment for a long time, as in *We don't know why Karl looks so angry; I think he's nursing a grudge against the family.* This expression uses *nurse* in the sense of "foster a feeling," a usage dating from the mid-1700s.

nut ♦ In addition to the idioms beginning with NUTS, also see DRIVE SOMEONE CRAZY (NUTS); FROM SOUP TO NUTS; HARD NUT TO CRACK.

nuts about, be Be extremely enthusiastic; also, be extremely fond of. For example, *Ellen is nuts about opera,* or *Kevin has been nuts about Megan since he met her.* This seemingly new slangy expression began life in the late 1700s as *nuts on* or *upon; about* began to be substituted about 1940.

nuts and bolts, the The essential or basic aspects of something, as in *They have lofty goals but don't specify the nuts and bolts of how to achieve them.* This expression alludes to basic working components of machinery. [Mid-1900s]

nutshell ♦ See IN A NUTSHELL.

nutty as a fruitcake Crazy, idiotic, as in *Mary's nutty as a fruitcake if she thinks she can get away with that.* The adjective *nutty* meaning "insane" was first recorded in 1821; the similarity to *fruitcake,* which literally contains nuts as well as fruit, was first recorded in 1935.

O

oar ♦ See PUT ONE'S OAR IN.

oats ♦ See FEEL ONE'S OATS; SOW ONE'S WILD OATS.

object ♦ See MONEY IS NO OBJECT.

objection ♦ See RAISE AN OBJECTION.

occasion ♦ See ON OCCASION; RISE TO THE OCCASION.

occur to one Come to mind, as in *It never occurred to me that he might refuse.* [Early 1600s]

odd couple ♦ See under STRANGE BEDFELLOWS.

odd man out 1. A person who is left out of a group for some reason, as in *The invitation was for couples only, so Jane was odd man out.* [Mid-1800s] 2. Something or someone who differs markedly from the others in a group, as in *Among all those ranch-style houses, their Victorian was odd man out.* [Late 1800s]

odds ♦ In addition to the idioms beginning with ODDS, also see AGAINST ALL ODDS; AT ODDS; BY ALL ODDS; LAY ODDS.

odds and ends Miscellaneous items, fragments and remnants, as in *I've finished putting everything away, except for a few odds and ends.* This expression may have originated as *odd ends* in the mid-1500s, meaning "short leftovers of some material" (such as lumber or cloth). It had acquired its present form and meaning by the mid-1700s.

odds are, the The chances are, as in *The odds are that they'll serve turkey for Thanksgiving.* Replacing *it is odds* by the late 1600s, this phrase refers to betting.

odor of sanctity Exaggerated or hypocritical piety, an assumption of moral superiority, as in *This candidate puts off some voters with his odor of sanctity.* This expression, originating in the medieval idea that the dead body of a saintly individual gives off a sweet smell, was used to describe saintliness in the mid-1700s. Today it is generally used ironically.

of age 1. Old enough, according to the law, to be eligible for something, as in *In this state he's not of age for buying liquor, but he may vote,* or *Next year Jane's coming of age and will get her driver's license.* This usage was first recorded about 1430. The term **under age** signifies being too young to be eligible, as in *It's against the law to serve alcohol to anyone under age.* 2. **come of age.** Mature or develop fully, as in *The school's bilingual program has finally come of age.*

of a kind 1. Of some sort, but not a typical or perfect specimen. For example, *They have a backyard of a kind, but it's tiny.* This usage was first recorded in 1895. For a synonym, see OF SORTS. 2. **one of a**

kind. A unique instance, as in *There are no others like it; this hybrid daylily is one of a kind,* or *She's extremely generous, one of a kind.* Also see TWO OF A KIND.

of all things From all the possibilities, as in *I said I'd help in any way I can, and of all things they want me to handle publicity.* This term, generally expressing surprise, was first recorded in 1925.

of a piece Also, **all of a piece.** Of the same kind, as in *This legislation is of a piece with the previous bill,* or *Her rude behavior was all of a piece.* The *piece* in this idiom alludes to a single mass of material. [Early 1600s]

of a sort ♦ See OF SORTS.

of choice Preferred above others, as in *A strike is the union's weapon of choice.* Used with other prepositions (*by, for, with*), all meaning "by preference," this idiom dates from about 1300. Also see BY CHOICE.

of consequence Important, as in *For all matters of consequence we have to consult the board,* or *Only scientists of consequence have been invited to speak.* This idiom was first recorded in 1489.

of course 1. In the customary or expected order, naturally, as in *The new minister did not, of course, fire the church secretary.* This usage, first recorded in 1548, employs *course* in the sense of "ordinary procedure." 2. Certainly, as in *Of course I'll answer the phone,* or *Are you going to the meeting? — Of course.* [Early 1800s] Also see MATTER OF COURSE.

off ♦ In addition to the idioms beginning with OFF, also see BACK OFF; BAD OFF; BEAT OFF; BEAT THE PANTS OFF; BEG OFF; BE OFF; BETTER OFF; BITE OFF MORE THAN ONE CAN CHEW; BITE SOMEONE'S HEAD OFF; BLAST OFF; BLOW OFF; BLOW OFF STEAM; BLOW THE LID OFF; BORE TO DEATH (THE PANTS OFF); BRANCH OFF; BREAK OFF; BRING OFF; BROWNED OFF; BRUSH OFF; BUG OFF; BUMP OFF; BURN OFF; BUY OFF; BUZZ OFF; CALL OFF; CAP IT ALL (OFF); CARRY OFF; CART OFF; CAST OFF; CHANGE OFF; CHARGE OFF; CHECK OFF; CHEESED OFF; CHIP OFF THE OLD BLOCK; CHOKE OFF; CLEAR OUT (OFF); COME OFF; COME OFF IT; COOL DOWN (OFF); COOL OFF; COUNT OFF; CRY OFF; CUT OFF; CUT OFF ONE'S NOSE; DASH OFF; DAY OFF; DIE OFF; DOZE OFF; DROP OFF; DUST OFF; EASE OFF; EASY AS PIE (ROLLING OFF A LOG); FALL AWAY (OFF); FAT OF THE LAND, LIVE OFF THE; FIGHT OFF; FIRE OFF; FIRST OFF; FISH OR CUT BAIT (SHIT OR GET OFF); FLY OFF THE HANDLE; FOB OFF; FUCK OFF; GET OFF; GET OFF ON; GET OFF ONE'S TAIL; GET OFF THE DIME; GET OFF THE GROUND; GIVE OFF; GIVE THE SHIRT OFF ONE'S BACK; GO OFF; GO OFF THE DEEP END; GOOF OFF; HANDS OFF; HATS OFF TO; HAUL OFF; HAVE IT (OFF); HEAD OFF; HIGH OFF THE HOG; HIT IT OFF; HOLD OFF; HOT OFF THE PRESS; JERK OFF; JUMPING-OFF PLACE; KEEP OFF; KICK OFF; KILL OFF; KISS OFF;

KNOCK IT OFF; KNOCK OFF; KNOCK SOMEONE'S BLOCK OFF; KNOCK THE SOCKS OFF; LAUGH OFF; LAY OFF; LEAD OFF; LEAVE OFF; LET OFF; LEVEL OFF; LIFT OFF; LIKE A CHICKEN WITH ITS HEAD CUT OFF; LIKE WATER OFF A DUCK'S BACK; LOAD OFF ONE'S MIND; LOG IN (OFF); MAKE OFF; MOUTH OFF; NOD OFF; NO SKIN OFF ONE'S NOSE; ON (OFF) CAMERA; ON (OFF) DUTY; ON THE (OFF) CHANCE; PACK OFF; PAIR OFF; PALM OFF; PANTS OFF; PASS OFF; PAY OFF; PEEL OFF; PICK OFF; PISS OFF; PLAY OFF; POLISH OFF; PULL OFF; PUSH OFF; PUT OFF; PUT SOMEONE OFF; QUICK OFF THE MARK; RAKE OFF; RATTLE OFF; RIGHT AWAY (OFF); RIP OFF; ROUND OFF; RUB OFF; RUN AWAY (OFF); RUN OFF; RUN OFF AT THE MOUTH; RUN OFF WITH; RUSH OFF ONE'S FEET; SEAL OFF; SEE SOMEONE OFF; SELL OFF; SEND OFF; SET OFF; SHAKE OFF; SHOOT OFF ONE'S MOUTH; SHOW OFF; SHRUG OFF; SHIT OFF; SIGN OFF; SLACK OFF; SLEEP OFF; SLIP OUT (OFF); SOUND OFF; SPIN OFF; SPLIT ONE'S SIDES (LAUGH ONE'S HEAD OFF); SPONGE ON (OFF); SQUARE OFF; SQUEEZE OFF; STAND OFF; STAVE OFF; STOP OFF; STRAIGHT OFF; SWEAR OFF; SWITCH ON (OFF); TAIL OFF; TAKE OFF; TAKE OFF AFTER; TAKE THE EDGE OFF; TAKE UP WHERE ONE LEFT OFF; TALK SOMEONE'S ARM OFF; TAPER OFF; TEAR OFF; TEE OFF; TELL OFF; TELL SOMEONE WHERE TO GET OFF; THROW OFF; THROW OFF; TRADE OFF; WIPE OFF THE MAP. Also see under ON.

off, be ♦ See BE OFF.

off again, on again ♦ See OFF AND ON, def. 2.

off and on Also, **on and off.** 1. Intermittently, from time to time. For example, *I read his column off and on,* or *We've been working on the garden all summer, on and off.* [Early 1500s] 2. Also, **off again, on again;** or **on again, off again.** Uncertain, vacillating, as in *Theirs is an off again, on again relationship,* or *The peace talks are on again, off again.* Some believe this term originally referred to minor railroad accidents, where a train went off track and then on again. [Mid-1800s]

off and running Making a good start, progressing well, as in *After the first episode the new soap opera was off and running.* Originating in horse racing, as the traditional announcement at the beginning of a race ("They're off and running"), this phrase began to be used more broadly in the second half of the 1900s.

off balance 1. Out of equilibrium, unsteady, as in *When learning how to ride a two-wheeler, it's easy to get off balance and fall,* or *She stood up and threw the canoe off balance.* [Mid-1900s] 2. Surprised, unprepared, as in *The teacher gives unannounced tests to keep the class off balance.* [Second half of 1900s]

off base Wrong, relying on a mistaken premise, as in *His description of the accounting system was*

totally off base. This metaphoric term originated in baseball, where a runner who steps off a base can be put out. [c. 1940]

off duty ♦ See under ON DUTY.

offense ♦ See NO OFFENSE; TAKE OFFENSE.

of few words, man of. Also, **woman of few words.** A person who does not speak much; also, a person of action rather than words. For example, *A woman of few words, Susan hardly seemed like a successful lawyer,* or *Harry's a man of few words but he gets things done.* This characteristic has been considered praiseworthy since Homer's time, but the precise idiom dates only from about 1600. Shakespeare had it in *Henry V* (3:2): "Men of few words are the best men."

off guard Also, **off one's guard.** Not watchful, easily surprised. It is often put as **catch** (or **be caught**) **off guard,** meaning "take (or be taken) by surprise." For example, *The securities analyst was caught off guard by that financial report,* or *With any luck the boss will be off guard when I come in late.* [Late 1600s] The antonym, **on guard** or **on one's guard,** meaning "watchful or prepared, especially to defend oneself," was first recorded in 1577. For example, *In this crowd we must be on guard against pickpockets,* or *I'm always on my guard when I'm asked how I voted.*

office ♦ See BOX OFFICE; FRONT OFFICE; LAND-OFFICE BUSINESS; TAKE OFFICE.

offing ♦ See IN THE OFFING.

off of Away from, from, as in *Don't take your eyes off of the road,* or *Can I borrow ten dollars off of you?* This seemingly ungrammatical idiom has been used since the 1500s and remains current, but more in oral than written communications. Also see under GET OFF, def. 8.

off one's chest, get Relieve one's mind by confessing or saying something that has been repressed. For example, *I've got to get this off my chest—I can't stand his parents,* or *He admitted taking the dollar and said he was glad to get it off his chest.* This expression uses *chest* for the seat of the emotions. [c. 1900]

off one's feed Have no desire to eat, have lost one's appetite, as in *Even though Mom's gone only for a week, her absence puts Dad off his feed.* Originating in the early 1800s and first used only for animals, this colloquial term later was applied to humans as well.

off one's guard ♦ See OFF GUARD.

off one's head Also, **off one's nut** or **rocker** or **trolley** or **chump.** Crazy, out of one's mind, as in *You're off your head if you think I'll pay your debts,* or *I think Jerry's gone off his nut over that car,* or *When she said we had to sleep in the barn we thought she* *was off her rocker,* or *The old man's been off his trolley for at least a year.* The expression using *head* is colloquial and dates from the mid-1800s; *nut* has been slang for "head" since the mid-1800s; *rocker,* dating from the late 1800s, may allude to an elderly person falling from a rocking chair; *trolley,* also dating from the late 1800s, may be explained by George Ade's use of it in *Artie* (1896): "Any one that's got his head full of the girl proposition's liable to go off his trolley at the first curve." The last, *chump,* is also slang for "head" and was first recorded in 1859.

off one's high horse ♦ See ON ONE'S HIGH HORSE.

off one's rocker Also, **off one's nut** or **trolley.** ♦ See OFF ONE'S HEAD.

off someone's back Also **off someone's case.** No longer harassing or bothering someone. It is often put as **get off someone's back** or **case,** as in *I told her to get off my back—I'll mow the lawn tomorrow,* or *I wish Dad would get off my case about grades.* The first of these slangy terms dates from the 1880s although it became frequent only in the 1940s, and its antonym, **on one's back** (as in *He's been on my back about that report all morning*) dates from about 1960. The variant **off someone's case** was first recorded only in 1970, and its antonym, **on someone's case** (as in *He's always on my case*) in 1971. Also see GET OFF, def. 8.

off someone's feet 1. **sweep** or **carry** or **knock off someone's feet.** Overwhelm someone emotionally; infatuate someone; make a very favorable impression on someone. For example, *Winning first prize knocked her off her feet,* or *With his little gifts and gallant behavior, he swept her off her feet,* or *That fine speech carried him off his feet.* The term using *sweep* dates from about 1900, *carry* from the mid-1800s, and *knock* from the early 1900s. 2. **run** or **rush someone off his** or **her feet.** Work someone to the point of exhaustion, hurry or pressure someone, as in *With all the preparations, they've been running me off my feet,* or *The waiters were rushed off their feet.* These hyperbolic expressions allude to running or hurrying so much that one falls down. The first dates from the mid-1800s; the second was first recorded as *rushed off one's legs* in 1916.

off someone's hands Out of or removed from someone's charge, possession, or responsibility. It is often put as **take off someone's hands,** as in *We hoped that once they saw the kittens they would take them off our hands,* or *I'm glad that swing set is finally off our hands.* [First half of 1600s]

off the air Not being broadcast, as in *Once they knew they were off the air, the panelists burst out laughing.* This idiom, along with the antonym **on the air** ("being broadcast"), dates from the 1920s, *air* being considered a medium for radio-wave transmission.

off the beam Off course, on the wrong track, as in *He's way off the beam with that argument.* This colloquial term and its antonym, **on the beam,** meaning "on the right track," allude to directing aircraft by means of radio beams. [Colloquial; mid-1900s]

off the beaten track An unusual route or destination, as in *We found a great vacation spot, off the beaten track.* This term alludes to a well-worn path trodden down by many feet and was first recorded in 1860, although the phrase *beaten track* was recorded in 1638 in reference to the usual, unoriginal way of doing something.

off the cuff Impromptu, extemporaneous, as in *His speech was entirely off the cuff.* This term supposedly alludes to the practice of speakers making last-minute notes on the cuff of a shirtsleeve. [1930s]

off the deep end ♦ See GO OFF THE DEEP END.

off the ground ♦ See GET OFF THE GROUND.

off the handle ♦ See FLY OFF THE HANDLE.

off the hook Also, **get** or **let off the hook.** Released (or be released) from blame or annoying obligation, as in *He was out of town during the robbery so he was off the hook,* or *I don't know how the muggers got off the hook,* or *Once they found the real culprit, they let Mary off the hook.* This idiom alludes to the fish that manages to free itself from the angler's hook and get away. [Mid-1800s]

off the mark Also, **wide of the mark.** Inaccurate, wrong, as in *The forecast was off the mark, since unemployment is down,* or *His answers on the test were just wide of the mark.* It is also put as **miss the mark,** meaning "be mistaken," as in *The minister missed the mark when he assumed everyone would contribute to the supper.* All these terms allude to *mark* in the sense of "a target," as do the antonyms **on the mark** and **hit the mark,** meaning "exactly right," as in *He was right on the mark with that budget amendment,* or *Bill hit the mark when he accused Tom of lying.* [Mid-1300s]

off the rack Ready-made, as in *She has all her clothes made; she never buys a dress off the rack.* The *rack* here is a frame from which clothes are hung. [Mid-1900s] A British synonym is **off the peg,** similarly alluding to a knob from which clothes are hung and dating from the late 1800s. Also see OFF THE SHELF.

off the rails In an abnormal or malfunctioning condition, as in *Her political campaign has been off the rails for months.* The phrase occurs commonly with *go,* as in *Once the superintendant resigned, the effort to reform the school system went off the rails.*

This idiom alludes to the rails on which trains run; if a train goes off the rails, it stops or crashes. [Mid-1800s]

off the record Unofficially, in confidence, not for publication, as in *What he was about to say, he told the reporters, was strictly off the record.* Probably alluding to striking evidence from a court record (because it is irrelevant or improper), this term came into wide use in the mid-1900s, especially with reference to persons who did not wish to be quoted by journalists. For antonyms, see GO ON RECORD; JUST FOR THE RECORD.

off the shelf Ready-made, available from merchandise or in stock, as opposed to a special order. For example, *Sometimes you can get a better discount by buying an appliance off the shelf.* [First half of 1900s] Also see OFF THE RACK; ON THE SHELF.

off the top of one's head In an impromptu way, without much thought, as in *Off the top of my head I'd say we'll double our profits in a year.* This idiom suggests one has not used the inside of one's head before making some statement. [Mid-1900s]

off the track Away from one's objective, train of thought, or a sequence of events, It is often put as **get** or **put** or **throw off the track**, as in *Your question has gotten me off the track,* or *The interruption threw Mom off the track and she forgot what she'd already put into the stew.* This term comes from railroading, where it means "derailed." Its figurative use was first recorded in 1875.

off the wagon ♦ See ON THE WAGON.

off the wall Eccentric, unconventional, as in *That idea of opening a 100-seat theater is off the wall.* This expression probably originated in baseball or some other sport in which the ball can bounce off a wall in an erratic way. [Colloquial; 1960s]

of it ♦ See COME TO THINK OF IT; FOR FUN (THE FUN OF IT); FOR THE HELL OF IT; FULL OF IT; HAVE A GOOD TIME (OF IT); LONG AND SHORT OF IT; MAKE A DAY OF IT; ON THE FACE OF IT; OUT OF IT; SNAP OUT OF IT; THAT'S ABOUT THE SIZE OF IT; THE HALF OF IT; WHAT OF IT.

of late Recently, lately, as in *She's been very quiet of late; is something wrong?* This idiom uses *late* as a noun instead of an adjective, a usage dating from about 1250. The idiom dates from the early 1400s.

of necessity Also, **out of necessity.** As an inevitable consequence, unavoidably, as in the New Testament: "Of necessity he must release one unto them at the Feast" (Luke 23:17). [Late 1300s]

of note Important, of distinction, famous, as in *I have nothing of note to report,* or *The speaker was a man of note.* This idiom uses *note* in the sense of "importance" or "fame." [Late 1500s]

of old Formerly, long since, at an earlier time, as in *In days of old the whole town turned out to watch the parade.* This somewhat archaic idiom dates from about 1400.

of one's life Being the greatest, worst, or best occasion of a lifetime, as in *She was having the time of her life at the party,* or *The threatened takeover of the company put the president in the fight of his life.*

of one's own accord Also, **of one's own free will.** Voluntarily, without prompting or coercion, as in *The entire audience rose of their own accord,* or *No, I'm climbing this mountain of my own free will.* The first term dates from about 1450, the variant from about 1600.

of service to someone, be Help someone, as in *How can I be of service to you?* This idiom uses *service* in the sense of "supplying someone's needs." [c. 1700]

of sorts Also, **of a sort.** Of a kind, especially a mediocre or somewhat different kind. For example, *He was wearing a jacket of sorts but no tie,* or *They established a constitutional government of a sort.* [c. 1900]

often ♦ See EVERY NOW AND THEN (SO OFTEN); MORE OFTEN THAN NOT.

often as not ♦ See under MORE OFTEN THAN NOT.

of the devil ♦ See SPEAK OF THE DEVIL.

of the essence Of the greatest importance, crucial, as in *Time is of the essence.* This idiom, which uses *essence* in the sense of "the most important element of something," was first recorded in 1873, although the phrase *the essence of . . .* was already being used in the mid-1600s.

of the first water Of the finest quality, as in *That was a play of the first water.* This idiom refers to a grading system for diamonds for their color or luster (compared to the shininess of water). The system is no longer used but the term, used figuratively since the early 1800s, has survived it.

of the kind ♦ See NOTHING OF THE KIND.

of the moment Of importance at this time, as in *The issue of the moment is dealing with our budget deficit.* This expression gave rise in succeeding decades to **the man of the moment,** meaning "the most important person at this time," as in *When Alan hit a home run and broke the tie, he was the man of the moment.* [c. 1930]

of two minds, be Be undecided, vacillate between two alternatives, as in *She's of two minds about her new job—it's much closer to home but also less challenging.* Put as *in two minds,* this idiom was first recorded in 1853, but variants such as *diverse minds* and *twenty minds* date back to the early 1500s.

oil ♦ See BANANA OIL; BURN THE MIDNIGHT OIL; GREASE (OIL) SOMEONE'S PALM; GREASE (OIL) THE WHEELS; POUR OIL ON TROUBLED WATERS; STRIKE IT RICH (OIL).

ointment ♦ See FLY IN THE OINTMENT.

old ♦ In addition to the idioms beginning with OLD, also see ANY OLD; CHIP OFF THE OLD BLOCK; COMFORTABLE AS AN OLD SHOE; DIRTY JOKE (OLD MAN); GET THE AIR (OLD HEAVE-HO); NEW WINE IN OLD BOTTLES; NO FOOL LIKE AN OLD FOOL; OF OLD; RIPE OLD AGE; SAME OLD STORY; SETTLE A SCORE (OLD SCORES); STAMPING GROUND, OLD; TEACH AN OLD DOG NEW TRICKS; UP TO ONE'S OLD TRICKS.

old as Adam Also, **old as the hills.** Ancient, as in *He must be as old as Adam by now,* or *That joke is as old as the hills.* The first term, alluding to the first human created by God, according to the Bible, was first recorded only in 1867. The variant, referring to geological time (when mountains were created), dates from about 1800.

old chestnut A stale joke, story, or saying, as in *Dad keeps on telling that old chestnut about how many psychiatrists it takes to change a light bulb.* This expression comes from William Dimond's play, *The Broken Sword* (1816), in which one character keeps repeating the same stories, one of them about a cork tree, and is interrupted each time by another character who says "Chestnut, you mean . . . I have heard you tell the joke twenty-seven times and I am sure it was a chestnut."

old college try, the One's best effort, as in *Come on, if we give it the old college try we just might be able to cut down this tree.* This slangy expression, originally a cheer to urge a team on, dates from the 1930s when college football films were very popular.

old saw A proverb or maxim, as in *Mom's always repeating the old saw, "Haste makes waste."* This term uses *saw* in the sense of "saying," and *old* in the sense of "wise" rather than old-fashioned. [Second half of 1400s]

old shoe ♦ See COMFORTABLE AS AN OLD SHOE.

old stamping ground ♦ See STAMPING GROUND.

old story, an A common occurrence or excuse. For example, *Karen's mood swings are an old story.* [c. 1700] Also see SAME OLD STORY.

old wives' tale A superstition, as in *Toads cause warts? That's an old wives' tale.* This expression was already known in ancient Greece, and a version in English was recorded in 1387. Despite invoking bigoted stereotypes of women and old people, it survives.

olive branch A symbol of peace, an offering of good will, as in *They feuded for years, but finally the Hatfields came over bearing an olive branch.* This term is alluded to in the Bible (Genesis 8:11), where the dove comes to Noah after the flood with an olive leaf in its mouth. [c. 1600]

omega ♦ See ALPHA AND OMEGA.

on, be ♦ See BE ON.

on account In part payment of a debt, as in *He paid half the amount on account.* [Early 1600s]

on account of Owing to, because of the fact that, as in *We canceled the beach picnic on account of the bad weather forecast.* This idiom was first recorded in 1936.

on a dime In a very small space, suddenly, as in *That horse is so well trained it can turn on a dime.* This expression alludes to the fact that the dime is the smallest-size U.S. coin. [Early 1900s]

on a first-name basis Quite familiar and friendly, as in *Practically all the guests were on a first-name basis.* This idiom alludes to the fact that using a person's given name betokens familiarity. [Second half of 1900s]

on again ♦ See under OFF AND ON.

on a limb ♦ See OUT ON A LIMB.

on all fours On one's hands and knees, as in *Seven of us were on all fours, looking for the lost earring in the sand.* In this idiom *fours* refers to the four limbs. [1300s]

on and off ♦ See OFF AND ON.

on and on Continuously, persistently, without stopping, as in *On and on they rode for three whole days.* Also see GO ON AND ON.

on an even keel Stable, balanced, as in *She had the knack of keeping us on an even keel in any emergency.* This term, used figuratively since the mid-1800s, alludes to keeping a vessel's keel in a level position, assuring smooth sailing.

on a par with As good as, equal to, as in *This violinist may be an amateur but he's on a par with professional orchestral players.* The noun *par* has meant "that which is equal" since the mid-1600s; the idiom here was first recorded in 1832.

on a pedestal, put Also, **set on a pedestal.** Greatly admire, magnify in importance, as in *Youngsters tend to put rock stars on a pedestal, forgetting that they're human.* This expression alludes to the raised position of a statue on a pedestal. [Mid-1800s]

on approval To be returned if not satisfactory, as in *They're offering custom-made shoes, manufactured from a computer design, on approval.* This expression, applied nearly always to the purchase of goods, was first recorded in 1870.

on a rampage Behaving violently, as in *There was a near riot after the game, when some of the spectators went on a rampage.* This term comes from the Old Scots verb *ramp,* meaning "to storm and rage." [Mid-1800s]

on a roll On a streak of success or intense activity, as in *The team's scored three runs in the last inning and they're really on a roll,* or *Once the experiment succeeded, Tim was on a roll.* This slangy term, alluding to the momentum in the act of rolling, dates from the second half of the 1900s, but *roll* alone has been used in this sense since the early 1800s.

on a shoestring With very limited financial means, as in *The newlyweds were living on a shoestring.* The precise allusion in this term is unclear. One fanciful theory is that debtors in British prisons would lower a shoe by its laces from a window so as to collect funds from visitors or passers-by. A more likely theory is that it alludes to the slender shape of a shoelace, likening it to slender resources. [Late 1800s]

on a string Under someone's control, as in *She'll drop everything whenever Sam asks for something—he's got her on a string.* This expression, alluding to pulling an animal on a leash, dates from the late 1500s, when it was put as *in a string.*

on a tangent On a sudden digression or change of course, as in *The professor's hard to follow; he's always off on a tangent.* This phrase often occurs in the idioms **fly off** or **go off on a tangent,** as in *The witness was convincing until he went off on a tangent.* This expression alludes to the geometric tangent—a line or curve that touches but does not intersect with another line or curve. [Second half of 1700s]

on balance Taking everything into consideration, as in *On balance I think we've had a very good year.* This expression, which in effect means "balancing all the factors involved," was first recorded in 1719.

on behalf of ♦ See IN BEHALF OF.

on bended knee Humbly, pleading, as in *They're desperate for funds; they're asking for contributions on bended knee.* This expression alludes to a traditional attitude of supplication. *Bended,* the past tense of *bend,* survives only in this idiom, elsewhere having been replaced by *bent.* [Mid-1600s]

on board Joining in or participating; as in *The department head addressed the new employees, saying "Welcome on board,"* or *The opera company has a new vocal coach on board to help the soloists.* This expression alludes to being on or in a vessel, airplane, or other vehicle. [Colloquial; second half of 1900s]

on borrowed time, live Outlive reasonable expectations, as in *Our twenty-year-old car is living on borrowed time,* or *The vet said our dog is living on borrowed time.* This expression alludes to time borrowed from death. [Late 1800s]

on call Available if summoned, as in *Medical residents are required to be on call at least three nights a week.* This expression originated as *at call* in

the late 1500s. Also see AT SOMEONE'S BECK AND CALL.

on camera Being filmed, as in *When the talk-show host began, I wasn't sure if we were on camera.* This usage dates from the first half of the 1900s, soon after the birth of motion-picture and television filming. The same is true of the antonym **off camera,** meaning "outside the view of a movie or TV camera," as in *Go ahead and scratch—we're off camera now.*

once ♦ In addition to the idioms beginning with ONCE, also see ALL AT ONCE; AT ONCE; EVERY NOW AND THEN (ONCE IN A WHILE); GIVE SOMEONE THE ONCE-OVER; YOU'RE ONLY YOUNG ONCE.

once and for all As a settled matter, finally, permanently, as in *Once and for all, we're not hiring that organist again,* or *We've settled that question once and for all.* This expression is in effect an abbreviation for "one time and for all time." [Late 1400s]

once bitten, twice shy Once hurt, one is doubly cautious in the future, as in *He was two days late last time, so she's not hiring him again—once bitten, twice shy.* This seemingly old observation, presumably alluding to an animal biting someone, was first recorded in 1894.

once in a blue moon Rarely, once in a very long time, as in *We only see our daughter once in a blue moon.* This term is something of a misnomer, because an actual blue moon—that is, the appearance of a second full moon in the same calendar month—occurs every 32 months or so. Further, the moon can appear blue in color at any time, depending on weather conditions. [Early 1800s]

once in a lifetime Extremely rare, especially as an opportunity. For example, *An offer like that will come just once in a lifetime.* This phrase, often used hyperbolically, was first recorded in 1854. Also see OF ONE'S LIFE.

once in a while Occasionally, not very often, as in *Once in a while I enjoy going fishing.* [Mid-1800s] Also see EVERY NOW AND THEN; FROM TIME TO TIME.

once over lightly Cursorily, quickly, as in *I did go over the program once over lightly, but perhaps I should read it more carefully.* [Colloquial; mid-1900s]

once upon a time On some past occasion, as in *I may have sung this piece once upon a time, but I don't really remember it.* This phrase, first recorded in 1595, is frequently used as the opening line of fairy tales and stories told to children, as in *Once upon a time there was a king who had three beautiful daughters.*

on cloud nine Blissfully happy, as in *Ever since he proposed to her, her parents have been on cloud nine.* The exact allusion of *nine* in this term is unclear, and different figures, especially seven (perhaps alluding to SEVENTH HEAVEN), are sometimes substituted. [Colloquial; mid-1900s]

on commission Making money based on sales or services rendered, as in *Real estate agents rarely get a salary; they work largely on commission.* This use of the noun *commission*, which generally refers to a percentage of the total price, dates from the early 1700s.

on condition that Provided that, with the restriction that, as in *She said she'd help with the costumes on condition that she would get ten free tickets to the play.* The use of the noun *condition* in the sense of "stipulation" dates from the late 1300s, and the precise phrase from the early 1500s.

on consignment Turning over goods for an agent to sell, with the provision that payment is made only on completed sales and that unsold goods may be returned to the consignor. For example, *This secondhand shop accepts items of clothing on consignment.* [c. 1700]

on deck 1. Available, ready for action, as in *We had ten kids on deck to clean up after the dance.* [Slang; second half of 1800s] 2. In baseball, scheduled to bat next, waiting near home plate to bat, as in *Joe was on deck next.* [1860s] Both usages allude to crew members being on the deck of a ship, in readiness to perform their duties.

on demand When needed or asked for, as in *She's always ready to sing on demand,* or *Nowadays infants are generally fed on demand.* This usage is a broadening of this phrase's meaning in finance, that is, "payable on being requested or presented," as in *This note is payable on demand.* [Late 1600s]

on draft Drawn from a large container, such as a keg (as opposed to bottles). For example, *We much prefer the taste of beer on draft.* [Mid-1800s]

on duty At one's post, at work, as in *The new nurse was on duty that evening,* or *The watchman was fired because he was drunk on duty.* [Mid-1600s] The antonym, **off duty**, means "not engaged in one's work," as in *Captain Smith was much more amiable when he was off duty.* [Mid-1800s]

one ♦ In addition to the idioms beginning with ONE, also see ALL IN ONE PIECE; ALL THE SAME (ONE); A-1 (A-ONE); AS ONE; AT ONE; AT ONE STROKE; AT ONE TIME; AT ONE TIME OR ANOTHER; BACK TO THE DRAWING BOARD (SQUARE ONE); EACH AND EVERY (LAST ONE); EACH OTHER (ONE ANOTHER); FAST ONE; FOR ONE, I; GO ONE BETTER; HANG (ONE) ON; HARP ON (ONE STRING); HOLE IN ONE; IN ONE EAR AND OUT THE OTHER; IN THE SAME (IN ONE) BREATH; IRONS IN THE FIRE, MORE THAN ONE; IT TAKES ONE TO KNOW ONE; JUST ONE OF THOSE THINGS; LOOK OUT FOR (NUMBER ONE); MORE THAN ONE WAY TO SKIN A CAT; NOT ONE IOTA; NUMBER ONE; ON THE ONE HAND; (ONE) PICTURE IS WORTH A THOUSAND WORDS; PUT ALL ONE'S EGGS IN ONE BASKET; QUICK ONE; SEEN ONE, SEEN THEM ALL; SIX OF ONE, HALF DOZEN OF THE OTHER; THAT'S ONE ON ME; TIE ONE ON; WEAR ANOTHER (MORE THAN ONE) HAT; WITH ONE ARM TIED BEHIND ONE'S BACK; WITH ONE VOICE; WORDS OF ONE SYLLABLE. (Note that this listing does not include those idioms where ONE is a personal pronoun meaning "someone" or "oneself.")

one and all Everyone, as in *She's told one and all about their quarrel.* [c. 1375]

one and only One's only love; one's only sweetheart. For example, *He swore she was his one and only, but the detective following him knew better.* [c. 1900]

one and the same Identical, as in *Gloria's grandfather had been, at one and the same time, a physician at the court and a general in the army.* This expression is an emphatic form of "the same." [Mid-1800s]

one another ♦ See EACH OTHER.

one-armed bandit A slot machine, as in *It's amazing how many people think they can make money playing a one-armed bandit.* This term refers to both appearance and function: the operating lever looks like an arm, and the machine in effect robs players, since it "wins" and keeps the player's money in an overwhelming majority of instances. [c. 1930]

on earth 1. Also, **in creation; in the world.** Ever, anywhere, of all possible things. These phrases are all used for emphasis in questions or, less often, in a negative context. For example, *What on earth is he doing with a spade?* or *Where in creation did that child go?* or *How in the world do you expect me to carry all those bags?* [Late 1700s] 2. **like nothing on earth.** Incomparable. For example, *That perfume smells like nothing on earth,* or *Her new hair color is like nothing on earth.* [c. 1900]

on easy street ♦ See EASY STREET.

one by one Also, **one at a time.** Individually in succession, as in *The ducklings jumped into the pond one by one,* or *One at a time they went into the office.* Formerly also put as *one and one* and *one after one,* this idiom dates from about A.D. 1000.

on edge Tense, nervous, irritable, as in *We were all on edge as we waited for the surgeon's report.* This expression transfers the edge of a cutting instrument to one's feelings. [Late 1800s] Also see ON THE EDGE; SET ONE'S TEETH ON EDGE.

one eye on Paying some but not full attention to, as in *He ran the rehearsal with one eye on the clock.* Also see HAVE ONE'S EYE ON; OUT OF THE CORNER OF ONE'S EYE; SEE WITH HALF AN EYE.

one fell swoop, in Also **at one fell swoop.** All at once, in a single action, as in *This law has lifted all the controls on cable TV in one fell swoop.* This term was used and probably invented by Shakespeare in *Macbeth* (4:3), where the playwright likens the murder of Macduff's wife and children to a hawk swooping down on defenseless prey. Although *fell* here means "cruel" or "ruthless," this meaning has been lost in the current idiom, where it now signifies "sudden."

one foot in the grave, have Be close to death or in terrible condition, as in *Jane looks as though she has one foot in the grave.* This picturesque hyperbolic phrase was first recorded in 1566.

one for the books Also, **one for the book.** An outstanding or unusual achievement or event, as in *All of the main awards went to one picture—that's one for the books.* This expression originally alluded to record books kept for sports but soon was applied to other endeavors. [Colloquial; c. 1900]

one for the road A final drink before leaving, as in *Won't you have just one for the road?* This term always alludes to an alcoholic drink and a practice that, if the person is going to drive away, is not only frowned on but in many places illegal. [First half of 1900s]

one good turn deserves another A favor should be returned in kind, as in *I'll give you a ride next time—one good turn deserves another.* This maxim was first recorded about 1400, and the converse, *One bad turn deserves another,* about 1500.

one-horse town A small and unimportant place, as in *Ours was just a one-horse town until the nuclear plant was built.* This expression, first recorded in 1857, presumably alluded to a town so small that a single horse would suffice for its transportation needs.

one in a million Also, **one in a thousand** or **billion.** Extraordinary, rare, as in *She's the kindest soul—she's one in a million,* or *This ring is one in a thousand.* All these terms are hyperbolic.

one jump ahead Anticipating and prepared for what will happen, as in *We have to keep one jump ahead of the opposition.* [First half of 1900s] Also see GET THE JUMP ON.

one-man show Also, **one-man band.** A person who does or manages just about everything, as in *This department is a one-man show—the chairman runs it all,* or *John conducts the interviews, writes the articles, solicits ads, deals with the printer—he's a one-man band.* This idiom alludes to the actor or artist responsible for the entire performance or exhibit, or the musician who plays every instrument in the group. [First half of 1900s]

one man's meat is another man's poison What is good for or enjoyed by one is not necessarily so for someone else. This adage, first recorded in 1576, is so well known it is often shortened, as in *Pat loves to travel to remote areas but that's not for Doris—one man's meat, you know.* Also see NO ACCOUNTING FOR TASTES.

on end 1. Continuously, without interruption, as in *It's been raining for days on end.* 2. Upright, having one end down, as in *Set this carton on end.* It also appears in **one's hair stands on end,** meaning the hair sticks up instead of lying flat. Both usages date from about 1300.

one of a kind ♦ See under OF A KIND.

one of these days Also, **one day; some day.** On some day in the future, as in *One of these days I'm going to clean out my desk,* or *One day you'll see what it's like to have your child insult you,* or *They hoped to buy a brand-new car some day.* [Mid-1500s] Also see ONE OF THOSE DAYS.

one of those days Also, **just one of those days.** A day when everything goes wrong, as in *The car wouldn't start, I lost my glasses—it was one of those days.* This expression was first recorded in 1936.

one on one A direct encounter between two persons, especially a conflict, as in *The two department heads went one on one regarding shelf space.* This slangy expression almost certainly comes from sports. It is commonly used to refer to a two-person basketball game, but is also applied to the interaction of two players on opposing teams in football, soccer, and similar team sports. [c. 1960]

one picture is worth a thousand words ♦ See PICTURE IS WORTH A THOUSAND WORDS.

oneself ♦ See AVAIL (ONESELF) OF; BE ONESELF; BESIDE ONSELF; BURN (ONESELF) OUT; BY ONESELF; COVER ONE'S ASS (ONESELF); CRANK (ONESELF) UP; DO ONESELF IN; EXCUSE ME (ONESELF); EXERT ONESELF; EXPLAIN ONESELF; EXPRESS ONESELF; FALL ALL OVER (ONESELF); FEEL LIKE ONESELF; FIND ONESELF; FLATTER ONESELF; FLING ONESELF AT; FORGET ONESELF; FULL OF ONESELF; GET A GRIP ON (ONESELF); GIVE A GOOD ACCOUNT OF ONESELF; GIVE OF ONESELF; GIVE (ONESELF) AWAY; GIVE ONESELF UP; HAVE ONESELF; HEAR ONESELF THINK; HELP ONESELF; KEEP TO ONESELF; KICK ONESELF; KNOCK ONESELF OUT; LAW UNTO ONESELF; LAY (ONESELF) OPEN; LEAVE (ONESELF) OPEN; LET (ONESELF) GO; LIVE WITH (ONESELF); LOSE ONESELF IN; MAKE A LAUGHINGSTOCK OF ONESELF; MAKE A NAME FOR ONESELF; MAKE AN EXHIBITION OF ONESELF; MAKE A NUISANCE OF ONESELF; MAKE A PIG OF ONESELF; MAKE ONESELF AT HOME; MAKE ONESELF SCARCE; NOT ONESELF; PAINT ONESELF INTO A CORNER; PLUME ONESELF; PRIDE ONESELF ON; PULL ONESELF TOGETHER; PULL ONESELF UP; PUT ONESELF OUT; RELIEVE ONESELF; REPEAT ONESELF; RESIGN ONESELF TO; SHIFT FOR ONESELF; SHOOT ONESELF IN THE FOOT; SPREAD ONESELF TOO THIN; SUIT ONESELF;

SURE OF ONESELF; TAKE IT UPON ONESELF; THROW ONESELF AT; THROW ONESELF ON THE MERCY OF; TIE ONESELF IN KNOTS; TROUBLE ONE'S HEAD (ONESELF) ABOUT.

one-track mind A mind limited to only one line of thought or action, as in *All you think about is sex—you have a one-track mind.* This expression, alluding to a train that runs only on one track or in one direction, was first recorded in 1928.

one up Having an advantage or lead over someone, as in *Sara is one up on Jane because she passed algebra in summer school.* This expression comes from sports, where it means to be one point ahead of one's opponents. It was transferred to general use about 1920.

one way or another Also, **one way or the other.** Somehow, in some fashion, as in *One way or another I'm sure we'll meet again,* or *He wasn't sure how to build a wall, but he would manage in one way or the other.* [Mid-1500s]

on faith, take it Trust, accept without proof, as in *I have no firm evidence that Bob's responsible for the errors—you'll just have to take it on faith.* This idiom employs *faith* in the sense of "belief or confidence in something," a usage dating from about 1300.

on file In or as if in a record for easy reference. For example, *There's no job open right now, but we'll keep your résumé on file.* The use of *file* in the sense of "a collection of papers stored for ready reference" dates from the early 1600s.

on fire ‣ See SET ON FIRE; SET THE WORLD ON FIRE.

on foot Walking or running, not using a vehicle. For example, *There's no road to the lodge; we have to get there on foot.* [c. 1300] Also see HOOF IT; ON ONE'S FEET; ON THE RIGHT FOOT.

on good terms On a friendly footing, as in *I'm on good terms with the manager, so I'll ask him to help you.* Shakespeare used the phrase slightly differently in *King Lear* (1:2): "Parted you in good terms?" The precise current usage was first recorded in 1669. Also see ON SPEAKING TERMS.

on guard ‣ See under OFF GUARD.

on hand 1. In one's possession, available, as in *The business needs to have enough cash on hand.* [c. 1100] 2. Present, as in *Jim was always on hand to help.* [Mid-1800s] 3. Soon, imminent. See AT HAND, def. 2.

on high 1. Up in the sky; also, in heaven. For example, *They fixed their eyes on high, looking for the comet,* or, in the Bible (Psalms 63:5), "The Lord our God who dwelleth on high." [c. 1200] 2. In a position of authority, as in *Those on high have decreed that we work every other weekend.* This us-

age is an ironic transfer from def. 1. Also see POWERS THAT BE.

on hold 1. In a state of temporary interruption, but not disconnection, during a telephone call, as in *While I was on hold, I checked my calendar for when I could schedule a meeting,* or *They had to put me on hold while they looked up my account.* [c. 1960] 2. In a state of postponement or delay, as in *When she was transferred, they had to put their romance on hold.* This figurative usage is a broadened sense of def. 1. [Colloquial; c. 1970]

on ice 1. In reserve or readiness. This idiom often occurs with *put,* meaning "to place in reserve," as in *Let's put that proposal on ice until we have the funds to implement it.* This usage alludes to putting things in cold storage for preservation. [Slang; late 1800s] 2. In prison, as in *He's been on ice for ten years.* This usage may be derived in part from the slang term *cooler* for "jail." [slang; c. 1930] 3. With a good chance of success, as in *I'm sure she'll win—it's on ice.* [slang; early 1900s]

on in years ‣ See ALONG IN YEARS.

onion ‣ See KNOW ONE'S STUFF (ONIONS).

on its merits Also, **on one's merits** or **according to one's merits.** With regard only to the intrinsic quality of something or someone. For example, *Who supports it doesn't matter; we have to consider the idea solely on its merits,* or *The agency doesn't care about her references but wants to hire candidates according to their merits.* [Late 1800s]

on line 1. See IN LINE, def. 2. 2. Actively linked to or operating a computer, as in *They haven't got the printer on line yet,* or *Mark's been on line all morning.* [Late 1900s] Also see GO ON, def. 9.

only ‣ In addition to the idioms beginning with ONLY, also see BEAUTY IS ONLY SKIN DEEP; HAVE AN EYE (EYES ONLY) FOR; IF ONLY; IN NAME ONLY; NOT THE ONLY FISH IN THE SEA; ONE AND ONLY; YOU'RE ONLY YOUNG ONCE

only game in town, the The only choice, which one must accept for want of a better one. For example, *Out here, this bank is the only game in town when it comes to financial services.* This term, dating from the early 1900s, originally alluded to a gambler looking for a game in a strange town.

only too 1. At the very least, as a matter of fact, as in *I know only too well that I can't win the lottery.* This usage was first recorded in 1817. 2. Very, extremely, as in *I am only too glad to help.* This usage was first recorded in 1899.

on no account Also, **not on any account.** Under no circumstances, certainly not, as in *On no account should you put a metal utensil in the microwave oven,* or *Dad said we can't go, not on any account.* [Mid-1800s]

on occasion From time to time, now and then, as in *Nell has been known to eat meat on occasion.* This usage, first in the form of **upon occasion,** replaced *by occasion* about 1600.

on one hand ♦ See ON THE ONE HAND.

on one's ♦ In addition to the following idioms beginning with ON ONE'S, also see under ON SOMEONE'S.

on one's account ♦ See ON ACCOUNT; ON ONE'S OWN ACCOUNT.

on one's behalf ♦ See IN BEHALF OF.

on one's best behavior Also, **on one's good behavior.** Very polite, as in *Mother told the children to be on their best behavior during Grandma's visit,* or *The whole staff were on their good behavior while the client inspected the premises.* [Late 1600s]

on one's doorstep ♦ See AT ONE'S DOOR.

on one's ear ♦ See SET ON ONE'S EAR.

on oneself ♦ See TAKE IT UPON ONESELF.

on one's feet ♦ In addition to the idiom (see the next entry) ON ONE'S FEET, also see DEAD ON ONE'S FEET; FALL (LAND) ON ONE'S FEET; GET TO ONE'S FEET; SET ONE BACK ON ONE'S FEET; STAND ON ONE'S FEET; THINK ON ONE'S FEET.

on one's feet **1.** Standing, as in *I'm tired—I've been on my feet all day.* [Mid-1400s] Also see GET TO ONE'S FEET. **2.** Also, **back on one's feet.** Healthy, returned to good health, as in *I hope you get back on your feet very soon.* [c. 1800]

on one's good behavior ♦ See ON ONE'S BEST BEHAVIOR.

on one's guard ♦ See under OFF GUARD.

on one's hands **1.** In one's possession or care, often as a responsibility, as in *As long as she had three children on her hands she couldn't get very much accomplished,* or *They had two houses on their hands because they hadn't sold the first before having to move.* This term was first recorded in 1528. For the antonym, see OFF ONE'S HANDS. **2. time on one's hands.** Time in which one has nothing necessary to do, free time, as in *She has a lot of time on her hands now that the kids have moved out.* Also see IN ONE'S HANDS.

on one's head Also, **on one's own head.** As one's responsibility or fault, as in *If the police catch you speeding it's on your own head.* This idiom, dating from the 1300s, conjures up the image of blame or guilt falling on someone's head. Also see OFF ONE'S HEAD.

on one's heels ♦ See AT ONE'S HEELS.

on one's high horse In an arrogant or condescending manner. For example, *When they started talking about music, David got on his high horse* and said that classical music was only fit for museums and archives. This expression, alluding to the use of tall horses by high-ranking persons, dates from the late 1700s. Similarly, **off one's high horse** means "less arrogantly, more humbly," as in *I wish she'd get off her high horse and be more friendly.* It dates from the early 1900s, but is heard less often today.

on one's home ground Where one has the advantage of familiarity. For example, *Teams generally find it easier to win on their home ground,* or *The candidate from Maine was speaking on his home ground.*

on one's honor Entrusted to behave honorably and honestly without supervision. For example, *The students were on their honor not to consult notes during the exam.* Originally alluding to a solemn oath, this idiom dates from the mid-1400s.

on one's last legs Extremely tired, close to collapsing, as in *We've been cleaning house all day and I'm on my last legs.* This hyperbolic expression originally meant "close to dying," and in John Ray's 1678 proverb collection it was transferred to being bankrupt. Soon afterward it was applied to the end of one's resources, physical or otherwise. It is sometimes applied to things, as in *That furnace is on its last legs.*

on one's mind Also, **on the brain.** In one's thoughts, preoccupying one. For example, *The book prize has been on my mind, but I haven't been able to discuss it with you.* It is often put as **have something on one's mind** (or **the brain**) meaning "be preoccupied with something," as in *I didn't mean to be rude; I just have a lot on my mind right now,* or *John has nothing but girls on the brain.* [Mid-1800s]

on one's own **1.** By one's own efforts or resources, as in *He built the entire addition on his own.* [Mid-1900s] **2.** Responsible for oneself, independent of outside help or control, as in *Dave moved out last fall; he's on his own now.* [Mid-1900s]

on one's own account Also, **on one's own hook** or **initiative.** For oneself; also, by one's own efforts, as in *I've gone into business on my own account,* or *He called the police on his own book,* or *She went job-hunting on her own initiative.* The first term, first recorded in 1801, transfers the financial sense of *account* to one's own interest or risk. The *book* variant, a colloquialism, was first recorded in 1812 and the precise analogy is unclear. The second variant, using *initiative* in the sense of "enterprise," was first recorded in 1858.

on one's own time During non-working hours, especially when one is not being paid. For example, *Marcia wrote poetry evenings and weekends, on her* *own time.* This expression implies that the time one spends working for someone else is no longer one's possession.

on one's part ♦ See FOR ONE'S PART.

on one's say-so According to one's authority, as in *I'm reorganizing the files on the boss's say-so,* or *You can skip the exam? On whose say-so?* The noun *say-so,* dating from about 1630, originally meant simply "saying something," that is, an assertion (without authority or proof). By the early 1800s it had acquired its present meaning.

on one's shoulders As one's responsibility, as in *The king carries his entire country on his shoulders,* or *The success of the conference rests on Nancy's shoulders.* This metaphoric use of *shoulders* as the burden-bearing part of the body dates from the late 1300s.

on one's soapbox Expressing one's views passionately or self-importantly, as in *Dexter can't resist getting on his soapbox about school expenditures.* This expression comes from the literal use of a soapbox as an improvised platform for a speaker, usually outdoors. [Mid-1600s]

on one's tail ♦ See GET OFF ONE'S TAIL; ON SOMEONE'S COATTAILS.

on one's toes Alert, ready to act, as in *Orchestra players must be on their toes all the time, so as not to miss an entrance.* This metaphoric expression probably alludes to boxers or runners who must be on their toes in order to move or start quickly. It gained currency with Richard Rodgers' and Lorenz Hart's extremely popular musical, *On Your Toes* (1936). [Early 1900s]

on one's uppers Poor, in reduced circumstances, as in as in *The Smiths try to hide the fact that they're on their uppers.* First recorded in 1886, this metaphoric term alludes to having worn out the soles of one's shoes so badly that only the top portions remain.

on one's way 1. See ON THE WAY. 2. Also, **be on one's way.** Leave, get going, as in *"On your way,"* said the officer, trying to move the crowd, or *It's been a wonderful party but we must be on our way now.* [Early 1900s]

on order Requested but not yet delivered, as in *Our new sofa is on order.* This term is always used for goods of some kind, the noun *order* having been used in the sense of "a commission for goods" since the early 1800s.

on pain of Also, **under pain of.** Subject to the penalty of a specific punishment. For example, *The air traffic controllers knew that going on strike was on pain of losing their jobs.* At one time this idiom often invoked death as the penalty, a usage that is largely hyperbolic today, as in *We'd*

better be back on time, under pain of death. [Late 1300s]

on paper In theory, hypothetically, as in *Considering casualties, on paper the Americans won the Vietnam War,* or *They are a good team on paper but not so in the field.* This metaphoric expression contrasts something written down with concrete reality. [Late 1700s]

on pins and needles Nervously anxious, as in *He was on pins and needles, waiting for the test results.* The graphic expression *pins and needles* for the tingling sensation experienced in recovering from numbness was transferred to a feeling of marked mental uneasiness about 1800.

on principle 1. On moral or ethical grounds. As James Russell Lowell wrote about Alexander Pope in 1871, "There was a time when I could not read Pope, but disliked him on principle." [First half of 1800s] 2. According to a fixed rule or practice. For example, *The police were locking up the demonstrators on principle.* [First half of 1800s] 3. **on general principle.** For no special reason, in general, as in *Dean won't touch broccoli on general principle.* [First half of 1800s]

on purpose 1. Deliberately, intentionally, as in *He left the photo out of the story on purpose.* Shakespeare's use of this idiom was among the earliest; it appears in *The Comedy of Errors* (4:3): "On purpose shut the doors against his way." 2. **accidentally on purpose.** Seemingly accidentally but actually deliberately, as in *She stepped on his foot accidentally on purpose.* This generally jocular phrase was first recorded in 1862.

on record ♦ See GO ON RECORD.

on relief Also, **on welfare; on the dole.** Receiving public financial assistance, as in *Half the people in this town are on relief,* or *Don hated the idea of going on welfare.* The first two terms originated in the United States in the 1930s, when government assistance of this kind was first instituted. **On the dole,** used mainly in Britain but occasionally in America, dates from the 1920s, although the use of *dole* for a charitable gift dates from about 1200.

on request When asked for, as in *The agreement states that the rights on this book revert to the author on request.* [c. 1800] Also see BY REQUEST.

on sale At a reduced price, as in *These rugs have been on sale for a month.* The use of *sale* for disposing of goods at lowered prices dates from about 1860.

on schedule At the announced or expected time, as in *Her first baby arrived right on schedule.* Originally alluding to published railroad timetables, this expression dates from the late 1800s.

on second thought Resulting from a revised opinion or change of mind, as in *I thought I'd go to the movies, but on second thought I'd rather stay home.* Similarly, **have second thoughts** means "change one's mind," as in *I've had second thoughts about moving to Florida.* This idiom alludes to ideas that come later. [Mid-1600s]

on sight Also, **at sight.** Immediately upon seeing, as in *The soldiers threatened to shoot looters on sight,* or *He's able to multiply those three-digit figures at sight.* [Second half of 1400s]

on someone's ♦ In addition to the following idioms beginning with ON SOMEONE'S, also see under ON ONE'S.

on someone's back Also, **on someone's case.** ♦ See under OFF SOMEONE'S BACK.

on someone's coattails Also, **on the coattails of.** Owing to another person's popularity or merits. For example, *He won the cabinet post by hanging on the senator's coattails,* or *He was elected to office on the coattails of the governor.* This expression, with its graphic image, dates from the mid-1800s, when coats with tails were in fashion.

on someone's nerves ♦ See GET ON SOMEONE'S NERVES.

on someone's side In support of someone's views or interests, as in *I'm glad you're on my side in this debate,* or *With the Canadians on our side, we should be able to persuade the Mexicans of a North American policy.* [1300s]

on speaking terms 1. Friendly enough to exchange superficial remarks, as in *We're on speaking terms with the new neighbors.* 2. Ready and willing to communicate, not alienated or estranged. For example, *We are on speaking terms again after the quarrel.* Both senses of this idiom commonly occur in the negative, as in *Brett and his brother haven't been on speaking terms for years.* The idiom was first recorded in 1786.

on spec Done on a speculative basis; with no assurance of profit. For example, *We didn't design our house; the builder built it on spec.* The use of *spec* as an abbreviation for *speculation* dates from the late 1700s.

on standby Ready and waiting, as in *We've got three more painters on standby.* This expression originated in the navy in the 1940s, where it referred to someone being ready to come on duty as soon as required. From about 1960 it began to be widely used in aviation for a passenger waiting to take the first available seat on a full flight.

on strike Engaged in a work stoppage, as in *The auto workers were on strike for the entire summer.* The use of *strike* for a concerted labor stoppage undertaken to gain concessions from employers dates from the early 1800s. Today it is also used more loosely, as in *Where washing dishes is concerned, Mom has announced that she's on strike.* Also see GO OUT, def. 4.

on sufferance Barely tolerated; agreed to but unwillingly. For example, *They rarely put a non-academic on the panel, so obviously I was there on sufferance.* This expression uses *sufferance* in the sense of "toleration," a usage obsolete except in this idiom. [Mid-1500s]

on tap Available for immediate use, ready, as in *We have two more trumpeters on tap for the parade.* This metaphoric expression alludes to a beverage such as beer that is ready to be drawn from a cask. [Mid-1800s]

on target Completely accurate, wholly valid, as in *Our cost estimates were right on target,* or *His criticisms were on target.* This seemingly old expression dates only from the mid-1900s, and the colloquial use of *target* for a goal one wishes to achieve dates from about 1940.

on tenterhooks In a state of painful suspense, as in *We were on tenterhooks all through the game, hoping against hope that our team would win.* This expression alludes to hooks that formerly were used to hold newly woven cloth that was being stretched on a frame. Their name has long survived this method of manufacture. [Mid-1700s]

on the air ♦ See under OFF THE AIR.

on the alert Watchful, fully prepared, as in *The inspectors are always on the alert for a manufacturing error.* [Late 1700s]

on the average As a rule, usually, as in *On the average, about 15 percent of the freshmen class will drop out before graduation.* This expression uses *average* in the sense of "a norm or standard." [First half of 1700s]

on the ball, be Also, **have something on the ball.** Be especially capable or efficient, as in *These programmers really have a lot on the ball.* This term originated in baseball, where it was used for throwing a pitch with exceptional speed, spin, or some other deceptive motion. [Slang; early 1900s]

on the bandwagon, get Also, **climb** or **hop** or **jump on the bandwagon.** Join a cause or movement, as in *More and more people are getting on the bandwagon to denounce cigarette smoking.* This expression alludes to a horsedrawn wagon carrying a brass band, used to accompany candidates on campaign tours in the second half of the 1800s. By about 1900 it was extended to supporting a campaign or other cause.

on the barrel ♦ See CASH ON THE BARREL.

on the beam ♦ See under OFF THE BEAM.

on the bench 1. Presiding as judge in a law court, as in *Lawyers are very careful when Judge Brown is on the bench.* This usage alludes to the seat occupied by a judge. [Late 1200s] **2.** Waiting for a chance to participate; also, removed from participation. For example, *Mary complained that all her colleagues were going to the sales conference while she was left on the bench.* This usage comes from baseball and other sports, where players not deemed ready or competent to play sit on a bench watching the game. [Early 1900s]

on the blink Also, **on the bum** or **fritz.** Malfunctioning, out of order, broken, as in *The TV is on the blink again*, or *You drive—our car's on the bum.* The first of these slangy expressions dates from the late 1800s and possibly alludes to an electric light that flickers on and off ("blinks"); the second, from the same period, possibly is derived from *bum* in the sense of "a contemptible person"; the third, *fritz*, dating from about 1900, is of unknown origin.

on the block 1. put or **go on the block.** Offer for sale, as in *These paintings will all be put on the block.* This usage alludes to the auction block, the platform from which the auctioneer sells, so called since the mid-1800s. **2. put one's head on the block.** Take a great risk, make oneself vulnerable, as in *I'm not going to put my head on the block just to save her reputation.* This usage alludes to the executioner's block, on which victims are beheaded, so called since the mid-1500s.

on the brain ♦ See ON ONE'S MIND.

on the bum ♦ See under ON THE BLINK.

on the button Exactly right, precisely, as in *Her review of the book was right on the button*, or *We're supposed to be there at six o'clock on the button.* This term may come from boxing, where a punch on the *button* means "a punch on the chin." [Colloquial; c. 1900] Also see ON THE DOT.

on the carpet ♦ See CALL ON THE CARPET.

on the chance that On the possibility that, as in *I came early on the chance that we might have time to chat.* This phrase uses *chance* in the sense of "a possibility or probability for some event," a usage dating from the late 1700s. It is sometimes put as **on the off chance,** meaning "on the slight but unlikely possibility," as in *I came late on the off chance that I could avoid Thomas.* The addition of *off* in the sense of "remote" dates from the mid-1800s.

on the cheap Economically, at very little cost, as in *We're traveling around Europe on the cheap.* [Colloquial; mid-1800s]

on the chin ♦ See TAKE IT ON THE CHIN.

on the contrary It's the opposite, as in *Is his shoulder hurting?—On the contrary, it's all better*, or *We thought you didn't like opera.—On the contrary, I love it.* This phrase, at first put as *by* or *for* or *in the contrary*, dates from the late 1300s; *on* has been used since the mid-1800s.

on the cuff 1. On credit, as in *He tried to hire a detective on the cuff.* It is sometimes put as **put on the cuff,** meaning "extend credit to," as in *They asked to be put on the cuff until they got their monthly check.* This usage probably alludes to the practice of recording bar tabs on the bartender's cuff. Also see OFF THE CUFF. [Slang; 1920s] **2.** Free of charge, as in *We hope these drinks are on the cuff.* [Slang; 1920s] Also see ON THE HOUSE.

on the defensive Prepared for withstanding aggression or attack, as in *The debate team's plan was to keep their opponents on the defensive*, or *This teacher put students on the defensive about their mistakes.* [c. 1600]

on the dot Exactly on time, as in *We had to be there at eight on the dot.* The *dot* in this idiom is the mark appearing on the face of a watch or clock indicating the time in question. It may come from the earlier *to a dot*, meaning "exactly" since the early 1700s but no longer heard today. [c. 1900] Also see ON THE BUTTON.

on the double Very quickly, as in *You'd better get here on the double.* This expression, also put as *at the double*, came from the military, where it means "double time"—that is, marching twice as fast as normally. [Early 1800s]

on the edge 1. In a precarious position; also, in a state of keen excitement, as from danger or risk. For example, *When the stock market crashed, their whole future was on the edge*, or *Skydivers obviously must enjoy living on the edge.* **2. on the edge of.** On the point of doing something, as in *He was on the edge of winning the election when the sex scandal broke.* [c. 1600] Both def. 1 and 2 allude to the danger of falling over the edge of a precipice.

on the eve of Just prior to, as in *On the eve of the conference the main speaker backed out.* This expression uses *eve*, literally "the night before," more loosely. [Late 1700s]

on the face of it Seemingly, based on available evidence, as in *On the face of it this project should break even in six months.* This idiom uses *face* in the sense of "a superficial view." [Early 1700s]

on the fence, be Also, **straddle the fence.** Be undecided, not committed, as in *I don't know if I'll move there; I'm still on the fence*, or *He's straddling the fence about the merger.* This picturesque expression, with its implication that one can jump to either side, at first was applied mainly to political commitments. [Early 1800s]

on the fly In a hurry, on the run, as in *I picked up some groceries on the fly.* The transfer of this expression, which literally means "in midair or in flight," dates from the mid-1800s.

on the fritz ♦ See under ON THE BLINK.

on the go In constant activity, very busy, as in *I'm exhausted—I've been on the go since eight this morning.* [Mid-1800s]

on the heels of Also, **hard on the heels of.** Directly behind, immediately following, as in *Mom's birthday comes on the heels of Mother's Day,* or *Hard on the heels of the flood there was a tornado.* The *hard* in the variant acts as an intensifier, giving it the sense of "close on the heels of". [Early 1800s] Also see AT ONE'S HEELS.

on the horizon Within view, not too far away, as in *The analysts see a huge rise in the stock market on the horizon.*

on the horns of a dilemma ♦ See HORNS OF A DILEMMA.

on the hour At every hour exactly; one o'clock, two o'clock, and so on. For example, *The shuttle to New York departs on the hour.* An extension of this idiom is **every hour on the hour**, meaning every time the clock's big hand reaches twelve, as in *The bus passes by the house every hour on the hour.*

on the house At the expense of the establishment, as in *This hotel serves an afternoon tea that's on the house.* This idiom uses *house* in the sense of "an inn, tavern, or other building serving the public." [Late 1800s]

on the in, be Have inside information, as in *She was too new to the firm to be on the in for policy changes.* [Colloquial; c. 1930] Also see IN ON; GET AN IN WITH.

on the increase Growing, especially in frequency of occurrence, as in *Violent crime is on the increase.* [Mid-1700s]

on the inside In a position of confidence or influence, as in *The new reporter said he got his facts from at least one official on the inside.* [c. 1930]

on the job 1. At work, busy, as in *We've got three men on the job.* [Late 1800s] 2. Paying close attention, alert, as in *Trust Jim to find out the details—he's always on the job.*

on the lam Running away, especially from the police, as in *He's always in some kind of trouble and perpetually on the lam.* The origin of this slangy term of the 1800s is not known.

on the level Honest, straightforward, sincere, as in *You can believe her—she's on the level.* This expression may have come from Freemasonry, where the carpenter's level symbolizes integrity. [Late 1800s]

on the line ♦ See LAY ON THE LINE.

on the lines of ♦ See ALONG THE LINES OF.

on the lookout Also, **on the watch.** Vigilant, alert, as in *Be on the lookout for the twins—they're somewhere on this playground,* or *He was on the watch for her arrival.* Both phrases were originally used with *upon.* **Upon the lookout** was originally nautical usage, meaning "on duty being watchful" (as for another ship, rocks, or land); it appeared in the mid-1700s, and *on* replaced *upon* about a century later. **Upon the watch** was first recorded in Daniel Defoe's *Robinson Crusoe* (1719), and **on the watch** in Jane Austen's *Sense and Sensibility* (1797).

on the loose 1. At large, free, as in *That dog of theirs is on the loose all the time.* [Second half of 1800s] 2. Acting without restraint, as in *After the game the players were in town, on the loose.* [Mid-1700s]

on the make 1. Seeking personal gain, as in *Tom's a young man on the make—he doesn't care whom he offends.* [Slang; second half of 1800s] 2. Looking for sexual conquest, as in *After several affairs, Peter got the reputation of being a man on the make.* [Slang; c. 1920]

on the map ♦ See PUT ON THE MAP.

on the mark ♦ See under OFF THE MARK.

on the market For sale; also, available for buying. For example, *We've put the boat on the market,* or *This is the only tandem bicycle on the market right now.* This phrase, first put as *in the market,* dates from the late 1600s; the first recorded use of the phrase with *on* was in 1891. Also see DRUG ON THE MARKET.

on the mend Recovering one's health, as in *I heard you had the flu, but I'm glad to see you're on the mend.* This idiom uses *mend* in the sense of "repair." [c. 1800]

on the money Also, **right on the money.** Exact, precise, as in *Your estimate is right on the money.* This term alludes to a winning bet in horse racing. [Slang; 1940s]

on the move 1. Busily moving about, very active, as in *A nurse is on the move all day long.* [Mid-1800s] Also see ON THE GO. 2. Going from one place to another, traveling, as in *Our troops are on the move again,* or *Ruth and Dick are always on the move, never staying put for more than a month or two.* [Late 1700s] 3. Making progress, advancing, as in *Their technology is clearly on the move.*

on the nail 1. Immediately, without delay, as in *He paid us back on the nail.* [c. 1600] 2. Under discussion or consideration, as in *The subject of the budget deficit has been on the nail for some time.* [Late 1800s] The precise allusion in these expressions has been lost. Neither has any connection to **hit the nail on the head** (see under HIT THE BULL'S-EYE).

on the nose Exactly, precisely; especially, at the appointed time or estimated amount. For example,

The busload of students arrived at the museum at ten o'clock right on the nose, or *He guessed the final score on the nose.* This term, like ON THE BUTTON, may come from boxing, where the opponent's nose is a highly desired target. [c. 1930]

on the off chance ♦ See under ON THE CHANCE THAT.

on the one hand Also, **on one hand.** As one point of view, from one standpoint. This phrase is often paired with **on the other hand** to indicate two sides of an issue. For example, *On the one hand this car is expensive; on the other hand, it's available and we need it right now.* [First half of 1600s]

on the order of 1. Approximately, as in *We need on the order of three cases of wine for the reception.* 2. Like, of a kind similar to, as in *Their house is on the order of a colonial saltbox.* [c. 1900]

on the other foot ♦ See SHOE IS ON THE OTHER FOOT.

on the other hand ♦ See under ON THE ONE HAND.

on the outs No longer on friendly terms, as in *They've been on the outs with their in-laws for years.* This idiom appeared in the early 1900s and derives from the synonymous **at outs,** first recorded in 1824.

on the part of ♦ See FOR ONE'S PART.

on the point of Also, **at the point of.** On the verge of, close to, as in *I was on the point of leaving when the phone rang.* The first term dates from the late 1200s, the second from the first half of the 1500s.

on the prowl Actively looking for something, as in *Their underpaid computer programmers are always on the prowl for better jobs.* This idiom transfers an animal's search for prey to human pursuits that are usually less blood-thirsty. [c. 1800]

on the qui vive On the alert, vigilant, as in *The police have been warned to be on the qui vive for terrorists.* This expression, containing the French words for "[long] live who?" originated as a sentinel's challenge to determine a person's political sympathies. The answer expected of allies was something like *vive le roi* ("long live the king"). It was taken over into English with its revised meaning in the early 1700s, the first recorded use being in 1726.

on the Q.T. Secretly, as in *They told her on the Q.T. that she was being promoted.* This slangy term, in which *Q.T.* is an abbreviation for "quiet," was first recorded in 1884.

on the rack Under great stress, as in *I was on the rack while I waited for the test results.* This expression, alluding to a medieval instrument of torture to which the victim was fastened and stretched, has been used figuratively since the late 1500s. Shakespeare had it in *The Merchant of Venice* (3:2): "Let me choose, for as I am I live upon the rack."

on the rebound Reacting to or recovering from an unhappy experience, especially the end of a love affair. For example, *A month after breaking up with Larry, Jane got engaged to Bob, a classic case of being on the rebound.* This metaphoric term, alluding to the bouncing back of a ball, has been used in the present sense since the mid-1800s, although *rebound* alone had been used figuratively for much longer.

on the receiving end In the situation of recipient, especially of something unpleasant, as in *It seems I'm always on the receiving end of his bad moods.* [c. 1930]

on the right foot, get off Also, **start off on the right foot.** Make a good beginning, establish good relations, as in *It's important to get off on the right foot in this new job.* This usage, alluding to walking correctly, was first recorded in 1909; the antonym, **get off on the wrong foot,** as in *I'm afraid we got off on the wrong foot with our daughter's in-laws,* was first recorded in 1925.

on the right tack Also, **on the right track.** Proceeding satisfactorily; also, following the correct line of reasoning. For example, *He thinks the housing market is improving, and he's on the right tack there* or *That's not exactly so, but you're on the right track.* The first term alludes to the direction of a sailboat, the second to the direction of a path. The same is true of the antonyms, **on the wrong tack** and **on the wrong track,** indicating an erroneous assumption or course of action. For example, *He's on the wrong tack for finding a solution,* or *The researchers were on the wrong track altogether when they assumed the virus was transmitted by mosquitoes.* The expressions using *tack* date from about 1900; those using *track* date from about 1880.

on the road 1. Traveling, as in *Our salesmen are on the road five days a week.* [Mid-1600s] 2. **on the road to.** On the way to, following a course that will end in. For example, *We could see Mary was on the road to recovery,* or *The business obviously was on the road to ruin.* [Mid-1600s]

on the rocks 1. Ruined, spoiled, as in *Six months after the wedding, their marriage was on the rocks.* This expression, alluding to a ship running aground on rocks and breaking apart, has been used figuratively for other disasters since the late 1800s. 2. Served over ice only, as in *He always drinks whiskey on the rocks.* The "rocks" here are the ice cubes. [Mid-1900s] 3. Destitute, bankrupt, as in *Can I borrow next month's rent? I'm on the rocks.* This usage, from the late 1800s, is heard more often in Britain than America.

on the ropes On the verge of defeat or collapse, helpless, as in *They acknowledged that their cam-*

paign was on the ropes, and they could not possibly win the election. This expression, alluding to a boxer forced back to the ropes of the ring and leaning against them for support, has been used figuratively since the mid-1900s.

on the run 1. In rapid retreat; also, attempting to escape from pursuers. For example, *The guerrillas were on the run after the ambush,* or *The burglars were on the run from the police.* [Early 1800s] 2. Hurrying from place to place, as in *The company officers were always on the run from New York to Los Angeles and back.* [Late 1800s]

on the safe side Avoiding danger, with a margin for error, as in *Just to be on the safe side, let's order another hundred chairs.* This idiom was first recorded in 1811.

on the same wavelength In complete accord, in rapport, as in *Conductor, orchestra members, soloists, and chorus all were on the same wavelength, making for a wonderful performance.* This term alludes to radio waves that carry a broadcast. [First half of 1900s]

on the scene, be Also, **arrive** or **come on the scene.** Be or arrive where an action or event occurs, as in *They won't have a wild party because their parents will be on the scene,* or *Once Bob arrives on the scene, you can expect fireworks.* Alluding to the theatrical scene, where a drama is being played, this phrase has been used more loosely since the early 1700s.

on the shelf 1. Inactive, not employed, as in *With mandatory retirement at 65, many useful employees are put on the shelf.* [Second half of 1500s] 2. In a state of disuse, as in *We'll have to put her proposal on the shelf until we have more funds.* [Late 1800s] 3. Without prospects of marriage. For example, *After she broke her third engagement, her parents were sure she'd be on the shelf.* This usage is always said of a woman and today considered offensive. It is probably obsolescent. [Early 1800s] All these usages allude to an article left on the shelf of a store, bookcase, or the like.

on the side 1. In addition to the main portion of something; also, in addition to one's regular job. For example, *He ordered some French fries on the side,* or *She often prepared tax returns on the side.* [Second half of 1800s] 2. See ON SOMEONE'S SIDE; ON THE SIDE OF THE ANGELS.

on the sidelines Observing rather than taking part, out of the action, as in *Bolivia's neighbors remained on the sidelines, waiting to see which faction in the dispute would prevail.* This idiom comes from sports. The *sidelines* are the two lines defining the sides of the court or playing field and the area immediately beyond them where, in such

sports as football, the non-playing team members sit. [First half of 1900s]

on the side of the angels Supporting the good side, as in *Whatever you may think of him, on important issues he's usually on the side of the angels.* This expression was coined by Benjamin Disraeli in 1864 in a speech about Darwin's theory that man is descended from apes: "The question is this: Is man an ape or an angel? Now I am on the side of the angels." Before long it was extended to broader use, specifically to the moral view.

on the skids In the process of decline or ruin, as in *If she quit now, her career would be on the skids.* The *skids* here are runners such as those on a sled, enabling one to go downhill quickly. [c. 1920]

on the sly Furtively, secretly, as in *She's always eating cookies on the sly.* The adjective *sly,* which means "cunning" or "crafty," is here used as a noun. [c. 1800]

on the spot 1. At once, without delay, as in *When the boss learned Tom had been lying, he fired him on the spot.* This usage suggests that one does not have time to move away from a particular spot. [Late 1600s] 2. At the scene of action, as in *Whenever there's a bad accident or fire, you can be sure the station will have a reporter on the spot.* This usage also employs *spot* in the sense of "a particular location." [Late 1600s] 3. Under pressure or in trouble, as in *He's on the spot, because he can't pay back the loan.* It is also phrased as **put on the spot,** meaning "put under pressure." For example, *The reporter's question put her on the spot; she didn't want to lie or to admit her part in the scandal.* [First half of 1900s]

on the spur of the moment Impulsively, without prior preparation, as in *He decided to join a tour to England on the spur of the moment.* This expression alludes to the goading action of a spur to a horse. [Late 1700s]

on the square Honestly and openly, as in *Our dealings with them have always been on the square.* This expression literally means "at right angles." Similarly the antonym **out of square,** literally signifying "not at right angles," figuratively means "not in agreement" or "irregular." For example, *The lab's report is out of square with the x-ray.* The first recorded use of this term was in 1542.

on the street Also, **in the street.** 1. Without a job, unemployed, as in *After they fired her she was on the street for two years.* [First half of 1900s] 2. Without a regular place of residence, homeless, as in *It's terrible to be on the street in winter.* [Mid-1800s] 3. Released from prison, as in *One more year and he'll be back in the street.* [First half of 1900s]

on the strength of On the basis of, as in *She was hired on the strength of her computer skills.* [Early 1600s]

on the surface Superficially, to all outward appearances, as in *On the surface he appeared brave and patriotic, but his troops knew better.* [Early 1700s]

on the table 1. Up for discussion as in *There are two new proposals on the table.* [Mid-1600s] **2.** Postponed or put aside for later consideration, as in *When they adjourned, three items were put on the table until the next meeting.* [First half of 1700s] The *table* in both idioms is a figurative conference table. Also see LAY ONE'S CARDS ON THE TABLE.

on the take Accepting bribes or other illegal income, as in *The commission found a number of police officers on the take.* [Colloquial; first half of 1900s]

on the tip of one's tongue Ready to utter something but unable to remember it at the moment, as in *I met him last year and his name is on the tip of my tongue—it'll come to me in a minute.* [Early 1700s]

on the town Also, **out on the town.** In spirited pursuit of entertainment offered by a town or city, as in *We went out on the town last night.* [Early 1700s]

on the up-and-up Open and honest, as in *Dad has always been on the up-and-up with them.* The precise allusion in this term is unknown. [Colloquial; c. 1860]

on the uptake In understanding or comprehension. This term is most often put as **quick on the uptake,** for readily understanding something, and **slow on the uptake,** for being slow to comprehend. For example, *Shirley will have no trouble learning that new computer program—she's very quick on the uptake.* It alludes to absorbing ("taking up") information. [Early 1800s]

on the verge of Close to, on the brink of, as in *I was on the verge of calling the doctor when he suddenly got better,* or *Sara was on the verge of tears when she heard the news.* This term uses *verge* in the sense of "the brink or border of something." [Mid-1800s]

on the wagon Abstaining from drinking alcoholic beverages, as in *Don't offer her wine; she's on the wagon.* This expression is a shortening of *on the water wagon,* referring to the horse-drawn water car once used to spray dirt roads to keep down the dust. Its present meaning dates from about 1900. The antonym **off the wagon,** used for a resumption of drinking, dates from the same period. B.J. Taylor used it in *Extra Dry* (1906): "It is better to have been on and off the wagon than never to have been on at all."

on the warpath Furious and on a hostile course of action, as in *When the meat wasn't delivered, the chef went on the warpath.* This expression was an English translation of a Native American term that literally means "a path used by a war party." **Go on the warpath** thus meant "go to battle." It was used in this way by James Fenimore Cooper in *The Deerslayer* (1841); its present hyperbolic use dates from the late 1800s.

on the watch ♦ See ON THE LOOKOUT.

on the way 1. Also, **on one's way.** In the process of coming, going, or traveling; also, about to come. For example, *The mail plane is on the way,* or *She is on her way out the door,* or *Winter is on the way.* **2.** On the route of a journey, as in *I met him on the way to town,* or *We ran into them on the way.* [c. A.D. 1000] **3. on the way to; well on the way to.** On the point of experiencing or achieving, as in *James is on the way to becoming a full professor,* or *Nancy is well on her way to a nervous breakdown.* [Late 1800s] Also see ON THE WAY OUT.

on the way out 1. About to go out, as in *We were on our way out when the phone rang.* **2.** Going out of fashion, becoming obsolete, as in *Full-size cars are on their way out.*

on the whole Considering everything, as in *On the whole we enjoyed our vacation, although the hotel was not perfect by any means.* [Late 1600s] Also see the synonyms BY AND LARGE; FOR THE MOST PART.

on the wing 1. In flight, usually referring to a bird as opposed to a plane. For example, *Louise is very good at identifying birds on the wing.* [Late 1400s] **2.** Active, in motion, as in *Coaches are always on the wing, trying to recruit talented athletes.* This usage may be obsolescent. [c. 1500]

on the wrong foot ♦ See ON THE RIGHT FOOT.

on the wrong side of bed ♦ See GET UP ON THE WRONG SIDE.

on the wrong tack Also, **on the wrong track.** ♦ See under ON THE RIGHT TACK.

on thin ice In a precarious or risky position, as in *After failing the midterm, he was on thin ice with his math teacher.* This metaphor is often rounded out as **skate on thin ice,** as in *He knew he was skating on thin ice when he took his rent money with him to the racetrack.* This idiom, which alludes to the danger that treading on thin ice will cause it to break, was first used figuratively by Ralph Waldo Emerson in his essay *Prudence* (1841): "In skating over thin ice our safety is in our speed."

on time 1. Punctually, according to schedule, as in *I hope the plane will be on time.* [Early 1800s] **2.** By paying in installments, on credit, as in *They are buying their car on time.* The *time* here refers to the designated period in which payments must be made. [Mid-1800s]

on tiptoe 1. Eagerly anticipating something, as in *The children were on tiptoe before the birthday* *party.* [Late 1500s] **2.** Moving stealthily, warily, as in *They went down the hall on tiptoe.* [Mid-1700s] Both usages transfer standing on one's toes to a particular reason for doing so; def. 2 alludes to moving more quietly in this fashion.

on to ♦ See BE ON TO.

on top In a dominant or successful position. It is also put as **come out on top,** as in *As we expected, Paul again came out on top in the chess tournament.* [Mid-1500s] Also see ON TOP OF.

on top of 1. In control of, fully informed about, as in *The weeds were terrible, but the new gardener was soon on top of them,* or *Our senator always manages to be on top of the issues.* **2.** In addition to, following closely on, as in *Several other benefits are being offered on top of a better salary,* or *On top of the flu Jane caught her sister's measles.* [c. 1600] **3.** Also, **on top of one another.** Very close to, crowded, as in *I didn't see her until she was right on top of us,* or *In these condominiums people are living right on top of one another.* [Mid-1900s]

on top of the world Feeling very happy, delighted, as in *She was on top of the world after her roses won first prize.* This idiom alludes to the peak of success or happiness. [c. 1920]

on trial 1. In the process of being tried, especially in a court of law. For example, *He would be put on trial for the murder of his wife.* [Early 1700s] **2.** As a test of something, on probation, as in *They said we could take the vacuum cleaner on trial and return it if it was too noisy.* [Early 1700s]

on view So as to be seen, as in *They will put the antiques on view an hour before the auction begins.* [Mid-1800s]

on welfare ♦ See ON RELIEF.

on your life ♦ See NOT ON YOUR LIFE.

open ♦ In addition to the idioms beginning with OPEN, also see KEEP A WEATHER EYE (OPEN); KEEP ONE'S EYES OPEN; LAY OPEN; LEAVE OPEN; LEAVE THE DOOR OPEN; NOT OPEN ONE'S MOUTH; OUT IN THE OPEN; THROW OPEN; WIDE OPEN; WITH ONE'S EYES OPEN; WITH OPEN ARMS.

open and aboveboard Also, **honest and aboveboard.** Candid and fair, without deceit or trickery, as in *I'll join you, but only if everything remains open and aboveboard.* Both versions of this expression are redundancies, since they use *open* and *aboveboard* in the sense of "honest." The latter word, dating from the early 1600s, comes from gambling and alludes to the fact that card players who do not keep their hands on the table (board) may be suspected of changing their cards under the table.

open and shut Simple, straightforward, easily solved, as in *With three eyewitnesses, the prosecutor said*

this case was open and shut. This term suggests that one has immediate access to the facts of a situation. [c. 1840]

open book Something or someone that can be readily examined or understood, as in *His entire life is an open book.* This metaphoric expression is often expanded to **read someone like an open book,** meaning "to discern someone's thoughts or feelings"; variations of this metaphor were used by Shakespeare: "Read o'er the volume of young Paris' face," (*Romeo and Juliet*, 1:3) and "O, like a book of sport thou'lt read me o'er" (*Troilus and Cressida*, 4:5). [Mid-1800s] For an antonym, see CLOSED BOOK.

open doors ♦ See OPEN THE DOOR TO.

open fire Begin a verbal attack, as in *In her second letter to the editor she opened fire, saying the reporter had deliberately misquoted her.* This idiom alludes to discharging a firearm. [Mid-1800s]

open house, keep Provide hospitality for visitors, as in *They loved company and kept open house virtually all summer long.* This usage differs from the plain *open house,* which refers to a particular occasion or period when a home or institution is open to visitors or prospective buyers. [First half of 1500s]

open mind A mind receptive to different opinions and ideas, as in *Her open mind could see merit in the new method.* This phrase is often put as **keep an open mind,** as in *The judge cautioned the jury to keep an open mind while hearing the evidence.* [First half of 1800s]

open one's eyes Become or make someone aware of the truth of a situation, as in *It's time you opened your eyes to the politics of this office,* or *The trip to Zimbabwe opened her eyes to the difficulties faced by developing nations.* [Second half of 1800s]

open one's heart to Confide in, reveal one's thoughts and feelings to, as in *Last night Meg opened her heart to her sister concerning her marriage.* This expression uses *heart* in the sense of "the seat of thought and emotion," a usage dating from the 9th century.

open one's mouth ♦ See NOT OPEN ONE'S MOUTH.

open question An unresolved issue, one that has not been finally determined. For example, *Whether the town should pave all the unpaved roads remains an open question.* In the mid-1800s this term acquired a specific meaning in the British Parliament, that is, "an issue on which members may vote independently, without respect to their party affiliation."

open season on A period of unrestrained criticism or attack on something or someone, as in *During an election year it's open season on all officeholders.*

This expression alludes to the period during which one may legally hunt or fish. [Colloquial; c. 1900]

open secret Something that is supposedly clandestine but is in fact widely known, as in *It's an open secret that both their children are adopted.* This expression originated as the title of a Spanish play by Calderón, *El Secreto a Voces* ("The Noisy Secret"), which was translated by Carlo Gozzi into Italian as *Il pubblico secreto* (1769). In English the term came into general use during the 1800s.

open the door to Also, **open doors.** Create an opportunity for, as in *Legalizing marijuana may open the door to all kinds of abuse,* or *Her statement opened the door to further discussion,* or *Dad's connections at the hospital have opened doors for Richard's colleagues at medical school.* [Late 1600s]

open up 1. Spread out, unfold, as in *A green valley opened up before us.* [Early 1800s] 2. Begin operation, as in *The new store opens up next month.* [Late 1700s] 3. Begin firing, begin attacking, as in *The artillery opened up at dawn,* or, figuratively, *The speaker opened up fiercely on the opposition.* [1930s] Also see OPEN FIRE. 4. Speak freely and candidly, as in *At last the witness opened up and told what happened.* [Colloquial; c. 1920] 5. Make an opening by cutting, as in *the surgeon opened up the patient's chest.* 6. Become available or accessible, as in *With new markets opening up all the time we hope to see our revenues increase dramatically.* [Mid-1800s] 7. Increase the speed of a vehicle, as in *Let's see how fast the car will go if you open it up.* [Colloquial; c. 1920] 8. Open the door, let me (or us) in, as in *Open up! This is the police.* [Mid-1900s] Note that in all of these usages except def. 4 and 7, *up* serves as an intensifier, that is, it emphasizes the verb *open.*

open with Begin with, as in *The concert season opens with the Symphony performing Mahler's Ninth.* This idiom uses *open* in the sense of "begin," a usage dating from the late 1600s.

opinion ♦ See FORM AN OPINION; MATTER OF OPINION.

opposite number, one's One's counterpart, as in *He's my opposite number in the California office.* This expression is generally used for a person's equivalent in another organization or system (*number* alluding to their position in a hierarchy). [c. 1900]

opt out Choose not to participate, as in *Our school opted out of the state competition.* [Slang; mid-1900s]

oranges ♦ See APPLES AND ORANGES.

orbit ♦ See IN ORBIT.

order ♦ In addition to the idioms beginning with ORDER, also see APPLE-PIE ORDER; BACK ORDER; CALL TO ORDER; IN ORDER; IN SHORT ORDER; JUST WHAT THE DOCTOR ORDERED; LAW AND ORDER; MADE TO ORDER; MARCHING ORDERS; ON ORDER; ON THE ORDER OF; OUT OF ORDER; PECKING ORDER; PUT ONE'S HOUSE IN ORDER; SHORT ORDER; STANDING ORDERS; TALL ORDER; TO ORDER.

order of the day, the The prevailing or expected mode, the current agenda, as in *Volatility is the order of the day in high-tech stocks,* or *T-shirts and blue jeans were the order of the day for the picnic.* This expression, dating from the late 1600s, originally alluded to the subject of debate in a legislature on a particular day, as well as to specific commands given to troops. Its figurative use dates from the second half of the 1700s.

order someone about Give peremptory commands to someone, be domineering, as in *That teacher had better learn not to order us about.* [Mid-1800s]

ordinary ♦ See OUT OF THE ORDINARY.

or else 1. Otherwise, in different circumstances, as in *Present your case now, or else you won't have a chance.* [c. 1300] 2. Regardless of any extenuating circumstances, no matter what, as in *Be there on time or else!* [Second half of 1800s]

or other One besides the one mentioned. This phrase is used to emphasize indefinite words beginning with *some,* such as *someone, somehow, sometime, somewhere.* For example, *Someone or other will be taking tickets at the door,* or *I can't remember where I put the lawn rake, but it's somewhere or other in the garage,* or *Somehow or other be found one that matched.* [c. 1600]

or so Approximately, especially alluding to a number, as in *Four hundred or so guests are invited.* [Late 1500s]

or what? A phrase following a statement that adds emphasis or suggests an option. For example, in *Is this a good movie or what?* the phrase asks for confirmation or agreement. However, it also may ask for an alternative, as in *Is this book a biography or what?* In the 1700s it generally asked for a choice among a series of options, and it still has this function, as in *In what does John excel? imagination? in reasoning powers? in mathematics? or what?*

or whatever Whatnot, or any other thing that might be mentioned, as in *They've stocked wine, beer, soda, or whatever,* or *You can stay or leave, or whatever.* [Early 1900s]

other ♦ In addition to the idioms beginning with OTHER, also see AT EACH OTHER'S THROATS; DO UNTO OTHERS; EACH OTHER; EVERY OTHER; IN ONE EAR AND OUT THE OTHER; IN SOMEONE'S POCKET (LIVE IN EACH OTHER'S POCKETS); IN OTHER WORDS; LAUGH OUT OF THE OTHER SIDE OF ONE'S MOUTH; LOOK THE OTHER WAY; MADE FOR (EACH OTHER); NONE OTHER THAN; ON THE ONE (THE OTHER) HAND; OR OTHER; RIGHT (OTHER) SIDE OF THE TRACKS; SHOE IS ON THE OTHER FOOT; SIX OF ONE, HALF A DOZEN OF

THE OTHER; THE OTHER DAY; THIS AND THAT (AND
THE OTHER); TURN THE OTHER CHEEK; WAIT FOR
THE OTHER SHOE TO DROP.

other day, the One day recently, a short time ago,
as in *I saw her in the museum the other day.* This
term originally meant either "the next day" or
"the preceding day" (tomorrow or yesterday). In
its current meaning it was first recorded in 1421.

other fish to fry Also, **better** or **bigger fish to fry.**
More important matters to attend to, as in *They
asked me to help with the decorations, but I have
other fish to fry.* [Mid-1500s]

other good fish in the sea ♦ See NOT THE ONLY
FISH IN THE SEA.

other side of the coin The opposite aspect, as in *I
know you'd like to go but the other side of the coin is
that someone has to stay with the baby,* or *The subscription is expensive, but the other side of the coin
is that it's an excellent publication.* This term replaced the older *other side of the medal* or *other side
of the shield* about 1900.

other side of the tracks ♦ See RIGHT SIDE OF THE
TRACKS.

other than 1. Different from, besides, as in *They
were shocked to find she has a lover other than her
husband.* [1250] **2.** In a different manner than;
otherwise than, as in *How could she be other than
happy with the new house?* [Late 1800s] **3. other
than that.** Except that, as in *Other than that the
nearest store was five miles away, it was a perfect
location.*

other things being equal Also, **all else being equal.**
Given the same circumstances, as in *Other things
being equal, I prefer the green sofa.* This term is a
translation of the Latin phrase *ceteris paribus,*
which was widely used until the 18th century,
when in began to be replaced by the English
equivalent.

other way round, the In the reverse direction, as
in *I don't think the sofa will go through the door this
way; let's try it the other way round.*

ounce ♦ In addition to the idiom beginning with
OUNCE, also see MORE BANG FOR THE BUCK (BOUNCE
FOR THE OUNCE).

**ounce of prevention is worth a pound of cure,
an** It is easier to forestall a disaster than to deal
with it. For example, *The new law makes all children
under twelve wear bicycle helmets—an ounce of
prevention.* This ancient proverb is first recorded
in Latin in Henry de Bracton's *De Legibus* (c.
1240) and has been repeated ever since, often in
shortened form.

out ♦ In addition to the idioms beginning with
OUT, also see ACE OUT; ACT OUT; ALL OUT; ASK OUT;
BACK OUT; BAIL OUT; BANG OUT; BAWL OUT; BEAR
OUT; BEAT ONE'S BRAINS OUT; BEAT OUT; BELT OUT;

BENT OUT OF SHAPE; BLACK OUT; BLISS OUT; BLOT
OUT; BLOW ONE'S BRAINS OUT; BLOW OUT; BLURT
OUT; BOTTOM OUT; BOW OUT; BRANCH OUT; BRAVE
OUT; BREAK OUT; BREAK OUT OF; BRING OUT; BUG
OUT; BUM OUT; BURN OUT; BURST INTO (OUT); BUY
OUT; CALL OUT; CAMP OUT; CANCEL OUT; CARD IN
(OUT); CARRY OUT; CAST OUT; CHECK OUT; CHEW
OUT; CHICKEN OUT; CHILL OUT; CHURN OUT; CLEAN
OUT; CLEAR OUT; CLOCK IN (OUT); CLOSE OUT;
COME OUT; COME OUT AHEAD; COME OUT IN THE
WASH; COME OUT OF; COME OUT WITH; CONK OUT;
COOL OFF (OUT); COP OUT; COUNT OUT; CRANK
OUT; CRAP OUT; CROP OUT; CRY (OUT) FOR; CUT IT
OUT; CUT OUT; DAY AFTER DAY (DAY IN, DAY OUT);
DEAL OUT; DECK OUT; DIE OUT; DIG OUT; DINE OUT
ON; DISH OUT; DO OUT OF; DOPE OUT; DOWN AND
OUT; DRAG ON (OUT); DRAW OUT; DROP OUT;
DROWN OUT; DRUM OUT; DRY OUT; DUCK OUT; EASE
OUT; EAT SOMEONE OUT OF HOUSE AND HOME; EAT
ONE'S HEART OUT; EAT OUT OF ONE'S
HAND; EDGE OUT; EKE OUT; FADE OUT; FALL OUT;
FARM OUT; FAR OUT; FEEL OUT; FERRET OUT; FIGHT
IT OUT; FIGURE OUT; FILL OUT; FIND OUT; FISH OUT;
FISH OUT OF WATER; FIT OUT; FIZZLE OUT; FLAKE
OUT; FLAT OUT; FLESH OUT; FLIP ONE'S LID (OUT);
FLUNK OUT; FOLLOW OUT; FOR CRYING OUT LOUD;
FORK OVER (OUT); FREAK OUT; FREEZE OUT; FRESH
OUT OF; GET OUT; GET OUT OF; GET THE LEAD OUT;
GIVE OUT; GO OUT; GO OUT OF ONE'S WAY; GROSS
OUT; GROW OUT OF; GUT IT OUT; HAMMER OUT;
HAND OUT; HANG OUT; HANG OUT ONE'S SHINGLE;
HANG OUT TO DRY; HASH OVER (OUT); HAVE AN
OUT; HAVE IT OUT; HAVE ONE'S WORK CUT OUT;
HEAD OUT; HEAR OUT; HEART GOES OUT TO; HELP
OUT; HIDE OUT; HIRE OUT; HIT OUT; HOLD OUT; IN
(OUT OF) FAVOR; IN ONE EAR AND OUT THE OTHER;
IN (OUT OF) ONE'S ELEMENT; IN (OUT OF) ONE'S
HAIR; IN (OUT OF) PRINT; IN (OUT OF) REACH; INS
AND OUTS; INSIDE OUT; INTO (OUT OF) THIN AIR; IN
(OUT OF) TUNE; IRON OUT; JURY IS STILL OUT; KEEP
AN EYE OUT; KICK OUT; KNOCK OUT; KNOCK THE
BOTTOM OUT; LASH OUT; LAY OUT; LEAVE OUT; LET
OUT; LET THE CAT OUT OF THE BAG; LIGHT OUT; LIKE
A BAT OUT OF HELL; LIVE OUT; LOCK OUT; LOG IN
(OUT); LOOK OUT; LOOK OUT FOR; LOSE OUT; LUCK
OUT; MAKE A MOUNTAIN OUT OF A MOLEHILL; MAKE
CAPITAL OUT OF; MAKE OUT; MAX OUT; MELLOW
OUT; MISS OUT ON; MURDER WILL OUT; MUSTER IN
(OUT); NOSE OUT; NOSE OUT OF JOINT; ODD MAN
OUT; ON THE OUTS; ON THE WAY OUT; OPT OUT; PAN
OUT; PARCEL OUT; PASS OUT; PAY OUT; PETER OUT;
PHASE IN (OUT); PICK OUT; PIG IT (OUT); PLAYED
OUT; PLAY OUT; POINT OUT; POOP OUT; POUND OUT;
POUR OUT; PRICE OUT OF THE MARKET; PRINT OUT;
PROVE OUT; PSYCH OUT; PULL OUT; PULL OUT ALL
THE STOPS; PULL OUT OF A HAT; PULL THE RUG OUT;
PUNCH IN (OUT); PUT ONE OUT; PUT ONESELF OUT;
PUT OUT; PUT OUT FEELERS; PUT SOMEONE OUT OF

HIS OR HER MISERY; PUT OUT TO GRASS; PUZZLE OUT; RACK OUT; RAIN OUT; READ OUT OF; RIDE OUT; RIGHT OUT; RIGHT-SIDE OUT; ROLL OUT; ROOT OUT; ROUND OFF (OUT); ROUGH OUT; RUB OUT; RULE OUT; RUN OUT OF; RUN OUT ON; RUN OUT THE CLOCK; SACK IN (OUT); SCARE OUT OF ONE'S WITS; SCREW SOMEONE OUT OF; SEE OUT; SELL OUT; SET OUT; SETTLE (WIPE OUT) OLD SCORES; SHELL OUT; SHIP OUT; SHOOT OUT; SHUT OUT; SIGN OUT; SING OUT; SINGLE OUT; SIT OUT; SKIP OUT; SLEEP OUT; SLIP OUT; SMOKE OUT; SNAP OUT OF IT; SNIFF OUT; SNUFF OUT; SOUND OUT; SPACE OUT; SPELL OUT; SPIN OUT; STAKE OUT; STAMP OUT; STAND OUT; START OUT; STEP OUT; STICK ONE'S NECK OUT; STICK OUT; STRAIGHTEN OUT; STRESS OUT; STRIKE OUT; STRING OUT; STRUNG OUT; SWEAR OUT; SWEAT OUT; TAKE A LEAF OUT OF SOMEONE'S BOOK; TAKE IT OUT ON; TAKE OUT; TAKE THE WIND OUT OF SOMEONE'S SAILS; TALKED OUT; TALK OUT; TALK OUT OF; TEASE OUT; TELL TALES (OUT OF SCHOOL); THINK OUT; THRASH OUT; THROW OUT; TIME OUT; TIRED OUT; TOP OUT; TRICK OUT; TROT OUT; TRUTH WILL OUT; TRY OUT; TUCKERED OUT; TUNE OUT; TURN OUT; WAIT OUT; WALK OUT; WANT IN (OUT); WASHED OUT; WASH OUT; WEAR OUT; WEASEL OUT; WEAVE IN AND OUT; WEED OUT; WELL OUT OF; WHACKED OUT; WIG OUT; WIN OUT; WIPE OUT; WORK OUT; WORM OUT OF; WRITE OUT; YEAR IN, YEAR OUT; ZAP OUT.

out and about Well enough to come and go, especially after an illness. For example, *I'm glad to see you're out and about again.* [Late 1800s] Also see UP AND ABOUT.

out and away By far, surpassing all others, as in *He's out and away the best pitcher in the league.* [First half of 1800s]

out at the elbows Also, **out at the heels** or **knees.** Wearing clothes that are worn out or torn; poor. For example, *When we last saw Phil be was out at the elbows.* These expressions, dating from the late 1500s and early 1600s, can refer to clothes worn through at these points as well as to a person too poor to replace them.

out back ♦ See under OUT FRONT.

out cold Also, **out for the count; out like a light.** Unconscious; also, asleep. For example, *He crashed into the wall and was out cold,* or *Willie punched him too hard, and he was out for the count* or *Don't call Jane; she's out like a light by ten every night.* The adjective *cold* refers to the lack of heat in a dead body and has been used to mean "unconscious" since the second half of the 1800s. The first variant comes from boxing, where a fighter who is knocked down must get up before the referee counts to ten or be declared defeated; it dates from about 1930. The last variant alludes to turning out a light and dates from the first half of the 1900s.

outdoors ♦ See BIG AS LIFE (ALL OUTDOORS).

out for, be 1. Be intent on, want, as in *The management is mostly out for bigger growth in sales.* [c. 1900] 2. **out for blood.** Intent on revenge, ready to fight with someone, as in *When Tom heard they'd outbid him, he was out for blood.* This hyperbolic term uses *blood* in the sense of "bloodshed" or "violent confrontation." Also see GO OUT FOR.

out for the count ♦ See under OUT COLD.

out from under Free from difficulties, especially from a burden of debts or work. For example, *They've been using credit cards for everything and don't know how they'll get out from under,* or *We have loads of mail to answer, but we'll soon get out from under.* This idiom uses *under* in the sense of "in a position of subjection." [Mid-1800s]

out front In front of a building or house, as in *We really need to put another light out front,* or *I'll meet you at the museum, out front.* The antonym, referring to the back of a building, is **out back,** as in *John's out back fixing his bike.* The noun *front* has been used for the side of a building where the main entrance is located since the mid-1300s; *back* for the rear of a building dates from the late 1300s.

out in left field Also, **out of left field.** Eccentric, odd; also, mistaken. For example, *The composer's use of dissonance in this symphony is way out in left field,* or *His answer was out of left field; he was totally wrong.* This idiom refers to baseball's left field but the precise allusion is disputed. Among the theories proposed is that in some ballparks the left field wall is farther from the batter than the wall in right field. Another is that in early ballparks, left field was often larger than right field and therefore was home to more lost balls and general confusion. [Mid-1900s] Also see FAR OUT.

out in the cold Excluded from benefits given to others, neglected, as in *Her stand on abortion left her out in the cold with the party.* This idiom alludes to being left outdoors without shelter. [Mid-1800s] Also see COME IN FROM THE COLD.

out in the open Also, **out into the open.** In or into public view or knowledge, as in *I wish he wouldn't talk behind our backs but bring his complaints out in the open,* or *It's important to bring the merger plans out into the open.* This term uses *open* to mean "an unconcealed state." [c. 1940]

out like a light ♦ See under OUT COLD.

out loud Audibly, aloud, as in *I sometimes find myself reading the paper out loud,* or *That movie was hilarious; the whole audience was laughing out loud.* First recorded in 1821, this synonym for *aloud* was once criticized as too colloquial for formal writing, but this view is no longer widespread.

Moreover, *aloud* is rarely used with verbs like *laugh* and *cry*. Also see FOR CRYING OUT LOUD.

out of, be Be lacking, as in *We're out of sugar and coffee.* Shakespeare used this idiom in *Henry V* (3:7): "These English are . . . out of beef." [Late 1500s] Also see RUN OUT OF.

out of a clear blue sky Also, **out of the blue.** Without warning, suddenly, as in *Her offer to help us with the fundraising came out of a clear blue sky,* or *We got a check from Aunt Ruby out of the blue.* These metaphoric terms allude to something dropping unexpectedly from the sky. [Late 1800s] Also see OUT OF NOWHERE.

out of bounds Beyond established limits, breaking the rules, unreasonable. For example, *Calling the teacher a liar—that's out of bounds.* This expression alludes to the boundaries of the playing area in numerous sports and to the rules applying to them. Its figurative use dates from the 1940s. [Early 1800s] Also see WITHIN BOUNDS.

out of breath Breathing with difficulty, panting, gasping. For example, *After five flights of stairs I'm out of breath.* This slightly hyperbolic term (since literally running out of breath means one is dead) dates from the late 1500s. Also see CATCH ONE'S BREATH.

out of business 1. No longer carrying on commercial transactions, as in *He's decided to go out of business when he turns sixty-five,* or The supermarkets are putting the small grocers out of business. 2. Not in working order, inoperative, as in *It looks as though the merry-go-round is out of business tonight.* Also see OUT OF COMMISSION; GO OUT, def. 5.

out of character ♦ See IN CHARACTER.

out of circulation ♦ See under IN CIRCULATION.

out of commission Not in working order, unable to function. For example, *The drawbridge is out of commission so we'll have to take the tunnel.* This idiom originally referred to a ship that was laid up for repairs or held in reserve. Similarly, the antonym, **in commission,** referred to a ship armed and ready for action. The latter term is also used in more general contexts today, as in *My car's back in commission now, so we can drive to the theater.* [Late 1800s]

out of condition Also, **out of shape.** ♦ See under IN CONDITION.

out of control Also, **out of hand.** No longer under management, direction, or regulation; unmanageable or unruly. For example, *Housing costs are out of control,* or *The children were getting out of hand again.* The first term uses *control* in the sense of "restraint," a usage dating from the late 1500s; the variant uses hand in the sense of "power" or "authority," and dates from the late 1800s.

out of date 1. Too old to be used, past the point of expiration, as in *This milk is out of date.* [Early 1600s] 2. Old-fashioned, no longer in style, as in *Dean has three suits but they're all out of date.* [Early 1800s]

out of fashion Also, **out of style.** ♦ See GO OUT, def. 5.

out of favor ♦ See under IN FAVOR.

out of gas ♦ See under RUN OUT OF.

out of hand 1. See OUT OF CONTROL. 2. At once, immediately, as in *The second surgeon rejected the doctor's treatment plan out of hand.* [1300s]

out of harm's way In a safe condition or place, as in *We fenced the yard to keep the children out of harm's way.* This idiom was first recorded about 1661.

out of humor ♦ See OUT OF SORTS.

out of it 1. Not participating in or knowledgable about a particular trend, pursuit, or group. For example, *Dad looked really out of it, riding his bike in bathing trunks and long black socks,* or *Mary sometimes felt out of it because she didn't know anyone in the most popular crowd.* [Early 1800s] 2. Confused or disoriented. For example, *Two or three beers and she was out of it,* or *He had no idea where he was or had been; he was totally out of it.* [Colloquial; mid-1900s]

out of joint 1. Dislocated, as in *Trying to break his fall, he put his shoulder out of joint.* [Late 1300s] 2. See NOSE OUT OF JOINT. 3. Out of order, inauspicious or unsatisfactory, as in *The entire lineup of our team is out of joint.* Shakespeare had this term in *Hamlet* (1:5): "The time is out of joint." [Early 1400s]

out of key ♦ See under IN KEY.

out of keeping ♦ See IN KEEPING.

out of kilter Also, **out of whack.** Not properly adjusted, not working well, out of order. For example, *This whole schedule is out of kilter with the rest of our projects,* or *The wheels on the trailer are out of whack.* The first term, also spelled *kelter,* dates from the early 1600s and its origin is not known. The precise allusion of the variant, a colloquial term dating from the late 1800s, is also unclear. Possibly it relates to a *whack,* or blow, throwing something off, or, some suggest, to *wacky,* that is, "crazy."

out of line 1. Uncalled for, improper; inappropriate. For example, *His remarks were totally out of line.* It is often put as **get out of line** or **step out of line,** meaning "behave improperly," as in *She really stepped out of line when she called him incompetent in front of his boss.* [Late 1700s] 2. Not in agreement with general practice, as in *Their prices are way out of line with other hotels.* Both def. 1 and 2 are metaphoric expressions that transfer being out of alignment to various kinds of behavior. 3. **out of one's line; not in one's line.** Not in one's occupation or field of interest. For example, *He offered a generous salary, but the work was out of her line*, or *I'd love to help, but telephone solicitation is not in my line.* This usage alludes to *line* in the sense of "a business or occupation." [Mid-1800s]

out of luck Having bad fortune, experiencing a misfortune, as in *You're out of luck if you want a copy; we just sold the last one.* This expression, first recorded in 1867, assumes that good fortune is a finite quantity that one can run out of. However, it generally applies to more temporary circumstances than being DOWN ON ONE'S LUCK.

out of nowhere Suddenly, unexpectedly, as in *That anonymous letter turned up out of nowhere.* It is often put as **come out of nowhere,** as in *Their team came out of nowhere and won the state championship.* This term uses *out of* in the sense of "from," and *nowhere* in the sense of "an unknown place." For a synonym, see OUT OF A CLEAR BLUE SKY.

out of one's ◆ In addition to the following idioms beginning with OUT OF ONE'S, also see under IN ONE'S.

out of one's depth Also, **beyond one's depth.** Outside one's understanding or competence, as in *He was out of his depth in that advanced calculus class*, or *The conductor realized that playing the fugue at the right tempo was beyond their depth.* This expression alludes to being in water so deep that one might sink. [c. 1600] Also see OVER ONE'S HEAD.

out of one's element ◆ See under IN ONE'S ELEMENT.

out of one's hair ◆ See under IN SOMEONE'S HAIR.

out of one's mind ◆ See GO OUT, def. 5; also, IN ONE'S RIGHT MIND.

out of one's shell ◆ See under IN ONE'S SHELL.

out of one's system Out of one's thoughts or inclinations. It is often put as **get something out of one's system,** as in *You need to get your ex-husband out of your system* or *At the annual all-chocolate buffet I try everything, which gets it out of my system for at least a month*, or *Let him complain as much as he wants so he'll get it out of his system.* This idiom uses *system* in the sense of "all one's physical and mental functions." [c. 1900]

out of one's way ◆ See GO OUT OF ONE'S WAY; also, OUT OF THE WAY.

out of order 1. Not functioning well, not operating properly or at all, as in *The oil burner is out of order again.* [Mid-1500s] 2. Unsuitable, inappropriate, as in *Her comments about the management were out of order.* Also see OUT OF LINE, def. 1. 3. Not following parliamentary procedure, as in *The chair called him out of order.*

out of phase Also, **out of sync.** In an unsynchronized or uncorrelated way. For example, *Inventory control and shipping are out of phase, so we can't rely on their figures*, or *The lights are out of sync and keep flashing at random.* For dates, see the antonym IN PHASE.

out of place Not in the proper situation, not belonging; inappropriate for the circumstances or location. For example, *A high school graduate, she felt out of place among all these academics with advanced degrees*, or *This velvet sofa is out of place on the porch.* This idiom uses *place* in the sense of "a fitting position." [First half of 1800s]

out of pocket 1. Lacking money; also, having suffered a financial loss, as in *We can't go; I'm out of pocket right now.* William Congreve had it in *The Old Bachelor* (1693): "But egad, I'm a little out of pocket at present." [Late 1600s] 2. Referring to actual money spent, as in *I had to pay the hotel bill out of pocket, but I know I'll be reimbursed.* This expression sometimes occurs as a hyphenated adjective mainly in the phrase *out-of-pocket expenses*, as in *My out-of-pocket expenses for business travel amounted to more than a thousand dollars.* [Late 1800s]

out of practice No longer used to doing something, no longer adept for lack of doing something, as in *Mom hadn't baked a cake in years—she said she was out of practice.* [Late 1800s] Also see IN PRACTICE.

out of print ◆ See under IN PRINT; also see GO OUT, def. 6.

out of proportion Also, **out of all proportion.** Not in proper relation to other things, especially by being the wrong size or amount. For example, *This vase looks out of proportion on this small table*, or *Her emotional response was out of all proportion to the circumstances.* The noun *proportion* means "an agreeable or harmonious relationship of one thing relative to another." [Early 1700s] The antonym **in proportion** dates from the late 1600s and also refers either to physical size or appropriate degree, as in *The bird's wings are huge in proportion to its body*, or *Her willingness to believe him stands in direct proportion to her love for intrigue.*

out of reach ◆ See under IN REACH.

out of season ◆ See under IN SEASON.

out of shape ◆ See under IN CONDITION; also, BENT OUT OF SHAPE.

out of sight 1. Also, **out of someone's sight.** Out of the range of vision, as in *Stay out of sight while they're visiting*, or *Don't let the baby out of your sight in the yard.* [c. 1200] This idiom is also used in the phrase **get out of someone's sight,** meaning "go away"; for example, *Jean was furious with Bill and told him to get out of her sight at once.* 2. Unreasonable, excessive, as in *Our bill for the wine* *was out of sight.* [Colloquial; late 1800s] **3.** Excellent, superb, as in *The graduation party was out of sight.* This phrase is also used as an interjection meaning "Wonderful!" as in *Do I like it? Out of sight!* [Slang; second half of 1900s] **4. out of sight, out of mind.** What is absent is soon forgotten, as in *I don't think of them unless they send a Christmas card—out of sight, out of mind, I guess.* This phrase has been proverbial since Homer's time; the earliest recorded use in English was about 1450.

out of sorts Irritable, grouchy, as in *Don't ask him today—he's out of sorts.* This expression also implies that one's poor spirits result from feeling slightly ill. [Early 1600s] The synonym **out of humor**, on the other hand, used more in Britain than America, simply means "ill-tempered" or "irritable." [Mid-1600s]

out of square ‣ See under ON THE SQUARE.

out of step ‣ See under IN STEP.

out of stock ‣ See under IN STOCK.

out of the blue ‣ See OUT OF A CLEAR BLUE SKY.

out of the corner of one's eye Glancing casually or surreptitiously, as in *Out of the corner of my eye I saw Justin walking out the door.* This expression refers to looking sideways at something rather than directly.

out of the frying pan into the fire From a bad situation to one that is much worse. For example, *After Karen quit the first law firm she went to one with even longer hours—out of the frying pan into the fire.* This expression, a proverb in many languages, was first recorded in English in 1528.

out of the hole ‣ See under IN THE HOLE.

out of the loop ‣ See under IN THE LOOP.

out of the mouths of babes Young and inexperienced persons often can be remarkably wise, as in *She's only six but she said, quite rightly, that Harry was afraid of the sitter—out of the mouths of babes, Mother said.* This expression is a shortening and revision of expressions in the Old and New Testaments of the Bible. In Psalms 8:2, God ordains strength out of the mouth of babes and sucklings; in Matthew 21:16, praise comes from this source. Later generations changed strength and praise to wisdom.

out of the ordinary Unusual, uncommon, exceptional, as in *The venison they served was certainly out of the ordinary.* This expression sometimes, but not always, indicates that something is better than the usual. However, the negative version, **nothing out of the ordinary**, usually indicates that something is *not* special or outstanding, as in *It was an interesting lecture, but nothing out of the ordinary.*

out of the picture ‣ See IN THE PICTURE.

out of the question Impossible, not worth considering, as in *Starting over again is certainly out of the question.* This term uses *question* to refer to what is being talked or asked about. [c. 1700]

out of the rain ‣ See COME IN OUT OF THE RAIN.

out of the running ‣ See under IN THE RUNNING.

out of the way **1.** Not obstructing, hindering, or interfering, as in *This chair is out of the way now, so you won't trip.* This phrase also appears in **get out of the** (or **one's**) **way**, as in *Would you please get your coat out of the way?* or *Get your car out of my way.* [Mid-1500s] **2.** Taken care of, disposed of, as in *I'm glad we got these details out of the way.* **3.** In a remote location, as in *This restaurant is a little out of the way.* [Mid-1300s] **4.** Unusual, remarkable, as in *It was out of the way for him to praise his staff.* [Second half of 1500s] **5.** Amiss, in error, improper, as in *The security guard checked all the locks and saw nothing out of the way.* [Early 1200s] Also see GO OUT OF ONE'S WAY.

out of the window Discarded, tossed out. This term is often used in the phrase **go out the window**, as in *For the town planners past experience seems to have gone out the window.* It alludes to unwanted items being hurled out of the window. [First half of 1900s]

out of the woods Out of difficulties, danger or trouble, as in *We're through the worst of the recession—we're out of the woods now,* or *That pneumonia was serious, but Charles is finally out of the woods.* This expression, alluding to having been lost in a forest, dates from Roman times; it was first recorded in English in 1792. The British usage is *out of the wood.*

out of the woodwork Emerging from obscurity or a place of seclusion. It often is put as **come** (or **crawl**) **out of the woodwork,** as in *The candidates for this job were coming out of the woodwork.* The expression alludes to insects crawling out of the interior wooden fittings of a house, such as baseboards and moldings. [Colloquial; mid-1900s]

out of thin air ‣ See INTO THIN AIR.

out of this world Extraordinary, superb, as in *Her carrot cake is out of this world.* This colloquial term refers to something too good for this world. [Early 1900s]

out of touch No longer in contact or communication, as in *John and Mark have been out of touch for years,* or *That speech showed he's out of touch with his constituency.* This metaphoric expression alludes to physical contact. [Late 1800s] Also see IN TOUCH.

out of town Away from the town or city under consideration; away from home. For example, *In his new job Tom will be going out of town nearly* *every week,* or *He's out of town but I'll have him call you when he gets back.* [Late 1300s]

out of turn 1. Not in the proper order or sequence, as in *When her doubles partner began to serve out of turn, their opponents called the umpire.* [Late 1800s] 2. In an inappropriate manner or at an inappropriate time, as in *I may be out of turn telling you, but shorts are not permitted in the restaurant.* [First half of 1900s] Also see SPEAK OUT OF TURN.

out of wedlock Of parents not legally married, as in *Over the centuries many royal children were born out of wedlock.* The noun *wedlock,* for the state of being married, is rarely heard today except in this phrase, first recorded in 1675; its converse, **in wedlock,** dates from the 1300s and is even more rarely used.

out of whack ♦ See under OUT OF KILTER.

out of whole cloth From pure fabrication or fiction. This expression is often put as **cut** (or **made**) **out of whole cloth,** as in *That story was cut out of whole cloth.* In the 15th century this expression referred to something fabricated from cloth that ran the full length of the loom. However, by the 1800s it was common practice for tailors to deceive their customers and, instead of using whole cloth, actually make garments from pieced goods. Their advertising slogan, "cut out of whole cloth," thus came to mean "made up, false."

out of work Unemployed; also, having no work to do. For example, *He lost his job a year ago and has been out of work ever since,* or *They don't give her enough assignments—she's always out of work.* Shakespeare used this expression in *Henry V* (1:2): "All out of work and cold for action."

out on a limb In a difficult, awkward, or vulnerable position, as in *I lodged a complaint about low salaries, but the people who had supported me left me out on a limb.* This expression alludes to an animal climbing out on the limb of a tree and then being afraid or unable to retreat. [Late 1800s]

out on bail Released from custody on the basis of bail being posted, as in *The lawyer promised to get him out on bail.* This expression alludes to a payment made to the court as surety that the accused will appear for trial.

out on one's ear Dismissed, thrown out in disgrace, as in *In this company you get only one chance, and if you fail you're out on your ear.* This term alludes to being physically thrown out head first. [Slang; early 1900s]

out on the town ♦ See ON THE TOWN.

outs ♦ See INS AND OUTS; ON THE OUTS.

outset ♦ See AT THE OUTSET.

outside ♦ In addition to the idiom beginning with OUTSIDE, also see AT MOST (THE OUTSIDE).

outside of Except for, aside from, as in *Outside of a little lipstick, she wore no makeup.* [Colloquial; mid-1800s]

out to lunch Not in touch with the real world, crazy; also, inattentive. For example, *If he believes that story, he's really out to lunch,* or *Anne hasn't heard a word you said—she's out to lunch.* This expression transfers a temporary physical absence for the purpose of eating to a temporary or permanent mental absence. [Slang; mid-1900s]

out with it Say it, as in *Tell us what you really think—out with it!* Used as an imperative, this idiom uses *out* in the sense of "public."

over ♦ In addition to the idioms beginning with OVER, also see ALL OVER (and entries beginning with ALL OVER); BEND OVER BACKWARD; BIND OVER; BLOW OVER; BOIL OVER; BOWL OVER; CARRY OVER; CHECK ON (OVER); CHEW THE CUD (OVER); CLOUD OVER; COME OVER; CROSS OVER; CROW OVER; CRY OVER SPILT MILK; DO OVER; DRAW A VEIL OVER; DROP BY (OVER); FALL ALL OVER; FORK OVER; FUCK OVER; GET OVER; GET THE ADVANTAGE OF (OVER); GIVE OVER; GLOSS OVER; GO OVER; HAND OVER; HAND OVER FIST; HANG OVER; HASH OVER; HAVE A HOLD OVER; HAVE IT (ALL OVER SOMEONE); HEAD OVER HEELS; HOLD OVER; HONEYMOON IS OVER; IN DEEP WATER (OVER ONE'S HEAD); IT'S ALL OVER WITH; JUMP ALL OVER; KEEL OVER; KEEP WATCH (OVER); KICK OVER THE TRACES; KNOCK FOR A LOOP (OVER WITH A FEATHER); KNOCK OVER; LAY OVER; LOOK LIKE DEATH (WARMED OVER); LOOK OVER; LORD IT OVER; LOSE SLEEP OVER; MAKE OVER; MIND OVER MATTER; MULL OVER; ONCE OVER LIGHTLY; PAPER OVER; PARTY'S OVER; PASS OVER; PICK OVER; PULL OVER; PULL THE WOOL OVER SOMEONE'S EYES; PUT OVER; RAKE OVER THE COALS; RIDE ROUGHSHOD OVER; ROLL OVER; ROOF OVER ONE'S HEAD; RUN ONE'S EYES OVER; RUN OVER; SCOOT OVER; SIGN OVER; SLEEP OVER; SMOOTH OVER; STAND OVER; START OVER; STOP OFF (OVER); TAKE OVER; TALK OVER; THINK OVER; THROW OVER; TIDE OVER; TILL HELL FREEZES OVER; TURN IN (OVER) ONE'S GRAVE; TURN OVER; TURN OVER A NEW LEAF; WALK ALL OVER; WATCH OVER; WATER OVER THE DAM; WIN OVER; WORK OVER.

over a barrel In a weak or difficult position, as in *Once the competitors found a flaw in our product, they had us over a barrel.* This slangy expression, first recorded in 1938, supposedly alludes to reviving a drowning victim by placing the body head down over a barrel and rolling it back and forth, so as to empty the lungs of water. The expression survives, although happily the practice does not.

over again Once more, as in *The conductor had them start the symphony over again.* [Mid-1500s]

over against As opposed to, contrasted with, as in *Over against the Smiths, the Johnsons were well off.* [c. 1500]

over and above In addition to, besides, as in *Over and above travel expenses he was given a daily allowance.* [Early 1500s]

over and done with Completed, finished, as in *That argument's over and done with, so drop the subject.* This usage is somewhat redundant but more emphatic than OVER WITH. [First half of the 1900s]

over and over Also, **over and over again.** Repeatedly, many times, as in *I've told you over and over that he can't eat spicy food.* [Late 1500s] Also see AGAIN AND AGAIN.

overboard ♦ See GO OVERBOARD.

over my dead body In no way, under no circumstances, as in *Over my dead body will you drop out of high school.* This hyperbolic expression is often used jokingly. [Early 1800s]

over one's head 1. To a position higher than another's, as in *She was furious when her assistant was promoted over her head.* Similarly, **go over someone's head** means "appeal to a higher authority," as in *Since she couldn't help me, I decided to go over her head and talk to her supervisor.* [Mid-1500s] 2. Beyond one's understanding or competence, as in *The math required to complete these figures is way over my head.* [Early 1600s] For a synonym, see OUT OF ONE'S DEPTH. Also see IN DEEP (OVER ONE'S HEAD).

over the edge Insane, as in *I think he's gone over the edge.* This expression alludes to the edge of sanity. [1920s]

over the hill Past one's prime, as in *I'm a little over the hill to be playing contact sports.* This term, alluding to a climber who has reached a mountaintop and is now descending, has been used figuratively for the decline caused by aging since the mid-1900s.

over the hump Past the most difficult part, as in *She's over the hump with her dissertation; she'll soon be done.* This expression alludes to a barrier that impedes progress. [Colloquial; 1920s]

over the top 1. Surpassing a goal or quota, as in *The new salesmen are excellent; they were over the top within the first six months.* [Mid-1900s] 2. Over the parapet of a military trench, as in *The lieutenant sent fresh troops over the top.* This usage dates from World War I. 3. Extreme, outrageous, as in *This comedian's style goes over the top.* [Slang; late 1900s]

over with Done, finished, as in *I'll be glad when exams are over with.* [Colloquial; second half of 1900s] Also see OVER AND DONE WITH.

owl ♦ See NIGHT OWL.

own ♦ In addition to the idioms beginning with OWN, also see AFRAID OF ONE'S OWN SHADOW; AFTER ONE'S OWN HEART; BEAT SOMEONE AT HIS OR HER OWN GAME; BLOW ONE'S OWN HORN; CALL ONE'S OWN; CLOSE TO HOME; COME INTO (ONE'S OWN); DIG ONE'S OWN GRAVE; DO ONE'S (OWN) THING; DOSE OF ONE'S OWN MEDICINE; GET (ONE'S OWN) BACK; GET ONE'S (OWN) WAY; GO ONE'S (OWN) WAY; HOLD ONE'S OWN; IN ONE'S (OWN) INTEREST; IN ONE'S OWN BACKYARD; IN ONE'S OWN RIGHT; IN ONE'S OWN WORLD; KEEP ONE'S OWN COUNSEL; KNOW ONE'S OWN MIND; LEAVE TO SOMEONE'S OWN DEVICES; MIND OF ONE'S OWN; MIND ONE'S OWN BUSINESS; OF ONE'S OWN ACCORD; ON ONE'S (OWN) FEET; ON ONE'S OWN; ON ONE'S OWN ACCOUNT; ON ONE'S OWN TIME; PADDLE ONE'S OWN CANOE; PAY BACK IN ONE'S OWN COIN; PAY ONE'S (OWN) WAY; PICK ON (SOMEONE YOUR OWN SIZE); PULL ONE'S (OWN) WEIGHT; SIGN ONE'S OWN DEATH WARRANT; STEW IN ONE'S OWN JUICE; TAKE INTO ONE'S (OWN) HANDS; UNDER ONE'S OWN STEAM; WRITE ONE'S OWN TICKET.

own person, be one's Also, **be one's own man** or **woman.** Be independent, be responsible for oneself. For example, *We can't tell Jerry what to do—he's his own person.* Chaucer used this idiom in *Troilus and Cressida:* "I am my own woman, well at ease." [Late 1300s]

own medicine ♦ See DOSE OF ONE'S OWN MEDICINE.

own up Confess, make a full admission, as in *Come on, Tim, you'd better own up that you lost the car keys.* This idiom uses the verb *own* in the sense of "acknowledge." [Colloquial; mid-1800s]

oyster ♦ See WORLD IS ONE'S OYSTER.

p

p ♦ See MIND ONE'S P'S AND Q'S.

pace ♦ See CHANGE OF PACE; KEEP PACE; PUT SOMEONE THROUGH HIS OR HER PACES; SET THE PACE; SNAIL'S PACE.

pack ♦ In addition to the idioms beginning with PACK, also see JOE SIX-PACK; SEND SOMEONE ABOUT HIS OR HER BUSINESS (PACKING).

pack a punch Also, **pack a wallop.** 1. Be capable of a forceful blow; also, deliver a forceful blow. For example, *Knowing Bob could pack a wicked punch, they were careful not to anger him,* or *She swung her handbag, really packing a wallop.* [Colloquial; c. 1920] 2. Have a powerful effect, as in *That vodka martini packed a wallop.* Thomas Wolfe had this figurative usage in a letter (c. 1938): "I think my play, *The House,* will pack a punch."

packed in like sardines Extremely crowded, as in *I could barely breathe—we were packed in like sar-*

dines. This term, alluding to how tightly sardines are packed in cans, has been applied to human crowding since the late 1800s.

pack it in Stop working or abandon an activity, as in *Let's pack it in for the day*. This usage alludes to packing one's things before departing, and during World War I became military slang for being killed. It also is used as an imperative ordering someone to stop, as in *Pack it in! I've heard enough out of you*. In Britain it is also put as **pack it up**. [Colloquial; early 1900s]

pack off Also, **pack someone** or **something off**. Send someone (or something) away unceremoniously, as in *As soon as the children are packed off to bed, I'll call you back*, or *She told Anne she'd pack her things off as soon as she had a chance*. [First half of 1700s]

pack them in Attract a large audience, as in *A big star will always pack them in*. This idiom alludes to tightly filling a hall. [c. 1940]

paddle ◆ In addition to the idiom beginning with PADDLE, also see UP THE CREEK (WITHOUT A PADDLE).

paddle one's own canoe Be independent and self-reliant, as in *It's time Bill learned to paddle his own canoe*. This idiom alludes to steering one's own boat. [c. 1800]

paid ◆ See under PAY.

pain ◆ In addition to the idioms beginning with PAIN, also see AT PAINS; FEEL NO PAIN; FOR ONE'S PAINS; GROWING PAINS; NO PAIN, NO GAIN; ON PAIN OF.

pain in the neck Also, **pain in the ass** or **butt**. A source of annoyance, a nuisance, as in *Joan is a real pain in the neck, with her constant complaining*, or *Jack told his brother to stop being a pain in the ass*. The first of these colloquial expressions dates from about 1900 and originated as a euphemism for the two less polite variants.

paint black Represent someone or something as evil or harmful. This idiom is most often used in a negative context, as in *He's not so black as he's been painted*. [Late 1500s]

paint oneself into a corner Get oneself into a difficulty from which one can't extricate oneself. For example, *By volunteering to do more work in the office and then taking a freelance job, George has painted himself into a corner*. This idiom uses the graphic image of painting all of the floor except for the corner one stands in, so that one cannot leave without stepping on wet paint.

paint the town red Go on a spree, as in *Whenever they go to New York they want to paint the town red*. The precise allusion of this term is disputed. Some believe it refers to setting something on fire; others point to a vague association of the color red with violence. [Late 1800s]

pair ◆ In addition to the idiom beginning with PAIR, also see SHOW ONE'S (A CLEAN PAIR OF) HEELS.

pair off 1. Put two persons together; also, become one of a couple, as in *Jean mentally paired off her guests whenever she planned a party*, or *All the tennis players had to pair off for a round of doubles matches*. [Late 1600s] **2.** Also, **pair up**. Make a pair of, match, as in *I always have trouble pairing up their socks*. [Early 1900s]

pal around Associate as friends or chums, as in *Bill and Jim have been palling around for years*. This expression makes a verb of the noun *pal*, which comes from the Gypsy word for "brother." [c. 1900]

pale ◆ See BEYOND THE PALE.

palm ◆ In addition to the idiom beginning with PALM, also see CROSS SOMEONE'S PALM; GREASE SOMEONE'S PALM; ITCHY PALM.

palm off Pass off by deception, substitute with intent to deceive, as in *The salesman tried to palm off a zircon as a diamond*, or *The producer tried to palm her off as a star from the Metropolitan Opera*. This expression alludes to concealing something in the palm of one's hand. It replaced the earlier *palm on* in the early 1800s.

pan ◆ In addition to the idiom beginning with PAN, also see FLASH IN THE PAN; OUT OF THE FRYING PAN.

pancake ◆ See FLAT AS A PANCAKE.

pandora's box A source of unforeseen trouble, as in *Revising the tax code is opening a Pandora's box*. This equivalent for the modern CAN OF WORMS comes from the Greek legend in which Pandora, entrusted with a box containing the world's ills, is overcome by curiosity and opens it, thereby releasing them. [Late 1500s]

panic ◆ See PUSH THE PANIC BUTTON.

pan out Turn out well, succeed, as in *If I don't pan out as a musician, I can always go back to school*. This expression alludes to washing gold from gravel in a pan. [Mid-1800s]

pants ◆ In addition to the idiom beginning with PANTS, also see ANTS IN ONE'S PANTS; BEAT THE PANTS OFF; CAUGHT WITH ONE'S PANTS DOWN; GET THE LEAD OUT OF (ONE'S PANTS); KICK IN THE PANTS; SEAT OF THE PANTS; TALK SOMEONE'S ARM (PANTS) OFF; WEAR THE PANTS.

pants off, the This phrase is used to intensify the meaning of verbs such as **bore, charm, kid, scare**, or **talk**. For example, *That speech bored the pants off us*, or *It was a real tornado and scared the pants off me*. Playwright Eugene O'Neill used it in *Ah, Wilderness!* (1933): "I tell you, you scared the pants off him," and Evelyn Waugh, in *A Handful of Dust* (1934), had a variation, "She bores my pants off." [Colloquial; early 1900s] Also see BORE TO DEATH; BEAT THE PANTS OFF.

paper ♦ In addition to the idiom beginning with PAPER, also see ON PAPER; PUSH PAPER; WALKING PAPERS.

paper over Also, **paper over the cracks.** Repair superficially, conceal, especially flaws. For example, *He used some accounting gimmicks to paper over a deficit,* or *It was hardly a perfect settlement, but they decided to paper over the cracks.* The German statesman Otto von Bismarck first used this analogy in a letter in 1865, and the first recorded example in English, in 1910, referred to it. The allusion is to covering cracked plaster with wallpaper, thereby improving its appearance but not the underlying defect.

par ♦ In addition to the idiom beginning with PAR, also see BELOW PAR; ON A PAR WITH; UP TO PAR.

parade ♦ See HIT PARADE; RAIN ON ONE'S PARADE.

paradise ♦ See FOOL'S PARADISE.

parcel ♦ In addition to the idiom beginning with PARCEL, also see PART AND PARCEL.

parcel out Divide into parts and distribute, as in *She parceled out the remaining candy among the children.* This idiom uses *parcel* in the sense of "divide into small portions." [Mid-1500s]

pardon ♦ See BEG TO DIFFER; EXCUSE ME.

par for the course An average or normal amount; just what one might expect. For example, *I missed three questions, but that's par for the course.* This term comes from golf, where it refers to the number of strokes needed by an expert golfer to finish the entire course. Its figurative use for other kinds of expectation dates from the second half of the 1900s.

part ♦ In addition to the idioms beginning with PART, also see BEST PART OF; BETTER HALF (PART OF); DISCRETION IS THE BETTER PART OF VALOR; DO ONE'S BIT (PART); FOOL AND HIS MONEY ARE SOON PARTED; FOR ONE'S PART; FOR THE MOST PART; IN GOOD PART; IN PART; TAKE PART; TAKE SOMEONE'S PART.

part and parcel An essential or basic element, as in *Traveling is part and parcel of Zach's job.* Used since the 15th century as a legal term, with *part* meaning "a portion" and *parcel* "something integral with a whole," this idiom began to be used more loosely from about 1800. Although both nouns have the same basic meaning, the redundancy lends emphasis.

part company Go separate ways; also, disagree about something. For example, *After they reached the park Jeff and Jane parted company,* or *They parted company on their views of foreign policy.* [Early 1700s]

particular ♦ See IN PARTICULAR.

parting of the ways A point of divergence, especially an important one, as in *When Jim decided to travel with the band and Jill wanted a more normal home life, they came to a parting of the ways.* This term, which transfers a fork in a road to alternative courses of action, appears in the Bible (Ezekiel 21:21), where the king of Babylon must decide whether or not to attack Jerusalem: "[He] stood at the parting of the way." [c. 1600]

parting shot A final insult or last word in an argument, as in *As she stalked out, Jane hurled as a parting shot, "And I quit!"* This idiom apparently originated as a corruption of *Parthian shot,* referring to the practice of ancient Parthian warriors of turning back to shoot at their pursuers. [Late 1800s]

part with Give up, let go of, relinquish, as in *Janice hated to part with her cat, but the landlord wouldn't allow pets.* [Mid-1300s]

party ♦ In addition to the idioms beginning with PARTY, also see LIFE OF THE PARTY.

party line The official policy of an organization or government, as in *The current party line opposes legalized abortion in all cases.* This term, dating from about 1830, was originally used for a political party's official policy but in the mid-1900s was almost exclusively applied to the rigid dicta of the Soviet Communist Party. Since then it has returned to looser use.

party's over, the It's time to be serious; carefree times have ended. For example, *Now that he's been promoted the party's over; he has to write a report every week.* This expression uses *party* in the sense of "a pleasant social gathering." [c. 1930]

pass ♦ In addition to the idioms beginning with PASS, also see BRING ABOUT (TO PASS); COME ABOUT (TO PASS); CROSS (PASS THROUGH) ONE'S MIND; HAND (PASS) IN ONE'S CHIPS; HEAD SOMEONE OFF (AT THE PASS); IN PASSING; MAKE (TAKE) A PASS AT; SHIPS THAT PASS IN THE NIGHT.

pass away Also, **pass on** or **over.** Die, as in *He passed away last week,* or *After Grandma passes on we'll sell the land,* or *I hear he's about to pass over.* All these terms are euphemisms for dying, although the verb *pass* alone as well as *pass away* have been used in the sense of "pass out of existence, die" since the 1300s. The two variants — adding *on* [c. 1800] and *over* [c. 1900] — allude to moving to some other-worldly realm.

pass by 1. Proceed past something, as in *If you pass by a white house, you've gone too far.* [c. 1300] 2. Also, **pass over.** Disregard, overlook, as in *Just pass by the first few pages and you'll get to the basics,* or *Ralph was passed over for promotion.* [1300s]

pass for Be accepted as or believed to be, usually something that is not so. For example, *Jean is 23 but could pass for a teenager,* or *They thought that copy would pass for an original.* [Late 1500s]

pass muster Meet a required standard, as in *That yard cleanup won't pass muster with Mom.* This expression originally meant "to undergo a military review without censure," *muster* referring to an assembling of troops for inspection or a similar purpose. [Late 1500s]

pass off 1. Misrepresent something or someone, as in *They tried to pass off that piece of glass as a gemstone,* or *Bill passed her off as his sister.* [Late 1700s] Also see PALM OFF. 2. Be completed or carried out, take place, as in *The meeting passed off without incident.* [Late 1700s]

pass on 1. See PASS AWAY. 2. Transfer something, as in *Sign the card and then pass it on to the others,* or *Grandpa passed his tools on to his favorite grandson.* Also see PASS THE TORCH.

pass one's lips Speak, utter, as in *Not a word of it will pass my lips, I promise.* [Mid-1700s]

pass out 1. Distribute, as in *He passed out the papers.* [Early 1900s] 2. also, **pass out cold.** Faint, as in *When she heard the news she passed out cold.* [Early 1900s] Also see OUT COLD.

pass over 1. See PASS BY, def. 2. 2. See PASS AWAY.

pass the buck Shift responsibility or blame elsewhere, as in *She's always passing the buck to her staff; it's time she accepted the blame herself.* This expression dates from the mid-1800s, when in a poker game a piece of buckshot or another object was passed around to remind a player that he was the next dealer. It acquired its present meaning by about 1900.

pass the hat Ask for financial contributions, as in *Let's pass the hat so we can get her a nice going-away gift.* This expression alludes to the actual practice of passing a hat around a gathering, but it is also used more figuratively, as in *The board decided to pass the hat again among the corporate sponsors.* [Late 1800s]

pass the time 1. Occupy oneself for an interval, as in *The plane was six hours late but I passed the time reading a book.* 2. **pass the time of day.** Exchange greetings, engage in pleasantries, chat, as in *Whenever I met her we would stop to pass the time of day.* [First half of 1800s]

pass the torch Also, **hand on the torch.** Relinquish responsibilities, a tradition, practice, or knowledge to another. For example, *When the company's founder became too ill to continue, he passed the torch to his nephew.* This metaphoric expression alludes to the ancient Greek torch race, in which a lighted torch was passed from one runner to the

next. A translation from both Greek and Latin, the English version dates from the late 1800s.

pass through one's mind ♦ See CROSS ONE'S MIND.

pass up Let go by, reject, as in *I can't believe Betty passed up the chocolate cake,* or *This opportunity is too good to pass up.* [Colloquial; late 1800s]

pass with flying colors ♦ See WITH FLYING COLORS.

past ♦ In addition to the idioms beginning with PAST, also see LIVE IN (THE PAST); NOT PUT SOMETHING PAST SOMEONE.

past master A person who is thoroughly experienced or exceptionally skilled in some activity or craft. For example, *We're lucky to get Ella, because she's a past master at fundraising.* This expression probably alludes to the original literal meaning, that is, one who formerly held the post of master in a lodge or other organization. Although *past mistress* was used for an exceptionally skilled woman in the mid-1800s, it is heard less often today, *master* serving for both sexes. [Mid-1800s]

past one's prime Beyond the peak of one's powers, as in *Jean still plays tennis but at 79 she's obviously past her prime.* Also see the synonym OVER THE HILL; PRIME OF LIFE.

pasture ♦ See PUT OUT TO GRASS (PASTURE).

pat ♦ In addition to the idiom beginning with PAT, also see STAND PAT.

patch up Mend or repair, make whole. For example, *He managed to patch up the lawn mower so it's running,* or *John cut his hand badly, but they patched him up in the emergency room,* or *Mike and Molly have patched up their differences.* This term alludes to mending something by putting patches of material on it. [Second half of 1500s]

path ♦ See BEAT A PATH TO SOMEONE'S DOOR; CROSS SOMEONE'S PATH; LEAD DOWN THE GARDEN PATH; LEAST RESISTANCE, PATH OF; ON THE WARPATH.

patience ♦ See TRY ONE'S PATIENCE.

pat on the back A word or gesture of support, approval, or praise, as in *The bonus she gave her assistant was a pat on the back for doing a good job.* [Early 1800s]

Paul ♦ See ROB PETER TO PAY PAUL.

pause ♦ See GIVE PAUSE.

pavement ♦ See POUND THE PAVEMENT.

pave the way Make progress or development easier, as in *Her findings paved the way for developing a new vaccine.* This expression alludes to paving a road so it is easier to travel on. [Late 1500s]

pawn off Dispose of by deception, as in *They tried to pawn off a rebuilt computer as new.* This expression may have originated as a corruption of PALM OFF, although it was also put as **pawn upon** in the 1700s, when it originated.

pay ♦ In addition to the idioms beginning with PAY, also see (PAY THE PIPER) CALL THE TUNE; CRIME DOES NOT PAY; DEVIL TO PAY; HELL TO PAY; LIP SERVICE, PAY; ROB PETER TO PAY PAUL; YOU GET WHAT YOU PAY FOR.

pay a call Also, **pay a visit; pay one's respects.** Make a short visit, especially as a formal courtesy or for business reasons. For example, *Bill asked her to pay a call to his ex-mother-in-law,* or *Each salesman was told to pay a visit to every new doctor in town,* or *We went to the wake to pay our respects.* Also see CALL ON, def. 2.

pay a compliment Express praise or commendation to someone, as in *Meredith wanted to pay Christopher a compliment so she told him she liked his new haircut.* This expression uses *pay* in the sense of "give something that is due." [c. 1700]

pay as you go Pay for purchases immediately instead of deferring payment. For example, *Ruth and Bob had no credit cards; they believed in paying as you go.* [First half of 1800s]

pay attention Heed, be attentive to, as in *Now pay attention to these instructions.* [Second half of 1700s]

pay a visit ♦ See PAY A CALL.

pay back 1. Repay a debt or a loan, as in *I'll pay you back next month.* 2. Also, **pay back in someone's own coin.** Revenge oneself, repay in kind, as in *He thought he could get away with copying my plans, but I'll pay him back in his own coin.* This expression refers to repaying a debt in exactly the same currency in which the money had been lent. [c. 1600]

pay court to Solicit the favors or affection of, as in *If you want to win the daughter, you'll have to pay court to her mother.* [Late 1500s]

pay dirt, hit Also, **strike pay dirt.** Make a valuable discovery or large profit, as in *We've been researching the source of that quotation for a month and we finally hit pay dirt in the Library of Congress.* This idiom, from the mid-1800s, refers to a miner's finding gold or other precious metals while sifting soil. By the late 1800s it had been transferred to other lucrative discoveries.

pay for 1. Cover the expenses of, defray the cost of, as in *I'll pay for your movie ticket,* or *This truck will pay for itself within a year.* [Mid-1300s] 2. Atone for, suffer for, as in *He may have looked like a good manager, but his successor will end up paying for his mistakes.* [Late 1600s]

pay off 1. Pay the full amount on a debt or on wages, as in *The car's finally paid off,* or *Les pays off the workers every Friday evening.* [Early 1700s] 2. Produce a profit, as in *That gamble did not pay off.* [Mid-1900s] 3. Also, **pay off an old score.** Get

revenge on someone for some grievance, require, as in *Jerry was satisfied; he'd paid off his ex-partner when he bought him out at half-price,* or *Amy went out with her roommate's boyfriend, but she was paying off an old score.* 4. Bribe, as in *The owner of the bar paid off the local police so he wouldn't get in trouble for serving liquor to minors.* [Colloquial; c. 1900]

pay one's dues Earn something through hard work, long experience, or suffering. For example, *She'd paid her dues in small-town shows before she finally got a Broadway part.* This expression transfers the cost of being a paid-up member in an organization to that of gaining experience in an endeavor. [Mid-1900s]

pay one's respects ♦ See PAY A CALL.

pay one's way 1. Also, **pay one's own way.** Pay in full for one's expenses, as in *She paid her way through college by working in the library.* 2. **pay someone's way.** Pay someone's expenses, as in *Dad offered to pay my way if I went to Spain with him.*

pay out 1. Distribute money, disburse, as in *He paid out the full amount.* [Mid-1800s] 2. Let out a rope by slackening, as in *She paid out the rope until it was long enough to tie the canoe onto the car.* This nautical expression dates from the late 1700s.

pay the piper ♦ See under CALL THE TUNE.

pay through the nose Pay an excessive amount for something, as in *We paid through the nose for that vacation.* The origin of this term has been lost. Possibly it alludes to the Danish nose tax, imposed in Ireland in the 9th century, whereby delinquent taxpayers were punished by having their noses slit. [Second half of 1600s]

pay up Pay in full, discharge all that is owing, as in, *It's late—let's pay up and go home.* [c. 1800] Also see PAY OFF, def. 1.

pay your money and take your choice Also, **you pays your money and takes your choice.** Since you're paying, it's your decision, as in *We can take the train or the bus—you pays your money and takes your choice.* This term first appeared in the English humor magazine *Punch* in the mid-1800s and has been repeated ever since.

PC Also, **p.c.** An abbreviation for POLITICALLY CORRECT.

pea ♦ See LIKE AS TWO PEAS IN A POD.

peace ♦ In addition to the idiom beginning with PEACE, also see AT PEACE; HOLD ONE'S TONGUE (PEACE); KEEP THE PEACE; LEAVE SOMEONE IN PEACE; MAKE ONE'S PEACE WITH; MAKE PEACE.

peace and quiet Tranquillity and freedom from disturbance. This phrase's redundancy—*quiet* here does not mean "lack of sound" but "peaceful-ness" — gives added emphasis. It often is used in wishes for this condition, as in *All I want is a little peace and quiet.* [Mid-1800s]

peacock ♦ See PROUD AS A PEACOCK.

pearls ♦ See CAST PEARLS BEFORE SWINE.

pebble ♦ See NOT THE ONLY FISH IN THE SEA (PEBBLE ON THE BEACH).

pecking order The hierarchy of authority in a group, as in *On a space mission, the astronauts have a definite pecking order.* This expression, invented in the 1920s by biologists who discovered that domestic poultry maintain such a hierarchy with one bird pecking another of lower status, was transferred to human behavior in the 1950s.

pedal ♦ See SOFT PEDAL.

pedestal ♦ See ON A PEDESTAL.

peel ♦ In addition to the idiom beginning with PEEL, also see KEEP ONE'S EYES OPEN (PEELED).

peel off 1. Remove an outer layer of skin, bark, paint, or the like; also, come off in thin strips or pieces. For example, *Peeling off birch bark can kill the tree*, or *Paint was peeling off the walls.* [Late 1500s] 2. Remove or separate, as in *Helen peeled off her gloves and got to work*, or *Al peeled off a ten-dollar bill and gave it to the driver.* [First half of 1900s] 3. Also, **peel away**. Depart from a group, as in *Ruth peeled off from the pack of runners and went down a back road.* This expression originated in air force jargon during World War II and was used for an airplane or pilot that left flight formation, a sight that suggested the peeling of skin from a banana.

peep ♦ See HEAR A PEEP OUT OF.

peeping Tom A person who secretly watches others, especially for sexual gratification; a voyeur. For example, *The police caught a peeping Tom right outside their house.* This expression, first recorded in 1796, alludes to the legend of the tailor Tom, the only person to watch the naked Lady Godiva as she rode by and who was struck blind for this sin.

peg ♦ In addition to the idiom beginning with PEG, also see SQUARE PEG IN A ROUND HOLE; TAKE DOWN A NOTCH (PEG).

peg away at Also, **plug away at**. Work steadily, persist, as in *She pegged away at the tax return until she'd finished*, or *If we keep plugging away at it, the painting will soon be done.* These idioms allude to the persistence required to fasten something by driving pegs or seal something by driving a plug. **Peg away** dates from the early 1800s, **plug away** from the mid-1900s.

pen ♦ See SLIP OF THE LIP (PEN).

penchant ♦ See HAVE A PENCHANT FOR.

pencil ♦ See PUT LEAD IN ONE'S PENCIL.

pennies from heaven Unexpected good fortune, a windfall, as in *They sent back our check — pennies from heaven.* This expression may have originated with a song and motion picture so named (1936), popularized by Bing Crosby.

penny ♦ In addition to the idioms beginning with PENNY, also see IN FOR A PENNY, IN FOR A POUND; PINCH PENNIES; PRETTY PENNY; TURN UP (LIKE A BAD PENNY).

penny for your thoughts, a What are you thinking about? For example, *You've been awfully quiet — a penny for your thoughts.* This expression dates from the 1500s and was in John Heywood's 1546 collection of proverbs.

penny pincher ♦ See PINCH PENNIES.

penny saved is a penny earned, a What one does not spend, one will have. This maxim for thrift is so familiar that it often appears in shortened form, as in *Although they can afford to buy a house right now, they're putting if off, on the principle of "a penny saved."* It appeared in slightly different form in George Herbert's *Outlandish Proverbs* (1640). Whether or not it originally suggested that savings earn interest is not known.

penny wise and pound foolish Stingy about small expenditures and extravagant with large ones, as in *Dean clips all the coupons for supermarket bargains but insists on going to the best restaurants — penny wise and pound foolish.* This phrase alludes to British currency, in which a pound was once worth 240 pennies, or pence, and is now worth 100 pence. The phrase is also occasionally used for being very careful about unimportant matters and careless about important ones. It was used in this way by Joseph Addison in *The Spectator* (1712): "A woman who will give up herself to a man in marriage where there is the least Room for such an apprehension ... may very properly be accused ... of being penny wise and pound foolish." [c. 1600]

people ♦ In addition to the idiom beginning with PEOPLE, also see TELL (PEOPLE) APART.

people who live in glass houses shouldn't throw stones One who is open to criticism should not criticize others, as in *It's stupid of Mike to mention his opponent's accepting donations from lobbyists — people who live in glass houses!* This proverb is so well known that it is often shortened. [Late 1300s] Also see POT CALLING THE KETTLE BLACK.

pep someone up Invigorate someone or cheer someone up, as in *This drink will pep you up*, or *The good news about his recovery pepped us up.* [1920s] Both the verb *pep* and the noun *pep*, denoting vigor and energy since about 1910, are abbreviations for *pepper,* a spice with a pungent, biting quality. They also have given rise to **pep rally,** a meeting to inspire enthusiasm [c. 1940], and **pep talk,** a speech meant to instill enthusiasm or bolster morale [1920s].

perish ♦ In addition to the idiom beginning with PERISH, also see PUBLISH OR PERISH.

perish the thought Don't even think of it. This expression is used as a wish that what was just mentioned will never happen. For example, *He's going to give another speech? Perish the thought!* This phrase appeared in Handel's oratorio *Joshua* (1748; text by Thomas Morell): "It never shall be said that our allies in vain implor'd our aid. Perish the thought!" Also see GOD FORBID.

perk up Restore to good spirits, liveliness, or good appearance, as in *You're exhausted, but a cup of tea will perk you up,* or *The flowers perked up the whole room.* [Mid-1600s]

person ♦ In addition to the idiom beginning with PERSON, also see FEEL LIKE ONESELF (A NEW PERSON); IN PERSON; OWN PERSON, ONE'S.

person of color A nonwhite person, such as someone of African or Native American descent. For example, *They have made a genuine effort to promote persons of color to executive positions.* This seemingly modern euphemism actually dates from the late 1700s and was revived in the late 1900s.

pet ♦ In addition to the idiom beginning with PET, also see TEACHER'S PET.

Pete Also, **Peter.** ♦ See FOR ONE'S (PETE'S) SAKE; HONEST TO GOD (PETE); ROB PETER TO PAY PAUL.

peter out Dwindle or diminish and come to an end, as in *Their enthusiasm soon petered out.* The origin of this usage is unknown, but one authority suggests it may refer to the apostle Peter, whose enthusiastic support of Jesus quickly diminished so that he denied knowing him three times during the night after Jesus's arrest. [Mid-1800s]

pet peeve A particular or recurring source of irritation, as in *My pet peeve is that neighbor's cat running through my herb garden.* [Early 1900s]

physical ♦ See GET PHYSICAL.

phase in Introduce one stage at a time. For example, *New technology must be phased in or the office will be overwhelmed.* The antonym is **phase out,** meaning "to bring or come to an end, one stage at a time," as in *The department is phasing out all the older computers.* [Mid-1900s]

Philadelphia lawyer A shrewd attorney, adept at dealing with legal technicalities, as in *It would take a Philadelphia lawyer to get him off.* This expression dates from the late 1700s and, as lexicographer Richard H. Thornton observed: "Why members of the Philadelphia bar should be credited with superhuman sagacity has never been satisfactorily explained."

pick ♦ In addition to the idioms beginning with PICK, also see BONE TO PICK; SLIM PICKINGS.

pick a bone with ♦ See BONE TO PICK.

pick and choose Select with great care, as in *John and Kate loved to go to the pastry shop, especially if they had time to pick and choose.* Despite its redundancy (*pick* and *choose* are synonyms), this phrase has survived since the 1400s.

pick apart Also, **pick holes in** or **pick to pieces.** Find flaws in something by close examination, criticize sharply, as in *The lawyer picked apart the testimony,* or *He found it easy to pick holes in their argument,* or *The new editor picked her manuscript to pieces.* These expressions use *pick* in the sense of "pierce" or "poke," a usage dating from the 1300s; *pick holes in* dates from the mid-1600s, *pick to pieces* from the mid-1800s.

pick a quarrel Also, **pick an argument** or **fight.** Seek an opportunity to quarrel or argue with someone. For example, *I don't want to pick a quarrel with you,* or *Jason was always in trouble for picking fights.* These terms use *pick* in the sense of "select." [Mid-1400s]

pick at 1. Pluck or pull at, especially with the fingers, as in *She was always picking at her skirt with her nails.* [1600s] 2. Eat sparingly and without appetite, as in *He was just picking at his dinner.* [Late 1500s] 3. Nag, badger, as in *He's picking at me all day long.* [Colloquial; second half of 1600s]

picked over ♦ See PICK OVER.

pick holes in ♦ See under PICK APART.

pickle ♦ See IN A FIX (PICKLE).

pick off Shoot after singling out, as in *The hunter picked off the ducks one by one.* [Early 1800s]

pick of the litter The best of a group, as in *He was first in the ticket line so he had the pick of the litter.* This term, alluding to the most desirable one from a litter of puppies or kittens, supplanted such earlier variants as *pick of the market, pick of the parish,* and *pick of the basket.* [Early 1900s]

pick on Tease, bully, victimize, as in *She told Mom the boys were always picking on her.* [Second half of 1800s] This expression is sometimes put as **pick on someone your own size,** meaning "don't badger someone who is younger, smaller, or weaker than yourself but do so only to an equal."

pick one's way Find and move through a passage carefully, as in *She picked her way through the crowd outside the theater,* or, more figuratively, *He picked his way through the mass of 19th-century journals, looking for references to his subject.* [Early 1700s]

pick out 1. Choose, select, as in *She picked out the best piece of fabric.* [Early 1500s] 2. Distinguish, discern from one's surroundings, as in *They managed to pick out their mother from the crowd.* [Mid-1500s] 3. Identify the notes of a tune and play it on an instrument, as in *When she was four she could pick out folk songs on the piano.* [Late 1800s]

pick over Sort out, examine item by item, as in *Dad hates to pick over the beans one by one.* This term is sometimes put as **picked over**, describing something that has already been selected from (as in *They have almost nothing left; the stock of bathing suits has been picked over*). [First half of 1800s]

pick someone's brain Obtain ideas or information from another person, as in *I'm out of ideas for decorating—let me pick your brain.* This term alludes to picking clean a carcass. [Mid-1800s]

pick to pieces ♦ See PICK APART.

pick up 1. Lift, take up by hand, as in *Please pick up that book from the floor.* [Early 1300s] 2. Collect or gather, as in *First they had to pick up the pieces of broken glass.* 3. Tidy, put in order, as in *Let's pick up the bedroom,* or *I'm always picking up after Pat.* [Mid-1800s] 4. Take on passengers or freight, as in *The bus picks up commuters at three stops.* 5. Acquire casually, get without great effort or by accident. For example, *I picked up a nice coat at the sale,* or *She had no trouble picking up French.* This usage is even extended to contracting diseases, as in *I think I picked up the baby's cold.* [Early 1500s] 6. Claim, as in *He picked up his laundry every Friday.* 7. Buy, as in *Please pick up some wine at the store on your way home.* 8. **pick up the bill** or **check** or **tab.** Accept a charge in order to pay it, as in *They always wait for us to pick up the tab.* [Colloquial; mid-1900s] 9. Increase speed or rate, as in *The plane picked up speed,* or *The conductor told the strings to pick up the tempo.* 10. Gain, as in *They picked up five yards on that pass play.* 11. Take into custody, apprehend, as in *The police picked him up for burglary.* [Colloquial; second half of 1800s] 12. Make a casual acquaintance with, especially in anticipation of sexual relations, as in *A stranger tried to pick her up at the bus station.* [Slang; late 1800s] 13. Come upon, find, detect, as in *The dog picked up the scent,* or *They picked up two submarines on sonar,* or *I can't pick up that station on the car radio.* 14. Resume, as in *Let's pick up the conversation after lunch.* 15. Improve or cause to improve in condition or activity, as in *Sales picked up last fall,* or *He picked up quickly after he got home from the hospital,* or *A cup of coffee will pick you up.* [1700s] 16. Gather one's belongings, as in *She just picked up and left him.* 17. **pick oneself up.** Recover from a fall or other mishap, as in *Jim picked himself up and stood there waiting.* [Mid-1800s]

Also see the subsequent entries beginning with PICK UP.

pick up on Become aware of, notice, as in *The teacher picked up on her nervousness right away.* [Colloquial; mid-1900s]

pick up the pieces Redeem a bad situation, restore matters to normal, as in *Once fighting ended, the task force picked up the pieces and restored democracy.* [Late 1800s]

picnic ♦ See NO PICNIC.

picture ♦ In addition to the idiom beginning with PICTURE, also see GET THE MESSAGE (PICTURE); IN THE PICTURE; PRETTY AS A PICTURE; TAKE A PICTURE; THE PICTURE.

picture is worth a thousand words, one A graphic illustration conveys a stronger message than words, as in *The book jacket is a big selling point— one picture is worth a thousand words.* This saying was invented by an advertising executive, Fred R. Barnard. To promote his agency's ads he took out an ad in *Printer's Ink* in 1921 with the headline "One Look Is Worth a Thousand Words" and attributed it to an ancient Japanese philosopher. Six years later he changed it to "Chinese Proverb: One Picture Is Worth Ten Thousand Words," illustrated with some Chinese characters. The attribution in both was invented; Barnard simply believed an Asian origin would give it more credibility.

pie ♦ In addition to the idiom beginning with PIE, also see APPLE-PIE ORDER; EASY AS PIE; EAT CROW (HUMBLE PIE); FINGER IN THE PIE; SLICE OF THE PIE.

piece ♦ In addition to the idioms beginning with PIECE, also see ALL IN ONE PIECE; CONVERSATION PIECE; GO TO PIECES; MUSEUM PIECE; OF A PIECE; PICK APART (TO PIECES); PICK UP THE PIECES; PUFF PIECE; SAY ONE'S PIECE; THINK PIECE; THRILL TO PIECES; TO PIECES; VILLAIN OF THE PIECE.

piece by piece In stages, gradually, as in *He took the clock apart piece by piece,* or *Let's go over your exam paper, piece by piece.* Also see BIT BY BIT.

piece of ass Also, **piece of tail.** Sexual intercourse, as in *He was out for a piece of ass.* [Vulgar slang; mid-1900s]

piece of cake Something easily accomplished, as in *I had no trouble finding your house—a piece of cake.* This expression originated in the Royal Air Force in the late 1930s for an easy mission, and the precise reference is as mysterious as that of the simile EASY AS PIE. Possibly it evokes the easy accomplishment of swallowing a slice of sweet dessert.

piece of change A sum of money, especially a considerable amount, as in *That car is worth a piece of change.* [Slang; early 1900s]

piece of one's mind Frank and severe criticism, censure, as in *Chuck was furious and gave him a piece of his mind.* The word *piece* here is used in the sense of "portion," but the portion of the mind alluded to always has a negative opinion. [Second half of 1500s]

piece of the action A share in an activity or in the profits, as in *They wanted a piece of the action in this land deal.* [Slang; mid-1900s]

piece together Join or combine parts into a whole, as in *With information from several observers, she pieced together an account of what had actually taken place.* [Late 1500s]

pie in the sky An empty wish or promise, as in *His dream of being hired as a sports editor proved to be pie in the sky.* This expression was first recorded in 1911 in a rallying song of a union, the International Workers of the World (or "Wobblies"): "Work and pray, live on hay, you'll get pie in the sky when you die."

pig ♦ In addition to the idioms beginning with PIG, also see IN A PIG'S EYE; LIKE PIGS IN CLOVER; MAKE A PIG OF ONESELF; WHEN PIGS FLY.

pigeon ♦ See CLAY PIGEON; STOOL PIGEON.

pig in a poke An object offered in a manner that conceals its true value, especially its lack of value. For example, *Eric believes that buying a used car is buying a pig in a poke.* This expression alludes to the practice of substituting a worthless object, such as a cat, for the costly suckling pig a customer has bought and wrapping it in a *poke,* or sack. It dates from a time when buyers of groceries relied on a weekly farmers' market and, unless they were cautious enough to check the poke's contents, would not discover the skullduggery until they got home. The word *poke* dates from the 13th century but is now used mainly in the southern United States. The idiom was first recorded in John Heywood's 1562 collection of proverbs. Also see LET THE CAT OUT OF THE BAG.

pig it Live in a slovenly way, as in *Ten roommates shared that small house, and as you might guess they were pigging it.* [Slang; late 1800s]

pig out Eat ravenously, gorge oneself, as in *The kids pigged out on the candy they had collected on Halloween.* [Slang; early 1970s]

pile ♦ In addition to the idioms beginning with PILE, also see MAKE A BUNDLE (PILE).

pile into Move in a disorderly group into, crowd into, as in *The team piled into the bus.* The related expression **pile in** takes no object, as in *Jack opened the car door and yelled, "Pile in!"* [First half of 1800s]

pile up 1. Accumulate, as in *The leaves piled up in the yard,* or *He piled up a huge fortune.* In this idiom

pile means "form a heap or mass of something." [Mid-1800s] 2. Be involved in a crash, as in *When the police arrived, at least four cars had piled up.* [Late 1800s]

pill ♦ See BITTER PILL TO SWALLOW; SUGAR THE PILL.

pillar to post ♦ See FROM PILLAR TO POST.

pimple ♦ See GOOSE PIMPLES

pin ♦ In addition to the idioms beginning with PIN, also see HEAR A PIN DROP; ON PINS AND NEEDLES.

pin back one's ears ♦ See PIN SOMEONE'S EARS BACK.

pinch ♦ In addition to the idioms beginning with PINCH, also see FEEL THE PINCH; IN A PINCH; WITH A GRAIN (PINCH) OF SALT.

pinch hitter A substitute for another person, especially in an emergency. For example, *Pat expected her mother to help with the baby, but just in case, she lined up her mother-in-law as pinch hitter.* This expression comes from baseball, where it is used for a player substituting for another at bat at a critical point or in a tight situation (called a *pinch* since the late 1400s). [Late 1800s]

pinch pennies Be thrifty or miserly, as in *There's no need to pinch pennies now that you're working full-time.* This term was first recorded in 1942.

pin down 1. Fix or establish clearly, as in *The firefighters finally were able to pin down the source of the odor.* [Mid-1900s] 2. Force someone to give precise information or opinions, as in *The reporter pinned down the governor on the issue of conservation measures.* [c. 1700]

pink ♦ See IN THE PINK; TICKLED PINK.

pin money Small amounts of money for incidental expenses, as in *Grandma usually gives the children some pin money whenever she visits.* This expression originally signified money given by a husband to his wife for small personal expenditures such as pins, which were very costly items in centuries past. A will recorded at York in 1542 listed a bequest: "I give my said daughter Margarett my lease of the parsonage . . . to buy her pins." [Early 1500s]

pin on Attribute to someone, especially a wrongdoing or crime. For example, *They pinned the murder on the wrong man.* This expression uses *pin* in the sense of "attach." [First half of 1900s]

pin one's heart on ♦ See WEAR ONE'S HEART ON ONE'S SLEEVE.

pin one's hopes on Also, **pin one's faith on.** Put one's hope or trust in someone or something, as in *She'd pinned her hopes on an early acceptance to the college but it didn't materialize.* This term, dating from the 1500s, originated as *pin one's faith on another's sleeve* and may have alluded to the practice of soldiers wearing their leader's insignia on their sleeves. By the 1800s, however, it acquired its present form.

pin someone's ears back Defeat overcome, punish, as in *The Red Sox had their ears pinned back by the Yankees*, or *You'll get your ears pinned back if you're late*. [c. 1940]

pipe ♦ In addition to the idioms beginning with PIPE, also see IN THE PIPELINE; LEAD-PIPE CINCH; PUT THAT IN YOUR PIPE.

pipe down Stop talking, be quiet, as in *I wish you children would pipe down*. This idiom is also used as an imperative, as in *Pipe down! We want to listen to the opera*. It comes from the navy, where the signal for all hands to turn in was sometimes sounded on a whistle or pipe. By 1900 it had been transferred to more general use.

pipe dream A fantastic notion or vain hope, as in *I'd love to have one home in the mountains and another at the seashore, but that's just a pipe dream*. Alluding to the fantasies induced by smoking an opium pipe, this term has been used more loosely since the late 1800s.

piper ♦ See CALL THE TUNE (PAY THE PIPER).

pipe up Speak up, as in *Finally she piped up, "I think I've got the winning ticket,"* or *Pipe up if you want more pancakes*. This term originally referred to a high, piping tone. [Mid-1800s]

piping hot Very hot, as in *These biscuits are piping hot*. This idiom alludes to something so hot that it makes a piping or hissing sound. [Late 1300s]

piss away Squander, waste, as in *They've pissed away a fortune on those horses*. This term uses *piss* in the sense of "discharge something as though it were urine." [Vulgar slang; first half of 1900s]

piss off 1. Make very angry, as in *That letter pissed me off*, or *She was pissed off because no one had called her*. [Vulgar slang; 1940s] 2. Go away, as in *Piss off and stop bothering me*. [Vulgar slang; mid-1900s]

pit ♦ In addition to the idiom beginning with PIT, also see THE PITS.

pit against Set in direct opposition or competition, as in *The civil war pitted brother against brother*. This idiom alludes to setting fighting cocks or dogs against one another in a pit. [Mid-1700s]

pitch ♦ In addition to the idioms beginning with PITCH, also see BLACK AS NIGHT (PITCH); IN THERE PITCHING; MAKE A PITCH FOR; SALES PITCH; WILD PITCH.

pitched battle, a An intense conflict, as in *Their disagreement turned into a pitched battle between the nurses and the physicians' assistants*. This term, dating from about 1600, originally alluded to a military battle in which the array of forces and battleground are predetermined (as opposed to a hasty skirmish).

pitcher ♦ See LITTLE PITCHERS HAVE BIG EARS.

pitch in 1. Set to work vigorously, as in *We pitched right in and started mowing the field*. [Colloquial; second half of 1800s] 2. Join forces with others; help, cooperate. For example, *We were hoping you'd pitch in and sort the books*. Also see PITCH INTO.

pitch into Attack, assault, either physically or verbally. For example, *Aunt Sally pitched into Uncle Rob when he forgot to go to the bank*. [Colloquial; first half of 1800s]

pitch on Also, **pitch upon**. Choose, decide on, as in *He pitched on the ideal solution*. This idiom uses *pitch* in the sense of "arrange or set something in order." [Early 1600s]

pitch woo Court, make love to, flatter, as in *They sat on the porch swing, pitching woo*, or *He's an excellent salesman, adept at pitching woo*. This idiom, which may be obsolescent, uses *pitch* in the sense of "talk." [Slang; early 1800s]

pity ♦ See FOR ONE'S (PITY'S) SAKE; TAKE PITY ON.

place ♦ In addition to the idiom beginning with PLACE, also see ALL OVER THE PLACE; BETWEEN A ROCK AND A HARD PLACE; FALL IN PLACE; FRIEND IN COURT (HIGH PLACES); GO PLACES; HAVE ONE'S HEART IN THE RIGHT PLACE; IN PLACE; IN SOMEONE'S SHOES (PLACE); INSTEAD (IN PLACE) OF; IN THE FIRST PLACE; JUMPING-OFF PLACE; KNOW ONE'S PLACE; OUT OF PLACE; PRIDE OF PLACE; PUT SOMEONE IN HIS OR HER PLACE; RUN IN PLACE; TAKE PLACE; TAKE SOMEONE'S PLACE.

place in the sun A dominant or favorable position or situation, as in *The Nobel prizewinners really enjoyed their place in the sun*. This term may have been coined about 1660 by the French philosopher Blaise Pascal but became well known only in the late 1800s, when it was applied to Germany's position in world affairs, especially concerning its desire for more lands.

plague ♦ See AVOID LIKE THE PLAGUE.

plain ♦ In addition to the idioms beginning with PLAIN, also see IN PLAIN ENGLISH.

plain as day Also, **plain as the nose on your face**. Very obvious, quite clear, as in *It's plain as day that they must sell their house before they can buy another*, or *It's plain as the nose on your face that she's lying*. These similes have largely replaced the earlier *plain as a packstaff* or *pikestaff*, from the mid-1500s, alluding to the stick on which a peddler carried his wares over his shoulder. The first term, from the late 1800s, is probably a shortening of *plain as the sun at midday*; the variant dates from the late 1600s.

plain sailing Easy going; straightforward, unobstructed progress. For example, *The first few months were difficult, but I think it's plain sailing from here on*. Alluding to navigating waters free of hazards, such as rocks or other obstructions, this term was transferred to other activities in the early 1800s.

plan ♦ In addition to the idiom beginning with PLAN, also see BEST-LAID PLANS.

plank ♦ See WALK THE PLANK.

plan on 1. Have as an aim or purpose, as in *We had planned on going to the movies after dinner.* 2. Anticipate, prepare for, as in *We planned on you to make a speech,* or *They hadn't planned on such a big crowd.* [Early 1900s]

plate ♦ See HAND TO ON A SILVER PLATTER (SERVE UP ON A PLATE); HAVE A LOT ON ONE'S PLATE.

platter ♦ See under HAND TO ON A SILVER PLATTER.

play ♦ In addition to the idioms beginning with PLAY, also see ALL WORK AND NO PLAY; CHILD'S PLAY; DEVIL'S ADVOCATE, PLAY; FAIR PLAY; FOUL PLAY; GAME THAT TWO CAN PLAY; GRANDSTAND PLAY; IN PLAY; MAKE A PLAY FOR; MUSICAL CHAIRS, PLAY; SQUEEZE PLAY; TRUMP CARD, PLAY ONE'S.

play along Cooperate or pretend to cooperate, as in *They decided to play along with the robbers, at least for a while.* [Colloquial; 1920s]

play a losing game ♦ See under LOSING BATTLE.

play around Act playfully or irresponsibly, especially in having a casual or extramarital sexual relationship. For example, *She got tired of his playing around and filed for divorce.* [1920s]

play at Do or take part in half-heartedly, as in *She was just playing at keeping house, letting the others do all the work.* [Mid-1800s]

play a waiting game Delay an action or decision so as to force an opponent to move or to gain additional information. For example, *The lawyer advised her to play a waiting game and see if her husband would come up with more alimony.* [Late 1800s]

play back Replay, especially a recorded performance; also, repeat. For example, *When we played back the tape of the concert we noticed a lot of missed notes,* or *He uses the same material again and again, playing back his old speech.* [Early 1900s]

play ball 1. Cooperate, as in *The opposing attorneys refused to play ball with us.* [Slang; c. 1900] 2. Get going, start, as in *It's time to get a move on; let's play ball.* This usage comes from the baseball umpire's call to start a game. [Slang; late 1800s]

play both ends against the middle Also, **play one off against another.** Gain an advantage by setting opposing parties or interests against one another. For example, *Some children are adept at manipulating their parents, playing both ends against the middle,* or *Aunt Jane had a nasty habit of playing the twins off against each other.* The first term may come from a cheating practice used in faro. Minute strips were cut off certain cards, so that one could tell where they lay in the deck. When

the cards were cut convex or concave, it was called "both ends against the middle." The figurative use of the term dates from the first half of the 1900s. The variant originated in the mid-1600s as *play against one another,* with *off* being added in the late 1800s.

play by ear 1. Play a musical instrument without the aid of written music, as in *By the time she was four, she could play a dozen songs by ear.* [Late 1600s] 2. **play it by ear.** Proceed gradually, depending on the circumstances; improvise. For example, *I'm not sure how much we should say about our plans, so let's play it by ear.* [Mid-1900s]

play cat and mouse Amuse oneself or trifle with, toy with, as in *She loved to play cat and mouse with an admirer, acting by turns friendly, indifferent, and jealous.* The analogy of a cat toying with a helpless mouse was drawn centuries earlier, but the precise term dates only from the early 1900s.

play down 1. Make little of, minimize the importance of, as in *A skillful salesman plays down the drawbacks of the product and emphasizes its good features.* [First half of 1900s] 2. **play down to.** Lower one's standards to meet the demands of someone, as in *Some stand-up comics deliberately play down to the vulgar taste of their audiences.* [Late 1800s]

played out 1. See PLAY OUT. 2. Exhausted, worn out, as in *This was the third trip the mules had made, and they were utterly played out.* [Mid-1800s]

play fair Behave honestly and honorably, obey the rules, as in *Not every supplier we deal with plays fair,* or *We can't just leave them to find their own way back—that's not playing fair.* Although this idiom conjures up playing by the rules in some game or sport, it actually has been used in this figurative way since the mid-1400s. Also see PLAY THE GAME.

play false Deceive or betray one, as in *If my memory does not play false, I met them years ago in Italy.* [Late 1500s]

play fast and loose Be recklessly irresponsible, unreliable, or deceitful, as in *This reporter is known for playing fast and loose with the facts.* This term probably originated in a 16th-century game called "fast and loose," played at country fairs. A belt was doubled and held with the loop at table's edge, and the player had to catch the loop with a stick as the belt was unrolled—an impossible feat. The term was already used figuratively by the late 1500s, especially for trifling with someone's affections.

play footsie 1. Behave coyly, flirt with, especially secretly. For example, *Get to the point, there's no need to play footsie with us.* This expression alludes to two persons surreptitiously rubbing each other's feet together. [1940s] 2. Cooperate or curry favor with in a sly or secret way, as in *The mayor's been playing footsie with various neighborhood councils.* [Mid-1900s]

play for 1. Take part for a particular reason, as in *We're not playing for money, just for fun.* A special usage of this idiom is **play for laughs,** that is, with the aim of arousing laughter. 2. **play someone for.** Manage someone for one's own ends, make a fool of, dupe or cheat. For example, *I resent your playing me for a fool,* or *He suddenly found out she'd been playing him for a sucker.* This usage employs *play* in the sense of "exhaust a hooked fish," that is, manage it on the line so that it exhausts itself. [Mid-1600s]

play for keeps ♦ See FOR KEEPS.

play for laughs ♦ See PLAY FOR, def. 1.

play for time Use delaying tactics, temporize, as in *The defense attorney decided to play for time while they searched for an eyewitness.* [c. 1940]

play games Be evasive or deceptive, as in *Don't play games with me—I want an honest answer.* Also see PLAY THE GAME.

play hardball Act aggressively and ruthlessly, as in *It's only a month before the election, and I'm sure they'll start to play hardball.* This term originated in baseball, where it alludes to using the standard ball as opposed to the slightly larger and minimally softer ball of softball. It was transferred to describe aggressive behavior only in the 1970s.

play hard to get Pretend to be inaccessible or uninterested; act coy, especially with the opposite sex. For example, *I know he has no appointments tomorrow; he's just playing hard to get,* or *Nicole is very popular, perhaps because she plays hard to get.* [Mid-1900s]

play havoc Also, **raise** or **wreak havoc.** Disrupt, damage, or destroy something, as in *The wind played havoc with her hair,* or *The fire alarm raised havoc with the children,* or *The earthquake wrought havoc in the town.* The noun *havoc* was once used as a command for invaders to begin looting and killing, but by the 1800s the term was being used for somewhat less aggressive activities. For a synonym, see PLAY THE DEVIL WITH.

play hide and seek Evade or seem to evade someone. For example, *Bill is hard to pin down—he's always playing hide and seek.* This expression alludes to the children's game in which one player tries to find others who are hiding. It has been used figuratively since the mid-1600s.

play hooky Be absent from school or some other obligation without permission, as in *It was such a beautiful day that Herb played hooky from work.* In this term, the noun *hooky* may have come from the phrase *hook it,* meaning "escape." [Mid-1800s]

play in Peoria Be acceptable to the average consumer or constituent. For example, *We've tested this new soup in several markets, but will it play in Peoria?* This expression originated among touring theater companies trying to make sure their productions would win favor in America's heartland, symbolized by the small city of Peoria, Illinois.

play into the hands of Act so as to give an advantage to an opponent, as in *The senator played right into the hands of her opponents when she backed that unpopular amendment to the tax bill.* [c. 1700]

play it close to one's chest Be secretive or cautious, give nothing away, as in *We've no idea how many tickets they sold; they play it close to their chests.* This expression, which is also put as **play one's cards close to one's chest,** alludes to holding one's cards up against one's chest, so that no one else can see them. [Slang; mid-1900s]

play it cool 1. Act cautiously and shrewdly, as in *When they asked how much she earned, she played it cool.* [Slang; 1940s] 2. Become or remain calm, as in *When they start to tease you, just play it cool.* [Slang; 1940s]

play it safe Also, **play safe.** Avoid extreme risks, as in *I played it safe and bet only a dollar,* or *Let's play safe and get a backup in case the announced speaker gets sick.* [c. 1900]

play musical chairs ♦ See MUSICAL CHAIRS.

play off 1. See under PLAY BOTH ENDS AGAINST THE MIDDLE. 2. Break a tie by playing an additional game or period, as in *Each team had won three games so they had to play off the tie to decide the championship.*

play on Also, **play upon.** Take advantage of or make use of for a desired effect, as in *These health care ads are meant to play on our fears.* This idiom uses *play* in the sense of "performing on an instrument." Shakespeare used it in *Hamlet* (3:2): "You would play upon me; you would seem to know my stops." [Late 1500s]

play one's cards close to one's chest ♦ See PLAY IT CLOSE TO THE CHEST.

play one's cards right Make good use of one's resources or strategies, as in *She played her cards right and got a promotion.* [Mid-1700s]

play one's trump card ♦ See TRUMP CARD.

play on words A word or turn of phrase with a double meaning, a pun or other humorous use of language. For example, *Shakespeare was a master at plays on words—his dramas are full of puns.* [First half of 1700s]

play out 1. Finish, run out, as in *This extreme fashion will soon play out,* or *The tension between factions will surely play itself out by next year.* [Late 1500s]

2. Unwind, unreel, as in *They slowly played out the cable.* Also see PLAYED OUT.

play politics Act for personal or political gain rather than principle, as in *I don't think this judge is fair—he's playing politics.* [Mid-1800s]

play possum Pretend to be dead or asleep, as in *Max always plays possum when it's time to clean up his room.* This expression alludes to the fact that the opossum falls into an apparent coma when caught, giving the appearance of death. [1820s]

play safe ♦ See PLAY IT SAFE.

play second fiddle Assume a subsidiary role to someone, as in *Mary resented always playing second fiddle to her older sister.* This term alludes to the part of second violin in an orchestra. Although many would argue it is as important as first violin, it is the idea of subordinacy that was transferred in the figurative term, so used since about 1800.

play the devil with Upset, ruin, make a mess of, as in *This weather plays the devil with my aching joints,* or *Wine stains play the devil with a white tablecloth.* This allusion to diabolical mischief is heard more in Britain than in America. [Mid-1500s] Also see the synonym PLAY HAVOC.

play the field Date more than one person; avoid an exclusive commitment. For example, *All of Joe's friends are married now, but he continues to play the field.* This term originated in British horse-racing, where it meant "to bet on every horse in a race except the favorite." It was transferred to other activities about 1930.

play the fool Act in a silly or stupid way, as in *Helen deliberately played the fool so they wouldn't realize she understood their strategy.* [First half of 1500s]

play the game Behave according to accepted customs, obey the rules. For example, *Not every foreign company can be counted on to play the game.* The *game* here alludes to a sport with a set of rules. [Late 1800s] Also see PLAY GAMES.

play the heavy Act the part of a villain; take the blame for unkind behavior. For example, *She can't bear firing an employee, so she relies on Jim to play the heavy.* This colloquial term comes from the theater, where *heavy* has been used for a stern, serious role or that of a villain since the early 1800s.

play the market Trade in securities in order to make money, as in *He is always playing the market with only mixed results.* This term uses *play* in the sense of "gamble," a usage dating from about 1500.

play to the gallery Appeal to spectators for maximum approval, as in *He peppers his speeches with humor and wisecracks about his opponent, clearly playing to the gallery.* In this term *gallery* refers to the cheapest seats in a British theater and hence the least sophisticated audience. [Late 1800s]

play up Emphasize or publicize, as in *In the press interview, the coach played up the importance of having a strong defense.* [c. 1900] Also see PLAY DOWN; PLAY UP TO.

play upon ♦ See PLAY ON.

play up to Curry favor with, flatter, as in *There's no use playing up to the boss; it doesn't influence him.* This expression originated about 1800 in the theater, where it meant "to support or assist another actor." Within a couple of decades it was being used in other venues.

play with fire Take part in a dangerous undertaking, as in *You're playing with fire if you go behind his back and commit his department.* Although the idea behind this metaphor is ancient, it was first recorded only in 1655.

plea ♦ See COP A PLEA.

please ♦ See AS YOU PLEASE.

pleased as Punch Delighted, as in *We were pleased as Punch when they asked us to be godparents.* This term alludes to the character Punch in Punch and Judy shows, who is always very happy when his evil deeds succeed. [Mid-1800s]

plenty ♦ See under NOT THE ONLY FISH IN THE SEA.

plot thickens, the Circumstances are becoming very complex or mysterious. Today this term is often used ironically or half-humorously, as in *His companion wasn't his wife or his partner—the plot thickens.* Originally (1671) it described the plot of a play that was overly intricate, and by the late 1800s it was used for increasingly complex mysteries in detective stories.

plow back Reinvest earnings or profits in one's business, as in *This company plows back half its profits every year.* This term transfers the farming practice of turning the soil from top to bottom to financial enterprises. [First half of 1900s]

plow into Strike with force, crash into; also, attack vigorously. For example, *The truck plowed into the retaining wall,* or *Carol plowed into the pile of correspondence.* This expression transfers the force of the farmer's plow to other enterprises. [Late 1800s]

plow under Cause to vanish, overwhelm, as in *The independent bookstores are being plowed under by the large chains.* This term alludes to the farmer's burying vegetation by turning it into the soil with a plow. [Second half of 1900s]

pluck up one's courage Also, **screw up one's courage.** Force oneself to overcome fear or timidity, as in *He was really afraid of slipping on the ice, but he plucked up his courage and ventured down the driveway,* or *I screwed up my courage and dove off the high board.* The first term uses *pluck* in the sense of "make a forcible effort"; Shakespeare put it as "Pluck up the spirits" (*The Taming of the Shrew*, 4:3). The variant derives from the use of *screw* to mean "force or strain by means of a screw."

plug ♦ In addition to the idiom beginning with PLUG, also see PEG (PLUG) AWAY AT; PULL THE PLUG ON.

plug away at ♦ See PEG AWAY AT.

plugged in, be Be closely attuned or responsive, as in *He couldn't make any important social connections because he just wasn't plugged in.* The related expression **be plugged into** takes an object, as in *These connoisseurs are plugged into the local art scene.* These terms allude to inserting a plug into an electrical socket. [Colloquial; c. 1970]

plume oneself Congratulate oneself, boast, as in *He plumed himself on his victory.* This idiom transfers the bird's habit of dressing its feathers to human self-satisfaction. [First half of 1600s]

plunge ♦ See TAKE THE PLUNGE.

plunk down Throw or place or drop heavily, as in *He plunked down the money and walked out,* or *It was hot work, so after an hour we plunked ourselves down in the shade.* [Late 1800s]

pocket ♦ In addition to the idioms beginning with POCKET, also see DEEP POCKETS; IN ONE'S POCKET; IN POCKET; LINE ONE'S POCKETS; MONEY BURNS A HOLE IN ONE'S POCKET; OUT OF POCKET.

pocket money Also, **spending money.** Cash for incidental or minor expenses, as in *They don't believe in giving the children pocket money without asking them to do chores,* or *Can I borrow a dollar? I'm out of all my spending money.* The first term, dating from the early 1600s, alludes to keeping small sums in one's pocket; the second alludes to money that may be spent (as opposed to saved) and dates from the late 1500s.

pocket veto The implied veto of a bill by the President of the United States or by a state governor or other executive who simply holds the bill without signing it until the legislature has adjourned. For example, *The President used the pocket veto to kill the crime bill.* This expression dates from the 1830s and alludes to putting the unsigned bill inside one's pocket.

poetic justice An outcome in which virtue is rewarded and evil punished, often in an especially appropriate or ironic manner. For example, *It was poetic justice for the known thief to go to jail for the one crime he didn't commit.* [Early 1700s]

poetic license Also, **artistic license.** The liberty taken by a writer or artist in deviating from conventional form or fact to achieve an effect. For example, *I've never seen grass or a tree of that color, but that's artistic license.* [Late 1700s]

point ♦ In addition to the idioms beginning with POINT, also see AT SWORD'S POINT; AT THAT POINT; AT THIS POINT; BELABOR THE POINT; BESIDE THE POINT; BOILING POINT; BROWNIE POINTS; CASE IN POINT; GET TO THE POINT; HIT THE HIGH SPOTS (POINTS); IN (POINT OF) FACT; IN POINT; JUMPING-OFF PLACE (POINT); MAKE A POINT OF; MAKE ONE'S POINT; MISS THE POINT; MOOT POINT; ON THE POINT OF; POSSESSION IS NINE POINTS OF THE LAW; SORE POINT; STRETCH A POINT; STRONG POINT; TAKE SOMEONE'S POINT; TO THE POINT; UP TO A POINT; WIN ON POINTS.

point in time A particular moment, as in *At no point in time had they decided to leave the country,* or *The exact point in time when he died has not been determined.* Critics say this usage is wordy since in most cases either *point* or *time* will suffice. However, it has survived since the mid-1700s. Also see AT THIS POINT.

point of no return The place in a course of action beyond which reversal is not possible. For example, *Once the contract is signed, we've reached the point of no return.* This expression comes from aviation, where it signifies the point where an aircraft does not have enough fuel to return to the starting point. [c. 1940]

point of view An attitude or standpoint, how one sees or thinks of something. For example, *From the manufacturer's point of view, the critical issue is cost.* This expression, originally alluding to one's vantage point in seeing a building or painting or other object, dates from the early 1700s.

point out Identify or bring to notice, as in *He pointed out the oldest buildings in the city,* or *She pointed out an error in our reasoning.* [Late 1400s]

point the finger at Attach blame to, accuse, as in *When they asked her who broke the window, she pointed the finger at Tom.* Also see PUT THE FINGER ON.

point up Emphasize, draw attention to, as in *Her comments point up the need for more security at the store.* [First half of 1900s]

poison ♦ In addition to the idiom beginning with POISON, also see ONE MAN'S MEAT IS ANOTHER MAN'S POISON.

poison-pen letter A letter, usually anonymous, that makes malicious statements about the recipient or a third party. For example, *She told the police about the poison-pen letters, but they said they couldn't pursue the matter.* [Early 1900s]

poke ♦ In addition to the idioms beginning with POKE, also see MAKE FUN OF (POKE FUN AT); PIG IN A POKE; TAKE A POKE AT.

poke around Also, **poke about.** Look through things; also, make an investigation. For example, *I was poking around the attic when I found these old photos,* or *The detective was poking about, tracking where she went on that fatal day.* [Early 1800s] Also see NOSE ABOUT; POKE ONE'S NOSE INTO.

poke fun at ♦ See under MAKE FUN OF.

poke one's nose into Pry into or meddle in another's affairs, as in *I told her to stop poking her nose into our business.* This usage replaced the earlier *thrust one's nose into* in the mid-1800s.

poker ♦ In addition to the idiom beginning with POKER, also see STIFF AS A BOARD (POKER).

poker face A visage lacking any expression that can be interpreted, as in *Whenever Betty attended one of her children's performances, she managed to keep a poker face.* This term alludes to the facial expression of a poker player who is expert at concealing his feelings about his hand. [c. 1880]

pole ♦ See LOW MAN ON THE TOTEM POLE; NOT TOUCH WITH A TEN-FOOT POLE.

poles apart In complete opposition, as in *The two brothers were poles apart in nearly all their views.* This expression alludes to the two extremities of the earth's axis, the North and South poles. [Early 1900s]

polish ♦ In addition to the idioms beginning with POLISH, also see SPIT AND POLISH.

polish off Finish or dispose of, especially quickly and easily. For example, *We polished off the pie in no time,* or *If everyone helps, we can polish off this job today.* This usage, dating from the early 1800s, came from boxing, where it originally meant "to defeat an opponent quickly and easily." By the 1830s it was used more generally.

polish the apple Try to win favor through flattery, as in *It may help your standing with the boss if you polish the apple.* This expression gave rise to the phrase **apple polishing.** The idiom alludes to the practice of schoolchildren bringing their teacher the gift of a bright, shiny apple. [c. 1920]

politically correct Also, **PC** or **p.c.** Showing an effort to make broad social and political changes to redress injustices caused by prejudice. It often involves changing or avoiding language that might offend anyone, especially with respect to gender, race, or ethnic background. For example, *Editors of major papers have sent out numerous directives concerning politically correct language.* This expression was born in the late 1900s, and excesses in trying to conform to its philosophy gave rise to humorous parodies.

politics ♦ See PLAY POLITICS.

pond ♦ See BIG FISH IN A SMALL POND; LITTLE FROG IN A BIG POND.

pony ♦ In addition to the idioms beginning with PONY, also see DOG-AND-PONY SHOW.

pony up Pay money that is owned or due, as in *Come on, it's time you ponied up this month's rent.* The allusion in this expression is unclear. [c. 1820]

poop out 1. Tire out, exhaust, as in *I ran about ten miles, but then I was too pooped out to go on.* 2. Quit, decide not to participate, especially at the last minute. For example, *We had about twenty signed up for the seminar, but then half of them pooped out.* [Slang; late 1800s]

poor as a churchmouse Having little or no wealth and few possessions, as in *She's poor as a churchmouse, so you can't expect her to donate anything.* The reason for this long-used simile is unclear, but most believe that, since churches are not known for storing food, a mouse inside one would fare poorly. It has survived such earlier phrases as *poor as Job.* [Second half of 1600s]

poor relation An inferior member of a group, as in *Many regard Turkey as the poor relation in the European alliance.* This expression, first recorded in 1720 for a family member in humble circumstances, began to be used figuratively in the mid-1900s.

poor taste, in Also, **in bad taste.** Not suitable, unseemly, offensive, as in *His criticism of the Pope was in poor taste,* or *That television interview was in very bad taste.* These idioms use *taste* in the sense of "discernment of what is appropriate."

pop off 1. Leave abruptly or hurriedly, as in *I'm just going to pop off and mail some letters.* 2. Die suddenly, as in *No one expected her to pop off like that.* [Colloquial; second half of 1700s] 3. Speak thoughtlessly in an angry outburst, as in *Don't pop off at me—complain to whoever's responsible.* [Slang; c. 1930] 4. **pop someone off.** Kill someone, as in *The sniper popped off at least three men.* [Slang; early 1800s] All four usages transfer *pop* in the sense of "explode" to other kinds of sudden or violent behavior.

pop the question Propose marriage, as in *He picked Valentine's Day to pop the question.* [Early 1700s]

pop up question Suddenly appear, as in *After a brief warm spell all the flowers popped up,* or *He's constantly popping up where he's least expected.*

pork barrel Government funding of something that benefits a particular district, whose legislator thereby wins favor with local voters. For example, *Our senator knows the value of the pork barrel.* This expression alludes to the fatness of pork, equated with political largesse since the mid-1800s. [c. 1900]

port ♦ See ANY PORT IN A STORM.

possessed by Driven by, obsessed with, as in *He was possessed by the idea of becoming a millionaire.* This idiom employs *possess* in the sense of "dominate one's thoughts or ideas," a usage dating from the late 1500s.

possession is nine points of the law Actually holding something is better than merely claiming it. For example, *When Karen told John he must return the sofa he'd borrowed, he said possession is nine points of the law.* This term originally alluded to nine elements that would aid someone's lawsuit, among them a good lawyer, good witnesses, a good jury, a good judge, and good luck. In time, however, the term was used more for squatter's rights. [Late 1500s]

possible ♦ See AS FAR AS POSSIBLE; AS SOON AS POSSIBLE.

possum ♦ See PLAY POSSUM.

post ♦ See DEAF AS A POST; FROM PILLAR TO POST; KEEP POSTED.

pot ♦ In addition to the idiom beginning with POT, also see FISH OR CUT BAIT (SHIT OR GET OFF THE POT); GO TO POT; HIT THE JACKPOT; SWEETEN THE KITTY (POT); TAKE POTLUCK; TEMPEST IN A TEAPOT; WATCHED POT NEVER BOILS.

potato ♦ See HOT POTATO; MEAT AND POTATOES; SMALL BEER (POTATOES).

pot calling the kettle black, the Accusing someone of faults that one has oneself, as in *Tom's criticizing Dexter for dubious line calls is a case of the pot calling the kettle black, since Tom's about the worst line judge I've ever seen.* This expression dates from the days of open-hearth cooking, which blackens practically all the utensils used. [Early 1600s]

potluck ♦ See TAKE POTLUCK.

pound ♦ In addition to the idioms beginning with POUND, also see IN FOR A PENNY, IN FOR A POUND; PENNY WISE, POUND FOOLISH.

pound of flesh A debt whose payment is harshly insisted on, as in *The other members of the cartel all want their pound of flesh from Brazil.* This expression alludes to the scene in Shakespeare's *The Merchant of Venice* (4:1) where the moneylender Shylock demands the pound of flesh promised him in payment for a loan, and Portia responds that he may have it but without an ounce of blood (since blood was not promised). [c. 1600]

pound out Produce, especially on a keyboard, as in *I can pound out another résumé,* or *She was pounding out song after song on the piano.* [c. 1900]

pound the pavement Walk the streets, especially in search of employment. For example, *He was fired last year and he's been pounding the pavement ever since.* A similar usage is **pound a beat,** meaning "to walk a particular route over and over"; it is nearly always applied to a police officer. [Early 1900s]

pour ♦ In addition to the idioms beginning with POUR, also see IT NEVER RAINS BUT IT POURS.

pour cold water on Also, **throw cold water on.** Discourage or deter, as in *Cutting my year-end bonus poured cold water on my loyalty to the company,* or *Hearing about the outbreak of cholera threw cold water on our plans to visit Bolivia.* This term, with its image of putting out a fire with water, at one time meant "defame" or "slander"; the modern meaning dates from about 1800.

pour oil on troubled waters Soothe or calm down something or someone, as in *The twins are quarreling so I'd best go pour oil on troubled waters.* This term alludes to an ancient practice of pouring oil on ocean waves to calm their turbulence, which was mentioned in the eighth century. [Mid-1800s]

pour on the coal Speed up, as in *They keep passing us so pour on the coal, Mom!* or *We can get this issue of the paper out on time if we pour on the coal.* This slangy expression originated in aviation in the 1930s but must have been an allusion to the coal-burning engines of trains and ships, since aircraft were never so powered. It has since been transferred to other vehicles and other endeavors.

pour out one's heart Express one's innermost thoughts and feelings to someone else, as in *Upset over the breakup, she poured out her heart to her mother.* Also see OPEN ONE'S HEART.

powder ♦ See KEEP ONE'S POWDER DRY; SITTING ON A POWDER KEG; TAKE A POWDER.

power ♦ In addition to the idioms beginning with POWER, also see CORRIDORS OF POWER; MORE POWER TO SOMEONE; STAYING POWER.

power behind the throne A person with great influence who stays behind the scenes and has no apparent authority. For example, *Harry may be the CEO, but it's obvious that his wife is the power behind the throne.* [Mid-1800s]

powers that be, the Those in control, the authorities, as in *Our plan was vetoed by the powers that be.* This expression appeared in William Tyndale's 1526 translation of the Bible (Romans 13:1): "The powers that be are ordained of God."

practical ♦ See TO ALL INTENTS AND (FOR ALL PRACTICAL) PURPOSES.

practice ♦ In addition to the idioms beginning with PRACTICE, also see IN PRACTICE; MAKE A PRACTICE OF; OUT OF PRACTICE; PUT INTO PRACTICE; SHARP PRACTICE.

practice makes perfect Frequently doing something makes one better at doing it, as in *I've knit at least a hundred sweaters, but in my case practice hasn't made perfect.* This proverbial expression was once put as *Use makes mastery,* but by 1560 the present form had become established.

practice what you preach Behave as you would have others behave, as in *You keep telling us to clean up, but I wish you'd practice what you preach.* This idiom expresses an ancient idea but appeared in this precise form only in 1678. Also see DO AS I SAY.

praise ♦ In addition to the idiom beginning with PRAISE, also see DAMN WITH FAINT PRAISE; SING SOMEONE'S PRAISES.

praise to the skies Commend lavishly or excessively, as in *The critics praised the new soprano to the skies.* This expression, alluding to lofty praise, was in the 1600s put as **extol to the skies** but acquired its present form in the early 1800s. Also see SING ONE'S PRAISES.

prayer, not a ♦ See under NOT A HOPE IN HELL.

preach ♦ In addition to the idiom beginning with PREACH, also see PRACTICE WHAT YOU PREACH.

preach to the converted Try to convince someone who is already convinced, as in *Why tell me smoking is bad when I gave it up years ago? You're preaching to the converted.* [Mid-1800s]

precedent ♦ See SET A PRECEDENT.

precious few Also, **precious little**. Very few, very little, as in *There are precious few leaves left on the trees,* or *We have precious little fuel left.* In these idioms *precious* serves as an intensive, a colloquial usage dating from the first half of the 1800s.

premium ♦ See AT A PREMIUM; PUT A PREMIUM ON.

presence of mind The ability to act sensibly, promptly, and appropriately, especially in a difficult situation or emergency. For example, *Distraught about losing her wallet and passport, she had the presence of mind to notify the authorities at once.* This idiom in effect says that one's mind is present and functioning. [Second half of 1600s]

present ♦ See ALL PRESENT AND ACCOUNTED FOR; AT PRESENT; FOR THE MOMENT (PRESENT); NO TIME LIKE THE PRESENT.

press ♦ In addition to the idioms beginning with PRESS, also see HARD PRESSED; HOT OFF THE PRESS; PUSH (PRESS) ONE'S LUCK; PUSH (PRESS) SOMEONE'S BUTTONS. Also see under PUSH.

pressed for time In a hurry, as in *How long will it take? I'm really pressed for time.* This idiom uses *press* in the sense of "subject to pressure," a usage dating from the late 1600s.

press into service Force someone or something to perform or function, as in *Can I press you into service to help people find their coats?* or *The funeral drew such a large crowd that more chairs were pressed into service.* This idiom transfers *press* in the sense of "seize and force someone to serve," as

seamen once were, to other activities. It was first recorded in 1871.

press on ♦ See PUSH ON.

press one's luck ♦ See PUSH ONE'S LUCK.

press the flesh Shake hands and mingle with people, especially when running for public office. For example, *The candidate went through the crowd, pressing the flesh.* [1920s]

pretty ♦ In addition to the idioms beginning with PRETTY, also see IN A FIX (PRETTY PICKLE); KETTLE OF FISH, PRETTY; SITTING PRETTY.

pretty as a picture Very attractive, as in *She looked pretty as a picture in her new hat.* The noun *picture* alone was used to describe beautiful objects from the early 1800s on; this locution, however, dates from about 1900.

pretty much Almost, nearly, approximately, as in *Our homework was pretty much finished.* This adverbial usage differs from the use of *pretty* for "considerable" (as in PRETTY PENNY). [c. 1800]

pretty penny, a A considerable sum of money, as in *That fur coat must have cost a pretty penny.* [Early 1700s]

prevail on Successfully persuade or influence, as in *They prevailed on me to speak at their annual luncheon.* This term uses *prevail* in the sense of "exert superior force." It replaced **prevail with** in the mid-1600s.

prey on 1. Plunder or pillage; also, make a profit at someone else's expense, victimize. For example, *Vikings preyed on the coastal towns of England,* or *The rich have been preying on the poor for centuries.* [Late 1500s] 2. Hunt, especially in order to eat, as in *Their cat preys on all the rodents in the neighborhood.* [c. 1600] 3. Exert a baneful or injurious effect, as in *Guilt preyed on his mind.* [c. 1700]

price ♦ In addition to the idioms beginning with PRICE, also see AT ALL COSTS (AT ANY PRICE); CHEAP AT TWICE THE PRICE; EVERY MAN HAS HIS PRICE.

price is right, the The price is very reasonable, it is a good value. This term is often used jokingly to describe something that is free but otherwise not particularly praiseworthy. For example, *These golf balls we found in the pond may not look new, but the price is right.* [Second half of 1900s]

price on one's head A reward for capturing or killing someone, usually someone guilty of a crime. For example, *He was a serial killer, and they put a price on his head.* The *head* in this term presumably alludes to the older punishment of beheading. [Mid-1700s]

price out of the market Charge so much for a product or service that no one will buy it, as in

Asking $10 each for those old records is pricing yourself out of the market. [First half of 1900s]

prick up one's ears Listen carefully, pay close attention, as in *When she heard them mention her boyfriend she pricked up her ears.* This term alludes to horses raising their ears at a sudden noise. [Late 1500s]

pride ♦ In addition to the idioms beginning with PRIDE, also see BURST WITH (PRIDE); SWALLOW ONE'S PRIDE.

pride and joy The object of one's great pleasure, as in *Our new grandson is our pride and joy,* or *Dana's car is his pride and joy.* This term was probably invented by Sir Walter Scott in his poem *Rokeby* (1813), where he described children as "a mother's pride, a father's joy."

pride of place The highest or most prominent position, as in *His trophy had pride of place on the mantelpiece.* [Early 1600s]

pride oneself on Also, **take pride in**. Be proud of, take satisfaction in, as in *We pride ourselves on always being punctual,* or *She took pride in her flower garden.* The first term dates from the late 1300s, the second from the late 1500s.

prime ♦ In addition to the idioms beginning with PRIME, also see PAST ONE'S PRIME.

prime mover The initial source of energy directed toward a goal, someone or something that sets others in motion. For example, *Jean was the prime mover in getting us more laboratory space,* or *Patriotism was the prime mover of the revolution.* [Late 1600s]

prime of life The best years of one's life, when one is at the peak of one's powers, as in *She was in the prime of life when she began to lose her sight.* The related phrase **in one's prime** can be applied to objects as well as persons. For example, *The roses were in their prime when you last saw them.* In both idioms *prime* means "first in quality or character." [Early 1700s] Also see PAST ONE'S PRIME.

prime the pump Encourage the growth or action of something, as in *Marjorie tried to prime the pump by offering some new issues for discussion.* In the late 1800s this expression originally was used for pouring liquid into a pump to expel the air and make it work. In the 1930s it was applied to government efforts to stimulate the economy and thereafter was applied to other undertakings.

principle ♦ See IN PRINCIPLE; ON PRINCIPLE.

print ♦ In addition to the idiom beginning with PRINT, also see GO OUT (OF PRINT); IN PRINT; SMALL PRINT.

print out 1. Write by drawing letters as opposed to cursive writing, as in *Please print out your name above your signature.* 2. Use a computer printer,

as in *This manuscript is too long to print out, so let's continue using floppy disks.* [Second half of 1900s]

private ♦ In addition to the idiom beginning with PRIVATE, also see FREE (PRIVATE) ENTERPRISE; GO PRIVATE; IN PRIVATE.

private eye A privately employed detective, as opposed to one working for the police or another authority. For example, *The children loved stories about private eyes, and Janey wanted to become one.* This expression comes from the term *private investigator,* the "i" of investigator being changed to "eye," which plays on the idea of a person looking into things. [1930s]

probability ♦ See IN ALL PROBABILITY.

problem ♦ See NO PROBLEM.

profile ♦ See KEEP A LOW PROFILE.

progress ♦ See IN PROGRESS.

promise ♦ See LICK AND A PROMISE.

proof of the pudding, the Results are what count, as in *Let's see if this ad actually helps sales — the proof of the pudding, you know.* The full expression of this proverb, dating from about 1600, is **The proof of the pudding is in the eating,** but it has become so well known that it is often abbreviated.

prop ♦ See KNOCK THE BOTTOM (PROPS) OUT FROM.

proportion ♦ See OUT OF PROPORTION.

pros and cons Arguments or considerations for and against something, as in *We'd best weigh all the pros and cons before we decide to add a new wing to the library.* This idiom is taken from the Latin *pro* for "for" and *con* for "against." [Late 1500s]

proud ♦ In addition to the idiom beginning with PROUD, also see DO SOMEONE PROUD.

proud as a peacock Having a very high opinion of oneself, filled with or showing excessive self-esteem. For example, *She strutted about in her new outfit, proud as a peacock.* This simile alludes to the male peacock, with its colorful tail that can be expanded like a fan, which has long symbolized vanity and pride. Chaucer used it in *The Reeve's Tail:* "As any peacock he was proud and gay." [1200s]

prove ♦ In addition to the idiom beginning with PROVE, also see EXCEPTION PROVES THE RULE.

prove out Succeed, turn out well, as in *Farm-raised trout has proved out so well that the fish industry plans to experiment with other species.* [Mid-1900s]

prune ♦ See FULL OF BEANS, def. 2.

psych out 1. Analyze or understand something; also, anticipate the intentions of someone, as in *It's hard to psych out the opposition's thinking, but we have to try.* 2. Undermine the confidence of, intimidate. For example, *The basketball team managed to psych out their opponents' guards.* This expression is often used in the passive and can mean "lose one's nerve," as in *After I learned that he had two doctorates in the field, I was completely psyched out.* Both slangy usages date from the second half of the 1900s and allude to influencing someone psychologically.

psych up Excite emotionally, as in *The chorus was really psyched up for performing in Symphony Hall.* [Slang; c. 1970]

public ♦ See GO PRIVATE (PUBLIC); IN PUBLIC; IN THE PUBLIC EYE; JOHN DOE (Q. PUBLIC); WASH ONE'S DIRTY LINEN IN PUBLIC.

publish or perish Produce published work or fall into disfavor. For example, *The younger members of the department have a heavier teaching load, but they also know it's publish or perish.* This expression is nearly always used for college or university teachers, for whom advancement frequently is predicated on publishing research in their field. [Mid-1900s]

pudding ♦ See PROOF OF THE PUDDING.

puff piece An approving or flattering article, as in *That was really a puff piece about the conductor, written by her cousin.* The use of *puff* for "exaggerated praise" dates from about 1600; *piece* was added in the mid-1900s.

pull ♦ In addition to the idioms beginning with PULL, also see FAST ONE, PULL A; HAVE PULL WITH; LIKE PULLING TEETH.

pull a boner Make a blunder, as in *I pulled an awful boner when I mentioned his ex-wife.* This expression is derived from the noun *bone head,* for "blockhead" or "stupid person." [Slang; early 1900s]

pull a fast one Also, **put over a fast one**. Engage in a deceitful practice or play an unfair trick. For example, *He pulled a fast one when he gave me that fake employment record,* or *She tried to put over a fast one, but we found out in time to stop her.* [Slang; c. 1920]

pull away 1. Move away or withdraw, as in *The car pulled away from the curb.* [Mid-1900s] 2. Move ahead or forward, as in *His horse pulled away and took the lead.*

pull back Retreat, as in *The troops gradually pulled back.* [Mid-1500s]

pull down 1. Demolish, destroy, as in *They pulled down several old office buildings downtown.* [Early 1500s] 2. Lower, reduce; also, depress in health or spirits. For example, *The bumper wheat crop is bound to pull down prices,* or *The flu really pulled him down.* [Late 1500s] 3. Draw as wages, as in *He pulled down a hefty salary.* [Colloquial; early 1900s]

pull in 1. Arrive at a destination, as in *The train pulled in right on time.* [c. 1900] 2. Rein in, restrain, as in *She pulled in her horse,* or *The executives did not want to pull in their most aggressive salesmen.*

[c. 1600] 3. Arrest a suspect, as in *The police said they could pull him in on lesser charges.* [Late 1800s]

pulling teeth ♦ See LIKE PULLING TEETH.

pull in one's horns Also, **draw in one's horns**. 1. Retreat, back down, restrain oneself, as in *The town manager wanted higher taxes but public reaction made him draw in his horns.* This expression alludes to the snail's habit of drawing in the soft projecting parts of its body when it is threatened. The idea was first expressed in the 15th century as *shrink one's horns,* and the idiom with *draw* developed about the same time. The idiom with *pull* did not appear until a century later. 2. Reduce expenses, as in *That drop in profits will force the company to pull in its horns.* [Late 1800s]

pull no punches Behave unrestrainedly, hold nothing back, as in *The doctor pulled no punches but told us the whole truth.* This expression comes from boxing, where to **pull one's punches** means "to hit less hard than one can." This idiom, too, has been applied more generally, as in *They decided to pull their punches during these delicate negotiations.* [First half of 1900s]

pull off Accomplish, bring off, especially in the face of difficulties or at the last minute. For example, *I never thought we'd ever stage this play, but somehow we pulled it off.* [Colloquial; second half of 1800s]

pull oneself together Regain one's composure or self-control, as in *After that frightening episode, it took her a while to pull herself together.* [Second half of 1800s]

pull oneself up by the bootstraps Succeed by one's own efforts, as in *She was homeless for nearly two years, but she managed to pull herself up by the bootstraps.* This expression alludes to pulling on high boots by means of the straps or loops attached to them at the top. [Early 1900s]

pull one's punches ♦ See PULL NO PUNCHES.

pull one's weight Also, **pull one's own weight**. Do one's share, as in *We have a small organization, so we all must pull our own weight.* This term comes from rowing, where each crew member must pull on an oar at least enough to propel himself or herself. Its figurative use dates from about 1900.

pull out 1. Leave, depart, as in *The bus pulled out at noon.* [Mid-1800s] 2. Withdraw from an undertaking, as in *After the crash many investors pulled out of the market.* [Late 1800s]

pull out all the stops Use all the resources or force at one's disposal, as in *The police pulled out all the stops to find the thief.* This term comes from organ-playing, where it means "bring into play every rank of pipes," thereby creating the fullest possible sound. It has been used figuratively since about 1860.

pull out of a hat Produce suddenly and surprisingly, as if by magic. For example, *We can't just pull the answers out of a hat.* This expression alludes to the magician's trick of pulling some unexpected object out of a hat. That object is often a rabbit, and the expression **pull a rabbit out of a hat** is often used to mean "get magical results," as in *Much as I would like to be able to pull a rabbit out of a hat, I doubt if I can find further funding for this project.*

pull over Bring a vehicle to the side of the road; also, instruct a motorist to stop. For example, *We pulled over to ask a passerby for directions,* or *The state trooper pulled the speeding motorist over.* [First half of 1900s]

pull rank Use one's higher status to compel obedience or obtain privileges, as in *She hated pulling rank in the office, but sometimes it was necessary.* This term comes from the military. [c. 1920]

pull round Restore or be restored to good health, as in *It was good nursing that pulled him round so quickly,* or *Once on antibiotics, he pulled round quickly.* [Late 1800s]

pull someone's chain 1. Make someone speak out of turn, as in *Who pulled your chain?—It's none of your business.* [1920s] 2. Make someone angry, especially deliberately, as in *Teenagers really know how to pull their parents' chains.* [c. 1960] Both usages allude to the literal sense of chain-pulling, that is, "causing someone to do something, as though activated by a chain."

pull someone's leg Play a joke on, tease, as in *Are you serious about moving back in or are you pulling my leg?* This term is thought to allude to tripping someone by so holding a stick or other object that one of his legs is pulled back. [Late 1800s]

pull something Play a trick, deceive someone, as in *We thought he was trying to pull something when he claimed he had never picked up our tickets.* It is often put as **pull something on someone**, as in *I knew he was pulling something on me when he told me the wrong date.* Also see PULL A FAST ONE.

pull strings Also, **pull wires**. Use one's influence, as in *By pulling strings he got us house seats to the opening,* or *His father pulled some wires and got him out of jail.* Both terms allude to manipulating a marionette. The first dates from the second half of the 1800s, the second from the early 1800s.

pull the plug on 1. Discontinue, end, as in *The government pulled the plug on that program.* [First half of 1900s] 2. Remove all life-supporting equipment, as in *The family debated whether it was time to pull the plug on him.* [Second half of 1900s] Although this idiom undoubtedly alludes to cut-

ting off electricity to an electrical device, it originally referred to the removal of a stopper that flushed an old-style toilet.

pull the rug out from under Remove all support and assistance from, usually suddenly. For example, *Stopping his allowance pulled the rug out from under him, forcing him to look for a job.* This metaphoric term alludes to pulling on a rug a person is standing on so that he or she falls. [Mid-1900s]

pull the wool over someone's eyes Deceive or hoodwink someone, as in *His partner had pulled the wool over his eyes for years by keeping the best accounts for himself.* This term alludes to the former custom of wearing a wig, which when slipping down can blind someone temporarily. [c. 1800]

pull through Survive a difficult situation or illness, as in *We've had to declare bankruptcy, but I'm sure we'll pull through.* [Mid-1800s]

pull together 1. Make a joint effort, cooperate, as in *If we pull together, I'm sure we'll meet our quota.* [Late 1700s] 2. **pull something together**. Assemble or gather together, as in *Once we pull together all the facts, we'll understand the situation.* [Late 1800s] Also see PULL ONESELF TOGETHER.

pull up 1. Stop or cause to stop, as in *He pulled up his horse,* or *They pulled up in front of the door.* [Early 1600s] 2. Catch up, advance in relation to others, as in a race. For example, *She was behind at the start, but she quickly pulled up.* [Late 1800s] Also see PULL ONESELF UP BY ONE'S BOOTSTRAPS.

pull up stakes Move away, leave one's home, job, or country. For example, *We've lived here for years, but now it's time to pull up stakes.* This expression alludes to the stakes that mark property boundaries. [Early 1800s]

pull wires ♦ See PULL STRINGS.

pulse ♦ See TAKE THE PULSE OF.

pump iron Lift weights, as in *She's started pumping iron three times a week.* This idiom was born with the late-20th-century stress on physical fitness. [Second half of 1900s]

pump up 1. Inflate with gas or air, as in *This tire needs pumping up.* [Late 1800s] 2. Fill with enthusiasm, strength, and energy, as in *The lively debate pumped us all up.* Mary Wollstonecraft used this idiom in slightly different form in *The Rights of Women* (1792): "Lover-like phrases of pumped-up passion."

punch ♦ In addition to the idioms beginning with PUNCH, also see BEAT TO IT (THE PUNCH); CAN'T PUNCH ONE'S WAY OUT OF A PAPER BAG; PACK A PUNCH; PLEASED AS PUNCH; PULL NO PUNCHES; ROLL WITH THE PUNCHES; SUCKER PUNCH; THROW A PUNCH.

punch in 1. Also, **punch a** or **the clock**. Check in at a job upon arrival, as in *You have to punch in or you won't get paid*, or *In this office no one has to punch a clock*. This usage alludes to the use of a time clock, which has a button an employee punches or strikes to record the time of arrival on a card. [1920s] Also see PUNCH OUT, def. 1. 2. Keyboard data into a computer, as in *He was careful about punching in all the payments*. [Mid-1900s]

punch out 1. Record one's time of departure from work, as in *We never punch out at exactly five o'clock*. This usage, dating from the 1920s, alludes to the use of a time clock. Also see PUNCH IN, def. 1. 2. Eject from a military aircraft, as in *The pilot punched out just before the plane blew up*. [Slang; 1960s]

punishment ♦ See GLUTTON FOR PUNISHMENT.

puppy love Also, **calf love**. Adolescent love or infatuation, especially one that is not expected to last, as in *Beth is besotted with him, but we think it's just puppy love*, or *He's got a bad case of calf love*. [First half of 1800s]

pure and simple No more and no less, plainly so, as in *This so-called educational video is really a game, pure and simple*. This expression is very nearly redundant, since *pure* and *simple* here mean "plain" and "unadorned." Oscar Wilde played on it in *The Importance of Being Earnest* (1895): "The truth is rarely pure and never simple." [Second half of 1800s]

pure as the driven snow Morally unsullied, chaste, as in *She's just sixteen and pure as the driven snow*. This simile dates from the late 1500s, although *driven*, which means "carried by the wind into drifts," was occasionally omitted. It is heard less often today.

purpose ♦ See AT CROSS PURPOSE; FOR ALL INTENTS AND PURPOSES; ON PURPOSE; SERVE A PURPOSE; TO GOOD PURPOSE; TO LITTLE OR NO PURPOSE.

purse ♦ In addition to the idiom beginning with PURSE, also see CAN'T MAKE A SILK PURSE OUT OF A SOW'S EAR.

purse strings Financial resources or control of them, as in *His mother doesn't want to let go of the purse strings because he may make some foolish investments*. This expression is often extended to **hold** or **tighten** or **loosen the purse strings**, as in *As long as Dad holds the purse strings, we have to consider his wishes*, or *The company is tightening the purse strings and will not be hiring many new people this year*. The *purse strings* in this idiom are the means of opening and closing a drawstring purse. [Early 1400s]

push around Treat or threaten to treat roughly, bully, domineer, as in *I won't let him push me around*. [Colloquial; c. 1920]

push comes to shove, if Also, **when push comes to shove**. When matters must be confronted, when a crucial point is reached, as in *If push comes to shove, the Federal Reserve Board will lower the interest rate*, or *They supposedly support equality, but when push comes to shove they always seem to promote a man instead of a woman*. This term comes from rugby, where, after an infraction of rules, forwards from each team face off and push against one another until one player can kick the ball to a teammate and resume the game. Its figurative use dates from the 1950s. Also see the synonym IF WORST COMES TO WORST.

push it Be overly insistent or forward, as in *I promise to think over your proposal, but don't push it*. This idiom uses *push* in the sense of "force some activity or issue." [First half of 1800s]

push off Also, **shove off**. Leave, set out, depart, as in *The patrol pushed off before dawn*, or *It's time to shove off*. This usage alludes to the literal meaning of a person in a boat pushing against the bank or dock to move away from the shore. [Colloquial; early 1900s]

push on 1. Also, **press on**. Continue or proceed along one's way, as in *The path was barely visible, but we pushed on*, or *It's time to push on to the next item on the agenda*. [Early 1700s] 2. **push something on someone**. Thrust something on someone for acceptance or attention, as in *She's always pushing second helpings on her guests*. [Early 1700s]

push one's luck Also, **press one's luck**. Risk one's good fortune, often by acting overconfidently, as in *We've gotten all but one of the concessions we asked for; demanding that last one would be pushing our luck*, or *You've done very well so far, but don't press your luck*. [Early 1900s]

push paper Do administrative, often petty, paperwork. For example, *She spent the whole day pushing paper for her boss*. [Colloquial; second half of 1900s]

push someone's buttons Also, **press someone's buttons**. Draw a strong emotional reaction from someone, especially anger or sexual arousal. For example, *My mother-in-law really knew how to push my buttons*, or *A good-looking redhead, she always seemed to press his buttons*. This metaphoric expression transfers activating some mechanism by pushing buttons to human emotions. [Slang; 1920s]

push the envelope Exceed the limits of what is normally done, be innovative, as in *They are pushing the envelope in using only new fabrics for winter clothing*. This idiom comes from aviation, the *envelope* alluding to the technical limits of a plane's performance, which, on a graph, appear as a rising slope as limits of speed and stress are approached and falls off when the capacity is exceeded and the pilot loses control; safety lies within these limits, or *envelope,* and exceeding them exposes pilot and plane to risk. [Slang; late 1960s]

push the panic button Also, **press the panic button.** Overreact to a situation, as in *Don't worry; Jane is always pushing the panic button, but I'm sure the baby's fine.* This term originated during World War II, when certain bombers had a bell-warning system so that the crew could bail out if the plane was severely hit. Occasionally a pilot would push the button in error, when there was only minor damage, causing the crew to bail out unnecessarily. By 1950 the expression had been transferred to other kinds of overreaction.

push up daisies Be dead and buried, as in *There is a cemetery full of heroes pushing up daisies.* This slangy expression, alluding to flowers growing over a grave, was first recorded about 1918, in one of Wilfred Owen's poems about World War I.

put ♦ In addition to the idioms beginning with PUT, also see (PUT) AT EASE; (PUT ON A) BRAVE FACE; CART BEFORE THE HORSE, PUT THE; CLAMP DOWN (PUT THE CLAMPS ON); FLESH OUT (PUT FLESH AND BONE ON); FOR (PUT IN ONE'S) TWO CENTS; (PUT ON A) HAIR SHIRT; HARD PUT; (PUT) IN EFFECT; (PUT) IN THE PICTURE; LAY (PUT) ONE'S CARDS ON THE TABLE; LAY (PUT) ONE'S HANDS ON; LAY (PUT) THE BLAME ON; (PUT SOMEONE'S) NOSE OUT OF JOINT; NOT PUT SOMETHING PAST SOMEONE; (PUT) OFF THE TRACK; (PUT) ON A PEDESTAL; (PUT) OUT OF BUSI-NESS; PULL (PUT OVER) A FAST ONE; PUT ONE'S HEAD ON THE BLOCK; THROW (PUT) OFF THE SCENT. Also see under SET.

put a bug in someone's ear Give someone a hint about something, as in *Janet put a bug in her husband's ear about getting the children a dog for Christmas.* This idiom presumably likens the buzzing about of an insect to a hint, although the exact analogy is not clear. [c. 1900]

put across 1. Cause to be understood or accepted, as in *She put her views across very well.* [c. 1920] 2. Attain or carry through by deceit, as in *You can't put anything across this teacher.* [c. 1920] Also see PUT OVER, def. 3.

put a damper on Discourage, dishearten, deter, as in *Grandpa's death put a damper on our Christmas holidays.* This idiom employs the noun *damper* in the sense of "something that damps or depresses the spirits," a usage dating from the mid-1700s.

put all one's eggs in one basket Risk all of one's resources in a single venture, as in *He had warned Peter about investing heavily in a single stock; it was putting all his eggs in one basket.* This proverb, first recorded in 1710, has largely replaced the much older *trust all one's goods to one ship.* Mark Twain

played on it in *Pudd'nhead Wilson* (1894): "The fool saith, 'Put not all thy eggs in one basket' . . . but the wise man saith, 'Put all your eggs in one basket, and *watch that basket!*'"

put an end to Also, **put a stop to.** Terminate, abolish, as in *It's time they put an end to their feud,* or *The police chief vowed to put a stop to prostitution.* This locution is more emphatic than the plain verbs *end* or *stop.* [Mid-1600s]

put an idea in one's head ♦ See PUT IDEAS INTO SOMEONE'S HEAD.

put a premium on Value more highly than usual, as in *Her employer put a premium on honesty and hard work.* First recorded in 1907, this term is almost always used figuratively.

put aside 1. Also, **put by** or **away.** Save, store up for future use, as in *We put aside all the toys for our grandchildren,* or *James put by dozens of cans of tomatoes this year,* or *She put away some of her salary every month.* The first two terms date from the late 1700s, the third from the late 1800s. 2. Also, **set aside.** Place out of the way, as in *The clerk put the bruised fruit aside to sell at reduced price;* or *We set aside the outdoor furniture before we water the lawn.* [Late 1800s]

put a spin on Give a certain meaning or interpretation to. *Spin* is usually modified by an adjective in this expression, as in *Robert was adept at putting positive spin on weak financial reports,* or *This chef has put a new spin on seafood dishes.* Also see SPIN DOCTOR. [1980s]

put at ease ♦ See AT EASE.

put at someone's disposal Allow one to use, as in *They put their car at our disposal for our entire stay.* This idiom employs *disposal* in the sense of "the liberty or power to use something," a usage dating from the early-1600s.

put away 1. Place in a designated spot for storage; also, place out of reach. For example, *Please put away your clothes,* or *This young tennis player can really put away the ball.* Also see SET ASIDE, def. 1. 2. Renounce, discard, as in *Put away all those negative thoughts.* [Late 1300s] 3. Consume quickly, ingest readily, as in *He put away his dinner in just a few minutes.* [Colloquial; late 1800s] 4. Confine to a mental health facility, as in *The doctor said we had to put her away.* [Colloquial; late 1800s] 5. Kill, as in *The vet put our old cat away.* [Colloquial; late 1500s]

put back the clock ♦ See SET BACK, def. 3.

put behind one 1. Try to forget, make an effort not to be bothered by, as in *He had to put that failed negotiation behind him and make a fresh start.* [Mid-1800s]

put by ♦ See SET ASIDE, def. 1.

put down 1. Write down; also, enter in a list. For example, *Please put down my name for a free ticket*, or *Put me down as a subscriber*. [Second half of 1500s] **2**. Bring to an end, repress, as in *They managed to put down the rebellion in a single day*, or *We've got to put down these rumors about a takeover*. [c. 1300] **3**. Kill a sick animal, as in *The vet said the dog must be put down*. [Mid-1500s] Also see PUT AWAY, def. 5. **4**. Belittle, disparage, criticize, as in *Her husband was always putting her down*. [c. 1400] Also see RUN DOWN, def. 6. **5**. Ascribe, attribute, as in *We put her poor performance down to stage fright*. [Late 1700s] **6**. Regard, classify, as in *We put her down as a hypochondriac*. [Mid-1800s] **7**. Pay a deposit, as in *We put down $2,000 for the car*. **8**. Store for future use, as in *David put down ten cases of this year's Chablis*. [Mid-1800s] **9**. Land in an aircraft; also, land an aircraft, as in *What time will we put down at Heathrow?* or *She put the plane down exactly on the runway*. [c. 1930] **10**. Put a child to bed, as in *The sitter said she'd put Brain down at 8:30*. [Second half of 1900s]

put down roots Settle somewhere, become established, as in *We've put down roots here and don't want to move away*. This metaphoric expression, first recorded in 1921, likens the rooting of a plant to human settlement.

put forth 1. Grow, as in *This bush puts forth new shoots each spring*. [First half of 1500s] **2**. Bring to bear, exert, as in *We'll have to put forth a great deal more effort*. [c. 1400] **3**. Also, **set forth**. Offer for consideration, as in *She put forth at least three new ideas*. [Mid-1300s] **4**. Bring to notice, publish, as in *The appendix puts forth a fresh analysis of events*. [Mid-1500s] **5**. See SET FORTH.

put forward Propose for consideration, as in *His attorney put forward a claim on the property*, or *They put me forward for the post of vice-chair*. [Mid-1800s]

put hair on one's chest ♦ See PUT LEAD IN ONE'S PENCIL.

put heads together ♦ See PUT OUR HEADS TOGETHER.

put ideas into someone's head Also, **put an idea in someone's head**. Suggest something to someone, as in *No, we're not moving—what put that idea in your head?* [Mid-1800s]

put in 1. Make a formal offer of, as in a court of law. For example, *He put in a plea of not guilty*. [Mid-1400s] **2**. Interpose, interject; see PUT IN A GOOD WORD; PUT ONE'S OAR IN. **3**. Spend time at a location or job, as in *He put in three years at hard labor*, or *She put in eight hours a day at her desk*. [Mid-1800s] **4**. Plant, as in *We put in thirty new trees*. [Early 1800s] **5**. Enter a port or harbor, as in *The yacht will put in here for the night*. [Early

1600s] **6. put in for**. Request or apply for something, as in *I put in for a raise*, or *John put in for department supervisor*. [c. 1600]

put in a good word Make a supportive remark or favorable recommendation. For example, *Please put in a good word for me with the supervisor*, or *When you see her, put in a good word for the department*. The use of *good word* for a laudatory utterance dates from about 1200.

put in an appearance Also, **make an appearance**. Be present, especially for a short time, as in *We were hoping the rock star would put in an appearance, but she didn't show up*, or *She was tired and didn't want to go to the party, but decided she had to make an appearance*. [Second half of 1600s]

put in mind of ♦ See PUT ONE IN MIND OF.

put in mothballs Defer indefinitely or for a very long time, as in *We've put the plans for a new library in mothballs*. This expression alludes to storing woolen clothing or other items with marble-size balls of naphthalene or camphor to prevent them from being damaged by moths. [1940s]

put in one's place ♦ See PUT SOMEONE IN HIS OR HER PLACE.

put in one's two cents ♦ See under FOR TWO CENTS.

put in order Arrange in proper sequence; see IN ORDER, def. 1; also PUT ONE'S HOUSE IN ORDER.

put in the way of Also, **put in one's way. 1**. Obstruct or impede, as in *The police put a traffic barrier in the way of northbound motorists*, or *I don't want to put anything in the way of your advancement*. [c. 1500] **2**. See IN ONE'S WAY, def. 2.

put into effect ♦ See IN EFFECT, def. 2.

put into practice Also, **put in practice**. Carry out in action, as in *It's time we put these new ideas into practice*. Shakespeare used this idiom in *Two Gentlemen of Verona* (3:2): "Thy advice, this night, I'll put in practice." [Mid-1500s]

put into words Express verbally, as in *I find it hard to put my feelings into words*. [Late 1800s]

put it mildly Understate, say without exaggeration, as in *It's a fairly long way to walk, to put it mildly—twenty miles or so*. [First half of 1900s]

put it to 1. Present for consideration, as in *Let's put it to a vote*, or *I put it to you, I did the best I could under the circumstances*. [Mid-1700s] **2**. Present something in a forceful, candid manner to someone, as in *I can't put it to you any more clearly—stay away from the electrical equipment*. **3**. Overburden with tasks or work, as in *They really put it to him, expecting to do all the packing*. **4**. Blame on, as in *They didn't know who broke the window so they put it to Sam*. **5**. Take unfair advantage, cheat, as in *That used-car dealer really put it to Betty*.

put lead in one's pencil Enhance or restore sexual vigor, as in *Try one of these hot peppers; that'll put lead in your pencil.* This phrase, a euphemism for causing an erection, is considered far more vulgar than the contemporary synonym **put hair on one's chest**, alluding to a secondary male sex characteristic. [Colloquial; c. 1900]

put money on Also, **put one's money on.** Bet on; also, consider likely or nearly certain, expect. For example, *Jean put her money on Contender but the horse came in last,* or *I'm sure the President will speak to the crowd; I'd put money on it.* This idiom was first recorded in 1931.

put off Delay or postpone, as in *He always puts off paying his bills.* This idiom, dating from the late 1300s, gave rise to the proverb **Never put off until tomorrow what you can do today**, first recorded in the late 1300s (in Chaucer's *Tale of Melibee*) and repeated ever since. Also see PUT ONE OFF.

put on 1. Clothe oneself with, as in *I put on my socks.* [Mid-1400s] 2. Apply, activate, as in *He put on the brakes.* [Mid-1700s] 3. Assume affectedly, pretend to, as in *He put on a British accent.* This idiom is sometimes put as **put it on**, as in *He's not really asleep; he's putting it on.* [Late 1600s; late 1800s] 4. **put someone on.** Tease or mislead another, as in *I don't believe you! You're putting me on.* [Slang; mid-1900s] 5. Add to, gain, as in *Please put this on our bill,* or *I've put on some weight.* 6. Cause to be performed, produce, as in *I hear they're putting on Shakespeare this summer.* [Late 1800s]

put on a brave face ♦ See BRAVE FACE.

put on a brave front ♦ See BRAVE FRONT.

put on airs Assume a haughty manner, pretend to be better than one is, as in *I'm sick of Claire and the way she puts on airs. Airs* here means "a manner of superiority." [c. 1700]

put on an act Pretend, especially in order to deceive; also, show off. For example, *We were afraid Charlie had hurt himself, but he was just putting on an act,* or *We know you're a good swimmer—stop putting on an act.* [c. 1930]

put on a pedestal ♦ See ON A PEDESTAL.

put one in mind of Remind one, as in *You put me in mind of your grandmother.* This idiom was first recorded in 1530. For a synonym see CALL TO MIND.

put one into the picture ♦ See IN THE PICTURE.

put one off 1. Repel or repulse someone, as in *His bad manners put her off,* or *They were put off by the bad smell.* [c. 1900] 2. **put someone off.** Persuade someone to delay further action, as in *He put off the creditors, promising to pay next week,* or *They managed to put him off from suing.* [Early 1600s]

put one off one's stride Also, **put one off one's stroke.** Interfere with one's progress, distract or disturb one, as in *The interruption put her off her stride for a moment, and she took several seconds to resume her train of thought,* or *The noise of the airplanes overhead put her off her stroke, and she missed the next ball.* The first term, first recorded in 1946, alludes to the regular pace of a walker or runner; the variant, first recorded in 1914, alludes to the regular strokes of a rower. Also see THROW OFF THE TRACK.

put one out 1. Inconvenience one, as in *Will it put you out if we arrive early?* Also see PUT ONESELF OUT. [Mid-1800s] 2. Offend or irritate one, as in *His watching television while I visited put me out.* [Early 1800s] Also see PUT OUT.

put one's back into it Make a strenuous effort, as in *If you put your back into that report, you'll soon be done.* This idiom alludes to physical labor involving the strength of one's back. It was first recorded in 1882.

put one's back up ♦ See GET ONE'S BACK UP.

put one's best foot forward Try for the best possible impression, make a good start, as in *Come on, let's put our best foot forward for this interview.* The allusion in this idiom is unclear, though it may concern marching. One theory is that *best foot* means "the right foot," the left being regarded as unlucky. [Late 1500s]

put one's cards on the table ♦ See LAY ONE'S CARDS ON THE TABLE.

put oneself in someone's place ♦ See PUT SOMEONE IN HIS OR HER PLACE, def. 2.

put oneself out Make a considerable effort, go to a lot of trouble, as in *Laura put herself out trying to make everyone feel at home.* [Mid-1800s] Also see PUT ONE OUT.

put one's face on Apply makeup, as in *Helen won't stir out of the house before she puts her face on.* [Colloquial; second half of 1900s]

put one's feet up Rest, as in *After a day of gardening I'm ready to put my feet up.*

put one's finger on Also, **lay one's finger on.** 1. Identify, as in *I can't put my finger on the man in that photo.* [Late 1800s] 2. See LAY A FINGER ON.

put one's foot down Take a firm stand, as in *She put her foot down and said we could not go to the carnival.* This idiom alludes to setting down one's foot firmly, representing a firm position. [Late 1800s]

put one's foot in it Make a blunder, as in *I didn't know it was a surprise party; I guess I put my foot in it.* This expression presumably alludes to setting one's foot down in mud or excrement. [Late 1700s] Also see FOOT IN ONE'S MOUTH.

put one's hand to ♦ See TURN ONE'S HAND TO.

put one's head on the block ♦ See ON THE BLOCK, def. 2.

put one's house in order Arrange one's affairs, as in *Stop meddling in your daughter's business and put your own house in order.* This metaphoric term appears in slightly different form in the Bible (Isaiah 38:1): "Set thine house in order." [Late 1500s]

put one's mind to Also, **set one's mind on**. Concentrate on or be determined to achieve, as in *She's put her mind to improving her test results*, or *I've set my mind on finding a job I really like.* [First half of 1800s]

put one's money where one's mouth is Back up one's opinion with action, as in *He goes on and on about helping the homeless; I wish he'd put his money where his mouth is.* This idiom, alluding to contributing cash to support one's stated views, has been broadened to include any kind of action. [First half of 1900s]

put one's nose out of joint ♦ See NOSE OUT OF JOINT.

put one's oar in Interfere with something or insert one's opinion, as in *I'll thank you not to put your oar in when we're discussing a private matter.* This term, referring to helping to row a boat, was first recorded in Charles Coffey's 1731 play *The Devil to Pay*: "I will govern my own house without your putting in an oar."

put one's shoulder to the wheel Work hard, make a strenuous effort, as in *We'll have to put our shoulder to the wheel to get this job done.* This metaphoric term, alluding to pushing a heavy vehicle that has bogged down, has been used figuratively since the late 1700s.

put on hold ♦ See ON HOLD.

put on ice ♦ See ON ICE, def. 1.

put on one's thinking cap Think or reflect seriously, as in *A new slogan? I'll have to put on my thinking cap for that.* This term originated in the late 1800s and replaced *considering cap*, which dates from the early 1600s.

put on the dog Also, **put on the ritz**. Behave in an elegant, extravagant manner, as in *We'll have to put on the dog when our daughter's in-laws visit*, or *They really put on the ritz for the wedding reception.* The allusion in the first of these slangy terms, first recorded in 1865, is unclear, although it has been suggested that the newly rich displayed their wealth by keeping pampered lapdogs. The second term, from the 1920s, alludes to the large, luxurious hotels founded by and named for César Ritz (1850–1918), which still exist in Paris, London, and many other major cities.

put on the feed bag Also, **tie on the feed bag**. Eat a meal, as in *Come on, it's time to put on the feed bag.* This slangy term, alluding to a horse's feed bag that is literally tied on, dates from the early 1900s.

put on the map Make famous, publicize, as in *The incident got on the national news and put our com-munity on the map.* This expression, alluding to a locality that formerly was too small to put on a map, dates from the early 1900s.

put on the spot ♦ See ON THE SPOT.

put on weight ♦ See PUT ON, def. 5.

put our heads together Also, **put their heads together**. Discuss or plan something among ourselves (or themselves), as in *Let's put our heads together and figure out what we can give him for his birthday.* This idiom, alluding to combining mental forces, originated in the late 1300s as *lay our heads together* and acquired its current form in the second half of the 1800s.

put out 1. Extinguish, as in *We put out the fire before we turned in.* [Early 1500s] 2. Also, **put to sea**. Leave a port or harbor, as in *They put out yesterday morning.* [Late 1500s] 3. Publish, as in *They put out a weekly newsletter.* [Early 1500s] 4. Engage in sex. This usage is applied solely to women, as in *She had a reputation for putting out.* [Vulgar slang; mid-1900s] Also see PUT ONE OUT.

put out feelers Discreetly try to learn something, as in *They put out feelers to see if anyone was interested in buying the company.* This idiom alludes to an animal's feelers, such as antennae or tentacles, used to find food. [First half of 1800s]

put out of business ♦ See OUT OF BUSINESS.

put out of one's mind Make oneself forget or overlook, as in *You've lost, but put that out of your mind and concentrate on the job.*

put out to grass Also, **put out to pasture**. Cause to retire, as in *With mandatory retirement they put you out to grass at age 65*, or *She's not all that busy now that she's been put out to pasture.* These idioms refer to farm animals sent to graze when they are no longer useful for other work.

put over 1. Make successful, bring off, as in *Do you think we can put over this play?* [Early 1900s] 2. Make something or someone be understood or accepted, as in *The public relations staff helped put our candidate over to the public.* [Early 1900s] 3. **put over on**. Fool, deceive, as in *We can't put anything over on Tom.* [Early 1900s] 4. Delay, postpone, as in *The meeting was put over until tomorrow.* [Early 1500s] Also see PUT OFF.

put paid to Finish off, end, as in *We'd best put paid to this issue.* [Early 1900s]

put right Fix, make amends, correct, as in *The wheel's come off, but we can put that right in no time*, or *Victor thought we were moving out, but we put him right.* [Late 1800s]

put someone away ♦ See PUT AWAY, def. 3.

put someone down ♦ See PUT DOWN, def. 4.

put someone in his or her place 1. Rebuke someone, remind someone of his or her position, as in *Alice is entirely too rude; it's time you put her in her* *place.* The noun *place* here denotes one's rank or position. [Mid-1900s] **2.** Also, **put oneself in someone's place.** Imagine being someone else, as in *Just put yourself in my place—how would you deal with it?* [Mid-1600s]

put someone on ♦ See PUT ON, def. 4.

put someone out of his or her misery 1. Kill a wounded or suffering animal or person, as in *When a horse breaks a leg, there is nothing to do but put it out of its misery.* [Late 1700s] **2.** End someone's feeling of suspense, as in *Tell them who won the tournament; put them out of their misery.* [c. 1920] Both usages employ *put out of* in the sense of "extricate" or "free from."

put someone right ♦ See PUT RIGHT.

put someone through his or her paces Test thoroughly to see what someone can do, as in *We put the new programmer though her paces, and she passed with flying colors.* The idiom can refer to things as well, as in *When we put the electrical system through its paces, we blew a fuse.* The expression alludes to testing a horse's ability in the various paces (trot, canter, and gallop). Its use referring to horses dates from the late 1700s; its figurative use was first recorded in 1871.

put someone up ♦ See PUT UP, def. 5.

put someone up to Incite someone to do something, especially a mischievous or malicious act. For example, *My brother put me up to making those prank telephone calls,* or *They didn't think of it on their own; someone put them up to it.* [Early 1800s]

put someone wise ♦ See PUT WISE.

put that in your pipe and smoke it Take that information and give it some thought, as in *I'm quitting at the end of the week—put that in your pipe and smoke it.* This term alludes to the thoughtful appearance of many pipe smokers. [Colloquial; early 1800s]

put the arm on Also, **put the bite** or **touch on.** Ask for or demand money, as in *He's the youngest and he's always putting the arm on Dad.* The first of these slangy usages, first recorded in 1939, alludes to a robber assaulting someone by yoking his arm around the victim's throat. The *bite* variant, first recorded in 1919, similarly alludes to a violent attack. The last, *touch,* has been slang for "theft" since the mid-1800s.

put the blame on ♦ See under LAY ON, def. 3; PUT IT TO, def. 3.

put the cart before the horse ♦ See CART BEFORE THE HORSE.

put the fear of God into Terrify someone, as in *The school counselor put the fear of God into the girls when she talked about AIDS.* This phrase alludes to a time when most people had a mingled feeling of dread and reverence toward the deity. [Late 1800s]

put the finger on Inform on, as in *The witness put the finger on the defendant.* [Slang; c. 1920] Also see PUT ONE'S FINGER ON.

put the heat on ♦ See TURN UP THE HEAT.

put their heads together ♦ See PUT OUR HEADS TOGETHER.

put the kibosh on Restrain or check something, as in *The rain put the kibosh on our beach party,* or *The boss put the kibosh on the whole project.* The word *kibosh* has been used in English since the first half of the 1800s and its origin is unknown.

put the lid on Also, **keep the lid on.** Suppress, as in *I don't know how but we'll have to put the lid on that rumor about her,* or *Let's keep the lid on our suspicions.* The word *lid* here is used in the sense of "a cover for a container." [Early 1900s]

put the make on Make sexual advances to, as in *He's always putting the make on his wife's friends.* This slangy expression, dating from the second half of the 1900s, uses *make* in the sense of "sexual overtures."

put the screws on ♦ See under TURN UP THE HEAT.

put the skids on Bring to a halt, as in *The school committee put the skids on the idea of a dress code.* The word *skid* here probably refers to a shoe or drag that applies pressure to the wheel of a vehicle to prevent it from moving.

put the skids under Bring about the failure or defeat of, as in *It was lack of funds that put the skids under the new senior center.* The *skids* here are runners or rollers on which a heavy object may be moved. [Colloquial; early 1900s]

put through 1. Bring to a successful conclusion, as in *We put through a number of new laws.* [Mid-1800s] **2.** Make a telephone connection, as in *Please put me through to the doctor.* [Late 1800s] **3.** Cause to undergo, especially something difficult or troublesome, as in *He put me through a lot during this last year.* The related expression, **put someone through the wringer,** means "to give someone a hard time," as in *The lawyer put the witness through the wringer.* The *wringer* alluded to is the old-fashioned clothes wringer, in which clothes are pressed between two rollers to extract moisture. [First half of 1900s]

put through the wringer ♦ See PUT THROUGH, def. 3.

put to bed Complete something and either set it aside or send it on to the next step, as in *We put the magazine to bed at ten,* or *They said they'd put the whole project to bed at least a month ago.* This expression, transferring nighttime retirement to other kinds of completion, was first applied to a newspaper, where it meant "send to press," that is, start to print. [Mid-1900s]

put to death Kill, execute, as in *Another convicted murderer was put to death last night.* [c. 1400]

put to flight Cause to run away, as in *The bombs put the civilians to flight.* [Mid-1800s]

put together 1. Build, assemble, create, as in *We put together the new bookcase,* or *This writer can't put together a coherent sentence.* [First half of 1500s] 2. Combine mentally, as in *Once she put this and that together she knew exactly what had happened.* [First half of 1600s] Also see PUT OUR HEADS TOGETHER; PUT TWO AND TWO TOGETHER.

put to good use Employ to the best advantage, as in *I'm sure this dictionary will be put to good use.*

put to it, be Be confronted with a severe difficulty, as in *I was put to it to finish this book on time.* This usage is derived from the active sense of *put to it,* that is, "force or challenge someone to something." [c. 1600]

put to rights ♦ See SET TO RIGHTS; also PUT RIGHT.

put to sea ♦ See PUT OUT, def. 2.

put to shame Outdo, eclipse, as in *Jane's immaculate kitchen puts mine to shame.* This idiom modifies the literal sense of *put to shame,* that is, "disgrace someone," to the much milder "cause to feel inferior." [Mid-1800s]

put to sleep 1. Bore utterly, as in *That show put me to sleep.* This hyperbolic term implies that something is so dull one could fall asleep. 2. Kill, especially as a kindness, as in *We had to put the cat to sleep.* This euphemism dates from the mid-1900s. 3. Subject to anesthesia, as in *This injection will put you to sleep so you won't feel any pain.*

put to the test Try or check out something or someone, as in *This tall grass will put our new lawnmower to the test,* or *Let's put Harry to the test and see if he knows the last 20 World Series winners.* [Mid-1600s]

put two and two together Draw the proper inference from existing evidence, as in *Putting two and two together, it's not hard to guess who will be chosen for the lead role in the play.* [Mid-1800s]

putty in someone's hands A person who is easily influenced or malleable, as in *Dean adored his little granddaughter; he was putty in her hands.* This metaphoric term, first recorded in 1924, transfers the malleable quality of putty to human behavior. Also see TWIST AROUND ONE'S FINGER.

put up 1. Erect, build; also, lift to a higher position. For example, *They put up three new houses on our street,* or *She looks more grownup when she puts up her hair in a bun.* [c. 1600] 2. Preserve, can, as in *She put up countless jars of jam.* [Early 1800s]

3. Nominate, as in *Tom put up Peter for president.* [Late 1500s] 4. Provide funds, especially in advance, as in *They put up nearly a million for the new museum.* 5. **put someone up.** Provide lodgings for, as in *We can put you up for the night.* [Mid-1700s] 6. Startle game from cover, as in *The hunter put up three grouse.* [Late 1400s] 7. Offer for sale, as in *They had to put up their last antiques.* [Early 1700s] 8. Make a display or appearance of, as in *They were actually broke but put up a good front.* [First half of 1800s] 9. Do well in a contest, as in *They put up a good fight.* [Late 1800s] 10. Stake money for a bet, as in *Each player put up ten dollars.* [Mid-1800s]

put-up job A prearranged conspiracy, especially a crime such as a burglary. For example, *The police suspected that the butler was in on it—it was a put-up job.* This colloquial phrase was first recorded in 1810.

put upon, be Be taken advantage of, be imposed on, as in *Bob was always put upon by his friends, who knew he couldn't say no.* It also is put as **feel put upon,** as in *We felt quite put upon because the entire family insisted on spending every holiday at our house.* [Mid-1800s]

put up or shut up Act on what you are saying or stop talking about it, as in *You've been citing evidence for months but never presented it—now put up or shut up.* This somewhat impolite term, often put as a command, is believed to come from gambling, in which a card player is told to ante up or withdraw. A second theory maintains that it means either put up your fists to fight or back down. [1870s] Also see PUT ONE'S MONEY WHERE ONE'S MOUTH IS.

put up with Endure without complaint, as in *She's been very patient, putting up with all kinds of inconvenience.* [Mid-1700s]

put wise Inform or enlighten someone, as in *You'd better put Arthur wise about the protocol before he visits them.* [Colloquial; early 1900s]

put words in someone's mouth Tell what someone should say, as in *Give Janey a chance to answer my question; don't put words in her mouth.* This graphic term appeared in the Bible (II Samuel 14:3): "So Joab put words in her mouth." Also see TAKE THE WORDS OUT OF ONE'S MOUTH.

puzzle out Clarify or solve something, as in *It took him a while to puzzle out the significance of the statement.* [Late 1700s]

Pyrrhic victory A victory that is offset by staggering losses, as in *The campaign was so divisive that even though he won the election it was a Pyrrhic victory.* This expression alludes to King Pyrrhus of Epirus, who defeated the Romans at Asculum in

A.D. 279, but lost his best officers and many of his troops. Pyrrhus then said: "Another such victory and we are lost." In English the term was first recorded (used figuratively) in 1879.

q

q ♦ See MIND ONE'S P'S AND Q'S.

Q.T. ♦ See ON THE Q.T.

quake in one's boots Also, **shake in one's boots; quake** or **shake like a leaf.** Tremble with fear, as in *The very thought of a hurricane blowing in makes me quake in my boots.* Both *quake* and *shake* here mean "tremble." These idioms were preceded by the alliterative phrase *shake in one's shoes* in the late 1800s. The idioms with *leaf* allude to trembling leaves, as in *He was shaking like a leaf when the exams were handed back.* A similar expression was used by Chaucer, who put it as *quake like an aspen leaf,* a particularly apt comparison since aspen leaves have flattened stems that cause the leaves to quiver in the gentlest breeze.

quantity ♦ See UNKNOWN QUANTITY.

quantum leap A dramatic advance, especially in knowledge or method, as in *Establishing a central bank represents a quantum leap in this small country's development.* This term originated as *quantum jump* in the mid-1900s in physics, where it denotes a sudden change from one energy state to another within an atom. Within a decade it was transferred to other advances, not necessarily sudden but very important ones.

quarrel ♦ See PICK A QUARREL.

quarter ♦ See AT CLOSE QUARTERS; DRAW AND QUARTER.

queen it Act like a queen, domineer, as in *She queened it over the family, treating her siblings like servants.* This female counterpart of LORD IT OVER was used by Shakespeare in *The Winter's Tale* (4:4). [c. 1600]

quest ♦ See under IN SEARCH OF.

question ♦ See ASK A STUPID QUESTION; BEG THE QUESTION; BESIDE THE POINT (QUESTION); BEYOND QUESTION; BURNING QUESTION;CALL IN QUESTION; IN QUESTION; LEADING QUESTION; LOADED QUESTION; OPEN QUESTION; OUT OF THE QUESTION; POP THE QUESTION; RHETORICAL QUESTION; WITHOUT QUESTION.

quick ♦ In addition to the idioms beginning with QUICK, also see CUT TO THE QUICK; (QUICK) ON THE UPTAKE.

quick and the dead The living and the dead, as in *The explosion was loud enough to wake the quick and the dead.* Although *quick* has been used for "living" since the 9th century A.D., it survives only in this idiom and in CUT TO THE QUICK, and may be obsolescent.

quick as a wink Also, **quick as a bunny** or **a flash.** Very speedily, as in *He was out of here quick as a wink,* or *She answered, quick as a bunny.* These similes have largely replaced the earlier *quick as lightning,* although *quick as a flash* no doubt alludes to it (also see LIKE GREASED LIGHTNING), and *quick as thought,* now obsolete. The *bunny* variant dates from the mid-1800s, the others from the late 1800s.

quicker than you can say Jack Robinson ♦ See BEFORE YOU CAN SAY JACK ROBINSON.

quick off the mark Fast to start or try something, as in *This physician is quick off the mark in trying the newest medications.* This expression comes from various kinds of races, where *mark* indicates the starting point. It was being used figuratively from the mid-1900s on.

quick one, a An alcoholic drink to be consumed rapidly, as in *We have time for a quick one before we board the plane.* [c. 1920]

quick on the draw Also, **quick on the trigger.** Rapid in acting or reacting, as in *You have to be quick on the draw if you want to find low-rent housing here,* or *Bruce was quick on the trigger when it came to answering questions.* The first expression came from the American West's gunslingers and was broadened to mean "a quick reaction" in the first half of the 1900s. The variant originated about 1800.

quick on the uptake ♦ See ON THE UPTAKE.

quid pro quo An equal exchange or substitution, as in *I think it should be quid pro quo—you mow the lawn and I'll take you to the movies.* This Latin expression, meaning "something for something," has been used in English since the late 1500s.

quiet ♦ In addition to the idiom beginning with QUIET, also see KEEP QUIET; PEACE AND QUIET.

quiet as a mouse Also, **still as a mouse.** Silent, without noise, as in *She sneaked into the house, quiet as a mouse,* or *When he heard the news he was still as a mouse.* The first of these similes dates from the mid-1500s, the second from the 1300s.

quit ♦ In addition to the idiom beginning with QUIT, also see CALL IT QUITS.

quit a bit Also, **quite a few; quite a lot.** A considerable or moderate amount, as in *There's still quite a bit of snow on the ground,* or *Quite a few parking spaces are open.* [Second half of 1800s]

quit while one's ahead Don't try to improve on something that is already accomplished, as in *Those drapes we hung are even enough—let's quit while* *we're ahead*. This idiom also implies that further action runs the risk of spoiling something. Also see LEAVE WELL ENOUGH ALONE.

r

R ♦ See THREE R'S.

rabbit ♦ See PULL (A RABBIT) OUT OF A HAT.

race ♦ See RAT RACE; SLOW BUT SURE (STEADY WINS THE RACE).

rack ♦ In addition to the idioms beginning with RACK, also see ON THE RACK.

rack and ruin, go to Also, **go to wrack and ruin.** Become decayed, decline or fall apart, as in *After the founder's death the business went to rack and ruin*. These expressions are emphatic redundancies, since *rack* and *wrack* (which are actually variants of the same word) mean "destruction" or "ruin." [Mid-1500s]

rack one's brain Also, **cudgel one's brains.** Strain to remember or find a solution, as in *I've been racking my brain trying to recall where we put the key*, or *He's been cudgeling his brains all day over this problem*. The first term, first recorded in 1583 as *rack one's wit*, alludes to the *rack* that is an instrument of torture, on which the victim's body was stretched until the joints were broken. The variant, from the same period, uses *cudgel* in the sense of "beat with a cudgel" (a short thick stick). Shakespeare used it in *Hamlet* (5:1): "Cudgel thy brains no more about it, for your dull as will not bend his pace with beating." Also see BEAT ONE'S BRAINS OUT.

rack out Go to sleep, as in *I racked out about midnight*. This slangy expression, as well as the related **rack time,** for sleeping or snooze time, use *rack* to refer to being laid out on a framework, here a bed.

rack up Accumulate or score, as in *Last night's episode of that new sitcom racked up at least fifteen points in the ratings*. [Colloquial; mid-1900s]

rag ♦ In addition to the idiom beginning with RAG, also see CHEW THE FAT (RAG); FROM RAGS TO RICHES; GLAD RAGS; RUN RAGGED.

rag doll A limp, ineffectual person, as in *You won't get a decision from her; she's a rag doll when it comes to making up her mind*. This expression transfers the limpness of a soft doll made from scraps of cloth to human behavior. [Mid-1800s]

rage ♦ See ALL THE RAGE.

ragged ♦ See RUN ONE RAGGED.

rail ♦ See OFF THE RAILS; THIN AS A RAIL; THIRD RAIL.

rain ♦ In addition to the idioms beginning with RAIN, also see COME IN OUT OF THE RAIN; IT NEVER RAINS BUT IT POURS; RIGHT AS RAIN.

rain cats and dogs Also, **rain buckets.** Rain very heavily, as in *It was raining cats and dogs so I couldn't walk to the store*, or *It's been raining buckets all day*. The precise allusion in the first term, which dates from the mid-1600s, has been lost, but it probably refers to gutters overflowing with debris that included sewage, garbage, and dead animals. Richard Brome used a version of this idiom in his play *The City Wit* (c. 1652), where a character pretending a knowledge of Latin translates wholly by ear, "*Regna bitque*/and it shall rain, *Dogmata Polla Sophon*/dogs and polecats and so forth." The variant presumably alludes to rain heavy enough to fill pails.

rain check A promise that an unaccepted offer will be renewed in the future, as in *I can't come to dinner Tuesday but hope you'll give me a rain check*. This term comes from baseball, where in the 1880s it became the practice to offer paying spectators a rain check entitling them to future admission for a game that was postponed or ended early owing to bad weather. By the early 1900s the term was transferred to tickets for other kinds of entertainment, and later to a coupon entitling a customer to buy, at a later date and at the same price, a sale item temporarily out of stock.

rain on one's parade Spoil one's plans, as in *The minority party in the legislature has tried hard to rain on the speaker's parade, but so far his agenda has prevailed*. This expression conjures up the image of a downpour ruining a celebration such as a parade. [c. 1900]

rain or shine No matter what the circumstances, as in *We promised we would finish the project tomorrow, rain or shine*. This term, first recorded in 1905, still refers to weather, as well as other uncertainty, and always implies that an activity will be carried out, no matter what. For a synonym, see HELL OR HIGH WATER.

rain out Force the cancellation or postponement of some event owing to bad weather. For example, *Our picnic was rained out, but we hope to have it next week*. [1920s]

rainy day, a A time of need or trouble, as in *We knew a rainy day would come sooner or later*. This idiom is often used in the context of **save for a rainy day,** which means to put something aside for a future time of need. [Late 1500s]

raise ♦ In addition to the idioms beginning with RAISE, also see CAUSE RAISED EYE-BROWS; CURTAIN RAISER; MAKE (RAISE) A STINK; PLAY (RAISE) HAVOC.

raise a hand against Also, **lift one's hand against.** Threaten to hit or actually hit, as in *She's never raised a hand against the children*. [First half of 1500s]

raise an objection Protest, as in *I'll raise no objections to your proposed bill if you promise to support me next time.* The use of *raise* in the sense of "bring up" or "mention" dates from the mid-1600s.

raise a stink ◆ See MAKE A STINK.

raise Cain Also, **raise hell** or **the devil.** Behave in a rowdy or disruptive way, as in *He said he'd raise Cain if they wouldn't give him a refund,* or *The gang was out to raise hell that night,* or *The wind raised the devil with our picnic.* The first term alludes to the son of Adam and Eve who killed his brother, Abel. It was first recorded in the *St. Louis Daily Pennant* (May 2, 1840): "Why have we every reason to believe that Adam and Eve were both rowdies? Because . . . they both raised Cain." This statement makes a pun on *raise,* meaning "bring up" or "nurturing." The two variants, alluding to bringing hell or the devil up to this world, are older, the first from about 1700, the second from about 1800.

raise eyebrows ◆ See CAUSE RAISED EYE-BROWS.

raise havoc ◆ See PLAY HAVOC.

raise hell ◆ See under RAISE CAIN.

raise one's hackles Make one very angry, as in *That really raised my hackles when he pitched straight at the batter's head. Hackles* are the hairs on the back of an animal's neck, which stick up when the animal feels fearful or angry. [Late 1800s]

raise one's sights Establish higher goals for oneself, as in *She seemed content as a paralegal, but we thought she should raise her sights and get a law degree.* This idiom uses *sights* in the sense of "a device on a gun or optical instrument that helps one take aim." [Mid-1900s] For the antonym, see LOWER ONE'S SIGHTS.

raise one's voice Talk louder, either to be heard more clearly or in anger, as in *You'll have to raise your voice if you expect the audience to hear you,* or *Don't you raise your voice at me!* [Late 1300s]

raise the ante Increase the price or cost of something, as in *We'd hoped to invest in some land, but they've raised the ante and now we can't afford it.* This term alludes to the *ante* or stakes of gambling. [Slang; late 1800s]

raise the curtain Also, **lift the curtain.** 1. Begin or start, as in *It's time to raise the curtain, guys—start shoveling.* 2. Make something public, disclose. In this sense, both terms often occur with *on,* as in *We won't know what the new design is until they lift the curtain on it.* Both usages, from the mid-1700s, allude to the curtain raised at the beginning of a theatrical performance, revealing the stage.

raise the devil ◆ See under RAISE CAIN.

raise the roof 1. Be extremely noisy and boisterous, as in *They'd had a lot to drink and were really raising the roof last night.* 2. Complain loudly and angrily, as in *When the landlord increased the rent, the tenants raised the roof about his lack of repairs and maintenance.* Both usages convey the image of the roof being lifted because it cannot contain either noise or rage. [Slang; mid-1800s] Also see HIT THE CEILING.

rake off Make an unlawful profit, as in *They suspected her of raking off some of the campaign contributions for her personal use.* This expression alludes to the raking of chips by an attendant at a gambling table. [Late 1800s]

rake over the coals Also, **haul over the coals.** Reprimand severely, as in *When Dad finds out about the damage to the car, he's sure to rake Peter over the coals,* or *The coach hauled him over the coals for missing practice.* These terms allude to the medieval torture of pulling a heretic over red-hot coals. [Early 1800s]

rake up Revive, bring to light, especially something unpleasant, as in *She was raking up old gossip.* [Late 1500s]

rally around Join in a common effort, as in *When Mom broke her leg the entire family rallied around to help.* This idiom gained currency with George F. Root's famous Civil War song, "The Battle Cry of Freedom," which urges troops to rally round the flag that goes with them into battle. [Early 1800s]

ramble on Speak or write at length and with many digressions, as in *As the speaker rambled on for at least two hours, the audience became restless.* This idiom was first recorded in 1710.

ram down someone's throat Also, **shove down someone's throat.** Compel to accept or consider, as in *That salesman tried to ram a life insurance policy down my throat,* or *She has a way of shoving her political views down your throat.* These terms transfer forcing one to swallow something to forcing acceptance of an object or idea.

rampage ◆ See ON A RAMPAGE.

random ◆ See AT RANDOM.

range ◆ See AT CLOSE RANGE.

rank ◆ In addition to the idiom beginning with RANK, also see BREAK RANKS; CLOSE RANKS; PULL RANK; RISE THROUGH THE RANKS.

rank and file Followers, the general membership, as in *This new senator really appeals to the rank and file in the labor unions.* This expression comes from the military, where a *rank* denotes soldiers standing side by side in a row, and *file* refers to soldiers standing behind one another. The first recorded figurative use of this term was in 1860.

ransom ◆ See KING'S RANSOM.

rant and rave Talk loudly and vehemently, especially in anger, as in *There you go again, ranting and raving about the neighbor's car in your driveway.* This idiom is a redundancy, since *rant* and *rave* mean just about the same thing, but probably survives on account of its alliterative appeal.

rap ♦ In addition to the idiom beginning with RAP, also see BEAT THE RAP; BUM RAP; NOT GIVE A DAMN (RAP); TAKE THE RAP.

rap someone's knuckles Reprimand, as in *If I'd seen John take that last piece of cake, I'd have rapped his knuckles.* This term transfers a physical punishment to a verbal one. [Late 1600s]

rare bird, a An exceptional individual, a unique person, as in *That wife of yours is a rare bird; you're lucky to have her.* This idiom, generally used as a compliment, is a translation of the Latin *rara avis*, which itself was used from about 1600 on and began to be translated only in the late 1800s.

rarely ever ♦ See HARDLY EVER.

raring to go Very eager to begin, as in *The children were all dressed and raring to go.* This idiom uses *raring* for *rearing*, and alludes to a horse's standing on its hind legs when it is anxious to get moving. [Early 1900s]

rat ♦ In addition to the idioms beginning with RAT, also see LIKE A DROWNED RAT; SMELL A RAT.

rate ♦ See AT ANY RATE; AT THIS RATE; X-RATED.

rather ♦ See HAD RATHER.

rat on Betray a comrade by giving information, as in *He ratted on his best friend to the police.* [Slang; early 1900s]

rat race Fierce competition to maintain or improve one's position in the workplace or social life. For example, *You may not realize what a rat race it is to get research grants.* This term presumably alludes to the rat's desperate struggle for survival. [Colloquial; first half of 1900s]

rattle off Also, **reel off.** Utter or perform rapidly or effortlessly, often at length. For example, *The treasurer rattled off the list of all those who had not paid their dues,* or *She reeled off song after song.* The verb *rattle* has been used for fast talking since the late 1300s and for other kinds of fast production since the late 1800s (George Bernard Shaw wrote of "men who rattle off their copy" in a letter of 1896). The verb *reel off,* which alludes to unwinding from a reel, has been used figuratively since about 1830.

rave ♦ See RANT AND RAVE; STARK RAVING MAD.

raw ♦ In addition to the idiom beginning with RAW, also see IN THE ALTOGETHER (RAW).

raw deal An instance of unfair or harsh treatment, as in *After 25 years with the bank Bob got a raw deal—no pension, no retirement benefits of any*

kind, just a gold watch. Raw here means "crude" or "unfair." [First half of 1900s]

razor ♦ See SHARP AS A TACK (RAZOR).

reach ♦ In addition to the idiom beginning with REACH, also see BOARDINGHOUSE REACH; GET TO (REACH) FIRST BASE; IN REACH.

reach for the sky **1.** Set very high goals, aspire to the best, as in *I'm sure they'll make you a partner, so reach for the sky.* The *sky* here stands for high aspirations. Also see SKY'S THE LIMIT. **2.** Put your hands up high, as in *One robber held the teller at gunpoint, shouting "Reach for the sky!"* This usage is always put as an imperative. [Slang; mid-1900s]

read ♦ In addition to the idioms beginning with READ, also see DO YOU READ ME; OPEN BOOK, READ LIKE AN.

read a lecture Also, **read a lesson.** Issue a reprimand, as in *Dad read us a lecture after the teacher phoned and complained.* The first term dates from the late 1500s, the variant from the early 1600s. Also see READ THE RIOT ACT; TEACH A LESSON.

read between the lines Perceive or detect a hidden meaning, as in *They say that everything's fine, but reading between the lines I suspect they have some marital problems.* This term comes from cryptography, where in one code reading every second line of a message gives a different meaning from that of the entire text. [Mid-1800s]

read into Find an additional hidden or unintended meaning in something that is said or written, as in *What I read into that speech on foreign policy is that the Vice President plans to run for President.* [Late 1800s]

read like an open book ♦ See OPEN BOOK.

read out of Expel from a group by proclamation, as in *After he was convicted for embezzling their funds, the members read him out of the investment club.* [First half of 1800s]

read someone's mind Discern what someone is thinking or feeling, as in *He often finished her sentences for her, almost as though he could read her mind.* [Late 1800s]

read the riot act Warn or reprimand forcefully or severely, as in *When he was caught throwing stones at the windows, the principal read him the riot act.* This term alludes to an actual British law, the Riot Act of 1714, which required reading a proclamation so as to disperse a crowd; those who did not obey within an hour were guilty of a felony. [First half of 1800s]

read up Study or learn by reading, as in *I don't know much about childhood illnesses, but I can always read up on them.* [First half of 1800s]

ready ♦ In addition to the idiom beginning with READY, also see AT THE READY; GET READY; GOOD AND (READY); ROUGH AND READY.

ready, willing, and able Well prepared and eager to do something, as in *Any time you want me to babysit, I'm ready, willing, and able.*

real ♦ In addition to the idiom beginning with REAL, also see FOR REAL; GET REAL.

reality check An assessment to determine if one's circumstances or expectations conform to reality, as in *Time for a reality check—wasn't this supposed to be a money-making enterprise?* [Slang; second half of 1900s]

real McCoy, the Also, **the McCoy.** The genuine thing, as in *That painting's not a reproduction—it's the real McCoy.* This idiom has a disputed origin, but the most likely source is its use to distinguish welterweight champion "Kid McCoy," the name used by Norman Selby (1873–1940), from other boxers using his name to capitalize on his popularity. [c. 1900]

rear ♦ In addition to the idioms beginning with REAR, also see BRING UP THE REAR.

rear end 1. The back part of anything, especially a vehicle, as in *There's a large dent in the rear end of the car.* 2. The buttocks, as in *I'm afraid these pants don't fit my rear end.* The noun *rear* alone has been used in both these senses, the first since the late 1700s and the second since the mid-1900s. The addition of *end* occurred in the first half of the 1900s.

rear its ugly head Appear. This phrase is used only of something undesirable or unpleasant, as in *The interview went very well until a question about his academic record reared its ugly head.* This expression was first recorded in slightly different form in Anthony Trollope's *Barchester Towers* (1857): "Rebellion had already reared her hideous head."

reason ♦ See BY REASON OF; IN REASON; IT STANDS TO REASON; LISTEN TO REASON; LOSE ONE'S MIND (REASON); RHYME OR REASON; SEE REASON; STAND TO REASON; WITH REASON.

reasonable ♦ See BEYOND A (REASONABLE) DOUBT.

rebound ♦ See ON THE REBOUND.

recall ♦ See BEYOND RECALL.

receiving ♦ See ON THE RECEIVING END.

reckon ♦ In addition to the idiom beginning with RECKON, also see FORCE TO BE RECKONED WITH.

reckon with 1. Take into account, be prepared for, as in *The third-party movement is a force to be reckoned with during the primaries.* This usage was first recorded in 1885. 2. Deal with, as in *Your lost wallet isn't the only problem we have to reckon with.* Also see TAKE INTO ACCOUNT.

record ♦ See BREAK THE RECORD; GO ON RECORD; JUST FOR THE RECORD; OFF THE RECORD; SET (THE RECORD) STRAIGHT; TRACK RECORD.

red ♦ In addition to the idioms beginning with RED, also see CATCH RED-HANDED; IN THE RED; NOT WORTH A DIME (RED CENT); PAINT THE TOWN RED; SEE RED.

red carpet Honorary treatment, lavish hospitality, as in *We'll have to get out the red carpet for the President's visit.* This term comes from the literal practice of rolling out a carpet to welcome a royal or other esteemed guest, and indeed is often put as **roll out the red carpet.** [Early 1900s]

red cent ♦ See under NOT WORTH A DIME.

redeeming feature A good quality or aspect that makes up for other drawbacks, as in *The house isn't very attractive, but the garden is the redeeming feature.* This idiom, first recorded in 1827, uses *redeem* in the sense of "compensate."

red herring Something that draws attention away from the central issue, as in *Talking about the new plant is a red herring to keep us from learning about downsizing plans.* The *herring* in this expression is red and strong-smelling from being preserved by smoking. The idiom alludes to dragging a smoked herring across a trail to cover up the scent and throw off tracking dogs. [Late 1800s]

red in the face, be Suffer embarrassment or shame; also, exert oneself to the utmost. For example, *He was red in the face from all of the mistakes he made while announcing the winners' names,* or *You can try until you're red in the face, but you still won't get straight A's.* The phrase *red face* was already used in the late 1300s to refer to blushing on account of shame. However, the interjection **Is my face red!** meaning "I am very embarrassed or ashamed," dates only from about 1930.

red-letter day A special occasion, as in *When Jack comes home from his tour of duty, that'll be a red-letter day.* This term alludes to the practice of marking feast days and other holy days in red on church calendars, dating from the 1400s. [c. 1700]

redress the balance Readjust matters, restore equilibrium, as in *If our party wins in a few big cities, it will redress the balance of urban and rural interests in the House.* [Mid-1800s]

red tape Official forms and procedures, especially those that are complex and time-consuming. For example, *There's so much red tape involved in approving our remodeling that we're tempted to postpone it indefinitely.* This expression alludes to the former British custom of tying up official documents with red ribbon. [Early 1800s]

reed ♦ See BROKEN REED.

reel off ♦ See RATTLE OFF.

reference ♦ See IN REGARD (REFERENCE) TO.

reflect on 1. Consider or think carefully about, as in *She reflected on her country's role in history.*

[c. 1600] A closely related phrase is **on due reflection,** meaning "after careful consideration." For example, *On due reflection I decided to vote for the incumbent.* **2. reflect on one.** Give evidence of one's qualities, as in *The hasty preparation of this report will reflect on you.* [Second half of 1600s]

regard ♦ See IN REGARD TO.

region ♦ See IN THE NEIGHBORHOOD (REGION) OF.

regular as clockwork ♦ See LIKE CLOCKWORK.

regular guy Also, **regular fellow.** A nice or agreeable person, as in *Luke's a regular guy,* or *Hilda's a regular fellow.* [Colloquial; first half of 1800s]

rein ♦ See DRAW IN THE REINS; FREE HAND (REIN); TIGHT REIN ON.

reinvent the wheel Do something again, from the beginning, especially in a needless or inefficient effort, as in *School committees need not reinvent the wheel every time they try to improve the curriculum.* This expression alludes to the invention of a simple but very important device that requires no improvement. [Second half of 1900s]

rejoice in Have or possess something highly desirable, as in *He rejoices in a keen mind.* [Late 1400s]

relation ♦ See POOR RELATION; RELATIVE (IN RELATION) TO.

relative to Correspondent or proportionate to, as in *Relative to its size, Boston has a great many universities,* or *It's important to get all the facts relative to the collision.* Another form of this idiom is in or **with relation to,** meaning "in reference or with regard to," as in *Demand is high in relation to supply,* or *That argument changes nothing with relation to our plans for hiring workers.* The usages with *relative* date from the second half of the 1700s, those with *relation* from the late 1500s.

relieve oneself Urinate or defecate, as in *The puppy relieved itself in the middle of the floor.* The use of *relieve* for these bodily functions dates from the mid-1800s.

relieve someone of 1. Take something away from someone, rob someone of something, as in *The pickpocket relieved Dean of his wallet.* 2. Take away a burden or responsibility, as in *The doorman relieved her of her packages,* or *He was relieved of all his duties.* [Early 1800s]

religion ♦ See GET RELIGION.

repeat oneself Express oneself in the same way or with the same words, as in *Grandma forgets she has told us this story before and repeats herself over and over,* or *This architect tends to repeat himself—all his houses look alike.* A well-known version of this idiom is the proverb **History repeats itself,** first recorded (in English) in 1561. For example, *Her mother also married when she was 18—history repeats itself.* [Mid-1800s]

request ♦ See AT SOMEONE'S REQUEST; BY REQUEST; ON REQUEST.

requirement ♦ See MEET THE REQUIREMENTS.

resistance ♦ See LEAST RESISTANCE.

resort ♦ See LAST RESORT.

resources ♦ See LEAVE SOMEONE TO HIS OR HER RESOURCES.

respect ♦ See IN REGARD (RESPECT) TO; PAY A CALL (ONE'S RESPECTS); WITH ALL DUE RESPECT.

rest ♦ In addition to the idioms beginning with REST, also see AT REST; LAY AT REST; LAY TO REST; SET ONE'S MIND AT REST.

rest assured You can be sure, as in *Rest assured that the police will recover your diamonds.* This expression uses *assured* in the sense of "certain" or "confident," a usage dating from the early 1500s.

rest on one's laurels Rely on one's past achievements, especially as a way of avoiding the work needed to advance one's status. For example, *Now that Julian's in his eighties, he's decided to rest on his laurels and let some of the younger agents do the work.* This term alludes to the crown of laurels awarded in ancient times for a spectacular achievement. [Late 1800s]

retreat ♦ See BEAT A RETREAT.

return ♦ In addition to the idioms beginning with RETURN, also see IN RETURN; MANY HAPPY RETURNS; POINT OF NO RETURN.

return the compliment Also, **return the favor.** Repay someone in kind, as in *Her political opponent came out with a smear campaign, and she returned the compliment.* Neither the *compliment* nor the *favor* in this idiom is necessarily desirable. [First half of 1700s]

return to the fold Come back to a group after an absence, as in *Matthew taught for a number of years, but now he's returned to the fold as vice-president of the firm.* This term employs *fold* in the sense of "an enclosure for sheep," which has been used figuratively since the first half of the 1300s.

rev up Increase the speed or rate of, enliven, stimulate, as in *Bill revved up the motor,* or *They looked for ways to rev up the ad campaign.* The verb *rev* is an abbreviation for *revolution,* alluding to the rate of rotation of an engine. The idiom dates from about 1920 and has been used figuratively since the mid-1900s.

rhetorical question A question asked without expecting an answer but for the sake of emphasis or effect. The expected answer is usually "yes" or "no." For example, *Can we improve the quality of our work? That's a rhetorical question.* [Late 1800s]

rhyme or reason, no An absence of common sense or reasonableness, as in *This memo has no rhyme or reason.* Closely related variants are **without rhyme or reason,** as in *The conclusion of her paper* was without rhyme or reason, and **neither rhyme nor reason,** as in *Neither rhyme nor reason will explain that lawyer's objections.* This term originated in French about 1475 and began to be used in English about a century later. Sir Thomas More is credited with saying of a mediocre book that a friend had put into verse, "Now it is somewhat, for now it is rhyme; whereas before it was neither rhyme nor reason."

rib ♦ See STICK TO THE RIBS.

rich ♦ In addition to the idiom beginning with RICH, also see EMBARRASSMENT OF RICHES; FROM RAGS TO RICHES; STRIKE IT RICH.

rich as Croesus Very wealthy, as in *They're rich as Croesus, with their penthouse, yacht, and horses.* This term alludes to Croesus, the legendary King of Lydia and supposedly the richest man on earth. The simile was first recorded in English in 1577.

rid ♦ See GET RID OF.

riddance ♦ See GOOD RIDDANCE.

ride ♦ In addition to the idioms beginning with RIDE, also see ALONG FOR THE RIDE; GO ALONG (FOR THE RIDE); GRAVY TRAIN, RIDE THE; HITCH A RIDE; LET RIDE; TAKE SOMEONE FOR A RIDE.

ride for a fall Court danger or disaster, as in *I think that anyone who backs the incumbent is riding for a fall.* This idiom alludes to the reckless rider who risks a bad spill. [Late 1800s]

ride hellbent for leather ♦ See HELLBENT FOR LEATHER.

ride herd on Keep close watch or tight control over, as in *Aunt Martha is always riding herd on her bridge club, making sure they follow the rules.* This idiom alludes to the cowboy who rides around a herd of cattle to keep them together. [Late 1800s]

ride high Enjoy success, as in *He's been riding high ever since they made him vice president.* The *high* here alludes to both elevated and elated status. [First half of 1800s]

ride out Survive, outlast, as in *They rode out the storm,* or *Times were hard during the depression, but we managed to ride it out.* [First half of 1500s]

ride roughshod over Act without regard for the feelings or interests of others, as in *She just forget on, riding roughshod over her colleagues.* This term alludes to the practice of arming horses with horseshoes mounted with projecting nails or points, which both gave them better traction and served as a weapon against fallen enemy soldiers. By 1800 it was being used figuratively for bullying behavior.

ride shotgun Guard someone or something while in transit, as in *The reporter found himself in the odd position of riding shotgun for an accused mob-*ster. This term alludes to the armed defender of a stagecoach who sat beside the driver to protect against marauders and bandits. Later it was transferred to anyone riding in the front passenger seat of a motor vehicle, as well as to the more general function of protection. [Mid-1900s]

ride up Gradually move upward from a normal position, as in *This skirt is too tight and it constantly rides up.* [Mid-1800s]

ridiculous ♦ See FROM THE RIDICULOUS TO THE SUBLIME.

rid of ♦ See GET RID OF.

right ♦ In addition to the idioms beginning with RIGHT, also see ALL RIGHT; ALL RIGHT FOR YOU; ALL RIGHT WITH ONE; BY RIGHTS; COME (RIGHT) OUT WITH; DEAD TO RIGHTS; GET RIGHT; GIVE ONE'S EYE-TEETH (RIGHT ARM); GO RIGHT; GO (RIGHT) THROUGH ONE; HANG A LEFT (RIGHT); HAVE A RIGHT TO; HAVE A SCREW LOOSE (ONE'S HEAD SCREWED ON RIGHT); HEART IN THE RIGHT PLACE; HIT (RIGHT) BETWEEN THE EYES; IN ONE'S OWN RIGHT; IN ONE'S RIGHT MIND; IN THE RIGHT; LEFT HAND DOESN'T KNOW WHAT THE RIGHT HAND IS DOING; MIGHT MAKES RIGHT; NOT RIGHT IN THE HEAD; (RIGHT) ON THE MONEY; ON THE RIGHT FOOT; ON THE RIGHT TACK; PLAY ONE'S CARDS RIGHT; PRICE IS RIGHT; PUT RIGHT; SAIL (RIGHT) THROUGH; SERVE ONE RIGHT; SET RIGHT; SET TO RIGHTS; STEP IN THE RIGHT DIRECTION; STRIKE THE RIGHT NOTE; THAT'S RIGHT; TURN OUT ALL RIGHT; TWO WRONGS DO NOT MAKE A RIGHT; WHEN IT COMES (RIGHT DOWN) TO.

right and left In or from all directions, on every side, as in *Questions were coming right and left,* or *She was giving orders right and left.* This idiom, first recorded in 1839, uses the directions *right* and *left* to signify all sides.

right as rain In good order or good health, satisfactory, as in *He was very ill, but he's right as rain now,* or *If she'd only worked on it another week everything would have been as right as rain.* The allusion in this simile is unclear, but it originated in Britain, where rainy weather is a normal fact of life, and indeed W.L. Phelps wrote, "The expression 'right as rain' must have been invented by an Englishman." It was first recorded in 1894.

right away Also, **right off.** Without delay, immediately, as in *Can you bring our dinners right away? We're in a hurry,* or *We liked her right off.* This idiom uses *right* as an intensifier and *away* in the sense of "at once," the latter usage dating from the 1500s and surviving only in such phrases as this one and FIRE AWAY. It was first recorded in 1818. Also see RIGHT OFF THE BAT.

right-hand man Also, **right-hand woman.** A trusted helper, as in *Give it to Jill, she's my right-hand man.*

Based on the idea that in most people the right hand is the stronger of the two, this idiom today usually disregards gender, as in the example. However, in the 17th and 18th centuries it also meant a soldier in a post of command on the right side of a cavalry unit, and then always denoted a man. [c. 1800]

right in the head ♦ See NOT RIGHT IN THE HEAD.

right off ♦ See RIGHT AWAY.

right off the bat Instantly, immediately, as in *I can't tell you how many right off the bat, but I can find out.* This term alludes to a baseball being hit by a bat. [First half of 1900s]

right of way 1. The right of one person or vehicle to travel over another's property, as in *The new owner doesn't like it, but hikers have had the right of way through these woods for decades.* [Mid-1700s] 2. The right to precede another person or vehicle, as in *Sailboats always have the right of way over motorboats, and swimmers do over any kind of boat.* [Early 1900s]

right on An exclamation of enthusiasm or encouragement, as in *You've said it really well—right on!* This interjection has a disputed origin. Some believe it comes from African-American slang (it was recorded in Odum and Johnson's *The Negro and His Songs*, 1925); others feel it is a shortening of *right on target*, used by military airmen, or *right on cue*, theatrical slang for saying the right lines at the right time. [Slang; first half of 1900s] Also see WAY TO GO.

right out Also, **straight out**. Plainly, without holding back, as in *He told her right out that he couldn't run for another term*, or *When Jan told us she wanted to study medicine, Dad said straight out that he couldn't afford medical school.*

right side, on someone's Also, **on someone's good side**. In someone's favor. It is often put as **get, keep,** or **stay on someone's right side**, as in *We must get on Bill's right side if we're to get approval of our plans*, or *Jane had a hard time staying on the good side of her difficult supervisor.* The antonym **on someone's wrong side**, means "in someone's disfavor," as in *I got on her wrong side by opening my mouth once too often.* Also see WRONG SIDE.

right side of the tracks The desirable part of town, as in *They were relieved to learn that his fiancée came from the right side of the tracks.* This expression alludes to the fact that when a railroad ran through a town, it often divided the prosperous neighborhoods from the poor ones. The latter district was called the **wrong side of the tracks,** as in *The children from the wrong side of the tracks often came to school without having eaten breakfast.* Today these terms are considered snobbish. [Second half of 1800s]

right-side out Turned correctly, with the outer side on the outside, as opposed to INSIDE OUT, def. 1. For example, *I turned the sweater right-side out before putting it on.*

right-side up With the top facing upward, as in *Please keep the box holding the china right side up*, or *He turned his cards right-side up.* [Early 1500s]

right tack ♦ See ON THE RIGHT TACK.

right up one's alley Also, **right down one's alley**. In one's specialty, to one's taste, as in *Writing press releases is right up her alley*, or *He loved opera, so this program of arias was right down his alley.* These idioms use *alley* in the sense of "one's own province," a usage dating from the early 1600s. [First half of 1900s] Also see CUP OF TEA.

Riley ♦ See LIFE OF RILEY.

ring ♦ In addition to the idioms beginning with RING, also see BRASS RING; GIVE SOMEONE A RING; HAVE A FAMILIAR RING; RUN RINGS AROUND; THREE-RING CIRCUS; THROW ONE'S HAT IN THE RING.

ring a bell Arouse an indistinct memory, remind one of something, as in *That name rings a bell—I think I've met him.* The *bell* here summons up a memory. [1930s]

ring down the curtain on Bring something to an end, as in *We'd best get to that grand old hotel before they ring down the curtain on it.* This idiom alludes to the old practice of signaling that a theater curtain be lowered at the ring of a bell. Similarly, **ring up the curtain on** refers to a bell rung to begin a performance and came to mean starting anything, as in *Their contribution rang up the curtain on the fund drive.* The figurative use of these terms dates from the early 1900s.

ring false Also, **have a false** or **hollow ring; strike a false note**. Seem wrong or deceitful, as in *Her denial rings false—I'm sure she was there when it happened*, or *His good wishes always seem to have a hollow ring*, or *Carol's congratulatory phone call really struck a false note.* **Ring false** and the antonym, **ring true**, which means "seem genuine," allude to the old practice of judging a coin genuine or fake by the sound it gives out when tapped. This practice became obsolete when coins ceased to be made of precious metals, but by then the idioms were being used to refer to other matters. [Mid-1800s]

ring one's chimes Arouse one's attention, excite one, as in *That kind of music really rings my chimes.* [Slang; 1970]

ringside seat A place providing a close view of something, as in *We lived right next door, so we had ringside seats for their quarrels.* This term presumably came from boxing, where it denotes the seats just outside the boxing ring. [c. 1860]

ring the changes Keep varying how one performs an action or says something, as in *She went on and on, ringing the changes on the joy of computers.* This expression alludes to the art of change-ringing, where a series of church bells are rung in as many sequences, or *changes,* as possible. [Early 1600s]

ring true ◆ See under RING FALSE.

ring up 1. Record, especially by means of a cash register, as in *They had already rung up the sale so I decided not to get the extra items.* [c. 1930] Although older cash registers usually signaled a recorded sale with the ringing of a bell, the idiom survives in the age of computers. 2. Accomplish, achieve, as in *They rang up an impressive string of victories.*

riot ◆ See READ THE RIOT ACT; RUN AMOK (RIOT).

riotous living An extravagant, dissolute lifestyle, as in *Two years of riotous living, and they'd squandered the entire inheritance.* This term was first recorded in 1389.

rip ◆ In addition to the idioms beginning with RIP, also see LET IT RIP.

ripe ◆ In addition to the idiom beginning with RIPE, also see TIME IS RIPE.

ripe old age An age advanced in years, as in *I expect to live to a ripe old age.* The adjective *ripe* here means "fully developed physically and mentally," but the current use of the idiom usually just signifies a long lifespan. [Second half of 1300s]

rip into Also, tear into. Attack or criticize vehemently, as in *She ripped into her opponent's voting record.* These expressions allude to the literal senses of the verbs *rip* and *tear,* that is, "cut" or "slash."

rip off 1. Steal, as in *They fired him when they caught him ripping off some of the merchandise.* 2. Cheat, defraud, as in *These advertising claims have ripped off a great many consumers.* 3. Copy, plagiarize, as in *He was sued for ripping off someone else's thesis.* All three usages are slang from the second half of the 1900s.

rise ◆ In addition to the idioms beginning with RISE, also see COME UP (RISE IN THE WORLD); GET A RISE OUT OF; GIVE BIRTH (RISE) TO.

rise and shine An expression used when waking someone up, as in *It's past seven, children—rise and shine!* Originating as a military order in the late 1800s, *shine* here means "act lively, do well."

rise from the ashes Emerge as new from something that has been destroyed, as in *A few months after the earthquake large sections of the city had risen from the ashes.* This expression alludes to the legendary phoenix, a bird that supposedly rose from the ashes of its funeral pyre with renewed youth.

rise in the world ◆ See COME UP, def. 4.

rise through the ranks Also, rise from the ranks; come up through the ranks. Work one's way to the top, as in *He's risen through the ranks, starting as a copy boy and ending up as senior editor.* Originally this term was used for an officer who had worked his way up from the rank of private, a rare feat. It was being applied to nonmilitary advances by the mid-1800s. Also see COME UP, def. 4.

rise to the bait Be tempted by or react to an enticement, as in *We told him there'd be lots of single young women at the party, and he rose to the bait.* Likening a fish rising to bait to human behavior dates from the late 1500s.

rise to the occasion Show unexpected skill in dealing with a difficulty that arises, as in *The leading man broke his leg in the first act but his understudy rose to the occasion and was rewarded with excellent reviews.* [Mid-1800s]

risk ◆ In addition to the idiom beginning with RISK, also see AT RISK; CALCULATED RISK; RUN A RISK.

risk life and limb Also, risk one's neck. Take dangerous chances, as in *There he was on the roof, risking life and limb to rescue the kitten,* or *I don't want to risk my neck contradicting him.* The first hyperbolic expression, dating from the early 1600s, doesn't make sense, since if one loses one's life one also loses the use of one's limbs. The variant, used for risky undertakings of all kinds, physical and nonphysical, presumably alludes to being hanged or beheaded. Also see STICK ONE'S NECK OUT.

river ◆ See SELL DOWN THE RIVER; UP THE RIVER.

road ◆ In addition to the idioms beginning with ROAD, also see ALL ROADS LEAD TO ROME; DOWN THE LINE (ROAD); END OF THE LINE (ROAD); GET THE SHOW ON THE ROAD; HIT THE ROAD; ONE FOR THE ROAD; ON THE ROAD.

road hog A motorist whose vehicle straddles two traffic lanes, as in *Stay in your own lane, you road hog!* This expression uses *hog* in the sense of "a greedy or selfish person." [Colloquial; late 1800s]

road show A tour made for a particular purpose, especially a political campaign. For example, *It was primary season, and every would-be candidate was planning a road show.* This term originated about 1900 for touring theatrical productions and in the mid-1900s began to be transferred to other endeavors.

road to hell is paved with good intentions, the Well-intended acts can have disastrous results, as in *She tried to help by defending Dad's position and they haven't spoken since—the road to hell is paved with good intentions.* This proverbial idiom probably derives from a similar statement by St. Bernard of Clairvaux about 1150, *L'enfer est plein de bonnes volontés ou désirs* ("Hell is full of good intentions or wishes"), and has been repeated ever since. [Late 1500s]

robbery ♦ See DAYLIGHT ROBBERY; HIGHWAY ROBBERY.

robinson ♦ See BEFORE YOU CAN SAY JACK ROBINSON.

rob Peter to pay Paul Take from one to give to another, shift resources. For example, *They took out a second mortgage on their house so they could buy a condo in Florida—they're robbing Peter to pay Paul.* Although legend has it that this expression alludes to appropriating the estates of St. Peter's Church, in Westminster, London, to pay for the repairs of St. Paul's Cathedral in the 1800s, the saying first appeared in a work by John Wycliffe about 1382.

rob someone blind Cheat someone in an unusually deceitful or thorough fashion, as in *The nurse was robbing the old couple blind.* This idiom may allude to robbing a blind beggar, who cannot see that the cup collecting donations is being emptied. [Mid-1900s]

rob the cradle Have a romantic or sexual relationship with someone much younger than oneself, as in *The old editor was notorious for robbing the cradle, always trying to date some young reporter.* [Colloquial; first half of 1900s]

rob the till ♦ See HAND IN THE TILL.

rock ♦ In addition to the idioms beginning with ROCK, also see BETWEEN A ROCK AND A HARD PLACE; ON THE ROCKS; STEADY AS A ROCK.

rock bottom The lowest possible level, absolute bottom, as in *Wheat prices have reached rock bottom.* This idiom alludes to the presence of bedrock that prevents digging farther down. [Late 1800s]

rocker ♦ See OFF ONE'S HEAD (ROCKER).

rocks in one's head, have Show poor judgment, act stupidly, as in *If you think that's an accurate summary, you've got rocks in your head.* The rocks in this idiom are a supposed substitute for brains. [Slang; 1940s]

rock the boat Disturb a stable situation, as in *An easygoing manager, he won't rock the boat unless it's absolutely necessary.* This idiom alludes to capsizing a small vessel, such as a canoe, by moving about in it too violently. [Colloquial; early 1900s]

rod ♦ See HOT ROD; SPARE THE ROD.

rogues' gallery A police collection of pictures of criminals and suspects kept for identification purposes. For example, *The detective went through the entire rogues' gallery but couldn't find a match with the suspect.* [Mid-1800s]

roll ♦ In addition to the idioms beginning with ROLL, also see EASY AS PIE (ROLLING OFF A LOG); GET ROLLING; GET THE BALL ROLLING; HEADS WILL ROLL; ON A ROLL; RED CARPET.

roll around Return or recur, as in *When income tax time rolls around, Peggy is too busy to play tennis.* [Late 1600s]

roll back Decrease, cut back, or reduce, especially prices, as in *Unless they roll back oil prices, this summer's tourist traffic will be half of last year's.* [c. 1940]

roll in 1. Retire for the night, as in *It's time to roll in—we'll see you in the morning.* **2.** Add, as in *She tried to roll in several new clauses, but the publisher would not agree.* **3.** Arrive, flow, or pour in, as in *The football fans have been rolling in since this morning.* **4.** Enjoy ample amounts of, especially of wealth, as in *Ask the Newmans for a donation—they're rolling in money.* This idiom alludes to having so much of something that one can roll around in it (as a pig might roll in mud). It is sometimes put as **rolling in it,** the *it* meaning money. [Late 1700s] Also see ROLL IN THE AISLES; ROLL IN THE HAY.

rolling stone A person who moves about a great deal and never settles down, as in *Kate's lived in ten cities in as many years—she's a real rolling stone.* This expression is a shortening of the proverb **a rolling stone gathers no moss,** first recorded in 1523, which indicates that one who never settles anywhere will not do well. After some 300 years of this interpretation, in the mid-1800s the value of gathering moss (and staying put) began to be questioned, and in current usage the term is most often used without any particular value judgment.

roll in the aisles Laugh very hard, as in *The comedian's new book had them rolling in the aisles.* This hyperbolic idiom alludes to a performance that causes an audience to laugh so hard that they might well roll about in the theater's aisles. [First half of 1900s]

roll in the hay Sexual intercourse, as in *The main character in the movie was always looking for a roll in the hay.* This phrase alludes to secret lovemaking in a hayloft. [Slang; mid-1900s]

roll out 1. Get out of bed, as in *I rolled out around six o'clock this morning.* [Colloquial; late 1800s] **2.** Introduce, disclose, as in *They rolled out the new washing machine with great fanfare.*

roll over Reinvest profits from one investment back into that investment or into another, as in *Our broker advised us to roll over the proceeds into a tax shelter.* [Mid-1900s]

roll the bones Cast dice, especially in the game of craps, as in *Let's go to the casino and roll the bones tonight.* This slangy term was first recorded in 1897, but the noun *bones* has referred to dice since the late 1300s (Chaucer used it in *The Pardoner's Tale*).

roll up 1. Accumulate, as in *He rolled up a fortune in commodity trading,* or *She rolled up a huge number* *of votes in this district.* [Mid-1800s] **2.** Arrive in a vehicle, as in *They rolled up in a taxi at exactly eight o'clock.*

roll up one's sleeves Prepare to work, as in *When he saw how much snow had fallen he simply rolled up his sleeves and went to find the shovel.* This expression, alluding to turning one's sleeves upward to avoid getting them wet or dirty, is used both literally and more loosely, as in the example here.

roll with the punches Cope with and withstand adversity, especially by being flexible. For example, *She'd had three different editors for her book, each with a different style, but she'd learned to roll with the punches.* This term alludes to the boxer's ability to deflect the full force of an opponent's blow by adroitly moving his body. [Mid-1900s]

Roman ♦ See WHEN IN ROME DO AS THE ROMANS DO.

Rome ♦ In addition to the idiom beginning with ROME, also see ALL ROADS LEAD TO ROME; FIDDLE WHILE ROME BURNS; WHEN IN ROME DO AS THE ROMANS DO.

Rome wasn't built in a day Important work takes time. This expression functions as an injunction or plea for someone to be patient. For example, *You can't expect her to finish this project in the time allotted; Rome wasn't built in a day.* This phrase was a French proverb in the late 1100s but was not recorded in English until 1545.

roof ♦ In addition to the idiom beginning with ROOF, also see GO THROUGH THE ROOF; HIT THE CEILING (ROOF); LIKE A CAT ON HOT BRICKS (A HOT TIN ROOF); RAISE THE ROOF.

roof over one's head, a A shelter, especially a home, as in *I can barely afford to put a roof over my head, my salary is so low.*

rooftop ♦ See SHOUT FROM THE ROOFTOPS.

room ♦ In addition to the idiom beginning with ROOM, also see NOT ENOUGH ROOM TO SWING A CAT; TAKE UP SPACE (ROOM).

room and board Lodging and meals, as in *The university's price for room and board has increased by another 10 percent.* [Mid-1900s]

roost ♦ See CHICKENS COME HOME TO ROOST; RULE THE ROOST.

root ♦ In addition to the idioms beginning with ROOT, also see PUT DOWN ROOTS; TAKE ROOT.

root and branch Utterly, completely, as in *The company has been transformed root and branch by the new management.* Alluding to both the underground and aboveground parts of a tree, this idiom was first recorded in 1640.

rooted to the spot Not moving, especially owing to some strong emotion. For example, *When the truck bore down on the dog, he was terrified and stood rooted to the spot.* This idiom likens the roots of a plant to a strong feeling that keeps one from moving.

root for Cheer on, give moral support to, as in *The fans were out rooting for their team,* or *I've been rooting for you to get that promotion.* This expression may come from the British verb *rout,* which is used of cattle and means "bellow." [Late 1800s]

root of the matter The essential part or cause of something, as in *We still don't understand what happened; we must get to the root of the matter.* This expression was first recorded in the Bible (Job 19:28).

root out Search for, seek to discover, as in *He was trying to root out the reason for her long absence.* This idiom alludes to the way hogs dig by using their snouts. [Mid-1800s]

rope ♦ In addition to the idiom beginning with ROPE, also see END OF ONE'S ROPE; ENOUGH ROPE; (SHOW SOMEONE) KNOW THE ROPES; ON THE ROPES.

rope in Also, **rope into.** Lure or entice someone into doing something, as in *We didn't want to spend the night there, but we got roped in by my lonely aunt,* or *The salesman tried to rope us into buying some worthless real estate.* These expressions allude to catching an animal by throwing a rope around it. [Mid-1800s]

rose ♦ See BED OF ROSES; COME UP ROSES; SEE THROUGH ROSE-COLORED GLASSES.

rote ♦ See BY HEART (ROTE).

rotten apple A bad individual among many good ones, especially one that spoils the group. For example, *The roommates are having problems with Edith—she's the one rotten apple of the bunch.* This expression is a shortening of the proverb **a rotten apple spoils the barrel,** coming from a 14th-century Latin proverb translated as "The rotten apple injures its neighbors." The allusion in this idiom is to the spread of mold or other diseases from one apple to the rest. In English the first recorded use was in Benjamin Franklin's *Poor Richard's Almanack* (1736).

rotten egg ♦ See under BAD EGG.

rotten to the core Thoroughly bad, as in *It seems that this police unit is rotten to the core, involved in numerous extortion schemes.* The noun *core* here denotes the central part or heart of anything or anyone. The idiom was first recorded in 1804.

rough ♦ In addition to the idioms beginning with ROUGH, also see DIAMOND IN THE ROUGH; RIDE ROUGHSHOD OVER; TAKE THE ROUGH WITH THE SMOOTH; WHEN THE GOING GETS ROUGH.

rough and ready Unrefined or makeshift but available for use or action, as in *The agenda is somewhat rough and ready, but it covers the main issues.* [First half of 1800s]

rough and tumble Disorderly scuffling or infighting, as in *She had some reservations about entering the rough and tumble of local politics*. This expression originated in the late 1700s in boxing, where it referred to a fight without rules. [Mid-1800s]

rough it Do without the usual comforts and conveniences, as in *We spent our vacation roughing it in a log cabin*. This idiom was first recorded in 1768. Mark Twain used it as the title of an account of his experiences in Nevada (*Roughing It*, 1872).

rough on, be 1. Be harmful to or difficult for, as in *The harsh winter has been rough on the highways*, or *Their divorce was rough on the whole family*. 2. Treat harshly, be severe with, as in *The police have been very rough on housebreakers*, or *Don't be too rough on Sam; he's only a child*. Both colloquial usages date from the second half of the 1800s.

rough out Also, **rough in**. Prepare or indicate in unfinished form, as in *He roughed out several different plans for a merger*, or *They roughed in where the doors and windows would go without checking with the architect*. [Second half of 1700s]

rough up Manhandle, subject to physical abuse, as in *The gang was about to rough him up when the police arrived*. [First half of 1900s]

round ♦ In addition to the idioms beginning with ROUND, also see ALL YEAR ROUND; BRING AROUND (ROUND); COME AROUND (ROUND); GET AROUND (ROUND); IN ROUND NUMBERS; IN THE ROUND; MAKE THE ROUNDS; OTHER WAY ROUND; PULL ROUND; RALLY AROUND. Also see under AROUND.

round and round Also, **around and around**. In circles, as in *You've gone round and round with the same argument and we still have no solution*. This idiom transfers moving in a circle to mental or verbal activities. [Second half of 1800s]

round figures ♦ See IN ROUND NUMBERS.

round off 1. Change a number to the closest whole number or the closest multiple of 10. For example, *Rounding it off, I expect the new school addition will cost a million dollars*. 2. Also, **round out**. Finish, complete, especially in a neat or perfect way. For example, *They rounded off the dinner with a magnificent liqueur*, or *That stamp rounded out his collection*. [Mid-1700s; variant, mid-1800s] Also see ROUND OUT.

round on Turn on, assail, especially verbally. For example, *They all rounded on Jake for not upholding the party line*. [Mid-1800s]

round out 1. See ROUND OFF, def. 2. 2. Grow or develop to a round form, as in *The tree was spindly when first planted, but it has since rounded out nicely*. [c. 1900]

round peg in a square hole ♦ See SQUARE PEG IN A ROUND HOLE.

round robin 1. A petition or other document signed by several persons in sequence, so that no one can tell who was the first to sign it. For example, *We decided to send a round robin to management to protest the new rules about work hours*. This term originally referred to a grievance presented by seamen to their captain, called *round* because of the circular sequence of names, but the source of *robin* has been lost. [Early 1700s] 2. In sports, a tournament in which each player or team plays against all of the others in turn. For example, *The club always holds a tennis round robin on the weekend before the Fourth of July*. [Late 1800s]

round the bend ♦ See AROUND THE BEND, def. 2.

round trip A journey to a given place and back again, usually over the same route; also, a ticket for such a trip. For example, *The fare for a round trip is generally lower than for two one-way journeys*. [Mid-1800s]

roundup ♦ See HEAD FOR (THE LAST ROUNDUP). Also see ROUND UP.

round up Collect or gather in a body, as in *We'll have to round up some more volunteers for the food drive*, or *The police rounded up all the suspects*. This term comes from the West, where since the mid-1800s it has been used for collecting livestock by riding around the herd and driving the animals together. By about 1875 it was extended to other kinds of gathering together.

row ♦ See GET ONE'S DUCKS IN A ROW; KICK UP A FUSS (ROW); SKID ROW; TOUGH ROW TO HOE.

rub ♦ In addition to the idioms beginning with RUB, also see THE RUB.

rubber check A check drawn on an account without the funds to pay it, as in *He's been handing out rubber checks right and left, but the police have caught up with him*. The *rubber* alludes to the fact that, like rubber, the check "bounces," in this case back from the bank. [Slang; c. 1920]

rubber stamp A person or organization that automatically approves or endorses a policy without assessing its merit; also, such an approval or endorsement. For example, *The nominating committee is merely a rubber stamp; they approve anyone the chairman names*, or *The dean gave his rubber stamp to the recommendations of the tenure committee*. This metaphoric term alludes to the rubber printing device used to imprint the same words over and over. [Early 1900s]

rubbish ♦ See GOOD RIDDANCE (TO BAD RUBBISH).

rub down Briskly rub the body, as in a massage. For example, *The trainer rubs down marathon runners*, or *That horse needs rubbing down*. This expression was first used (and still is) for rubbing away dust and sweat from a horse. [Late 1600s]

rub elbows with Also, **rub shoulders with.** Mix or socialize with, as in *There's nothing like rubbing elbows with the rich and famous,* or *At the reception diplomats were rubbing shoulders with heads of state.* Both of these terms allude to being in close contact with someone. [Mid-1800s]

Rubicon ♦ See CROSS THE RUBICON.

rub in Also, **rub it in.** Harp on something, especially an unpleasant matter, as in *She always rubs in the fact that she graduated with honors and I didn't,* or *I know I forgot your birthday, but don't keep rubbing it in.* This idiom alludes to the expression **rub salt into a wound,** an action that makes the wound more painful; it dates from medieval times and remains current. [Mid-1800s] Also see RUB SOMEONE'S NOSE IN IT.

rub off on Become transferred to another, influence through close contact, as in *We hoped some of their good manners would rub off on our children.* This idiom alludes to transferring something like paint to another substance by rubbing against it. [Mid-1900s]

rub one's hands Experience or exhibit pleased anticipation or self-satisfaction, as in *The owner rubbed his hands as the customer picked out item after item.* This metaphoric term alludes to the actual rubbing together of one's hands to express pleasure.

rub out 1. Obliterate or erase by, or as if by, rubbing. For example, *Bill was so busy rubbing out the old markings that he forgot to put in new ones.* [Mid-1600s] 2. Murder, kill, as in *They threatened to rub him out if he didn't pay up.* [Slang; mid-1800s]

rub someone's nose in it Bring something, especially an error or fault, repeatedly and forcefully to someone's attention. For example, *I know I was wrong, but don't rub my nose in it.* This expression alludes to the unkind practice of housebreaking a dog by rubbing its nose in its feces. [Mid-1900s]

rub the wrong way Irritate, annoy, as in *His remarks about welfare rubbed a great many people the wrong way.* This idiom alludes to rubbing an animal's fur in the wrong direction. [Mid-1800s] Also see RUFFLE SOMEONE'S FEATHERS.

rub up on Refresh one's knowledge, as in *I must rub up on my French before we leave for Paris.* [Second half of 1700s] Also see BRUSH UP, def. 2.

ruffle someone's feathers Annoy or offend someone, as in *Calling him a tightwad really ruffled his feathers.* This term alludes to the stiffened, upright feathers of an angry bird. [Mid-1800s]

rug ♦ See PULL THE RUG OUT FROM UNDER; SWEEP UNDER THE RUG. Also see under CARPET.

ruin ♦ See RACK AND RUIN.

rule ♦ In addition to the idioms beginning with RULE, also see AS A RULE; EXCEPTION PROVES THE RULE; GROUND RULES.

rule of thumb A rough and useful principle or method, based on experience rather than precisely accurate measures. For example, *His work with the youth group is largely by rule of thumb.* This expression alludes to making rough estimates of measurements by using one's thumb. [Second half of 1600s]

rule out 1. Eliminate from consideration, exclude, as in *The option of starting over again has been ruled out.* [Second half of 1800s] 2. Prevent, make impossible, as in *The snowstorm ruled out our weekly rehearsal.* [First half of 1900s]

rule the roost Be in charge, boss others, as in *In our division the chairman's son rules the roost.* This expression originated in the 15th century as *rule the roast,* which was either a corruption of *rooster* or alluded to the person who was in charge of the roast and thus ran the kitchen. In the barnyard a rooster decides which hen should roost near him. Both interpretations persisted for 200 years. Thomas Heywood (c. 1630) put it as "Her that ruled the roast in the kitchen," but Shakespeare had it in *2 Henry VI* (1:1): "The new-made duke that rules the roast," which is more ambiguous. In the mid-1700s *roost* began to compete with *roast,* and in the 1900s *roost* displaced *roast* altogether. Also see RUN THE SHOW.

run ♦ In addition to the idioms beginning with RUN, also see BEAT (RUN) ONE'S HEAD AGAINST THE WALL; CUT AND RUN; DRY RUN; EAT AND RUN; END RUN; GO (RUN) AROUND IN CIRCLES; GREAT MINDS (RUN IN THE SAME CHANNEL); HOME RUN; IN THE LONG RUN; LIKE CLOCKWORK, RUN; MAKE A BREAK (RUN) FOR; MAKE ONE'S BLOOD RUN COLD; (RUN) OFF SOMEONE'S FEET; ON THE RUN; STILL WATERS RUN DEEP; TIGHT SHIP, RUN A; WELL'S RUN DRY. Also see under RUNNING.

run across ♦ See COME ACROSS, def. 1.

run a fever Also, **run a temperature.** Suffer from a body temperature higher than normal, as in *She was running a fever so I kept her home from school.* These idioms use *run* in the sense of "cause to move," in this case upward. [Early 1900s]

run afoul of Also, **run foul of.** Come into conflict with, as in *If you keep parking illegally you'll run afoul of the police.* This expression originated in the late 1600s, when it was applied to a vessel colliding or becoming entangled with another vessel, but at the same time it was transferred to nonnautical usage. Both senses remain current.

run after Also, **chase after.** 1. Follow, pursue with haste, as in *Our dog loves to run after the mail* *truck,* or *The children were chasing after the geese in the park.* [c. 1300] **2.** Seek the company or attention of, especially aggressively. For example, *He's run after her for a year, but she just ignores him.* [Early 1500s]

run against 1. Also, **run up against** or **run into.** Encounter something, especially a difficulty, unexpectedly. For example, *We didn't know we'd run up against so much opposition,* or *He ran into trouble with his taxes.* [Late 1300s] **2.** Work against, as in *Public sentiment ran against her.* [Late 1300s] **3.** Oppose for elective office, as in *Susan decided to run against a very popular incumbent.* This usage is a figurative application of running in a footrace. [First half of 1800s]

run along Go away, leave, as in *I'll be running along now; I'm already late.* This expression is also used as an imperative to tell someone to go away, as in *Run along, children, I have work to do.* [Early 1800s]

run amok Also, **run riot** or **wild.** Behave in a frenzied, out-of-control, or unrestrained manner. For example, *I was afraid that if I left the toddler alone she would run amok and have a hard time calming down,* or *The weeds are running riot in the lawn,* or *The children were running wild in the playground. Amok* comes from a Malay word for "frenzied" and was adopted into English, and at first spelled *amuck,* in the second half of the 1600s. *Run riot* dates from the early 1500s and derives from an earlier sense, that is, a hound's following an animal scent. **Run wild** alludes to an animal reverting to its natural, uncultivated state; its figurative use dates from the late 1700s.

run an errand Go to perform a commission, as in *I spent the morning running household errands—to the cleaners, the supermarket, the hardware store.* [c. 1500]

run a risk Also, **run the risk.** Be subjected to danger, as in *Hiding anything from customs means running a risk that you'll be caught,* or *Without the right postage and address, this package runs the risk of being lost.* [Mid-1600s]

run around 1. Go about hurriedly here and there, as in *I have been running around all day so I want to stay home tonight and relax.* [Early 1900s] **2.** Also, **run around with.** Associate or consort with socially, as in *At college she began to run around with a very liberal group.* [Late 1800s] **3.** Be sexually unfaithful, as in *She caught him running around just once too often and finally sued for divorce.* [Early 1900s]

run around ♦ See GET THE RUNAROUND.

run around in circles ♦ See GO AROUND, def. 4; RUN RINGS AROUND.

run around like a chicken ♦ See CHICKEN WITH ITS HEAD CUT OFF.

run around with ♦ See RUN AROUND, def. 2.

run a temperature ♦ See RUN A FEVER.

run a tight ship ♦ See TIGHT SHIP.

run away 1. Flee, escape, as in *Our dog is no watchdog; he runs away from strangers,* or *Our six-year-old said he'd run away from home.* [Late 1300s] **2.** Also, **run off.** Leave secretly, especially to elope, as in *She ran away from home when she was only thirteen,* or *They ran off to Maryland and got married by a justice of the peace.* [Early 1600s] **3.** **it won't run away.** An object, activity, or issue will not disappear, as in *You can leave, but when you come back the mess in the kitchen will still be there—it won't run away, you know!* This jocular assurance of permanence dates from the late 1800s. Also see RUN AWAY WITH.

run away with 1. Also, **run off with.** Hurriedly make off with someone or something, as in *She ran away with the boy next door,* or *The children ran off with the ball.* [Early 1600s] **2.** Win handily, as in *The film ran away with all the important awards.* [Early 1800s] **3.** Get the better of, as in *Sometimes his enthusiasm runs away with him.* [Late 1600s]

run by someone Try out on someone, as in *Let me run this idea by you and see what you think of it.* [Colloquial; 1900s]

run circles around ♦ See RUN RINGS AROUND.

run counter to Be in conflict with, oppose, as in *Practice often runs counter to theory.* This idiom, first recorded in 1843, uses *counter* in the sense of "in an opposite direction."

run down 1. Stop because of lack of power or force, as in *The alarm clock finally ran down.* [Mid-1700s] **2.** Make or be tired, cause to decline or be declined in health or vigor, as in *His long illness ran him down, leaving him with no energy,* or *After that huge assignment his strength ran down.* [First half of 1800s] **3.** Collide with and knock over, as in *The speeding motorist ran down a pedestrian.* [Second half of 1500s] **4.** Chase and capture, as in *Police detectives ran down the suspects.* [Second half of 1600s] **5.** Trace the source of, as in *She ran down all the references at the library.* **6.** Disparage, as in *Don't run him down, he's a talented actor.* [Second half of 1600s] Also see PUT DOWN, def. 4. **7.** Also, **run one's eyes over.** Look over, review, as in *Let's run down the membership list again and see if we can pick a delegate,* or *She ran her eyes over the crowd, looking for her husband.* **8.** In baseball, tag out a runner between bases, as in *We might have won but in the last inning they ran down two of our runners.*

run dry ♦ See WELL'S RUN DRY.

run for it Also, **run for one's life.** Depart as fast as possible, either to escape danger or to reach something quickly. For example, *You'd better run for it before the teacher catches you,* or *The bully is coming after you—run for your life!* The *for it* in the first term almost certainly means "for one's life"—that is, to save one's life, a usage that can be literal or hyperbolic. Also see FOR DEAR LIFE; MAKE A BREAK FOR IT.

run for one's money, a A close contest or a strong competition, as in *We may not win the game, but let's give them a run for their money.* This term probably comes from horse racing, where one may get considerable pleasure from watching the race even if one does not win much. Its first recorded use was in 1874.

run foul ♦ See RUN AFOUL OF.

run high Be intense, as in *Feelings are running high on the issue of raising taxes.* This expression, first recorded in 1711, transfers the strong currents or tides that make for high waves to human concerns.

run in 1. Insert or include something extra, as in *Can you run this map in with the text?* [Early 1800s] 2. Also, **run on.** In printing, make a solid body of text without a paragraph or other break, as in *The quotation should be run in rather than set as a paragraph.* 3. Also, **run someone in.** Take someone into custody, as in *The police were going to run him in, but he got away.* [Slang; mid-1800s] 4. Visit someone briefly, as in *If I have time, I'll run in to see Aunt Mary.* [Second half of 1800s] 5. Break something or someone in, as in *Let's run in the new model on a short flight.* [Early 1900s] Also see RUN INTO.

run in place Work or exert oneself without noticeable change or progress. For example, *I've worked on this project for months but feel I'm running in place.* This idiom employs *in place* in the sense of "on one spot," a usage dating from the late 1200s.

run interference Handle problems or help clear the way for another, as in *The press secretary runs interference for the governor.* This term comes from football, where it refers to the blocking of defensive players by offensive players to let the ball carrier advance. Its figurative use dates from the mid-1900s.

run in the blood Also, **run in the family.** Be characteristic of a family or passed on from one generation to the next, as in *That happy-go-lucky trait runs in the blood,* or *Big ears run in the family.* The first term dates from the early 1600s, the second from the late 1700s.

run into 1. Meet or find by chance, as in *I ran into an old friend at the concert.* [c. 1900] 2. See RUN

AGAINST, def. 1. 3. Collide with, as in *The car ran straight into the retaining wall.* [c. 1800] 4. Incur, as in *We've run into extra expenses with the renovation,* or *James said they've run into debt.* [c. 1400] 5. Mount up, increase to, as in *Her book may well run into a second volume.* 6. Follow without interruption, as in *What with one day running into the next, we never knew just what day it was!* or *He spoke so fast his words ran into one another.* [Late 1600s] Also see RUN INTO A STONE WALL; RUN INTO THE GROUND.

run into a stone wall Also, **run into a brick wall.** Encounter an insurmountable barrier to progress, as in *We tried to get faster approval from the town and ran into a stone wall,* or *For Allan, learning a foreign language amounted to running into a brick wall.*

run into the ground 1. Pursue a topic until it has been thoroughly discussed or exhausted, as in *They've run the abortion issue into the ground.* 2. Ruin or destroy, as in *During her brief time as chief executive Marjorie just about ran the company into the ground.* Both usages allude to pushing something so far that it is, in effect, buried. [Early 1800s]

run its course Proceed to its logical or natural conclusion, as in *The doctor said the cold would probably run its course within a week.* This idiom employs *course* in the sense of "an onward movement in a particular path." [Second half of 1500s]

run like clockwork ♦ See LIKE CLOCKWORK.

running ♦ In addition to the idioms beginning with RUNNING, also see HIT THE GROUND RUNNING; IN THE RUNNING; METER IS RUNNING; OFF AND RUNNING.

running on empty At the end of one's resources, out of money, as in *I don't know how much longer we can live this way—we're running on empty with no jobs in sight.* This idiom refers to a car running when the gas gauge indicates it is out of fuel. [Second half of 1900s]

running start An initial advantage, as in *His background in biochemistry gave him a running start in the field of genetics.* This expression alludes to track events such as the running broad jump, in which one begins moving before reaching the actual take-off point. [1920s] Also see under GET OFF THE GROUND.

run off 1. Escape; see RUN AWAY, def. 2. 2. Flow off, drain, as in *By noon all the water had run off the driveway.* [Early 1700s] 3. Print, duplicate, or copy, as in *We ran off 200 copies of the budget.* [Late 1800s] 4. Decide a contest or competition, as in *The last two events will be run off on Tuesday.* [Late 1800s] 5. Also, **run someone out.** Force or drive someone away, as in *The security guard ran off the trespassers,* or *They ran him out of town.* [Early

1700s] **6.** Produce or perform quickly and easily, as in *After years of practice, he could run off a sermon in a couple of hours.* [Late 1600s]

run off at the mouth Talk incessantly, babble, as in *Wilbur is always running off at the mouth about his investments.* This idiom transfers a flow of water to an unending flow of words. [Slang; c. 1900]

run off with **1.** Make off with; see RUN AWAY WITH, def. 1. **2.** Capture or carry off, as in *The debaters ran off with the state championship.*

run of luck Also, **run of bad luck.** A continued spell of good (or bad) fortune, as in *The builder had a run of luck with day after day of good weather,* or *Nothing was going right; he was having a long run of bad luck.* Originally used mainly in games of chance, this idiom was first recorded in 1782, but the use of *run* for a continued spell of something dates from the late 1600s.

run of the mill Ordinary, average, as in *There's nothing special about these singers—they're just run of the mill.* This expression alludes to fabrics coming directly from a mill without having been sorted or inspected for quality. It has survived such similar phrases as *run of the mine* and *run of the kiln,* for the products of mines and kilns. [Late 1800s]

run on **1.** Keep going, continue; also, remain in effect. For example, *That murder trial has been running on for months,* or *How much longer can this debt be allowed to run on?* [Late 1500s] **2.** Talk at length; see GO ON, def. 5. **3.** Continue a text without a break; see RUN IN, def. 2.

run someone off his or her feet ⊁ See OFF SOMEONE'S FEET, def. 2.

run one ragged Exhaust one, as in *I've run myself ragged with this project.* This idiom alludes to working so hard that one's appearance is reduced to rags. [c. 1920]

run one's eyes over ⊁ See RUN DOWN, def. 7.

run one's head against the wall ⊁ See BEAT ONE'S HEAD AGAINST THE WALL.

run one's own show ⊁ See under RUN THE SHOW.

run out **1.** Become used up or exhausted, as in *Our supplies have run out.* [Late 1600s] **2.** Compel to leave; see RUN OFF, def. 5. **3.** Become void, expire, as in *Our renter's insurance ran out last month.* [c. 1300] Also see RUN OUT OF; RUN OUT ON.

run out of Exhaust a supply or quantity of, as in *We're about to run out of coffee and sugar.* This expression, dating from about 1700, can be used both literally and figuratively. Thus **run out of gas** may mean one no longer has any fuel, but it has also acquired the figurative sense of exhausting a supply of energy, enthusiasm, or support, and hence causing some activity to come to a halt. For

example, *After running ten laps I ran out of gas and had to rest to catch my breath,* or *The economic recovery seems to have run out of gas.* On the other hand, **run out of steam,** originally alluding to a steam engine, today is used only figuratively to indicate a depletion of energy of any kind.

run out on Desert, abandon, as in *He's run out on the family.* [First half of 1900s]

run over **1.** Knock down and, often, pass over, as in *The car ran over our dog.* [First half of 1900s] **2.** Review quickly, as in *I'll run over the speech one more time.* [Early 1600s] **3.** Overflow, as in *This pot's running over.* This usage appears in the well-known Twenty-third Psalm: "My cup runneth over [with God's bounty]." **4.** Go beyond, exceed, as in *I've run over the allotted time, but there are still questions.* [Early 1500s]

run rings around Also, **run circles around.** Be markedly superior to, as in *Ethan runs rings around David in chess,* or *In spelling, Karen runs circles around her classmates.* The first term, dating from the late 1800s, alludes to a horse running around a riding ring much faster than the others.

run riot ⊁ See RUN AMOK.

run scared Become intimidated or frightened. For example, *The polls don't look too good for our candidate and he's running scared,* or *The shrinking market has many businesses running scared.* [Mid-1900s]

run short Use something up so that a supply runs out or becomes insufficient, as in *We ran short of envelopes,* or *The organization is running short of money.* [Mid-1700s]

run someone in ⊁ See RUN IN, def. 3.

run the gamut Extend over an entire range, as in *His music runs the gamut from rock to classical.* This expression alludes to the medieval musical scale of Guido d'Arezzo, *gamut* being a contraction of *gamma* and *ut,* the lowest and highest notes respectively. [Mid-1800s]

run the gauntlet Be exposed to danger, criticism, or other adversity, as in *After he was misquoted in the interview, he knew he would have to run the gauntlet of his colleagues' anger.* This term, dating from the first half of the 1600s, comes from the word *gantlope,* which itself comes from the Swedish word *gatlopp,* for "lane-course." It referred to a form of military punishment where a man ran between two rows of soldiers who struck him with sticks or knotted ropes. Almost as soon as *gantlope* appeared, it was replaced by *gauntlet.* The word was being used figuratively for other kinds of punishment by 1661, when Joseph Glanvill wrote, "To print, is to run the gantlet, and to expose oneself to the tongues strapado" (*The Vanity of Dogmatizing, or Confidence in Opinion*).

run the show Take charge, assume control, as in *Ever since Bill retired from the business, his daughter's been running the show.* The word *show* here simply means "kind of undertaking." [First half of 1900s] A similar usage is **run one's own show,** meaning "exert control over one's own activities" or "act independently." For example, *The high school drama club didn't ask permission to perform that play—they want to run their own show.* [Mid-1900s]

run through 1. Pierce, as in *The soldier was run through by a bayonet.* [c. 1400] **2.** Use up quickly, as in *She ran through her allowance in no time.* [c. 1600] **3.** Practice, review or rehearse quickly, as in *Let's run through the first movement again,* or *The crew ran through the rescue procedures,* or *The attorney ran through the defense witness's testimony.* [Mid-1400s]

run to 1. Amount to, as in *The total will run to thousands of dollars.* This usage employs *run* in the sense of "extend." [Mid-1500s] **2.** Lean toward, favor, as in *My taste runs to chocolate desserts.* [Colloquial; second half of 1800s] Also see RUN TO EARTH; RUN TO FORM; RUN TO SEED.

run to earth Also, **run to ground.** Track down, find, as in *Somehow we have to run those relatives of hers to earth,* or *It won't be easy, but I'm sure we can run that jewelry to ground.* This expression comes from hunting, where hounds run their quarry to the earth or ground, that is, to their lair. Its figurative use dates from the mid-1800s.

run to form Also, **run true to form.** Act as one expects, especially in keeping with previous behavior. For example, *She ran to form, arriving an hour late,* or *The door-to-door campaign was running true to form, with solicitors always arriving at dinnertime.* This term originally was used for race horses running as expected from their previous record; it was transferred to human behavior in the late 1800s.

run to seed Also, **go to seed.** Become devitalized or worn out; deteriorate, as in *I went back to visit my old elementary school, and sadly, it has really run to seed,* or *The gold medalist quickly went to seed after he left competition.* This term alludes to plants that, when allowed to set seed after flowering, either taste bitter, as in the case of lettuce, or do not send out new buds, as is true of annual flowers. Its figurative use dates from the first half of the 1800s.

run up 1. Make or become greater or larger, as in *That offer will run up the price of the stock.* [Late 1500s] **2.** Accumulate, as in *She ran up huge bills at the florist.* [First half of 1700s] **3.** Sew rapidly, as in *I can run up some new curtains for the kitchen.* [Mid-1800s] **4.** Raise a flag, as in *Let's run up the flag in time for the holiday.* This usage, originating

in the navy about 1900, gave rise to the slangy phrase, **Let's run it up the flagpole and see if anybody salutes,** meaning, "Let's try this out." The latter originated about 1960 as advertising jargon.

run wild ♦ See RUN AMOK.

run with 1. Also, **run around with.** Socialize with; see RUN AROUND, def. 2. **2.** Take as one's own, adopt; also, carry out enthusiastically. For example, *He wanted to run with the idea and go public immediately.* **3. run with the hare, hunt with the hounds.** Support two opposing sides at the same time, as in *He wants to increase the magazine's circulation along with its price—that's trying to run with the hare and hunt with the hounds.* This expression, alluding to being both hunter and hunted at the same time, dates from the 1400s and was already a proverb in John Heywood's 1546 collection.

rush ♦ See BUM'S RUSH; FOOLS RUSH IN WHERE ANGELS FEAR TO TREAD; MAD RUSH; (RUSH) OFF SOMEONE'S FEET.

rustle up Get together food or some other needed item with some effort, as in *I don't know what we have but I'll rustle up a meal somehow,* or *You boys need to rustle up some wood for a campfire.* The verb *rustle* here means "to assemble in a hurry." [Late 1800s]

rut ♦ See IN A RUT.

S

saber rattling A flamboyant display of military power; also, aggressive blustering. For example, *There had been a great deal of saber rattling between the two nations but hostilities had never broken out.* This term, originating about 1920 and alluding to an officer indicating he would draw his saber, at first referred to threatening military force but later was extended to more general use, as in *Both candidates engaged in pre-debate saber rattling.*

sack ♦ In addition to the idiom beginning with SACK, also see GET THE AX (SACK); HIT THE HAY (SACK); SAD SACK.

sackcloth and ashes Mourning or penitence, as in *What I did to Julie's child was terrible, and I've been in sackcloth and ashes ever since.* This term refers to the ancient Hebrew custom of indicating humility before God by wearing a coarse cloth, normally used to make sacks, and dusting oneself with ashes. In English it appeared in William Tyndale's 1526 biblical translations (Matthew 11:21), "They [the cities Tyre and Sidon] had repented long ago in sackcloth and ashes."

sack out Go to sleep, go to bed, as in *We sacked out about midnight.* This slangy idiom is a verbal use of the noun *sack,* slang for "bed" since about 1940; it alludes to a sleeping bag and appears in such similar phrases as **in the sack,** in bed, and **sack time,** bedtime.

sacred cow A person or thing immune to criticism or questioning, as in *The rules governing the press conference have become a sacred cow in this administration.* This term alludes to the honored status of cows in Hinduism, where they are a symbol of God's generosity to humankind. It has been used figuratively since about 1900.

sadder but wiser Unhappy but having learned from one's mistakes, as in *Sadder but wiser, she's never going near poison ivy again.* The pairing of these two adjectives was first recorded in Samuel Coleridge's *The Rime of the Ancient Mariner* (1798).

saddle ◆ In addition to the idiom beginning with SADDLE, also see IN THE DRIVER'S SEAT (SADDLE).

saddle someone with Burden someone with, as in *Before he left on vacation, he saddled his assistant with many tasks he hadn't time to do himself.* [Late 1600s]

sad sack A singularly inept person, as in *Poor George is a hopeless sad sack.* This term alludes to a cartoon character, Sad Sack, invented by George Baker in 1942 and representing a soldier in ill-fitting uniform who failed at whatever he tried to do. It was soon transferred to clumsily inept civilians.

safe ◆ In addition to the idioms beginning with SAFE, also see BETTER SAFE THAN SORRY; ON THE SAFE SIDE; PLAY IT SAFE.

safe and sound Out of danger and unharmed, as in *It was a challenging climb, so I'm relieved they got home safe and sound.* [c. 1300]

safe as houses Totally secure, as in *If you buy Treasury bonds, your money will be safe as houses but you won't get a large return.* In today's security-conscious climate, where alarm systems to deter housebreaks have become increasingly common, this simile may seem puzzling. Presumably it uses *house* in the sense of "a shelter from the elements." [Late 1800s]

safety in numbers, there's A group has more protection against harm than an individual, as in *Her parents won't allow her to date but do let her go to parties, saying there's safety in numbers.* This phrase comes from the Latin proverb, *Defend it numerus,* presumably alluding to a military situation. It was first recorded in English about 1550.

said ◆ See EASIER SAID THAN DONE; ENOUGH SAID; NO SOONER SAID THAN DONE; WHEN ALL'S SAID AND DONE; YOU SAID IT. Also see under SAY.

sail ◆ In addition to the idioms beginning with SAIL, also see (SAIL UNDER) FALSE COLORS; PLAIN SAILING; SET SAIL; SMOOTH SAILING; TAKE THE WIND OUT OF ONE'S SAILS; TRIM ONE'S SAILS.

sail close to the wind Be on the verge of doing something illegal or improper, as in *She was sailing pretty close to the wind when she called him a liar.* This term alludes to the danger incurred when literally sailing too close to (that is, in the direction of) the wind. Its figurative use dates from the first half of the 1800s.

sail into Attack or criticize vigorously, as in *It was part of his technique to sail into the sales force at the start of their end-of-the-year meeting.* This term derives from *sail* in the sense of "move vigorously." [Mid-1800s]

sail through Also, **sail right through.** Accomplish quickly and easily, make easy progress through, as in *He sailed through the written test in no time,* or *We sailed right through customs.* This expression alludes to a boat moving quickly and easily through the water. [Mid-1900s]

sail under false colors ◆ See under FALSE COLORS.

sake ◆ See FOR THE SAKE OF.

salad days The time of youth, innocence, and inexperience, as in *Back in our salad days we went anywhere at night, never thinking about whether it was safe or not.* This expression, alluding to the greenness of inexperience, was probably invented by Shakespeare in *Antony and Cleopatra* (1:5), when Cleopatra, now enamored of Antony, speaks of her early admiration for Julius Caesar as foolish: "My salad days, when I was green in judgment, cold in blood."

sale ◆ See CLOSE THE SALE; ON SALE; WHITE SALE.

sales pitch A line of talk that attempts to persuade someone of something, as in *Let's hear your latest sales pitch for energy conservation.* This term uses the noun *pitch* in the sense of "a talk," or more literally, a throwing of words at one. [Slang; late 1800s]

salt ◆ In addition to the idioms beginning with SALT, also see BACK TO THE SALT MINES; WITH A GRAIN OF SALT.

salt away Also, **salt down.** Keep in reserve, store, save, as in *He salted away most of his earnings in a bank account.* This idiom alludes to using salt as a food preservative. [Mid-1800s]

salt of the earth, the The best or noblest of their kind, as in *These campers are the salt of the earth.* This metaphoric term was used by Jesus for those who were persecuted for being loyal to him (Matthew 5:13) and has been repeated ever since.

Samaritan ◆ See GOOD SAMARITAN.

same ◆ In addition to the idioms beginning with SAME, also see ALL THE SAME; AMOUNT TO THE SAME THING; AT THE SAME TIME; BY THE SAME TOKEN; CAST IN THE SAME MOLD; GREAT MINDS (RUN IN THE SAME CHANNEL); IN THE SAME BOAT; IN THE SAME

BREATH; IN THE SAME LEAGUE; ONE AND THE SAME; ON THE SAME WAVELENGTH.

same difference No difference at all, the same thing, as in *She's my sister, or stepsister—same difference.* This jocular colloquial phrase dates from about 1940.

same here Also, **the same with me.** Me too, I agree, as in *I think she was lying all along.—Same here,* or *I couldn't sleep because of the noise.—The same with me.* The first phrase is also used in an order for food or drink to indicate one wants the same thing as the previous person ordering; for example, *One more beer, please.—Same here.* [Colloquial; late 1800s]

same old story, the Also, **the same old rigmarole.** A frequently recurring event or situation, as in *It's the same old story—they won't hire you without experience but how can you get experience if you're not hired?* Both these expressions originally alluded to a tiresome, rambling discourse but today are used mainly for an irksome recurrence. The first gained currency during World War II with a song, "As Time Goes By," popularized in the film *Casablanca* (1942).

same to you I wish you the same (as you have wished me), as in *Merry Christmas!—Same to you.* [Late 1800s]

sanctity ♦ See ODOR OF SANCTITY.

sand ♦ See BUILD ON SAND; HIDE ONE'S HEAD IN THE SAND.

sardine ♦ See PACKED IN LIKE SARDINES.

sauce ♦ In addition to the idiom beginning with SAUCE, also see HIT THE BOTTLE (SAUCE).

sauce for the goose is sauce for the gander, what's What applies to one applies to both, especially to both male and female. For example, *After her husband went off with his fishing buddies for a week, she decided to take a vacation without him—what's sauce for the goose, you know.* This proverbial expression, often shortened as in the example, was cited and described as "a woman's proverb" in John Ray's *English Proverbs* (1678).

save ♦ In addition to the idioms beginning with SAVE, also see PENNY SAVED IS A PENNY EARNED; RAINY DAY, SAVE FOR A; SCRIMP AND SAVE; TO SAVE ONE'S LIFE.

saved by the bell Rescued from a difficulty at the last moment, as in *I couldn't put off explaining his absence any longer, but then Bill arrived and I was saved by the bell.* This expression alludes to the bell rung at the end of a boxing round, which, if it rings before a knocked-down boxer has been counted out, lets him get up and continue fighting in the next round. Its figurative use dates from the mid-1900s.

save face Avoid humiliation or embarrassment, preserve dignity, as in *Rather than fire him outright, they let him save face by accepting his resignation.* The phrase, which uses *face* in the sense of "outward appearances," is modeled on the antonym LOSE FACE. [Late 1800s]

save for a rainy day ♦ See RAINY DAY.

save one's bacon Also, **save one's neck** or **skin.** Rescue one from a difficult situation or harm, as in *I was having a hard time changing the flat tire but along came Bud, who saved my bacon,* or *The boat capsized in icy waters, but the life preservers saved our skins.* The allusion in the first term is no longer clear. It may simply be a comical way of referring to one's body or one's life. At the time it was first recorded, in 1654, bacon was a prized commodity, so perhaps saving one's bacon was tantamount to keeping something precious. Both variants allude to saving one's life, the one with *skin* dating from the early 1500s, and with *neck,* alluding to beheading, from the late 1600s.

save one's breath Refrain from arguing about a lost cause, as in *You can save your breath; I'm not going to change my mind.* This term was also put as **save your breath to cool your porridge** (or **broth**), that is, by not blowing on the too hot liquid. The idea of not expending one's breath to say something another person doesn't want to hear dates from the early 1700s.

save the day Prevent a misfortune, as in *They had forgotten the knife to cut the wedding cake, but Elizabeth arrived with one and saved the day.*

save up Accumulate something for a particular purpose, as in *Jan had been saving up her allowance for a new bicycle.* [First half of 1800s]

saving grace, a A redeeming quality, especially one compensating for drawbacks or negative characteristics. For example, *She may not be too knowledgeable, but her saving grace is that she doesn't pretend to be.* This term, dating from the late 1500s, at first referred to the concept of being saved from eternal damnation, and was used more loosely only from the late 1800s on.

saw ♦ See OLD SAW.

say ♦ In addition to the idioms beginning with SAY, also see BEFORE YOU CAN SAY JACK ROBINSON; CRY (SAY) UNCLE; DO AS I SAY; GET ONE'S SAY; GIVE (SAY) THE WORD; GO WITHOUT (SAYING); HAVE A SAY IN; I DARE SAY; I'LL SAY; NEEDLESS TO SAY; NEVER SAY DIE; NEVER SAY NEVER; NOT TO MENTION (SAY NOTHING OF); ON ONE'S SAY-SO; STRANGE TO SAY; SUFFICE IT TO SAY; THAT IS (TO SAY); TO SAY THE LEAST; YOU CAN SAY THAT AGAIN; YOU DON'T SAY. Also see UNDER SAID.

say a mouthful Utter something important or meaningful, as in *You said a mouthful when you* *called him a fine musician.* This term is often used to express agreement, much as YOU CAN SAY THAT AGAIN is. It was first recorded in 1790.

say grace Pronounce a short prayer before a meal, as in *Before we started in on the turkey, we asked Liz to say grace.* The word *grace* here signifies asking for God's blessing or giving thanks for the food being served. [Early 1300s]

say one's piece ♦ See SPEAK ONE'S PIECE.

says who? Who claims the truth of this statement, which I don't believe? For example, *That horse of yours will never win a race. — Says who?* This slangy expression of disagreement or disbelief may also be put in declarative form, **says you!**, meaning "I disagree with what you just said." For example, *It was an accident, I didn't mean to break it. — Says you! You've always hated that vase.* [First half of 1900s]

say the word ♦ See GIVE THE WORD.

say uncle ♦ See CRY UNCLE.

scale ♦ In addition to the idiom beginning with SCALE, also see TIP THE BALANCE (SCALE); TURN THE TABLES (SCALES).

scale down Reduce the size or cost of, as in *The owners decided to scale down wages.* This expression, along with the related **scale up**, which refers to an increase, alludes to *scale* in the sense of "a fixed standard." [Late 1800s]

scarce ♦ In addition to the idiom beginning with SCARCE, also see MAKE ONESELF SCARCE.

scarce as hen's teeth Also, **scarcer than hen's teeth.** Exceptionally rare, as in *On a rainy night, taxis are as scarce as hen's teeth.* Since hens have no teeth, this term in effect says that something is so scarce as to be nonexistent. [Mid-1800s]

scarcely ever ♦ See HARDLY EVER.

scare ♦ In addition to the idioms beginning with SCARE, also see RUN SCARED.

scare out of one's wits Also, **frighten out of one's wits; scare stiff** or **silly** or **to death** or **the living daylights out of** or **the pants off.** Terrify, make one panic, as in *When the lights went out, she was scared out of her wits,* or *I was scared stiff that I would fail the driver's test.* The first of these hyperbolic terms, *scare out of one's wits,* is the oldest and, like *silly,* suggests one is frightened enough to lose one's mind. The verb *scare* dates from about 1200, and *out of one's wits* was first recorded in William Tyndale's translation of the Bible in 1526 (I Corinthians 14:23): "Will they not say that ye are out of your wits?" They were first put together in 1697, the same period from which came *scare out of one's seven senses,* a usage now obsolete. The variant using *daylights,* which sometimes occurs

without *living,* dates from the 1950s. *Daylights* at one time referred to the eyes but here means "vital organs." *Frighten to death* was first recorded in Charles Dickens's *Barnaby Rudge* (1840) and *scare to death* probably appeared about the same time. However, *to death* used as an intensifier dates from the 1500s. These terms allude to the fact that a sudden fright can precipitate cardiac arrest. *Scare stiff,* first recorded in 1905, alludes to the temporary paralysis that can accompany intense fear. For the last variant, see also under PANTS OFF.

scare up Also, **scrape together** or **up.** Assemble or produce with considerable effort, as in *We managed to scare up extra chairs for the unexpectedly large audience,* or *He managed to scrape together enough cash to buy two more tickets.* The first term alludes to *scare* in the sense of "flush game out of cover" and dates from the mid-1800s; the variant, alluding to scratching or clawing for something, was first recorded in 1549. Also see SCRAPE UP AN ACQUAINTANCE.

scarlet woman A prostitute, an immoral woman, as in *Malicious gossip had it that she was a scarlet woman, which was quite untrue.* This expression first appeared in Revelation 17:5, describing Saint John's vision of a woman in scarlet clothes with an inscription on her forehead, "Mystery, Babylon the Great, the mother of harlots and abominations of the earth." Some interpreters believe she stood for Rome, drunk with the blood of saints, but by about 1700 the term was being used more generally for a woman with loose morals.

scene ♦ See BEHIND THE SCENES; MAKE A SCENE; MAKE THE SCENE; ON THE SCENE; SET THE SCENE FOR.

scent ♦ See THROW OFF, def. 3.

schedule ♦ See ON SCHEDULE.

scheme ♦ See BEST-LAID PLANS (SCHEMES).

school ♦ In addition to the idiom beginning with SCHOOL, also see TELL TALES (OUT OF SCHOOL).

schoolgirl complexion Fresh, glowing, unblemished skin, as in *She's fifty but she still has her schoolgirl complexion.* This expression, alluding to the beauty of young skin, was invented for an advertising campaign for Palmolive Soap, which ran from about 1923 through the 1930s and claimed to preserve one's schoolgirl complexion.

school of hard knocks The practical experience of life, including hardship and disappointments. For example, *A self-made man, he never went to college but came up through the school of hard knocks.* This idiom uses *knock,* "a blow," as a metaphor for a setback. [Mid-1800s]

scoot over Move to the side, especially to make room. For example, *If you scoot over a little I'll have room to sit down.* [Colloquial; first half of 1900s]

score ♦ See BOX SCORE; KNOW THE SCORE; PAY OFF (AN OLD SCORE); SETTLE A SCORE.

scoring position, in About to succeed, as in *The publisher is in scoring position with that instant book about the trial.* This term comes from sports, where it signifies being in a spot where scoring is likely. In baseball it refers to a situation in which a runner is on second or third base. The figurative use of the term dates from the second half of the 1900s.

scot ♦ See GET OFF (SCOT-FREE).

scout ♦ See GOOD EGG (SCOUT).

scrape ♦ See (SCRAPE THE) BOTTOM OF THE BARREL; BOW AND SCRAPE; SCARE (SCRAPE) UP.

scrape together ♦ See SCARE UP.

scrape up an acquaintance Make an effort to become familiar with someone, especially for one's own benefit. For example, *He scraped up an acquaintance with the college president in hopes of getting his son admitted.* This term uses *scrape* in the sense of "gather with difficulty" (also see under SCARE UP). Originally put as *scrape acquaintance,* it was first recorded in 1600.

scratch ♦ In addition to the idioms beginning with SCRATCH, also see FROM SCRATCH; UP TO PAR (SCRATCH).

scratch one's head Express puzzlement or perplexity, think hard, as in *They scratched their heads over this vexing question, but no one knew the answer.* Although literally scratching one's head may simply betoken the fact that it itches, it also may indicate mental mystification or bewilderment. The term's figurative use dates from the first half of the 1900s.

scratch someone's back Do someone a favor in hopes that a favor will be returned. For example, *I don't mind driving this time—she's scratched my back plenty of times.* It also is put as **you scratch my back and I'll scratch yours,** as in *If you do the laundry I'll do the cooking—you scratch my back and I'll scratch yours.* This idiom was first recorded in 1704.

scratch the surface Investigate or treat something superficially, as in *This feed-the-hungry program only scratches the surface of the problem,* or *Her survey course barely scratches the surface of economic history.* This metaphoric term transfers shallow markings made in a stone or other material to a shallow treatment of a subject or issue. [Early 1900s]

scream bloody murder Angrily protest as loudly as possible, as in *When Jimmy took her teddy bear, Lauren screamed bloody murder,* or *Residents are screaming bloody murder about the increase in property taxes.* The *scream* here may be either literal (as in the first example) or figurative, which is also true of invoking *murder* as though one were in danger of being killed. Versions of this term, such as **cry murder,** date from the 1400s.

screw ♦ In addition to the idioms beginning with SCREW, also see HAVE A SCREW LOOSE; PLUCK (SCREW) UP ONE'S COURAGE; TIGHTEN THE SCREWS; TURN UP THE HEAT (PUT THE SCREWS ON).

screw around 1. Fool around aimlessly, accomplishing nothing, as in *If you boys would stop screwing around we'd have the fence painted in an hour.* It is also put as **screw around with,** as in *Stop screwing around with the new camera.* The idiom probably derives from *screw* in the sense of "turn" or "twist." [Slang; second half of 1900s] 2. Be sexually promiscuous, as in *He's been screwing around behind her back for years.* [Vulgar slang; first half of 1900s]

screw loose ♦ See HAVE A SCREW LOOSE.

screw someone out of Cheat, deceive, or defraud someone, as in *They screwed me out of my overtime pay again.* It is often rendered in the passive, **be** or **get screwed,** meaning "be cheated, deceived, or defrauded." For example, *We're getting screwed by this new income tax regulation.* [Slang; c. 1900]

screw up 1. Muster or summon up; see PLUCK UP ONE'S COURAGE. 2. Make a mess of an undertaking; also, make a mistake, as in *I really screwed up this report,* or *She said she was sorry, admitting that she had screwed up.* Some authorities believe this usage is a euphemism for FUCK UP. [Slang; c. 1940] 3. Injure, damage, as in *I screwed up my back lifting all those heavy books.* [Slang] 4. Make neurotic or anxious, as in *Her family really screwed her up, but her therapist has helped her a lot.* [Slang; mid-1900s]

screw up one's courage ♦ See PLUCK UP ONE'S COURAGE.

screw you Go to hell, as in *You won't help after all? Well, screw you!* A euphemism for the still ruder FUCK YOU, this slangy term dates from the mid-1900s.

scrimp and save Economize severely, spend as little as possible, as in *For years we had to scrimp and save, but now we can enjoy life more.* [Mid-1800s]

scrounge around Forage about in an effort to obtain something at no cost, as in *We scrounged around their kitchen looking for a snack.* It derives from the dialectal *scrunge,* "steal." [Colloquial; c. 1900]

scrounge up Find or round up something, as in *I'll have to scrounge up another microphone for today's speaker.* [Colloquial; c. 1900]

scrub up Thoroughly wash one's hands and forearms, as before performing surgery. For example,

The residents had to scrub up in case they were called on to assist with the operation. [c. 1900]

Scylla ♦ See BETWEEN A ROCK AND A HARD PLACE (SCYLLA AND CHARYBDIS).

sea ♦ In addition to the idiom beginning with SEA, also see AT SEA; BETWEEN A ROCK AND A HARD PLACE (DEVIL AND THE DEEP BLUE SEA); HIGH SEAS; NOT THE ONLY FISH IN THE SEA; PUT OUT (TO SEA).

seal ♦ In addition to the idioms beginning with SEAL, also see LIPS ARE SEALED; SET ONE'S SEAL ON; SIGNED, SEALED AND DELIVERED.

sea legs The ability to adjust to a new situation or difficult conditions, as in *She's only spoken in public a few times; she hasn't found her sea legs yet.* This expression was first recorded in 1712 and then referred to, as it still does, the ability to walk steadily on board ship, especially in rough seas. By the late 1800s it was being transferred to other challenging situations.

seal of approval An endorsement of something or someone, as in *Our candidate doesn't have the governor's seal of approval,* or *The new management gave the old refund policy their seal of approval.* This idiom was used, and perhaps invented, as an advertising gimmick of *Good Housekeeping Magazine,* which gave its so-called "seal of approval" to products it endorsed; the products' packaging in turn bore a small emblem attesting to this endorsement. The noun *seal* here is used in the same sense as in SET ONE'S SEAL ON.

seal off Also, **seal up.** Close tightly or barricade to prevent entry or exit. For example, *We're sealing off the unused wing of the building,* or *The jar is tightly sealed up.* Dating from the first half of the 1900s, this idiom uses *seal* in the sense of "close securely," as one used to do with a seal of wax.

seal one's fate Decide what will become of one, as in *The letter of rejection sealed his fate; he'd have to apply to other medical schools.* This term employs *seal* in the sense of "permanently fix or fasten something," a usage dating from the mid-1600s.

seam ♦ See BURST AT THE SEAMS; COME APART AT THE SEAMS.

seamy side The sordid or base aspect of something, as in *This nightclub certainly shows you the seamy side of the community.* This term refers to the wrong side of a garment, revealing the stitched seams. Shakespeare used it figuratively in *Othello* (4:2): "That turn'd your wit the seamy side without."

search ♦ In addition to the idiom beginning with SEARCH, also see HIGH AND LOW, SEARCH; IN SEARCH OF.

search me I don't know the answer to that, as in *Where's John?—Search me. I haven't seen him for*

weeks. This expression in effect means "you can investigate me completely for the information you want but you won't find it." [Slang; c. 1900]

season ♦ See IN SEASON; OPEN SEASON.

seat ♦ In addition to the idiom beginning with SEAT, also see BACKSEAT DRIVER; CATBIRD SEAT; HOT SEAT; IN THE DRIVER'S SEAT; RINGSIDE SEAT; TAKE A BACK SEAT.

seat of the pants, by the Using intuition and improvisation rather than method or experience, as in *He ran the business by the seat of his pants.* This expression was invented by World War II fliers, who used it to describe flying when instruments were not working or weather interfered with visibility. It was transferred to broader use soon after the war.

second ♦ In addition to the idioms beginning with SECOND, also see AT SECOND HAND; COME OFF (SECOND BEST); IN A FLASH (SECOND); IN THE FIRST (SECOND) PLACE; ON SECOND THOUGHT; PLAY SECOND FIDDLE; SPLIT SECOND; TOP (SECOND) BANANA.

second banana ♦ See under TOP BANANA.

second best Also, **second class.** Next after the first in rank or quality, inferior to the best, as in *We aren't satisfied with being second best in sales,* or *This hotel is obviously second class.* The first term dates from the first half of the 1400s, the variant from about 1800. Also see COME OFF, def. 2; SECOND CLASS.

second childhood The dotage of old age; also, childlike playfulness in an adult. For example, *Grandpa needs full-time care, now that he's in his second childhood,* or *Since he retired and started learning to fly, he's been in his second childhood.* Depending on the context, this term may allude either to such problems of old age as losing one's mental or physical capacities or to delighting in new pleasures in a childlike fashion. [c. 1900]

second class 1. Inferior; see SECOND BEST. 2. Travel accommodations ranking below the highest or first class, as in *Traveling second class on European trains is not only cheaper but gives you more contact with local people.* [c. 1840] 3. In the United States and Canada, a category of mail consisting of periodicals and newspapers. [c. 1870] 4. **second-class citizen.** An individual regarded or treated as inferior to others in status or rights, an underprivileged person. For example, *In many countries women still are considered second-class citizens.* This term uses *second class* in the sense of "inferior." [c. 1940]

second cousin Something that is related or similar but not quite the same, as in *This beef stew is second cousin to boeuf bourguignon.* This expression transfers the literal sense of *second cousin*—that is, the child of the first cousin of one's mother or father—a usage dating from the mid-1600s.

second fiddle ♦ See PLAY SECOND FIDDLE.

second hand ♦ See AT SECOND HAND.

second nature A habit or mode of behavior so long practiced that it seems innate, as in *Driving in heavy traffic is second nature to Chris*. This expression is a shortened form of an ancient proverb, *Custom* (or *usage*) *is a second nature*, first recorded in 1390. It alludes to the fact that very frequently repeating something makes it seem completely natural or inborn.

second sight Clairvoyance, as in *Jane must have second sight; she knew exactly where Dad had mislaid his keys*. This expression, alluding to the supposed power of someone to perceive an event in the future or distance as though actually present, dates from the early 1600s.

second thoughts ♦ See ON SECOND THOUGHT.

second to none The best, as in *Mom's chocolate cake is second to none*. Shakespeare was among the first to use this term in *The Comedy of Errors* (5:1), when Angelo speaks warmly of Antipholus of Syracuse: "Of credit infinite, highly belov'd, second to none that lives here."

second wind Restored energy or strength, enabling one to continue an activity or task. For example, *I wasn't sure how far they'd get in a week, but now they seem to have gotten their second wind and are making good progress painting the mural*. This expression, dating from the late 1800s, was at first (and still is) used for returned ease in breathing after becoming out of breath during physical exertion such as running. It soon began to be applied to nonphysical efforts as well.

secret ♦ See IN SECRET; OPEN SECRET.

security ♦ In addition to the idiom beginning with SECURITY, also see LULL INTO (FALSE SENSE OF SECURITY).

security blanket Something that dispels anxiety, as in *I always carry my appointments calender; it's my security blanket*. This colloquial term, dating from about 1960, was at first (and still is) used for the blanket or toy or other object held by a young child to reduce anxiety.

see ♦ In addition to the idioms beginning with SEE, also see AS FAR AS I CAN SEE; BEGIN TO SEE DAYLIGHT; CAN'T SEE BEYOND THE END OF ONE'S NOSE; CAN'T SEE THE FOREST FOR THE TREES; I'LL BE SEEING YOU; I SEE; LET ME SEE; LONG TIME NO SEE; SO I SEE; WAIT AND SEE. Also see under SEEN.

see about 1. Also, **see to**. Attend to, take care of, as in *I'll see about the refreshments if you'll handle the tickets*, or *Will you see to the outdoor chores?* The variant is also put as **see to it**, as in *Yes, I'll see to it that everything's done*. [First half of 1800s] 2. Investigate, as in *I'm not sure, but I'll see about the cost of renting a van*. Also see LOOK INTO.

see after ♦ See LOOK AFTER.

see a man about a dog Excuse oneself without giving the real reason for leaving, especially to go to the toilet or have an alcoholic drink. For example, *Excuse me, I have to see a man about a dog*. This euphemistic term dates from the Prohibition days of the 1920s, when buying liquor was illegal, and, after repeal, was transferred to other circumstances.

see beyond one's nose ♦ See CAN'T SEE BEYOND THE END OF ONE'S NOSE.

seed ♦ See RUN TO SEED.

see daylight ♦ See BEGIN TO SEE DAYLIGHT.

see double See two images of one object, either as an illusion or owing to some visual aberration, especially one caused by intoxication. For example, *Those twins look so much alike they make me think I'm seeing double*, or *One more drink and I'll be seeing double*. This idiom was first recorded in 1628.

see eye to eye Agree completely, as in *I'm so glad we see eye to eye on whom we should pick for department head*. This expression appears in the Bible (Isaiah 52:8). [c. 1600]

see fit Deem appropriate, as in *He's entitled to divide up his property as he sees fit*, or *If we see fit to attend, we'll be there*. This expression uses *see* in the sense of "view as," a usage dating from about 1325.

seeing is believing Only physical or concrete evidence is convincing, as in *She wrote us that she's lost twenty pounds, but seeing is believing*. This idiom was first recorded in this form in 1639.

seeing that Also, **seeing as** or **seeing as how**. In view of, inasmuch as. For example, *Seeing that you're coming anyhow, I decided not to take notes for you*, or *Seeing as they liked her first book, they were sure to make a good offer for the second one*. The first expression was used by Shakespeare in *Julius Caesar* (2:2): "Seeing that death, a necessary end, will come when it will come." The variants are colloquialisms and are recorded from the second half of the 1900s, although they probably have been in much longer use orally.

seeing things Experiencing hallucinations or delusions, as in *I thought I saw my father, but I must have been seeing things; he died twenty years ago*. [First half of 1900s]

see into 1. Investigate; see LOOK INTO. 2. Understand the true character or nature of, as in *Mother could see into Mary very well and knew exactly what she was up to*. Shakespeare used this idiom in *2 Henry VI* (3:1): "Well hath your Highness seen into this duke."

seek ♦ See PLAY HIDE AND SEEK.

seen better days, have Be worn out, have fallen into a state of decline, as in *This chair has seen better days*, or *The family business has seen better days*. This term was first used by Shakespeare to describe a decline of fortune (*Timon of Athens*, 4:2) but soon was broadened to describe aging or deterioration in both humans and objects.

seen one, seen them all One example suffices, as in *I'm afraid I don't care for home movies—seen one, seen them all*. This world-weary expression was first recorded in 1811. A newer idiom expressing a very similar view is **been there, done that**, indicating that it is boring to repeat an experience once it has lost its novelty. For example, *No, I don't want to climb Mount Washington; been there, done that*. This idiom was first recorded in Australia in 1983 and was popularized in America in the 1990s through a widely aired commercial for a soft drink.

see one's way to Also, **see one's way clear to.** Find it possible or feel free to do something, as in *Can you see your way to lending me the car for the week?* or *I finally saw my way clear to taking a vacation in Costa Rica.* This expression, which transfers seeing one's path to something unobstructed, was first recorded in 1774.

see out 1. Also, **see someone out; see someone to the door.** Escort someone to the door, as in *The butler saw him out*, or *She refused to see him to the door.* This usage was first recorded in Shakespeare's *Coriolanus* (3:3): "Come, come, let's see him out at gates." Also see SEE SOMEONE OFF. **2.** Remain with an undertaking to the end; see SEE THROUGH, def. 2.

see reason Adopt a sensible course of action, let oneself be persuaded, as in *At ninety Grandma finally saw reason and gave up driving her car.* This expression, which uses *reason* in the sense of "good sense," was first recorded in Shakespeare's *1 Henry IV* (1:2).

see red Become very angry, as in *I saw red when I learned they had not invited Tom and his family.* The precise allusion in this term is not known, but it probably refers to the longstanding association of the color red with passion and anger. [Colloquial; c. 1900]

see someone off Take leave of someone, as in *We saw our guests off at the door*, or *They came to the airport to see us off.* This expression was first recorded in 1809. Also see SEE OUT, def. 1.

see stars Perceive flashing lights, especially after a blow to one's head. For example, *A swinging door hit me and I really saw stars.* [Late 1800s]

see the back of Be finished with, as in *I hope we've seen the back of Betsy; she is terribly rude.* This idiom transfers literally seeing someone's back because they are leaving to a more figurative and permanent departure. Also see SEE THE LAST OF.

see the color of one's money ♦ See COLOR OF ONE'S MONEY.

see the elephant Experience more than one wants to, learn a hard lesson; also, see combat, especially for the first time. For example, *After the expedition lost two climbers in an avalanche, they had seen the elephant and turned back*, or *On his first tour of duty he saw the elephant.* This slangy expression, first recorded in 1835, alludes to having seen all the sights one can see, including that rare beast, and returning home unimpressed or disappointed.

see the last of End one's dealings with someone or something, as in *I hope I've seen the last of those boring ice shows*, or *We haven't seen the last of Jerry—he'll be back.* [Early 1800s]

see the light Also, **begin to see the light.** Understand or begin to understand something; also, see the merit of another's explanation or decision. For example, *Dean had been trying to explain that tax deduction for fifteen minutes when I finally saw the light*, or *Pat was furious she and her friends were not allowed to go hiking on their own in the mountains, but she began to see the light when a group got lost up there.* This term, dating from the late 1600s, originally referred to religious conversion, the *light* meaning "true religion." By the early 1800s it was used more broadly for any kind of understanding. Also see LIGHT AT THE END OF A TUNNEL; SEE THE LIGHT OF DAY.

see the light of day Be published, brought out, or born. For example, *I wonder if her book will ever see the light of day*, or *The family reunion was a disaster, and I wish the idea for it had never seen the light of day*, or *When we visited Pittsburgh, we saw where Mom had first seen the light of day.* [Early 1700s]

see the sights View noteworthy features or objects, especially when visiting a place. For example, *It's impossible to see all the sights of Paris in just a week.* [Mid-1700s]

see things ♦ See SEEING THINGS.

see through 1. see through someone or **something.** Understand the true character or nature of someone or something, as in *We saw through his superficial charm: he was obviously a liar.* [c. 1400] **2.** Also, **see out.** Remain with an undertaking to the end; also, provide steadfast support to. For example, *I saw the reorganization through and then I left the company*, or *We'll see out the year in Florida and then decide if the move is permanent*, or *We'll see you through medical school but then you're on your own.*

see through rose-colored glasses Also, **look through rose-colored glasses**. Take an optimistic view of something, as in *Kate enjoys just about every activity; she sees the world through rose-colored glasses,* or *If only Marvin wouldn't be so critical, if he could look through rose-colored glasses once in a while, he'd be much happier.* The adjectives *rosy* and *rose-colored* have been used in the sense of "hopeful" or "optimistic" since the 1700s; the current idiom dates from the 1850s.

see to Also, **see to it.** ♦ See under SEE ABOUT.

see with half an eye Notice the obvious, tell at a glance, as in *I could see with half an eye that he was sleeping through the entire concert.* This hyperbolic expression, which presumably alludes to an eye that is only half-open, was first recorded in 1579.

seize on Also, **seize upon. 1.** Grab or take hold of suddenly, as in *He seized on the bell rope and started to pull vigorously,* or *She seized upon every opportunity to present her side of the story.* [Late 1600s] **2.** Resort to some action, especially out of dire necessity, as in *He seized upon any excuse, no matter how farfetched.*

seize up Come to a halt, as in *The peace talks seized up and were not rescheduled.* Originally, from about 1870 on, this term was applied to a machine of some kind that jammed or locked, owing to excessive heat or friction. Its figurative use dates from about 1950.

sell ♦ In addition to the idioms beginning with SELL, also see HARD SELL; LIKE HOT CAKES, SELL.

sell a bill of goods Deceive, swindle, take unfair advantage of, as in *He was just selling you a bill of goods when he said he worked as a secret agent,* or *Watch out if anyone says he wants to trade bikes with you; he's apt to be selling you a bill of goods.* The *bill of goods* here means "a dishonest offer." [c. 1920]

sell down the river Betray, as in *They kept the merger a secret until the last minute, so the employees who were laid off felt they'd been sold down the river.* This expression, dating from the mid-1800s, alludes to slaves being sold down the Mississippi River to work as laborers on cotton plantations. Its figurative use dates from the late 1800s.

sell like hot cakes ♦ See LIKE HOT CAKES.

sell off Get rid of by selling, often at reduced prices. For example, *The jeweler was eager to sell off the last of the diamond rings.* [c. 1700] Also see SELL OUT, def. 1.

sell oneself 1. Convince another of one's merits, present oneself in a favorable light, as in *A job interview is an ideal opportunity to sell oneself to a prospective employer.* Originally this idiom, dating from the second half of the 1700s, alluded to sell-

ing one's services for money, but it was being used more loosely by the mid-1800s. **2.** Compromise one's principles for monetary gain. An early version was **sell oneself (or one's soul) to the devil,** which alluded to enlisting the devil's help in exchange for one's soul after death. It is embodied in the legend of Faust, first recorded in the late 1500s.

sell out 1. Dispose of entirely by selling. For example, *The rancher finally sold out to the oil company,* or *The tickets to the concert were sold out a month ago.* [Late 1700s] **2.** Betray one's cause or colleagues, as in *He sold out to the other side.* [Slang; late 1800s]

sell short 1. Contract for the sale of securities or commodities one expects to own at a later date and at a lower price, as in *Selling short runs the risk of a market rise, forcing one to pay more than one expected.* [Mid-1800s] **2. sell someone short.** Underestimate the true value or worth of someone, as in *Don't sell her short; she's a very able lawyer.* [First half of 1900s]

sell someone on Convince or persuade someone of the worth or desirability of something, as in *They were hoping to sell enough legislators on their bill so that it would pass easily,* or *Dave was really sold on that new car.* [Colloquial; early 1900s]

send away Also, **send off. 1.** Dispatch someone or something, as in *We send the children away to camp every summer,* or *I sent off that letter last week.* The first term dates from the first half of the 1500s, the variant from the late 1700s. **2.** Order an item, as in *I sent away for those gloves last month but they haven't arrived yet.* Also see SEND FOR, def. 2.

send down Suspend or dismiss from a university, principally a British one. For example, *He's done very poorly ever since he was sent down from Oxford.* [Mid-1800s]

send flying Cause to be knocked or scattered about, as in *She bumped into the table and sent all the papers flying.* This somewhat hyperbolic idiom was first recorded in 1789.

send for 1. Summon someone, request that someone come, as in *She sent for all the children when their father lay dying.* [Late 1500s] **2.** Order a delivery of something, as in *The king sent for a bottle of wine.* Also see SEND AWAY, def. 2; SEND OUT, def. 2.

send in 1. Cause to be dispatched or delivered, as in *Let's send in a letter of protest to the hiring committee.* [Early 1700s] **2.** Cause someone to become involved in a particular undertaking, as in *This disagreement is serious; it's time to send in the lawyers,* or *In the final few minutes the coach sent in Richard on right wing.* [Mid-1800s]

send off ♦ See SEND AWAY, def. 1.

send on 1. Forward something, as in *He's moved; I'll send on this letter to his new address.* [First half of 1800s] 2. **send someone on.** Cause someone to go on an errand or path, as in *I sent your brother on an errand but he should be back soon,* or *They've sent us on a wild goose chase.* [Second half of 1800s]

send out 1. Issue or dispatch, as in *We sent out the wedding invitations last month,* or *When did you send out that message?* [c. 1400] 2. **send out for.** Order a delivery of something, as in *Every Wednesday we send out for Chinese food.*

send round Circulate widely, as in *A copy of the new bylaws is being sent round to all union members.* [First half of 1800s]

send someone about his or her business Also, **send someone packing.** Dismiss someone abruptly, as in *They always ring the bell at suppertime, asking for signatures, but I send them about their business,* or *The owner caught Jack taking small items from the store and sent him packing.* The first term, which in effect tells people to tend to their own affairs, was first recorded in 1768; the variant, alluding to telling people to pack their bags and leave, was first recorded in 1594. Also see SEND AWAY.

send someone packing ♦ See SEND SOMEONE ABOUT HIS OR HER BUSINESS.

send up 1. Put in prison, as in *He'll be sent up for at least ten years.* [Mid-1800s] 2. Cause to rise, as in *The emissions sent up by that factory are clearly poisonous.* [Late 1500s] 3. Satirize, make a parody of, as in *This playwright has a genius for sending up suburban life.* [First half of 1900s] 4. **send up a trial balloon.** See TRIAL BALLOON.

sense ♦ See COME TO ONE'S SENSES; HORSE SENSE; IN A SENSE; LULL INTO (A FALSE SENSE OF SECURITY); MAKE SENSE; SIXTH SENSE; TAKE LEAVE OF (ONE'S SENSES); TALK SENSE.

separate but equal Relating to or affected by a policy whereby two groups may be segregated if they are given equal facilities and opportunities. For example, *They've divided up the physical education budget so that the girls' teams are separate but equal to the boys'.* This idiom comes from a Louisiana law of 1890, upheld by the U.S. Supreme Court in Plessy v. Ferguson, "requiring all railway companies carrying passengers on their trains in this state, to provide equal but separate accommodations for the white and colored races." Subsequently it was widely used to separate African-Americans from the white population through a general policy of racial segregation. In 1954, in a unanimous ruling to end school segregation, the Supreme Court finally overturned the law (in Brown v. Board of Education).

separate the men from the boys Distinguish between mature, experienced individuals and novices, as in *The picket line will separate the men from the boys in the union.* The idiom is used without respect to gender. [c. 1930]

separate the sheep from the goats Distinguish between good and bad individuals, or superior and inferior ones. For example, *In a civil war where both sides commit atrocities, you can't separate the sheep from the goats.* This term refers to Jesus's prophecy in the New Testament (Matthew 25:32) that the sheep (that is, the compassionate) will sit on God's right hand (and find salvation), and the goats (the hard-hearted) will sit on the left (and be sent to damnation).

separate wheat from chaff Sort the valuable from the worthless, as in *I hope we'll get a preview of the auction so we can separate the wheat from the chaff.* This idiom alludes to the ancient practice of winnowing grain.

serve ♦ In addition to the idioms beginning with SERVE, also see BREAK SOMEONE'S SERVE; FIRST COME, FIRST SERVED; HAND TO ON A SILVER PLATTER (SERVE UP ON A PLATE).

serve a purpose Also, **serve one's** or **the purpose.** Be useful, meet the needs or requirements, satisfy, as in *I don't know why they've added all this information but it probably serves a purpose,* or *It often serves his purpose to be vague,* or *We don't have a spading fork but this shovel should serve the purpose.* This idiom was first recorded in 1513.

serve one right Be deserved under the circumstances. For example, *That punishment serves him right after what he's done to you.* It is also put as **serves you right,** as in *It wasn't accepted? Serves you right for applying so late.* These idioms use *serve* in the sense of "treat in a specified manner," in this case, justly. [Late 1500s]

serve time Undergo a prison sentence; also, work at a particular task, especially an undesirable one. For example, *We couldn't hire him when we learned that he had served time for robbery,* or *I applied for a transfer after serving time in that chaotic department.* [Late 1800s]

serve up 1. Dish out food, as in *Next they served up some oysters.* [First half of 1400s] 2. Provide, as in *He served up joke after joke, delighting his audience.* [First half of 1600s] Also see HAND TO ON A SILVER PLATTER.

service ♦ See AT SOMEONE'S SERVICE; BREAK SOMEONE'S SERVE (SERVICE); LIP SERVICE; OF SERVICE TO SOMEONE; PRESS INTO SERVICE.

session ♦ See BULL SESSION.

set ♦ In addition to the idioms beginning with SET, also see ALL SET; DEAD SET AGAINST; GET SET; GET (SET) SOMEONE'S BACK UP; GET (SET) THE BALL ROLLING; LAY (SET) EYES ON; LET (SET) LOOSE; ON A PEDESTAL, SET; SMART SET; TONGUES WAGGING, SET. Also see under PUT.

set about Begin, start, as in *How do we set about solving this puzzle?* [c. 1600]

set against Be or cause someone to be opposed to, as in *Civil wars often set brother against brother,* or *The police chief's critics were set against his officers.* [Late 1200s] Also see DEAD SET AGAINST.

set an example Also, **set a good** or **bad example.** Behave in a way that should (or will) be imitated, as in *Dad was always telling Bill to set a good example for his younger brother,* or *They were afraid of setting a bad example for the other nations.* [Late 1700s]

set apart 1. Reserve for a specific use, as in *One group of tissue samples was set apart for incubation.* [c. 1600] 2. Make noticeable, as in *Certain traits set her apart from her peers.* [Late 1400s]

set a precedent Establish a usage, tradition, or standard to be followed in the future. For example, *He set a precedent by having the chaplain lead the academic procession.* The word *precedent* here signifies a previous instance or legal decision upon which future instances are based, a usage dating from the early 1400s. In British and American law it more specifically refers to a legal decision that may be used as a standard in subsequent cases.

set aside 1. Separate and reserve for a special purpose, as in *We have to set aside some chairs for latecomers.* [Early 1700s] Also see SET BY. 2. Discard or reject, as in *Setting aside all health considerations, do you believe this law is fair to smokers?* [Early 1400s] 3. Declare invalid, annul, or overrule, as in *The higher court set aside the conviction.* [Mid-1700s] Also see LAY ASIDE.

set at Also, **set upon.** Attack or assail, as in *The dog set at the postman,* or *The hyenas set upon the wounded lion.* The first term dates from the early 1400s, the variant from the late 1300s.

set at rest ♦ See LAY AT REST.

set back 1. Slow down the progress of, hinder, as in *The project was set back by the frequent absences of staff members.* [First half of 1500s] 2. Cost, as in *That car set me back twenty thousand dollars.* [Colloquial; c. 1900] 3. Change to a lower level or earlier time, as in *We set back the thermostat whenever we go on vacation,* or *On October 10 we have to set back the clocks.* [First half of 1600s] **Set back the clock** is also used figuratively to mean "return to an earlier era," as in *He wished he could set back the clock to those carefree high-school days.* Also see SET FORWARD.

set back on one's heels Surprise, shock, or disconcert, as in *The news of their divorce set us back on our heels.* This idiom, with its graphic image of someone being pushed back, dates from the first half of the 1900s.

set back the clock ♦ See SET BACK, def. 3.

set by Put aside for future use, as in *She had shelves and shelves of cans set by for some imagined food emergency.* [Late 1500s] Also see SET ASIDE, def. 1; SET STORE BY.

set down 1. Place in a lower position, as in *Set the baby down here,* or *Set the bags down on the hall table.* [Late 1400s] 2. Put in writing, record, as in *Just set down all the facts as you remember them.* [Second half of 1500s] 3. Regard, consider, as in *Just set him down as a fool.* [Late 1700s] 4. Assign to a cause, ascribe, as in *Let's set down his error to inexperience.* [Early 1800s] 5. Land an aircraft, as in *The pilot set the plane down hard on the runway.* Also see PUT DOWN.

set eyes on ♦ See LAY EYES ON.

set fire to ♦ See SET ON FIRE.

set foot 1. **set foot in.** Enter, as in *I'll never set foot in this house again.* 2. **set foot on.** Step on, as in *We were so happy to set foot on dry land.* [c. 1600]

set forth 1. Also, **put forth.** Start a journey, as in *We plan to set forth at daybreak,* or *They put forth for France tomorrow.* [c. 1400] 2. Present for consideration; also, express in words, as in *She set forth a very sensible plan,* or *We need to set forth our ideas clearly.* [Early 1500s] 3. See PUT FORTH, def. 3.

set forward Also, **set ahead.** Turn a clock to a later time, as in *For daylight-saving time we set the clocks forward.* [1600s]

set in 1. Insert, put in, as in *I still have to set in the sleeves and then the sweater will be done.* [Late 1300s] 2. Begin to happen or become apparent, as in *Darkness was setting in as I left.* [c. 1700] 3. Move toward the shore, said of wind or water, as in *The tide sets in very quickly here.* [Early 1700s]

set in motion Start something moving, give impetus to something, as in *A press conference set the new project in motion.* It is also put as **set the wheels in motion,** as in *Let's set the wheels in motion for the new library wing.* This idiom dates from about 1800. It was preceded by **put in motion,** which dates from the mid-1600s.

set in one's ways, be Be inflexible, fixed in one's habits, as in *She's too set in her ways to go out and buy a dog.* This idiom uses *set* in the sense of "in a rigid position," a usage dating from about 1300.

set loose ♦ See LET LOOSE.

set off 1. Give rise to, cause to occur, as in *The acid set off a chemical reaction.* [Early 1600s] 2. Cause to explode, as in *They set off a bomb.* [Late 1800s] 3. Distinguish, show to be different, contrast with, as in *That black coat sets him off from the others in the picture,* or *Italics set this sentence off from the rest of the text.* [Late 1500s] 4. Enhance, make more attractive, as in *That color sets off her blonde hair.* [Early 1600s] 5. Begin a journey, leave, as in *When do you set off for Europe?* [Second half of 1700s]

set on Also, **set upon**. 1. Attack; see SET AT. 2. Instigate, urge one to engage in action, as in *The older boys set on the young ones to get in trouble.* [Early 1500s] 3. **be set on** or **upon**. Be determined to, as in *He's set on studying law.*

set on a pedestal ♦ See ON A PEDESTAL.

set one back ♦ See SET BACK, def. 1; 2.

set one back on one's feet Help restore one's position, reestablish one, as in *The outplacement office promised to help set the displaced workers back on their feet.* This idiom uses an upright position as a metaphor for being active and productive.

set one's back up ♦ See PUT ONE'S BACK UP.

set one's cap for Pursue someone romantically, as in *We all thought Anne had set her cap for Joe, but we were wrong.* In the 1700s this term, which may have alluded to donning one's best headgear, was applied to members of either sex, but by the early 1800s it generally described a woman chasing a man. It is probably obsolescent.

set one's face against Strongly disapprove, as in *Her parents set their faces against her eloping.* The term *set one's face* has been used in the sense of "assume a fixed facial expression" since the mid-1500s.

set one's heart on Also, **have one's heart set on**. Strongly desire something, as in *I'd set my heart on a vacation in New Mexico but got sick and couldn't go,* or *Harry had his heart set on a new pickup truck.* [Late 1300s]

set one's mind at rest Also, **put one's mind at rest**. Stop worrying, allay one's anxiety. For example, *Your car's been found undamaged, so set your mind at rest.* Also see LAY AT REST.

set one's mind on ♦ See under PUT ONE'S MIND TO.

set one's seal on Also, **put one's seal on**. Authorize, give one's approval to, as in *We can go ahead as soon as the boss sets his seal on it.* This idiom alludes to the old-time practice of affixing a seal on a document as a form of verification. It also began to be used more loosely in the early 1600s.

set one's sights on Have as a goal, as in *She's set her sights on law school.* This expression alludes to the device on a firearm used for taking aim. [Mid-1900s]

set one's teeth on edge Irritate, annoy, make one cringe, as in *That raucous laugh sets my teeth on edge.* This expression alludes to the shuddering feeling evoked by a grating noise or similar irritation. It appears in several books of the Bible and was also used by Shakespeare. [c. 1600]

set on fire 1. Also, **set fire to**. Cause to ignite and burn, as in *The drought and high wind combined to set the woods on fire.* [c. 1400] 2. Cause to become excited, as in *The music set the audience on fire.* Also see CATCH FIRE; SET THE WORLD ON FIRE.

set out 1. Begin an earnest attempt, as in *He set out to prove his point,* or *We accomplished what we set out to do.* [Late 1800s] 2. Lay out systematically, as in *She set out all the reports in chronological order.* [Second half of 1500s] 3. Display for exhibition or sale, as in *The Japanese restaurant set out samples of all the different kinds of sushi.* [c. 1300] 4. Plant, as in *It was time to set out the seedlings.* [Early 1800s] 5. Begin a journey, as in *They set out at dawn.* [Late 1500s]

set right Also, **put right**. 1. Place something in proper position; also, repair something. For example, *Your tie is lopsided; let me set it right,* or *The faucets were in backwards but the plumber will soon put them right.* [Second half of 1500s] 2. Correct someone, as in *They thought he was married but he quickly set them right.* 3. Make something accurate or fair, as in *He offered to pay for the meal to put things right.* Also see SET STRAIGHT.

set sail Also, **make sail**. Begin a voyage on water, as in *Dad rented a yacht, and we're about to set sail for the Caribbean,* or *We'll make sail for the nearest port.* These expressions, dating from the early 1500s, originally meant "put the sails in position to catch the wind," and hence cause the vessel to move.

set store by Also, **set great store by**. Regard as valuable or worthwhile, as in *I don't set much store by her judgment,* or *He sets great store by his good name.* The word *store* here is used in the sense of "something precious," a usage that is obsolete except in these terms.

set straight Correct someone by providing accurate information; also, make an arrangement honest or fair. For example, *Let me set you straight about Lisa; she's never actually worked for us,* or *To set matters straight I'll pay you back Monday.* It is sometimes put as **set the record straight**, meaning "correct an inaccurate account," as in *Just to set the record straight, we arrived at ten.* [First half of 1900s]

set the pace Establish a standard for others to follow, as in *Jim has set the pace for the department, exceeding the monthly quota every time.* This expression comes from racing, where it is said of a horse that passes the others and leads the field. It was transferred to other activities in the early 1900s.

set the record straight ♦ See SET STRAIGHT.

set the scene for Also, **set the stage for.** Provide the underlying basis or background for, make likely or inevitable, as in *Their fights about money set the scene for a divorce,* or *The comptroller's assessment of the firm's finances set the stage for a successful bond issue.* These expressions allude to arranging a play's actors and properties on a theatrical stage. The first term dates from the late 1700s, the variant from the late 1800s.

set the table Also, **lay the table.** Arrange a cloth, plates, glasses, silverware and the like for a meal, as in *Please set the table for eight tonight.* [Late 1300s]

set the wheels in motion ♦ See SET IN MOTION.

set the world on fire Perform an outstanding feat and win fame, as in *An ambitious man, be longed to set the world on fire with his inventions.* This hyperbolic expression uses *set on fire* in the sense of "arouse excitement in." Also see SET ON FIRE, def. 2.

settle a score Also, **settle** or **wipe out an old score** or **scores.** Get even, avenge a grievance or an injury. For example, *Wendy settled an old score with Bill when she made him wait for half an hour in the rain.* These expressions, dating from the mid-1800s to early 1900s, all use *score* in the sense of "an account" or "bill." Also see PAY OFF, def. 3.

settle down 1. Begin living a stable, orderly life; also, marry. For example, *After traveling all over the world for years, he decided to settle down in his home town,* or *Her parents wished she would settle down and raise a family.* [Early 1600s] 2. Become calm, less nervous, or less restless, as in *Come on, children, it's time to settle down.* [Mid-1800s] 3. Apply oneself seriously, as in *If you don't settle down to your homework, you'll never get it done.* [First half of 1800s]

settle for Accept or be satisfied with as a compromise, as in *He really wanted a bigger raise but decided to settle for what they offered.* [Mid-1900s]

settle on Also, **settle upon.** 1. Decide something, as in *They finally settled on Bermuda for their vacation.* [Second half of 1700s] 2. Give property or a title to someone, as in *She settled an annuity on her husband.* [Mid-1600s]

settle someone's hash Subdue or get rid of someone, deal with a troublemaker, as in *If John starts another argument we know just how to settle his hash.* This term, dating from about 1800, uses *hash* in the sense of "a mess."

settle up Also, **settle with someone.** Pay a debt or one's share of the cost, as in *When can you settle up for the tickets I bought for us?* or *Jean said she'd settle with the bank next month.*

set to 1. Apply oneself, begin, work energetically, as in *We set to revamping our policy on child care,* or *She set to studying for the bar exam.* [Early 1400s] 2. Begin fighting, as in *Both of them were furious, and they set to immediately.* [First half of 1700s]

set tongues wagging ♦ See TONGUES WAG.

set to rights Also, **put to rights.** Place in proper condition or order. For example, *The caterer promised to set the room to rights before he left,* or *Don't worry, the lawyer will put the will to rights.* These terms date from the second half of the 1600s, although *to rights* in the sense of "in proper order" was first recorded about 1330. Also see SET RIGHT.

set up 1. Place in an upright position, as in *I keep setting up this lamp but it won't stay up.* [c. 1200] 2. Elevate, raise; also, put in a position of authority or power, as in *They set him up as their leader.* [Late 1300s] 3. Put oneself forward, claim to be, as in *He set himself up as an authority on the banking system.* [Mid-1800s] 4. Assemble, erect, make ready for use, as in *They set up the sound system last night.* [c. 1200] 5. Establish, found, as in *They set up a new charity for the homeless.* [Early 1400s] 6. Establish in business by providing capital or other backing, as in *His father set her up in a new dental practice.* [First half of 1500s] 7. Treat someone to drinks, pay for drinks, as in *Please let us set you up tonight.* [Colloquial; late 1800s] 8. Stimulate or exhilarate, as in *That victory really set up our team.* [c. 1600] 9. Lay plans for, as in *I think they set up the kidnapping months ago.* [First half of 1900s] 10. Prepare someone for a deception or trickery or joke, as in *They set up their victim for the usual real estate scam,* or *Her friends set her up so that she was the only person in costume.* [Mid-1900s] 11. Cause, bring about, as in *The new taxes set up howls of protest.* [Mid-1800s]

set up housekeeping Move in together, as in *Couples today often set up housekeeping long before they marry.* [Mid-1800s]

set upon ♦ See SET ON.

set up shop Open a business, start a profession, as in *Now that you've got your degree, where do you plan to set up shop?* This idiom was first recorded about 1570.

seven ♦ See AT SIXES AND SEVENS; IN SEVENTH HEAVEN.

sew up 1. Complete successfully, as in *Our team has sewn up the championship.* [Colloquial; c. 1900] 2. Gain complete control of, monopolize, as in *Our restaurant hopes to sew up the town's takeout business.* [Colloquial; first half of 1900s]

sex ♦ See FAIR SEX.

shack up 1. Sleep together or live in sexual intimacy without being married. For example, *They had been dating for two months and then decided to* *shack up.* [Slang; first half of 1900s] **2.** Stay or reside with, as in *I'm shacking up with my cousin till I find a place of my own.* [Slang; first half of 1900s]

shades of A reminder of a person or situation in the past. For example, *He really played a fine game for a fifty-year-old—shades of his high school triumphs,* or *They found themselves alone on the beach—shades of their childhood summers together.* [Mid-1800s]

shadow ♦ In addition to the idiom beginning with SHADOW, also see AFRAID OF ONE'S OWN SHADOW; BEYOND A (SHADOW OF A) DOUBT.

shadow of one's self Also, **shadow of one's former or old self.** A person, group, or thing that has become weaker in physical or mental capacities or in power or authority. For example, *After that long battle with the flu, he was just a shadow of his old self,* or *This new administration is but a shadow of itself,* or *The revised constitution is a shadow of its former self.* The use of *shadow* for an emaciated person dates from the late 1500s, and by about 1800 the word began to be used for other kinds of attenuation.

shaggy-dog story A long drawn-out anecdote with an absurd or anticlimactic ending. For example, *At first he had us laughing wildly at his shaggy-dog stories, but after the third or fourth we found them tiresome.* The term alludes to a well-known series of such stories, which involved a talking dog. [c. 1940]

shake ♦ In addition to the idioms beginning with SHAKE, also see ALL SHOOK (SHAKEN) UP; FAIR SHAKE; IN TWO SHAKES; MORE THAN ONE CAN SHAKE A STICK AT; MOVERS AND SHAKERS; NO GREAT SHAKES; QUAKE (SHAKE) IN ONE'S BOOTS.

shake a leg 1. Dance, as in *Whenever there was music he was eager to shake a leg.* [Colloquial; first half of 1800s] **2.** Hurry up, as in *Shake a leg or we'll miss the plane.* [Colloquial; first half of 1800s]

shake a stick at ♦ See MORE THAN ONE CAN SHAKE A STICK AT.

shake down 1. Extort money from, as in *They had quite a racket, shaking down merchants for so-called protection.* [Slang; second half of 1800s] **2.** Make a thorough search of, as in *They shook down all the passengers, looking for drugs.* [Slang; early 1900s] **3.** Subject a new vehicle or machine to a tryout, as in *We'll shake down the new model next week.* **4.** Become acclimated or accustomed, to a new place, job, or the like, as in *Is this your first job? You'll soon shake down.* [Mid-1800s]

shake hands 1. Also, **shake someone's hand.** Clasp another's hand in greeting, farewell, or congratulation or as a sign of friendship or goodwill. For example, *Stop fighting, boys; shake hands and be done with it,* or *You won first prize? Let me shake your hand.* [Early 1500s] **2. shake hands on.** Con-

firm a promise or bargain, as in *We didn't sign a contract; we simply shook hands on our agreement.* [Early 1900s]

shake in one's boots ♦ See QUAKE IN ONE'S BOOTS.

shake off Free oneself or get rid of something or someone, as in *I've had a hard time shaking off this cold,* or *She forged ahead, shaking off all the other runners.* It is also put as **give someone the shake,** as in *We managed to give our pursuers the shake.* The first term dates from the late 1300s; the slangy variant dates from the second half of the 1800s.

shake one's head Express disapproval, dissent, or doubt, as in *That announcement had us shaking our heads in dismay.* This expression, which can be used both literally (for moving one's head from side to side) and figuratively, dates from about 1300.

shaker ♦ See MOVER AND SHAKER.

shake someone's tree Arouse to action or reaction, disturb, as in *He really shook Hollywood's tree.*

shake the dust from one's feet Depart in a hurry, especially from an unpleasant situation; also, leave forever. For example, *I couldn't wait to shake the dust from my feet; I never wanted to see either of them again.* This metaphoric term, alluding to moving one's feet fast enough to shake off dust, appears in several books of the Bible. [c. 1600]

shake up 1. Agitate in order to mix or loosen, as in *This cough medicine needs to be thoroughly shaken up,* or *Please shake up these pillows.* **2.** Upset greatly, as in *Even though no one was hurt, he was greatly shaken up by the accident.* This usage alludes to being agitated like a liquid being shaken. Also see ALL SHOOK UP. [Late 1800s] **3.** Subject to drastic rearrangement or reorganization, as in *New management was bent on shaking up each division.*

shake with laughter Convulse with the humor of something, as in *When asked if he was planning to give away the bride, he shook with laughter at the very thought.* [Early 1700s]

shame ♦ In addition to the idiom beginning with SHAME, also see CRYING SHAME; FOR SHAME; PUT TO SHAME.

shame on you ♦ See under FOR SHAME.

shape ♦ In addition to the idiom beginning with SHAPE, also see BENT OUT OF SHAPE; IN CONDITION (SHAPE); LICK INTO SHAPE; TAKE SHAPE.

shape up 1. Turn out, develop; see TAKE SHAPE. **2.** Improve so as to meet a standard, as in *The coach told the team that they'd better shape up or they'd be at the bottom of the league.* This usage was first recorded in 1938. **3. shape up or ship out** Behave yourself or be forced to leave, as in *The new supervisor told Tom he'd have to shape up or ship out.* This expression originated in the 1940s, during World War II, as a threat that if one didn't behave in an appropriate military manner one would be sent overseas to a combat zone. After the war it was transferred to other situations calling for improved performance.

share ♦ In addition to the idiom beginning with SHARE, also see FAIR SHARE; LION'S SHARE.

share and share alike Mete out or partake of something equally, as in *Mom told the children to share and share alike with their Halloween candy.* This term, first recorded about 1566, alluded to the equal apportioning of spoils and soon was broadened to include equal sharing in the costs of a venture and other undertakings or possessions.

sharp ♦ In addition to the idioms beginning with SHARP, also see KEEP AN EYE (A SHARP LOOKOUT) FOR; LOOK SHARP.

sharp as a tack Also, **sharp as a razor.** Mentally acute. For example, *She's very witty — she's sharp as a tack.* These similes are also used literally to mean "having a keen cutting edge" and have largely replaced the earlier *sharp as a needle* or *thorn.* The first dates from about 1900, the variant from the mid-1800s.

sharp practice Crafty or deceitful dealings, especially in business. For example, *That firm's known for its sharp practice, so I'd rather not deal with them.* This expression, first recorded in 1836, uses *sharp* in the combined sense of "mentally acute" and "cutting."

shave ♦ See CLOSE CALL (SHAVE).

shed blood Also, **spill blood.** Wound or kill someone, especially violently. For example, *It was a bitter fight but fortunately no blood was shed,* or *A great deal of blood has been spilled in this family feud.* Both of these terms allude to causing blood to flow and fall on the ground. The first dates from the 1200s. The variant amplifies the verb *spill,* which from about 1300 to 1600 by itself meant "slay" or "kill"; it was first recorded about 1125.

shed light on Also, **throw light on.** Clarify or explain, as in *I was hoping the professor would shed light on how he arrived at his theory,* or *Can anyone throw some light on where these plants came from?* Originally, from about 1200, these expressions were used literally, in the sense of "illuminate," but they soon were used figuratively as well.

sheep ♦ See BLACK SHEEP; HANGED FOR A SHEEP; SEPARATE THE SHEEP FROM THE GOATS; WOLF IN SHEEP'S CLOTHING.

sheet ♦ See THREE SHEETS TO THE WIND; WHITE AS A SHEET.

shelf ♦ See OFF THE SHELF; ON THE SHELF.

shell ♦ In addition to the idiom beginning with SHELL, also see IN ONE'S SHELL.

shellacking ♦ See TAKE A SHELLACKING.

shell out Pay, hand over, as in *We had to shell out $1,000 for auto repairs.* This expression transfers taking a seed such as a pea or nut out of its pod or shell to taking money out of one's pocket. [Colloquial; c. 1800]

shift for oneself Also, **fend for oneself.** Provide for one's own needs, as in *Don't worry about Anne; she's very good at shifting for herself,* or *The children had to fend for themselves after school.* The first term, using *shift* in the now obsolete sense of "manage," was first recorded about 1513; the variant, using *fend for* in the sense of "look after," was first recorded in 1629.

shilling ♦ See CUT OFF (WITH A SHILLING).

shine ♦ In addition to the idiom beginning with SHINE, also see MAKE HAY WHILE THE SUN SHINES; RAIN OR SHINE; RISE AND SHINE; TAKE A FANCY (SHINE) TO.

shine up to Try to impress or please, be attentive to, as in *George was always shining up to the teacher,* or *Her father warned her about men shining up to her for her money.* [Colloquial; late 1800s]

shingle ♦ See HANG OUT ONE'S SHINGLE.

ship ♦ In addition to the idioms beginning with SHIP, also see DESERT A SINKING SHIP; ENOUGH TO SINK A SHIP; SHAPE UP (OR SHIP OUT); TIGHT SHIP; WHEN ONE'S SHIP COMES IN.

ship of state The nation, as in *We can't help but wonder who will be steering our ship of state a hundred years from now.* This metaphoric expression was first recorded in English in a translation of Niccolò Machiavelli's *The Prince* (1675).

ship out 1. Leave, especially for a distant place, as in *The transport planes carried troops shipping out to the Mediterranean.* Although this usage originally meant "depart by ship," the expression is no longer limited to that mode of travel. [c. 1900] 2. Send, export, especially to a distant place, as in *The factory shipped out many more orders last month.* [Mid-1600s] 3. Quit a job or be fired; see SHAPE UP, def. 3.

ships that pass in the night Individuals who are rarely in the same place at the same time. For example, *Jan works the early shift and Paula the late shift — they're two ships that pass in the night.* This metaphoric expression comes from Henry Wadsworth Longfellow's poem "The Theologian's Tale" (published in *Tales of a Wayside Inn,* 1873).

shirt ♦ See GIVE THE SHIRT OFF ONE'S BACK; HAIR SHIRT; KEEP ONE'S SHIRT ON; LOSE ONE'S SHIRT; STUFFED SHIRT.

shit on Treat with malice or disrespect, as in *I'm tired of all these administrators shitting on me every* *time I want to try something new.* This usage is vulgar slang.

shit or get off the pot ♦ See under FISH OR CUT BAIT.

shit will hit the fan, the Also, **when** or **then the shit hits the fan.** There will be major trouble, often following the disclosure of a piece of information. For example, *When they find out they were firing on their own planes, the shit will hit the fan.* This idiom calls up the graphic image of feces spread by a rapidly revolving electric fan. [Vulgar slang; c. 1930]

shock ♦ See CULTURE SHOCK.

shoe ♦ In addition to the idiom beginning with SHOE, also see COMFORTABLE AS AN OLD SHOE; FILL SOMEONE'S SHOES; GOODY-TWO-SHOES; IF THE SHOE FITS; IN SOMEONE'S SHOES; STEP INTO SOMEONE'S SHOES; WAIT FOR THE OTHER SHOE TO DROP.

shoe is on the other foot, the The circumstances have reversed, the participants have changed places, as in *I was one of his research assistants, subject to his orders, but now that I'm his department head the shoe is on the other foot.* This metaphoric term first appeared in the mid-1800s as *the boot is on the other leg.* Literally wearing the right shoe on the left foot would be quite uncomfortable, and this notion is implied in this idiom, which suggests that changing places is not equally beneficial to both parties.

shoestring ♦ See ON A SHOESTRING.

shook up ♦ See ALL SHOOK UP.

shoot ♦ In addition to the idioms beginning with SHOOT, also see LIKE SHOOTING FISH IN A BARREL; SURE AS SHOOTING; WHOLE BALL OF WAX (SHOOTING MATCH). Also see under SHOT.

shoot down 1. Ruin the aspirations of, disappoint, as in *Bill was hoping Sharon would go out with him, but she shot him down.* 2. Reject, defeat; also, expose as false. For example, *It was the best idea I could come up with, but they unanimously shot it down,* or *It was inevitable that they would shoot down any claim made by the opposing candidate.* This colloquial expression, which alludes to bringing down an aircraft or game bird by shooting, is sometimes intensified as **shoot down in flames,** originally (in World War I) referring to bringing down enemy aircraft but by the late 1950s extended to decisively defeating anyone or anything.

shoot for Strive or aim for, as in *We're shooting for higher production by spring.* This term, alluding to aiming at something with a weapon, has largely replaced the earlier *shoot at,* which dates from the 1400s.

shoot from the hip Speak or act recklessly or impulsively, as in *Steve isn't very tactful; indeed, he's known for shooting from the hip.* This expression

transfers the fast shooting accomplished by drawing a gun from a holster and shooting without raising it to quick speaking or acting. [Slang; mid-1900s] For a similar transfer, see SHOOT OFF ONE'S MOUTH.

shoot off one's mouth Speak indiscreetly; also, brag or boast. For example, *Now don't go shooting off your mouth about it; it's supposed to be a surprise,* or *Terry is always shooting off his mouth about how many languages he speaks.* [Slang; mid-1800s]

shoot one's bolt Also, **shoot one's wad.** Do all within one's power; exhaust one's resources or capabilities. For example, *They were asking for more ideas but Bob had shot his bolt and couldn't come up with any,* or *Don't shoot your wad with that article or you won't have any material for the sequels.* The first expression comes from archery and referred to using up all of one's bolts (short, heavy arrows fired with a crossbow); it was a proverb by the 1200s. The colloquial variant, dating from about 1900, comes from gambling and refers to spending all of a wad of rolled-up banknotes. Also see SHOOT THE WORKS.

shoot oneself in the foot Foolishly harm one's own cause, as in *He really shot himself in the foot, telling the interviewer all about the others who were applying for the job he wanted.* This colloquial term alludes to an accidental shooting as opposed to a deliberate one done so as to avoid military service.

shoot straight Also, **shoot square.** Deal fairly and honestly, as in *You can't trust most car salesmen, but Jim always shoots straight,* or *We always shoot square with our customers.* These colloquial terms use *straight* and *square* in the sense of "straightforward and honest," and *shoot* in the sense of "deal with."

shoot the breeze Also, **shoot** or **throw the bull.** Talk idly, chat, as in *They've been sitting on the porch for hours, just shooting the breeze,* or *The guys sit around the locker room, throwing the bull.* The first of these slangy terms, alluding to talking into the wind, was first recorded in 1919. In the variant, first recorded in 1908, *bull* is a shortening of *bullshit,* and means "empty talk" or "lies."

shoot the works Expend all one's efforts or capital, as in *He's broke after shooting the works on that new office building.* [Colloquial; first half of 1900s] Also see THE WORKS.

shoot up 1. Grow or get taller very rapidly, as in *She's really shot up in the last year, and now she's taller than her mother.* [First half of 1500s] 2. Riddle with bullets; damage or terrorize with gunfire. For example, *I liked the scene in which the cowboy stomps into the saloon, gets drunk, and shoots the place up.* [Late 1800s] 3. Inject a drug intravenously, especially an illegal drug. For example,

The police caught him shooting up and arrested him. [Slang; first half of 1900s]

shop ♦ In addition to the idiom beginning with SHOP, also see BULL IN A CHINA SHOP; CLOSE UP (SHOP); SET UP (SHOP); SHUT UP (SHOP); TALK SHOP.

shop around 1. Look for the best bargain, opportunity, or the like, as in *This job offers only minimum wage so she decided to shop around for one with better pay.* This expression alludes to looking in different stores in search of bargains or a particular item. [c. 1920] 2. Look for a buyer for, offer for sale to various parties, as in *The company is now being actively shopped around.* [Second half of 1900s]

shore up Support, prop, as in *The new law was designed to shore up banks in danger of failure.* This expression derives from the noun *shore*, meaning "prop," a beam or timber propped against a structure to provide support. The verb *shore* dates from 1340 and was first recorded in a figurative context in 1581.

short ♦ In addition to the idioms beginning with SHORT, also see BY THE SHORT HAIRS; CAUGHT SHORT; CUT SHORT; FALL SHORT; FOR SHORT; IN BRIEF (SHORT); IN SHORT ORDER; IN SHORT SUPPLY; IN THE LONG (SHORT) RUN; LIFE IS TOO SHORT; LONG AND SHORT OF IT; LONG (SHORT) HAUL; MAKE A LONG STORY SHORT; MAKE SHORT WORK OF; NOTHING SHORT OF; RUN SHORT; SELL SHORT; STOP SHORT.

short and sweet Satisfyingly brief and pertinent, as in *When we asked about the coming merger, the chairman's answer was short and sweet—it wasn't going to happen.* This expression was already proverbial in 1539, when it appeared in Richard Taverner's translation of Erasmus's *Adagia.* Over the years it was occasionally amplified, as in James Kelly's *Scottish Proverbs* (1721): "Better short and sweet than long and lax."

short end of the stick, the The inferior part, the worse side of an unequal deal. For example, *Helen got the short end of the stick when she was assigned another week of night duty.* The precise analogy in this term, first recorded in the 1930s, has been lost. Some believe it comes from *worse end of the staff,* used since the early 1500s, which in the mid-1800s became, in some instances, *short* or *shitty end of the stick,* allegedly from a stick poked up one's rectum by another in command of the situation. Others believe it alludes to fighting with sticks, where having a shorter stick is a disadvantage. Also see WRONG END OF THE STICK.

short for ♦ See FOR SHORT.

short haul ♦ See under LONG HAUL.

short notice, on Also, **at short notice.** With little advance warning or time to prepare, as in *They told us to be ready to move out on short notice.* The noun *notice* here is used in the sense of "information" or "intelligence." [Late 1700s]

short of 1. Having an inadequate supply of, as in *We're short of cash right now.* [Late 1600s] Also see FALL SHORT OF. 2. Less than, inferior to, as in *Nothing short of her best effort was needed to make the team.* [Mid-1500s] 3. Other than, without resorting to, as in *Short of yelling, I had no other way of getting his attention.* 4. See STOP SHORT, def. 3.

short order 1. Quickly; see IN SHORT ORDER. 2. An order of food to be prepared and served quickly, as in *It's just a diner, serving short orders exclusively.* This expression, dating from about 1890, gave rise to the adjective **short-order,** used not only in **short-order cook,** a cook specializing in short orders, but in other terms such as **short-order divorce,** a divorce quickly obtained owing to liberal divorce laws.

short run ♦ See under LONG RUN.

short shrift, give Also, **get short shrift.** Give (or receive) cursory attention or little time. For example, *The architect made elaborate plans for the entry but gave short shrift to the back of the house.* Literally, *shrift* refers to confession to a priest, who gives absolution and penance, and *short shrift* to the brief time allowed for this sacrament to a prisoner before execution. Shakespeare so used it in *Richard III* (3:4), but it came to be used more loosely in succeeding centuries. [Late 1800s]

shot ♦ In addition to the idioms beginning with SHOT, also see BIG CHEESE (SHOT); CALL THE SHOTS; CHEAP SHOT; GIVE IT ONE'S BEST SHOT; HAVE A CRACK (SHOT) AT; LIKE A SHOT; LONG SHOT; PARTING SHOT. Also see under SHOOT.

shotgun ♦ In addition to the idiom beginning with SHOTGUN, also see RIDE SHOTGUN.

shotgun wedding An agreement or compromise made through necessity, as in *Since neither side won a majority, the coalition government was obviously a shotgun wedding.* This expression alludes to a marriage precipitated by a woman's pregnancy, causing her father to point a literal or figurative gun at the responsible man's head. Its figurative use dates from the mid-1900s.

shot in the arm, a A stimulus or booster, something vitalizing or encouraging, as in *Getting a new concertmaster was a real shot in the arm for the orchestra.* This colloquial expression alludes to a stimulant given by injection. [c. 1920]

shot in the dark A wild, unsubstantiated guess; also, an attempt that has little chance for success. For example, *It was a shot in the dark, but the engineers had a hunch that replacing the value would make the system work,* or *You can try looking for your key on the beach, but I think it's a shot in the dark.* [Colloquial; late 1800s]

shot to hell Worn out, ruined, as in *This carpet is shot to hell,* or *My privacy's been shot to hell, what* *with all these reporters.* This term alludes to being shot by gunfire. [Slang; late 1800s]

shot up 1. Severely wounded by gunfire; see SHOOT UP, def. 2. 2. Drugged; see SHOOT UP, def. 3.

should ◆ In addition to the idiom beginning with SHOULD, also see (SHOULD) GET ONE'S HEAD EXAMINED.

shoulder ◆ In addition to the idiom beginning with SHOULDER, also see BROAD SHOULDERS; CHIP ON ONE'S SHOULDER; COLD SHOULDER; CRY ON SOMEONE'S SHOULDER; GOOD HEAD ON ONE'S SHOULDERS; HEAD AND SHOULDERS ABOVE; ON ONE'S SHOULDERS; PUT ONE'S SHOULDER TO THE WHEEL; RUB ELBOWS (SHOULDERS) WITH; SHRUG ONE'S SHOULDERS; SQUARE ONE'S SHOULDERS; STRAIGHT FROM THE SHOULDER; WEIGHT OF THE WORLD ON ONE'S SHOULDERS.

shoulder to shoulder In close proximity or co-operation, as in *The volunteers worked shoulder to shoulder in the effort to rescue the miners.* This expression originated in the late 1500s in the military, at first signifying troops in close formation. Its figurative use dates from the late 1800s.

should have stood in bed, I I've had such a bad day that I should never have gotten up at all. For example, *And then I got rear-ended at the stop sign—I should have stood in bed.* This ungrammatical colloquial phrase—properly put as *stayed in bed*—is ascribed to fight manager Joe Jacobs, who in 1935 saw his first baseball game, the opening game of the World Series between the Detroit Tigers and Chicago Cubs. It was a very cold day, and when asked what he thought of baseball, Jacobs replied, "I should have stood in bed."

shout ◆ In addition to the idioms beginning with SHOUT, also see ALL OVER BUT THE SHOUTING.

shout down Overwhelm or silence by yelling or jeering, as in *The audience went wild and shouted down the speaker.* [c. 1920]

shout from the rooftops Announce publicly, as in *Just because I won first prize you needn't shout it from the rooftops.* This term alludes to climbing on a roof so as to be heard by more people. A similar phrase, using *housetops*, appears in the New Testament (Luke 12:3): "That which ye have spoken . . . shall be proclaimed upon the housetops." [c. 1600]

shove ◆ See PUSH COMES TO SHOVE; PUSH (SHOVE) OFF; RAM (SHOVE) DOWN SOMEONE'S THROAT; STICK (SHOVE) IT.

show ◆ In addition to the idioms beginning with SHOW, also see BARE (SHOW) ONE'S TEETH; DOG-AND-PONY SHOW; FALSE COLORS, SHOW; FOR SHOW; GET THE SHOW ON THE ROAD; GO TO SHOW; KNOW (SHOW) THE ROPES; ONE-MAN SHOW; ROAD SHOW; RUN THE SHOW; STEAL THE SHOW; (SHOW ONE'S) TRUE COLORS.

show and tell A public presentation or display, as in *It was a terrible bore, what with their show and tell of every last detail about their trip around the world.* This expression originated in the 1940s to describe a learning exercise for young children, in which each child in a group brings some object to show the others and talks about it.

shower ◆ See COLD SHOWER.

show must go on, the The proceedings must continue, no matter what unfortunate event has occurred, as in *The chairman died yesterday but the show must go on.* This expression is a theatrical credo dating from the 1800s and was transferred to other situations in the first half of the 1900s.

show off Display in an ostentatious, conspicuous way; also, seek attention by displaying one's accomplishments, abilities, or possessions. For example, *I'm wearing shorts to show off my Florida tan,* or *Karen loved showing off her new baby to her friends,* or *There's no need to show off, Fred; we all know you're a good dancer.* [Early 1800s]

show of hands An informal vote made by participants holding up one hand each to indicate a choice, as in *Let's have a show of hands—how many want the next meeting on a Sunday?* [Late 1700s]

show one's colors ◆ See under FALSE COLORS; also SHOW ONE'S TRUE COLORS.

show one's face Appear, as in *She was so upset that we were sure she'd never show her face at the theater again.* This idiom has appeared in slightly different forms, such as *show one's neck* or *visage* or *nose,* since about 1225.

show one's hand Reveal one's plans, intentions, or resources, especially when they were previously hidden. For example, *We have to be careful not to show our hand to our competitors.* The *hand* here refers to a hand of cards, and showing them means turning them face up. [Late 1800s]

show one's heels Also, **show a clean pair of heels.** Run away, flee, as in *He wanted to ask her out but she showed her heels before he had a chance,* or *As soon as the burglar alarm went off, the housebreaker showed a clean pair of heels.* The backs of one's heels are exactly what is seen when one is running away, but the allusion of *clean* is a bit puzzling, unless it is meant in the colloquial sense of "thorough," as in a *clean getaway.* [First half of 1500s]

show one's teeth ◆ See BARE ONE'S TEETH.

show one's true colors Reveal oneself as one really is, as in *We always thought he was completely honest, but he showed his true colors when he tried to use a stolen credit card.* This expression alludes to the antonym, FALSE COLORS, that is, sailing under a flag other than one's own. [Late 1700s]

show signs of Exhibit indications or hints of, as in *She definitely shows signs of accepting the appointment,* or *Terry's health shows no signs of improvement.* [Late 1400s]

show someone a good time Entertain someone, as in *I know Aunt Dorothy will show us a good time when we visit San Francisco.* This idiom uses the verb *show* in the sense of "accord or grant something," a usage dating from about 1200.

show someone out Also, **show someone to the door.** Escort someone who is leaving to the exit door, as in *Thanks for coming; please excuse me for not showing you out,* or *Please show Mr. Smith to the door.* [Second half of 1700s] Also see SEE OUT, def. 1; SHOW SOMEONE THE DOOR.

show someone the door Order someone to leave, as in *I never should have listened to him; I should have shown him the door at once.* This expression, first recorded in 1778, is not the same as **show someone to the door** (see under SHOW SOMEONE OUT).

show someone the ropes ◆ See under KNOW THE ROPES.

show the way Guide, as in *This division has shown the way to bigger profits.* This expression transfers the physical sense of guiding one in a particular direction. [Early 1500s] Also see LEAD THE WAY.

show the white feather Display cowardice, as in *The minute Bob put up his fists, Bill showed the white feather and backed down.* This expression comes from cockfighting, where a white feather in a bird's tail is considered a sign of inferior breeding. [Early 1800s]

show to advantage Also, **show to good** or **one's advantage.** Display in a flattering way, benefit, as in *This lighting shows the paintings to advantage,* or *Your extensive use of quotations shows your learning to good advantage.* [Mid-1300s]

show up 1. Be clearly visible, as in *The print doesn't show up against this dark background.* [Late 1800s] 2. Put in an appearance, arrive, as in *I wonder if he'll show up at all.* [Late 1800s] 3. Expose or reveal the true character of, as in *This failure showed up their efforts as a waste of time.* [Early 1800s] 4. Also, **show someone up.** Surpass someone in ability, outdo someone, as in *John's high score on that math test really showed up the rest of the class.* [Colloquial; first half of 1900s]

shrift ◆ See SHORT SHRIFT.

shrinking violet, a An extremely shy person, as in *She was a shrinking violet until she went away to college.* This metaphoric idiom refers to the flower, but the precise allusion is unclear, since violets thrive under a variety of conditions and often are considered a garden weed. [Early 1900s]

shrug off 1. Minimize the importance of, as in *That nasty review didn't bother him at all; he just shrugged it off.* [Early 1900s] 2. Get rid of, as in *She managed to shrug off her drowsiness and keep driving.* [Mid-1900s] 3. Wriggle out of a garment, as in *He shrugged off his coat.* [First half of 1900s]

shrug one's shoulders Show indecision or indifference, as in *When I asked her if she minded staying home, she just shrugged her shoulders.* This redundant idiom—*shrug* means "to raise and contract the shoulders"—dates from about 1450.

shuffle off 1. Get rid of, act evasively, as in *They've tried to shuffle off public inquiries about the safety of their planes.* This usage, dating from about 1600, also appears in the oft-quoted **shuffle off this mortal coil,** from Shakespeare's *Hamlet* (3:1), where it means "become freed from the turmoil of life," that is, "die." 2. Move away reluctantly, dragging one's feet, as in *The prisoners shuffled off to their work detail.* [Late 1500s]

shut ◆ In addition to the idioms beginning with SHUT, also see CLOSE (SHUT) DOWN; CLOSE (SHUT) ONE'S EYES TO; CLOSE (SHUT) THE DOOR ON; KEEP ONE'S MOUTH SHUT; OPEN AND SHUT CASE; PUT UP OR SHUT UP.

shut down 1. See CLOSE DOWN, def. 1. 2. Stop or switch off machinery, as in *They shut down all the machines for one week a year.* [Late 1800s]

shut off 1. Stop the flow or passage of, as in *They shut off the water while repairs were being made.* [Early 1800s] 2. Close off, isolate, as in *Loners shut themselves off from the community.* [First half of 1800s]

shut one's eyes to ◆ See CLOSE ONE'S EYES TO.

shut out 1. Exclude, deny entry to, block, as in *Anyone convicted of a crime is shut out from the legal profession,* or *These curtains shut out all the light.* [Late 1300s] 2. Prevent an opponent from scoring, as in *They were shut out of the last two games,* or *Reagan shut out Ford in the Texas primary in 1976.* Originating in baseball about 1880, this usage was later transferred to other sports and then even broader usage.

shut the door ◆ See CLOSE THE DOOR.

shut up 1. Imprison, confine, enclose, as in *The dog was shut up in the cellar for the night,* or *She shut up her memories and never talked about the past.* [c. 1400] 2. Close completely, as in *The windows were shut up tightly so no rain came in.* [Early 1500s] This usage also occurs in **shut up shop,** meaning "close the premises of a business," as in *It's late, let's shut up shop now.* [Late 1500s] Also see CLOSE UP, def. 3. 3. Cause someone to stop speaking, silence someone, as in *It's time someone* *shut him up.* [Early 1800s] **4.** Stop speaking, as in *I've told you what I think and now I'll shut up.* This usage also occurs as a rather rude imperative, as in *Shut up! You've said enough.* [First half of 1800s]

shy ♦ In addition to the idiom beginning with SHY, also see BRICKS SHY OF A LOAD; FIGHT SHY OF; ONCE BITTEN, TWICE SHY.

shy away from Avoid, evade, as in *He shied away from all questions concerning his private life.* [Late 1700s]

sick ♦ In addition to the idiom beginning with SICK, also see CALL IN SICK; GET SICK; MAKE ONE SICK; WORRIED SICK.

sick and tired Also, **sick** or **tired to death.** Thoroughly weary or bored, as in *I'm sick and tired of these begging phone calls,* or *She was sick to death of that endless recorded music.* These hyperbolic expressions of exasperation imply one is weary to the point of illness or death. The first dates from the late 1700s, the first variant from the late 1800s, and the second variant from the first half of the 1700s.

sick as a dog Very ill, especially from a stomach malady. For example, *I don't know what was in that stew but I was sick as a dog all night.* This simile was first recorded in 1705. Why a dog should be viewed as particularly sick remains unclear.

sick at heart Grieving, very disappointed, dejected, as in *We were sick at heart when we learned of her predicament.* This idiom, which transfers heart disease to unhappiness, was first recorded in 1581.

sick in bed ♦ See LAID UP, def. 1.

sick joke An anecdote intended to be humorous but actually in very bad taste, as in *His stories turn out to be sick jokes about people who are handicapped in some way.* [Colloquial; mid-1900s]

sick to one's stomach Also, **sick at one's stomach.** Nauseated, vomiting, as in *I always get sick to my stomach in the back seat of a car.* [Mid-1600s]

sic transit gloria mundi Nothing on earth is permanent, as in *His first three novels were bestsellers and now he can't even find an agent—sic transit gloria mundi.* This expression, Latin for "Thus passes the glory of the world," has been used in English since about 1600, and is familiar enough so that it is sometimes abbreviated to **sic transit.**

side ♦ In addition to the idioms beginning with SIDE, also see BLIND SPOT (SIDE); BRIGHT SIDE; CAN'T HIT THE BROAD SIDE OF A BARN; CHOOSE UP (SIDES); GET ON SOMEONE'S GOOD SIDE; GET UP ON THE WRONG SIDE OF BED; IN GOOD WITH (ON SOMEONE'S GOOD SIDE); KNOW WHICH SIDE OF BREAD IS BUTTERED; LAUGH OUT OF THE OTHER SIDE OF ONE'S MOUTH; LET SOMEONE (THE SIDE) DOWN; ON SOMEONE'S SIDE; ON THE SAFE SIDE; ON THE SIDE; ON THE SIDE OF THE ANGELS; OTHER SIDE OF THE COIN; RIGHT SIDE OF THE TRACKS; RIGHT-SIDE OUT; RIGHT-SIDE UP; SEAMY SIDE; SPLIT ONE'S SIDES; SUNNY SIDE UP; TAKE ASIDE (TO ONE SIDE); TAKE SIDES; THIS SIDE OF; THORN IN ONE'S FLESH (SIDE); WORK BOTH SIDES OF THE STREET; WRONG SIDE OF.

side against Refuse to support, oppose in a dispute, as in *The older club members sided against the new program director and her strenuous exercise programs.* [First half of 1700s] For the antonym, see SIDE WITH.

side by side Next to each other, close together, as in *They were walking down the street side by side when the taxi jumped the curb,* or *In the new Russia communism and capitalism are trying to live side by side.* [c. 1200]

sidelines ♦ See ON THE SIDELINES.

side of the tracks ♦ See under RIGHT SIDE OF THE TRACKS.

side street A minor thoroughfare that carries little traffic, as in *Our favorite hotel is on a quiet little side street.* The *side* in this idiom means "off to one side, away from the main street." [c. 1600] Also see BACK STREET.

sideways ♦ See KNOCK FOR A LOOP (SIDEWAYS); LOOK SIDEWAYS AT.

side with Support or favor, as in *The Armenians traditionally side with the Greeks against the Turks.* This idiom was first recorded in 1600. For the antonym, see SIDE AGAINST.

sight ♦ In addition to the idioms beginning with SIGHT, also see AT FIRST BLUSH (SIGHT); AT SIGHT; CAN'T STAND THE SIGHT OF; CATCH SIGHT OF; HEAVE INTO SIGHT; IN SIGHT; KNOW BY SIGHT; LOSE SIGHT OF; LOVE AT FIRST SIGHT; LOWER ONE'S SIGHTS; ON SIGHT; OUT OF SIGHT; RAISE ONE'S SIGHTS; SECOND SIGHT; SEE THE SIGHTS; SET ONE'S SIGHTS ON; TWENTY-TWENTY HINDSIGHT.

sight for sore eyes, a One whom it is a relief or joy to see, as in *Linda, who had not seen him in 15 years, told him he was a sight for sore eyes.* This idiom implies an appearance so welcome that it heals ailing eyes. [First half of 1700s]

sight unseen Without having viewed the object in question, as in *He bought the horse sight unseen.* This seeming oxymoron—how can a *sight,* which means something seen, be not seen?—dates from the late 1800s.

sign ♦ In addition to the idioms beginning with SIGN, see HIGH SIGN; SHOW SIGNS OF.

signed, sealed, and delivered Completed satisfactorily, as in *The house is sold—signed, sealed, and delivered.* This idiom refers to a legal deed, which to be valid had to be signed by the seller, sealed with a wax seal, and delivered to the new owner. It began to be used more loosely in the first half of the 1900s.

sign in Record one's arrival by signing a register, as in *He signed in both himself and his wife.* [c. 1930] For the antonym, see SIGN OUT.

sign off 1. Announce the end of a communication, especially a broadcast. For example, *There's no one there now; the station has signed off for the night.* [c. 1920] 2. Stop talking, become silent, as in *Every time the subject of marriage came up, Harold signed off.* [Colloquial; mid-1900s] 3. Express approval formally or conclusively, as in *The President got the majority leader to sign off on the tax proposal.* This usage is colloquial.

sign on 1. Enlist oneself as an employee, as in *Arthur decided to sign on with the new software company.* [Late 1800s] 2. Begin radio or television broadcasting, especially at the beginning of the day, as in *What time does the station sign on?* [c. 1920]

sign one's own death warrant Bring about one's own downfall, do oneself irreparable harm, as in *In taking his secretary to a risqué nightclub, the parish priest was signing his own death warrant.* This expression may refer to acts that ensure someone's later murder, as when, in 1921, the Irish revolutionary leader Michael Collins signed the peace treaty he had negotiated with England and said, "I tell you, I have signed my death warrant." Thirteen months later Collins was assassinated by political opponents. The expression is also used hyperbolically, however, for severe repercussions or punishments. [First half of 1900s] Also see SHOOT ONESELF IN THE FOOT.

sign on the dotted line Agree formally or fully, as in *The deal is just about fixed; all they have to do is sign on the dotted line.* This idiom refers to the broken line traditionally appearing at the bottom of a legal document, indicating the place for one's signature. [Early 1900s]

sign out Record the departure of a person or the removal of an object, as in *He turned in his room key and signed out about an hour ago,* or *I asked the librarian how many books I could sign out.* [c. 1930]

sign over Legally dispose of or make over to a different owner, as in *She signed over nearly all of her property to the church.* [Early 1700s]

sign up Enlist in an organization; also, register or subscribe to something. For example, *He signed up for four years in the navy,* or *Are you planning to sign up for that pottery class?* [Early 1900s]

silence is golden Keeping one's mouth shut is a great virtue, as in *Don't tell anyone else about it—silence is golden.* Although this precise phrase was first recorded only in 1848, it is part of a much older proverb, "Speech is silver and silence is golden."

silent majority A group that makes up a majority of voters but does not widely express its views through marches or demonstrations. For example, *They thought they had a convincing case, but they hadn't counted on the silent majority.* This idiom was first recorded in 1874 but gained currency in the 1960s, when President Richard Nixon claimed that his policies were supported by a majority of citizens who did not bother to make their views known.

silk ♦ See CAN'T MAKE A SILK PURSE OUT OF A SOW'S EAR; SMOOTH AS SILK.

silver ♦ In addition to the idiom beginning with SILVER, also see BORN WITH A SILVER SPOON; CROSS SOMEONE'S PALM WITH SILVER; HAND TO ON A SILVER PLATTER.

silver lining An element of hope or a redeeming quality in an otherwise bad situation, as in *The rally had a disappointing turnout, but the silver lining was that those who came pledged a great deal of money.* This metaphoric term is a shortening of **Every cloud has a silver lining**, in turn derived from John Milton's *Comus* (1634): "A sable cloud turns forth its silver lining on the night."

simmer down Become calm after anger or excitement, as in *Simmer down, Mary; I'm sure he'll make it up to you,* or *I haven't time to look at your report now, but I will when things have simmered down a bit.* This idiom derives from *simmer* in the sense of "cook at low heat, below the boiling point." [Second half of 1800s]

simon pure Absolutely genuine, quite authentic, as in *That laboratory test was simon pure; none of the specimens was adulterared.* This expression comes from the name of a character in a play, Susannah Centilivre's *A Bold Stroke for a Wife* (1717), who is the victim of an impersonation but turns up in the end and proves that he is "the real Simon Pure."

simple ♦ See PURE AND SIMPLE.

sin ♦ See LIVE IN SIN; MORE SINNED AGAINST THAN SINNING; MULTITUDE OF SINS; UGLY AS SIN; WAGES OF SIN.

since ♦ See GREATEST THING SINCE SLICED BREAD.

sine qua non An essential element or condition, as in *A perfect cake is the sine qua non of a birthday party.* This phrase is Latin for "without which not" and has been used in English since about 1600. It appears more in writing than in speech.

sing a different tune Also, **sing another tune.** ♦ See CHANGE ONE'S TUNE.

sing for one's supper Work for one's pay or reward, as in *Entertaining visiting scientists is part of the job; you know I have to sing for my supper:* This metaphoric term alludes to wandering minstrels who performed in taverns and were paid with a meal. First recorded in 1609, it gained currency with the familiar nursery rhyme, "Little Tommy Tucker, sings for his supper" (c. 1744).

single ♦ In addition to the idioms beginning with SINGLE, also see EACH AND EVERY (EVERY SINGLE).

single file, in Also, **in Indian file.** Aligned one behind the other, as in *We have to bike in single file here*, or *The children were told to march in Indian file.* Both usages are associated with military formations; the first term was first recorded in 1670; the variant, alluding to the usual marching order of Native Americans, was first recorded in 1758.

single out Choose or distinguish from others, as in *We singled him out from all the other applicants.* This idiom was first recorded in 1629.

sing out Call out loudly, shout, as in *One of them fell in the stream and sang out for help.* [Early 1800s]

sing someone's praises Commend someone, especially to others, as in *They were singing her praises to the entire community.* [Mid-1500s] Also see PRAISE TO THE SKIES.

sink ♦ In addition to the idioms beginning with SINK, also see DESERT A SINKING SHIP; ENOUGH TO SINK A SHIP; EVERYTHING BUT THE KITCHEN SINK; HEART SINKS.

sinker ♦ See HOOK, LINE, AND SINKER.

sink in Penetrate the mind, be absorbed, as in *The news of the crash didn't sink in right away.* [Late 1300s]

sinking feeling, a A sense of dread or apprehension, as in *I had a sinking feeling that I'd forgotten my ticket.* This expression employs *sink* in the sense of "become depressed," a usage dating from the early 1600s.

sink one's teeth into Also, **get one's teeth into.** Become fully engaged in, as in *He couldn't wait to sink his teeth into that problem.* This metaphoric expression alludes to an animal biting vigorously into its prey. [Early 1900s]

sink or swim Succumb or succeed, no matter what, as in *Now that we've bought the farm, we'll have to make a go of it, sink or swim.* This expression alludes to the former barbaric practice of throwing a suspected witch into deep water, often weighted down. In case of sinking, the victim died; in case of swimming, the victim was considered in league with the devil and therefore was executed. A related idiom, **float or sink,** was used by Chaucer in the late 1300s; Shakespeare had the current form in *1 Henry IV* (1:3): "Or sink or swim."

sink through the floor Suffer extreme embarrassment, as in *When she called our name on the list of those who owed dues, I sank through the floor.* This hyperbolic term dates from the early 1900s.

sit ♦ In addition to the idioms beginning with SIT, also see AT A SITTING.

sit at one's feet ♦ See AT ONE'S FEET.

sit back 1. Relax, as in *Now that the work's finished, we can just sit back.* 2. Refrain from interfering or taking part, as in *Mom and Dad just sat back and watched Meg try to decide whether or not she should tell on her friends.* [Mid-1900s] Also see SIT BY.

sit bolt upright ♦ See BOLT UPRIGHT.

sit by Also, **sit idly by.** Refrain from interfering, remain passive, as in *I can't just sit by and let her get in trouble.*

sit down 1. Take a seat, as in *Won't you sit down? I won't be long.* [c. 1200] 2. **sit down to.** Prepare to eat a meal, as in *At six we all sat down to dinner.* [Late 1500s]

sit in 1. Attend or take part as a visitor, as in *My son's jazz group asked me to sit in tonight.* It is often put as **sit in on,** as in *They asked me to sit in on their poker game.* [Mid-1800s] 2. Take part in a sit-in, that is, an organized protest in which seated participants refuse to move. For example, *The students threatened to sit in unless the dean was reinstated.* [c. 1940] 3. **sit in on.** Visit or observe, as in *I'm sitting in on his class, but not for credit.* [Early 1900s] 4. **sit in for.** Substitute for a regular member of a group, as in *I'm just sitting in for Harold, who couldn't make it.*

sit on Also, **sit upon.** 1. Confer about or deliberate over, as in *Another attorney was called to sit on the case.* [Mid-1400s] 2. Suppress or repress, as in *I know they were sitting on some evidence.* [Early 1900s] 3. Postpone action or resolution regarding, as in *I don't know why the city council is sitting on their decision.* [Early 1900s] 4. Rebuke sharply, reprimand, as in *If he interrupts one more time I'm going to sit on him.* [Slang; second half of 1800s]

sit on one's hands Take no action; also, fail to applaud. For example, *Instead of making a new will, George is sitting on his hands*, or *The matinee audience was apathetic, sitting on their hands for the whole performance.* Both usages of this metaphor for passivity date from the first half of the 1900s.

sit out 1. Also, **sit through.** Stay until the end of, as in *We decided to sit out the lecture instead of leaving early*, or *He was only eight when he sat through an entire opera—and it lasted nearly five hours.* [Early 1700s] 2. Refrain from taking part in, as in *Jane's foot hurt so she sat out the last three dances.* [Mid-1600s] 3. Outlast, outstay, as in *He sat out all the other guests, hoping to get a word alone with the host.* [Mid-1700s]

sit pretty ♦ See SITTING PRETTY.

sit through ♦ See SIT OUT, def. 1.

sit tight Be patient, take no action, as in *If you just sit tight I'm sure your passport will be returned to you.* [Colloquial; first half of 1700s]

sitting duck An easy target, as in *If you park in front of a fire hydrant, you're a sitting duck for a ticket.* This term alludes to the ease with which a hunter can shoot a duck that remains in one spot, in contrast to one in flight. [First half of 1900s]

sitting on a powder keg In imminent danger, in an explosive situation, as in *Our office is sitting on a powder keg while management decides whether or not to close us down.* This metaphoric term alludes to sitting on a keg of gunpowder that could go off at any moment. [First half of 1900s]

sitting pretty In an advantageous position; also, financially well off. For example, *The terms of the will left Mary sitting pretty.* Although the use of *pretty* in the sense of "advantageous" is much older, this colloquialism dates only from the early 1900s. It was given extra currency as the title of two different musicals, *Sittin' Pretty* (M. Moore, 1921) and *Sitting Pretty* (G. Bolton and P.G. Wodehouse, 1924).

situation ♦ See NO-WIN SITUATION.

sit up **1.** Rise to a sitting position from lying down, as in *The sick child sat up and asked for a drink of water.* [Early 1200s] **2.** Stay up later than usual, as in *The nurse sat up with her all night long.* [Mid-1500s] **3.** Sit with the spine erect, as in *She was always telling the students to sit up.* [Early 1700s] **4.** Become suddenly alert, as in *The students sat up when he brought up the test.* The same sense appears in the related **sit up and take notice,** as in *When he mentioned the arrival of a movie star, they all sat up and took notice.* [Late 1800s]

sit well with Please, fit or suit, be acceptable to, as in *I don't think that explanation sits well with the headmaster,* or *His sense of humor does not sit well with this elderly audience.* [Early 1700s]

six ♦ In addition to the idioms beginning with SIX, also see AT SIXES AND SEVENS; DEEP SIX; JOE SIX-PACK.

six feet under Dead and buried, as in *No, you can't read my diary—not until I'm six feet under.* Although this expression alludes to what has long been the traditional depth of a grave, that is, approximately the same as the length of the coffin, it dates only from the mid-1900s.

six of one, half a dozen of the other The two alternatives are the same, as in *Either Route 2 or Long Avenue will get you there—it's six of one, half a dozen of the other.* This term simply equates two different ways of saying "six." [First half of 1800s]

sixth sense Keen intuition, as in *She had a sixth sense that they would find it in the cellar.* This term alludes to a sense in addition to the five physical senses of sight, hearing, smell, taste, and touch. [c. 1800]

size ♦ In addition to the idiom beginning with SIZE, also see CUT DOWN (TO SIZE); PICK ON (SOMEONE YOUR OWN SIZE); TAKE DOWN A NOTCH (TO SIZE); THAT'S ABOUT THE SIZE OF IT; TRY ON (FOR SIZE).

size up Make an estimate, opinion, or judgment of, as in *She sized up her opponent and decided to withdraw from the election.* This usage transfers measuring the size of something to broader meaning. [Late 1800s]

skate ♦ In addition to the idiom beginning with SKATE, also see CHEAP SKATE; ON THIN ICE, SKATE.

skate over Treat superficially or hurriedly, avoid mentioning, as in *He concentrated on the main points of the contract and skated over the details.* This idiom transfers the gliding motion of skating to dealing with something in a cursory way. [Mid-1900s]

skeleton in the closet A shameful secret, as in *Both her parents were alcoholics; that was the skeleton in her closet.* This metaphoric term alludes to a murder victim long concealed in a closet, possibly based on some true incident that is now forgotten. [Early 1800s]

skid ♦ In addition to the idiom beginning with SKID, also see ON THE SKIDS; PUT THE SKIDS ON; PUT THE SKIDS UNDER.

skid row A squalid district inhabited by derelicts and vagrants; also, a life of impoverished dissipation. For example, *That part of town is our skid row,* or *His drinking was getting so bad we thought he was headed for skid row.* This expression originated in the lumber industry, where it signified a road or track made of logs laid crosswise over which logs were slid. Around 1900 the name *Skid Road* was used for the part of a town frequented by loggers, which had many bars and brothels, and by the 1930s the variant *skid row,* with its current meaning, came into use.

skin ♦ In addition to the idioms beginning with SKIN, also see BEAUTY IS ONLY SKIN DEEP; BY THE SKIN OF ONE'S TEETH; GET UNDER SOMEONE'S SKIN; JUMP OUT OF ONE'S SKIN; MAKE ONE'S FLESH CREEP (SKIN CRAWL); MORE THAN ONE WAY TO SKIN A CAT; NO SKIN OFF ONE'S NOSE; SAVE ONE'S BACON (SKIN); SOAKED TO THE SKIN; THICK SKIN.

skin alive Punish severely, as in *If I find the guy who slashed my tire I'll skin him alive.* This hyperbolic expression transfers the barbaric practice of flaying a live prisoner to other forms of punishment. [Colloquial; mid-1800s]

skin and bones Painfully thin, emaciated. This phrase often is expanded to **nothing but skin and**

bones, as in *She came home from her trip nothing but skin and bones.* This hyperbolic expression — one could hardly be alive without some flesh — dates from the early 1400s.

skin deep ♦ See BEAUTY IS ONLY SKIN DEEP.

skin off one's nose ♦ See NO SKIN OFF ONE'S NOSE.

skin of one's teeth ♦ See BY THE SKIN OF ONE'S TEETH.

skip ♦ In addition to the idioms beginning with SKIP, also see HEART MISSES (SKIPS) A BEAT; HOP, SKIP, AND A JUMP.

skip bail Also, **jump bail.** Fail to appear in court for trial and thereby give up the bail bond (paid to secure one's appearance). For example, *I can't afford to skip bail—I'd lose half a million,* or *We were sure he'd jump bail but he finally showed up.* This idiom uses *skip* and *jump* in the sense of "evade." The first dates from about 1900, the variant from the mid-1800s. Also see MAKE BAIL.

skip it Drop the subject, ignore the matter, as in *I don't understand what you mean. — Oh, skip it for now.* This interjection uses *skip* in the sense of "pass over." [Colloquial; c. 1930]

skip out Leave hastily, abscond, as in *They just skipped out of town.* It is also put as **skip out on,** meaning "desert, abandon" as in *He skipped out on his wife, leaving her with the four children.* [Colloquial; second half of 1800s]

sky ♦ In addition to the idiom beginning with SKY, also see BLOW SKY-HIGH; OUT OF A CLEAR BLUE SKY; PIE IN THE SKY; REACH FOR THE SKY.

sky's the limit, the There is no limit (to ambition, aspirations, expense, or the like). For example, *Order anything you like on the menu — the sky's the limit tonight,* or *He's so brilliant he can do anything — the sky's the limit.* This metaphoric idiom was first recorded in 1920.

slack off Decrease in activity or intensity, as in *If business ever slacks off we can go on vacation,* or *When the project fell behind schedule again, she thought we were slacking off.* [Second half of 1800s]

slam dunk A forceful, dramatic move, as in *That indictment was a slam dunk if ever there was one.* This expression is also often put as a verb, **slam-dunk,** meaning "make a forceful move against someone," as in *This is a great chance for us to slam-dunk the opposition.* The idiom comes from basketball, where it refers to a dramatic shot in which the ball is thrust into the basket from above the rim. It was transferred to other activities from about 1980 on.

slap down Restrain or correct emphatically, as in *They thought he was getting far too arrogant and needed to be slapped down.* This idiom, which literally means "inflict a physical blow," began to be used figuratively in the first half of the 1900s.

slap in the face A sharp rebuke or rebuff, as in *Being criticized in front of my staff was a real slap in the face,* or *We thought it quite a slap in the face when they returned our letter unopened.* The figurative use of this term, which can also refer to a literal blow, dates from the late 1800s.

slap on the back A gesture of congratulation, as in *The coach gave him a slap on the back for coming in first.* [Early 1800s]

slap on the wrist A mild reproof, as in *We were fined heavily, and all she got from the judge was a slap on the wrist.* [Early 1900s]

slate ♦ In addition to the idiom beginning with SLATE, also see CLEAN SLATE.

slated for, be Be planned or scheduled, as in *The history test is slated for Thursday,* or *He's slated for a second round of auditions.* [Late 1800s]

slaughter ♦ See LIKE A LAMB TO THE SLAUGHTER.

sleaze factor The element in a political party, administration, or other organization that is corrupt, controversial, or tainted by scandal. For example, *I can't see myself making a campaign contribution to them — there's too much of a sleaze factor.* This slangy expression derives from the adjective *sleazy,* which means "vulgar" or "tawdry." The idiom was first used in politics in the 1980s.

sledding ♦ See EASY SLEDDING; TOUGH SLEDDING.

sleep ♦ In addition to the idioms beginning with SLEEP, also see LET SLEEPING DOGS LIE; LOSE SLEEP OVER; PUT TO SLEEP. Also see under ASLEEP.

sleep around Engage in sex promiscuously, as in *Fortunately, no one mentioned that both of them had slept around in their younger days.* [Colloquial; 1920s]

sleep a wink, not Not sleep at all, as in *I couldn't sleep a wink last night.* This expression, in which *wink* alludes to closing the eyes for sleep, was first recorded about 1325.

sleep in 1. Sleep at one's place of employment, as in *They have a butler and maid who both sleep in.* [First half of 1800s] 2. Sleep late, either accidentally or deliberately. For example, *I slept in and missed my usual train,* or *On weekends we like to sleep in.* [Late 1800s]

sleep like a log Also, **sleep like a top.** Sleep very soundly, as in *I slept like a log,* or *She said she slept like a top.* Both of these similes transfer the immobility of an object to that of a person who is sound asleep (since a top spinning quickly looks immobile). The first dates from the late 1600s; the variant is newer.

sleep on something Consider something overnight before deciding, as in *I don't know if I want to go on such a long hike; let me sleep on it.* This usage was first recorded in 1519 in the state papers of

King Henry VIII: "His Grace ... said that he would sleep and dream upon the matter."

sleep out 1. Sleep at home, as opposed to one's place of employment, as in *We have a full-time nurse for her, but she sleeps out*. [Mid-1800s] 2. Sleep away from one's own home, as in *She's not here; she's sleeping out*.

sleep over Spend the night as a guest in another's home, as in *Karen's friend Wilma is going to sleep over tonight*. [Second half of 1800s]

sleep through 1. Sleep without waking for a period of time, usually the night, as in *At three months many babies have learned to sleep through*. [Mid-1900s] 2. **sleep through something**. Fail to pay attention, as in *We all slept through the explanation and then had trouble getting the machines started*.

sleep with Be sexually intimate with, as in *The playwright had made several attempts to sleep with the maid*. The related phrase **sleep together** means "have sexual relations," as in *We wondered if they were sleeping together but didn't dare to ask them*. The verb *sleep* has been associated with sex since the 10th century. **Sleep with** dates from the 1300s; **sleep together** was first recorded a century later.

sleeve ♦ See CARD UP ONE'S SLEEVE; LAUGH UP ONE'S SLEEVE; ROLL UP ONE'S SLEEVES; WEAR ONE'S HEART ON ONE'S SLEEVE.

sleight of hand Trickery, deviousness, as in *By some sleight of hand they managed to overlook all bonuses*. This term alludes to the performance of magic tricks with the hands. Its figurative use dates from about 1700.

slice ♦ In addition to the subsequent idiom beginning with SLICE, also see GREATEST THING SINCE SLICED BREAD; NO MATTER HOW YOU SLICE IT.

slice of the pie Also, **slice of the cake**. A share of the proceeds or benefits, as in *It's reasonable for a heavy contributor to ask for a big slice of the pie*. This metaphor for a division of the spoils dates from the late 1800s. Also see the synonym PIECE OF THE ACTION.

slick as a whistle Very smooth and neat; also, smoothly, quickly, easily. For example, *That salesman is as slick as a whistle*, or *The fence post went in place slick as a whistle*. The allusion in this simile, first recorded in 1830, is not totally clear, but presumably it refers either to the ease of producing a whistle or to its clear tone.

slide ♦ See LET RIDE (SLIDE); LET SLIP (SLIDE).

slight ♦ See IN THE LEAST (SLIGHTEST).

slim pickings A small amount left after others have taken a share. For example, *After each of the children took what they wanted of Mother's things,*

it was slim pickings for the rest of the family. This expression alludes to animals devouring a carcass. [Early 1600s]

sling ♦ In addition to the idioms beginning with SLING, also see ASS IN A SLING.

sling hash Serve food in a restaurant, especially a cheap establishment. For example, *The only job she could find was slinging hash in the neighborhood diner*. This term alludes to the inelegant presentation and nature of the food, in effect, tossing hash before a customer. [Slang; mid-1800s]

sling mud at Insult or discredit someone, as in *The paper became famous for slinging mud at movie stars*. This term replaced *throw mud at*, which dates from the second half of the 1700s.

slink away Also, **slink off**. Depart furtively, as in *The shoplifter slipped an item into his coat pocket and slunk away*, or *After that severe scolding, she slunk off*. This term employs *slink* in the sense of "move stealthily," a usage dating from the late 1300s.

slip ♦ In addition to the idioms beginning with SLIP, also see GIVE THE SLIP; LET SLIP.

slip a cog Also, **slip a gear** or **one's gears**. Lose one's ability to reason soundly or make correct judgments, as in *She must have slipped a cog or she would never have gone out barefoot in December*, or *What's the matter with him? Has he slipped his gears?* These slangy usages allude to a mechanical failure owing to the cog of a gear or a gear failing to mesh. The first dates from about 1930, the variant from the 1960s.

slip of the lip Also, **slip of the tongue** or **pen**. An inadvertent mistake in speaking (or writing), as in *It was just a slip of the lip that made me say the wrong name*, or *She didn't mean it; it was a slip of the tongue*, or *He intended to write "the honorable" but a slip of the pen turned it into "reverend."* The usage with *pen* dates from the mid-1600s; the others are a century or so younger.

slip one's mind Be overlooked or forgotten, as in *I meant to pick up the wine but it slipped my mind*. This idiom was first recorded about 1340.

slip out 1. See LET SLIP OUT. 2. Also, **slip away** or **off**. Leave quietly and unobtrusively, as in *She slipped out without telling a soul*, or *Let's slip away before the sermon*, or *Jason and Sheila slipped off to Bermuda*. The use of *slip* with *away* dates from about 1450; *out* from the first half of the 1500s; *off* from the mid-1800s.

slippery as an eel Elusive, devious, as in *When it comes to talking about his investments, Jim's slippery as an eel*. This simile, first recorded about 1412, alludes to the eel's skin, which has tiny scales and is quite slippery when wet.

slippery slope A dangerous course, one that leads easily to catastrophe, as in *He's on a slippery slope, compromising his values to please both the bosses and the union.* This metaphoric expression alludes to traversing a slick hillside, in constant danger of falling. [Mid-1900s]

slip something over on Hoodwink, trick, as in *Her lawyer tried to slip one over on him, but his lawyer wouldn't let him get away with it,* or *Don't trust Dan—he's always slipping something over on his customers.* [c. 1900]

slip through one's fingers ♦ See LET SLIP, def. 3.

slip up Make a mistake, blunder, as in *I slipped up and gave the invitations to the wrong people.* [Mid-1900s]

slow ♦ In addition to the idioms beginning with SLOW, also see MILLS OF THE GODS GRIND SLOWLY; ON THE UPTAKE, SLOW.

slow burn Slowly increasing anger. It is often put as **do a slow burn,** meaning "gradually grow angrier," as in *I did a slow burn when he kept me waiting for three hours.* The *burn* in this idiom comes from *burn up* in the sense of "make furious." The term was first cited in 1938 and was closely associated with comedian Edgar Kennedy.

slow but sure Gradual or plodding but certain to finish, as in *Slow but sure this book's getting written.* This idiom was first recorded in 1562, although the idea is much older. A related phrase appears in the proverb **slow and steady wins the race,** which is the moral of Aesop's fable about the race between a tortoise and a hare, which stopped to nap during the race and therefore lost.

slow down 1. Delay, retard, reduce speed, as in *She slowed down the sled by dragging her foot,* or *Slow down, Bill; you're driving much too fast.* [First half of 1800s] Also see SLOW UP. 2. Become less active or vigorous, as in *Now that I'm in my seventies I find I've slowed down quite a bit.* [Second half of 1800s]

slow on the uptake ♦ See ON THE UPTAKE.

slow up Slacken or cause to slacken in speed, as in *The train slowed up as it approached the curve,* or *Come on, you're slowing me up.* [Late 1800s] Also see SLOW DOWN, def. 1.

sly ♦ See ON THE SLY.

small ♦ In addition to the idioms beginning with SMALL, also see BIG FISH IN A SMALL POND; (SMALL) COG IN THE WHEEL; GIVE THANKS FOR SMALL BLESSINGS; IT'S A SMALL WORLD; LITTLE (SMALL) FROG IN A BIG POND; MAKE A (SMALL) FORTUNE; NO (SMALL) WONDER; STILL SMALL VOICE.

small beer Also, **small potatoes.** Of little importance, as in *Don't listen to Henry; he's small beer,* or

It's silly to worry about that bill; it's small potatoes. The first term alludes to a beer of low alcoholic content (also called *light beer* today) and was used metaphorically by Shakespeare in several plays. The variant may have been invented by frontiersman Davy Crockett; it was first recorded in 1836. Also see SMALL FRY, def. 2.

small cog in a large wheel ♦ See COG IN THE WHEEL.

small frog in a big pond ♦ See LITTLE FROG IN A BIG POND.

small fry 1. Young children, as in *This show is not suitable for small fry.* 2. Persons of little importance or influence, as in *She wasn't about to invite the Washington small fry to the reception.* Both usages allude to *fry* in the sense of "young or small fish." [Late 1800s]

small hours Also, **wee hours.** The hours following midnight, as in *I stayed up working through the small hours,* or *The parents didn't come home until the wee hours.* The adjectives *small* and *wee* both refer to the low numbers of those hours (one o'clock, two o'clock, etc.). [c. 1830]

small print Also, **fine print.** The details in a contract or other document, often indicating restrictions or other disadvantages. For example, *Be sure you read the small print before you sign your name to it,* or *They had the warranty terms in fine print, so you'd overlook the fact that it was only good for a month.* This idiom alludes to the fact that such material is often printed in smaller type than the rest of the document. [Mid-1900s]

small talk Casual or trivial conversation, chitchat, as in *We stood around making small talk until the guest of honor arrived.* The *small* in this expression alludes to unimportant subjects of conversation, as opposed to serious or weighty ones. [Mid-1700s]

small time A modest or minor level of achievement, as in *Her success took her out of the small time to prime-time television.* This expression was originally used in vaudeville for second-rate theaters and productions. [Early 1900s] Also see BIG TIME, def. 2.

small wonder ♦ See NO WONDER.

smart aleck An impudent or obnoxiously self-assertive individual, a wise guy, as in *New teachers often have a hard time coping with the smart alecks in their classes.* This expression, dating from the mid-1800s, probably alluded to a person of this description who was named Alec or Alexander, but his identity has been lost.

smart as a whip Very intelligent or clever, as in *Little Brian is smart as a whip; he's only three and already learning to read.* This simile alludes to the sharp crack of a whip. [Mid-1900s] Also see MIND LIKE A STEEL TRAP.

smart set A fashionable social group, as in *This restaurant has been discovered by the smart set.* This idiom may be obsolescent. [Late 1800s]

smash hit An outstanding success, as in *She was a smash hit in the role of the governess,* or *His first book was a smash hit but this one isn't doing well.* [c. 1920]

smear campaign An attempt to ruin a reputation by slander or vilification, as in *This press agent is well known for starting smear campaigns against her clients' major competitors.* This phrase was first recorded in 1938 and uses *smear* in the sense of "an attempt to discredit" or "slander."

smell ♦ In addition to the idioms beginning with SMELL, also see COME UP (SMELLING LIKE) ROSES; STINK (SMELL) TO HIGH HEAVEN.

smell a rat Suspect something is wrong, especially a betrayal of some kind. For example, *When I didn't hear any more from my prospective employer, I began to smell a rat.* This expression alludes to a cat sniffing out a rat. [c. 1550]

smell fishy Be suspect or suspicious, as in *His explanation definitely smells fishy; my guess is that he's lying.* This idiom alludes to the fact that fresh fish have no odor but stale or rotten ones do. [Early 1800s]

smell to high heaven ♦ See STINK TO HIGH HEAVEN.

smell up Also, **stink up.** Cause a bad odor, as in *These onions smell up the whole house,* or *Your old sneakers are stinking up the closet; throw them out.* [Mid-1900s]

smile ♦ In addition to the idiom beginning with SMILE, also see CRACK A SMILE.

smile on Look with favor or approval on, as in *The current administration smiles on anyone who gives it helpful publicity.* [c. 1400]

smithereens ♦ See BLOW TO SMITHEREENS.

smoke ♦ In addition to the idiom beginning with SMOKE, also see CHAIN SMOKER; GO UP IN FLAMES (SMOKE); HOLY COW (SMOKE); NO SMOKE WITHOUT FIRE; WATCH ONE'S DUST (SMOKE).

smoke out Expose, reveal, bring to public view, as in *Reporters thrive on smoking out a scandal.* This expression alludes to driving a person or animal out of a hiding place by filling it with smoke. [Late 1500s]

smoking gun Something that serves as indisputable evidence or proof, especially of a crime. For example, *There is no smoking gun in the Oval Office; the President had no role in tampering with the evidence.* This expression alludes to the smoke coming from a recently discharged firearm, a normal occurrence until the invention of smokeless powder. [Mid-1900s]

smooth ♦ In addition to the idioms beginning with SMOOTH, also see TAKE THE ROUGH WITH THE SMOOTH.

smooth as silk Lacking impediments or obstacles, unhindered, as in *The negotiations went smooth as silk.* This simile alludes to the slippery quality of silk. [c. 1900] Also see SMOOTH SAILING.

smooth over Rid of obstructions or difficulties, as in *We tried to smooth things over between the families before the wedding but did not succeed.* [Late 1600s]

smooth sailing Easy progress, as in *We had a hard time setting up the new computer system but it'll be smooth sailing from here on.* The *smooth* in this idiom alludes to calm waters, free from big waves or roughness, a usage dating from the late 1300s. The transfer to other kinds of easy progress dates from the second half of the 1900s. Also see PLAIN SAILING.

snag ♦ See HIT A SNAG.

snail mail Ordinary postal service, as opposed to electronic communications. For example, *He hasn't taken to his computer so he's still using snail mail.* This slangy idiom, alluding to the alleged slowness of the snail, caught on at least partly for its rhyme. [1980s]

snail's pace A very slow pace, as in *They're making progress with testing the new vaccine, but at a snail's pace.* [c. 1400]

snake in one's bosom ♦ See VIPER IN ONE'S BOSOM.

snake in the grass A treacherous person, as in *Ben secretly applied for the same job as his best friend; no one knew he was such a snake in the grass.* This metaphor for treachery, alluding to a poisonous snake concealed in tall grass, was used in 37 B.C. by the Roman poet Virgil (*latet anguis in herba*). It was first recorded in English in 1696 as the title of a book by Charles Leslie.

snake oil ♦ See under BANANA OIL.

snap at Speak irritably or abruptly to someone, as in *This teacher was always snapping at the children.* This use of *snap* transfers an animal's sudden bite at something to a verbal attack. [Late 1500s]

snap back Rebound from a setback, recover quickly, as in *I think we'll snap back quickly from this business downturn.* This idiom transfers the sudden release of tension on, for example, a branch to other kinds of recovery. [First half of 1900s]

snap judgment A hurried or impetuous decision or finding, as in *George was known for making snap judgments on personnel questions; he rarely bothered to investigate further.* This expression, which uses *snap* in the sense of "quick," was first recorded in 1841.

snap one's fingers at Treat with contempt, scorn, disregard, as in *Peter just snapped his fingers at the* *speed limit and drove as fast he liked,* or *Joanne snapped her fingers at the rumor about their bankruptcy.* This expression alludes to the gesture of striking one's finger against one's thumb, thereby making a sharp noise. [Early 1800s]

snap out of Suddenly recover, as in *You can't expect an entire economy to snap out of the doldrums overnight.* This expression is also put as an imperative, **Snap out of it!** telling someone to return to his or her normal state of mind from an undesirable condition such as grief, self-pity, or depression; for example, *Snap out of it, Stella; it's over and done with.* [1920s]

snappy ♦ See under MAKE HASTE.

snap someone's head off ♦ See BITE SOMEONE'S HEAD OFF.

snap to Move swiftly and smartly to an action, as in *The troops snapped to attention.* This phrase is sometimes expanded to **snap to it,** as in *You'd better snap to it if we're going to finish today.* [Early 1900s]

snap up Snatch for one's own use, as in *As soon as they lower the price we intend to snap up the house; it's exactly what we want.* [Mid-1500s]

sneak preview An advance showing of something, as in *It was supposed to be bad luck but she gave the bridegroom a sneak preview of her wedding gown.* This expression originated in the 1930s for a single public showing of a motion picture before its general release, and in succeeding decades was transferred to other undertakings.

sneeze at ♦ See NOT TO BE SNEEZED AT.

sniff out Uncover, as *If there's anything to that rumor, Gladys will sniff it out.* This expression alludes to an animal sniffing for prey. [First half of 1900s]

snit ♦ See IN A SNIT.

snow ♦ In addition to the idioms beginning with SNOW, also see PURE AS THE DRIVEN SNOW.

snowball's chance in hell, a No chance at all, as in *He hasn't a snowball's chance in hell of getting there in two hours.* This idiom, nearly always used negatively, alludes to the traditional view of hell as extremely hot, causing snow to melt at once. [Late 1800s]

snow job An effort to deceive, persuade, or overwhelm with insincere talk. For example, *Peter tried to give the officer a snow job about an emergency at the hospital but he got a speeding ticket all the same.* This slangy expression, originating in the military during World War II, presumably alludes to the idiom SNOW UNDER.

snow under Overwhelm, overpower, as in *I can't go; I'm just snowed under with work,* or *We were snowed under by more votes than we could have anticipated.* This expression alludes to being buried in snow. [Late 1800s]

snuff ♦ In addition to the idiom beginning with SNUFF, also see UP TO PAR (SNUFF).

snuff out 1. Extinguish, put a sudden end to, as in *Three young lives were snuffed out in that automobile accident.* This usage alludes to *snuff* in the sense of "put out a candle by pinching the wick," an area itself called *snuff* from the late 1300s on. [Mid-1800s] 2. Kill, murder, as in *If he told the police, the gang would snuff him out.* [Slang; first half of 1900s] 3. Also, **snuff it.** Die or be killed, as in *He looked very ill indeed, as though he might snuff out any day,* or *Grandpa just snuffed it.* [Slang; second half of 1800s]

snug as a bug in a rug Very cozy and comfortable, as in *During the blizzard we had plenty of firewood and stayed in the cottage, snug as a bug in a rug.* This expression, thought to allude to a moth larva happily feeding inside a rolled-up carpet, was first recorded in 1769 and probably owes its long life to the rhyme.

so ♦ In addition to the idioms beginning with SO, also see AND SO FORTH (AND SO ON); AS (SO) FAR AS; AS (SO) FAR AS POSSIBLE; AS (SO) FAR AS THAT GOES; AS (SO) LONG AS; AS (SO) MUCH AS; EVERY NOW AND THEN (SO OFTEN); GO SO FAR AS TO; HOW COME (SO); IN SO MANY WORDS; IS THAT A FACT (SO); I TOLD YOU SO; JUST SO; NEVER HAD IT SO GOOD; NOT (SO) BAD; ON ONE'S SAY-SO; OR SO; TAKE IT (JUST SO MUCH); WITHOUT SO MUCH AS.

soaked to the skin Also, **soaked through.** Drenched, extremely wet, as in *What a downpour; I'm soaked to the skin,* or *She fell in the stream and was soaked through.* The implication in this idiom implies that water has penetrated one's clothing, so one is thoroughly wet. The phrase *to the skin* has been so used since about 1600; it and the variant were combined in Randle Cotgrave's *Dictionary* (1611) as "Wet through, or (as we say) to the skin."

soak up 1. Absorb, take in, as in *I lay there, soaking up the sun,* or *She often went to hear poets read their work, soaking up every word.* This usage, alluding to absorbing a liquid, dates from the mid-1500s. 2. Drink to excess, as in *She can really soak up her beer.*

soap ♦ In addition to the idiom beginning with SOAP, also see NO DICE (SOAP); ON ONE'S SOAPBOX; SOFT SOAP.

soap opera 1. A radio or television serial with stock characters in domestic dramas that are noted for being sentimental and melodramatic. For example, *She just watches soap operas all day long.* This term originated in the mid-1930s and was so called because the sponsors of the earliest such radio shows were often soap manufacturers. 2. Real-life situation resembling one that might occur in a soap opera, as in *She just goes on and on* about her various medical and family problems, one long soap opera. [1940s]

so as to In order to, as in *We took off our shoes so as to avoid scratching the newly finished floors.* This idiom is always followed by an infinitive. For a synonym, see IN ORDER TO, def. 5.

so be it Let it be so, I accept it as it is. For example, *If you can't change the reservation, so be it; I'll travel on Monday.* This phrase, often given as a translation of the Hebrew (and Greek and Latin) *amen,* has been employed in the current sense since about 1600.

sober as a judge Not at all intoxicated, quite clear-headed, as in *Even after three drinks he was sober as a judge.* Why judges should be equated with sobriety is not known, but the simile was first recorded in 1694.

sob story A tale of personal hardship, true or invented, that is intended to arouse pity in the listener. For example, *She always came up with some sob story to excuse her absences, but no one believed her.* [Early 1900s]

society ♦ See under MUTUAL ADMIRATION SOCIETY.

sock away Put money in a safe place for future use, as in *I've got about $2,000 socked away for a new car.* This usage presumably alludes to putting one's savings in a sock. [Colloquial; first half of 1900s]

sock in Close down an airport or other facility due to thick fog or other weather conditions impeding visibility, as in *The airport was socked in all morning and air traffic was at a standstill,* or *We finally got to the peak and were totally socked in—there was no view at all.* The *sock* referred to here is probably a *windsock,* as decisions to close an airport are made in part on the basis of observations of windsocks, which indicate wind direction. The expression was first recorded in 1944.

sock it to Deliver a physical blow, forceful comment, or reprimand to, as in *The judge often socks it to the jury in a murder case.* This idiom uses *sock* in the sense of "strike hard." It is also put as an imperative, as in *Sock it to them, kid!* or *Sock it to me!,* which is sometimes used to give encouragement but can also have sexual overtones. [Second half of 1800s]

so far Also, **thus far.** Up to this point, as in *So far we haven't seen him in the crowd,* or *They've made very little progress on their report thus far.* [c. 1300]

so far as ♦ See under AS FAR AS.

so far, so good Matters are satisfactory up to this point, as in *You've knitted the main portion of the sweater but not the sleeves? Well, so far, so good.* This idiom was first recorded in James Kelly's *Scottish Proverbs* (1721), where it is defined: "So far, so good. So much is done to good purpose."

soft ♦ In addition to the idioms beginning with SOFT, also see HARD (SOFT) SELL.

soften up Reduce resistance, as in *His sales motto was: a fine lunch and a few drinks often will soften up a prospective customer.* This expression transfers lessening of physical hardness to lessening mental resistance. It was first used, however, in World War II, where it meant "reduce the enemy's defenses by preliminary bombing." [c. 1940]

soft in the head Mentally deficient; also, silly, foolish. For example, *He's nice enough but a bit soft in the head.* The *soft* in this idiom, first recorded in 1775, alludes to a weakness in mental capacity.

soft job An easy job or task, as in *He really has a soft job—his assistants do nearly all the work.* This colloquial expression uses *soft* in the sense of "involving little or no hardship or discomfort." It was first put as *soft employment* in 1639.

soft on 1. Attracted to or emotionally involved with, as in *He's been soft on Margaret for years.* This usage was first recorded in 1840. 2. Not stern, lenient, especially too much so. For example, *Some think the court has been soft on violent protesters.* This usage was first recorded in 1883.

soft pedal Something that de-emphasizes, restrains, or plays down, as in *The mayor put a soft pedal on this potentially explosive situation.* This expression alludes to the una corda or soft pedal of the piano, which reduces the volume of the sound. It gave rise to the verb *soft-pedal,* meaning both "reduce the volume of" or "make less emphatic, downplay." [Early 1900s]

soft sell ♦ See HARD SELL, def. 1.

soft soap Flattery, cajolery, as in *She's only six but she's learned how to get her way with soft soap.* This colloquial expression alludes to liquid soap, likening its slippery quality to insincere flattery. Its figurative use was first recorded in 1830.

soft spot 1. A weak or vulnerable point, as in *That's the soft spot in his argument.* [Mid-1900s] 2. **have a soft spot for.** Have a tender or sentimental feeling for, as in *Grandpa had a soft spot for Brian, his first grandson.* This expression, first recorded in 1753 as "a soft place in one's heart," uses *soft* in the sense of "tender."

soft touch Someone easily persuaded or taken advantage of, especially in giving away money. For example, *Ask Dan for the money; he's always a soft touch.* [First half of 1900s]

so help me Also, **so help me God.** I swear that what I am saying is true, as in *So help me, I haven't enough cash to pay for the tickets,* or *I wasn't there, so help me God.* This idiom became a formula for swearing a formal oath and is still so used in courts of law for swearing in a witness (*I swear to tell the truth, the whole truth, and nothing but the* *truth, so help me God*). It was first recorded in 1508 as "So help me, our Lord."

soil one's hands ♦ See DIRTY ONE'S HANDS.

sold on, be ♦ See SELL SOMEONE ON.

sold out ♦ See SELL OUT.

so long Good-bye, as in *So long, we'll see you next week.* The allusion here is puzzling; *long* presumably means "a long time" and perhaps the sense is "until we meet again after a long time," but the usage has no such implication. [Colloquial; first half of 1800s]

so long as ♦ See AS LONG AS, def. 1 and 2.

so many 1. Such a large number, as in *There were so many guests that we didn't have enough chairs.* [First half of 1200s] 2. An unspecified number, as in *There allegedly are so many shrimp per pound, but of course the exact number depends on their size and weight.* [First half of 1500s] 3. Forming a group, as in *The reporters turned on the speaker like so many tigers let loose.* [c. 1600]

some ♦ See AND THEN SOME; CATCH SOME RAYS; CATCH SOME Z'S; DIG UP (SOME DIRT); IN A (SOME) SENSE; IN SOME MEASURE; ONE OF THESE DAYS (SOME DAY); TAKE SOME DOING; TO SOME DEGREE; WIN SOME, LOSE SOME.

somebody up there loves me I am having very good luck right now; also, someone with influence is favoring me. For example, *I won $40 on that horse—somebody up there loves me,* or *I don't know how I got that great assignment; somebody up there loves me.* This idiom, generally used half-jokingly, alludes either to heavenly intervention or to the help of a temporal higher authority. [Colloquial; mid-1900s] Also see FRIEND IN COURT.

somehow ♦ See under OR OTHER.

something ♦ In addition to the idioms beginning with SOMETHING, also see BUY SOMETHING; GET (HAVE) SOMETHING ON SOMEONE; GET SOMETHING STRAIGHT; HAVE SOMETHING AGAINST; HOLD SOMETHING AGAINST; HOLD (SOMETHING) OVER; LOOK LIKE SOMETHING THE CAT DRAGGED IN; MAKE SOMETHING OF; NOT PUT SOMETHING PAST ONE; ON THE BALL, HAVE SOMETHING; (SOMETHING) OR OTHER; PULL SOMETHING ON; START SOMETHING; TAKE SOMETHING; YOU KNOW SOMETHING?

something else A person, thing, or event that is quite remarkable, as in *That pitcher is something else,* or *Her new film is something else.* The *else* in this idiom means "other than ordinary." [Colloquial; early 1900s]

something else again A different case entirely, as in *If he'd called to cancel, we wouldn't mind, but not showing up, that's something else again.* [Mid-1800s]

something in the wind A secret plan or undertaking, as in *I think there's something in the wind for Mom and Dad's anniversary.* This expression alludes to the carrying of a scent by the wind. [First half of 1500s]

something like Similar to, resembling, as in *They want a flower garden something like the ones they saw in England.* [Mid-1600s]

something of a To some extent, as in *Our professor is something of an eccentric.* [Early 1700s]

something or other ♦ See under OR OTHER.

something tells me I suspect, I have an intuition, as in *Something tells me that she's not really as ill as she says,* or *Something told him that it was going to snow.*

something thing, a Something occasional or transient, as in *For most free-lance musicians, work is a sometime thing.* This idiom gained currency in the title of a song by George Gershwin, "A Woman Is A Sometime Thing" (1935), introduced in the folk opera *Porgy and Bess.*

somewhere ♦ In addition to the idiom beginning with SOMEWHERE, also see GET SOMEWHERE; (SOMEWHERE) OR OTHER.

somewhere along the line At some point in time, as in *Somewhere along the line I'm sure I climbed that mountain.* [Mid-1900s]

so much An unspecified amount or cost, as in *They price the fabric at so much per yard.* [Late 1300s] Also see AS MUCH AS; SO MUCH FOR; SO MUCH THE.

so much as ♦ See AS MUCH AS, def. 3.

so much for We have sufficiently treated or are finished with something, as in *So much for this year's sales figures; now let's estimate next year's.* [Late 1500s]

so much the To that extent or degree, as in *You decided to stay home? So much the better, for now we won't need a second car.* This usage is always followed by a comparative adjective, such as *better* in the example. [Early 1200s]

son ♦ In addition to the idiom beginning with SON, also see FAVORITE SON; LIKE FATHER, LIKE SON.

song ♦ In addition to the idiom beginning with SONG, also see FOR A SONG; SWAN SONG.

song and dance An elaborate story or effort to explain and justify something, or to deceive and mislead someone. For example, *Do you really believe his song and dance about the alarm not going off, being stopped for speeding, and then the car breaking down?* or *At every annual meeting the chairman goes through the same song and dance about the company's great future plans.* This term originally referred to a vaudeville act featuring song and dance. [Late 1800s]

son of a bitch Also, **SOB; son of a gun.** A mean, dis-agreeable individual, as in *He was regarded as the worst son of a bitch in the industry,* or *He ran out on her? What an SOB,* or *He's a real son of a gun when it comes to owing you money.* The first of these terms, calling a man the son of a female dog, dates from the early 1300s and is considered vulgar enough to have given rise to the two variants, both euphemisms. The first variant, an abbrevia-tion, dates from World War I. The second, first recorded in 1708, gave rise to the theory that it originally applied to baby boys born at sea (in the days when women accompanied their husbands on long voyages). The explanation seems un-likely, especially since presumably some of the babies were girls. It also once meant the illegiti-mate son of a soldier (or "gun"). More probably, however, *son of a gun* evolved simply as a eu-phemism for the first term and appealed because of its rhyme. Both it and *son of a bitch* are also put as interjections expressing surprise, amazement, disgust, or disappointment, as in *Son of a bitch! I lost my ticket,* or *I'll be a son of a gun! That must be the governor.*

soon ♦ See AS SOON AS; FOOL AND HIS MONEY ARE SOON PARTED; HAD RATHER (SOONER); JUST AS SOON; NO SOONER SAID THAN DONE; SPEAK TOO SOON.

sooner or later Eventually, at some unspecified future time, as in *Sooner or later we'll have to an-swer that letter,* or *It's bound to stop raining sooner or later.* This term, which generally implies that some future event is certain to happen, was first recorded in 1577.

sooner the better, the As quickly or early as pos-sible, as in *As for stopping that check, the sooner the better.* This idiom was first recorded in 1477.

sore ♦ In addition to the idiom beginning with SORE, also see SIGHT FOR SORE EYES; STICK OUT (LIKE A SORE THUMB).

sore point, a A sensitive or annoying issue, as in *Don't mention diets to Elsie; it's a sore point with her.* This idiom was first recorded as *a sore place* in 1690.

sorrow ♦ See DROWN ONE'S SORROWS; MORE IN SOR-ROW THAN IN ANGER.

sorry ♦ See BETTER SAFE THAN SORRY.

sort ♦ See AFTER A FASHION (SORT); ALL KINDS (SORTS) OF; BAD SORT; IT TAKES ALL SORTS; KIND (SORT) OF; NOTHING OF THE KIND (SORT); OF SORTS; OUT OF SORTS.

so that 1. In order that, as in *I stopped so that you could catch up.* 2. With the result or consequence that, as in *Mail the package now so that it will arrive on time.* 3. **so . . . that.** In such a way or to such an extent that, as in *The line was so long that I could scarcely find the end of it.* All three usages date from A.D. 1000 or earlier, and the first two are some-

times put simply as **so,** as in *I stopped so you could catch up,* or *Mail it now so it will arrive on time.*

so to speak Phrased like this, in a manner of speaking, as in *He was, so to speak, the head of the family, although he was only related by marriage to most of the family members.* This term originally meant "in the vernacular" or "lower-class lan-guage" and was used as an aristocrat's apology for stooping to such use. [Early 1800s] Also see AS IT WERE.

sought after Also, **much sought after.** Very popu-lar, in demand, as in *He was much sought after as a throat specialist, particularly by singers.* This ex-pression uses the past participle of *seek* in the sense of "desired" or "searched for." [Late 1800s]

soul ♦ In addition to the idiom beginning with SOUL, also see BARE ONE'S SOUL; HEART AND SOUL; KEEP BODY AND SOUL TOGETHER; KINDRED SPIRIT (SOUL); LIVING SOUL.

soul of, the The essence of some quality, as in *You can trust her; she's the soul of discretion,* or *He's the very soul of generosity but he can be cranky at times.* This idiom was first recorded in 1605.

sound ♦ In addition to the idioms beginning with SOUND, also see SAFE AND SOUND.

sound as a bell In excellent condition, as in *Now that the brakes have been relined, the car is sound as a bell,* or *The surgery went well and now he's sound as a bell.* This simile rests on the assump-tion that the bell in question is not cracked (which would make it useless). First recorded in 1565, it has survived numerous other similes (*sound as a top* or *roach* or *dollar*), probably owing to its pun on "sound."

sound bite A short, striking, quotable statement well suited to a television news program. For example, *He's extremely good at sound bites, but a really substantive speech is beyond him.* This slangy expression, first recorded in 1980, origi-nated in political campaigns in which candi-dates tried to get across a particular message or get publicity by having it picked up in news-casts.

sound off Express one's views vigorously and loudly, as in *Dad's always sounding off about higher taxes.* This expression probably comes from the original meaning, that is, "strike up a military band." [Early 1900s]

sound out Seek the views or intentions of, as in *We'd better sound out Mom about who's using the station wagon,* or *Let's sound out the staff before we decide which week we should close for vacation.* This expression derives from *sound* meaning "to measure the depth of water by lowering a line or lead." It was transferred to other kinds of inquiry in the late 1500s, but *out* was not added for several centuries.

soup ♦ In addition to the idiom beginning with SOUP, also see DUCK SOUP; FROM SOUP TO NUTS; IN THE SOUP; THICK AS THIEVES (PEA SOUP).

soup up Make something more powerful; especially, add speed to an engine. For example, *He was riding around in that car he'd souped up*, or *They had to soup up the sound system for the outdoor concert*. [Slang; c. 1930]

sour grapes Disparaging what one cannot obtain, as in *The losers' scorn for the award is pure sour grapes*. This expression alludes to the Greek writer Aesop's famous fable about a fox that cannot reach some grapes on a high vine and announces that they are sour. In English the fable was first recorded in William Caxton's 1484 translation, "The fox said these raisins be sour."

sour on Become disenchanted with, take a dislike to, as in *At first they liked the new supervisor, but now they've soured on her*. [c. 1860]

south ♦ See GO SOUTH.

sow ♦ In addition to the idiom beginning with sow, also see CAN'T MAKE A SILK PURSE OUT OF A SOW'S EAR.

so what Who cares? What does it matter? For example, *You're not going to the beach today? Well, so what, you can go tomorrow*, or *So what if she left without saying goodbye—she'll call you, I'm sure*. [First half of 1900s] Also see WHAT OF IT.

sow one's wild oats Behave foolishly, immoderately or promiscuously when young, as in *Brad has spent the last couple of years sowing his wild oats, but now he seems ready to settle down*. This expression alludes to sowing inferior wild oats instead of good cultivated grain, the verb *sowing*— that is, "planting seed"—in particular suggesting sexual promiscuity. [Mid-1500s]

space ♦ In addition to the idiom beginning with SPACE, also see BREATHING SPACE; TAKE UP SPACE.

space out Stupefy or disorient, as if or from a drug. For example, *This medication spaces me out so I can't think clearly*, or *I wonder what those kids are on—they look totally spaced out*. [1960s] Also see ZONE OUT.

spade ♦ See CALL A SPADE A SPADE; DO THE SPADE-WORK; IN SPADES.

Spain ♦ See CASTLES IN THE AIR (SPAIN).

span ♦ See SPICK AND SPAN.

spare ♦ In addition to the idioms beginning with SPARE, also see TO SPARE.

spare the rod and spoil the child Discipline is necessary for good upbringing, as in *She lets Richard get away with anything—spare the rod, you know*.

This adage appears in the Bible (Proverbs 13:24) and made its way into practically every proverb collection. It originally referred to corporal punishment. It is still quoted, often in shortened form, and today does not necessarily mean physical discipline.

spare tire Fat around one's middle, as in *He's determined to lose ten pounds and that spare tire he's acquired*. This expression transfers the term for an extra tire carried in cars in case of a flat tire to excess fat around the waist. [Colloquial; mid-1900s]

spark ♦ See MAKE THE SPARKS FLY.

sparring partner An individual with whom one enjoys arguing, as in *Jim's my best sparring partner*. This expression alludes to boxing, where since about 1900 it has denoted the person one practices or trains with. [Mid-1900s] Also see SPAR WITH.

spar with Argue or debate with, as in *You'd never know they were happily married, because they're constantly sparring with each other*. [Early 1600s]

speak ♦ In addition to the idioms beginning with SPEAK, also see ACTIONS SPEAK LOUDER THAN WORDS; IN A MANNER OF SPEAKING; NOTHING TO SPEAK OF; NOT TO MENTION (SPEAK OF); ON SPEAKING TERMS; SO TO SPEAK; TO SPEAK OF.

speak down to ♦ See TALK DOWN TO.

speak for 1. Intercede for, recommend, as in *He spoke for the young applicant, commending her honesty.* [c. 1300] 2. Express the views of, as in *I can't speak for my husband but I'd love to accept*, or *I don't care what Harry thinks—Speak for yourself, Joe.* [c. 1300] 3. **speak for itself**. Be significant or self-evident, as in *They haven't called us in months, and that speaks for itself.* [Second half of 1700s] 4. **spoken for**. Ordered, engaged, or reserved, as in *This lot of rugs is already spoken for*, or *Is this dance spoken for? This usage comes from the older verb, bespeak*, meaning "to order." [Late 1600s]

speak of the devil The person just mentioned has appeared, as in *Why, speak of the devil—there's Jeannie*. This expression is a shortening of the older *Speak of the devil and he's sure to appear*, based on the superstition that pronouncing the devil's name will cause his arrival on the scene. The figurative use was already explained in James Kelly's *Scottish Proverbs* (1721).

speak one's mind Also, **speak out**. Say what one really thinks, talk freely and fearlessly, as in *Will you give me a chance to speak my mind or am I supposed to agree with everything you say?* or *Jan welcomed the chance to speak out about abortion*. The first term dates from about 1600, the variant from the late 1600s. Also see SPEAK ONE'S PIECE.

speak one's piece Also, **say one's piece**. Say what one thinks, or what one usually says or is expected to say. For example, *All right, you've spoken your piece; now let someone else have a turn.* The *piece* in this expression alludes to a memorized poem or speech of the kind recited in a classroom. [Mid-1900s]

speak out ♦ See SPEAK ONE'S MIND; SPEAK UP, def. 1.

speak out of turn ♦ See OUT OF TURN, def. 2.

speak the same language Understand one another very well, agree with each other, as in *Negotiations went on for days, but finally both sides realized they weren't speaking the same language.* This term, alluding to literal understanding of spoken words, dates from the late 1800s.

speak too soon Assume something prematurely, as in *I guess I spoke too soon about moving to Boston; I didn't get the job after all.*

speak up 1. Also, **speak out**. Talk loudly, so as to be heard, as in *Speak up, child, I can't hear you,* or *He should speak out so that those in back can hear him.* The first term dates from the early 1700s, the variant from the early 1500s. 2. Also, **speak up for**. Express one's opinion or one's support for someone or something. For example, *When it comes to speaking up about the town's needs, you can rely on Mary,* or *I'm glad you spoke up for me in that meeting.* [c. 1700]

speak volumes Be significant, indicate a great deal, as in *That house of theirs speaks volumes about their income.* This idiom uses *volumes* in the sense of "the information contained in volumes of books." [c. 1800]

spec ♦ See ON SPEC.

species ♦ See ENDANGERED SPECIES.

speed ♦ In addition to the idiom beginning with SPEED, also see FULL SPEED AHEAD; UP TO PAR (SPEED).

speed up Accelerate, expedite, increase the rate, as in *The car speeded up as it went downhill,* or *It's difficult to speed up production without new equipment.* [Late 1800s]

spell ♦ In addition to the idiom beginning with SPELL, also see COLD SNAP (SPELL); UNDER SOMEONE'S SPELL.

spell out 1. Make plain, clarify, as in *We asked her to spell out her objectives.* [c. 1940] 2. Read slowly and laboriously, as in *He was only six but he managed to spell out the instructions.* [Early 1800s] 3. Puzzle out, manage to understand with some effort, as in *It took years before anyone could spell out the inscriptions on the Rosetta Stone.* [Late 1600s] All three usages transfer *spell* in the sense of "proceed letter by letter."

spend ♦ See POCKET (SPENDING) MONEY.

spice ♦ See VARIETY IS THE SPICE OF LIFE.

spick and span Neat and clean, as in *When Ruth has finished cleaning, the whole house is spick and*

span. This term combines two nouns that are now obsolete, *spick,* "a nail" or "spike," and *span,* "a wooden chip." In the 1500s a sailing ship was considered *spick and span* when every spike and chip was brand-new. The transfer to the current sense took place in the mid-1800s.

spill ♦ In addition to the idiom beginning with SPILL, also see SHED (SPILL) BLOOD; TAKE A SPILL.

spill the beans Disclose a secret or reveal something prematurely, as in *You can count on little Carol to spill the beans about the surprise.* In this colloquial expression, first recorded in 1919, *spill* means "divulge," a usage dating from the 1500s.

spin ♦ In addition to the idioms beginning with SPIN, also see GO INTO A TAILSPIN; MAKE ONE'S HEAD SPIN; PUT A SPIN ON.

spin a yarn Tell a story, especially a long drawn-out or totally fanciful one, as in *This author really knows how to spin a yarn,* or *Whenever he's late he spins some yarn about a crisis.* Originally a nautical term dating from about 1800, this expression probably owes its life to the fact that it embodies a double meaning, *yarn* signifying both "spun fiber" and "a tale."

spin control Manipulation of news, especially political news, as in *The White House press secretary is a master of spin control.* This idiom uses *spin* in the sense of "interpretation," that is, how something will be interpreted by the public (also see PUT A SPIN ON). [c. 1980] Also see SPIN DOCTOR.

spin doctor An individual charged with getting others to interpret a statement or event from a particular viewpoint, as in *Charlie is the governor's spin doctor.* This term, born about 1980 along with SPIN CONTROL, uses *doctor* in the colloquial sense of "one who repairs something."

spin off Derive or produce from something else, especially a small part from a larger whole. For example, *The corporation decided to spin off the automobile parts division,* or *Her column was spun off from her book on this subject.* The expression transfers the throwing off by centrifugal force, as in spinning, to other enterprises. [Mid-1900s]

spin one's wheels Expend effort with no result, as in *We're just spinning our wheels here while management tries to make up its mind.* This idiom, with its image of a vehicle in snow or sand that spins its wheels but cannot move, dates from the mid-1900s.

spin out 1. Protract or prolong, as in *They spun out the negotiations over a period of months.* This idiom alludes to drawing out a thread by spinning. [c. 1600] 2. Rotate out of control, as in *The car spun out and crashed into the store window.* [Mid-1900s]

spirit ♦ In addition to the idioms beginning with SPIRIT, also see KINDRED SPIRIT.

spirit away Carry off mysteriously or secretly, as in *The police found that the documents had been spirited away from the office.* This term derives from the noun *spirit*, in the sense of "a supernatural being such as a ghost." [Second half of 1600s]

spirit is willing but the flesh is weak, the One would like to undertake something but hasn't the energy or strength to do so. For example, *Another set of tennis? The spirit is willing but the flesh is weak.* Today often used as a rueful admission of weariness or other physical weakness, this idiom was first recorded in the New Testament (Matthew 26:41), where Jesus tells his disciples: "Watch and pray, that ye enter not into temptation: the spirit indeed is willing, but the flesh is weak." A modern equivalent is **I would if I could but I can't.**

spit and polish Close attention to appearance and order, as in *With a little spit and polish this house will sell very quickly.* This expression originated in the military, presumably alluding to literally shining up something with the aid of a little saliva. There it also came to mean "too much attention to appearance, and not enough to more important concerns," as in *The commander is so concerned with spit and polish that he overlooks the crew's morale.* [Late 1800s]

spite ♦ See IN SPITE OF.

spitting distance A very short distance, as in *We were in spitting distance of winning the pennant but then we lost three games in a row.* Alluding to the relatively short distance over which one's spit will carry, this idiom was first recorded in 1895 as *within spitting range.*

spitting image A precise resemblance, especially in closely related persons. For example, *Dirk is the spitting image of his grandfather.* This idiom alludes to the earlier use of the noun *spit* for "likeness," in turn probably derived from an old proverb, "as like as one as if he had been spit out of his mouth" (c. 1400). The current idiom dates from about 1900.

spit up Vomit, as in *Infants often spit up part of their milk.*

splash down Land in water, as in *The spacecraft splashed down within a few hundred yards of the pickup point.* The *splash* in this idiom alludes to the impact of a solid body on water. [c. 1960]

spleen ♦ See VENT ONE'S SPLEEN.

splinter group A part of an organization that breaks away from the main body, usually owing to disagreement. For example, *Perot's supporters at first constituted a splinter group but soon formed a third political party.* This idiom alludes to the

noun *splinter*, a fragment of wood or some other material that is split or broken off. [Mid-1900s]

split hairs Make trivial distinctions, quibble, as in *Let's not split hairs about whose turn it is; I'll close up today and you do it tomorrow.* This metaphoric idiom transfers dividing so fine an object as a single hair to other petty divisions. [Second half of 1600s]

split one's sides Also, **laugh one's head off.** Be extremely amused, laugh uproariously. For example, *That comedian had us splitting our sides,* or *Jane laughed her head off when she saw Rob's costume.* The first of these hyperbolic terms dates from about 1700.

split second An instant, a fraction of a second, as in *Our best swimmer came in a split second before theirs.* This expression alludes to a stop watch that has two second hands, one above the other, for timing more than one athlete or intervals of a race by a single athlete. Each hand can be stopped independently of the other, so a second can be "split" when one second hand stops a fraction of a second after the other. [c. 1880]

split the difference Compromise between two close figures, divide the remainder equally. For example, *You're asking $5,000 for the car and I'm offering $4,000; let's split the difference and make it $4,500.* [c. 1700]

split ticket A ballot cast for candidates of more than one party, as in *I'm registered as an Independent, and indeed I usually vote a split ticket.* This idiom uses *ticket* in the sense of "a list of nominees for office," a usage dating from the late 1700s. Also see STRAIGHT TICKET.

spoil ♦ In addition to the idioms beginning with SPOIL, also see SPARE THE ROD AND SPOIL THE CHILD; TOO MANY COOKS SPOIL THE BROTH; TO THE VICTOR BELONG THE SPOILS.

spoil for Be eager for, as in *He's just spoiling for a fight.* This idiom nearly always refers to some kind of altercation. It may allude to *spoil* in the sense of "deteriorate over a period of time." [Mid-1800s]

spoken for ♦ See SPEAK FOR, def. 3.

sponge ♦ In addition to the idiom beginning with SPONGE, also see THROW IN THE SPONGE.

sponge on Also, **sponge off.** Impose on another's hospitality or generosity, as in *He's been sponging on relatives for the past year.* This expression uses *sponge* in the sense of "to soak up something." [Late 1600s]

spoon ♦ See BORN WITH A SILVER SPOON; GREASY SPOON.

sporting blood Willingness to take risks, as in *His sporting blood won't let him stay away from the races.* This idiom uses *sporting* in the sense of "associated with gambling."

sporting chance, a A fair chance for success, as in *She thinks she has a sporting chance for being named bureau chief.* [Colloquial; late 1800s]

spot ♦ See BLIND SPOT; HIT THE HIGH SPOTS; HIT THE SPOT; IN A BIND (TIGHT SPOT); IN A FIX (SPOT); JOHNNY-ON-THE-SPOT; KNOCK THE SOCKS (SPOTS) OFF; LEOPARD CANNOT CHANGE ITS SPOTS; ON THE SPOT; ROOTED TO THE SPOT; SOFT SPOT; X MARKS THE SPOT.

spotlight ♦ See IN THE LIMELIGHT (SPOTLIGHT); STEAL THE SHOW (SPOTLIGHT).

spread like wildfire Disseminate or circulate very quickly, as in *The rumor about their divorce spread like wildfire.* The noun *wildfire* means "a raging, rapidly spreading conflagration." [c. 1800]

spread oneself too thin Overextend oneself, undertake too many different enterprises. For example, *Tom's exhausted; what with work, volunteer activities, and social life he's spread himself too thin.* This expression alludes to smearing something (like butter on bread) in such a thin layer that it does not cover the surface. Jonathan Swift used **spread thin** in a positive sense, that is, something should occur less often (*Polite Conversation, 1731–1738*): "They [polite speeches] ought to be husbanded better, and spread much thinner."

spring chicken ♦ See NO SPRING CHICKEN.

spring for Pay another's expenses, treat, as in *I'll spring for the dinner this time.* [Slang; c. 1900]

spring on someone ♦ Present or make known unexpectedly, as in *They sprung the news of their engagement on the family last night.* This idiom uses *spring* in the sense of "make a sudden move." Mark Twain used it in *Tom Sawyer* (1876): "Old Mr. Jones is going to try to spring something on the people here tonight."

spruce up ♦ Make neat and trim, as in *She spruced up the chairs with new cushions.* This idiom originated in the late 1500s as simply *spruce* but had acquired *up* by 1676.

spur ♦ In addition to the idiom beginning with SPUR, also see ON THE SPUR OF THE MOMENT; WIN ONE'S SPURS.

spur on Goad or urge ahead, as in *The thought of winning a Pulitzer Prize spurred the reporter on.* This expression transfers using spurs to make a horse go faster to incentives of other kinds. [Late 1500s]

spy on Secretly or furtively observe someone or something, as in *The children loved spying on the grownups,* or *The company sent him to spy on the competitor's sales force.* [Early 1600s]

square ♦ In addition to the idioms beginning with SQUARE, also see BACK TO THE DRAWING BOARD (SQUARE ONE); FAIR AND SQUARE; ON THE SQUARE; ROUND PEG IN A SQUARE HOLE; SHOOT STRAIGHT (SQUARE).

square away Put in order; also, get ready for. For example, *Once we've got the files squared away, we can decide on next year's repertory,* or *She had to square away the house before leaving town.* This expression uses *square* in the sense of "arrange in accordance with some principle," indirectly alluding to the geometric square. [Early 1800s]

square deal A just, equitable arrangement or transaction, as in *I know I'll get a square deal if I work with that supplier.* This idiom uses *square* in the sense of "fair" or "honest," a usage dating from the 1300s. [Late 1800s]

square meal, a A substantial or complete meal, as in *These airlines never feed you; I haven't had a square meal on one yet.* [Mid-1800s]

square off Take a fighting stance, prepare to fight, as in *As they squared off, the teacher came out and stopped them,* or *The ambassador said the two countries were squaring off.* [First half of 1800s]

square one's shoulders Prepare to face adversity, as in *She knew it wouldn't be easy but she squared her shoulders and faced the hostile audience.* This expression transfers standing erect with the shoulders pulled back, forming an angle much like a square's right angle, to the situations calling for this stance. It was first recorded in 1819.

square peg in a round hole Also, **round peg in a square hole.** A misfit, especially a person unsuited for a position or activity. For example, *Ruth doesn't have the finesse for this job; she's a round peg in a square hole.* This idiom, with its graphic image of something that cannot fit, dates from about 1800.

square the circle Try to do the impossible, as in *Getting that bill through the legislature is the same as trying to square the circle.* This idiom alludes to the impossibility of turning a circle into a square. John Donne may have been the first to use it (*Sermons,* 1624): "Go not thou about to square either circle (God or thyself)."

square up Settle a bill or debt, as in *The others went to get the car while he squared up with the waiter.* This idiom derives from *square* in the sense of "set straight." [Early 1800s]

square with 1. Correspond to, agree with, as in *His story doesn't square with what the witness saw.* [Late 1500s] 2. Settle a disagreement or account with someone, put a matter straight, as in *We've squared it with the management to bring our own wine.* [Mid-1800s]

squeak by Also, **squeak through.** Manage barely to pass, win, survive, or the like, as in *They are just squeaking by on their income,* or *He squeaked through the driver's test.* This idiom transfers *squeak* in the sense of "barely emit a sound" to "narrowly manage something." [First half of 1900s] Also see SQUEEZE THROUGH.

squeaky wheel gets the grease The loudest complaints get the most attention, as in *No matter what table they give her, Helen generally insists on a better one and gets it—the squeaky wheel gets the grease.* The current version of this idiom, with its allusion to a wagon wheel that needs oiling, is ascribed to American humorist Josh Billings (1818–1885) in a poem, "The Kicker": "I hate to be a kicker [complainer], I always long for peace, But the wheel that does the squeaking Is the one that gets the grease." However, the idea of the idiom is much older. A manuscript from about 1400 had: "Ever the worst spoke of the cart creaks." Similar sayings were repeated over the succeeding centuries.

squeeze ♦ In addition to the idioms beginning with SQUEEZE, also see MAIN SQUEEZE; PUT THE ARM (SQUEEZE) ON; TIGHT SQUEEZE.

squeeze off fire a gun, as in *He squeezed off one shot after another but didn't bring down a single crow.* The idiom alludes to squeezing the trigger. [Mid-1900s]

squeeze play A situation in which pressure exerted to obtain a concession or achieve a goal, as in *Workers sometimes feel caught in a squeeze play between union and management.* This expression, dating from about 1900, originated in baseball, where it refers to a prearranged play in which the runner on third base breaks for home plate on the pitch, and the batter bunts. [c. 1915]

squeeze through Also, **squeeze by.** Manage to pass, win, or survive by a narrow margin, as in *We squeezed through the second round of playoffs,* or *There was just enough food stored in the cabin for us to squeeze by until the hurricane ended.* This idiom uses *squeeze* in the sense of "succeed by means of compression." [c. 1700] Also see SQUEAK BY.

squirrel away Hide or store, as in *She squirreled away her savings in at least four different banks.* This expression alludes to the squirrel's habit of hiding nuts and acorns in the ground. [First half of 1900s]

stab ♦ In addition to the idiom beginning with STAB, also see MAKE A STAB AT.

stab in the back, a A betrayal of trust, an act of treachery, as in *Voting against our bill at the last minute was a real stab in the back.* It is also put as **stab someone in the back,** meaning "betray someone." For example, *Don't trust George; he's been known to stab his friends in the back.* Both the noun and verb forms of this idiom, alluding to a physical attack when one's back is turned, date from the early 1900s.

stable ♦ See LOCK THE BARN (STABLE) DOOR AFTER THE HORSE HAS BOLTED.

stack ♦ In addition to the idioms beginning with STACK, also see BLOW ONE'S TOP (STACK); CARDS ARE STACKED; NEEDLE IN A HAYSTACK; SWEAR ON A STACK OF BIBLES.

stack the cards ♦ See CARDS ARE STACKED.

stack up 1. Measure up, equal, as in *Their gift doesn't stack up against mine.* This usage alludes to piling up one's chips at poker, and comparing them to those of the other players. [Early 1900s] 2. Make sense, seem plausible, as in *Her explanation just doesn't stack up.* Also see ADD UP, def. 2.

staff of life A staple or necessary food, especially bread. For example, *Rice is the staff of life for a majority of the earth's people.* This expression, which uses *staff* in the sense of "a support," was first recorded in 1638.

stag ♦ In addition to the idiom beginning with STAG, also see GO STAG.

stage ♦ In addition to the idioms beginning with STAGE, also see AT THIS STAGE; SET THE SCENE (STAGE) FOR.

stage fright Acute nervousness when performing or speaking before an audience, as in *When John first had to present his findings to the board of directors, stage fright made him stutter.* [Second half of 1800s]

stage whisper A whisper loud enough to be overheard, as in *Our three-year-old behaved beautifully at the ceremony, but then he asked in a stage whisper, "Why does that lady have blue hair?"* This expression alludes to an actor's whisper on stage, which is meant to be heard by the audience. [Mid-1800s]

stag party A social gathering for men exclusively, often involving entertainment considered unsuitable for women. For example, *They wanted to give him a stag party before the wedding but John wasn't interested.* This idiom uses *stag* in the sense of "a man unaccompanied by a woman." [c. 1850]

stake ♦ In addition to the idioms beginning with STAKE, also see AT STAKE; BURN AT THE STAKE; HAVE A STAKE IN; PULL UP STAKES.

stake a claim Also, **stake out a claim.** Indicate something as one's own, as in *I'm staking a claim to the drumstick,* or *She staked out a claim for herself in the insurance business.* This term, dating from the mid-1800s, originally meant "register a claim to land by marking it with stakes." It was being used figuratively by the late 1800s.

stake out Keep an area or person under police surveillance; also, assign someone to conduct such a surveillance. For example, *They staked out the house,* or *He was staked out in the alley, watching for drug dealers.* [c. 1940]

stamp ♦ In addition to the idiom beginning with STAMP, also see RUBBER STAMP.

stamping ground Also, **old stamping ground**. A habitual or favorite haunt, as in *Whenever we visit, we go back to our old stamping ground, the drugstore nearest the high school*. This term alludes to a traditional gathering place for horses or cattle, which stamp down the ground with their hooves. [Early 1800s]

stamp out Extinguish or destroy, as in *The government stamped out the rebellion in a brutal way*, or *The police were determined to stamp out drug dealers*. This metaphoric expression alludes to extinguishing a fire by trampling on it. [Mid-1800s]

stand ♦ In addition to the idioms beginning with STAND, also see CAN'T STAND THE SIGHT OF; HEART MISSES A BEAT (STANDS STILL); (STAND) IN AWE OF; IT STANDS TO REASON; KNOW WHERE ONE STANDS; MAKE A STAND; MAKE ONE'S HAIR STAND ON END; NOT HAVE (STAND) AN EARTHLY CHANCE; TAKE A STAND; WITHOUT A LEG TO STAND ON.

stand a chance Have a possibility or a hope of success, as in *Do you think Mary stands a chance of finishing the marathon?* or *I think we stand a fair chance of seeing the Queen arrive at Buckingham Palace*. This idiom was first recorded in 1796. Also see NOT HAVE AN EARTHLY CHANCE.

stand at ease ♦ See AT EASE, def. 2.

stand by 1. Be ready or available to act, as in *I'm almost ready for you to carve the turkey, so please stand by*. [Mid-1200s] 2. Wait for something to resume, as in *We are all standing by until the power is restored*. Also see ON STANDBY. 3. Be present but remain uninvolved, refrain from acting, as in *I can't stand by and see these kids shoplifting*. [Late 1300s] 4. Remain loyal, as in *She's my friend and I'll stand by her, no matter what*. [Early 1500s] Also see STICK BY. 5. Adhere to, abide by, as in *I'm going to stand by what I said yesterday*. [Late 1300s]

stand corrected Agree that one was wrong, as in *I stand corrected—we did go to Finland in 1985*. This idiom was first recorded in John Dryden's *The Maiden Queen* (1668): "I stand corrected, and myself reprove."

stand down 1. Leave a witness stand, as in *The judge told her to stand down*. [Late 1600s] 2. Withdraw, as from a political contest or a game or race, as in *Harry decided to stand down as a candidate for mayor*. [Late 1800s] 3. Go off duty, as in *The American forces were ordered to stand down*. [Early 1900s]

stand fast ♦ See STAND ONE'S GROUND.

stand for 1. Represent, symbolize, as in *The stars and stripes stands for our country*. [Early 1600s] 2. Advocate, support, uphold, as in *The National Writers Union stands for freedom of the press*. [c. 1300] Also see STAND UP FOR. 3. Put up with,

tolerate. This usage is generally in a negative context, as in *Mother will not stand for rude behavior*. [Late 1800s] Also see HOLD STILL FOR. 4. **stand for something**. Have some value or importance, as in *She realized that appearances do stand for something*. This usage dates from the mid-1800s but was preceded by **stand for nothing**, meaning "be worthless," dating from the late 1300s. Also see STAND IN FOR.

stand guard Watch over, act as a lookout, as in *We'll climb the tree and get the apples if Josh will stand guard*, or *There's a parking space; stand guard while I make a U-turn and get to it*. This term alludes to the military defense of posting guards to watch for the enemy.

stand in awe ♦ See IN AWE OF.

stand in for Substitute for, as in *He's kindly agreed to stand in for me at the reception*. [Early 1900s]

standing joke Something that is always funny even though it is often repeated. for example, *Mary's "Dennis who?" when her husband is mentioned is a standing joke around here*. This idiom employs *standing* in the sense of "established" or "regular," a usage dating from the mid-1500s.

standing on one's head ♦ See under DO BLINDFOLDED.

stand in good stead Be extremely useful, as in *That umbrella stood me in good stead on our trip; it rained every day*. [c. 1300]

standing order A regulation that is in force until it is specifically changed or withdrawn, as in *The waiters have standing orders to fill all glasses as they are emptied*. This idiom began life in the mid-1600s as *standing rule;* the word *order* began to be used about 1800 for such military orders and gradually was extended to other areas.

stand off 1. Stay at a distance remain apart, as in *Carol stood off from the others*. [First half of 1600s] This usage gave rise to the adjective *standoffish* for "aloof" or "reserved in a haughty way." 2. Put off, keep away, as in *The police stood off the angry strikers*. [Second half of 1800s]

stand on 1. Be based on, depend on, as in *Our success will stand on their support*. [c. 1600] 2. Insist on observance of, as in *Let's not stand on ceremony*. This usage today is nearly always put in a negative context. [Mid-1500s]

stand one's ground Also, **hold one's ground; stand fast**. Be firm or unyielding, as in *You've got to respect him for standing his ground when all the others disagree*, or *I'm going to hold my ground on this issue*, or *No matter how he votes, I'm standing fast*. This idiom, dating from the early 1600s, originally was applied to an army holding its territory against the enemy, but was being used figuratively as well by the end of the 1600s.

stand on one's own feet Act or behave independently, as in *You've got to learn to stand on your own feet and not always listen to your peers.* [Mid-1500s]

stand out 1. Protrude, project, as in *Those reliefs stand out from the building walls.* [First half of 1500s] 2. Be conspicuous, distinctive, or prominent, as in *He's so tall that he always stands out in a crowd.* [Mid-1800s] 3. Refuse to comply, remain opposed, as in *The one juror is standing out against a guilty verdict.* [Late 1500s]

stand over 1. Watch or supervise closely, as in *I hate to cook when you're standing over me.* [First half of 1300s] 2. Postpone, as in *We'll have to let this budget item stand over till next year.* [Early 1800s]

stand pat Refuse to change one's position or opinion, as in *We're going to stand pat on this amendment to the bylaws.* This expression may be derived from the verb *pat* in the sense of "strike firmly and accurately." [Late 1800s]

standstill ♦ See COME TO A HALT (STANDSTILL).

stand still for ♦ See HOLD STILL FOR.

stand the gaff Take severe criticism or other adversity in stride, as in *If you can't stand the gaff, don't try running for office.* [Slang; late 1800s]

stand the sight of ♦ See CAN'T STAND THE SIGHT OF.

stand to reason Be logical or rational, as in *It stands to reason that if you don't like hot weather you shouldn't move to Florida.* [Early 1600s]

stand up 1. Remain valid, sound, or durable, as in *His claim will not stand up in court,* or *Our old car stood up well over time.* [Mid-1900s] 2. Fail to keep a date or appointment with, as in *Al stood her up twice in the past week, and that will be the end of their relationship.* [Colloquial; c. 1900] Also see STAND UP FOR; STAND UP TO; STAND UP WITH.

stand up and be counted Reveal one's convictions or opinions, especially when it requires courage to do so. For example, *Stop muttering your complaints about the music; stand up and be counted if you want something changed.* The counted in this expression alludes to having one's vote on a matter acknowledged. [c. 1900]

stand up for Also, **stick up for.** Side with, defend, as in *Paul always stands up for what he thinks is right,* or *Ginny has learned to stick up for her family.* The first recorded use of the first term is by Shakespeare in *King Lear* (1:2), when Edmund, Gloucester's bastard son, says: "Now gods, stand up for bastards!" The colloquial variant was first recorded in 1837.

stand up to Confront fearlessly, oppose boldly, as in *You've got to stand up to the boss if you want him to respect you.* [Early 1600s]

stand up with Be the principal witness at a wedding, that is, act as best man or maid or matron of honor. For example, *Jane asked her sister to stand up with her.*

star ♦ In addition to the idiom beginning with STAR, also see BORN UNDER A LUCKY STAR; SEE STARS; THANK ONE'S LUCKY STARS.

starch ♦ See TAKE THE STARCH OUT OF.

stare down Cause someone to waver or give in by or as if by being stared at. For example, *Insisting on a better room, he stared down the manager until he got it.* This expression alludes to staring at someone without being the first to blink or lower one's gaze. [Mid-1800s]

stare in the face Also, **look in the face.** Be glaringly obvious, although initially overlooked, as in *The solution to the problem had been staring me in the face all along,* or *I wouldn't know a Tibetan terrier if it looked me in the face.* [Late 1600s]

stark raving mad Totally crazy, as in *The constant uncertainty over his job is making him stark raving mad.* This term, meaning "completely wildly insane," is used both hyperbolically and literally. Versions of this expression appear to have sprung from the minds of great literary figures. **Stark mad** was first recorded by poet John Skelton in 1489; **stark raving** was first recorded by playwright John Beaumont in 1648; **stark staring mad** was first used by John Dryden in 1693. The current wording, **stark raving mad,** first appeared in Henry Fielding's *The Intriguing Chambermaid* in 1734.

stars in one's eyes, have Be dazzled or enraptured, especially with romance; also, be naively idealistic or optimistic. For example, *Thinking about their coming marriage, they both had stars in their eyes,* or *Kit had stars in her eyes when she talked about the millions who would buy her recording.* This idiom transfers the shining of stars to eyes shining with love or enthusiasm. [c. 1900]

start ♦ In addition to the idioms beginning with START, also see FALSE START; FITS AND STARTS; FOR OPENERS (STARTERS); (START) FROM SCRATCH; FROM SOUP TO NUTS (START TO FINISH); GET OFF THE GROUND (TO A FLYING START); HEAD START; RUNNING START; TO START WITH.

starters ♦ See under FOR OPENERS.

start from scratch ♦ See FROM SCRATCH.

start in Begin, as in *He started in serving, without taking any practice.* [Late 1800s] Also see START OUT.

start in on 1. Begin doing something, as in *We started right in on the repairs.* Also see START IN. 2. Attack, especially verbally, as in *Nancy keeps starting in on Carl, complaining about the errors in his work.* [Early 1900s]

start off 1. Set out on a trip, as in *We plan to start off in the morning.* [Early 1800s] Also see START

OUT. **2. start someone off.** Cause someone to set out or to begin something, as in *Mother packed their lunches and started them off,* or *Paul started them off on their multiplication tables.* [Early 1700s] For **start off on the right foot,** see GET OFF ON THE RIGHT FOOT.

start out Set out on a trip, as in *The climbers started out from base camp shortly after midnight.* [Early 1900s]

start over Begin again, as in *This article is no good; I'll have to start over.* [Early 1900s]

start something Cause trouble, especially a quarrel or fight, as in *Stop bringing that up — do you want to start something?* [Colloquial; early 1900s]

start up **1.** Begin to operate, especially a machine or engine, as in *Start up the motor so we can get going.* [First half of 1900s] **2.** Move suddenly or begin an activity, as in *When the alarm rang I started up.* [Early 1200s] **3.** Organize a new enterprise, as in *Starting up a business requires considerable capital.* [Second half of 1900s]

state ◆ In addition to the idiom beginning with STATE, also see IN A LATHER (STATE); IN STATE; SHIP OF STATE.

state of the art The highest level of development, very up-to-date, as in *This new television set reflects the state of the art in screen technology.* Despite including the word *art,* this term originated in technology, and its first recorded use appears in a 1910 book on the gas turbine. Today it is often used adjectivally, as in *This is a state-of-the-art camera,* and sometimes very loosely, as in *That movie is state-of-the-art Woody Allen.*

status quo The existing condition or state of affairs, as in *We don't want to admit more singers to the chorus; we like the status quo.* This term, Latin for "state in which," has been used in English since the early 1800s.

status symbol A position or activity that allows one's social prestige to be displayed, as in *She doesn't even drive; that car of hers is purely a status symbol.* [Mid-1900s]

stave off Keep or hold away, repel, as in *The Federal Reserve Board is determined to stave off inflation.* This metaphoric expression transfers beating something off with a staff or stave to nonphysical repulsion. [c. 1600]

stay ◆ In addition to the idioms beginning with STAY, also see HERE TO STAY; (STAY) IN TOUCH; (STAY ON ONE'S) RIGHT SIDE; SHOULD HAVE STOOD (STAYED) IN BED; STICK (STAY) WITH.

staying power The ability to endure or last, as in *I'm not sure that this young novelist will have staying power,* or *Our candidate definitely has staying power.* This expression comes from racing, where

it means "the strength to maintain speed through a race." [Second half of 1800s]

stay over Remain overnight, as in *We hadn't planned to stay over but the bad weather changed our plans.* [Late 1800s]

stay put Remain in a fixed or established position, as in *I can't get that trellis to stay put,* or *I'm coming, just stay put till I get there.* [First half of 1800s]

stay the course Hold or persevere to the end, as in *No, he's not resigning; he's going to stay the course.* This metaphoric expression, alluding to a horse running an entire race, was first recorded in 1916.

stay with **1.** Remain in one's mind or memory, as in *That song has stayed with me all these years.* [Late 1500s] **2.** Keep up with; also, concentrate on, continue with. For example, *The runner from Kenya stayed with Mark almost to the finish line,* or *She has an amazing talent for staying with a problem.* [Late 1800s] Also see STICK WITH.

stead ◆ See IN SOMEONE'S SHOES (STEAD); STAND IN GOOD STEAD. Also see under INSTEAD.

steady ◆ In addition to the idiom beginning with STEADY, also see GO STEADY; SLOW BUT SURE (STEADY WINS THE RACE).

steady as a rock Firm, dependable, as in *Betty always knows her part; she's steady as a rock.* This simile uses *rock* in the sense of "something that affords a sure support," a usage dating from the early 1500s.

steal a march on Gain an advantage over unexpectedly or secretly, as in *Macy's stole a march on their rival department store with their Thanksgiving Day parade.* This metaphoric expression comes from medieval warfare, where a *march* was the distance an army could travel in a day. By quietly marching at night, a force could surprise and overtake the enemy at daybreak. Its figurative use dates from the second half of the 1700s.

steal someone blind Also, **rob someone blind.** Rob or cheat someone mercilessly, as in *Ann always maintained that children would steal their parents blind.* The allusion here is unclear. Possibly it means stealing everything, including someone's sight. [Mid-1900s]

steal someone's heart Win someone's love, as in *That puppy stole Brian's heart.* [Late 1500s]

steal someone's thunder Use or appropriate another's idea, especially to one's advantage, as in *It was Harold's idea but they stole his thunder and turned it into a massive advertising campaign without giving him credit.* This idiom comes from an actual incident in which playwright and critic John Dennis (1657–1734) devised a "thunder machine" (by rattling a sheet of tin backstage) for his play, *Appius and Virginia* (1709), and a few days later discovered the same device being used in a performance of *Macbeth*, whereupon he declared, "They steal my thunder."

steal the show Also, **steal the spotlight**. Be the center of attention, as in *The speeches were interesting but Eliza's singing stole the show*. This idiom alludes to unexpectedly outshining the rest of the cast in a theatrical production. [First half of 1900s]

steam ♦ See BLOW OFF STEAM; FULL SPEED (STEAM) AHEAD; GET UP STEAM; RUN OUT OF STEAM; UNDER ONE'S OWN STEAM.

steamed up Stirred up, aroused with ardor, excitement, anger, or other strong emotion, as in *She was all steamed up about the results*. The precise meaning depends on the context. [Colloquial; early 1900s]

steel ♦ In addition to the idiom beginning with STEEL, also see MIND LIKE A STEEL TRAP.

steel one's heart against Also, **harden one's heart**. Suppress one's feelings for, as in *He finally steeled his heart against them and refused the loan*, or *You'll just have to harden your heart and tell them the truth*. This metaphoric idiom transfers making something hard to rendering oneself insensible or unfeeling. Versions of it date from the late 1500s. Also see HEART OF STONE.

steer ♦ In addition to the idiom beginning with STEER, also see BUM STEER.

steer clear of Stay away from, avoid, as in *Dad warned us to steer clear of Dr. Smith and his poor advice*. This idiom alludes to guiding a vessel away from some obstacle. Its figurative use was first recorded in 1723.

stem ♦ In addition to the idiom beginning with STEM, also see FROM SOUP TO NUTS (STEM TO STERN).

stem the tide Stop the course of a trend or tendency, as in *It is not easy to stem the tide of public opinion*. This idiom uses *stem* in the sense of "stop" or "restrain." [Mid-1800s]

stem to stern ♦ See under FROM SOUP TO NUTS.

step ♦ In addition to the idioms beginning with STEP, also see FALSE STEP; IN STEP; (STEP) OUT OF LINE; TAKE STEPS; WATCH ONE'S STEP.

step aside 1. Move out of the way, as in *Please step aside—I've got my arms full of groceries*. This usage was first recorded in 1530. 2. Withdraw, make room for a replacement, as in *The senior researcher decided to step aside for a younger colleague*. [Second half of 1900s]

step by step By degrees, as in *You'll have to go through this recipe step by step*. This idiom transfers putting one foot in front of the other to other kinds of progress. [c. 1700]

step down 1. Resign from office, as in *He threatened to step down if they continued to argue with him*. [Late 1800s] 2. Reduce, especially in stages, as in *They were stepping down the voltage*. [c. 1900] Also see STEP UP, def. 1.

step in Enter into an activity or situation; also, intervene. For example, *The business was doing poorly until Stan stepped in*, or *They are going to make a mess of the mailing unless someone steps in and shows them what to do*. [Late 1400s] Also see STEP INTO.

step in the right direction, a A move that advances a course of action, as in *Asking Bill to resign is a step in the right direction*. This idiom was first recorded in 1871.

step into Involve oneself or intervene, as in *He knew he'd be able to step into a job in his father's firm*, or *Jane asked Mary to step into the matter and settle it*. Also see STEP IN.

step into someone's shoes Take someone's place, as in *He's groomed Harriet to step into his shoes when he resigns*. Also see FILL SOMEONE'S SHOES; IN SOMEONE'S SHOES.

step on it Hurry up, go faster, as in *Step on it or we are going to be late*. This idiom alludes to stepping on a vehicle's gas pedal. [Colloquial; c. 1920]

step on someone's toes Also, **tread on someone's toes**. Hurt or offend someone. For example, *Be careful what you say about her losing weight; don't step on her toes*, or *Would I be stepping on someone's toes if I asked to help out with the party arrangements?* This metaphoric idiom transfers physical to emotional pain. [Late 1300s]

step out 1. Walk briskly, as in *He stepped out in time to the music*. [c. 1800] 2. Also, **step outside**. Go outside briefly, as in *He just stepped out for a cigarette*. [First half of 1500s] 3. Go out for an evening of entertainment, as in *They're stepping out again tonight*. 4. **step out with**. Accompany or consort with a person as when going on a date, as in *She's been stepping out with him for a month*. [Colloquial; early 1900s]

step out of line ♦ See OUT OF LINE, def. 1.

step up 1. Increase, especially in stages, as in *We've got to step up production*. [Early 1900s] Also see STEP DOWN, def. 2. 2. Come forward, as in *Step up to the podium, folks, and I'll show you how it works*. [Mid-1600s]

stern ♦ See FROM SOUP TO NUTS (STEM TO STERN).

steven ♦ See EVEN STEVEN.

stew ♦ In addition to the idiom beginning with STEW, also see IN A STEW.

stew in one's own juice Suffer the consequences of one's actions, as in *He's run into debt again, but this time we're leaving him to stew in his own juice*.

This metaphoric term alludes to cooking something in its own liquid. Versions of it, such as **fry in one's own grease**, date from Chaucer's time, but the present term dates from the second half of the 1800s.

stick ♦ In addition to the idioms beginning with STICK, also see CARROT AND STICK; GET ON THE STICK; MAKE STICK; MORE THAN ONE CAN SHAKE A STICK AT; SHORT END OF THE STICK; STAND (STICK) UP FOR; WRONG END OF THE STICK. Also see under STUCK.

stick around Remain, linger, as in *I hope you'll stick around till the end.* This idiom uses *stick* in the sense of "stay." [Colloquial; early 1900s]

stick at Scruple or hesitate, as in *She sticks at nothing to gain her ends.* This idiom, nearly always used in a negative context, was first recorded in 1525. Also see STOP AT NOTHING.

stick by Also, **stick to.** Remain loyal to, as in *The brothers said they'd stick by one another, no matter what,* or *Phyllis promised to stick to Bert.* This idiom derives from *stick* in the sense of "adhere." [Early 1500s] Also see STAND BY, def. 4.

stick in one's craw Also, **stick in one's throat. 1.** Be unable to say something, as in *I meant to apologize but the words stuck in my craw.* [Early 1600s] **2.** Be so offensive that one can't tolerate it, as in *That obscene art exhibit stuck in my throat.* [Late 1600s]

stick it 1. Continue what one is doing, endure something to the end, as in *I hate large parties but I promised her I'd stick it to the end.* [Early 1900s] Also see STICK OUT, def. 2. **2.** Also, **stick it** or **shove it up one's ass.** Do whatever you like with it, I don't want it, as in *Do that job all over again? Why don't you stick it?*, or *Tell the chef he can take this fish and shove it up his ass.* This vulgar slangy idiom, which uses *stick* in the sense of "thrust inward or upward," also functions as a variant of UP YOURS. [Second half of 1800s]

stick it to someone Treat someone badly or unfairly, as in *The head nurse really stuck it to Judy when she made her take all three shifts.* This slangy usage may be derived from STICK IT, def. 2.

stick one's neck out Make oneself vulnerable, take a risk, as in *I'm going to stick my neck out and ask for a raise.* This expression probably alludes to a chicken extending its neck before being slaughtered. [Colloquial; early 1900s]

stick out 1. Also, **stick out a mile** or **like a sore thumb.** Be very prominent or conspicuous, as in *Dad's funny hat made him stick out in the crowd,* or *That purple house sticks out a mile,* or *John's lie sticks out like a sore thumb.* The first term dates from the mid-1500s, the variants from the first half of the 1900s. The variant using *thumb* alludes to the propensity for holding an injured thumb stiffly, making it stand out (and thereby risking

further injury). **2.** Continue doing something, endure something, as in *I know you don't like it but you have to stick out the job for another month.* [Late 1600s] A variant is **stick it out,** as in *His new play's boring, but since he's my cousin we'd better stick it out.* [Late 1800s] Also see STICK IT, def. 1.

stick to 1. Remain loyal; see STICK BY. **2.** Persist in or continue applying oneself to, as in *I'm sticking to my opinion that he's basically honest,* or *The music teacher told John to stick to the clarinet, at least until the end of the year.* [First half of 1500s] Also see STICK TO ONE'S GUNS; STICK TO ONE'S LAST.

stick together Remain united, as in *It's important that we stick together on this issue.* [Mid-1500s]

stick to one's guns Hold fast to a statement, opinion, or course of action, as in *The witness stuck to her guns about the exact time she was there.* This expression, originally put as *stand to one's guns,* alluded to a gunner remaining by his post. Its figurative use dates from the mid-1800s.

stick to one's last Keep to what you know and don't interfere out of your province, as in *Let me handle the defense in this suit; you stick to your last and track down more eyewitnesses.* This adage comes from an ancient story about a shoemaker criticizing a work by a Greek painter named Apelles, saying that the shoe in the picture was not correctly portrayed. After the painter corrected it, the shoemaker pointed out an error in the leg, whereupon the painter said, "Shoemaker, do not go above your last." Over the centuries the story was repeated, and the expression still is sometimes put as **cobbler, stick to your last,** even though cobblers are nearly obsolete.

stick to the ribs Be substantial or filling, as in *It may not be health food but steak really sticks to the ribs.* This idiom was first recorded in 1603.

stick up 1. Project from a surface, as in *That little cowlick of his sticks up no matter what you do.* [Early 1400s] **2.** Put up a poster or notice, as in *Will you stick up this announcement on the bulletin board?* [Late 1700s] **3.** Rob, especially at gunpoint, as in *The gang concentrated on sticking up liquor stores and gas stations.* This usage, dating from the mid-1800s, gave rise to the colloquial phrase, **stick 'em up,** a robber's order to a victim to raise his or her hands above the head. [1930s]

stick up for ♦ See STAND UP FOR.

stick with Continue to support or be faithful to, as in *They stuck with us through all our difficulties.* [Colloquial; early 1900s]

sticky fingers A propensity to steal, as in *You'd better not leave any cash around; she's known for her sticky fingers.* This metaphor makes it seem as if valuables adhere naturally to a thief's fingers. [Colloquial; late 1800s]

stiff ◆ In addition to the idioms beginning with STIFF, also see BORE TO DEATH (STIFF); KEEP A STIFF UPPER LIP; SCARE OUT OF ONE'S WITS (STIFF).

stiff as a board Also, **stiff as a poker**. Inflexible, rigidly formal, unbending, as in *This cloth is stiff as a board; what happened to it?* or *There he stood, stiff as a poker, unwilling to give an inch*. The *board* in the first simile for rigidity is a slab of wood; the second, alluding to the iron implement used to push around logs in open fires, dates from the late 1700s.

stiff upper lip ◆ See KEEP A STIFF UPPER LIP.

still ◆ In addition to the idioms beginning with STILL, also see HEART MISSES A BEAT (STANDS STILL); HOLD STILL; JURY IS STILL OUT; KEEP QUIET (STILL); QUIET (STILL) AS A MOUSE.

still and all Nevertheless, all the same, as in *But still and all, trekking in Nepal is an expensive undertaking*. Although critics believe this idiom is an unnecessarily long form of the adverb *still*, it has been used since the early 1800s and remains current.

still small voice One's conscience, as in *I'd love to go but a still small voice tells me I really have to stay home and work*. The term comes from the Bible (I Kings 19:12), where Elijah hears his own inner voice: "And after the earthquake a fire . . . and after the fire a still small voice."

still waters run deep A quiet person may be very profound, as in *Susie rarely says much, but still waters run deep*. The physical observation in this term dates from ancient times, but it has been used figuratively since about 1400. Anthony Trollope amplified it in *He Knew He Was Right* (1869): "That's what I call still water. She runs deep enough. . . . So quiet, but so—clever."

sting ◆ See TAKE THE STING OUT OF.

stink ◆ In addition to the idiom beginning with STINK, also see BIG STINK; MAKE A STINK; SMELL (STINK) UP.

stink to high heaven Also, **smell to high heaven**. Be of very poor quality; also, be suspect or in bad repute. For example, *This plan of yours stinks to high heaven*, or *His financial schemes smell to high heaven; I'm sure they're dishonest*. This expression alludes to something so rank that it can be smelled from a great distance. [c. 1600]

stir ◆ In addition to the idioms beginning with STIR, also see CAUSE A COMMOTION (STIR).

stir up 1. Mix together the ingredients or parts, as in *He stirred up some pancake batter*, or *Will you stir up the fire?* [Mid-1300s] 2. Rouse to action, incite, provoke, as in *He's always stirring up trouble among the campers*, or *If the strikers aren't careful*

they'll stir up a riot. [First half of 1500s] Also see STIR UP A HORNETS' NEST.

stir up a hornets' nest Make trouble, cause a commotion, as in *Asking for an audit of the treasurer's books stirred up a hornets' nest in the association*. This metaphoric term, likening hornets to angry humans, dates from the first half of the 1700s.

stitch ◆ In addition to the idiom beginning with STITCH, also see IN STITCHES; WITHOUT A STITCH ON.

stitch in time, a A prompt action will avert more serious trouble. For example, *Changing the car's oil every 7,000 miles is a stitch in time*. The complete form of this adage, **a stitch in time saves nine**, appeared in Thomas Fuller's 1732 proverb collection, *Gnomologia*, and is so well known that it often is stated in shortened form. Ogden Nash played with it in the title for his verse collection, *A Stitch Too Late Is My Fate* (1938).

stock ◆ See IN STOCK; LOCK, STOCK, AND BARREL; MAKE A LAUGHING STOCK OF; TAKE STOCK; TAKE STOCK IN.

stocking feet Wearing socks or stockings, but not shoes, as in *I got locked out of the house in my stocking feet*. [First half of 1800s]

stomach ◆ See BUTTERFLIES IN ONE'S STOMACH; CAN'T STAND (STOMACH) THE SIGHT OF; EYES ARE BIGGER THAN ONE'S STOMACH; NO STOMACH FOR; SICK TO ONE'S STOMACH; TURN ONE'S STOMACH.

stone ◆ In addition to the idioms beginning with STONE, also see CAST IN STONE; CAST THE FIRST STONE; FLAT (STONE) BROKE; HEART OF STONE; LEAVE NO STONE UNTURNED; ROLLING STONE GATHERS NO MOSS; RUN INTO A STONE WALL.

stone cold Unfeeling, insensible, as in *That sad story left her stone cold*. This analogy was already used by Shakespeare in *Henry V* (2:3): "Cold as any stone."

stone deaf Totally unable to hear, as in *Poor Grandpa, in the last year he's become stone deaf*. [First half of 1800s]

stone's throw, a A very short distance, as in *They live just a stone's throw from us*. This metaphoric term alludes to how far one can toss a stone. [Second half of 1500s]

stood ◆ See SHOULD HAVE STOOD IN BED.

stool ◆ In addition to the idiom beginning with STOOL, also see FALL BETWEEN THE CRACKS (TWO STOOLS).

stool pigeon A decoy or informer, especially a police spy. For example, *Watch out for Doug; I'm sure he's a stool pigeon for the supervisor*. This term alludes to a bird tied to a stool or similar perch in order to attract other birds, which will then be shot. However, one writer believes that *stool* is a variant for *stale* or *stall*, both nouns used for a decoy bird before 1500 or so. [c. 1820]

stoop labor Back-bending manual work, especially farm work. For example, *They had us picking peas all day, and that's too much stoop labor:* [First half of 1900s]

stoop to Condescend to something beneath one's dignity, as in *She wouldn't stoop to listening to that obnoxious gossip.* [Second half of 1500s]

stop ♦ In addition to the idioms beginning with STOP, also see BUCK STOPS HERE; PULL OUT ALL THE STOPS; PUT AN END (A STOP) TO.

stop at nothing Do everything in one's power, be prevented by no obstacle, as in *She'll stop at nothing to get her revenge.* This expression was first recorded in John Dryden's *Aurengzebe* (1676): "The World is made for the bold impious man; Who stops at nothing, seizes all he can."

stop by Also, **stop in.** Pay a brief visit, as in *I hope you'll stop by this afternoon,* or *He stopped in at Martha's whenever he came to New York on business.* The first term dates from about 1900, the variant from the mid-1800s.

stop cold Also, **stop dead** or in **in one's tracks** or **on a dime.** Halt suddenly, come to a standstill, as in *When a thread breaks, the machine just stops cold,* or *He was so surprised to see them in the audience that he stopped dead in the middle of his speech,* or *The deer saw the hunter and stopped in its tracks,* or *An excellent skateboarder, she could stop on a dime.* The first term uses *cold* in the sense "suddenly and completely," a usage dating from the late 1800s. The first variant was first recorded in 1789 and probably was derived from the slightly older, and still current, **come to a dead stop,** with the same meaning. The second variant uses *in one's tracks* in the sense of "on the spot" or "where one is at the moment"; it was first recorded in 1824. The third variant alludes to the *dime* or ten-cent piece, the smallest-size coin.

stop in ♦ See under STOP BY.

stop off Also, **stop over.** Interrupt a journey for a short stay somewhere, as in *When we drove through Massachusetts we stopped off for a few days at Cape Cod,* or *When you're in the area try to stop over and see our new house.* [Mid-1800s]

stop payment Instruct a bank not to honor a check one has drawn, as in *If that check was lost, we'll have to stop payment on it before issuing another.* This usage was first recorded in 1722.

stop short 1. Also, **stop one short.** Check abruptly, as in *When we tried to cross the street, the barrier stopped us short.* [Early 1300s] 2. Cause someone to stop speaking, as in *I was about to tell them the date when my father stopped me short.* [Late 1800s] 3. **stop short of.** Not go so far as to do or say something. For example, *He may embroider*

the truth but he stops short of actually lying. This usage was first recorded in 1818.

stop someone's clock Kill someone, as in *They threatened to stop his clock if he appeared on the witness stand.* This expression transfers the ticking of a clock to the progress of one's life. [Slang; 1940s]

stop the clock Postpone a deadline by not counting the elapsing hours. For example, *Management agreed to stop the clock so that a new contract could be negotiated before the present one expired.* [Mid-1900s]

stop up Fill a hole or gap, block an opening or passage. For example, *We need to stop up the chinks in the walls,* or *The sink is stopped up; it won't drain.* This idiom was at first put simply as *stop,* the adverb *up* being added only in the early 1700s.

storage ♦ See IN COLD STORAGE.

store ♦ See IN STORE; MIND THE STORE; SET STORE BY; VARIETY STORE.

storm ♦ See ANY PORT IN A STORM; KICK UP A FUSS (STORM); RIDE OUT (THE STORM); TAKE BY STORM; WEATHER THE STORM.

story ♦ In addition to the idiom beginning with STORY, also see COCK AND BULL STORY; COVER STORY; FISH STORY; HARD LUCK STORY; MAKE A LONG STORY SHORT; OLD STORY; SAME OLD STORY; SHAGGY DOG STORY; SOB STORY; UPPER STORY.

story of my life, the What typically happens to me, as in *I rushed through the meeting to get to the airport, and then the plane was three hours late—that's the story of my life.* This hyperbolic expression is generally used ruefully to describe some mishap or misfortune. [Mid-1900s]

stow away 1. Put aside or store something until needed, as in *We generally stow away the lawn furniture in the toolshed.* [Late 1700s] 2. Hide oneself aboard ship or in a vehicle in order to get free transportation, as in *The youngsters planned to stow away on a freighter but they never even got to the waterfront.* This usage gave rise to the noun *stowaway.* [Mid-1800s] 2. Greedily consume food or drink, as in *Bob sure can stow away a lot in a short time.* [Colloquial; mid-1800s]

straddle the fence ♦ See ON THE FENCE.

straight ♦ In addition to the idioms beginning with STRAIGHT, also see (STRAIGHT) FROM THE HORSE'S MOUTH; GET SOMETHING STRAIGHT; GIVE IT TO (SOMEONE STRAIGHT); GO STRAIGHT; KEEP A STRAIGHT FACE; RIGHT (STRAIGHT) OUT; SET STRAIGHT; SHOOT STRAIGHT.

straight and narrow, the The honest and upright way of living, as in *He led a wild life when he was young, but he's been on the straight and narrow for some years.* This expression is widely thought to come from confusion of *straight,* "not crooked," with *straight*, "narrow," owing to a misinterpretation of a passage from the New Testament: "Strait is the gate, and narrow is the way, which leadeth unto life" (Matthew 7:14). The current phrase dates only from the first half of the 1800s.

straight as an arrow Honest, genuine, as in *You can trust Pat with the money; he's straight as an arrow*. This simile alludes to the arrow's undeviating flight through the air. [Second half of 1900s]

straighten out 1. Clear up disorder, a confusion, or a misunderstanding, as in *This is an awful mess; I hope you'll straighten it out*, or *I don't understand; please straighten me out*. [Late 1800s] 2. Adopt an honest, upright course, as in *He's only sixteen; I'm sure he'll straighten out before long*. [First half of 1900s]

straighten up Make tidy, as in *Let's get this room straightened up*. [Second half of 1800s]

straight face ♦ See KEEP A STRAIGHT FACE.

straight from the horse's mouth ♦ See FROM THE HORSE'S MOUTH.

straight from the shoulder In a direct, forthright manner, as in *I'll tell you, straight from the shoulder, that you'll have to do better or they'll fire you*. This expression comes from boxing, where it describes a blow delivered with full force. Its figurative use dates from the late 1800s.

straight goods The truth, as in *Is that straight goods about how much you still owe?* or *I'm giving you the straight goods about Monica*. [Slang; late 1800s]

straight off Also, **straight away**. Immediately, as in *I knew straight off that he was lying*, or *I'll get to the dishes straight away*. The first term dates from the late 1700s, the variant from the mid-1600s.

straight out ♦ See RIGHT OUT.

straight talk Plain, honest speaking, as in *We have to have some straight talk with Harry before he goes away to college*. [Late 1800s]

straight ticket All the candidates of a single political party, as in *Are you going to vote a straight ticket again?* [Mid-1800s] Also see SPLIT TICKET.

straight up Served without ice, generally said of an alcoholic drink, as in *He ordered a martini straight up*. *Straight* was first recorded with this meaning in 1874.

strange bedfellows A peculiar alliance or combination, as in *George and Arthur really are strange bedfellows, sharing the same job but totally different in their views*. Although strictly speaking *bedfellows* are persons who share a bed, like husband and wife, the term has been used figuratively since the late 1400s. This particular idiom may have been invented by Shakespeare in *The Tempest* (2:2), "Misery acquaints a man with strange bedfellows." Today a common extension is **politics**

makes strange bedfellows, meaning that politicians form peculiar associations so as to win more votes. A similar term is **odd couple**, a pair who share either housing or a business but are very different in most ways. This term gained currency with Neil Simon's Broadway play *The Odd Couple* and, even more, with the motion picture (1968) and subsequent television series based on it, contrasting housemates Felix and Oscar, one meticulously neat and obsessively punctual, the other extremely messy and casual.

strange to say Also, **strangely enough**. Surprisingly, curiously, unaccountably, as in *Strange to say, all the boys in his class are six feet tall or taller*, or *I've never been to the circus, strangely enough*. This idiom was first recorded in 1697 as *strange to relate*.

strapped for In need of, as in *We're strapped for cash this week*. Originating in the mid-1800s as simply *strapped*, meaning "in need of money," the term acquired *for* in the first half of the 1900s. Now the term is also used for other needs, as in *I can't give you any more firewood; I'm strapped for it myself*.

straw ♦ In addition to the idioms beginning with STRAW, also see DRAW STRAWS; GRASP AT STRAWS; LAST STRAW; MAKE BRICKS WITHOUT STRAW; NOT WORTH A DIME (STRAW).

straw boss A subordinate boss, a worker who supervises other workers as well as performing regular duties. For example, *Jim was pleased when he was promoted to straw boss*. This term alludes to the person's position as a **straw man**, that is, a front or cover for the real boss and of only nominal importance. [Late 1800s]

straw in the wind A slight hint of the future, as in *The public unrest is a straw in the wind indicating future problems for the regime*. This expression alludes to a straw showing in what direction the wind blows, an observation also behind the idiom STRAW VOTE.

straw that breaks the camel's back ♦ See LAST STRAW.

straw vote Also, **straw poll**. An unofficial vote or poll indicating how people feel about a candidate or issue. For example, *Let's take a straw poll on the bill and see how it fares*. This idiom alludes to a straw used to show in what direction the wind blows, in this case the wind of public opinion. O. Henry joked about it in *A Ruler of Men* (1907): "A straw vote only shows which way the hot air blows." [c. 1885]

streak ♦ See LIKE GREASED LIGHTNING (A BLUE STREAK); TALK SOMEONE'S ARM OFF (A BLUE STREAK); WINNING STREAK.

stream ♦ See CHANGE HORSES IN MIDSTREAM; SWIM AGAINST THE CURRENT (STREAM).

street ♦ See BACK STREET; EASY STREET; MAN IN THE STREET; ON THE STREET; SIDE STREET; WORK BOTH SIDES OF THE STREET.

strength ♦ See BRUTE FORCE (STRENGTH); ON THE STRENGTH OF; TOWER OF STRENGTH.

stress out Subject to or undergo extreme pressure or strain, as from working. For example, *I badly need a vacation; I'm just plain stressed out from this job and its aggravations.* The verb *stress* has meant "afflict with hardship" or "distress" since the 16th century, but the phrase **stress out**, alluding to psychological stress, dates only from the 1940s.

stretch ♦ In addition to the idioms beginning with STRETCH, also see AT A STRETCH; BY ANY STRETCH.

stretch a point Extend or enlarge beyond the usual limits, exaggerate, as in *It would be stretching a point to say this novel is the work of a great writer.* [Mid-1600s]

stretch one's legs Stand up or go for a walk, especially after a prolonged period of sitting. For example, *Let's go stretch our legs at intermission.* [c. 1600]

stride ♦ See HIT ONE'S STRIDE; MAKE GREAT STRIDES; TAKE IN STRIDE.

strike ♦ In addition to the idioms beginning with STRIKE, also see GO OUT (ON STRIKE); HAPPY MEDIUM, STRIKE A; LIGHTNING NEVER STRIKES TWICE; ON STRIKE; TWO STRIKES AGAINST.

strike a balance Find a compromise, as in *We have to strike a balance between what we want and what we can afford.* This expression alludes to accounting, where it signifies finding a profit or loss by weighing income versus outlay. [Mid-1800s]

strike a bargain Reach an agreement, as in *They finally struck a bargain after weeks of wrangling over who would get what.* [Mid-1700s]

strike a chord Trigger a feeling or memory, as in *That poem strikes a chord in all those touched by the Holocaust.* This term alludes to striking the strings or keys of a musical instrument. [First half of 1800s] Also see STRIKE THE RIGHT NOTE.

strike a happy medium ♦ See HAPPY MEDIUM.

strike down 1. Fell with a blow or misfortune, as in *The tree was struck down by lightning,* or *He was struck down by tuberculosis while in his twenties.* [Late 1400s] 2. Render ineffective, cancel, especially in a legal context. For example, *The appeals court struck down the verdict.* [Late 1800s]

strike it rich Also, **strike oil** or **strike it lucky.** Experience sudden financial success, as in *He never dreamed that he'd strike it rich this soon,* or *They really struck oil with that investment,* or *One of these days we'll strike it lucky.* The first of these idioms originated in mining, where it referred to finding a rich mineral deposit. [Colloquial; second half of 1800s]

strike out 1. Cancel or erase, as in *Strike out that last sentence, please.* [Early 1500s] 2. Begin a course of action, set out energetically, as in *Elaine was determined to strike out on her own.* [Early 1700s] 3. Fail in an endeavor, as in *His latest business venture has struck out.* This usage originated in baseball, where it refers to a batter's failure to put the ball in play (*Williams struck out three times in yesterday's game*), as well as to a pitcher's success in eliminating a batter (*Clemens struck him out again in the fourth inning*). [Late 1800s]

strike the right note Say or do what is especially appropriate, as in *She struck the right note when she complimented the new parents on their baby.* This expression alludes to playing the correct note on an instrument.

strike while the iron is hot Take advantage of favorable conditions, as in *They just made a huge profit, so let's strike while the iron is hot and ask for some money.* This adage alludes to the blacksmith's forge. [Late 1300s] Also see MAKE HAY WHILE THE SUN SHINES.

string ♦ In addition to the idioms beginning with STRING, also see HARP ON (ONE STRING); NO STRINGS ATTACHED; ON A SHOESTRING; ON A STRING; PULL STRINGS; PURSE STRINGS; TIED TO APRON STRINGS; TWO STRINGS TO ONE'S BOW.

string along 1. Go along with someone, accompany or follow, as in *I decided to string along with them, just to see what might happen.* [Colloquial; first half of 1900s]. 2. Agree, as in *We knew that three committee members would string along with us for now.* [Colloquial; first half of 1900s] 3. **string someone along.** Keep someone waiting or in a state of uncertainty; also, fool or deceive someone. For example, *We were stringing them along, hoping that we'd get a better offer,* or *She was in tears when she found out that he'd just been stringing her along.* [Colloquial; c. 1900]

string out 1. Stretch, extend; also, prolong. For example, *The parade strung out for miles,* or *The meetings strung out over weeks instead of days.* [First half of 1800s] 2. **strung out.** Addicted to, stupefied by, or debilitated by drug use, as in *She was completely strung out when they found her.* [Second half of 1900s]

strings attached ♦ See NO STRINGS ATTACHED.

string together Compose, assemble, as in *There's more to devising an effective slogan than stringing together some words.* This expression alludes to threading beads on a string. [First half of 1800s]

string up Hang; also, kill by hanging. For example, *They strung up their Christmas lights in October,* or *The mob wanted to string him up on the nearest tree.* [Early 1800s]

stroke ♦ See AT ONE STROKE; NO ACCOUNTING FOR TASTE (DIFFERENT STROKES FOR DIFFERENT FOLKS); PUT ONE OFF ONE'S STRIDE (STROKE).

strong ♦ In addition to the idioms beginning with STRONG, also see COME ON STRONG.

strong point Also, **strong suit**. An area in which someone or something excels, as in *That beautiful lobby is the building's strong point*, or *Writing is her strong suit*. The first term was first recorded in 1840; the variant alludes to various card games, in which it signifies the suit with the highest or most cards.

strong silent type A man of action who is reserved and masks his feelings. For example, *Paula always preferred the strong silent type to more extroverted men*. Almost never used for a woman, this expression may be obsolescent. [c. 1900]

strong suit ♦ See STRONG POINT.

strung out ♦ See STRING OUT, def. 2.

strut one's stuff Behave or perform in an ostentatious manner, show off, as in *The skaters were out, strutting their stuff*. This expression uses *strut* in the sense of "display in order to impress others." [Slang; first half of 1900s]

stubborn as a mule Extremely obstinate, as in *He's stubborn as a mule about wearing a suit and tie*. This simile evokes the proverbial stubbornness of mules, whose use as draft animals was once so common that the reputation for obstinacy can hardly be as warranted as the term indicates. [Early 1800s]

stuck for, be Be unable to obtain or think of, as in *We're stuck for a fourth for bridge*, or *In this course I'm always stuck for an answer*. [Colloquial; first half of 1900s]

stuck on, be Be very fond of, as in *She's been stuck on him ever since first grade*. [Slang; late 1800s]

stuck with Saddled or burdened with; also, unable to get rid of. For example, *Once again Dean was stuck with the check for all of the dinner guests*, or *She's my sister-in-law so I'm stuck with her*. [Mid-1800s]

study ♦ See BROWN STUDY.

stuff ♦ In addition to the idioms beginning with STUFF, also see GET STUFFED; HOT NUMBER (STUFF); KID STUFF; KNOW ONE'S STUFF; STRUT ONE'S STUFF.

stuff and nonsense Utter foolishness or absurdity, as in *Stuff and nonsense, of course I can pack a suitcase*. Often used as an interjection, this idiom employs *stuff* in the sense of "rubbish." It was first recorded in 1749.

stuffed shirt An overly formal or pompous person, as in *She's such a stuffed shirt that I'm surprised you'd invite her to a barbecue*. This expression alludes to a shirt filled with paper (instead of a real person). [c. 1900]

stuff it Take back something, as in *As for that memo of yours, you can just stuff it*. This idiom is used, often as an interjection, to express contempt or defiance. Presumably it is short for "Stuff it up your ass." [Vulgar slang; 1950s]

stuff one's face ♦ See FEED ONE'S FACE.

stuff the ballot box Put fraudulent votes in a ballot box, or otherwise cheat in an election. For example, *The only way he'll win is if we stuff the ballot box*. [Second half of 1800s]

stumble across Also, **stumble on**. Find by chance, discover or meet with unexpectedly. For example, *When we were hiking up the mountain we stumbled across a few abandoned shepherd's huts*, or *At the flea market Alfred stumbled on a quite valuable old lithograph*. This idiom uses *stumble* in the sense of "accidentally trip." [Mid-1500s]

stumbling block A hindrance or obstacle, as in *His lack of a degree is a real stumbling block to his advancement*. This term originally meant "a tree stump over which one trips." Its figurative use dates from the early 1500s.

style ♦ See CRAMP SOMEONE'S STYLE; GO OUT (OF STYLE); IN FASHION (STYLE).

subject ♦ In addition to the idiom beginning with SUBJECT, also see CHANGE THE SUBJECT.

subject to, be 1. Be under the control or authority of, as in *All citizens in this nation are subject to the law*. [First half of 1300s] 2. Be prone or disposed to, as in *This child has always been subject to colds*. [Late 1300s] 3. Be likely to incur or receive, as in *This memo is subject to misinterpretation*. [Late 1300s] 4. Depend on, be likely to be affected by, as in *Our vacation plans are subject to the boss's whims*. [Early 1800s]

subscribe to 1. Contract to receive and pay for a given number of issues of a periodical, for tickets to a series of performances, or for a utility service. For example, *We subscribe to the local paper*, or *Betty and I have been subscribing to this concert series for years*, or *We have no choice; we have to subscribe to the local power company*. 2. Feel or express approval of, as in *I subscribe to your opinion but I don't think Donald does*. [Mid-1500s] 3. Promise to pay or contribute money to, as in *We subscribe to many charities*. [Mid-1600s] All of these usages come from *subscribe* in the sense of "sign one's name to something, such as a pledge."

substance ♦ See IN SUBSTANCE; SUM AND SUBSTANCE.

such and such Not specified, unnamed and undetermined, as in *They agreed to meet at such and such a time and place*. [Mid-1500s]

such as For example, as in *She adores the English novels of manners, such as those by Austen and Trollope*. [Late 1600s]

such as it is In the form that it has, which is not very good but all that's available, as in *Of course you can stay for supper, such as it is.* This expression is generally used apologetically, indicating that the item in question isn't very good or worth much. [Late 1300s]

sucker list A list of names of likely prospects for making purchases or donations, as in *Some charities raise money by selling their sucker lists to other organizations.* This term uses *sucker* in the sense of "dupe," a usage that in turn alludes to the naiveté of a baby suckling at its mother's breast. [Colloquial; 1940s]

sucker punch An unexpected blow, as in *They felt that suddenly raising the interest rate was a sucker punch to the administration.* This expression comes from boxing, where it is used for a punch delivered unexpectedly; boxing great Jack Dempsey wrote, "The right lead [for a right-handed boxer] is called a sucker punch." [Slang; mid-1900s]

suck in 1. Also, **suck into**. Draw into a course of action, as in *They sucked me into helping them raise money.* [Second half of 1700s] 2. Take advantage of, cheat, swindle, as in *That used-car salesman sure sucked in my uncle and aunt.* This usage employs *suck* in the sense of "take in." [First half of 1800s]

suck up to Behave obsequiously towards, ingratiate oneself with, as in *Now that he's the boss they're all sucking up to him, hoping to get big raises.* [Vulgar slang; mid-1800s]

sudden ♦ See ALL OF A SUDDEN.

suffer ♦ See NOT SUFFER FOOLS GLADLY.

suffice it to say It is enough to say this and no more, as in *Suffice it to say that the judge was furious when the invitation was withdrawn.* [Late 1600s]

sugar daddy A wealthy, usually older man who gives expensive gifts to someone much younger in return for companionship or sexual favors. For example, *The aspiring young actress and the sugar daddy are a classic combination in Hollywood.* The *sugar* in this term alludes to the sweetening role of the gifts, and *daddy* to the age difference between the pair. [Early 1900s]

sugar the pill Make something unpleasant more palatable, as in *There would be no Christmas bonus this year but management sugared the pill by giving workers extra vacation time over the holidays.* [Late 1700s]

suit ♦ In addition to the idioms beginning with SUIT, also see BIRTHDAY SUIT; EMPTY SUIT; FOLLOW SUIT; LONG SUIT; STRONG POINT (SUIT).

suitcase ♦ See LIVE OUT (OF A SUITCASE).

suit down to the ground ♦ See under DOWN TO THE GROUND.

suit oneself Do as one pleases, as in *We had expected you, but if you don't want to come, suit yourself.* This idiom, which uses *suit* in the sense of "be agreeable or convenient," is often put as an imperative. [Late 1800s]

suit up Put on clothes for a particular activity, as in *Come on, fellows, it's time to suit up for the hockey game.* [Mid-1900s]

sum and substance The essence or gist of something, as in *The sum and substance of their platform is financial conservatism.* This redundant expression—both *sum* and *substance* here mean "essence"—has probably survived owing to alliteration. Shakespeare used it in *The Two Gentlemen of Verona* (4:1): "My riches are these poor habiliments [clothes], Of which if you should here disfurnish me, You take the sum and substance that I have."

sum total The entirety, everything, as in *I spent all day in the kitchen and the sum total of my efforts is this cake.* [Mid-1600s]

sum up Present the substance of, summarize, as in *They always sum up the important news in a couple of minutes,* or *That expletive sums up my feelings about the matter.* [Early 1600s]

sun ♦ In addition to the idiom beginning with SUN, also see EVERYTHING BUT THE KITCHEN SINK (UNDER THE SUN); MAKE HAY WHILE THE SUN SHINES; NOTHING NEW UNDER THE SUN; PLACE IN THE SUN.

sun belt The southern and southwestern United States, as in *Retirees have been moving to the sun belt for years.* It is so called for its warm climate. [Mid-1900s]

Sunday ♦ In addition to the idiom beginning with SUNDAY, also see MONTH OF SUNDAYS.

Sunday best One's finest clothes, as in *They were all in their Sunday best for the photographer.* This expression alludes to reserving one's best clothes for going to church; indeed, an older idiom is *Sunday-go-to-meeting clothes* (*meeting* here meaning "prayer meeting"). [Mid-1800s]

sundry ♦ See ALL AND SUNDRY.

sunny side 1. The pleasant or cheerful aspect of something, as in *Beth always sees the sunny side of events like graduations.* This idiom alludes to the area on which sunlight falls. [First half of 1800s] 2. **on the sunny side of.** At an age less than, younger than, as in *He's still on the sunny side of forty.* [Second half of 1800s] 3. **sunny-side up.** Fried so that the yolk remains intact and uppermost, as in *I ordered my eggs sunny-side up and you brought me scrambled eggs.* This expression transfers the appearance of the sun to that of an egg yolk. [c. 1900]

supper ♦ See SING FOR ONE'S SUPPER.

supply ♦ See IN SHORT SUPPLY.

suppose ♦ See I SUPPOSE SO.

supposed to 1. Intended to; also, believed to, expected to. For example, *This pill is supposed to relieve your pain*, or *You're supposed to be my partner*. [Early 1300s.] 2. Required to, as in *He is supposed to call home*. [Mid-1800s] 3. **not supposed to**. Not permitted to, as in *You're not supposed to smoke in here*.

sure ♦ In addition to the idioms beginning with SURE, also see FOR CERTAIN (SURE); MAKE SURE; SLOW BUT SURE; TO BE SURE.

sure as shooting Most certainly, as in *It's going to snow tonight, sure as shooting*, or *That grizzly is sure as shooting going to make dinner out of us*. This idiom has replaced the older *sure as a gun*, dating from the mid-1600s, a time when guns fired with far less certainty. [Second half of 1800s]

sure cure A remedy that won't fail, as in *Hard work is a sure cure for brooding*. Originating in the late 1800s as an advertising slogan (*Dr. Keck's Sure Cure for Catarrh*; first recorded in 1881), this rhyming phrase was soon extended to other matters.

sure enough Actually, as one might have thought, as in *Sure enough, the plane was three hours late*. [Mid-1500s]

sure of oneself Self-confident, as in *Now that Mary's graduated she's much more sure of herself*. This expression uses *sure* in the sense of "confident" or "secure," a usage dating from the mid-1400s.

sure thing 1. **a sure thing**. A certainty, as in *Making the bestseller list has been a sure thing for Stephen King*. This usage originally alluded to a bet that one could not lose. [First half of 1800s] 2. Yes indeed, certainly, as in *Are you coming tonight?—Sure thing!* This use of the idiom as an interjection dates from the late 1800s.

surface ♦ See ON THE SURFACE; SCRATCH THE SURFACE.

surprise ♦ See TAKE BY SURPRISE.

survival of the fittest Those best adapted to particular conditions will succeed in the long run, as in *They've had to close a dozen of their stores, but the ones in the western part of the state are doing well—it's the survival of the fittest*. This phrase was invented by Herbert Spencer in *Principles of Biology* (1864) to describe Charles Darwin's theory of natural selection of living species. By the early 1900s it was being transferred to other areas.

suspicion ♦ See ABOVE SUSPICION.

swallow ♦ In addition to the idioms beginning with SWALLOW, also see BITTER PILL TO SWALLOW.

swallow one's pride Humble oneself, as in *She decided to swallow her pride and apologize*. This idiom employs *swallow* in the sense of "refrain from expressing," a usage dating from the early 1600s.

swallow one's words Take back what one said, as in *If they win I'll have to swallow my words*. George Farquhar used this idiom in *The Inconstant* (1702): "I have swallowed my words already; I have eaten them up." For a synonym, see EAT ONE'S WORDS.

swan song A final accomplishment or performance, one's last work. For example, *I'm resigning tomorrow; this project was my swan song*. This term alludes to the old belief that swans normally are mute but burst into beautiful song moments before they die. Although the idea is much older, the term was first recorded in English only in 1890.

swap horses ♦ See CHANGE HORSES IN MIDSTREAM.

swath ♦ See CUT A WIDE SWATH.

sway ♦ See HOLD SWAY.

swear at Curse, use abusive, violent, or blasphemous language against, as in *He has a way of swearing at all the other drivers on the road*. [Late 1600s]

swear by 1. Have great reliance on or confidence in, as in *She swears by her personal physician*. [Early 1800s] 2. Also, **swear to**. Have reliable knowledge of, be sure of, as in *I think she was going to the library but I can't swear to it*. [Mid-1700s] 3. Take an oath by, as in *I swear by all the saints in heaven*. [Early 1200s]

swear in Administer a legal or official oath to, as in *The new mayor will be sworn in tomorrow*. [c. 1700]

swear like a trooper Freely utter profanity or obscenity, as in *The teacher was shocked when she heard one of the fathers begin to swear like a trooper*. The *troopers* in this term were the cavalry, who were singled out for their swearing from the early 1700s on.

swear off Pledge to renounce or give up, as in *I've sworn off cigarettes*. This expression was first used for abjuring liquor in the first half of the 1800s but has since been broadened to just about anything.

swear on a stack of Bibles Promise solemnly that what one is about to say is true, as in *I swear on a stack of Bibles that I had nothing to do with his dropping out*. This term alludes to the practice of placing one's hand on a sacred object while taking an oath, which dates from the mid-10th century. It is still followed in courts of law where a witness being sworn to tell the truth places a hand on the Bible. [Mid-1800s]

swear out Obtain a warrant for arrest by making a charge under oath, as in *The school principal swore out a warrant for the arrest of the vandals*. [Late 1800s]

swear to ♦ See SWEAR BY, def. 2.

sweat ♦ In addition to the idioms beginning with SWEAT, also see BY THE SWEAT OF ONE'S BROW; IN A COLD SWEAT; NO PROBLEM (SWEAT).

sweat blood 1. Also, **sweat one's guts out.** Work diligently or strenuously, as in *The men were sweating blood to finish the roof before the storm hit.* The phrase using *guts* was first used about 1890, and that with *blood* shortly thereafter. 2. Suffer mental anguish, worry intensely, as in *Waiting for the test results, I was sweating blood.* This usage was first recorded in a work by D.H. Lawrence in 1924. Both usages are colloquial, and allude to the agony of Jesus in Gethsemane (Luke 22:44): "And being in an agony he prayed more earnestly: and his sweat was as it were great drops of blood falling down to the ground."

sweat bullets Perspire profusely; also, suffer mental anguish. For example, *We were sweating bullets, sitting in the sun through all those graduation speeches,* or *It was their first baby, and David was sweating bullets while Karen was in labor.* The *bullets* in this expression allude to drops of perspiration the size of bullets. [Slang; mid-1900s]

sweat of one's brow ♦ See BY THE SWEAT OF ONE'S BROW.

sweat out Endure or await something anxiously, as in *He sweated out that last final exam,* or *I don't know if I made the team—I'm still sweating it out.* This idiom, often expanded to **sweat it out,** was first recorded in 1876.

sweep ♦ In addition to the idioms beginning with SWEEP, also see MAKE A CLEAN SWEEP; NEW BROOM SWEEPS CLEAN; (SWEEP) OFF SOMEONE'S FEET.

sweep off someone's feet ♦ See OFF SOMEONE'S FEET.

sweep under the rug Hide something, as in *Their attempts to sweep the scandal under the rug were not very successful.* This idiom alludes to sweeping dust under the rug, so it won't be seen. [Mid-1900s]

sweet ♦ In addition to the idioms beginning with SWEET, also see SHORT AND SWEET; TAKE THE BITTER WITH THE SWEET.

sweet dreams Sleep well, as in *Good night, children, sweet dreams.* [c. 1900]

sweeten the kitty Also, **sweeten the pot** or **deal.** Make something financially more attractive, as in *I am unable to give you the new title but I could sweeten the kitty a little by giving you a raise.* This idiom comes from card games such as poker, where it means "add money to the pool," and uses *sweeten* in the sense of "make more agreeable." [Slang; c. 1900]

sweetness and light Ostentatious amiability and friendliness, as in *One day she has a temper tantrum, the next day she's all sweetness and light.* This phrase was coined by Jonathan Swift in his *Battle of the Books* (1704), where it referred literally to the products of bees: honey and light from beeswax candles. But in Matthew Arnold's *Culture and Anarchy* (1869), the term meant "beauty and intelligence." In the 20th century, however, it was applied to personal qualities of friendliness and courtesy and to the general pleasantness of a situation, as in *Working with him isn't all sweetness and light, you know.* Today it is generally used ironically, indicating lack of trust in a person's seeming friendliness or for a difficult situation.

sweet nothings Endearments, often whispered, between lovers. For example, *They sat in a corner all evening, whispering sweet nothings.* [c. 1900] Also see SWEET TALK.

sweet on, be Enamored of, in love with, as in *I think Barbara's sweet on Nick.* This colloquial idiom was first recorded in 1740.

sweet talk Flattery, cajolery, as in *She uses sweet talk to get her way.* [First half of 1900s]

sweet tooth A love for sugary foods, as in *You can always please Nell with cake or ice cream; she has a big sweet tooth.* This expression dates from the late 1300s, although it then referred not only to sweets but other delicacies as well.

swelled head, have a Be conceited, as in *Winning all those prizes has not given her a swelled head, at least not yet.* This idiom began as *be swellheaded,* first recorded in 1817. The present form dates from about 1860. For a synonym see BIG HEAD.

swim ♦ In addition to the idioms beginning with SWIM, also see IN THE SWIM; SINK OR SWIM.

swim against the current Also, **swim against the stream** or **tide.** Go against prevailing opinion or thought, as in *I'm voting for him even if that is swimming against the current.* Shakespeare used a similar metaphor in 2 *Henry IV* (5:2): "You must now speak Sir John Falstaff fair, which swims against your stream." For the antonym, see SWIM WITH THE TIDE.

swim with the tide Go along with prevailing opinion or thought, as in *Irene doesn't have a mind of her own; she just swims with the tide.* In the late 1600s this idiom was also put as *swim down the stream,* a usage not much heard today. The present form was first recorded in 1712. For the antonym, see SWIM AGAINST THE CURRENT.

swine ♦ See CAST PEARLS BEFORE SWINE.

swing ♦ In addition to the idiom beginning with SWING, also see GET INTO THE SWING OF THINGS; IN FULL SWING; NOT ENOUGH ROOM TO SWING A CAT.

swing into action Energetically start doing something, as in *Come on, let's swing into action before the others arrive.* This idiom uses *swing* in the sense of "move vigorously."

switch ♦ In addition to the idioms beginning with SWITCH, also see ASLEEP AT THE SWITCH; BAIT AND SWITCH.

switch off Stop paying attention, lose interest, as in *Whenever he starts in on economics, I switch off automatically.* This metaphoric expression transfers turning off a light switch or similar device to diverting one's attention. [c. 1860] Also see SWITCH ON.

switch on Produce as if operating by a control, as in *She switched on the charm as soon as he walked in.* [Mid-1900s] Also see SWITCH OFF.

swoop ♦ See ONE FELL SWOOP.

sword ♦ In addition to the idiom beginning with SWORD, also see AT SWORD'S POINT; CROSS SWORDS.

sword of Damocles Also, **Damocles' sword.** Impending disaster, as in *The likelihood of layoffs has been a sword of Damocles over the department for months.* This expression alludes to the legend of Damocles, a servile courtier to King Dionysius I of Syracuse. The king, weary of Damocles' obsequious flattery, invited him to a banquet and seated him under a sword hung by a single hair, so as to point out to him the precariousness of his position. The idiom was first recorded in 1747. The same story gave rise to the expression HANG BY A THREAD.

syllable ♦ See WORDS OF ONE SYLLABLE.

symbol ♦ See STATUS SYMBOL.

system ♦ See ALL SYSTEMS GO; OUT OF ONE'S SYSTEM.

t

T ♦ See DOT THE I'S AND CROSS THE T'S; TO A T.

tab ♦ See KEEP TABS ON.

table ♦ See CLEAR OUT (THE TABLE); LAY ONE'S CARDS ON THE TABLE; ON THE TABLE; SET THE TABLE; TURN THE TABLES; UNDER THE TABLE; WAIT AT TABLE.

tack ♦ See GET DOWN TO BRASS TACKS; ON THE RIGHT TACK; SHARP AS A TACK.

tail ♦ In addition to the idioms beginning with TAIL, also see BRIGHT-EYED AND BUSHY-TAILED; CAN'T MAKE HEAD OR TAIL OF; GET OFF ONE'S TAIL; HEADS OR TAILS; IN TWO SHAKES (OF A LAMB'S TAIL); ON SOMEONE'S COATTAILS; TIGER BY THE TAIL; TURN TAIL; WORK ONE'S FINGERS TO THE BONE (TAIL OFF).

tail between one's legs, with one's Dejected, cowed, ashamed, especially after a defeat or being proven wrong. For example, *After bragging about her great musical ability, she lost the competition and went off with her tail between her legs.* This idiom alludes to a dog's slinking away in this manner. [First half of 1800s]

tail end 1. The rear or hindmost part, as in *Douglas was at the tail end of the academic procession.* [Mid-1700s] 2. The very end, the conclusion, as in *Only at the tail end of his speech did he thank his sponsors.* [Mid-1800s]

tail off Also, **tail away.** Diminish gradually, subside, as in *The fireworks tailed off into darkness.* [Mid-1800s]

tailor-made for ♦ See MADE TO MEASURE.

tailspin ♦ See GO INTO A TAILSPIN.

tail wagging the dog, the A small or unimportant factor or element governing an important one; a reversal of the proper roles. For example, *She found herself explaining the new therapy to her doctor—a real case of the tail wagging the dog.* [c. 1900]

take ♦ In addition to the idioms beginning with TAKE, also see AT (TAKE) PAINS; DEVIL TAKE THE HINDMOST; DOUBLE TAKE; GIVE AND TAKE; GIVE OR TAKE; GO TO (TAKE) THE TROUBLE; HAVE (TAKE) A CRACK AT; HAVE (TAKE) A FIT; IN (TAKE) EFFECT; (TAKE) IN GOOD PART; IN TOW, TAKE; IT TAKES ALL SORTS; IT TAKES GETTING USED TO; IT TAKES ONE TO KNOW ONE; (TAKE) OFF ONE'S HANDS; (TAKE) ON FAITH; ON THE TAKE; PAY YOUR MONEY AND TAKE YOUR CHOICE; PRIDE ONESELF (TAKE PRIDE IN); (TAKE A) RAIN CHECK; SIT UP AND TAKE NOTICE; THAT'S (TAKES CARE OF) THAT; WHAT DO YOU TAKE ME FOR; WHAT IT TAKES; (TAKE) WITH A GRAIN OF SALT; YOU CAN LEAD (TAKE) A HORSE TO WATER; YOU CAN'T TAKE IT WITH YOU.

take aback Surprise, shock, as in *He was taken aback by her caustic remark.* This idiom comes from nautical terminology of the mid-1700s, when *be taken aback* referred to the stalling of a ship caused by a wind shift that made the sails lay back against the masts. Its figurative use was first recorded in 1829.

take a back seat Occupy an inferior position; allow another to be in control. For example, *Linda was content to take a back seat and let Nancy run the meeting.* This idiom uses *back seat* in contrast to the driver's seat, that is, the one in control. [Mid-1800s]

take a bath Experience serious financial loss, as in *The company took a bath investing in that new product.* This idiom, which originated in gambling, transfers washing oneself in a bathtub to being "cleaned out" financially. [Slang; first half of 1900s]

take a bow Acknowledge praise or applause, as in *The conductor asked the composer to take a bow.* This idiom uses *bow* in the sense of "inclining the body or head as a token of salutation." [c. 1800]

take a break Interrupt one's activity briefly, as in *We've been working for two hours; let's take a break.* Also see TAKE FIVE.

take account of ♦ See TAKE INTO ACCOUNT.

take a chance Risk something, gamble, as in *I'll take a chance that he'll be on the next plane.* [c. 1900]

take a crack at ♦ See HAVE A CRACK AT.

take a dim view of Regard disapprovingly, as in *I take a dim view of meeting every single week.* This idiom, which uses *dim* in the sense of "unfavorable," was first recorded in 1947.

take advantage of Put to good use; avail oneself of; also, profit selfishly by, exploit. For example, *Let's take advantage of the good weather and go hiking,* or *They really take advantage of her good nature, getting her to do all the disagreeable chores.* [Late 1300s]

take a fall 1. Also, **take a spill.** Suffer a fall, fall down, as in *You took quite a fall on the ski slopes, didn't you?* or *Bill took a spill on the ice.* 2. Be arrested or convicted, as in *He's taken a fall or two and spent some years in jail.* [Slang; 1920s]

take a fancy to Also, **take a liking** or **shine to.** Be attracted to someone or something, as in *They took a fancy to spicy foods after their Mexican vacation,* or *I'm hoping he'll take a liking to the water, now that we have a cottage on a lake,* or *We think Bill's taken a shine to Betsy.* The first term was first recorded in 1541, the first variant in 1570, and the last, a colloquialism, in 1850.

take a fit ♦ See HAVE A FIT.

take after Follow the example of; also, resemble in appearance, temperament, or character. For example, *Bill took after his uncle and began working as a volunteer for the Red Cross.* [Mid-1500s]

take a gander at Look at, glance at, as in *Will you take a gander at that woman's red hair!* This slangy idiom, dating from the early 1900s, presumably came from the verb *gander,* meaning "stretch one's neck to see," possibly alluding to the long neck of the male goose. For a synonym, see TAKE A LOOK AT.

take a hand in ♦ See HAVE A HAND IN.

take a hike Go hiking; also, go away. For example, *We asked Jim to take a hike with us but he didn't want to,* or *I've had enough of you—take a hike!* The latter usage is a slangy imperative. Also see TAKE A WALK.

take a hint Also, **take the hint.** Accept an indirect or covert suggestion, as in *Evelyn took the hint and quietly left the room.* This idiom was first recorded in 1711.

take aim Direct a missile or criticism at something or someone, as in *Raising his rifle, Chet took aim at the squirrel but missed it entirely,* or *In his last speech the President took aim at the opposition leader.* [Late 1500s]

take a joke Accept teasing at one's own expense, as in *Sam really couldn't take a joke.* This idiom, often put negatively, was first recorded in 1780. Also see TAKE IT.

take a leaf out of someone's book Imitate or follow someone's example, as in *Harriet took a leaf out of her mother's book and began to keep track of how much money she was spending on food.* This idiom alludes to tearing a page from a book. [c. 1800]

take a leak Urinate, as in *Excuse me, I've got to take a leak.* [Vulgar slang; c. 1930]

take a load off one's mind ♦ See LOAD OFF ONE'S MIND. Also see TAKE THE LOAD OFF.

take a look at Turn your attention to, examine, as in *Take a look at that new building,* or *The doctor took a look at Gene's throat and swollen glands.* For a synonym, see TAKE A GANDER AT.

take amiss ♦ See TAKE THE WRONG WAY.

take an interest 1. Be concerned or curious, as in *She really takes an interest in foreign affairs,* or *I wish he'd take an interest in classical music.* 2. Share in a right to or ownership of property or a business, as in *He promised to take an interest in the company as soon as he could afford to.*

take apart 1. Dismantle or disassemble, as in *They had to take apart the stereo before they could move it.* This usage was first recorded in 1936. 2. Examine thoroughly, analyze or dissect, as in *The teacher embarrassed Tom by taking his thesis apart in front of the class.* [Mid-1900s] 3. Beat up, thrash, as in *You'd better be careful; those boys will take you apart.* [Slang; mid-1900s]

take a picture Photograph, as in *I'd love to take a picture of your garden.* This idiom was first used in the 1600s for making a drawing or other portrayal. It was transferred to photography in the mid-1800s.

take a poke at Hit with one's fist, as in *If you don't quit teasing I'll take a poke at you.* [Colloquial; c. 1930]

take a powder Make a speedy departure, run away, as in *I looked around and he was gone—he'd taken a powder.* This slangy idiom may be derived from the British dialect sense of *powder* as "a sudden hurry," a usage dating from about 1600. It may also allude to the explosive quality of gunpowder.

take a rain check ♦ See RAIN CHECK.

take as gospel Also, **take for gospel.** Believe absolutely, regard as true, as in *We took every word of his as gospel, but in fact he was often mistaken.* This idiom, first recorded in 1496, uses *gospel* in the sense of the absolute truth. Also see GOSPEL TRUTH.

take a shellacking Be soundly beaten or defeated, as in *Our team took quite a shellacking last night.* Why being coated with shellac should suggest defeat is not clear. [Slang; c. 1930]

take a shine to ♦ See TAKE A FANCY.

take aside Also, **take to one side.** Talk to another privately or away from others, as in *The doctor took Pat aside to explain what she had to do,* or *The boss took William to one side rather than criticize his work in front of his colleagues.*

take a spill ♦ See TAKE A FALL.

take a stand Adopt a firm position about an issue, as in *She was more than willing to take a stand on abortion rights.* This idiom alludes to the military sense of *stand,* "hold one's ground against an enemy." [Mid-1800s] Also see MAKE A STAND.

take at face value ♦ See AT FACE VALUE.

take a turn for the better Improve, as in *We thought she was on her deathbed but now she's taken a turn for the better.* The antonym is **take a turn for the worse,** meaning "get worse, deteriorate," as in *Unemployment has been fairly low lately, but now the economy's taken a turn for the worse.* This idiom employs *turn* in the sense of "a reversal," a usage dating from about 1600.

take a walk Leave abruptly, walk out. For example, *If she's rude again I'm just going to take a walk,* or *The director would not put up with tantrums and ordered the young actress to take a walk.* [Colloquial; late 1800s] Also see TAKE A HIKE; WALK OUT, def. 2.

take away from Detract, as in *Her straggly hair takes away from her otherwise attractive appearance.* [Second half of 1800s]

take a whack at ♦ See HAVE A CRACK AT.

take back 1. Retract a statement, as in *I said you weren't much of a cook but after that dinner I take it all back.* This usage was first recorded in 1775. 2. **take one back.** Return in thought to a past time, as in *That music takes me back to the first dance I ever went to.* [Late 1800s]

take by storm Make a vivid impression on, quickly win popular acclaim or renown, as in *The new rock group took the town by storm.* This usage transfers the original military meaning of the phrase, "assault in a violent attack," to more peaceful endeavors. [Mid-1800s]

take by surprise Encounter unexpectedly, as in *The rainshower took us by surprise.* [Late 1600s]

take care 1. Be careful, use caution, as in *Take care or you will slip on the ice.* [Late 1500s] 2. Goodbye, as in *I have to go now; take care.* This apparent abbreviation of **take care of yourself** is used both orally and in writing, where it sometimes replaces the conventional *Sincerely* or *Love* in signing off correspondence. [Colloquial; 1960s]

take care of 1. Attend to, assume responsibility for, as in *Go ahead to the movies, I'll take care of parking the car,* or *They've hired someone to take*

care of the children for a week. [Late 1500s] 2. Beat up or kill someone, as in *If he didn't pay up they threatened to take care of him and his family.* [Slang; c. 1930]

take charge Assume control, command, or responsibility, as in *I'll take charge of selling the tickets if you'll do the publicity,* or *They're not happy about the counselor who took charge of the children.* [Late 1300s]

take cover Seek protection, find a hiding place, as in *It started to pour so we took cover under the trees,* or *He wanted to avoid the reporters so we said he could take cover in our summer cottage.* This term uses *cover* in the sense of "shelter" or "concealment," a usage dating from the 1400s.

take doing Require considerable effort, as in *It'll take doing to get the whole house painted in a week.* This expression sometimes is put as **take some doing,** as in *You want the President to come? That'll take some doing!* [First half of 1900s]

take down 1. Bring from a higher position to a lower one, as in *After the sale they took down all the signs.* [c. 1300] 2. Take apart, dismantle, as in *They took down the scaffolding.* [Mid-1500s] 3. Humble or humiliate; see TAKE DOWN A NOTCH. 4. Record in writing, as in *Please take down all these price quotations.* [Early 1700s]

take down a notch Also, **take down a peg.** Deflate or humble someone, as in *He's so arrogant that I wish someone would take him down a notch,* or *That defeat took them down a peg.* Both *notch* and *peg* in this idiom allude to a series, the former of indentations, the latter of knobs, used to raise or lower something. Specifically, *peg* alludes to the pegs used to lower a ship's colors. Their figurative use dates from the second half of the 1600s. Also see CUT DOWN, def. 4.

take effect ♦ See IN EFFECT, def. 2.

take exception to Disagree with, object to, as in *I take exception to that remark about unfair practices.* This idiom, first recorded in 1542, uses *exception* in the sense of "objection," a meaning obsolete except in a few phrases.

take five Relax, take some time off from what one is doing, as in *We've been at it long enough; let's take five.* This term is short for "take five minutes off." [Slang; first half of 1900s] For a synonym, see TAKE A BREAK.

take flight Also, **take wing.** Run away, flee, go away, as in *When the militia arrived, the demonstrators took flight,* or *The tenant took wing before paying the rent.* The first idiom derives from the earlier **take one's flight,** dating from the late 1300s, and was first recorded in 1435. The variant was first recorded in 1704.

take for 1. Regard as, as in *Do you take me for a fool?* [First half of 1400s] 2. Consider mistakenly, as in *Don't take our silence for approval,* or *I think they took us for foreigners.* [Second half of 1500s] Also see TAKE FOR GRANTED; WHAT DO YOU TAKE ME FOR.

take for a ride ♦ See TAKE SOMEONE FOR A RIDE.

take for gospel ♦ See TAKE AS GOSPEL.

take for granted 1. Consider as true or real, anticipate correctly, as in *I took it for granted that they'd offer to pay for their share but I was wrong.* [c. 1600] 2. Underestimate the value of, become used to, as in *The editors felt that the publisher was taking them for granted.*

take heart Be confident, be brave, as in *Take heart, we may still win this game.* This idiom uses *heart* in the sense of "courage." [First half of 1500s]

take hold 1. Grasp, as in *Take hold of this end of the rope.* [Late 1500s] 2. Become established, as in *The new vines quickly took hold,* or *This idea will never take hold with the voters.* [c. 1300]

take ill ♦ See GET SICK.

take in 1. Admit, receive as a guest or employee, as in *They offered to take in two of the orphaned children.* [First half of 1500s] 2. Reduce in size, make smaller or shorter, as in *I've lost some weight so I'll have to take in my clothes.* [Early 1500s] 3. Include or constitute, as in *This list takes in all the members, past and present.* [Mid-1600s] 4. Understand, as in *I couldn't take in all that French dialogue in the movie.* [Second half of 1600s] 5. Deceive, swindle, as in *That alleged fundraiser took me in completely.* [First half of 1700s] 6. Look at thoroughly, as in *We want to take in all the sights.* [First half of 1700s] 7. Accept work to be done at home, as in *His grandmother took in washing to support her children.* [First half of 1800s] 8. Receive as proceeds, as in *We had a good audience; how much did we take in?* [Late 1800s] Also see the following entries beginning with TAKE IN.

take in good part ♦ See IN GOOD PART.

take in hand Deal with, assume control of, as in *He's going to take their debts in hand and see if they need to declare bankruptcy,* or *Once the new teacher takes them in hand this class will do much better.* [c. 1300] Also see IN HAND, def. 2.

take in stride Accept something as a matter of course, not allow something to interrupt or disturb one's routine. For example, *There were bound to be setbacks but Jack took them in stride.* This idiom alludes to a horse clearing an obstacle without checking its stride. [c. 1900]

take into account Also, **take account of; take into consideration.** Bear in mind, consider, allow for, as in *We have to take into account that ten of the musicians were absent,* or *It's important to take ac-count of where the audience is coming from,* or *When you take into consideration the fact that they were founded only a year ago, they've done very well.* *Take into consideration* is the oldest of these expressions, dating from the mid-1500s. *Take into account* and *take account of* date from the late 1600s. The antonyms, **leave out of account** or **take no account of,** mean "ignore, pay no attention to," as in *They've left the most important item out of ac-count.* [Second half of 1800s] All of these idioms use *account* in the sense of "reckoning" or "calculation," and *consideration* in the sense of "regard for the circumstances."

take into one's confidence Trust someone with a secret, as in *She took me into her confidence and admitted that she was quitting next month.* This idiom uses *confidence* in the sense of "trust," a usage dating from the late 1500s.

take into one's head ♦ See GET INTO ONE'S HEAD.

take into one's own hands ♦ See TAKE THE LAW INTO ONE'S OWN HANDS.

take issue with Disagree with, as in *I take issue with those figures; they don't include last month's sales.* This idiom comes from legal terminology, where it was originally put as to **join issue,** meaning "take the opposite side of a case." [Late 1600s]

take it 1. Understand, as in *I take it they won't ac-cept your proposal.* [Early 1500s] 2. Endure abuse, criticism, harsh treatment, or unpleasantness, as in *Tell me what you really think of me—I can take it.* [Mid-1800s] This phrase is sometimes modified as **take just so much,** meaning "endure only up to a point." For example, *I can take just so much of this nonsense before I lose patience.* Also see TAKE IT ON THE CHIN; TAKE LYING DOWN. 3. Accept or believe something, as in *I'll take it on the doctor's say-so.* Also see the subsequent entries beginning with TAKE IT.

take it easy Don't hurry, proceed at a comfortable pace, relax. For example, *Take it easy—we don't have to be there till noon,* or *Bruce decided to take it easy this weekend and put off working on the house.* [Mid-1800s]

take it from here Also, **take it from there.** Continue from a certain point onwards, as in *I've done what I could with correcting the blatant errors; you'll have to take it from here.* [Mid-1900s]

take it from me Also, **you can take it from me.** Rest assured, believe me, as in *You can take it from me, we've been working hard on it.* This idiom was first recorded in 1622 in slightly different form, *take it upon my word.* The current form appeared in 1672.

take it on the chin Suffer adversity or defeat, as in *Paul really took it on the chin today when he got fired* for missing a deadline. This idiom alludes to taking a physical blow on the chin. [First half of 1900s]

take it or leave it Accept or reject unconditionally, as in *I'm asking $1,000 for this computer— take it or leave it.* This term, used to indicate one's final offer, was first recorded in 1576.

take it out of one Exhaust or fatigue one, as in *This construction job really takes it out of me.* This idiom alludes to depleting one's energy. [Mid-1800s]

take it out on Also, **take something out on.** Vent one's frustration or anger on a person or object. For example, *I know you're furious about your grades but don't take it out on me.* [First half of 1800s]

take its toll Be damaging or harmful, cause loss or destruction, as in *The civil war has taken its toll on both sides,* or *The heavy truck traffic has taken its toll on the highways.* This expression transfers the taking of *toll,* a tribute or tax, to exacting other costs. [Late 1800s]

take it upon oneself Also, **take on oneself.** Undertake something, as in *I took it upon myself to count the precise number of children in the audience,* or *She took it on herself to enter a convent.* [Second half of 1400s]

take kindly to Be receptive to, attracted by, or pleased with, as in *He'll take kindly to the criticism if it's constructive,* or *Henry won't take kindly to your stepping on his newly planted grass.* This idiom uses *kindly* in the sense of "in a pleasant or agreeable manner." [c. 1800]

take leave of 1. Also, **take one's leave of.** Depart from, say good-bye to. For example, *Sorry but I have to take leave of you now,* or *After the movie we'll take our leave of you.* [Mid-1200s] 2. **take leave of one's senses.** Behave irrationally, act crazy, as in *Give them the keys to the house? Have you taken leave of your senses?* [Late 1800s] Also see COME TO ONE'S SENSES.

take liberties 1. Behave improperly or disrespectfully; also, make unwanted sexual advances. For example, *He doesn't allow staff members to take liberties, such as calling clients by their first names,* or *She decided that if Jack tried to take liberties with her she would go straight home.* This idiom uses *liberties* in the sense of "an overstepping of propriety," and thus differs markedly from TAKE THE LIBERTY OF. [c. 1700] 2. Make a statement or take an action not warranted by the facts or circumstances, as in *Their book takes liberties with the historical record.*

take lying down Submit to an insult, rebuke, or other harsh treatment without resisting, as in *He won't take that snub lying down.* This idiom uses *lying down* in the sense of "passively." [Late 1800s] Also see TAKE IT, def. 2.

taken aback ♦ See TAKE ABACK.

take no for an answer, not Not accept a refusal, be persistent in demanding something, as in *I want you to show me the statements and I won't take no for an answer.* This idiom was first recorded in 1930 in Winston Churchill's *My Early Life:* "Don't take no for an answer, never submit to failure."

take note Also, **take notice.** Pay attention, as in *Take note, not one man here is wearing a tie,* or *The aide took notice of the boys throwing spitballs and reported them.* An antonym is **take no notice of,** meaning "ignore," as in *Take no notice of them and they'll stop teasing you.* [Late 1500s] Also see TAKE NOTES.

take notes Also, **make notes.** Record one's observations or what one hears in order to help recall them later. For example, *Jim never takes notes in class and I think he'll regret it,* or *The decorator made notes of window measurements and other dimensions.* [Mid-1500s] Also see TAKE NOTE.

taken with, be Be attracted to or charmed by, as in *I was quite taken with those watercolors,* or *The composer seemed to be taken with the young soprano who performed his songs.* [First half of 1500s]

take off 1. Remove, as in *Take off your coat and stay for a while,* or *I took my foot off the brake.* [c. 1300] 2. Deduct, decrease, as in *He took 20 percent off the original price,* or *I want you to trim my hair, but please don't take off too much.* [c. 1700] 3. Carry or take away, as in *The passengers were taken off one by one.* [Late 1800s] 4. Also, **take oneself off.** Leave, go away, as in *I'm taking off now,* or *We take ourselves off for China next month,* or, as an imperative, *Take yourself off right now!* [First half of 1800s] 5. Move forward quickly, as in *The dog took off after the car.* 6. Become well known or popular, or achieve sudden growth, as in *That actor's career has really taken off,* or *Sales took off around the holidays.* [Mid-1900s] 7. Rise in flight, as in *The airplane took off on time.* [Mid-1800s] 8. Discontinue, as in *The railroad took off the commuter special.* [Mid-1700s] 9. Imitate humorously or satirically, as in *He had a way of taking off the governor that made us howl with laughter.* [Mid-1700s] 10. Withhold service, as in *I'm taking off from work today because of the funeral.* [First half of 1900s]

take offense Feel resentment or emotional pain, as in *I didn't realize he'd take offense when he wasn't invited.* [Mid-1800s]

take office Assume an official position or employment, as in *The new chair takes office after the first of the year.* [Mid-1800s]

take off one's hands ♦ See OFF ONE'S HANDS.

take off one's hat to ♦ See TAKE ONE'S HAT OFF.

take on 1. Undertake or begin to deal with, as in *I took on new responsibilities,* or *She took on too much when she accepted both assignments.* [Early 1300s] **2.** Hire, engage, as in *We take on extra workers during the busy season.* [Early 1600s] **3.** Oppose in competition, as in *This young wrestler was willing to take on all comers.* [Late 1800s] **4.** Display strong emotion, as in *Don't take on so.* [Colloquial; early 1400s] **5.** Acquire as, or as if, one's own, as in *He took on the look of a prosperous banker.* [Late 1700s]

take one's breath away Astonish or shock one, with pleasure, surprise, or some other emotion. For example, *That beautiful display just takes my breath away.* This idiom alludes to the way one holds one's breath when overcome with sudden emotion. [Mid-1800s]

take one's chances Accept the risks, resign oneself to whatever happens, as in *I've no idea whether this scheme will work; I'll just take my chances.* [Early 1300s]

take one's cue from Follow the lead of another, as in *I'm not sure what to bring, so I'll take my cue from you.* This expression, first recorded in 1622, alludes to the cue giving an actor a signal to speak.

take one's hat off to Also, **take off one's hat to.** Express one's admiration, as in *I take off my hat to you—you've done very well indeed.* [Mid-1800s] Also see HATS OFF TO.

take one's leave ♦ See TAKE LEAVE OF.

take one's medicine Put up with unpleasantness, learn one's lesson. For example, *After failing math, he had to take his medicine and go to summer school.* This idiom uses *medicine* in the sense of "a bitter-tasting remedy." [Mid-1800s]

take one's time Act slowly or at one's leisure, as in *You can take your time altering that dress; I don't need it right away.* [Late 1700s]

take one's word for ♦ See TAKE SOMEONE AT HIS OR HER WORD.

take on faith ♦ See ON FAITH.

take on oneself ♦ See TAKE IT UPON ONESELF.

take out 1. Extract, remove, as in *He should take out that splinter.* [c. 1300] **2.** Secure by applying to an authority, as in *She took out a real estate license.* [Late 1600s] **3.** Escort on a date, as in *He's been taking out a different girl every night of the week.* [c. 1600] **4.** Give vent to; see TAKE IT OUT ON. **5.** Carry away for use elsewhere, as in *Can we get some pizza to take out?* **6.** Obtain as an equivalent in different form, as in *We took out the money she owed us by having her babysit.* [Early 1600s] **7.** Set out, as in *Jan and Herb took out for the beach,* or *The police took out after the suspects.* [Mid-1800s] **8.** Kill, destroy, as in *Two snipers took out a*

whole platoon, or *Flying low, the plane took out the enemy bunker in one pass.* [1930s] **9.** See under TAKE OUT OF.

take out of ♦ See TAKE A LEAF OUT OF SOMEONE'S BOOK; TAKE IT OUT OF ONE; TAKE THE BREAD OUT OF SOMEONE'S MOUTH; TAKE THE HEAT OUT OF; TAKE THE STARCH OUT OF; TAKE THE STING OUT OF; TAKE THE WIND OUT OF SOMEONE'S SAILS; TAKE THE WORDS OUT OF SOMEONE'S MOUTH.

take over Assume control, management, or possession of, as in *The pilot told his copilot to take over the controls,* or *There's a secret bid to take over our company.* [Late 1800s]

take pains ♦ See AT PAINS.

take part Play a role in, share in, participate, as in *Will you be taking part in the wedding?* or *He did not take part in the discussion.* [Late 1300s] Also see TAKE ONE'S PART.

take pity on Also, **have pity on.** Show compassion or mercy to, as in *Take pity on the cook and eat that last piece of cake,* or, as Miles Coverdale's 1535 translation of the Bible has it (Job 19:21), "Have pity upon me, have pity upon me, O ye, my friends." This idiom may be used half-jokingly, as in the first example, or seriously. [Late 1200s]

take place 1. Happen, occur, as in *Let me know where the ceremony will take place.* [Second half of 1700s] **2. take the place of.** Substitute for, as in *These glasses will have to take the place of wine goblets,* or *Jane took her sister's place in line.* [Second half of 1800s]

take potluck Come to eat whatever happens to be served; also, take one's chances. For example, *You're welcome to join us for supper but you'll have to take potluck,* or *When the flight was canceled, passengers had to take potluck on other airlines.* This idiom alludes to accepting whatever happens to be in the cooking pot. [Second half of 1700s]

take pride in ♦ See PRIDE ONESELF ON.

take root Become established or fixed, as in *We're not sure how the movement took root, but it did so very rapidly.* This idiom transfers the establishment of a plant, whose roots settle into the earth, to other matters. [Late 1500s]

take shape Also, **shape up.** Turn out, develop, acquire a distinctive form, as in *Her reelection campaign is already taking shape, two years before the election,* or *Can you tell us how the book is shaping up?* The first term dates from the mid-1700s and the variant, originally put as *shape out,* from about 1600.

take sick ♦ See GET SICK.

take sides Also, **take someone's side.** Support or favor one party in a dispute, as in *Parents shouldn't take sides in their children's quarrels,* or *Thanks for* *taking my side concerning the agenda.* [c. 1700] Also see TAKE SOMEONE'S PART.

take some doing ♦ See TAKE DOING.

take someone at his or her word Also, take someone's word for. Accept what someone says on trust, as in *Since he said he'd agree to any of my ideas, I'll take him at his word,* or *She said she wanted to help out and I took her word for it.* This idiom appeared in Miles Coverdale's translation of the Bible: "He said . . . he is my brother. And the men took him shortly at his word" (I Kings 22:33). It is still so used. [1535]

take someone for a ride 1. Cheat or deliberately mislead someone, as in *Car salesmen will take you for a ride in more ways than one!* [Colloquial; c. 1920] 2. Murder someone, as in *The gang threatened to take him for a ride.* [Slang; 1920] Both usages allude to taking a person for an automobile ride.

take someone in ♦ See TAKE IN, def. 5.

take someone's life 1. Kill someone, as in *They argued about invoking the death penalty for taking someone's life.* [c. 1300] 2. **take one's own life.** Commit suicide, as in *Most churches have long opposed taking one's own life.* [First half of 1900s] 3. **take one's life in one's hands.** Take a serious risk, as in *Climbing without oxygen is really taking your life in your hands.*

take someone's measure Also, take the measure of someone. Size someone up, evaluate someone or something, as in *At their first meeting, heads of state generally try to take each other's measure,* or *The voters are taking the measure of the union's demands.* [Mid-1600s]

take someone's name in vain Speak casually or idly of someone, as in *There he goes, taking my name in vain again.* This idiom originated as a translation from the Latin of the Vulgate Bible (Exodus 20:7), "to take God's name in vain," and for a time was used only to denote blasphemy and profanity. In the early 1700s it began to be used more loosely as well.

take someone's part Stand up for or support someone, as in *Thanks for taking my part against the supervisor.* This idiom uses *part* in the sense of "side in a dispute." It was first recorded in 1732, although a different version, take part with, dates from the early 1400s. Also see TAKE SIDES; TAKE PART.

take someone's point Understand what someone is saying, concede the truth of what someone said, as in *Am I taking your point correctly when you say you disagree but do not object?* [Late 1800s]

take someone's word for ♦ See TAKE SOMEONE AT HIS OR HER WORD.

take something ♦ See under TAKE IT.

take something on faith ♦ See ON FAITH.

takes one to know one ♦ See IT TAKES ONE TO KNOW ONE.

take steps Begin a course of action, as in *The town is taking steps to provide better street lights,* or *They took steps to keep their plans secret.* [Early 1600s]

take stock Make an estimate or appraisal, as in *We have to take stock of our finances before we can undertake a new project,* or *The career counselor advised Mark to take stock before changing his plans.* This expression transfers making an inventory of goods (*stock*) to other kinds of appraisal. [Early 1800s]

take stock in Trust, believe, attach importance to, as in *He exaggerates so much that I don't take stock in anything he says.* This term uses *stock* in the sense of "capital." [Second half of 1800s]

takes two ♦ See IT TAKES TWO TO TANGO.

take the bit in one's mouth Also, take the bit between one's teeth. Throw off restraints and proceed on a headlong course, take control. For example, *My partner took the bit in his mouth and bid a grand slam,* or *Jane took the bit between her teeth and now there's no stopping her.* This idiom alludes to the *bit,* the metal mouthpiece of a bridle whereby a rider controls a horse. [c. 1600]

take the bitter with the sweet Accept adversity as well as good fortune, as in *Although he got the job, he hadn't counted on having to work with Matthew; he'll just have to take the bitter with the sweet.* This idiom uses *bitter* for "bad" and *sweet* for "good," a usage dating from the late 1300s. It was first recorded in John Heywood's 1546 proverb collection. For a synonym, see TAKE THE ROUGH WITH THE SMOOTH.

take the bread out of someone's mouth Deprive someone of his or her livelihood, as in *Lowering wages is taking the bread out of the workers' mouths.* [c. 1700]

take the bull by the horns Confront a problem head-on, as in *We'll have to take the bull by the horns and tackle the Medicare question.* This term most likely alludes to grasping a safely tethered bull, not one the matador is fighting in the ring. [c. 1800]

take the cake Be the most outstanding in some respect, either the best or the worst. For example, *That advertising slogan really took the cake,* or *What a mess they made of the concert—that takes the cake!* This expression alludes to a contest called a *cakewalk,* in which a cake is the prize. Its figurative use, for something either excellent or outrageously bad, dates from the 1880s.

take the edge off Ease or assuage, make less severe, as in *That snack took the edge off our hunger,* or *Her kind manner took the edge off her refusal.*

This term alludes to blunting the edge of a cutting instrument. Shakespeare used it figuratively in *The Tempest* (4:1): "To take away the edge of that day's celebration." The precise wording of the idiom dates from the first half of the 1900s.

take the fall Incur blame or censure for another's misdeeds, as in *She's taken the fall for you in terms of any political damage,* or *A senior official took the fall for the failed intelligence operation.* This expression originated in the 1920s as underworld slang. It began to be extended to less criminal kinds of blame in the second half of the 1900s. Also see TAKE A FALL, def. 2; TAKE THE RAP.

take the field Enter a competition, as in *The country's best spellers took the field in the national spelling bee.* This term originated around 1600 when it meant "to open a military campaign." The *field* here is the field of battle. The term has been used figuratively almost as long, the first recorded use being in 1614.

take the Fifth Refuse to answer on the grounds that one may incriminate oneself, as in *He took the Fifth on so many of the prosecutor's questions that we're sure he's guilty.* This idiom refers to the Fifth Amendment to the U.S. Constitution, which states that no person shall be compelled to be a witness against himself or herself. [Mid-1900s]

take the floor Rise to speak formally to an assembled group, as in *After that long introduction, the treasurer took the floor.* This idiom uses *floor* in the sense of "right: to speak," in turn derived from its meaning as the part of the legislature from which members address the group. [c. 1800]

take the heat Endure severe censure or criticism, as in *He was known for being able to take the heat during a crisis.* This idiom uses *heat* in the sense of "intense pressure," as in IF YOU CAN'T STAND THE HEAT GET OUT OF THE KITCHEN. [First half of 1900s]

take the initiative Begin a task or plan of action, as in *The boss was on vacation when they ran out of materials, so Julie took the initiative and ordered more.* This term uses *initiative* in the sense of "the power to originate something," a usage dating from the late 1700s.

take the law into one's hands Also, **take the law into one's own hands.** Replace the established authority with one's own, as in *While the captain was on shore the sailors took the law into their own hands and sneaked the prisoner off the ship.* Generally indicating disapproval of doing something forbidden, this idiom was first recorded in 1606.

take the liberty of Act on one's own authority without permission from another, as in *I took the liberty of forwarding the mail to his summer address.* It is also put as **take the liberty to,** as in *He took the liberty to address the Governor by her first name.* This rather formal locution was first recorded in 1625 and does not imply the opprobrium of the similar-sounding TAKE LIBERTIES.

take the load off Sit down, relax, as in *I wish you'd take some time and take the load off.* A shortening of **take the load off one's feet,** this colloquial phrase dates from about 1940. It is sometimes put as **take a load off.**

take the plunge Venture something, commit oneself, as in *You're been living together for a year, so when are you going to take the plunge and get married?* It is also put as **make the plunge,** *plunge* alluding to diving in a body of water. [Mid-1800s]

take the pulse of Also, **feel the pulse of.** Try to determine the intentions or sentiments of a person or group, as in *These exit polls allegedly take the pulse of the voters, but I don't believe they're very meaningful.* [First half of 1600s] Also see FEEL OUT.

take the rap Be punished or blamed for something, as in *I don't want to take the rap for Mary, who forgot to mail the check in time,* or *Steve is such a nice guy that he's always taking the rap for his colleagues.* This slangy idiom originally used *rap* in the sense of "a criminal charge," a usage still current. By the mid-1900s it was also used more broadly.

take the rough with the smooth Accept the bad along with the good, as in *You can't expect to close a lot of sales every week—you have to take the rough with the smooth.* This adage was first recorded about 1400. Also see TAKE THE BITTER WITH THE SWEET.

take the starch out of Deflate or ridicule someone, as in *That practical joke at the office party really took the starch out of Nick.* This expression, first recorded in 1840, alludes to the starch used to stiffen a shirt.

take the sting out of Lessen the severity or unpleasantness of something, as in *That senior citizen discount took the sting out of the airfares.* [Mid-1800s]

take the trouble ◆ See GO TO THE TROUBLE.

take the wind out of one's sails Hamper or stop one, put one at a disadvantage, as in *When they announced they were doing the same study as ours, it took the wind out of our sails,* or *The applause for the concertmaster took the wind out of the conductor's sails.* This expression alludes to sailing to windward of another ship, thereby robbing it of wind for its sails. [Early 1800s]

take the words out of someone's mouth Anticipate what someone is about to say; also, completely agree with someone. For example, *When* *you mentioned her dislike of fish you took the words right out of my mouth,* or *You took the words out of my mouth when you said he was stupid.* This idiom was first recorded in 1574.

take the wrong way Also, **take amiss**. Misunderstand, misinterpret, especially so as to take offense. For example, *I don't want you to take this the wrong way, but you have to give others a chance to speak,* or *Please don't take their criticism amiss; they mean well.* The variant dates from the late 1300s. Also see GET SOMEONE WRONG.

take to 1. Have recourse to, go to, as in *They took to the woods.* [c. 1200] 2. Develop as a habit or steady practice, as in *He took to coming home later and later.* [c. 1300] 3. Become fond of, like, as in *I took to him immediately,* or *The first time she skied she took to it.* This expression, from the mid-1700s, is sometimes expanded to **take to it like a duck to water,** a simile dating from the late 1800s. 4. **take to be.** Understand, consider, or assume, as in *I took it to be the right entrance.* [Mid-1500s] Also see the subsequent entries beginning with TAKE TO.

take to heart Be deeply moved or affected or upset by, as in *I know you'll take these comments about your story to heart,* or *She really took that college rejection to heart.* [c. 1300]

take to one's heels Run away, as in *When the burglar alarm went off they took to their heels.* This expression alludes to the fact that the heels are all one sees of a fugitive running away fast. Although similar expressions turned up from Shakespeare's time on, the exact idiom dates only from the first half of the 1800s. Also see SHOW ONE'S HEELS.

take to task Upbraid, scold; blame or censure. For example, *The teacher took Doris to task for turning in such a sloppy report.* This term, dating from the mid-1700s, at first meant either assigning or challenging someone to a task. Its current sense dates from the late 1800s.

take to the cleaners 1. Take or cheat one out of all of one's money or possessions, as in *Her divorce lawyer took him to the cleaners,* or *That broker has taken a number of clients to the cleaners.* [Slang; early 1900s] 2. Drub, beat up, as in *He didn't just push you—he took you to the cleaners.* [Slang; early 1900s]

take turns Alternate, as in *Since there is only one horse, Beth and Amanda are taking turns riding.* This phrase uses *turn* in the sense of "one of a series of actions done in succession." [Late 1300s] Also see IN TURN.

take umbrage Feel resentment, take offense, as in *Aunt Agatha is quick to take umbrage at any suggestion to do things differently.* This expression features one of the rare surviving uses of *umbrage,* which now means "resentment" but comes from the Latin *umbra,* for "shade," and presumably alludes to the "shadow" of displeasure. [Late 1600s]

take up 1. Raise, lift, as in *We have to take up the old carpet and sand the floor.* [c. 1300] 2. Reduce in size, shorten, tighten, as in *I have to take up the hem of this coat,* or *You have to take up the slack in that reel or you'll never land a fish.* [c. 1800] 3. Station oneself, settle in, as in *We took up our positions at the front.* [Mid-1500s] 4. Accept an option, bet, or challenge, as in *No one wanted to take up that bet.* This usage is often expanded to **take someone up on,** as in *You're offering to clean the barn? I'll take you up on that.* **Take up** dates from about 1700, the variant from the early 1900s. 5. Develop an interest in, begin an activity, as in *Jim took up gardening.* [Mid-1400s] Also see GO INTO, def. 3. 6. Use up or occupy entirely, as in *The extra duties took up most of my time,* or *This desk takes up too much space in the office,* or *How much room will your car take up?* [c. 1600] 7. Begin again, resume, as in *I'll take up the story where you left off.* [Mid-1600s] 8. Deal with, as in *Let's take up these questions one at a time.* [c. 1500] 9. Absorb, as in *These large trees are taking up all the water in the soil.* [Late 1600s] 10. Support, adopt as a protégé, as in *She's always taking up one or another young singer.* [Late 1300s] Also see the subsequent entries beginning with TAKE UP.

take up a collection Request and gather donations, as in *They were taking up a collection for the church that burned down,* or *The veterans' group takes up a collection every month of household goods and furniture.* This idiom was first recorded in 1849.

take up arms Also, **take up the cudgels.** Become involved in a conflict, either physical or verbal, as in *The Kurds took up arms against the Iranians at least two centuries ago,* or *Some believe it's the vice-president's job to take up the cudgels for the president.* The first term originated in the 1400s in the sense of going to war. The variant, alluding to cudgels as weapons, has been used figuratively since the mid-1600s and is probably obsolescent.

take up for Support in an argument, as in *To our surprise her father took up for her fiancé.* [Second half of 1800s]

take up on ◆ See TAKE UP, def. 4.

take up space Also, **take up room** or **time.** ◆ See TAKE UP, def. 6.

take up where one left off ◆ See TAKE UP, def. 7.

take up with Begin to associate with, consort with, as in *She took up with a fast crowd.* [Early 1600s]

take wing ◆ See TAKE FLIGHT.

take with a grain of salt ♦ See WITH A GRAIN OF SALT.

tale ♦ See OLD WIVES' TALE; TALL TALE; TELL TALES; THEREBY HANGS A TALE.

talk ♦ In addition to the idioms beginning with TALK, also see ALL TALK; DIRTY JOKE (TALK DIRTY); DOUBLE TALK; HEART TO HEART (TALK); LOOK WHO'S TALKING; MONEY TALKS; NOW YOU'RE TALKING; SMALL TALK; STRAIGHT TALK; SWEET TALK.

talk around Also, **talk round**. Persuade, as in *I talked him around to my point of view,* or *He had a hard time talking them round, but they finally agreed to postpone the tournament.* Also see TALK INTO.

talk at Speak to someone without regard for or interest in his or her reaction or response. For example, *She had a way of talking at us that was quite unpleasant.* [First half of 1800s]

talk back Also, **answer back**. Reply rudely or impertinently, as in *She was always in trouble for talking back,* or *The teacher won't allow anyone to answer back to her.* [Second half of 1800s]

talk big Brag, boast, as in *I don't believe he's ever shot even a duck, but he sure talks big about hunting.* This colloquial idiom was first recorded in 1699.

talk dirty ♦ See under DIRTY JOKE.

talk down 1. Belittle, depreciate, as in *They talked down the importance of the move.* 2. Silence someone by speaking loudly and persistently, as in *They talked down whatever objections she brought up.* [Early 1800s] 3. Help an aircraft to land by giving directions via radio, as in *The fog was so thick the control tower had to talk us down.* [c. 1940] 4. See TALK DOWN TO.

talk down to Also, **speak down to**. Address someone with insulting condescension, patronize, as in *Just because she's editor-in-chief doesn't give her the right to talk down to her staff,* or *Children hate teachers who speak down to them.*

talked out Weary from speaking, as in *I haven't another thing to say; I'm all talked out.* [c. 1900] Also see TALK OUT.

talk into Persuade, as in *They talked me into going swimming with them.* This idiom was first recorded in 1697. The antonym is **talk out of,** meaning "dissuade," as in *They tried to talk me out of going swimming.* It is almost a century newer, first recorded in Jane Austen's *Sense and Sensibility* (1797–1798).

talk of the town, the A subject of considerable gossip, as in *Turning up drunk at the debutante ball will certainly make you the talk of the town.* Already mentioned in two Latin sources, this expression surfaced in English in the mid-1600s.

talk out 1. Discuss a matter exhaustively, as in *We talked out our marital problems with the therapist.* [c. 1900] Also see TALKED OUT. 2. Resolve or settle by discussion, as in *Karen felt she and her father should talk out their differences.* [Mid-1800s]

talk out of ♦ See under TALK INTO; also see OUT OF TURN, def. 2.

talk over 1. Discuss thoroughly, as in *Let's talk over the entire plan and see if we discover any flaws.* [First half of 1700s] 2. Win someone over by persuasion, as in *We talked them over to our point of view.* [First half of 1800s] Also see TALK AROUND.

talk sense Speak rationally and coherently, as in *Ranting and raving won't help; it's time we talked sense,* or *I wish you'd talk some sense into that son of yours.* Shakespeare used this idiom in slightly different form in *The Merry Wives of Windsor* (2:1): "Believe it, Page, he speaks sense."

talk shop Converse about one's business or profession, as in *Whenever John and his dad get together, they talk shop.* [Mid-1800s]

talk someone's arm off Also, **talk someone's ear** or **head** or **pants off; talk a blue streak; talk until one is blue in the face; talk the bark off a tree** or **the hind leg off a donkey** or **horse**. Talk so much as to exhaust the listener, as in *Whenever I run into her she talks my arm off,* or *Louise was so excited that she talked a blue streak,* or *You can talk the bark off a tree but you still won't convince me.* The first four expressions imply that one is so bored by a person's loquacity that one's arm (or ear or head or pants) fall off; they date from the first half of the 1900s (also see PANTS OFF). The term *like a blue streak* alone simply means "very quickly," but in this idiom, first recorded in 1914, it means "continuously." The obvious hyperboles implying *talk* that takes *the bark off a tree,* first recorded in 1831, or *the hind leg off a horse,* from 1808, are heard less often today. Also see under BLUE IN THE FACE.

talk through one's hat Talk nonsense; also, hold forth about something one knows very little about. For example, *He was talking through his hat when he described the shipwreck,* or *Mother went on and on about various screwdrivers but in fact she was talking through her hat.* The allusion in this idiom makes no sense either, which may be the point. [Late 1800s]

talk to Also, **give a talking to**. Scold, reprimand, as in *The teacher said he'd have to talk to Jeff after school,* or *Dad gave us both a good talking to.* [Colloquial; second half of 1800s] For **talk to like a Dutch uncle,** see DUTCH UNCLE.

talk turkey Speak plainly, get to the point, as in *Don't call me until you're ready to talk turkey.* This expression allegedly comes from a tale about an Indian and a white man who hunted together and divided the game. When the white man said, "I'll take the turkey and you the buzzard, or you take the buzzard and I the turkey," the Indian replied, "Talk turkey to me." Whether or not this tale had a true basis, the term was recorded in its present meaning by about 1840.

talk up Speak in favor of, promote, as in *They were talking up their candidate all over the state.* [Second half of 1800s]

talk ♦ In addition to the idioms beginning with TALL, also see WALK TALL.

tall order A goal that is hard to fulfill or achieve, as in *Getting a thousand new subscribers is a tall order indeed.* This expression uses *tall* in the sense of "impressively great" or "difficult." [c. 1900]

tall tale A fanciful or greatly exaggerated story, as in *Some youngsters love tall tales about creatures from outer space coming to earth.* This idiom uses *tall* in the sense of "exaggerated." [Mid-1800s]

tamper with 1. Interfere or meddle, especially in a harmful way. For example, *If you tamper with that lock it's sure to break.* [c. 1600] 2. Engage in improper or secret dealings, as in *He was accused of tampering with the jury.* [c. 1600]

tangent ♦ See ON A TANGENT.

tank ♦ In addition to the idiom beginning with TANK, also see THINK TANK.

tank up 1. Fill a gas tank with fuel, as in *As soon as we tank up the car we can leave.* [First half of 1900s] 2. Drink to the point of intoxication. F. Scott Fitzgerald used this expression in *The Great Gatsby* (1926): "I think he'd tanked up a good deal at luncheon." This expression often is put in the passive, meaning "be or become intoxicated," as in *My roommate really got tanked up last night.* [Slang; c. 1900]

tan someone's hide Also, **have someone's hide.** Spank or beat someone, as in *Dad said he'd tan Billy's hide if he caught him smoking,* or *I'll have your hide if you take something without paying for it.* This term uses *hide* in the sense of "skin." The allusion in the first expression is to a spanking that will change one's skin just as chemicals tan animal hide (convert it into leather). [Second half of 1600s]

tap ♦ See ON TAP.

tape ♦ See RED TAPE.

taper off 1. Become thinner or narrower at one end, as in *The road began to taper off until it was just a narrow path.* [c. 1600] 2. Diminish or lessen gradually, end by degrees, as in *The storm finally tapered off.* [Mid-1800s]

tar ♦ In addition to the idiom beginning with TAR, also see BEAT THE LIVING DAYLIGHTS (TAR) OUT OF.

tar and feather Criticize severely, punish, as in *The traditionalists often want to tar and feather those who don't conform.* This expression alludes

to a former brutal punishment in which a person was smeared with tar and covered with feathers, which then stuck. It was first used as a punishment for theft in the English navy, recorded in the Ordinance of Richard I in 1189, and by the mid-1700s had become mob practice. The figurative usage dates from the mid-1800s.

target ♦ See ON TARGET; SITTING DUCK (TARGET).

tarred with the same brush Having the same faults or bad qualities, as in *He may be lazy, but if you ask me his friends are all tarred with the same brush.* This term is thought to come from sheep farming, where the animals' sores were treated by brushing tar over them, and all the sheep in a flock were treated in the same way. The term was transferred to likeness in human beings in the early 1800s.

task ♦ See TAKE TO TASK.

taste ♦ See ACQUIRED TASTE; DOSE (TASTE) OF ONE'S OWN MEDICINE; LEAVE A BAD TASTE IN ONE'S MOUTH; NO ACCOUNTING FOR TASTES; POOR TASTE.

tat ♦ See TIT FOR TAT.

tax ♦ In addition to the idiom beginning with TAX, also see DEATH AND TAXES.

tax with Charge, accuse, as in *He was taxed with betraying his fellows.* [Mid-1600s]

tea ♦ See CUP OF TEA; NOT FOR ALL THE TEA IN CHINA; TEMPEST IN A TEAPOT.

teach a lesson Punish in order to prevent a recurrence of bad behavior. For example, *Timmy set the wastebasket on fire; that should teach him a lesson about playing with matches.* This term uses *lesson* in the sense of "a punishment or rebuke," a usage dating from the late 1500s. Also see LEARN ONE'S LESSON.

teach an old dog new tricks Change longstanding habits or ways, especially in an old person. For example, *His grandmother avoids using the microwave oven—you can't teach an old dog new tricks.* This expression, alluding to the difficulty of changing one's ways, was first recorded in 1523 in a book of husbandry, where it was used literally. By 1546 a version of it appeared in John Heywood's proverb collection.

teacher's pet A person who has gained favor with authority, as in *Al has managed to be teacher's pet in any job he has held.* This expression transfers the original sense of a teacher's favorite pupil to broader use. [1920s]

team up with Form an association with, as in *Our pediatrician is teaming up with specialists in such areas as orthopedics and cardiology.* This expression alludes to the harnessing together of draft animals, such as oxen. [First half of 1900s]

teapot ♦ See TEMPEST IN A TEAPOT.

tear ♦ In addition to the idioms beginning with TEAR, also see RIP (TEAR) INTO; WEAR AND TEAR. Also see under TEARS; TORN.

tear apart 1. Upset or make distraught, as in *The parents' divorce tore apart the grandparents.* [Second half of 1800s] 2. Criticize severely, as in *The professor tore her paper apart.* [Mid-1900s] 3. Search some place completely, as in *The police tore the house apart.* [Second half of 1900s] 4. Separate, especially unwillingly, as in *The war tore many families apart.*

tear around Move about in excited or angry haste, as in *He tore around the house, looking for the dog.* [Second half of 1700s]

tear at 1. Pull at or attack violently, as in *Jane eagerly tore at the wrapping paper,* or *The dog tore at the meat.* [Mid-1800s] 2. Distress, as in *Their plight tore at his heart.*

tear away Remove oneself unwillingly or reluctantly, as in *I couldn't tear myself away from that painting.* [Late 1700s]

tear down 1. Demolish, take apart, as in *They tore down the old tenements,* or *He loved to tear down old engines.* [Early 1600s] 2. Vilify or discredit, as in *He's always tearing down someone or other.* [First half of 1900s]

tear into ♦ See RIP INTO.

tear it Ruin something, spoil one's chances, as in *She knew she'd torn it when she lost the address.* It is often put as **that tears it,** as in *He's a whole week late—well, that tears it for the September issue.* [Colloquial; early 1900s]

tear off 1. Produce hurriedly and casually, as in *He tore off a poem a day for an entire month.* 2. Leave in a hurry, as in *She tore off to the store because it was about to close.* [c. 1900]

tear one's hair Also, **tear out one's hair.** Be greatly upset or distressed, as in *I'm tearing my hair over these errors.* This expression alludes to literally tearing out one's hair in a frenzy of grief or anger, a usage dating from A.D. 1000. Today it is generally hyperbolic.

tears ♦ See BORE TO DEATH (TEARS); BURST INTO (TEARS); CROCODILE TEARS. Also see under TEAR.

tease out Lure out, obtain or extract with effort, as in *We had a hard time teasing the wedding date out of him.* This term alludes to the literal sense of *tease,* "untangle or release something with a pointed tool." [Mid-1900s]

tee off 1. Start or begin, as in *We teed off the fundraising drive with a banquet.* This usage is a metaphor taken from golf, where **tee off** means "start play by driving a golf ball from the tee." [Second half of 1900s] 2. Make angry or irritated, as in *That rude comment teed him off,* or *I was teed*

off *because it rained all weekend.* [Slang; mid-1900s] Also see TICK OFF.

teeth ♦ See ARMED TO THE TEETH; BARE ONE'S TEETH; BY THE SKIN OF ONE'S TEETH; CUT ONE'S TEETH ON; FED TO THE GILLS (TEETH); FLY IN THE FACE (TEETH) OF; GIVE ONE'S EYETEETH; GNASH ONE'S TEETH; GRIT ONE'S TEETH; IN THE TEETH OF; KICK IN THE PANTS (TEETH); LIE THROUGH ONE'S TEETH; LIKE PULLING TEETH; SCARCE AS HEN'S TEETH; SET ONE'S TEETH ON EDGE; SINK ONE'S TEETH INTO; TO THE TEETH. Also see under TOOTH.

tell ♦ In addition to the idioms beginning with TELL, also see DO TELL; KISS AND TELL; SHOW AND TELL; SOMETHING TELLS ME; THERE'S NO TELLING; THING OR TWO, TELL A; TIME WILL TELL; WHICH IS WHICH, TELL; YOU NEVER CAN TELL; YOU'RE TELLING ME. Also see under TOLD.

tell apart Discern or distinguish, as in *It's hard to tell the twins apart.* [First half of 1900s]

tell a thing or two ♦ See THING OR TWO.

tell it like it is Speak the truth, no matter how unpleasant. For example, *We're obligated to tell it like it is to the stockholders.* [Slang; second half of 1900s]

tell it to the Marines Go fool someone else because I won't believe that. For example, *He's a millionaire? Tell it to the Marines!* This term originated among British sailors, who regarded marines as naive and gullible. [c. 1800]

tell me Also, **tell me about it.** I know, I agree with you, as in *Since the layoffs I have been overloaded with work—Tell me!* or *We had a hard time finding the place.—Tell me about it! It took me all morning.* Identical to a literal request to be told about something, this expression must be distinguished from it by the context and the speaker's tone. [Colloquial; second half of 1900s]

tell off Rebuke severely, reprimand, as in *It's time someone told her off about her behavior.* There is also a synonymous expression, **tell someone where to get off,** as in *When he called back a third time, I told him where to get off.* [Colloquial; early 1900s] Also see GET OFF, def. 7.

tell on Tattle on, inform on, as in *Marjorie said she'd tell on him if he pulled her hair again.* This seemingly modern term appeared in a 1539 translation of the Bible (I Samuel 27:11): "David saved neither man nor woman . . . for fear (said he) lest they should tell on us."

tell someone where to get off ♦ See TELL OFF.

tell tales Divulge secrets, as in *Don't trust him; he's apt to tell tales.* This expression was first recorded about 1350. A variant, **tell tales out of school,** first recorded in 1530, presumably alluded to schoolchildren gossiping but was soon broadened to revealing secret or private information. Both may be obsolescent.

tell time Keep track of the hours; also, know how to read a clock or watch. For example, *This old clock still tells time quite accurately,* or *He taught his niece to tell time by using a cuckoo clock.* This expression uses *tell* in the sense of "reckon" or "calculate," a usage dating from about A.D. 1000.

temper ♦ See HOLD ONE'S TEMPER; LOSE ONE'S TEMPER.

temperature ♦ See RUN A FEVER (TEMPERATURE).

tempest in a teapot Also, **tempest in a teacup.** A great disturbance or uproar over a matter of little or no importance. For example, *All that because a handful of the thousand invited guests didn't show up? What a tempest in a teapot!* This expression has appeared in slightly different forms for more than 300 years. Among the variations are *storm in a cream bowl, tempest in a glass of water,* and *storm in a hand-wash basin.* The British prefer **storm in a teacup.** The current American forms were first recorded in 1854. For a synonym, see MUCH ADO ABOUT NOTHING.

tempt fate Also, **tempt the fates.** Take a severe risk, as in *It's tempting fate to start up that mountain so late in the day,* or *Patrice thought driving that old car was tempting the fates; it was sure to break down.* This expression uses *tempt* in the sense of "test in a way that involves risk or danger." Earlier idioms with a similar meaning were *tempt God,* dating from the 1300s, and *tempt fortune,* first recorded in 1603, with *fate* appearing about 1700.

ten ♦ See COUNT TO TEN; NOT TOUCH WITH A TEN-FOOT POLE.

tender ♦ See LEAVE TO SOMEONE'S TENDER MERCIES.

tender age A young age, as in *It's a great advantage to learn languages at a tender age.* [Early 1300s]

tender loving care Also, **TLC.** Solicitous and compassionate care, as in *These houseplants sure have had tender loving care,* or *Older house for sale, needs some renovation and TLC.* Originally used to describe the work of caregivers such as nurses, this term today is often used ironically or euphemistically. [Second half of 1900s]

tender mercies ♦ See LEAVE TO SOMEONE'S TENDER MERCIES.

tend to 1. Apply one's attention, as in *We should tend to our business, which is to teach youngsters.* This term uses *tend* in the sense of "attend." [1300s] **2.** Be disposed or inclined, as in *We tend to believe whatever we are told.* This term uses *tend* in the sense of "have a tendency." [c. 1600]

tenterhooks ♦ See ON TENTERHOOKS.

terms ♦ See BRING TO TERMS; COME TO TERMS WITH; CONTRADICTION IN TERMS; IN NO UNCERTAIN TERMS; IN TERMS OF; ON GOOD TERMS; ON SPEAKING TERMS.

territory ♦ See COME WITH THE TERRITORY; COVER THE FIELD (TERRITORY).

terror ♦ See HOLY TERROR.

test ♦ See ACID TEST; PUT TO THE TEST.

tether ♦ See END OF ONE'S ROPE (TETHER).

than ♦ See ACTIONS SPEAK LOUDER THAN WORDS; BARK IS WORSE THAN ONE'S BITE; BETTER LATE THAN NEVER; BETTER SAFE THAN SORRY; BETTER THAN; BITE OFF MORE THAN ONE CAN CHEW; BLOOD IS THICKER THAN WATER; EASIER SAID THAN DONE; EYES ARE BIGGER THAN ONE'S STOMACH; IN (LESS THAN) NO TIME; IRONS IN THE FIRE, MORE THAN ONE; LESS THAN; MORE DEAD THAN ALIVE; MORE FUN THAN A BARREL OF MONKEYS; MORE IN SORROW THAN IN ANGER; MORE OFTEN THAN NOT; MORE SINNED AGAINST THAN SINNING; MORE THAN MEETS THE EYE; MORE THAN ONE BARGAINED FOR; MORE THAN ONE CAN SHAKE A STICK AT; MORE THAN ONE WAY TO SKIN A CAT; NONE OTHER THAN; NO SOONER SAID THAN DONE; OTHER THAN; QUICKER THAN YOU CAN SAY JACK ROBINSON; WEAR ANOTHER (MORE THAN ONE) HAT.

thank ♦ In addition to the idioms beginning with THANK, also see GIVE THANKS FOR SMALL BLESSINGS.

thank God Also, **thank goodness** or **heaven.** I'm grateful, as in *Thank God you arrived safely,* or *We didn't, thank goodness, run out of food,* or *Thank heaven the book arrived on time.* These ejaculations originally expressed gratitude to divine providence but today tend to be used in a more casual way. [c. 1200]

thank one's lucky stars Be grateful for good fortune, as in *I thank my lucky stars that I wasn't on that plane that crashed.* This phrase, which reflects the ancient belief in the influence of stars over human destinies, appeared in slightly different form in Ben Jonson's play *Every Man Out of His Humour* (1599): "I thank my Stars for it." The exact locution dates from the 1800s and is more a general expression of relief than of belief in the stars' protection. Also see THANK GOD.

thanks to On account of, because of, as in *Thanks to your help, we'll be done on time.* This phrase alludes to gratitude being due to someone or something. It is also put negatively, **no thanks to,** meaning "without the benefit of help from," as in *We finally found your house, no thanks to the confusing map you drew.* This usage, first recorded in 1633, is about a hundred years older than the first term, recorded only in 1737.

that ♦ In addition to the idioms beginning with THAT, also see ALL'S WELL THAT ENDS WELL; ALL THAT; ALL THAT GLITTERS IS NOT GOLD; AND ALL (THAT); AS FAR AS THAT GOES; AT THAT POINT; AT THIS (THAT) RATE; AT THIS (THAT) STAGE; BE THAT AS IT MAY; BITE THE HAND THAT FEEDS YOU; CROSS A

(THAT) BRIDGE; FOR THAT MATTER; GAME THAT TWO CAN PLAY; HOW ABOUT THAT; HOW DOES THAT GRAB YOU; HOW'S THAT; IN ORDER (THAT); IN THAT; IS THAT A FACT; IT (THAT) FIGURES; JUST LIKE THAT; JUST THE (THAT'S THE) TICKET; LAST STRAW (THAT BREAKS); LIKE THAT; LOOK LIKE THE CAT THAT ATE THE CANARY; NOT ALL THAT; NOT BUILT THAT WAY; NOW THAT; ON CONDITION THAT; ON THE CHANCE (THAT); POWERS THAT BE; PUT THAT IN YOUR PIPE; SEEING THAT; SHIPS THAT PASS IN THE NIGHT; SO THAT; SUFFICE IT TO SAY THAT; TEAR (THAT TEARS) IT; THIS AND THAT; TO THAT EFFECT; WHEN IT COMES TO (THAT); WOULD THAT; YOU CAN SAY THAT AGAIN.

that ain't hay That's a great deal, especially of money; also, that's important. For example, *He's making ten thousand a month, and that ain't hay.* Originally used to describe a sum of money that is large, this phrase was later extended to other circumstances, as in *She married a titled lord, and that ain't hay.* [Colloquial; first half of 1900s]

that does it Also, **that does the trick.** The last requirement has been fulfilled; that accomplishes it. For example, *That does it; we're ready to send in the application now,* or *That last screw does the trick—it's fully assembled.* Grose's *Dictionary of the Vulgar Tongue* (1823) defines *do the trick* as "accomplish a robbery or other business successfully," and presumably the *it* in the first term stands for *the trick.* [Early 1800s] Also see THAT'S THAT.

that is Also, **that is to say.** To explain more clearly, in other words, as in *It's on the first floor, that is, at street level,* or *We're coming next month, that is to say, in November.* [Early 1600s] Also see under THAT'S.

that'll be the day That will never happen, that's very unlikely, as in *You think I'll win the lottery? That'll be the day!* Presumably this phrase is short for *that will be the day worth waiting for,* but it is nearly always used ironically, as in the example. [Mid-1900s]

that makes two of us I agree, me too, as in *I'm sure it's going to rain.—That makes two of us.* [First half of 1900s]

that's about the size of it That sums up the situation; that's how things are. For example, *So he's going to resign next month?—Yes, that's about the size of it,* or *Mary's applying to all those colleges?—That's about the size of it.* A mid-19th century British expression that soon crossed the Atlantic, it appeared in Mark Twain's *Tramp Abroad* (1880): "'Bloodshed!' 'That's about the size of it,' I said."

that's ____ for you This is the way something or someone is, as in *She's changed her mind again; that's Mary for you,* or *They came close to winning but they lost; that's tennis for you.*

that's how the ball bounces Also, **that's the way the ball bounces** or **the cookie crumbles.** That is the way matters have worked out and nothing can be done about it. For example, *I'm sorry you got fired but that's how the ball bounces,* or *They wanted a baby girl but got a third boy—that's the way the cookie crumbles.* These phrases allude to an odd bounce or a crumbled cookie that cannot be put back together. [Colloquial; mid-1900s]

that's one on me That's a joke at my expense, as in *And after all that discussion they didn't show up—that's one on me.* This phrase must be distinguished from **that's a new one on me,** which means "this is the first time I've heard of or seen that" (as in *A checkerboard rug—that's a new one on me*). Both idioms can be used with other personal pronouns (for example, **that's one on you**) and date from the early 1900s.

that's right Yes; that's correct; I agree. For example, *Are you leaving early?—That's right, I have to go now,* or *So you were classmates?—That's right.* [c. 1900]

that's that Also, **that takes care of that.** There's no more to be said or done; the matter is finished, the issue is settled. For example, *Dad's not buying you a television set, and that's that,* or *We've paid all we owe, and that takes care of that.* [Early 1800s]

that's the beauty of This is the most satisfactory feature of, as in *And our vacations fall at the same time; that's the beauty of working in different law practices.* [Mid-1700s]

that's the ticket ♦ See JUST THE TICKET.

that will do That is enough, that will suffice, as in *Please don't give me more peas; that will do,* or *That will do, children! There's to be no running near the pool.* [Late 1800s]

the beauty of ♦ See under THAT'S THE BEAUTY OF.

the bigger they come ♦ See BIGGER THEY COME.

the breaks Pieces of luck, turns of events, as in *No matter how well he pitches, the team always makes fielding errors—that's the breaks, I guess,* or *There's not much you can do if the breaks are against you.* In the singular and modified forms, this term becomes **good** or **bad** or **lucky break.** In the plural form, only the context determines its favorable or unfavorable meaning. [Slang; early 1900s] Also see TOUGH BREAK.

the business 1. Verbal abuse, scolding, or teasing; also, a beating. For example, *At boarding school new kids always get the business,* or *The boxer faked and then gave his opponent the business.* [Slang; c. 1940] 2. A harsh interrogation, as in *The detectives gave each suspect the business.* [Slang; c. 1940] 3. Dismissal from work or jilting, as in *Once the new management takes over I'm sure to* *get the business,* or *Dorothy gave him the business and married someone else.* [Slang; c. 1940]

the creeps Also, **the willies.** A sensation of horror or repugnance, as in *That weird man gives me the creeps,* or *I get the willies when I hear that dirge music.* The first of these colloquial terms alludes to a sensation of something crawling on one's skin. Charles Dickens used it in *David Copperfield* (1849) to describe a physical ailment: "She was constantly complaining of the cold and of its occasioning a visitation in her back, which she called 'the creeps.'" But soon after it was used to describe fear and loathing. The variant dates from the late 1800s, and both its allusion and origin are unclear.

the damage The cost or price of something, as in *So what's the damage for this outfit?* This seemingly modern slangy phrase, with *damage* alluding to the harm done to one's pocketbook, was first recorded in 1755.

the hell with ♦ See TO HELL WITH.

the horse's mouth ♦ See FROM THE HORSE'S MOUTH.

the idea Also, **the very idea.** ♦ See under WHAT'S THE IDEA.

the latest Also, **the latest thing.** The most recent development, as in fashion or the news. For example, *Wearing straw hats to the beach is the latest thing,* or *Have you heard the latest about the royal family?* [Colloquial; late 1800s] Also see THE THING.

the likes of ♦ See LIKES OF.

the limit The most extreme; someone or something that irritates, delights, or surprises to the ultimate degree. For example, *Hiring and firing someone the same day—that's the limit in employee relations!* or *That excuse of yours for missing the wedding, that's the limit,* or *He's done wonders before but this last one is the limit.* This idiom uses *limit* as "the last possible point or boundary." [Colloquial; c. 1900]

the long and the short of it ♦ See LONG AND SHORT OF IT.

the lowdown on The whole truth about something, as in *We're waiting to hear the lowdown on what happened after we left.* This term uses *lowdown* in the sense of "the basic or fundamental part." [Slang; early 1900s]

the masses The body of common people, or people of low socioeconomic status, as in *TV sitcoms are designed to appeal to the masses.* This idiom is nearly always used in a snobbish context that puts down the taste, intelligence, or some other quality of the majority of people. W.S. Gilbert satirized this view in the peers' march in *Iolanthe* (1882), in which the lower-middle class and the masses are ordered to bow down before the peers.

Prime Minister William Gladstone took a different view (Speech, 1886): "All the world over, I will back the masses against the [upper] classes." [First half of 1800s]

the matter ♦ See WHAT'S THE MATTER.

the more the merrier ♦ See MORE THE MERRIER.

them's fighting words ♦ See FIGHTING WORDS.

then ♦ In addition to the idioms beginning with THEN, also see AND THEN SOME; EVERY NOW AND THEN.

then again Also, **but then.** On the other hand, an opposite possibility. For example, *I think it'll arrive tomorrow; then again, it may not,* or *We think you'll like this restaurant, but then again, not everyone does,* or *The play was a bit dull, but then she's a great actress.*

then and there Also, **there and then.** At that precise time and place; on the spot. For example, *When the board questioned his judgment again, he resigned then and there.* The first term was first recorded in 1442, the variant in 1496.

the other day ♦ See OTHER DAY.

the other way round ♦ See OTHER WAY ROUND.

the picture ♦ See IN THE PICTURE.

the pits The worst possible situation, as in *Spending your birthday working alone is the pits,* or *That job is the pits.* The allusion in this term is unclear. Some think it refers to coal pits, others to armpits, and still others to the area beside an auto racecourse, also called *the pits,* where cars are serviced during a race. [Second half of 1900s]

there ♦ In addition to the idioms beginning with THERE, also see ALL THERE; GET THERE; HANG IN (THERE); HERE AND THERE; HERE; THERE, AND EVERYWHERE; IN THERE PITCHING; NEITHER HERE NOR THERE; NO SMOKE WITHOUT (WHERE THERE'S SMOKE THERE'S) FIRE; NOTHING TO IT (THERE'S); SOMEBODY UP THERE LOVES ME; TAKE IT FROM HERE (THERE); THEN AND THERE; WHERE THERE'S A WILL; WHILE THERE'S LIFE THERE'S HOPE.

there but for the grace of God go I I also could be in that terrible situation, as in *Seeing him with two flat tires on the highway, she said "There but for the grace of God go I."* This expression has been attributed to John Bradford, who so remarked on seeing criminals being led to their execution (c. 1553) and who in fact was executed himself as a heretic a few years later. A number of religious leaders, including John Bunyan, have been credited with it as well.

thereby hangs a tale That detail or incident reminds one of another story, as in *So he went without supper, but thereby hangs a tale.* This expression, embodying the pun on *tail* and *tale,* was used by Shakespeare in at least four of his plays and presumably was well known before that. [1500s]

there's no accounting for tastes ♦ See NO AC-COUNTING FOR TASTES.

there's no fool like an old fool ♦ See NO FOOL LIKE AN OLD FOOL.

there's no smoke without fire ♦ See NO SMOKE WITHOUT FIRE.

there's no telling It's impossible to determine, as in *There's no telling how many children will come down with measles,* or *There's no telling what will happen in the next episode of that soap opera.* This idiom uses *telling* in the sense of "reckoning," a usage dating from the late 1300s.

there's no time like the present ♦ See NO TIME LIKE THE PRESENT.

the ropes ♦ See KNOW THE ROPES; ON THE ROPES.

the rub The difficulty or problem, as in *We'd love to come but there's the rub—we can't get reservations.* This expression may come from lawn bowling, where *rub* refers to an unevenness in the ground that impedes the ball. Its most famous use is in one of Hamlet's soliloquies (*Hamlet,* 3:1): "To sleep, perchance to dream—ay, there's the rub, For in that sleep of death what dreams may come . . . Must give us pause." [Late 1500s]

the score ♦ See KNOW THE SCORE.

these ♦ See ONE OF THESE DAYS.

the soul of ♦ See SOUL OF.

the stake ♦ See BURN AT THE STAKE.

the thing Also, **the in thing.** Something in style or vogue, the latest trend. For example, *Wearing over-sized clothes is the thing these days,* or *Vans and sports utility vehicles have been the in thing for some time now.* The first term dates from the mid-1700s; the second, which uses *in* in the sense of "popular," dates from the mid-1900s. Also see THE LATEST.

the thing is The issue, main point, or problem is, as in *The thing is, we haven't enough money for the tickets.* [Colloquial; late 1800s]

the ticket ♦ See JUST THE TICKET.

the wiser ♦ See NONE THE WISER.

the works 1. Everything, the full range of possibilities, as in *He ordered a pizza with the works,* or *All right, tell me, give me the works on it.* This usage derives from *works* in the sense of "a complete set of parts for a machine or mechanism." [Colloquial; late 1800s] 2. A beating or other severe treatment. This usage is often put as **give someone the works,** as in *They took him outside and gave him the works.* [Slang; first half of 1900s]

they ♦ See BIGGER THEY COME; LET THE CHIPS FALL WHERE THEY MAY.

thick ♦ In addition to the idioms beginning with THICK, also see BLOOD IS THICKER THAN WATER; LAY IT ON THICK; PLOT THICKENS; THROUGH THICK AND THIN.

thick and fast Rapidly crowding, coming so fast they run together, as in *The questions came at him thick and fast.* This term originated in the second half of the 1500s as *thick and threefold* and was replaced by the current version about 1700. For a synonym, see FAST AND FURIOUS.

thick and thin ♦ See THROUGH THICK AND THIN.

thick as thieves Intimate, closely allied, as in *The sisters-in-law are thick as thieves.* This term uses *thick* in the sense of "intimate," a usage that is obsolete except in this simile. [Early 1800s]

thick skin Insensitivity to criticism or insult, as in *You can tell him exactly what you think of his new piece; unlike most composers he has a thick skin.* This term transfers an impervious outer coating to mental or emotional toughness. [Mid-1500s]

thief, thieves ♦ See IT TAKES ONE TO KNOW ONE (A THIEF TO CATCH A THIEF); THICK AS THIEVES.

thin ♦ In addition to the idioms beginning with THIN, also see INTO THIN AIR; ON THIN ICE; SPREAD ONESELF TOO THIN; THROUGH THICK AND THIN; WEAR THIN.

thin as a rail Very slender, as in *I do not know why she's dieting; she's thin as a rail already.* This simile, which uses *rail* in the sense of "a narrow bar," has largely replaced such other versions as *thin as a lath* or *rake,* although the latter is still common in Britain. [Second half of 1800s]

thin edge of the wedge A minor change that begins a major development, especially an undesirable one. For example, *First they asked me to postpone my vacation for a week, and then for a month; it's the thin edge of the wedge and pretty soon it'll be a year.* This term alludes to the narrow wedge inserted into a log for splitting wood. [Mid-1800s]

thing ♦ In addition to the idiom beginning with THING, also see ALL THE RAGE (THING); ALL THINGS TO ALL MEN; AMOUNT TO THE SAME THING; DO ONE'S THING; FIRST THING; FIRST THINGS FIRST; FOR ONE (THING); GET (A THING) GOING; GET INTO THE SWING OF THINGS; GREATEST THING SINCE SLICED BREAD; HAVE A GOOD THING GOING; HAVE A THING ABOUT; JUST ONE OF THOSE THINGS; KNOW ALL THE ANSWERS (A THING OR TWO); LITTLE KNOWLEDGE IS A DANGEROUS THING; NEAR THING; NO SUCH THING; NOT KNOW BEANS (THE FIRST THING); OF ALL THINGS; OTHER THINGS BEING EQUAL; SEEING THINGS; SURE THING; THE LATEST (THING); THE THING; THE THING IS; TOO MUCH OF A GOOD THING; VERY THING.

thing or two Quite a lot, as in *You can count on Bob to tell you a thing or two about Iran.* This term is nearly always an understatement. [Mid-1800s] Also see under KNOW ALL THE ANSWERS.

things are looking up Matters are improving; see under LOOK UP.

think ◆ In addition to the idioms beginning with THINK, also see COME TO THINK OF IT; HAVE ANOTHER GUESS (THINK) COMING; HEAR ONESELF THINK; NOT THINK MUCH OF; PUT ON ONE'S THINKING CAP; WISHFUL THINKING. Also see under THOUGHT.

think a lot of Also, **think highly** or **well** or **the world of**. Have a good opinion of, regard very favorably, as in *I think a lot of my daughter-in-law,* or *He didn't think highly of this company,* or *Dean thought the world of his youngest.* These expressions use *think* in the sense of "regard" or "value," a usage dating from the late 1300s. For antonyms, see NOT THINK MUCH OF; THINK LITTLE OF.

think aloud Speak one's thoughts audibly, as in *We need flour, sugar, butter—I'm just thinking aloud.* [Early 1700s]

think back Recall or reflect on, as in *When I think back on my days as a summer camper, I really had a good time,* or *As he thought back to his father, long dead, tears came to his eyes.* [Mid-1900s]

think better of Reconsider, change one's mind about, as in *I hope you'll think better of it before you quit your job.* [c. 1600]

think big Be ambitious, as in *There's no point in moving to a place the same size; we have to think big and plan for expansion.* [Colloquial; mid-1900s]

thinking cap ◆ See PUT ON ONE'S THINKING CAP.

think little of Have a poor opinion of, as in *I think little of moving to Florida since none of us likes heat or humidity.* This term uses *think* in the sense of "regard" or "value," a usage dating from the 1300s. Also see NOT THINK MUCH OF.

think nothing of 1. Give little consideration to, regard as routine, as in *He thinks nothing of driving 100 miles to see a new movie.* [c. 1800] 2. **think nothing of it**. It's not important, as in *Thanks for the lift.—Think nothing of it.* This way of saying YOU'RE WELCOME dates from the late 1800s.

think on one's feet React quickly, be mentally agile, as in *Reporters bombarded him with difficult questions, but Bill was very good at thinking on his feet.* This expression uses *on one's feet* in the sense of "wide awake, alertly." [First half of 1900s]

think out ◆ See THINK THROUGH.

think over Ponder, reflect about, especially with a view to making a decision. For example, *I'll have to think it over carefully before I can say yes or no.* [Mid-1800s]

think piece An article that presents news analysis, background material, and the author's opinions, as in *Her goal was to write think pieces but the editor kept assigning crime stories.* [c. 1940]

think positive Be optimistic, concentrate on the good rather than the bad, as in *It's true you were fired but think positive—now you can look for a job you really like.* This expression comes from the psychological doctrine of *positive thinking,* which gained currency with Norman Vincent Peale's popular book, *The Power of Positive Thinking* (1953). [Second half of 1900s]

think tank A group or organization dedicated to problem-solving and research, especially in such areas as technology, social or political strategy, and the military. For example, *The congressional leaders rely too heavily on that conservative think tank.* This term originated about 1900 as a facetious colloquialism for *brain* and was given its new meaning about 1950.

think the world of ◆ See under THINK A LOT OF.

think through Also, **think out**. Arrive at a thorough understanding of; devise or contrive thoroughly. For example, *That answer doesn't work; I don't believe you've thought the problem through,* or *He thought out a far more efficient method.* The first term dates from the early 1900s, the variant from the mid-1800s. Also see THINK UP.

think twice 1. Reconsider something, weigh something carefully, as in *I've got to think twice before spending that much on a car.* [Late 1800s] 2. **not think twice**. Take no notice, not worry about, as in *She didn't think twice about flying off to Europe with a day's notice.* [Mid-1900s]

think up Devise, contrive by thinking, as in *She's an expert at thinking up interesting programs.* [Mid-1800s]

thin on top Becoming bald, as in *I notice that he's getting a little thin on top.* The *top* in this euphemism refers to the top of the head. [Second half of 1800s]

third degree Intensive questioning or rough treatment used to obtain information or a confession, as in *The detectives gave her the third degree,* or *Jim gave her the third degree when she came home so late.* This term comes from freemasonry, where a candidate receives the third or highest degree, that of master mason, upon passing an intensive test. Dating from the 1770s, the phrase was transferred to other kinds of interrogation in the late 1800s.

third rail Something that is dangerous to tamper with, as in *Anything concerning veterans is a political third rail.* This term alludes to the rail that supplies the high voltage powering an electric train, so called since 1918. On the other hand, **grab hold of the third rail** means "become energized." Both shifts from the original meaning date from the late 1900s.

third world Underdeveloped or developing countries, as in *The conditions in our poorest rural areas resemble those in the third world.* This expression originated in the mid-1900s, at first denoting those countries in Asia and Africa that were not aligned with either the Communist bloc nations or the non-Communist Western nations. Because they were for the most part poor and underdeveloped, the term was transferred to all countries with those characteristics, and later still to poorer groups within a larger prevailing culture.

this ♦ In addition to the idioms beginning with THIS, also see AT THIS POINT; AT THIS RATE; AT THIS STAGE; FROM THIS DAY FORWARD; IN THIS DAY AND AGE; OUT OF THIS WORLD; SHUFFLE OFF (THIS MORTAL COIL).

this and that Also, **this, that, and the other.** Various miscellaneous items, one thing and another, as in *He said this and that about the budget, but nothing new or of great substance,* or *We spent all evening chatting about this, that, and the other.* The first idiom was first recorded in 1581; the variant dates from the early 1900s.

this is where I came in This is where I began, my knowledge dates from this point. For example, *Do you have anything more to add, because if not, this is where I came in.* This idiom, dating from the 1920s, originally alluded to the continuous showing of a motion picture, with customers entering the theater at any stage while the film was running and leaving when it reached the point where they had started.

this side of Short of, before, as in *I think she's still this side of forty,* or *I doubt they'll arrive this side of noon.* [First half of 1400s]

thither ♦ See HITHER AND THITHER.

Thomas ♦ See DOUBTING THOMAS.

thorn in one's flesh Also, **thorn in one's side.** A constant source of irritation, as in *Paul's complaining and whining are a thorn in my flesh,* or *Mother's always comparing us children—it's a thorn in our sides.* This metaphoric expression appears twice in the Bible. In Judges 2:3 it is enemies that "shall be as thorns in your sides"; in II Corinthians 12:7 Paul says his infirmities are "given to me a thorn in the flesh."

those ♦ See JUST ONE OF THOSE THINGS; ONE OF THOSE DAYS.

though ♦ See AS IF (THOUGH).

thought ♦ See FOOD FOR THOUGHT; LOST IN THOUGHT; ON SECOND THOUGHT; PENNY FOR YOUR THOUGHTS; PERISH THE THOUGHT; TRAIN OF THOUGHT. Also see under THINK.

thousand ♦ See BAT A THOUSAND; BY THE DOZEN (THOUSAND); ONE IN A MILLION (THOUSAND); PICTURE IS WORTH A THOUSAND WORDS.

thrash about Also, **thrash around.** Move wildly or violently, as in *He thrashed about all night, unable to sleep,* or *The fish thrashed around on the dock, so Meg threw it back in the water.* [Mid-1800s]

thrash out Discuss fully, especially to resolve a problem, as in *We'll just have to thrash out our ideas about where to go on vacation.* [Late 1800s]

thread ♦ See HANG BY A THREAD; LOSE THE THREAD.

threat ♦ See TRIPLE THREAT.

three cheers for Good for, hurrah for, congratulations to, as in *Three cheers for our mayor! Hip, hip, hooray!* Why one should shout one's encouragement or approbation three times rather than two or four is unclear. A shouted cheer presumably originated as a nautical practice, if we are to believe Daniel Defoe in *Captain Singleton* (1720): "We gave them a cheer, as the seamen call it." *Three cheers* was first recorded in 1751. The term is also used sarcastically, when one is not really offering congratulations, as in *So you finally passed; well, three cheers for you.*

three-ring circus A situation of complete confusion, as in *It was a three-ring circus, with the baby crying, the dog barking, both telephones ringing, and someone at the front door.* This term alludes to a circus where three rings or arenas are featuring performances simultaneously. Perhaps invented by show business impresario P.T. Barnum, the term was extended to other confused situations by about 1900.

three R's The fundamentals of education, as in *It's a terrible school; the children are not even taught the three R's.* It is widely believed that Sir William Curtis, an alderman who became Lord Mayor of London, once presented a toast to the three R's— reading, riting, and rithmetic—thereby betraying his illiteracy. In any event, the term was picked up by others and so used from the early 1800s on.

three's a crowd Also, **two's company, three's a crowd.** A third person spoils the ideal combination of a couple, as in *No, I won't join you— three's a crowd.* This expression, alluding to a third person spoiling the privacy of a pair of lovers, was already a proverb in 1546. For a synonym, see FIFTH WHEEL.

three sheets to the wind Also, **three sheets in the wind.** Drunk, inebriated, as in *After six beers he's three sheets to the wind.* This expression is generally thought to refer to the sheet—that is, a rope or chain—that holds one or both lower corners of a sail. If the sheet is allowed to go slack in the wind, the sail flaps about and the boat is tossed about much as a drunk staggers. Having three sheets loose would presumably make the situation all the worse. Another explanation holds that with two or four sheets to the wind the boat is balanced, whereas with three it is not. [Mid-1800s]

thrill to pieces Also, **thrill to death.** Give great pleasure, delight, as in *I was just thrilled to pieces with our new grandson,* or *He was thrilled to death* *when he first saw the Himalayas.* Both of these hyperbolic terms use *thrill* in the sense of "affect with sudden emotion," a usage dating from the late 1500s. Also see TICKLED PINK.

throat ♦ See AT EACH OTHER'S THROATS; CUT SOMEONE'S THROAT; FROG IN ONE'S THROAT; JUMP DOWN SOMEONE'S THROAT; LUMP IN ONE'S THROAT; RAM (SHOVE) DOWN SOMEONE'S THROAT; STICK IN ONE'S CRAW (THROAT).

throe ♦ See IN THE THROES.

throne ♦ See POWER BEHIND THE THRONE.

through ♦ In addition to the idioms beginning with THROUGH, see BREAK THROUGH; CARRY THROUGH; COME THROUGH; COME UP (THROUGH); CROSS (PASS THROUGH) ONE'S MIND; FALL BETWEEN (THROUGH) THE CRACKS; FALL THROUGH; FOLLOW THROUGH; GET THROUGH; GET THROUGH ONE'S HEAD; GO THROUGH; GO THROUGH CHANNELS; GO THROUGH THE MOTIONS; GO THROUGH THE ROOF; JUMP THROUGH HOOPS; LEAF THROUGH; LET DAYLIGHT THROUGH; LET SLIP (THROUGH THE FINGERS); LIE THROUGH ONE'S TEETH; LIVE THROUGH; MUDDLE THROUGH; PAY THROUGH THE NOSE; PULL THROUGH; PUT THROUGH; PUT SOMEONE THROUGH HIS OR HER PACES; RISE THROUGH THE RANKS; RUN THROUGH; SAIL THROUGH; SEE THROUGH; SEE THROUGH ROSE-COLORED GLASSES; SINK THROUGH THE FLOOR; SIT OUT (THROUGH); SLEEP THROUGH; SQUEAK BY (THROUGH); SQUEEZE THROUGH; TALK THROUGH ONE'S HAT; THINK THROUGH; WIN THROUGH; WORK ONE'S WAY INTO (THROUGH).

through and through In every part or aspect, throughout. For example, *I was wet through and through,* or *He was a success through and through.* This idiom originally was used to indicate literally penetration, as by a sword. The figurative usage was first recorded in 1410.

through one's hat ♦ See TALK THROUGH ONE'S HAT.

through one's head ♦ See GET THROUGH ONE'S HEAD.

through one's mind ♦ See CROSS ONE'S MIND.

through rose-colored glasses ♦ See SEE THROUGH ROSE-COLORED GLASSES.

through the mill Hardship or rough treatment, as in *They put him through the mill, making him work at every one of the machines,* or *Jane was exhausted; she felt she'd been through the mill.* This term alludes to being ground down like grain in a mill. [Late 1800s]

through the motions ♦ See GO THROUGH THE MOTIONS.

through thick and thin Despite all obstacles or adversities, as in *She promised to stand by him through thick and thin.* This term alludes to penetrating a forest with both thick and sparse undergrowth. Today it is nearly always used with the idea of supporting something or someone in all circumstances, as in the example. [Late 1300s]

throw ♦ In addition to the idioms beginning with THROW, also see CAST (THROW) ONE'S LOT WITH; CAST (THROW) THE FIRST STONE; HAVE (THROW) A FIT; (THROW) IN ONE'S FACE; KNOCK (THROW) FOR A LOOP; POUR (THROW) COLD WATER ON; SHED (THROW) LIGHT ON; STONE'S THROW.

throw a curve Surprise or outwit someone, as in *They threw me a curve when they said that our department would be combined with yours.* This colloquial term comes from baseball, where a pitcher tries to fool the batter by using a *curve ball,* which is thrown with sufficient spin to make it veer from its expected path. The term was transferred to other kinds of surprise, not necessarily unpleasant, in the mid-1900s.

throw a fit ♦ See HAVE A FIT.

throw a monkey wrench into Sabotage or frustrate a project or plans, as in *The boss threw a monkey wrench into our plans when he said we'd have to work Saturday.* This transfer of industrial sabotage—that is, throwing a tool inside machinery—to other subjects dates from the early 1900s.

throw a party Put on or hold a social gathering, as in *They're throwing a party to introduce their nephew to the neighbors,* or *She threw a party every Saturday night.* [Colloquial; first half of 1900s]

throw a punch Deliver a blow with the fist, as in *He was furious enough to throw a punch at the other driver.* This term originated in boxing but has been extended to less formal fisticuffs as well. [First half of 1900s]

throw away 1. Also, **throw** or **toss out.** Dispose of, discard, as in *This coat is too good to throw away,* or *Did you throw out the rest of the milk?* or *She tossed out all his old letters.* [First half of 1500s] 2. Waste, fail to use, as in *She's thrown away her inheritance on all kinds of foolish enterprises,* or *He's thrown away his chances for an engineering job.* [Mid-1600s] 3. Also, **throw out.** Utter or perform in an offhand, seemingly careless way, as in *He threw away the news that their summer cottage had been broken into,* or *She threw out some suggestions for changing the bylaws.* [First half of 1900s]

throw back 1. Hinder the progress of, check, as in *His illness threw his schooling back a year,* or *The troops were thrown back by a barrage of fire.* [First half of 1800s] 2. Revert to an earlier type or stage, as in *That dog throws back to his wolf ancestors.* This usage gave rise to the noun **throwback,** a reversion to a former stage or type. [Second half of 1800s] 3. **throw back on.** Cause to depend on, make reliant on, as in *When the violinist didn't show up, they were thrown back on the pianist.* [Mid-1800s]

throw caution to the winds Also, **throw discretion to the winds.** Behave or speak very rashly, as in *Throwing caution to the winds, he ran after the truck,* or *I'm afraid she's thrown discretion to the winds and told everyone about the divorce.* This expression uses *to the winds* in the sense of "utterly vanishing" or "out of existence," a usage dating from the mid-1600s. The first recorded use of *throw to the winds* was in 1885.

throw cold water on ◆ See POUR COLD WATER ON.

throw down the gauntlet Declare or issue a challenge, as in *The senator threw down the gauntlet on the abortion issue.* This expression alludes to the medieval practice of a knight throwing down his gauntlet, or metal glove, as a challenge to combat. Its figurative use dates from the second half of the 1700s, as does the less frequently heard **take up the gauntlet,** for accepting a challenge.

throw dust in someone's eyes Mislead someone, as in *The governor's press aide threw dust in their eyes, talking about a flight at the airport when he was heading for the highway.* This metaphoric expression alludes to throwing dust or sand in the air to confuse a pursuing enemy. [Mid-1700s]

throw for a loop ◆ See KNOCK FOR A LOOP.

throw good money after bad Waste more money in hopes of recouping previous losses, as in *Hiring him to improve that software is throwing good money after bad; it's based on an older operating system and will soon be obsolete.* [Late 1800s]

throw in 1. Insert or introduce into the course of something, interject, as in *He always threw in a few jokes to lighten the atmosphere.* [c. 1700] 2. Add something with no additional charge, as in *The salesman said he'd throw in the carpet padding.* [Second half of 1600s] 3. **throw in with.** Enter into association with, as in *His friends warned him against throwing in with the notorious street gang.* [Second half of 1800s] Also see CAST ONE'S LOT and the subsequent idioms beginning with THROW IN.

throw in one's hand Give up, abandon, as in *I'm through trying to assemble it; I'm throwing in my hand.* This expression comes from card games such as poker, where it is used to retire from the game. Its figurative use dates from the 1920s.

throw in one's lot with ◆ See CAST ONE'S LOT.

throw in someone's face Confront or upbraid someone with something, as in *Dean keeps throwing her poor driving record in her face.* [c. 1600]

throw in the sponge Also, **throw in the towel.** Give up, acknowledge defeat, as in *I can't move this rock; I'm throwing in the sponge,* or *Bill decided to throw in the towel and resign from his job.* This

idiom comes from boxing, where formerly a fighter (or his second) conceded defeat by throwing the sponge or towel used to wipe his face into the ring. [c. 1900]

throw light on ◆ See SHED LIGHT ON.

throw off 1. Cast out, rid oneself of, as in *He threw off all unpleasant memories and went to the reunion.* [Early 1600s] 2. Give off, emit, as in *The garbage was throwing off an awful smell.* [First half of 1700s] Also see THROW OUT, def. 1. 3. Also, **throw** or **put off the scent.** Distract, divert, or mislead, as in *A mistaken estimate threw off her calculations,* or *These clues were designed to throw the detective off the scent.* The variant comes from hunting, where the quarry may try to put pursuing hounds off the scent. Its figurative use dates from the mid-1800s. Also see OFF THE TRACK. 4. Perform in a quick, spontaneous, or casual manner, as in *He threw off one sketch after another.* [Mid-1700s]

throw off balance ◆ See OFF BALANCE.

throw off the track ◆ See OFF THE TRACK.

throw oneself at Also, **throw oneself at someone's head.** Try to attract someone's interest, attention, or love, as in *He always had women throwing themselves at his head.* [Late 1700s]

throw oneself into Enter or engage in a project with enthusiasm, as in *Nora threw herself into making the invitations.* This idiom uses *throw* in the sense of "fling impetuously," a usage dating from about 1200.

throw one's hat in the ring Also, **toss one's hat in the ring.** Announce one's candidacy or enter a contest, as in *The governor was slow to throw his hat in the ring in the senatorial race.* This term comes from boxing, where throwing a hat in the ring formerly indicated a challenge; today the idiom nearly always refers to political candidacy. [c. 1900]

throw one's weight around Wield power or authority, especially in a heavyhanded way. For example, *One doesn't make oneself popular by throwing one's weight around.* [Colloquial; early 1900s]

throw open Make more accessible, especially suddenly or dramatically, as in *His withdrawal threw open the nomination to all comers.* [Mid-1800s]

throw out 1. Give off, emit, as in *That flashlight throws out a powerful beam.* [Mid-1700s] Also see THROW OFF, def. 2. 2. Reject, as in *We threw out her proposal.* [Early 1600s] 3. Get rid of, discard; see THROW AWAY, def. 1. 4. Offer a suggestion or plan, as in *The nominating committee threw out names for our consideration.* [Early 1600s] Also see THROW AWAY, def. 3. 5. Forcibly eject, force the departure of, as in *The bartender threw out the drunk,* or

He was thrown out of the country club for failing to pay his dues. [Early 1500] **6.** Put out of alignment, as in *Lifting that sofa threw out my back.* **7.** In baseball or cricket, put a player out by throwing the ball. In baseball, the throw is to a base before the batter reaches it; in cricket, the throw must hit the batsman's wicket. [Second half of 1800s]

throw out the baby with the bath water Discard something valuable along with something not wanted. For example, *I know you don't approve of that one item in the bill but we shouldn't throw out the baby with the bath water by voting the bill down.* This expression, with its vivid image of a baby being tossed out with a stream of dirty water, is probably translated from a German proverb, *Das Kind mit dem Bade ausschütten* ("Pour the baby out with the bath"). It was first recorded in English in 1853 by Thomas Carlyle, who translated many works from German.

throw over Reject, abandon, as in *They'd lived together for a year when she suddenly threw him over and moved out.* This idiom, possibly alluding to throwing something or someone overboard, was first recorded in 1835.

throw someone Cause someone to be confused or perplexed, disconcert someone, as in *We didn't let our worries throw us,* or *That unfavorable review threw her.* [Colloquial; mid-1800s] Also see KNOCK FOR A LOOP.

throw the book at Punish or reprimand severely, as in *I just knew the professor would throw the book at me for being late with my paper.* This expression originally meant "sentence a convicted person to the maximum penalties allowed," the *book* being the roster of applicable laws. Its figurative use dates from the mid-1900s.

throw together **1.** Assemble hurriedly, as in *I just threw together some salad and took it along.* [Early 1700s] **2.** Cause to associate, as in *Their parents were always throwing the young couple together hoping they would like each other.* [Early 1800s]

throw to the wolves Also, **throw to the dogs** or **lions.** Send to a terrible fate; sacrifice someone, especially so as to save oneself. For example, *Leaving him with hostile reporters was throwing him to the wolves,* or *If Bob doesn't perform as they expect, they'll throw him to the lions.* All three hyperbolic terms allude to the ravenous appetite of these animals, which presumably will devour the victim. The first term comes from Aesop's fable about a nurse who threatens to throw her charge to the wolves if the child does not behave. [First half of 1900s]

throw up **1.** Vomit, as in *The new drug makes many patients throw up.* [First half of 1700s] **2.** Aban-

don, relinquish, as in *After the results of the poll came in, she threw up her campaign for the Senate.* **3.** Construct hurriedly, as in *The builder threw up three houses in a matter of a few months.* [Late 1500s] **4. throw it up to.** Criticize, upbraid, as in *Dad was always throwing it up to the boys that they were careless and messy.* [Early 1800s]

throw up one's hands Indicate or express utter hopelessness. For example, *Jim was getting nowhere so he threw up his hands and abandoned the argument.* This idiom alludes to a traditional gesture for giving up.

throw up to ♦ See THROW UP, def. 5.

thumb ♦ In addition to the idioms beginning with THUMB, also see ALL THUMBS; GREEN THUMB; RULE OF THUMB; STICK OUT (LIKE A SORE THUMB); TWIDDLE ONE'S THUMBS; UNDER SOMEONE'S THUMB.

thumb a ride ♦ See HITCH A RIDE.

thumbnail sketch A brief outline or cursory description, as in *Let me give you a thumbnail sketch of the situation.* This idiom alludes to drawing a picture no larger than a thumbnail. [Mid-1800s]

thumb one's nose Express scorn or ridicule. For example, *I'm sure the members of the school committee thumb their noses at any suggestion we make.* This expression alludes to the traditional gesture of contempt, that is, placing the thumb under the nose and wiggling the fingers. [c. 1900]

thumbs up An expression of approval or hopefulness, as in *The town said thumbs up on building the elderly housing project.* The antonym **thumbs down** indicates disapproval or rejection, as in *Mother gave us thumbs down on serving beer at our party.* Alluding to crowd signals used in Roman amphitheaters, these idioms were first recorded in English about 1600. In ancient times the meaning of the gestures was opposite that of today. Thumbs down indicated approval; thumbs up, rejection. Exactly when the reversal occurred is not known, but the present conventions were established by the early 1900s.

thunder ♦ See under STEAL SOMEONE'S THUNDER.

thus far ♦ See under SO FAR.

tick ♦ In addition to the idiom beginning with TICK, also see CLOCK IS TICKING; TIGHT AS A TICK; WHAT MAKES ONE TICK.

ticket ♦ See JUST THE TICKET; MEAL TICKET; SPLIT TICKET; STRAIGHT TICKET; WRITE ONE'S OWN TICKET.

tickled pink Also, **tickled to death.** Delighted, as in *I was tickled pink when I got his autograph,* or *His parents were tickled to death when he decided to marry her.* The first term, first recorded in 1922, alludes to one's face turning pink with laughter when one is being tickled. The variant, clearly a hyperbole, dates form about 1800.

tickle one's fancy Appeal to one, be to one's liking, as in *That joke tickled my fancy.* This term uses *fancy* in the sense of "liking" of "taste." [Second half of 1700s]

tickle the ivories Play the piano, as in *He went on tickling the ivories until three in the morning.* This expression alludes to a piano's keys, traditionally made of ivory. [Colloquial; first half of 1900s]

tick off Infuriate, make angry. For example, *That article ticked me off.* [Colloquial; second half of 1900s] For a vulgar synonym, see PISS OFF.

tide ♦ In addition to the idiom beginning with TIDE, also see STEM THE TIDE; SWIM AGAINST THE CURRENT (TIDE); SWIM WITH THE TIDE; TIME AND TIDE; TURN OF THE TIDE.

tide over Support through a difficult period, as in *I asked my brother for $100 to tide me over until payday.* This expression alludes to the way the tide carries something. [Early 1800s]

tie, tied ♦ In addition to the idioms beginning with TIE and TIED, also see FIT TO BE TIED; PUT (TIE) ON THE FEED BAG; WITH ONE ARM TIED BEHIND ONE'S BACK.

tie down Constrain, confine, or limit, as in *As long as the children were small, she was too tied down to look for a job.* [Late 1600s]

tied to apron strings Wholly dependent on or controlled by a woman, especially one's mother or wife. For example, *At 25, he was still too tied to her apron strings to get an apartment of his own.* This expression, dating from the early 1800s, probably alluded to *apron-string tenure,* a 17th-century law that allowed a husband to control his wife's and her family's property during her lifetime.

tied up ♦ See TIE UP.

tie in Connect closely with, coordinate, as in *They are trying to tie in the movie promotion with the book it is based on,* or *His story does not tie in with the facts.* [First half of 1900s]

tie into Attack energetically, as in *They tied into the buffet as though they hadn't eaten in months.* [Colloquial; c. 1900]

tie into knots Confuse, upset, or bewilder, as in *He tied himself into knots when he tried to explain how the engine works.* This metaphoric idiom transfers a knotted tangle to mental confusion. [Late 1800s]

tie one on Become intoxicated; go on a drinking spree. For example, *They went out and really tied one on.* The precise allusion here—what it is one ties on—is unclear. [Slang; mid-1900s]

tie one's hands Prevent one from acting, as in *I can't help you this time; my hands are tied by the*

club's rules. This metaphoric term transfers physical bondage to other kinds of constraint. It was first recorded in 1642.

tie the knot Get married; also perform a marriage ceremony. For example, *So when are you two going to tie the knot?* or *They asked their friend, who is a judge, to tie the knot.* [Early 1700s]

tie up 1. Fasten securely; also, moor a ship. For example, *Can you help me tie up these bundles?* or *The forecast was terrible, so we decided to tie up at the dock and wait out the storm.* The first usage dates from the early 1500s, the nautical usage from the mid-1800s. 2. Impede the progress of, block, as in *The accident tied up traffic for hours.* [Late 1500s 3. Keep occupied, engage, as in *She was tied up in a meeting all morning.* [Late 1800s] 4. Make funds or property inaccessible for other uses, as in *Her cash is tied up in government bonds.* [Early 1800s]

tiger by the tail Something too difficult to manage or cope with, as in *You know nothing about the commodities market; you'll end up catching a tiger by the tail.* This colorful metaphor conjures up the image of grabbing a powerful but fierce animal by the tail, only to have it turn on one. [Second half of 1900s]

tight ♦ In addition to the idioms beginning with TIGHT, also see IN A BIND (TIGHT CORNER); SIT TIGHT.

tight as a drum Taut or close-fitting; also watertight. For example, *That baby's eaten so much that the skin on his belly is tight as a drum,* or *You needn't worry about leaks; this tent is tight as a drum.* Originally this expression alluded to the skin of a drumhead, which is tightly stretched, and in the mid-1800s was transferred to other kinds of tautness. Later, however, it sometimes referred to a drumshaped container, such as an oil drum, which had to be well sealed to prevent leaks, and the expression then signified "watertight."

tight as a tick Drunk, as in *She was tight as a tick after just one glass of wine.* This expression alludes to a tick engorged with the blood of the animals it feeds on. [Slang; mid-1800s]

tighten one's belt Spend less, be more frugal, as in *Business has been bad, so we'll have to tighten our belts.* This metaphoric term alludes to pulling in one's belt after losing weight from not having enough to eat. [First half of 1900s]

tighten the screws ♦ See under TURN UP THE HEAT.

tight rein on, a Strict control over, as in *We told them to keep a tight rein on spending for the next year.* This expression alludes to the narrow strap (rein) attached to a bit and used to control a horse's movements. *Rein* has been used to refer to any kind of restraint since the first half of the 1400s.

tightrope ♦ See WALK A TIGHTROPE.

tight ship A well-managed organization, as in *The camp director runs a tight ship.* This metaphoric term alludes to a ship in which the ropes are taut and by extension the ship is strictly managed. [Second half of 1900s]

tight spot ♦ See under IN A BIND.

tight squeeze A difficulty caused by too little time or space, or too little credit or funds. For example, *It will be a tight squeeze to get there on time*, or *I don't know if the sofa will go through the door; it's a tight squeeze*, or *The company's in a tight squeeze because of poor cash flow*. This idiom uses *tight* in the sense of "too narrow or constricted." [c. 1900]

till ♦ In addition to the subsequent idioms beginning with TILL, also see HAND IN THE TILL; UNTIL.

till all hours ♦ See ALL HOURS.

till hell freezes over Forever, as in *They said they'd go on searching till hell freezes over, but I'm sure they'll give up soon.* This hyperbolic expression dates from the early 1900s. So does its antonym, **not till hell freezes over**, meaning "never," as in *I'm not giving it, not until hell freezes over.*

till the cows come home Also, **when the cows come home**. For a long time, as in *you can keep asking till the cows come home, but you still may not go bungee-jumping*. This term alludes to when the cows return to the barn for milking. [Late 1500s]

tilt at windmills Engage in conflict with an imagined opponent, pursue a vain goal, as in *Trying to reform campaign financing in this legislature is tilting at windmills.* This metaphoric expression alludes to the hero of Miguel de Cervantes' *Don Quixote* (1605), who rides with his lance at full tilt (poised to strike) against a row of windmills, which he mistakes for evil giants.

time ♦ In addition to the idioms beginning with TIME, also see ABOUT TIME; AGAINST THE CLOCK (TIME); AHEAD OF ONE'S TIME; AHEAD OF TIME; ALL THE TIME; AT ALL TIMES; AT ONE TIME; AT ONE TIME OR ANOTHER; AT THE SAME TIME; AT THIS POINT (IN TIME); AT TIMES; BEAT TIME; BEHIND IN (TIME); BEHIND THE TIMES; BIDE ONE'S TIME; BIG TIME; BUY TIME; CALL ONE'S (TIME ONE'S) OWN; CHOW DOWN (TIME); CRUNCH TIME; DO TIME; EVERY TIME ONE TURNS AROUND; FOR THE MOMENT (TIME BEING; FROM TIME TO TIME; GOOD-TIME CHARLIE; HALF THE TIME; HARD TIME; HAVE A GOOD TIME; HIGH TIME; IN BETWEEN TIMES; IN DUE COURSE (OF TIME); IN GOOD TIME; IN NO TIME; IN THE FULLNESS OF TIME; IN THE NICK OF TIME; KEEP TIME; KEEP UP (WITH THE TIMES); KILL TIME; LESS THAN (NO TIME); LONG TIME NO SEE; LOSE TIME; MAKE GOOD TIME; MAKE TIME; MAKE UP FOR LOST TIME; MANY IS THE (TIME); MARK TIME; NOT GIVE SOME-ONE THE TIME OF DAY; NO TIME FOR; NO TIME LIKE THE PRESENT; OF ONE'S LIFE, TIME; ON BORROWED TIME; ONCE UPON A TIME; ONE BY ONE (AT A TIME); ON ONE'S OWN TIME; ON TIME; PASS THE TIME; PLAY FOR TIME; POINT IN TIME; PRESSED FOR TIME; SERVE TIME; SHOW SOMEONE A GOOD TIME; SMALL TIME; STITCH IN TIME; TAKE ONE'S TIME; TAKE UP SPACE (TIME); TELL TIME; WHALE OF A TIME.

time after time Also, **time and again; time and time again**. Repeatedly, again and again, as in *Time after time he was warned about the river rising*, or *We've been told time and time again that property taxes will go up next year.* The first idiom dates from the first half of the 1600s, the variants from the first half of the 1800s.

time and a half A rate of pay for overtime work that is one and one-half times higher than the regular hourly wage, as in *I don't mind working Sunday so long as I get time and a half.* This expression uses *time* in the sense of "the number of hours worked." [c. 1885]

time and tide wait for no man One must not procrastinate or delay, as in *Let's get on with the voting; time and tide won't wait, you know.* This proverbial phrase, alluding to the fact that human events or concerns cannot stop the passage of time or the movement of the tides, first appeared about 1395 in Chaucer's *Prologue to the Clerk's Tale*. The alliterative beginning, *time and tide*, was repeated in various contexts over the years but today survives only in the proverb, which is often shortened (as above).

time bomb A situation that threatens to have disastrous consequences at some future time, as in *That departmental dispute is a time bomb just waiting to go off.* This term alludes to an explosive device that is set to go off at a specific time. [First half of 1900s]

time flies Time passes quickly, as in *It's midnight already? Time flies when you're having fun*, or *I gues it's ten years since I last saw you—how time flies.* This idiom was first recorded about 1800 but Shakespeare used a similar phrase, "the swiftest hours, as they flew," as did Alexander Pope, "swift fly the years."

time hangs heavy Also, **time hangs heavy on one's hands**. Time passes slowly, as in *She adjusted quite well to the nursing home, except that she says time hangs heavy on her hands.* This metaphoric term, first recorded in the late 1760s, likens the passage of time to a burdensome weight.

time immemorial Also, **time out of mind**. Long ago, beyond memory or recall, as in *These ruins have stood here since time immemorial*, or *His office has been on Madison Avenue for time out of mind.* The first expression comes from English law, where it signifies "beyond legal memory," specifically before the reign of Richard I (1189–1199), fixed as the legal limit for bringing certain kinds of lawsuit. By about 1600 it was broadened to its present sense of "a very long time ago." The variant, first recorded in 1432, uses *mind* in the sense of "memory" or "recall."

time is money One's time is a valuable commodity, as in *I can't stay home and wait any longer; time is money, you know.* This proverbial term goes back to one first recorded in 1572, **time is precious**, in a discourse on usury.

time is ripe This is the right moment for something, as in *The time is ripe for a revival of that play.* Shakespeare used this term (and may have originated it) in *1 Henry IV* (1:3): "Letters shall direct your course when time is ripe."

time is up The period of time allowed for something is ended, as in *Turn in your papers, students; time is up.* This idiom uses *up* in the sense of "completed" or "expired," a usage dating from about 1400.

time of day The hour shown on a clock; also, a stage in any activity or period. For example, *What time of day is the repairman coming?* or *This is hardly the time of day to ask for another installment when he's just turned one in.* [Late 1500s] Also see NOT GIVE SOMEONE THE TIME OF DAY.

time off A break from one's employment or school, as in *I need some time off from teaching to work on my dissertation,* or *He took time off to make some phone calls.* [First half of 1900s]

time of one's life An extremely pleasurable experience; see under OF ONE'S LIFE.

time on one's hands An interval with nothing to do; see under ON ONE'S HANDS; TIME HANGS HEAVY.

time out A short break from work or play; also, a punishment for misbehavior in young children in which they are briefly separated from the group. For example, *People rush around so much these days that I think everyone should take some time out now and then,* or *We don't throw food, Brian; you need some time out to think about it.* This expression comes from a number of sports in which it signifies an interruption in play where the officials stop the clock, for purposes of rest, making a substitution, or consultation. Its figurative use dates from the mid-1900s.

time out of mind ♦ See TIME IMMEMORIAL.

time warp A stoppage in the passage of time; also, a distortion of time whereby an event or person could hypothetically move from one era to another. For example, *Nothing in their lives has changed since the sixties; they're in a time warp,* or *Having a seventy-year-old actress portray a*

teenager—*that was some time warp!* This term originated in science fiction, where it signifies "a supernatural movement from one era to another," and came to be used more loosely. [c. 1950]

time was Formerly, in the past, as in *Time was, the city streets were perfectly safe at night.* [Mid-1500s]

time will tell Sooner or later something will become known or be revealed, as in *I don't know whether or not they'll like the reconstruction; only time will tell.* This proverbial phrase dates from the early 1500s.

tin god A self-important, dictatorial, petty person who imposes ideas, beliefs, and standards on subordinates. For example, *The officials in these small towns often act like tin gods.* The *tin* in this expression alludes to the fact that tin is a base metal with relatively little value. [Late 1800s]

tinker ♦ In addition to the idiom beginning with TINKER, also see NOT WORTH A DAMN (TINKER'S DAMN).

tinker with Try to repair, work aimlessly or unskillfully with, as in *He tinekered with the engine all day but it still wouldn't start.* This idiom, first recorded in 1658, alludes to working as a tinker, that is, mending metal utensils.

tip ♦ In addition to the idioms beginning with TIP, also see FROM HEAD (TIP) TO TOE; ON THE TIP OF ONE'S TONGUE.

tip off Supply with secret or private information; also, warn or alert. For example, *The broker often tipped her off about stocks about to go down in price,* or *Somehow they were tipped off and left the country before the police could catch them.* [Colloquial; late 1800s]

tip of the iceberg Superficial evidence of a much larger problem, as in *Laying off a hundred workers is only the tip of the iceberg.* This idiom alludes to the structure of an iceberg, most of whose bulk lies underwater. [Mid-1900s]

tip one's hand Accidentally reveal one's intentions, as in *He avoided any comments on birthdays for fear of tipping his hand about the surprise party.* This idiom probably alludes to holding one's hand in such a way that others can see the cards one is holding. [Colloquial; early 1900s]

tip the balance Also, **tip the scales; turn the scale.** Offset the balance and thereby favor one side or precipitate an action. For example, *He felt that affirmative action had tipped the balance slightly in favor of minority groups,* or *New high-tech weapons definitely tipped the scales in the Gulf War,* or *Just one more mistake will turn the scale against them.* Shakespeare used **turn the scale** literally in *Measure for Measure* (4:2): "You weigh equally; a feather will turn the scale." The idioms with *tip* are much younger, dating from the first half of the 1900s.

tiptoe ♦ See ON TIPTOE.

tired ♦ In addition to the idiom beginning with TIRED, also see DEAD ON ONE'S FEET (TIRED); SICK AND TIRED.

tired out Also, **tired to death**. Exhausted, as in *She looked tired out after that trip*, or *He came home tired to death*. The first term dates from the second half of the 1500s; the second, a hyperbole, was first recorded in 1740. Also see SICK AND TIRED; TO DEATH.

tit for tat Repayment in kind, retaliation, as in *If he won't help with the beach clean-up, I won't run a booth at the bake sale; that's tit for tat*. This term is believed to be a corruption of *tip for tap*, which meant "a blow for a blow." Its current form dates from the mid-1500s.

to a degree Also, **to an extent**. ♦ See TO SOME DEGREE.

to advantage ♦ See SHOW TO ADVANTAGE.

to a fare-thee-well To the most extreme degree, especially a condition of perfection. For example, *We've cleaned the house to a fare-thee-well*, or *He played the part of martyr to a fare-thee-well*. This term first appeared as **to a fare-you-well** in the late 1800s, and the more archaic-sounding present form replaced it about 1940.

to a fault Excessively, extremely, as in *He was generous to a fault*. This phrase, always qualifying an adjective, has been so used since the mid-1700s. Indeed, Oliver Goldsmith had this precise usage in *The Life of Richard Nash* (1762).

to all intents and purposes Also, **for all intents and purposes; for all practical purposes**. In every practical sense, virtually. For example, *For all intents and purposes the case is closed*, or *For all practical purposes the Vice-President is the chief executive while the President is in the hospital*. The first phrase, dating from the 1500s, originated in English law, where it was *to all intents, constructions, and purposes*. A shorter synonym is IN EFFECT, def. 1.

to a man Unanimously, without exception, as in *The committee voted against the proposal to a man*. This expression, first recorded in 1712, uses *man* in the sense of "everyone." It continues to be so used despite its sexist tone. **To a woman** is very occasionally used for unanimous actions in groups that include only women. Also see AS ONE; WITH ONE VOICE.

to and fro Back and forth, as in *He was like a caged animal, pacing to and fro*. Strictly speaking, *to* means "toward" and *fro* "away from," but this idiom is used more vaguely in the sense of "moving alternately in different directions." [First half of 1300s]

toast ♦ See WARM AS TOAST.

to a T Also, **to a turn**. Perfectly, exactly right, as in *The description fitted him to a T*, or *The roast was done to a turn*. The first expression, dating from the late 1600s, may allude to the T-square, used for accurate drawing, but some think it refers to crossing one's T's. The variant alludes to meat being turned on a spit until it is cooked to the proper degree. The variant was first recorded in 1780.

to beat the band Also, **to beat all**. to the greatest possible degree. For example, *The baby was crying to beat the band*, or *The wind is blowing to beat the band*, or *John is dressed up to beat all*. This idiom uses *beat* in the sense of "surpass." The first term may, according to one theory, allude to a desire to arrive before the musicians who led a parade, so as to see the entire event. Another theory holds that it means "make more noise than (and thereby beat) a loud band." [Colloquial; late 1800s]

to be sure Undoubtedly, certainly, of course, as in *The coat is expensive, to be sure, but it's bound to last longer than a cheap one*. This idiom was first recorded in 1657.

to blame, be Be responsible for or guilty of something wrong or bad, as in *Obviously the teacher was to blame for the chaos in the classroom*, or *Mary was not to blame for these errors*. [Early 1200s]

to boot Besides, in addition. For example, *It rained every day and it was cold to boot*, or *He said they'd lower the price of the car by $1,000 and throw in air conditioning to boot*. This expression has nothing to do with footwear. *Boot* here is an archaic noun meaning "advantage," and in the idiom has been broadened to include anything additional, good or bad. [c. A.D. 1000]

to burn ♦ See MONEY TO BURN.

to date Up to now, until the present time, as in *to date we've received no word from them*. [First half of 1900s]

today ♦ See HERE TODAY, GONE TOMORROW.

to death To an extreme or intolerable degree, as in *I am tired to death of these fundraising phone cals*, or *That movie just thrilled me to death*. This hyperbolic phrase is used as an intensifier. Also see SICK AND TIRED; TIRED OUT. [c. 1300]

toe ♦ In addition to the idiom beginning with TOE, also see DIP ONE'S TOES INTO; FROM HEAD TO TOE; ON ONE'S TOES; STEP ON SOMEONE'S TOES; TURN UP ONE'S TOES.

to each his own One has a right to one's personal preferences, as in *I'd never pick that color, but to each his own*. Versions of this maxim appeared in the late 1500s but the modern wording was first recorded in 1713.

toe the line Also, **toe the mark.** Meet a standard, abide by the rules, as in *The new director will make us toe the line, I'm sure,* or *At daycare Brian has to toe the mark, but at home his mother's quite lenient.* This idiom refers to runners in a race placing their toes on the starting line and not moving until the starting signal. Its figurative use dates from the early 1800s.

together ♦ In addition to the idiom beginning with TOGETHER, also see GET ONE'S ACT TOGETHER; GET TOGETHER; GO TOGETHER; HANG TOGETHER; KEEP BODY AND SOUL TOGETHER; KNOCK TOGETHER; LIVE TOGETHER; PIECE TOGETHER; PULL ONESELF TOGETHER; PULL TOGETHER; PUT OUR HEADS TO-GETHER; PUT TOGETHER; PUT TWO AND TWO TO-GETHER; SCARE UP (SCRAPE TOGETHER); STICK TOGETHER; STRING TOGETHER; THROW TOGETHER.

together with In the company of; also, in addition to. For example, *He arrived at the theater together with his girlfriend,* or *The lawyer found the will, together with other papers, in the murdered man's files.* [Late 1400s] For a synonym, see ALONG WITH.

to good purpose To effective use, as in *A donation to the homeless shelter will be put to good purpose.* This idiom was first recorded in 1553. Also see TO LITTLE OR NO PURPOSE.

to hand 1. Also, **at hand.** Nearby, accessible as in *I don't have the right tools to hand but asked her to get them for me.* [c. 1300] 2. Also, **in hand.** In one's possession, as in *He had their letter to hand,* or *She had the money in hand.* The first term dates from the mid-1700s, the second from about 1200. Also see HAND TO HAND.

to heel 1. Close behind someone, as in *The dog started chasing the car but Miriam called him to heel.* This expression is used almost solely in reference to dogs. The *heel* in this idiom, first recorded in 1810, is the person's. 2. Under control or discipline, as in *By a series of surprise raids the police brought the gang members to heel.* This expression alludes to controlling a dog by training it to follow at one's heels. [Late 1800s]

to hell and gone Far away, forever, as in *I don't know where it is—to hell and gone,* or *I can keep talking to hell and gone but it will do no good.* This hyperbolic term dates from the first half of the 1900s.

to hell with Also, **the hell with.** I'm disgusted with, get rid of, as in *To hell with that plan; it's ridiculous,* or *The hell with that so-called genius; he's made a serious mistake in this report.* [Early 1900s]

token ♦ See BY THE SAME TOKEN; IN TOKEN OF.

told ♦ See ALL TOLD; I TOLD YOU SO; LITTLE BIRD TOLD ME. ALSO SEE UNDER TELL.

to little purpose Also, **to no purpose.** Of little or no use, in vain, as in *Hiring a new lawyer will be to little purpose.* The related phrases are sometimes combined in **to little or no purpose** and used as a general indicator of futility. *To little purpose* was first recorded in 1560. For a synonym, see TO NO AVAIL; also see TO GOOD PURPOSE.

toll ♦ See TAKE ITS TOLL.

Tom ♦ See EVERY TOM, DICK, AND HARRY; PEEPING TOM.

tomorrow ♦ In addition to the idiom beginning with TOMORROW, also see HERE TODAY, GONE TO-MORROW; PUT OFF (UNTIL TOMORROW).

tomorrow is another day One may not accomplish everything today but will have another chance. For example, *We've stuffed hundreds of envelopes and still aren't done, but tomorrow is another day.* This comforting maxim was first put as *Tomorrow is a new day* about 1520, was widely repeated, and changed to its present form in the mid-1800s.

to my mind As I see it, in my opinion, as in *To my mind we have enough money to start building now.* [First half of 1500s]

ton ♦ See LIKE A TON OF BRICKS.

tone down Make less vivid, harsh, or violent; moderate. For example, *That's a little too much rouge; I'd tone it down a bit,* or *Do you think I should tone down this letter of complaint?* This idiom uses *tone* in the sense of "adjust the tone or quality of something," as does the antonym, **tone up,** meaning "brighten or strengthen." For example, *These curtains will tone up the whole room,* or *This exercise is said to tone up the triceps.* [Mid-1800s]

tong ♦ See HAMMER AND TONGS.

tongue ♦ In addition to the idioms beginning with TONGUE, also see BITE ONE'S TONGUE; CAT GOT SOMEONE'S TONGUE; HOLD ONE'S TONGUE; KEEP A CIVIL TONGUE; ON THE TIP OF ONE'S TONGUE; SLIP OF THE LIP (TONGUE).

tongue hangs out, one's One is eagerly anticipating something, as in *Their tongues were hanging out at the thought of seeing the movie stars in person.* This expression alludes to an animal's tongue hanging out of its mouth in anticipation of food. [Late 1800s]

tongue in cheek, with Ironically or as a joke, as in *Was he speaking with tongue in cheek when he said Sally should run for president?* This term probably alludes to the facial expression produced by poking one's tongue in one's cheek, perhaps to suppress a smile. [First half of 1800s]

tongues wag People are gossiping. For example, *Tongues wagged when another police car was parked in front of their house,* or *Their arrival in a* *stretch limousine set the neighbors' tongues wagging.* This metaphoric expression transfers the rapid movement of the tongue to idle or indiscreet chatter. [Late 1500s]

to no avail Also, **of little or no avail.** Of no use or advantage, ineffective, as in *All his shouting was to no avail; no one could hear him,* or *The life jacket was of little or no avail.* This idiom uses *avail* in the sense of "advantage" or "assistance," a usage dating from the mid-1400s. Also see TO LITTLE PURPOSE.

too ♦ In addition to the idioms beginning with TOO, also see CARRY TOO FAR; (TOO) CLOSE TO HOME; EAT ONE'S CAKE AND HAVE IT, TOO; GO TOO FAR; IRONS IN THE FIRE, TOO MANY; LIFE IS TOO SHORT; NONE TOO; NOT (TOO) BAD; ONLY TOO; SPEAK TOO SOON; SPREAD ONESELF TOO THIN; TAKE ON (TOO MUCH).

too bad Unfortunate, as in *Too bad the shoes don't fit you.* [Late 1500s]

too big for one's britches Also, **too big for one's boots.** Conceited, self-important, as in *Ever since he won that tournament he's gotten too big for his britches,* or *there's no talking to Jill anymore—she's just too big for her boots.* This metaphoric idiom alludes to becoming so "swollen" with conceit that one's pants or boots no longer fit. [Late 1800s]

too close for comfort Also, **too close to home.** Dangerously nearby or accurate, as in *That last shot was too close for comfort,* or *Their attacks on the speaker hit too close to home, and he left in a huff.*

too close to call Resulting in too narrow a margin to make a decision, as in *That ball didn't miss by much but it was too close to call,* or *The election was too close to call, so they decided to have a runoff.* This expression comes from sports, where *call* has signified "a judgment" since the mid-1600s. In the 1960s it began to be applied to pre-election polls and then to the outcome of elections.

too good to be true So excellent that it defies belief, as in *She loves all her in-laws? That's too good to be true.* This term expresses the skeptical view that something so seemingly fine must have something wrong with it. The term was part of the title of Thomas Lupton's *Sivquila; Too Good to be True* (1580).

too little, too late Inadequate as a remedy and not in time to be effective, as in *The effort to divert the stream into a corn field was too little too late—the houses were already flooded.* This term originated in the military, where it was applied to reinforcements that were insufficient and arrived too late to be of help. [First half of 1900s]

tool up 1. Provide the equipment for a particular task, as in *Now that we're all tooled up let's repair the boat.* This term originated in industry, where it is used for supplying a factory with machinery or other equipment for production. [1920s] **2.** Arm oneself, as in *They tooled up for their encounter with the rival gang.* [Second half of 1900s]

too many cooks spoil the broth Too many persons involved in managing an activity can ruin it, as in *Without a conductor, every player had an idea for how the music should go—too many cooks spoil the broth.* This expression alludes to each of many cooks adding something to a soup, which finally tastes awful. It was already considered a proverb in 1574 (by George Gascoigne in *The Life of P. Care*).

too much of a good thing Too large an amount of a beneficial or useful thing or activity can be harmful or excessive. For example, *The indoor decorations are fine but the outdoor Santa, sled, reindeer, gnomes—it's just too much of a good thing.* Expressed in slightly different form even earlier, Shakespeare used this precise wording in praise of moderation in *As You Like It* (4:1): "Can one desire too much of a good thing?"

to oneself ♦ See KEEP TO ONESELF.

to one's face Openly, directly, as in *I do not have the nerve to tell him to his face that he wasn't invited and shouldn't have come.* This idiom alludes to a direct confrontation. [Mid-1500s]

to one's feet ♦ See GET TO ONE'S FEET.

to one's heart's content To one's complete satisfaction, without limitation, as in *I've been eating strawberries to my heart's content,* or *The youngsters played in the sand to their hearts' content.* Shakespeare used this expression in a number of his plays. [Late 1500s]

to one's name Owned by one, as in *He has not got a nickel to his name,* or *She has only one pair of shoes to her name.* This idiom was first recorded in 1876.

to order ♦ See MADE TO ORDER.

tooth ♦ In addition to the idiom beginning with TOOTH, also see FIGHT TOOTH AND NAIL; FINE-TOOTH COMB; LONG IN THE TOOTH; SWEET TOOTH. Also see under TEETH.

tooth fairy a mythical source of bounty, as in *So who will finance this venture—the tooth fairy?* This expression refers to the fairy credited with leaving money under a child's pillow in place of a baby tooth that has fallen out, a practice popular with American parents since the first half of the 1900s.

top ♦ In addition to the idioms beginning with TOP, also see AT THE TOP OF ONE'S LUNGS; AT THE TOP OF THE HOUR; BIG TOP; BLOW ONE'S TOP; BRASS HAT (TOP BRASS); FROM HEAD TO TOE (TOP TO TOE); OFF THE TOP OF ONE'S HEAD; ON TOP; ON TOP OF; ON TOP OF THE WORLD; OVER THE TOP; SLEEP LIKE A LOG (TOP); THIN ON TOP.

top banana Also, **top dog.** The principal person in a group, organization, or undertaking, as in *His* plan was to be *top banana* within ten years, or *Now that she's top dog you can't get hold of her at all.* The first term comes from show business, where from the early 1900s it has signified the leading comedian (possibly the original allusion was to Frank Lebowitz, a burlesque comedian who used bananas in his act). It also gave rise to **second banana**, for a supporting actor, usually a straight man. Both were transferred to more general use in the second half of the 1900s, as in executive Peter Barton's statement, "There is a certain pain to being a second banana, but you have to have an ability to sublimate your ego," quoted in *the New York Times,* May 15, 1996. The variant, *top dog,* originated in sports in the late 1800s and signified the odds-on favorite or winner in a contest; it alludes to the dog who wins (comes out on top) in a dogfight.

top brass ♦ See UNDER BRASS HAT.

top dog ♦ See TOP BANANA.

top dollar The highest price, as in *They'll have to pay top dollar at that resort.* [Second half of 1900s]

top drawer Of the highest quality, importance, or rank, as in *The musicians in this pick-up orchestra were top drawer.* It probably alludes to the uppermost drawer in a bureau or chest, where the most valuable objects (such as jewelry) are usually kept. [c. 1900]

to pieces Into fragments, disorganized, or confused, as in *I tore his argument to pieces.* This metaphoric term has been so used since about 1600. Also see GO TO PIECES; PICK APART (TO PIECES); THRILL TO PIECES.

top off 1. Fill a container, especially when it is almost full to begin with. For example, *I don't need much gas; just top off the tank, please.* [First half of 1900s] 2. Finish, especially in a spectacular way, as in *They topped off their trip with a visit to the White House.* [First half of 1800s]

top out 1. Complete the top portion of a building, as in *They were scheduled to top out the dome next week.* This idiom was first recorded in 1834. 2. Fill up a ship or complete its cargo, as in *The ship was topped out with scrap iron.* This idiom was first recorded in 1940. 3. Cease rising, as in *Interest rates topped out at 10 percent.* [Second half of 1900s] 4. Retire just as one becomes very successful, as in *He decided that at sixty it was time to top out.* [Colloquial; second half of 1900s]

top to toe ♦ See FROM HEAD TO TOE.

torch ♦ See CARRY A TORCH; PASS THE TORCH.

to rights ♦ See DEAD TO RIGHTS; SET TO RIGHTS.

torn between, be Be distracted by two conflicting choices, be in a dilemma, as in *I'm torn between going to the mountains or going to the*

seashore; each appeals to me. This idiom was first recorded in 1871.

to save one's life Even if one's life depended on it, as in *I couldn't eat another bite to save my life,* or *Betty wouldn't climb a mountain to save her life.* This hyperbolic expression nearly always follows a negative statement that one wouldn't or couldn't do something. Anthony Trollope used a slightly different wording in *The Kellys and the O'Kellys* (1848): "I shan't remain long, if it was to save my life and theirs; I can't get up small talk for the rector and his curate."

to say nothing of ♦ See under NOT TO MENTION.

to say the least Not to exaggerate, as in *When the ring turned up in the lost and found, she was delighted, to say the least.* This idiom was first recorded in 1809.

to some degree Also, **to a certain degree; to some** or **a certain extent; to a degree** or **an extent.** Somewhat, in a way, as in *To some degree we'll have to compromise,* or *To an extent it's a matter of adjusting to the colder climate.* The use of *degree* in these terms, all used in the same way, dates from the first half of the 1700s, and *extent* from the mid-1800s.

to spare In addition to what is needed, extra, left over, as in *We paid our bills and still had money to spare.* This expression uses *spare* in the sense of "leftover" or "unused," a usage dating from the late 1500s.

to speak of Worth mentioning; see NOTHING TO SPEAK OF; NOT TO MENTION.

toss ♦ In addition to the idioms beginning with TOSS, also see THROW AWAY (TOSS OUT); THROW (TOSS) ONE'S HAT IN THE RING.

toss off 1. Do readily or without effort, as in *Asimov was amazing, tossing off book after book.* [Mid-1800s] 2. Also, **toss down.** Consume quickly, especially a drink in one draft. For example, *He tossed off the beer and headed for the door,* or *She tossed down one glass after another.* [Late 1500s]

toss one's cookies Vomit, as in *A roller-coaster ride may make her toss her cookies.* This slangy euphemism dates from the first half of the 1900s.

to start with Also, **to begin with.** In the first place, initially, as in *We'll notify him by e-mail to start with,* or *To begin with, they haven't paid their taxes in years.* The first term dates from the second half of the 1800s, the variant from the mid-1500s. Also see FOR OPENERS.

totem ♦ See LOW MAN ON THE TOTEM POLE.

to that effect With that basic or general meaning, as in *He said he was very worried, or words to that effect.* This term is also put as **to the effect that** when introducing a clause, as in *She was a little* *vague but said something to the effect that she'd re-pay the loan very soon.* [Mid-1600s]

to the best of To the utmost extent of, especially of one's ability, knowledge, or power. For example, *I'm sure he'll do it to the best of his ability,* or *To the best of my knowledge, they arrive tomorrow.* [c. 1500]

to the bitter end ♦ See BITTER END.

to the bone ♦ See CHILLED TO THE BONE; CUT TO THE BONE; WORK ONE'S FINGERS TO THE BONE.

to the contrary To the opposite effect, in denial, as in *No matter what they say to the contrary, I am positive that he was present.* This idiom was first recorded in 1512. Also see ON THE CONTRARY.

to the core ♦ See ROTTEN TO THE CORE.

to the effect that ♦ See TO THAT EFFECT.

to the ends of the earth ♦ See ENDS OF THE EARTH.

to the fore In into, or toward a position of prominence, as in *A new virtuoso pianist has come to the fore.* [First half of 1800s]

to the full Also, **to the fullest.** To the maximum extent, completely, as in *He had always lived life to the full.* [Late 1300s]

to the good Also, **all to the good.** To an advantage or profit, as in *We've got extra material and that's all to the good, I think.* This idiom was first recorded in 1882.

to the hilt Also, **up to the hilt.** Completely, to the maximum degree, as in *The house was mortgaged up to the hilt.* This idiom alludes to the handle (*hilt*) of a sword, the only portion that remains out when the weapon is plunged all the way in. The figurative use of the term was first recorded in 1687.

to the last To the end, especially to the end of one's life. For example, *The defenders held out to the last but the bombs finished them.* [c. 1600]

to the letter Precisely, as in *If you follow the directions to the letter, you can't go wrong. Letter* here refers to the exact terms of some statement. [c. 1800]

to the life Resembling exactly, as in *She's her sister to the life,* or *The play's so realistic; the murder is acted out to the life.* This idiom uses *life* in the sense of "a lifelike semblance." [c. 1600]

to the manner born Accustomed from birth to a particular behavior or lifestyle, as in *At a high-society function she behaves as though to the manner born, but we know she came from very humble circumstances.* This term was invented by Shakespeare in *Hamlet.* Referring to the King's carousing in Danish style, Hamlet says (1:4): "Though I am native here And to the manner born, it is a custom More honor'd in the breach than the observance." The *manner* in this expression was later sometimes changed to *manor,* "the main house of

an estate," and the idiom's sense became equated with "high-born" (and therefore accustomed to luxury), a way in which it is often used today.

to the nines To perfection, to the highest degree; see under DRESSED TO KILL.

to the nth degree To the utmost, as in *They'd decked out the house to the nth degree.* This expression comes from mathematics, where *to the nth* means "to any required power" (n standing for any number). It was first recorded in 1852.

to the point 1. Relevant, concerning the matter at hand, as in *Her remarks were brief and to the point,* or *He rambled on and on, never speaking to the point.* [Early 1800s] For an antonym, see BESIDE THE POINT. 2. Concerning the important or essential issue, as in *More to the point, she hasn't any money.* This usage is often put as **come** or **get to the point,** meaning "address the important issue." For example, *Please come to the point; we haven't much time,* or *Do you suppose he'll ever get to the point of all this?* [Late 1300s]

to the teeth 1. Completely, fully, as in *Obviously new to skiing, they were equipped to the teeth with the latest gear.* This idiom dates from the late 1300s. Also see ARMED TO THE TEETH; FED TO THE GILLS. 2. Also, **up to the** or **one's teeth.** Fully committed, as in *We're in this collaboration up to our teeth.* [First half of 1900s] Both of these hyperbolic usages allude to being fully covered or immersed in something up to one's teeth.

to the tune of To the sum or extent of, as in *They had profits to the tune of about $20 million.* This idiom transfers *tune,* a succession of musical tones, to a succession of figures. [First half of 1700s]

to the victor belong the spoils The winner gets everything, as in *He not only won the tournament but ended up with numerous lucrative endorsements—to the victor belong the spoils.* This expression alludes to the spoils system of American politics, whereby the winner of an election gives desirable jobs to party supporters. [First half of 1800s]

to the wall ♦ See BACK TO THE WALL; GO TO THE WALL.

touch ♦ In addition to the idioms beginning with TOUCH, also see COMMON TOUCH; FINISHING TOUCH; HIT (TOUCH) BOTTOM; IN TOUCH; LOSE ONE'S TOUCH; LOSE TOUCH; NOT TOUCH WITH A TEN-FOOT POLE; OUT OF TOUCH; PUT THE ARM (TOUCH) ON; SOFT TOUCH.

touch and go Extremely uncertain or risky, as in *It was touch and go after the surgery; we were not sure he'd survive it,* or *It was touch and go but they finally gave me a seat on the plane.* This idiom implies that a mere touch may cause a calamity. [Early 1800s]

touch base with Make contact or renew communications with, as in *I'll try to touch base with you when I'm in Ohio,* or *The candidate touched base with every ethnic group in the city.* This idiom comes from baseball, where a runner must touch each base without being tagged before a run can be scored.

touch bottom Reach the lowest point, as in *During the recession the economists kept saying that we hadn't touched bottom yet.* This metaphor for reaching the ground under a body of water has been used since the mid-1800s.

touch down Land on the ground, as in *The spacecraft touched down on schedule.* This idiom was first recorded in 1935.

touched by, be Also, **be touched with.** Be affected by some emotion, especially a tender feeling like gratitude, pity, or sympathy. For example, *She was very touched by his concern for her welfare.* This idiom alludes to touching or reaching one's heart, the seat of emotions. [First half of 1300s]

touched in the head Also, **touched.** A little bit crazy, somewhat deranged, as in *I think the war left him a little touched in the head.* [Late 1800s]

touch off 1. Cause to explode or fire; also, initiate, trigger. For example, *The boys touched off a whole line of firecrackers,* or *These disclosures will touch off a public uproar.* This idiom comes from early firearms, which were set off by putting a light to the touch-hole. Its figurative use dates from the late 1800s. 2. Depict very precisely, as in *He touched off Teddy Roosevelt as well as it's ever been done.* [Mid-1700s]

touch on Also, **touch upon.** 1. Mention briefly or casually in passing, as in *He barely touched on the subject of immigration.* [First half of 1600s] 2. Approach closely, verge on, as in *This frenzy touched on clinical insanity.* [Early 1800s]

touch up Make minor changes or improvements, as in *This wall needs some touching up but not complete repainting.* [Early 1700s]

tough ♦ In addition to the idioms beginning with TOUGH, also see GET TOUGH; GUT (TOUGH) IT OUT; HANG TOUGH; HARD (TOUGH) ACT TO FOLLOW; HARD (TOUGH) NUT TO CRACK.

tough break Also, **tough luck.** A trying or troublesome circumstance, bad luck, as in *He got a tough break when he was denied a raise,* or *Tough luck for the team last night.* This idiom uses *tough* in the sense of "difficult," a usage dating from the early 1600s. The variant is also used as a sarcastic interjection, as in *So you didn't make straight A's— tough luck!* A slangy variant of this interjection is **tough beans,** and a ruder version is **tough shit.** [Colloquial; c. 1900]

tough it out ♦ See GUT IT OUT.

tough nut ♦ See HARD NUT TO CRACK.

tough row to hoe Also, **hard row to hoe.** A difficult course, hard work to accomplish, as in *He knew he'd have a tough row to hoe by running against this popular incumbent.* [First half of 1800s]

tough sledding Difficult work or progress, as in *This bill faces tough sledding in the legislature.* This idiom transfers the route on which a sled can travel to other kinds of progress toward a goal. It was first recorded as *hard sledding* in 1839. For the antonym, see EASY SLEDDING.

tow ♦ See IN TOW.

to wake the dead, loud enough Very loud, as in *That band is loud enough to wake the dead.* This hyperbolic expression dates from the mid-1800s.

toward ♦ See GO A LONG WAY TOWARD.

towel ♦ See CRYING TOWEL; THROW IN THE SPONGE (TOWEL).

tower ♦ In addition to the idiom beginning with TOWER, also see IVORY TOWER

tower of strength A dependable person on whom one can lean in time of trouble, as in *After Dad died Grandma was a tower of strength for the whole family.* This expression, first recorded in 1549, originally was used most often to refer to God and heaven, but Shakespeare had it differently in *Richard III* (5:3): "Besides, the King's name is a tower of strength."

to whom it may concern To the appropriate recipient for this message, as in *I didn't know who was responsible for these complaints so I just addressed it "to whom it may concern."* This phrase is a formula used in letters, testimonials, and the like when one does not know the name of the proper person to address. [Second half of 1800s]

to windward Toward an advantageous position, as in *We were hoping to get to windward of the situation.* This expression transfers the nautical meaning of the phrase, "move in the direction from which the wind blows," to other kinds of undertaking. Its figurative use dates from the late 1700s.

to wit That is to say, namely, as in *There are three good reasons for not going, to wit, we don't want to, we don't have to, and we can't get a reservation.* This expression comes from the now archaic verb *to wit,* meaning "know or be aware of," not heard except in this usage. [Late 1500s]

town ♦ In addition to the idiom beginning with TOWN, also see ALL OVER THE PLACE (TOWN); GHOST TOWN; GO TO TOWN; MAN ABOUT TOWN; ONE-HORSE TOWN; ONLY GAME IN TOWN; ON THE TOWN; OUT OF TOWN; PAINT THE TOWN RED; TALK OF THE TOWN.

town and gown The inhabitants of a college or university town and the students and personnel of the college, as in *There used to be friction between* *town and gown but the new parking lots have eased it.* The *gown* in this expression alludes to the academic robes traditional in British universities. [Early 1800s]

toy with 1. Amuse oneself idly with, trifle, as in *He teased her, toying with her as a cat toys with a mouse.* [Early 1500s] 2. Treat casually or without seriousness, as in *I'm toying with the idea of writing a novel.* [Early 1800s]

traces ♦ See KICK OVER THE TRACES.

track ♦ In addition to the idioms beginning with TRACK, also see COVER ONE'S TRACKS; DROP IN ONE'S TRACKS; FAST TRACK; FOLLOW IN SOMEONE'S FOOTSTEPS (TRACKS); INSIDE TRACK; JUMP THE TRACK; KEEP (LOSE) TRACK; MAKE TRACKS; OFF THE BEATEN TRACK; OFF THE TRACK; ONE-TRACK MIND; ON THE RIGHT TACK (TRACK); RIGHT SIDE OF THE TRACKS; STOP COLD (IN ONE'S TRACKS).

track down Follow successfully, locate, as in *I've been trying to track down that book but haven't had any luck.* This term alludes to the literal use of *track,* "follow the footsteps of." [Second half of 1800s]

track record A record of actual performance or achievements, as in *This applicant has an excellent track record.* This term probably comes from horse racing, where it signifies the best time a horse has ever achieved at a particular track or over a particular distance. However, some believe it alludes to track and field records. Its figurative use dates from the late 1940s.

trade ♦ In addition to the idioms beginning with TRADE, also see TRICKS OF THE TRADE.

trade down Exchange for something of lower value or price, as in *They bought a smaller boat, trading down for the sake of economy.* Similarly, **trade up** means "make an exchange for something of higher value or price," as in *They traded up to a larger house.* [First half of 1900s]

trade in Give or sell an old or used item and apply the value or proceeds to a new item. For example, *Some people prefer to trade in their old car to the dealer, but we feel we'll do better by simply selling it.* [First half of 1900s]

trade off Exchange one thing for another, especially as a compromise. For example, *They were willing to trade off some vacation for the freedom to work flexible hours.* This idiom gave rise to *tradeoff* for "an exchange." [First half of 1800s]

trade on Profit by, exploit, as in *The children of celebrities often trade on their family names.* [Late 1800s]

trade up ♦ See under TRADE DOWN.

trail ♦ See BLAZE A TRAIL.

train ♦ In addition to the idiom beginning with TRAIN, also see GRAVY TRAIN.

train of thought A succession of connected ideas, a path of reasoning, as in *You've interrupted my train of thought; now what was I saying?* This idiom, which uses *train* in the sense of "an orderly sequence," was first recorded in 1651, in philosopher Thomas Hobbes's *Leviathan.*

trap ♦ See FALL INTO A TRAP; MIND LIKE A STEEL TRAP.

travel light Take little baggage; also, be relatively free of responsibilities or deep thoughts, as in *I can be ready in half an hour; I always travel light,* or *I don't want to buy a house and get tied down; I like to travel light,* or *It's hard to figure out whom they'll attack next, because ideologically they travel light.* The literal use dates from the 1920s, the figurative from the mid-1900s.

tread ♦ In addition to the idioms beginning with TREAD, also see FOOLS RUSH IN WHERE ANGELS FEAR TO TREAD; STEP (TREAD) ON ONE'S TOES.

tread the boards Act on the stage, as in *Her main ambition was to tread the boards in a big city.* This idiom uses *boards* in the sense of "a theatrical stage," a usage dating from the mid-1700s. It dates from the mid-1800s but was preceded by the idiom *tread the stage,* first recorded in 1691.

tread water Expend effort that maintains one's status but does not make much progress toward a goal, as in *He was just treading water from paycheck to paycheck.* This idiom alludes to the term's literal meaning, that is, "keep one's head above water by remaining upright and pumping the legs."

treat ♦ In addition to the idiom beginning with TREAT, also see DUTCH TREAT; TRICK OR TREAT.

treat like dirt Behave badly or show contempt toward, as in *Her boss treats all the secretaries like dirt.* This idiom uses *dirt* in the sense of "something worthless," a usage dating from the mid-1300s.

treatment ♦ See RED CARPET (TREATMENT).

tree ♦ See BARK UP THE WRONG TREE; CAN'T SEE THE FOREST FOR THE TREES; TALK SOMEONE'S ARM OFF (THE BARK OFF A TREE); UP A TREE.

trial ♦ In addition to the idioms beginning with TRIAL, also see ON TRIAL.

trial and error An attempt to accomplish something by trying various means until the correct one is found. For example, *The only way to solve this problem is by trial and error.* The *error* here alludes to the failed means or attempts, which are discarded until the right way is found. [c. 1800s]

trial balloon An idea or plan advanced tentatively to test public reaction, as in *Let's send up a trial balloon for this new program before we commit ourselves.* This expression alludes to sending up balloons to test weather conditions. [c. 1930]

trail by fire A test of one's abilities to perform well under pressure, as in *Finishing this huge list of* *chores in time for the wedding is really a trial by fire.* This expression alludes to the medieval practice of determining a person's guilt by having them undergo an ordeal, such as walking barefoot through a fire.

trials and tribulations Tests of one's patience or endurance, as in *She went through all the trials and tribulations of being admitted to law school only to find she couldn't afford to go.* This redundant expression—*trial* and *tribulation* here both mean the same thing—is also used semi-humorously, as in *Do you really want to hear about the trials and tribulations of my day at the office?*

triangle ◆ See ETERNAL TRIANGLE.

trick ◆ In addition to the idioms beginning with TRICK, also see BAG OF TRICKS; CONFIDENCE GAME (TRICK); DIRTY TRICKS; DO THE TRICK; HAT TRICK; HOW'S TRICKS; NOT MISS A TRICK; TEACH AN OLD DOG NEW TRICKS; THAT DOES IT (THE TRICK); TURN A TRICK; UP TO ONE'S OLD TRICKS.

trick or treat A greeting by children asking for treats on Halloween and threatening to play a trick on those who refuse to give them. For example, *The children went from house to house, shouting "Trick or treat!"* [c. 1940]

trick out Ornament or adorn, especially ostentatiously or garishly, as in *She was all tricked out in beads and fringe and what-have-you.* This term uses *trick* in the sense of "dress up" or "decorate," a usage dating from about 1500. [Early 1700s]

tricks of the trade Clever ways of operating a business or performing a task or activity, especially slightly dishonest or unfair ones. For example, *Alma knows all the tricks of the trade, cutting the fabric as close as possible,* or *The butcher weighs meat after it's wrapped; charging for the packaging is one of the tricks of the trade.*

tried and true Tested and proved to be worthy or reliable, as in *Let me deal with it—my method is tried and true.* [Mid-1900s]

trigger ◆ In addition to the idiom beginning with TRIGGER, also see QUICK ON THE DRAW (TRIGGER).

trigger happy Inclined to act violently at the slightest provocation, as in *They feared that the President was trigger happy and would send in troops at the drop of a hat.* This expression alludes to being too eager to fire a gun. [c. 1940]

trim one's sails Modify one's stand, adapt to circumstances, as in *His advisers told him to trim his sails before he alienated voters and bungled the election completely.* This metaphoric expression alludes to adjusting a ship's sails to take full advantage of prevailing winds. [Late 1700s]

trip ◆ In addition to the idioms beginning with TRIP, also see BAD TRIP; EGO TRIP; ROUND TRIP.

triple threat A person who is adept in three areas, as in *She's a triple threat on the editorial staff—she can edit, write, and design pages.* This term comes from football, where it signifies a player who is good at running, passing, and kicking. [c. 1920] Also see HAT TRICK.

trip the light fantastic Dance, as in *Let's go out tonight and trip the light fantastic.* This expression was originated by John Milton in *L'Allegro* (1632): "Come and trip it as ye go, On the light fantastick toe." The idiom uses *trip* in the sense of "a light, tripping step," and although *fantastick* was never the name of any particular dance, it survived and was given revived currency in James W. Blake's immensely popular song, *The Sidewalks of New York* (1894).

trip up Make or cause someone to make a mistake, as in *The other finalist tripped up when he was asked to spell "trireme,"* or *They tripped him up with that difficult question.* [Second half of 1700s]

Trojan ◆ See under WORK LIKE A BEAVER (TROJAN).

trolley ◆ See OFF ONE'S HEAD (TROLLEY).

trooper ◆ See SWEAR LIKE A TROOPER.

trot ◆ In addition to the idiom beginning with TROT, also see HOT TO TROT.

trot out Bring out and show for inspection and admiration, as in *He trotted out all his old war medals.* This expression alludes to leading out a horse to show off its various paces, including the trot. [Colloquial; first half of 1800s]

trouble ◆ In addition to the idioms beginning with TROUBLE, also see BORROW TROUBLE; FISH IN TROUBLED WATERS; GO TO THE TROUBLE; IN TROUBLE WITH; POUR OIL ON TROUBLED WATERS.

trouble one's head with Also, **trouble oneself about**. Bother or worry about, as in *Don't trouble your head with these details; I'll take care of it,* or *It seems to me that teachers should trouble themselves more about teaching and less about manners.* The first term dates from the mid-1600s, the variant from the early 1500s.

trouble someone for Politely ask for something, as in *May I trouble you for a drink of water?* This idiom uses *trouble* in the sense of "disturb." [Mid-1800s]

trowel ◆ See under LAY IT ON THICK.

truck ◆ See HAVE NO TRUCK WITH.

true ◆ In addition to the idioms beginning with TRUE, also see COME TRUE; COURSE OF TRUE LOVE; DREAM COME TRUE; FIND TRUE NORTH; HOLD GOOD (TRUE); RING FALSE (TRUE); RUN (TRUE) TO FORM; TOO GOOD TO BE TRUE; TRIED AND TRUE.

true blue Loyal, faithful, as in *You can count on her support; she's true blue.* This expression alludes to the idea of blue being the color of constancy, but the exact allusion is disputed. One theory holds it alludes to the unchanging blue sky, another to the fastness of a blue dye that will not run. Blue has been the identifying color of various factions in history. In the mid-1600s the Scottish Covenanters, who pledged to uphold Presbyterianism, were called *true blue* (as opposed to *red*, the color of the royalists). In the 1800s the same term came to mean "staunchly Tory," and in America, "politically sound."

true colors ♦ See under SHOW ONE'S TRUE COLORS.

true to 1. Loyal or faithful to, as in *She knew he'd be true to his marriage vows*, or, as Shakespeare had Polonius tell Hamlet, "This above all, to thine own self be true" (*Hamlet*, 1:3). [c. 1200] 2. Conforming to or consistent with, as in *The speech was true to the party platform*, or *True to type, he died while working at his desk*. 3. **true to life.** Consistent with reality, realistically represented, as in *This painting is very true to life*. [Early 1800s] For *true to form*, see under RUN TO FORM.

trump ♦ In addition to the idioms beginning with TRUMP also see HOLD ALL THE ACES (TRUMPS); TURN UP TRUMPS.

trump card A key resource to gain an advantage at the opportune moment, as in *That surprise witness was the defense's trump card*, or *She played her trump card, announcing that the Senator would speak*. This expression transfers the trump card of games such as bridge, which can win over a card of another suit, to other kinds of advantage. [Early 1800s]

trump up Concoct fraudulently, fabricate, as in *They trumped up a charge of conspiracy*, or *She had trumped up another excuse for not doing the work*. This expression, first recorded in 1695, uses *trump* in the sense of "devise fraudulently," a usage otherwise obsolete.

trust ♦ See BRAIN TRUST; IN TRUST.

truth ♦ In addition to the idioms beginning with TRUTH, also see GOSPEL TRUTH; HOME TRUTH; MOMENT OF TRUTH; NAKED TRUTH; UNVARNISHED TRUTH.

truth is stranger than fiction Real life can be more remarkable than invented tales, as in *In our two-month trip around the world we ran into long-lost relatives on three separate occasions, proving that truth is stranger than fiction*. This expression may have been invented by Byron, who used it in *Don Juan* (1833).

truth will out The facts will be known, as in *She thought she could get away with it, but truth will out, and I'm sure she'll get caught*. Shakespeare used this idiom in *The Merchant of Venice* (2:2): "But in the end truth will out." Also see MURDER WILL OUT.

try ♦ In addition to the idioms beginning with TRY, also see OLD COLLEGE TRY. Also see under TRIED.

try on 1. Test the fit or look of a garment by putting it on, as in *Do you want to try on this dress?* This expression is also put as **try on for size,** which is sometimes used figuratively, as in *The teacher wanted to try the new method on for size before agreeing to sue it*. [Late 1600s] 2. Test the effectiveness or acceptability of something, as in *The actors decided to try on the new play out of town*. [Late 1800s] Also see TRY OUT.

try one's hand 1. Attempt to do something for the first time, as in *I thought I'd try my hand at snorkeling*. This idiom uses *try* in the sense of "ascertain by experiment or effort," a usage dating from the late 1500s. 2. Also, **try one's luck.** Take a chance doing something, as in *We thought we'd try our luck at getting a hotel room at the last minute*.

try one's patience Put one's tolerance to a severe test, cause one to be annoyed, as in *Putting these parts together really tries my patience*, or *Her constant lateness tries our patience*. This idiom uses *try* in the sense of "test," a usage dating from about 1300.

try out 1. Undergo a qualifying test, as for an athletic team. For example, *I'm trying out for the basketball team*. [Mid-1900s] 2. Test or use experimentally, as in *They're trying out new diesels*, or *We're trying out this new margarine*. [Late 1800s]

tube ♦ See DOWN THE TUBES.

tuck ♦ In addition to the idioms beginning with TUCK, also see NIP AND TUCK.

tuck away 1. Eat heartily, as in *He tucked away an enormous steak*. [Colloquial; mid-1800s] Also see TUCK INTO. 2. Hide, put in storage, as in *She had several hundred dollars tucked away*. [c. 1900]

tucker ♦ See BEST BIB AND TUCKER.

tuckered out Exhausted, very tired, as in *I was all tuckered out after that game*. The precise origin of this usage is not known. [Colloquial; 1820s]

tuck in Thrust in the edge of or end of something, such as bed linens or a shirt; also, make a child secure in bed by folding in the bedclothes. For example, *Tuck in your shirt; it looks awful hanging out of your pants*, or *Mother went upstairs to tuck in the children*. [First half of 1600s]

tuck into Eat heartily or greedily, as in *For a two-year-old he really tucked into his food*. [Early 1800s]

tug of war A struggle for supremacy, as in *There's a constant political tug of war between those who favor giving more power to the states and those who want a strong federal government*. Although there is an athletic contest also so named, in which participants holding either end of a rope try to pull each other across a dividing line, the present usage, first recorded in 1677, predates it by about two centuries. The noun *tug* itself means "a strenuous contest between two sides," and *war* refers to fighting, either physical or figurative.

tumble ◆ See ROUGH AND TUMBLE.

tune ◆ In addition to the idioms beginning with TUNE, also see CALL THE TUNE; CARRY A TUNE; CHANGE ONE'S TUNE; DANCE TO ANOTHER TUNE; IN TUNE; TO THE TUNE OF.

tune in 1. Adjust a receiver to receive a particular program or signals at a particular frequency, as in *Tune in tomorrow, folks, for more up-to-date news.* [Early 1900s] 2. Be aware or responsive, as in *She's really tuned in to teenagers.* [1920s] For an antonym, see TUNE OUT.

tune out 1. Adjust a receiver so as not to receive a signal, as in *Let's tune out all this interference.* [Early 1900s] 2. Dissociate oneself from one's surroundings; also, disregard, ignore. For example, *The average reader, used to seeing lots of color images, tunes out when confronted with big blocks of text,* or *Some mothers are expert at tuning out the children's whining and quarreling.* [1920s] For an antonym, see TUNE IN.

tune up Adjust machinery so it is in proper condition, as in *I took the car in to be tuned up.* [Early 1900s]

tunnel ◆ See LIGHT AT THE END OF THE TUNNEL.

turkey ◆ See COLD TURKEY; TALK TURKEY.

turn ◆ In addition to the idioms beginning with TURN, also see AT EVERY TURN; BY TURNS; EVERY TIME ONE TURNS AROUND; GOOD TURN; IN TURN; LET (TURN) LOOSE; NOT KNOW WHERE TO TURN; ONE GOOD TURN DESERVES ANOTHER; OUT OF TURN; TAKE A TURN FOR THE BETTER; TAKE TURNS; TO A T (TURN); TWIST (TURN) AROUND ONE'S FINGER; WHEN SOMEONE'S BACK IS TURNED. Also see under UNTURNED.

turn a blind eye to Deliberately overlook, ignore, as in *She decided to turn a blind eye to her roommate's going-on.* This expression is believed to come from the siege of Copenhagen (1801), in which Lord Horatio Nelson, second in command of the English fleet, was ordered to withdraw but pretended not to see the flagship's signals to do so by putting his glass to the eye that had been blinded in an earlier battle. His attack led to a major victory. Also see TURN A DEAF EAR.

turnabout is fair play Taking alternate or successive turns at doing something is just and equitable. For example, *Come on, I want to sit in the front seat now—turnabout is fair play.* This justification for taking turns was first recorded in 1755.

turn a deaf ear Refuse to listen, as in *You can plead all day but he's turning a deaf ear to everyone.* This

expression dates from the first half of the 1400s and was in most proverb collections from 1546 on. Also see FALL ON DEAF EARS.

turn against Become or make antagonistic to, as in *Adolescents often turn against their parents, but only temporarily,* or *She turned him against his colleagues by telling him they were spying on him.* [First half of 1800s]

turn a hair, not Not become afraid or upset, remain calm, as in *She didn't turn a hair during the bank robbery.* This term, also put as **without turning a hair,** comes from horse racing. After a race, a horse often has roughened, outward-turned hair. Its figurative use, nearly always in the negative, dates from the late 1800s.

turn around Reverse the direction or course of something or someone, as in *He has a way of turning around a failing business,* or *If someone doesn't turn him around he's headed for trouble.* [Late 1800s]

turn around one's finger ◆ See TWIST AROUND ONE'S FINGER.

turn a trick Engage in sex for pay, as in *A young prostitute may turn a dozen tricks in a few hours.* This idiom uses *trick* in the sense of "a sexual act." [Slang; mid-1900s]

turn away 1. Send away, dismiss, as in *They ran short and had to turn away many customers.* [Late 1500s] 2. Repel, as in *The high prices turned away prospective buyers.* 3. Avert, deflect, as in *She managed to turn away all criticism.* [Late 1300s]

turn back 1. Reverse one's direction, as in *We had to turn back earlier than expected.* [First half of 1500s] 2. Drive someone back or away, as in *They turned back anyone who didn't have an invitation,* or *Our forces soon turned back the enemy.* [First half of 1500s] 3. Fold down, as in *Turn back the page you're on to keep your place in the magazine.* [Second half of 1800s] Also see TURN ONE'S BACK ON.

turn down 1. Fold or double down, as in *They always turn down your bed here,* or *Turn down your collar.* [c. 1600] 2. Invert, as in *She turned down her cards,* or *They turn down the glasses in the cupboard.* [Mid-1700s] 3. Reject, fail to accept, as in *They turned down his proposal,* or *Joe was turned down at four schools before he was finally accepted.* [Late 1800s] 4. Diminish in volume, brightness, or speed. For example, *Please turn down the radio; it's too loud,* or *They turned down the lights and began to dance.* [Second half of 1800s]

turn for the better Also, **turn for the worse.** ◆ See under TAKE A TURN FOR THE BETTER.

turn in 1. Hand in, give over, as in *I turned in my exam and left the room.* [c. 1300] 2. Surrender or inform on, especially to the police, as in *The shoplifter turned herself in.* [1920s] 3. Produce, as in *He turned in a consistent performance every day.* [Mid-1900s] **4.** Go to bed, as in *I turned in early last night.* [Colloquial; late 1600s]

turn in one's grave Also **turn over in one's grave.** Be very upset. This idiom is used only of a dead person, who in all likelihood would have been upset by developments in question, as in *If she knew you'd sold her jewelry, she'd turn over in her grave.* [Late 1800s]

turn loose ▸ See LET LOOSE.

turn off 1. Stop the operation, activity, or flow of; shut off, as in *Turn off the lights when you leave.* [Mid-1800s] **2.** Affect with dislike, revulsion, or boredom; cause to lose interest. For example, *That vulgar comedian turned us off completely,* or *The movie was all right for an hour or so, but then I was turned off.* [Slang; mid-1900s]

turn of phrase A particular arrangement of words, as in *I'd never heard that turn of phrase before,* or *An idiom can be described as a turn of phrase.* This idiom alludes to the turning or shaping of objects (as on a lathe), a usage dating from the late 1600s.

turn of the century The beginning or end of a particular century, as in *That idiom dates from the turn of the century, that is to say, about 1900.* This expression was first recorded in 1926.

turn of the tide A reversal of fortune, as in *This last poll marked the turn of the tide, with our candidate gaining a sizable majority.* Similarly, **to turn the tide** means "reverse a situation," as in *The arrival of reinforcements turned the tide in the battle.* This idiom transfers the ebb and flow of the ocean's tides to human affairs. Although the idea is much older, the precise idiom dates from the first half of the 1800s.

turn on 1. Cause to begin the operation, flow, or activity of, as in *Turn on the lights, please,* or *Don't turn on the sprinkler yet.* [First half of 1800s] **2.** Begin to display, employ, or exude, as in *He turned on the charm.* [Late 1800s] **3.** Also, **get high** or **on.** Take or cause to take a mind-altering drug, as in *The boys were excited about turning on,* or *They tried to get her high,* or *I told them I wouldn't get on tonight.* [Slang; mid-1900s] **4.** Be or cause to become excited or interested, as in *His mother was the first to turn him on to classical music.* [c. 1900] **5.** Be or become sexually aroused, as in *He blushed when she asked him what turned him on.* [Second half of 1900s] **6.** Also, **turn upon.** Depend on, relate to, as in *The entire plot turns on mistaken identity.* This usage, first recorded in 1661, uses *turn in* the sense of "revolve on an axis or hinge." **7.** Also, **turn upon.** Attack, become hostile toward, as in *Although normally friendly, the dog suddenly turned on everyone who came to the door.* Also see TURN AGAINST.

turn one's back on Deny, reject; also abandon, forsake. For example, *I can't turn my back on my own daughter, no matter what she's done,* or *He simply turned his back on them and never gave it a second thought.* [c. 1400] Also see WHEN ONE'S BACK IS TURNED.

turn one's hand to Also, **put one's hand to.** Apply oneself to, begin working at, as in *Next she turned her hand to staring her dissertation,* or *He was so lazy he wouldn't put his hand to anything.* [c. 1700]

turn one's head 1. Cause to become infatuated, as in *The new teacher turned all the girls' heads.* [Mid-1800s] **2.** Cause to become conceited, as in *Winning that prize has turned his head.* A 16th-century translator of Seneca used this phrase: "His head was turned by too great success" (*Ad Lucullus,* 1571).

turn one's stomach Nauseate one, disgust one, as in *That mess of spoiled food turns my stomach.* This idiom alludes to being so nauseated that one vomits—that is, the stomach in effect turns around and brings up food. It was first recorded in 1622.

turn on one's heel Leave, as in *When I inquired about his sister, he turned on his heel and walked away.* This idiom alludes to making a sharp about-face similar to a military step but here usually implies a sudden departure. It was first recorded in 1751.

turn on the waterworks Start to weep, as in *Whenever Dad refuses a request of hers she turns on the waterworks.* This term implies that one begins to weep deliberately, as though switching on a system of pipes connected to reservoirs.

turn out 1. Shut off, as in *He turned out the light.* [Late 1800s] **2.** Arrive or assemble for an event, as in *A large number of voters turned out for the rally.* [Mid-1700s] **3.** Produce, as in *They turn out three thousand cars a month.* [Mid-1700s] **4.** Be found to be in the end; also, end up, result, as in *The rookie turned out to be a fine fielder,* or *The cake didn't turn out very well.* [First half of 1700s] Also see TURN OUT ALL RIGHT. **5.** Equip, outfit, as in *The bride was turned out beautifully.* [First half of 1800s] **6.** Get out of bed, as in *Come on, children; time to turn out.* [Colloquial; early 1800s] **7.** Evict, expel, as in *The landlord turned out his tenant.* [Early 1500s]

turn out all right Also, **work out all right.** Succeed, as in *The new cover turned out all right,* or *We're hoping their vacation will work out all right.* The first term uses *turn out* in the sense of "result"; the variant uses *work out* in the sense of "proceed so as to produce a certain outcome," a usage dating from the later 1800s. Also see PAN OUT; WORK OUT.

turn over 1. Invert, bring the bottom to the top, as in *We have to turn over the soil before we plant anything.* [Second half of 1300s] **2.** Shift position, as by rolling from side to side. For example, *This bed is so narrow I can barely turn over.* [First half of 1700s] **3.** Rotate, cycle, as in *The engine turned over but the car wouldn't start.* [Early 1900s] **4.** Think about, consider; as in *She turned over the idea in her mind.* [Early 1800s] **5.** Transfer to another, surrender, as in *I turned over the funds to the children.* [Mid-1500s] **6.** Do business to the extent or amount of, as in *We hoped the company would turn over a million dollars the first year.* [Mid-1800s] **7.** Seem to lurch or heave convulsively, as in *The plane hit an air pocket and my stomach turned over.* [Second half of 1800s] **8.** Replace or renew the constituent parts, as in *Half of our staff turns over every few years.* [Mid-1900s] Also see TURN OVER A NEW LEAF.

turn over a new leaf Make a fresh start, change one's conduct or attitude for the better, as in *He promised the teacher he would turn over a new leaf and behave himself in class.* This expression alludes to turning the page of a book to a new page. [Early 1500s]

turn over in one's grave ♦ See TURN IN ONE'S GRAVE.

turn tail Run away, as in *When they heard the sirens, the boys turned tail.* This term alludes to an animal's turning its back in flight. [Mid-1500s]

turn the clock back ♦ See SET BACK, def. 3.

turn the corner Pass a milestone or critical point, begin to recover. For example, *Experts say the economy has turned the corner and is in the midst of an upturn,* or *The doctor believes he's turned the corner and is on the mend.* This expression alludes to passing around the corner in a race, particularly the last corner. [First half of 1800s]

turn the other cheek Respond meekly or mildly to insult or injury without retaliating. For example, *There's no point in arguing with that unreasonable supervisor; just turn the other cheek.* This expression comes from the New Testament, in which Jesus tells his followers to love their enemies and offer their other cheek to those who have struck one cheek (Luke 6:29).

turn the scale ♦ See TIP THE BALANCE.

turn the tables Reverse a situation and gain the upper hand, as in *Steffi won their previous three matches but today Mary turned the tables and prevailed.* This expression alludes to the former practice of reversing the table or board in games such as chess, thereby switching the opponents' positions. [c. 1600]

turn the tide ♦ See TURN OF THE TIDE.

turn the trick ♦ See DO THE TRICK; TURN A TRICK.

turn thumbs down ♦ See under THUMBS UP.

turn to **1.** Begin work, apply oneself to, as in *Next he turned to cutting wood for the fire.* This usage was first recorded in 1667. **2.** Refer to, consult, as in

She turned to the help-wanted ads. This usage was first recorded in 1631. **3.** Appeal to, apply to for help, as in *At a time like this one turns to one's closest friends,* or *We'll have to turn to the French consulate for more information.* This usage was first recorded in 1821. Also see TURN TO GOOD ACCOUNT.

turn to good account Use for one's benefit, as in *He turned the delay to good account, using the time to finish correspondence.* This idiom, first recorded in 1878, uses *account* in the sense of "a reckoning."

turn turtle Capsize, turn upside down, as in *When they collided, the car turned turtle.* This expression alludes to the helplessness of a turtle turned on its back, where its shell can no longer protect it. [First half of 1800s]

turn up **1.** Increase the volume, speed, intensity, or flow of, as in *Turn up the air conditioning; it's too hot in here.* [Late 1800s] **2.** Find or be found, as in *She turned up the missing papers,* or *Your coat turned up in the closet.* **3.** Appear, arrive, as in *His name turns up in the newspaper now and then,* or *Some old friends turned up unexpectedly.* [c. 1700] This usage gave rise to **turn up like a bad penny,** meaning that something unwanted constantly reappears, as in *Ken turns up like a bad penny whenever there's free liquor. Bad* here alludes to a counterfeit coin. **4.** Fold or be capable of being folded, as in *I'll just turn up the hem,* or *He preferred cuffs that turn up.* [c. 1600] **5.** Happen unexpectedly, as in *Something turned up so I couldn't go to the play.* Also see the following idioms beginning with TURN UP.

turn up like a bad penny ♦ See TURN UP, def. 3.

turn up one's nose Regard with disdain or scorn, as in *She turned up her nose at the broccoli.* This idiom was first recorded in 1779.

turn up one's toes Die, as in *He turned up his toes last week.* This expression alludes to the position of the toes when one lies flat on one's back without moving. It may be obsolescent. [Mid-1800s]

turn upside down Put in disorder, mix or mess up, as in *He turned the whole house upside down looking for his checkbook.* This metaphoric phrase transfers literally inverting something so that the upper part becomes the lower (or vice versa) to throwing into disorder or confusion. [First half of 1800s]

turn up the heat on Also, **put the heat** or **screws** or **squeeze on; tighten the screws on.** Pressure someone, as in *The cops turned up the heat on drivers who show signs of drunkenness,* or *They said they'd tighten the screws on her if she didn't confess.* All of these slangy terms allude to forms of physical coercion or torture. The first dates from about 1930, the variants using *screws* from the mid-1800s, and *squeeze* from the late 1700s.

turn up trumps End well, succeed, as in *Some brief courtships and hasty marriages turn up trumps.* This expression alludes to card games in which trump cards are superior to cards of other suits. [Late 1700s]

turtle ♦ See TURN TURTLE.

tweedledum and tweedledee Two matters, persons, or groups that are very much alike, as in *Bob says he's not voting in this election because the candidates are tweedledum and tweedledee.* This term was invented by John Byrom, who in 1725 made fun of two quarreling composers, Handel and Bononcini, and said there was little difference between their music, since one went "tweedledum" and the other "tweedledee." The term gained further currency when Lewis Carroll used it for two fat little men in *Through the Looking-Glass* (1872). For a synonym, see SIX OF ONE, HALF DOZEN OF THE OTHER.

twenty-twenty hindsight Knowledge after the fact, as in *With twenty-twenty hindsight, I wouldn't have bought these tickets.* This idiom uses *twenty-twenty* in the optometrist's sense, that is, "indicating normal vision," and *hindsight* in the sense of "looking back" or "reconsidering." [First half of 1900s]

twice ♦ See CHEAP AT TWICE THE PRICE; LIGHTNING NEVER STRIKES TWICE; ONCE BITTEN, TWICE SHY; THINK TWICE.

twiddle one's thumbs Be bored or idle, as in *There I sat for three hours, twiddling my thumbs, while he made call after call.* This expression alludes to the habit of idly turning one's thumbs about one another during a period of inactivity. [Mid-1800s]

twinkling ♦ See IN THE TWINKLING OF AN EYE.

twist around one's finger Also, **turn** or **wind** or **wrap around one's finger**. Exert complete control over someone, do as one likes with someone, as in *Alison could twist just about every man around her finger.* This hyperbolic term dates from the mid-1800s.

twist in the wind Be abandoned to a bad situation, especially be left to incur blame, as in *The governor denied knowing it was illegal and left his aide to twist in the wind.* It is also put as **leave twisting in the wind**, meaning "abandon or strand in a difficult situation," as in *Sensing a public relations disaster, the President left the Vice-President twisting in the wind.* This expression, at first applied to a President's nominees who faced opposition and were abandoned by the President, alludes to the corpse of a hanged man left dangling and twisting in the open air. [Slang; early 1970s] Also see OUT ON A LIMB.

twist someone's arm Coerce or persuade someone, as in *If you twist my arm I'll stay for another drink,* or *She didn't really want to go to the theater but he twisted her arm.* Originally alluding to physical coercion, this term is now generally used more loosely and often jocularly. [Mid-1900s]

two ♦ In addition to the idioms beginning with TWO, also see BETWEEN TWO FIRES; FALL BETWEEN THE CRACK (TWO STOOLS); FOR TWO CENTS; GAME THAT TWO CAN PLAY; GOODY-TWO-SHOES; IN TWO SHAKES; IT TAKES TWO; KILL TWO BIRDS WITH ONE STONE; KNOW ALL THE ANSWERS (A THING OR TWO); LESSER OF TWO EVILS; LIKE AS TWO PEAS IN A POD; NO TWO WAYS ABOUT IT; OF TWO MINDS; PUT TWO AND TWO TOGETHER; THAT MAKES TWO OF US; THING OR TWO; WEAR TWO HATS.

two bits ♦ See under FOR TWO CENTS.

two can play at that game ♦ See GAME THAT TWO CAN PLAY.

two cents ♦ See FOR TWO CENTS.

two left feet, have Be clumsy, as in *I'll never get the hang of this dance; I've got two left feet.* This expression conjures up an image of feet that are not symmetrical, as left and right are, therefore causing imbalance or stumbling. It was first recorded in 1915.

two of a kind Very similar individuals or things, as in *Patrice and John are two of a kind—they're true hiking enthusiasts.* This idiom uses *kind* in the sense of "a class with common characteristics," a usage dating from about A.D. 1000.

two's company ♦ See THREE'S A CROWD.

two shakes of a lamb's tail ♦ See IN TWO SHAKES OF A LAMB'S TAIL.

two strikes against Strong factors opposing, as in *There are two strikes against her possibility of a promotion.* This term comes from baseball, where a batter is allowed three strikes at a fairly pitched ball before being called out; thus, a batter with two strikes has but one more chance to hit a fair ball. The figurative use dates from the early 1900s.

two strings to one's bow More than one means of reaching an objective, as in *Louise hasn't heard yet, but she's got two strings to her bow—she can always appeal to the chairman.* This expression alludes to a well-prepared archer, who carries a spare string in case one fails. [Mid-1400s]

two ways about it ♦ See NO TWO WAYS ABOUT IT.

two wrongs do not make a right A second misdeed or mistake does not cancel the first, as in *Don't take his ball just because he took yours—two wrongs do not make a right.* This proverbial adage sounds ancient but was first recorded in 1783, as *Three wrongs will not make one right.*

typhoid Mary A carrier or spreader of misfortune, as in *I swear he's a typhoid Mary; everything at the office has gone wrong since he was hired.* This expression alludes to a real person, Mary Manson, who died in 1938. An Irish-born servant, she transmitted typhoid fever to others and was referred to as "typhoid Mary" from the early 1900s. The term was broadened to other carriers of calamity in the mid-1900s.

u

ugly ◆ In addition to the idioms beginning with UGLY, also see REAR ITS UGLY HEAD.

ugly as sin Physically or morally hideous, as in *I can't think why she likes that dog; it's ugly as sin.* This simile, first recorded in 1801, replaced the earlier *ugly as the devil.*

ugly customer An ill-natured or vicious individual, as in *Watch out for Charlie when he's drinking; he can be an ugly customer.* This phrase uses *ugly* in the sense of "mean" or "dangerous." [c. 1800]

ugly duckling A homely or unpromising individual who grows into an attractive or talented person, as in *She was the family ugly duckling but blossomed in her twenties.* This term alludes to Hans Christian Andersen's fairy tale about a cygnet hatched with ducklings that is despised for its clumsiness until it grows up into a beautiful swan. The tale was first translated into English in 1846, and the term was used figuratively by 1871.

uncalled for Not justified, undeserved, as in *That rude remark was uncalled for.* [Early 1800s] Also see CALL FOR, def. 3.

uncertain ◆ See IN NO UNCERTAIN TERMS.

uncle ◆ See CRY UNCLE; DUTCH UNCLE.

under ◆ In addition to the idioms beginning with UNDER, also see BELOW (UNDER) PAR; BORN UNDER A LUCKY STAR; BUCKLE UNDER; COME UNDER; CUT THE GROUND FROM UNDER; DON'T LET THE GRASS GROW UNDER ONE'S FEET; EVERYTHING BUT THE KITCHEN SINK (UNDER THE SUN); FALL UNDER; FALSE COLORS, SAIL UNDER; GET UNDER SOMEONE'S SKIN; GO UNDER; HIDE ONE'S LIGHT UNDER A BUSHEL; HOT UNDER THE COLLAR; KEEP UNDER ONE'S HAT; KNOCK THE BOTTOM OUT (PROPS OUT FROM UNDER); KNUCKLE UNDER; LIGHT A FIRE UNDER; NOTHING NEW UNDER THE SUN; OF (UNDER) AGE; OUT FROM UNDER; PLOW UNDER; PULL THE RUG OUT FROM UNDER; PUT THE SKIDS UNDER; SIX FEET UNDER; SNOW UNDER; SWEEP UNDER THE RUG; WATER OVER THE DAM (UNDER THE BRIDGE).

under a cloud Under suspicion, in trouble, or out of favor, as in *Ever since his brother was accused of fraud, he's been under a cloud.* This metaphoric expression calls up the image of a single black cloud hanging over an individual. [c. 1500]

under age ◆ See under OF AGE.

under any circumstances Also, **under no circumstances.** ◆ See UNDER THE CIRCUMSTANCES.

under arrest In police custody, as in *They put him under arrest and charged him with stealing a car.* [Late 1300s]

under consideration Being thought about or discussed, as in *Your application is under considera-*

tion; we'll let you know next week. This idiom was first recorded in 1665.

under cover 1. Protected by a shelter, as in *It began to pour but fortunately we were under cover.* [c. 1400] 2. **under cover of.** Also, **under the cover of.** Hidden or protected by, as in *They sneaked out under cover of darkness,* or, as it was put in a sermon in 1751: "Presumption which loves to conceal itself under the cover of humility" (John Jortin, *Sermons on Different Subjects*).

under false colors ◆ See FALSE COLORS.

under fire Criticized or held responsible, as in *The landlord is under fire for not repairing the roof.* This expression originally referred to being within range of enemy guns; its figurative use dates from the late 1800s.

underground railroad A secret network for moving and housing fugitives, as in *There's definitely an underground railroad helping women escape abusive husbands.* This term, dating from the first half of the 1800s, alludes to the network that secretly transported runaway slaves through the northern states to Canada. It was revived more than a century later for similar escape routes.

under lock and key Securely locked up, as in *He keeps the wine under lock and key.* [First half of 1500s]

under one's belt Experienced or achieved, as in *Once a medical student has anatomy under her belt, she'll have much less to memorize.* This metaphoric expression likens food that has been consumed to an experience that has been digested. [Colloquial; first half of 1800s]

under one's breath Softly, in an undertone or whisper, as in *"I can't stand one more minute of that music," she muttered under her breath.* This idiom, first recorded in 1832, is probably a hyperbole, alluding to a sound that is softer than breathing.

under one's feet In one's path or in one's way, as in *Come on, children, get out from under my feet.*

under one's hat ◆ See KEEP UNDER ONE'S HAT.

under one's nose Right there, in plain view, as in *Your keys are on the table, right under your nose.* This expression is generally a reminder that something one cannot find is actually there. [c. 1600]

under one's own steam Independently, without help, as in *For two years I published the quarterly newsletter under my own steam.* This expression uses *steam* in the sense of "driving power," as in a steam engine. [Early 1900s]

under one's skin ◆ See GET UNDER ONE'S SKIN.

under pain of ◆ See ON PAIN OF.

under par ◆ See BELOW PAR.

under someone's spell Fascinated or influenced by someone, as in *I think he has our daughter* *under his spell.* This idiom derives from the literal meaning of *spell,* "a word or formula that has magical power." [Mid-1800s]

under someone's thumb Controlled or dominated by someone, as in *He's been under his mother's thumb for years.* The allusion in this metaphoric idiom is unclear, that is, why a thumb rather than a fist or some other anatomic part should symbolize control. [Mid-1700s]

under someone's wing Guided or protected by someone, as in *The department head asked Bill to take Joe under his wing during his first few weeks with the firm.* This metaphoric term alludes to the mother hen sheltering her chicks. [1200s]

understand ◆ See GIVE TO UNDERSTAND.

under the aegis of Also, **under the auspices of.** Protected or sponsored by, as in *The fund drive for the new field is under the aegis of the Rotary Club,* or *He was admitted to the club under the auspices of Mr. Leonard.* The first term comes from Greek myth, where the *aegis* was the protective shield of Zeus. *Auspices* originally meant "observations of birds made to obtain omens." It then came to be used for a sign or omen, and still later for a favorable influence. [Late 1700s]

under the circumstances Also, **in the circumstances.** Given these conditions, such being the case, as in *Under the circumstances we can't leave Mary out.* This idiom uses *circumstance* in the sense of "a particular situation," a usage dating from the late 1300s. It may also be modified in various ways, such as **under any circumstances** meaning "no matter what the situation," as in *We'll phone her under any circumstances;* **under no circumstances,** meaning "in no case, never," as in *Under no circumstances may you smoke;* **under any other circumstances,** meaning "in a different situation," as in *I can't work under any other circumstances;* and **under the same circumstances,** meaning "given the same situation," as in *Under the same circumstances anyone would have done the same.*

under the counter Secretly, surreptitiously, as in *I'm sure they're selling liquor to minors under the counter.* This expression most often alludes to an illegal transaction, the *counter* being the flat-surfaced furnishing or table *over* which legal business is conducted. It was first recorded in 1926. Also see UNDER THE TABLE.

under the gun Under pressure to solve a problem or meet a deadline, as in *The reporter was under the gun for that article on taxes.* This idiom alludes to a gun being pointed at a person to force him or her to act. [Colloquial; c. 1900]

under the hammer For sale, as in *These paintings and Oriental rugs must come under the hammer if we're to pay the mortgage.* This expression alludes

to the auctioneer's hammer, which is rapped to indicate a completed transaction. [Mid-1800s]

under the impression Thinking, assuming, or believing something, as in *I was under the impression that they were coming today.* This idiom often suggests that the idea or belief one had is mistaken. [Mid-1800s]

under the influence Impaired functioning owing to alcohol consumption, as in *He was accused of driving under the influence.* This expression, from legal jargon, is short for *under the influence of intoxicating liquor* and implies that one is not completely drunk. Since it is nearly always applied to drivers suspected or so accused, it has given rise to the police acronym *DUI,* for "driving under the influence." [Second half of 1800s]

under the knife Undergoing surgery, as in *He was awake the entire time he was under the knife.* The phrase is often put as **go under the knife,** meaning "be operated on," as in *When do you go under the knife? Knife* standing for "surgery" was first recorded in 1880.

under the sun ◆ See under EVERYTHING BUT THE KITCHEN SINK; NOTHING NEW UNDER THE SUN.

under the table In secret, as in *They paid her under the table so as to avoid taxes.* This term alludes to money being passed under a table in some shady transaction, such as a bribe. [Mid-1900s] Also see UNDER THE COUNTER.

under the weather Ailing, ill; also, suffering from a hangover. For example, *She said she was under the weather and couldn't make it to the meeting.* This expression presumably alludes to the influence of the weather on one's health. [Early 1800s] The same term is sometimes used as a euphemism for being drunk, as in *After four drinks, Ellen was a bit under the weather.*

under the wire Barely, scarcely, just within the limit, as in *This book will be finished just under the wire.* This term comes from horse racing, where the wire marks the finish line. [First half of 1900s] Also see DOWN TO THE WIRE.

under way 1. In motion, as in *The ship got under way at noon.* [c. 1930] 2. Already started, in progress, as in *Plans are under way to expand.* [c. 1930]

under wraps Concealed or secret, as in *The design for the new plant is under wraps.* This idiom frequently is put as **keep under wraps,** meaning "keep secret," as in *Let's keep this theory under wraps until we've tested it sufficiently.* It alludes to covering something completely by wrapping it up. [1930s]

unglued ◆ See under COME APART AT THE SEAMS.

unheard of Very unusual, extraordinary, as in *It's unheard of to have all one's money refunded two* *years after the purchase.* This expression alludes to a circumstance so unusual that it has never been heard of. [Late 1500s]

unkindest cut The worst insult, ultimate treachery, as in *And then, the unkindest cut of all—my partner walks out on me just when the deal is about to go through.* This expression was invented by Shakespeare in describing Julius Caesar's stabbing to death by his friends in *Julius Caesar* (3:2): "This was the most unkindest cut of all."

unknown quantity An unpredictable person or thing, as in *We don't know how the new pitcher will do—he's an unknown quantity.* This expression comes from algebra, where it signifies an unknown numerical value. Its figurative use dates from the mid-1800s.

unlikely ♦ See IN THE UNLIKELY EVENT.

unseen ♦ See SIGHT UNSEEN.

unstuck ♦ See under COME APART AT THE SEAMS.

until ♦ See PUT OFF UNTIL TOMORROW; TALK ONE'S ARM OFF (UNTIL BLUE IN THE FACE). Also see under TILL.

untimely ♦ See COME TO AN (UNTIMELY) END.

unto ♦ See DO UNTO OTHERS; LAW UNTO ONESELF.

unturned ♦ See LEAVE NO STONE UNTURNED.

unvarnished truth The plain facts without embellishment, as in *Let's just have the unvarnished truth about the sale.* This idiom was first recorded in 1883, although *unvarnished* had been used to describe a direct statement since Shakespeare's time.

unwritten law An accepted although informal rule of behavior, as in *It's an unwritten law that you lock the gate when you leave the swimming pool.* [Mid-1400s]

up ♦ In addition to the idioms beginning with UP, also see ACT UP; ADD UP; ADD UP TO; ALL SHOOK UP; ALL UP; ANTE UP; BACK UP; BALL UP; BANG UP; BARK UP THE WRONG TREE; BEAR UP; BEAT UP; BEEF UP; BID UP; BLOW UP; BOB UP; BONE UP; BOOT UP; BOTTLE UP; BOUND UP IN; BRACE UP; BREAK UP; BRING UP; BRING UP THE REAR; BRING UP TO DATE; BRUSH UP; BUCKLE UP; BUCK UP; BUDDY UP; BUILD UP; BUMP UP; BURN UP; BUTTER UP; BUTTON UP; BUY UP; CALL UP; CAMP IT UP; CARD UP ONE'S SLEEVE; CATCH UP; CHALK UP; CHARGE UP; CHAT UP; CHEER UP; CHOKE UP; CHOOSE UP; CLAM UP; CLEAN UP; CLEAR UP; CLOCK UP; CLOSE UP; CLOUD OVER (UP); COME (UP) FROM BEHIND; COME UP; COME UP AGAINST; COME UP ROSES; COME UP WITH; COOK UP; COUGH UP; COVER UP; COZY UP; CRACKED UP; CRACK UP; CRANK UP; CRAP UP; CREEP UP ON; CROP UP; CROSS UP; CURL UP; CUT UP; DEAD FROM THE NECK UP; DIG UP; DOLL UP; DOUBLE UP; DO UP; DRAW UP; DREAM UP; DRESS UP; DRUM UP; DRY UP; EASE OFF (UP); EAT OUT (SOMEONE UP); EAT UP; END UP; FACE UP TO; FED TO THE GILLS (UP); FEEL UP; FEEL UP TO; FIGURE UP; FIRE UP; FIT OUT (UP); FIX UP; FIX UP WITH; FLARE UP; FOLD UP; FOLLOW UP; FOUL UP; FROM THE GROUND UP; FUCK UP; GAME IS UP; GANG UP; GAS UP; GEAR UP; GET SOMEONE'S BACK UP; GET UP; GET UP ON THE WRONG SIDE OF BED; GET UP STEAM; GIVE ONESELF UP; GIVE UP; GIVE UP THE GHOST; GO BELLY UP; GOOF UP; GO UP; GO UP IN FLAMES; GROW UP; GUM UP; HAM UP; HANDS UP; HANG UP; HARD UP; HAUL UP; HAVE HAD IT (UP TO HERE); HEADS UP; HEAD UP; HEAT UP; HIT UP; HOLD ONE'S END UP; HOLD ONE'S HEAD HIGH (UP); HOLD UP; HOLE UP; HOOK UP; HOPPED UP; HURRY UP AND WAIT; HUSH UP; JACK UP; JAZZ UP; JUICE UP; KEEP IT UP; KEEP ONE'S CHIN UP; KEEP (SOMEONE) UP; KEY UP; KICK UP; KICK UP A FUSS; KICK UP ONE'S HEELS; KISS AND MAKE UP; KNOCK UP; LAID UP; LAND IN (UP); LAP UP; LARK IT UP; LAUGH UP ONE'S SLEEVE; LAY IN (UP); LEAD DOWN (UP) THE GARDEN PATH; LEAD UP TO; LEG UP; LET UP; LIGHTEN UP; LIGHT UP; LINE UP; LIVE IT UP; LIVE UP TO; LOCK UP; LOOK OVER (UP AND DOWN); LOOK UP; LOUSE UP; MAKE UP; MAKE UP FOR LOST TIME; MAKE UP ONE'S MIND; MAKE UP TO; MARK UP; MEASURE UP; MEET UP WITH; MESS UP; MIX IT UP; MIX UP; MOP UP; MOP UP THE FLOOR WITH; MOVE UP; MUCK UP; NOT ALL IT'S CRACKED UP TO BE; NUMBER'S UP; ONE UP; ON THE UP-AND-UP; OPEN UP; OWN UP; PAIR OFF (UP); PASS UP; PATCH UP; PAY UP; PEP SOMEONE UP; PERK UP; PICK UP; PICK UP ON; PILE UP; PIPE UP; PLAY UP; PLAY UP TO; PLUCK UP; POINT UP; PONY UP; POP UP; PRICK UP ONE'S EARS; PSYCH UP; PULL ONESELF UP; PULL UP; PULL UP STAKES; PUMP UP; PUSH UP DAISIES; PUT ONE'S FEET UP; PUT SOMEONE UP TO; PUT UP; PUT-UP JOB; PUT UP OR SHUT UP; PUT UP WITH; RACK UP; RAKE UP; READ UP; REV UP; RIDE UP; RIGHT-SIDE UP; RIGHT UP ONE'S ALLEY; RING UP; ROLL UP; ROLL UP ONE'S SLEEVES; ROUGH UP; ROUND UP; RUB UP ON; RUN (UP) AGAINST; RUN UP; RUSTLE UP; SAVE UP FOR; SCARE UP; SCRAPE UP AN ACQUAINTANCE; SCREW UP; SCROUNGE AROUND (UP); SCRUB UP; SEAL OFF (UP); SEIZE UP; SEND UP; SERVE UP; SETTLE UP; SET UP; SET UP HOUSEKEEPING; SEW UP; SHACK UP; SHAKE UP; SHAPE UP; SHINE UP TO; SHOOT UP; SHORE UP; SHOT UP; SHOW UP; SHUT UP; SIGN UP; SIT UP; SIT UP AND TAKE NOTICE; SIZE UP; SLIP UP; SLOW UP; SMELL UP; SNAP UP; SOAK UP; SOFTEN UP; SOMEBODY UP THERE LOVES ME; SPEAK OUT (UP); SPEED UP; SPIT UP; SPRUCE UP; SQUARE UP; STACK UP; STAND UP; STAND UP AND BE COUNTED; STAND UP FOR; STAND UP TO; STAND UP WITH; START UP; STEAMED UP; STEP UP; STICK UP; STIR UP; STIR UP A HORNETS' NEST; STOP UP; STRAIGHTEN UP; STRAIGHT UP; STRIKE UP; STRING UP; SUCK UP TO; SUIT UP; SUM UP; TAKE UP; TAKE UP A COLLECTION; TAKE UP ARMS; TAKE UP FOR;

TAKE UP ON; TAKE UP SPACE; TAKE UP WHERE ONE LEFT OFF; TAKE UP WITH; TALK UP; TANK UP; TEAM UP WITH; THINK UP; THROW UP; THROW UP ONE'S HANDS; THUMBS UP; TIE UP; TIME IS UP; TONE DOWN (UP); TOOL UP; (UP) TO THE HILT; TOUCH UP; TRADE DOWN (UP); TRIAL BALLOON, SEND UP A; TRIP UP; TRUMP UP; TUNE UP; TURN UP; TURN UP ONE'S NOSE; TURN UP ONE'S TOES; TURN UP THE HEAT; TURN UP TRUMPS; WAIT UP; WAKE-UP CALL; WARM UP; WASH UP; WHAT'S COOKING (UP); WHAT'S (UP) WITH; WHIP UP; WHOOP IT UP; WIND UP; WISE UP; WORKED UP; WORK ONE'S WAY (UP); WORK UP; WRAPPED UP; WRAP UP; WRITE UP. Also see under UPPER.

up a creek Also, **up shit creek; up the creek (without a paddle).** In trouble, in a serious predicament, as in *If the check doesn't arrive today I'm up a creek,* or *The car wouldn't start, so I was up the creek without a paddle.* This slangy idiom conjures up the image of a stranded canoeist with no way of moving (paddling) the canoe. President Harry S. Truman used the first term in a letter in 1918. The first variant is considered vulgar.

up against Contending or confronted with, as in *I'm up against a strong opponent in this election.* This idiom is also put as **up against it,** which means "in serious difficulty, especially in desperate financial straits." For example, *When the collection agency called again, we knew we were up against it.* [Late 1800s]

up and about Also, **up and around; up and doing.** Active again, especially after an illness or rest, as in *They had her up and about just one day after surgery,* or *I'm so glad you're up and around; we need your help,* or *It's time to be up and doing.* [Early 1800s]

up and at 'em Get going, get busy, as in *Up and at 'em—there's a lot of work to be done.* This colloquial idiom, often uttered as a command, uses *at 'em* (for "at them") in the general sense of tackling a project, and not in reference to specific persons.

up a tree In a difficult situation, as in *They found the drugs in his suitcase, so he was up a tree.* This expression alludes to an animal, such as a raccoon or squirrel, that climbs a tree for refuge from attackers, which then surround the tree so it cannot come down. [Colloquial; early 1800s]

up for grabs Available to anyone, as in *Now that he's resigned, his job is up for grabs.* This term alludes to something being thrown in the air for anyone to grasp or catch. [Colloquial; 1920s]

up front 1. In the forward section, as of an airplane or theater. For example, *We'd like two seats as far up front as possible.* [First half of 1900s] 2. Paid in advance, as in *We need at least half of the money for the production up front.* [Colloquial; c. 1930]

3. Candid, direct, as in *Now tell me straight up front what you think of this outfit.* [Second half of 1900s]

up in arms Angry, rebellious, as in *The town was up in arms over the state's plan to allow commercial flights at the air base.* This idiom originally referred to an armed rebellion and was so used from the late 1500s. Its figurative use dates from about 1700.

up in the air Not settled, uncertain, as in *The proposal to build a golf course next to the airport is still up in the air.* This metaphoric expression likens something floating in the air to an unsettled matter. Put as *in the air* from the mid-1700s, it acquired *up* in the first half of the 1900s.

upon ♦ See ACT ON (UPON); CALL ON (UPON); CHANCE ON (UPON); COME ACROSS (UPON); COME ON (UPON); COUNT ON (UPON); DAWN ON (UPON); DWELL ON (UPON); ENTER ON (UPON); FALL BACK ON (UPON); FALL ON (UPON); GROW ON (UPON); HARD ON (UPON); HIT ON (UPON); INCUMBENT UPON; LIGHT ON (UPON); ONCE UPON A TIME; PITCH ON (UPON); PLAY ON (UPON); PUT UPON; SEIZE ON (UPON); SET AT (UPON); TAKE IT UPON ONESELF; WAIT ON (UPON); WEIGH ON (UPON); WORK ON (UPON).

up one's alley ♦ See under RIGHT UP ONE'S ALLEY.

up one's sleeve ♦ See CARD UP ONE'S SLEEVE.

up on something, be Be well informed or up-to-date about something, as in *I'm not up on the latest models of cars.* [Colloquial]

upper ♦ In addition to the idioms beginning with UPPER, also see KEEP A STIFF UPPER LIP; ON ONE'S UPPERS.

upper crust The highest social class, as in *She wanted badly to be one of the upper crust but it wasn't going to happen.* This term alludes to the choicest part of a pie or loaf of bread. [First half of 1800s]

upper hand Also, **whip hand.** A dominating or controlling position, as in *Once you let Jeff get the upper hand there'll be no stopping him,* or *When it comes to checkers, my son-in-law generally has the whip hand.* The first term alludes to an ancient game in which each player in turn grasps a stick with one hand, beginning from the bottom, and the last who can put his hand at the top wins. Its figurative use dates from the late 1400s. The variant alludes to the driver who holds the whip in a horse-drawn vehicle; it was being used figuratively by the late 1600s.

upper story The head or brain, as in *He's not all there in the upper story.* This expression transfers the literal sense of a higher floor in a multistory building to the top portion of the human body. Richard Bentley used it in *A Dissertation on the*

Epistles of Phalaris (1699), where he compares a man with "brains . . . in his head" to a man who has "furniture in his upper story."

upright ◆ See BOLT UPRIGHT.

uproar ◆ See MAKE A SCENE (AN UPROAR).

ups and downs Good times and bad times, successes and failures, as in *We've had our ups and downs but things are going fairly well now.* This term was first recorded in 1659.

upset the applecart Spoil carefully laid plans, as in *Now don't upset the applecart by revealing where we're going.* This expression started out as *upset the cart,* used since Roman times to mean "spoil everything." The precise idiom dates from the late 1700s.

upside ◆ In addition to the idiom beginning with UPSIDE, also see TURN UPSIDE DOWN.

upside the head Against the side of someone's head, as in *With those nightsticks the police are known for knocking suspects upside the head.* [Slang; second half of 1900s]

upstairs ◆ See KICK UPSTAIRS.

uptake ◆ See ON THE UPTAKE.

up the creek Also, **up shit creek.** ◆ See UP A CREEK.

up the river To or in prison, as in *They sent him up the river for five years.* This phrase originally referred to Sing-Sing Prison, on the Hudson River about 30 miles north of New York City. So used from about 1890 on, it was broadened to apply to any prison by the early 1900s.

up the wall ◆ See under DRIVE SOMEONE CRAZY.

up to 1. As far as or approaching a certain point. For example, *The water was nearly up to the windowsill,* or *They allowed us up to two hours to finish the test,* or *This seed should yield up to 300 bushels per acre.* [c. A.D. 950] 2. **be up to.** Be able to do or deal with, as in *When I got home, she asked if I was up to a walk on the beach.* This usage is often put negatively, that is, **not be up to something,** as in *He's not up to a long drive.* [Late 1700s] 3. Occupied with, engaged in, as in *What have you been up to lately?* This usage can mean "devising" or "scheming," as in *We knew those two were up to something.* It also appears in **up to no good,** meaning "occupied wit or devising something harmful," as in *I'm sure those kids are up to no good.* [First half of 1800s] 4. Dependent on, as in *The success of this project is up to us.* [c. 1900] Also see the following idioms beginning with UP TO.

up to a point To some extent, somewhat, as in *I can work weekends up to a point, but after a month or so I get tired of it.* This phrase uses *point* in the sense of "a definite position." [Early 1800s]

up to date ◆ See BRING UP TO DATE.

up to no good ◆ See UP TO, def. 3.

up to one's ears Also, **in up to one's eyes** or **eyeballs** or **neck.** Deeply involved; also, oversupplied, surfeited. For example, *I'm up to my ears in work,* or *He's in up to his eyes with the in-laws.* This hyperbolic and slangy idiom implies one is flooded with something up to those organs. The first was first recorded in 1839; *up to the eyes* in 1778; *to the eyeballs* in 1911; *to the neck* in 1856.

up to one's old tricks Behaving in one's usual deceitful or mischievous fashion, as in *She's up to her old tricks, telling her parents one thing and her teachers another,* or *He's up to his old tricks, teasing his sisters until they're in tears.* Put as *at his old tricks,* this idiom was first recorded in 1823.

up to par Also, **up to scratch** or **snuff** or **speed** or **the mark.** Satisfactory, up to a given standard, as in *She didn't feel up to par today so she stayed home,* or *I'm sure he'll come up to scratch when the time comes,* or *She's up to snuff again.* Nearly all the versions of this idiom come from sports, *par* from golf, *scratch* and *mark* from boxing (after being knocked down a fighter had eight seconds to make his way to a mark scratched in the center of the ring), and *speed* from racing. However, the allusion in the variant with *snuff,* which dates from the early 1800s, has been lost.

upwards of Also, **upward of.** More than, in excess of, as in *Upwards of 30,000 spectators filled the ballpark.* [c. 1600]

up yours A vulgar exclamation of contempt, as in *So you think you can beat me? Well, up yours!* This expression, a shortening of the even more vulgar **stick it up your ass,** is sometimes accompanied by an obscene gesture (see GIVE THE FINGER). [Vulgar slang; mid-1900s]

use ◆ In addition to the idioms beginning with USE, also see HAVE NO USE FOR; MAKE USE OF; NO USE; PUT TO GOOD USE. Also see under USED.

used ◆ In addition to the idiom beginning with USED, also see IT TAKES GETTING USED TO. Also see under USE.

used to 1. Accustomed or habituated to. This expression is often put as **be** or **get used to,** as in *I'm not used to driving a manual-shift car,* or *She can't get used to calling him Dad.* [Early 1500s] 2. Formerly. This sense is used with a following verb to indicate a past state, as in *I used to ride my bicycle to the post office,* or *This used to be the best restaurant in town.* [Late 1800s]

use one's head Think, have common sense, as in *Use your head, Martin. No one's coming out in this weather.* This idiom uses *head* in the sense of "brain" or "intellect," a usage dating from the late 1300s.

use up 1. Consume completely, as in *The kids used up all their money playing video games.* [Late

1700s] **2.** Exhaust, tire out, as in *I'm totally used up from digging that hole.* [Colloquial; mid-1800s]

usual ◆ See AS USUAL; BUSINESS AS USUAL.

utter a word ◆ See under NOT OPEN ONE'S MOUTH.

V

vain ◆ See IN VAIN; TAKE SOMEONE'S NAME IN VAIN.

valor ◆ See DISCRETION IS THE BETTER PART OF VALOR.

value ◆ See AT FACE VALUE.

vanish ◆ See under INTO THIN AIR.

variety is the spice of life Diversity makes life interesting, as in *Jim dates a different girl every week—variety is the spice of life, he claims.* This phrase comes from William Cowper's poem, "The Task" (1785): "Variety is the very spice of life, That gives it all its flavor."

variety store A retail shop that carries a large selection of usually inexpensive merchandise, as in *What this town needs is a good variety store.* [Second half of 1700s]

various and sundry Of different kinds, miscellaneous, as in *Various and sundry items did not sell, so they'll probably hold another auction.* This expression is a redundancy, the two adjectives meaning just about the same thing.

veil ◆ See DRAW A VEIL OVER.

velvet ◆ See under IRON HAND.

vengeance ◆ See WITH A VENGEANCE.

vent ◆ In addition to the idiom beginning with VENT, also see GIVE VENT TO.

vent one's spleen Express one's anger, as in *Some people see town council meetings as a place where they can vent their spleen.* This expression uses *vent* in the sense of "air," and *spleen* in the sense of "anger," alluding to the fact that this organ was once thought to be the seat of ill humor and melancholy. [First half of 1600s]

venture ◆ See NOTHING VENTURED, NOTHING GAINED.

verge ◆ In addition to the idiom beginning with VERGE, also see ON THE VERGE OF.

verge on **1.** Approach, come close to, as in *Her ability verges on genius.* [Early 1800s] **2.** Be on the edge or border of, as in *Our property verges on conservation land.* [Late 1700s]

verse ◆ See CHAPTER AND VERSE.

very ◆ In addition to the idioms beginning with VERY, also see ALL VERY WELL; WHAT'S THE (THE VERY) IDEA.

very thing, the Exactly what is needed or wanted, as in *That hat's the very thing to complete the cos-*

tume. This idiom, which uses *very* to denote exact identity, was first recorded in 1768.

very well **1.** Exceedingly healthy, as in *How are you?—Very well, thank you.* **2.** Extremely skillfully or properly, as in *He manages that sailboat very well.* **3.** All right, I agree to, as in *Will you take her hand?—Very well, but only to cross the street.* Also see ALL VERY WELL.

vested interest A personal stake in something, as in *She has a vested interest in keeping the house in her name.* This term, first recorded in 1818, uses *vested* in the sense of "established" or "secured."

vicious circle A series of events in which each problem creates another and worsens the original one. For example, *The fatter I get, the unhappier I am, so I eat to cheer myself up, which makes me fatter yet—it's a vicious circle.* This expression comes from the French *circle vicieux*, which in philosophy means "a circular proof"—that is, the proof of one statement depends on a second statement, whose proof in turn depends on the first. One writer suggests that the English meaning of "vicious" helped the expression acquire its more pejorative present sense, used since 1839.

victor ◆ See TO THE VICTOR BELONG THE SPOILS.

victory ◆ See PYRRHIC VICTORY.

view ◆ See BIRD'S EYE VIEW; IN (VIEW) THE LIGHT OF; IN VIEW; ON VIEW; POINT OF VIEW; TAKE A DIM VIEW; WITH A VIEW TO.

vigor ◆ See VIM AND VIGOR.

villain of the piece, the The person to blame for what is bad or wrong, as in *I'm afraid the caterer is the villain of the piece—the food wasn't ready for hours.* The *piece* in this term alludes to a play in which the villain is the character whose evildoing is important to the plot. [Mid-1800s]

vim and vigor Ebullient vitality and energy, as in *He was full of vim and vigor after that swim.* This redundant expression uses both *vim* and *vigor* in the sense of "energy" or "strength."

vine ◆ See CLINGING VINE; WITHER ON THE VINE.

violet ◆ See SHRINKING VIOLET.

viper in one's bosom Also, **snake in one's bosom.** An ungrateful or treacherous friend, as in *I got him dozens of freelance jobs, and then he told everyone I was a lousy musician—nothing like nourishing a viper in one's bosom.* This metaphoric expression, often put as **nourish a viper** (or **snake**) **in one's bosom,** comes from Aesop's fable about a farmer who shelters a snake dying from the cold, which then fatally bites him after it recovers. It was referred to by Chaucer and Shakespeare, and appeared in numerous proverb collections.

virtue ◆ See BY VIRTUE OF; MAKE A VIRTUE OF NECESSITY.

visit ♦ See PAY A CALL (VISIT).

voice ♦ See AT THE TOP OF ONE'S LUNGS (VOICE); GIVE VOICE TO; HAVE A SAY (VOICE) IN; RAISE ONE'S VOICE; STILL SMALL VOICE; WITH ONE VOICE.

void ♦ See NULL AND VOID.

volume ♦ See SPEAK VOLUMES.

vote down Defeat a candidate or measure, as in *The new amendment was voted down by a narrow margin.* This idiom was first recorded in 1642.

vote with one's feet Indicate one's disapproval by walking out or emigrating, as in *The service was so bad that we decided to vote with our feet,* or *Thousands of Hong Kong residents voted with their feet and left before the Chinese takeover.* [Slang; mid-1900s]

voyage ♦ See MAIDEN VOYAGE.

W

wade in Also, **wade into.** Plunge into, begin or attack resolutely and energetically, as in *She waded into that pile of correspondence.* This idiom transfers entering water to beginning some action. [Mid-1800s]

wag ♦ See TAIL WAGGING THE DOG; TONGUES WAG.

wages of sin, the The results or consequences of evildoing, as in *She ate all of the strawberries and ended up with a terrible stomachache—the wages of sin, no doubt.* This expression comes from the New Testament, where Paul writes to the Romans (6:23): "The wages of sin is death." Today it is often used more lightly, as in the example.

wagon ♦ See FIX SOMEONE'S WAGON; HITCH ONE'S WAGON; ON THE BANDWAGON; ON THE WAGON.

wail like a banshee Scream shrilly, as in *Terrified, she wailed like a banshee.* In Irish folklore, a *banshee* is a spirit in the form of a wailing woman whose appearance is an omen that one member of a family will die. The simile dates from the late 1800s.

wait ♦ In addition to the idioms beginning with WAIT, also see CAN'T WAIT; HURRY UP AND WAIT; IN WAITING; LIE IN WAIT; PLAY A WAITING GAME.

wait a minute 1. Stop, I want to say something, as in *Wait a minute—he wasn't there yesterday.* 2. What a surprise, as in *Wait a minute! It was you who called the police?* For a similar phrase, see HOLD EVERYTHING.

wait and see Bide one's time for events to run their course, as in *Do you think they'll raise taxes?—We'll have to wait and see.* This expression was first recorded in Daniel Defoe's *Robinson Crusoe* (1719): "We had no remedy but to wait and see." In Britain the phrase became asso-

ciated with Prime Minister H.H. Asquith, who in 1910 so often said it to the opposition regarding an impending bill that he became known as "Old Wait and See."

wait at table Also, **wait on table.** Serve at a meal, as in *She got a summer job at a resort waiting at table,* or *Waiting on table usually does not pay very well.* [Mid-1500s] Also see WAIT ON.

wait for the other shoe to drop Await a seemingly inevitable event, as in *Now that she has a good enough job to leave her husband, we're just waiting for the other shoe to drop.* This expression alludes to a person awakened by a neighbor who loudly dropped one shoe on the floor and is waiting for the second shoe to be dropped. [Early 1900s]

waiting game ♦ See PLAY A WAITING GAME.

waiting in the wings ♦ See IN THE WINGS.

wait on 1. Also, **wait upon.** Serve, minister to, especially for personal needs or in a store or restaurant. For example, *Guests at the Inn should not expect to be waited on—they can make their own beds and get their own breakfast.* [Early 1500s] 2. Make a formal call on, as in *They waited on the ambassador.* [c. 1500] 3. Also, **wait upon.** Await, remain in readiness for, as in *We're waiting on their decision to close the school.* This usage, a synonym of **wait for,** dates from the late 1600s but in the mid-1800s began to be criticized by many authorities. However, by the late 1900s it had come into increasingly wider use and is again largely accepted.

wait on hand and foot Do everything for someone, serve someone's every need, as in *Her mother has always waited on her hand and foot.* [First half of 1300s]

wait out Delay until the end of something, as in *They waited out the war in Paris.* This expression comes from baseball, where it alludes to the batter refraining from swinging at pitches in the hope of being walked (getting to first base on balls). It was first recorded in 1909 and was transferred to other activities by the 1930s.

wait up 1. Postpone going to bed in anticipation of someone or something, as in *My parents always wait up until I get home, no matter how late it is.* [Mid-1800s] 2. Stop or pause so that another can catch up, as in *Let's wait up for the stragglers,* or *Don't walk so fast; wait up for me.* [Colloquial]

wake ♦ In addition to the idioms beginning with WAKE, also see IN THE WAKE OF; TO WAKE THE DEAD.

wake-up call A portentous event, report, or situation that brings an issue to immediate attention. For example, *The rise in unemployment has given a wake-up call to state governments,* or *The success of the online subscription is a wake-up call to publishers.* This metaphoric term originated in the second half of the 1900s for a telephone call arranged in advance to awaken a sleeper, especially in a hotel. Its figurative use dates from about 1990.

walk ♦ In addition to the idioms beginning with WALK, also see COCK OF THE WALK; HANDS DOWN (IN A WALK); WORSHIP THE GROUND SOMEONE WALKS ON.

walk all over Also, **walk over.** Treat contemptuously, be overbearing and inconsiderate to, as in *I don't know why she puts up with the way he walks all over her,* or *Don't let those aggressive people in sales walk over you.* This idiom transfers physically treading on someone to trampling on one's feelings. [Second half of 1800s]

walk a tightrope Also, **be on a tightrope.** Take or be on a very precarious course, as in *A university press must walk a tightrope to publish scholarly books and still make money,* or *The general was on a tightrope as to whether he should advance or retreat.* This idiom transfers the balancing act performed by tightrope or high-wire acrobats to other concerns. [First half of 1900s]

walk away from 1. Survive an accident with little injury, as in *They were lucky to walk away from that collision.* [Second half of 1900s] 2. Refuse to deal with or become involved, abandon, as in *No parent finds it easy to walk away from a child in trouble.* [Second half of 1900s] 3. Outdo, outrun, or defeat with little difficulty, as in *The Packers are walking away from the other teams in their division.* [Slang] Also see WALK OVER.

walk away with ♦ See WALK OFF WITH.

walking encyclopedia A very knowledgeable person, as in *Ask Rob—he's a walking encyclopedia of military history.* A similar expression, *a walking dictionary,* was used by George Chapman in his poem "Tears of Peace" (c. 1600).

walking papers A dismissal, as in *They're downsizing, and I got my walking papers last week.* This slangy expression, first recorded in 1835, refers to a written notice of dismissal.

walk off with 1. Also, **walk away with.** Win easily, as in *Our team walked off with the pennant,* or *He expected a tough opponent, but to his surprise he walked away with first place.* [First half of 1800s] 2. Steal, as in *Someone walked off with my suitcase.* [Early 1700s]

walk of life A trade, profession, or occupation, as in *He'll do well in whatever walk of life he chooses.* This expression uses *walk* in the sense of "line of work." [c. 1800]

walk on air Feel elated or exuberantly joyful, as in *She was walking on air after she found out she'd won the teaching award.* This metaphoric term likens feeling happy to floating. [Late 1800s]

walk on eggs Proceed very cautiously, as in *I knew I was walking on eggs when I asked about the department's involvement in the lawsuit.* This

metaphoric idiom transfers walking on fragile eggs to discussing or investigating a dangerous subject. [First half of 1700s]

walk out 1. Go on strike, as in *The union threatened to walk out if management would not listen to its demands.* [Late 1800s] 2. Leave suddenly, especially as a sign of disapproval. For example, *The play was so bad we walked out after the first act.* [First half of 1800s] 3. Also, **walk out on.** Desert, abandon, as in *He walked out on his wife and five children.* [Late 1800s]

walk over 1. See WALK ALL OVER. 2. Defeat easily, as in *We walked over them in that practice game but don't know how we'll do in the real thing.* [Second half of 1900s]

walk tall Show pride and self-confidence, as in *The most important thing she taught us was to walk tall.* [Colloquial; mid-1900s]

walk the floor Pace up and down, as in *In former times expectant fathers walked the floor, but now they often are labor coaches,* or *The baby was colicky, so she walked the floor with him all night.*

walk the plank Be forced to resign, as in *We were sure that Ted hadn't left of his own accord; he'd walked the plank.* This metaphoric idiom alludes to a form of execution used in the 17th century, mainly by pirates, whereby a victim was forced to walk off the end of a board placed on the edge of the ship's deck and so drown. [Second half of 1800s]

walk through 1. Perform in a perfunctory fashion, as in *She was just walking through her job, hoping to quit very soon.* This idiom originally referred to practicing parts in a play at an early rehearsal. It was applied more broadly from the late 1800s. Also see GO THROUGH THE MOTIONS. **2. walk someone through.** Instruct someone carefully, one step at a time, as in *He was very helpful, walking me through all the steps in this complex computer program.*

wall ♦ In addition to the idioms beginning with WALL, also see BACK TO THE WALL; BEAT ONE'S HEAD AGAINST THE WALL; BETWEEN YOU AND ME AND THE LAMPPOST (FOUR WALLS); CLIMB THE WALLS; DRIVE SOMEONE CRAZY (UP THE WALL); FLY ON THE WALL; GO TO THE WALL; HANDWRITING ON THE WALL; HOLE IN THE WALL; OFF THE WALL; RUN INTO A STONE WALL.

wallop ♦ See PACK A PUNCH (WALLOP).

walls have ears, the The conversation is easily overheard, someone is listening, as in *Be careful what you say; the walls have ears.* This saying may come from a story about Dionysius of Syracuse (430–367 B.C.), who had an ear-shaped cave cut and connected between the rooms of his palace so that he could hear what was being said from another room. Similar listening posts were installed in other palaces over the centuries, including the

Louvre in Paris. In English the phrase was first recorded in its present form in 1620.

Walter Mitty A person, generally quite ordinary or ineffectual, who indulges in fantastic daydreams of personal triumphs. For example, *He's a Walter Mitty about riding in a rodeo but is actually afraid of horses.* This term comes from James Thurber's short story, *The Secret Life of Walter Mitty* (1939), describing just such a character.

wane ♦ See WAX AND WANE.

want ♦ In addition to the idioms beginning with WANT, also see WASTE NOT, WANT NOT.

want for nothing Not lack any necessities or comforts, as in *He saw to it that his mother wanted for nothing.* This term uses *want* in the sense of "lack." [Mid-1600s]

want in 1. Desire to enter, as in *The cat wants in.* The antonym is **want out**, as in *The dog wants out.* [First half of 1800s] 2. Wish to join a business, project, or other undertaking, as in *Some investors want in but have not yet been admitted.* Again, the antonym is **want out**, as in *Many Quebec residents want out of Canada.* [Mid-1900s]

war ♦ In addition to the idioms beginning with WAR, also see ALL'S FAIR IN LOVE AND WAR; AT WAR; BEEN TO THE WARS; DECLARE WAR; TUG OF WAR.

ward off 1. Turn aside, parry, as in *He tried to ward off her blows.* [Second half of 1500s] 2. Try to prevent, avert, as in *She took vitamin C to ward off a cold.* [Mid-1700s]

war horse Also, **old war horse**. A dependable, frequently performed attraction, as in *The opera company is doing nothing but old war horses this season, like Aïda and La Bohème.* This term originated in the mid-1600s for a military charger that had been through many battles. In the 1800s it began to be used for human veterans, and in the mid-1900s for popular productions, especially of musical works.

warm ♦ In addition to the idioms beginning with WARM, also see COLD HANDS, WARM HEART; LOOK LIKE DEATH (WARMED OVER).

warm as toast Comfortably warm, as in *It was freezing outside, but we were warm as toast in front of the fire.* Despite the British custom of serving toasted bread in a rack that rapidly cools it, this idiom originated in England, at first as *hot as toast* (c. 1430) and by the mid-1800s in its present form.

warm heart ♦ See COLD HANDS, WARM HEART.

warm the bench Also, **ride the bench**. Be a secondary or substitute participant; wait one's turn to participate. For example, *I can't wait till the head of accounting retires; I've been warming the bench for years.* This expression comes from such

sports as baseball and football, and their standard practice of having substitute players sit on a bench in case they are needed in a game. [Slang; early 1900s]

warm the cockles of one's heart Gratify one, make one feel good, as in *It warms the cockles of my heart to see them getting along so well.* This expression uses a corruption of the Latin name for the heart's ventricles, *cochleae cordis.* [Second half of 1600s]

warm up 1. Prepare for exercise or an athletic event by stretching or practicing beforehand, as in *It's important to warm up before you play any sport.* The idiom is also applied to musicians getting ready to perform. [Late 1800s] 2. Make enthusiastic, excited, or animated, as in *He was good at warming up an audience for the main speaker.* [Mid-1800s] 3. Also, **warm up to**. Become friendlier or more receptive toward, as in *I had a hard time warming up to my mother-in-law.* [Early 1800s] 4. Reach a temperature high enough to work efficiently, as in *I'll go out and warm up the car.* [Mid-1900s] 5. Reheat food, as in *If we warm up the leftovers, we'll have enough for everyone* [Mid-1800s] 6. Approach a state of violence or confrontation, as in *Racial tension was rapidly warming up.* Also see HEAT UP.

warm welcome A hearty, hospitable reception or greeting, as in *We got a very warm welcome when we finally arrived.* This expression, dating from the mid-1700s, should not be confused with the similar **warm reception**, which from about 1700 signified a hostile welcome, as in *His rivals were planning a warm reception for him.*

war of nerves A conflict characterized by psychological pressure such as threats and rumors, aiming to undermine an enemy's morale. For example, *Her lawyer said the university had waged a war of nerves to persuade his client to resign.* This expression alludes to tactics used in World War II. [Late 1930s]

warp ♦ In addition to the idiom beginning with WARP, also see TIME WARP.

warp and woof The underlying structure or foundation of something, as in *He foresaw great changes in the warp and woof of the nation's economy.* This expression, used figuratively since the second half of the 1500s, alludes to the threads that run lengthwise (*warp*) and crosswise (*woof*) in a woven fabric.

warpath ♦ See ON THE WARPATH.

warrant ♦ See SIGN ONE'S OWN DEATH WARRANT.

warts and all Including all blemishes, faults, and shortcomings, as in *Rather unwisely, they decided to buy the house, warts and all.* This expression supposedly alludes to Oliver Cromwell's instruction to portrait painter Sir Peter Lely to "remark all these roughness, pimples, warts, and everything as you see me, otherwise I will never pay a farthing for it." [First half of 1600s]

wash ♦ In addition to the idioms beginning with WASH, also see COME OUT IN THE WASH; WON'T WASH.

wash down 1. Clean by washing from top to bottom, as in *He always washes down the walls before painting.* [Second half of 1800s] 2. Drink a liquid after eating food or taking medicine, as in *He washed down the pills with a glass of water.* [c. 1600]

washed out Faded in color; also, lacking animation. For example, *This carpet is all washed out from the sun,* or *He looks all washed out.* [Late 1700s; early 1800s] Also see WASH OUT, def. 3.

washed up ♦ See WASH UP, def. 3.

wash one's dirty linen in public Also **air one's dirty linen** or **laundry**. Expose private matters to public view, especially unsavory secrets. These metaphors are reworkings of a French proverb, *Il faut laver son linge sale en famille* ("One should wash one's dirty linen at home"), which was quoted by Napoleon on his return from Elba (1815). It was first recorded in English in 1867.

wash one's hands of Refuse to accept responsibility for; abandon or renounce. For example, *I've done all I can for him, and now I'm washing my hands of him.* This expression alludes to Pontius Pilate's washing his hands before having Jesus put to death, saying "I am innocent of the blood of this just person" (Matthew 27:24).

wash out 1. Remove or be removed by washing; also, cause to fade by laundering. For example, *Give it to me; I'll wash out that stain,* or *The bleach has really washed out that bright print.* [Mid-1700s] 2. Wear away or be worn away by the flow of water, as in *The river rose and washed out the dam,* or *The road has completely washed out.* [Mid-1700s] 3. Deplete or be depleted of energy, as in *Working on her feet all day just washed her out,* or *I just washed out after that long tennis match.* [Mid-1800s] 4. Eliminate or be eliminated as unsatisfactory, as in *He washed out of medical school after just one year,* or *After only two months as chairman I washed out.* [Colloquial; early 1900s] 5. Cancel owing to bad weather, as in *The picnic was washed out.* [Colloquial; early 1900s] Also see WASHED OUT.

wash up 1. Wash one's hands and face, as in *It's time to wash up for dinner.* [First half of 1900s] Also see CLEAN UP, def. 2. 2. Clean the utensils after a meal, as in *I'll cook dinner if you promise to wash up.* [Mid-1700s] Also see DO THE DISHES. 3. Bring about the end or ruin of; finish. This usage is often used put in the passive, **be washed up,**

as in *She's all washed up as a singer.* [Colloquial; early 1900s]

waste ♦ In addition to the idioms beginning with WASTE, also see GO TO WASTE; HASTE MAKES WASTE; LAY WASTE.

waste away Lose energy and vigor, become enfeebled and weak, as in *She was wasting away before our eyes.* [Late 1300s]

waste not, want not Wise use of one's resources will keep one from poverty. For example, *I just hate to throw out good food—waste not, want not.* This proverbial saying was first recorded in 1772 but had an earlier, even more alliterative version, *willful waste makes woeful want* (1576).

waste one's breath Speak in vain (because no one agrees), as in *Don't waste your breath complaining to the supervisor—it won't help.* This notion was first recorded about 1400 as *wasting words.* The exact idiom was first recorded in 1667. Also see SAVE ONE'S BREATH.

watch ♦ In addition to the idioms beginning with WATCH, also see KEEP WATCH; LOOK (WATCH) OUT; ON THE LOOKOUT (WATCH).

watched pot never boils, a Anxious waiting does not speed up matters, as in *Stop running downstairs for every mail delivery—a watched pot never boils, you know.* This hyperbolic adage reflects the experience of anyone who has ever been in a hurry to bring water to a boil, which eventually occurs but can seem to take forever. [Mid-1800s]

watch it Also, **watch out**. Be careful, as in *Watch it as you go down that ladder,* or *Watch out, there are a lot of cars on this road.* The first term dates from the early 1900s, the variant from the mid-1800s. Also see LOOK OUT.

watch like a hawk Observe very closely, as in *I was watching him like a hawk, but I never did see him take your wallet.* This simile alludes to the hawk's exceptionally keen sight.

watch my dust Also, **watch my smoke**. See how fast I am, or how quickly I'll succeed. For example, *I'm going to turn that investment into my first million, just you watch my dust,* or *I'll make it, just watch my smoke.* The first term alludes to the dust raised by a galloping horse, the second to the smoke generated by an engine. [Colloquial; late 1800s]

watch one's step Exercise caution, as in *You'd better watch your step talking to them about a merger.* Often put as an admonition, this phrase transfers taking care in walking to other kinds of caution. [First half of 1900s]

watch out ♦ See LOOK OUT; WATCH IT.

watch over Guard for protection or safekeeping, as in *There were only two aides watching over that* *large group of children.* This idiom was first recorded in 1526.

water ♦ In addition to the idioms beginning with WATER, also see ABOVE WATER; BACKWATER; BLOOD IS THICKER THAN WATER; BLOW OUT (OF THE WATER); COME ON IN (THE WATER'S FINE); DEAD IN THE WATER; FISH IN TROUBLED WATERS; FISH OUT OF WATER; HEAD ABOVE WATER; HELL OR HIGH WATER; HIGH-WATER MARK; HOLD WATER; HOT WATER; IN DEEP (WATER); KEEP ONE'S HEAD (ABOVE WATER); LIKE WATER OFF A DUCK'S BACK; MAKE ONE'S MOUTH WATER; MUDDY THE WATERS; OF THE FIRST WATER; POUR COLD WATER ON; POUR OIL ON TROUBLED WATERS; STILL WATERS RUN DEEP; TAKE TO (LIKE A DUCK TO WATER); THROW OUT THE BABY WITH THE BATH WATER; TREAD WATER; YOU CAN LEAD A HORSE TO WATER.

water down Dilute or weaken, as in *He watered down that unfavorable report with feeble excuses.* [Mid-1800s]

waterfront ♦ See COVER THE FIELD (WATERFRONT).

Waterloo ♦ See MEET ONE'S WATERLOO.

water over the dam Also, **water under the bridge.** Something that is over and done with, especially an unfortunate occurrence. For example, *Last year's problems with delivery are water over the dam,* or *Never mind that old quarrel; that's water under the bridge.* These metaphoric phrases allude to water that has flowed over a spillway or under a bridge and thus is gone forever. The first term was first recorded in 1797; the variant dates from the late 1800s.

waterworks ♦ See TURN ON THE WATERWORKS.

wave ♦ See MAKE WAVES.

wax ♦ In addition to the idiom beginning with WAX, also see WHOLE BALL OF WAX.

wax and wane Increase and decrease, as in size, number, strength, or intensity, as in *Enrollments in these programs wax and wane from year to year.* This expression alludes to the phases of the moon, with its periodic changes in size. It was first recorded in the 1300s.

way ♦ In addition to the idioms beginning with WAY, also see ALL THE WAY; BY THE WAY; BY WAY OF; CAN'T PUNCH ONE'S WAY OUT OF A PAPER BAG; COME A LONG WAY; COME ONE'S WAY; CUT BOTH WAYS; DOWNHILL ALL THE WAY; EVERY WHICH WAY; FEEL ONE'S WAY; FIND ONE'S WAY; FROM WAY BACK; GET ONE'S WAY; GIVE WAY; GO ALL THE WAY; GO A LONG WAY TOWARD; GO ONE'S WAY; GO OUT OF ONE'S WAY; GO THE WAY OF ALL FLESH; HARD WAY; HAVE A WAY WITH; HAVE IT BOTH WAYS; HAVE ONE'S WAY WITH; IN A BAD WAY; IN A BIG WAY; IN A WAY; IN ONE'S WAY; IN THE FAMILY WAY; IN THE WAY; IN THE WORST WAY; KNOW ALL THE ANSWERS (ONE'S WAY AROUND); LAUGH ALL THE WAY TO THE BANK; LEAD

THE WAY; LOOK THE OTHER WAY; MAKE ONE'S WAY; MAKE WAY; MEND ONE'S WAYS; MORE THAN ONE WAY TO SKIN A CAT; NOT BUILT THAT WAY; NO TWO WAYS ABOUT IT; NO WAY; ONE WAY OR ANOTHER; ON ONE'S WAY; ON THE WAY; ON THE WAY OUT; OTHER WAY ROUND; OUT OF THE WAY; PARTING OF THE WAYS; PAVE THE WAY; PAY ONE'S WAY; PICK ONE'S WAY; PUT IN THE WAY OF; RIGHT OF WAY; RUB THE WRONG WAY; SEE ONE'S WAY TO; SET IN ONE'S WAYS; SHOW THE WAY; TAKE THE WRONG WAY; THAT'S HOW (THE WAY) THE BALL BOUNCES; UNDER WAY; WEND ONE'S WAY; WORK ONE'S WAY.

wayside ♦ See FALL BY THE WAYSIDE.

way the wind blows, which Also, **how the wind blows.** How matters stand, as in *Let's see which way the wind blows before we decide,* or *He's going to find out how the wind blows concerning a promotion.* This metaphoric term for the course of events first appeared in John Heywood's proverb collection of 1546.

way to go Well done, as in *That was a great lecture—way to go!* This exclamation of approval and encouragement originated in sports, addressed to athletes who are performing well. In the 1960s it began to be used for any kind of achievement.

weak ♦ In addition to the idioms beginning with WEAK, also see SPIRIT IS WILLING BUT THE FLESH IS WEAK.

weak as a kitten Feeble and fragile, as in *After that bout with flu she was weak as a kitten.* This simile has largely replaced **weak as a cat,** from the early 1800s.

weak link The least dependable member of a group, as in *The shipping department, slow in getting out orders, is our weak link in customer service,* or *They're all very capable designers except for Ron, who is clearly the weak link.* This expression alludes to the fragile portion of a chain, where it is most likely to break. [Mid-1800s]

weak moment, in a At a time of weakness or little resistance, as in *In a weak moment I agreed to let our son rent a truck.*

weakness ♦ See HAVE A WEAKNESS FOR.

wear ♦ In addition to the idioms beginning with WEAR, also see HAIR SHIRT, WEAR A; IF THE SHOE FITS, WEAR IT; NONE THE WORSE FOR (WEAR); WORSE FOR WEAR.

wear and tear Damage and deterioration resulting from ordinary use and exposure, as in *This sofa shows a lot of wear and tear; we should replace it.* [Second half of 1600s]

wear another hat Also, **wear a different hat** or **two hats; wear more than one hat.** Function in a different or more than one capacity or position, as in *I'm wearing another hat today; yesterday I was a* *housewife, today I'm an attorney,* or *I wear two hats—are you asking me as a member of the city council or as a storeowner?* This metaphoric expression alludes to headgear worn for different occupations. [Mid-1900s]

wear down Diminish, weaken, or tire by relentless pressure, as in *The heels of these shoes are quite worn down,* or *Her constant nagging about getting a new car wore down his resistance.* [First half of 1800s]

wear off Diminish gradually, lose effectiveness, as in *We'll wait till the drug wears off.* [Late 1600s]

wear one's heart on one's sleeve Also, **pin one's heart on one's sleeve.** Openly show one's feelings, especially amorous ones. For example, *You can't help but see how he feels about her; he wears his heart on his sleeve.* This expression alludes to the former custom of tying a woman's favor to her lover's sleeve, thereby announcing their attachment. Shakespeare had it in *Othello* (1:1): "But I will wear my heart upon my sleeve for daws to peck at."

wear out 1. Become or cause to become unusable through long or heavy use, as in *She wears out her shoes in no time,* or *The coupling in this device has worn out.* [Early 1400s] 2. Exhaust, tire, as in *I was worn out from packing all those books.* Also see TIRED OUT. [First half of 1500s]

wear out one's welcome Visit for longer than one's host wants, as in *She wanted to stay another few days but feared she would wear out her welcome.* This expression uses *wear out* in the sense of "exhaust" or "use up." [Mid-1800s]

wear the pants Exercise controlling authority in a household, as in *Grandma wears the pants at our house.* This idiom, generally applied to women and dating from the mid-1500s, a time when they wore only skirts, equates pants with an authoritative and properly masculine role. Originally put as *wear the breeches,* it remains in use despite current fashions.

wear thin 1. Be weakened or diminished gradually, as in *My patience is wearing thin.* [Late 1800s] 2. Become less convincing, acceptable, or popular, as in *His excuses are wearing thin.* [First half of 1900s] Both usages transfer the thinning of a physical object, such as cloth, to nonmaterial characteristics.

wear two hats ♦ See WEAR ANOTHER HAT.

wear well Last under continual or hard use; also, withstand criticism or the test of time. For example, *These boots have worn well,* or *His poetry wears well.* [Mid-1500s]

weasel out Back out of a situation or commitment, especially in a sneaky way. For example, *I'd love to weasel out of serving on the board.* This expression alludes to the stealthy hunting and nest-

ing habits of the weasel, a small, slender-bodied predator. [Colloquial; mid-1900s]

weasel word A word used to deprive a statement of its force or evade a direct commitment, as in *Calling it "organized spontaneity" is using a weasel word; "organized" has sucked the meaning out of "spontaneity."* This idiom may allude to the weasel's habit of sucking the contents out of a bird's egg, so that only the shell remains. [Late 1800s]

weather ♦ In addition to the idiom beginning with WEATHER, also see FAIR-WEATHER FRIEND; HEAVY GOING (WEATHER); KEEP A WEATHER EYE OUT; UNDER THE WEATHER.

weather the storm Survive difficulties, as in *If she can just weather the storm of that contract violation, she'll be fine.* This expression alludes to a ship coming safely through bad weather. [Mid-1600s]

weave in and out Move by twisting and turning or winding in and out, as in *The motorcycle wove in and out of traffic, leaving us far behind.* This expression is a redundancy, since *weave* literally means "intertwine strands of thread."

wedding ♦ See SHOTGUN WEDDING.

wedge ♦ See THIN EDGE OF THE WEDGE.

wedlock ♦ See OUT OF WEDLOCK.

weed out Eliminate as inferior, unsuited, or unwanted, as in *She was asked to weed out the unqualified applicants.* This expression transfers removing weeds from a garden to removing unwanted elements from other enterprises. [First half of 1500s]

wee hours ♦ See SMALL HOURS.

weep buckets Cry copiously, as in *That sad tale of unrequited love always made her weep buckets.* [Colloquial]

weepers ♦ See FINDERS KEEPERS, LOSERS WEEPERS.

weigh down Burden, oppress, as in *Their problems have weighed them down.* This expression transfers bowing under a physical weight to emotional burdens. [c. 1600]

weigh in Be weighed; also, be of a particular weight. For example, *Because it was such a small plane, the passengers and their luggage had to weigh in before takeoff,* or *The fish weighed in at 18 pounds.* [Late 1800s]

weigh on Also, **weigh upon.** Depress, as in *His criticism weighed on her,* or *The long silence began to weigh upon us.* This idiom was first recorded in 1775.

weigh one's words Speak or write with deliberation or considerable care, as in *The doctor weighed his words as he explained her illness.* This term was first recorded in 1340.

weight ♦ See BY WEIGHT; CARRY WEIGHT; DEAD WEIGHT; PULL ONE'S WEIGHT; PUT ON WEIGHT;

THROW ONE'S WEIGHT AROUND; WORTH ONE'S WEIGHT IN GOLD.

welcome ♦ See WARM WELCOME; WEAR OUT ONE'S WELCOME; YOU'RE WELCOME.

welcome mat A friendly welcome, as in *They put out the welcome mat for all new members.* This expression alludes to a doormat with the word "Welcome" printed on it. [Mid-1900s]

welcome to, be Be cordially or freely allowed to, as in *You're most welcome to join us,* or *You're welcome to borrow my boat whenever you like.* [1300s] Also see YOU'RE WELCOME.

well ♦ In addition to the idioms beginning with WELL, also see ALIVE AND KICKING (WELL); ALL'S WELL THAT ENDS WELL; ALL VERY WELL; AS WELL; AS WELL AS; AUGUR WELL FOR; DAMN WELL; DO WELL; FULL WELL; GET WELL; HAIL FELLOW WELL MET; HANGED FOR A SHEEP, MIGHT AS WELL BE; LEAVE WELL ENOUGH ALONE; ONLY TOO (WELL); SIT WELL WITH; THINK A LOT (WELL) OF; TO A FARE-THEE-WELL; VERY WELL; WEAR WELL.

well and good Acceptable, all right, as in *If you can get a better discount elsewhere, well and good.* This redundant phrase was first recorded in 1699.

well off In fortunate circumstances, especially wealthy or prosperous, as in *They're quite well off now.* This phrase may be a shortening of *come well off,* that is, "emerge in good circumstances." [First half of 1600s]

well out of, be Be lucky not to be involved with, as in *You're well out of that marriage; he was never right for you.* This expression is a shortening of *well to be out of.*

well preserved Aging gracefully, still in good condition, as in *I can't believe she's 65; she's certainly well preserved.* [Mid-1800s]

well's run dry, the A supply or resource has been exhausted, as in *There's no more principal left; the well's run dry,* or *There's not another novel in her; the well's run dry.* This expression likens an underground water source to other plentiful sources. Benjamin Franklin used it in *Poor Richard's Almanack* (1757).

wend one's way Proceed along a course, go, as in *It's getting late; we had best wend our way home.* [c. 1400]

west ♦ See GO WEST.

wet ♦ In addition to the idioms beginning with WET, also see ALL WET; GET ONE'S FEET WET; LIKE (WET AS) A DROWNED RAT; MAD AS A HORNET (WET HEN).

wet behind the ears Also, **not dry behind the ears.** Immature, inexperienced, as in *How can you take instructions from Tom? He's still wet behind the ears,* or *Jane's not dry behind the ears yet.* This term

alludes to the fact that the last place to dry in a newborn colt or calf is the indentation behind its ears. [Early 1900s]

wet blanket A person who discourages enjoyment or enthusiasm, as in *Don't be such a wet blanket—the carnival will be fun!* This expression alludes to smothering a fire with a wet blanket. [Early 1800s]

wet one's whistle Have a drink, as in *I'm just going to wet my whistle before I go out on the tennis court.* This expression uses *whistle* in the sense of "mouth" and may allude to the fact that it is very hard to whistle with dry lips. [Late 1300s]

we wuz robbed Also, **we was robbed** or **we were robbed.** We were cheated out of a victory; we were tricked or outsmarted. For example, *That ball was inside the lines—we wuz robbed!* This expression, with its attempt to render nonstandard speech, has been attributed to fight manager Joe Jacobs (1896–1940), who uttered it on June 21, 1932, after his client, Max Schmeling, had clearly outboxed Jack Sharkey, only to have the heavyweight title awarded to Sharkey. It is still used, most often in a sports context.

whack ♦ In addition to the idioms beginning with WHACK, also see HAVE A CRACK (WHACK) AT; OUT OF KILTER (WHACK).

whacked out 1. Tired out, exhausted, as in *They were whacked out after that long flight.* [Slang; mid-1900s] 2. Crazy, especially under the influence of drugs. For example, *She looked whacked out when the police picked her up.* [Slang; mid-1900s]

whack off 1. Cut off, as in *The cook whacked off the fish's head with one blow,* or *The barber whacked off more hair than I wanted him to.* [Slang; first half of 1900s] 2. Masturbate, as in *He went to his room and whacked off.* [Vulgar slang; mid-1900s]

whale away Attack physically or verbally, as in *Our boys whaled away at the enemy,* or *The talk-show host whaled away at the hostile critics.* The word *whale* here does not allude to the ocean mammal, but means "flog" or "thrash." [Mid-1800s]

whale of a time A very enjoyable experience, as in *We had a whale of a time in Puerto Rico.* This idiom alludes to the largest mammal to describe something very large and impressive. [Colloquial; early 1900s]

what ♦ In addition to the idioms beginning with WHAT, also see COME WHAT MAY; FOR ALL ONE IS (WHAT IT'S) WORTH; GET WHAT'S COMING TO ONE; IT'S (WHAT) A ZOO; JUST WHAT THE DOCTOR ORDERED; KNOW THE SCORE (WHAT'S WHAT); LEFT HAND DOESN'T KNOW WHAT THE RIGHT HAND IS DOING; NO MATTER (WHAT); ON EARTH, WHAT; OR WHAT?; PRACTICE WHAT YOU PREACH; SAUCE FOR THE GOOSE IS SAUCE FOR THE GANDER, WHAT'S; SO

WHAT; WHERE'S (WHAT'S) THE BEEF?; YOU KNOW SOMETHING (YOU KNOW WHAT).

what about 1. Would you like, as in *What about another beer?* or *What about a game of bridge?* **2.** What do you think of, as in *So what about renting that white house on the corner?* **3.** Why, concerning what, as in *I need your frank opinion.— What about?* **4. what about it?** What should we do, what course of action should be taken. For example, *We're supposed to be there at noon and bring two sandwiches each—now what about it?* [First half of 1900s] Also see HOW ABOUT.

what do you know What a surprise, as in *What do you know, our suitcases are the first off the plane.* [Early 1900s]

what do you take me for? What sort of person do you think I am? For example, *What do you take me for, an idiot?* This expression dates from the mid-1800s.

whatever ◆ See OR WHATEVER.

what for 1. For what purpose or reason, why, as in *I know you're going to England, but what for?* [Mid-1700s] **2.** A punishment or scolding, as in *You'll get what for from Mom if she catches you smoking,* or *The teacher really gave Bud what for.* [Colloquial; second half of 1800s]

what gives ◆ See WHAT'S COOKING; WHAT'S WITH.

what goes around comes around ◆ See FULL CIRCLE.

what have you What remains and need not be mentioned; and the like. For example, *The display room is full of stereos, TV's, and what have you.* Although first recorded in 1920, this expression uses an archaic form of putting a question (using *have you* instead of *do you have*) as a noun clause, and *what* in the sense of "anything that." The synonym **who knows what** is much older, dating from about 1700; for example, *When we cleaned out the tool shed we found old grass seed, fertilizer, and who knows what other junk.* Also see OF WHATEVER.

what if Suppose that, as in *What if the speaker doesn't get here in time?* This expression is in effect a shortening of "what would happen if." It was first recorded about 1420.

what in the world ◆ See under ON EARTH.

what is more Also, **what's more.** In addition, furthermore, as in *I never got there; what's more, I never really intended to go.* [First half of 1800s]

what it takes The necessary expertise or qualities, as in *She's got what it takes to make a good doctor,* or *Inherited wealth is what it takes to maintain that lifestyle.* This idiom uses *what* in the sense of "that which" and *take* in the sense of "require." [1920s]

what makes one tick What makes one function characteristically, what motivates one, as in *We've never figured out what makes these chess players*

tick. This expression alludes to *tick* in the sense of "function as an operating mechanism, such as a clock." [Colloquial; first half of 1900s]

what of it? Also, **what's it to you?** What does it matter? Also, how does it concern or interest you? For example, *I know I don't need another coat but what of it?—I like this one,* or *What's it to you how many hours I sleep at night?* The first term, a synonym of so WHAT, dates from the late 1500s; the second, another way of saying "mind your own business," dates from the early 1900s.

what's cooking Also, **what's new (with you); what's up; what gives.** What's going on, what is happening, as in *What's cooking at the office these days?* or *What's new at your house?* or *Why are all those cars honking their horns? What's up?* or *Are you really going to France next week? What gives?* The first expression, slang from about 1940, transfers the process of preparing food to other processes. The first variant, a version of "what news are there," dates from the same period and was given added currency by a popular film and song, *What's New, Pussycat?* (1965); the title itself became an idiom for a time, **what's new, pussycat?** The second variant, a colloquialism from the first half of the 1900s, gained currency in the 1940s from *Bugs Bunny* cartoons in which the rabbit repeatedly says "What's up, Doc?" The last variant, **what gives,** may derive from the German equivalent, *Was gibt's?* Slang from about 1940, it is also used to mean "how are you," as in *Hello Jack—what gives?* Also see WHAT'S WITH.

what's done is done There is no changing something; it's finished or final. For example, *I forgot to include my dividend income in my tax return but what's done is done—I've already mailed the form.* This expression uses *done* in the sense of "ended" or "settled," a usage dating from the first half of the 1400s.

what's eating you Also, **what's bugging you.** What is annoying or bothering you? For example, *We've conceded just about every point, so what's eating you now?* or *You're in a terrible mood—what's bugging you?* The first slangy term, dating from the late 1800s, presumably uses *eat* in the sense of "consume"; the colloquial variant, from about 1940, uses *bug* in the sense of "annoy." Also see WHAT'S WITH.

what's it to you ◆ See WHAT OF IT.

what's new ◆ See WHAT'S COOKING.

what's the good of Also, **what's the use of.** What purpose or advantage is there in, as in *What's the good of crying when you can't do anything about it?* or *What's the use of getting a doctorate in philosophy when you won't be able to get a job afterward?* This idiom was first recorded in 1701.

what's the idea Also, **what's the big idea; the very idea.** What do you think you are doing? What foolishness do you have in mind? For example, *What's the idea of taking the car without permission?* or *You've invited yourself along? What's the big idea?* or *Take a two-year-old up Mount Washington? The very idea!* These phrases, all implying the speaker's disapproval, use *idea* in the sense of "what one has in mind." The first two date from about 1900; the third is heard more in Britain than America.

what's the matter What is the difficulty or problem? What troubles or ails you? For example, *You look upset—what's the matter?* or *Can you tell me what's the matter with my car?* This idiom uses *matter* in the sense of "the essence of something," in this case a problem. It was first recorded in 1469. Also see WHAT'S WITH.

what's up ♦ See WHAT'S COOKING.

what's what ♦ See KNOW WHAT'S WHAT.

what's with Also, **what's up with; what gives with.** What is going on with; tell me about or explain it. For example, *What's with all the food they're giving away?* or *What's up with Lee these days?* or *What gives with Jack? Why is he so glum?* This idiom is also sometimes used as a substitute for *how are you* or *what's wrong,* as in *Hi, Pam, what's with you?* or *What gives with you—why are you yelling?* [Colloquial; c. 1940]

what the hell 1. It's not important, who cares, as in *It cost a lot more, but what the hell, we can afford it.* [Second half of 1800s] Also see WHAT OF IT. 2. An intensive of *what,* as in *What the hell do you think you're doing?* [First half of 1800s] Also see under ON EARTH.

what with Taking into consideration, because of, as in *What with all you have to carry, we should take a taxi.* This usage replaced the earlier *what for.* [c. 1600]

wheel ♦ In addition to the idioms beginning with WHEEL, also see ASLEEP AT THE SWITCH (WHEEL); AT THE WHEEL; BIG CHEESE (WHEEL); COG IN THE WHEEL; FIFTH WHEEL; GREASE (OIL) THE WHEELS; HELL ON WHEELS; PUT ONE'S SHOULDER TO THE WHEEL; REINVENT THE WHEEL; SET (WHEELS) IN MOTION; SPIN ONE'S WHEELS; SQUEAKY WHEEL GETS THE GREASE.

wheel and deal Operate or manipulate for one's own interest, especially in an aggressive or unscrupulous way. For example, *Bernie's wheeling and dealing has made him rich but not very popular.* This term comes from gambling in the American West, where a *wheeler-dealer* was a heavy bettor on the roulette wheel and at cards. [Colloquial; c. 1940]

wheels in motion ♦ See under SET IN MOTION.

wheels within wheels Complex interacting processes, agents, or motives, as in *It's difficult to find out just which government agency is responsible; there are wheels within wheels.* This term, which now evokes the complex interaction of gears, may derive from a scene in the Bible (Ezekiel 1:16): "Their appearance and their work was as it were a wheel in the middle of a wheel." [c. 1600]

when ♦ In addition to the idioms beginning with WHEN, also see CROSS A BRIDGE WHEN ONE COMES TO IT; PUSH COMES TO SHOVE, WHEN.

when all's said and done Also, **after all is said and done.** In the end, nevertheless, as in *When all's said and done, the doctors did what they could for Gordon, but he was too ill to survive.* This term was first recorded in 1560.

when in Rome do as the Romans do Follow local custom, as in *Kate said they'd all be wearing shorts or blue jeans to the outdoor wedding, so when in Rome—we'll do the same.* This advice allegedly was Saint Ambrose's answer to Saint Augustine when asked whether they should fast on Saturday as Romans did, or not, as in Milan. It appeared in English by about 1530 and remains so well known that it is often shortened, as in the example.

when it comes to Also, **if** or **when it comes right down to.** As regards, when the situation entails. For example, *When it comes to renting or buying, you'll spend about the same amount.* It is also put as **when it comes down to it** or **that,** as in *If it comes right down to it, they said you could visit any time you're able to,* or *When it comes to that, we can lend you the fare.* This idiom uses *come to* in the sense of "amount to" or "be equivalent to." [Second half of 1700s]

when least expected When something is not awaited, as in *My brother always calls when least expected,* or *You might know that the furnace would break down when least expected—we just had it overhauled.*

when one's back is turned When one is away or not looking, as in *You can count on the children to misbehave when the teacher's back is turned,* or *I don't dare go on vacation; he'll take my job when my back is turned.* Also see WHEN THE CAT'S AWAY, THE MICE WILL PLAY.

when one's ship comes in When one has made one's fortune, as in *When my ship comes in I'll get a Mercedes or better.* This term alludes to ships returning from far-off places with a cargo of valuables. It may be obsolescent. [Mid-1800s]

when pigs fly Never, as in *Sure he'll pay for the drinks—when pigs fly.* Equating the flight of pigs with something impossible dates from the early

1600s, when several writers alleged that pigs fly with their tails forward. The idiom is also put as **pigs may fly.**

when the cat's away, the mice will play Without supervision, people will do as they please, especially in disregarding or breaking rules. For example, *As soon as their parents left, the children invited all their friends over—when the cat's away, you know.* This expression has been a proverb since about 1600 and is so well known it is often shortened, as in the example.

when the chips are down When a situation is urgent or desperate, as in *When the chips were down, all the children came home to help their mother.* This expression comes from poker, where *chips* represent money being bet. When all the bets have been made, and the chips put down, the hand is over and the players turn up their cards to see who has won. [Late 1800s]

when the dust has settled Also, **after** or **once the dust settles.** When matters have calmed down, as in *The merger is complete, and when the dust has settled we can start on new projects.* This idiom uses *dust* in the sense of "turmoil" or "commotion," a usage dating from the first half of the 1800s.

when the going gets tough, the tough get going ♦ See under GET GOING, def. 2.

when the shit hits the fan ♦ See SHIT WILL HIT THE FAN.

where ♦ In addition to the idioms beginning with WHERE, also see CLOSE TO HOME (HIT WHERE ONE LIVES); FOOLS RUSH IN WHERE ANGELS FEAR TO TREAD; GIVE CREDIT (WHERE CREDIT IS DUE); KNOW WHERE ONE STANDS; LET THE CHIPS FALL WHERE THEY MAY; NOT KNOW WHERE TO TURN; PUT ONE'S MONEY WHERE ONE'S MOUTH IS; TAKE UP WHERE ONE LEFT OFF; TELL SOMEONE WHERE TO GET OFF; THIS IS WHERE I CAME IN.

where do we go from here Given the present situation, what should we do next? For example, *Unemployment's rising and numerous banks have failed; where do we go from here?* This phrase originated about 1945 and is most often applied to a political, economic, social, or moral state of the country, of a business, or the like.

wherefore ♦ See WHYS AND WHEREFORES.

where it's at Also, **where the action is.** The key center of activity; where important things are happening. For example, *He decided to set up his store here, convinced that this is where it's at,* or *I'm going into the brokerage business; that's where the action is these days.* The action or activity in this phrase can relate to just about anything—financial, political, social, or commercial. [Slang; c. 1960]

where one is coming from What one means, from one's point of view, based on one's background or prior experience. For example, *I don't believe in capital punishment, but as a pacifist you know where I'm coming from.* [Second half of 1900s]

where one lives ♦ See under CLOSE TO HOME.

where's the beef? 1. Also, **what's the beef?** What is the source of a complaint, as in *Where's the beef? No one was hurt in the accident.* This usage employs *beef* in the sense of a "complaint" or "grudge," also appearing in the phrase **have no beef with,** meaning "have no quarrel with." [Slang; late 1800s] **2.** Where is the content or substance, as in *That was a very articulate speech, but where's the beef?* This usage was originally the slogan for a television commercial for a hamburger chain attacking the poor quality of rival chains. (1984) The phrase was almost immediately transferred to other kinds of substance, especially in politics.

where's the fire What's the big hurry, as in *We've got to finish up.—Why, where's the fire?* This phrase, generally addressed to someone in an unseemly rush (such as a speeding motorist pulled over by a police officer), alludes to firemen hurrying to put out a fire. [Slang; 1920]

where there's a will, there's a way If one really wants to do something, one can. For example, *Max has no idea of how to get the money to repair his boat, but where there's a will.* This proverb was stated slightly differently in 1640 (*To him that will, ways are not wanting*) but has been repeated in its present form since the early 1800s. It is so well known it is often shortened, as in the example.

where there's smoke ♦ See NO SMOKE WITHOUT FIRE.

whether ♦ In addition to the idiom beginning with WHETHER, also see NOT KNOW WHETHER.

whether or not Also, **whether or no.** Regardless of whether, no matter if. For example, *Whether or not it rains, we're going to walk to the theater,* or *She plans to sing at the wedding, whether or no anyone asks her to.* The negative element in these constructions may also follow the subject and verb, as in *I have to attend, whether I want to or not.* [c. 1600]

whet one's appetite Arouse one's interest or eagerness, as in *That first Schubert piece whetted my appetite; I hope she sings some others.* This idiom, first recorded in 1612, transfers making one hungry for food to other kinds of eagerness.

which ♦ In addition to the idioms beginning with WHICH, also see EVERY WHICH WAY; KNOW WHICH SIDE OF BREAD IS BUTTERED; (WHICH) WAY THE WIND BLOWS.

which is which What particular one is what particular one, or what is the difference between different ones. For example, *These twins look so much alike I can't tell which is which,* or *Both our raincoats are tan; do you know which is which?* This idiom was first recorded about 1412.

which way the wind blows ◆ See WAY THE WIND BLOWS.

while ◆ In addition to the idioms beginning with WHILE, also see ALL THE TIME (WHILE); A WHILE BACK; EVERY NOW AND THEN (ONCE IN A WHILE); FIDDLE WHILE ROME BURNS; GET OUT WHILE THE GETTING IS GOOD; IN A WHILE; MAKE HAY WHILE THE SUN SHINES; ONCE IN A WHILE; QUIT WHILE YOU'RE AHEAD; STRIKE WHILE THE IRON'S HOT; WORTH ONE'S WHILE.

while away Spend time idly or pleasantly, as in *It was a beautiful day and we whiled away the hours in the garden.* This expression is the only surviving use of the verb *while,* meaning "to spend time." [First half of 1600s]

while back ◆ See A WHILE BACK.

while there's life there's hope Also, **where there's life there's hope.** So long as someone or something ailing is alive, there is hope for recovery. For example, *The company has survived previous recessions; while there's life there's hope.* A statement made about dying individuals since ancient times, it was cited in numerous proverb collections from 1539 on. Today it is also applied to inanimate matters.

whip ◆ In addition to the idiom beginning with WHIP, also see CRACK THE WHIP; LICK (WHIP) INTO SHAPE; SMART AS A WHIP; UPPER (WHIP) HAND.

whipping boy A scapegoat, as in *This department's always been the whipping boy when things don't go well.* This expression alludes to the former practice of keeping a boy to be whipped in place of a prince who was to be punished. [Early 1900s]

whip up 1. Arouse, excite, as in *The speaker whipped up the mob.* [Early 1800s] **2.** Prepare quickly, as in *I can easily whip up some lunch.* This usage was first recorded in 1611.

whirl ◆ See GIVE SOMETHING A WHIRL.

whisker ◆ See BY A HAIR (WHISKER); WIN BY A NOSE (WHISKER).

whisper ◆ See STAGE WHISPER.

whispering campaign A deliberate spreading of derogatory rumors about a candidate, as in *That whispering campaign destroyed his chances for election.* [c. 1920]

whistle ◆ In addition to the idioms beginning with WHISTLE, also see BLOW THE WHISTLE ON; CLEAN AS A WHISTLE; SLICK AS A WHISTLE; WET ONE'S WHISTLE.

whistle Dixie Engage in unrealistic, hopeful fantasizing, as in *If you think you can drive there in two hours, you're whistling Dixie.* This idiom alludes to the song "Dixie" and the vain hope that the Confederacy, known as *Dixie,* would win the Civil War.

whistle for Ask for or expect without any prospect of success, as in *If you want a cash refund, you can just whistle for it.* [Mid-1700s]

whistle in the dark Summon up courage in a frightening situation, make a show of bravery. For example, *They knew they were lost and were just whistling in the dark.* This expression alludes to a literal attempt to keep up one's courage. [First half of 1900s]

white ◆ In addition to the idioms beginning with WHITE, also see BLACK AND WHITE; BLEED SOMEONE WHITE; GREAT WHITE HOPE; SHOW THE WHITE FEATHER.

white as a sheet Very pale in the face, as in *She was white as a sheet after that near encounter.* This simile, dating from about 1600, survives despite the fact that bedsheets now come in all colors.

white elephant An unwanted or useless item, as in *The cottage at the lake had become a real white elephant—too run down to sell, yet costly to keep up,* or *Grandma's ornate silver is a white elephant; no one wants it but it's too valuable to discard.* This expression comes from a legendary former Siamese custom whereby an albino elephant, considered sacred, could only be owned by the king. The king would bestow such an animal on a subject with whom he was displeased and wait until the high cost of feeding the animal, which could not be slaughtered, ruined the owner. The story was told in England in the 1600s, and in the 1800s the term began to be used figuratively.

white feather ◆ See SHOW THE WHITE FEATHER.

white flag, show the Also, **hang out** or **hoist the white flag.** Surrender, yield, as in *Our opponents held all the cards tonight, so we showed the white flag and left early.* This expression alludes to the white flag indicating a surrender in battle, a custom apparently dating from Roman times and adopted as an international symbol of surrender or truce. [Late 1600s]

white lie An untruth told to spare feelings or from politeness, as in *She asked if I liked her dress, and of course I told a white lie.* This term uses *white* in the sense of "harmless." [First half of 1700s]

white sale A special offering of towels, bed linens and similar goods, not necessarily white-colored. For example, *The big stores always have white sales in January.* [c. 1900]

within reach ◆ See IN REACH.

who knows what ◆ See under WHAT HAVE YOU.

whole ◆ In addition to the idioms beginning with WHOLE, also see AS A WHOLE; GO WHOLE HOG; ON THE WHOLE; OUT OF WHOLE CLOTH.

whole ball of wax, the Also, **the whole enchilada** or **shooting match** or **shebang**. Everything, all the elements, the entire affair. For example, *The union demanded higher wages, a pension plan, job security—the whole ball of wax,* or *The contract includes paperback rights, film rights, electronic media—the whole enchilada,* or *She lost her job, her pension, her health-care coverage, the whole shooting match.* Not all the allusions in these slangy terms are clear. *Ball of wax* may refer to a 17th-century English legal practice whereby land was divided among heirs by covering scraps of paper representing portions of land with wax, rolling each into a ball, and drawing the balls from a hat. An *enchilada* combines several foods inside a tortilla; a *shooting match* denotes a shooting competition; and a *shebang* is a rude hut or shelter. The first two of these slangy terms date from the second half of the 1900s, the last two from the late 1800s. For synonyms, see WHOLE KIT AND CABOODLE; WHOLE MEGILLAH.

whole hog ◆ See GO WHOLE HOG.

whole kit and caboodle, the Everything, every part, as in *He packed up all his gear, the whole kit and caboodle, and walked out.* This expression is a redundancy, for *kit* has meant "a collection or group" since the mid-1700s (though this meaning survives only in the full idiom today), and *caboodle* has been used with the same meaning since the 1840s. In fact *caboodle* is thought to be a corruption of the phrase *kit and boodle,* another redundant phrase, since *boodle* also meant "a collection."

whole megillah Also, **whole schmeer**. Everything, every aspect or element, as in *The accountant went through the whole megillah all over again,* or *Her divorce lawyer took him for the house, the car, the whole schmeer.* The first term alludes to the *Megillah,* five books of the Bible read on certain Jewish feast days and considered by some to be very long and tedious. *Schmeer* is Yiddish for "smear" or "smudge." [Slang; second half of 1900s]

whole new ballgame, a A completely altered situation, as in *It will take a year to reassign the staff, and by then some will have quit and we'll have a whole new ballgame.* This expression comes from baseball, where it signifies a complete turn of events, as when the team that was ahead falls behind. [Colloquial; 1960s]

whole nine yards, the Everything that is relevant; the whole thing. For example, *He decided to take everything to college—his books, his stereo, his computer, his skis, the whole nine yards.* The source of this expression is not known, but there are several possibilities: the amount of cloth required to make a complete suit of clothes; the fully set sails of a three-masted ship where each mast carries three yards, that is, spars, to support the sails; or the amount of cement (in cubic yards) contained in a cement mixer for a big construction job. [Colloquial]

whole shebang Also, **whole shooting match**. ◆ See WHOLE BALL OF WAX.

whoop it up 1. Also, **make whoopee**. Celebrate noisily, as in *After exams they decided to whoop it up at their apartment,* or *Down in the basement the residents were making whoopee.* The variant may be dying out. [Slang; late 1800s] 2. Arouse enthusiasm, especially politically, as in *The volunteers' job is to whoop it up for the candidate.* [Slang; late 1800s]

who's who The outstanding or best-known individuals of a group, as in *Tonight's concert features a veritable who's who of musicians.* This expression comes from the name of a famous reference work, *Who's Who,* first published in 1849, which contains biographical sketches of famous individuals and is regularly updated. Its name in turn was based on **who is who,** that is, the identity of each of a number of persons, a phrase dating from the late 1300s. [Early 1900s]

whys and wherefores All the underlying causes and reasons, as in *She went into the whys and wherefores of the adoption agency's rules and procedures.* This idiom today is a redundancy since *why* and *wherefore* mean the same thing. Formerly, however, *why* indicated the reason for something and *wherefore* how it came to be. [c. 1600]

wide ◆ In addition to the idioms beginning with WIDE, also see ALL WOOL AND A YARD WIDE; CUT A WIDE SWATH; FAR AND WIDE; GIVE A WIDE BERTH TO; LAY (ONESELF WIDE) OPEN; LEAVE (WIDE) OPEN; OFF (WIDE OF) THE MARK.

wide awake Fully awake; also, very alert. For example, *He lay there, wide awake, unable to sleep,* or *She was wide awake to all the possibilities.* The *wide* in this idiom alludes to the eyes being wide open. [Early 1800s]

wide open 1. Unresolved, unsettled, as in *The fate of that former colony is still wide open.* [Mid-1900s] 2. Unprotected or vulnerable, as in *That remark about immigrants left him wide open to hostile criticism.* This expression originated in boxing, where it signifies being off one's guard and open to an opponent's punches. It began to be used more broadly about 1940. Also see LEAVE OPEN.

widow ◆ See GRASS WIDOW.

wife ◆ See under WIVES.

wig ◆ In addition to the idiom beginning with WIG, also see FLIP ONE'S LID (WIG).

wig out Become or make wildly excited or irrational, as in *He'll wig out when he gets the bill for that party.* This idiom probably alludes to the earlier *flip one's wig* (see under FLIP ONE'S LID). [Slang; c. 1950] also see FREAK OUT, def. 2.

wild ♦ In addition to the idioms beginning with WILD, also see GO HOG WILD; GO WILDING; RUN AMOK (WILD); SOW ONE'S WILD OATS.

wild about, be Be highly excited or enthusiastic about, as in *She was just wild about that jazz band.* This usage replaced the slightly earlier *wild after.* [Second half of 1800s]

wild card An unpredictable person or event, as in *Don't count on his support—he's a wild card,* or *A traffic jam? That's a wild card we didn't expect.* This expression comes from card games, especially poker, where it refers to a card that can stand for any rank chosen by the player who holds it. The term was adopted in sports for an additional player or team chosen to take part in a contest after the regular places have been taken. It is also used in computer terminology for a symbol that stands for one or more characters in searches for files that share a common specification. Its figurative use dates from the mid-1900s.

wildfire ♦ See SPREAD LIKE WILDFIRE.

wild goose chase A futile search or pursuit, as in *I think she sent us on a wild goose chase looking for their beach house.* This idiom originally referred to a form of 16th-century horseracing requiring riders to follow a leader in a particular formation (presumably resembling a flock of geese in flight). Its figurative use dates from about 1600.

wild horses couldn't drag me Nothing could induce or persuade me, as in *Wild horses couldn't drag me to that nightclub.* This idiom, always in negative form, is believed to have replaced *wild horses couldn't draw it from me,* referring to the medieval torture of using horses to stretch a prisoner and thereby force a confession. [First half of 1800s]

wild oats ♦ See SOW ONE'S WILD OATS.

wild pitch A careless statement or action, as in *Calling comic books great literature—that's a wild pitch.* This term comes from baseball, where it signifies a pitched ball so far off target that the catcher misses it, enabling a base runner to advance. [Mid-1900s]

will ♦ In addition to the idiom beginning with WILL, also see AGAINST ONE'S WILL; AT WILL; BOYS WILL BE BOYS; HEADS (WILL) ROLL; MURDER WILL OUT; OF ONE'S OWN ACCORD (FREE WILL); SHIT WILL HIT THE FAN; THAT WILL DO; TIME WILL TELL; TRUTH WILL OUT; WHEN THE CAT'S AWAY, MICE WILL PLAY; WHERE THERE'S A WILL; WITH A WILL; WITH THE BEST WILL IN THE WORLD; WONDERS WILL NEVER CEASE.

willies ♦ See under THE CREEPS.

willing ♦ See READY, WILLING, AND ABLE; SPIRIT IS WILLING BUT THE FLESH IS WEAK.

will not hear of ♦ See NOT HAVE IT.

win ♦ In addition to the idioms beginning with WIN, also see (WIN) HANDS DOWN; NO-WIN SITUATION; SLOW BUT SURE (STEADY WINS THE RACE); YOU CAN'T WIN; YOU CAN'T WIN 'EM ALL.

win by a nose Also, **win by a whisker.** Just barely succeed, as in *Sally's political cartoon came in first in the contest, but I heard that she won by a nose.* This term comes from horseracing, where from about 1900 on it referred to a finish so close that only a portion of the horse's nose reached the finish ahead of the second horse. *A whisker*—that is, a hair—is a narrower margin yet. [Second half of 1900s]

wind ♦ In addition to the idioms beginning with WIND, also see BEFORE THE WIND; BREAK WIND; GET WIND OF; GONE WITH THE WIND; ILL WIND; IN THE WIND; LIKE GREASED LIGHTNING (THE WIND); SAIL CLOSE TO THE WIND; SECOND WIND; SOMETHING IN THE WIND; STRAW IN THE WIND; TAKE THE WIND OUT OF ONE'S SAILS; THREE SHEETS TO THE WIND; THROW CAUTION TO THE WINDS; TWIST IN THE WIND; WAY THE WIND BLOWS.

wind down Diminish gradually, draw to a close, as in *By midnight the party had wound down.* [Mid-1900s] Also see WIND UP.

windmill ♦ See TILT AT WINDMILLS.

window ♦ See OUT THE WINDOW.

wind up 1. Come or bring to a finish, as in *The party was winding up, so we decided to leave,* or *Let's wind up the meeting and get back to work.* [Early 1800s] Also see WIND DOWN. 2. Put in order, settle, as in *She had to wind up her affairs before she could move.* [Late 1700s] 3. Arrive somewhere following a course of action, end up, as in *We got lost and wound up in another town altogether,* or *If you're careless with your bank account, you can wind up overdrawn.* [Colloquial; early 1900s]

wine ♦ In addition to the idiom beginning with WINE, also see NEW WINE IN OLD BOTTLES.

wine and dine Entertain someone or treat someone to a fine meal, as in *The company likes to wine and dine visiting scientists.* [Colloquial; mid-1800s]

wing ♦ In addition to the idiom beginning with WING, also see CLIP SOMEONE'S WINGS; IN THE WINGS; LEFT WING; ON THE WING; SPREAD ONE'S WINGS; TAKE FLIGHT (WING); UNDER SOMEONE'S WING.

wing it Improvise, as in *The interviewer had not read the author's book; he was just winging it.* This expression comes from the theater, where it alludes to an actor studying his part in the wings (the areas to either side of the stage) because he has been suddenly called on to replace another. First recorded in 1885, it eventually was extended to other kinds of improvisation based on unpreparedness.

win hands down Also, **win in a walk** or **breeze.** ♦ See under HANDS DOWN.

wink ♦ In addition to the idiom beginning with WINK, also see FORTY WINKS; QUICK AS A WINK; SLEEP A WINK.

wink at Deliberately overlook, pretend not to see, as in *Sometimes it's wise to wink at a friend's shortcomings.* This idiom, first recorded in 1537, uses *wink* in the sense of "close one's eyes."

winning streak A series of consecutive successes, a run of good luck, as in *Our son-in-law has been on a winning streak with his investment.* This expression comes from gambling. [Mid-1900s]

win one's spurs Gain a position or attain distinction through hard work or some special accomplishment. For example, *After two years of freelancing, she won her spurs as a programmer and was hired for the top job.* This expression originally alluded to being knighted for some act of bravery and was being used figuratively by the mid-1500s.

win on points Succeed but barely, especially by a technicality. For example, *Both sides were forceful in that argument about the embargo, but I think the senator won on points.* This term comes from boxing, where in the absence of a knockout the winner is decided on the basis of points awarded for each round. Its figurative use dates from the mid-1900s.

win out Succeed, prevail, as in *She was sure she'd win out if she persisted.* [Late 1800s]

win over Persuade, gain one's support, as in *It won't be easy to win him over to our point of view.* [Late 1800s]

win some, lose some It's not possible to win all the time, as in *The coach was philosophical about our being shut out, saying "Win some, lose some."* This expression, generally uttered about a loss, originated in the early 1900s among gamblers who bet on sporting events. A variant, **win some, lose some, some rained out**, suggests that the idiom comes from baseball. Its figurative use dates from the 1940s. Also see YOU CAN'T WIN 'EM ALL.

win through Also, **win the day.** End successfully, be victorious, as in *We didn't know until the very end if they would win through,* or *It seems that hard work won the day.* The first term dates from the late 1800s and today is more often put as COME THROUGH (def. 1). The variant originally alluded to the outcome of a battle and dates from the late 1500s.

wipe ♦ In addition to the idioms beginning with WIPE, also see MOP UP (WIPE) THE FLOOR WITH; SETTLE (WIPE OUT) AN OLD SCORE.

wipe off the map Also, **wipe off the face of the earth.** Eliminate completely, as in *Some day we*

hope to wipe malaria off the map. This idiom uses *wipe* in the sense of "obliterate," and *map* and *face* of the earth in the sense of "everywhere."

wipe out 1. Destroy, as in *The large chains are wiping out the independent bookstores.* Originally put simply as *wipe*, the idiom acquired *out* in the first half of the 1800s. **2.** Kill; also, murder. For example, *The entire crew was wiped out in the plane crash,* or *The gangsters threatened to wipe him and his family out.* [Late 1800s]

wipe the slate clean ♦ See under CLEAN SLATE.

wire ♦ See DOWN TO THE WIRE; GET ONE'S WIRES CROSSED; LIVE WIRE; PULL STRINGS (WIRES); UNDER THE WIRE.

wise ♦ In addition to the idioms beginning with WISE, also see GET WISE TO; NONE THE WISER; PENNY WISE AND POUND FOOLISH; PUT WISE; SADDER BUT WISER; WORD TO THE WISE.

wise guy An obnoxious know-it-all, a person who makes sarcastic or annoying remarks, as in *The teacher was delighted that the worst wise guy in the class was moving out of town.* [Slang; second half of 1800s] Also see SMART ALECK.

wise up to Make or become aware, informed or sophisticated, as in *It's time someone wised you up to Mary; she's an incorrigible first,* or *As soon as Tony wised up to what the company was doing, he quit.* [Slang; early 1900s] Also see PUT WISE.

wish ♦ In addition to the idiom beginning with WISH, also see IF WISHES WERE HORSES.

wishful thinking Interpreting matters as one would like them to be, as opposed to what they really are. For example, *Matthew wanted to be a basketball player, but with his height that was wishful thinking.* This term comes from Freudian psychology of the mid-1920s and soon began to be used more loosely.

wish on Foist or impose something on another, as in *I wouldn't wish this job on my worst enemy.* [Early 1900s]

wit ♦ See AT ONE'S WIT'S END; HAVE ONE'S WITS ABOUT ONE; LIVE BY ONE'S WITS; SCARE OUT OF ONE'S WITS; TO WIT.

witching hour Midnight, as in *They arrived just at the witching hour.* This term alludes to older superstitions concerning a time appropriate to witchcraft and other supernatural occurrences. Shakespeare and others wrote of "the witching time of night." The precise phrase was first recorded in 1835.

with ♦ In addition to the idioms beginning with WITH, also see ALIVE WITH; ALL OVER WITH; ALL RIGHT WITH; ALL UP (WITH); ALONG WITH; AT HOME (WITH); AT ODDS (WITH); AT ONE (WITH); BEAR WITH; BORN WITH A SILVER SPOON; BOTH BARRELS, WITH; BOUND UP IN (WITH); BREAK WITH; BURST WITH; CAN DO WITH; CAN'T DO ANYTHING WITH;

CAST ONE'S LOT WITH; CAUGHT WITH ONE'S PANTS DOWN; CHARGE WITH; CLEAR WITH; COME DOWN WITH; COME OUT WITH; COME TO GRIPS WITH; COME TO TERMS WITH; COME UP WITH; COME WITH THE TERRITORY; COOK WITH GAS; DAMN WITH FAINT PRAISE; DEAL WITH; DIE WITH ONE'S BOOTS ON; DISPENSE WITH; DO AWAY WITH; DOWN WITH; FALL IN WITH; FENCE WITH; FIGHT FIRE WITH FIRE; FIT IN (WITH); FIX UP WITH; GET ALONG WITH; GET AN IN WITH; GET AWAY WITH; GET EVEN WITH; GET INVOLVED WITH; GET IN WITH; GET ON (WITH IT); GET OVER (WITH); GET TOGETHER (WITH); GET TOUGH WITH; GO ALONG (WITH); GO HALVES WITH; GO HARD WITH; GONE WITH THE WIND; GO OUT (WITH); GO THROUGH (WITH); GO TO BED WITH; GO WITH; GO WITH THE FLOW; GREEN WITH ENVY; HANDLE WITH GLOVES; HAVE A BRUSH WITH; HAVE A WAY WITH; HAVE A WORD WITH; HAVE DONE (WITH); HAVE NO TRUCK WITH; HAVE PULL WITH; HAVE TO DO WITH; HAVE WORDS WITH; HOLD WITH; IN BAD WITH; IN GOOD WITH; IN LEAGUE WITH; IN (WITH) REGARD TO; IN TROUBLE WITH; IN WITH; IT'S ALL OVER WITH; KEEP UP WITH; KILL WITH KINDNESS; LAUGH AND THE WORLD LAUGHS WITH YOU; LEAD WITH ONE'S CHIN; LEARN TO LIVE WITH; LEVEL WITH; LIE WITH; LIKE A CHICKEN WITH ITS HEAD CUT OFF; OVER AND DONE WITH; OVER WITH; PAL AROUND WITH; PART WITH; PLAY BALL (WITH); PLAY THE DEVIL WITH; PLAY WITH FIRE; PUT UP WITH; RECKON WITH; ROLL WITH THE PUNCHES; RUB ELBOWS WITH; RUN AROUND (WITH); RUN AWAY WITH; RUN OFF WITH; RUN WITH; SADDLE SOMEONE WITH; SEE WITH HALF AN EYE; SETTLE WITH; SHAKE HANDS WITH; SHAKE WITH LAUGHTER; SIDE WITH; SIGN ON WITH; SIT WELL WITH; SLEEP WITH; SPAR WITH; SQUARE WITH; STAND UP WITH; STAY WITH; STICK WITH; STUCK WITH; SWIM WITH THE TIDE; TAKE ISSUE WITH; TAKEN WITH; TAKE THE BITTER WITH THE SWEET; TAKE THE ROUGH WITH THE SMOOTH; TAKE UP WITH; TAMPER WITH; TARRED WITH THE SAME BRUSH; TAX WITH; TEAM UP WITH; TINKER WITH; TOGETHER WITH; TO HELL WITH; TOP OFF (WITH); TO START WITH; TOY WITH; TROUBLE ONE'S HEAD WITH; VOTE WITH ONE'S FEET; WALK OFF WITH; WHAT'S WITH; WHAT WITH; YOU CAN'T TAKE IT WITH YOU.

with a grain of salt Also, **with a pinch of salt.** Skeptically, with reservations. For example, *I always take Sandy's stories about illnesses with a grain of salt—she tends to exaggerate.* This expression is a translation of the Latin *cum grano salis,* which Pliny used in describing Pompey's discovery of an antidote for poison (to be taken with a grain of salt). It was soon adopted by English writers.

with all due respect Although I think highly of you, as in *With all due respect, you haven't really answered my question,* or *With all due respect, that ac-*

count doesn't fit the facts. This phrase always precedes a polite disagreement with what a person has said or brings up a controversial point. [c. 1800]

with all one's heart With great willingness or pleasure; also, with the deepest feeling or devotion. For example, *I wish you well with all my heart.* [Late 1400s]

with an eye to ♦ See HAVE ONE'S EYE ON, def. 2.

with a vengeance With great violence or energy; also, to an extreme degree. For example, *The cottage was filthy and Ruth began cleaning with a vengeance,* or *December has turned cold with a vengeance.* This expression was first recorded in 1533. Also see WITH A WILL.

with a view to For the purpose of, aiming toward, as in *A-frame houses were designed with a view to shedding heavy snow.* This idiom was first recorded in 1728.

with a will Vigorously, energetically, as in *He started pruning with a will.* This term, first recorded in 1848, uses *will* in the sense of "determination."

with bad grace Reluctantly, rudely, as in *He finally agreed to share the cost, but with bad grace.* [Mid-1700s] Also see WITH GOOD GRACE.

with bated breath Eagerly or anxiously, as in *We waited for the announcement of the winner with bated breath.* This expression literally means "holding one's breath" (*bate* means "restrain"). Today it is also used somewhat ironically, indicating one is not all that eager or anxious. [Late 1500s] Also see HOLD ONE'S BREATH, def. 2.

with bells on Ready to celebrate, eagerly, as in *Of course I'll come; I'll be there with bells on.* This metaphoric expression alludes to decorating oneself or one's clothing with little bells for some special performance or occasion. A well-known nursery rhyme has: "See a fine lady upon a white horse, Rings on her fingers and bells on her toes, And she shall have music wherever she goes" (in *Gammer Gurton's Garland,* 1784).

wither on the vine Fail to come to fruition, as in *This building project will wither on the vine if they don't agree on a price.* This expression alludes to grapes shriveling and drying up because they were not picked when ripe.

with flying colors, pass with Also, **come through with flying colors.** Win, succeed, as in *She came through the bar exam with flying colors.* This expression alludes to a victorious ship sailing with its flags high. [Late 1600s]

with good grace Willingly, pleasantly, as in *They had tried hard to win but accepted their loss with good grace.* [Mid-1700s] Also see WITH BAD GRACE.

with half a heart ♦ See HALF A HEART.

within ♦ In addition to the idioms beginning with WITHIN, also see IN (WITHIN) REASON; SPITTING DISTANCE, WITHIN; WHEELS WITHIN WHEELS.

within an ace of Also, **within an inch of.** Very close to, within a narrow margin of, as in *We were within an ace of calling you, but we'd lost your phone number,* or *We were within an inch of buying tickets for that concert.* The first term refers to the *ace* of dice, that is, the one pip on a die. The lowest number one can throw with a *pair* of dice is two (two aces), a throw that is within an ace of one. The term began to be used for other kinds of near miss by about 1700.

within bounds Reasonable and allowable, up to a certain point, as in *It's all right to play your stereo, but please keep the volume within bounds.* Like its antonym, OUT OF BOUNDS, this term originally referred to the boundaries of a playing area or field.

within call Also, **within hail.** Near enough to hear a summons, as in *Tommy's allowed to play outside but only within call of his mother,* or *We told them they could bike ahead of us but to stay within hail.* The first term was first recorded in 1668, the variant in 1697.

within reason ♦ See IN REASON.

with interest With more than what one should receive, extra, and then some. For example, *Mary borrowed Jane's new dress without asking, but Jane paid her back with interest—she drove off in Mary's car.* This idiom alludes to *interest* in the financial sense. Its figurative use dates from the late 1500s.

with it, be Also, **get with it.** Be or become knowledgeable about the current or latest trends, fashions, or ideas, as in *She just turned 60, but she's still very much with it,* or *Get with it, Dad, that kind of razor hasn't been made for years.* [Slang; 1920s]

with one arm tied behind one's back Also, **with one hand; with one's eyes closed.** Very easily, as in *I can assemble that chair with one arm tied behind my back,* or *I could make a better dinner with one hand,* or *He can do that puzzle with his eyes closed.* All these phrases are hyperbolic. Also see DO BLINDFOLDED.

with one's eyes open Fully aware, as in *We started this project with our eyes open and are not surprised at the results.* [First half of 1900s] Also see KEEP ONE'S EYES OPEN.

with one's pants down ♦ See CAUGHT WITH ONE'S PANTS DOWN.

with one voice Unanimously, in complete agreement, as in *The board rejected the proposal with one voice.* [Late 1300s] For synonyms, see AS ONE; TO A MAN.

with open arms Enthusiastically, warmly, as in *They received their new daughter-in-law with* open arms. This term alludes to an embrace. [Mid-1600s]

without ♦ In addition to the idioms beginning with WITHOUT, also see ABSENT WITHOUT LEAVE; DO WITHOUT; GET ALONG WITHOUT; GO WITHOUT SAYING; NO SMOKE WITHOUT FIRE; WORLD WITHOUT END.

without a leg to stand on With no chance of success, as in *He tried to get the town to change the street lights, but because there was no money in the budget he found himself without a leg to stand on.* A related idiom is **not have a leg to stand on,** as in *Once the detective exposed his false alibi, he didn't have a leg to stand on.* This metaphoric idiom transfers lack of physical support to arguments or theories. [Late 1500s]

without a stitch on Naked, as in *They let their baby run around outside without a stitch on.* A related phrase is **not have a stitch on.** These expressions use *stitch* in the sense of "a piece of clothing," a usage dating from the early 1800s.

without batting an eye Showing no emotion, acting as though nothing were unusual. For example, *Richard ate the snails without batting an eye.* A related phrase is **not bat an eye,** as in *He didn't bat an eye when she told him he was being laid off.* These expressions, which use *bat* in the sense of "blink," date from about 1900.

without doubt Also, **without a doubt.** ♦ See NO DOUBT.

without fail For certain, as in *That check will arrive tomorrow morning without fail.* This idiom today is used mainly to strengthen a statement. [Early 1700s]

without further ado Also, **without more ado.** Without more work, ceremony, or fuss. For example, *Without further ado they adjourned the meeting and went home,* or *And now, without more ado, here is our speaker of the day.* This idiom has one of the few surviving uses of the noun *ado,* meaning "what is being done." (Another is MUCH ADO ABOUT NOTHING.) [Late 1300s]

without question Certainly, undoubtedly, as in *Without question he's the best editor we've ever had.* [Late 1600s]

without so much as With not even, as in *She stormed out without so much as a goodbye.* [Mid-1600s]

with reason For a ground or cause, justifiably, as in *He turned down their offer, but with reason—he didn't want to move his family to a big city.* [c. 1600]

with reference to Also, **with regard** or **respect to.** ♦ See IN REGARD TO.

with the best of them As well as anyone, as in *Donna can pitch a ball with the best of them.* This idiom was first recorded in 1748.

with the best will in the world No matter how much one wants to or tries, as in *I couldn't eat another bite, not with the best will in the world.* [Mid-1800s]

with the exception of ♦ See EXCEPT FOR.

with the gloves off With or ready to dispense rough treatment, as in *Prepared to oppose the council, the mayor marched into the meeting with the gloves off.* This idiom alludes to old-style boxing, when gloves were not used. [Early 1800s]

wives ♦ See OLD WIVES' TALE.

wolf ♦ In addition to the idiom beginning with WOLF, also see CRY WOLF; KEEP THE WOLF FROM THE DOOR; LONE WOLF.

wolf in sheep's clothing An enemy disguised as a friend, as in *Dan was a wolf in sheep's clothing, pretending to help but all the while spying for our competitors.* This term comes from the ancient fable about a wolf that dresses up in the skin of a sheep and sneaks up on a flock. This fable has given rise to a rich history of allusions as in the Sermon on the Mount when Jesus speaks of false prophets in sheep's clothing, "but inwardly they are ravening wolves" (Matthew 7:15).

woman ♦ See FEEL LIKE ONESELF (NEW WOMAN); MARKED MAN (WOMAN); (WOMAN) OF FEW WORDS; OWN PERSON (WOMAN); RIGHT-HAND MAN (WOMAN); SCARLET WOMAN.

wonder ♦ In addition to the idiom beginning with WONDER, also see FOR A WONDER; NO WONDER; WORK WONDERS.

wonders will never cease What a surprise, as in *He's on time—wonders will never cease.* This expression is generally used ironically. [Late 1700s]

won't hear of ♦ See under NOT HAVE IT.

won't wash Will not stand up to examination, is unconvincing, will not work, as in *That excuse about your sick aunt just won't wash.* This expression originally alluded to a fabric that would not stand up to washing but by the late 1800s was used figuratively for other kinds of failure.

woo ♦ See PITCH WOO.

wood, woods ♦ See BABE IN THE WOODS; CAN'T SEE THE FOREST (WOOD) FOR THE TREES; DEAD WOOD; KNOCK ON WOOD; NECK OF THE WOODS; OUT OF THE WOODS.

wool ♦ See ALL WOOL AND A YARD WIDE; PULL THE WOOL OVER SOMEONE'S EYES.

word ♦ In addition to the idioms beginning with WORD, also see ACTIONS SPEAK LOUDER THAN WORDS; AT A LOSS (FOR WORDS); AT A WORD; BREAK ONE'S WORD; EAT ONE'S WORDS; FAMOUS LAST WORDS; FIGHTING WORDS; FOUR-LETTER WORD; FROM THE WORD GO; GET A WORD IN EDGEWISE; GIVE THE WORD; GO BACK ON (ONE'S WORD); GOOD AS ONE'S WORD; HANG ON SOMEONE'S WORDS; HAVE A WORD WITH; HAVE WORDS WITH; IN BRIEF (A WORD); IN OTHER WORDS; IN SO MANY WORDS; KEEP ONE'S WORD; LAST WORD; LEAVE WORD; MAN OF HIS WORD; MARK MY WORDS; MINCE MATTERS (WORDS); MUM'S THE WORD; NOT BREATHE A WORD; NOT OPEN ONE'S MOUTH (UTTER A WORD); OF FEW WORDS; PICTURE IS WORTH A THOUSAND WORDS; PLAY ON WORDS; PUT IN A GOOD WORD; PUT INTO WORDS; PUT WORDS IN SOMEONE'S MOUTH; SWALLOW ONE'S WORDS; TAKE SOMEONE AT HIS OR HER WORD; TAKE THE WORDS OUT OF SOMEONE'S MOUTH; TRUE TO (ONE'S WORD); WEASEL WORD; WEIGH ONE'S WORDS.

word for word Exactly as written or spoken, as in *That was the forecast, word for word.* Chaucer used this idiom in the late 1300s.

word of honor A pledge of one's good faith, as in *On his word of honor he assured us that he was telling the truth.* [Early 1800s]

word of mouth, by Orally, by one person telling another, as in *They don't advertise; they get all their customers by word of mouth.* [Mid-1500s]

words fail me I can't put my thoughts or feelings into words, especially because of surprise or shock, as in *When she showed up at the wedding with all three ex-husbands—well, words fail me.* [Second half of 1900s]

words of one syllable, in In simple terms, as in *I don't understand financial derivatives—can you explain them in words of one syllable?* [Colloquial; 1920s]

words stick in one's throat ♦ See STICK IN ONE'S THROAT.

words to that effect ♦ See TO THAT EFFECT.

word to the wise, a Here's good advice, as in *A word to the wise: don't walk alone here because these streets are not safe at night.* A shortening of *A word to the wise is enough,* as it was put by Roman writers, this phrase in English dates from the mid-1500s.

work ♦ In addition to the idioms beginning with WORK, also see ALL IN A DAY'S WORK; ALL WORK AND NO PLAY; AT WORK; BUSY WORK; DIRTY WORK; GET DOWN TO (WORK); GOOD WORKS; GUM UP (THE WORKS); HAVE ONE'S WORK CUT OUT; IN THE WORKS; MAKE SHORT WORK OF; MANY HANDS MAKE LIGHT WORK; OUT OF WORK; SHOOT THE WORKS; THE WORKS; TURN (WORK) OUT ALL RIGHT.

work both sides of the street Engage in double-dealing, be duplicitous, as in *The real estate agent was known for working both sides of the street, advising first the buyer and then the seller.* This metaphoric term transfers opposite sides of a street to opposite sides of a negotiation.

worked up, be Also, **get all worked up.** Be or become excited or upset, as in *She got all worked up about the idea of adopting a baby.* [Late 1600s] Also see WORK UP.

work in 1. Insert or introduce, as in *As part of their presentation they worked in a request for funding the exhibit.* Similarly, **work into** means "insert or introduce into something else," as in *She worked more flour into the mixture.* [Late 1600s] 2. Make time for in a schedule, as in *The dentist said he would try to work her in this morning.* Here, too, **work into** is sometimes used, as in *She had to work two emergency cases into her morning schedule.* [Mid-1700s]

work it Arrange, bring about, as in *We'll try to work it so that the board meets tomorrow.* [Colloquial; late 1800s]

work like a beaver Also, **work like a dog** or **horse** or **Trojan.** Work very energetically and hard, as in *She worked like a beaver to clean out all the closets,* or *I've been working like a dog weeding the garden,* or *He's very strong and works like a horse.* The first of these similes is the oldest, first recorded in 1741; the variants date from the second half of the 1800s. Also see WORK ONE'S FINGERS TO THE BONE.

work like a charm Function very well, have a good effect or outcome, as in *That knife-sharpener works like a charm,* or *Her deferential manner worked like a charm; he agreed to everything they'd asked for.* This expression uses *charm* in the sense of "a magic spell." [Mid-1800s] Also see WORK WONDERS.

work off Get rid of by work or effort, as in *They worked off that big dinner by running on the beach,* or *It'll take him months to work off that debt.* [Second half of 1600s]

work on Also, **work upon.** Exercise influence on, as in *If you work on him, he might change his mind,* or *She always worked upon their feelings by pretending to be more ill than she really was.* [Early 1600s]

work one's fingers to the bone Also, **work one's tail** or **butt off.** Exert oneself, labor very hard, as in *She's working her fingers to the bone to support her children,* or *I work my tail off and then the government takes half my income in taxes.* The first hyperbole, with its image of working the skin and flesh off one's fingers, dates from the mid-1800s; the less polite variants date from the first half of the 1900s.

work one's way Exert oneself to proceed in a particular direction; also, finance a project by working. For example, *The painters are working their way from the top floor to the basement,* or *I'm trying to work my way into the publishing world,* or *She's working her way through college.* [Second half of 1800s]

work out 1. Accomplish by work or effort, as in *I think we can work out a solution to this problem.*

[1500s] For **work out all right,** see TURN OUT ALL RIGHT. 2. Find a solution for, solve, as in *They hoped to work out their personal differences,* or *Can you help me work out this equation?* [Mid-1800s] 3. Formulate or develop, as in *We were told to work out a new plan,* or *He's very good at working out complicated plots.* [Early 1800s] 4. Discharge a debt by working instead of paying money, as in *She promised she'd work out the rest of the rent by babysitting for them.* [Second half of 1600s] 5. Prove effective or successful, as in *I wonder if their marriage will work out.* 6. Have a specific result, add up, as in *It worked out that she was able to go to the party after all,* or *The total works out to more than a million.* [Late 1800s] 7. Engage in strenuous exercise for physical conditioning, as in *He works out with weights every other day.* [1920s] 8. Exhaust a resource, such as a mine, as in *This mine has been completely worked out.* [Mid-1500s]

work over Beat up, as in *The secret police worked him over and he's never been the same.* [c. 1920]

work up 1. Arouse emotions; see WORKED UP. 2. Increase one's skill, status, or responsibility through effort, as in *He worked up to 30 sit-ups a day,* or *She worked up to bank manager.* Also see WORK ONE'S WAY. [Second half of 1600s] 3. Intensify gradually, as in *The film worked up to a thrilling climax.* [Second half of 1600s] 4. Develop or produce by effort, as in *Swimming always works up an appetite.* [Second half of 1600s]

work wonders Succeed, produce a good outcome, as in *The new coat of paint works wonders with this bedroom,* or *The physical therapy has worked wonders with these patients.* Literally meaning "perform miracles," this term has been used somewhat more loosely since the 1700s. Also see WORK LIKE A CHARM.

world ♦ In addition to the idioms beginning with WORLD, also see ALL OVER THE PLACE (WORLD); BEST OF BOTH WORLDS; BRING INTO THE WORLD; COME UP (IN THE WORLD); DEAD TO THE WORLD; FOR ALL THE WORLD; GO OUT (OF THE WORLD); IN ONE'S OWN WORLD; IT'S A SMALL WORLD; LAUGH AND THE WORLD LAUGHS WITH YOU; MAN OF THE WORLD; MOVE UP (IN THE WORLD); NOT FOR ALL THE TEA IN CHINA (FOR THE WORLD); ON EARTH (IN THE WORLD), WHAT; ON TOP OF THE WORLD; OUT OF THIS WORLD; SET THE WORLD ON FIRE; THINK A LOT (THE WORLD) OF; THIRD WORLD; WITH THE BEST WILL IN THE WORLD.

world is one's oyster, the Everything is going well, as in *I was younger then, and the world was my oyster.* In this term the oyster is something from which to extract great profit (a pearl). It was probably invented by Shakespeare in *The Merry*

Wives of Windsor (2:2): "Why then, the world's mine oyster, which I with sword will open."

world of good, a A great benefit, as in *A vacation will do you a world of good.* This expression uses *world* in the sense of "a great deal," a usage dating from the 1400s. [Late 1800s]

worm ♦ In addition to the idioms beginning with WORM, also see CAN OF WORMS; EARLY BIRD CATCHES THE WORM.

worm into Insinuate oneself subtly or gradually, as in *He tried to worm into her confidence.* This idiom alludes to the sinuous path of a worm. [Early 1600s]

worm out of Elicit or make one's way by artful or devious means. For example, *He tried to worm the answer out of her,* or *She can't worm out of this situation.* This expression alludes to the sinuous passage of a worm. [Early 1700s]

worm turns, the Also, **the worm has turned.** Even a very tolerant person will one day lose patience. For example, *He bullied his assistant for years, but one day the worm turned and he walked out without notice, taking along his best clients.* This expression comes from the proverb *Tread on a worm and it will turn,* first recorded in John Heywood's 1546 collection.

worn out ♦ See WEAR OUT.

worn to a frazzle In a state of nervous exhaustion, as in *The very idea of moving again has us worn to a frazzle.* This expression transfers *frazzle,* which means "a frayed edge," to one's feelings. [Late 1800s]

worried sick Also, **worried to death.** Extremely anxious, as in *Her parents were worried sick when she didn't come home all night,* or *We've been worried to death about the drop in the stock market.* These somewhat hyperbolic phrases (one could conceivably feel ill from worrying but would hardly die from it) date from the second half of the 1800s.

worse ♦ In addition to the idiom beginning with WORSE, also see ALL THE (WORSE); BARK IS WORSE THAN ONE'S BITE; FATE WORSE THAN DEATH; FOR BETTER OF FOR WORSE; FROM BAD TO WORSE; IF WORST COMES TO WORST; NONE THE WORSE; TAKE A TURN FOR THE BETTER (WORSE). Also see UNDER WORST.

worse for wear Also, **the worse for the wear.** In poor physical condition owing to long use; also, drunk. For example, *This television set is really worse for the wear; we'll have to replace it,* or *He'd better not drive home; he's definitely the worse for the wear.* [c. A.D. 1000] For an antonym, see NONE THE WORSE FOR.

worship the ground someone walks on Regard someone reverently, as in *Jim just worships the ground his father walks on.* This hyperbole for

deep admiration or romantic feeling was first recorded in 1848.

worst ♦ See AT WORST; GET (HAVE) THE WORST OF IT; IF WORST COMES TO WORST; IN THE WORST WAY. Also see under WORSE.

worth ♦ In addition to the idioms beginning with WORTH, also see FOR ALL ONE IS WORTH; GAME IS NOT WORTH THE CANDLE; GET ONE'S MONEY'S WORTH; NOT WORTH A DAMN; PICTURE IS WORTH A THOUSAND WORDS.

worth one's weight in gold Also, **worth its weight in gold.** Very valuable, as in *John's been extremely helpful; he's worth his weight in gold,* or *That tractor's been worth its weight in gold.* This metaphoric term dates from Roman times and appeared in English by the early 1300s.

worth one's while 1. Merit one's time or efforts, as in *It's hardly worth your while to count the transactions; it can be done by computer.* [Late 1600s] 2. **make something worth one's while.** Compensate one for one's time or efforts, as in *If you take care of our yard while we're away, I'll make it worth your while.* [Mid-1800s] Both usages employ *while* in the sense of "a period of time spent."

worthy of the name Deserving a name or description, as in *Any artist worthy of the name can draw better than that.* This expression uses *worthy of* in the sense of "deserving by reason of merit," a usage dating from about 1300.

would ♦ In addition to the idioms beginning with WOULD, also see AS LUCK WOULD HAVE IT; FLY ON THE WALL, WOULD LIKE TO BE A. Also see under WOULDN'T.

wouldn't ♦ In addition to the idiom beginning with WOULDN'T, also see BUTTER WOULDN'T MELT; CAUGHT DEAD, WOULDN'T BE; NOT (WOULDN'T) LIFT A FINGER. Also see under NOT.

wouldn't dream of Also, **not dream of.** Not occur to one, not consider, as in *Even if it were lying open on my desk, I wouldn't dream of reading another person's letter.* This expression uses *dream of* in the sense of "remotely think of." [First half of 1500s]

would rather Prefer to, as in *We would rather eat dinner before the movie.* [Mid-1500s]

would that I wish that, as in *Would that I could stop working and go hiking with you.* For a synonym, see IF ONLY.

wound ♦ See LICK ONE'S WOUNDS; RUB IN (SALT INTO A WOUND).

wrack ♦ See under RACK.

wrap ♦ In addition to the idiom beginning with WRAP, also see TWIST (WRAP) AROUND ONE'S FINGER; UNDER WRAPS.

wrapped up in Completely preoccupied by or absorbed in, as in *She is wrapped up in her studies.* [c. 1600] Also see WRAP UP.

wrap up 1. Bring to a conclusion, settle successfully, as in *As soon as we wrap up this deal, we can go on vacation.* [First half of 1900s] 2. Summarize, recapitulate, as in *To wrap up, the professor went over the three main categories.* [First half of the 1900s]

wreak havoc ♦ See PLAY HAVOC.

wrench ♦ See THROW A MONKEY WRENCH.

wringer ♦ See under PUT THROUGH (THE WRINGER).

wrist ♦ See SLAP ON THE WRIST.

write ♦ In addition to the idioms beginning with WRITE, also see NOTHING TO WRITE HOME ABOUT. Also see under WROTE.

write down 1. Set down in writing, record, as in *Please write down your new address and phone number.* [Late 1500s] 2. Reduce in rank, value, or price, as in *They've written down their assets.* [Late 1800s] 3. Write in a simple or condescending style, as in *These science texts are written down for high-school students.* [Second half of 1800s]

write in 1. Cast a vote by inserting a name not listed on the ballot, as in *He asked them to write in his name as a candidate.* [c. 1930] 2. Insert in a text or document, as in *Please don't write in your corrections on the printed pages, but list them separately.* [Late 1300s] 3. Communicate with an organization by mail, as in *Listeners are being asked to write in their requests.* [1920s]

write off 1. Reduce an asset's book value to zero because it is worthless, as in *The truck was wrecked completely, so we can write it off.* [Late 1600s] 2. Cancel from an account as a loss, as in *Since they'll never be able to pay back what they owe, let's just write off that debt.* [Late 1800s] Also see CHARGE OFF, def. 2, 3. Regard as a failure or worthless, as in *There was nothing to do but write off the first day of our trip because of the bad weather,* or *She resented their tendency to write her off as a mere housewife.* [Late 1800s] 4. Amortize, as in *We can write off the new computer network in two years or less.* Also see CHARGE OFF, def. 2.

write one's own ticket Set one's own conditions or course of action according to one's wishes or needs. For example, *This generous grant lets recipients write their own tickets.* This term uses *ticket* in the sense of "something entitling the holder to a privilege." [Colloquial; 1920s]

write out 1. Express in writing, especially in full form. For example, *Write out your request on this form,* or *No abbreviations allowed; you have to write everything out.* [Mid-1500s] 2. **write oneself out.** Exhaust one's energies or abilities by writing too much, as in *He's been doing a novel a year for ages, but now he's written himself out.* [Early 1800s]

write up 1. Write a report or description, as for publication, as in *She's been writing up these local concerts for years.* [Early 1400s] 2. Overvalue an

asset, as in *That accountant is always writing up our equipment, forgetting depreciation.*

writing on the wall ♦ See HANDWRITING ON THE WALL.

writ large Signified, expressed, or embodied with greater magnitude, as in *That book on Lincoln is simply an article writ large.* [Mid-1600s]

wrong ♦ See BACK THE WRONG HORSE; BARK UP THE WRONG TREE; DO SOMEONE WRONG; GET SOMEONE WRONG; GET UP ON THE WRONG SIDE OF BED; GO WRONG; IN THE WRONG; ON THE RIGHT (WRONG) FOOT; ON THE RIGHT (WRONG) TACK; RIGHT (WRONG) SIDE OF THE TRACKS; RUB THE WRONG WAY; TAKE THE WRONG WAY; TWO WRONGS DO NOT MAKE A RIGHT.

wrong end of the stick, the A misunderstanding or distortion, as in *We ordered a "full quart" of rice, but the clerk got hold of the wrong end of the stick and sent us "four quarts" instead.* This expression refers to a walking stick held upside down, which does not help a walker much. It originated in the 1400s as *worse end of the staff* and changed to the current wording only in the late 1800s. Also see SHORT END OF THE STICK

wrong-foot Deceive by moving differently from what one expects, as in *He won quite a few points by wrong-footing his opponent.* This expression comes from tennis, where it means to hit the ball in the direction the opponent is moving away from. It was transferred to other applications in the late 1900s, as in Susan Larson's review of a concert: "Music wrong-footing and deceiving the ear" (*Boston Globe*, November 1, 1994).

wrong scent, on the On a false trail or track, as in *He managed to put the police on the wrong scent and got away.* This term alludes to hunting with hounds. [c. 1600]

wrong side of someone ♦ See under RIGHT SIDE, ON SOMEONE'S.

wrong side of the tracks ♦ See under RIGHT SIDE OF THE TRACKS.

wrote the book on Knows nearly everything about, as in *Ask Dr. Lock; he wrote the book on pediatric cardiology,* or *I wrote the book on job-hunting; I've been looking for two years.* This expression is always put in the past tense. [Colloquial; second half of 1900s]

xyz

X marks the spot This mark shows the location, as in *On the postcard, X marks the spot where we picked blueberries.* Although the use of a cross or X is probably much older, this term was first recorded in 1813.

X-rated Sexually explicit, vulgar, or obscene, as in *This film should be X-rated; it's not suitable for children.* This expression alludes to a rating system established for motion pictures, in which films rated X may not be viewed by persons under the age of 17. [c. 1970]

yard ♦ See ALL WOOL AND A YARD WIDE; IN ONE'S OWN BACK YARD; WHOLE NINE YARDS.

yarn ♦ See SPIN A YARN.

year ♦ In addition to the idiom beginning with YEAR, also see ALL YEAR ROUND; ALONG IN YEARS; BY THE DAY (YEAR); DONKEY'S YEARS.

year in, year out Regularly, every year, as in *We've been going to the Cape, year in, year out, ever since we were children.* This expression was first recorded in 1830.

yen ♦ See HAVE A YEN FOR.

yes and no In some ways and not others, as in *Did you enjoy yourself?—Yes and no, I liked the music itself but hated the conductor.* This idiom, always a reply to a question, was first recorded in 1873.

yesterday ♦ See NOT BORN YESTERDAY.

yet ♦ See AS YET.

yon ♦ See HITHER AND THITHER (YON).

you ♦ In addition to the idioms beginning with YOU, also see ALL RIGHT FOR YOU; AS YOU PLEASE; BEFORE YOU CAN SAY JACK ROBINSON; BEFORE YOU KNOW IT; BETWEEN YOU AND ME; BITE THE HAND THAT FEEDS YOU; DO YOU READ ME; FOR SHAME (ON YOU); FUCK YOU; GOOD FOR (YOU); HOW DOES THAT GRAB YOU; HOW DO YOU DO; IF YOU CAN'T BEAT THEM, JOIN THEM; I'LL BE SEEING YOU; I TOLD YOU SO; LOOK BEFORE YOU LEAP; MIND YOU; MY HEART BLEEDS FOR YOU; NO MATTER HOW YOU SLICE IT; NOT IF YOU PAID ME; NOW YOU'RE TALKING; PAY AS YOU GO; PRACTICE WHAT YOU PREACH; QUIT WHILE YOU'RE AHEAD; SAME TO YOU; SAYS WHO (YOU); SCREW YOU; THAT'S—FOR YOU; WHAT DO YOU KNOW; WHAT DO YOU TAKE ME FOR; WHAT HAVE YOU; WHAT OF IT (WHAT'S IT TO YOU); WHAT'S EATING YOU.

you better believe it ♦ See YOU'D BETTER BELIEVE IT.

you bet your ass Also, **you bet** or **you can bet your bottom** or **bottom dollar** or **(sweet) life.** You can be absolutely sure, as in *You bet your ass I'll be there,* or *You can bet your sweet life that was Bill with another woman,* or *Are you coming?—You bet I am.* All these phrases in effect mean that you can be so sure of something that you can wager your body or life or valuables on it; *ass* is considered vulgar, and *bottom dollar* means "last dollar." [Colloquial; second half of 1800s]

you can lead a horse to water but you can't make it drink Even favorable circumstances won't force one to do something one doesn't want

to, as in *We've gotten all the college catalogs but he still hasn't applied—you can lead a horse to water.* This metaphoric term dates from the 12th century and was in John Heywood's proverb collection of 1546. It is so well known that it is often shortened, as in the example.

you can say that again Also, **you said it.** I totally agree with what you said, as in *What a relief that Brian didn't get hurt.—You can say that again!* or *This is a huge house.—You said it.* [Colloquial; first half of 1900s]

you can't take it with you Enjoy material things while you're alive, as in *Go ahead and buy the fancier car; you can't take it with you.* This phrase gained currency as the title of a very popular play (1936) by George S. Kaufman and Moss Hart and of the 1938 film based on it. [First half of 1800s]

you can't win Also, **you just can't win.** Whatever one does is wrong or not enough, as in *Every time I block one of the woodchuck's holes, I find another; you just can't win.* [First half of 1900s] For a synonym, see DAMNED IF I DO, DAMNED IF I DON'T.

you can't win 'em all Success is not inevitable, as in *They published your article but not your rebuttal to the reviewer? Well, you can't win 'em all.* [First half of 1900s] For a synonym, see WIN SOME, LOSE SOME.

you could cut it with a knife Alluding to something very thick, such as muggy air or a heavy accent; also, a very tense atmosphere. For example, *The smoke was so thick you could cut it with a knife,* or *When I walked in they all stopped talking and you could cut the air with a knife.* [Colloquial; late 1800s]

you'd better believe it Also, **you better believe it.** You may be assured, as in *You walk ten miles every day?—You'd better believe it!* This imperative is almost synonymous with YOU BET YOUR ASS. [Colloquial; mid-1800s]

you don't say How surprising, is that true? Also, I find that hard to believe. For example, *I've been working on this project for two years.—You don't say,* or *The man who runs this soup kitchen is a real saint.—You don't say!* This expression, a shortening of **you don't say so,** may be used straightforwardly or ironically. [Late 1800s]

you get what you pay for Inexpensive goods or services are likely to be inferior, as in *That vacuum cleaner fell apart in a year—I guess you get what you pay for,* or *The volunteers take three times as long with the mailing, but you get what you pay for.* This economic observation probably dates from ancient times but is disputed by those who do not equate high price with high quality.

you just don't get it ♦ See under GET IT, def. 2.

you know You are aware, you see, do you remember, as in *She's very lonely, you know, so do go and visit*, or *You know, this exhibit ends tomorrow*, or *You know that black dog our neighbors had? She was run over a year ago*. This phrase is also quite often a conversational filler, equivalent to "um" and occasionally repeated over and over (as in *It's a fine day for, you know, the beach, and, you know, we could leave now*); this usage is more oral than written, and many consider it deplorable. [Late 1500s]

you know something? Also, **you know what?** Listen to what I'm going to tell you, as in *You know something? He's always hated spicy food*, or *You know what? They're not getting married after all.* Both these colloquial expressions are shortenings (Of *Do you know something?* or *Do you know what?*) and are used to emphasize the following statement or to introduce a surprising fact or comment. The first dates from the mid-1900s. The variant, from the late 1800s, should not be confused with WHAT DO YOU KNOW or YOU KNOW.

you name it Everything one can think of, as in *We've got a crib, highchair, diapers—you name it.* [Colloquial; mid-1900s]

you never can tell Also, **you never know.** Perhaps, possibly, one can't be certain, as in *You never can tell, it might turn into a beautiful day*, or *You may yet win the lottery—you never know.* The first term uses *tell* in the sense of "discern," a usage dating from the late 1300s; the variant dates from the mid-1800s.

young at heart Having a youthful outlook, especially in spite of one's age. For example, *She loves carnivals and fairs; she's a grandmother but she's young at heart.*

you're telling me I'm well aware of that, as in *She's a terrific dancer.—You're telling me! I taught her how*, or *You're telling me, the prices are sky-high here.* [Early 1900s]

you're welcome Also, **don't mention it.** No thanks are needed, I was glad to do it. For example, *Thanks for picking me up.—You're welcome*, or *I appreciate what you did for Mother.—Don't mention it.* Both phrases are polite formulas for responding to thanks. The first dates from about 1900; the variant was first recorded in 1841. For

synonyms, see FORGET IT; NO PROBLEM, def. 2. Also see WELCOME TO.

your guess is as good as mine I don't know any more than you do, as in *As for when he'll arrive, your guess is as good as mine.* [1920s]

yours truly 1. A closing formula for a letter, as in *It was signed "Yours truly, Mary Smith."* [Late 1700s] 2. I, me, myself, as in *Jane sends her love, as does yours truly.* [Colloquial; mid-1800s]

you said it ♦ See YOU CAN SAY THAT AGAIN.

you scratch my back and I'll scratch yours ♦ See SCRATCH ONE'S BACK.

you've lost me I can't follow what you're saying, I'm puzzled or bewildered. For example, *Please explain it again; you've lost me.* This turn of phrase transfers losing one's way to discourse. [c. 1960]

z ♦ See FROM SOUP TO NUTS (A TO Z).

zap out Interrupt or delete unwanted parts of a television program or video, as in *We've taped the show and now we can zap out all the commercials.* [c. 1980]

zero in on 1. Aim precisely at a target, as in *They zeroed in on the last snipers.* [c. 1940] 2. Direct one's attention to, concentrate or focus on, as in *We must zero in on the exact combination of ingredients*, or *The whole class zeroed in on the new assignment.* This usage transfers aiming a firearm to directing one's attention. [Mid-1900s] 3. Converge on, close in on, as in *The children zeroed in on the electric train display.* [Mid-1900s]

zone out Stop paying attention, dissociate oneself from a situation. Also, engage in a mindless activity. For example, *When Felicia starts talking about her ailments and her friends' ailments, I totally zone out.* This idiom also occurs in the passive, **be zoned out.** It originally alluded to narcotic intoxication and then was broadened to other kinds of dissociation. For a near synonym, see TUNE OUT, def. 2. [Slang; second half of 1900s]

zoo ♦ See IT'S A ZOO.

zoom in on 1. Obtain a closeup view of the subject with a camera, as in *The TV people zoomed in on the Olympic gold medalist.* [Mid-1900s] 2. Focus on, examine closely, as in *The moderator got the panelists to zoom in on the health-care issue.* [Second half of 1900s]